GunDigest®
2025
79th EDITION

EDITED BY

PHILIP P. MASSARO

Published by

Gun Digest® Books, an imprint of Caribou Media Group, LLC
5583 W. Waterford Ln., Suite D, Appleton, WI, 54913
gundigest.com

To order books or other products call 920.471.4522 ext.104
or visit us online at gundigeststore.com

CAUTION: Technical data presented here, particularly technical data on handloading and on firearms adjustment and alteration, inevitably reflects individual experience with particular equipment and components under specific circumstances the reader cannot duplicate exactly. Such data presentations therefore should be used for guidance only and with caution. Caribou Media accepts no responsibility for results obtained using these data.

ISBN-13: 978-1-959265-25-2

Edited by Phil Massaro and Corey Graff
Cover Design by Gene Coo
Interior Design by Jon Stein

Printed in the United States of America

10 9 8 7 6 5 4 3 2 1

John T. Amber
LITERARY AWARD

The John T. Amber Literary Award is named for the editor of *Gun Digest* from 1950 to 1979, a period that could be called the heyday of gun and outdoor writing. Amber worked with many of the legends in the business during his almost 30 years with the book, including the great shooting and hunting writer Townsend Whelen. In 1967, Amber instituted an annual award, which he named for Whelen, to honor an outstanding author from the previous year's *Gun Digest* edition. In 1982, three years after Amber's retirement, the award was renamed in his honor.

A writer must be intimately familiar with their subject matter to be effective and authentic. Few have the level of experience in shooting and firearms evaluation as W.F. "Bill" Vanderpool. To begin his long and storied career in law enforcement, Vanderpool started as a State Beverage Agent in his native state of Florida, hunting rogue stills and the 'shiners who ran them. After earning a degree from Florida State University, he was made Special Agent at the FBI and soon became a SWAT Team sniper, working out of the Washington Field Office.

In 1979, Vanderpool transferred to the FBI Academy at Quantico, Virginia, and became a member of the Firearms Training Unit (FTU), responsible for training new FBI agents and instructors. During that time, he developed the FBI's training courses, evaluated the chosen issue ammunition, and selected the Bureau's firearms; these efforts all led to the development of the FBI Ballistic Research Facility.

The adage that "those who can, do; those who can't, teach" doesn't apply to Bill Vanderpool. He has the honor of being the only FBI agent in the history of the Bureau *and* the National Academy to have fired a "Possible": an official perfect score. He has his opinions and prides himself on receiving a fortnight's leave (without pay, mind you) for his resistance to the FBI's adoption of the S&W 10mm pistol. It turns out he was correct in the end.

Bill Vanderpool

In his retirement, Vanderpool worked for Sigarms for a decade and regularly contributed to the *Sigarms Quarterly* newsletter. After a second retirement, he has lowered himself to the ranks of us lowly gun writers (editor's tongue planted firmly in cheek) and, not surprisingly, has found his stride as an author. He has contributed to *Gun Digest the Magazine*, the NRA's *American Rifleman*, and the *Gun Digest* annual book, among other publications. His first book, *Guns of the FBI: A History of the Bureau's Firearms and Training*, is in its second printing (available at gundigeststore.com). Last year's feature, "Make the Shot: A History of Exhibition Shooting, Then and Now," was his first

original contribution to the *Gun Digest*, though it hopefully will not be his last.

After such an esteemed career, Vanderpool has a wealth of knowledge and expertise to share, and I look forward to reading more of his work in the coming years, as will our readers. It isn't often that a gentleman with such a distinguished background is willing to share a lifetime's worth of knowledge. Thank you, Bill, for all your efforts. Oddly enough, as he and I were communicating about his background for this award, he told me that when he was young, he phoned *Gun Digest's* editor, John Amber—in honor of whom this Award is named—with a question about a firearm. Things have come full circle!

It's my pleasure to bestow upon Bill Vanderpool the John T. Amber Literary Award for his excellent article "Make the Shot" in the 78th Edition of the *Gun Digest*. While well-known for his FBI exploits, the article showcased another side of Vanderpool's persona. He took readers on a fun-filled trip back through time with exhibition shooters Ad and Plinky Toepperwein, showmen William "Buffalo Bill" Cody and Capt. A. H. Bogardus, and sharpshooters Annie Oakley, Ed McGivern, Bill Jordan, and others. Stories like this remind us that while guns are always serious business, they can be fun and inspiring, too. It's the sort of yarn that would make Amber proud. Congratulations, Bill, on a well-written story.

Phil Massaro, Editor-in-Chief

GunDigest
2025

3   **John T. Amber Literary Award**

6   **Introduction: 79th Edition**

8   **About the Cover**

FEATURES

14   **Straightwall Revival!**
BY RON SPOMER

22   **The .270 Winchester Celebrates a Century**
BY CRAIG BODDINGTON

32   **Gunsite Service Pistols**
BY DICK WILLIAMS

40   **The 9.3x62 Mauser on Three Continents**
BY PHIL MASSARO

52   **Does Size Matter?**
BY FRANK MELLONI

64   **Campfire Handguns**
BY RICK HACKER

72   **The Great .22 Comparison**
BY MICHAEL PENDLEY

80   **Custom & Engraved Guns—Tom Turpin Tribute**
BY PHIL MASSARO

90   **The .300 H&H: First. Still Best?**
BY WAYNE VAN ZWOLL

100   **Browning Sweet Sixteen**
BY NICK HAHN

112   **A Trio of Czech Firearms**
BY GEORGE LAYMAN

126   **The Pigeon-Grade Mystery**
BY TERRY WIELAND

140   **Three Great New Gobbler Guns**
BY BRAD FITZPATRICK

150   **They Never Made the Big Time**
BY PIERRE VAN DER WALT

164   **The 1911 Situation**
BY BOB CAMPBELL

176   **Guns of the Alaskan Guides**
BY PHIL SHOEMAKER

186   **Rethinking the .22 Magnum**
BY WILL BRANTLEY

194   **M1 Garand Restoration**
BY JOSH WAYNER

208   **Sako: Finnish Soul in Steel and Wood**
BY JENS ULRIK HØGH

218   **Bryan Coleman, PH: High Stakes in Africa**
BY JOE COOGAN

232   **Advancing the .410 Bore**
BY L.P. BREZNY

240   **Red, White & Blue-Collar Gunbuilders**
BY KRISTIN ALBERTS

252   **70 Years of Buck Fever**
BY LARRY WEISHUHN

262   **Gun Store Museum Reveals Historical Gems**
BY ALAN CLEMONS

276   **Too Much Gun?**
BY THOMAS GOMEZ

284   **Maximum Leverage**
BY PATRICK MCCARTHY & TOM MARSHALL

292   **The .44 Magnum ... One Year Later**
BY ELMER KEITH

Photo: Weatherby

TESTFIRE

305 **Parkwest Arms SD-76**
BY FRED ZEGLIN

310 **The Anschutz Model 1761**
BY STAN TRZONIEC

315 **Mossberg 940 Pro Series Shotguns**
BY BRAD FENSON

319 **Franchi Momentum in .350 Legend**
BY MIKE DICKERSON

325 **Weatherby's 307 Alpine CT**
BY PHIL MASSARO

ONE GOOD GUN

329 **A Model 700 Named Elvira**
BY BILL GABBARD

335 **Remembering Dad and the Walther PP**
BY BRADLEY JOHNSON

340 **Marlin 336RC**
BY TRENT MARSH

344 **The Winchester Model 69A**
BY STEVE GASH

REPORTS FROM THE FIELD

348 **New Rifles**
BY TRENT MARSH

360 **New AR-15s/AR-10s**
BY TODD WOODARD

368 **New Semi-Auto Pistols**
BY ROBERT SADOWSKI

376 **New Revolvers and Others**
BY SHANE JAHN

382 **New Shotguns**
BY KRISTIN ALBERTS

390 **New Muzzloaders**
BY BRAD FENSON

394 **New Optics**
BY JOE ARTERBURN

401 **New Airguns**
BY JIM HOUSE

407 **New Ammo**
BY PHIL MASSARO

417 **New Reloading**
BY PHIL MASSARO

2025 FIREARMS CATALOG

RIFLES
Centerfire – Autoloaders 421
Centerfire – ARs 423
Centerfire – Levers & Slides 439
Centerfire – Bolt Actions 443
Centerfire – Single Shots 457
Drillings, Combination/Double Guns 459
Rimfire – Autoloaders 460
Rimfire – Lever, Slide, Bolt-Actions & Others 462
Competition – Centerfires & Rimfires 466

HANDGUNS
Autoloaders 468
Competition 501
Double-Action Revolvers 503
Single-Action Revolvers 517
Miscellaneous 524

SHOTGUNS
Autoloaders 527

Pumps 534
Over/Unders 537
Side-by-Sides 544
Bolt Actions, Single Shots & Lever Actions 548
Military & Police 550

BLACKPOWDER
Single-Shot Pistols 553
Revolvers 555
Muskets & Rifles 559

AIRGUNS
Handguns 565
Long Guns 577

BALLISTICS TABLES
Average Centerfire Rifle Cartridge Ballistics 590
Centerfire Handgun Cartridge Ballistics 599
Rimfire Ammunition Ballistics 603
Shotshell Loads 604

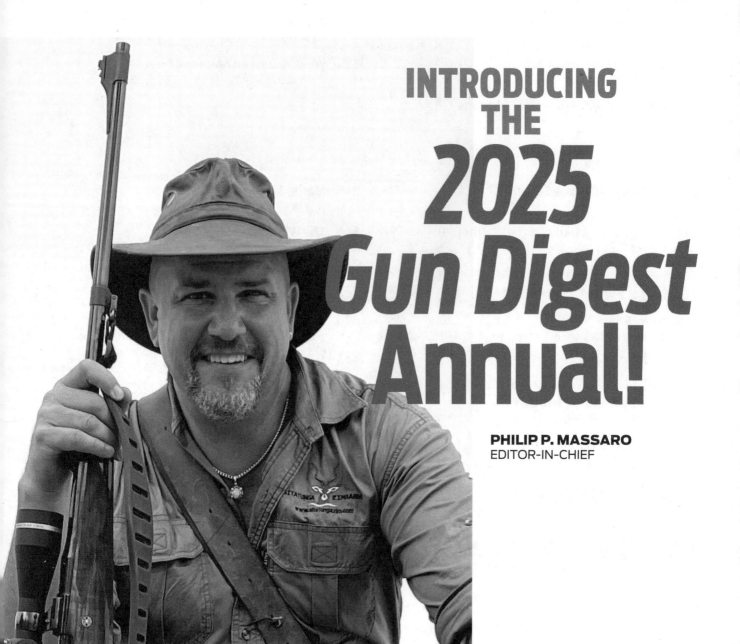

INTRODUCING THE
2025
Gun Digest
Annual!

PHILIP P. MASSARO
EDITOR-IN-CHIEF

Welcome all to the 79th Edition of *Gun Digest*, the World's Greatest Gun Book! We have a bunch to celebrate this year and some tough news to be sad about. In 2025, two wonderful centerfire cartridges will celebrate their 100th birthdays: the venerated and still universally popular .270 Winchester has a hundred candles on its cake, and my favorite .30-caliber—the .300 Holland & Holland Magnum—also turns 100 this year. Craig Boddington and Wayne van Zwoll, respectively, handle the party planning for those two cartridges in their excellent feature pieces. So be sure and give those a read.

On a sad note, the *Gun Digest* family and the shooting world at large lost a patriarch. Tom Turpin, the maestro of the annual Custom & Engraved Guns feature, has passed away. Long associated with the custom gun industry and revered among members of the American Custom Gunmaker's Guild, Turpin was a gentleman, well-versed in firearms of all types, and as you'll read in our tribute to him in the Custom & Engraved Guns section, instrumental in keeping certain types of rifles and cartridges alive.

Shooters continue to embrace the classic firearm and cartridge designs while readily accepting the latest cartridges—Hornady's .22 ARC is a prime example—and many modern twists on old themes. The lever-action rifle, while traditionally blued steel and walnut-stocked, has recently become a popular platform for weatherproof coatings, polymer stocks, and tactical garb. Who knows where things will lead? One thing is true: there doesn't seem to be any slowdown in consumers' appetites.

INSIDE THE 79TH EDITION
Long embracing historical feature articles, Nick Hahn tackles the Browning Sweet Sixteen's lineage, Jens Ulrik Hogh brings us the history of Sako rifles, and Terry Wieland delivers a dissertation on the scatterguns used for live pigeon shoots. In the cartridge department, Will Brantley revisits the classic .22 Winchester Magnum Rimfire, Pierre van der Walt highlights those cartridges of yesteryear that didn't make it far off the drawing board, Ron Spomer tackles the wide variety of straight-walled cartridges (including the newest developments) and Yours Truly makes his best attempt at shedding some light on Otto Bock's 9.3x62mm Mauser cartridge.

For those who prefer to spend their money on rifles made here in the United States, our own Kristin Alberts takes the time to outline those rifle manufacturers who still operate on home soil. For handgun fans, Bob Campbell brings us up to date on the latest developments of the Browning-designed 1911 pistol, and first-time contributor Frank Melloni tackles everyday carry handgun sizes and how each appeals to different-sized shooters.

We have new cartridges, ammunition, and many innovative firearms; for example, Smith & Wesson makes a foray into the lever-action market. Fred Zeglin takes a look at the Parkwest rifle—a modern variant of the classic Dakota Model 76—and Dick Williams sheds light on the Gunsite Glock Service Pistol. Brad Fitzpatrick highlights a trio of new shotguns specially purposed for the turkey woods; there is plenty of coverage of new firearm models. My old pal L.P. Brezny delves deep into the resurgence of the .410-bore, giving an honest overview of what it will and won't do.

For those who like nostalgic stories (I'm as big a fan as there is), you'll find Joe Coogan's piece on the guns and storied life of African Professional Hunter Bryan Coleman. Bradley Johnson shares his late father's Walther PP handgun, Bill Gabbard highlights his favorite Remington 700, and Trent Marsh relates hunting tales with his vintage Marlin 336 in the classic .30-30 Winchester. If you want to learn about a particular topic, seek out those who have spent a lifetime doing that thing. Case in point: Alaskan Master Guide Phil Shoemaker takes us through a topic he has all sorts of expertise: the guns of the Alaskan hunting guides.

My good friend Larry Weishuhn—Mr. Whitetail himself—looks back on his 70-year history of pursuing America's favorite game animal, the good old whitetail deer. I suspect Weishuhn has it figured out after seven decades of hunting deer. For the fans of vintage military rifles, George Layman introduces us to a trio of Czechoslovakian rifles that challenged the Russian gear of the day. And hearkening back to the glory days of *Gun Digest*, we've reprinted an Elmer Keith classic feature, with EK giving his thoughts on the .44 Magnum one year after its release.

Always popular with readers, our Reports from the Field section highlights the latest developments in firearms, optics, ammunition and reloading supplies to keep you abreast of what's been released since last we met. And our catalog section gives a comprehensive overview of what's currently available in the shooting world; all put together, there shouldn't be much question as to why the *Gun Digest* proudly wears the title of The World's Greatest Gun Book! Whether you're passionate about personal carry handguns, big-bore hunting guns, proper scatterguns, or just a good old deer rifle, the 79th Edition of the *Gun Digest* has something for you. Please enjoy. **GD**

GUN DIGEST STAFF

JIM SCHLENDER | Group Publisher
PHILIP P. MASSARO | Editor-In-Chief
COREY GRAFF | Features Editor

DEPARTMENT CONTRIBUTORS

Trent Marsh | Rifles
Todd Woodard | AR Rifles
Robert Sadowski | Semi-Auto Pistols
Shane Jahn | Revolvers & Others
Kristin Alberts | Shotguns

Brad Fenson | Muzzleloaders
Joe Arterburn | Optics
Jim House | Airguns
Philip P. Massaro | Ammo, Reloading & Ballistics

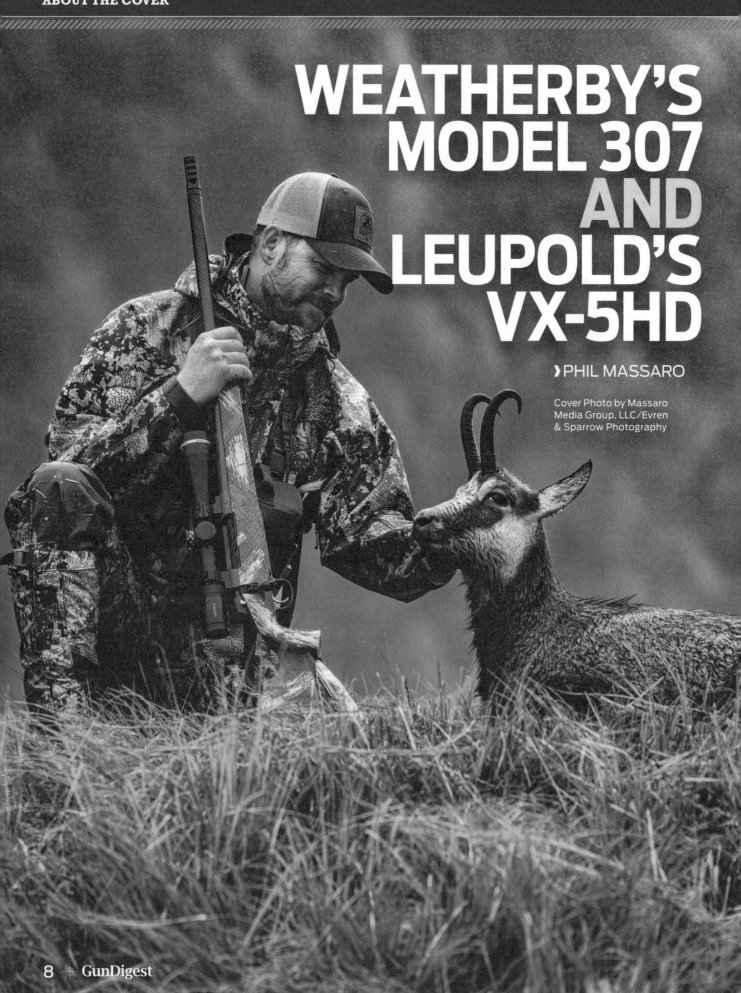

WEATHERBY'S MODEL 307 AND LEUPOLD'S VX-5HD

›PHIL MASSARO

Cover Photo by Massaro
Media Group, LLC/Evren
& Sparrow Photography

Roy Weatherby built his company in Southern California with not only the rifles that bore his name but also a series of cartridges that remain among the speediest on record. Building on the post-WWII boom in both hunters and shooters, Weatherby became a name associated with higher-end performance. Roy handed the reins to his son Ed, who in turn (and in my time) seated his son Adam on the Weatherby throne. I wasn't exactly shocked when I heard Adam Weatherby moved his company from the West Coast to Sheridan, Wyoming. Adam made some rather innovative and bold moves shortly after the relocation, including the first Weatherby cartridges without a belt or the signature double-radius shoulder, namely the RPM or Rebated Precision Magnums.

The Weatherby Model 307 bridges that gap between target and hunting gun, and field reports show outstanding accuracy.

The new Weathery Model 307 Alpine MDT Carbon with folding stock.

THE WEATHERBY MODEL 307

The latest rifle to come out of Sheridan, Wyoming, is the Model 307, which is quite a far stretch from the classic Mark V design, but it might seem immediately familiar. Where the Weatherby actions have traditionally used six- or nine-lug actions, the new Weatherby 307 (named for the area code of Sheridan, Wyoming) uses a dual-lug push-feed design and a cylindrical receiver; it can be seen as a first-cousin to the Remington 700. In fact, the vast majority of parts and accoutrements designed for the 700 fit the Model 307, enhancing the versatility of the design. Unlike the 700, the 307's right lug has a groove that rides along an anti-bind rail in the receiver, and the bolt body is fluted. The 307 features an M16-style extractor and the familiar plunger ejector on the bolt face. Weatherby designed the 307's bolt to be easily disassembled without tools; depress the rear bolt shroud, remove the bolt handle (held in place with the spring pressure), and the bolt assembly comes apart. There is a two-position rocker safety on the right side of the receiver, and the rifle can be unloaded with the safety engaged. The bolt release is located at the left rear of the receiver. Weatherby has opted for a TriggerTech trigger that is user-adjustable and crisp.

The 307 rifle line offers a half-dozen options—including a wood-stocked model, a pair featuring the MDT folding stock, and a MeatEater signature version—but our cover features the new Alpine CT.

Wearing a BSF carbon-fiber barrel and Weatherby's Accubrake muzzle brake, the Alpine CT is stocked in the Peak 44 Bastion carbon-fiber stock. The Bastion stock has a forend with a flat profile, is equipped with two sling swivels at the front and one at the rear, and is finished in an attractive green/light gray pattern. There is no checkering on the stock, but that isn't an issue: the carbon-fiber design and slightly raised texture of the hand-painted camouflage finish affords a positive grip, even with hunting gloves. Weighing a mere 24 ounces, the Bastion stock gives rigidity without weight. Though the vertical grip profile might not fit in among the classic hunting rifles of the early 20th century, it is undeniably ergonomic. A Peak 44 honeycombed recoil pad takes the sting out of even the magnum cartridges.

The Alpine CT is offered in 14 different chamberings, including many Weatherby classics, the new PRC family, 6.5 Creedmoor, and 6.5 Weatherby RPM.

The VX-5HD 3-15x44 CDS-ZL2 shown on the cover has a 5x magnification level, and the elevation turret uses Leupold's CDS or Custom Dial System. Editor Massaro believes it strikes the best value balance between quality, weight, and price.

LEUPOLD'S VX-5HD SERIES RIFLESCOPES

While Leupold has always had an impeccable reputation in the sporting optics market, the latest releases in the VX-5HD and VX-6HD are real show-stoppers. With a proprietary lens coating that results in a bright and crisp edge-to-edge image, these lines offer great value and weight that won't ruin the balance of a fine hunting rifle. I am particularly partial to the VX-5HD line, as the windage turret is under a cap, unlike the VX-6HD, which uses an exposed turret for windage.

The VX-5HD 3-15x44 CDS-ZL2 shown on the cover has a 5x magnification level, and the elevation turret uses Leupold's CDS or Custom Dial System; it comes shipped with an external turret marked in MOA, but Leupold offers a custom turret to the purchaser, marked in yardage for your particular load. Provide your cartridge, projectile (type, Ballistic Coefficient, and weight), muzzle velocity, zero range, and the elevation at which you intend to use the rifle most; Leupold will cut you a custom dial marked in yardage. So, with this simple conversion dial, you range the target, dial that particular distance on the elevation turret, and you've got a dead hold—except for wind deflection.

I've used this system with several different cartridges and bullet weights, and it is an absolute game-changer. Yes, you may have to experiment with different altitude densities if you travel from your 'home environment.' But boy, this sure makes holdover a breeze compared to the ballistic solutions offered by any other scope.

The adjustment on the left side of the housing has the adjustable objective (AO), allowing the shooter to fine-tune one of the crispest images on the market, removing the effects of parallax. Even old eyes like mine can be salvaged with the judicious use of an AO, and I've come to rely on it for my long-range rigs. In addition, the scope came with the FireDot reticle; push a button on the scope's left side, and a small illuminated dot lights up at the crosshair junction. The dot's intensity is adjustable by repeatedly pressing the button. In many hunting situations, that FireDot can be worth its weight in gold.

The VX-5HD line offers five magnification levels: 1-5x24mm, 2-10x42mm, 3-15x44mm (on our cover), 3-15x56mm, and, for those who like even more light, a 4-20x52mm and a 7-35x56mm. The first three sport 30mm maintubes, the latter two 34mm maintubes. Reticle choices range from the simple yet effective duplex to illuminated choices like the FireDot I'm so fond of to the TMOA, which offers many options for the long-range shooter.

Having used the three lower magnification models in a wide variety of shooting and hunting situations from Alaska to Zimbabwe, there are many reasons why I've put several VX-5HD scopes on top of my rifles, from long-range setups to the do-all rigs that can be asked to cover the majority of the bases, up to and including my dangerous game guns. In this editor's opinion, Leupold has found the optimal balance of features in the VX-5HD line.

Mount that 3-15x scope on a light-and-rigid rifle like Weatherby's 307, and you've got a rig that can handle the rigors of any backcountry hunt and the back 40.

See my TESTFIRE review in this edition for a more detailed review of this rifle and scope. **GD**

The Model 307 Alpine CT.

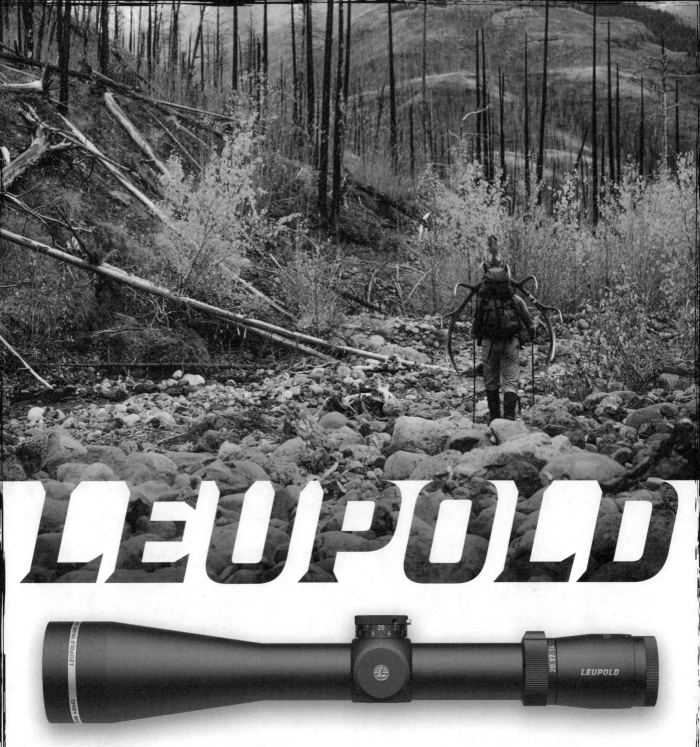

VX-5HD | EVERYTHING YOU NEED AND NOTHING YOU DON'T

BE RELENTLESS

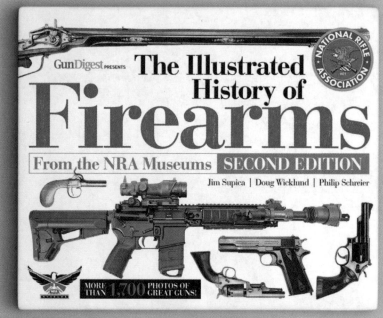

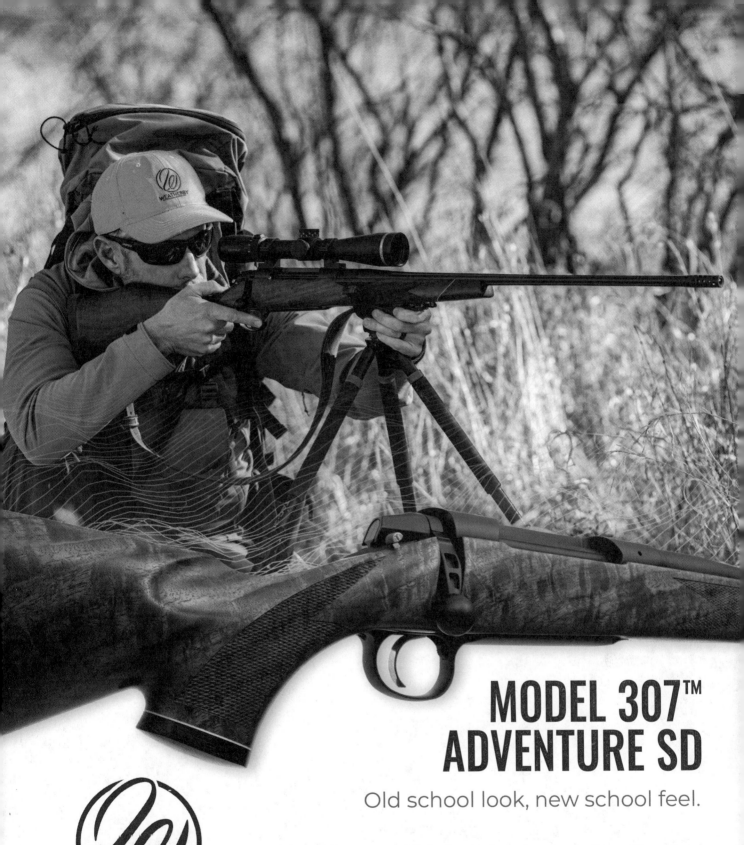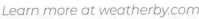

SHARPS PAT.
OCT 5th 1852

AM
BU

SUPERIOR
1320 Cedar
Sturgis, S

If gun fails to
opening, causing serious injury.
seconds. Carefully unload, avoiding
Wear proper hearing protection—re
hearing. Wear shooting glasses to
Improperly hand-loaded ammuniti
should be done only by competent
loadin
or hi

Straightwall Revival!

New straightwall cartridges fill a niche created by Game & Fish regulations enacted in several states.

❯ RON SPOMER

Why mess with Legends, Hammers, and Masters when Sharps rifles have launched .45 slugs from the .45-120 Sharps for more than 130 years? One reason might be that the .45-120 case is too long for some deer hunting jurisdictions.

The Scottish Reverend Alexander John Forsyth's explosive patent of a mercury fulminate detonation mechanism for firearms came three years too late to benefit the Lewis & Clark Expedition. The 33 soldiers on that 1804-06 Voyage of Discovery were stuck with flintlocks, trying to keep their priming pans charged in Montana's winds, and dry in Oregon's winter rains.

On the other hand, the mountain men who followed in the wake of Lewis and Clark enjoyed the convenience of setting off their muzzleloaders with fire from copper percussion caps patented in the U.S. in 1822. Firearm design and function evolve slowly, one advance feeding another, but sometimes they can change quickly and dramatically. The percussion cap, for example, didn't make flintlocks obsolete. It led rather quickly to the game-changing creation of the ultra-convenient, weather-resistant, self-contained, metallic centerfire cartridge. From 1857 to 1886, these handy capsules grew from one to dozens in calibers from .22 to .58, most rimmed cylinders until a French chemist applied sulfuric acid and nitric acid to cotton fibers. This potent, highly flammable mixture was called nitrocellulose, soon to be more universally known as smokeless powder.

Overnight, rifle cartridge power tripled. To take full advantage of this, ammo designers choked straightwall cases to narrower and narrower calibers, using velocity to offset and augment projectile energy. Within 20 years, bottlenecked cartridges had relegated straightwalls to the backseat, if not the trunk.

Given this reality and progress, one might ask why major ammunition manufacturers are unleashing new straightwall centerfire rifle cartridges in the 21st century. The .350 Legend in 2019. The .400 Legend and .360 Buckhammer in 2023. These are essentially late-19th-century cartridges masquerading as 21st-century advancements.

We might dig deeper into cartridge development history to appreciate this odd trajectory. Once the percussion cap made flintlock ignition obsolete, we were on the brink of major evolution. In 1845,

Flobert in France stuck a BB atop a cap to make the first self-contained metallic cartridge, but one without powder. The primer itself propelled the little pellet. That gave Horace Smith and Dan Wesson an idea. They stretched the copper cap to .421 inch, flared its base into a rim, filled it with the priming mix, added 4 grains of blackpowder, and topped it with a 29-grain round-nose lead bullet. They then slipped these rimfire capsules into their new revolving cylinder pistol's seven chambers and, bing, bang, boom. Americans had their first fully contained metallic cartridge, the .22 Short, and a firearm to shoot it. Signed, sealed, and delivered. It's yours.

Thus began a revolution in firearms and a flurry of new, self-contained, metallic cartridges, nearly all straightwall rimfires, until 1873. That was the year Oliver Winchester introduced the .44 Winchester Center Fire, America's first sporting centerfire cartridge. The U.S. Government released its military .45-70 centerfire in the same year, igniting another explosion of new, metallic cartridges. Between 1857 and 1895, the year the first commercial, smokeless sporting cartridge hit the market in the USA, some 140 self-contained cartridges were introduced to American shooters, all but a handful with cylinders tapering just enough toward their mouths to facilitate easy extraction from breech chambers. This was the era of the straightwall cartridge. Smokeless powder would end it. But before we jump too far ahead, let's investigate why most metallic blackpowder cartridges sport parallel walls.

It wasn't as if no one thought about necking down a straightwall case. The bottlenecked .56-46 Spencer came out in 1866. Winchester's bottlenecked .45-70 was designed to increase powder volume via a wider case. This gave .45-70 Govt. performance in a cartridge short enough to function in the M1876 Centennial lever-action rifle. Several other centerfires of the time were necked down, but they were mainly used for target shooting. It makes you wonder if hunters thought bottlenecks were weaker than straightwalls. Given the broad understanding that a large-caliber, heavy lead bullet was always the answer for higher

While the Winchester Legends and Bushmaster are aimed at AR and bolt-action shooters, Remington's .360 Buckhammer is an unabashed, old-school tubular magazine lever rifle cartridge.

With the old .35 Remington and .30-30 Winchester in the deer woods, why would anyone need a .350 Legend, .400 Legend, .360 Buckhammer, or .450 Bushmaster? It's probably because some states disallow bottlenecks and the bigger, longer, straightwalled .45-70 Govt. on the far right.

The .44 Remington Magnum, .357 Magnum, and 10mm Auto have taken whitetails for years. Still, as short handgun rounds, they don't max out potential velocity like the new straightwalls.

Nathan Robinson found the .400 Legend adequate for taking this 160-class Ohio whitetail. He was shooting the Winchester XPR in the new chambering.

Winchester recently answered the call of whitetail hunters who wanted more mass and diameter in their straightwall cartridges.

energy in blackpowder arms, this seems likely. Blackpowder's relatively low energy output per grain limited maximum velocity, so increasing bullet mass was the only route to more on-target punch.

Tradition might have favored straight-walls, too. For hundreds of years, every gun's powder reservoir had been the straightwall bottom of its barrel—a straightwall cartridge was just a reflection of that. And then there was the chimney syndrome. Like house chimneys, blackpowder barrels quickly fouled with soot. The narrower they were for a given powder volume, the faster they plugged up. Hunters likely did not want to waste time being chimney sweeps.

Ironically, smokeless powder relieved this bottleneck, making bottlenecked cartridges viable. With nitrocellulose generating three times more energy than an equivalent quantity of blackpowder *and* leaving in its wake virtually no unburned carbon, cartridge designers were free to throttle those old straight-walled cases and drive lighter, longer, more aerodynamically efficient bullets faster and farther. The bottle-shaped 8x50mm French Lebel did it first in 1886. The .303 British followed in 1887, the German 8x57mm Mauser and 8x50Rmm Austrian Mauser in 1888.

The U.S. joined the revolution in 1893, replacing its straightwall .45-70 with the .30-40 Krag. Two years later, Winchester

released America's first smokeless sporting cartridge, the .30 Winchester Center Fire, aka .30-30. The race was on. Savage countered with its .303 Savage in its revolutionary 1895 rotary magazine lever-action rifle, soon to become the enduring M99. The Navy joined the smokeless bottleneck party with a ridiculously small-bore 6mm cartridge that anticipated the .243 Winchester and .244 Remington by 60 years. The 6mm Lee Navy didn't last long on the open market, but it strongly foreshadowed things to come.

Of all these developments, two of the most influential were the 8x57 Mauser and its kissing cousin, the 7x57 Mauser. Both gave rise to arguably the most significant U.S. cartridge ever released—the .30-'06 Springfield.

The 7x57mm's part in this played out in Cuba, where Spanish soldiers atop Kettle and San Juan Hills rained 173-grain lead hail on U.S. troops. The rapidly firing 7x57mm Spanish Mausers knocked a sense of urgency in the U.S. military brass. Our recently ad-

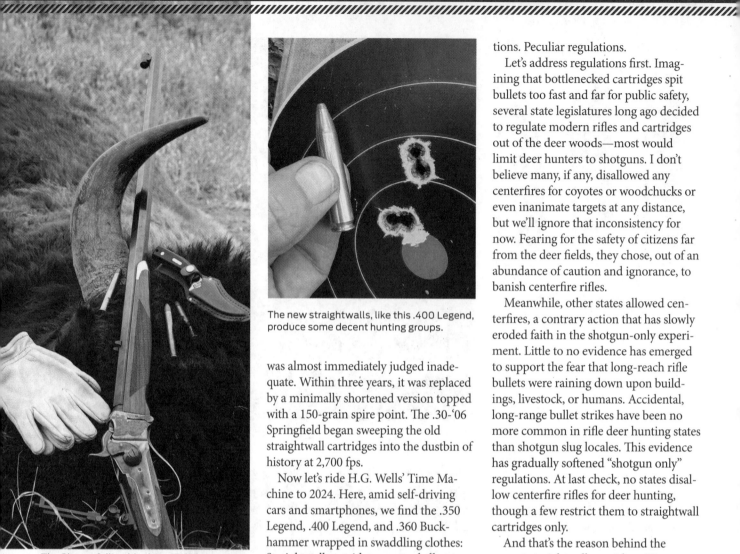

The new straightwalls, like this .400 Legend, produce some decent hunting groups.

The Sharps falling block in .45-120 was one of many that proved itself in the latter days of the unregulated bison slaughter. You'd think it more than adequate for today's deer hunter—and you'd be right, except some states do not allow it.

opted .30-40 Krags weren't keeping up. Teddy Roosevelt had to bring up .45-70 Gatling guns to overpower the Mausers. Engineers at Springfield Armory went back to the drawing board. Adhering to the enduring adage that imitation is the sincerest form of flattery, they stretched the 8x57 German Mauser case, necked it down to grip a .308-inch bullet, chambered it in a Mauser-like, controlled-round-feed bolt-action called the 1903 Springfield, and ignited a patent infringement lawsuit from the Germans. The case was primarily settled out of court on the battlefields of World War I.

The original .30-'03 Springfield pushed a 220-grain round nose at 2,300 fps and was almost immediately judged inadequate. Within three years, it was replaced by a minimally shortened version topped with a 150-grain spire point. The .30-'06 Springfield began sweeping the old straightwall cartridges into the dustbin of history at 2,700 fps.

Now let's ride H.G. Wells' Time Machine to 2024. Here, amid self-driving cars and smartphones, we find the .350 Legend, .400 Legend, and .360 Buckhammer wrapped in swaddling clothes: Straightwall cartridges one and all, yet none older than four years. Have Winchester and Remington forgotten the old news? With everything from a .17 HMR to a .30-378 Weatherby Magnum in the bottleneck arsenal, why would they create any new straightwall rifle cartridge?

One can excuse the creation of the .458 Winchester Magnum in 1956 because, at that time, the U.S. didn't have a big-bore dangerous game round to compete with the British .470 Nitro Express and .450 Nitro Express. The .444 Marlin in 1964 and .375 Winchester in 1978 are understandable straightwall creations. They were supposed to revive lagging interest in the old tubular magazine lever-actions. The .450 Marlin of 2000 enabled Marlin to safely chamber a higher energy version of the still-popular .45-70 Gov't. All of this made sense. But new straightwall cartridges in the 21st century? What's up with that?

AR-15 rifles and government regula-tions. Peculiar regulations.

Let's address regulations first. Imagining that bottlenecked cartridges spit bullets too fast and far for public safety, several state legislatures long ago decided to regulate modern rifles and cartridges out of the deer woods—most would limit deer hunters to shotguns. I don't believe many, if any, disallowed any centerfires for coyotes or woodchucks or even inanimate targets at any distance, but we'll ignore that inconsistency for now. Fearing for the safety of citizens far from the deer fields, they chose, out of an abundance of caution and ignorance, to banish centerfire rifles.

Meanwhile, other states allowed centerfires, a contrary action that has slowly eroded faith in the shotgun-only experiment. Little to no evidence has emerged to support the fear that long-reach rifle bullets were raining down upon buildings, livestock, or humans. Accidental, long-range bullet strikes have been no more common in rifle deer hunting states than shotgun slug locales. This evidence has gradually softened "shotgun only" regulations. At last check, no states disallow centerfire rifles for deer hunting, though a few restrict them to straightwall cartridges only.

And that's the reason behind the newest straightwall cartridges. However, based on the maxim that nothing is safe while the legislatures are in session, we can't guarantee that this regulatory information is still valid. Still, as of the 2023 hunting season, Iowa, parts of Michigan, Indiana, and Ohio have restrictions requiring one degree or another of straightwall compliance. We'll refer readers to their state's Fish & Game hunting regulations for clarification and use the rest of our allotted space to flatter the new straightwall cartridges and some of the golden oldies.

REVIVAL STRAIGHTWALLS

Many shooters appreciate the history, style, and function of 19th-century "buffalo guns," such as the Sharps Falling Block, Remington Rolling Block, and Winchester High Wall, all chambered for big straightwall cartridges. Several manufacturers (Sharps Rifle Co., Uberti, Pedersoli) are again building these classic rifles chambered .45-70, .45-90, .45-110, .45-120, etc.

Unfortunately, most old rounds do not qualify as legal in straightwall deer hunting jurisdictions. But some lever-action straightwalls might.

Despite the popularity of the bolt-action sporting rifle, millions of Americans have remained faithful to the lever-actions. Call it nostalgia, cowboy fantasy, hidebound tradition, but don't call it insignificant. The fit, feel, handling, and just plain tactile pleasure of carrying and cycling a lever-action make it an enduring classic.

Winchester has sold more than 7 million M94s. Marlin tried to die, but demand for the old 336 convinced Ruger to revive it with a new and improved version. The original Henry brass receiver Model 1860 lever-action sprang back to life at Henry Repeating Arms in 1996. A long line of lever-action models has since joined it. Winchester is still building its lever-action models 73, 76, 86, 92, and 95. There are various lever-action replicas and copies of 19th-century designs from Pedersoli and Rossi. This year, Smith & Wesson announced its new 1854 lever-action in .44 Magnum; the title, if not design, reflects the S&W patent Volcanic rifle of 1854, fewer than 10 of which were ever built.

Most of today's lever-actions are chambered for straightwall pistol cartridges, old and modern, or bottlenecked rounds like the .30-30 and .32 Special with the hoped-for revival of the .35 Remington. In old straightwall chamberings, you can find the Winchester M94 in .38-55 and .450 Marlin and the M86 in .45-70 and .45-90. Currently, and sadly, no one chambers for the .444 Marlin or .375 Winchester, but Winchester Repeating Arms is chambering its M95 in the big .405 Winchester, the most powerful straightwall round ever chambered in a lever-action. A Hornady load throws a 300-grain Interlock 2,200 fps for 3,224 ft-lbs of kinetic energy. Unfortunately, the .405 Winchester is, like the .38-55, .375 Winchester, and .45-70, too long to be legal in some states. And that's why the new straightwalls have popped up. Here's a look at the current crop of straightwall-compliant cartridges.

Sure, you can use a .45-120 Sharps to take a bison out west, but it might also be legal in the Midwest deer hunting states.

Of the more recent straightwall cartridges, these four are vying for the most attention. .350 Legend, .360 Buckhammer, .400 Legend, and .450 Bushmaster. Only the Buckhammer works with a rimmed case for optimum performance in traditional lever-actions with tubular magazines.

.350 LEGEND

Winchester was the first major ammo manufacturer to design a cartridge specifically to meet the restrictions of straightwall regulations. Because Michigan disallowed any cartridge with a case over 1.8 inches, Winchester made the .350 Legend case 1.8 inches long. Since Ohio mandated a minimum caliber of .35, Winchester fitted the round with a .357-inch bullet, the same diameter as used in the .357 Magnum. Then, thinking beyond government limitations, it imagined likely platforms for the new straightwall. Lever-actions would seem a natural choice for these Midwest whitetail states, but lever guns are relatively expensive compared to many entry-level bolt guns. In addition, AR-15 semi-autos appear to be increasingly popular. To accommodate them, Winchester engineers gave their new creation the .378-inch rim diameter of the .223 Remington, enlarged the base to .390 inch, tapered the body to .378 inch at the neck, headspaced off the mouth, and set the overall cartridge length the same as the .223 Remington: 2.26 inches to fit AR magazines.

The upshot is a versatile cartridge at home in any short-throw bolt-action, single-shot, or AR-style autoloader. It can work with lever-actions and, with moon clips, even revolvers. The .350 Legend factory loads run from 145 grains at 2,300 fps through 180 grains at 2,000 fps, plus a 255-grain suppressed load with recoil on

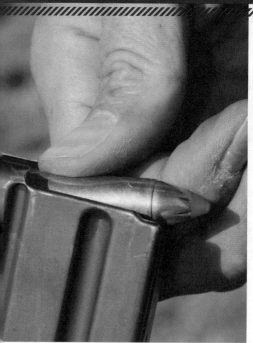

The .450 Bushmaster was designed to provide big-bore performance in the short magazine AR-15 format rifle.

Compared to the bottlenecked 6.8 SPC and .30-30 Winchester, the .45-70 and .400 Legend might be considered trajectory dinosaurs, but they more than hold their own in terminal performance.

par with or slightly below a .243 Winchester. The maximum point-blank range (MPBR) for Winchester's 150-gr. Copper Impact load for a 6-inch-diameter target stretches to 200 yards with a 175-yard zero. The retained energy at that distance is about 850 ft-lbs. The point-blank reach for Winchester's 180-grain Power Point load is 193 yards, with a 165-yard zero. Retained energy is 859 ft-lbs, and the heavier bullet carries more momentum.

With four hunting seasons behind it, the .350 Legend has proven a rousing success, employed not only in the states for which it was designed but also far afield in close-range deer hunting habitats across the continent. Feral pig hunters have embraced it for its wide frontal area combined with mild recoil and high-volume fire in AR rifles. New and small-framed shooters embrace it for its light recoil combined with .30-30-like terminal performance. This popularity has inspired Federal and Hornady to load it with 160- and 170-grain bullets.

.360 BUCKHAMMER

Not to be upstaged by Winchester, Remington joined the new straight-wall-compliant competition with a classic rimmed case ideal for chambering in single-shots and, especially, lever-actions. The .360 Buckhammer is basically the .30-30 case

necked up to hold a .358-inch bullet. It's a perfect candidate for chambering in traditional, tubular-magazine lever guns like the Marlin 336 and Henry Side-Gate. Winchester will not likely chamber its venerated M94 for the .360 Buckhammer, but you never know.

Remington launched with two initial loads: A 180-grain Core-Lokt round nose at 2,400 fps for 2,301 ft-lbs and a 200-grain round nose at 2,200 fps for 2,149 ft-lbs muzzle energy. The maximum point-blank range for the 180-grain bullet reaches 209 yards with a 180-yard zero. With a 169-yard zero, the MPBR for the 200-grain bullet is 197 yards, with a retained energy of 968 ft-lbs. Only Henry chambers lever-actions in a .360 Buckhammer; it also offers a break-action single-shot rifle in the round.

.400 LEGEND

The .400 Legend is Winchester's response to hunters wanting a bit more bullet diameter and power than the .350 Legend, but without the heavy recoil of the .450 Bushmaster or the long case of the .45-70, .450 Marlin, .375 Winchester, and other, older straightwalls. Like the .350 Legend, the .400 adheres to the AR magazine length of 2.26 inches, but the rim diameter is larger at .422 inch. It's also a rebated rim cartridge, its base spanning .440 inch and tapering to .4267 inch for headspacing on the mouth. SAAMI MAP for the .400 Legend is 45,000 psi, 10,000 psi less than the .350 Legend.

Like the .350 Legend, the .400 Legend is designed for bolt-actions, ARs, and single-shots, but if it catches on, it could be chambered in revolvers. Winchester's

initial 215-grain Power Point load departs 2,250 fps to carry 2,416 ft-lbs of muzzle energy. Zeroed at 174 yards, its point-blank range extends to 203 yards, where it retains 1,130 ft-lbs energy, about 175 more than a typical 170-grain .30-30.

Two new loads were introduced at the 2024 SHOT Show: a 190-grain Deer Season XP bullet for which no ballistic data was available at press time and a 300-grain Open Tip Range Super Suppressed load rated 1,060 fps for 748 ft-lbs and an obvious momentum boost over lighter bullets.

.450 BUSHMASTER

In 2007, the .450 Bushmaster straightwall-compliant big-bore was designed from a shortened .284 Winchester case to take the AR-15 to a new power level. A 1.7-inch case and 2.26-inch overall length drive 250-grain .352-inch bullets at 2,200 fps to generate roughly 2,600 ft-lbs. That power comes compliments of a case capacity of 59.5 grains of water. Most major ammo brands load .450 Bushmaster with bullets from 220 grains all-copper to 395 grains in subsonic loads.

A Hornady FTX load at 2,200 fps zeroed at 171 yards will extend MPBR to 200 yards, where that bullet's kinetic energy will still be 1,274 ft-lbs. That drops to 874 ft-lbs (still substantial) at 300 yards, where drop and wind deflection are about 25 inches.

While the Winchester and Remington cartridges recoil similarly to the .30-30 and .35 Remington, the .450 Bushmaster nudges it into .30-'06 range.

Various AR rifles are chambered in .450 Bushmaster, but so are many bolt-

The .450 Bushmaster fits the same ARs as the 5.56 NATO and .223 Remington.

actions from Ruger, Howa, CVA, Savage, Mossberg, Bergara, Christiansen Arms, and others.

.50 BEOWULF

Alexander Arms created the .50 Beowulf and made most AR-style rifles chambered for it. The severely rebated, 1.65-inch case is typically loaded with 300- to 500-grain bullets stepping out at 1,900 fps to 1,400 fps, respectively. Factory-loaded ammunition is available from Underwood and Alexander.

By driving a 300-grain Hornady FTX 1,900 fps, the .50 Beowulf puts out 2,400 ft-lbs, which is not the most among this group but is likely sufficient considering the projectile's diameter. This load will recoil about 2 ft-lbs more than the .450 Bushmaster and right with a 180-grain full-house load from a .30-'06. 𝕲𝕯

Cartridge/Year

Some popular straightwall cartridges and associates: .357 Mag., 10mm Auto, .44 Rem. Mag., .35 Rem., .30-30, .350 Legend, .360 Buckhammer, .400 Legend, .450 Bushmaster, .45-70, .450 Marlin, .38-55 WCF, .405 Winchester, .458 Winchester Magnum, .450 Nitro Express, and .45-120 Sharps.

.45-70 Gov't 1872	.375 Win. 1978	.450 Bushmaster 2009
.38-55 Win. 1884	.450 Marlin 2000	.350 Legend 2019
.405 Win. 1904	.50 Beowulf 2001	.360 Buckhammer 2023
.444 Marlin 1964	.50 Beowulf 2001	.400 Legend 2023

This .270, built by Joe Balickie decades ago, shoots holes in the myth that the cartridge isn't accurate. With its vintage scope, it's MOA with almost anything. With a load it likes, like Hornady's Superformance, top right, it cuts that in half.

The
.270
Winchester
Celebrates a Century

100 Years Later, It Remains Effective

›CRAIG BODDINGTON

100

years later, it remains effective. Although developed in 1923, the .270 Winchester was introduced in 1925 along with the new Winchester Model 54 rifle. The M54 was Winchester's first commercial centerfire bolt-action, initial chamberings including the hot new .270. It was not the first high-velocity sporting cartridge. A decade earlier, Charles Newton's cartridges were speedy. And in 1915, the Newton-designed .250-3000 (.250 Savage) was the first commercial cartridge to break 3,000 feet per second (fps). The .270 Winchester was the second commercial 3,000-fps merchant, possibly the third. Holland & Holland's Super .30, long called the .300 H&H Magnum, was also introduced in 1925.

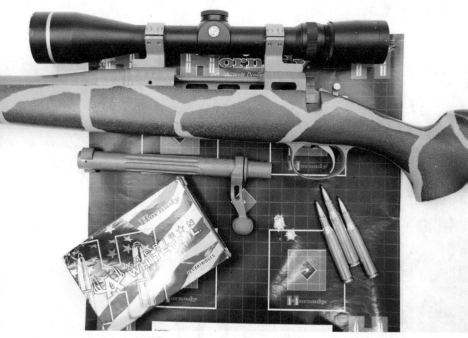

Donna Boddington's pet MGA .270 isn't finicky despite its light weight. It loves Hornady's "vanilla ice cream" American Whitetail load with 130-grain Interlock but shoots about this well with almost anything, even better with some loads.

The .270's original load featured a 130-grain bullet at 3,140 fps, red-hot for its day. It was so hot that the standard 130-grain load was soon downgraded to 3,060 fps, where it remains today. A 100-grain varmint load and a 150-grain load were added quickly. The "compromise" 140-grain load didn't come along until much later. The 140-grain load is standard at 2,950 fps; the 150-grain load at 2,850. All three loads produce just over 2,700 ft-lbs of muzzle energy.

Interestingly, the .270 Winchester didn't take off like a skyrocket. Post-WWI, surplus Springfields and 1917 U.S. Enfields were cheap and available. However, in America, lever-actions from Marlin, Savage, and Winchester were still dominant, and the bolt-action was starting to make inroads. Among bolt-action fans, the .30-'06 Springfield was king. Another two decades would pass before riflescopes came into widespread use, so the greater range and accuracy of the bolt-action was almost a moot point.

The M54 had a bolt handle that confounded scope mounting, so it was an iron-sight rifle. This may have had some impact on the initial .270 sales. Winchester fixed this in 1936 with its beloved Model 70. By then, the .270 Winchester

was gaining ground. I doubt it was ever more popular than the .30-'06, but it became a standard choice among American hunters. By then, Jack O'Connor (1902–1978), longtime Shooting Editor at *Outdoor Life*, was one of America's best-known gun writers. His unabashed admiration for the .270 had much to do with its success and lasting popularity.

In the postwar era, the .270 was chambered by virtually all manufacturers who offered a .30-'06-length action. Today, with so many fast new cartridges, it has slipped, but it is still a worldwide standard ... and a great hunting cartridge.

CASE AND CALIBER

The obvious intent for Winchester's engineers: Create a cartridge that produced higher velocity than the .30-'06 yet, with lighter bullets, developed less recoil. We say that the .270 Winchester is based on the .30-'06 case. Sort of, not exactly. It's actually based on the older .30-'03 case, which is longer: 2.54 inches versus the 2.494-inch case of the "Model of 1906." By 1925, the .30-'03 was no longer commercially loaded. One can only assume that, with 1925 propellants, Winchester's engineers tried wringing every scrap of velocity out of the new .270. Which, for

the day, they did.

The choice of its .277-inch bullet diameter isn't so obvious; it's not known precisely how or why they settled on that obscure diameter. Also in 1923, the .276 Pedersen, firing a .284-inch (7mm), was developed as a shorter, lighter-recoiling cartridge that could more easily be housed in a semi-automatic military rifle than the longer, more powerful .30-'06. The military wrestled with the .276 Pedersen for a decade before the Garand rifle was modified to handle the .30-'06.

Winchester's engineers were surely aware of the Pedersen project. Perhaps they didn't want a less powerful cartridge. The .25-06 was developed at Frankford Arsenal during WWI. Post-war, American wildcatters were hard at work, doing this and that with the popular and available .30-'06 case. It seems likely that Winchester's engineers looked at wildcat versions of the 6.5mm-06 and 7mm-06. Although never commercially adopted, the 6.5mm-06 is fast and a fairly popular wildcat. The 7mm-06 was also a standard wildcat, at least until Remington modified it into the .280 Rem. The .280 Rem is a "7mm-06," except Remington moved the shoulder forward so its cartridge could not be chambered in a .270.

In 1923, Winchester's engineers must have considered 6.5mm (.264) and 7mm (.284) bullet diameters. To be precise, .264 inch is not literally 6.5mm, nor is .284 inch literally 7mm. However, these diameters had long been established as standard for, respectively, "6.5mm" and "7mm" cartridges. With WWI fresh in our memory, perhaps Winchester rejected the 6.5mm and 7mm because they were "European calibers."

Indeed, they also looked at the .25-06. With 1923 propellants, it was probably overbore capacity but was becoming a standard wildcat. It would remain a well-known wildcat until 1969 when Remington adopted it as the .25-06 Remington. In 1923, Winchester's .25-35 was still popular, but Arthur Savage was doing great as his Savage 99 and bolt-action M20 were offered in both .250 Savage and the new .300 Savage. Possibly, they rejected the .25 caliber because rival Savage "owned" that bullet diameter.

So, why .277? Metrically, .277 is

Boddington's best-ever mule deer was taken in Alberta with a Kimber Mountain Ascent in .270 Win., firing a 130-grain Barnes X. He believes the old .270 Winchester is just about ideal for almost all North American deer hunting.

The MGA .270 weighs just 5.7 pounds with scope. At that weight, this little rifle has significant recoil. Add a pound or two, and the .270 Win. is wonderfully mild-mannered.

6.8mm—almost. The actual conversion for 6.8mm is .268 inch. Among Peter Paul Mauser's many experiments was a 6.8x57mm Mauser proposed to China. It was never produced and is so obscure that Frank Barnes' *Cartridges of the World* has no photograph or exact specifications. Not impossible Winchester knew about it, but why did it settle on it? Perhaps, through the sands of time, there's no answer.

There's a .007-inch (seven thousandths) difference in diameter between .277 and .284 (7mm). To me, that's not enough frontal area to matter. O'Connor was also a lifelong fan of the 7x57 Mauser. However, when the 7mm Rem. Mag. came out in 1962 he wrote that "it wouldn't do anything his .270 couldn't do." Mostly true, certainly from his standpoint as primarily a sheep/goat/deer hunter. Also, for unknown reasons, Winchester settled on a 1:10 rifling twist for its hot new cartridge, the same as standard for the '06. (Except in .30-caliber, a 1:10 twist stabilizes bullets from 130 grains to a round-nosed 220-grain.) In .277, a 1:10 twist is fine for 100 to 150 grains. Even then, the 150-grain bullet cannot be extremely long and aerodynamic.

Much hunting can be done effectively with a .270 Winchester and a good 150-grain bullet. O'Connor took many elk, moose, and larger African antelopes with his 270s. Even Elmer Keith, who hated the ground O'Connor walked on, conceded grudgingly (in a letter, never in print!) that the .270 Winchester was

Gun writing great Jack O'Connor with one of his last rams, a fine Stone sheep taken in the early 1970s with his beloved Biesen No. 2. Based on a Winchester M70 Featherweight .270 and stocked by Al Biesen, from 1960 onward this was O'Connor's favorite mountain rifle.

Some quality .277-inch bullets, left to right: 130-grain Swift Scirocco, 150-grain Nosler Partition, 162-grain Winchester Copper Extreme Point, 170-grain Berger Elite Hunter, 175-grain Sierra Tipped GameKing. The two left-hand ones are typical .270 Winchester bullets; the bullets on the right are longer, heavier options that require a faster-than-traditional .270 twist rate.

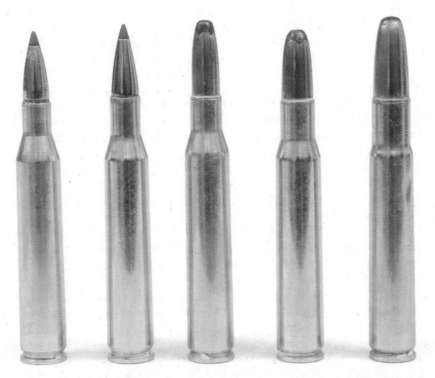

The .30-'06 family of factory cartridges. The .270 was the first factory cartridge based on the .30-'06 case, but good old American wildcatters had already been at work for years.

Outfitter Charlie Ren and Jack O'Connor, in Sonora, August 1935, on O'Connor's first sheep hunt. O'Connor may have owned a .270 at that time, but the rifle he carried was a 7x57. The truth is, O'Connor didn't get a ram on that hunt. The photo was taken by Boddington's uncle, Arthur C. ("Art") Popham Jr., then Professor O'Connor's student at the University of Arizona.

adequate for elk given good shot placement and a 150-grain Nosler Partition (the only premium hunting bullet in their day). O'Connor especially touted the .270 as ideal for wild sheep, and he was right. However, its bullet weight limitation has long been a concern for hunters pursuing game larger than deer.

THE O'CONNOR LEGACY

Although he hunted widely in Africa, Jack O'Connor loved his sheep hunting most of all. Today, it's often stated that Professor O'Connor took "all" of his wild rams with a .270. This is simply not true. In his Arizona days, it's unclear exactly how many desert rams he took by crossing over into Sonora. According to his friend Buck Buckner, only one Sonoran ram, his last, was taken with a .270. Several were taken with a 7x57, at least one with a .257 Roberts, and one with a .348 Winchester, when the .348 and M71 Winchester were brand new.

No known photo of this ".348" ram exists, and O'Connor only wrote about it briefly in passing. He was close to Winchester and perhaps had a typical gun writer obligation to use it. Amazing as it sounds, before WWII, desert sheep in Sonora were among his most available "test subjects."

O'Connor's lineage to the .270 goes back to the beginning. He bought an early M54 .270 in 1925 but didn't keep it long. That doesn't mean he didn't like it. On a pittance teacher's salary and a lesser pittance for gun-and-hunting articles written during the Great Depression, guns came and went.

My uncle, Art Popham, started college at the University of Arizona in 1935. Jack O'Connor was his English professor. In August 1936, before the next term started, they crossed into Sonora for Jack's (and my uncle's) first sheep hunt. August is not a good time to hunt in the Sonoran Desert. A tough, grueling hunt, combined with bad water that nearly killed my uncle, kept him out of school for a year. Shooting a custom Springfield .30-'06 with a Noske scope, Uncle Art got, well, more than one ram. His professor blanked. According to legend, O'Connor owned multiple .270s between 1925 and 1940. Maybe, but on that 1936 sheep hunt, he took a 7x57 and didn't get a ram. He returned in the fall when the weather cooled to take his first desert ram—with a 7x57.

By 1940, the Professor was coming around to the .270 Winchester. As his success grew, he was achieving the ability to travel. On early hunts into Canada, he typically took a .270 and a .30-'06, the former for sheep, the latter for larger game. O'Connor and my uncle remained friends, and he was godfather to my only male cousin. However, I only met him a couple of times and mostly knew him through my uncle and cousins. From biographies and personal accounts, his near-single-minded love for the .270 didn't reach the fore until he was in his fifties and dominant as the Dean of Gun Writers.

In 1959, he walked into a hardware store in Lewiston, Idaho, and purchased a Winchester M70 Featherweight .270. This factoid tells me some things. O'Connor quit teaching in 1945 to pur-

sue writing, but it's important to understand that he wasn't just a gun writer. He published three novels, two of which were developed into screenplays. Pure gun writers do not walk into gun shops and purchase current factory rifles. We call the manufacturer and request a test gun.

Anyway, on a whim and because he could, the Professor purchased this rifle. It turned out to be a sub-MOA rifle, uncommon back then. He turned it over to Al Biesen for restocking, and it became his beloved and famous "Biesen No. 2," which he used for much of his hunting for the rest of his life.

With an exceptionally accurate .270 stocked to fit him like a glove, O'Connor waxed increasingly eloquent on the .270. O'Connor passed away just before I went full-time in the business. Doesn't matter. Clear through the 1980s and beyond, the Professor had a profound influence on us young gun writers. I did my first hunting with a .270 in 1973; liked it. I

didn't write much about it. No way was a young writer going to write about Jack O'Connor's cartridge.

HUNTING CARTRIDGE

When considering the .270, it's essential to understand it was envisioned for hunting, not as a target or match cartridge. This fact is perhaps odd because, in 1925, North American big game was at a low ebb; the awesome recovery had just begun. Hunting opportunities were limited, and "High Power" rifle competition was at its most popular. Most serious gun writers, including O'Connor, participated. The .270 was not designed to play in this game. During WWII, game populations got a considerable rest. When the Greatest Generation came home, many started hunting again, with greater opportunities than before. It was in the postwar period that the .270 achieved its huge popularity.

Throughout my career, I have considered *Field & Stream's* Dave Petzal one

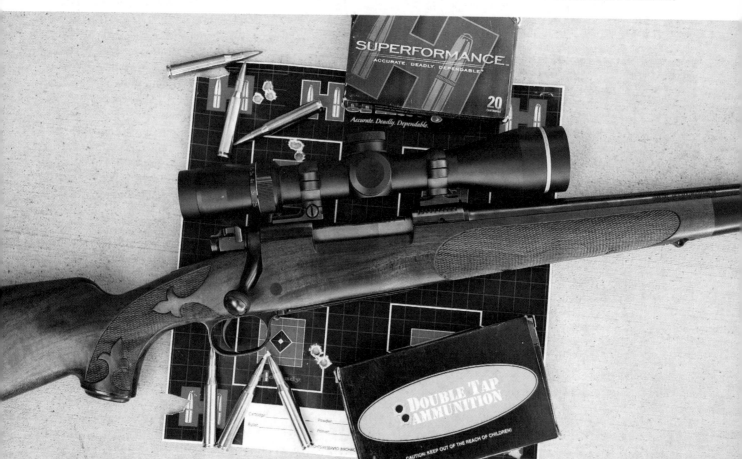

Winchester's Jack O'Connor Commemorative M70 Featherweight .270 was styled after O'Connor's famous Biesen No. 2, his go-to rifle in his latter years. Out of the box, this rifle produced half-inch groups with factory loads. So much for .270 Win. accuracy issues.

This Kimber Mountain Ascent .270 was sub-MOA out of the box with random factory ammo. Traditional .270 bullets were not developed for extreme accuracy, but Boddington has seen few issues with .270 Win. accuracy.

of our most astute rifle guys. Although Petzal likes the .270 and has hunted with it a lot, he once wrote that, in his experience, it wasn't especially accurate. As he pointed out, the .270's bullets were indeed hunting bullets—few match or target projectiles have been made in .277-inch diameter and no match factory loads. However, on raw accuracy, I differ with my old friend and fellow lefty: I've rarely seen a .270 Win. with accuracy problems. I've shot many that were spectacular right out of the box.

We must *caveat* this: .270 bullets and loads were never developed for benchrest accuracy. The rifling twist and bullet weight issue means that the .270 Win. doesn't fit into today's extreme-range shooting. That accepted, it remains an accurate, powerful, and flat-shooting hunting cartridge at the ranges most of us shoot game.

With the equipment we have today, the .270 is just fine to at least a quarter mile. Despite all the stuff about extreme-range

This excellent Montana bighorn was the first wild sheep Boddington took with a .270 using his Kimber with a handloaded 140-grain Ballistic Tip. Since then, he's used the round for numerous wild sheep and goats. It works fine, just like Professor O'Connor taught.

shots on game, 440 yards is a far poke; you'd better have good conditions and know what you're doing. For sure, the .270 Win. will reach farther than that. Stated or unstated, known or unknown, we all have limits. On game, my self-imposed limit kicks in somewhere on the far side of a quarter mile. That's still .270 Win. country.

I find the century-old .270 Winchester ideal for almost all deer hunting under any conditions. O'Connor found it

perfect for mountain game, essentially deer-sized. I mostly agree. For me, long shots on sheep and goats are to be avoided — too much risk. Mountain winds are tough to read. Huge effort to get a shot, and you must start all over if you blow it. And, let's face it, mountain hunts are expensive. Minimize risk by working as hard as necessary to get a certain shot. I have used .270s for a lot of North American and some Eurasian

Boddington took this kudu on the run at about 250 yards with his Joe Balickie .270. The .270 is a fine choice for nearly the entire run of African antelopes.

The "traditional" .270 hunting cartridges, with 1:10 twist, are, left to right: .270 Winchester, .270 WSM, and .270 Weatherby Magnum, now joined by the 6.8 Western and 27 Nosler, both specified with faster rifling twists, enabling heavier bullets than ever before offered in .277-inch diameter.

If there's any controversy surrounding the .270 as a hunting cartridge, it must be its suitability for game larger than deer, specifically elk. O'Connor genuinely thought it was plenty of gun for elk. Honestly, I've never been so sure. Donna and I have taken several elk with our .270s, never a problem. Even so, I don't think it's ideal. I'm okay with the bullet diameter and velocity, energy, and ranging ability. However, even though I've seen it work well on elk, I'm more comfortable with heavier bullets.

VERSUS THE NEW .270S

Unlike the proliferation of 6.5mm, 7mm, and .30 calibers, few cartridges use the .277-inch bullet. In 1944, Roy Weatherby created the .270 Weatherby Magnum; in 2002, Winchester introduced the .270 WSM. Also in 2002, Remington introduced the 6.8mm Special Purpose Cartridge. Designed as a military alternative for the AR-15, the 6.8 SPC is a nice little round for short-range use on deer and hogs. The AR-15 action limits it to light-for-caliber 120-grain bullets, so it isn't part of this discussion as a general-purpose hunting cartridge.

The .270 Weatherby and .270 WSM are significantly faster than the .270 Winchester. They generate more energy, and I believe this can be seen in the impact on game. However, I'm not convinced the extra energy puts them in a different class on larger game. In part, this is because both use the same 1:10 twist as the old .270. Thus, they have the same bullet weight limitation, maxing out at 150 grains.

Now we have two brand new .270s: Winchester's 6.8 Western and the 27 Nosler. These break the mold. Specified for faster rifling twists, they stabilize heavier bullets than possible in previous .270 cartridges, at least to 175 grains. Thanks to these cartridges, such bullets now exist, and these cartridges propel them to meaningful velocity.

American shooters are bound and determined to split hairs. Some of us like 6.5mms, others prefer .270s, and still others are 7mm fans. Frontal area matters, but it's hard to say precisely how much more bullet diameter makes a difference. Bullet weight also matters. With, say,

sheep and goat hunting. However, some Asian mountain ranges are big and open, tough to get close. Over there, I've usually carried more powerful cartridges with heavier bullets.

For unknown reasons, I've only taken a .270 on a few African safaris. My wife, Donna, is the .270 girl; she's taken much more African game with the cartridge than I have. She has found it ideal for the full run of plains game up to zebra, which

can weigh up to 800 pounds. In the African context, where you might shoot your "plains game rifle" daily, its modest recoil is a real plus. Donna's MGA .270 weighs just 5.7 pounds scoped. At that weight, it bounces pretty good, but Donna is one of those people who is nearly impervious to recoil. She shoots it well and doesn't think it kicks. It does, but a .270 of average weight, maybe 7½ pounds, is a pussycat.

140-grain bullets at a similar velocity, it's difficult to build a case between 6.5mm, .270, or 7mm. Step up to 175-grain bullets, and there's a difference. Bullets this heavy don't exist in 6.5mm and, until recently, have not existed in .277. 7mm fans have long argued the advantage of the 7mm's heavier bullets. Put a 175-grain .277 bullet in a 6.8 Western or 27 Nosler, and performance must be essentially the same as any 7mm at similar velocity with similar bullet weight and design.

So, are the new cartridges in fast-twist barrels *better* than the grand old .270 Win.? It depends on what you want to do. Donna and I have three .270 Winchester rifles: Her light MGA, a .270 barrel for our Blaser R8, and a gorgeous Joe Balickie custom rifle—all shockingly accurate. For larger game, including elk, the new .270s with heavy bullets are superior; maybe superior for the full run of African plains game. Last year, I used a 6.8 Western on safari, shooting 162-grain bullets. Not as heavy as they come, but heavier than I can get in my .270s. The result? Awesome performance on large antelopes. For the extreme-range shooting being done today, there's no question: today's long, heavy bullets with off-the-charts Ballistic Coefficients beat anything we could ever shoot in a .270 Win.

Whether .270 Win., Weatherby, or WSM, the only way to get that heavy-bullet performance is to rebarrel or start over. My .270 barrels shoot fine, so I'm not interested in rebarreling. Most owners of the myriad .270 Win. rifles currently in use probably feel much the same. Starting over is a different story. If you're looking for a rifle primarily for elk, or if you're in the extreme range club, then maybe one of these "new .270s" is right for you.

For me, understanding the game I generally hunt and the shots I'm comfortable taking, the .270 Win. remains a favorite cartridge. It shoots flat, doesn't kick, and does its job. In my case, I've only used it for fifty years, just half of this storied cartridge's history. The older I get, the more I think Professor O'Connor was right all along. The .270 Winchester is a cartridge to start with and stay with—for the hunting and field shooting most of us do. **GD**

Donna Boddington used her pet MGA .270 with 130-grain Interlocks to take this fine desert bighorn in Mexico. As O'Connor taught us, the .270 remains an excellent choice for most mountain hunting.

Boddington used his Joe Balickie .270 Winchester to take this fine desert mule deer in Far West Texas. One shot at 300 yards with a Federal Terminal Ascent 136-grain bullet did the trick.

Gunsite Service Pistols

A new Glock Gunsite Service Pistol joins the Fink's GSG 1911 at the storied shooting academy.

›DICK WILLIAMS

When Gunsite announced the availability of a new Gunsite Glock Service Pistol (GGSP) at the famed Academy's Pro Shop, there were some unconfirmed rumors that Jeff Cooper turned over in his grave! I suspect these rumors were started by folks who had not paid proper attention to the Colonel's teachings over the years.

Colonel Cooper was a man who based his opinions on observations of actual events, not speculations about what might happen in the future. During the Leather Slap Contests at Big Bear during the 1960s (the predecessor of today's action shooting games and the inspiration for Cooper founding the original American Pistol Institute in 1976), the John Browning-designed 1911 pistol dominated the winners' circle. Paying careful attention to the techniques used in achieving success with the handguns available, Cooper developed a teaching format for the modern service pistol.

Yes, there is a new Gunsite Glock Service Pistol available at the Academy. It has both the "Bird and the Word" on top of the slide to remind you that this is indeed a serious fighting pistol! The MSRP is $1,275 and includes everything on the gun but this beautiful custom leather rig from Simply Rugged Holsters. Simply Rugged goods are available in the Gunsite Pro Shop, and if you decide you want something with your personal touch, contact Rob Leahy at Simply Rugged. He will have all the leather you dreamed of in your hands before you finish your Gunsite class.

As Gunsite Academy (the renamed American Pistol Institute) enters its 48th successful year of teaching Americans how to defend themselves with firearms, those teaching techniques—along with updates incorporating the new breed of defensive pistols, rifles, and shotguns—are still being taught at both the original site in Paulden, Arizona and selected installations around the country. One of the big items on my bucket list is to attend Gunsite's 50th Anniversary festivities.

What Colonel Cooper didn't see on the firing line (because it didn't exist in 1976) was the Glock handgun and the incredible success it would have by the year 2000 and into the new millennium. The Austrian "Tupperware Pistol," as its detractors originally called it, has been sold by the millions and is used by more police and military institutions than any other handgun on the market. During that same period, ammunition companies have invested millions of dollars to improve the terminal ballistic effects of 9mm ammunition. Combine the Glock's incredible simplicity and reliability with a magazine capacity more than double that of the 1911, and you have a defensive pistol that can't be ignored.

When the Glock became the most prevalent pistol brought to Gunsite by students, it was definitely time to make a statement. While different handguns have been sold in the Academy Pro Shop since its opening, the Gunsite Service Pistol or GSP had always been a Browning-designed 1911 chambered for the .45 ACP. Enter the Gunsite Glock Service Pistol.

One good thing about Glocks is that anyone who knows anything about

Two of the special Glock modifications are in this picture. Note the slightly enlarged and rounded FBI Magazine Release behind the triggerguard. The Minus Connector that improves the trigger pull is located inside the gun's fire control system.

handguns knows precisely what the gun looks like simply by saying "Glock." And while Gunsite added some things to the GSSP, the new gun is still instantly recognized as a Glock. If you're a serious aficionado of the Austrian pistol and the GGSP strikes you as being slightly wrong dimensionally, it's because it utilizes the shorter slide of a Model 19 on the frame of the higher-capacity Model 17. Shorter length, higher ammo capacity: sounds like a win/win combination.

The most noticeable feature of the GSSP is the inclusion of a Holosun HE509T red-dot optic mounted on top of the slide just in front of the rear sight. This was not an afterthought on the part of the Gunsite Training staff. About half the students attending these days are

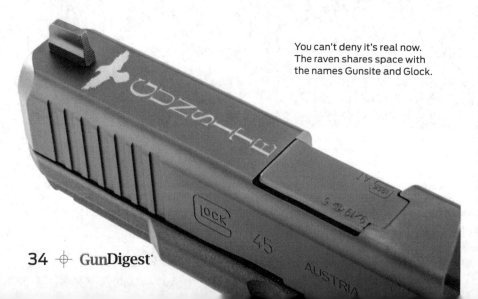

You can't deny it's real now. The raven shares space with the names Gunsite and Glock.

showing up with optics mounted on their pistols. More importantly, new shooters are performing better with guns so equipped compared to students with iron sights. In addition, police department trainers are reporting improved scores from the recruits coming through the various police academies. These are the real-world results that Colonel Cooper reviewed when he first codified the training doctrine for the modern service pistol. Upgrading one's training program to incorporate new developments in equipment and techniques is essential to maintaining proper skills, both for civilians and law enforcement/military personnel. So what if the enhanced performance is primarily the result of a generation of Americans that grew up playing video games using optics on their weapons? The improved skills demand recognition.

The Holosun 509T has a solid titanium frame for enhanced survivability and utilizes solar and battery power to run the optic. Unlike other optics, the Holosun does not use adaptor plates for mounting on the slide; it fits precisely into a slot machined into the top of the slide. The Holosun's mounting screws hold the optic to the slide; they do not see any shear loads because the Holosun frame is braced on both ends by the slide itself. Looking through the generous window

Hostage targets like this one on the Urban Scrambler do not allow misses; missing the perp can be a death sentence for the hostage.

of the 509T, you can have two presentations. One is a 32-MOA circle surrounding a conventional single 2-MOA dot. With a touch or two of the finger, you can change the presentation by eliminating the outer circle and leaving the more conventional center dot; it's your choice. When carried in your holster, the optic remains dormant. Drawing the pistol turns on the power, and it's "Bandits beware!" The tall iron sights designed to allow aimed fire over an installed suppressor are co-witnessed through the Holosun window, so the old-fashioned iron sights will always be available if needed to finish a fight.

The Gunsite Glock features a few other non-standard modifications that range from productive (i.e., improve your fighting skills) to cosmetic (i.e., gotta have that!). The fire control system

The GSSP has ambidextrous slide release (or slide lock) levers that make manual manipulations easier for left-handed shooters. Any lefty will much appreciate this in a week-long 1,000-round training class.

has a "Minus Connector." While using negative adjectives like "Minus" in describing a new gun feature is generally frowned upon in marketing circles, it's accurate. The connector reduces the trigger pull weight of the new Glock

The Lanyard Loop is a traditional feature of fighting handguns of yesteryear. Don't forget your Pith Helmet!

by something over a pound. It's still rather long and spongy, but you can feel the reduction in overall weight. I didn't do long-range precision shooting drills with the gun while at the Academy, but I think the newer, lighter trigger will be an advantage as engagement ranges increase.

The slightly enlarged and rounded FBI magazine release button was helpful in reloading drills. I can't offer any serious comment on the lanyard loop installed on the bottom rear of the grip frame. I know its purpose is to keep the gun in your possession in case you lose your grip, but I've never seen one used except in old movies featuring British troops posted in various countries around the world in the 19th and early 20th centuries. I guess the fact that I saw them used in old-time movies confirms Gunsite's "historic" rationale. And while the current and retro Gunsite logos and the word "GUNSITE" on the top of the slide and backplate may not improve your shooting skills, they always do wonders for my mood. Given the amount of Gunsite logo gear sold in the Academy Pro Shop, both the word and the bird belong on these guns!

THE 1911 GSP

Manufacturing arrangements differ for the .45 ACP GSP than the 9mm GGSP. Whereas the Gunsite Glock Service Pistols are built by Glock and delivered complete to the Gunsite Pro Shop, the 1911s are assembled onsite at the Gunsite Gunsmithy using purchased precision-built components. Seeing the first three items on the list of components for this newest standard-sized 1911 warmed my

The Holosun provides a generous viewing window, while the tall rear sight allows you to use your iron sights (that you've previously co-witnessed) in case the optics have been destroyed. Every time you present the gun, the retro raven on the backplate reminds you of your great time at Gunsite!

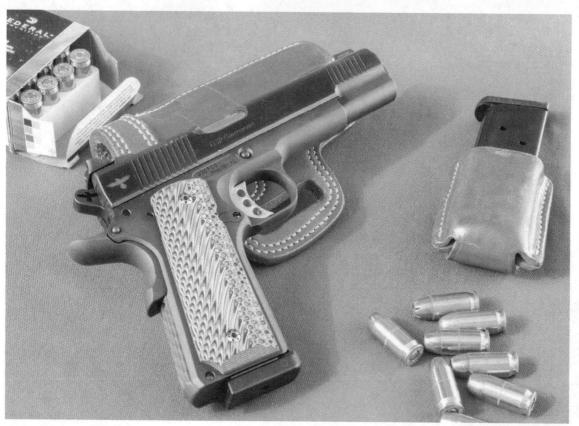

Roughly halfway through its first century of "field testing," including a couple of world wars, the 1911 was upgraded from seven rounds of FMJ ammo to eight rounds of jacketed hollow points, and it's still serving today. Does anyone care to challenge that resume?

heart: forged steel frame, forged steel slide, and hammer-forged match barrel. The Academy's on-site gunsmithy is Finks Custom Gunsmithing, and based on custom work I've had by the shop in the past, the new GSP couldn't be anything but a superb defensive pistol.

Sitting in the furnished transport case, the GSP was obviously (at least to this old 1911 shooter) a purpose-built handgun meant to save your life. An initial inspection of the weapon revealed many of the custom features I like. The extended beavertail grip safety with the oversized bulge at the base is essential for two reasons. First, any prolonged training session can result in multiple slide cuts to the web of your shooting hand without the wide flare at the top of the safety. Second, without the oversized bulge at the base of the safety, I have trouble fully disengaging the grip safety with a shooting grip that keeps my shooting hand thumb on top of the thumb safety. In an article in the late 1980s, Jeff Cooper pointed out that this phenomenon occurs with a relatively high percentage of shooters.

The iron sight setup is excellent, consisting of a Wilson Combat Battlesight with a blacked-out U-notch and a Novak front tritium yellow outline night sight. While shooting at Gunsite, Rangemaster Lew Gosnell ran us through some drills consisting of single, timed head-shots, each requiring an individual presentation from the holster. Engagement ranges began at 3 yards and backed up to 25 yards, with different times allowed at each distance. After six shots, I had five inside the snot box on the Gunsite silhouette targets and one just an inch above the dividing line. It was the best performance I've ever achieved on that exercise with any sight system—optics or irons.

I like the feel of G10 grips; they offer a rough surface without sharp edges, and a dished-out area behind the magazine release button that facilitates both speed and tactical reloads. Likewise, the scalloped main-

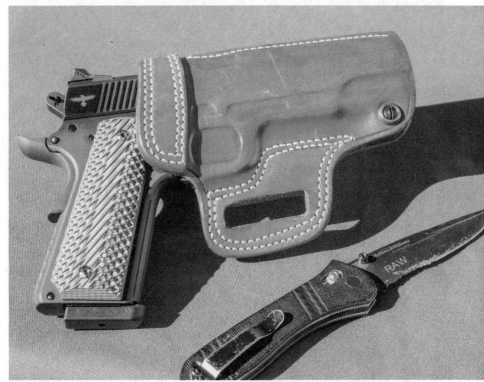

Even before the GSP, the Williams "Carry Kit" has remained small over the years, featuring just a couple of serious tools: a 1911 carried in a Galco Avenger holster and a well-worn Bladetech in a pocket.

There isn't a self-loading pistol in the world whose profile projects beauty, functionality, and simple elegance like the 1911. This Gunsite pistol's hammer skeletonized with the Academy's raven mascot takes the cool factor to another level!

Range Master Lew Gosnell and Gunsmithy owner Dave Fink give the new Gunsite Service Pistols a workout on the North Range. When handguns pass these guys' scrutiny, they are definitely serious defensive weapons.

The GSP 1911, as delivered, includes two eight-round magazines, cleaning and takedown tools, a manual, and a sample target fired at Finks Custom Gunsmith. Its MSRP is $1,799.

spring housing provided anti-slip protection and quicker shot-to-shot recovery without overly aggressive surfaces. Finally, the frontstrap's slightly rougher satin-finished surface and rather gentle vertical serrations help maintain control during recoil—a nicely done system to facilitate a faster rate of fire. Wilson Combat's single-side tactical thumb safety worked perfectly on every presentation and could easily be operated by my support hand. I can't make a case for an ambidextrous thumb safety on the GSP.

Other obvious and useful features on the GSP that most respected gunsmiths recommend include the lowered and flared ejection port, the triggerguard undercut to keep your shooting hand as close as possible to the bore axis, and throat and reliability work on a match barrel with a recessed target crown for those of us who are too clumsy to complete all our ballet lessons. Front and rear slide serrations make manual slide operations and chamber checks much easier, and a beveled mag well greatly facilitates reloads.

To paraphrase Dorothy in *The Wizard of Oz*, "There's no trigger like a 1911 trigger!" Dave Fink sets the GSP's skeletonized match trigger at 4.25 pounds with no creep. When you carry a fighting handgun with a trigger pull like this, precise shot placement becomes the predictable norm.

Fink's Custom dehorn package is a nice touch, something we're seeing less of in recent years as some custom gunsmiths seem to think that sharp edges are proof of precision machining. When you're getting close to the end of your first hundred rounds fired in a serious Gunsite handgun training class, you'll appreciate your dehorn package and the fact that you're the only student in the class who hasn't been whining at the instructor for some more bandaids and adhesive tape!

The cosmetic engraving on the 1911 GSP is slightly downsized and subdued compared to the Glock but just as pleasing. The left side of the slide has the words *Government Service Pistol* in large print. On the right side of the slide under the ejection port is the Finks gunsmithing logo and the letters *F.C.G. Paulden, AZ*, while the current Gunsite raven logo rests proudly just behind the rear slide serrations. But to me, the crown jewel is the Gunsite raven cut into the 1911's hammer. I mean, if you're going to skeletonize the hammer by making a hole in it, why should that hole be anything but the instantly recognizable (and dare I say

it) "World-famous duck of death?"

Since these are serious fighting handguns, I want to finish on defensive capabilities rather than discussing cosmetics. A group of gun writers spent three days at Gunsite with optics-equipped Glocks, going through several drills and training techniques offered in the school's classes. At my age, the winter temperatures kept me huddled over the heater in my truck until the afternoon sessions when the thermometer finally broke 40 degrees. In addition to being a California sissy, I didn't have the benefit of growing up on video games. Although I have used dot optics successfully on two of my hunting handguns, I'd never used one in a scenario where I was the prey and time was of the essence.

The 32-MOA outer circle seemed a little too busy for me, so I set the selector switch to the 2-MOA center red dot only. By the third day, I was still searching for the dot every time I pulled the Glock from the holster. Simple solution: I needed more coaching, practice, and warmer weather. A five-day Gunsite 250 class in March or April using a GGSP would sort things out. Meanwhile, knowing from handgun hunting experience the increased accuracy results you can get at ranges well beyond 25 yards, I have

installed a Holosun 509T on an extra slide for my Glock 19 and will be looking for more range time.

From my handgun hunts over the past few years, it's clear that I can make more precise shots with a handgun using red-dot optics than iron sights. However, hunting is a much different scenario than the defensive use of handguns. When hunting, you are the predator, not the prey, which allows you to choose when to take the first shot instead of reacting quickly to a threat against you or your loved ones.

I don't yet know whether or not I will switch to a red dot-equipped CCW gun full-time. I'm no Rob Leatham with a 1911, but I have acquired some reasonable skills at close range in fast-action/reaction engagements. Using an open-sight 1911 like the GSP with its superb trigger, I can make hits at longer ranges. My initial thoughts make me lean toward the ease of concealing an iron-sighted pistol, but today's holsters offer some excellent carry options that are relatively easy to hide. I suspect my decision may vary daily based on several other non-performance considerations. Regarding the choice between 9mm and .45 ACP? No, you're not sucking me into that black hole of lost discussions! **GD**

Forget the old arguments regarding 9mm vs. 45ACP; each gun has its advantages, and it's up to you to choose. Remember what's at stake.

The 9.3x62 Mauser

Otto Bock's Brainchild is a Cartridge for All Seasons

› PHIL MASSARO

Sitting a mere 60 paces from the bait tree, with the African light fading faster than my bank balance, Professional Hunter Tanya Blake and I watched the leopard climb toward its dinner. Doing my damnedest to stay calm, I settled into the rifle, took aim, and broke the trigger. Sending a 286-grain bullet from the custom 9.3x62 Mauser, I heard the projectile hit flesh, and my excitement level soared. It was my first leopard, though this was not my first experience with the 9.3x62 Mauser cartridge; it would not be my last.

on
Three Continents

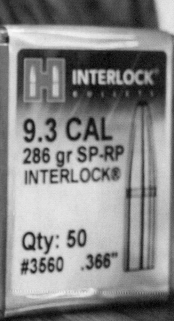

From steenbok to deer to buffalo, the 9.3x62 Mauser can do it all.

Otto Bock
(1856–1926),
inventor of the
9.3x62 Mauser.

Otto Bock †

Am 18. Mai verstarb unser langjähriges Mitglied, Herr Hoflieferant

Otto Bock

kurz vor Vollendung seines 70. Lebensjahres. In dem Verstorbenen betrauern wir einen treuen Anhänger unserer Organisation, der eine Reihe von Jahren unserem Vorstande, als Schatzmeister und 2. Vorsitzender angehört hat.

Das Andenken des lieben Kollegen werden wir stets in Ehren halten.

Der Vorstand:
Paul Schmidt, 1. Vorsitzender.

Bring up the classic cartridges taken on safaris across Eastern and Southern Africa in the early 20th century, and you'll hear names like Rigby, Jeffery, Holland & Holland, Westley Richards, and Gibbs. But despite the volumes written about those cartridges, the German 9.3x62mm handled a good portion of the hunting work. That's especially true in the colonies of German East Africa (later Tanganyika and ultimately Tanzania after independence) and German South West Africa (which would become Namibia in 1990). And much like the Mauser Model 98 bolt-action repeating rifle for which it was designed, in the spirit of German engineering, the 9.3x62mm Mauser cartridge shines in its combination of simplicity and effectiveness. Let's dig into the history and design of the 9.3x62 and see what it's good for and how it stacks up against its competition.

Otto Bock, riflemaker and taxidermist from Berlin, Ger-

Ron Petty and the author with the big-bodied "*keiler*" boar Massaro took in Poland. He used a Heym SR21 chambered in 9.3x62, loading Norma's 230-grain EcoStrike ammo.

HISTORIC
Cartridges
in Perspective

many (born 1856, died May 18, 1926), is credited with developing the 9.3x62mm cartridge, which, by all accounts, came onto the scene in 1905. The 8x57mm and 7x57mm cartridges, which were developed in the late 19th century, were undoubtedly revolutionary and, to this day, remain perfectly viable hunting rounds. But, they have a limit. While they are fine for everything on the European continent, they lack the bullet weight and diameter to handle the giant fauna of the African continent. Yes, I am well aware that both have been successfully used to take any and all game animals—W.D.M. 'Karamojo' Bell popularized the 7x57 for elephants—but there were also a good many unsuccessful ventures, especially with the big beasts. Bock aimed for a Mauser-esque design that could be taken to remote locations and reliably handle the world's biggest and baddest beasts.

In that first decade of the 20th century, with smokeless powder and jacketed bullets relatively new to the scene, the now long-accepted standards and minimums were yet to be established, as the heavy lead slugs and moderate-at-best velocities of the 19th-century sporting cartridges gave way to smaller bore diameters. Many European military powers had transitioned to much smaller cartridges, with Germany adopting the 8x57, Spain and others leaning on the 7x57, Scandinavia developing the 6.5x55, and America dumping the .45-70 Government for the .30-40 Krag, .30-'01 Springfield, .30-'03 Springfield, and ultimately the .30-'06 Springfield. Many traveling sportsmen of this era took advantage of the military cartridges, with U.S. President Theodore Roosevelt taking the .30-'03 Springfield on safari in 1909.

With the stage set for using smaller cartridges in military applications, it wouldn't be long before they were used in the hunting fields. Otto Bock took much from the design of the previous military rounds, especially the 7x57 and 8x57 Mauser. The 9.3x62mm Mauser uses a case length of—you guessed it—62mm, or 2.441 inches; coupled with a cartridge overall length of 3.291 inches, you have a round that sits perfectly in a Mauser 98 receiver. The bullet diameter is a nominal 9.3mm or .366 inch, and the rimless

The 9.3x62 was designed to fit the Mauser 98 rifle, sharing the same head diameter as the earlier 7x57 and 8x57 Mauser cartridges.

A quick note about the muzzle velocities of cartridges developed in this era: the velocity figures of many of our classic cartridges that have been adopted and regurgitated as 'absolute' are often skewed. First, the test barrels used for establishing the advertised velocities were sometimes longer than usual. I have seen test data from that era where barrels as long as 30 or 32 inches were used to establish muzzle velocities for a particular cartridge, and it isn't hard to see where those figures would drop off when a sporting rifle with a barrel of 24 or even 26 inches was employed. Second, the means of measuring velocity at the turn of the 20th century, when Bock was crafting the 9.3x62, were nowhere near as precise as today's tools. Ballistic pendulums and even the earliest electronic chronographs often gave erroneous data or, at best, an approximation of velocities. Lastly, the smokeless propellants used then were extremely sensitive to fluctuations in temperature, and a cartridge developed in the cooler climate of England or continental Europe might see a higher muzzle velocity when transported to the tropics of Africa or the heat of India.

As an interesting aside, my Zimbabwean friend, Dr. Kevin Robertson, known in hunting circles as "Doctari," obtained a supply of vintage .416 Rigby ammunition in sealed tins. Instead of generating the well-known muzzle velocity of 2,350 fps, the vintage ammunition measured just over 2,100 fps. So, while we know our forefathers used Cartridge X with a particular bullet weight at a specific speed, the truth is, quite often, they got the job done with less velocity and energy than even they knew.

cartridge uses a shoulder angle of 17.5 degrees for headspacing. That rim measures .470 inch—slightly smaller than the .473 of the 7x57, 8x57, and Springfield variants—which will still fit perfectly into a 98 Mauser bolt face. The case has minimal body taper, measuring .451 inch in diameter at the shoulder, yet feeds wonderfully from a box magazine.

The initial 9.3x62 factory loads included a 285-grain bullet at a muzzle velocity of 2,150 fps.

Bock's 9.3x62mm initially sent a 285-grain bullet at 2,150 fps, offering just shy of 3,000 ft-lbs of energy. That was mild recoil compared to the larger cartridges usually associated with dangerous game, especially considering it was housed in a lightweight rifle. Compared to the British-made sporting rifles chambered for medium bores like the .350 Rigby, .318 Westley Richards, and .333 Jeffery, the simplistic Mauser 98 chambered for the 9.3x62 must have had an attractive price tag to those German emigrants.

The cartridge was popular across Eastern and Southern Africa—again, affordability and availability played a role—and quietly took all varieties of game animals. In his excellent book *African Rifles and Cartridges*, John 'Pondoro' Taylor writes, "It was immediately acceptable and has ever since been the most widely used medium bore in Africa. This, of course, was because being German, it could be sold much more cheaply than could a similar Mauser-actioned weapon of British manufacture. It's a simply splendid general-purpose cartridge, and its shells could be bought in almost any store throughout the length and breadth of Africa … Men just take it for granted, and it goes steadily on its way like some honest old farm horse." Coming from Taylor, that is a ringing endorsement.

After the First World War, 285-grain ammunition for the 9.3x62 saw an increase in muzzle velocity to somewhere between 2,350 and 2,400 fps, where it stands today, increasing the muzzle energy to over 3,500 ft-lbs. Though the 285-grain

(and now 286-grain) slugs were the projectile that earned the 9.3x62mm Mauser cartridge its fine reputation, today, there are many bullet weights to choose from, both lighter and heavier, and in many different conformations.

Though I had handloaded many configurations of the 9.3x62mm for clients and friends over the years, my first personal hunting experience with the cartridge came on a driven hunt for wild boar in Poland. A driven hunt is a unique event and can be quite foreign to American hunters who are accustomed to either ambush from a blind or spot-and-stalk. On the driven hunt, hound dogs and beaters (each with their own unique "*whoop!*" or "*hai-yah!*" call) drive or beat a thick patch of vegetation, be it brush patches, thick woods, standing corn, or other crop fields where game animals might hide out.

With the hunters spread apart between 100 and 150 yards and cognizant of others' positions for safety reasons, most shots are at running game. Thus,

A Heym SR21 bolt-action in 9.3x62 on loan from Lukasz Dzierzanowski in Poland topped with an Aimpoint reflex sight. This setup is an excellent choice for the fast-action "driven hunts" popular across Europe.

Norma's EcoStrike 230-grain lead-free load is well suited to smaller game at longer distances.

the rifles are usually topped with a low-power scope, a red-dot reflex sight, or good old iron sights. The event was sponsored by Norma Ammunition, which had just released its TipStrike and EcoStrike ammunition lines, and my friend, Łukasz Dzierżanowski, provided the firearms. He had several interesting choices, including a handy little double rifle chambered for 8x57 IRS and a Heym Model 21 in 9.3x62mm, topped with an Aimpoint red-dot sight.

With that Heym 21 in hand, loaded with Norma's 230-grain EcoStrike load, and standing on the edge of an open field with the beaters and hounds in the thick stuff, the first wild boars broke cover. Like here in the U.S., Europe's wild boar (same genus and species as our feral hogs) are prolific breeders, and the land-owners prefer that the hunters take as many as possible. I took a sow and piglet with the straight-pull Heym, but when the *keiler* broke cover, he had my immediate attention. Twice the size of any other hog I'd seen to that point, he was the kind of boar anyone would be happy with; as Jack O'Connor so eloquently

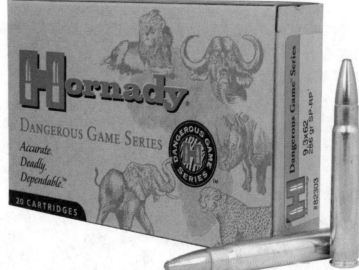

Hornady's 286-grain InterLock bullet in the Dangerous Game ammo line gives you a quality cup-and-core bullet at a moderate velocity. You might opt for a premium bullet for Cape buffalo and similar-sized game, but it's very effective for everything else. Photo: Hornady

stated: "the big ones look big."

The 150-yard running shot hit just at the back of the lungs, and the game-keeper dispatched the beast out in an open field (hunters aren't allowed to leave their station while the hunt is on); when I got to the boar, his actual size truly impressed me. He had good teeth, though one of his tusks was broken at the gum

line, and the keepers and beaters told me he weighed 330 pounds; he was an old warrior who'd been through the wringer, and his teeth are on my wall to this day. While I'm sure I could've killed a boar of that size with a smaller cartridge—say a .308 Winchester or .30-'06 Springfield—I sure didn't mind the extra bullet weight and diameter.

While the 230-grain bullet is on the lighter end of the spectrum, the Norma EcoStrike is a lead-free design and will hold together well on thick-skinned game, though it is too light for Cape buffalo, Asiatic water buffalo, and the like. It will make a sound choice for black bears, elk, and even moose. Cruising at a velocity of 2,625 fps, you can zero the 230- to 232-grain bullets at 200 yards, which strike just over 11 inches low at 300 yards. Norma discontinued the 230-grain EcoStrike, opting instead for a 250-grain variety of that bullet, but still lists the Oryx, Vulcan, and Jaktmatch bullets at that weight for the 9.3x62.

Sitting down to plan our safari at the Dallas Safari Club Convention in early 2023 with Tanya Blake (interestingly, the only fully licensed female Professional Hunter in Zimbabwe), I told her I was ready to try the chess game that is leopard hunting. Blake is a cat specialist–though she also handles the other dangerous game species swimmingly–in that she has an affinity for getting what may be the apex predator to believe that it has found and taken over another leopard's kill, and have that cat come back in

daylight to offer a shot. We decided to hunt the Chirisa Block, a National Parks concession I'd hunted back in 2018, as it offered a reasonable chance at a leopard and the potential for Cape buffalo and plains game species.

Our agreed-upon plan was to focus on the leopard, with her doing a few days of pre-baiting before my arrival, and perhaps try for buffalo or kudu and other plains game if time allowed. We'd made the deal, sorted the dates, and firmed up the plan.

It was three aisles over when a shrill whistle caught my attention, followed by the utterance of my last name. It was none other than Todd Ramirez, bespoke riflemaker, waving me over to his booth. "I'd love to have you hunt with one of my rifles; I think you'd appreciate the design and build." Todd, I couldn't possibly have agreed more. Discussing my upcoming safari and the possible species on the list, Ramirez recommended the 9.3x62mm. Its recoil level is low enough for the precision shots required for a leopard at last light, yet it possesses enough bullet weight and horsepower to take Cape buffalo, eland, zebra, and other plains game.

And while many other countries set the minimum caliber for any dangerous game species at the .375 bores, Zimbabwe accepts the 9.3mm cartridges for all species.

I settled on three different bullets for this safari, as I'd have several opportunities. With a tom leopard as the main focus, I wanted a projectile stiff enough to guarantee penetration at any angle yet soft enough up front to give the quick energy transfer that works so well on a thin-skinned cat. The Hornady InterLock checked all the boxes, and I handloaded that bullet in Lapua cases over a charge of 57.5 grains of Reloder 15, sparked by a Federal Gold Medal Match GM210M large rifle match primer. The Ramirez rifle would put three of those Hornady spitzers into a group measuring right around ¾ MOA, more than accurate enough for a shot on a cat in a bait tree, guaranteed to be less than 100 yards away. My Oehler 35P chronograph showed those Hornadys leaving the muzzle at 2,310 fps.

For the possibility of a Cape buffalo, I opted for a pair of factory loads: Federal Premium's 286-grain Barnes TSX load

Massaro handloaded 286-grain Hornady InterLocks in Lapua cases to use in the Todd Ramirez custom rifle for his leopard safari.

The fruits of the safari team's labor and the 9.3x62mm Mauser: one big, fully mature tom leopard and a hunter with an irremovable smile.

at 2,360 fps, in its Safari line as my soft point, and Nosler's 286-grain monolithic solid at 2,400 fps for backup. This rifle liked the Barnes TSX, making nice little ½-MOA groups, with Nosler solids printing just under 1 MOA. Sadly, the buffalo didn't read the script, and the allotted time for that hunt ran out without a shot opportunity.

The leopard was a different story. Four days into checking baits, we saw that one of the bait sites just off the Sengwa River had been hit; the zebra leg had been noticeably chewed, and we made a beeline for the trail cameras. The SD cards revealed not one, but two leopards had fed on that particular bait–a female had come in first, followed by a very good-sized male. We immediately built a

blind and prepared to sit on the bait that afternoon. Because the Chirisa Block is part of Zimbabwe's National Parks, leopards may be baited but not taken with artificial light. In other words, we could only shoot in daylight, which posed an additional challenge.

The second day after the cats showed up, the camera indicated that the big tom had stayed on the bait until almost 8:00 a.m. (a rarity), so after sitting in the blind that evening with no results, we decided to get up very early and sit the morning. No cat–he had climbed out of the tree a half-hour before dawn. But that evening, after not feeding all day (and as Blake had predicted), Mr. Spots came into the bait tree, making for one of the most intense encounters of my hunting career. At the

very last light, I got the green light to shoot and held the Leupold's crosshairs just behind the tom's shoulder. Blake saw the cat get knocked out of the tree, but she also saw him slowly trot away. To make a long story short, there was a harrowing follow-up into some very thick vegetation in the dark and the realization that it was wisest to mark the position and come back in the morning.

Would I lose the cat to the hyenas? There was significant blood, but that riverine bush was just too thick to guarantee that no one would get hurt. The following morning, Blake and her trackers belly crawled into that same matted inky-dark patch, with yours truly and our game scout waiting as tense as a bowstring on the other side of that patch for a wounded leopard to boil out. The report of her .416 Rigby was the sweetest sound I could've heard, and the cat–still alive but visibly on his last legs–was sorted. My bullet had gone just behind the lungs, passing through, and it was probably the fact that he was alive overnight that prevented the hyenas from tearing him apart. The celebration that ensued in camp was fantastic.

Heading home into the fall hunting season here in New York, I wanted to use the Ramirez 9.3x62 for our whitetail deer and black bear season. The Catskill Mountains are home to both large deer and black bears (though, admittedly, nei-

ther species would require a 9.3x62mm), and as I wanted to test the Federal Premium Barnes TSX load, I opted for that 286-grain monometal hollowpoint. While I had the largest set of black bear scat and spoor, I didn't have a crack at him, but a respectable eight-point buck offered a quartering-away shot at 160 yards through the open woods on the edge of a small meadow. Even in the rifle's recoil, I saw the deer fall out of the scope as if pole-axed.

While it's only happened on occasion, imagine my surprise when we recovered the bullet from the deer's front shoulder. Despite the monometal construction and the fantastic sectional density, the bullet

Want the best penetration from your 9.3x62? Use the Federal Safari load with the 286-grain Woodleigh Hydrostatically Stabilized Solid; it is one of the best choices for thick-skinned game. Photo: Federal Premium

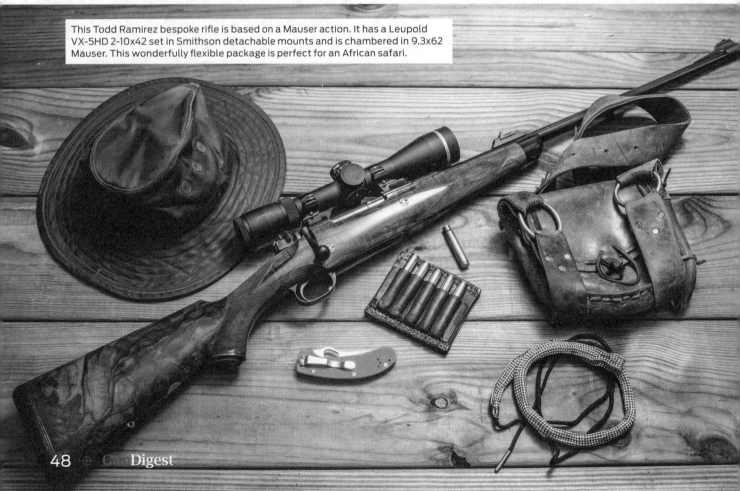

This Todd Ramirez bespoke rifle is based on a Mauser action. It has a Leupold VX-5HD 2-10x42 set in Smithson detachable mounts and is chambered in 9.3x62 Mauser. This wonderfully flexible package is perfect for an African safari.

Massaro used the Ramirez 9.3x62 for this New York whitetail buck; a 286-grain Barnes TSX quickly filled the tag.

expanded 1.68x its original diameter and retained 100 percent of its weight. I doubt I could repeat the exercise, but it was neat to see the recovered slug.

9.3X62 VS. CONTEMPORARIES

With a case similar in configuration to the .30-'06 family, immediate comparisons will be made to the .35 Whelen and, because of the similar bullet diameter, to the .375 H&H Magnum. Both are logical comparisons. The .35 Whelen is closer in appearance, yet like many of the .35-caliber cartridges, it uses a 1:16 twist rate, so the bullet weight for factory loads tends to top out at 250 grains, with many built around the 200- and 225-grain slugs.

I find very little difference between the .35 Whelen and the 9.3x62 in the recoil department. However, I find that the .375 H&H—while it has an undeniably universal appeal—ramps up the recoil significantly, which is to be expected with the 300- to 400-fps velocity increase. The .375 H&H also offers additional bullet weight, with the most popular choice

being the 300-grain slugs. And while the lovable belted cartridge remains the do-all choice globally, it requires a magnum-length receiver.

What about the .375 Ruger? It checks many of the same boxes as the 9.3x62 while offering the heavier slugs of the .375-inch bore, yet in a long-action rifle. It makes the caliber minimum for dangerous game that many countries, including Zambia and Tanzania, have implemented. Still, the 9.3x62 is easier on the shoulder. The 9.3x64 Brenneke is just a bit longer and 22 years younger but operates at a higher pressure and gives a decided velocity boost; trying to find any ammunition for the 9.3x64 is an impossibility these days, though. Designed for single-shots and double rifles, the 9.3x74R is a longer, rimmed cartridge and is the ballistic twin of the 9.3x62 Mauser. If you like a double, the 9.3x74R makes sense, but in a repeating rifle, the 9.3x62mm makes more sense. The .370 Sako, also known as the 9.3x66mm, performs like the .375 H&H Magnum but

has all but faded into obscurity; Federal Premium had two listed loads, but a recent search shows them as discontinued.

In Africa, the 9.3x62 might not be as popular as the .375 H&H Magnum or considered a stopping rifle among Professional Hunters whose duty is to clean up the messes we hunters make. But it's funny when you start speaking to local hunters in many African countries (especially those with a strong German influence) and seeing how many use the 9.3x62 as their personal rifle for hunting.

Here in America, the 9.3x62 Mauser is not a very popular cartridge for reasons I cannot explain. Its .366-inch bore diameter is close to our beloved .35s, and the cartridge will fit comfortably in the rifles we love most. I think a synthetic stock bolt-action, with a controlled round feed action and weather-proof metal, would make a great choice for an Alaskan rifle, black bear over bait, or an elk hunt. While not a speed demon, it's a perfectly viable 300-yard gun, and up close for brown bears in the thick stuff it has the

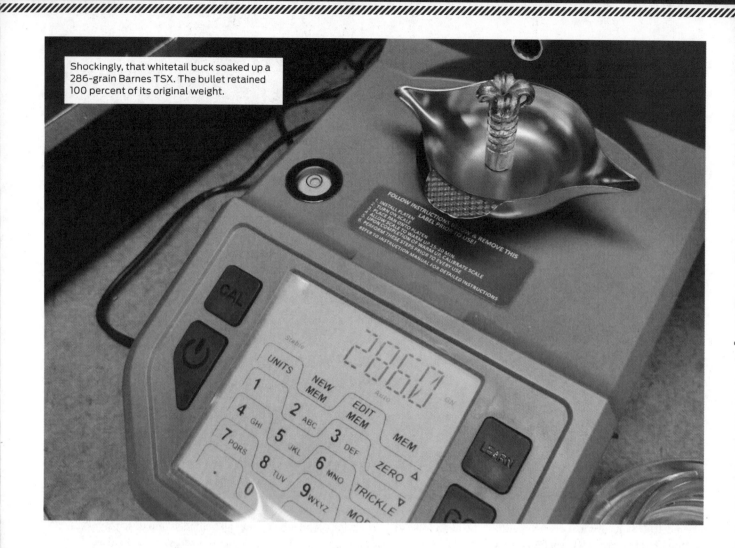

Shockingly, that whitetail buck soaked up a 286-grain Barnes TSX. The bullet retained 100 percent of its original weight.

payload to save your bacon, with a recoil level that allows you to get back on target quickly for a follow-up shot.

The 9.3x62 Mauser compares favorably to those other revered cartridges and pairs well with the larger dangerous game rounds. It is a perfect choice as a light rifle that could pull double duty on safari.

FACTORY LOADS AND HANDLOADS
There are many factory loads available for the 9.3x62mm, including the Hornady Custom 286-grain stuff, Federal Premium's Woodleigh Hydro and Swift A-Frame (both at 286 grains), a quartet of factory loads from Nosler, including 286-grain Partitions and Solids, and 250-grain AccuBond and lead-free E-Tip bullets. Norma loads the 250-grain EcoStrike, the Oryx at 232 and 286 grains, and the heavy 325-grain Oryx at a muzzle velocity of 2,231 fps, though I haven't seen much available here in the U.S. as of late. The latter load would

serve as a proper stopping cartridge in the 9.3x62.

If you handload your ammunition, the 9.3x62 Mauser opens all kinds of doors for you. Barnes has the 250- and 286-grain TSX, the 250-grain TTSX (the polymer-tipped variant), and the excellent Banded Solid at 250 and 286 grains. Hornady offers the 286-grain InterLock I took the leopard with, as well as the 300-grain DGS (Dangerous Game Solid), and Swift has its A-Frame soft point at 250 and 300 grains, as well as the Breakaway Solid at 286 grains. Nosler has its proven Partition bullet at 286 grains and the E-Tip and AccuBond at 250 grains. Woodleigh produces its Hydrostatically Stabilized Solid at 232 and 286 grains and the Weldcore soft point at 250, 286, and 320 grains, giving a flexible lineup for the 9.3mm bores.

The 9.3x62 likes powders in the medium to slower burn rate range, like Reloder 15, which served me so well.

However, I've also had great results with Hodgdon's H414, Varget, H4350, IMR 4064, IMR 4320, and Norma 202. I spark all my 9.3x62 loads with Federal's GM210M large rifle match primer or CCI's 200 large rifle primer. Quality cases are available from Nosler, Prvi Partizan, and Lapua.

IN CONCLUSION
Once a hunter wanders above .30 caliber, things can get confusing, as there is a lot of competition and overlap. You may ask yourself: Will my heavier cartridge make a safari to Africa? Or will my cartridge be asked to handle the bigger species of North America? Either way, even if we're talking about the .30-'06 Springfield, bullets weighing 220 grains can easily be employed, so choosing a cartridge that offers a bullet weight range starting where the .30s leave off would make sense.

Cartridges such as the .458 Winchester Magnum, .458 Lott, .450 Rigby, and .460

Weatherby Magnum play a prominent role as a stopping rifle for dangerous game species. Still, they don't offer much flexibility for other species. The .416s and .404s are a bit more flexible while retaining the possibility of 450-grain bullets and, therefore, can still be used as a stopping gun. But I think the 9.3x62—much like the .375 Holland & Holland Magnum—can wear two hats.

The 9.3x62 is used in Europe for moose, hogs, deer species and more; it is used in Africa for any plains game and functions as an all-around dangerous game cartridge. I have not personally used the 9.3x62 on Cape buffalo or elephants, but I have loaded ammunition for those purposes, and it worked just fine. Of course, the hunters who used the 9.3x62 had a Professional Hunter with a larger bore to back them up. Even so, for the last 120 years, Otto Bock's brainchild has been consistently putting even the largest mammals in the salt.

While I am an unabashed fan of the .375 H&H Magnum and have claimed it is the most useful cartridge ever designed, the 9.3x62 is perhaps only second by a nose. Had many of the game laws not decreed the .375-inch bore as the legal minimum, or perhaps if Winchester had picked up the 9.3x62 Mauser for the Model 70 in 1939 (making both American rifles and ammunition available), things might have been radically different.

I will confidently end with this: if I were without luggage or rifles on an African safari or Alaskan adventure and offered a 9.3x62mm Mauser to use, I wouldn't bat an eyelash. **GD**

On the left, the 9.3x62 Mauser, and on the right, the .375 H&H Magnum; these are two cartridges that can handle any big game species yet are surprisingly easy on the shoulder.

Three lead-free 9.3x62 factory loads: a 286-grain Barnes TSX Federal Premium, a 286-grain Nosler Solid monometal bullet, and a 250-grain Nosler Expansion Tip.

Does Size Matter?

A comprehensive look at the four quintessential EDC pistol sizes.

›FRANK MELLONI

Sometimes, I look back at my life and realize it's a series of ironic twists of fate. For instance, who would believe living in New York would position me to learn more about concealed carry equipment than in a less restrictive state? For as bountiful as they are, New York gun laws seem to be shrouded in a mystique akin only to the deepest-rooted secret society.

For instance, before the recent gun law changes, every pistol permit allowed some form of concealed carry. Nearly everywhere outside the five boroughs allowed you to carry a handgun on your way to or from the range and even make stops along the way. Without getting into too much detail, the description of these stops could be stretched to allow for everyday carry. Furthermore, daily pistol evaluations allowed me to test-carry hundreds of options, as my day-to-day operations always involved a trip to the range. Lastly, as the Northeast experiences all four seasons, I've also had ample opportunity to work on concealment in clothing for nearly every weather condition imaginable.

There's something to be said for a
firearm and cartridge conversion that
fits in the palm of your hand.

A GUN FOR EVERYONE

I mentioned a "recent change" to New York's laws, which only increased my time with concealed carry equipment. That change is the legendary *Bruen* decision, which overturned an unconstitutional law New York had on the books for over 100 years. In bitter defeat, the lawmakers enacted the Concealed Carry Improvement Act, which, like many recent bills, does something completely different from what it implies. This "improvement" replaced the "may issue" scheme with a laundry list of requirements, including the infamous 18-hour Mandatory Training Program.

As the owner of Renaissance Firearms Instruction, we rose to the state's call for instructors while using the proceeds to sue them over this equally unconstitutional set of laws. In the first year alone, we put hundreds of students through training and have seen and heard the many stories behind the decisions for their firearm purchases. Sadly, many of them ended up with the wrong handgun.

By "wrong" handgun, I mean that their dress or lifestyle didn't support the comfortable concealment of the gun. That pistol was often placed in their hands by a spouse, buddy, or a helpful gun store clerk whose firearms experience is limited to stretching pistols across a counter. The truth is, only one person can choose the best carry pistol for your needs—you. Now, there are brand and cartridge fanatics who make this claim as if it's part of their religion; our instructors don't fall into this dogma. No, not a single one of us believes that Gunmaker X is the "only" one you can trust your life to or that Thor himself made cartridge .XX that kills both the body and the soul.

YOUR BODY, YOUR CHOICE

First, consider the most critical factor: the handgun's general size. Before I go any further, let's digest that last line, as it's one of the few absolutes I write or teach. Before choosing a handgun brand, action style, and even chambering, you must ensure you can conceal it. Concurrently, this should be the only reason to consider carrying a minimalist firearm.

Compact guns are *not* made explicitly for compact people. That being said, if you are about to buy a pocket pistol or a snub-nosed revolver for your wife because it's a good "girl's gun," stop. She needs to be in the gun store when the decision is made. Moreover, holster options should be presented to her beforehand so she can start thinking about how and where she plans to carry it. Don't forget, she may have a compelling reason for off-body carry, and if that is the case, she can conceal just about anything. Therefore, don't immediately dismiss full-sized options and their numerous advantages.

As I type this, I remember a female student's delight when I replaced her ultra-compact magnum revolver with a government-profile 1911. Not only was she hitting her target, but she also enjoyed the mitigated recoil that comes

Many believe in the old dependable wheelgun. Improvements like moon-clip capability help level their capacity shortcomings.

BLACK HILLS AMMUNITION FACTORY NEW

.38 SPECIAL
125 Gr. JHP +P

The Ruger LCP Max is still easier to pocket than George Costanza's wallet.

with an extra pound of steel. On the other side of the spectrum, ditch any ego you might have to "carry like a man," as a gun that is too heavy or bulky often gets left at home. Having a good pocket pistol is a must for days like these. Naturally, there are classes of handguns in between these two extremes, and understanding them is the focus of this article.

With that, I've divided concealed carry handgun sizes into four easy-to-digest categories, each with a pair of my favorites to highlight their strengths and weaknesses.

FULL-SIZED HANDGUNS

Starting with the largest, consider the oft-overlooked benefits of the full-sized handgun. For argument's sake, I consider this any pistol with a barrel approaching the 5-inch mark.

The most obvious advantage of plus-sized handguns is their increased sight radius. The farther the sights are stretched out, the more inherently ac-

curate a firearm will be. To hammer this point home, barrel length is restricted in most pistol shooting sports, as it may present an unfair advantage. Think of sights as marks you made for drawing a straight and level line; the farther apart the dots, the better the chance of that happening.

Longer pistols also point better. Compare pointing with a ruler to pointing with a yardstick. The longer yardstick will get you on target faster and, in essence, become a crude way of aiming when you can't see your sights or forget to use them under stress.

GOD SPOKE, MOSES LISTENED

No discussion of fighting pistols would be complete without John Moses Browning. Responsible for the lion's share of modern firearms patents, many believe that handgun perfection was achieved in 1911 when the military adopted his famous design. Over 100 years later, the iconic 1911 pistol is still one of the best-

selling in the country, and rightfully so. Eight rounds (or more) of heavy-hitting .45 ACP will undoubtedly handle any two-legged threat, and its recoil is only marginally greater than 9mm Luger.

One of the best balances of cost to quality in 1911s is the Springfield Mil-Spec, which delivers the full 1911 experience without investing in all the extras. This makes it a great gun to tinker with, and some consider it a blank canvas. To that end, I butchered mine to the point of needing a professional to step in. Sending it off to Nighthawk for "the full treatment," returned a handgun with refined checkered front and backstraps, a tuned trigger, and an overall accuracy boost. When loaded with Hornady's 185-grain American Gunner load, I can expect 25-yard five-shot groups that measure less than 2 inches. That's impressive for a target pistol; however, considering these loads generate over 400 ft-lbs of energy at the muzzle, it becomes obvious why this firearm will live on forever.

THEY JUST HIT DIFFERENT

Although not the rule, larger guns are typically better suited to handle more powerful cartridges. Now, living in bear country, I realize that humans are not the only threat out there, and I am no longer at the top of the food chain. Whenever I think of John Browning, I envision him sharing a bottle of bourbon with Col. Jeff Cooper as they beam a ray of light down upon the gates at Gunsite Academy. The two men understood that handguns needed more energy, although they differed on the best way to achieve it.

Where Browning preferred the slow and heavy nature of the .45 ACP, Col. Cooper thought slender and fast was the ticket with his 10mm Auto. This spicy round is good medicine for black bears and can even defeat intermediate barriers, turning cover into mere concealment in a gunfight. Ironically, the go-to platform for this cartridge is an appropriately chambered 1911, but a few years ago, I think Smith & Wesson nailed it with its M&P 10mm 2.0.

Heavy is the nature of larger rounds, especially when you have 15+1 on deck, so the polymer frame of this beast makes it quite manageable. Through superior ergonomics and balancing, the recoil isn't half of what you'd expect, either. Like many other M&P pistols, it's built with interchangeable backstraps to tailor to your mitt. It even accepts a red-dot optic, making it an excellent late-night or early-morning hiking companion. Twenty-five-yard groups in the 2- to 3-inch range are the norm with this firearm, and I have found that Federal's 180-grain Trophy Bonded Bear Claw load can consistently meet this benchmark while producing 520 ft-lbs of muzzle energy. Loaded for bear has a new meaning.

THE RUB

Of course, there aren't any free lunches in life. Larger guns typically come with larger grips, which could present a few different problems. Abandon the adage "buy what feels comfortable" and get

Smith & Wesson's 10mm M&P is an excellent woods-carry gun, among other things.

Springfield makes 1911s from mil-spec to custom, while Nighthawk is all high-end.

what feels right instead. Most pistols feel comfortable, which is why salesmen love saying that. Take the handling opportunity to establish a proper two-handed grip. If you don't know what that is, a shooting lesson should be your initial investment. That means a lesson from a professional instructor, not going out with a friend who's "really into it."

Once you have your hands on the gun, see if you can activate the controls, rack the slide, and after ensuring it's unloaded, smoothly press the trigger. If not, keep looking.

Remember that you may be limited to outside-the-waistband (OWB) carry, a shoulder holster, or an off-body option. Go through your day and ensure you

wear the proper clothing to conceal a pistol carried in this fashion.

COMPACT HANDGUNS

The next step down in size brings us to what I consider the most ambiguous of them all: the compact handgun. Being somewhere in the middle, this class has a habit of swallowing up guns that many consider full-sized, as well as those that are better filed under the micro heading discussed next.

This category has changed how I look at things, thus bumping smaller revolvers into this class. As for categorizing semi-autos, it comes down to the grip more than the barrel for me. However, if you prefer to consider barrel length, it should

pass the 3-inch mark but shouldn't exceed 4.5 inches. Pistols that fit into this box can be carried in more ways than their larger brethren while offering excellent recoil mitigation and shot recovery. Let's dive in with a few options you might have missed.

THE ALUMI-GLOCK

I have a buddy who's in love with Glock pistols. However, before the romance matures, he must replace the sights, work on the trigger, and swap out the recoil spring, guide rod, and barrel. After this process, he modifies the grip and triggerguard before stippling the frame and Cerakoting the slide. Only then does he deem it perfect, save the grip angle

Compact handguns make excellent range companions and conceal fine for many people.

and frame flex. If you're like him, it's fair to say that you appreciate what Glock represents but feel there are better ways to get there.

If that's the case, the Live Free Armory AMP (Aluminum Match-Grade Pistol) is for you. As the name suggests, the frame is constructed from aircraft-grade aluminum, retaining the weight-saving properties of polymer without the flimsiness. It's angled to feel more like a 1911 in the hand, complete with interchangeable stocks and is compatible with Glock-style magazines. Unlike most of its Austrian inspirers, it comes milled for a red-dot right out of the box while featuring a sturdy fiber-optic front sight. If you choose a flush-fit G17 mag, the AMP's capacity is 15+1, putting it on par with other pistols in its class. Better still, you can pump the round count up to 34 or even 51 if you don't mind things looking a little crazy. I doubt you'd ever be able to conceal either of these options, but boy is that fun on the range!

The Live Free Armory (LFA) AMP or Aluminum Match-Grade Pistol combines the best features of a Glock with a 1911 grip angle.

In my experience, the AMP likes Remington's 147-grain Golden Saber Bonded the best of everything I've ever fed them. These fly below the sound barrier yet yield 329 ft-lbs of energy. I'd classify the recoil as more of a slow push than a snappy lift, making it enjoyable to shoot. The sights do an excellent job in the accuracy department, allowing for 2- to 2.75-inch groups at 25 yards when I do my part. Best of all, it fits in nearly any Glock 19 holster, so carry options are plentiful.

DO A WHEELIE
Although fading from popularity, there is still plenty of allure to carrying the classic snub-nose revolver. If you are fond of smaller grips, they meet that need and are simple to load and unload. The argument still stands that they are more reliable; however, it is losing ground as semi-autos have never been more dependable.

The test of time has always been the most powerful qualifier in my book, so it's hard to argue with the Smith & Wesson J-Frame. The latest rendition,

the Model 442 Pro Series, is a spin on the classic design and is cut for moon clips. Being able to drop five rounds in simultaneously hastens reload speeds to nearly a semi-auto level and makes range days a bit more productive, as you'll spend more time shooting. Using aluminum alloy for the frame, S&W delivers this worthy CCW option at a scant 14.6 ounces, making it one of the lightest .38 Special offerings on the market. The 442 Pro is rated for "continuous" +P use, so I like to practice with what I carry.

Black Hills Ammunition makes a fantastic 125-grain jacketed hollowpoint that clocks an acceptable velocity of 875 fps from the abbreviated 1.88-inch barrel. At the muzzle, this works out to 212 ft-lbs of energy, which is still adequate to handle a human threat; I just wouldn't count on it for the long shot. Aside from the anemic nature of .38 Special, stubbies are tough to group at extended distances. The Black Hills load is among the tightest shooting I've ever used in this gun, but sadly, at 25 yards, five-shot averages are in the 5- to 6-inch range.

JACK OF ALL TRADES?
Your personality will dictate whether a compact pistol is a perfect fit. Some general losses are accuracy and velocity, but most will agree they are marginal outside of a competition setting. The same can be said about concealability, but that comes down to the individual.

Guns of this size can be neatly tucked into an inside-the-waistband (IWB) holster, but some might argue that they are a touch cumbersome. Carrying one OWB will be more comfortable than a full-sized handgun, so it has that going for it. Lastly, the size reduction opens up a few more carry methods, such as on the ankle in the case of the J-Frame. A perpetual optimist, I feel you can't go wrong with having something from this class in your safe. If you inevitably choose not to carry it, their resale market is quite expansive, or you can shelf it as a loaner for a buddy who wants to join you at the range.

MICRO-COMPACT HANDGUNS
This next class of firearm is interesting, as it can be viewed as either a revolution-

Live Free Armory has a metallic answer to fantastic plastic striker-fired lovers.

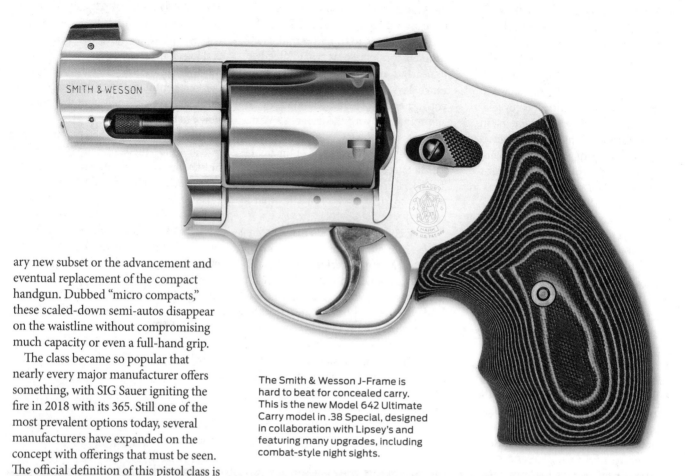

The Smith & Wesson J-Frame is hard to beat for concealed carry. This is the new Model 642 Ultimate Carry model in .38 Special, designed in collaboration with Lipsey's and featuring many upgrades, including combat-style night sights.

ary new subset or the advancement and eventual replacement of the compact handgun. Dubbed "micro compacts," these scaled-down semi-autos disappear on the waistline without compromising much capacity or even a full-hand grip.

The class became so popular that nearly every major manufacturer offers something, with SIG Sauer igniting the fire in 2018 with its 365. Still one of the most prevalent options today, several manufacturers have expanded on the concept with offerings that must be seen. The official definition of this pistol class is still being written. Still, I would consider anything with a barrel of less than 3.5 inches to qualify if it allows for a full grip and has a capacity of at least 10 rounds. Here are two that fit the description. I feel they fly far too low below the radar.

THE GX4 IS NO BULL

Taurus has always had a knack for making things less expensive, but as of late, we're also seeing some excellent feats in engineering and design mixed in. The 9mm GX4 carries an MSRP of just $399, making it the least expensive selection in this category. If you prefer having the option for a red-dot, $50 more puts you into the TORO (Taurus Optic Ready Option) edition. Even with the flush-fit 11-round magazine, I can manage to get my entire hand on it; however, when I slap in the 13-rounder, the gun feels like it is much, much larger. The trigger on this pistol is one of the best I've ever felt across all sizes and platforms, and the sights are large and intuitive.

Hornady's Critical Defense +P 9mm

load always yields excellent results in this firearm. It produces 297 ft-lbs of energy and groups five shots together as tight as 4 inches at 25 yards using just the iron sights.

MOSSBERG PUMPS OUT A HANDGUN

The industry took note when Mossberg released its second handgun in its 100+ year history. A victim of timing, the 9mm was just a little too short on capacity to compete with the others. Never to be beaten in a fight, the Connecticut manufacturer quickly re-spun the design and produced the enhanced capacity MC2sc.

I've used this gun extensively, including at several writer's events at Gunsite Academy. What impressed me most was its ability to take a beating in conditions as punishing as the hot, dry Arizona desert. Aside from being robust, it has one of the most unique and well-thought-out texturing patterns in the micro-compact category.

Federal's 9mm 124-grain HST load

nicely balances accuracy and downrange power with around 350 ft-lbs of energy at the muzzle and five-shot 25-yard groups measuring in the 3- to 4-inch range when equipped with a quality red-dot. For a pistol so small, I found it exceptionally cozy with a flush-fit mag installed. Inserting the 14-rounder adds enough length for even the most enormous hands and remains reasonably small for concealment in tighter clothes.

SMALL IN SIZE, BIG ON UTILITY

As previously mentioned, this pistol class is making compacts less relevant as time goes on. Weight and size savings are substantial, while the energy and accuracy loss are marginal. Using stack-and-a-half magazines sacrifices little capacity, if any, and makes spares more realistic to carry.

Using one on the range will be quite enjoyable, especially when you employ mags that allow for a complete grasp. Given their capacity is on par with their larger counterparts, your rhythm will remain minimally interrupted. Carrying a micro- or sub-compact in an OWB, IWB, or on an ankle is nearly unnoticeable, and if your pockets are large enough, they even lend themselves to limited carry in this manner.

POCKET HANDGUNS

The last category of carry pistol would be the polar opposite of the full-size class. Just as full-size handguns are designed for power, energy, and capacity at all costs, pocket pistols are built to be as tiny as possible. Concessions are made in every area, including shooting comfort, accuracy, and overall energy. While this might seem like an awful business model, it fills some rather significant gaps.

The definition of a pocket pistol is straightforward; if it can be hidden in a pocket, it qualifies. Essentially, the overall footprint shouldn't exceed that of a standard pocket accessory. Barrels will be the shortest on the market, and you shouldn't expect to be able to get your pinky on the frame. For those who like to carry a back-up gun, these are perfect for that role. The critical takeaway is to understand that you are not buying a target pistol, so keep practice realistic. That said, here is a pair that is by my side daily.

CONCEALMENT TO THE MAX

Ruger was onto something with its Lightweight Carry Pistol, or LCP. This small-framed .380 ACP is an easy carry

for restrictive dress, making it desirable to businessmen and bikers.

A recent upgrade incorporated a modern magazine design and increased capacity to 10+1 or 12+1 when the extender is installed. That's a lot of heat for a vest pocket, especially when you consider most prior designs in this class couldn't get there with diminutive .32 or .25 ACP. A pronounced tritium front sight and U-notched rear make it useful beyond bad breath range and functionally quick to acquire.

Ammunition is everything when it comes to .380 ACP lethality, so it pays to roll out the chronograph and crunch the numbers. In doing so, I've determined the top contender in this field to be Underwood's 68-grain Xtreme Defender load. It advertises 1,300 fps on the box, which I believe is realistic for longer barrels; however, the shorter, 2.8-inch barrel of the LCP Max loses about 100 fps off that rating. While I hate losing steam, I still have 221 ft-lbs of muzzle energy to deal with a threat.

Because everything is situational, determining an adequate self-defense threshold has never been a clear-cut science. Some camps believe anything over 100 ft-lbs will do

the job, while some say anything short of 300 isn't enough.

THE LAST RESORT

Surprisingly, the old "better than nothing" adage applies to firearms. While rimfire is not my first recommendation for general self-defense, it fits in where nothing else will, literally. Instances like jogging or lounging on the couch come to mind, earning this tiniest of handguns the moniker of "pajama gun."

My go-to for ultimate concealment is the North American Arms Ranger II. This single-action mini-revolver can fire both .22 LR and .22 WMR with the appropriate cylinder, leaving an easy-to-find practice option on the table. Realistically, the 1-5/8-inch barrel isn't long enough to realize most of the magnum's potential, but when you're trying to wring out as much energy as possible, every little bit helps.

Taurus's micro-compact GX4 9mm is fun to shoot, easy to carry, and costs less than a trip to the grocery store.

The Mossberg MC2sc was late to the race but delivered on function and comfort.

I've found CCI's 40-grain Maxi-Mag .22 WMR to be the best fit for this gun. It generates 60 ft-lbs of muzzle energy and is loud enough to register as a gunshot to an attacker. While seemingly unimportant, a threat's psychological response to gunfire might open things up enough for you to flee the area or make your way to your primary firearm. Of course, if applied to the head or heart, rimfire stands a good chance of neutralizing the altercation in a single shot.

Loading and unloading this little guy is expedited through the Webley-style break-open top, making it fun on the range and easy to get your rounds in. Its accuracy is sufficient for targets just outside of arm's length, but expect groups at 25 yards to be at least a foot across.

Pocket pistols are the answer for the gun owner who swears it's impractical to carry every day or in every outfit. As the name suggests, you only need a semi-generous pocket and a quality pocket

IWB carry is likely the most popular method of concealment. Just make sure your gun is appropriately sized.

If you're OK with wearing a jacket all day, shoulder holsters are superbly comfortable.

holster to keep a gun on you. I liken my LCP Max to my wallet and slip the entire package into my front pocket whenever I grab my keys and prepare to leave for the day.

Designs like the NAA Ranger II are even easier to leave with, as they are built with safety notches, allowing the hammer to rest between chambers. As the firing mechanism needs to be cocked for the trigger mechanism to be engaged, it is one of the only designs that is acceptable to carry without a holster. Lastly, pocket pistols don't need to be carried in pockets. They also feel great on the waistband and nearly disappear on an ankle, making them ever more suited as a backup gun.

Don't overlook something in the micro-compact category like the Ruger LCP II Lite Rack. Holding 10+1 rounds of .22 LR, it might not be a powerful manstopper, but it's better than nothing if a shooter has weak hands or can't conceal a larger pistol.

CONCLUSION

The synopsis of all of this is really no different than anything else in the world of firearms. While the human mind loves simple answers that blanket a subject, the best answer to the question "What gun should I buy?" is "It depends."

Start with how you dress; then, go shopping for the largest style of firearm you can conceal. Some capacity or ac-curacy—and enjoyability on the range—might be lost as things get smaller. However, remember that it's not a linear relationship, and an inch of barrel length may have little to no adverse effect on these criteria. Lastly, subscribe to the idea that you may need to buy more than one firearm, especially if you wear a lot of dif-ferent hats or experience drastic weather changes.

In instances where larger guns aren't realistic to carry, never shy away from carrying a sub-caliber. A .22 LR in a pants pocket will always be more effective than a .45 ACP locked in your gun safe. **GD**

Campfire HANDGUNS

Don't Leave Home Without Them

❯RICK HACKER

The night was bitterly cold and pitch black except for the faint silvery starlight that helped guide my horse and me down the steep mountainside. We made our way toward the distant glow of what I knew to be our base camp on this, my third unfruitful day of a Rocky Mountain elk hunt. Upon nearing the welcome glow and warmth of the campfire, I reined up, drew my still unfired .54-caliber Hawken from its saddle scabbard and dismounted just as the camp cook came running out of the tent screaming, "That gosh-darned, son-of-gun field mouse has been in the flour sack ag'in and they ain't gonna be no biscuits if this keeps up!"

Of course, he didn't say, "Gosh-darned, son-of-a-gun." He used words that were more of a colloquial nature. But the message was clear enough when I entered the tent and saw several small holes gnawed in the flour sack. And as if to torment poor "Cookie" further, the tiny field mouse poked its head out from around the flour sack at that very moment and stared at us.

Some might think this "C" engraved, blued, and casehardened Standard Manufacturing Single Action with *fleur-de-lis* grips might be too pretty to take on a hunting trip. However, Hacker finds it makes for an ideal campfire handgun, where it's not exposed to the scratching and dinging hazards of the trail and instead earns bragging rights during informal target practice afterward. Despite being collectible, he also finds his Randall Sportsman's Bowie just as useful. All Photos: Rick Hacker

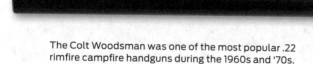

The Colt Woodsman was one of the most popular .22 rimfire campfire handguns during the 1960s and '70s.

"Let me handle this," I whispered as I silently sat down on a bench, quietly cocked the hammer of the Hawken, and set the rear trigger. Then, slowly raising the rifle to my shoulder and lining up the rear buckhorn sight with the front blade until it was perfectly positioned on the field mouse, I touched off the shot. The voluminous roar of the Hawken was accompanied by a thick, white tent-filled cloud of FFG smoke that momentarily obscured everything from sight. But as the haze slowly drifted out the open tent flap into the night, we could barely make out what little remained of our furry antagonist.

I admit this was a case of being over-gunned for the occasion, but at the time, the Hawken was all I had. Much later, I found myself lamenting that I hadn't brought my Smith & Wesson K-22 along on this hunt, as it clearly would have gotten the job done just as efficiently and much less dramatically. Since then, I have always packed a pistol along on any outdoor outing where it's legal to do so.

I'm not talking about hunting hand-guns here. In fact, it is just the opposite, as many of those big-bore bruisers are often too bulky for a hip holster and, outfitted with a scope or other sighting reticle as many of them are today, too awkward to toss in a backpack or tuck away in your bedroll. Rather, I'm referring to "campfire handguns," one essential tool many outdoorsmen and women never think about or take with them when hiking or hunting or just to accompany them on a picnic in the woods. And as such, they don't realize their omission until they need it. Or wish they had it. Or until it's too late.

More specifically, these are those handy sidearms—single-actions, double-actions, or semi-automatics—that many of us pack on our hips when we're back at camp and not otherwise lugging around a heavier and more cumbersome rifle or shotgun. Campfire handguns don't take up much room in a backpack yet are a source of comfort when outdoors, especially when unwanted critters—whether on four legs, two, or slither—invade our space. Yes, campfire handguns can be a definite source of self-protection and leisure-time enjoyment, such as après-hunt plinking. And while grabbing a .30-'06 to eradicate a food-nibbling squirrel (or using a big-bored muzzleloader as I did) may be the ultimate form of overkill, drawing a .22 and dispatching the little thief is not only more effective but, in many ways, can be a form of therapy, especially when we haven't pulled the trigger on anything else thus far on a hunting trip. This, again, brings to mind that particular elk hunt.

The campfire handgun concept actually started around the first part of the 20th century, with the growing practice of having a relatively easy-to-carry pistol, usually of a small caliber, to toss into your "kit," or portable stash of supplies that you carried for the day, which was often a saddle bag, fishing creel, tackle box, or even a lunch bucket. Although the term soon morphed into widespread usage, it got official recognition in 1936 when Smith & Wesson introduced the 22/32 Kit Gun, a .22 rimfire double-action revolver built on a slightly larger .32-caliber frame. Eventually discontinued due to lagging sales coupled with World War II, this style of handgun (me-

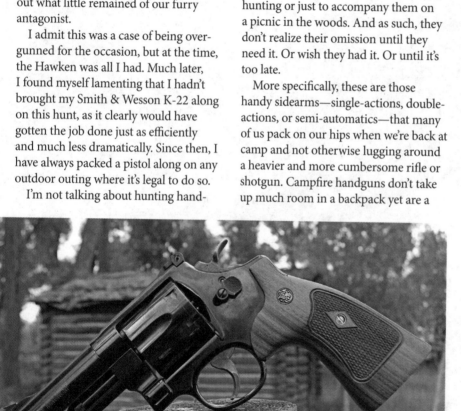

Hacker is a big fan of packing his 4-inch-barrel S&W Model 29 in camp when you don't know who or what might show up.

This Ruger Super Single Six Convertible, with its adjustable sights and extra .22 Mag cylinder, is an ideal campfire handgun.

dium frame, small caliber) was reintroduced in 1953 in an improved model as S&W's "22/32 Kit Gun, Model of 1953." Thus, the kit gun nomenclature was officially re-established for a new generation of shooters. Today, Smith & Wesson still makes a dramatically updated version of this trend-setting pistol as its eight-shot Model 317 Kit Gun. Of course, nowadays, numerous other handguns qualify for the title of kit gun. However, that term has matured to include some larger-framed and bigger-caliber versions to become campfire handguns.

But from the 1920s through the '50s, some .22 rimfire pistols seemed tailor-made for outdoor outings. Back then, various models of the Colt Woodsman and Hi-Standard semi-autos were some of the most popular guns with which to punch holes in tin cans, not to mention rabbits, squirrels, and prairie dogs. After all, if you didn't hit your target with the first shot, you would have a magazine full of repeat shots to continue trying your rapid-fire luck with low-cost .22 rimfire cartridges.

But beginning in 1949, these guns gradually gave way to ones like the more affordable Ruger Standard—the gun that launched Sturm, Ruger & Co. into the stratosphere of success. At the time, a High Standard G-B Hammerless was selling for $50, and Colt's fixed-sight Sport Model Woodsman went for approximately $69, but the original version of Ruger's first .22 semi-auto listed for only $37.50. Today, that gun is still in the line, although it has undergone several changes. As of this writing, it currently exists as the 75th Anniversary Mark IV and various Tactical and Competition models exist. But countless numbers of the original versions of Colt, Hi-Standard, and Ruger .22 semi-automatics are still found as regular staples in backpacks and camping gear throughout the country. However, some of these earlier guns have also attained collectible status.

The aforementioned S&W K-22 revolver is also in the category of campfire handguns turned collectible, as is the early Ruger Flatgate Single Six, which first appeared in 1953 and was initially priced

at $57.50. Many modern-day shooters don't even know of its existence, as it only lasted for four years, after which it began being made with a more traditionally styled rounded loading gate. To its credit, the Ruger Single Six is still in the line and, for me, is one of the best campfire guns you can take along on a fishing or hunting trip (especially the Super Single Six Convertible, which has an extra cylinder chambered in .22 Magnum). And let us not forget the Colt Frontier Scout, a scaled-down .22 rimfire version of the famed Single Action Army, produced from 1958 until 1986; it was a go-to thumb-buster for many who couldn't opt for the pricier SAA. Those vintage guns still serve that purpose today, although I have seen more than one three-digit offer being made to a fellow hunter who just happened to bring his Scout along as a campfire handgun.

In 1973, Ruger revamped its line to include the New Model Single Six, which features a transfer bar that enables the gun to be carried with six rounds instead of five. Now, there is even a New Model

The Lipsey's Ruger Shopkeeper is a limited edition of the Bearcat. It features a bird's-head grip and a shorter 3-inch barrel, making it an ideal close-range campfire handgun.

The single-action Ruger Blackhawk is a highly versatile campfire handgun. It's available in .357 Magnum (shown), .41 Remington Magnum, .45 Colt, and .30 Carbine and is compatible with certain rifles.

Single Seven and a New Model Single Nine, giving you even more thumb-cocking fun without reloading after the sixth shot. But for me, one of the most fun campfire guns is the Ruger Bearcat, a compact, fixed sight .22 sixgun that—especially in its stainless steel configuration—can be tossed in a tackle box or slid into a coat pocket with nary a care. And Ruger's new .22 Wrangler, which combines zinc and aluminum to keep costs and weight to a minimum, is one of the newest and most economical campfire revolvers yet.

Of course, .22 rimfire handguns are the most cost-effective ways to plink away at tin cans and sticks and, yes, even pieces of leftover fruit (hollowpoints and oranges at twenty paces, anyone?), but bigger-bored handguns, such as a .44 Special, .45 Colt, or even a .44 Magnum can be much more effective on larger furbearers and other unwanted visitors who may have more than a few nibbles of crackers on their mind.

For example, as the only non-Texan member of a ragtag deer hunting group known as the Rio Concho Association, I used to pack a .44 Special Smith & Wesson Second Model Hand Ejector on our annual deer hunts in Texas. Inasmuch as we were hunting on a ranch owned by one of the Association's members and since deer season overlapped with turkey season and javelinas were rampant, there was no telling what one might encounter as we traipsed through the scrub brush. On subsequent hunts, I often took one of my S&W Model 29s, usually loaded with .44 Specials but sometimes stoked with full-powered .44 Magnums, depending upon what I was hunting and where. In truth, I am rather partial to bigger-bored campfire handguns—or at least I was until the current availability and ammo cost have made me think twice about each campside shot I take.

In my opinion, double-action revolvers require a bit more care than single-actions as campfire guns, as cylinder latches can be accidentally opened on some DA guns as they are shoved into pouches and backpacks. So, I advise keeping these wheelguns in a holster, whether on your belt or stored in your pack, and a pistol case is ideal for transporting handguns safely to your campsite. Galco and 1791 both make revolver and semi-automatic leather holsters with quick on-again-off-again steel belt clips for those times when you want to shuck your handgun quickly and easily and, just as quickly, reattach it to your belt. For those occasions, I've recently been using 1791's new IWB Fair Chase Deer Hide Holster for my Smith & Wesson Model 36 with its rarely encountered 3-inch barrel.

Since semi-autos are sometimes more complicated to operate than revolvers, they require more diligence in their campsite use. For example, by simply swinging out the cylinder on a double-action revolver, one can quickly confirm whether or not the gun is loaded. However, an "empty" semi-automatic pistol might still have a round in the chamber even though the magazine has been removed. Leisure shooting is no time to let your guard down or ignore the basic rules of gun safety.

This might be a good place to caution picnickers and hunters who will be away from their campsites for any length of time to keep their handguns out of

Ruger's New Model Vaquero is an excellent knock-about single-action, especially in stainless steel (shown), known for its ruggedness. This gun has been outfitted with Eagle's Gunfighter Grips, which have a deeper, non-slip "Reactiv" checkering. John Bianchi made the buscadero rig for the author.

One of the author's favorite campfire handguns is his customized Ruger New Model Blackhawk Bisley in .44 Special (a Lipsey's limited edition), which has an aftermarket casehardened frame by Turnbull, Hamilton Bowen sights, and a tuned action by Andy Horvath. The elkhorn grips are from Eagle Grips.

The original Ruger Single Six Flatgate (top) and the post-1956 Single Six (bottom) set the stage for modern-day .22 camp guns. Both of these early .22 rimfires shoot to point-of-aim.

Kimber only made its excellent 1911-styled .22 Rimfire Super from 2004 to 2015 but currently produces the .22 Rimfire Compact and .22 Rimfire Target Conversion Kits for many of its .45 ACP pistols, turning them into economical guns for informal campfire plinking.

sight and secure them from unwanted access, as visitors to your camp may not be just "visiting," but are more intent on looting. It's a sad commentary, but some people steal things when you're not around. That means either taking the gun with you, locking it in the glove compartment of your car or truck, or, better yet, securing it in an attached gun safe that is permanently installed in your vehicle. But sometimes, this isn't always feasible in a wilderness camp where the terrain isn't conducive to four-wheel drive, or vehicles aren't allowed. In that case, the only other option is to clandestinely hide the handgun while away from your campsite. However, speaking from personal experience, there is such a thing as hiding it too well.

Once, on a deer hunt with one of my buddies in the rugged mountains on the eastern side of the Sierra Nevadas, we had to hike in for two hours to get to where the "big bucks" were. That meant packing in with all our gear, including my pre-64 Winchester Model 70. But I also took a 3-inch-barreled Third Model Colt Single Action Army Sheriff's Model for my campfire handgun, rationalizing that the shorter barrel would cut down weight. The fact is, I just wanted to have that gun along on this hunting trip.

When it came time to start hunting at the break of dawn, I began worrying about leaving that highly desirable Sheriff's Model in camp, even though we were in an extremely remote area. In fact, during our hunt, we discovered an old cowboy's grave from 1910 that had never been touched. Nonetheless, I hid the sixgun so well that I couldn't remember where I had hidden it when we returned to camp after a grueling day climbing over rocks and battling through blowdowns! I spent the better part of the night looking for that sixshooter and finally had to wait until daylight to continue my search when I found it securely ensconced in the crotch of an old, weathered tree. It cost me half a day's hunting, but I didn't lose my campfire handgun.

By far, the safest handgun to have in camp is a single-action revolver, as, assuming the hammer is resting over an empty chamber (on non-transfer bar models), there is no way the gun can be fired unless the hammer is manually pulled back and the trigger depressed. Naturally, one of my favorite single-action revolvers is the Colt Peacemaker, which, if you think about it, started as the first popular campfire handgun over a century ago. However, as the value and scarcity of these SAAs have grown over the years (have you priced a Third Generation Colt SAA lately?) I find myself opting for alternatives. One of the best is the extremely well-made Standard Manufacturing Single Action, an identically proportioned mirror image of the SAA. Yes, they cost about as much as a factory-new Colt SAA, but they are much more readily available and boast all-steel parts. It is a solid, quality gun in every respect, and my engraved .45 version, with its 4¾-inch barrel, is destined to continue with me on many of my campfire handgun adventures, maintaining a tradition I started over forty years ago.

In fact, the first campfire handgun I ever took with my hunting rifle was a first-generation Colt Single Action Army, which proved its value right out of the starting gate on a big game hunt in the Cedar Flats area of Arizona. Late one night, induced by nature's call, I was compelled to leave the sanctity of my warm sleeping bag. Not wishing to take my Winchester 71 on what would invariably be a two-handed endeavor, I grabbed the .45 Colt instead and ventured into the blackness outside my tent. The unmistakable "*whirr*" of a buzz-worm ("rattlesnake" to you flatlanders) prompted me to freeze in my tracks instinctively. My flashlight immediately confirmed my fears, for the culprit was starting to coil and getting ready to strike. Barely able to use the Peacemaker's rudimentary sights, I fired three quick shots as fast as my thumb could work the hammer. Honesty compels me to admit that only one of those shots hit its mark, but it made me a believer in the value of always taking a campfire handgun along on hunting and camping trips. **GD**

The author's 6-inch-barreled Model 29 may be a bit bulky for trail use but is quite adequate when strange noises are heard around the campsite—for intruders bigger than a ground squirrel.

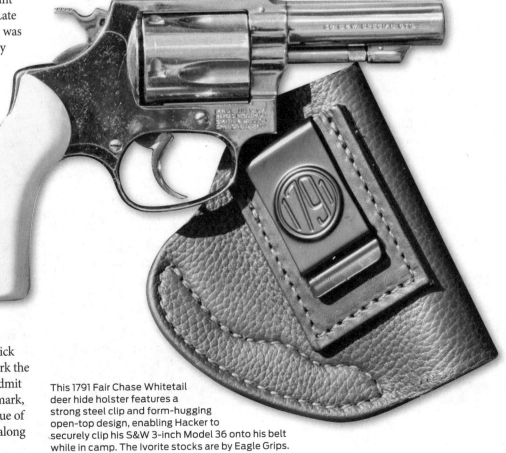

This 1791 Fair Chase Whitetail deer hide holster features a strong steel clip and form-hugging open-top design, enabling Hacker to securely clip his S&W 3-inch Model 36 onto his belt while in camp. The Ivorite stocks are by Eagle Grips.

The author wrings out a trio of modern rimfire rifles.

›MICHAEL PENDLEY

Some 40-plus years ago, my first rifle (a Winchester Model 67) was a single-shot .22. I'd bet the same goes for many folks reading this. You loaded a single round, closed the bolt, then cocked it by pulling back a spring-loaded knob at the rear of the receiver. That Model 67 was older, even back then. The cartridge had to be placed just right, and the bolt closed gently to get it to load without jamming. It rarely extracted, meaning my trusty pocket knife had to come into play to pull the empty case after a shot. The iron sights were barely adequate, but over time, I learned where to hold to make an accurate shot.

The Great .22 Comparison

The Henry Frontier's classic lines and feel make it natural for a trip to the woods to chase squirrels or other small game.

Looking back, I'm sure my dad entrusted me with that particular rifle for my first solo trips afield for several reasons, even though more modern .22 rifles were at his disposal. He knew it would teach me to make my first shot count since a follow-up would only occur several minutes later. It would teach me to use iron sights, a skill every hunter should have. And it was relatively safe for a young shooter. He knew I wouldn't spray bullets around the treetops as quickly as I could pull the trigger. It also saved him some ammo, as the small handful of rounds he would dole out would last me several trips.

Faults aside, that old gun eventually made life hard for the rabbits and squirrels along our family farm's hardwood ridges and bottomland fields. It also instilled a love of the .22 Long Rifle that remains today—one that I have passed down to my kids. There aren't many more fun and cost-effective ways to spend a family day afield than with rimfire rifles, a box of bulk ammo, and a few targets or a stand of hardwoods full of squirrels.

HISTORY OF THE .22 LR

Lots of shooters share the .22 Long Rifle passion. Year after year, the round is the most sold caliber in new guns and ammunition. So, how did this popular and versatile round come about? It started in 1857 as a cartridge designed for the Smith & Wesson Model 1, S&W's first firearm. The .22 Rimfire cartridge had a 4-grain blackpowder charge and a 29-grain bullet. That round became the .22 short, the oldest cartridge still in production today. Interestingly, the Model 1 was marketed as a close-range personal protection gun. Next came the .22 Long in 1871 with a slightly longer case and an extra grain of blackpowder for 5 grains. Then, the .22 Extra Long came about in 1880 with a 6-grain charge.

In 1887, the J. Stevens Arms & Tool Company introduced the quintessential .22 rimfire cartridge, the .22 Long Rifle (LR). It duplicated the performance of the .22 Extra Long in a shorter cartridge. Almost immediately, it became one of the most popular rounds sold. The change to smokeless powder further improved the performance, and today, numerous variations of different bullet styles and weights are manufactured worldwide.

PRESENT DAY

Why does the .22 LR remain so popular with today's shooters? For one, it's versatile. You can use it to hunt small game and predators, as a sidearm when working on the farm or running a trapline, and for fun and inexpensive range time. Like all ammo, recent years have seen a drastic jump in cost per round, even for the .22 LR, but it remains one of the least expensive ways to spend a day at the shooting bench. Ammo cost for the .22 LR ranges from around 9 cents per trigger pull to 15 cents for some specialty and target loads, a fraction of what even inexpensive centerfire rounds run these days.

Every hunter and shooter should own at least one .22 rimfire rifle. Modern manufacturers have embraced our love of the .22 and offer the round in almost every rifle style imaginable. Many of these guns are capable of single-hole accuracy and come in at a bargain price compared to similar centerfire versions. Gone are the days of handfed single-shot rifles that needed to be babied to get the round to feed. Today's guns will digest ammo of different styles and bullet weights and do it without a hiccup. Whether you prefer honing your skills at the shooting range or strolling through the hardwoods in search of small game for the dinner pot, a .22 rimfire will fit the bill.

I tested three action styles from leading manufacturers. All were a joy to shoot. And while the .22 LR isn't loud by any caliber standard, a lifetime of shooting, not always with hearing protection, has made me appreciate shooting quietly. All three guns in this test came with a factory-threaded barrel so that I could add a Banish 22 suppressor

A medium or high mount allows enough room to thumb the Henry Frontier's hammer with optics mounted.

from Silencer Central. No matter what style of gun you prefer, I guarantee there is a .22 LR version out there.

HENRY FRONTIER MODEL

The classic lever-action introduced in 1848 as the "Volition Repeating Rifle" earned the moniker "The Gun That Won the West." The ability to load and fire several rounds with just a short throw of the action made for fast follow-up shots, a novel concept then. For years, the lever-action .30-30 was synonymous with deer rifle. It could be found in deer camps from the southern swamps to the northern mountains. While other rifle actions

are popular across the globe, the lever-action remains a distinctly American style.

Add in hit TV shows like "The Rifleman" and "Winchester 73," and you have an entire generation of shooters who grew up dreaming of owning a lever-action. I was no different. My first real deer rifle was a Marlin 336 in .30-30.

I never really outgrew that love of the lever gun. Luckily, the action has experienced a resurgence in recent years, with several new guns being released in various calibers, including .22 LR. Rimfire shooters have long enjoyed the .22s produced by the Henry Rifle Company; I included Henry's Frontier Model Threaded Barrel in this comparison. The tubular magazine on many lever-actions prevents easy reloading when using a silencer. The suppressor would stop the magazine follower from sliding out, meaning you would have to remove the silencer each time you want to reload. Henry solved

The author tested each rifle with various ammunition, including the CCI Green Tag, Subsonic, and Quiet-22, for accuracy and noise level.

The Frontier's threaded barrel allows the easy addition of most silencers.

While the Frontier's long barrel provides clearance for the magazine tube to clear a suppressor, the rifle is ungainly in the field with a can attached.

this with the Frontier Model by adding a 24-inch barrel and shortening the magazine tube so that you can reload without removing the can. Even with the shortened tube, the rifle still holds eight rounds.

When you unbox this rifle, you first think, "Man, this is a pretty gun." The 24-inch octagonal barrel mated to the smooth, dark hardwood stock gives it a classic look that screams to be taken to the woods.

As expected from a Henry, the build quality is excellent, with careful metal-to-wood fit and an action as smooth as motor oil on ice. The muzzle end of the barrel uses industry-standard 1/2×28 threads that are .400-inch in length, making for an easy addition of most rimfire silencers. The trigger breaks at a crisp 3.8 pounds and feels smooth on the bench and in the woods. The length of pull runs 14 inches, a good compromise that lets shooters of all sizes handle and enjoy the rifle and shoot it comfortably.

The Frontier comes factory with an adjustable semi-buckhorn rear and a tall, brass-bead front sight on the octagon barrel in a dovetail fixture. The rear sight features a white diamond at the bottom of a traditional "U." While the open sights are serviceable, they are a little large for distant aiming. Luckily, the rifle comes from the factory with an integrated ⅜-inch dovetail, allowing the easy addition of a scope. I topped the Henry with a Leupold VX-Freedom 3x9 scope. As with most lever-actions, a taller scope mount is necessary for hammer clearance under the scope.

The safety is the traditional quarter-cock lever style, allowing the shooter to bring the hammer back about 1/8-inch until you hear a click, or, with the hammer fully cocked, hold the hammer with your thumb while releasing it by pressing on the trigger. Then, lower the hammer down to the "safe" position. As with all hammer guns, take extreme care when lowering the hammer.

The Frontier is a joy to shoot. The action is smooth enough to cycle without removing the rifle from your shoulder or taking your eye off the target while plinking away. The longer 24-inch barrel, while a bit ungainly with the

The Ruger 10/22 Takedown packs into an included storage pouch, making it easy to stash away in your truck or pack.

suppressor installed, was accurate, and it more than held its own on the bench against the other actions.

Accuracy with the Frontier was exceptional, with 50-yard groups hovering near a half-inch with most ammunition. The addition of the silencer opened up the group, but just slightly, with multiple ammo brands and bullet styles still printing under an inch. If classic styling and tradition are your cup of tea, the Frontier is the rifle for you. Its MSRP is $609.00.

RUGER 10/22 TAKEDOWN

Ruger first introduced its semi-auto 10/22 in 1964. To say the rifle design was a hit would be an understatement. Since then, Ruger has sold over 7 million of the popular little rifle. Third-party aftermarket parts like triggers, stocks, and barrels abound, making it one of the most easily customizable rifles today. I'd venture just about every avid shooter or hunter either owns one or has shot one at least once.

The original carbine came with a 10-round rotary magazine, but extended magazines are available.

Ruger now offers over a dozen varieties of the 10/22. In 2012, it introduced a takedown model that breaks down with an easy twist of the barrel to fit into a handy carry bag. The model (21133) I tested came with a precision-rifled, 16.12-inch barrel with a .920-inch-diameter barrel fluted for weight reduction. The shorter barrel is handy and easy to point and shoot, both as-is and with a suppressor. Before heading to the range, I topped the rifle with a Leupold VX-Freedom 3-9 scope.

Takedown is as simple as locking the bolt back and verifying that the rifle is unloaded, pushing a recessed lever, twisting the subassemblies and pulling them apart. No tools are required.

While some takedown rifles struggle to hold the point of impact (POI), Ruger came up with an ingenious way to lock the barrel into the exact position time after time by adding an "adjustment knob" locking system. Loosen the adjustment knob by turning it to the right as far as possible. Insert the barrel assembly by turning it to the

With the 10/22 Takedown, you can quickly go from carry case to the woods with the confidence that your bullets will still hit the same spot.

right 45 degrees with moderate inward pressure after insertion. Now, rotate it to the left (clockwise) until it locks in place. Finally, tighten the adjustment knob by turning it counterclockwise as far as possible with finger pressure. It works. I took the rifle down and put it back together several times, and the POI remained consistent.

Other than the takedown feature, the new 10/22 remains the same in other respects. The cross-bolt safety is located forward of the triggerguard and is set up for right-handed shooters. The factory-supplied magazine is the familiar 10-round rotary style. The bolt lock is found under the gun forward of

the safety. While the trigger broke at a relatively stiff 5.5 pounds, it was crisp with minimal creep, which made it easy to shoot accurately (several aftermarket triggers are available, if you prefer a lighter pull). The 10/22 Takedown Model features the Ruger Modular Stock System with interchangeable standard and high cheek pieces that snap on and off for a custom fit based on your shooting style and optics choice.

The 10/22 was near Hollywood quiet with CCI Clean-22 40-grain target loads at 1,070 fps but would not cycle the CCI Quiet-22 segmented hollowpoint at 710 fps. Perhaps after a long break-in, it might

The Frontier's long barrel maximized velocity and was highly accurate with various ammo brands and bullet weights.

The 10/22 Takedown's knurled adjustment ring allows the shooter to return to the same point of impact each time the rifle is taken down and reassembled.

The combination of carbon-fiber stock and barrel paired with a machined aluminum receiver make the Ranger both lightweight, at just a hair over 5 pounds, and blazingly accurate.

cycle the slower loads, but the new rifle would not. All other ammo tested fed reliably with each trigger pull.

Sub-1-inch groups at 50 yards were common on the bench with a wide range of ammo brands. With the suppressor installed, groups ran at 1 inch, and POI shifted slightly from the bare barrel. If a fast follow-up shot and ease of storage appeal to you, you will be happy with the 10/22 Takedown. The Ruger 10/22 Takedown's MSRP is $799.99, but I have seen them for considerably less in real-world pricing.

CHRISTENSEN ARMS RANGER .22

While bolt-action rimfire rifles have been around for a while, the Ranger .22 from Christensen Arms is not your grandfather's squirrel gun. From the company that pioneered carbon-fiber barrels and stocks, the Ranger is an affordable, super-accurate .22 equally at home on the bench or in the woods.

Its anodized black receiver is machined from aluminum. A two-lug steel bolt uses dual-locking lugs for reliable feeding. Dual extractors and a fixed ejector ensure reliable removal of spent rounds, and an anti-bind rail on the left side of the bolt aids smooth operation.

Mated to that action is a Christensen Arm's 18-inch barrel that begins with a hand-lapped 416R stainless-steel blank turned down to a narrow profile. A carbon-fiber sleeve is fitted over the steel with air space in between. Finally, a steel muzzle device is threaded on to form a stiff, lightweight, accurate barrel. The Ranger's muzzle is threaded 1/2x28, making direct installation of most rimfire suppressors easy. The action and barrel are mated with a Christensen Arms lightweight and strong carbon stock with a semi-tactical shape and a 13.75-inch length of pull, making the rifle easy to shoulder and shoot for just about anyone. The fully-rigged rifle weighs 5 pounds, so it's easy to tote around the woods.

The Ranger .22 comes from the factory with the excellent TriggerTech field trigger designed for the Remington 700, which is adjustable from 2.5 to 5 pounds. My test gun tripped the scale at just under 4 pounds before adjustments, with a crisp, clean break and no noticeable creep. The Ranger is a joy to shoot. As a bonus, it's compatible with most Remington 700 aftermarket triggers, so if you prefer another brand to match your big game rifle more closely, it's a simple swap.

Unlike the first two rifles in this test, the Ranger does not come with iron sights but instead has an integral (0 MOA) Picatinny-style rail for simple and rigid optics mounting. My test gun was topped with a Riton 3 Conquer in 3-15x44, making even long-range plinking a breeze.

The Ranger uses the proven Ruger 10/22 rotary-style magazine to feed reliably with each bolt turn, no matter how rushed. It also accepts any extended magazine designed for the 10/22 if you prefer more than 10 rounds. The magazine release is a paddle style actuated from the rear. The bolt release is mounted at 9 o'clock on the receiver, so bolt removal for cleaning is a simple task. Finally, the simple forward/back safety lever is located on the right side of the tang, just like many centerfire designs. You can work the bolt with the safety in the On position.

Just how accurate is the Ranger .22? Regardless of ammo brand and bullet style, it stacked group after 50-yard group under an inch, with several under .5 inch! Many groups should have been even tighter, but I could almost call the slight flyer when I felt the trigger break while the crosshairs hovered just off the aiming point. The CCI Target 40-grain Mini-Mag consistently turned in the tightest groups. With the Banish 22 suppressor attached, subsonic loads were whisper quiet, with the thud of the bullet striking the dirt backstop sounding much louder than the round firing.

With all these premium rifle features, you might expect the Ranger to come with a premium price tag. Instead, the suggested retail is just $849.99, a bargain for what you

Range time with the Christensen Arms Ranger .22 proved fun and near custom-rifle accurate.

The Ranger's carbon-fiber barrel mates well with the Banish 22 from Silencer Central without making the rifle overly long.

get. If you're looking for a benchrest-accurate .22 LR that is also light enough to carry on a hunt, the Ranger is the perfect choice.

Whether you prefer lever, bolt or semi-auto, a quality .22 rimfire is out there to fit your needs. Choose the model that closely matches your big game rifle for quality range time to improve your shooting without the extra cost and noise of a centerfire. Or pick more than one and switch back and forth; you won't find more bang for the buck than with any of these modern .22 LR choices. **GD**

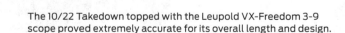

The 10/22 Takedown topped with the Leupold VX-Freedom 3-9 scope proved extremely accurate for its overall length and design.

Tom Turpin in his natural environment: with a gun in hand.

Custom & Engraved Guns

A Tribute to Tom Turpin

> PHIL MASSARO

On 17 January 2024, the *Gun Digest* family and the world lost a very good man; Lieutenant Colonel Thomas Turpin (Ret.) passed away in Sierra Vista, Arizona, at age 85. For years, Tom handled the Custom & Engraved Guns section of this esteemed tome, and he handled it well. Sadly, I never had the opportunity to meet Tom in person—our interactions were limited to telephone conversations primarily because we lived on opposite ends of the country—but I truly enjoyed our conversations, as we had much in common.

Tom Turpin would retire from the U.S. Army as a Lieutenant Colonel.

Massaro and Turpin shared an affinity for big-bore cartridges, and this Fred Wells rifle in .510 Wells certainly checks that box in spades. Turpin showed us this Wells rifle in his "On Custom Guns" feature in the 77th Edition.

In my writing and research, I discovered that Tom played a significant role in the resurgence of the .470 Nitro Express cartridge (one near and dear to me) and the double rifle itself. While stationed in the Army in Germany, he worked with Heym Rifles to bring back the classic side-by-side double rifle from the brink of extinction. Whenever I grab my Heym 89B double rifle, chambered in .470 NE, I think of Tom and our conversations about the rebirth of the classic African rifles.

Tom Turpin maintained a close relationship with the American Custom Gunmakers Guild (ACGG). Dave Norin, long-time professional gunsmith (now retired) and friend of Turpin's, had this to offer: "Tom's passion for custom guns was apparent in his many books and articles. He was a good and generous friend to all custom gunmakers and a real champion of the custom gun trade. Tom's legacy will reach beyond his books and articles; his influence will be found in the careers of the custom gunmakers of the current generation and of those yet to be inspired."

Guild member and custom riflemaker Jeff Tapp added: "Tom was a great friend, as well as a patron to the custom gunmakers and the Gunmaker's Guild. His books and magazine articles were instrumental in bringing customers and gunmakers together, as well as educating us all on the best-quality gunmaking in the United States. He will be sorely missed both as a professional and friend."

Corey Graff, our features editor here at the *Gun Digest*, reflected on his working relationship with Turpin.

"Tom Turpin always delivered something exceptional," Graff said. "I came to appreciate his professionalism and friendliness in our remote work interactions. He was a perfectionist. While many things give an editor uncontrollable shakes, searing heartburn, and the heebie-jeebies, Turpin made things easy. I never had to go back to him with questions about his writing for clarification or to ask for better photos. His annual submission of custom and engraved guns was as reliable as a Swiss watch—and he set the bar very high.

"Each summer, when the first copies of the *Gun Digest* arrived at the office, I'd quickly turn to Turpin's custom gun feature to check if the printer had mucked anything up and if the vivid colors were accurately reproduced. It was the highwater mark of the book and my favorite part. Nothing made your eyeballs water with delight, and your heart flutter faster than the otherworldly artisanship Turpin would find. It was just classy.

"Notably, during his several-decade streak, Turpin worked with possibly more *Gun Digest* editors than any other contributor. While I could not document precisely when he started contributing, he was behind at least some of the early "Custom Guns and Art of the Engraver" features before 2001. He worked directly with editor John T. Amber (whose editorship spanned from 1950 to 1979) and many editors who followed, including Ken Warner (1980–2000), Ken Ramage (2001–2009), Dan Shideler (2010–2012), Jerry Lee (2013–2020), and Phil Massaro (2021–present). The gun publishing industry is a meat grinder and not kind to those lacking discipline; many get churned out quickly or burn out. Turpin hung in there.

"I've been asked to pick a favorite from Turpin's features, which is almost impossible considering the hundreds of exquisite models he covered. While any metal engraving—be it on knives or guns—is a guilty pleasure, I'm struck by some of the firearms Turpin spotlighted with less obvious embellishment, which he dubbed 'custom afield.' An example might exhibit a crisp wood-to-metal fit, classic touches such as a safari-style barrel band, or other subtle details that only one with discernment tempered with age and experience could identify, let alone appreciate. Perfect execution and gun-to-owner-fit might qualify. They were beautiful works of art, but they seemed like something you could still hunt with and earn a few scratches to add character.

"For example, take the Reto Buehler-Gary Goudy '09 Argentine chambered in 9.3x64 Brenneke that Turpin featured in the *2024 Gun Digest* (which would be his final contribution). Writes Turpin: 'Seldom encountered in the U.S., the 9.3x64 Brenneke is an excellent big game cartridge comparable to the venerable .375 H&H. Swiss-born gunmaker Reto Buehler was selected as the metalsmith on this project because he was intimately familiar with this cartridge. The stock work was done by the author's old pal Gary Goudy, and this rifle perfectly embodies the concept of a 'custom afield.'

"What made Turpin's custom guns section so endearing? In his feature article, 'Collecting *Gun Digest*: The Greatest Gun Annual,' the late Dan Shideler understood the secret sauce: '*Gun Digest*

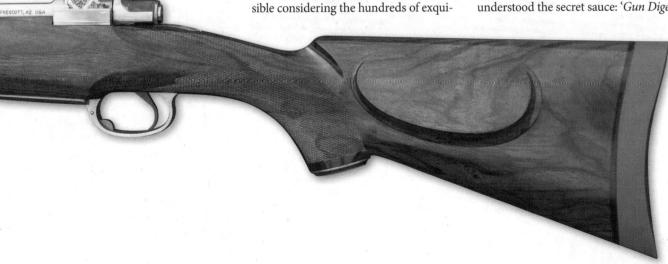

Turpin brought this beautiful bolt gun in .375 H&H Magnum—based on a Granite Mountain Arms action—by Ben Piper of Piper Rifles to light in the 76th Edition of *Gun Digest*. Massaro has often opined that a good Three-Seven-Five can do it all; this gun does it in style.

TIMELINE OF
Tom Turpin's
Contributions to
the *Gun Digest* Annual

We are very pleased to announce that the recipient of the 31st annual John T. Amber Literary Award [is] Tom Turpin. A long-time contributor [to] *Gun Digest*, Tom is being recognized [fo]r two reasons: first, for his story in the [201]th edition, "Fit For A Lady." This story [pr]ofiled Osa Johnson and a custom Mauser [th]at was made for her more than 80 years [a]go. Osa and her husband, Martin, were [a]dventurers who traveled the world filming [d]ocumentaries of their journeys to Africa, [M]alaysia, and the South Sea islands from [1]917 until the mid 1930s.

Tom is also being honored for his many years of devotion to the custom gun trade and his annual report in these pages—always well illustrated with excellent photography—of the finest examples of the gunmaker's art. He was a protégé of the great John Amber himself, editor of *Gun Digest* from 1950 to 1979, and for whom our Literary Award is named. Amber played a major role in promoting the art of the custom gun within these pages as the trade began to grow in the 1950s. We asked Tom to give us his thoughts on John Amber.

"I distinctly remember when I first met John T. Amber. It was in April, 1978, at Alexandria Palace in London, England. I had known who Amber was since the early 1950s, when I first discovered *Gun Digest*. I corresponded with him in the late 1970s about writing an occasional piece for him, which led to our meeting. John and his entourage consisted of a good bit of firearms history. I met John, William B. Ruger, Don and Norma Allen, Al Lind and his wife, and Jim Wilkinson of Rifle Ranch fame, all at the same time. I was truly a kid in the candy store that day.

For some reason, JTA took a liking to me, and took me under his wing, nurturing my budding outdoor writing career along nicely. In addition to publishing some of my early work in *Gun Digest*, he also introduced me around the industry, advising me about who I needed to know, and perhaps more importantly, those I needed to avoid like the plague. His help was invaluable. Over time, he became almost a surrogate father to me."

For this reason particularly, among many others, I am so deeply honored to receive this award carrying his name. I am also honored every year to provide, under my byline, John's favorite part of *Gun Digest*, the custom gun and engraving section."

Tom Turpin was born and raised in Kentucky. After graduating from what is now Eastern Kentucky University in 1959, thanks to the ROTC program, he was commissioned a 2nd Lt. in the United States Army. He entered active duty in the spring of 1960. Early in his army career, he shot competitively on several rifle teams, ending up shooting in the 3rd Army matches at Fort Benning, GA.

Tom's nationally published writing career began in 1972 when Petersen's *Guns & Ammo* published his first article. At the time, he was living in Alaska, during a tour of duty with the US Army. Not long after that, he had a few articles published in *Gun Digest* and *Guns Magazine*. During the seventies and eighties, Tom was very busy balancing a military career, including a couple of tours in Vietnam, an outdoor writing career, and raising a family. He also served as a design consultant to the German firearms manufacturer, F.W. Heym and, from time to time, assisted the German optics company, Schmidt & Bender. Tom's military career ended in retirement as a Lieutenant Colonel after 26 years active duty, at the beginning of 1986.

These days, after more than 40 years in the writing business, several hundred published articles, three books and substantial contributions to several more, he is still at the keyboard. In addition to being a contributing editor to *Gun Digest*, he is a freelance contributor to many other publications in the field. His book, *Artistry in Wood & Metal*, originally published by Safari Club International, was reprinted by Krause Publications in early 2012, and is now on the market.

An avid hunter, he has hunted on four continents. A great fan of the late Jack O'Connor, Tom has found the sage advice contained in O'Connor's writings to be very accurate. As such, his favorite hunting caliber for most situations is the .270 Winchester. Tom and his wife Pauline live and work in the wonderful high desert community of Sierra Vista, Arizona, along with their two Labradors, three German Shorthairs, and 22 Japanese Koi fish. The elk steaks still taste wonderful, the scotch still provides a tranquilizing effect adding to the pleasure of life, and at the ripe old age of 73, Tom is looking forward to his next hunt, and his next story.

- **1955 Edition**–First edition with a dedicated "Custom Rifles" section.
- **1959 Edition**-Artistry in Metal about engraving department with no byline.
- **1996 Edition**-"Custom Guns and Art of the Engraver" department with no byline.
- **2001 Edition**-Editor Ken Ramage introduces Turpin as a "long-time contributor" and his "The Art of the Engraver and Custom Guns" department in black & white.
- **2002 Edition**-The first time Turpin's "The Art of the Engraver and Custom Guns" feature appears in color.
- **2003 Edition**-Turpin's department is renamed to the "Engraved and Custom Gun Review."
- **2006 Edition**-Department renamed to "The Art of Engraved & Custom Guns."
- **2010 Edition**-Turpin's department is again renamed to the more concise "Custom & Engraved Guns." It is now a well-established and regular color feature, dubbed "Our Annual Review of the Finest Examples of Beauty and Artistry in the World of the Custom Gun."
- **2013 Edition**-Tom Turpin is awarded the 31st John T. Amber Award.
- **2022 Edition**-Following the disruptions from the COVID-19 pandemic, Turpin departs from his usual coverage and instead pens a less photo-intensive, more expositional feature, "Five Favored Custom Guns."
- **2023 Edition**-Another departure from his typical full-color photo essay, Turpin pens a shorter feature article, "On Custom Guns," with an in-depth sidebar by editor-in-chief Phil Massaro, titled "The 40th Anniversary of the American Custom Gun Makers Guild."
- **2024 Edition**-Turpin's Custom & Engraved Guns returns with a spectacular collection of high-grade photography. Sadly, it will be his final contribution.

While Turpin always provided plenty of tantalizing engraved firearms that drew your attention, *Gun Digest* features editor Corey Graff came to appreciate Turpin's more subtle selections, the "custom afield" guns, such as this Reto Buehler–Gary Goudy '09 Argentine chambered in 9.3x64 Brenneke.

was founded in 1944 by Milton P. Klein, owner of a major Chicagoland sporting goods store. Guns were in short supply in those World War II years, and Klein reasoned that if people couldn't buy new guns, perhaps they'd like to read about them.'

"Tom Turpin also covered guns many could never afford, but we liked looking at them. It was a wild, emotional roller-coaster ride that left you daydreaming about fancy guns that made the untouchable seem possible: You'd be quickly drawn in and seduced by a deep-blued, color-casehardened, pearl ivory-gripped Colt Single Action Army one minute and, turning the page, a pre-'64 Model 70 with Germanic scroll engraving in the next. He could transport you through time—from the Wild, Wild West to a driven boar hunt in the Black Forest to the African veldt with the flip of a page. Turpin was the Doctor Who of guns."

Jim Schlender, *Gun Digest's* publisher, worked with Tom the longest out of anyone presently involved with the book. He offered the following:

"One of the highlights of my work year has always been cracking open the package of custom and engraved firearms images Tom chose to feature in *Gun Digest*," said Schlender. "He clearly

enjoyed his work, but I'll use that word lightly because I think putting this feature together each year was more of a labor of love for him. During one of our chats, I muttered something about how I'm often disappointed with the game bird art on shotguns. I don't know if he took a cue from that comment or not, but a couple of years later, for the 2021 edition, he included some beautiful imagery created by Brian Hochstrat, presented on a superb Browning Superposed O/U. Instead of a flushing pheasant or quail, Hochstrat featured multiple images of a peregrine falcon, with each sideplate showing the elegant bird dive-bombing a flock of Hungarian partridges. That piece is still one of my favorites among the hundreds of examples he showcased for *Gun Digest*. Tom, I'm eternally grateful for your professionalism, insight and friendship. We'll miss you."

I think the measure of a man is often best found in the views of his sons. Tom's son, Jeff, has helped facilitate his father's submissions over the last few years (Tom and computers didn't quite get along), and I've gotten to know Jeff lately. He wrote the following about his father's legacy.

"As long as I can remember, my

father's passion was sporting rifles and their use in chasing game," Jeff Turpin said. "Sporting rifles is a broad category of firearms, and my father's specific passion was the classic, hunting, bolt-action rifle, with a specific preference for the Winchester pre-'64 Model 70 action. That being said, my father was never known to have kicked a good German Mauser action out of bed, or a classic double rifle, for that matter! It was the walnut, steel, and uncommon artistry that mattered. I inherited this passion for custom rifles and hunting and am forever grateful.

"From collaborating on custom rifle projects with artisans such as Gary Goudy and Reto Buehler to being with me on my first trophy bull elk hunt in Arizona, my father and I were a team. As his hunting years declined over the years, mine stepped up, and he eagerly participated in that transition. Our rituals were the same. Based on the type of game, geographic region, anticipated altitude, and weather, we would identify the short list of ideal calibers. If luck were on our side, we would have a favorite rifle or two in that caliber in our arsenal. Select

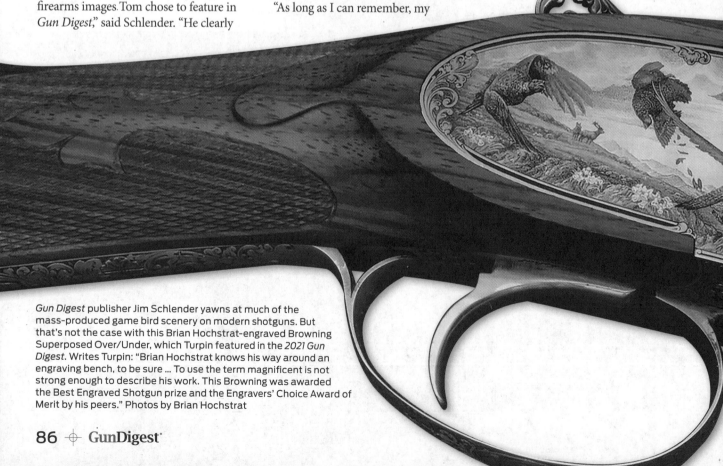

Gun Digest publisher Jim Schlender yawns at much of the mass-produced game bird scenery on modern shotguns. But that's not the case with this Brian Hochstrat-engraved Browning Superposed Over/Under, which Turpin featured in the *2021 Gun Digest*. Writes Turpin: "Brian Hochstrat knows his way around an engraving bench, to be sure ... To use the term magnificent is not strong enough to describe his work. This Browning was awarded the Best Engraved Shotgun prize and the Engravers' Choice Award of Merit by his peers." Photos by Brian Hochstrat

the rifle, then the ideal custom load to complement it. We then got to reloading, and range work, rinse, and repeat. I won't say my father and I were the most pedantic about the process, but rest assured, every rifle we hunted with was at its best, and we knew it inside and out.

"We shared many adventures together, my father and I, and for all the time we spent together, he never wavered from who he was at his core. My father was a 'good ol' boy' from Kentucky whose passion for custom rifles and hunting never waned. He saw it like it was and told it like it is. He loved his wife, Pauline, dearly, and they both shared a love for

In the 2001 edition of the *Gun Digest*, editor Ken Ramage officially introduced readers to Turpin's "The Art of the Engraver and Custom Guns" department, which would be a regular feature for the following 24 years. Ramage also reviewed Turpin's book, *Modern Custom Guns: Walnut, Steel, and Uncommon Artistry.*

About Our Covers...

ON THE OCCASION of this 55th Edition of GUN DIGEST, we illustrate our covers with striking examples selected from some of the finest firearms work by engravers and custom arms makers. The beauty, grace and craftsmanship evident in these arms is a joy to behold and an uplifting experience for all shooting sportsmen and collectors.

Of course, even the most beautifully-executed custom arm cannot be properly appreciated by the reading public unless its image has been captured by a highly talented artisan in the craft of arms photography. Within this 55th Edition, and filling the pages of three books you will shortly read more about, you will see the work of today's most skilled arms photographers.

We extend a special thanks to well-known author Tom Turpin for his part in the preparation of the front and back covers of this edition. He is a long-time contributor to GUN DIGEST, very knowledgeable in all aspects of custom firearms and is, in

fact, the author of two richly-illustrated hardcover books on engraving and custom firearms published recently by Krause Publications. Further, he is the author of the well-illustrated section entitled "The Art of the Engraver & Custom Guns," which begins on page 65 of this 55th Edition.

In coming editions, GUN DIGEST will continue to present selected works of custom arms makers, engravers and arms photographers. Readers seeking even more information on this fascinating class of firearms will be interested in the following commentary regarding three Krause hardcover titles which authoritatively – and beautifully – cover the subjects of custom arms-making and engraving. Two are by Tom Turpin; the third by Steven Dodd Hughes, an author whose talent as a custom gunmaker is matched by his talent as an arms photographer.

As always, feel free to contact me via letter or email (ramagek@krause.com). We hope you enjoy this edition. *KR*

Modern Custom Guns, by Tom Turpin

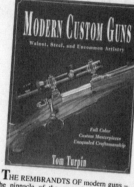

THE REMBRANDTS OF modern guns – the pinnacle of the gunmaker's art – are enjoyed by custom firearms enthusiasts throughout the world as works of art; utilitarian in function, yet exquisite in design. Now a full-color, hardcover book celebrates these creations, paying long-overdue tribute to

the best custom-made guns of today and yesterday.

Modern Custom Guns offers details not found elsewhere, along with more than 200 beautiful full-color photographs that capture perfectly the unique elements of each featured gun.

The book covers the top-of-the-line custom work of today's premier gunmakers, engravers, specialists and artisans – reporting on the detailed workmanship and embellishment of stocks, actions and barrels from expert firearms designers. Included are individual profiles of master craftspeople with detailed, close-up representations of their finest works; details on the custom work of some of the major manufacturers and an in-depth look back at custom firearms and custom arms makers of yesteryear.

From Chapter 8, 'Engraving, Carving, and Inlays' (pages 74&75); *Modern Custom Guns.*

Guns On The Covers

The Front Cover: With no frame of reference, this Farquharson looks to be a standard-size rifle. However, it is an original miniature that is less than half the size of a full-size model. This one has been totally rebuilt with Steve Heilmann doing the metalwork, Darwin Hensley crafting the exquisite stock and Terry Wallace adorning it with his superb engraving. *Photo by Turk's Head Productions, Inc.*

The Back Cover: One of the finest lever-action rifles that I have ever seen. This 1886 Winchester was stocked by Jerry Fisher and engraved by Robert Swartley. Both these artisans have been in the business for many years and each just keeps getting better and better. *Photo by David Wesbrook.*

Tom Turpin

Modern Custom Guns includes chapters covering ownership of custom guns; custom stocks; custom metalsmithing; actions; barrels; *bells and whistles;* sights and sight mounts; engraving, carving and inlays; custom gun guilds; factory custom guns; semi-custom guns and the state-of-the-art today. Featured are many of today's top custom engravers, including Winston Churchill, Mike Dubber, Ralph Ingle, Lynton McKenzie, Ron Smith, Lisa Tomlin and Claus Willig; such specialists as Ted Blackburn, Kathy Forster, Jim Hasson, Marvin Huey, Dave Talley, Doug Turnbull, and Jim Wisner; and top custom arms makers including Dietrich Apel, Mark Cromwell, Steve Heilmann, Jay McCament, the David Miller Co., Bruce Russell and Ed Webber. The book also includes a source directory of engravers, specialists, and custom makers.

"Both (*a custom rifle and a factory product*) will satisfactorily do the job for which they were designed," Turpin says in the book. "Factory rifles vary in sophistication from the mass-produced Remington 700 and its competitors to the more refined Dakota 76 and similar rifles. They are excellent rifles. Each can be relied upon to deliver a bullet on the target, with groups measuring two minutes-of-angle or less. For the hunter who uses a rifle merely as a tool, an assembly line model – identical to thousands of others – is usually plenty good enough.

"On the other hand, for those who want only the best, or who appreciate beauty and admire technical virtuosity above all else, a full custom job is the only way to go ... They can have precisely what they want and can rest assured that the finished rifle will be the best in the world."

Modern Custom Guns (208 full-color pages; 8 1/2x11; hardcover with full-color dust jacket): $49.95.

Art of the Engraver & Custom Gunmaker

by Tom Turpin

A Beretta 682 O/U shotgun stocked and extensively metalsmithed by gunmaker Jay McCament. The engraving is by Bob Evans and the photography by Turk's Head Productions.

Texan Terry Theis did the Germanically-styled engraving and gold inlay work on this floorplate. Terry studied under German Master Engraver and dear friend of mine, the late Erich Boessler. *Photo courtesy of the engraver.*

A magnificent 500 NE double rifle from Dakota Arms. The wonderful engraving was executed by Creative Arts of Italy, who also supplied the photography.

This lovely custom Mauser chambered for the 280 Remington is the work of young custom maker Shane Thompson. His work is clean and crisp and his styling and execution above reproach. This quality of work, coming from a relative youngster, is proof-positive that custom gunmaking is not a dying art. *Photo by Steven Dodd Hughes.*

56th EDITION, 2002 97

Turpin's custom gun feature was first printed in full color in the *2002 Gun Digest* edition. It would remain that way.

dogs. As the years went by, the pandemic hit, and my dad's hunting days were over, including his role as my hunting partner. Even though he couldn't participate actively, he never stopped mentoring and encouraging me and was always present.

"It's been five months or so since my father's passing, and I reflect on my time with him often. I find myself picking up my mobile phone to call him when I am on the road, to give him the latest updates, only to realize he won't answer. As I am sure many readers will know, this reality hits like a ton of bricks. Rest assured, the time I spent with him and the lessons I learned will never be forgotten. His passions live on in me and my family and, with luck, will pass on from generation to generation. Spend time with those you love, don't sweat the little stuff, and most importantly, never forget my father's words, "Life is too short to hunt with an ugly rifle!"

Jeff's twin brother, James (older by just five minutes), also offered some fitting words about his dad: "Our dad was born in Irvine, Kentucky, on August 10, 1938. He left us at Peppi's House Hospice in Tucson, Arizona, five minutes into January 17, 2024. Dad was a retired Lt. Colonel in the United States Army, an avid hunter, and an author of many books and magazine articles. He was also a wonderful husband, father, grandfather, and all-around great guy. I got my love of Porsche 911s from him. He had two in his life when we lived in Germany: an orange Targa and then, later, a beautiful white Carrera SC without AC (not so great when you get stationed in Arizona!). I will always appreciate his timely words of wisdom. I will also always appreciate that he spent many hours with me in the operating room waiting area while my pregnant wife in her 2nd trimester had to have emergency surgery. I will miss him and his piercing blue eyes, kindness, and his 'good ol' boy' humor. We will love and miss him always. Dad was right, though: 'Life is too short to hunt with an ugly rifle.'"

And lastly, Tom's third son, Steve, offered these thoughts: "I feel honored to call myself one of Tom Turpin's sons. It has been an overwhelming experience dealing with his loss, and it would have

been unbearable were it not for all of the fond memories he left behind. From the times we spent together when he coached my little league baseball team to the many times I caddied for him when he golfed with his buddies (including the time he saved me from a rattlesnake I almost stepped on), he was always a character. He never failed to entertain me with his humorous and witty Kentucky sayings, which we lovingly referred to as '*dadisms*.' My dad's true passion was hunting and firearms, and I watched him throughout my life studying and master-

ing the art and mechanics of all things outdoors and rifle! Growing up with him was something I will always treasure and a lesson in knowing that in anything you do, you need to do right. I will miss him forever and will always treasure the memories."

While I am honored to have my name on the cover of the World's Greatest Gun Book, I cherish the relationships built in the process most. Thank you, Tom, for the great chats, your vast knowledge of firearms, and your unique ability to bring the finest pieces to the forefront. ⊕

Tom Turpin and his three sons at James Turpin's wedding.

The great Tom Turpin, autographing one of his books in 2014. He will be missed by all.

The .300 H&H:
First.
Still Best?

It defined ".30 magnum," then sired others. Some hunters say none surpass it. Here's why.

›WAYNE VAN ZWOLL

This lovely Parkwest rifle, a follow-on to the Dakota 76, is chambered in .300 H&H—a superb pairing.

From the hem of a dusky Oregon meadow, I strained to see antlers on the elk cruising timber's edge opposite. Light leaked fast. Then, even the tree limbs merged, erasing the animal in the glade's dark rim. I exhaled and drew the rifle, tight against the sling, in over my knees. The urge to fire had almost trumped good sense. But wanting to see antlers won't make them appear. Attuned to evening's silence, I turned slowly before rising for a quick check of the forest behind.

Tobacconist Harris Holland began making guns in 1835. His nephew Henry apprenticed, then joined him in 1867. Nine years later, the firm became Holland & Holland. Harris signed checks until his death in 1896.

Stark against the dark lodgepoles, near as second base to home plate, stood an elk, eyes locked on me. My pulse skipped, then hammered. Ivory-tipped tines popped the rack from the shadows. A veritable candelabrum! I eased the rifle to my shoulder. The beast loomed large in the Lyman Alaskan. But to my dismay, its tiny dot had vanished in the gloom. I tried in vain to find it as if it were a faint star by looking a bit off to the side. No luck. Desperate, I aimed at a patch of bleached grass at the bull's feet. There! The rifle shook harder as the dot found the elk's shoulder—and vanished. Frantic now, I dipped the dot again into the grass, locked it in my vision and jerked it onto the bull's shoulder, firing as it disappeared.

The Henriksen-stocked Mauser in hand that evening left in an ill-advised trade years later. It was then my only rifle in .300 H&H Magnum. It was not my last.

There's something rangy and raw and, well, *American* about a .30-caliber magnum. Indeed, the first of commercial record was born stateside. Developed by the brilliant Charles Newton and called the .30 Adolph Express after gunmaker Fred Adolph, the big rimless round booted 180-grain bullets out the muzzle at 2,880 fps. In 1913, alas, few hunters were ready for such a rocket. To riflemen of that day, the .30-'06 packed the power of Zeus. Besides, Newton's .30 had no home except in rifles of that name. While of sound design—even pioneering features like the interrupted-thread lock-up Roy Weatherby would use in Mark V rifles 40 years later—Newton's rifles fell victim to the economic tumult triggered by the Great War. Evidently recognizing the cartridge for the gem that it was, Western Cartridge Co. loaded Newton's .30 well after his last attempt to build rifles, dropping it from the roster in 1938.

Meanwhile, the .300 Holland & Holland appeared in Western's catalog. It came from the London shop of Harris Holland and his nephew Henry. Harris had been a tobacconist before taking a career turn in 1835 that would make his shop famous for hunting rifles and

The .300 H&H appeared in London, with the .275 and .375 on the same case, in 1912. It came stateside in 1925. U.S. ammunition had more punch than early British loads, which only matched our .30-'06 in power.

cartridges. Henry became his apprentice in 1861, his partner six years later. In 1876, "Holland & Holland" replaced "H. Holland" as the firm's name of record. But Harris held tight to management decisions, signing all checks until his death in 1896.

A long belted cartridge designed for cordite powder, "Holland's Super .30," as it was called at its 1925 U.S. debut, duplicated .30 Newton performance. Actually, these two cartridges had appeared about the same time. Holland's shop listed the .300 in 1912, along with the .275 and .375 H&H. This trio share a belted case with a .532 rim, though the .275's hull is .35 shorter than the 2.85-inch brass of the .300 and .375. The .300 H&H has the same case taper as its .375 sibling but a more gradual 8½-degree shoulder. This long, gentle shoulder has much to do with the incomparably smooth glide of the leggy cartridges as they nose from magazine to chamber.

Besides bore/bullet diameters and the house of origin, designations for powerful British cartridges of the early 1900s bore such inspiring labels as "Belted Rimless Nitro Express." The "Magnum" moniker came of age then. "Flanged" (rimmed) versions, loaded to slightly lower pressures and velocities, suited hinged-breech rifles.

***

Initially, the .300 H&H was hardly a ballistic champ. The long, pale strands of cordite used by the British had high nitroglycerine content. Pressures climbed when temperature-sensitive cordite loads were exposed to tropical heat. Because

A fine elk cartridge, the Super .30 took Wayne's first elk. A lack of available rifles limited its popularity until Winchester's Model 70 and Remington's Model 721 appeared in 1937 and 1948, respectively.

East Africa was where many British hunting rifles of the day were likely to wind up, propellant charges were held to conservative levels. Velocities for 150-, 180- and 220-grain bullets in the .300 H&H hovered at 3,000, 2,700 and 2,400 fps, respectively, about what we expect of the .30-'06. Later loads by Winchester and Remington would launch 150-grain softpoints at nearly 3,200 fps.

A pointed 180-grain bullet at the American standard of 2,920 fps generates about 3,450 ft-lbs at the muzzle and brings more than 1,900 to 400 yards. Given a 200-yard zero, that bullet strikes 7 inches low at 300 steps, 20 inches low at 400. It flies about 15 percent flatter than if fired from a .30-'06 cartridge and carries a 10 percent advantage in wind.

Loaded stateside with 220- and

In 1937, the .300 H&H became a charter chambering in Winchester's Model 70, the first U.S. rifle to list it.

A fine plains-game cartridge, the .300 H&H has taken animals the world over. John Nosler favored it. His Partition bullet resulted from a bullet failure on a mud-encrusted moose he shot with a .300 H&H.

Driving bonded 150-grain bullets at over 3,150 fps, the .300 H&H shoots flat, takes down tough game.

225-grain bullets at around 2,600 fps, the .300 H&H matched the killing punch of its erstwhile rival, Rigby's .350 Rimless Magnum, introduced in 1908. The Rigby's case had no belt, but its .525 rim and 3.57-inch loaded length were close matches to the .532 and 3.60 measures of the .300. Bullets for the .350 Rigby were .357 in diameter, not .358, long standard in the U.S. Its 225-grain softpoints left the muzzle at an impressive 2,625 fps, pack-ing over 3,400 ft-lbs.

These days, modern powders give century-old cartridges new life, provided the rifles and hulls can bottle their enthu-siasm. To my eye, the most impressive current .300 H&H factory loads are from Nosler. It offers a 200-grain Partition or AccuBond at 2,700 fps for 3,360 ft-lbs of energy. The AccuBond carries over a ton of wallop past 400 yards!

Not until 1955 would Holland & Hol-land follow with another belted cartridge on what has become known as the .375 H&H case. In 1955, it announced the .244 H&H Magnum, its brass short-ened slightly to 2.78 inches. It was still clearly "overbore." That is, its capacity was greater than warranted by the bore, so it didn't burn powder efficiently. It used more than 70 grains of slow powder to give 100-grain bullets their listed velocity of 3,500 fps. The .244 H&H was a commercial flop. The short-action .243 Winchester and .244 Remington arrived stateside at the same time, using less powder to drive 100-grain bullets at 3,100 fps with less blast from lighter, less costly rifles.

Case length also applied the brakes to sales of .300 and .375 H&H rifles in the U.S. Rifle actions designed for the .30-'06, the U.S. infantry cartridge of that day, were too short for these British mag-nums. The .30-'06's 2.49-inch case brings the loaded length to 3.34. The loaded length for the .300 and .375 H&H: 3.60. Even after enlarging the bolt face and perhaps altering the extractor, a shooter wanting to make a magnum from a .30-'06 Springfield or an 8x57 Mauser Model

98 had to find room in the magazine and receiver for the longer cartridges. Some gunsmiths shaved metal from feed ramps. But this surgery imposed a steeper climb on bullets and reduced the strength of the abutment for the bolt's lower locking lug. The .300 H&H that took my first elk was so modified. It gave me no trouble.

During the 1920s and '30s, as surplus houses priced Krags, Mausers and Springfields at irresistible levels, hunters fell in love with the .30-'06. Those craving more power turned to the 1917 Enfield, a stout, if ungainly, action long enough to cycle .300 H&H cartridges. The machining needed to wrest a presentable profile from the 1917 action added considerably to cost—one reason why few svelte 1917 sporters of that era turn up at gun shows.

***

While parts of Europe starved, removing the rubble of WWI, the U.S. partied with barnstormers and flappers, endured Prohibition and gangsters and sent the stock market on a tear. Wealthy sportsmen of that day indulged with fine British magazine rifles on Magnum Mauser actions and custom sporters from New York's Griffin & Howe. The .300 H&H would survive in that rarified air until Winchester offered it as a charter chambering in its Model 70 bolt rifle in 1937.

Meanwhile, it got an unexpected boost from competitive marksman Ben Comfort, who in 1935 won the 1,000-yard Wimbledon Match at Camp Perry with a rifle in .300 H&H. It was built by Griffin & Howe on a Remington 30-S action (essentially a 1917 Enfield without the rear sight "ears"). Its heavy 30-inch Winchester barrel and a prone stock by G&H's Ernest Kerner brought the rifle weight to 13.2 pounds. Comfort added a 10x Lyman Super Targetspot scope to fire

his winning score of 100-14V. He used Western factory loads. During the 1940s, Western cataloged a 180-grain match load for the Super .30, claiming 3,030 fps with a boattail bullet. Subsequently, the .30 H&H would earn its keep mainly as a hunting cartridge.

Comfort's win came less than two years before Winchester introduced the Model 70. Early .375s wore a heavy 24-inch barrel, later replaced by a medium-weight 25-inch. The .300 H&H arrived with a slender 26-inch barrel and, like the 70s bored for lesser cartridges, an "egg-lump" for the rear sight dovetail. I think this is one of the most elegant Model 70s ever built. Winchester also chambered the cartridge in heavy-barreled target rifles for bullseye competitors of the day. In my experience, long barrels are well-suited to the .300 H&H. Remington thought likewise in 1948, fitting a 26-inch .300 H&H barrel to its new Model 721. Other rifles for this magnum would be offered with 24-inch barrels and launch bullets at listed speeds (derived, commonly, from

Stateside, these .30s gave hunters increasing reach in the early 20th century: .30-'06 (1906), .300 H&H Magnum (1925), .300 Weatherby Magnum (1945).

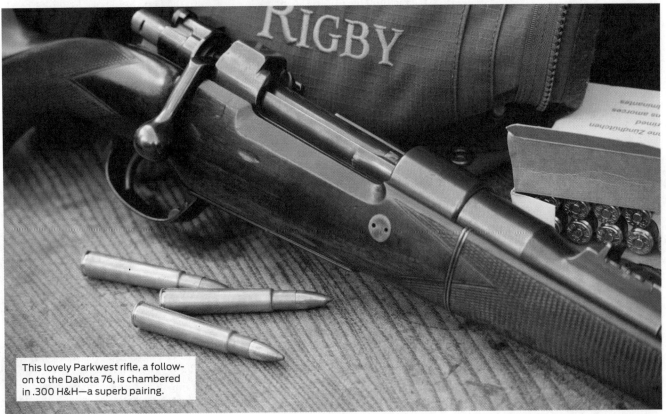

This lovely Parkwest rifle, a follow-on to the Dakota 76, is chambered in .300 H&H—a superb pairing.

EXAMPLES FROM THE NO. 1:

MANUFACTURER/BULLET WEIGHT AND TYPE	VELOCITY (FPS) AT 15 FEET	GROUP (INCHES) AT 100 YARDS
Nosler factory load, 150-gr. AccuBond	3,175	1.0
Federal factory load, 180-gr. TSX	2,993	1.0
Hornady factory load, 180-gr. InterBond	2,939	1.2
Handload: 69 gr. H4831, 200-gr. Nosler Partition	2,823	1.5

A belted magnum for .30-'06-length actions, the .308 Norma arrived stateside in 1960, though first only as unprimed brass! It edges the .300 H&H ballistically. Winchester's .300 Magnum buried both at market.

24-inch lab barrels). But my Model 70 and a Ruger No. 1 with a 26-inch barrel routinely beat those numbers.

Even as Winchester, then Remington, blessed the market with "magnum-length" actions in well-designed, affordable bolt rifles (on the eve of WWII, a Model 70 in .300 H&H listed at $61.80), hunters lusted after a .30 magnum cartridge to pair with mechanisms for the .30-'06. Meanwhile, Roy Weatherby announced a powerful .30 with radiused shoulders on a blown-out .300 H&H case. Initially a proprietary cartridge chambered only in costly Weatherby rifles, the .300 Weatherby Magnum would later earn broad acclaim as the most powerful .300 of a generation.

Oddly enough, the first .30-bore cartridge on a short magnum case hailed from Norma of Sweden. The .308 Norma Magnum hull measures 2.56 inches, slightly longer than the .338 Winchester Magnum's, so it doesn't chamber in barrels bored to .30-338,

developed by wildcatters tired of waiting on Winchester to come up with a .30 magnum. Alas, Norma blunted its entry into the U.S. by first selling only cartridge *cases*. A year and a half later, ammunition followed, "re" on the headstamps signifying reloadable Boxer-primed brass. To my recollection, only Browning then cataloged a rifle in .308 Norma Magnum among American gun companies. That lovely High Power, with FN Mauser action, was made from 1960 to 1974.

Not surprisingly, Norma's big .30 was also picked up by Sweden's own gunmaker, Sako.

***

Winchester's .300 Magnum cartridge arrived in 1963, partly in response to Remington's 7mm Magnum. Riflemen expected a necked-down .338. Winchester instead delivered a belted case with the same head but a length of 2.620 inches and a short .264 neck. Case capacity exceeded the .308 Norma's, but in .30-'06-length actions, deep bullet seating in the .300 Winchester case gave it no practical edge over the .308 Norma.

Both these short belted magnums, essentially re-shaped .30 Supers, are exceedingly versatile. The .300 Winchester has

Remington's Model 721 was designed to keep production costs below those of its 30-S and to best serve budget-minded hunters. Four years after its 1948 debut, the 721 in .300 H&H retailed for $103.90.

become one of the most popular North American big game cartridges. Powerful enough for all but the earth's biggest beasts, it has all the reach a hunter needs and as much recoil as most shooters can handle without flinching badly.

Incidentally, while recoil energy is determined by rifle weight, bullet weight, and exit velocity, "felt" recoil depends on several other variables: Does your rifle have a skinny steel buttplate or a broad Pachmayr pad? A low, sharp comb or one that babies your cheek and helps the rifle come straight back as the bullet leaves? Another factor seems to be case shape. Launching a 180-grain bullet at 2,970 fps from a .300 magnum cartridge in a 7¼-pound rifle, you'll get about 27 ft-lbs of recoil. Bump the rifle weight to 8¼ pounds, and recoil energy drops to 24 ft-lbs. Case shape doesn't affect those figures; but it seems to me—and to many other hunters, including African PHs—that sharp case shoulders bring sharper kick, that long sloping shoulders deliver a "push instead of a punch." This perception holds for cartridges of bigger bore, too, even among people who build dangerous game rifles.

In the 1980s, Don Allen, who founded Dakota Arms, created a series of rimless magnums on the .404 Jeffery case. Developed to fit .30-'06-length actions, the .300 Dakota has a 2.550-inch case of greater diameter than those fashioned on the belted .375 H&H Magnum. Rim and head diameters of the .300 Dakota are .545, trumping the .532 rim of the .375 and .300 H&H and offspring. The Dakota gives up little in diameter from its head to its 32-degree shoulder. Its beefy profile brings powder capacity well over that of the .300 H&H and short belted magnums. It packages the power of the .300 Weatherby Magnum in a 30-'06-length case.

About this time, I hied off to Zimbabwe with a Winchester 70 in .300 Magnum on my first safari. My handloads of 69 grains H4831 and 180-grain Speer and Remington Core-Lokt bullets breezily downed whatever game they struck. Once, after a long morning, I missed the shift in my tracker's body language as he bent over a new set of craters in the sand. He snaked after them through

Wayne prefers 180- and 200-grain bullets in the .300 H&H. These 200-grain Partitions can be launched at nearly 2,800 fps. A better load for elk and moose is hard to find.

Long enough for the .300 H&H, the Model 70 action controls feeding with a non-rotating extractor.

Don Allen borrowed from the Model 70 to design his Dakota action, now under the shingle of Parkwest Arms. Here: a Parkwest bolt face with signature Mauser claw and a slot for the mechanical ejector.

wait-a-bit thorn. A white-hot noon sun dried the blood cross-hatching my arms and legs. Taller trees spilled shadow into the bush ahead. Stumbling blindly on, I almost bumped Philip, still as a shorthair on point. Before I could follow his gaze, the bush erupted almost at our feet. A grenade blast of horn and hide, the tawny beast towered briefly in a vortex of limbs and dust. "Shoot!" Philip rarely spoke; this was no time to chat. The rifle swung itself. I fired as a shoulder the size of a truck door blocked all else behind the

crosswire. The earth seemed to shake as the animal fell. It did not move. I've since shot other Eland, but none closer. None are etched so clearly in memory as that first bull.

Like my first elk, it yielded to Holland & Holland's elegant .300, patriarch of what would become a great clan of .30 magnums. There are yet hunters who remember when ".300 Magnum" on the barrel of a Model 70 meant .300 H&H because there were no others to challenge it. We still wonder if any really do. **GD**

How Does the Super .30 Stack Up Today?

The .300 H&H gave way at market to a flood of more potent .30s. Arguments persist as to which is the "best." Higher velocity and heavier bullets impose more recoil as they deliver flatter flight and harder hits downrange. Here are some numbers:

.300 H&H MAGNUM
(HORNADY, 180-GRAIN INTERBOND)

	MUZZLE	100 YDS.	200 YDS.	300 YDS.
Velocity (fps)	2,870	2,678	2,493	2,316
Energy (ft-lbs)	3,292	2,865	2,484	2,144
Arc (in.)	-1.5	+1.7	0	-7.3

.300 WEATHERBY MAGNUM
(WEATHERBY, 180-GRAIN NOSLER PARTITION)

	MUZZLE	100 YDS.	200 YDS.	300 YDS.
Velocity (fps)	3,240	3,028	2,826	2,634
Energy (ft-lbs)	4,198	3,665	3,194	2,772
Arc (in.)	-1.5	+1.2	0	-5.5

.300 REMINGTON ULTRA MAG
(FEDERAL, 180-GRAIN BARNES TRIPLE-SHOCK X)

	MUZZLE	100 YDS.	200 YDS.	300 YDS.
Velocity (fps)	3,150	2,930	2,730	2,530
Energy (ft-lbs)	3,965	3,440	2,970	2,555
Arc (in.)	-1.5	+1.3	0	-6.0

.308 NORMA MAGNUM
(NORMA, 180-GRAIN ORYX)

	MUZZLE	100 YDS.	200 YDS.	300 YDS.
Velocity (fps)	2,953	2,630	2,330	2,049
Energy (ft-lbs)	3,486	2,766	2,170	1,679
Arc (in.)	-1.5	+1.8	0	-8.2

Limited runs of rifles in .300 H&H include a Ruger No. 1 single-shot built for Cabelas. It gave the author this group. The Super .30's gradual 8½-degree shoulder (foreground) makes it feed smoothly.

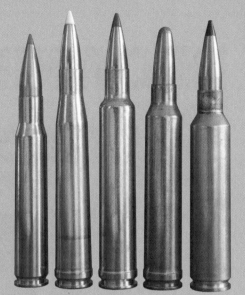

L-R: .30-'06, .300 H&H, .300 Weatherby (a "blown-out" .300 H&H), .300 Winchester and .300 Dakota. Like the Dakota, many powerful cartridges now (like the PRCs) lack a belt and headspace on the shoulder.

.300 WINCHESTER MAGNUM
(WINCHESTER, 180-GRAIN POWER MAX BONDED)

	MUZZLE	100 YDS.	200 YDS.	300 YDS.
Velocity (fps)	2,960	2,722	2,496	2,281
Energy (ft-lbs)	3,501	2,961	2,490	2,080
Arc (in.)	-1.5	+1.6	0	-7.2

.300 DAKOTA
(DAKOTA, 180-GRAIN SWIFT A-FRAME)

	MUZZLE	100 YDS.	200 YDS.	300 YDS.
Velocity (fps)	3,250	2,999	2,763	2,538
Energy (ft-lbs)	4,223	3,597	2,575	2,051
Arc (in.)	-1.5	+1.2	0	-5.8

.300 REMINGTON SHORT ACTION ULTRA MAG
(REMINGTON, 180-GRAIN CORE-LOKT ULTRA BONDED)

	MUZZLE	100 YDS.	200 YDS.	300 YDS.
Velocity (fps)	2,960	2,727	2,506	2,295
Energy (ft-lbs)	3,501	2,972	2,509	2,105
Arc (in.)	-1.5	+1.6	0	-7.1

.300 WINCHESTER SHORT MAGNUM
(WINCHESTER, 180-GRAIN POWER-POINT)

	MUZZLE	100 YDS.	200 YDS.	300 YDS.
Velocity (fps)	2,970	2,755	2,549	2,353
Energy (ft-lbs)	3,526	3,034	2,598	2,214
Arc (in.)	-1.5	+1.6	0	-7.0

.300 RUGER COMPACT MAGNUM
(HORNADY, 180-GRAIN SST)

	MUZZLE	100 YDS.	200 YDS.	300 YDS.
Velocity (fps)	3,040	2,840	2,649	2,466
Energy (ft-lbs)	3,693	3,223	2,804	2,430
Arc (in.)	-1.5	+1.4	0	-6.4

Here are a few important things to keep in mind with these comparisons:

1 The .300 H&H was designed for cordite powder and has pronounced case taper with a long neck. Its sibling "full-length" magnums (.300 Weatherby and .300 Remington Ultra Mag, with 2.85-inch cases) have less body taper and sharper shoulders, so greater case capacity. They were developed much later.

2 "Short belted magnums" (.308 Norma, .300 Winchester, also the rimless .300 Dakota, with 2.55- to 2.62-inch cases) have limited body taper and sharp shoulders to match the .300 H&H's powder capacity.

3 Short rimless magnums (.300 Remington SAUM, .300 Winchester WSM, .300 Ruger RCM, with cases about 2.10 inches long) have "fatter" bodies. Powder columns are shorter but greater in diameter.

4 Long-range velocity, energy, and drop figures depend a great deal on each bullet's ballistic coefficient and less and less on launch speed as distance increases.

5 While the factory loads listed are representative, new loads are ever replacing old. These may be more or less ambitious than their predecessors. The few .300 H&H factory loads still available have much more zip than original British loads, but not all equal the performance claimed for the frothiest U.S. loads.

BROWNING Sweet 16

Why the 16-gauge A-5 "Humpback" hit the sweet spot for generations of shooters.

❯ NICK HAHN

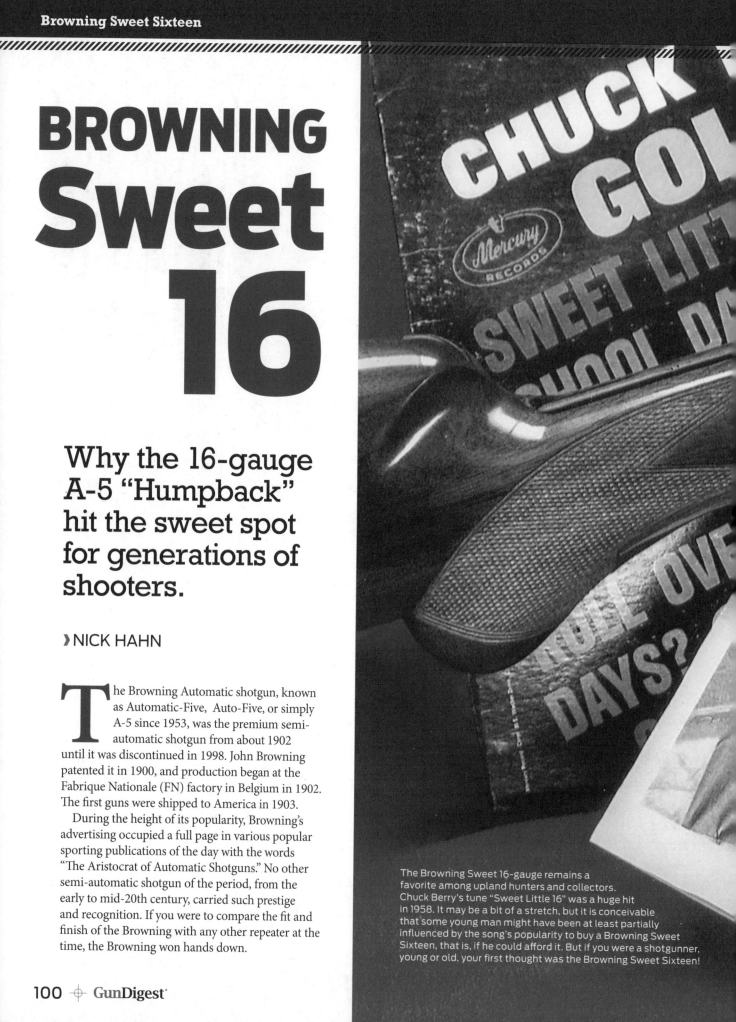

The Browning Automatic shotgun, known as Automatic-Five, Auto-Five, or simply A-5 since 1953, was the premium semi-automatic shotgun from about 1902 until it was discontinued in 1998. John Browning patented it in 1900, and production began at the Fabrique Nationale (FN) factory in Belgium in 1902. The first guns were shipped to America in 1903.

During the height of its popularity, Browning's advertising occupied a full page in various popular sporting publications of the day with the words "The Aristocrat of Automatic Shotguns." No other semi-automatic shotgun of the period, from the early to mid-20th century, carried such prestige and recognition. If you were to compare the fit and finish of the Browning with any other repeater at the time, the Browning won hands down.

The Browning Sweet 16-gauge remains a favorite among upland hunters and collectors. Chuck Berry's tune "Sweet Little 16" was a huge hit in 1958. It may be a bit of a stretch, but it is conceivable that some young man might have been at least partially influenced by the song's popularity to buy a Browning Sweet Sixteen, that is, if he could afford it. But if you were a shotgunner, young or old, your first thought was the Browning Sweet Sixteen!

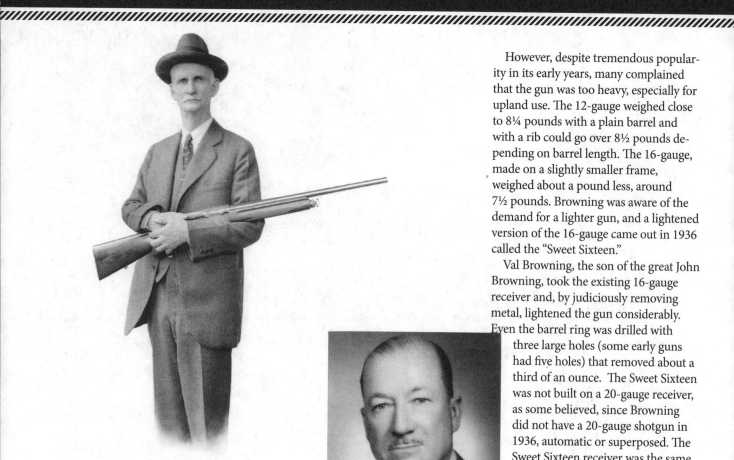

John Browning holding his favorite shotgun invention, the Automatic-Five. The gun he is holding is very early, a 12-gauge with no engraving and a straight grip stock. It was also regularly supplied with sling swivels. Later, the A-5 evolved with engraving and a rounded semi-pistol grip, and, for the American market, swivels were supplied only on request.

Val Browning, the son of the great John Browning, although overshadowed by his father, was a great firearms inventor in his own right. Val Browning's first great contribution was the redesigning/lightening of the 16-gauge to produce the Sweet Sixteen in 1936. He went on to design the single trigger mechanism for the Superposed and downsized it to a very successful 20-gauge, which appeared postwar in 1949.

This full-page advertisement for the Browning Automatic shotgun is from 1947 when Browning started importing Belgian guns after the war. The gun that is portrayed is a 16-gauge. Note its slender look and the ¼-inch milled step on the barrel at the receiver. However, the gun in the ad is not a Sweet Sixteen, which would have had the trigger and the front safety gold-plated.

However, despite tremendous popularity in its early years, many complained that the gun was too heavy, especially for upland use. The 12-gauge weighed close to 8¼ pounds with a plain barrel and with a rib could go over 8½ pounds depending on barrel length. The 16-gauge, made on a slightly smaller frame, weighed about a pound less, around 7½ pounds. Browning was aware of the demand for a lighter gun, and a lightened version of the 16-gauge came out in 1936 called the "Sweet Sixteen."

Val Browning, the son of the great John Browning, took the existing 16-gauge receiver and, by judiciously removing metal, lightened the gun considerably. Even the barrel ring was drilled with three large holes (some early guns had five holes) that removed about a third of an ounce. The Sweet Sixteen was not built on a 20-gauge receiver, as some believed, since Browning did not have a 20-gauge shotgun in 1936, automatic or superposed. The Sweet Sixteen receiver was the same on the outside as the Standard 16 model receiver.

All the internal lightening cuts made the gun lighter and livelier. Some early prototypes with radically "shaved" receivers weighed as little as 6¼ pounds. Ultimately, the gun offered to the public was a bit heavier, did not have the shaved appearance, and externally looked the same as the Standard 16, except for the gold-plated trigger and safety.

The Sweet Sixteen's serial numbering was the same as the Standard model until about mid-1953. Before World War II, all Browning automatics, 12- and 16-gauges, had serial numbers that began without a prefix letter. After the war, the serial numbers for the 16s began with the prefix X. In 1953, the serial numbers on the Sweet Sixteen changed to begin with the prefix S, while the Standard had the prefix R. The name Sweet Sixteen was engraved on the receiver's left side starting in 1948-49. Even before the name engraving and the change in serial number prefix, the iconic model always had the trigger and the front safety gold-plated. So, besides the lighter weight, you could always tell the Sweet Sixteen from the

Standard Model by the gold-plated parts.

The Sweet Sixteen was advertised as the ultimate upland shotgun. It weighed a pound less than its larger 12-gauge brother, so it appealed to many upland gunners. At about 6¾ pounds average with a plain barrel, it was not a lightweight by today's standards. But back in the day, when the Standard 16-gauge model tipped the scales at around 7¼ pounds or more, a gun weighing around half a pound less was a considerable improvement. Most semi-auto shotguns of that era tended to be heavy, and the Browning Sweet Sixteen was an exception—it was light in comparison.

In the 1950s, the new Remington Model 11-48 and the Savage Model 775 "Lightweight" were the only other semi-autos available in 16-gauge, but both weighed around 7 pounds or more, although the Remington Model 11-48 16-gauge was advertised as being at "about" 6¾ pounds. Still, it averaged 7 pounds. The Savage Model 775 Lightweight with its alloy receiver was listed at 7 pounds for the 16-gauge. The discontinued Remington Model 11 was still around but weighed over 7 pounds in 16-gauge. The Browning Sweet Sixteen averaged 6¾ pounds with a plain barrel.

Additionally, the Browning A-5 has always had the most compact receiver of all repeaters. A Sweet Sixteen with a 26-inch barrel has the same overall length as most double guns with 28-inch barrels! As far as 16-gauge semi-autos were concerned, nothing around could compare with the Sweet Sixteen, not in weight and certainly not in quality of make, fit, and finish.

The Sweet Sixteen became one of the most popular Browning shotguns. It became a massive success in Europe, where the 16-gauge was always liked. To paraphrase Matt Eastman, the author of *Matt Eastman's Guide to Browning Belgium Sporting Firearms*, "… the Sweet 16, one of the company's best sellers, did more to popularize the Auto-5 than any other model."

In 1953, HRH Crown Prince Akihito (Emperor of Japan from 1989–2019) went on a worldwide tour at age 20. Like most young men of his generation and social standing, Akihito was an avid sportsman. Being of small stature and

Many hunters in parts of the Midwest and the West considered the Sweet Sixteen the ultimate pheasant gun. It was light enough to carry all day yet could handle loads powerful enough to knock down those tough roosters. This is a mid-1950s-vintage gun that accounted for many ringnecks.

A 1955-vintage Browning Sweet Sixteen with proper loads made for a dandy duck gun. Even the well-known proponent of big bores, Elmer Keith, who was fond of the 10-gauge for duck shooting, stated that the 16 made for an excellent waterfowl gun over decoys. Many gunners used the 16-gauge for duck hunting, including Jack O'Connor, Elmer Keith's literary adversary!

The slogan "The Aristocrat of Automatic Shotguns" went a long way to convince many that the Browning was the best that you could get. This one is from 1957, possibly during the Sweet Sixteen's peak popularity. Although the 20-gauge appeared the following year, the Sweet Sixteen was still the best seller for several years. Note that the gun has a ventilated rib, which Browning began to push starting around the mid-1950s.

slightly built, he was known to shoot a 16, a better fit than the bigger 12.

During the world tour, Akihito visited Belgium's famous arms factory, Fabrique Nationale (FN), which was the maker of all Browning firearms at the time. The FN front office had arranged to present the Crown Prince with a special 20-gauge Superposed. But he upset those plans when casually remarking that the Browning Automatic was his favorite. The FN brass was caught by surprise and had no time to prepare a special automatic. Fortunately, they found a very nice high-grade Sweet Sixteen that had its order recently canceled, so that gun was presented to him. When the public learned that the Crown Prince had a Sweet Sixteen, Browning shotgun sales spiked significantly in Japan, even though money was very tight when it was still recovering from the devastation of WWII. Besides Japan's Crown Prince, many members of the world's royalty, rich and famous, owned and shot Browning A-5s.

Of all the Browning automatic shotguns, many consider the Sweet Sixteen to be the best handling of the lot. It has just the right amount

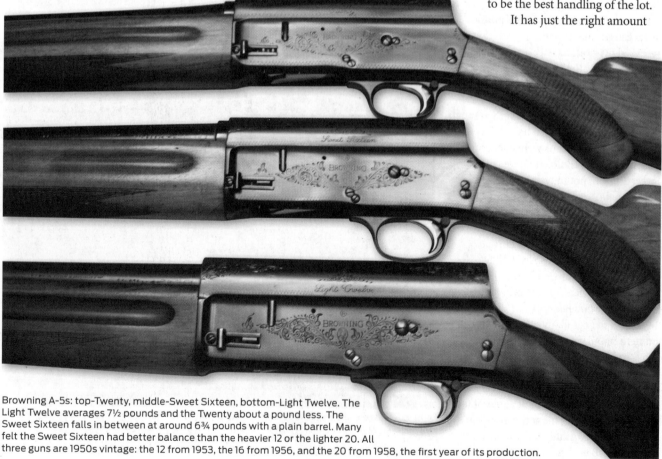

Browning A-5s: top-Twenty, middle-Sweet Sixteen, bottom-Light Twelve. The Light Twelve averages 7½ pounds and the Twenty about a pound less. The Sweet Sixteen falls in between at around 6¾ pounds with a plain barrel. Many felt the Sweet Sixteen had better balance than the heavier 12 or the lighter 20. All three guns are 1950s vintage: the 12 from 1953, the 16 from 1956, and the 20 from 1958, the first year of its production.

of heft, feel, and balance. The 20-gauge is lighter than the Sweet Sixteen on the average by about a ¼ pound. But for some, it lacks the dynamic feel of the Sweet Sixteen. The 20-gauge Magnum model, on the other hand, is heavier.

Many found the Browning Automatic shotgun not very appealing visually. The shape of the square stern receiver had much to do with this negative view. However, the old saying "handsome is as handsome does" applies here, for many shooters and collectors appreciated the Browning's square stern. There are certainly more modern-looking, sleeker, semi-automatic shotguns available today, at least in the opinion of some. Many criticized the old gun and welcomed its discontinuance in 1998. It's a relic, some said, an old-fashioned design that is almost a century old.

True, it was designed in the 19th Century and has that 19th-Century look. But there is something to be said about a solidly built gun with beautifully machined and precisely fitted parts, even if it is a repeater and not a double gun. No semi-auto shotgun on the market today has quite the charisma or the solid feel of the old Browning A-5.

John Browning originally designed the Auto-5 in 12-gauge. But when Browning Arms Company, headed by his son Val, decided to release the scaled-down version in the Sweet Sixteen, it seemed to have hit upon a magic formula. The lightened 16-gauge variant had the perfect size and weight combination for an ideal-handling semi-automatic shotgun, at least for the 16-gauge.

There is something about the Sweet Sixteen that feels just right. It is neither the lightest 16 by any stretch of the imagination nor the slimmest and sleekest. But compared to the 12, it looks slimmer and sleeker. Its receiver is 5/8 of an inch shorter in length, 1/10th of an inch thinner, and lower in height. That may not seem like much, but when combined with the slimmer 16's barrel, it reduces weight considerably and visually appears slimmer. Small wonder the Browning full-page ads of the past always showed the 16-gauge model rather than the 12-gauge—Browning's marketing people felt that the 16 was more "photogenic"

This is a 1975 Sweet Sixteen from the final year of Belgian manufacture. These models have a feel and pointability that is easier to experience than to describe. The Bicentennial Year 1976 saw the introduction of the first Japanese Miroku-made A-5s, and Sweet Sixteens were not in the lineup until they were resurrected in 1987.

than the 12. Just heft a Sweet Sixteen, and you will realize there is much more to this gun than its appearance.

The late Don Zutz said it best in a piece he wrote in 1998, in which he talked about the passing of an era and the discontinuance of the A-5 that year. He said the A-5 was outmoded, and the new gas-operated Browning Gold was taking over. Zutz favored the Remington Model 1100 throughout his gun writing career and considered the 1100 the best-handling semi-auto ever made. Yet, to quote him directly: "In my not-so-humble opinion, the Browning A-5 Sweet Sixteen was among the greatest upland guns … My own use of the Sweet Sixteen was very limited, but if I had to, I could spend my entire career with one and not complain." He wrote this in the "Gun Rack" column of the June/July 1998 issue of the former *Wing & Shot* magazine.

Those who read Zutz know he was somewhat critical of the A-5. He was a great promoter of modern gas-operated semi-autos such as the Remington 1100 and felt that the A-5's long recoil system was antiquated. Yet, all bets were off

when it came to the Sweet Sixteen.

The Browning Automatic underwent several mechanical and cosmetic changes throughout its production. The very early 12- and 16-gauges had straight-grip stocks. That is how John Browning designed the gun. However, in time, the rounded semi-pistol grip became the standard, and for a long time, it became a trademark of Browning shotguns, called the "round knob" by aficionados. The straight grip option was available until 1966. In fact, the full pistol grip option was available as well. In 1967, Browning switched to the full pistol grip, the so-called "flat knob," which lasted into Japanese production until the 1980s when the new version of the round knob was revived.

When the Sweet Sixteen first appeared in 1937, it was offered as a three- or a five-shot. The three-shot version was introduced in 1934 for the 12 and the 16 to answer the new legislation limiting magazine capacity for waterfowl. Ironically, Browning introduced the wooden plug two years later, in 1936, which easily converted the five-shot into a three-shot and then, if needed, just as easily changed it back to a five-shot by removing the plug. The plug made the three-shot model redundant, and Browning stopped importing it in 1940.

1940 was also the final year of Belgian Browning manufacture until the war ended. When Belgian Browning imports resumed in 1947, some three-shots were imported as "Browning Specials." But this lasted only for that first year in 1947 when imports resumed postwar. There were far more three-shots made in 12-gauge and Standard 16 than as Sweet Sixteens, and although Browning did not import three-shots after 1947, FN continued to make them well into the 1970s until Belgian production ceased.

The three-shot versions were popular in some regions of the world. Although the weight difference between the three- and five-shot was very slight, usually just a couple of ounces, the three-shot did have a livelier feel. The shorter magazine tube and forearm (about an inch) made for a different feel with a lighter front. Some Browning fans were upset that Browning stopped importing the three-shot. Despite the lack of additional shots,

they felt that it made for a better upland gun: lighter and better handling for the uplands than the standard five-shot Sweet Sixteen. Be that as it may, 1947 was the last year Browning imported the three-shot.

The following change occurred when the short 2 9/16-inch chambers were dropped in favor of the longer 2¾-inch chambers. This required the installation of a sliding ejector in the barrel extension. Cosmetically, the Grade I was initially without engraving. However, starting in 1938, Browning began to offer Grade I shotguns with an engraving pattern similar to the earlier Grade II. Pre-war Browning offered Grades I to IV. In 1940, Grades II to IV were dropped and available on special order only. The FN guns (non-Browning imports) were without engraving as Grade I. Specially engraved exhibition and presentation guns, as well as commemorative models, were produced throughout the years.

Postwar, the grip checkering pattern was shortened. The front sliding safety was replaced in

1950–51 with a rear crossbolt. The introduction of the so-called "speed loading" system, which Val Browning designed for the new two-shot Double Automatic, occurred in 1952. Simply put, the shooter didn't need to load the chamber first by chambering a round and then insert additional rounds into the magazine. The speed loading system allowed the gunner to stuff the round into the magazine (with the bolt open), and the first round would automatically feed into the chamber. To this day, Browning is the only company that has employed the system in its autoloading shotguns. No doubt its patent is still in effect.

That system was introduced into the five-shot semi-auto in about 1953. Browning and private gunsmiths also retrofitted many older guns with the system. So, you may come across a gun made before 1953, even some pre-war models with the feature.

While the change to crossbolt safety may not necessarily have been an im-

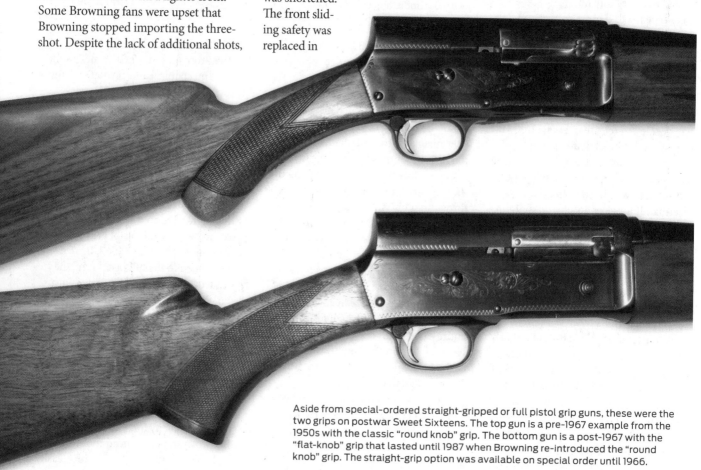

Aside from special-ordered straight-gripped or full pistol grip guns, these were the two grips on postwar Sweet Sixteens. The top gun is a pre-1967 example from the 1950s with the classic "round knob" grip. The bottom gun is a post-1967 with the "flat-knob" grip that lasted until 1987 when Browning re-introduced the "round knob" grip. The straight-grip option was available on special order until 1966.

provement, the introduction of the speed loading feature won approval from most. However, as with the safety, some didn't care. At this time, the name Automatic Five was introduced to differentiate the five-shot from the new two-shot Double Automatic. There were no other mechanical changes for the rest of its production life except for the introduction of choke tubes in the 1980s.

The receivers were all given deep satin rust blue until 1959-60 when the less expensive hot blue dipping was implemented to save costs. Although the rust-blued receiver looked richer, some considered the hot blue process attractive and durable. The wood had an oil finish during the prewar and early postwar periods, then switched to a hand-rubbed lacquer finish. But in the early 1960s, the shiny spray-on synthetic finish (used today) replaced the more costly oil and lacquer.

Another cost-saving change that took place was something most may not have noticed. Before the early 1960s, all Browning pins and screws were solid pieces. But sometime in the period between 1961 and 1962, the small cartridge stop, carrier latch, and magazine cut-off pins were changed from solid screws to hollow, rolled pins. Then, as already mentioned, starting in 1967, all Browning shotgun stocks were made with a flat bottom full pistol grip rather than the old, rounded semi-pistol style. The grip configuration change simplified the checkering pattern. All cosmetic changes were made to save costs, although Browning PR referred to them as "modernizing."

The buttplates were predominantly made of horn prewar and into the 1950s, although hard rubber ones were used during the same period. Around the early 1960s, plastic took over. The horn buttplates were notorious for getting badly disfigured with so-called 'worm holes' and cracks and chips, so some shooters preferred the plastic or earlier hard rubber type. The buttplates all had the FN logo surrounded by the words Browning Automatic in fancy script. This changed when the manufacturing switched to Japan. The plastic buttplates on Japanese-made guns were named Browning, like on the Superposed buttplates.

The Sweet Sixteen at the top is a 1956 vintage with crossbolt safety. At the bottom is a 1947 vintage (first postwar import) with a front safety. The name Sweet Sixteen was not initially engraved on the guns, although it was called that from the beginning in 1936. It wasn't until sometime in late 1948 to early 1949 that the name was engraved on the upper-left side of the receiver. Also, the front safety and trigger were always gold-plated on the Sweet Sixteen. The newer crossbolt-type safety was introduced around 1952. The Standard 16, along with the Standard 12, had plain-blued triggers, and both models were discontinued in 1968.

A pair of Sweet Sixteens from the 1950s. Many consider the mid-1950s the best years for Browning Automatic shotguns. The guns were made three years apart, the one on the left in 1953 and the one on the right in 1956. Everything else is all-original except for the wood, which was refinished on both guns (in oil, like the original). The older 1953 gun shows more blue wear, especially around the sharp edges.

A beautifully engraved Grade IV Sweet Sixteen. Before World War II, Browning offered higher grades, engraved and stocked with gorgeous wood. However, due to rising costs and a lack of demand, the high-grade A-5s were dropped in 1940. They were exquisite and ranged from Grade I to Grade IV. Of course, there were always special order, exhibition, and presentation models that were fabulously engraved and stocked.

The lavishly decorated 2-millionth Commemorative model was made only in 12-gauge in 1970. It was produced and engraved in Belgium since Browning had not started making A-5s in Japan yet. This engraving pattern was created 40 years earlier for the 1930 World's Fair Exhibition.

Another small change took place in 1976 with the switch to Japan. The barrel ring was no longer an integral part of the barrel but was a separate piece that was brazed on, and it lacked the three holes drilled for lightening. All these changes explain why die-hard Browning aficionados consider the best years for the Browning A-5 to be from the mid to late 1950s, after the introduction of the rear crossbolt safety and the speed-loading system and before the change to the synthetic wood finish and other cost-saving changes.

Also, the checkering on the grip and the engraving on the receiver were slightly increased sometime around 1954. But rather than the mid to late 1950s, the period should be expanded from around 1953 (when speed loading was incorporated) to about 1963 (when screws were replaced with rolled pins, wood finished with synthetic spray, and receivers no longer rust blued)—a decade or so that some refer to as the "golden age" for all Belgian-made Browning firearms. But, here again, it is all a matter of personal taste and opinion. There were those, for instance, who preferred the older front sliding safety over the newer crossbolt. This was especially true of those WWII and Korean War veterans who were used to the front safety of the M1 Garand.

Browning was always very accommodating to customers, and one could place a special order for just about any length barrel. For 12-gauge, a barrel as long as 34 inches with just about any choke could be ordered. Different stock dimensions, such as a straight grip and oil or synthetic finish, could also be had. The 16-gauge was available regularly in 26- or 28-inch barrel lengths but could be ordered with a longer 30- and the shorter 24-inch barrel with or without a rib. Because

Browning's current production A5 Sweet Sixteen. This 16-gauge autoloading shotgun with a humpback receiver sports a gloss walnut stock, fiber-optic sight, recoil-operated Kinematic Drive, and Invector-DS interchangeable choke tubes.

these barrels were cut to metric measurements, they came out short, for example, 25½ inches instead of 26 and 27½ inches instead of 28. They were cut to metric lengths of 65cm for the 25½ and 70cm for the 27½. Consequently, the longer 30-inch barrel was 29½ (75cm), and the shorter 24-inch barrel was 23½ inches (60cm). A 5cm difference separated each barrel length.

In 1963, when Browning offered the Buck Special barrels with rifle sights, they were listed as 23½ inches (60cm). However, Browning later listed them as 24 inches. These short barrels were also available on special order with or without a ventilated rib and choked improved cylinder or modified before 1963, they were just not cataloged as regular items. A Sweet Sixteen that typically weighed around 6¾ pounds with a plain 26- or 28-inch barrel could be ordered with a short 24-inch barrel (23½) that lowered the weight closer to 6½ pounds. So, the entire spectrum of 16-gauge barrel lengths ranged from 30 (29½) inches down to 24 (23½) inches. There are even some that were special ordered with much shorter 20- and 22-inch barrels.

The Sweet Sixteen was discontinued in 1976 when Belgian manufacture of the A-5 switched to Japan. However, in 1987, Browning brought it back following numerous requests for the model. Its return coincided with Browning introducing the Citori over/under in 16-gauge. The Japanese-made Sweet Sixteen was no different from its Belgian predecessor, except for the "Invector" choke tubes and the brazed barrel ring. The early Japanese-made guns, the 12s and 20s, did not have the choke tube barrels and had the flat bottom full pistol grip stocks. So, they were identical to the Belgian guns for all practical purposes. The only noticeable superficial

This is a 1956-vintage Sweet Sixteen that still retains most of its original rust blue on the receiver. It has very nice wood for a Grade I, and it hits the scale at 6¾ pounds with its plain 25½-inch barrel. Like all Sweet Sixteens, it's not a lightweight by today's standards, but certainly light enough to carry comfortably all day in the field. An excellent upland gun that truly "carries like a 20 and shoots like a 12!"

A Ducks Unlimited 1988 Sweet Sixteen made in Japan. Several high-grade Custom Shop A-5s were produced in the 1980s and '90s before the gun was discontinued. Some of these heavily engraved models were given old-grade designations with higher numbers, such as Grade V and VI, which did not exist prewar. Some were manufactured in Japan but engraved in Belgium, others entirely in Japan, and others entirely made and engraved in Belgium.

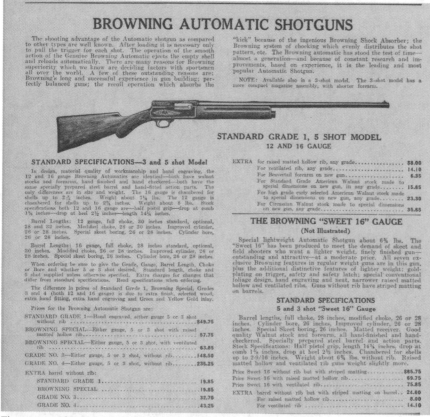

Three years after its introduction in 1936, the Sweet Sixteen was advertised in the 1939 Stoeger's catalog, the predecessor of today's *Shooter's Bible*. Note that the illustrated gun has that telltale milled step on the barrel by the receiver, indicating a 16-gauge. It was also in 1939 that Browning started to offer Grade I engraving. At $65.75 a copy, the author would have loved to have purchased about a dozen. Of course, that would be more like $2,500 in today's money.

difference was that the plastic buttplate was like the one on the Superposed, with just the name Browning on it.

Also, the magazine cap had three knurled bands or rings rather than two like the FN guns. However, some FN shotguns were made in the mid-1970s that had magazine caps with three bands. Then, perhaps to prop up flagging sales, Browning returned to the rounded semi-pistol grip configuration.

The Japanese Sweet Sixteens tended to be heavier than the Belgian guns. Wood density was one reason. Also, Japanese steel is heavier than Belgian. But, besides the heavier wood and steel, Japanese Sweet Sixteens were available only with a ventilated rib barrel, no plain barrel versions. Also, the Invector choke system required the barrels to be slightly thicker, adding more weight. When you combine all of these things, you can see why Japanese-made Sweet Sixteens would be heavier than Belgian. Finding a Japanese-produced Sweet Sixteen that is as light as the Belgian guns would be very difficult. However, the Japanese models are very well made, as good as the Belgian ones, and they have the advantage of steel shot-safe barrels.

Many gun writers dubbed the 16-gauge the "Queen of the Uplands," the perfect gauge for upland gunning. They believed Browning's Sweet Sixteen packaged the 16-gauge with an ideal balance, weight, and handling qualities to make it a perfect upland semi-auto.

The Belgian-made Sweet Sixteens were discontinued in 1976, and the model was not manufactured in Japan until 1987. The Japanese-made Sweet Sixteen had a short run, only about five years as a regular production, until 1992. There were some special small runs after 1992, but the entire A-5 line was discontinued in 1998.

In 2016, Browning brought out a new "Sweet Sixteen" A-5 that is inertia-operated and made in Portugal. With its alloy receiver, it weighs a wispy 6 pounds, almost a pound less than the old Sweet Sixteen. It has been around for almost a decade and has had a pretty favorable reception, according to gun reviews. Only time will tell if it has the staying power of the original. Its "modern-looking" design and sharp angular features may not appeal to everyone; however, to some who prefer a different appearance and think that the discontinued A-5 is old-fashioned, the new gun may suit their needs.

Ironically, not long ago, Browning announced the new Sweet Sixteen "Lightning" model. This version has the classic, traditional-looking stock and forearm with that round knob semi-pistol grip that was so popular on the old A-5. As the saying goes, *what's old is new*, and the old Sweet Sixteen has been at least somewhat resurrected superficially. But, despite its name, it is not the same Sweet Sixteen, not by a long shot.

To many who have shot and carried the old Sweet Sixteen in the field, there is nothing quite like it. The solid feel, yet relatively light weight, and good balance with a weight between the hands is something the newer guns cannot duplicate, even if they are made to resemble the old model. Who knows, maybe the old Browning A-5 and the Sweet Sixteen will be resurrected by someone or Browning. Look at what happened to the Browning Hi Power pistol: Browning discontinued it in 2018. However, different makers are now marketing several versions, and FN has brought it back. Perhaps the same thing will happen to the old A-5 and the classic Sweet Sixteen.

Incidentally, a clone of the Browning A-5 is still being made and sold in Japan. It is produced with both steel and alloy receivers by a couple of companies and is quite popular. It wouldn't be difficult for someone to start importing one of these Japanese-made A-5s or have Miroku resume production. Who knows, like the Hi Power, there may be a return of the old Browning A-5 and the wonderful Sweet Sixteen. How about one with an alloy receiver like the old Super Light A-5? That would be a real lightweight. In the meantime, for most Browning enthusiasts, the return of the old "original" Sweet Sixteen is good enough. GD

3" Mag. 12 Gauge   Light 12 Gauge   Sweet 16 Gauge   3" Mag. 20 Gauge   Buck Special 12 Gauge

A lineup of A-5s from Browning's 1975 catalog still includes the Sweet Sixteen. This was the last year of Belgian-made A-5s. Later, in the early 1980s, some Belgian A-5s appeared, assembled with leftover parts at the FN factory. These shotguns were poorly finished and avoided by knowledgeable Browning collectors.

A Trio of Czechs

Three primary military small arms that defied the Soviet Union from 1952 to 1984: the CZ52 pistol (top), the Vz 52 (center) and the Sa.Vz 58 (bottom). Author Collection

Guns that challenged the Russian Bear ... before the Berlin Wall fell and the party ended.

❯GEORGE LAYMAN

Of all post-World War II and Soviet satellites of the 1950s, the Czechoslovakian Socialist Republic became the epitome of non-conformists behind the Iron Curtain, whose military stuck to their guns! Following the Allied defeat of Nazi Germany, Axis member nations and former occupied territories of Eastern Europe marched in lockstep with the U.S.S.R. By late 1945, the Kremlin wasted no time installing its military commissars, with local communist partisans and their underground wartime leaders. The priority was reorganizing the military and regional police forces of the Eastern Bloc.

As early as 1947, Jan and Jaroslav Kratochvil had been working on a gas-operated semi-automatic rifle design: the Vz 52, a design sharing nothing with the SKS, including its "Z50" cartridge, more commonly known as the 7.62x45mm. Jude Steele Collection

Russia immediately began standardizing the re-armament of their new cadres within the expanded socialist paradise. Still, they were in no hurry to supply them with the latest technology. Hence, Russia was delighted to provide them with vast quantities of WWII-period Mosin-Nagant 7.62x54mm M1944 carbines, 7.62x25mm PPSh-41 submachine guns, and Tokarev TT-33 semi-automatic pistols. The ulterior motive, however, would be the in-country licensing of obsolescent guns at an inflated fee, and a mandatory option shortly, or so they thought. Not everyone "liberated" by the Red Army was on board with this, especially a proud country with pre-existing arms manufacturing capabilities.

From the early 1920s until the German occupation of March 1939, Czechoslovakia's First Republic, had a thriving economy of arms production and export business worldwide, known for exceptional quality, rivaling even Germany.

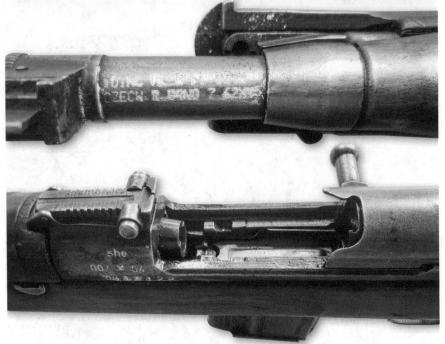

Though most Vz 52 rifles were imported in the 1990s from Latin America, the most recent find was in 2019 when Royal Tiger Imports located small quantities from Ethiopia. Note the steel-cased 7.62x45mm cartridge on the left is slightly larger than the 7.62x39 on the right. Author Collection

Before the Stalin-influenced rigged elections of 1948, Czechoslovak Communist leader Klement Gottwald was secretly installed into power while the Czech arms industry quietly resumed. The relatively intact, surrendered German arms machinery abandoned at the Zbrojovka Brno factory (Waffenwerke Brunn during occupation) boosted the restart even quicker. Ironically, well before 1939, Factory Brno was already tooled up for the Mauser Vz 24, with tolerances closely aligned to the standard German infantry rifle, the 7.92mm Mauser Model 98K.

Throughout 1947-48, the Czechs took large numbers of wartime 98K rifles in various stages of completion, assembling many and reigniting the export trade to customers such as Ethiopia, Israel, and Pakistan. The post-war Czech 98k rifles eventually saw some basic hardware such as barrel bands, triggerguards, and floorplates quickly dry up. Skilled Czech toolmakers reverse-engineered fixtures

A comparison of the AYM factory markings versus those of the SHE plant at CZUB. It is estimated that some 249,000 Vz 52 rifles in 7.62x45 were manufactured at AYM in Slovakia and the SHE factory at Uhersky Brod.

and jigs to produce these parts as steel stampings without the time-consuming machining process.

By late 1949, Gottwald's puppet regime halted arms exporting to non-communist states. The final export variants were those sold or bartered to East Germany in early 1950, and are quite scarce. The Czechs also issued these post-war Mauser 98K rifles on a limited basis, in 8mm Mauser. Around this time, Czechoslovakian defense minister Alexicja Ceppicka (Klement Gottwald's son-in-law) asked the Soviet Union for its latest technology in arms development, which was twice refused. To the industrious Czech mind, the Mosin-Nagant M1944, the PPSh-41, and the Tokarev were a crude step backward, though never explicitly saying so.

Fortunately, Joseph Stalin was amused by the Czech show trials and executions of several ranking communist apparatchiks accused of being Zionists or lukewarm socialists. The results saw Stalin

rewarding the Czechs with a relaxed, free hand to produce "indigenous arms of a national conception." However, Stalin never knew they were way ahead of him.

THE VZ 52 SEMI-AUTOMATIC RIFLE AND CZ 52 PISTOL

Beginning in 1948, Czech brothers Jan and Jaroslav Kratochvil, were designing the future Czech answer to the SKS that would become the "Samonabijeci Pushka Vz or.52," or Semi-Automatic Model 52 rifle. Commonly known in the United States as the Czech Vz 52, its adoption saw Czechoslovakia become the first member of the Eastern Bloc to issue an in-house, 10-shot, gas-operated rifle in the quasi-SKS vein. The greatest drawback of the Vz 52 was its chambering in a very odd 7.62x45mm caliber, a cartridge slightly more powerful than the standard Russian M43 7.62x39 of SKS and AK fame. The peculiar Czech cartridge, coded the "Z 50," would never again be

chambered in another weapon within the communist sphere.

The developmental stages of the Vz 52 saw Kratochvil's prototype coined the Vz-493. Using an annular, short-stroke gas piston system, it was anything but simple in concept. Its frontal tipping bolt and carrier were operated by the inertia of two lugs on a spring-charged sleeve surrounding the barrel, recessed at the front of the receiver, which actuated through residual gasses from the bore, returning in place by the recoil spring. Overall, it was a complicated system compared to the simpler SKS.

A final prototype of the new Czech service rifle, now coded as the CZ 502, was ready for field tests in early 1951. A few changes, such as a lighter alloy for the folding bayonet and eliminating a gas regulator, finalized Kratochvil's design. The official designation was the "Vz or 52," which the army adopted on March 20, 1952. Again, to put it lightly,

This CZ 27 pistol was made before the 1939 German occupation and is superbly constructed and finished. The Germans continued production, issuing them during World War II. Stuart Mowbray Collection

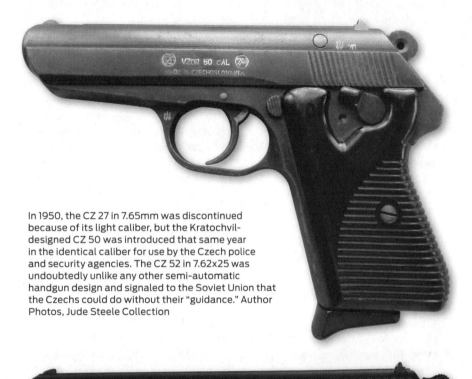

In 1950, the CZ 27 in 7.65mm was discontinued because of its light caliber, but the Kratochvil-designed CZ 50 was introduced that same year in the identical caliber for use by the Czech police and security agencies. The CZ 52 in 7.62x25 was undoubtedly unlike any other semi-automatic handgun design and signaled to the Soviet Union that the Czechs could do without their "guidance." Author Photos, Jude Steele Collection

the intent of this exceedingly unique weapon was to vainly impress the Soviet Union that "Czechoslovakia didn't need Russia's shared technology after all!" Even so, some Soviet engineers saw Czech innovation as "a fetish for the mechanically superior, to surpass the rules of practicality."

In a nutshell, the Vz 52 semi-automatic rifle became the first of three indigenously designed small arms to be domestically made without paying the Russians a single ruble in licensing fees.

The first 4,740 Vz 52 rifles were produced at Slovakia's Povazska Strojarne ammunition factory, coded "Factory 029 AYM." The initial manufacturing was plagued with issues, which was problematic given a lack of resources and an insufficiently trained workforce. Most of the labor force involved ammunition production, not small arms. In October 1953, Colonel General Vaclav Kratochvil ordered a second plant to manufacture the Vz 52 that would commence at the far better-equipped Ceska Zbrojovka Uhersky Brod, or CZUB factory, coded as the "007 SHE" plant. To the sharp eye, it can be seen that the final finish of those guns made at the AYM plant was not as well done as at CZUB.

Nevertheless, production continued there until 1956. In early 1955, following much tweaking and minor improvements at CZUB, the final bugs of the Vz 52 were worked out to the army's

satisfaction. On May 9, 1955, the new rifle was introduced publicly in Prague at the Tenth Anniversary Victory Parade. Also, that same month, pressure from the Kremlin again brought up the old Stalin-approved, non-standard caliber question. Russia's ultimatum was to either adopt the Eastern Bloc's official 7.62x39mm cartridge and purchase an SKS license or retool the Vz 52 to the standard infantry cartridge of the Warsaw Pact. Soviet Premier Nikita Khrushchev was fed up with the late Stalin's favoritism policies of the past, making it evident in his secret speech to the 20th Party Congress.

Thus, in 1956, modification of the Vz 52 was underway in compliance with this directive, and the first rechambered guns were issued the following year. The modified version became the Vz 52/57, with a total of about 97,000 guns in 7.62x39mm manufactured. They served for two years and were slated to be sold or distributed to third-world socialist clients by the 1960s. Inevitably, its replacement would herald a superbly designed Czech answer to the AK-47, which later shall be seen.

We must regress, however, to the late 1940s, as the Kratochvil brothers were doing double duty on another project, once again, in compliance with Soviet discontent.

Introduced in 1927, the highly popular CZ 27 semi-automatic pistol was discontinued in 1950 and used by the pre-war Czech military and police. Here again, was yet another popular export arm before the 1939 Nazi occupation, and German manufacture of the CZ 27 continued to war's end. In late 1945, it was back in production and made to pre-war standards of enviable workmanship. Chambered in the light 7.65mm Browning cartridge, the Gottwald regime was again read the riot act, as the Russians demanded a 7.62x25mm pistol be designed or purchase a license to build the TT 33 Tokarev.

Again ahead of the Soviets, the Kratochvil Brothers had been concurrently designing a new Czech service pistol together with the Vz 52 rifle project—naturally to avoid lining Moscow's pocketbook. Working steadily since 1948, they jointly introduced a prototype pistol in 1949, coined the Vz 491, but the Russians angrily nixed it, as it was adapted for the 9mm Parabellum and had to be modified for the standard 7.62x25mm Tokarev cartridge.

In 1951, they presented the reworked version to the Czech army for field testing. Labeled the Vz 513 in the Russian caliber, and unlike the boxy Tokarev, it was one of the sleekest semi-automatic pistols ever issued behind the Iron Curtain. Officially accepted in 1952, the new *Poloautomaticka pistol Vz or.52* or Semi-automatic Pistol Model 52 (identical in nomenclature to the Vz 52 rifle, it's known in the U.S. as the CZ 52 to avoid confusion), incorporated a unique roller-locked system. Fitted with a cam block behind the chamber, the vertical detent rollers lock the barrel on firing, similar in concept to the German MG 42 machine gun. The block at the rear of the barrel sacrificed chamber thickness, making for an arguably complex system. Its worn rollers required replacement over time unless the originals could be swapped out for more modern, hardened replacements. Thus, a maintenance program was scheduled every five years for the CZ 52, compared to a Tokarev that hardly required such a need.

Ergonomically, the slim width and high bore axis of the CZ 52 pistol increase felt recoil, and the peculiar height of the hammer makes for difficult thumb cocking with one hand. Regardless, it remained in the Czech military system for 30-plus years. The single-action CZ 52 also employs a hammer drop safety similar to the Walther P-38/PPK that works in unison with a firing pin block. However, CZ 52 parts were often subject to wear, and the reliability of this feature became dubious. During the 1980s, the army did not recommend carrying the nearly 30-year-old guns with a loaded chamber. Additionally, the CZ 52 was never intended to be dry-fired, as the original firing pins were brittle and could break off the nose when snapped on empty chambers**.

Without explanation, in 1950, the Kratochvil brothers introduced a scaled-down, 7.65mm (.32 ACP) version of the CZ 52 known as the CZ 50 (a hypocritical move, witness discontinuance of the excellent CZ 27 the same year!) for

The decock lever doubles as a safety. When pushing the latch upward, the disconnector block has been known to break or let go on a loaded chamber, thus inadvertently firing. Century Arms was the only known importer that replaced CZ 52 guns with worn or broken safeties that required a new firing block and marked such guns with a "Z" on the rear-left triggerguard flat. The author recommends not relying on this or carrying these guns with a loaded chamber.

Following extensive testing, the Samopal Vz 58 was on the production line by 1959 and, to this day, continues to serve countless militaries worldwide. For one final time, the Czechoslovak Socialist Republic had its way, defying the Soviet Union and the rest of the Warsaw Pact in adopting what peripherally appears as "AK" but is not.

ranking officers and police. The CZ 50 remained in production into the 1970s and is an excellent example of how communists lied to each other as they did to the West. This smaller version of the CZ 52 was far more practical than its larger counterpart, given the lower pressures of the 7.65mm cartridge and a simple blowback design. All in all, by 1952, the Czechoslovak military and police sidearm question was settled for more than three decades.

***

By 1958, the Czech general staff realized their primary infantry rifles, the Vz 52 and Vz 52/57 replacement, were in dire need of a serious upgrade. Witnessing Russian and Western arms technology moving rapidly, the Czechs had fortunately been preparing for this for nearly two years. The shortcomings of the Vz 52

taught many lessons, and by 1959, Czechoslovakia, almost overnight, tauntingly surprised the Soviet Union with a genuine "triumph of the Czech genius!"

THE 7.62X39 SAMOPAL VZ OR 58

As early as 1955, the Soviet Union was mulling the distribution of AK technology to Warsaw Pact members; however, China became the first to receive it in 1956. Introduced publicly in 1958, certain high-ranking Warsaw Pact flag officers knew about the heavily veiled AK-47. Without hesitation, Czechoslovakia had plans for such an arm, but as demonstrated in the past, it would be on their terms. Indeed, on a need-to-know basis, the Czech Defense Ministry had observed prototypes and drawings of

the radically configured Kalashnikov selective-fire assault rifle, with most Pact members anxiously willing to obtain licensing for domestic production.

In late 1956, the Czechs jumpstarted their version of an "AK platform" project out of nowhere. Research and development took place at the Konstrukta Brno plant under Jiri Cermak, a highly skilled engineer and machinist who took the reins of designing Czechoslovakia's version of "the AK-47 that wasn't." Aside from its Russian counterpart's most recognizable feature—a curved, 30-round magazine and 7.62x39 caliber—physical similarities were nil at best. What the Vz 52 was to the SKS nearly a decade earlier, the Czechs played a game changer to the AK, with an arm having internal mechanics all its own.

For four-plus years, the Russians strug-

gled to get the AK-47 (actually adopted 1949) just right, until 1951. The Czechs had theirs down pat in a little over a year and a half and nearly ready to produce by late 1958. Christened the Samopal Vz or.58*, it was a very well-thought-out design. Weighing less than 7 pounds and equipped with a 15.5-inch barrel, its machined steel receiver was lighter than the improved, stamped steel-framed AKM. Compared to the Russian AK, the Vz 58 has a short-stroke gas piston system versus the longer of the former—all in all, no components of the Vz 58 interchange with any of the various AK platforms.

Equipped with a press-fit barrel as the Vz 52, the new Czech reply to the AK was affectionately known by the infantry as the "Padlo," or paddle, due to its flat, narrow, board-like stock and slender frame. Its fire control system was com-

pletely original in concept. Compared to the Kalashnikov's rotating bolt, the Vz 58's breechblock has a hinged locking piece (with lugs) that drops during firing, engaging the shoulders of the receiver guardrails. The short travel of the gas piston pushes the carrier back, with the hinged breech piece returning upward, providing the required momentum during extraction. When disassembled, its hinged locking piece is reminiscent of the Walther P-38.

The Vz 58 also dispenses with the AK's conventional pivoting hammer, using the striker-fired concept. However, the firing pin is housed within the breechblock, separate from the cylindrical linear hammer. During rearward movement, the Vz 58's carrier and breechblock travel under the receiver cover, exposing the action much like the Vz 52 and SKS. Unlike

the AK, there is no ejection port, and the receiver cover houses the striker and the recoil spring. During extraction and feeding, the action is completely exposed, precluding any chance of spent cases hanging up the action in freak instances.

Other twists, such as a notched carrier, allow a magazine to be loaded with stripper clips while the mag remains in place. Unlike the AK, an empty magazine locks the bolt to the rear, plus the Vz 58 has a manual rear bolt stop. Using capture pins, one at the rear and one at the front, aids in quickly removing the receiver cover and handguard during disassembly. The two original basic versions of the Vz 58 are the *Pechotni* (Infantry Model), equipped with either an impregnated wood and plastic composition or beechwood stocks and the compact Paratrooper model or "*Vysadkovy*," which

This 1960s photo shows a Czech army advisor accompanying Congolese irregulars following a weapons delivery. This early 1960s full-color training schematic of the Sa.Vz 58 was used for military classroom instruction. Photos: Tomas Quis, Czech Small Arms, Jablunka, Czech Republic

is issued with a folding stock. As early as the mid-1960s, the Vz 58 was sold to other communist states or prospective countries sponsoring wars of liberation, such as Somalia, Libya, Burundi, Angola, Guatemala, and numerous others.

In 1965, North Vietnam received some 1,500 for evaluation in the humid jungle climate, and they were found to be ideally suited and eagerly accepted. The composition stock furniture was impervious to termites and superb for underground reserve caches. Being 1.5 pounds lighter than an AKM, the Vz 58 acquired great favor with the People's Republic of Vietnam, which obtained some 15,000 per year during the Vietnam War, with an estimated total of 90,000 delivered by 1975.

As opposed to the Vz 52, which lasted seven years in Czech service, the Vz 58 was the standard issue for the Czech army from 1959 to 1984 until it was replaced. More than 30 countries on five continents used the Vz 58, which remains active in many nations today. The Slovakian army still issues it as of this writing. No longer made by the state, the current private manufacturer of the Vz 58 is Czech Small Arms in Jablunka, Czech Republic, and it continues to fulfill contracts worldwide. The Sporter Model and seven different versions are imported in semi-automatic form to the United States, complying with legal barrel length.

RANGE TIME

Comparing the Vz 52 and Vz 58 on the firing line is quite a contrast, especially for offhand shooters. At slightly under 10 pounds, the former is truly old school and is not conducive for extended peri-

ods at the shoulder. Combined with its front-heavy metal furniture and bayonet and added weight, if the cleaning kit is in the butt, it truly makes for an arm's full. The biggest issue with the Vz 52 is finding reliable 7.62x45mm surplus ammunition. Czechoslovakia sold large quantities of rifles and ammunition to the United Arab Republic and later to Cuba in the 1970s when Havana upgraded to more modern weaponry.

About 1977, loads of Cuban Vz 52 rifles were supplied to Nicaraguan rebels and El Salvador's FMNLA. The Grenada operation found Cuba providing 1,125 of them in support of the New Jewel movement just before the 1983 U.S. invasion. Thus, most 7.62x45mm ammunition has been stored in wet, humid, tropical climates, which is less than ideal. Using 1964-dated "AZ" export-coded fodder

7,62mm SAMOPAL vz. 58
Řez

Poloha součástek spušťadla při střelbě jednotlivými ranami
(úderník napnut)

Poloha součástek spušťadla při střelbě dávkami
(úderník spuštěn)

1 Hlaveň
2 Nosič mušky
3 Muška
4 Chránítko závitu
5 Pojistka chránítka závitu se zpruhou
6 Plynový násadec
7 Píst
8 Zpruha pístu
9 Klopka hledí
10 Stiskátko hledí
11 Pouzdro závěru
12 Vyhazovač
13 Nosič závorníku
14 Závorník
15 Zápalník
16 Vytahovač
17 Opěrka vytahovače
18 Zpruha vytahovače
19 Závora
20 Úderník
21 Víko pouzdra závěru
22 Vodicí tyčinka úderné zpruhy
23 Úderná zpruha
24 Vodicí tyčinka vratné zpruhy
25 Vratná zpruha
26 Voditko vratné zpruhy
27 Uzávěra vratné zpruhy
28 Spoušť
29 Přerušovač
30 Spoušťová páka
31 Vypouštěcí páka
32 Záchyty úderníku (levý, pravý)
33 Pojistník
34 Péro spušťadla
35 Přeřaďovač (pojistka)
36 Lučík s lůžkem pro palbíčku
37 Patba
38 Botka
39 Šroub botky
40 Šroub pažby
41 Nadpažbí
42 Podpažbí
43 Palbíčka
44 Šroub palbíčky
45 Pouzdro zásobníku
46 Podavač
47 Zpruha podavače
48 Dno zásobníku

Součástky závěru

Vratné ústrojí

made by Sellier & Bellot seemed the most sure-fire ammo I obtained. The 123-grain jacketed bullets at 60 yards printed 3- to 4-inch or greater groups. But, it's nerve-wracking when squeezing off, and a mere "click" on dead primers did occur.

No commercial ammunition of this caliber has ever been produced, so it's merely a fact of life to be dealt with. Though not available for evaluation, a 7.62x39mm Vz 52/57 would have likely changed the entire picture. An out-of-the-ordinary design compared to the SKS, the Czechs also went beyond simplicity in their choice of a 7.62x25mm sidearm. Dislike for the time-tested Tokarev TT 33 was evident, with indigenous pride being the motivation.

The CZ 52 pistol has the physical characteristics of genuine Cold War, communist-era cosmetics, resembling

nothing made in the West. Its roller cam locking system is way out of the familiar and, admittedly, is not as user-friendly as the Browning-influenced Tokarev. Still, it is reliable and grabs an audience! As anticipated, using 1950s Eastern Bloc surplus ammo at 25 yards, I found the CZ 52 printing all over the silhouette. Contrarily, modern, non-corrosive, Sellier & Bellot, or PPU commercial ammo loaded with an 86-grain full-jacketed projectile makes up the difference, with 3-inch groups the norm.

Testing 1953 Bulgarian surplus ammunition regretfully gave some erratic performance, as the ammo shortage saw no commercial offerings available then. This dramatic session witnessed unburned powder, with tremendous muzzle flash, and shot placement printing at 7 o'clock in 4- to 5-inch groups. Despite its quirky,

unconventional traits, this author prefers the CZ 52 over the Tokarev: Its unique balance fits me like a glove despite a tendency to jump at the muzzle. The slender lines of the CZ 52 have had me carrying one as a CCW for years. However, remember that *the CZ 52 is not a concealed carry weapon well-suited to the unfamiliar,* given its peculiar characteristics that could go awry in a real-world situation. Familiarization and training are a must.

The Czechs underwent a long trial and error period during early Cold War-era arms design. However, the greatest accomplishment of this home-grown trio from the 1950s is the Sa.Vz 58 carbine. My introduction to it during the Vietnam War was love at first sight over any other Com Bloc small arms.

I fortunately located a Vz 58 during three TDY missions with the 1st Special

The author considers the Vz 58 to be the greatest success of the Czech trio. The CSA Sporter Model, in any of its six-plus configurations, is equipped with two polycarbonate transparent magazines, a big plus for eyeballing the remaining rounds in a magazine during serious confrontations. The Vz 58 magazines, both the original aluminum alloy and those out of the box, insert and extract far quicker than an AK. This grouping at 70 yards was shot in a rapid-fire sequence. Photos: Dianna Kelly

During the author's session with the CZ 52 pistol, there was a shortage of 7.62x25, so he used Bulgarian surplus, 1953 dated. Measurement of the 85-grain Bulgarian projectiles miked out to .308 diameter, some .002-inch smaller, and precisely the issue for poor shot placement. Commercial S&B Czech bullets measure .310 on the nose, which was learned a few weeks after finally obtaining a boxPhoto: Jude Steele

The only choice of ammunition for the 7.62x45mm Vz 52 is what's left of the remaining surplus. It has never been available from commercial manufacturers; thus, the shooter must examine ammunition before purchase. Jude Steele Photos and Collection

A pair of rarely seen Czech Vz rifles. At the top is the 7.62x39mm Vz 52/57, which the now-defunct German Transarms International imported with its TAI Minot, ND, original U.S. address on the right receiver ring. Also marked is 39 and the Schuss (shooting firearm) authorization markings. The left receiver ring shows the caliber marking, another Bundes eagle cartouche. Century Arms accounted for most of the 788 Vz 52/57 rifles brought into the United States. The 7.62x45mm Vz 52 (upper and lower two photos), at the bottom, with Arabic numerals on the buttstock, was brought back from Iraq in 2005 by a late U.S. Army Lt. Colonel.

Forces Group out of Okinawa. The closest I've been to the real deal in 52 years is the current Czech Small Arms (CSA) semi-automatic version imported as the Samopal.Vz.58 Sporter. The U.S.-legal import version fulfills the performance of its ancestor sans the 15-inch barrel and selective-fire capability. The light weight of the Vz 58 at 7 pounds with a full magazine allows for controllable long-term offhand firing. The chrome-lined, 1:7 right-hand twist barrels of the Czech Small Arms Vz 58 are made in Germany by Lothar Walther of steel and manganese and, at 16.4 inches, are fully U.S. compliant. The impregnated composition stock furniture is original surplus from the 1960s and '70s and provides a genuine taste of the past.

All shooting with the CSA Vz 58 was done at 60 yards using Red Army Standard 122-grain FMJ cartridges. The massive clusters printed ½- to 2-inch groups consistently during all sessions. Additionally, I was curious how some 1970s-vintage East German training ammunition with nylon and metal core would print. Performance was questionable at best and very corrosive. The CSA barrel rapidly heats the forearm, following two magazines in rapid succession. If needed, a padded shooting glove will protect you from this, or grasping the long, slender, aluminum or polycarbonate magazine as a vertical forearm.

It's easy to see how Czechoslovakia could avoid any kow tow to the Soviet Union regarding small arms adoption. They were steps ahead of the Russians and progressed accordingly when hard-line pressure from the Warsaw Pact demanded uniformity to the Soviet standard. The Czechs dealt with the Russian Bear on their turf through innovative and skilled gun-making. This region of Eastern Europe continues that longstanding tradition to this very day. In 1989, when the Wall tumbled down, and the Czechoslovak communist party was over, an old local adage, "*To Se Nevrati,*" continued to be true: "*They Won't Be Back*" … The Soviet Union, that is! **GD**

RESOURCES
- *Communist Bloc Handguns*, George Layman, Mowbray Publishing, 2018, Woonsocket, Rhode Island
- *The Collectors Guide to the SKS,* George Layman, Mowbray Publishing, 2023 Woonsocket, Rhode Island
- Czech Small Arms, *Vz 58 Sporter Manual,* 2021
- *Samopal* means submachine gun in Czech, but the Sa.Vz 58 uses a rifle cartridge. The idea was that it was intended to replace the PPSh 41, the Sa 25, and other submachine guns; hence, it was given this moniker.
- Modern replacements and other CZ 52 parts can be obtained from Harrington Products, Lafayette, Indiana. harringtonproducts@fpnmail.com

I am much obliged to Tomas Quis of CSA Jablunka, Czech Republic, and Kieran Reeves of Czech Small Arms USA, Knoxville, Tennessee, for their assistance. A round of thanks goes to my cousin Jude Steele for providing several arms featured here.

Purdey bar-in-wood hammer pigeon gun, built in 1881, with original Damascus barrels (top) and W&C Scott & Son "Monte Carlo B" from 1899.

The Pigeon-Grade Mystery

Cracking the code on live pigeon guns—mysterious gems from another era.

❭ TERRY WIELAND

It was 1964. My first Browning catalog had arrived in the mail, and I retired to my bedroom to devour it from cover to cover, alternately slavering over the lush illustrations and wallowing in a level of envious desire I've experienced only rarely since. Absorbed by the fabulous illustrations of the Browning Superposed, one thing puzzled me: What was "Pigeon Grade?" Why would a classy company like Browning name one of its best guns after the common pigeon? It was not even a game bird, like the pheasant or woodcock. Pigeons were town-square pests loathed by every sanitation department. So what gives?

H.J. Hussey's "Imperial Ejector" was his sidelock 'best,' and the best it was. All have serial numbers beginning with '14' (14xxx), and many are—or were—pigeon guns. Hussey was a bit of a rogue, but his guns were superb.

It was only some years later that I happened upon the explanation—that the sport of shooting live pigeons from traps was the forerunner of the game of trap shooting as we know it today. And, as practiced throughout Europe by wealthy aristocrats shooting some of the finest guns ever made competing for big money, box-pigeon shooting was—and is—the real aristocrat of the shotgun sports.

With serious money at stake and kings and princes involved, it's not surprising the specialized "pigeon gun" evolved, crafted by the finest gunmakers in the world, to help win the prizes and gain some of the glory.

Why, you may well ask, did it then take me several decades to learn what pigeon grade meant? The reason is that not much is written about it in the shooting press. Those who practice the game in places where it's still legal don't want to publicize it and draw down the hand-wringing indignation (and legislation) of those who wish to ban anything they disapprove.

Although live pigeon trap shooting is a very old sport—the earliest written records are from 1793, and it was widespread well before then—it has been outlawed in one country after another, ostensibly on humanitarian grounds. So, publicize it? Thank you, no.

Cyril Adams was a well-known American trap shooter. He once owned the English gun company Atkin, Grant & Lang and wrote a book called *Lock, Stock & Barrel* (Safari Press, 1996). He followed this in 2017 with *Live Pigeon Trap Shooting*, a history of the game throughout the world, with chapters on the birds, the traps, the clubs, the famous shooters, the guns, and the ammunition.

Adams wrote that live pigeon trap shooting originated in England and spread to the Continent and then around the world. Because the British were dominant among pigeon shooters for more than a century, it's not surprising that British gunmakers were at the forefront of refining the competitive pigeon gun.

Historically, Adams traced the origins of competitive shooting at live birds to the Greek siege of Troy, which involved one bird, a tall pole, and bows and arrows. Pigeon shooting, as we know it, however, probably began around 1760 in rural England and evolved over 200 years.

During that time, different species of birds were tried, and various methods were developed for holding and releasing them; some customs became standard, and others were discarded. Much depended on the available guns, and as shotguns were refined, pigeon shooting progressed. As well, such live bird shooting went in and out of fashion—an activity for aristocrats today, a practice for "the country pot house" tomorrow, and suddenly fashionable again a year from now, with beautifully groomed shooting clubs and elegant ladies in the stands.

If there was a golden age of pigeon shooting, it was from the invention of the centerfire cartridge in the 1860s to the outbreak of war in 1914. During that time, the practice became widespread, with substantial prizes, and everyone from kings on down competed for it. There were, naturally, different levels for varying social classes, just as there are million-dollar horse races at one end and ranch hands running races at the fairground at the other.

By about 1880, certain customs had become accepted practice, and rules were drawn up to govern competitions. The sport as it is known today is mainly based on those rules.

The action takes place inside a roughly egg-shaped ring, with the shooter standing on a line at the small end of the egg and five traps placed in a curved line across the large end. A fence about 2 feet high surrounds the whole thing. The fence is 17 yards to the left of trap one, 17 yards to the right of trap five, and 17 yards from trap three, in the center, to the fence at the rear. This is roughly speaking since rings are individual, like golf courses, not rigidly defined like a baseball diamond.

When the shooter calls for a bird, it can be sprung from any of the five traps—no one knows which. He then must react quickly and drop the bird inside the fence, or it will count as lost. Pigeons are strong fliers and can go from motionless to 45 or 50 miles per hour in a heartbeat, and you have no idea which way they might go—left, right, straight up, twisting to go with the wind, or right back toward you like a Spitfire on a strafing run.

Modern traps nestle the bird in a hammock, which launches it into the air as the sides of the trap collapse. This, combined with the clatter of the trap opening, puts birds into instant flight. The direction and manner in which the bird flies depends on many factors: wind direction and speed, the direction it was facing when the trap opened, or just pigeon whim.

Shooting these birds and "grassing" them solidly calls for a very specialized gun and ammunition. Early on, rules limited the shot and powder charge that could be used, gradually settling on the formula of "one and a quarter, three and a quarter" (1¼-3¼). This is the famous pigeon load, with 1¼ ounces of shot ahead of 3¼ drams of powder. It's a heavy load by any standard except modern waterfowl and turkey loads, and it can pound the shooter and the bird—one reason pigeon guns were 1 to 2 pounds heavier than a comparable game gun. A Purdey for pheasants might weigh 4 to 6 pounds, while a Purdey pigeon gun would be 7½ to 8½ pounds.

Modern practice allows the shooter two shots at each bird. This gives him a second shot if he misses or a chance to apply a *coup de grâce* to a wounded bird that's down inside the ring. A lightning-fast second shot, with the gun not solidly in the shoulder, is very punishing, and

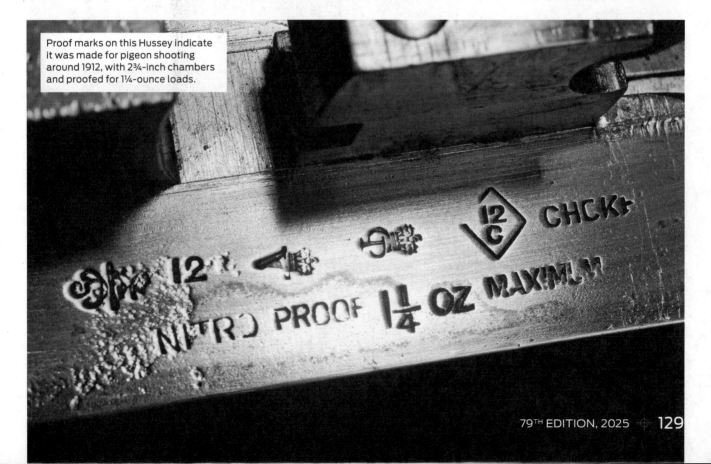

Proof marks on this Hussey indicate it was made for pigeon shooting around 1912, with 2¾-inch chambers and proofed for 1¼-ounce loads.

doing it over and over quickly adds up—another reason for a heavier gun.

But it can't be too heavy.

Compare it to a modern single-barrel trap gun: For a standard 16-yard trap, the gun may weigh 9 or 10 pounds, with much of the weight out in its 34-inch barrel and trap loads are powder puffs compared to pigeon loads. This formula can't work with a pigeon gun because a bird can come out of the trap and fly straight back toward the shooter—these are called "attack birds"—or circle and approach, and the pigeon gun has to be light and handy enough to deal with them.

A morning of box-pigeon shooting involves fewer birds than trap or skeet shooting. A typical morning's draw is 15 birds—five in each of three rings; this is repeated in the afternoon and then again the next day for 60 birds. Where a trap shooter must go 100 straight to make it to the next round, it's rare for a pigeon shooter to drop 15 out of 15. Scores of 12 to 14 are typical for even top-notch shooters.

One reason is that there is a built-in handicap system. If a shooter grasses all five birds at ring one, shooting from 29 yards, then on ring two, he moves back to the 30-yard line; if he goes five straight there, on ring three, he starts at 31. If, by the time he enters ring three in the afternoon, he has killed all 25 birds so far, he will be shooting his last five from the 34-yard line. And keep in mind he is *starting* from 2 yards farther back than the *longest* Handicap Trap distance (27 yards).

Another vital aspect is gambling. Everywhere it is practiced (and has been for 200 years), pigeon shooting is driven by gambling, just like horse racing. There are large cash prizes at every level, with ongoing side bets among competitors and spectators throughout the event. And we are talking big money. At a 60-competitor match, for example, with 60 birds each, the overall winner could take home $40,000 and considerably more if he wins his side bets.

For this reason, a great deal more is riding on each bird than even at the highest levels of trap or skeet. In Europe, touts and bookies would shout the odds on a shooter missing the next bird a few feet from his ear, with crowds for and against cheering or booing. Keeping your nerve and shooting coolly and well on a tough and demanding target, with half the crowd hoping you'll miss and cheering accordingly, calls for superhuman levels of *sangfroid*.

This brings us to the guns they used, and why, when these shotguns come on the auction block today, they are well worth grabbing because they were some of the finest ever made.

As we have seen, pigeon shooting involved serious money, and winners of big matches were reported in all the sporting periodicals of the day. Often, both the winner's name and the make of gun he used, and sometimes even his ammunition, were listed beside the prize money, and this became valuable publicity for the gunmakers involved.

At big matches, gunmakers sent representatives to the shooting grounds to assist clients, to look for ways to improve guns and, not least, to ensure their name got in the papers. (This often required a bribe to the journalist.) If competition among the shooters was intense, it was every bit as cutthroat among their makers. This could become a serious expense for the gunmakers, and some of the more prominent, established names,

Typical flat pigeon rib on a James Woodward hammer gun stippled to prevent glare.

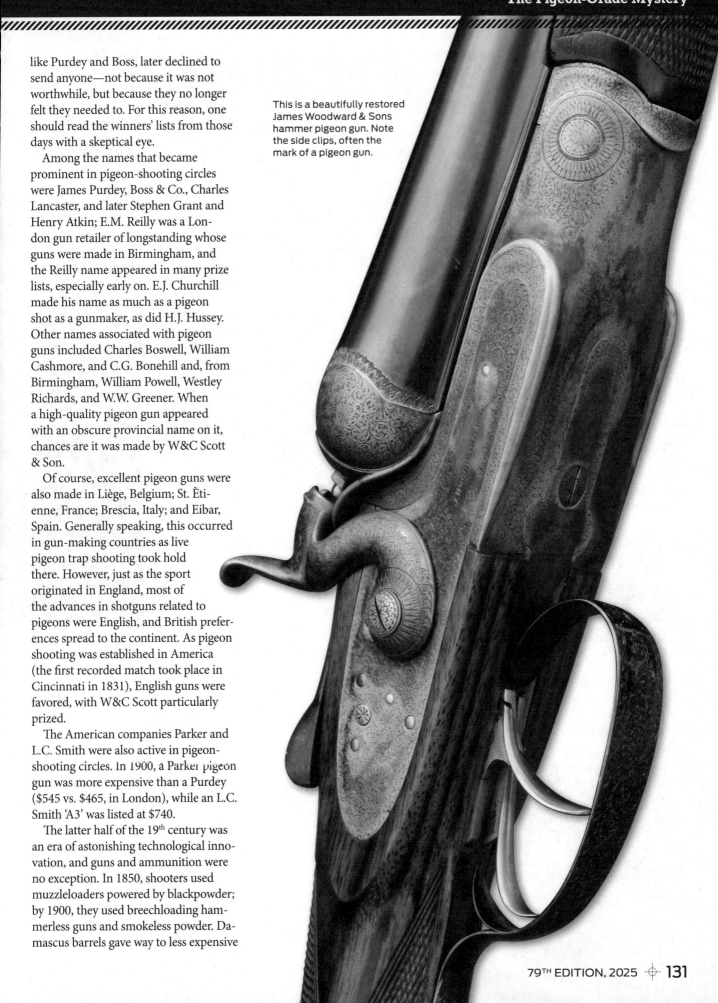

like Purdey and Boss, later declined to send anyone—not because it was not worthwhile, but because they no longer felt they needed to. For this reason, one should read the winners' lists from those days with a skeptical eye.

Among the names that became prominent in pigeon-shooting circles were James Purdey, Boss & Co., Charles Lancaster, and later Stephen Grant and Henry Atkin; E.M. Reilly was a London gun retailer of longstanding whose guns were made in Birmingham, and the Reilly name appeared in many prize lists, especially early on. E.J. Churchill made his name as much as a pigeon shot as a gunmaker, as did H.J. Hussey. Other names associated with pigeon guns included Charles Boswell, William Cashmore, and C.G. Bonehill and, from Birmingham, William Powell, Westley Richards, and W.W. Greener. When a high-quality pigeon gun appeared with an obscure provincial name on it, chances are it was made by W&C Scott & Son.

Of course, excellent pigeon guns were also made in Liège, Belgium; St. Ètienne, France; Brescia, Italy; and Eibar, Spain. Generally speaking, this occurred in gun-making countries as live pigeon trap shooting took hold there. However, just as the sport originated in England, most of the advances in shotguns related to pigeons were English, and British preferences spread to the continent. As pigeon shooting was established in America (the first recorded match took place in Cincinnati in 1831), English guns were favored, with W&C Scott particularly prized.

The American companies Parker and L.C. Smith were also active in pigeon-shooting circles. In 1900, a Parker pigeon gun was more expensive than a Purdey ($545 vs. $465, in London), while an L.C. Smith 'A3' was listed at $740.

The latter half of the 19th century was an era of astonishing technological innovation, and guns and ammunition were no exception. In 1850, shooters used muzzleloaders powered by blackpowder; by 1900, they used breechloading hammerless guns and smokeless powder. Damascus barrels gave way to less expensive

This is a beautifully restored James Woodward & Sons hammer pigeon gun. Note the side clips, often the mark of a pigeon gun.

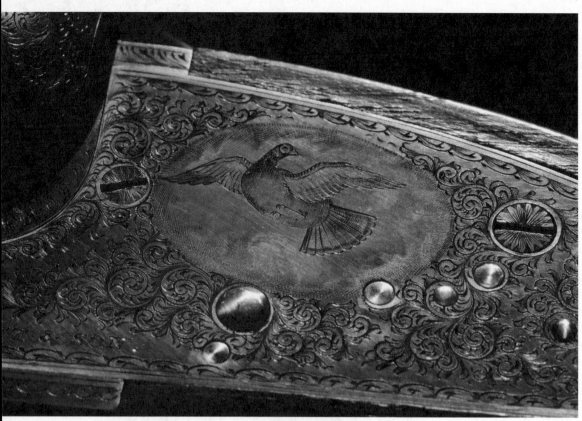

The sidelock of a Scott "Monte Carlo B" with its trademark pigeon. There's no mistaking the gun's purpose in life.

H.J. Hussey pigeon gun, newly restocked (its third) and with new ejectors, safety catch, and triggerguard. The expense was worth it to put the gun's superb Frank Squires barrels back in business. The author has shot everything from darting doves to Handicap Trap with this gun and its tulip chokes.

fluid steel, and these barrels ended the century with varying degrees of choke to make them more effective at close range and long range.

In London, there were a dozen truly great names in shotgun making, and with many lesser ones intent on making a name for themselves; competition was intense. Much of the credit for this frenzy of innovation goes to the passion for shooting driven birds, like red grouse and pheasants, but much is also owed to live pigeon trap shooting. In the same way, as many advances in automobiles were born on the race tracks, so much of the progress in guns and ammunition was proven on pigeons.

To put these advances in perspective, the 1850s saw the development of break-

A "Bogardus Club Gun" made for Captain Adam Bogardus by W&C Scott & Son. Note the thick fences and heavy-duty strikers. These were made for rugged use as pigeon guns.

action breechloaders; the 1860s, the centerfire cartridge; 1870s, hammerless actions; 1880s, ejectors and choke; 1890s, smokeless powder; 1900, single triggers and, by 1914, over/under guns (Boss, Woodward).

Not all of these innovations were seen as progress by live pigeon shooters, and many were adopted only reluctantly, much later. The demands of high-volume driven bird shooting, with two guns and a loader, are decidedly different than those for trap shooting, one bird at a time with big money on the line. Still, the two disciplines fed off each other, with gunmakers hurrying to meet every demand, correct every flaw, and perfect every innovation.

Three that were slow to gain ac-

ceptance among pigeon shooters were fluid-steel barrels, hammerless actions, and safety catches. In pigeon shooting, malfunctions are not always allowed, and a misfire can cost you a bird and a lot of money. Not only does your gun need to be absolutely reliable, but you also must have confidence that it is—since confidence is essential to doing well in the game.

Damascus barrels were expensive and difficult to produce, but they had advantages over even advanced fluid steel like Whitworth, mainly in strength for weight, which allowed finely tuned balance. Some pigeon shooters demanded Damascus until it became impossible to obtain after 1914 (some of the very best was produced in Belgium.)

Hammerless actions were slow to catch on, and this is true even of game guns since notables like Lord Ripon and King George V were using hammer guns into the 1920s. Early hammerless actions were less reliable than hammer guns, and being more complicated, they were also more prone to breakage or malfunction.

Safeties? Hammer guns don't need them, and a safety on a hammerless gun can either be slipped on accidentally or fail to come fully off, causing a stiff trigger pull or no pull at all. Even after hammerless guns became accepted, many pigeon guns were built with either the safety catch permanently pinned in place or without safety.

While fashions in barrel length came and went for game guns, pigeon shooters stuck to long barrels—30 inches minimum, generally—with barrels as long as 34 or even 36 inches on special orders. Pigeon shooters also took to choked barrels without hesitation once their effectiveness was proven, well-knowing the advantages of a more concentrated shot pattern.

Single triggers did not catch on immediately because they were not as reliable as the familiar double triggers and, despite the promotion given to them by Boss & Co., offered no real advantage. The same can be said of over/unders: These had been tried for years, but it was not until John Robertson, the brilliant gunmaker/owner of Boss & Co., unveiled his beautiful (and eminently efficacious) design in 1909 that shooters began to take notice.

The reputation of James Purdey notwithstanding, Boss & Co. was recognized as at least Purdey's equal in quality (and many thought better). The other London company in the same class was James Woodward, and Woodward's came out with its own over/under in 1913. To this day, there is debate as to which is better, Boss or Woodward, but, notably, Purdey acquired Woodward in 1949 specifically to get its hands on the over/under, and to this day, a Purdey over/under is a Woodward under another name.

By 1900, virtually every British gunmaker offered a specialized pigeon gun or insisted they could build one. One name prominent by its absence is Holland & Holland, but it did not build its own guns until 1893 when it built its factory on Harrow Road in London; until then, it's widely believed but never fully acknowledged that H&H guns and rifles were built in Birmingham, mainly by W&C Scott & Son, with some final finishing carried out in Holland's shop.

This is not to say that Holland guns were all built elsewhere, as were E.M. Reilly, William Evans, or W.J. Jeffery. Harris Holland, the founder of the company, was a tobacconist who was an enthusiastic pigeon shooter, and that's what got him into the business of buying and selling, and later making, guns. His nephew, Henry, later came into the business and was an active inventor and innovator, but mainly in the field of rifles. For whatever reason, Holland & Holland never became a big name in pigeon guns at the level of Boss or Stephen Grant.

How can you tell if a gun is or began life as a pigeon gun? After all, guns can be altered, barrels cut off, or re-barreled altogether, and certainly, they can be restocked.

Weight is the obvious first consideration. Find an English gun that is over 7

Capt. Bogardus had firm ideas about what made an excellent pigeon gun and a high regard for Scott guns.

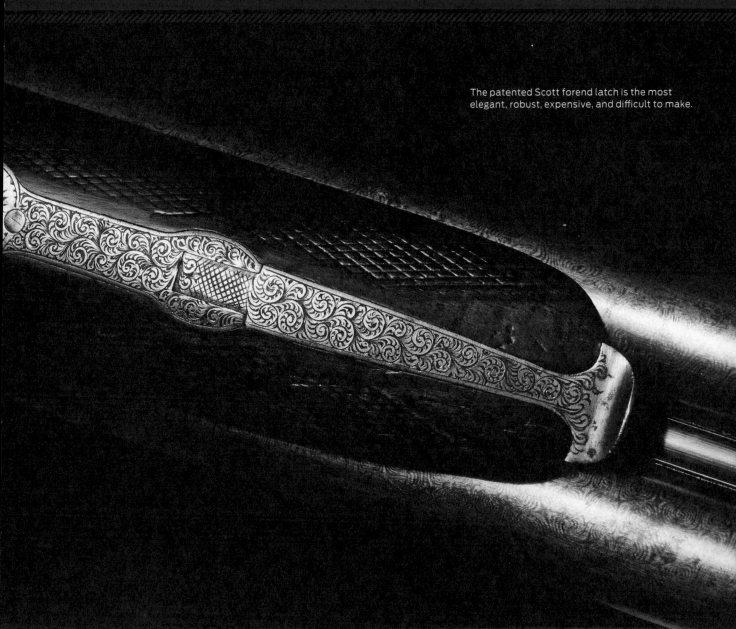

The patented Scott forend latch is the most elegant, robust, expensive, and difficult to make.

pounds; chances are it was a pigeon gun. By the 1890s, they'd settled on cartridge lengths for different purposes, discarding the old catch-all 2⅝-inch case in favor of 2½ inches for game guns, 3 inches for waterfowl, and 2¾ inches for pigeon guns. Since a pigeon gun would then be proofed for 1¼-ounce loads, it called for slightly heftier barrels at the breech end and a heavier frame to hold them. And the proof marks can tell you a lot.

Original, 2¾-inch chambers and 1¼-ounce loads? Undoubtedly (almost!) a pigeon gun. I say "almost" because one quickly learns with the English gun trade to never say never and never say always. There are exceptions to virtually everything.

If you come across a hammer gun that is unduly heavy and long-barreled, built years after hammerless designs had taken over, it too was likely a pigeon gun. Another indicator is the presence of side clips and a third fastener, such as the Greener crossbolt. You sometimes find Jones under-levers on pigeon guns long after the faster Purdey top-levers had replaced them because they are simple, strong, and foolproof.

With the side-by-side, the rib is also a good indicator. Pigeon guns had wide, flat ribs and were either matted or cross-hatched to eliminate glare. They also might have both a bead at the muzzle and one mid-barrel. Two beads were an almost certain indicator the gun was

intended to be shot gun-up, in the current parlance, versus gun-down. Rules were altered, not everywhere and not at the same time, in mid-century, to allow shooters to call for the bird with the gun already mounted. Two beads that could form a figure-8 when the gun was in position aided proper alignment.

A gun with long barrels choked Full & Full (or, earlier, Choke & Choke) is almost certainly a pigeon gun, and if it has a second set of barrels with more open chokes, that seals the deal.

A hammerless gun with no safety (like the great American single-barrel trap guns) is a sure indicator. A pinned safety, or evidence that one had been pinned, is also a good sign.

Ejectors? An unnecessary complication, and one that can go wrong when you least want it. An ejector breaking halfway through a five-bird round can render the gun unusable. Ask me how I know that.

Stock design is subject to fashion, but some characteristics of a pigeon stock versus a game stock are a pistol grip, sometimes combined with a broad (beavertail) forend. A pigeon stock is also straighter, causing the gun to naturally shoot high, which allows a full view of the bird while pulling the trigger.

According to Cyril Adams, an 1896 advertisement in a Boston newspaper is the earliest known reference to a Scott innovation called the "Monte Carlo" comb. It was named after the renowned pigeon ring and annual shoots at Monte Carlo in Monaco, the unofficial world championship for pigeon shooting. It allows a high, straight stock at the same time as

the butt is held securely in the shoulder. Monte Carlo stocks are now part of the universal gun lexicon, but this is where it originated.

Scott also named its famous live pigeon gun the Monte Carlo 'B.' It's a sidelock with a pigeon engraved on each lockplate and is usually depicted with a semi-pistol (Prince of Wales) grip. The Monte Carlo 'B' also had the rectangular Scott crossbolt, similar in function to the round Greener, for added strength.

The W&C Scott Monte Carlo 'B' is one of the earliest known models named for a particular shooting activity and was prized in the United States, where the Scott name was much better known than in England. In the U.K., few guns were sold under the Scott name, while thousands bore the names of other makers, like Holland & Holland.

Captain Adam Bogardus, the famous American market gunner, exhibition

shooter, and live pigeon shot, particularly liked Scott guns. When he decided to market a gun with his name on it—the "Bogardus Club Gun"—he commissioned W&C Scott to make it. The guns were stylish, with the superb Scott forend latch, extra-heavy fences, lovely hammers, and competition strikers. If you come across one on the dusty far end of a gun rack, grab it.

In 1897, W&C Scott & Son merged with P. Webley and Richard Ellis & Son to form Webley & Scott. However, it continued to make double guns in its old premises, under its old name, for the next 40 years, while Webley abandoned the shotgun market to concentrate on revolvers.

Lest anyone think a Scott gun is somehow lesser because it was made in Birmingham, here is Nigel Brown on the subject, quoting John and Tom Wilkes, "two of the most highly respected crafts-

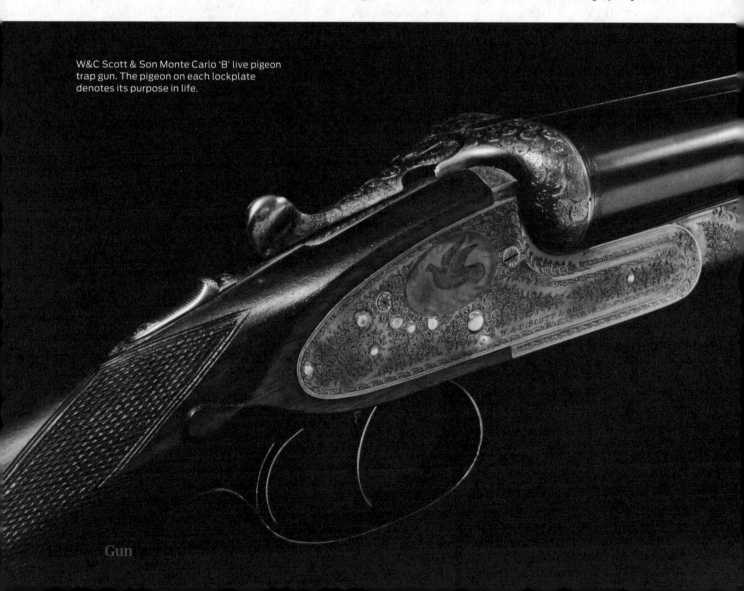

W&C Scott & Son Monte Carlo 'B' live pigeon trap gun. The pigeon on each lockplate denotes its purpose in life.

Gun

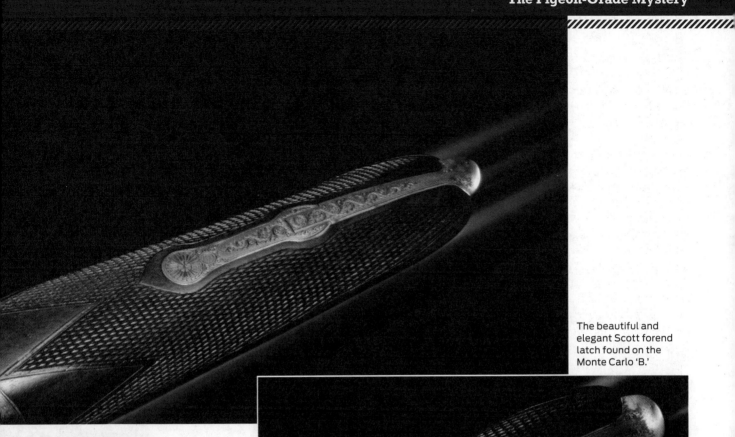

The beautiful and elegant Scott forend latch found on the Monte Carlo 'B.'

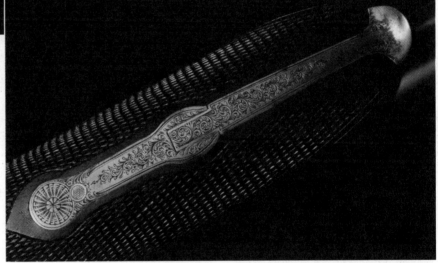

men in the London trade (who have) forgotten more about gunmaking than most others will ever know."

W&C Scott, they said, was "one of the finest gunmaking businesses in the British Isles. Not only could they produce the finest quality when requested, they could do so in quantity."

There is really nothing one can say about a Purdey pigeon gun or a Boss, Woodward, or Stephen Grant that has not been written many times. They are superb, and you know they will be wonderful before you pick one up. But there are also dark horses in the field, and searching auction catalogs and viewing halls will sometimes reveal one.

A couple of years ago, at Rock Island,

I was stalking a Purdey bar-in-wood hammer pigeon gun belonging to Robert Braden, Cyril Adams' co-author of *Lock, Stock & Barrel.* A gorgeous thing, it had two sets of barrels—original Damascus from when the gun was made in 1881 and a second fluid-steel set added by Purdey in 1883, with more open chokes. The latter set, I surmised, was for shooting the South American pigeon variant, *columbaire,* wherein professional bird-throwers throw the pigeon by hand.

Anyway, a William Cashmore gun with two sets of barrels was also on the card, but it was expected to bring a third of the Purdey's price. It had Cashmore's patented lock-up system that would put a Wells Fargo vault to shame. Steve Denny,

A James Purdey bar-in-wood action on a hammer pigeon gun. Bar-in-wood guns are complicated to make but are highly prized.

formerly of H&H, advised me that the Cashmore frames, although rare, were legendary for strength.

I landed the Purdey but, alas, not the Cashmore. Another guy of similar interests picked it up, fell in love, and we battled each other to the $9,000 mark, at which point I decided the Purdey would suffice.

There are other clues to pigeon aristocracy. In 1900, as now, London gunmakers relied on outworkers, and barrel maker Frank Squires was reputed to be the best. If you find a gun with long barrels and 'F.S.' stamped on them, you may have a hidden treasure.

Some years ago, I acquired an H.J. Hussey 'Imperial Ejector' with 30-inch barrels marked F.S. Hussey was a fine pigeon shot and an excellent gunmaker, so one would expect a Hussey pigeon gun to be first-rate. This one had been severely damaged, restocked at least once, ejectors replaced at least twice, and reduced to the

role of a waterfowl gun. I restored it to grandeur with a new stock, ejectors, and triggerguard and replaced the inappropriate safety catch with a proper one.

The safety catch was a puzzle. How do you break one? The answer was that it had either never had a safety (a pigeon gun clue) or was pinned and broken, so a later owner replaced it with a catch off a cheap Belgian gun.

All the work was well worth the effort. The Frank Squires barrels had "tulip" chokes—commonly called "jug" chokes in the U.S.—that throw beautiful even patterns from close in (think Skeet low-house one) to far out (Handicap Trap) and everything in between. With a tulip choke, the bore widens slightly several inches from the muzzle, then tightens again. By measurement, they would be classed as LM/IM, but in practice, they do everything well, so why worry? Perfect for a pigeon gun.

The vast majority of hammerless

English pigeon guns from the golden age (1880–1914) are sidelocks because there was a firm belief that a boxlock was not as good, and pigeon shooters demanded the best. The exception is W.W. Greener, a loud proponent of boxlocks, especially his "Facile Princeps" and "treble wedge-fast" mechanism. He advertised pigeon guns and, presumably, made some. Westley Richards, although the originator of the Anson & Deeley boxlock, seems to have built its pigeon guns on its sidelock action.

Pigeon guns from Purdey have always been a badge of status and one of the finest sidelock side-by-sides ever made. Ernest Hemingway mentions Purdey pigeon guns in a couple of his short stories. The Beesley patent self-opener from 1880, on which all Purdey sidelocks are built, is one of the most durable and dependable actions ever made—both qualities essential in a pigeon gun. For this reason, Purdey continued to build

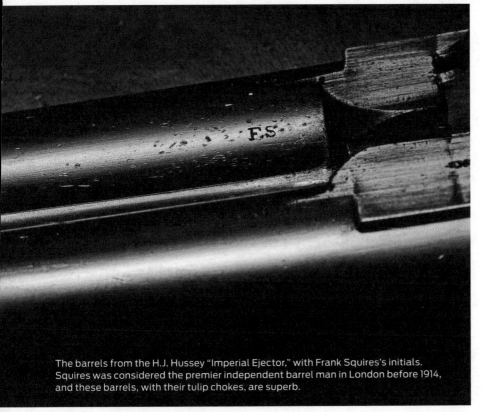

This is a James Purdey & Sons bar-in-wood hammer pigeon gun from 1881. Note the side clips. Guns do not come much more elegant than this.

1918. In 1921, it was banned in Great Britain, eradicating the domestic market for pigeon guns. The big names—Purdey and Boss—still provided guns to wealthy foreigners, but from that point on, the market shrank. After 1945, one European country after another banned pigeon shooting, until today only Spain remains.

As for the guns themselves, there was a gradual shift away from side-by-sides to over/unders. This was due to many factors, not because they were better for the purpose. Over/unders lend themselves to machine production, and gun-for-gun are heavier than side-by-sides. Some shoot-

pigeon guns for foreign clients long after box-pigeon shooting was banned in Britain in 1921.

On the subject of boxlocks, the new "Super Bird" from Connecticut Shotgun Manufacturing Co. is built on CSMC's very strong 'RBL' action. It's intended primarily for SxS events in sporting clays, but the name gives it away.

If it's difficult to know where to begin the story of live pigeon trap guns, it's equally difficult to know where to end.

Live pigeon trap shooting spread across Europe and worldwide during the 19th century and began to contract after

ers bought into the "single sighting plane" myth, but the drift was due more to cost than anything else.

The prominent British firms made great efforts to crack the American market during the '20s and '30s. Thanks to the Great War, that was where the money was. But with Browning's excellent Superposed available at a low price, it was an uphill battle.

Today, many of the wonderful SxS pigeon guns have been converted to other purposes, with barrels cut down, guns restocked, and some even fitted with detachable choke tubes. It says a lot about their intrinsic quality that shooters believe it's worth spending the money.

Still, unapologetic pigeon guns still come on the market and, not being of a modern configuration, often sell for relatively little. If you can pick up a Boss or Woodward or Grant or Purdey pigeon gun from before 1914—especially a hammer gun to drool over—they offer a chance to see what it's like to shoot a gun that was one of the finest ever made.

Pigeon grade. Now you know. **GD**

The barrels from the H.J. Hussey "Imperial Ejector," with Frank Squires's initials. Squires was considered the premier independent barrel man in London before 1914, and these barrels, with their tulip chokes, are superb.

Three Great New Gobbler Guns

We tested three new turkey guns from top manufacturers, but which one is the right option for your spring season?

> BRAD FITZPATRICK

Beretta's A300 Turkey is a well-thought-out gobbler gun. The crossbolt safety is easy to access and quiet to disengage, and the oversized controls are quick to access even with gloves. A Picatinny rail is included for optics mounting.

My, how the wild turkey's fortunes have changed over the last hundred years. In the early 20th century, wild turkey populations plummeted, and the birds were extirpated in 18 states. Unregulated hunting and habitat loss were to blame, but by the 1950s, dedicated restoration efforts were underway. In 1973, the National Wild Turkey Federation was established, and soon, turkey populations began to bounce back nationwide.

The author with a big Texas Rio Grande gobbler harvested with the Mossberg SA-28 Tactical Turkey. The Mossberg's reliable gas-operating system makes the light but lethal 28-gauge very soft shooting.

The Mossberg International SA-28 Tactical Turkey carries the lowest MSRP of any gun listed. Still, it's a lightweight, low-recoiling shotgun that reliably puts down large toms.

Today, an estimated 6.5 million wild turkeys roam 49 states, and spring turkey hunting has become a tradition for many. As the days lengthen and budding flowers herald the arrival of spring, tom turkeys begin battling for hens, and turkey hunters prepare to take to the woods.

Turkey hunting is a tradition in many parts of the country, but today's turkey hunting gear is more advanced than ever. The most dramatic shift has been the adoption of sub-gauge shotguns for turkey hunting, resulting from new non-toxic tungsten shot offerings like TSS that are far denser than lead. Not surprisingly, two of the guns in this roundup are chambered in 20-gauge, and one is a 28-gauge, but what is surprising is how effective smaller-bore shotguns have become thanks to the use of TSS.

Other changes have occurred in recent years, primarily a shift toward optics on turkey guns. Optics offer several advantages, such as a wider field of view when lining up your shot, but perhaps the greatest benefit is the capability to adjust your point of impact. If your turkey gun isn't throwing a pattern where you'd like, there's no longer a need to adjust the point of aim to the point of impact. Adjust your reflex optic, and the gun will shoot where it should.

The guns themselves have changed, too. Improved choke offerings, more ergonomic stocks, and new finishes make today's turkey guns even more effective, allowing hunters to drop birds at distances thought unimaginable only a few years ago. Forty yards was considered quite a long shot with a 12-gauge turkey gun. Today, experienced hunters with the right load, choke, and optic can cleanly harvest birds at even greater distances with .410s.

The wild turkey's fortunes have changed, as have those of turkey hunters. Today's gobbler guns are lighter to carry, lighter recoiling, more accurate, and even more lethal than just a few years ago. We're testing the best new turkey shotguns from Mossberg, Beretta, and Franchi to see what each offers.

Shannon Jackson patterns the Mossberg SA-28 Tactical Turkey before a South Texas turkey hunt. The Mossberg's pistol grip allows for a steady hold on the shotgun, and the included Picatinny rail makes it easy to add a reflex sight.

Franchi's Affinity 3 Turkey Elite is purpose-built for gobblers. The extended Rhino chokes throw excellent patterns, and the Gore Optifade Subalpine stock and Midnight Bronze Cerakote finish on the metalwork help this gun blend in and protect it from the worst elements.

The Franchi's pistol grip stock features sling attachment slots on the left and right sides. It's not a conventional sling attachment design, but it's convenient and rugged and allows the gun to ride comfortably against the hunter's back.

MOSSBERG INTERNATIONAL SA-28 TACTICAL TURKEY

The Mossberg SA-28 Tactical Turkey is a gas-operated semi-auto 28-gauge shotgun built in Turkey. As the name suggests, it offers some common features found on tactical shotguns. Chief among these is a vertical pistol grip that offers excellent control over the gun and allows for fast, subtle movement of the shotgun when birds are approaching. The gun also features a Picatinny rail up top for mounting optics; a pair of fiber-optic ghost ring sights are included. The 22-inch vent-rib barrel is threaded for chokes and has a single extended turkey tube.

As with most modern gobbler guns, the SA-28 Tactical Turkey sports a full camo dip. The Mossy Oak Greenleaf pattern is more retro than today's modern digital camo patterns, but it looks great

The Franchi has oversized controls and a Picatinny rail upon which the author mounted a Burris FastFire 4 optic—an ideal combo for turkey hunting. If you don't choose to use an optic, the Franchi's adjustable fiber-optic iron sights are excellent.

on the gun and is functional in various habitats. The browns and greens contrast nicely, allowing it to blend in. Turkeys live and die by their eyes, and a gun that disappears into the background might offer the extra half-second you need to get a shot.

Weighing in at just 5 pounds, 7 ounces, the Mossberg is indeed a light shotgun, even by 28-gauge standards. But even with heavy Apex 1 3/8-ounce loads of No. 9 TSS, the recoil was manageable and far less punishing than a 7-pound 12-gauge with magnum loads doles out.

The reduced perceived recoil is due to its gas piston system, wherein gas from the fired shells travels through vents to operate a piston that, in turn, cycles the action. It's not a particularly novel design, but it is effective. In addition to the Mossberg's light weight, it's relatively compact, measuring just 39 inches.

I tested the Mossberg's effectiveness on

The author and Adam Heggenstaller with opening day gobblers harvested in southern Ohio using Franchi's Affinity 3 Turkey Elite shotguns. Franchi shotguns and Fiocchi Golden Turkey TSS ammunition stopped both birds in their tracks.

The Beretta A300 with Leupold DeltaPoint optic and Fiocchi's 3-inch Golden Turkey TSS load proved a deadly combination on birds. Despite these powerful loads, the Kock-Off system and gas operation helped reduce recoil to manageable levels.

spring Rios in South Texas. The massive ranch covered several thousand acres of mesquite flats and oak forests carved up by sand two-tracks the birds used as thoroughfares and strutting grounds. That generally meant where the hunt began was not where it ended, and my hunting partner Linda Powell and I had to try to pin down the birds for a shot. That run-and-gun tactic can be taxing, but it's precisely the type of hunting for which the SA-28 Tactical was designed.

I killed my first bird of that trip as it slipped down a two-track on the back side of a lake. Linda and I expected the birds to pass to our right as they made their way toward a large open field ringed by oak trees, but as is so often the case, the birds didn't follow the script. Instead, two mature gobblers slipped out of heavy cover to our left. I slipped the shotgun slowly to my left, lined up with the closer bird's neck and head, and fired. The 1

3/8-ounce of No. 9 TSS pellets smothered the bird's head and dropped it where it stood.

My second turkey of the trip could be heard gobbling along a cattle fence, and Linda and I set up in the shade of a mesquite to the south of the field. I called softly, and the bird responded until it suddenly stopped vocalizing. I thought perhaps it had spooked or finally laid eyes on a hen. Later, I was blinking slowly in anticipation of an afternoon nap when, without warning, the bird walked out directly in front of me. It had crossed the field, circled the grove of trees where we set up, and walked down a road beside me. I had a second tag but didn't want to shoot since it was Linda's bird, but it became apparent the turkey had seen enough and smelled a rat. He let out that dreaded alarm *putt* and lifted his head to go, but not before I hit him with a load of Apex shot. He fell in a cloud of dust on

the road.

The Mossberg is a purpose-built turkey gun, and it's a fantastic sub-gauge gobbler-getter that's light and easy to carry. I do wish the controls were as large as those on the other guns listed, but otherwise it's a fantastic option if a hunter is willing to work to find 28-gauge turkey loads. There's certainly no doubt that a 28-gauge does indeed make a fine turkey shotgun, as the Mossberg demonstrated. MSRP: $902

FRANCHI AFFINITY 3 TURKEY ELITE

The Franchi Affinity 3 Turkey Elite is a semi-auto available in 12- and 20-gauge. However, unlike the other two shotguns on this list, it utilizes an inertia-operated action that relies on fewer moving parts than a gas gun. The system is simple: a rotating bolt head, a bolt body, and a return spring. When the shell is fired, the gun moves rearward with recoil, but the bolt remains free-floating and doesn't move with the rest of the shotgun. Recoil force compresses a spring in the bolt that, when released, shoves the bolt rearward to cycle the action. A return spring located on the magazine tube returns the bolt to battery. Since the Franchi relies on recoil from the shot to cycle the action, it operates cleanly, reducing maintenance requirements compared to gas guns.

The inertia-operated design has other benefits. Because it doesn't have a traditional gas-operating system mounted around the magazine tube, the forearm can be trimmed down. Positioning the return spring on the magazine tubes gives Franchi more liberty with stock designs and configurations than competing guns with return springs inside the buttstock. Like the Mossberg, the Franchi comes with a pistol grip (Steady-Grip), but the Affinity's 14.4-inch length of pull is substantially longer than the Mossberg's 12.8-inch LOP. The Affinity features side cutouts for attaching a sling to the forearm and buttstock.

Both 12- and 20-gauge versions come with 24-inch barrels, and the receiver and

barrel are coated with a Cerakote Midnight Bronze surface finish that protects the metal and reduces glare. Extended Rhino ported long, and extra-long range screw-in turkey chokes come standard. The Franchi's lengthened forcing cone and extended choke create tight, even patterns. Testing out to 50 yards with Fiocchi's 3-inch Golden Turkey TSS No.9 load showed consistent killing patterns that put dozens of pellets on target.

The Franchi offers adjustable sights, which is a benefit on a turkey gun for anyone who isn't planning to mount an optic on their firearm. The rear rifle-style sight allows you to adjust the point of impact, and the front dual-glow Tru-Glo bead has a hood to reduce glare. The combination of fiber-optic front and rear sights offers a clear sight picture, but like all the other guns on this list, the Franchi comes with a rail that simplifies optics mounting. The bolt handle and bolt release buttons have been enlarged for easy operation.

The 20-gauge version of the Affinity 3 Turkey Elite tested weighed 6.8 pounds, making it the heaviest gun on the list.

That's not all bad, though, because the Franchi's weight makes it manageable to shoot with 3-inch magnum loads. The TSA recoil pad also reduces recoil impact, and the heel of the pad is radiused so it won't hang up on a vest or jacket when shouldering the gun.

Last spring, I carried the Franchi topped with a Burris Fastfire 4 optic on my turkey hunt with Real McCoy Outdoors in southern Ohio. The lodge is best known for producing massive free-range whitetails, but its steps to bolster deer populations have also dramatically increased turkeys. When we arrived the evening before the hunt, the oak and poplar-covered hills were alive with gobbles.

It didn't take long to punch my tag, either. Chad McCoy told me to set up before sunrise at the end of a long finger of cropland bordered on both sides by steep, forested ravines. Before legal shooting light, gobblers were already calling, and when I gave a cluck to draw them in, I was afraid they'd pass by me before I could legally shoot. But the birds milled and gobbled just below me for

The Beretta A300 Turkey is available in either Mossy Oak DNA (shown here) or Realtree Edge camo, both of which effectively help conceal the gun from the sharp eye of gobblers. A shortened 24-inch barrel makes the A300 lighter and more maneuverable in the turkey woods.

Beretta's A300 gas-operated semi-auto has proven reliable and is an excellent choice for turkey hunters. It's available in 20-gauge (shown here) or 12-gauge.

twenty minutes before I looked to my left and saw one large gobbler standing in the open. I rotated the shotgun, centered the dot of the FastFire on the junction of the neck and body, and fired. The bird dropped when the swarm of Fiocchi TSS struck.

Like the Mossberg, the Franchi is a dedicated turkey gun, and it's heavier, longer (41.4 inches) and has a longer length of pull than the Mossberg. But the Franchi is a premium turkey gun with all the features you want and the reliability you'd expect at this price point. MSRP: $1,349

BERETTA A300 ULTIMA TURKEY

Beretta is the oldest name in the firearms business, yet the brand remains on the cutting edge of shotgun design, even after almost five centuries. The company's A300 Ultima shotguns are outstanding, and one of the latest additions to the family is the A300 Ultima Turkey.

The A300 Ultima is a gas-operated shotgun with a self-regulating gas system

MOSSBERG INTERNATIONAL SA-28 TURKEY TACTICAL

ACTION	GAS-OPERATED
Gauge	28
Weight	5.4 lbs.
Overall Length	39 in.
Barrel Length	22 in.
Chokes	Extra-full turkey extended
MSRP	$902

FRANCHI AFFINITY 3 TURKEY ELITE

ACTION	INERTIA-OPERATED
Gauge	12, 20 (tested)
Weight	6.8 lbs.
Overall Length	41 in.
Barrel Length	24 in.
Chokes	Long-range ported/extended, extra long-range ported/extended
MSRP	$1,349

BERETTA A300 ULTIMA TURKEY

ACTION	GAS-OPERATED
Gauge	12, 20 (tested)
Weight	6.6 lbs.
Overall Length	44 in.
Barrel Length	24 in.
Chokes	(2) Extra-full turkey extended, modified flush fit
MSRP	$999

that expels unused gas. It's a proven piston-operated design that cycles reliably and is easy to clean and maintain. Of course, the gas operating system also reduces felt recoil by prolonging the "push" of the gun, so we perceive that gas shotguns kick less, which makes them more comfortable to shoot. Further reducing recoil is Beretta's Kick-Off System, which incorporates shock absorbers into the stock, dropping recoil up to an additional 60 percent. That's hugely beneficial when firing heavy turkey loads.

The A300 Ultima is not as much a "dedicated" turkey gun as the other shotguns listed here. It doesn't come with a ghost ring or adjustable iron sights but a simple stepped rib with a red fiber-optic bead. It does, however, have a receiver that is drilled and tapped and a Picatinny rail, so mounting a reflex optic is quite simple. The stock has a more traditional profile than the Franchi or Mossberg and lacks the pistol grips found on those guns. It uses the Beretta Mobil Choke System, and the test gun came with an extended extra full turkey choke plus a flush-fit modified tube.

The Beretta's design makes it the most versatile gun in the group. With its 24-inch barrel, the gun's overall length is 44.5 inches, weighing 6.6 pounds. It's perfectly well-suited as a waterfowl gun and would be an excellent option for the northern grouse woods. I've been carrying the A300 Ultima Turkey while rabbit hunting with a pack of beagles, and its quick handling and short overall length make it an ideal bunny gun.

That's not to say that the A300 Ultima doesn't offer many great features that make it an ideal turkey gun. Sure, it lacks the pistol grip favored by many gobbler hunters, but the oversized controls are easy to access and operate. Camo options include Mossy Oak DNA and Realtree Edge, which offer excellent concealment, especially in dark timber during the early season. A soft-touch comb insert also goes a long way toward dampening perceived recoil. The sharp stab of a hard shotgun comb driving up and into the shooter's face is often the catalyst for a flinch.

Despite not having killed a bird (yet)

with the A300 Ultima, it is the gun on this list with which I've had the most experience simply because I've been able to range test it more extensively than the other samples. I've come to like the Beretta, especially the Kick-Off recoil reduction, which significantly reduces perceived recoil. If you mount an optic on it, be aware that you'll have to remove the front two thread protectors to mount the rail, and do so carefully; it's easy to mar the finish on the top of the gun. However, optics mounting is otherwise not an issue.

A Leupold DeltaPoint Pro red-dot mounted on the A300 Ultima proved very effective when pattern-tested using Fiocchi Golden Turkey 3-inch loads to 50 yards. The No.9 shot maintains full coverage to that distance, and I wouldn't hesitate to take a bird from there. The Beretta requires you to press the magazine release button (just ahead of the trigger-guard) to release a shell for chambering like the Franchi. The advantage is that it's very simple to unload and reload the gun's chamber. I prefer the Beretta's angled crossbolt manual safety that rides ahead of the trigger better than the other two safeties, but it's loud.

Overall, the A300 Ultima Turkey is an outstanding gobbler gun that's the most versatile and softest shooting on the list. Reliability was also excellent, and the Beretta is an excellent value. MSRP: $999 GD

They Never Made the Big Time

British and European cartridges that were years ahead of their time ... yet still failed.

❯PIERRE VAN DER WALT

I t should not be news to any reader that the British and European gun trades were highly active in cartridge conceptualization and design from the advent of the 20th century to the outbreak of World War II. Cartridge designs rode a near-permanent wave during this period, but not all progressed beyond the experimental or proposition stage. This article is about a few of those obscure bolt-action cartridge concepts of which we are aware. There are many more that are not covered here and even more that have disappeared in the fog of time, about which we will probably never know anything. An entire book could be written about them.

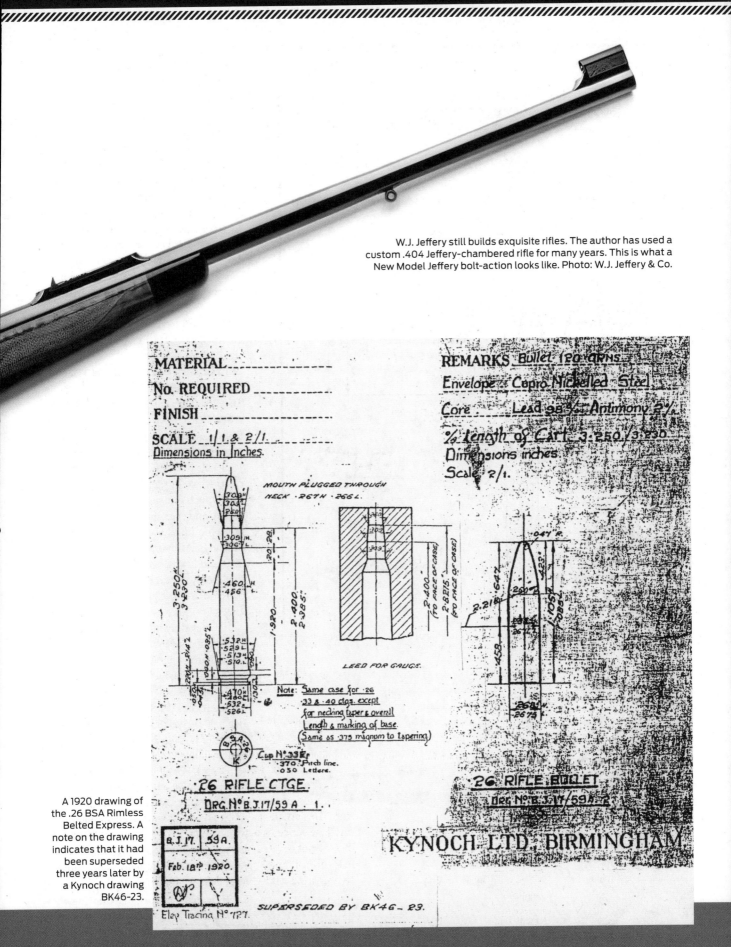

W.J. Jeffery still builds exquisite rifles. The author has used a custom .404 Jeffery-chambered rifle for many years. This is what a New Model Jeffery bolt-action looks like. Photo: W.J. Jeffery & Co.

A 1920 drawing of the .26 BSA Rimless Belted Express. A note on the drawing indicates that it had been superseded three years later by a Kynoch drawing BK46-23.

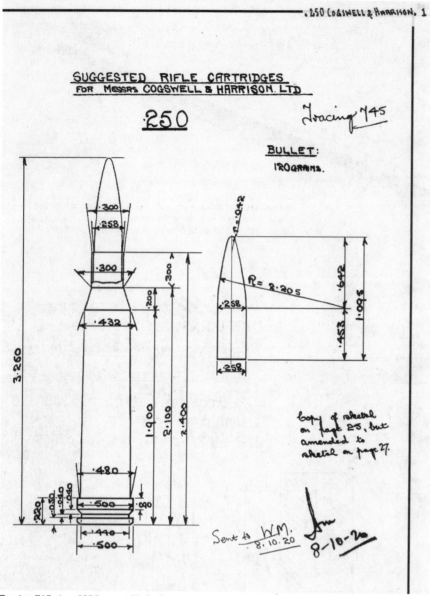

Tracing 745 circa 1920, most likely the conceptual drawing of the .250 Cogswell & Harrington cartridge. It was superseded in 1923.

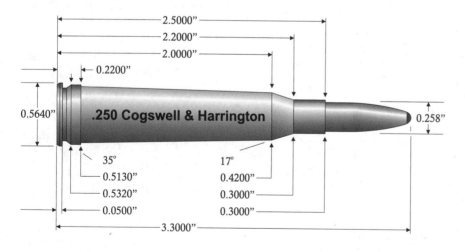

If I were a man of means, I would, just for the hell of it, have built a collection of British-style rifles chambered for some of these '*never*' cartridges on modern Granite Mountain Arms (GMA) or Prechtl custom Mauser 98 actions.

The disappearance or destruction of many European cartridge records during WWII and the recent closure of the historic Birmingham Proof House in the United Kingdom, followed by the sale of its records to an undisclosed collector, makes original research near impossible. I therefore relied on whatever sources of existing research I could find, sometimes almost verbatim. Sources will be acknowledged as best as possible, and where I omitted recognition, it is accidental, not intentional.

.250 COGSWELL & HARRINGTON SUPER HIGH VELOCITY

The .250 C&H cartridge was conceived around 1920. Two drawings exist: one from Eley dated October 8, 1920, and another from Kynoch (BJ17-71) of July 18, 1922. They differ materially. The cartridge color sketch image follows the Kynoch dimensions as it is the most recent, and even the 1920 sketch already notes modifications and refers to earlier drawings. Although I have never seen a .250 C&H cartridge, Fleming[1] speculates that it may have seen limited production by Kynoch as the primer was revised in 1928.

The Eley drawing[2] stipulates the case at 2.400 inches (60.96mm), while the Kynoch drawing[3] lists it as 2.500 inches (63.5mm). The Eley drawing shows a maximum commercial cartridge length of 3.26 inches (82.80mm) and the Kynoch 3.30 inches (83.82mm). The bullet diameter is given as .258 inch (6.55mm) and not the present-day .257 inch (6.53mm). For all practical purposes, we can use the same barrel specifications as the .250-3000 Savage: a groove diameter of .257 inch (6.53mm) and a caliber of .250 inch (6.35mm).

The .250 Cogswell & Harrison design is typically British period-related, but the final version's body taper was an excessive 2.991 degrees. The original drawing with the lesser body taper was the better of the two versions in my book, even with its

.250 COGSWELL & HARRINGTON DRAWING DIFFERENCES

IDENTIFICATION DATE	RIM Ø (R1) DIAMETER (IN.)	BELT Ø (R3) DIAMETER (IN.)	BASE Ø (P1) DIAMETER (IN.)	SHOULDER (P2) DIAMETER (IN.)	CASE (L3) LENGTH (IN.)	COAL
(L6) (in.)						
1920	.500	.500	.480	.432	2.400	3.250
1923 (Kynoch)	.564	.532	.513	.420	2.500	3.300

The cartridge is quite interesting because it is belted but semi-rimmed with a rim diameter of .564 inch (14.33mm).

odd belt diameter. Its neck measures .300 inch (7.62mm), constituting 120 percent of the caliber. The shoulder angle is a shallow, Cordite-charging-compatible 17 degrees. The case capacity is in the region of 62–65 grains of water.

I could not find a definitive pressure specification for the .250 Cogswell & Harrison. QuickLoad lists it as 50,763 psi, but obviously without substantiation, and I have no idea where that specification was sourced. The .240 H&H Apex, which hails from the same year, has a maximum average pressure limit of 60,191 psi. The .250-3000 Savage of 1914, a lever-action cartridge, has a Sporting Arms & Ammunition Manufacturers' Institute (SAAMI) maximum average pressure limit of 45,000 CUP (Copper Units Pressure), while the *Commission internationale permanente pour l'épreuve des armes à feu portatives* (CIP) limits it to 52,939 psi. Given that it is a post-WWI bolt-action cartridge design, I can see no reason the .250 Cogswell & Harrison cannot be loaded to .240 Apex levels. Thus, it compares to contemporary .257-inch rounds as detailed in the .250 C&H Performance Comparison Table.

In practical terms, the .250 Cogswell & Harrington would have performed somewhere between the rimless .25-'06 Remington and the .257 Weatherby Magnum. It was hailed as an excellent option for "Hill-Shooting in India, or for Deer-Stalking in Scotland.[4]"

In the 1924 Cogswell & Harrison brochure, the cartridge was offered in a Mauser 98 action, and the Cordite ballistics listed it as 3,000 fps with a 110-grain bullet, which would have been achieved at pressures around 45,000 psi.

Drawings of two other belted Cogswell & Harrington cartridges also exist but have not been included here due to space restrictions; that of the .370 (Kynoch

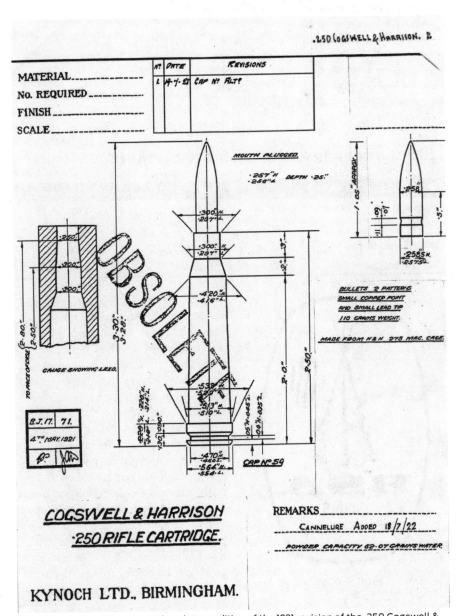

This Kynoch drawing seems to be a late rendition of the 1921 revision of the .250 Cogswell & Harrison cartridge since the notes and remarks date 1922 and 1928, respectively.

BJ17—71.4 dated May 5, 1921) and of a .380 (Eley 137.24 dated June 13, 1920) neither of which made it.

.26 BSA RIMLESS BELTED EXPRESS
BSA (Birmingham Small Arms Company, Ltd.) was established around 1861. It played a significant role in British small arms manufacture until about 1973, when it closed. It offered airguns, rifles, and cartridges of its own design, amongst which were the .26 and

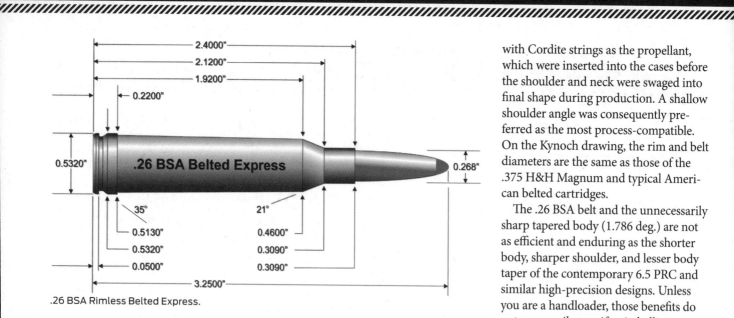

.26 BSA Rimless Belted Express.

.250 C&H PERFORMANCE COMPARISON TABLE
(26-IN. BARREL)

CARTRIDGE	BULLET (GR.)	MAP (PSI)	VELOCITY (FPS)
.257 Roberts	120	58,000	2,800
.25-'06 Remington	120	63,000	3,100
.250 Cogswell & Harrison	120	55,000	3,125
.257 Weatherby Magnum	120	53,500	3,300

The famous logo of the BSA company during its heyday. Photo: BSA

.40 BSA Rimless Belted Express. The earliest blueprint of the .26 BSA I have is Kynoch's drawing numbered BJ17-55A, dated February 18, 1920. It was superseded by Kynoch drawing BK46-23, which I am still trying to find. At the time of the .26 BSA's introduction, the company built its rifles on modified Enfield Pattern-14 bolt-action systems, not Mauser or Mannlicher actions common to other British gunmakers.

The .26 BSA Cartridge Comparison Table shows its closest ballistic rivals. The .264 Winchester Magnum could also have been included, but it is more powerful than the cartridges in the comparison. The .26 BSA's rivals are the 6.5 Remington Magnum and the recent 6.5 PRC. That is quite a revelation, given that this cartridge is over a century old.

Theoretically, the .26 BSA equals or marginally outperforms the highly touted 6.5 PRC cartridge if loaded to the same pressure levels. In practice, the 6.5 PRC is technically a much more sophisticated cartridge with better cartridge-to-chamber interface and combustion characteristics. (Not that the .260 BSA cartridge is the potentially better one; it already equaled the PRC's ballistic potential a century ago.)

The .260 BSA has a 2.400-inch (60,96mm) long case with a 107.69 percent long neck, which conforms to contemporary criteria. The shallow shoulder angle of 21 degrees is high for a British cartridge. British rounds were loaded with Cordite strings as the propellant, which were inserted into the cases before the shoulder and neck were swaged into final shape during production. A shallow shoulder angle was consequently preferred as the most process-compatible. On the Kynoch drawing, the rim and belt diameters are the same as those of the .375 H&H Magnum and typical American belted cartridges.

The .26 BSA belt and the unnecessarily sharp tapered body (1.786 deg.) are not as efficient and enduring as the shorter body, sharper shoulder, and lesser body taper of the contemporary 6.5 PRC and similar high-precision designs. Unless you are a handloader, those benefits do not necessarily manifest in ballistic or precision superiority. It also shows that Britain was at least 39 years ahead of the USA in terms of the .260-inch caliber cartridge design because the U.S. only introduced the belted .264 Winchester Magnum in 1959 and the 6.5mm Remington Magnum in 1966. The rimless 6.5 PRC wouldn't see the light of day until 2018—98 years later!

.280 JEFFERY (.33/.280 JEFFERY)

The .280 Jeffery originated with Kynoch drawing AY12-41 of November 19, 2013. It is a .333 Jeffery necked down to .287 inch (7.29mm), not the .284 inch (7.21mm) that later became the 7mm standard. W.J. Jeffery offered it in his Mauser 98 rifles. Most sources claim that it only went into production in 1915, but 1914 is more likely. As with the 7mm WSM and Remington's UltraMag cartridges, its parent case was the .404 Jeffery, except the British took this approach 88 years before the Americans did. Loaded with 57 grains of Cordite, it launched a 140-grain bullet at 3,000 fps.[5,6] Remember that the velocities listed for British cartridges were derived from 28-inch (711mm) proof barrels.

The .280 Jeffery is a forerunner of the modern 7mm Blaser Magnum, circa 2009. The Blaser, designed by my friend Christer Larsson, former Head of Ballistics at Norma Precision, has a marginally shorter case body (L1) and case length (L3) but less body taper and a sharper shoulder. These two cartridges have the same case water capacity and ballistics at

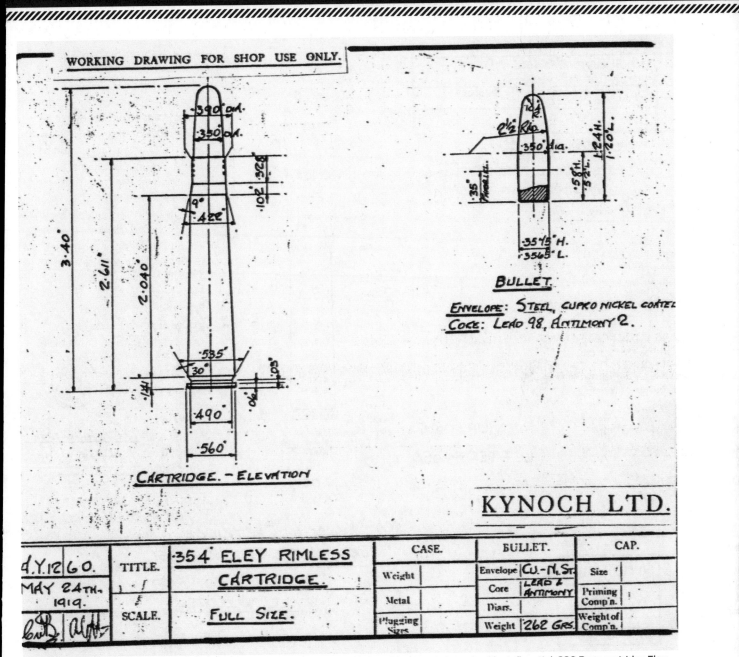

WORKING DRAWING FOR SHOP USE ONLY.

BULLET.

ENVELOPE: STEEL, CUPRO NICKEL COATED
CORE: LEAD 98, ANTIMONY 2.

CARTRIDGE. — ELEVATION

KYNOCH LTD.

A.Y.12 6 0.	TITLE.	.354 ELEY RIMLESS	CASE.		BULLET.		CAP.	
MAY 24TH. 1919.		CARTRIDGE.	Weight		Envelope	CU.-N. ST.	Size	
					Core	LEAD 2 ANTIMONY	Priming Comp'n.	
	SCALE.	FULL SIZE.	Metal		Diars.			
			Plugging Sizes		Weight	262 GRS.	Weight of Comp'n.	

Kynoch drawing AY12-60, dated 1919, shows the planned .354 Eley Rimless cartridge. It was based on the influential .280 Ross cartridge Eley also designed.

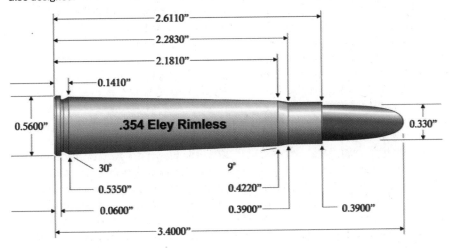

.354 Eley Rimless

2.6110"
2.2830"
2.1810"
0.1410"
0.5600"
0.330"
30°
9°
0.5350"
0.4220"
0.0600"
0.3900"
0.3900"
3.4000"

The accompanying comparison table details the contemporary cartridges most comparable to the .322 Rigby Nitro. Since the .322's modern adversaries are all loaded to maximum average pressures (MAP) exceeding 60,000 psi, I settled on the pressure level for the .322 Rigby for comparison in QuickLoad using a 24-inch (610mm) barrel. The average of five top-performing loads at 90 percent of maximum average pressure was used.

QuickLoad is not gospel, but it provides a solid comparative base for calculation. The 'wonder kid' .338 Lapua and Norma Magnums were essentially

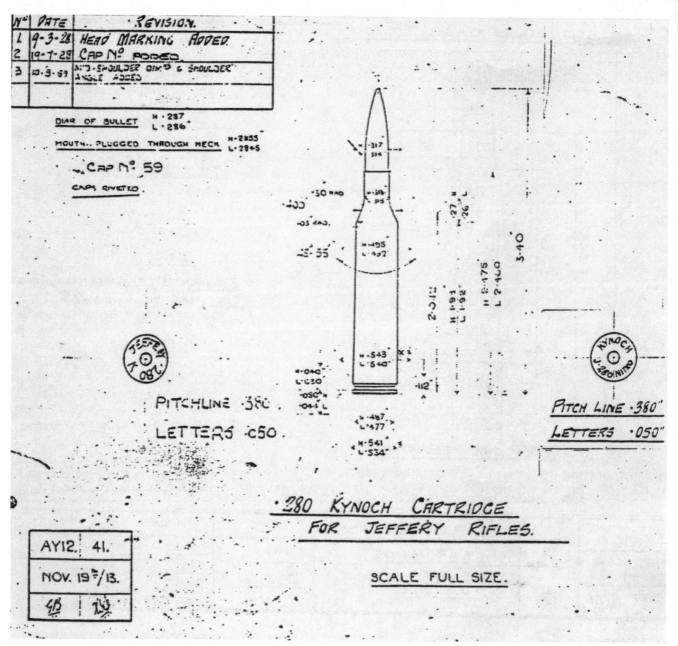

This is a poor-quality drawing of the .280 Jeffery. Although the original drawing dates back to 1913, this version lists modifications up to 1959.

identical pressure levels for all practical purposes.

Apart from bullet diameter, the minor dimensional differences are detailed in the accompanying .280 Jeffery Cartridge Comparison Table. Although the .280 was loaded hot in its day, modern propellants enable it to exceed original ballistics in 24-inch (610mm) barrels.

Loaded with modern propellants to contemporary pressure levels, the .280 Jeffery trades punches with the .280 Remington, 7x64mm Brenneke, 7mm WSM, 7mm Remington Magnum, and

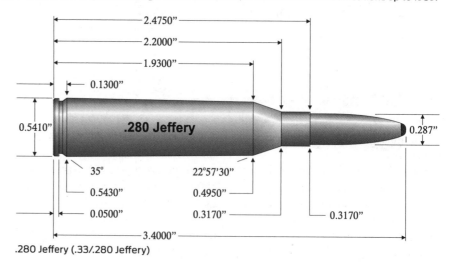

.280 Jeffery (.33/.280 Jeffery)

.26 BSA CARTRIDGE COMPARISON TABLE (26-IN. BARREL)

CARTRIDGE	YEAR	CAPACITY (GR.)	MAP (PSI)	BULLET (GR.)	VELOCITY (FPS)
.26 BSA	1920	69.0	50,763 (QL)	120	3,150
.26 BSA	1920	69.0	62,500 (CIP)	120	3,250
6.5 Remington Mag.	1966	68.0	63,901	120	3,000
6.5 PRC (Hornady)	2018	68.0	65,000	120	3,250

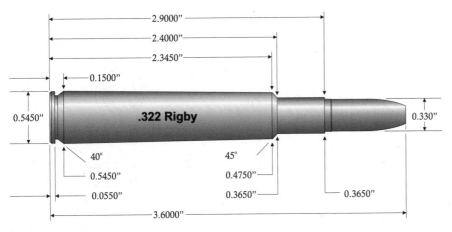

.322 Rigby Nitro.

.280 JEFFERY CARTRIDGE COMPARISON TABLE (24-IN. BARREL)

CARTRIDGE	BULLET (GR.)	90% MAP (PSI)	CAPACITY (GR.)	VELOCITY (FPS)
.280 (.33/.280) Jeffery	140	54,825	82.5	3,350
7mm Blaser Magnum	140	54,825	82.5	3,350

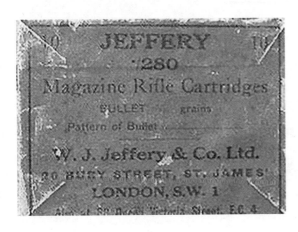

This worn box of .280 Jeffery ammunition in the collection of Paul Strydom invokes a sense of nostalgia to accompany a discussion of these forgotten old cartridges. Photo: Paul Strydom

the 7mm Blaser without ever taking to the canvas.

From a design perspective, its neck is a surprise for a British cartridge preceding WWI: It is short—around 98.2 percent of caliber. Even the .276 Enfield with which the British military experimented had a longer neck. The 22°57'30" shoulder was also rather sharp for a pre-WWI British round. The body taper is era-typical at a rather pronounced 1.687 degrees. It's interesting that a cartridge would fall by the wayside, only to essentially be revived 96 years later as a solution to real or perceived needs[7]. But that is the world of cartridges for you.

.322 RIGBY NITRO

In the 1914 history section of the famous John Rigby & Co. website, there is a sentence that reads: "John Rigby had further plans for his .416 cartridge case. When World War I began in June 1914, he was working with Kynoch to develop the Rigby .322 Nitro cartridge. They intended to use a .330 diameter bullet weighing 250 grains. The velocity should have been about 3,000 feet per second, which would have produced more than 5,000 foot pounds of energy at the muzzle. Completion of the project was delayed until after the war, but with John Rigby's death in 1916 all development ceased."

The .322 Rigby died with its conceiver and was never commercially produced. A few cartridges must have been made for experimental purposes because there are a few specimens in collectors' hands. The 250-grain .330-inch bullet made the .318 Westley Richards (circa 1910) famous. Many years ago, I wrote: "The .322 Rigby was not conceived as a .350 Rigby Magnum necked down, but an original design. The various sources list slightly differing dimensions for the cartridge, but performance levels hovered around 2,500 fps with 275-grain bullets from 24-in. (610mm) barrels."

However, John Rigby used the .404 Jeffery case as the basis for the .322, not his .416 case. That is abundantly clear from the March 17, 1914, letter posted on the Rigby website and the Kynoch drawing AY12-47 dated March 24, 1914. It is understandable because, as I explained in *African Dangerous Game Cartridges* (p. 277), he indirectly contributed to the creation of the .404 Jeffery.

Drawing AY12-47 shows the cartridge as having the same cartridge overall length of 3.75 inches (95.25mm) as the .416 Rigby (Mauser magnum-length action) rather than the 3.53 inches (89.66mm) of the .404 Jeffery. The latter can be fitted into a standard-length Mauser action with a stretched magazine box, as is commonly done to accommodate the .375 H&H Magnum (COAL 3.6 inches). Interestingly, this drawing does not specify the case body length (L1), but Ken Howell[8] determined it by using CAD software to 'reverse engineer' the dimension as 2.345 inches (59.56mm).

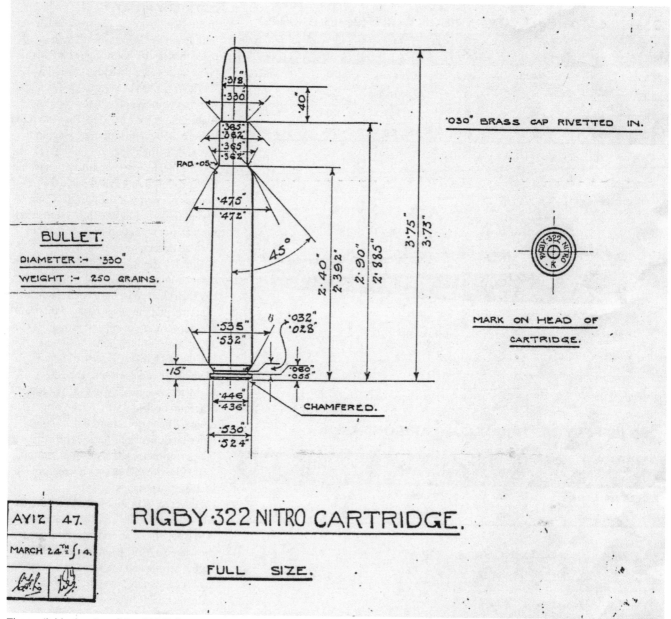

The available drawing of the .322 Rigby Nitro cartridge dated March 24, 1914.

Body taper has thus been calculated as 1.566 degrees.

The case water capacity of the .322 Rigby Nitro is in the region of 102–103 grains. Rigby specified the muzzle velocity at 3,000 fps with a 250-grain bullet using Cordite. I can only presume that this performance was to be derived from the typical 28-inch (711mm) test barrels standard in the British trade. Using QuickLoad and a British-style Woodleigh 250-grain .330-inch bullet, I derived an approximate pressure level of 62,500 psi, which is way above what would have been acceptable in 1914. I submit that Rigby's velocity expectation for the 250-grain bullet was optimistic.

If, however, I use a 275-grain bullet with a length of 1.34 inches (34mm), I can simulate 2,500 fps from a 24-inch (610mm) barrel at a mere 47,137 psi—identical to the pressure specification of the .416 Rigby.

.322 RIGBY CARTRIDGE COMPARISON TABLE
(24-IN. BARREL)

CARTRIDGE	BULLET (GR.)	90% MAP (PSI)	CAPACITY (GR.)	VELOCITY (FPS)
.318 Westley Richards	250	43,075	69.0	2,385
.322 Rigby Nitro	250	54,000	103.0	2,760
.338 Norma Magnum	250	57,436	105.5	2,864
.338 Lapua Magnum	250	54,824	118.0	2,864
.338 Remington UltraMag	250	57,435	110.0	2,807

conceived 99 years ago! Reinventing the wheel seems to be the current pastime.

.354 ELEY RIMLESS

The .354 Eley Rimless is a particularly obscure concept that never progressed beyond the drawing board. The drawing number, dY12-60, is especially odd. Even stranger is that it is a Kynoch drawing of an Eley cartridge marked '*Working Drawing for Shop Use Only.*' Its date is May 24, 1919, just more than six months after the end of WWI. I could not find any other reference to it except in Harding, but the timeframe Harding records raises more questions than answers.

He may be referring to yet another cartridge when he writes: "In 1906 Eley were to start the manufacture of cartridges for rifles designed by Sir Charles Ross, a Scotsman who had emigrated to Canada." At least three variants were made by Eley, including two distinctly different versions of the .280-inch rimless, together with the rimless .354 inch. Alternatively, an Eley drawing, which I have not been privy to, dating back to 1906, may exist.

The .354-inch Eley essentially is a .280 Rimless Nitro Express Ross necked up. Both cartridges share the .404 Jeffery parent case with the rim (R1) and base (P1) measuring .535 inch (13.59mm) and a common shoulder (P2) of .422 inch (10.72mm). The shoulder angle of the .354 Eley is much shallower than that of the Ross, a meager 9 degrees rather than 26°33'63", and it also reduces the body length (L1) by .141 inch (3.58mm) to a length of 2.040 inches (51.82mm). The water capacity of the .354 Eley case is in the region of 88–90 grains.

The .354 Eley's bullet diameter would have been .350 inch (8.89mm) rather than the .358 inch (9.09mm) that eventually became popular. Body taper would have been excessive, as on the .280 Ross, around 3.405 degrees. Such a sharp body taper will make it prone to case-head separation when reloading the case repeatedly and inhibits case water capacity. With less body taper, the .354 Eley would easily have outperformed the .358 Norma Magnum and the 9.3x64mm Brenneke cartridges.

Assuming it was intended for the same

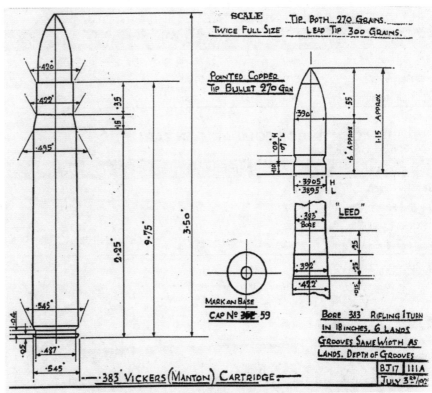

The drawing on which the .383 Vickers hunting cartridge was to be based. No information indicating that it progressed beyond this drawing seems to exist.

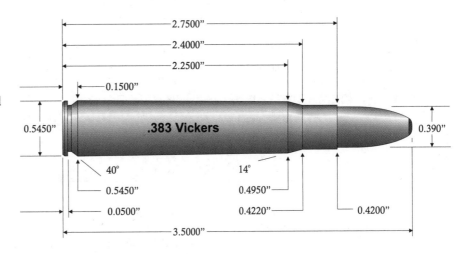

straight-pull design as the .280 Ross, ballistic calculations were based on the identical maximum average pressure specification of 47,137 psi. For its projected ballistics, refer to the .354 Eley Cartridge Comparison Table. The bullet specified for the .354 Eley weighed 262 grains.

.383 VICKERS

Who does not remember the images of the water-cooled Vickers machine gun hammering away at the German lines during World War I? Vickers Limited,

which produced that machine gun, also created several cartridges. An exciting one that never saw the light of day was the .383 Vickers. Harding[9] covers it as follows: "This is yet another experimental calibre produced by Kynoch Ltd, in 1927, presumably for Manton & Co. of Calcutta who must have rejected it, given their name is crossed out. To date I have yet to find a specimen of this calibre."

If Bill Harding has not seen a specimen, none probably exist because he was the historian and archivist to the

.383 VICKERS COMPARISON TABLE (300 GRAINS)

CARTRIDGE	BULLET (GR.)	90% MAP (PSI)	VELOCITY (FPS)
.375 H&H Magnum	300	54,000	2,610
.383 Vickers	300	54,000	2,650
.400 H&H Magnum	300	54,000	2,775

.354 ELEY CARTRIDGE COMPARISON TABLE (24-INCH BARREL)

CARTRIDGE	BULLET (GR.)	PRESSURE (PSI)	VELOCITY (FPS)
.354 Eley Rimless	262	47,137	2,575
.354 Eley Rimless	262	57,435	2,710
.358 Norma Magnum	262	57,435	2,715
9,3x64mm Brenneke	262	57,435	2,692

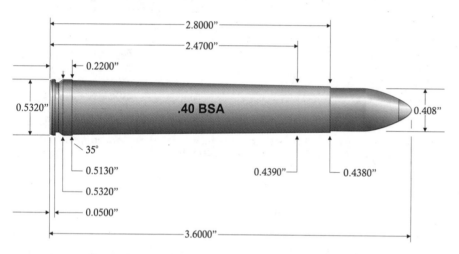

.40 BSA PERFORMANCE TABLE (24-INCH BARREL)

CARTRIDGE	BULLET (GR.)	90% MAP (PSI)	CAPACITY (GR.)	VELOCITY (FPS)
.40 BSA	260	57,435	104	2,925
.40 BSA	400	57,435	104	2,375

Birmingham Proof House (among many other related positions), and he has most probably seen it all.

According to the cartridge drawing BJ17-11A of July 3, 1929, the .383 Vickers would have been based on a slightly shortened (2.75 inches, 69.85mm) .404 Jeffery case given a 14-degree shallow angle and a short-for-the-era 91.38 percent of caliber neck. Bullets (270 and 300 grains) and groove diameters were to have been .390 inch (9.91mm), and the bore/caliber to measure .383 inch (9.73mm). The body taper was 1.35 degrees. The case water volume would have been around 103.5 grains.

This oddball caliber was most likely designed to compete with the .375 H&H Magnum, any bolt-action .40 prospects, and the venerable .450/400 in double rifles. The .400 H&H Rimless only came about 80 years later, but its groove diameter is .410 inch. I own both the .375 and .400 H&H cartridges, so I have a reasonable understanding of cartridges in the caliber bracket. To make a reasonable comparison, I used the SAAMI maximum average pressure specification of the .375 H&H Magnum of 62,000 psi (427 Mpa) as a baseline in the accompanying .383 Vickers Comparison Table from 24-inch (610mm) barrels.

The unusual bullet diameter could have been why Manton & Co. rejected the cartridge. It would have been a more capable design if Vickers had maintained the .404 Jeffery case length of 2.875 inches (73.02mm) and extended the cartridge length to equal that of the .375 H&H Magnum at 3.6 inches (91.44mm) and mated it to a .400–.410-inch bullet. Bear in mind that both the .404 Jeffery (1904) and the .416 Rigby (1911) had already established their reputations for the better part of 20 and 18 years, respectively. The .383 cartridge would not have brought anything new to the table.

.40 BSA

Although the .41 Roper (designed by Sylvester Howard Roper, the American inventor of the motorcycle), was the first belted cartridge, Holland & Holland in the UK cemented the concept with its .400/375 H&H in 1905, which the great .375 H&H Magnum later superseded. [Editor's note: In all my years of research, I had always understood the .400/375 H&H, or Velopex, to be the first belted cartridge. This shows that you never stop learning.]

In the world of double and top-break rifles, cartridges in the .400–.411-inch bracket have been very popular since about 1884. The .450/400 Nitro Express 3", introduced by Jeffery in 1902, is still highly regarded in Africa. This popularity has never migrated to bolt-action rifles and cartridges, but it is not for lack of trying. In America, Charles Newton, Kleinguenther, Townsend Whelen, and Art Alphin tried it and failed. British Sporting Arms (BSA) and Holland & Holland also tried and failed in the UK. It is just not a caliber that grips the imagination of the hunting public in the face of competition from the .375 H&H Magnum and the .416 Rigby.

BSA made one such UK attempt. Kynoch drawing BJ17-59, dated February 16, 1921, depicts the .40 BSA cartridge for which a light, copper-point .250-grain bullet of 408 inch (10.36mm) diameter was inexplicably specified. Bullets in the 400-grain class are preferred for cartridges in this performance bracket. The load was 69 grains of Cordite. It was a belted, stretched-length (2.8 inches, 71.12mm) straight-tapered wall cartridge geometrically comparable to the .458 Lott. BSA offered Enfield P14 rifles chambered for it.

Had the .40 BSA survived, its closest modern rivals would have been the .400 H&H Belted Magnum of 2002 and the .400 Pondoro. The BSA and H&H's case capacities are virtually identical, while the Pondoro has about 2 percent more capacity. Capacity differences are negligible.

.430 GIBBS NITRO

Although the .430 Gibbs Nitro, based on Kynoch drawing AY12-24 dated January 4, 1913, never went into production, a few specimens were specially created by my friend Otto Planyavski and are floating around collections. Planyavski even recreated the typical Gibbs .430 Nitro headstamp with the Kynoch K at the six o'clock position.

The .430 Gibbs Nitro was based on the full-length .416 Rigby case with a marginally shallower 37-degree shoulder and about 128–129 grains of water capacity. Its neck length is 129.4 percent of caliber, and its body taper is 1.2 degrees. The cartridge's overall length (L6) was 3.750 inches (95.25mm). Therefore, the .430 Gibbs would have required a Mauser magnum-length action.

The Kynoch drawing specifies a .435-inch (11.05mm) bullet weighing 410 grains. Its bullet diameter is identical to that of the .425 Westley Richards. The .425 Westley Richards, introduced in 1909, uses a 347-grain .435-inch (11.05mm) bullet and is based on the .404 Jeffery case shortened and modified to a rebated rim configuration. Its case's water capacity generally hovers in the region of 107 grains.[10] The .430 Gibbs concept had obviously been intended to compete with the .416 Rigby, the .404 Jeffery, and the 11.2x72mm Schüler rather than the more compact and sedate .425 Westley Richards.

The case water capacity of the .430 Gibbs Nitro is almost identical to the brand-dependent average of the .416. Gibbs had specified a maximum average pressure of just 39,160 psi for its even bigger .505 Magnum Gibbs introduced in 1911. Given a difference of only two years between the introduction of the .416 Rigby and the .430 Gibbs and sharing the same case, it is reasonable to assume that the .430 Gibbs would have had a similar

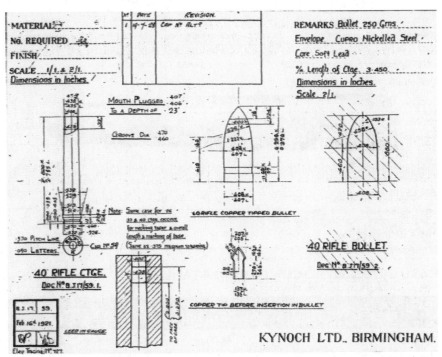

This cartridge, the .40 BSA, is highly sought after among collectors, and a premium specimen can easily cost US$1,500.00!

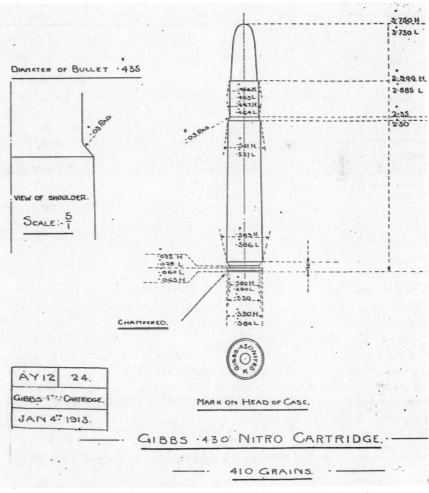

An early sketch of the .430 Gibbs Nitro cartridge dated 1913, most likely by Kynoch.

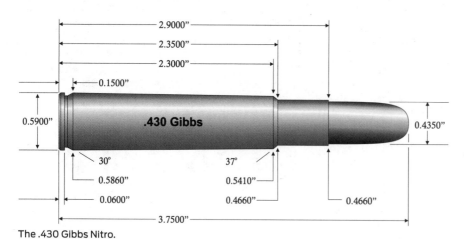

The .430 Gibbs Nitro.

.430 GIBBS NITRO COMPARISON TABLE
(410 GRAINS, 24-IN. BARREL)

CARTRIDGE	BULLET (IN.)	95% MAP (PSI)	CAPACITY (GR.)	VELOCITY (FPS)
.416 Rigby	.416	44,781	127.5	2,425
.404 Jeffery	.423	50,291	113.3	2,400
.425 Westley Richards	.435	41,335	107.0	2,255
.430 Gibbs Nitro	.435	44,781	128.2	2,480
11.2x7mm Schüler	.440	45,469	113.0	2,485

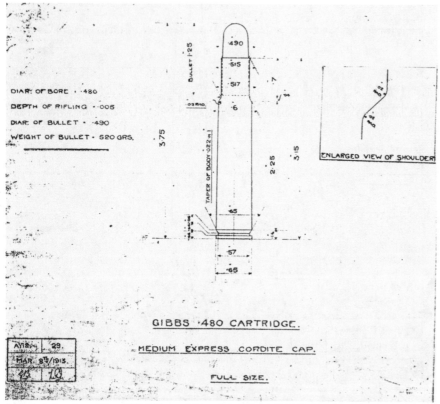

A Kynoch drawing of the .480 Gibbs cartridge dated March 8, 1913, designated AY12-29.

maximum average pressure specification to the .416 Rigby, namely 47,138 psi. Using the .425 Westley Richards barrel specifications, the .430 Gibbs can be recreated in QuickLoad to approximate its ballistic potential. Due to the low pressures of the group of cartridges, 95 percent of the specified maximum average pressure was used for the QuickLoad calculations.

The .430 Gibbs Nitro would have been a formidable cartridge. However, the outbreak of World War I in 1914 and the likelihood that Rigby would not have considered parting with irreplaceable Magnum Mauser actions in hand during hostilities most likely scuttled the concept. Its only bullet diameter competitor would have been the less powerful .425 Westley Richards and the oddball Schüler, which never made it to the big time.

.480 GIBBS

The .480 Gibbs was conceived shortly after the .430 Gibbs because the only drawing (Kynoch AY12-35) is dated July 29, 1913. Unlike the .430, it was based on Gibbs' massive proprietary case, the .505 Magnum Gibbs. Both cartridges require a magnum-length Mauser action and magazine box. The .505 Magnum Gibbs cartridge succeeded and is even more popular in Africa than in its heyday. However, the .480 Gibbs never made it out of the starting blocks.

Although the .480 Gibbs may be considered a .505 Magnum Gibbs necked down to fire a 520-grain bullet of .491-inch (12.47mm) diameter, the .480's case body length (L1) is .0498 inch (1.265mm) shorter. It shares the same 45-degree shoulder and case head configuration, but its body taper is .764 degrees, whereas the .505's is between .988 and 1.002 degrees, depending on whether CIP or Birmingham Proof House dimensions are used. Its neck length is 144 percent of caliber.

The water capacity of the .480 Gibbs case would have been around 168.2 grains. For practical purposes, and in the absence of data, the maximum average pressure of the .480 should be identical to that of the .505 Gibbs: 39,160 psi.

We will never know why Gibbs considered a cartridge so close to his existing .505 Magnum Gibbs and used an odd bullet diameter. He probably realized it was a bad idea from a commercial perspective and abandoned the design. The closest rivals to the .480 Gibbs Nitro would have been the more compact .500 Jeffery and the in-house .505 Magnum Gibbs. The .480 Gibbs Nitro Comparison Table shows how these three would have stacked up against each other.

SUMMARY

Countless other fascinating British and European cartridge designs never made it beyond the conceptual, experimental, or limited-production phases. Books could be written about them. The golden thread that runs through them all is that almost everything lately introduced as innovative or pioneering is nothing but a rehash of these abandoned old cartridges.

The most significant advance in cartridges, in my view, is not the changes in dimensions that turn obsolete designs into the modern counterparts lately hailed as the be-all-and-end-all. It's the American awakening to rim and base diameter dimensions for rounds above and beyond the .223 Remington, .30-'06 Springfield, and .300 Winchester Magnum that hampered American cartridges for a century. Now that the Americans have accepted the .404 Jeffery and .416 Rigby as parent cases and introduced the rimless .375 Ruger base and head geometry, a new world has opened up for cartridge design. Weatherby also recently contributed by stretching the .284 Winchester case. The only outstanding awakening still required for America is the 8x68mmS case head, once pursued by Charles Newton. **GD**

I must thank and acknowledge the assistance of my friends Casey Lewis, Will Reuter, Paul Strydom, and Nico Swart with material for this article.

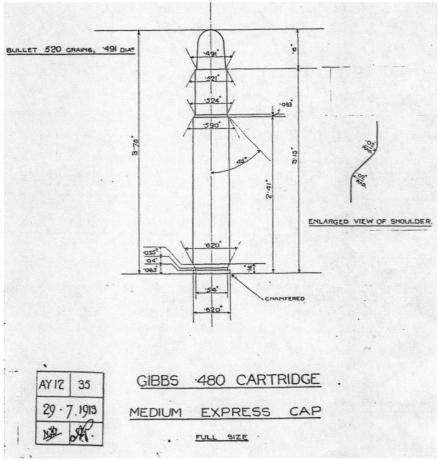

Another Kynoch drawing of the .480 Gibbs. This time dated July 29, 1913, and designated AY12-35.

.480 GIBBS NITRO COMPARISON TABLE

CARTRIDGE	BULLET (GR.)	87.5% MAP (PSI)	CAPACITY (GR.)	VELOCITY (FPS)
.480 Gibbs Nitro	520	34,265	168.2	2,340
.505 Magnum Gibbs	525	34,265	178.4	2,300
.500 Jeffery/12.7x70 Schüler	535	41,879	154.2	2,450

Endnotes

1 Fleming, Bill. British Sporting Rifle Cartridges. Armory Publications, 1993. Oceanside, USA

2 Fleming, Bill. British Sporting Rifle Cartridges. Armory Publications, 1993. Oceanside, USA

3 Ibid

4 Cogswell & Harrison catalog, 1924. Middlesex, UK

5 Barnes, Frank. Cartridges of the World 11th Ed. Gun Digest Books, 2006. Iola, USA

6 Hoyem, George. The History & Development of Small Arms Ammunition Vol III. Armory Publications, 2005. Missoula, USA

7 Van der Walt, Pierre. African Medium Game Cartridges. Pathfinder, 2018. Randburg, RSA.

8 Howell, Ken. Designing and Forming Custom Cartridges. The ICA, 1995. Stevensville, USA.

9 Harding, CW. Eley Cartridges. Quiller Publishing, 2009. Shrewsbury, UK.

10 Van der Walt, Pierre. African Dangerous Game Cartridges. Pathfinder, 2011. Randburg, RSA.

Nighthawk Custom offers
beautifully crafted 1911 handguns
famed for reliability and accuracy.
This is the .30 Super Carry version.

The 1911 Situation

Latest developments in the greatest handgun.

> BOB CAMPBELL

The 1911 handgun has been in service for more than 110 years. Many developments have occurred in the pistol, most of them beneficial. The past couple of years have been especially interesting, as the 1911 has found its way into the modern world. The gun is famously adaptable, something of a Mr. Potato Head. Easily accessorized and aggrandized, it also falls victim to those with a bad case of *tinkitis*: fixing what isn't broken.

Kimber has taken 1911 innovation up a notch while maintaining its excellent handling. The Rapide II shown here features lightening cuts in the slide, forward cocking serrations, superbly executed checkering, and a good barrel-to-slide fit.

Optics-ready handguns are a futuristic wave beneficial to many shooters. Optics make for real speed, allowing the shooter to concentrate on a single aiming point—put the dot on the target and press the trigger.

That aside, the 1911 pistol may also be elevated to a work of art by a craftsman. However, most of the work done with the 1911 in the past few years has been aimed at improving it for modern shooters with optics, light rails, and even suppressor-ready barrels. There was a race to the bottom among makers, with manufacturers striving to offer the least expensive 1911. That isn't a model of pride in manufacture, but someone had to win this dubious contest. Then, there is an earnest competition to manufacture a pistol with good features, performance, and reliability at a fair price.

At present, the sweet spot for a service-grade pistol seems just south of $1,000. For barely a fraction more, you get something even better, and for less, well, you get less. Let's look at the 1911. While the model has excellent longevity, I am not certain we can say the years have always been kind to the design. Some of the downgrades and odd modifications have been scandalous.

A LONG WAY WITH THE 1911

I have written three books on the 1911, and the pistol has also played a significant role in most of my other firearms-related books. I armed a protagonist in the *Hunter and the Hunted* thriller with a Colt .38 Super and another with a 1911 .45 ACP. I began reading about the 1911 in elementary school. I learned of the Colt 1911's service in the hands of Corporal Alvin York, Balloon Buster Frank Luke, and Lawrence of Arabia, among many others. Texas Rangers Frank Hamer and 'Lone Wolf' Gonzaullas carried it. I even enjoyed fictional depictions of the 1911.

Mike Hammer carried his 1911 in a shoulder holster, although in *The Goliath Bone,* he went to a hip holster in his 'old age.' The Shadow, the Phantom and Mr. Monster carried a pair of .45s. During a tense time in my own life when dealing with neo-Nazis, I carried a pair of 1911s. I was a pioneer in writing about dealing with hate groups on the Internet and in person. I told my story in *Law and Order,* and my adversary was featured on the cover of *Rolling Stone.* There was some irony in arresting a nazi while carrying a vintage 1911. While furthering my education and raising two boys and a red-headed-lightning-bolt-from-heaven in the form of my little girl, I sometimes was in a financial crunch.

A GI-Type 1911A1 from Auto Ordnance. It is a great shooting gun by GI standards.

No, it was financial strangulation!

But I always had at least one good example of the 1911 on hand. Books by C. B. Colby initially stirred my interest; these were clearly written and interesting children's books about guns. I hope you enjoy my work as much as I enjoyed his, and if you are not familiar with the 1911, Gun Digest's books are a great start.

I graduated to Cooper and Skelton soon enough after Colby. My first 1911 was a satin nickel Combat

This Steve Woods custom was top-of-the-line a generation ago, but today, it is a historical footnote.

Commander that served well. I did not become attached to a specific pistol, but as improvements came, I traded into superior handguns, beginning with the Series 80 Colt.

DON'T GO CHEAP

There have always been more cheap guns than good guns. The 1911 was designed to be a service-grade pistol. The Black Army and later Parkerized guns were not as nicely finished, and while some 1911s may rattle when shaken, the barrel locking lugs and barrel bushing were tight enough for good accuracy. A 5-inch group at 25 yards was the passing grade with 230-grain hardball ammunition. Most GI guns were more accurate than this.

The 1911's good attributes include a grip that fits most hands well and a low bore axis that limits muzzle flip, straight-to-the-rear trigger compression, and a combination of a slide lock safety and grip safety. The balance is ideal and makes the 1911 a superb combat pistol. The 1911 demands some care in manufacture. A requisite 1/32nd-inch gap between the two halves of the feed ramp ensures feed reliability. The slide should ride off the frame, and the rail and railways should properly fit.

Springfield Armory Releases
Blacked-Out
Emissary Model

The new Emissary Black series continues Springfield Armory's foray into ultra-futuristic-looking 1911s. The models—4.25- and 5-inch bull barrels in .45 ACP and 9mm—sport all the features shooters appreciate about the original Emissary line.

The bull barrels used in the Emissary Black models are fully supported and match-grade from the factory.

Building on the Emissary's success and appealing to those who appreciate a contemporary all-blacked-out aesthetic, Springfield's new Emissary Black screams "covert" and just made many 1911 shooters' heads explode with delight.

Available in four variants, including a 4.25- and 5-inch model in .45 Auto and 9mm, the Emissary Black 1911 from Springfield Armory is a hot-looking single-stack. Features include bull barrels, accessory rail, Cerakote blacked-out finish, and Tri-Top cut slide with light-diffusing 40 lpi flat-top serrations. The frames and slides are forged and built to last forever, even under +P pressures.

Bridging the gap between duty and custom handguns, the Emissary delivers a capable 1911 pistol with defense-minded features for serious use. With the addition of these all-black variants—and with the 4.25-inch model now featuring a full-length dustcover with a strip of Picatinny rail—there are even more options for the defense-minded user with a desire for custom-style features.

As with the original two-tone models, these new pistols are constructed with a forged steel frame and slide for strength and durability. Sporting a black Cerakote finish, the pistols feature a distinctive squared triggerguard that offers additional room for ease of operation with a gloved hand.

The slide's "Tri-Top" cut gives the Emissary custom styling, while a flattened topstrap is finished with 40 line-per-inch (lpi) serrations to diffuse light and reduce glare. The Emissary's tritium and luminescent front sight pairs with a Tactical Rack U-Dot rear sight for easy target acquisition in all lighting conditions.

Inside the slide, a bushingless stainless steel bull barrel with a black nitride finish delivers maximum accuracy while reducing felt recoil and muzzle flip. In addition, the skeletonized hammer delivers ultra-fast lock times and combines with a solid-body, flat-faced trigger for top-end performance.

The frame's frontstrap and mainspring housing are wrapped in a grenade-pattern texture for firm engagement in adverse conditions, which are matched with slim-line grip panels by VZ Grips machined from G10. Each pistol comes with two top-quality magazines with base pads. MSRP for each of the four new variants is $1,378.

"These four variants add a unique new look to the popular Emissary line of 1911 pistols," said Steve Kramer, Vice President of Marketing for Springfield Armory. "With this all-black finish, shooters now have four new appealing options for a defensive handgun with an additional measure of refinement."

The grip safety should be set to release the trigger about halfway into the grip safety's travel. Cheapened 1911s began appearing in the Basque region of Spain in the 1920s. Some were barely serviceable; many had soft steel. Some 1911s made cheap may be OK for recreation, but they are not good spear carriers for the 1911 community. However, not all GI-type guns are cheap guns. A GI .45 is recognizable by the original small sights, a small thumb safety, a grip safety, and no modern improvements. Where are GI guns today? I recently fired and examined the Auto Ordnance base gun, a proper modern rendition of the 1911A1. I found it reliable, well-fitted, finished, and a worthy modern example of the GI gun. While the sights are small, the pistol is more accurate than most original military 1911A1 handguns. If you want an original type 1911, they are far from dead, but most are cheap guns. The Auto Ordnance is a fitting tribute to the original as a well-made and reliable handgun. There isn't much to go wrong, and they serve a purpose.

I fire the 1911 better than any other handgun. By better, I mean more accurately, faster to a center-punched first shot hit, and with a faster run on a combat course. I understand the concept of differential achievement and realize that some shooters may fire a dissimilar handgun better. I get it. But I also think perhaps they simply have not fired the 1911 enough! You can get into a mental pretzel comparing handguns and the different voices.

Despite my allegiance to the 1911, my advice is, if you are betting your life on the gun, don't get a cheap 1911; choose a Glock or SIG. They are reliable. A cheap 1911 handgun with a terrible trigger and junk parts will ruin your opinion of the 1911. If you can afford a good 1911, it will be a joy forever and a good companion. Understand the maintenance requirements. That said, there have been several genuine innovations in the past few years. Let's look at some of these.

SPRINGFIELD EMISSARY

The Emissary from Springfield Armory is about as far from an original 1911 as it gets and yet still deserving to be called a

Springfield's Emissary 1911 is a far cry from the pistols that went over the top in World War I. Its frame is narrower, and it sports a squared triggerguard to assist with a solid support hand grip.

1911. The pistol was created with a slightly narrower grip frame. It measures 1.09 inches in width at the grips compared to the Springfield Mil-Spec at 1.12 inches. The Mil-Spec doesn't stretch my average-size hands; just the same, the Emissary's role in concealed carry is enhanced. The slide is a well-polished bright blue, and the frame is stainless. The slide is the more distinctive feature to the eyes.

Springfield created the Tri-Cut slide with two angled flats and a flat top. The forward-cocking serrations are shallow and slip in and out of leather holsters without taking a bite. The leverage gained by placing the cocking serrations atop the slide is noticeable in handling the pistol. The squared triggerguard allows for hooking a forefinger on it in a style that seems to be coming back into vogue. This squared-off triggerguard affects the fit in some holsters. The front sight is a reversed ramp, dovetailed in place, and features a fluorescent yellow border surrounding a tritium insert. The rear sight is a wedge type, allowing the slide to be racked if jammed against a boot heel or heavy belt. This seems to be a requirement for modern 1911s intended for defense use. The rear sight features a white-outline U-notch. This setup is among the finest on the planet for fast re-active combat shooting. The Emissary is a 1911, but it has a different appearance.

Time will tell on the Emissary, but after range time with two examples, I find the piece reliable, accurate, and a well-defined improvement over many 1911 handguns. The Emissary seems designed for personal defense over competition and range work. It is a great-looking and excellent shooting pistol.

SIG 1911S

SIG makes excellent 1911 handguns and uses a distinctive slide cut resembling the SIG P-Series with the original Granite Series 1911. To remain competitive, SIG introduced the Classic, a 1911 with standard contours.

KIMBER OFFERINGS

Addressing the newest advances in optical sights is a move afoot in the 1911 community. At present, these handguns are few and far between. Among the most interesting is the Kimber KHX. Like all Kimber Custom Shop pistols, the KHX is a distinctive firearm. I have extensive experience with a steel gray and a black finish example. Reliability is evident, and Kimber's crisp trigger action is also there.

When I tested a red-dot sight (RDS)-equipped 1911, I sent an RSVP and was pleasantly surprised. The setup is capable and offers a good combination of speed and accuracy. Some folks have Ferrari

Optics-ready 1911 handguns, such as this Springfield Armory, have been a trend for some time.

hands and work practically any handgun fast, very fast. Any of my students can grasp the basics, but a few become virtuosos. An optics-equipped 1911 provides both-eyes-open speed shooting and increased accuracy for those who practice. I have not changed over to daily carry (yet), as my handful of 1911 handguns are long-serving and do not need replacement. Just the same, a young person starting out may well wish to examine the KHX. Or anyone willing to be open-minded and train with the red-dot sight. The KHX is an affordable means of going red-dot capable.

COLT OPTIONS

The Colt Competition has existed for many years, which isn't new. I went into mental pretzels considering which 1911 handguns to include in this roundup, and the Colt got an 'OK' because, in several meaningful ways, it is a new pistol.

Colt has experience with 1911 handguns, and the pistol illustrated clearly exhibits modern features that make it a good shooter. The original Colt Competition Model was good, while the new pistol differs in some details. The front sight of the original issue featured blue fiber optics. While it was fashionably matched

to the pistol's trademark blue grips, blue isn't a high-visibility color. We now have a red fiber-optic front sight.

More significantly, the lockwork is now Series 70. There is no firing pin block. This makes for a superior trigger action from the factory. Safety is retained with a heavy-duty firing pin spring. If you don't drop the 1911 directly on the muzzle from six feet, all are drop-safe! Even so, we like to have a margin of safety. It isn't impossible to obtain a good trigger action in a Series 80 gun, but if you tune to the Nth degree or use a factory gun, get

a Series 70. That said, I no longer touch a trigger action in a 1911. Too many good trigger components were originally set for a superb trigger pull to take a chance and file on a trigger and sear engagement. This is especially true in handguns of mediocre quality with poor-quality internal components. I have fired two exceptional groups with .45 ACP pistols, about 33 years apart. The best group fired (with Speer 230-grain Gold Dot ammunition) was with the Colt illustrated. The Colt Competition pistol is the single most accurate 1911 I have owned. All

Savage's new 1911 has turned in credible accuracy.

Colt Compeition 1911 handguns may be similar; I may have a Wednesday gun. I am no stranger to high-end 1911s, and I had just as soon have this Colt. Colt got it right, and modern production looks like they are continuing to get it right. In the past few years, the makers have been listening to the buying public, and the Colt Competition has made an exclamation point for this.

Having been too close for comfort with felons intent on doing harm, I regard reliability as the primary requirement of a good-quality handgun. While a break-in period may be allowable, most modern 1911 handguns are manufactured to tight tolerance and don't need it. I have seen progression without progress across the board in many consumer goods, and it takes a lot to impress me favorably.

A SAVAGE 1911?

Savage isn't known for handguns, but it makes some of my favorite rifles, including the radical straight-pull Impulse rifle. The Savage 1911 isn't breaking down any doors, but it is a credible rendition of the 1911 with standard features.

The pistol is offered with a slick dust

The new Savage 1911 is going through its paces.

cover or a rail mount in black-coated and stainless versions. It features the newly designed Novak rear sight, which is compact but adjustable for elevation. A tritium bar graces the rear sight to complement a single front dot set into the Novak sight. Many professionals regard the Bar Dot setup as superior. There is little you cannot get anywhere else, but there is some novelty in owning a Savage 1911.

The pistol is a full-size Government Model with a 5-inch barrel. There is no full-length guide rod and no checkered frontstrap. The tritium sight component is by Night Fision, and Greider manufactures the trigger. The package seems well put together. The Savage 1911 is quite accurate. New guns sometimes have problems, and the Savage magazines rubbed the trigger bow (Wilson Combat and MecGar magazines did not). I did

Kimber's new KDS9C is among last year's most attractive and useful innovations. A commander-size 1911 with an aluminum frame, the KDS9c has been designed to accept a 15-round magazine. This light and easily concealed 9mm is a joy to fire.

A true innovation is the optics-ready Kimber.

We have had a great 1911 on hand for decades, so modern introductions had best be credible to bring in new buyers. The 1911 feeling isn't like any other incipient crush. No one who gets the bug can own just one. The Springfield Loaded is an excellent example of what a 1911 should be.

The 9mm 1911 has been around almost as long as the 1911. The original Commander was a 9mm. The Kimber KDS9c is a marvel of engineering. A commander-size 1911 with an aluminum frame, the KDS9c has been designed to accept a 15-round magazine. This light and easily concealed 9mm is a joy to fire. My example has proven reliable and more accurate than expected. It is among the more nicely made and attractive of the new 1911 handguns. Eliminating the grip safety from the design may be a plus or minus, but it is necessary given the compact, high-capacity grip frame. This is a credible 1911 that is well worth its price. It is easy to use and so accurate. I can confidently state that if you miss, it is the archer, not the arrow! This pistol is going places.

not like the grip safety adjustment, and the extractor needed re-tuning after a few hundred cartridges. On the other hand, a stainless steel example sailed through an evaluation. Perhaps my Savage was made on Friday when everyone wanted to go home. The Savage has promise, and quality control will make or break it. Folks are forgiving of new introductions with a great deal of bling.

AFFORDABLE 1911 QUALITY

I recently purchased a stainless steel Springfield Loaded. When I was much younger, you either got by with factory guns with small sights and controls or you spent a small fortune in a custom shop. Kimber set the world on its heels with its Custom and Custom II pistols. The 1911 can be its own advocate, and the Custom II convinced many buyers to enter the 1911 world.

Springfield launched the Loaded Model, now just called the Loaded, as a worthy competitor. It features Novak sights, an ambidextrous safety, a target-grade trigger, a smooth trigger action with rapid reset, nicely checkered grips, and forward-cocking serrations. This pistol is among the best put-together 1911 handguns and has been a best buy for

many years. I gave my oldest son a Loaded Target, and he has been very pleased. My younger son is an Army Major, and his stainless GI Springfield went to Novak's Gun Shop. These are exceptional handguns.

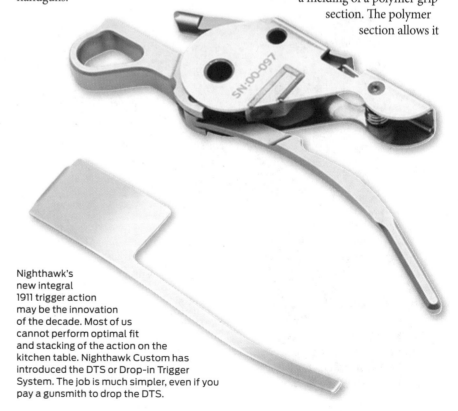

Nighthawk's new integral 1911 trigger action may be the innovation of the decade. Most of us cannot perform optimal fit and stacking of the action on the kitchen table. Nighthawk Custom has introduced the DTS or Drop-in Trigger System. The job is much simpler, even if you pay a gunsmith to drop the DTS.

The Springfield Prodigy is a blend of a traditional 1911 in terms of controls and a melding of a polymer grip section. The polymer section allows it to accept 17- and 20-round magazines. The Prodigy is optics-ready and very easy to shoot well. This is a full-size 1911 pistol with modest recoil and excellent accuracy potential. It is a thoroughly modern 1911 making its way into competition. The standard 1911 calibers are 9mm Luger and .45 ACP. The 9mm offers less recoil and less expense, even in these uncertain times. After all, you will spend more money over time than the original purchase price of the handgun for ammunition. The .45 ACP offers a combination of excellent wound potential and a self-loading handgun. The .38 Super is very much a gun crank's gun, with few of these in active service. The 10mm is enjoying one of its time-to-time comebacks.

There are .22-caliber pistols that look much like a 1911 and handle similarly. They are a great deal of fun and useful for training, but they aren't really 1911s, as they feature a fixed barrel. An unusual introduction is the Federal Cartridge .30 Super Carry. This is a hot little round with energy in the low-end 9mm spectrum. Far superior to the .380 ACP, the .30 Super Carry is an interesting development. Ballistics-wise, it's similar to the old 7.65mm French loading. I don't see dropping caliber for a few rounds in capacity, but the .30 Super isn't a weak sister.

Nighthawk Custom makes some of the nicest 1911 handguns on the planet. Nighthawk is a well-known name because of its accuracy, reliability, pride of ownership, and even heirloom investments. It has a 12+1-capacity .30 Super Carry pistol available, and it is a 1911. I am sure it has merit as a thing of value. Beyond question, some will be well pleased with a pistol of this quality chambered for a cartridge with minimal recoil.

1911 EXTRAS

While the handguns are varied, 1911 accessories and parts are always interesting. Many folks like to build a 1911 from quality frame and slide makers. Some like to upgrade existing firearms. The 1911 is more complicated to build than the Glock or AR-15. One of our most respected makers just made things much simpler. There are differences in 1911 pistols, and it is sometimes difficult to fit a trigger. After three books on the 1911, working 1911s for 40 years, and writing a university-level curriculum for a gunsmith program, I would never attempt to do a 'trigger job' on an existing 1911.

Too many modern pistols use MIM parts. Once the coating is gone, wear is rapid. It is easy to ruin a trigger action and create a dangerous situation. Modern drop-in trigger components are far superior in every way. Optimal fit and stacking of the action isn't something for most of us to perform on the kitchen table. Nighthawk Custom has introduced the DTS or Drop-in Trigger System. The job is much simpler, even if you pay a gunsmith to install the DTS. This closed system is similar in many ways to the AR-15 cassette-type trigger.

The Springfield Prodigy is a high-capacity 9mm 1911 with a mounted optic that may be used in competition and carried for personal defense.

This barrel is an Ed Brown suppressor-ready. The superbly crafted barrel enhances accuracy, and many shooters desire to add a suppressor.

Brownell's offers plates for optics-ready 1911 handguns for the popular models.

A modern 1911 needs a good holster. This is the Galco Combat. Molding to the individual handgun is good, with excellent stitching. The draw angle allows for a sharp presentation.

Among the 1911's advantages is its straight-to-rear trigger press. This trigger was usually set at 6 to 8 pounds of compression on military pistols. Good work could be done in combat shooting with that trigger, although there is a vast difference between a smooth, tight, but heavy trigger and a rough, heavy one typically found on cheap pistols. Shooters want a smooth and lighter trigger action, especially for accuracy work. This is achievable, provided the gunsmith doing the work is skilled. Quality trigger actions can be expensive, considering the time involved in fitting parts by hand. Even purchasing a trigger set from a maker doesn't guarantee that fitting isn't needed, and some parts require more fitting than others.

The Nighthawk DTS is compact, well-made, and easy to install. Mark Dye, the Director of the Gunsmithing Program at Montgomery Community College, invented it. A trained gunsmith will find the DTS a great option compared to ordering an ignition set and then installing it. While the home hobbyist is discouraged from working trigger actions, a gunsmith skilled with the 1911 and its function will find the DTS a workable system with minimum experience.

OPTICS, SUPPRESSORS, AND HOLSTERS

Another trend in 1911 handguns that is likely to become even more popular

The author wringing out a long-slide Rock Island Armory 1911 .45. The author finds the 6-inch-barrel 1911, commonly referred to as a 'long slide,' to be a good-shooting 1911. With a longer sight radius and muzzle bias, muzzle flip is limited, and the overall feel is excellent.

is the availability of optics-ready 1911 slides on factory handguns. Wilson Combat offers an optics-ready version of its Close Quarters Battle pistol. It doesn't get any better than that. Kimber offers the KHX, and even economy makers offer an optics-ready 1911 in 'get your feet wet with the 1911' grades. Springfield's DS Prodigy is a high-capacity optics-ready handgun.

Brownells is a good source for optics plates for modern 1911 handguns. The optics-ready 1911 is an option that many of us should try—it may be the fastest handgun in the world on a series of targets, as proven in competition.

Another trend that isn't going away is the suppressor-ready handgun. 1911s are not going to be left out of this game. Ed Brown has offered excellent 1911 parts for decades. Among the most modern of these is a threaded barrel for the 1911. The superbly crafted barrel makes for an accuracy-enhancing upgrade, and adding a suppressor is desirable for many shooters. Brownells.com offers these parts.

Just when you think 1911 holsters were highly evolved, Ryan Grizzle has updated the inside the waistband (IWB) holster to new heights. The Southern Draw Reinforced illustrated has moved the belt loops about on the body of the holster to cinch the rig in tight against the body, offering superior concealed carry. It is constructed of first-class leather in vintage brown. Galco has met the challenge of optics-ready handguns in factory holsters. The redesign must shift the reinforcement to accommodate the optics cut. As there are increasingly

Ryan Grizzle's antique leather finished holster is a work of art that will last for many years.

more 1911 handguns with a frame rail to accommodate combat light, holsters must be redesigned. The Galco Concealable is a top-quality holster accommodating optics-ready and rail guns. The draw is sharp, and the balance of speed and retention is outstanding. Quality continues.

SUMMARY

Optics-ready, suppressor-ready, and continuing quality have been watchwords in recent years. Accessories and holsters are keeping pace with modern developments. The newest introductions are interesting and exciting as the 1911 enters its eleventh decade. **GD**

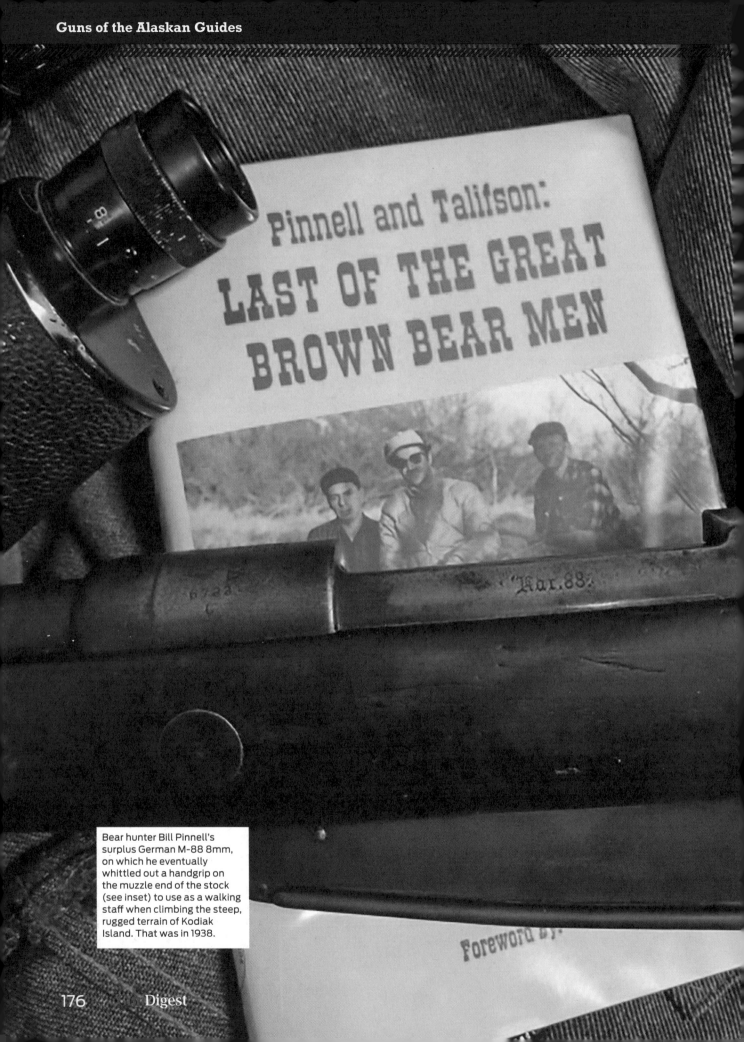

Pinnell and Talifson:
LAST OF THE GREAT
BROWN BEAR MEN

Bear hunter Bill Pinnell's surplus German M-88 8mm, on which he eventually whittled out a handgrip on the muzzle end of the stock (see inset) to use as a walking staff when climbing the steep, rugged terrain of Kodiak Island. That was in 1938.

Guns of the Alaskan Guides: When failure is not an option

"Alle Kunst ist umsunt, wen nein Engel auf das Zündloch brunzt."

(All of your skills are of no avail if an angel pisses in the flash hole.)

❯PHIL SHOEMAKER

Two centuries before the discovery of Alaska, shooters in Germany were well aware of the vagaries confronting hunters and their choices of weaponry. Today, even with modern rifles and ammunition, hunters in Alaska's vast, rugged, and remote wilderness remain vulnerable to unanticipated problems of demons befouling their flash holes.

Bush (remote) Alaskans are intimately familiar with the KISS (keep it simple, stupid) adage. When mechanical problems occur, the more complex items are typically afflicted. As a hunting guide, I find that triggers and riflescopes are most often the culprits today.

Hunter Bob Gibbs and guide Taj Shoemaker with an Alaskan brown bear that fell to a Turnbull .475.

A Turnbull 1886 .475 and a client's custom sporting Mauser.

Half a century ago, it was unusual to hear of hunters having problems with triggers, as a high percentage of bolt-action rifles were either military surplus or modern manifestations with robust, simple firing mechanisms. In our ongoing quest for accuracy, triggers have evolved toward ultra-crisp, lightweight, complex target-shooting ones that are more fragile.

Modern riflescopes have evolved into powerful optics marvels, but most are massively oversized and overweight for a hunting rifle. Their weight and mechanical complexities render them vastly more expensive and prone to the shooter's misinterpretation or failure with hard-recoiling calibers.

Most early Alaskan hunters chose ubiquitous lever-action rifles from Winchester or Marlin or the brutally rugged bolt-action designs derived from military guns. Both designs proved boringly effective in the territory's perpetually damp, saltwater-infused coastal areas or its remote and often frigid interior.

Allen Hasselborg, "The Bear Man of Admiralty Island," was an early fan of Winchester lever-actions. Over the years, he carried the 1886 .45-70 and the M-95 .405 for guiding hunters and photographers from his homestead at Mole Harbor in the dense rainforest of Southeast Alaska. When Winchester updated the M1886 and brought out the Model 71 in .348 Winchester, it became another popular option from the rainforested areas in Southeast Alaska on through Kodiak Island.

Lever-actions remain excellent choices today. I have carried my 1886 Winchester .45-70 loaded with Buffalo Bore hardcast 430-gr. bullets many miles in the big bear country of the Alaskan Peninsula, and my son Taj often carries his Turnbull .475 while guiding bear hunters.

Lever-action rifles dominated the hunting scene until the end of WWI, and returning GIs, now familiar with the rugged reliability of modern bolt-actions, realized their value.

In 1938, two down-on-their-luck roustabouts, Bill Pinnell and Morris Talifson, left Montana and arrived on Kodiak Island, hoping to improve their lot by gold mining on the island's Southwest coast. Pinnell arrived with a surplus German M-88 8mm and eventually whittled out a handgrip on the muzzle end of the stock to use as a walking staff when climbing the steep, rugged terrain of the island. Talifson chose a sporterized Enfield .30-'06. It wasn't until 10 years later that they began guiding Kodiak bear hunters, and the soon-to-be-famous duo purchased new Winchester M70 .375 H&H rifles for guiding brown bear hunters on Kodiak. A few years later, they purchased scope-sighted .300 H&H rifles to guide sheep hunters in the Brooks Range.

The Winchester M70 .375 H&H was the *sine qua non* of Alaskan guide rifles for the next half-century. Alaska's first Master Guide, the legendary Hal Waugh, was somewhat of a rifle crank, as they were called in those days. He had his Model 70 rechambered to the .375 Weatherby and christened it "Big Nan." After he passed, the rifle rested for years at the foot of a massive Kodiak Brown bear mounted in the museum lobby at the University of Alaska in Fairbanks.

My five decades-long quest for a singular perfect Alaskan rifle began with the .30-'06 I owned when I first moved to Alaska and began guiding hunters. It was an inexpensive Sears & Roebuck J.C. Higgins brand with a cheap wooden stock and excellent FN Mauser action.

During my first three decades of guiding for sheep, moose, caribou and brown bears, the rifle went through several metamorphoses. I quickly discovered that its cheap American walnut stock had a propensity to warp when it got wet, so I replaced it with a synthetic one and wrote about it (*Rifle* magazine, 1984, Issue 94).

Over the passing years, the rifle became sort of a guide's version of a Barbie doll. It wore three different barrels—two .30-'06 and a .35 Whelen—six stocks, four triggers, three different sets of bottom metal and an untold number of scopes and mounts. Finally, for my 60th birthday, my good friend Lon Paul and Arizona barrel maker Danny Peterson

offered to build me a custom rifle using my "original" rifle. After agonizing over caliber choice, I realized what two generations of previous Alaskan hunters had already discovered: The .30-'06 remains the single most useful and practical cartridge for Alaskan hunters.

Although I liked the smooth, reliable dependability of the carbon steel Mauser M98 action, I also admired the attributes of stainless steel barrels. Danny outdid himself using one of his stainless steel blanks and built one with an integral quarter rib, sling attachment, and front sight base. Lon had it black chrome-plated to match the blued finish on the rest of the rifle. Jerry Fisher provided one of his

sleek, rounded bottom metal units that rendered the rifle a pleasure to carry in the hand all day. Lon then sorted through his collection of fine wood and chose a dense, stable, and exceptionally righteous blank of Circassian walnut.

Since I primarily hunt large game, I had requested the barrel be built with a 1-in-8 twist to stabilize the 200- and 220-grain bullets I prefer to use in Alaska. It still shoots exceptionally well with Barnes TSX and Hornady GMX bullets as light as 150 grains. I have since used my .30-'06 on virtually every species of Alaskan game, including Dall rams at over 500 yards and charging brown bears at less than 5 yards. I have preached

Working Alaskan guide rifles, left to right: G-Series stainless M70 .375 H&H, pre-64 M70 9.3x62, .375 Ruger, Ruger MkII .375 H&H built by Bill Atkinson.

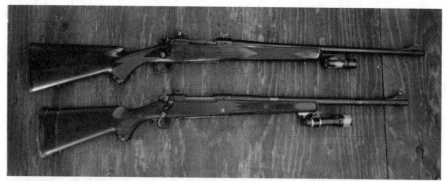

Guide rifles with lights mounted for things that go bump in the night.

Guide Tia Shoemaker's .416
Remington made by D'Arcy Echols.

for decades that anyone who claims the .30-'06 is ineffective has never used one or is unwittingly commenting on their marksmanship.

Although the .30-'06 and heavy Nosler Partition bullets had served me well as an incorrigible rifle fanatic with a few seriously close calls with wounded brown bears, I wondered if a larger caliber might offer a slightly better insurance policy with a lower deductible. So, I purchased a Mark X Mauser barreled action in .458 Win. and bedded it in a Brown Precision fiberglass stock. Like the guns I carried in Vietnam, I built the rifle purely for performance, without any aspirations or affectations of beauty. It quickly earned the moniker of "Old Ugly."

I submitted another feature for *Rifle* magazine about building the rifle (1985, Issue 101), and nearly two decades later, the editor asked for an update for the July 2003 issue. After forty years of hard use in Alaska and one trip to Africa, Old Ugly remains my serious, go-to rifle when things absolutely need to die. In the 45 years I have been guiding in Alaska, I have killed big bears with numerous calibers, from the 9mm handgun to the massive .505 Gibbs, and the more experience I gathered with other large bores, the more I came to appreciate the benefits and performance of the standard .458 Win. Like the .45 ACP in handguns, it's not the largest, nor most powerful, but has a long and distinguished history of getting the job done.

The balance of a rifle is also a critical factor affecting both performance and speed of handling. I modified Old Ugly's weight and balance with judicious placement of steel bedding compound mixed with iron filings and lead shot. The preponderance of weight is centered between my hands. Mounted with a 2½-power Leupold scope and a short overall length of 41 inches, it weighs just over nine pounds loaded. Its short

13-inch LOP and 21-inch barrel allow me to get on target quickly, even wearing heavy clothes in the thickest pucker brush.

The abbreviated little rifle pivots quickly around its center of gravity, much as a figure skater spins faster when they pull in their arms. It is, in effect, more of a CQB (close-quarter battle) carbine, like our military M4, rather than a full-length battle rifle. While full-sized battle rifles have many theoretical advantages, speed of operations in confined spaces is not one of them. A right-handed hunter wrinkling a wounded beast out of a dense thicket and stepping forward with their right foot the moment they are charged from the same side does not need any extraneous length of pull. In thick brush, I can carry my little .458 muzzle down, high across my chest like a SWAT entry team, and get it into action faster than any other rifle I own.

I was somewhat surprised to see that Hal Waugh's favorite bear rifle, "Big Nan," has the same short length of pull as Old Ugly, even though Hal was much taller. However, we spent years jousting with the prehistoric-sized bears in the same terrain.

Professionals serious about using their rifles—target shooters, dangerous game hunters, or military Spec-Op types—tend to look at their equipment more with a function/goal-oriented pragmatic eye than amateurs, hobbyists, or enthusiasts. Real-world lessons have a nasty habit of contradicting established practices of gun manufacturers, advertising agents and the dogma espoused by dilettantes long on theory but short on experience.

During the late 1990s, I did a lot of writing for shooting publications, and the European 9.3x62 was the popular "newly discovered" caliber by American gun writers. Having previously carried the .35 Whelen while guiding sheep and bear hunters and been given a 9.5x62 (aka .375 Scovill) to experiment with and write about, I couldn't resist the temptation to try a 9.3x62. Finding a pre-64 Winchester M70 .30-'06 with a worn-out bore incentivized me to proceed.

I called a few industry contacts about having the rifle re-bored. Norm Johnson at High Plains Reboring and Barrels offered to install a new 22-inch stainless steel 9.3x62 barrel in exchange for the original Winchester barrel. A few months later, rifle builder D'Arcy Echols asked if

Other Alaskan guide gun mods include taping the barrel, which helps when using the rifle as a walking and wading staff.

The author, while guiding sheep and bear hunters with an FN .35 Whelen carbine.

One hundred-year-old lever-actions remain viable and popular in the Alaskan bush.

Popular guide rifles include a M70 .338, a pre-64 9.3x62, and two .375 H&H M70s.

I was interested in testing one of his new carbon-fiber stocks for a review and generously offered to fit the stock if I would also be interested in testing the durability of various metal treatments and coatings. So, the entire rifle ended up in D'Arcy's hands, and he had the various metal parts coated with different techniques. We figured comparing all the finishes on one rifle would give us an honest test.

Weighing a bit less than 7 pounds with a peep sight and an additional 13 oz. with a 1.5x5 Leupold scope, the rifle has turned out to be one of the most carried rifles in my rack. It rests by the door of our lodge due to its lightweight, rugged durability, and performance on game. It's the rifle I find myself picking up most often when heading out to the field. Having used the 9.3x62 to stop several bears wounded by clients, I have not noticed any detectable difference in performance between it and the .375 H&H.

Another rifle in my fleet of "perfect Alaskan rifles" is a 1917 Eddystone Enfield that I found in a local pawnshop. It was typical of the once common, ubiquitous "sporterized" WWII military rifles. It captured my attention due to its full-length, Mannlicher-style Fajen stock with the ostentatious 1960s-style rollover cheekpiece. However, the forearm to the end of the 22-inch barrel was slim and attractive, the rear of the receiver nicely reshaped and blued, the ungainly stepped bottom metal expertly cut and straightened, and the massive bolt stop spring seat removed and the spring reshaped. The rifle's price was a fraction of what the action work alone would currently cost. I thought someday it might make a nice .375 H&H.

Years later, I was telling my gunmaking friend Lon Paul about the rifle, and he suggested sending it to him for a professional opinion. He then suggested sending it to Danny Peterson in Prescott, Arizona, to be bored to 9.3x62 as it would be much cheaper than a new barrel and modifying the action to work with the long .375 H&H. After Danny had returned the barreled action to Lon, I gave him full rein on the project. Within

The author carried a Zoli O/U .450/400 for several years.

Master Guide Hal Waugh's "Big Nan" 1947 Win. M70 rechambered to .375 Weatherby and "Old Ugly," the author's Mauser .458.

a few months, the "Pig" was born! The rifle was so christened after the Bob Akin quote that, while one may not be able to make a racehorse out of a pig, with some effort, they could make a very fast pig.

The Pig, indeed, turned out to be fast. Lon is a master at crafting superbly balanced rifles for hunters, guides and African professionals who often need to shoot quickly from the offhand position. He also straightened the awkwardly bent military bolt handle and added a bolt knob reminiscent of the original Mauser

sporting rifles. We decided to retain the original cock-on-closing feature for its proven reliability and speed. It seems awkward for those used to slowly operating modern bolt-actions. Still, one never notices when quickly operating the bolt from the shoulder with the alacrity required when hunting dangerous game.

With the peep sight, the rifle weighs an even 8 pounds, and with a vintage Leupold 3X scope and QD mounts, it weighs 13 ounces more. On moose hunts and during salmon fishing trips when bears are daily companions, I carry it with a Williams peep sight, and during spring brown bear season, where there is a likely chance I might have to take long-range shots, I mount the scope on it.

While those four rifles are the primary distillate of my decades-long quest for the perfect all-around Alaskan guide rifle, numerous other qualifying guns reside in my rack. They are typically used throughout the season by myself, my guides and packers, or loaned to hunters. At the beginning of each season, I usually play the game of musical chairs with each rifle

to speculate which one might best serve my purpose that season.

I was immediately intrigued when rifle manufacturer Ruger and ammunition giant Hornady announced their corroboration on a new .375 cartridge. Creating a cartridge with the same length and industry-standard .535 rim diameter as popular magnum rounds like the 7mm Remington and .300 and .338 Winchester and exchanging the useless belt for additional powder space was simple genius. I expected industry gun writers to fawn

over the new concept but was surprised at the general malaise. Most writers simply mentioned how it was nothing more than the old Newton case or used it as a means to expound on the greatness of the original H&H magnum.

One writer who did understand the concept was my late friend Chub Eastman. He was an exceptionally experienced and knowledgeable gun writer. Chub immediately had Pac Nor install a .375 Ruger barrel on an old FN Mauser action and tested it while I ordered one of the first Ruger Alaskan carbines. Ruger promptly sent me two rifles, the stainless steel 20-inch barrel Alaskan version with a Hogue stock and the African variant with blued steel 22-inch barrel and a wooden stock. That fall, I loaned the Alaskan Ruger to my second bear hunter of the year, Floridian Wayne Simmons, who used it to take a massive, old record book boar.

Later that year, Chub offered to sell me his rifle at the annual SHOT Show, and Texas rifle builder Charley Sisk offered to use it to build me a tough, no-nonsense guide rifle. Charlie reworked the action for reliability and re-barreled it with a stainless steel Shilen. Bedded in an early Borden Rimrock stock, the rifle is one of the lightest, shortest and best-balanced rifles in my rack. It has also proven to be superbly accurate and a camp favorite.

"Pointer" is another rifle popular with all my guides. It was so christened because everything they point it at seems to die. Pointer began life as a standard .338 Ruger MkII that the late Bill Atkinson, the famed gunsmith and barrel maker from Prescott, Arizona, re-barreled and modified to work with the .375 H&H. Bill Ruger considered Atkinson his personal gunsmith. I do not doubt that Pointer was instrumental in developing the current .375 Ruger cartridge and Ruger Alaskan models. It is a rugged and powerful rifle perfect for Alaskan hunters. The only possible drawback is that the rugged Ruger bolt stop must be thinned to fit the longer H&H round. However, due to the superb design of the Ruger spring-buffered bolt stop, the rifle continues to take the abuse for which Rugers are famous. The MkII action seems to come to life after being slicked up with

A few of the author's favorites: .458, 9.3x62, and .30-'06.

Wayne Simmons with the first bear taken with the then-new .375 Ruger.

The .375 H&H and the .375 Ruger are two of the best Alaskan guide rounds.

use or properly honed. When operating the bolt with speed, the bolt stop plunger spring not only buffers the bolt stop but also gives a noticeable amount of forward assistance by bumping the bolt forward to chamber another round.

When I received the rifle, the original wood stock was cracked, so I installed one of Bill Ruger's favorite Zytel "canoe paddle" stocks. Besides being well-balanced and tougher than a woodpecker's lips, it will house a Ruger peep sight under the grip panel. With a Leupold 1-4x scope in Ak Arms rings, Pointer weighs 8 lbs., 7oz. The exceptional balance and handling qualities inspired me to install another Zytel stock on my .416 Ruger Alaskan. The weights are the same.

Other rifles in my rack are a couple of stainless steel G-Series Winchester M70s in .338 Win. Both wear Borden stocks, 4x Leupold scopes and are superbly accurate. But since the introduction of the .375 Ruger, they have spent more time in the rack than in the field.

A few other camp rifles that get serious usage are my son Taj's Ruger Mk II .375. It wears a cut, chopped, sliced, diced, and taped Hogue stock and makes Old Ugly .458 look positively pretty by comparison. It also has a proven track record for outstanding performance.

At the opposite end of the aesthetic spectrum is my daughter Tia's .416 Remington, which legendary gun-maker D'Arcy Echols built for her. With a 22-inch barrel and 2.5x Leupold scope, it weighs 7½ pounds and performs as expected from one of the world's best rifle builders. Her favorite hunting load uses 300-grain Barnes TSX bullets. She not only carries it when guiding brown bear and moose hunters but has used it on game as varied as Dall sheep in the Brooks Range to Cape buffalo in Zimbabwe.

I have been a student and collector of serious-use rifles my entire life. Over the past 45 years, I've actively guided in Alaska and have enjoyed experimenting

Double-barreled rifles have seen some use in Alaska. Kodiak Guide Joe Want used an H&H Royal .500 Nitro for many years.

Shoemaker's Old Ugly, Taj's New Ugly, and Tia's .375 Ruger. Function is king in Alaska!

with calibers and designs, both old and new. I always wanted to give double rifles a fair chance and knew my friend and long-time Kodiak guide Joe Want loved his Best Grade, Holland & Holland Royal .500 Nitro, when trailing wounded brown bears. I purchased and carried a nice Zoli O&U .450/400 3" NE while guiding bear hunters for a few years. But I didn't find the rough, wide-open country I primarily hunt on the Alaskan peninsula conducive

to carrying a rifle with constantly loaded chambers.

I also particularly enjoy finding and using older rifles that Alaskan hunters and guides have used, as it gives me insights into the mechanics and their hunting techniques. If there is a singular fact that I can address about the rifles chosen by successful guides over the past century, it would be their rugged and reliable simplicity. **GD**

Rethinking the .22 Magnum

For rimfire chores, does it beat the .22 LR?

WILL BRANTLEY

I n each annual edition of this *Gun Digest*, you are regaled by tales of exotic places full of stories about trophy bull elk or dangerous African game. You read about rifles that, if they're not modern and sexy, are at least classic and classy. And then there are my assignments, which are here to keep you grounded.

With that in mind, let me tell you about a skunk I killed the other day on a muddy trail in Kentucky with a .22 Magnum. It wasn't the first skunk I've taken with the legendary rimfire cartridge. In fact, I killed a different skunk only the day before. And if history is any indicator, I'll shoot another one or two before the year is out—and I'll use the heralded .22 Magnum to handle all the heavy lifting.

This skunk was dispatched from 120 yards—guessed but not confirmed with a rangefinder—with the rifle rested across the handlebars of a Honda four-wheeler. Only a single bullet was required, and the results were swift and, as skunk killings go, mostly odor-free.

What brought me into the situation was that from late December through February each year, I run a line of about two dozen predator traps. My primary targets are coyotes, bobcats, raccoons, and foxes. To dispatch them in a trap and preserve their furs, I mostly use a .22 Long Rifle handgun loaded with standard-velocity 40-grain bullets.

But now and then, a striped polecat (that's Southern for skunk; I realize true polecats are living elsewhere) finds its way into one of my Bridger footholds. I trap partly for the fun of it but primar-

ily for predator control. I've learned that removing some predators in the late winter equates to more turkey poults and deer fawns in the spring and summer. As skunks are documented nest predators, they get no quarter from me on the trapline.

Not that I'd be brave enough to approach and release one. Being caught in a foothold trap seems to activate a hair trigger for the skunk's primary defense, which is quite noxious and something you'll learn all about if you get too close. That is one reason why, in addition to my .22 LR handgun, I never check a trapline without a scoped and highly accurate .22 WMR rifle close by with which I can kill skunks instantly and from well out of reach of their spray.

Another reason for the rifle? Not every shot you get at a predator while run-

ning a trapline happens because you've caught one. Every season, I get chance opportunities at critters, from coyotes and bobcats to armadillos. The .22 WMR is the perfect cartridge for incidental varmint work because it offers more effective range and power than the .22 LR without the ear-ringing report and fur-wrecking properties of a .22 centerfire.

My go-to rifle on the line is a Bergara Micro Rimfire Carbon with a threaded, 20-inch carbon-fiber barrel and match-grade chamber. Mine's fitted with a SilencerCo Sparrow suppressor, and I have it topped with a 30mm Hawke Vantage 3-9x42 IR scope. The illuminated reticle really shines, pun intended, for low-light shooting at slinky predators. The rifle weighs just 5 pounds, and with the scope and suppressor added, the finished weight can't be much more than 7 pounds. It's impervious to the weather and grime that guns are exposed to on a trapline, and it shoots lights out.

Yet, that rifle is far from the only .22 Magnum I own and shoot regularly. There's the worn Marlin bolt gun I still use for killing groundhogs at my folks' cabin, the new Ruger Precision Rimfire that has become a go-to squirrel sniper, and the scratched-and-battered Ruger Single Six revolver that's my companion for summer frog hunting.

Since my teenage years, the .22 WMR has been a favorite cartridge for hunting and varmint shooting. Given its utility in rifles and handguns, I think it's one of the best cartridges a serious outdoorsperson can own. Better factory ammunition, premium bullets, and outstanding new rifles and handguns have also given the .22 WMR a resurgence in popularity.

ORIGINS AND REPUTATION

The .22 Winchester Magnum Rimfire—.22 WMR or .22 Magnum for short—was introduced in 1959. It is an elongated version of the .22 Winchester Rimfire (WRF), introduced in 1890 and still factory-loaded by Winchester and CCI today. Though the .22 WRF offered ballistic advantages over the .22 LR loads of the day, it had little advantage over today's high-velocity Long Rifle ammunition and is basically obscure.

But the .22 Magnum is another matter.

The .22 WMR is an incredibly versatile hunting cartridge, and the author much prefers it over the standard .22 Long Rifle.

Though it uses bullets of the same diameter, WMR cases are longer in length and larger in diameter than .22 LR. From a rifle barrel, published ballistics show a 40-grain CCI Gamepoint .22 WMR leaves the muzzle at 1,875 feet per second, 615 fps faster than a 36-grain CCI Mini-Mag .22 LR. The magnum rimfire also carries almost twice the muzzle energy at 312 foot-pounds. For perspective, that's more energy than a 130-grain .38 Special +P fired from a handgun.

Though public opinion seems more favorable now, the .22 Magnum suffered a mixed reputation for decades, particularly among some gun writers. Field & Stream Rifles Editor David Petzal included it in his 10 Most Overrated Cartridges Ever Made roundup. He summarized the .22 WMR by saying:

"It's been around since 1959, and is by any account a commercially successful cartridge, but I'm damned if I can see why. On the one hand, it's more powerful than the .22 LR, but on the other, it gives you only 25 yards (or so) more effective range. It has neither the low cost of the .22 LR or its accuracy."

Now, to give credit where due, Petzal is one of history's great gun writers who knows more about rifles than I do. As a hunting editor of *Field & Stream* myself, I know him personally. He's a nice guy (despite the gruff persona) who happens to be wrong about the .22 Magnum.

Of course, if you compare the merits of the .22 WMR to the .22 LR, the cost is a natural consideration, and the magnum cartridge is indeed more expensive. CCI Maxi-Mags are about 25 cents per shot in 2024, compared to 8 cents for Mini-Mag .22 LR. Yet, compared to cheap centerfire

rifle ammunition, the .22 WMR remains economical to shoot. For perspective, .223 Remington American Eagle 55-grain FMJ is about 62 cents per round.

If your idea of a rimfire's role is primarily burning up ammunition by the brick at targets and maybe shooting a squirrel on occasion, then sure, the cost savings of the .22 LR is a big consideration. But the .22 Magnum is not a plinking or training round; it's a hunting cartridge.

The flatter trajectory from the added velocity is a decisive advantage. Sighted in at 50 yards, the .22 WMR hits a half-inch low at 75 yards and 8 inches low at 150 yards. The .22 LR, sighted in at the same distance, drops 1.8 inches at 75 yards and 20 inches at 150. For perspective, a squirrel's head is about 2 inches in diameter, and a coyote's vitals are about 6 inches in diameter. So, with the

.22 WMR, you can hold dead-on and clip a squirrel's noggin out to 75+ yards or dump a coyote at 150 yards without holding off fur. You simply cannot do the same with a .22 LR.

Besides that, the .22 WMR carries more energy at 100 yards than the .22 LR does at the muzzle—and that creates a dramatic difference in the terminal effect on critters and is the primary reason behind the .22 WMR's fanbase. Those

who regularly use this cartridge know it punches above its fighting weight.

My buddy Ryan usually keeps a Ruger American Rimfire in .22 WMR in his truck. It's not only his go-to squirrel gun but also his pick for coyotes, opossums, and any other critters he comes upon in a day of countryside turd-kicking. Ryan's also a part-time cattle farmer, which isn't always a pleasant business. Sick and injured cattle frequently have to be put

down, and he makes no bones about what works best to do the job humanely. "I've tried to put cows down with pistols, like 9mms and .380s, and it's not good," he says. "Those pistol bullets will not always penetrate a cow's skull. But the .22 Magnum between the eyes is a different story. It's one and done about every time."

I've shot hundreds of predators, both called and trapped, with the .22 LR, .17 HMR and .22 WMR. I've also hunted squirrels extensively with each of the cartridges. There is no question in my mind that the .22 Mag is the most decisive killer of the bunch. The .17 has the edge in velocity, but the .22 Mag's bullets weigh about twice as much. They penetrate deeper and do a better job of anchoring tough coyotes quickly—though they're not always as friendly on fur. I like the .17 HMR slightly better for squirrel hunting because, with the right bullet, it's less destructive on meat. But the .22 WMR works excellently if you take headshots.

If I had to choose just one all-purpose rimfire rifle for everything from small game hunting to 100-yard coyote calling, it would unquestionably be a .22 Magnum. Fortunately, I'm not in such dire straits, and I have great rifles chambered for all three cartridges.

The Ruger Precision Rimfire in .22 WMR has become one of the author's go-to squirrel guns.

ACCURACY

All that power is great, but it doesn't do a squirrel hunter any good if the guns don't shoot. For a time, the .22 WMR's reputation for inaccuracy may have been warranted. My dad has an old bolt-action Marlin with a tubular magazine, perhaps a 783, that I used when I was a kid for shooting groundhogs in the neighbor's pasture. It worked well enough, but good 50-yard groups for that gun were around an inch. I need a squirrel rifle to shoot better. (To be fair to the old Marlin, it wore a cheap 4x scope, and the bolt handle had been broken off and welded back on.)

I've shot several new .22 Mags from various manufacturers over the past decade, and I rarely find one now that doesn't shoot very well. Take my Ruger Precision Rimfire, for example. Topped with a Leupold VX Freedom 4-12x40, it will put five CCI Gamepoints into a tiny, ragged hole at 50 yards. That's not just headshooting accuracy for squirrel hunting; it's eyeball accuracy. My "skunk rifle," the Bergara BMR, doesn't shoot quite that well, but it nonetheless groups well under an inch at 50 yards with CCI Maxi-Mag hollowpoints.

Rifle manufacturing processes have improved (not just for rimfires but also for rifles). Factory triggers are much improved and often adjustable. As I understand from folks in the know, chamber tolerances have improved for the .22 WMR. That .22 Mag rifles aren't capable of outstanding accuracy is not true anymore. Many of them will shoot just as well as .22 LR guns.

Besides that, factory ammunition is far better. I was limited to a few 40-grain jacketed hollowpoint options when I was a teenager, hunting groundhogs. Today, manufacturers are loading .22 WMR with a variety of premium bullets. CCI offers the polymer-tipped 30-grain V-Max and VNT, the 40-grain Maxi-Mag Jacketed Hollowpoint, the 40-grain Gamepoint Jacketed Soft Point (my personal favorite), and the 46-grain Polymer-Coated Segmented Hollowpoint. Winchester has 10 .22 WMR options, including a 30-grain Varmint High-Velocity JHP, a 30-grain V-Max, and a pair of defensive offerings, including a 40-grain Silvertip and 40-grain Defender JHP. Hornady has a load with its signature 30-grain V-Max and a defensive option with the 45-grain FTX (Flex Tip).

The lighter-weight bullets tend to bump velocities up by 200 fps and provide a more explosive effect on smaller critters. For my use, I usually lean toward 40-grain bullets with more controlled expansion. They don't always "blow up" when they contact a squirrel, meaning better weight retention and deeper penetration on predators. They exit coyotes more often than not.

A FEW FAVORITE RIFLES

Plenty of excellent .22 Magnum rifles are on the market now, but I have firsthand experience with all these or guns very close to them. None are cheap, but they won't break your budget.

RUGER PRECISION RIMFIRE

I was skeptical of this "chassis rifle" when I first carried it into the squirrel woods, but I quickly came around. With a Quick-Fit precision adjustable stock, free-floating handguard, threaded target barrel and adjustable trigger, it's built for competitive shooters. Still, it is also right at home in the oaks and hickories. The rifle uses Ruger's dead-nuts-reliable rotary mag (like the 10/22), which is the best rimfire rifle magazine made if you ask me. Mine is the most accurate .22 WMR I've ever shot, too.

BERGARA BMR

The Bergara is the .22 Mag I reach for, if not daily, at least weekly during the fall

and winter. It's my truck gun, ATV gun, and out-the-back-window-of-the-house gun. As mentioned, it won't quite shoot with my Ruger Precision, but it is still more than capable of headshooting accuracy in the squirrel woods. With a traditionally styled stock and No. 6 carbon-fiber barrel, it's also ultra-lightweight and impervious to the weather.

My only critique of it is the magazine system. It feeds well enough, but the mag release lever is large and obnoxious, and the mags (both five- and 10-rounders are supplied) require some finagling to seat properly into the rifle.

SAVAGE A22 MAGNUM

Over the years, semi-automatic .22 Magnums have come and gone, but few of them have worked reliably. Savage figured it out with the A22 Magnum, which uses a delayed-blowback action to cycle the magnum cartridges reliably without splitting cases. The rifle works exceptionally well with CCI's complementary A22 Magnum ammunition, which uses a 35-grain version of my favorite Gamepoint bullet.

The A22 Magnums I've shot, and there have been several, wouldn't quite group with the Ruger or Bergara listed above, but they were ahead of my dad's old Marlin, and reliability was excellent. If I were

looking for a dedicated predator hunting rifle where report and over-penetration were concerns, this would be tops.

HENRY LEVER-ACTION .22 MAGNUM EXPRESS

Once upon a time, Winchester and Marlin ruled the lever-gun roost, but not anymore. Henry Repeating Arms has more top-shelf lever guns in its lineup than anyone else. The rifles are made in America with classic bluing and walnut furniture, and I've yet to shoot one that I didn't want to keep and hand down to my son one day.

I have two Henry Single-Shots and a Big Boy in my centerfire collection, but the Lever-Action .22 Magnum Express would be next on my wishlist. It has the lines of a classic lever gun with an 11-round tubular magazine but with a Picatinny optics rail pre-installed and a Monte Carlo buttstock with a raised comb. There's no sense in having a quality .22 Magnum rifle without a solid scope on top.

HANDGUNS

The .22 Magnum is a rifle cartridge that shines in handguns, too. It's outstanding for the trail and campsite. It also offers potential for defensive use, particularly with new ammunition like Speer Gold

Dot, optimized for performance in shorter handgun barrels. Expect a louder report than a .22 LR handgun but identical recoil (none) and far better terminal performance.

RUGER NEW MODEL SINGLE SIX

The Ruger New Model Single Six single-action revolver was originally meant to capitalize on the popularity of the Colt Single Action Army. Still, it's become a classic in its own right. It has interchangeable cylinders, one for shooting .22 Long Rifle (or .22 Shorts or Longs), and the other for .22 Magnum. My first handgun was a Single Six with a 5.5-inch barrel that my dad bought used, and it only came with the magnum cylinder. That's all I've ever needed. There's no telling how many critters have been befallen by that gun, and it still rides on my hip on many an excursion to this day.

SMITH & WESSON MODEL 48

I like single-action revolvers, but I *love* a classic double-action, and Smith & Wesson in particular. The K-frame Model 48 is available in S&W's Classic series. It's a steel beauty with wood grips and Patridge sights but with modern enhancements like a transfer bar safety. If I wanted a top-of-the-line .22 Magnum double-action as an all-purpose handgun

The Bergara BMR Carbon is lightweight, and shoots lights out. It could be the perfect truck gun.

for hunting, target shooting, and defense in a pinch, this would be it.

KEL-TEC PMR 30

I love revolvers but won't go full Fudd on you in the handgun section. A few other companies now offer high-capacity .22 WMR semi-autos, but the Kel-Tec PMR 30 was among the first that worked. My buddy Ryan (mentioned earlier) has one,

and he says that any problem that can't be solved with 30 rounds of .22 Magnum is a real problem indeed. The gun is a bit finicky if magazines are not loaded correctly, but when they are, it's a reliable little blaster that's easy to hit with, a ball to shoot, and not terribly expensive. ·

CONCLUSION

The .22 WMR is many things, but over-

rated ain't one of them. That it is capable of pinpoint accuracy worthy of precision small game hunting, has the punch to anchor coyotes, and works nearly as well in revolvers as it does in rifles makes it a cartridge worth keeping around, perhaps in a few different guns.

There's maybe no finer round for dispatching those striped polecats, either. **GD**

The .22 WMR is a fine revolver cartridge. The author has carried this worn Super Single Six for decades.

M1 Garand Restoration

Fulton Armory transforms a tired old warhorse into a thoroughbred fit for the winner's circle.

❯ JOSH WAYNER

A special, miserable heat exists in northern Ohio during those long, late summer days. It may be the humidity that sits over Lake Erie, a lesser Great Lake, or perhaps just the area's ecology. Low-hanging clouds blocked the sun but seemed to create a ceiling of moisture that made wearing my shooting coat just about the last thing I wanted to do. But here I was, at the 2023 Camp Perry National Matches, lamenting the weather just as I had for nearly twenty years. In my hands was a rifle that I intended to shoot a medal score with, an M1 Garand. Though this was not just any old M1, it was a rifle reborn from a junk pile into a work of art thanks to Fulton Armory's expert gunsmiths.

The M1, as the author bought it. Note that it is in less-than-ideal condition and has a 'lock bar' rear sight.

The metal finish displays the characteristic coloration of inferior zinc-based remedies.

RIGHT TYPE OF TRASH

My initial plan for this project was to do a scratch build on a 1903 Springfield to use at the National Matches. My goal was relatively simple: I wanted to do a restoration project and run an article to show that it could be done. However, those hopes were soon dashed. That's because, during my research, I only kept finding beautiful, complete 1903 rifles for the same relative price as buying all the parts and trying to cobble them together. I ended up with some fine examples, including a mint condition Mark 1 in unissued condition. The owner had thought it was trash because it "was wrapped in wax paper and covered in gunk, and the gunk was too thick to remove." Well, that was false, and I bought it for a song, only lamenting that it had been removed from its original wrapper. I stripped the hardened cosmoline, and underneath it was a brand-new gun from 1919.

I gave up on the quest to find a suitable 1903 after I wound up with enough pristine examples to make a museum green with envy. I then decided to look at the much more common rifle, the M1 Garand. As a reader of these prestigious pages, you may assume that all of us esteemed writers are also gunsmiths, ballistics experts, and generally the smartest people in the room. This is false. I know next to nothing about rebuilding an M1 Garand. Buying a good action and fitting a stock is too easy; a hobby blogger could

Note the poor wood and metal finish. The handguards on this rifle rattled severely.

do that. I needed to look into an expert solution that would result in a good final product, one to which you, dear reader, could send your own rifle. I immediately turned my attention to Fulton Armory, the last company in the country that is truly working on and restoring the M1 Garand.

I contacted Fulton Armory in the spring of 2023 and talked to Rich Hall, General Manager. The project was green-lit, and Fulton Armory wanted to work with me to produce this article. I was to find the worst possible M1 rifle I could get my mitts on, and FA would make it into the most accurate rifle on the line at Camp Perry. With the mission in hand, I looked for a truly defiled gun, one that no reasonable person would ever pay cash for.

Again, as it turns out, most of the rifles I found were at least in functional condition, just not great to look at. I perused gun shows but quickly found that most people there put up nice rifles at exorbitant prices but were more interested in selling beef jerky and Chinese-made Trijicon knockoffs. I hunted and hunted but came up empty-handed each time. I resorted to posting ads online, hoping to catch someone's attention who wanted to offload some truly bad stuff. I cast a wide net and was instantly rewarded with what I sought. A person replied to my ad with the caveat, "This is a parts gun; I wouldn't fire it if I were you." Later that day, I saw the gun in person, and the action was solid; the rest was pretty terrible. We made a deal, and I was proud to walk away with what I hoped would be the base for my Fulton Armory rebuild.

The rifle itself was in sorry condition. I scrubbed it up a bit for these pages so you wouldn't cringe at the thought of me paying American currency for it. The wood condition was regrettable. The barrel was shot out. I noted upon disassembly that most of the parts were heavily worn, likely from overzealous cleaning at the hands of recruits.

The rifle retained an original 'lock bar' rear sight, a feature most people remove as the sighting system was refined and made simpler. Some collectors add value for an 'original' lock bar sight; if you pay extra for that, you're a rube. Anyone can install a lock bar sight on an M1. There is no special code or serial number range to make it more correct than the standard rear sight. I've been a military rifle collector for more than twenty years, and I believe this lock bar rear sight is the actual one issued on this rifle or original to the receiver. The rest of the parts were a mixed bag, as is typical on all Garands.

Knowing this was probably the worst M1 rifle I could find that still could yield me a functional receiver, I went about the next steps with Fulton Armory to get

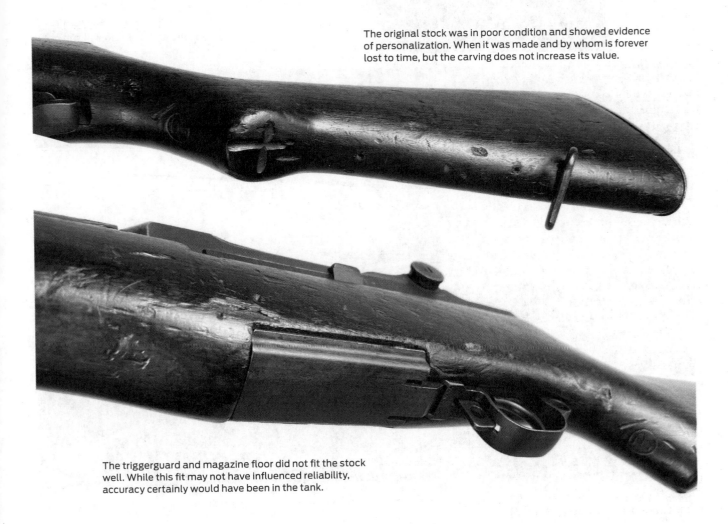

The original stock was in poor condition and showed evidence of personalization. When it was made and by whom is forever lost to time, but the carving does not increase its value.

The triggerguard and magazine floor did not fit the stock well. While this fit may not have influenced reliability, accuracy certainly would have been in the tank.

The rifle's original muzzle. Note the excessive wear and the 'poppet' gas plug. Fulton Armory installs a new gas plug because the original is designed to launch grenades.

this travesty back in shooting condition. Hall asked me to do a test fire with the rifle to showcase how much the accuracy improved, but upon detailed inspection, I deemed it unsafe. I probably could have fired it … once. Not that the receiver was in danger of splitting, but that the rest of the parts were in such poor condition that they may have caused damage to the action. I had no faith that the op rod or the spring were in serviceable condition, nor did I believe that the gas port was the correct diameter.

I wanted to avoid a situation where the stressed and over-gassed system would cause the op rod to blow off its rail and bend. While bent op rods are not as common as online experts would have you believe, in this case, I didn't want to destroy the chances of the salvageable parts having to be remade. The Garand is famously known as one of the best battle implements ever devised. However, it is a relatively delicate design that needs to operate in a fairly specific range of pressures; not all .30-'06 ammo will suffice.

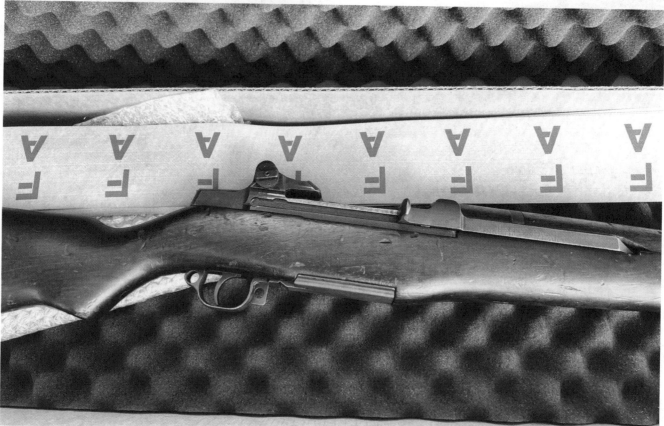

The concierge packaging the M1 rifle will ship in. Fulton Armory boxes are custom, padded, and come with their own tape. Everything you need to ship your rifle is included in the box.

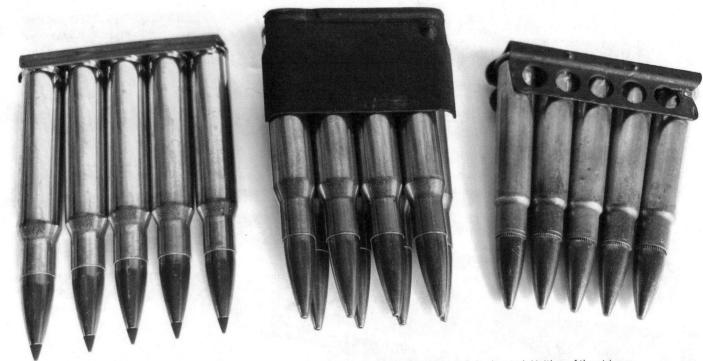

Stripper clips (M1903, left, and Enfield, right) are distinct from the en-bloc M1 Garand clip (center). Neither of the stripper clips here is fully inserted into their respective rifles, where the M1 clip is. It is ejected upon the last shot fired. Ping!

Rich Hall instructed me on the procedures surrounding the Fulton process. FA offers a concierge service for the guns wherein they send you an approved box that contains the necessary tape and instructions. It is a streamlined process; ultimately, you won't need to go through an FFL dealer to get your gun sent out and returned. The U.S. Postal Service will return it to you when Fulton finishes it. I advise contacting Fulton Armory directly and reviewing what you want to be done to your specific rifle. I let the company do as it wished with mine to showcase its efforts for the CMP sports and National Matches. There are other things Fulton can do with your M1 rifle; review the website or ask. As it is the world's premier gunsmithing enterprise for the M1 rifle, it's worth discussing your options. The concierge service was excellent and simple, and it was the best experience I have had for an out-of-state gunsmith service. With my rifle sent off, I began to source the other supplies I would need for my National Match venture.

SLINGS AND THINGS

The M1 rifle is somewhat picky regarding what pressure ranges it will operate in. It's designed for Government M2 Ball ammo and its associated variants: a 150-gr. bullet at approximately 2,700 fps. This isn't especially awe-inspiring by today's measure, but it was considered an excellent and powerful cartridge for the time.

The common conception is that the M1 rifle needs to use a 150-gr. bullet, but this is not true. The fear, again, is bending the op rod, a seemingly deadly thing that will destroy a rifle. I have never encountered an M1 owner who bent an op rod in two decades of CMP shooting. I've seen some thumbnails ripped off, plenty of cuts and bruises, flat primers, and worn-out locking lugs, but I have never seen a bent op rod. If you go online, you'll immediately be treated to the "If you shoot a 168-gr. bullet in that rifle, it's toast" claim, but this is complete nonsense.

The old guard online who stew on the forums would have you believe that op rods are bent simply by looking at the incorrect ammunition; this is just not true. You can safely fire bullets up to and over 175 grains in the M1 Garand with no ill effect as long as you are not hot-rodding it. The bullet weight is only a factor in the pressure calculation: the M1 is not as concerned with projectile weight as it is with the operating pressure of the cartridge itself. If you're not mindful of operating pressure, you can create a bad situation with bullets as light as 125 grains. The M1 rifle operates well within a happy medium of bullet weight and chamber pressure. Ideally, you will not want to push it.

Fulton Armory said that I should shoot factory ammo in the finished rifle. I'm a prolific handloader and did my best to avoid the temptation to play around with various loads in the restored gun. As recently as last summer, there was some difficulty due to ammunition shortages. Since then, the industry has been cranking out tens of millions of cartridges to the point the American population is arguably sitting on billions and billions of rounds. But my task was more specific. I needed a factory load for .30-'06 that was safe in the Garand.

I contacted several companies to see if I could snag some ammo, but no dice. The M1-specific loads were not in demand, and I was out of luck ... until

The Fulton M1 rifle (bottom) is comparable in size and weight to many other popular CMP-legal guns, such as the M1903 Springfield (rare Mark 1 variant pictured here), Swiss K31 7.5x55, and British No.4 Mk2 .303.

my friend Seth Swerczek at Hornady came through for me at the last minute. I've come to rely on him for these oddball projects over time, and, wouldn't you know it, a case of 168-gr. M1 Match ammo appeared on my doorstep just a few weeks before Camp Perry.

Factory-loaded ammunition for the M1 Garand is not uncommon, but it is a bit of a specialty. The specs on the rifle itself demand a slightly lower pressure than today's standard .30-'06 loads, as the M1 operates at about 50,000 PSI. In contrast, today's general loads hover in the territory of 60,000 PSI. So, will it immediately destroy your rifle to fire a modern factory load? Probably not. But don't do it on purpose. Most 150-gr. ammo is safe in the M1.

In my younger years, I was less concerned about this and shot a wide range of factory and surplus loads in my Garand to no ill effect. As a disclaimer, I'd take the time to secure what you can that

is rated for the M1. Some have said that even the common 150-gr. Remington UMC load is unsafe in the M1, but it has never shown me issues, and it is equivalent to the old Greek HXP loads in terms of velocity.

Next up was a suitable, American-made match sling to accompany the finished M1 rifle. I began looking around to see if I could find the Holy Grail: an original Les Tam sling. These slings are widely regarded as the best service rifle slings ever made, and in all my two decades of competition experience, I failed to get one made by the man himself. As it happens in this life, he's retired, so I had to look elsewhere, and luckily, I found a well-recommended sling maker that lives up to the same quality as Tam, one Joel S. Berlin.

A match sling is one of those things you can't skimp on if you want to do well in competition: it is far from a simple carry strap, which is sadly the primary

function that today's slings have been reduced to. A quality sling can dramatically increase your scores if you know how to use it. (An excellent book on this topic is *Service Rifle Slings* by Glen Zediker.)

After reaching out, I found myself with three of Berlin's slings. The quality of this leather is simply top-notch, and there are many options to pick from regarding colors and fittings. The military M1907 sling is regarded as one of the best positional shooting slings ever devised, and it is correct for use on the M1 rifle and most American military rifles. In WWII, the more common fabric slings took over, but these are dubious at best for match shooting and don't have fixed adjustment points like the M1907. You can adjust the M1907-pattern slings for the shooter and position repeatably, which few other sling designs can do. Think of it as 'dialing in' your sling tension in a similar way you would zero your optics. Once you have your desired tension, you can practice and compete without guesswork.

Clips are next up for discussion. The Fulton M1 rifle is an accuracy machine, but poor-quality clips can lead to malfunctions. While I'm sure it has been beaten to death over the generations, the M1 does not feed from what we today call a 'magazine;' it uses an en-bloc clip that physically 'clips' the rounds in place inside the gun. The M1 has a magazine comprising the triggerguard assembly and receiver, similar to the Mauser or 1903 Springfield. While the clip-fed magazine is distinct from the detachable mags we know and love today, it is not the same as a stripper clip, which does not (usually) get inserted into the gun itself.

Make sure your clips are in working order and, ideally, in like-new condition. Watch for excessive wear, tension, and bending. A good M1 clip should be rigid and uniform. When loading to eight rounds, the last one inserted should be somewhat difficult to get in but not bulge out the walls of the clip; if that happens, it may cause a feed issue that can be difficult to clear.

The minutiae of the M1 is something lost on many people. The old guys used to go so far as to make gauges for their clips. They had special tools for each part of the gun and, overall, had a truly unique and deep knowledge of the gun that so many Americans and their allies relied on. The little tips and tricks are lost on the current generation, and many people have, either by accident or simple necessity, begun to rediscover them. For instance, new clips can be 'fuzzy' with

Parkerizing. I bought a ton of clips from Fulton, and they were minty but a bit too abrasive on the outside. A simple fix is to give them a tumble in a brass polisher to knock off the textured surface. You'd be surprised how much smoothing up clips can influence the rifle's reliability.

THE FULTON ARMORY M1 GARAND

I received notice from Rich that my M1 rifle was ready to return to me. Again, it shipped right to me through USPS, and I didn't need to endure the pain of visiting my local FFL. When I opened that box, well, let me tell you, I was floored. The rifle I sent was corroded trash, a wallhanger at best. The rifle in front of me was, without a doubt, the best-looking M1 I've ever gazed upon. The wood smelled of oil, and the metal finish was the most satisfying shade of gray. The uniformity of the finished product was breathtaking, and even now, months and months later, I enjoy looking at the rifle as much as I love firing it. Fulton Armory's gunsmiths indeed rendered me speechless with the incredible detail they delivered. Folks, this is the real deal.

The main thing I noticed about the rifle was the quality of the wood-to-metal fit. Compared to the original, this rifle was another animal entirely. Some of the

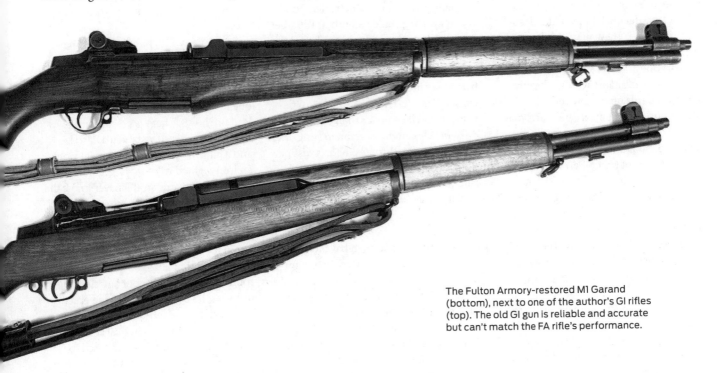

The Fulton Armory-restored M1 Garand (bottom), next to one of the author's GI rifles (top). The old GI gun is reliable and accurate but can't match the FA rifle's performance.

The finish of the Fulton Armory M1 is extraordinarily beautiful.

FA's minutia may seem unnecessary, but when you can get a rifle like this shooting 1.5 inches off the bench, you'll quickly become a believer, but more on M1 accuracy later.

Fulton armorers receive the rifle and then do an extremely detailed inspection. When I say detailed, I mean like clean-room-detailed. These guys check out every part, nook, cranny, plug, and pin. If a part doesn't meet spec, it returns to you in a bag of shame with all the other sub-par boards on our proverbial Ship of Theseus. These out-of-spec parts may not even be that out of spec, but they are not good enough for a rifle that will end up on the line at Camp Perry. A notable external example is the change to the standard rear sight. The lock bar rear sight is cumbersome and unnecessary, and Fulton's armorers installed a new, easier-to-use sight assembly. The 'collector' value here wasn't a factor; shooting for medals was the order of the day.

New parts aren't just swapped in willy-nilly, either. A much more detailed process is executed on the rebuild that sees these parts assembled with the utmost care. For instance, the bolt and receiver lugs are lapped for full contact and final

headspace. The company says this ensures even wear and bolt alignment. A new barrel—24 inches, 1:10 twist, chambered in .30-'06 Government, is installed to meet match specs. The barrel installed on my rifle for this article was manufactured by Criterion out of chrome-moly and has a chrome-lined bore.

You may be wondering why anyone would want a chrome-lined barrel for match shooting when that has been allegedly proven to be a detriment to accuracy. The simple fact is that I'd rather have a chromed barrel for long barrel life and ease of maintenance. It is something of an 'old guard' myth that chrome-lined barrels are incapable of match-grade accuracy. For what we are using this type of rifle for, you'll be better than fine.

To make matters more interesting, the chamber is also chrome-lined. A distinction must be made here from other M1 rifles: this barrel is incredibly difficult to install. Most rifle barrels are installed, and the chamber is reamed to the final headspace. Not so here. FA armorers install the barrel and then have to ensure it's correctly timed and headspace it to the receiver and bolt, which are three separate headspacing measurements. You can't ream a chromed chamber: doing so would destroy the lining and the barrel. This detail is one of the most important things to understand about Fulton Armory's work; these aren't simply slapped

together out of a parts bin. When I say that they fit every part, they fit every part.

This chromed barrel and its accompanying installation are of high importance to me. In some years, I have put as many as 3,000 rounds through my CMP rifles. A Swedish Mauser I shoot regularly has seen over 12,000 rounds in a decade of use. Yes, it could be argued that I am shooting out historic barrels, and in many cases, I am. The aught-six isn't a barrel burner, but the rifle gets hot and dirty, and I want something that I won't have to send in every few years for a new tube.

Some of my PRS buddies have a new barrel installed every calendar year. I ponder how it could be worth it to go through that kind of effort, but I'm no one to talk, treating vintage bolt guns like lead fire hoses. There is no substantial difference between a standard barrel and a chrome-lined one—especially on an iron-sighted rifle—at typical ranges inside of 600 yards. You'll never know the difference on paper. The enhanced barrel life and durability are more important to me, and I know I'll be shooting this barrel for the next couple of decades. In the latter half of 2023, I put nearly 2,000 rounds through it without any cleaning or issues. It's still shooting to the exact point of aim.

The M1 has lots of physical contact with the barrel. Today, we are used to free-floating barrels on most of our rifles, and this is decidedly not one of those types. The M1 has a three-piece stock design, arguably the most critical factor in making it accurate. Fulton has you covered in this regard, and fitting the stock and handguards is an art form. Shooters have, for nearly a century (the M1 was officially adopted in 1936 but was in testing in both .276- and .30-caliber variants since 1928), been trying to tweak the most accuracy possible from it.

The officially adopted M1 was suitably accurate for combat, but like everything, tinkerers wanted more out of it. Fulton Armory takes advantage of our combined ancestral knowledge and skill but executes it so the gun remains legal for National Match as-issued competition. In short, Fulton takes the rattle out of your rifle.

The stock is oversized and fitted lovingly to the receiver. CMP rules prevent bedding or other means of mating metal to wood, so Fulton armorers painstakingly fit the individual stock and metal parts together so that the fit is incredibly tight and precise. This isn't a file job your uncle does while crushing Natty Lights in his garage; no, Fulton does this with utmost precision. The finished product is tight but easily disassembled.

Experienced M1 shooters will know that, when putting the rifle back together, there should be some pressure when closing the triggerguard (the disassembly process on the M1 starts with pulling on and swinging out the triggerguard to remove the trigger and hammer assembly).

Receiver detail.

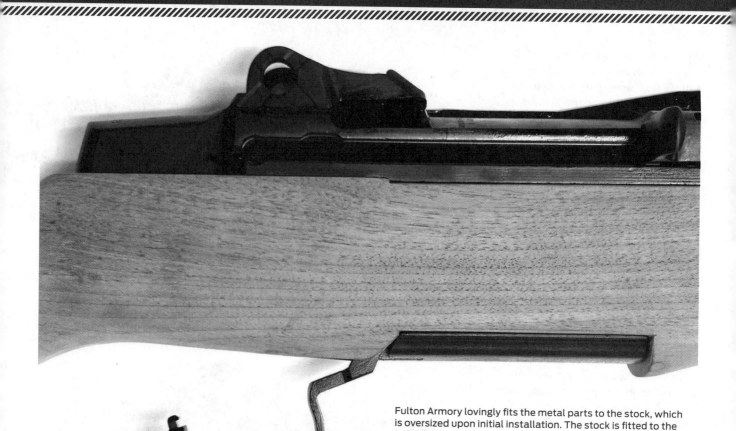

Fulton Armory lovingly fits the metal parts to the stock, which is oversized upon initial installation. The stock is fitted to the individual receiver ... painstakingly. Photo: Fulton Armory

Too much pressure and you'll have stress on the stock. Too little, and you'll have a sloppy gun. Fulton executes this minutia of National Match culture so incredibly well that I could have wept.

The old timers I used to shoot with, many long gone to their great reward, used to tell young Josh just what to look for in a good M1. It is this appreciation of the culture that I love about Fulton: these guys genuinely get it. There may be far fewer of us than there were even a decade ago, but the fact that Fulton captured what I would call the perfect M1 lockup means a lot and this little tidbit of shooting culture isn't going to be lost to time.

In addition to the fit of the stock, the handguards and their accompanying metal components take advantage of

Close-up detail of charging handle and op rod.

all we know about M1 accuracy. Fitting these parts is complex, and many moving components interact with them. The op rod moves underneath the barrel, and the handguard retainers along the barrel can run afoul on it. Handguard rattle has always been a problem on the Garand, specifically the forward handguard. This piece tends to slide back to front, applying uneven pressure on the barrel and getting knocked about by the op rod. Fulton addresses this tactfully and subtly so as not to hinder any moving parts. On the Fulton gun, you'd think this puppy was glued in place. It is so solid: there is no wiggle at all. Remarkably, it still comes apart with little effort, further validating the build quality.

The wood isn't the only thing that gets a loving treatment. If suitable to be rebuilt into the complete rifle, the metal parts are stripped of their previous surfaces and given a proprietary manganese phosphate Parkerizing job. While it's hard to tell, the rifle in its original condition likely had an earlier type of Parkerizing that used zinc, which is considered inferior to manganese phosphate. The earlier types of Parkerizing would display the light gray and greenish finished color, which is correct if you find it today, but by the end of WWII and beyond, the type of finish you see on the final rifle here is the idealized standard. Fulton Armory's method is a guarded secret, and I can see why; the results are incredibly even, and the finish immediately identifies it as a Fulton gun. On the line at the matches, I was asked if the rifle was from FA, and I was surprised by how many people could tell.

THE FA M1 IN ACTION

Fulton test-fired the Garand before returning it to me, and everything was checked out. I was eager to get the rifle and sling broken in, so I immediately loaded up my clips and got my range gear. The old method of zeroing an M1 Garand is to click the rear sight down all the way, then come up eight or nine clicks for 100 or 200 yards. I did just that and sent the first Hornady and Remington factory loads downrange. I was stunned. Not only did the rifle drop UMC 150-gr. loads into 2 inches off the

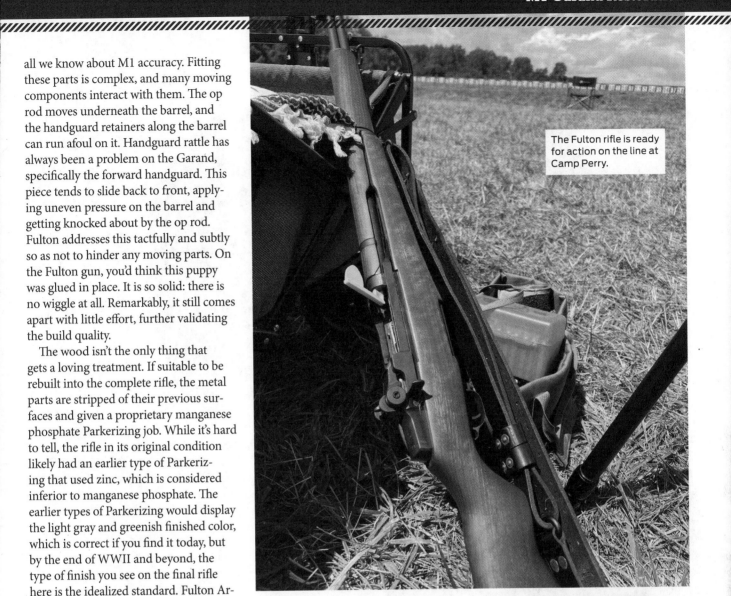

The Fulton rifle is ready for action on the line at Camp Perry.

A small cutout for the firing pin. This relief cut prevents the firing pin from slamming into the stock, which can result in a crack or worse. Photo: Fulton Armory

The bolt lugs are lapped to ensure complete contact. Note that the headspace is a three-part equation, with the bolt being headspaced in addition to the chromed barrel and refinished receiver. It is not beginner work. Photo: Fulton Armory

The front handguard tenon is oversized, so the lower band is form-fitted, eliminating accuracy-robbing movement. Photo: Fulton Armory

Fulton Armory centers the op rod on the looser band to ensure clearance and to align the action with the stock. Photo: Fulton Armory

bench at 100, it plunked the 168-gr. Hornady loads into a sweet 1.5-inch group for five shots. This precision is incredible for an M1, and I knew I had an X-Ring rifle. The accuracy at 200 yards was just as good—the rifle is easily capable of exceptional scores.

Slinging up and beginning practice is a bit different. Anyone can fire the M1 well off the bench, but things get more challenging with only a sling and coat as support. Firing prone at 200, the rifle was easily a 10-ring gun if I did my part. Thanks to FA's exceptional trigger job, I could easily control my trigger pull, which is not always easy on GI rifles, which tend to be sloppier, leading to problems in the offhand portion of firing. Bear in mind that firing at my home range in cool Michigan weather is one thing. Camp Perry was another.

I shot in four matches in the 2023 events at Camp Perry. The weather was oppressive, hot, and rainy. Northerners of Dutch stock like me tend to avoid the heat, and I almost single-handedly kept Gatorade in business while trying to remain hydrated. Like everyone on that line, I was in my padded coat over a thick sweater, pretending I enjoyed it. Despite my discomfort, the FA M1 landed me a silver score in the match, a bit less than the gold I was hoping for, but considering the conditions, I felt I did well. I shot a 276-4X, an average of 9.2/10 points per shot, so I kept all shots average inside a foot from prone, rapid fire, and standing at 200 yards. The Hornady loads kept virtually all my prone shots inside the 10-ring, with a couple of nines in there. Standing, well, I pulled my average down a bit. I was extremely pleased with the FA M1, and aside from my fatigue, it performed as well as I could have hoped. Perry is a graveyard of expectations, and I have to say that it was humbling to be back after a four-year hiatus. Had I a GI

The author (left) with the Fulton Armory crew at Camp Perry.

Many people are familiar with the metallic sights on the Viale Range at Camp Perry. Sometimes, it feels like a second home.

The author firing the Fulton Armory M1 rifle at the 2023 National Matches.

M1, I would have been lucky to have shot close to a medal score; the Fulton rifle was accurate enough to give me an edge I probably didn't deserve against better shooters.

SEND IT! (TO FULTON ARMORY)

When this was submitted for publication, the expected lead time for a National Match legal Fulton Armory M1 was around four months. Fulton Armory may deliver faster than that, but don't count on it. FA offers other services, and you don't necessarily need to follow the package I did for this article. But, if you want your own M1 worked on or to restore Grandpa's gun to its former glory, you should send it in.

The service isn't cheap, with most work packages averaging $2,500 or so, depending on options. However, this is as good as it gets for the devoted. Before you start, call and explain what you want and go from there. Fulton Armory was simply a joy to work with, and I am tremendously excited to have been able to take this project from idea to parking lot deal to the line at Camp Perry. These guys do it right. **GD**

The author lowers his score from the standing position. Offhand shooting is very tough, and after 20 years of CMP shooting, it hasn't become any easier. If there is one thing to practice for CMP, this is it.

After a fun time at the games, the author with the Fulton Armory M1 and his CMP medals.

Sako:
Finnish Soul in

Sako's original factory buildings in Riihimäki, a small town in the Finnish countryside, served it for decades.

Steel and Wood

›JENS ULRIK HØGH

The Pystykorva m/28-30 is widely recognized as one of the finest military repeating rifles ever made. It excelled in shooting competitions and on the ice-cold battlefields of the Winter War.

Sako, including the Tikka brand, sells more hunting rifles yearly than any other European rifle manufacturer. Its qualities mirror the Finnish people's soul, its history linked closely to Finland's.

I acquired my first hunting license in the mid-1980s at 16 when the big game opportunities in Denmark were limited. However, I was fascinated with exploring the world and experiencing exotic hunting adventures. I read all the hunting and firearms literature I could find to prepare for the day when this dream would become a reality. I wanted to learn everything about hunting, to train my shooting skills, and to save enough money to purchase the best hunting equipment. After extensive research, I purchased a .338 Winchester in a Sako rifle, which I believed was the ideal shooting tool. Even though today, after 36 years of hunting experience, I would opt for a .375 H&H, but that .338 Sako remains at the top of my quality barometer. It's still one of the best factory-made European rifles, matched by few others and only surpassed by hand-built guns. Scandinavian hunters highly regarded the Sako's quality and reliability, and it was considered the most sought-after rifle.

SAKO'S DNA

Simple, functional, and durable designs characterize Finnish production. "Made in Finland," like "Made in Switzerland" or "Made in Sweden," is recognized as a seal of quality around the world. Finland, along with the other Nordic countries, is one of the northernmost inhabited regions on the planet, which means long, dark, cold winters, where temperatures often reach -20 or -30 degrees Celsius. The Finnish landscape is endlessly beautiful and brutally unforgiving, which has always been the primary challenge for the country's people. Careful planning, craftsmanship, and hard work are fundamental requirements for living here. In such circumstances, there is no room for tools to fail. Equipment needs to be efficient and durable; otherwise, it's completely useless. The Finns are known

as people made from a unique mold.

For centuries, the land that is now Finland was a poor part of the Swedish kingdom. In 1809, Russian Tsar Alexander I conquered the country, making Finland an autonomous principality under his Russian empire. In 1917, a century later in the wake of the Russian Revolution, the Finnish people declared independence. A civil war ensued. The 'whites' (right-wingers) won over the 'reds' (pro-Soviet communists), Finland became independent, and it was in this young nation plagued by unrest and uncertainty that Sako was born. Sako began as a repair shop for the Finnish Civil Guard's weapons. The Civil Guard consisted of around 100,000 volunteer soldiers, and their armament consisted primarily of captured Russian and Japanese rifles in a dilapidated state.

The L46 was Sako's first rifle for the civilian market.

In the early years, the Sako factory and workshop were busily upgrading the rifles of the Finnish army.

The Sako products are characterized by their design, materials, craftsmanship, finish, and function, all of which leave a clear impression of reliability, durability, and functionality. I've never shot a Sako that wasn't accurate. Then and now, hunters in the U.S., Canada, Australia, New Zealand, and South Africa, the best customers of the Finnish brand, endorsed Sako quality. These hunters needed superb rifles for their challenging big game hunts, which confirms the first-hand impression that Sako is a solid shooting tool.

Most of these weapons had been through both the Russo-Japanese War in 1905 and World War I in 1914–1918, and the wear and tear was so severe that most of the barrels had virtually no rifling left in them. Since the newborn nation didn't have the means or ability to replace the worn-out rifles with new ones, the only solution was to repair and upgrade what it had.

In 1919, Under the leadership of a dedicated engineer, a gunsmithing workshop was set up in an old brewery building in Helsinki. Initially, eight employees repaired the firearms that came in. The operation quickly had to be scaled up because there were so many firearms to repair. By the end of 1920, 23 employees worked in the shop, and the machine park was greatly expanded. On April 1, 1921, the workshop was separated from the Civil Guard organization as an

One of the main ingredients in the Sako success story is the functional design of the rifles.

independent unit, and this date has since been considered Sako's birthday. "Sako" derives from the original name Suojel-uskuntain Ase- ja Konepaja Osakeyhtiö, which means Civil Guard Gun and Machining Works Ltd.

In the early years, the company grew and moved to other premises in Helsinki before moving to its current address in Riihimäki in 1927. The new buildings were the premises of a failed ammunition plant.

INTO THE FIRE
Within a few years of Sako's founding, it became clear that the military firearms the workshop refurbished were too worn out to be worth repairing. So, in 1923, the factory imported new Swiss barrels for the Mosin-Nagant and Arisaka rifles. After minor modifications, additional barrels were ordered, and the modified Mosin-Nagants were named m/24—a far better rifle than the originals. Sako's gunsmiths further developed the design

and made improvements to the magazine and sights, and by 1928, it had been refined enough to warrant a new model designation. The m/28 was nicknamed Pystykorva, Finnish for the hunting dog breed finspitz (the front sight was shaped like the dog breed's head).

After minor improvements, they settled on the m/28-30, recognized as one of the world's finest military repeating rifles. In 1931, Sako began production of rifle barrels on refurbished German machinery. In connection with the World Shooting Championships held in Helsinki in 1937, the Finnish organizers sent two m/28-30s to all participating countries' delegations before the match. The international competitors received the rifles exceptionally well, accounting for several World Records in the shooting events. Sako's reputation for quality had become global.

However, over the years, Sako had less and less to do as the Civil Guard's firearms were upgraded. The worldwide depression of the late 1920s also hit the

company, which was desperately short of orders. The factory increasingly turned to refurbishing military equipment and producing ammunition—primarily for submachine guns—for the Finnish forces. Further development of the m/28-30 rifle resulted in the military rifle model designated m/39. In 1939, Sako began production, manufacturing all parts of the rifle. Many consider it one of the finest military repeating rifles ever produced.

THE RUSSIANS CAME
On November 30, 1939, Russia attacked Finland with the stated goal of conquering the entire country. The invasion was expected to take a few days. The Russian forces numbered around one million men, more than 6,500 tanks, and nearly 4,000 aircraft. The Finnish army, with around 250,000 men, 30 tanks, and 130 aircraft, faced this enormous force. On paper, the war seemed lost before it began. However, the fact that the Finns were highly motivated to defend

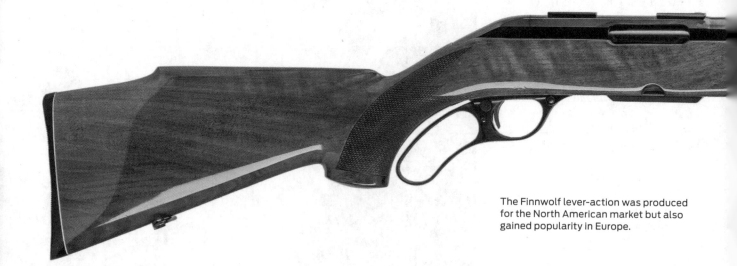

The Finnwolf lever-action was produced for the North American market but also gained popularity in Europe.

the freedom of their still relatively new nation made the Russian victory much more difficult to achieve than expected. By the time an armistice was signed on March 13, 1940, after just three and a half months of winter warfare, the Russians had lost more than 126,000 men, while Finnish casualties amounted to just over 26,000.

The Finns primarily fought with Sako repeating rifles. This was especially true of the infamous Finnish snipers, who, hidden in the snow, cost the Russians huge losses. Best known of these was the 160cm-tall Simo Häyhä—also known as "The White Death." He was armed with a Sako-produced m28-30 Pystykorva (with iron sights) and took out more than 500 Russian soldiers, making him the deadliest sniper in world history.

It wasn't long before the Russians attacked again. In the summer of 1941, Russian planes bombed Finnish cities, prompting Finland—by then allied with Germany—to declare war on the Soviet Union and launch an offensive to reclaim the land Finland had lost in the previous war. The Continuation War lasted for three years, during which wartime production was in full swing at Sako, primarily in the form of 9mm machine gun ammunition for the Finnish troops. The machines ran around the clock and were only stopped and serviced 8 hours weekly. No fewer than 275 million

military rounds and four million hunting cartridges were produced. In addition, the factory produced more than 70,000 m/39 rifles during the war years.

Although the wars were formally lost, resulting in the loss of a small part of Finland's territory, the outcome was a huge moral victory and a testament to the toughness of the Finnish people, not least because the Finns had maintained their freedom against all odds.

THE PRICE OF PEACE

Despite Sako's enormous war effort, the company nevertheless found itself in serious trouble at the war's end. The ceasefire with the Russians meant that all military orders were canceled, and the many male employees who went to war as rifle makers returned from the front with no work to do. As part of the ceasefire agreement with the Soviet Union, the Finnish Civil Guard, of which Sako had been a part until then, was dissolved. As a result, the shares in Sako were hastily transferred to the Finnish Red Cross, which owned the company for the next several years.

Sako was in crisis. Its production was hurriedly switched to alternative products, such as machines for the Finnish textile industry, tools for watchmakers and jewelers, telephone parts, cable shoes, shoemaking leather, axe handles, and cigarette lighters—anything to keep the wheels turning. The company also

suffered because it now had to pay taxes. Things were looking bleak for Sako.

In 1946, Elias Hydén was appointed the CEO of Sako. From the start, he planned for the company to return to its roots and produce rifles. It had the expertise, machinery, and everything else in place. Still, the market for military weapons had dried up, so it focused on the civilian market, and Sako had neither experience nor products ready to sell. However, there was hope.

During the war, some of Sako's employees had been working on a new rifle design. A fine-caliber small rifle tailor-made for Nordic winter hunting of capercaillie (a member of the grouse family) and black grouse. It used a small action designed around the diminutive 7x33 caliber, which was relatively popular in Finland but largely unknown in the rest of the world. The little L46 rifle worked brilliantly and was highly accurate, but it wasn't easy to sell outside of Finland. There was very little interest in the new gun in Sweden, where forest birds are similarly hunted. In Denmark and Norway, interest was greater, and soon, France and Belgium also started buying the rifles, but sales were too slow to sustain the company.

USA LENDS A HAND

The turning point came in 1948 when Jan Winter, an American gun importer, came

across a lightly used L46 for around $60 at Abercrombie & Fitch in New York. He bought the rifle and showed it to some of his more gun-savvy friends in the industry, including Julian Hatcher, Col. Townsend Whelen, and Warren Page. They agreed that the rifle was technically promising but needed several changes to make it attractive to American hunters.

First and foremost, it would need to be available in popular American calibers such as .222 Rem. and .218 Bee; the safety would need to be moved from the left to the right side of the bolt carrier, the sheet iron triggerguard would need to be replaced with a properly milled steel one, and the birchwood stock replaced with walnut. Jan Winter traveled to Riihimäki to negotiate the cosmetic details of the design with the Finns at Sako. Although they listened politely, they were highly skeptical of the many suggestions. In particular, the walnut stocks seemed ridiculous to the Finns. After all, how could the Yankees suggest that a company in a timber country like Finland import wood for the stocks when they had so much excellent wood in their forests?

Nevertheless, Sako eventually agreed to refine the L46 rifle for the U.S. market, and soon after, everyone involved was surprised by the reaction. Sales skyrocketed. In 1952, the U.S. became its largest export market. In 1953, the American market grew larger than the Finnish domestic market. The mood was ecstatic; Sako quickly built a growing fanbase worldwide. North America, Europe, Southern Africa, and Australia/New Zealand became significant export markets in the 1950s.

EXPORT SUCCESS

1957 growth gained momentum when Sako scaled its rifle to fit the new .308 Winchester caliber. True to form, the new

The Finnish sniper Simo Häyhä officially killed more than 200 Russian soldiers during the Winter War from 1939–40 using iron sights to stay as low as possible. Unofficially, the number was around 500, and on top of that, more than 200 were killed with submachine guns. He was awarded a Sako M/28-30 for his service but continued to use his refurbished Sako throughout the war.

gun was dubbed the "L57" and received an ecstatic reception (after a few cosmetic inputs from the U.S.). Sales were brisk. These were good years for Sako. Within two years of its introduction, the L57 was upgraded to the L579, and the L46 became the L461, with design changes made possible by Sako's investment in a high-tech investment casting foundry.

The L579 was soon followed by a similar bolt-action rifle based on an even larger action—the L61R—accommodating .30-'06-class cartridges. Then, a lever-action rifle designed for the U.S. (the VL63) hit the market.

Recognizing that the name Sako was perceived as Japanese in export markets and that the rifles' cryptic model names didn't mean much to hunters, the various models were given sexier designations. The L461 became known as the "Vixen," and the L579 as the "Forester," the L61R as "Finnbear," and the VL63 as "Finnwolf."

VARIOUS OWNERS

1962 Finnish Red Cross ownership ended when Suomen Kaapelitehdas (Finnis Cable Factory) acquired Sako. A few years later, both companies became part of the Nokia Group. Throughout the 1960s, Sako grew steadily, and a large order for military rifles for the Finnish defense forces followed. Unfortunately, the trend reversed in the 1970s. Sako's military production became unprofitable, and the oil crisis severely dampened the civilian market. The company ran into losses and had to lay off staff yearly. In 1985, an agreement was reached to merge the three Finnish arms factories, Valmet (which until then was state-owned), Tikka, and Sako.

In 1986, the new company—Sako-Valmet—was operational. However, the business could have done better, and its owners were looking for a buyer. Despite the business challenges, the development of new products did not stop. In 1996—the year Sako celebrated its 75th anniversary—the Sako 75 was introduced. The model was met with great enthusiasm in the hunting press, as it was created after extensive research into what modern hunters demanded. The rifles were groundbreaking in many ways. The Model 75 was also a big hit with customers: So much so that, just one year after its introduction, Sako stopped production of all previous model series in light of the Model 75's success. The fact that the Sako 75 rifles were very high quality from the

A box of Sako 7x33 rifle ammo was developed for the winter hunt of capercaillies and black grouses in the Nordic countries.

Sako's success is based on stringent quality control. Each rifle is test-shot, and Sako guarantees an accuracy of 1 MOA with five shots.

The current Sako headquarters reflects decades of growth but remains in the same location in Riihimäki.

beginning made them no less legendary. To this day, a Sako 75 is a state-of-the-art rifle and a modern classic.

From a business perspective, however, Sako took a few more years to reach its full potential. A giant step in that direction happened at the beginning of the new millennium when the Italian family-owned company Beretta bought Sako with plans to invest large sums of money in its future. The results were immediate. Product development, sales, and production were accelerated. Under Beretta's ownership, Sako has seen nothing but progress. New model series have been added, and old ones have broken records. In 2013, the Finnish maker produced more than 100,000 rifles for the first time, and in 2020, it announced that it had just produced the one-millionth Tikka T3, making it the only European-made hunting rifle ever sold in such numbers.

The Sako 90 Peak action with integral Picatinny bases.

First Sako 90 Kill

The Sako 90 Bavarian is as traditional as a European rifle gets. Blued steel. Iron sights. Walnut stock in traditional German shape. It's the choice of pipe-smoking grandpas … and traditional quality connoisseurs in general.

After a long and comprehensive briefing, the local forester assigned us to our stands in the vast Finnish forest area—a private property with a relatively large whitetail deer and moose population. There were even a few roe deer on the property, which is unusual in Finland.

I got a stand about 100 meters into the forest along a tractor track. From there, I could safely shoot in all directions. To my right, a rocky forest hill. Straight ahead, a strip of older forest, and to my left, a large clearing with a clear view of a forest edge 300 meters out. Behind me was a 50-meter wide ravine, and a ridge between me and the neighboring post to that side ensured the safety of shooting in that direction.

It looked promising (in retrospect, my posts always look promising). I had been handed Sako's new Model 90 Bavarian prototype to hunt with that day, chambered for the universal .300 Winchester Magnum. It is the "grandfather model" of the 90 series with a beautiful wooden walnut and Bavarian stock design. It's a lovely rifle ideally suited to combine with pipe smoking and, thus, another good reason for me to get started with that discipline. All joking aside, I appreciate a beautiful classic rifle far more than one with a plastic stock. This preference seems to be growing directly proportional to the percentage of white hairs in my beard.

I loaded the magazine and put an extra one in the chamber (you can quickly run out of ammo on a driven hunt). Then, it was just a matter of waiting and enjoying the magnificent Finnish countryside on a foggy, calm day in the forest.

LIFE AND DEATH

I didn't have to wait long. First, I heard a dog in the distance. Then, stomping steps on the forest floor. A movement caught my attention. Down the hill came a bouncing animal about the size of a fallow deer. I'd never seen a whitetail on a hunt before, so it took a second before the penny dropped, and I realized that the strangely moving animal was actually of the species we were hunting. I saw the sun glinting briefly on the antlers between the ears and knew it was a buck.

I found the animal in the scope and tried to swing with a suitable lead. The shot broke with the buck at a distance of about 30 meters. The deer didn't flinch at all but immediately picked up the pace. I repeated and shot again. I'm pretty sure the second shot only hit a Finnish pine tree. The following shot was quickly fired and also ended up in the flora. But when the deer had sprinted about 70 meters, it stopped momentarily on a small rocky knoll. My fourth shot put it down.

The 10 seconds of firing must have sounded belligerent to the neighboring hunters. I reported on the phone that I had killed a deer and (after explaining the other three shots had missed) was told to continue the hunt. However, nothing more happened at my stand that morning.

I rushed up the hill to see my deer when the drive ended. A final leap had taken the buck over the small hilltop,

The author with a 10-point whitetail buck shot on a driven hunt in Finland at the introduction event for the new Sako Model 90.

where it fell on the spot. It was an old 10-pointer with broken tips and worn-down teeth. Two fatal shots in the engine room (my first and my last), confirming that a little extra firepower is valuable when you are shooting at running game on a driven hunt. This deer was probably the first animal killed with a Sako 90. I found it quite fitting that an old gray-bearded gentleman killed an old gray-bearded buck with a traditional grandfather rifle.

NEW MODEL SERIES

In 2006, Sako's engineers found room for improvement and introduced the Model 85. The differences between the 85 and the 75 are primarily found in the details, and the same can largely be said of the leap from the Model 85 to the Model 90, which is now the name for top-tier Finnish rifles.

TECHNICAL UPDATES

The most noticeable difference between the Sako 90 and the 85 is the different profile on the top of the action. On the Model 90, the company moved away from the integral Sako mounting base that has accompanied its rifles for decades. Instead, there are now two different integral mounting base solutions. On models with a wooden stock (and the option of iron sights), the mounting base is a 17mm groove like the Tikka, an ultra-low mounting base that is optimal for use with iron sights. On models

The Sako 90 comes in many configurations. This is the stainless steel Sako 90 Peak with synthetic stock.

with a synthetic or laminate stock, standard Picatinny bases are machined into the action, giving you almost unlimited choices in mount selection.

Also, on the Sako 90, there is more steel between the two action rings. That's because the ejection port has a different profile. This design results in a stiffer action with an inherently higher accuracy potential. A new solution for the ejector system makes the smaller ejection port possible. The Model 85 used a fixed ejector (as on a Mauser 98), which sometimes caused problems with the ejection of long

The SAKO Vixen was the refined version of the L46, first known as the L461. After the model names were upgraded, it became the Sako Vixen—one of the most beautiful little bolt-action rifles ever produced.

cases. Now, they have switched to two spring-loaded ejectors in the bolt head. According to Sako, this provides a more consistent and reliable ejection, as user error is eliminated. To prevent potential misoperation, Sako has introduced a safety button on the Model 90's bolt, which must be activated if you want to disassemble it for cleaning.

A more significant but less conspicuous change is that the entire trigger group has been redesigned from the ground up. The trigger pull is adjustable in five steps with a Torx key through the triggerguard. In addition, the trigger blade can now be moved longitudinally to fine-tune the ergonomics to each shooter. The safety has also been upgraded to lock the firing pin in the safe position. So far, only

the Bavarian model is unaffected by the changes to the trigger group, as it comes standard with a set trigger, which is an entirely different design.

Most Sako 85 model configurations continue with the addition of upgraded Model 90 technology. However, some of the models are renamed. The Sako Hunter (models with wooden stocks and either stainless or blued steel parts) retains its name. So does the traditional Bavarian model. The Carbon Light Model in the 85 series will now be called the Peak. The Carbon Wolf becomes the Quest. The Finnlight II becomes the Adventure. There's little doubt that the models with synthetic stocks will be the best sellers. However, if I had to choose an all-round rifle from the range, I would prefer a Hunter, probably in stainless steel, or a Varmint Stainless, which is heavier and has Picatinny bases.

The Sako 90 is a significant technical upgrade from the Model 85. Much has been done to the design than first impressions suggest. Sako has always been an excellent brand, and the new Model 90 has become even better. **GD**

High Stakes and High Jinx

Hunting the biggest game with the largest rifle, Professional Hunter Bryan Coleman always found the humor in most situations—even the dangerous ones.

Coleman (right) and a safari client take a break after a successful buffalo hunt. Coleman holds his John Harper .577 NE double, his primary heavy rifle for backing up clients hunting dangerous game.

in Africa

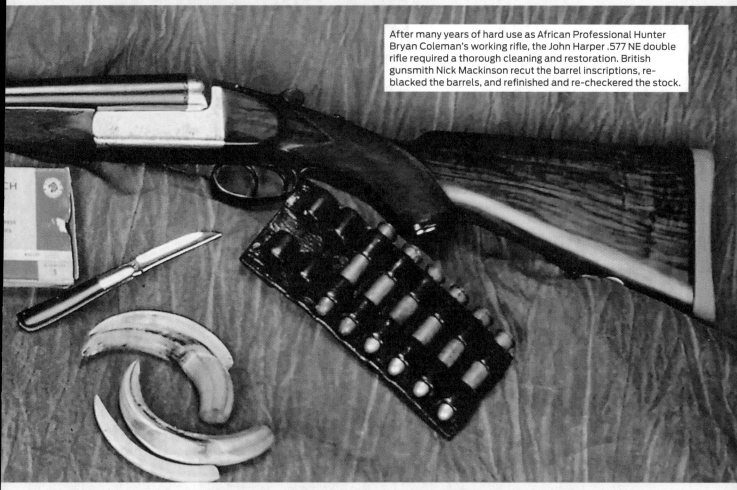

After many years of hard use as African Professional Hunter Bryan Coleman's working rifle, the John Harper .577 NE double rifle required a thorough cleaning and restoration. British gunsmith Nick Mackinson recut the barrel inscriptions, re-blacked the barrels, and refinished and re-checkered the stock.

❯JOE COOGAN

A relentless sense of humor compels Bryan Coleman to wring the joke out of almost everything he sees, says or does—consequences be damned. If you were lucky enough to be on safari with Coleman, you learned to sleep with one eye open and keep a sharp ear out for things that go bump in the night. Clients were mostly tolerant of his pranks because, as one of East Africa's top-rated white hunters, Coleman routinely delivered exceptional results—and a fun time to boot.

Coleman occasionally pushed the limits of his unsuspecting victims' good nature, but he could also take a good prank when aimed in his direction. Former colleague and friend Robin Hurt did many safaris with Coleman over the years and remembers one of the "Prince of Pranksters'" tried-and-true safari tricks. After dinner, when everyone had retired for the evening, he'd tie a hunk of zebra haunch to the tent pole of an unsuspecting victim's tent—or even worse, to the leg of their bed. When a hyena or two grabbed the meat and viciously yanked and shook the tent, Coleman found the ungodly commotion highly amusing as the screams and shouts from inside the tent competed with the maniacal sniggers and chortles of the hyenas tugging on the meat outside the tent.

Police Work

Coleman's legendary jesting is just one facet of the man's remarkable personality and life spent mainly in Africa, where, at different times, he hunted man and beast with equal determination and success. Coleman's father was Inspector J.C. Coleman, a pioneer policeman in Kenya Colony, British East Africa. As a decorated 21-year veteran, Inspector Coleman survived many dangerous scrapes, including one incident that happened when he tracked a gang of suspected murderers. During the ensuing fight, he was struck with a poisoned arrow but miraculously survived the usually fatal wound.

Young Coleman's early years were steeped in outdoor adventures and big game hunting. While still in his teens, he took his first elephant. He became particularly adept at hunting Kenya's mountain game, especially the spiral-horned bongo, which is considered the most challenging and spectacular of the mountain species. By the time Coleman finished school, he'd accumulated an impressive amount of mountain hunting experience, which, combined with proficient gun handling, made him a natural to follow in his father's footsteps. He joined the ranks of the Kenya Police Force in 1949.

When the Mau Mau Insurrection flared up in 1952, those with specialized knowledge of the montane forests were often called upon to lead tracker teams

During the Mau Mau atrocities, a British army officer who had served in India and retired to Kenya handed in his John Harper .577 Nitro Express (NE) to the Central Firearms Bureau in Nairobi to avoid falling into the wrong hands. The mint-condition rifle had only been fired four times.

Coleman relaxes in a 1960s Kenyan tented camp from which he conducted hunting and photographic safaris with the East African outfitter, Hunters Africa, Ltd. from 1962 until Kenya closed safari hunting in 1977.

patrolling at altitudes between 5,000 and sometimes above 10,000 feet, often in freezing rain and heavy mists. Coleman's tracking skills, as well as his expertise and familiarity with the forested areas of Mt. Kenya and the Aberdares, were critical to surviving skirmishes with the mountain-based terrorists and bringing them to justice.

During Coleman's Kenya Police service, he carried various firearms, including a .45 Webley and .38 Smith & Wesson revolvers, a 12-gauge Greener shotgun, and a Sten or Patchett submachine gun. But, the real irony was that during one of the most dangerous situations Coleman ever encountered in police work (see sidebar: Unarmed & Dangerous), he

was unarmed. It was an abrupt wake-up call that could have ended with dire consequences but served instead as a life lesson. Coleman has never been without a gun, either in his hands or within easy reach, no matter where he is or what he is doing.

JOHN HARPER .577 NE

Coleman discovered that one of the perks of a Kenyan policeman was being privy to information about guns coming into the Central Firearms Bureau in Nairobi that were destined to be sold or destroyed. Many of these firearms had either been confiscated or recovered from thefts and burglaries throughout the colony. Occasionally, guns were turned in

by license holders or possibly by relatives of someone who had recently passed, and the family had no further need or interest in keeping the firearm. Coleman kept a sharp eye out for any interesting rifles that might show up.

During the Mau Mau atrocities, a British army officer who had served in India and retired to Kenya handed in his double rifle to the Central Firearms Bureau to keep it from falling into the wrong hands. It was a leather-cased John Harper .577 Nitro Express (NE) in mint condition, having only previously been fired four times. When Coleman learned of the rifle, he bought it as soon as possible, planning to use it when hunting elephants.

John Harper was a skilled Birmingham, England gunmaker who crafted fine-quality boxlock double rifles. One of those rifles was Coleman's .577 NE, made for Peter Orr & Sons, a Scottish merchant operating in Madras and Rangoon, India, where the British officer had originally purchased it.

The John Harper .577 NE rifle was built on a color case-hardened boxlock action, featuring an automatic safety with the safe indicator inlaid in gold and a pivoting third fastener that engaged a doll's head barrel extension. It also featured bushed strikers and double triggers with an articulated front trigger to minimize the chances of finger injury during recoil. Eighty percent of the action was engraved with cut scroll engraving of varying sizes covering the top lever, trigger plate, floor plate, and triggerguard.

Attractive shaded scroll engraving surrounds game scenes depicting two of the Big Five—a lion (right) and an elephant (left) in tall grass. A Bengal tiger is depicted on the front of the floor plate and the triggerguard bow. The serial number is engraved on the triggerguard tang, which extends to the buttstock's steel pistol grip cap.

The rifle weighs 12 pounds and 12 ounces and is fitted with 26-inch chopper lump barrels that feature a matted

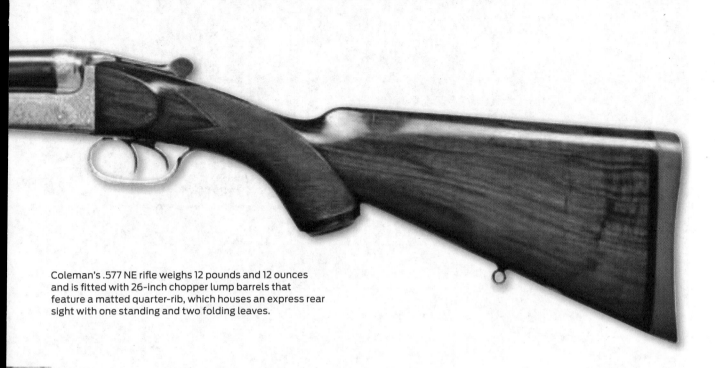

Coleman's .577 NE rifle weighs 12 pounds and 12 ounces and is fitted with 26-inch chopper lump barrels that feature a matted quarter-rib, which houses an express rear sight with one standing and two folding leaves.

Coleman next to a large elephant taken in Kenya's Hunting Block 11, located in the Northern Frontier District (NFD). Coleman believes hunting the super-tuskers was the most challenging and exciting big game.

quarter-rib, housing an express rear sight with one standing and two folding leaves. A silver bead adorns the front ramp sight. The barrels are engraved with the wording, Made by "John Harper for . P. Orr & Sons . Ltd . Madras & Rangoon ." appearing on the right barrel and ".577 Cartridge 3 Inch Case." displayed on the left barrel. The barrel flats are stamped with Birmingham nitro proofmarks indicating it was proofed for 90 grains of cordite and a 650-grain bullet.

The stock is cut from lightly streaked and nicely figured European walnut. It has a 15¾-inch length of pull and a Silver-type solid red recoil pad. The drop at the heel measures approximately 2 5/8 inches, while the drop at the comb measures approximately 2 inches, with a ¼-inch cast-off. The checkering on the pistol grip and matching splinter forearm features a closely spaced point pattern.

The .577 NE cartridge utilizes a straight-rimmed .584-inch caliber case designed for single-shot and double rifles. The .577 NE cartridge case is made in three different lengths based on the respective .577 Black Powder Express cartridge from which it originated. The most popular case length for the .577 NE is the 3-inch case firing a 750-grain bullet at over 2,050 feet per second (fps) and generating over 7,000 foot-pounds (ft-

lbs) of energy with recoil to match. The penetration of the .577 bullet is excellent and considered much better than the 900-grain slug of the .600 NE.

One of Coleman's most memorable encounters carrying his .577 NE involved a showdown with a puff adder, which resulted in a casualty of a different nature. When confronted by the large, highly dangerous snake, Coleman brought his big .577 into play—not to shoot the snake (ammo was too expensive and hard to find), but rather to anchor the head with the buttstock to hack it off with a panga (machete). Unfortunately, as he did so, his aim was off, and Coleman managed to nick a chunk of wood out of the buttstock's comb but also dispatched the snake simultaneously. Upon his return to Nairobi, Coleman enlisted Len Bull, Shaw and Hunter's resident gunsmith, to repair the damaged stock by inletting a matched piece of walnut into the damaged area, which is still in place today.

In 1995, Coleman, with regret, made the gut-wrenching decision to let go of his big .577 double rifle. During the 24 years he'd carried the rifle, he'd fired it approximately 50 times and, given its sentimental value, he felt like he was bidding goodbye to an old friend.

Coleman consigned the rifle to Dallas gun dealer Mims Reed, who remembers

When Coleman tried to anchor a large puff adder with the buttstock of his 577 to chop off the snake's head with a panga (machete), he nicked a chunk out of the buttstock's comb. Shaw & Hunter's gunsmith, Len Bull, repaired the damaged stock with an inletted piece of matching walnut. Photo Credit: Lauren Dean

well the day the rifle was brought into his shop. "While the bores and chambers were 'up to snuff,' the outside looked as if it had been 'rode hard and put up wet!'" Reed said. "It was a working gun, and it looked like it. The metal finish was missing, the checkering was worn smooth, and the stock was slick black with a combination of oil, age, and bull dust."

Reed soon found a buyer for the British double who decided that after many years of use in Africa as an honest, hard-core, Professional Hunter's work-

ing rifle, everything needed to be cleaned and checked out. The rifle was shipped to British gunsmith Nick Mackinson, who lived in Canada, with instructions to "bring it back to life."

Mackinson recut the barrel inscriptions so they wouldn't be lost with polishing and re-blacked the barrels. He polished the action body, which was originally color case-hardened, to a bright coin finish and painstakingly heat-treated the walnut stock to draw out as much oil as possible. Mackinson completed his

work by re-checkering the pistol grip and forearm.

Once cleaned and relieved of excess oil, the walnut stock's beautiful color and grain were highlighted with a hand-rubbed oil finish. The buyer wished to keep Len Bull's inletted piece of walnut intact as a badge of honor and a source of conversation around the campfire.

Over the years, Coleman's .577 NE has changed hands a few times. In May 2022, it was sold at a Poulin Auction that showcased it in a Youtube video

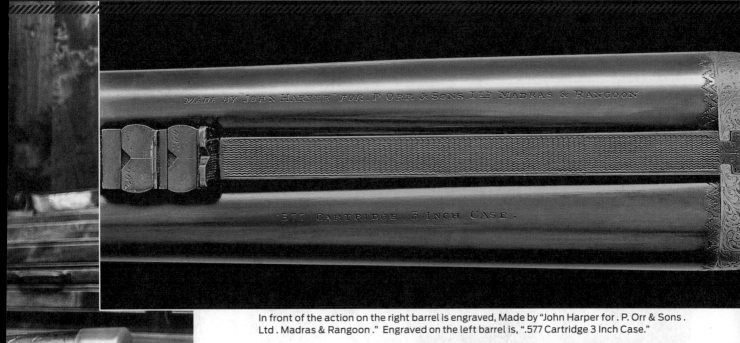

In front of the action on the right barrel is engraved, Made by "John Harper for . P. Orr & Sons . Ltd . Madras & Rangoon ." Engraved on the left barrel is, ".577 Cartridge 3 Inch Case."

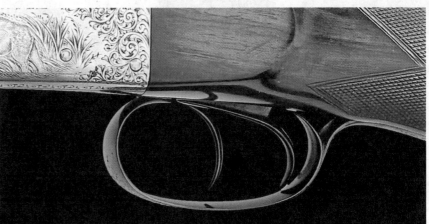

In keeping with the features of big-bore double rifles, Coleman's .577 NE has bushed strikers and double triggers. The front trigger is articulated to minimize the chances of finger injury during recoil.

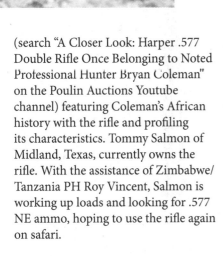

(search "A Closer Look: Harper .577 Double Rifle Once Belonging to Noted Professional Hunter Bryan Coleman" on the Poulin Auctions Youtube channel) featuring Coleman's African history with the rifle and profiling its characteristics. Tommy Salmon of Midland, Texas, currently owns the rifle. With the assistance of Zimbabwe/ Tanzania PH Roy Vincent, Salmon is working up loads and looking for .577 NE ammo, hoping to use the rifle again on safari.

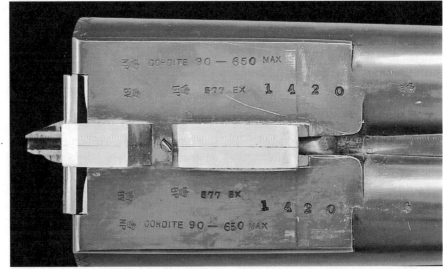

The barrel flats are stamped with Birmingham nitro proofmarks indicating the .577 NE is proofed for 90 grains of cordite with a 650-grain bullet, although Coleman always used Kynoch's 750-grain loads.

Coleman cultivated a safari clientele that shared his passion for elephant hunting during his safari years. Throughout his safari career, Coleman averaged at least one 100-pounder per season.

SAFARI WORK

By the latter part of 1956, the Mau Mau Rebellion was ending, and Coleman found himself reevaluating his role as a colonial law enforcement officer. Having decided he'd had his fill of manhunts, he decided to resign from the police force and considered other career options. He wanted to trade the "asphalt jungle" for the real jungle to pursue his hunting passion.

In 1957, Coleman was issued a restricted assistance permit (PH license). He soon approached a grizzled, old-school white hunter named Louis Woodruff who agreed to tutor him in the ways of conducting professional safaris. Under the old white hunter's experienced eye, Coleman served a strict apprenticeship with Woodruff, making it clear that professional hunting safaris were very different from the personal hunting he

had done on his own. Woodruff stressed the importance of putting clients of varying capabilities into position to make an effective shot on game.

"This will be much more difficult and challenging," Woodruff told the young Coleman. "Much more than if you were doing the shooting yourself."

At the same time, Woodruff emphasized how much the safety and well-being of the clients would depend on Coleman's skills and know-how. Woodruff pointed out that the actual "trigger-pulling" on safari would account for less than 10 percent of the experience. A safari's success would not only be a matter of knowing the game and the country but, more importantly, hinge on how well Coleman could handle the quirks and foibles of human nature. Coleman's sense of humor would go a long way toward helping him navigate the tricky terrain of satisfying

his clients while keeping them safe. He would also be leading a retinue of native crew, maintaining vehicles and equipment, and, last but not least, producing the quality of trophies that his clients would expect.

Despite his fun-loving spirit, Coleman took his white hunter apprenticeship seriously. The second part involved joining the famous white hunter J.A. Hunter on a culling scheme in the Kibwezi district near Tsavo N.P. This added greatly to Coleman's already extensive Big Five experience. Satisfying Woodruff's and Hunter's expectations and requirements as an aspiring white hunter was no easy task, but Coleman did so with flying colors. Both white hunters signed off on his unrestricted PH license.

In 1958, with the ink on his assistance permit still wet, Coleman worked as an independent PH. He was now qualified to conduct safaris for all of the dangerous game and could PH for any Kenya-registered safari company that needed a second or third hunter on larger outfits. Coleman was also appointed honorary game warden by the Kenya Game Department.

It wasn't long before Coleman was invited to join Safariland, a long-established and well-respected Nairobi-based outfitting firm employing some of the brightest stars in the safari world at that time. Safariland's roster of PHs after WWII included proven hands such as Tom Murray-Smith, Bob Foster, Bunny Ray, Geoff Lawrence-Brown, Owen McCallum, Bill Jenvy, and Douglas Collins. Coleman was honored and proud to be listed among their ranks.

But when a number of the old guard white hunters began retiring, the number of safaris Safariland undertook was reduced. It became obvious to Coleman that he needed to make other plans, so he started his own safari outfit, *Bryan Coleman Safaris.* He'd operated for about a year on his own when he was approached by White Hunters, Ltd. and offered a directorship in the company. Later, the company was renamed Hunters Africa, Ltd. in deference to the political proclivities of the newly independent Kenya. Coleman spent the rest of his time in Kenya conducting safaris with Hunters Africa.

During this time, one of Coleman's clients acquired a late '50s-issue Win-

For size comparison, a .577 NE round stands between a .700 H&H cartridge (left) and a .500 NE (right), all developed and intended for hunting the world's largest game.

Kynoch's .577 NE cartridges became a popular standard round for hunting African elephants in the early 20th century. Double rifle cartridges' case heads are typically rimmed, allowing them to be extracted or ejected from the chambers.

chester Model 70 Super Grade in .458 Winchester Magnum for hunting an elephant. Winchester had introduced the .458 Winchester Magnum cartridge in 1956, and this Model 70 was one of the first rifles chambered for that caliber. Shaw & Hunter, the Nairobi gun shop, imported the .458 rifle to rent it out to safari clients. Coleman handled and shot the rifle during the safari and liked it well enough to buy it. He added it to his battery of safari rifles, which included a Springfield .30-'06 magazine rifle with a 4x Redfield scope. The .458 served as a second big-bore to his heavy .577 double, partaking in plenty of big game action over the years. The rifle's accumulated history and sentimental value have ensured it remains with the Coleman family and will be passed down to his son, Carl.

CLOSE CALLS

During his safari years, Coleman survived numerous near-fatal encounters with dangerous game, but the closest call came when a wounded buffalo ambushed him in a thick Lolgorian forest. The bull charged suddenly and seemingly from nowhere, knocking Coleman's .577 double out of his hands before he could shoot. As the bull lowered his head to toss him, Coleman jumped onto the horns and held on for dear life. The bull continued charging toward Coleman's gunbearer, Sungura, while Coleman clung to the horns with everything he was worth.

Sungura, who carried Coleman's spare .458 rifle, shot the buff as it passed him, very fortunately without hitting Coleman. Even at this death-defying moment, Coleman found it humorous enough to yell out "*adios!*" to Sungura and Howard Chow, his shocked client, as he went past them riding the buffalo's horns. Fortunately, Sungura's shot took quick effect, causing the buff to drop and fall on top of Coleman. Sungura and Chow rushed up to roll the buffalo off Coleman, who escaped the wild encounter with scrapes, bruises, and a few cracked ribs.

For real fun, Coleman enjoyed the challenge of sneaking up to sleeping

rhinos to touch them on the backside. Learning to dodge black rhinos as a youngster in the Kenya highlands and then observing them as much as he did on safari, he became familiar with their habits and behaviors, which were fairly predictable. For instance, Coleman observed that rhinos could not get to their feet quickly after a nap. And as quick as they were once on their feet, they were slow to turn around, compared to a buffalo that can swap ends in a flash.

After discussing it with his trackers, who were also savvy to rhino habits, Coleman decided to try to sneak close enough to a sleeping rhino to touch him. The trackers said the rhino would need to be facing into the wind, which they usually were, and be completely asleep in the right kind of cover. They also warned that touching the rhino would instantly wake him up. Once Coleman accomplished this feat, proving to himself that it could be done under the right circumstances, he often bet his clients $100 that he could do it—and never lost.

UP CLOSE AND PERSONAL

Coleman liked getting close to game animals and enjoyed the close approach to elephants. He was particularly intrigued by super-size bulls carrying tusks weighing 100 pounds or more, which he found to be the most challenging and exciting big game to hunt. During his safari years,

he cultivated a safari clientele that shared his passion for elephant hunting and averaged at least one 100-pounder (100 pounds per tusk) per season, often more.

One client who shared Coleman's passion for hunting big tuskers was Flavy Davis from Houston, Texas. Davis first hunted with Coleman in the early '60s and became a repeat client over the next ten years, devoting his time and energy toward collecting a 100-pounder.

In June 1970, Davis' determination and persistence finally paid off. Coleman and Davis were wrapping up the last part of a 21-day safari in Block 12, located directly north of Garissa in northern Kenya. It was a block that could produce big ivory, but it was not easy terrain to navigate and posed the risk of confronting *Shifta*, the "sure-enough" Somali bad guys. The Somalis were tough, ruthless men who could walk 100 miles, shoot an elephant with an AK-47, hack out the tusks and then walk 100 miles back carrying the tusks—one man by himself. Killing a white man was nothing for a Somali with that mindset.

On the first day in the block, Coleman located a herd of 19 bull elephants with several tuskers carrying respectable ivory. But it almost became too much of a good thing because working in close to that many elephants meant the chances of being detected by one or more of the pachyderms was likely. Looking for the

Coleman's Winchester Model 70 was one of the first rifles chambered for the .458 Winchester Magnum cartridge. The rifle was imported by the Nairobi gun shop Shaw & Hunter and available for rental to safari clients. Coleman liked the rifle well enough to buy it after a client used it on an elephant hunt.

Facing Danger Unarmed

The author (left) recently visited Coleman, now 92 years old, at his home in Texas. Guns are still a part of Coleman's daily life, as evidenced by a 100-yard target that allows him to take a shot just by stepping out his back door.

In his book *White Hunters, The Golden Age of Safaris*, Brian Herne describes an incident illustrating Coleman's cool head and determination in the face of grave danger.

"… a well-armed gang of five murderous thugs had been wreaking havoc among residents of a Nairobi suburb. Coleman was among the security forces called together on a stormy evening at the Muthaiga police station to hear a detailed briefing about the terrorists. Like everyone in the armed forces at that time, Coleman wore a revolver and carried a Sten or Patchett submachine gun. When he went off duty later that night, Coleman hurriedly changed out of his khaki police tunic and short pants for civilian clothes. He mounted his Harley-Davidson motorcycle to head for home. Because of the rain, Coleman wore the full-length navy wool greatcoat of the Kenya police.

"Coleman had not traveled far in the darkness when he saw a Ford Zephyr car with five African men in it. His sixth sense kicked in, and he leapt into action. 'I instinctively knew it was them,' Bryan later commented. 'I don't know how I knew, but I just knew.' He swung his big motorcycle into a U-turn and roared after the Ford, and reached for the Smith & Wesson .38 that was usually holstered at his thigh. The .38 was not there. Coleman froze. It was then that he recalled unstrapping his Sam Browne belt and revolver holster as he changed clothes. His Sten gun had also been left behind. As he roared along in tandem with the speeding Ford, Bryan could see the faces of the armed Mau Mau gangsters. It was too late to back off, so Coleman reached over and smashed his fist against the suspects' car window, signaling with all the ferocity he could muster for the vehicle to pull over. For better or worse they did.

"Coleman's sharp instincts, developed during other types of pursuit, had been correct. The occupants of the car were the same dangerous terrorists who had been the subject of the police briefing. Coleman later recalled, 'I kept one hand under my greatcoat, as if I was holding a gun. I told them to drive to the Muthaiga police station, and I would ride along beside them. I said if there was any monkey business I would shoot the lot of them. To his amazement the gangsters, perhaps awed by his command of the Kikuyu language, or perhaps because they figured the lone motorcyclist must have some angle or reinforcements they did not know about, promptly went with him, docilely marching into the police station with their hands above their heads."

"It was unbelievable," Coleman says, "because they were armed to the teeth with automatic weapons."

largest bull among so many was tough, dangerous work. Spotting a big bull and keeping him in sight long enough to get off a shot and not get trampled to death in the stampede afterward made it risky business, indeed.

Eventually, a large-bodied bull was spotted, which they thought might be the one. But the thick brush where he stood hid the tusks from view. The seconds ticked away, seeming to take hours, but the sight took everyone's breath away when the bull finally stepped clear of the brush. Weighing heavy on the bull's head was a magnificent pair of long, thick, perfectly matched tusks. This elephant was the largest-tusked bull Coleman had ever seen, and at a glance, he knew the tusks bettered the hoped-for 100-pound mark by a wide margin.

They kept the bull in sight and hoped the wind would hold steady to have any chance of getting close to it. Coleman risked a quick dash to get close and allow Davis to take a shot at the big bull. They scurried up to within 20 yards of the bull standing broadside, and Davis wasted no time raising his Winchester M70 .375 H&H Magnum and firing. Coleman followed with an insurance shot from his .577 to reduce the risk of losing the extraordinary elephant. The bull covered 25 yards with a few quick steps before collapsing onto his right side.

As expected, all hell broke loose with the sound of the shots—bulls trumpeted and scattered in every direction. When the dust settled, one askari (guard) bull remained, refusing to leave the downed monarch. Coleman did not want to pressure the askari and be forced to shoot him, so the group backed away from the scene to allow the younger bull to move off of his own accord. The sun was close to setting when the party reached the vehicle for the drive back to camp.

That evening, the memorable occasion was celebrated by Davis, Coleman, and the whole safari crew, who raised several toasts to the magnificent tusker they had worked so hard to find. The next morning, they were relieved to find the askari bull had left the downed bull. They could now admire the huge tusks and take photos as they ran their hands over the long tusks to feel their smoothness and soak in the spectacular success of the hunt.

When the tusks were weighed and registered with the game department in Nairobi, they tipped the scales at 128 and 130 pounds, making them Coleman's largest client-collected tusker ever. Even

Back at camp, Flavy Davis (left) and Bryan Coleman display Davis' incredible tusks, which weighed 128 and 130 pounds and measured nearly 10 feet in length—the largest elephant Coleman's clients ever took.

In the late 1950s, Coleman added a Winchester Model 70 .458 Winchester Magnum to his safari rifles as a second heavy to his .577 NE. That rifle, one of the first .458 Winchesters made, holds sentimental value for him and remains with his family.

industry and affecting thousands of Kenyans who depended upon and benefited directly from it. The country suffered from the hasty and ill-conceived decision, eliminating significant income from selling hunting licenses, game permits, and area and trophy fees. Money that could have been used for implementing effective anti-poaching and conservation programs was eliminated, while ivory and rhino poaching accelerated to unprecedented levels. The real tragedy, though, was that corrupt government officials at the highest levels who should have been protecting wildlife were instrumental in decimating it.

In 1981, Coleman retired from safari work and settled in Texas to concentrate on wildlife conservation projects and game ranching. His gravitating to Texas was no surprise as it was the closest thing to Africa this side of the Atlantic. Given the wildlife and the look and feel of the terrain, South Texas was a natural choice for him. Minus cowboy hat and boots, he felt right at home.

Today, at 92, he and Joan live between Houston and Austin, near their son Carl and his family. Coleman built the house where he lives on a small lake fed by a flowing creek in an area that allows him to step out his back door and see deer, hear coyotes, or squeeze off a shot with a handgun or rifle at a 100-yard target.

On a recent visit to see him at his Texas home, I can confirm that Coleman still adheres to a philosophy of always being armed, which he's lived by for most of his life. When I asked him what he carries these days, he reached into his pocket to produce a well-worn Smith & Wesson Model 642 Airweight in .38 Special. Coleman chuckled at the irony, pointing to the diminutive J-frame revolver in his hand compared to the behemoth .577 NE he carried on his shoulder for so many years in Africa.

"They both serve a similar purpose appropriate to the size of the threat they're designed to stop," Coleman said. "These days, in this patch of bush, the threat doesn't require the knockdown power and penetration of a .577—but as always, it still takes a steady hand and a sharp eye. That, I can do with this little Smith," he said, with a wink and a smile. **GD**

today, 53 years later, Coleman can still picture in his mind the amazing herd of bull elephants, and he's quick to state that nothing compares to the anticipation and exhilaration of the first glimpse of dreamed-of ivory as you creep in amongst several big bulls with your heart in your throat.

CHANGING TIMES

By the early 1970s, the hunting situation in Kenya had deteriorated dramatically, with poachers running rampant throughout many of the best elephant areas. It was widely known that high-level government officials were enabling and personally benefitting from much of the poaching. With his future in Kenya looking more bleak, Coleman relocated. His wife, Joan, was a registered nurse,

which qualified the family for fast-track immigration to the States in 1973.

With the family settled in the U.S., Coleman continued doing safari work for a few more years to accommodate the wishes of his long roster of clients. He completed his last safari in Kenya in 1974 but continued conducting safaris in other countries, which included Sudan, Tanzania, Zambia, and Zimbabwe. Spending around eight months a year on safari, Coleman traveled back and forth between Africa and the U.S.. He worked in cooperation with other respected PHs, including Robin Hurt, Danny McCallum, Dave Ommanney, and Soren Lindstrom, to name a few.

In 1977, Kenya suddenly and without warning banned all safari hunting, shocking an established and proven

Advancing the .410 BORE

Tungsten shot is the variable that turns the diminutive .410 bore into a valid small game and turkey gun.

❯ L.P. BREZNY

Many brands within the industry have been getting into the TSS game recently. Why? Because the stuff works.

T he constructive development of the .410 bore arguably started sometime during the mid-1800s and was associated with the Indian Wars throughout the western United States. In those days, the U.S. Cavalry chased Indians around the land west of the Missouri River and, as mounted on horseback, carried Springfield trapdoor carbines chambered in .45-70 Government.

The author's Mossberg Model 500 .410 bore with Metro choke and suppressed extension.

During one of my many excursions digging deep into piles of old rifles in western states' off-the-grid gun shops, I located no fewer than three Springfield carbines that retained no rifling whatsoever. The barrels were not burned out but had been drilled clean of rifling to turn them into sub-gauge shotguns. One idea was to have a few of these smoothbore Springfields packed into the field to allow the horse troops some ability to hunt small game and upland birds, thereby living at least part-time off the land as they traveled across hundreds of square miles of prairie in search of the crafty Lakota and others. The second idea was a firearm capable of hitting fast-moving targets, such as the Plains Indians galloping on bare horseback.

The spread between a .45-70 rifle cartridge and a 2¾-inch .410 shotshell is not so different in that the former measured out to a case diameter of .499 inch, while the brass base of the latter's hull stands at .472 inch. We see this compatibility with handgun chambers shooting .45 Colt Long and .410 bore shotshells from the same wheel gun cylinder or even fixed single-shot chambers. With this information, it's not difficult to understand how the U.S. Army armorers converted the Springfield carbines into bird and small game guns. Thus, to my way of thinking, this could be regarded as one of the first uses directed at smallbore shotgunning. The .45-70 government, as a straightwall cartridge, retained ample room for powder, base wad, lead charge, and some card or wax crimp.

In terms of exact dates regarding the development of the .410 shotshell, I could only find that the first 2½-inch one came about in, or close to, 1857 by Eley Ammunition England. Much of the other information regarding the little gun's shotshell is sketchy and somewhat clouded by speculation. The .410 bore is a fairly young cartridge compared to other historically based rounds. However, it is evident that very little has been done to date, save for the 3-inch variant of the shotshell, to make it more serviceable for additional work beyond barn rat reduction or clay target shooting.

Not only have .410 loads advanced drastically as of late, but today's shotguns and combination rifle/shotgun systems have vastly improved. For purposes of this review, I've selected several .410-bore shotguns from my inventory here at Ballistics Research & Development, including the Tristar LR94 2½-inch .410, a single-shot built expressly for the new ammunition now available in the turkey load market as offered currently by Rossi, and the ever-lovin' old school Mossberg Model 500 pump-action field gun.

The other test guns were a Browning BPS, Chiappa Tri Barrel, and Rossi shoulder-stocked wheelgun, all using threaded choke tubes. Choke tubes are critical in developing high-performance .410-bore firearms because the lack of the ability to control pattern density and performance at different ranges limits the discussion, regardless of the type of ammunition or firearm employed in the field.

.410 PERFORMANCE LEVELS

During the past several years, while working with my associate at Shot Data Systems, we formalized detailed ballistics tables that show the running profile of different shot sizes in tungsten metal. (The data presented here are unique as generated by Shot Data Systems Minnesota and include the pre-computer-generated data produced by Ballistics Research & Development, Piedmont, South Dakota, from real-time downrange chronograph data.)

Shooting rounds across chronograph screens and then having those raw numbers normalized by Shotdata computer programs has taught us that .18-density tungsten (18 gram/cc), the second-heaviest metal on Earth, is a total game-changer in smoothbore ballistics. Its super-heavy and dense weight means extended energy at longer ranges. Also, less velocity is required to move this "super mass," and the damage inflicted by even a No. 10 "dust" pellet is incredibly effective on game.

As a general rule, being labeled "The rule of six hundred," a shotgun pellet requires at least 600 fps in terminal or at-target velocity to gain adequate penetration. Moving to pure tungsten shot, a force multiplier comes into play because the massive density associated with this heavy metal compounds the

The author with a .410-harvested gobbler using the Mossberg 500 with Metro extension.

TABLE 1. NO. 9 TUNGSTEN IRON SHOT

"TSS" No. 9
STANDARD METRO
PELLET WEIGHT (GR.): 1.200 EFFECTIVE SD: 0.0273
PELLET DIAMETER (IN.): 0.07924 Average

RANGE (YDS.)	VELOCITY (FPS)	ENERGY (FT-LBS)	TIME OF FLIGHT (SEC.)	DROP (INS.)	WIND DEF 45 MPH (IN/10 MPH)	LEAD (FT.)
0	1,220	4.0	0.0000	0.0	0.0	0
10	1,028	2.8	0.0279	0.1	0.2	1.8
20	889	2.1	0.0595	0.6	1.4	3.9
30	783	1.6	0.0957	1.5	3.4	6.3
40	701	1.3	0.1364	3.0	6.1	9.0
50	630	1.1	0.1817	5.2	9.9	12.0
60	567	0.9	0.2321	8.3	15.0	15.3

The above data are derived from a small sample and involve some assumptions. Chronograph data is difficult due to the nature of the ultra-fine shot.

TABLE 2.

Pattern Test: Wind 0, Temp. 60 F, Elevation 3,400 feet above sea level (tripod rest). Metro Gun TM extension choke/suppressor. Rossi Single Shot Tuffy, Handload .410 bore, 3-inch No. 9 tungsten shot 190 pellets. 12X12-inch rifle target.

DISTANCE (YDS.)	AREA COVERAGE (%)	HITS TOTAL	TURKEY HEAD/ NECK HITS TOTAL
Tuffy factory full choke. Mossberg factory-threaded custom choke by Rossi.			
30	97	184	39
35	88	167	33
40	71	135	30
Factory full choke. Rossi Tuffy:			
*30			
*Pattern 9 inches low	78	138	19
30	80	152	26
Factory full choke. Mossberg 500:			
30	77	146	34

A second test run using the 12X12-inch rifle target at reasonable ranges (30-40 yards) with 3-inch Federal .410 tungsten TSS 9/16-oz. loads, along with the Hevi-Shot 9/16 oz., produced the following results.

TABLE 3.

DISTANCE (YDS.)	AREA COVERAGE (%)	HITS TOTAL	TURKEY HEAD/ NECK HITS TOTAL
Factory full choke Rossi Tuffy test gun. Bushnell optics.			
40	68	—	34
30	58	—	40

(Tight patterns based on special-choked Metrogun TM, barrel extension, and full-choke Rossi factory-threaded systems.)

The Rossi Brat single-shot .410 bore with the hunting Metro extension.

net kinetic energy striking effect and, as such, damages vitals not even contacted directly by a pellet strike. As to where this rule came from? With untold numbers of waterfowl, turkeys, and related game put to rest with everything from light steel, ITX, Hevi-Shot, and tungsten blends by several manufacturers, plus hands-on test shooting, measuring and running live-fire test loads over chronograph screens produced detailed pictures of just what speed and performance are all about in the world of shotgun pellet lethality. Recorded data and effects kept coming up with the same 600 fps as the cutoff point in a pellet's lethal energy effect downrange.

At about 1,300 fps, a pellet made of lead and sized to No. 9 shot will run out of energy (600 fps) at 35 yards. The same pellet in tungsten shot? Based on our findings, the hard, heavy material is very workable to 55 yards. Even in velocity-reduced subsonic loads (980 fps muzzle), that same tungsten pellet will take out a heavy target (turkey) from 35 to 40 yards. Based on actual events during testing, I will show results obtained with the 2½- and 3-inch .410 bore that seal this theory and physically observed-based conclusion in stone.

If tungsten is so good, why not increase the shot size and gain the benefits of increased weight, size, and speed? In the small .410 hull, the volume-to-pellet count is always an issue, and moving up to even a No. 6 pellet can spell impending disaster. Pattern payload control is a requirement here, and testing shows that very fine shot in mass, even at low payload weight (1/2 oz., 180 pellets), tends to own the performance package every time with tungsten in the small-bore shotgun.

PATTERNING FOR PERFORMANCE

Regardless of how hard a given load hits downrange, the pattern delivered by a firearm must be considered. In the case of the .410, those newer screw-in chokes can be a real game-changer for effective performance on birds and small game. I have found that, in terms of a turkey gun, you should keep the constriction numbers as tight as possible with any given choke tube system offered by a manufacturer. This applies to .410-bore shotguns

Performance? Four-bird 2023 spring season. The load was ½ oz. No. 9 TSS. Backridge Ammunition load development.

used for waterfowl or even upland hunting. Yes, both areas are coming into their own due to the increased performance level of advanced shot types.

Shooting test handloads consisting of 8.5 grains of Lil'Gun and ½ oz. of .18 pure tungsten shot in a No. 9 pellet, or full-house 11 grains of Lil'Gun (previously listed in Table 1), the following results were observed on the two-dimensional pattern boards.

FIELD RESULTS

Regardless of the ballistics numbers on paper, the real-world results on game seal the deal regarding good, bad, or just flat-out ugly results. My research and hands-on testing using tungsten shot in sub-gauge shotguns started over four years ago in the .410 bore and 28-gauge shotguns.

A mom-and-pop garage operation sent me tungsten in a No. 7 shot size better than ten years ago, but at that time, few were in the tungsten club. While working with the product was interesting, it didn't go very far in development then. Today, however, tungsten shot has been recognized by many shotgunners as the magic material to get the most performance out of a shotgun shell.

TABLE 4. PELLET RECOVERY EFFECTS.

DISTANCE (YDS.)	RECOVERED PELLETS & NOTES
1. Gobbler 23 lbs., .410 bore, 3-in. No. 6 lead:	
33	Recovered pellets. Seven head-neck hits. Penetration skull/brain: Two pellets (the skull stopped them both). Neck upper body spine: Five pellet strikes. Kinetic energy displacement contributed to sustained kinetic energy shock. Penetration moderate.
2. Gobbler 24½ lbs., .410 bore, No. 9 tungsten (.18 density handloads):	
37	Recovered pellets 14. Three pellets in the wing butt; the shot moved across the breast, penetrating 1 inch and breaking the wing bone clean through. Two pellets embedded in the breastplate with no effect on vitals. Eight pellets in the neck, with penetration to the spinal core center, no pass-through (killing hits). Two pellets in the skull recovered across and through the brainpan (killing hits).
3. Gobbler 19¾ lbs. No. 9 tungsten (.18 density Backridge Ammunition manufactured on custom bases). Load: Metrogun Specs ½ oz., 3-inch hull, subsonic velocity: 850 fps	
28	Seven pellet hits. Three pellets with head penetration to the brainpan and five to the neck. Three pellets penetrated to the spinal cord (kill hits). Two pellets hit the neck, but no primary damage. Note: silent shot.
4. Gobbler 20½ lbs. No. 9 tungsten (.18 density Backridge Ammunition, custom subsonic 3-in. ½-oz. load.)	
27	Five recovered pellets. Four pellets for head penetration deep enough for kill hits. One pellet neck. One slicing hit (non-lethal).

From the spring and fall of 2018 through the spring of 2023, I harvested 11 turkeys with tungsten-based .410 loads, five of which were trophy gobblers. One bird was hit and required a second very fast backup shot from my Browning BPS pump-action .410. This season, the first bird lost to a seemingly direct head-neck hit, which resulted in no recovery.

Did the load fail? No, I had a shot that was marginal at best. In other words, my bad. After shooting the first Minnesota season record gobbler in 1978, I have recorded over 100 kills with four losses. This was the one loss I didn't expect, but it shows that even super-grade tungsten can't overcome it when the gunner fails in their task.

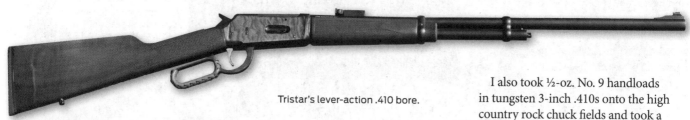

Tristar's lever-action .410 bore.

TABLE 5. NO. 7½ TSS SHOT

STANDARD METRO
PELLET WEIGHT (GR.): 2.010 EFFECTIVE SD: 0.0318
PELLET DIAMETER (IN.): 0.095 STANDARD SD: 0.0318

RANGE (YDS.)	VELOCITY (FPS)	ENERGY (FT-LBS)	TIME OF FLIGHT (SEC.)	DROP (INS.)	WIND DEF 45 MPH (IN/10 MPH)	LEAD (FT.)
0	1,220	6.6	0.0000	0.0	0.0	0.0
10	1,052	4.9	0.0275	0.1	0.2	1.8
20	925	3.8	0.0581	0.6	1.2	3.8
30	825	3.0	0.0927	1.5	2.9	6.1
40	745	2.5	0.1311	2.8	5.3	8.7
50	680	2.1	0.1734	4.8	8.3	11.4
60	621	1.7	0.2198	7.6	12.4	14.5

Tristar lever-action .410 as a chuck-control system. The TSS .410 loads can be a game-changer in the performance department.

I also took ½-oz. No. 9 handloads in tungsten 3-inch .410s onto the high country rock chuck fields and took a couple of chucks inside 40 yards with TriStar's new lever-action 94-410. These critters never knew what hit them from that full choke.

Here at Ballistics Research & Development, we don't just shoot birds and run standard butchering methods on recovered subjects. We want to learn from every harvested game animal in the field.

Be advised that tungsten, commonly called TSS, is not magic and can not do it all for the hunter, but it comes in a close second to perfection.

My ballistics data and field applications clearly show that even in the small .410-bore loads, when used inside 40 yards—the best range is 30 yards—TSS in a No. 8, No. 9, or even No. 10 shot is very effective. Shooting a double pair of gobblers early in the season this last spring, it was a case of 'shoot and pull over to bird number two with ease' at about 35 yards. The .410 bore is best applied in gunning work by turkey callers who know their business or are willing to work at calling. The range is still a major issue with small sub-loaded ammunition, even with TSS shot. While the high-impact shot will kill cleanly well beyond the indicated range limits, the patterns from small payloads will not maintain an effective game-harvesting profile.

For the most part, save for my own designed TSS No. 9 shot load provided to me as a factory load by Backridge Ammunition TN, I had an RCBS 12-gauge reloading press converted by West River Machine, Rapid City, South Dakota, to .410. Then I loaded 8.5 grains Lil'Gun and ½ oz. of No. 9 tungsten, or No. 10 shot when I could get my hands on it. Since almost all tungsten on this rockpile called Earth comes from China, and only two sources cover the market even at that, most of the raw shot is all just about alike regardless of what you pay for it. Consulting with several TSS sources in ballistics development,

I've learned a great deal about this product and have come to respect what it can do and how much it drives up the effectiveness of the .410-bore shotgun.

Need to cover rough country or long distances on foot? The .410 in a lightweight model can do the deal quite well if the hunter understands the little gun's limitations. Tungsten is just about 56 percent denser than pure, black lead shot. That means where lead dies downrange, tungsten is just getting started. Control the payload on a pattern board first, and the rest of the story will take care of itself.

Tungsten shot is so effective that we have started to design 2¾ 12-gauge loads at a single ounce in weight using No. 9 and No. 7½ shot. The results are dead birds at ranges as great as 63 yards. Why so light a payload? It cuts the cost of a high-priced game load almost in half and still gets positive results.

Finally, I have customers buying my Metro Systems who are professional animal control experts and, as such, are ballistics experts. Shooting No. 2 TSS has resulted in up to four geese hit by a shoot-through when coming in as a line or standing with heads and bodies aligned. It is not sporting at all, but it is required in that line of work (bang for the buck, as such). This says that .18-density TSS (pure) is off-the-charts good—it turns the .410 bore into a monster. **GD**

TABLE 6. NO. 8 TUNGSTEN SHOT
STANDARD METRO MINOR CHOKE VELOCITY INCREASE IGNORED
PELLET WEIGHT (GR.): 1.833 EFFECTIVE SD: 0.0316
PELLET DIAMETER (IN.): 0.091 STANDARD SD: 0.0316

RANGE (YDS.)	VELOCITY (FPS)	ENERGY (FT-LBS)	TIME OF FLIGHT (SEC.)	DROP (INS.)	WIND DEF 45 MPH (IN/10 MPH)	LEAD (FT.)
0	1,400	8.0	0.0000	0.0	0.0	0
10	1,183	5.7	0.0242	0.1	0.2	1.6
20	1,023	4.3	0.0517	0.5	1.2	3.4
30	902	3.3	0.0831	1.2	2.9	5.5
40	806	2.6	0.1185	2.3	5.3	7.8
50	730	2.2	0.1578	3.9	8.4	10.4
60	666	1.8	0.2010	6.2	12.2	13.3
70	608	1.5	0.2483	9.3	17.1	16.4

Note: Even with an excess velocity of 600+ fps and TSS energy, patterns must be considered when assessing performance profiles downrange. High-performance chokes and aftermarket payload control systems are seriously recommended.

Patterns with No. 7, ½ oz. pure .18 tungsten (dust) at 25 yards.

Rossi single-shot on a tripod rest for downrange accuracy. The TSS in ½ oz. shoots softball-sized patterns at 35 yards.

Examples of guns representing the author's favorite all-American gun companies are Magnum Research, Ruger, Savage, Henry, Colt, and Bond Arms.

Red, White & Blue-Collar Gunbuilders:
America's Thriving Firearms Manufacturers

KRISTIN ALBERTS

A t a time when it is becoming increasingly difficult to find American-made products, from vehicles to appliances to apparel, one of the most critical of all our freedoms finds its base alive and well on Old Glory's soil. This is the backbone of the American firearms industry.

WHAT WE'RE UP TO

Before any feathers ruffle unnecessarily, this is no knock on firearms made in other countries. In fact, some of my most prized possessions are a family heirloom Belgian-Browning A5 and High Power. Likewise, there's no disputing the longstanding quality of Italian shotguns nor pocketbook savings rolling out of Turkey.

Instead, the purpose here is to celebrate the craftsmanship still found just down the road from any one of us. So, it's especially uplifting to see gun manufacturers digging in their proverbial heels and keeping things—and jobs—domestic.

THE GUIDELINES

Let's set some ground rules. This list is far from comprehensive. To include the story and details on every U.S.-based gunbuilder would take up most of the pages in this book. We posed the question to over 30 companies of how many of their firearms are made on American

turf. Included herein are only those with which I've had positive personal experiences, but also directly confirmed the source of parts and percentage of the firearms produced here.

Some are loud and proud about being 100% American-made, from the most minuscule screws to walnut and finishes. Several are based here and split production domestically and internationally, while others snag specific components from distant locales. What follows is a mix of budget brands, premium customs, and young start-ups alongside those celebrating a hundred years in business. Cue the patriotic music.

BIGHORN ARMORY

Few firearms companies can claim they have no direct competition, but that's a true statement for Bighorn Armory (BHA). The Cody, Wyoming-based operation has created a niche market around unique, big-bore firearms. Known primarily for its hulky lever guns, Bighorn

caters to hunters and shooters who adore large holes in their muzzles—and who recognize that firing those high-pressure rounds requires firearms constructed to endure. That quality is never in question when buying Bighorn.

The flagship Model 89 blends features from John Browning's Models 1886 and 1892 but adds a twist of modern metallurgy to overbuild—and yes, that's the term BHA Founder and President Greg Buchel uses—a lever-action that can handily and safely launch rounds like the .500 S&W and .460 S&W.

It's not all lever guns, either. On quiet Blackburn Street, Bighorn also touts premium modern sporting rifles in unexpected chamberings. Pulling the trigger on the company's AR-500 semi-automatic .500 Automax—the most powerful AR in the world—is empowering, surprisingly manageable, and just like the Model 89, capable of harvesting any game on the planet. If that's not enough, there's even a pistol variant for those bent on harness-

The Bighorn Armory Black Thunder.

ing T-Rex-bagging power in the hand.

Buchel never missed a beat when asked what percentage of BHA firearms and parts are made in the States. "All of it. Every last bit. The majority is done in-house, and the few processes we outsource are all done in the U.S."

BOND ARMS

American innovation is the name of the game at Bond Arms, the largest manufacturer of derringers in the firearms industry. The Granbury, TX, operation revered for its interchangeable-barreled derringers is making major waves with recent additions to its lineup. It catalogs 40 model variants of derringers, a lever gun with AR tendencies, a beastly single-barrel pocket piece, and an ultra-compact 9mm pistol.

Calibers range from .22 LR to .45-70. Yes, you read that correctly—.45-70. Bond's single-barrel, break-action Cyclops in .45-70 Government—and .44 Mag for the fainter of heart—is a ball of fire. To be fair, I've fired one extensively and found it remarkably controllable with lighter loads. I mean, who doesn't want to own a palm-sized pocket gun firing a 150-plus-year-old rifle round? Call me crazy, but here we are. Plus, the engraved Cyclops unibrow face engraved on the muzzle adds a playful edge to a serious weapon.

Bond Arms is unveiling a tactical lever-action rifle called the LVRB. It uses a proprietary and patented lever-action in conjunction with a magazine-fed frame matched with an AR-style upper. This concept allows users to have a high-capacity rifle in areas where semi-automatic use and ownership are prohibited. Further, the lever mechanism strips full-size rifle cartridges from the magazine, not just shorter pistol ammunition. This feature gives the LVRB a significant advantage over other tactical lever-actions. Current chamberings include .223 Wylde, .300 Blackout, .450 Bushmaster, and .350 Legend.

All that said, let's not overshadow the stainless steel, break-action, stacked-barrel derringers that drove the gunmaker to fame. Owner Gordon Bond, who took the reins from his brother Greg, eschews the term "derringer," preferring instead

The Bond Arms duo.

The Henry Long Ranger Deluxe Engraved .308.

a double-barreled handgun. No matter the terminology or barrel count, Bond Arms is all business. With this being the 2025 edition of *Gun Digest*, let's wish Bond Arms—always "Made in Texas by Texans"—a happy 30th anniversary.

Connecticut Shotgun Manufacturing Company

Some firearms exude an aura of pure class; others rough-and-tumble. Connecticut Shotgun (CSMC) handily merges those divergent categories. Its forte is an expanding contingent of finely crafted double shotguns under the company name; however, they grow alongside wild, high-capacity tactical arms bearing the Standard Manufacturing mark. The latter includes the DP-12 double-barreled pump shotgun, Jackhammer drum-fired rimfire pistol, a series of 1911s, a folding Switch-Gun revolver, and a S333 Thunderstruck double-barreled revolver.

CSMC operates a 140,000-square-foot building in New Britain, CT, where it manufactures high-grade firearms. Gunsmithing Manager Rich Wilson says, "It's an all-encompassing facility where we manufacture everything ourselves—the stock, springs, wood finish, hardening, barrel making—we do it all here in one building, so it's 100%."

Connecticut Shotgun Manufacturing Company/Galazan's was started in 1975 by President Antony Galazan, the namesake of many firearms. The most well-known and popular seller for CSMC, though, is the company's A-10, an exquisite O/U sidelock with exhibition-grade wood, deep relief engraving, and all desirable accoutrements for serious uplanders and discerning clay busters.

"What sets us apart is we're dedicated to gunmaking and do everything in one place … everything!" Wilson says. "I don't know another company that does this." CSMC designs, engineers, fabricates and holds a portfolio of patents. At the time of this writing, the company was preparing to launch a Standard Mfg. Model 2311 pistol chambered in 9mm that accepts Glock magazines and a full host of small-frame Galazan double shotguns—boxlock and sidelock—dedicated to 28- and .410 bores.

HENRY REPEATING ARMS

Name a gun company, any gun company, that comes to mind with the tagline "Made in America or Not Made at All." It's Henry Repeating Arms. From American Walnut to American steel, fit and finishes, it's all from and done in the States.

Founder & CEO Anthony Imperato and current President Andy Wickstrom have driven—in some cases quite literally—the cowboy action brand to fame. Known primarily for lever-actions from high polish to austere, they've even branched into racing. If there's a blue-collar, heart-on-the-sleeve market, Henry has been there. From backing race cars at your local dirt or Nascar track to multi-million-dollar charitable donations, alongside support for veterans, Henry has made its name synonymous with the everyday American hero.

There are rimfires and centerfires, Golden Boys and Silver, youth models, single-shots, U.S. Survival rifles, a 9mm Homesteader semi-auto carbine, and even a burgeoning family of single-action revolvers. That's all in addition to the extensive catalog of lever-driven tribute editions honoring what it considers America's finest, including law enforcement, firefighters, EMS, truckers, farmers, military, Eagle Scouts, fathers,

and mothers.

Headquarters and manufacturing facilities remain in New Jersey, though most production moved to Wisconsin, with facilities humming in Rice Lake and Ladysmith. I've stood eye to eye with Cape buffalo in Africa with nary but a Henry All-Weather .45-70 lever gun between us, so it's safe to say I trust the quality. There's American pride from the coasts to the cheese curd heartland.

HERITAGE MANUFACTURING CO.

Looking broadly at American firearms companies means not necessarily associating American-made with having to pay more. No company exemplifies that value-forward ethic more than Heritage. Value hits first and foremost, making the brand instantly accessible to every buyer.

Though known predominantly for single-action rimfire wheelguns, many with interchangeable cylinders from .22 LR to .22 WMR, Heritage has also been expanding into other markets. These

The Heritage Rancher and Rough Rider Buntline.

Magnum Research's Desert Eagle tiger stripe models.

include Rancher revolving carbines, Settler lever-actions, and even a Badlander double-barreled coach scattergun, each named to pay homage to the spirit of the American West. Every last one of Heritage's rimfire revolvers is sourced, manufactured, and assembled in the United States—Bainbridge, GA, to be exact—and the same holds for its other firearms.

Heritage is the market's largest seller of rimfire single-action revolvers, occupying a niche that immediately appeals to the nostalgia of the wild frontier and the desire for affordable training tools and backyard plinkers. After all, who among us hasn't fond recollections of knocking pop cans from a fencepost? If companies like Heritage keep the next generation creating those same kinds of good, honest outdoor memories, there's ample hope for our future.

KAHR ARMS

In the scope of American history, Kahr Arms is a relative youngster. Founded in 1995 by CEO Justin Moon, Kahr started with the K9 semi-automatic pistol and continues generating a full contingent of concealable duty-minded pistols. The company's CCWs include models in value and premium categories, creating a market accessible to various price points and consumer feature demands.

Per the company's website, "all Kahr Arms products are proudly made in the USA." Not only Kahr but also affiliate brand Auto Ordnance—of Tommy Gun gangster fame—operate out of Greeley, PA. That Kahr name evolved into the Kahr Firearms Group, formed in 2012 after the Auto Ordnance acquisition of 1999, followed by Magnum Research in 2010, all strong U.S. brands.

Location is not taken lightly by the Kahr brass. "The decision to move manufacturing away from states that infringe on our rights was a direct statement of our resolve," Moon says. "Kahr's leadership has become active in political efforts to preserve the Second Amendment and all the fundamental rights guaranteed by the Constitution. American shooters can be confident that they have a partner in the Kahr Firearms Group who will stand firm for freedom and the American way of life. This is our history, and we are proud to be a part of America's history."

MAGNUM RESEARCH, INC.

Alphabetical order be darned. Here's Magnum Research, Inc. (MRI), the wild and wooly stepchild of the Kahr group. The current Magnum Research name holds such a prominent place in American consciousness, from film to field, that it gets some real estate here. Jim Skildum and John Risdall founded MRI in 1979, well before the Kahr Group buyout in 2010.

The allure is right there in the name. Magnum chamberings done in uniquely engineered ways. A .45-70 or similarly seriously-chambered, long-barreled hunting revolver? Check. Wicked big semi-automatic pistols housing rounds like .50 Action Express? Check. That's the BFR—Biggest Finest, Revolver, and the storied Desert Eagle. Even if you haven't hoisted the hulkish Desert Eagle gas-operated, rotating-bolt pistol, surely you've seen its cameo on the silver screen in flicks such as "Boondock Saints," "Goldmember," "Robocop," or "The Matrix." Call me a crow if you must, but the bling and flash of finish options like the tiger-stripe Desert Eagles attract me. Yes, this is the same Desert Eagle that was

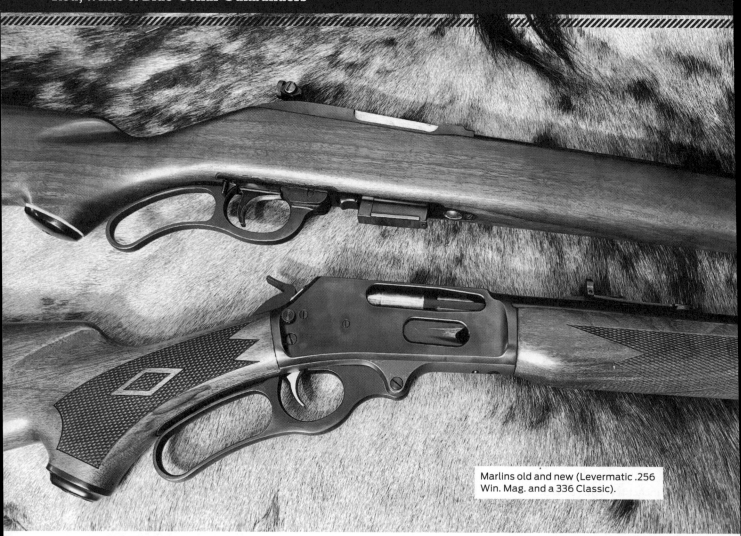

Marlins old and new (Levermatic .256 Win. Mag. and a 336 Classic).

once built in Israel. Still, since 2009, those flashy pop culture icons have been sharing production space with the company's other finery in .

Though overshadowed, the "others" deserve more than passing mention, including a burgeoning line of rimfire and centerfire rifles. The Magnum Lite and Switchbolt occupy rimfire territory, while Mountain Eagle bolt-actions claim space in lightweight and target categories. All these gems—save the MRI 1911 manufactured by BUL in Israel—emerge from the Pillager, MN, HQ.

MARLIN

Like a phoenix rising from the ashes—not ironically Ruger's longtime logo—so blazes forward a recharged Marlin brand under Sturm, Ruger, and Co. ownership. Since I was a youngster watching westerns and my first working of a well-loved original Marlin Model 39, I've admired the brand that has been around since 1870. That horse-and-rider brand has

seen the country through some tumultuous times, born to a country recovering from the Civil War. Still, one thing has remained constant—the production of trusted lever-actions, among other sidelight models.

Just as the Model 39 and subsequent 39A set the standard for American-made rimfires, so the 336 lever gun in .30-30 Win. or .35 Rem. claimed more whitetails than most other rifles combined. From innovations like the solid-top side eject to microgroove rifling to those short-throw Levermatics seemingly run with a flip of the fingers, Marlin always seemed to be galloping forward—until it wasn't.

When the 2020 bankruptcy sale broke, which also rolled names such as Remington, Barnes, Bushmaster, and Dakota Arms, we all wondered how the country could lose such a storied icon. Yet, since Ruger grabbed the reins, Marlin is back on track and better than ever in Mayodan, NC. First came the re-introduced Model 1895 big bore, followed quickly by

the 1894 and 336 Classic. What will nip their heels is up in the air when this went to print, but 'twere we gamblers casting dice, the odds are high for a rimfire return. If we get a gun even half as good as those early 39s, it'll be a keeper. Until then, all is right in the American firearms world once again, with Marlin back in business.

MONTANA RIFLE COMPANY

The high-end rifle market in America is a well-fed machine, so to stand out from the competition takes something special. That's the sweet spot Montana Rifle tickles. A quick chat with thrice-retired industry professional and former Montana CEO Ron Petty reveals the passion, innovation, and hunters' heart that drives the brand created in Kalispell but now located in Memphis, MI, and owned by Grace Engineering.

The Montana bolt-action rifle grabs the strongest features of two revered designs in the Mauser 98 and early Winchester

Montana Rifle Company.

Model 70—and then manages to improve on them. It's only recently that I've had the pleasure—and believe me, it's a pleasure—to spend time with the latest Junction model, with its exceptional walnut dress, reliable feeding system, and ½ MOA guarantee. All the desirables are checked—adaptive controlled round feed, billet-machined solid stainless receiver, adjustable trigger, hand-lapped button-rifled barrels, and the list rolls on.

Montana Rifle does one thing—bolt-action rifles—and it does it well. All critical parts are blueprinted and built in-house, and the entire firearm is made in America, except walnut stocks sourced from Italian gun furniture powerhouse

Minelli. The degree of precision displayed in the paired operations at Grace and Montana Rifle reflects the quality of workmanship still found in the good old US of A.

MOSSBERG

O.F. Mossberg & Sons, in operation since 1919, holds the title of oldest family-owned firearms manufacturer in the United States. To be clear, not all Mossberg firearms are all-American these days, but core products are. To clarify, those wearing the Mossberg name are built in the USA, with most parts either crafted or sourced domestically. Firearms under the Mossberg International brand

are made to company specs by international partners, then imported and warranted by Mossberg.

A recent example came on a spring Gould's Turkey hunt in Sonora, Mexico. Our hunting party of four shared a Mossberg SA-28 Tactical Turkey autoloader, built in Turkey and a Mossberg 940 Pro Turkey 12-gauge made in North Haven, CT. Both repeaters functioned flawlessly, looked the part in full camo dress, and bagged gobblers.

In addition to Connecticut, the company also maintains a manufacturing facility in Eagle Pass, TX. The name of the Mossberg game is, per Director of Media Relations Linda Powell, "to provide con-

The author with her Sonora Mexico Goulds Turkey with Outfitter Ted Jaycox and the Mossberg 940 Pro Turkey 12-gauge.

sumers with the highest quality firearms at an affordable price so everyone can enjoy our hunting and shooting sports traditions." And that's where Mossberg has thrived.

Customers find a high cost-benefit ratio when they spend their hard-earned cash. Probabilities are high that you have—or know someone who does—an old Model 500 pump that's still going strong. Still not sold on the gold-and-blue brand? Says Powell, "Mossberg has supplied all five branches of the U.S. military, law enforcement agencies, and militaries worldwide with our field-proven 500/590/590A1 pump-action shotguns." The pairing of pride in its craft and family-driven ownership shines through, no matter the price point.

NORTH AMERICAN ARMS

The saying that good things come in small packages might just as well have been written about North American Arms (NAA). In business for over 30 years, the company's itsy-bitsy firearms—revolvers in most cases—may be described as mini, adorable, or micro, but they're fully functional short guns built for the long haul. Most are rimfires, from .22 Shorts to Mags, though NAA also offers a couple of stainless steel semi-auto pocket pistols in .32 and .380 ACP.

Several curios, customs, and collectibles include the coolest belt buckle in all the land and limited-run cased collector sets. NAA's role in the market may primarily be seen as a novelty, but it's clearly setting a standard of "being the ultimate in concealability" with a target market of those who require a most discreet companion.

Operations are located in Provo—Utah's most-eldest city and home to Brigham Young University. All NAA firearms are assembled in the United States, but we never received a clear answer on the source of every last part. Of particular note, NAA has been, since 2022, an employee-owned company.

NOSLER

Ask most shooters what they love about Nosler; the most common answer will center around the outfit's bullets or am-

munition lines. Born of John Nosler's 1948 bullet performance displeasure on a moose hunt, the elder Nosler set out to create a better bullet. The Nosler Company was born around Partition projectiles.

Yet, the now nearly 80-year-old Oregon company that today calls Bend home puts a heavier emphasis on its firearms—and related proprietary chamberings—with each passing year. From the single-shot Model 48 Handgun to the more traditional Model 48 bolt-actions, Nosler continues to set itself apart as a premium American manufacturer. Recent product announcements include serious ultralight and specialty rifles, with the Model 21 alongside the fully customizable Carbon Chassis Hunter.

The company clearly states that all rifles are hand-assembled at its plants in Oregon "using the finest components," but details on the source of all parts are still unclear. Regardless of the answer, I've had only positive experiences with Nosler's firearms. It was quite a painful endeavor to part ways with a test-model handgun that shot ½ MOA all day.

What could be more American than a North American Arms belt buckle?

Firearm production has spread to Redmond, OR, and though the footprint expands, the Nosler family remains at the wheel. Nosler's name is associated with quality, whether bullets, reloading manuals, ammunition, or firearms.

PARKWEST ARMS

In the town best known for its wild annual motorcycle rally, one of the coun-

try's most distinguished custom firearms manufacturers quietly turns out some gems. The address is Industry Road, the town of Sturgis, SD. Even if you don't yet know the name Parkwest Arms, President/CEO Steve Rabackoff is confident it's one you won't forget once you handle its firearms. Half work of art, half functional workhorse, each rifle is 100% built and assembled in Sturgis, and every component is produced in the USA.

Nestled in the heart of the Black Hills, Parkwest occupies what was once the revered Dakota Arms. My storied Dakota Model 76, once owned by the Gunny himself, R. Lee Ermey, remains a purposeful masterpiece. I may have added a few dings and tangible memories to the .416 Rigby, but that rifle has a pretty firm hold on the category of the most beautiful and badass gun I own. Thus, it was with great sadness that I watched Remington acquire, dismantle, and subsequently lose what was once an American icon in South Dakota.

While I've yet to hunt with a Parkwest rifle, the specimens I've handled bear striking resemblance in form and quality to their predecessors. Moreover, the Parkwest team has even expanded into tactical, single-shot, and an intriguing rimfire rifle. Dakota, and now Parkwest, pieces may be an investment, but regret is never one of the outcomes for those making the commitment.

REMARMS/REMINGTON

The "new" Remington—or technically RemArms—is shrouded in mystery. I've yet to handle or fire the flagship Model 700 Alpha 1, born of the renowned American darling Model 700 bolt-actions. I do adore my old-school 700 BDL

The Parkwest Arms 76 Dark Continent.

hunting rifle and the tales that haggard .30-'06 could tell. When the now-historical 2020 bankruptcy separated the namesake's holding brands, once-powerhouse Remington disappeared from view, but almost every brand has come back better than ever.

Remington Firearms, now under Roundhill Group ownership, is not to be confused with Remington, the ammunition brand under a distinctly different proprietorship. The firearms maker maintains its corporate office and main manufacturing facility in LaGrange, GA, where, per verification with the company, "the majority of components are made in the USA, with all firearm models built and assembled here." At the time of this writing, current models include the 700, 870, 1100, V3, and 783, with additional models in the works. No matter the hands on the wheel, the country wouldn't seem complete without Big Green.

RUGER

When I line up my great-grandfather's Ruger Standard pistol, dating to 1950, alongside my newish small game master Mark IV Hunter, I can't help but marvel at how much Ruger has grown while at once remaining the same. Though features and finishes innovate, the familiar feel and reliability remain constant.

Having celebrated 75 years of American firearms manufacturing in 2024, Sturm, Ruger, and Co. is barreling forward with a full head of steam into the next three-quarter century. Continued new and updated product announcements flow with each turn of the calendar, with recent additions including second-generation American bolt-action hunting rifles, a freshened Mini-14 stainless folder, CCW handguns galore, and even a .22 Hornet Super Redhawk, signaling the company's continued march forward whilst maintaining a firm foothold in the past.

When asked how many of its firearms parts are sourced here and assembled in the states, the one-word answer was "all." Ruger's operations have now spread to three domestic locations: Newport, NH; Prescott, AZ; and Mayodan, NC. The final location shares space with Ruger's rapidly expanding Marlin production.

SAVAGE ARMS

Ask me about my favorite firearms, and the Savage 99 lever-action, with its hammerless design, early internal rotary magazine, brass round counter, and oh-so-comfortable-to-carry shapely rounded receiver, ranks high among them. Though long out of production and unlikely to return—no matter how

much I plead—that degree of innovation and quality reflects what has kept Savage Arms in production for more than 125 years. Those traditional numbers have given way to modernized demands, with Savage's bolt-action 110 and budget-priced Axis series leading sales.

Astute firearms historians will recall the 1907 United States Army Trials to select a service pistol. Though Mr. Browning's M1911 design was crowned, Savage's own .45-caliber contender held its own, though the downsized Savage Model 1907 in .32-caliber is better known with collectors today. The sidearm circle of life came full circle when Savage introduced its own Model 1911 in 2022.

Savage manufactures its centerfire firearms—handguns, shotguns, and rifles—at company headquarters in Westfield, MA, though it operates a significant rimfire facility in Lakefield, Ontario, while simultaneously importing from abroad under its Stevens division. The grandiose variety of models, variants, price points, and shooting styles is impressive. From the affordable Axis to more recent innovations in Impulse straight pulls, Stance pistols, Renegauge shotguns, and the latest 110 Ultralite Elite, Savage holds a steady finger on the pulse of today's workaday shooters, hunters, and competitors.

The new RemArms Alpha 1 rifle.

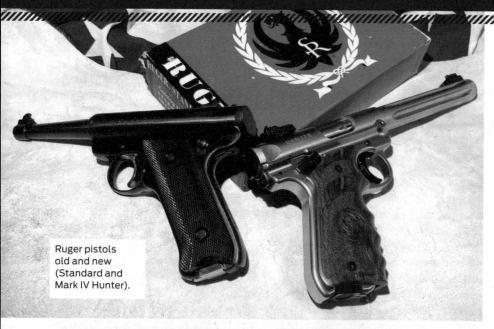

Ruger pistols old and new (Standard and Mark IV Hunter).

Savage old and new (110 Predator and Model 99).

VOLQUARTSEN

From its headquarters in Carroll, IA, a city of 10,000 along the Middle Raccoon River, the Volquartsen team turns out precision products. They're quick to point out that everything is 100% American-made. Not only are the firearms assembled from start to finish in Carroll, but all parts are CNC-machined or wire-EDM cut at the location.

Believe it or not, the brand has been around for 50 years, with the second generation now leading after their father started it all in the basement of a rental house. The family-oriented American dream sets the tone for excellence and core values. From an initial broader focus in the gun world, 'tis ultra-accurate rimfires that now define the company. After spending quality time with Volquartsen's Black Mamba pistol, customized around a Ruger Mk IV 22/45 frame, I'm hooked. Despite its 6-inch compensated barrel, the piece weighs less than 2 pounds, packs an exceptional trigger, and shoots lights out. The same can be said for most every rifle and pistol bearing Volquartsen's name.

"While every manufacturer has access to the same machines and finishes, it's truly our people behind the machines that set us apart," says Marketing Director Chad Wittrock. "Our team's attention to detail requires individual commitment not to take shortcuts. Would it be easier to be content with 'if it's not broke, don't fix it?' It absolutely would be! That way of thinking isn't who we are, though."

WEATHERBY

Following a family lineage in gunmaking has seldom been simpler than it is with Weatherby. From founder Roy to son Ed to current leader and grandson Adam, the Weatherby name has been syn-

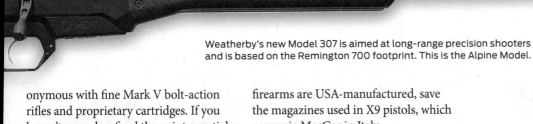

Weatherby's new Model 307 is aimed at long-range precision shooters and is based on the Remington 700 footprint. This is the Alpine Model.

Weatherby Headquarters in Sheridan, Wyoming.

onymous with fine Mark V bolt-action rifles and proprietary cartridges. If you haven't owned or fired the quintessential .300 Weatherby or founder-favorite .257 Weatherby Mark V rifle, have you fully lived an American life?

For decades, the company called South Gate, CA, home, but Second Amendment enthusiasts toasted the 2018 decision to pack up and relocate to gun-friendly Sheridan, WY. While we'd like to report that more of the company's firearms were made in the states, the Vanguard rifle and all current shotguns are of international manufacture. However, the crux remains. That Mark V that started it all, with its rock-solid nine-locking lug action, continues to be crafted with American pride. There's even a fledgling Model 307 modernized bolt gun, its name paying homage to the Sheridan area code, crafted with that Wyoming rollmark on the receiver.

WILSON COMBAT

I freely admit to knowing little about Bill Wilson and his Wilson Combat brand—until recently speaking with him and reading his autobiography. The man is a modern American firearms legend, and under his guidance, Wilson Combat was founded in 1977 and has since evolved into one of the country's dynamos. Wilson is proud to report that all components of his

firearms are USA-manufactured, save the magazines used in X9 pistols, which come via MecGar in Italy.

What started as a one-man band customizing 1911s has exploded into multiple modern manufacturing plants that employ over 200 Americans and a handful of brands. According to Wilson, each company's niche is high-end products. Wilson recently acquired New Ultralight Arms (NULA), Melvin Forbes's brainchild, which is now crafted in-house at Wilson Combat, sharing square footage in Berryville, AR.

But it's not just Wilson and NULA. Lehigh Defense and Chip McCormick Custom, ammunition and magazine/accessory makers, respectively, fall under Wilson's umbrella. Both operate in Texas, the former in Clarksville and the latter in Bogata.

A BRIGHT FUTURE

For more than 200 years, Americans have been crafting quality firearms. Many have come and gone over those decades, and many more have been omitted here due to space constraints alone. As gun enthusiasts and freedom lovers, we should take joy in knowing American arms manufacturers are standing their ground with the talent, ingenuity, craftsmanship, and confidence to lead us into the next century. **GD**

These are original U.S. Army 1911 and Savage 1907 pistols.

The NULA Model 20 is now manufactured by Wilson Combat.

70 Years of Buck Fever

Mr. Whitetail Shares His Many Deer Rifles Throughout the Years

❯LARRY WEISHUHN

"**R**emember, aim right behind the shoulder and be sure it's a buck with at least two points on one side," said Dad, turning to walk toward his stand. Before disappearing, he turned and said, "Stay awake!" He knew I was not about to go to sleep. It was his way of saying, "Pay attention to all things going on around you." I nodded, tightly clutched a single .22 Long Rifle hollowpoint cartridge in my right hand and my maternal grandfather's single-shot Remington Model 33 in my left. The Model 33 was the first bolt-action rimfire rifle Remington, introduced in 1932. I used that rifle to shoot my first squirrel the previous spring. "I'll let you sit in a deer stand by yourself after you show me you can safely handle a rifle and you shoot your first squirrel," was my dad's response when I asked him about hunting deer on my own, rather than sitting in the same tree as him. I shot that first squirrel just before turning six.

An awesome Texas Hill Country deer taken on the FTW Ranch with a Ruger Guide Gun in .375 Ruger, the round Weishuhn proclaims would be his choice if he could only have one with which to hunt the world.

The author's first deer guns were chambered in .22 Long Rifle, 12-gauge 00 Buck, .30-30 Winchester, and .257 Roberts.

The author's father, Lester Weishuhn, hunted with a Winchester Model 94 .30-30, initially shooting open sights but adding a Weaver K4 later.

As soon as Dad walked out of sight, I loaded the .22 Long Rifle hollowpoint in the chamber; should a deer appear, I would pull back the cocking knurl to cock the rifle, but not before!

Deer were few and far between in our rural area just north of the Colorado River and Texas Gulf Coast in the 1950s. It was something to brag about if you saw a deer during those years. Should a hunter be so fortunate as to take a buck, he or she would be a local hero. Yes, women hunted then, at least in our part of Texas!

For three years, I hunted with that Remington Model 33; .22 rimfires were legal. Hunting at every opportunity behind our rural home for those three years, I saw six deer, which were all does. Not so secretly, I longed for and dreamed of hunting with a real deer rifle, a Winchester Model 94 .30-30 Winchester, like those carried by my dad and my uncle Herbert Aschenbeck. By then, I had started reading *Outdoor Life*, *Field & Stream* and *Sports Afield*, as well as an occasional issue of *American Rifleman*. One of my uncles passed his issues to me. I treasured them! In their pages, Jack O'Connor touted the accuracy of bolt-action rifles chambered for such rounds as .270 Winchester and .30-'06 Springfield. Still, in our rural community, most hunted with either a Model 94 .30-30, Savage Model 99, or 12-gauge shotguns.

I drooled over many rifles, particularly the bolt-actions, and dreamed of taking my first whitetail deer. I tried to convince Dad to buy me a Winchester Model 54 or Model 70 .270 Winchester so I could be like my hero, Jack O'Connor, but the money was tight.

Then came the 1961 hunting season. Screw-worm flies, which ate live flesh at the larval stage, significantly suppressing deer herds, were finally being controlled. With that pestilence under control, deer populations across Texas increased. For the first time ever, bucks with spike antlers were legal.

For years, I had been saving to buy my own deer rifle. Unfortunately, as the hunting season approached, I was still shy of affording a rifle. My dad suggested I use Grandpa Aschenbeck's Bridge Gun Company single-shot 12-gauge, loaded with 00 Buck, which he had called "The Roar." He knew any shot would be close. On opening day morning, I took my first whitetail, a spike buck, the taking of which I have told and written about many times. (For the complete story, read the "My First Buck" chapter in one of my latest books, *Deer Addictions*.) After eight years of hunting at every opportunity, I finally became a successful deer hunter.

Bridge Gun Company was the trademark used by Shapleigh Hardware in St. Louis, Missouri. Its guns were made by Crescent Fire Arms Company, founded in 1888. Savage Arms eventually bought the company. The guns were sold through Sears, Montgomery Ward and Western Auto. I am uncertain where or how my granddad acquired the shotgun.

After years of saving, I finally had enough money to buy a Savage Model 340 bolt-action .30-30 Win. topped with a Weaver K4 scope. I was thrilled to finally have my own "real deer rifle." With it, I shot several whitetails using Remington 170-grain Core-Lokt ammunition. It continued to help provide venison for my wife, Mary Anne, and me during our early years. We got married a year out of high school. Her Dad, E.V. Potter, spent most of his adult life in law enforcement. He loved to hunt and owned several guns, including, among others, a Winchester Model 88 lever-action in .243 Winchester, as well as numerous handguns, including a .22 LR Harrington & Richardson revolver and a Remington Model 1911 .45 ACP, both of which I hunted with, the latter for deer.

From early on, I wanted to experience as many hunting rifles and handguns as possible, even muzzleloaders. Little did I realize that just out of college in 1970, I was setting the stage for a lifetime of hunting with a lot of different guns.

Fresh out of Texas A&M University and working with the Texas Parks & Wildlife Department and Texas A&M Department of Veterinary Pathology's Wildlife Disease Project, I went on my first mule deer hunt. Doubting my .30-30 Win. was sufficient for mule deer, I talked my brother Glenn into letting me use his Savage Model 99 lever-action chambered in .300 Savage. I took my first mule deer high on a ridge in western Texas with

Weishuhn's first deer rifles (left to right) included a Remington Model 33 single-shot .22, a Savage Model 340 in .30-30 topped with a Weaver K4 scope, and a Remington Model 722 (customized by him) chambered in .257 Roberts with a Weaver K4 scope.

that rifle, then grudgingly returned it to my brother.

A few months later, I bought a used Remington Model 722 in .257 Roberts, on which I mounted a K4 Weaver scope. Working for the Wildlife Disease Project, part of my job was collecting animals for research purposes. Once I had that rifle, I ordered a semi-inletted Claro Walnut stock from Herter's and re-stocked it. After trying several handloads, I settled on

87-grain bullets. With that combination, I shot many, many whitetails.

In time, I added a couple of Remington Model 700s, both in .270 Winchester. In these, I used a variety of 130-grain bullets, commercial and handloads. Shortly after Ruger introduced its Model 77, I added a 7x57 Mauser and a .30-'06, which wore Leupold 3-9x variables.

During those years, I did a whole lot of "collecting." I used not only my own rifles

Early on, Larry became enamored with handgun hunting. He shows a respectable 8-point taken with a T/C Contender chambered in .309 JDJ.

For several years, the author hunted a considerable amount with various handguns, including this T/C Encore chambered in .30-'06, which he not only used on deer but elk, moose, caribou, pronghorn, and African plains game.

hunting publications shortly out of college, but most were penned under various "pseudonyms" after I sold my first national article and cover photo in 1970. During my years with the Texas Parks & Wildlife Department, the agency frowned on writing for any publication other than the Department's. That eventually led to me leaving State employment and starting my own wildlife management consultant company, which created more writing, television, and public relations opportunities.

When I started hunting in the early 1950s, guns were blued steel with walnut stocks. To me, guns were, then and continue to be, hunting tools, but they are also objects of beauty. I loved "finely figured" wood stocks back then. I still do! "Plastic," aka synthetic, and "fancy plywood," aka laminated stocks, had not yet arrived on the scene. Shooting long-range meant taking pokes out to 300 yards. Hunting with a "modern sporting rifle" equated to using a round propelled by smokeless rather than blackpowder.

THEN THINGS STARTED CHANGING.
In the early 1970s, thanks to the movie *Jeremiah Johnson,* there was renewed interest in muzzleloading rifles. Like others, I was swept up in the muzzleloader craze and soon owned .50-caliber Hawken rifles by T/C and CVA. At about the same time, Clint Eastwood introduced viewers to "the world's most powerful handgun," the .44 Magnum, created by Elmer Keith and Smith & Wesson several years before. Dirty Harry popularized the cartridge and handguns. I had started seriously shooting and hunting with Ruger Blackhawk revolvers a few years earlier, initially a .357 Magnum.

The modern muzzleloader era got a huge shot in the arm in 1985 when my dear friend, the late Tony Knight, created and introduced his MK-85 .50-caliber in-line muzzleloader. This led to the opening of muzzleloader seasons in just about every state. I shot numerous muzzleloaders by Knight and Thompson/Center Arms during those years. Most were stocked in beautiful wood initially, but laminated wood and synthetic stocks soon replaced them. We also started using blackpowder substitutes such as

but many others. Those included rifles chambered in nearly everything from .222 Remington to .45-70 Government, and handguns chambered in .357 Magnum, .44 Magnum, .45 Colt and others.

During those years, I recorded each shot taken at game, whether I was collecting or hunting. I kept records of caliber and round, bullet and load, rifle or handgun, sights, distance to the target, wind conditions and temperature, the game's body position when shot, reaction to the shot and distance traveled after the shot. I completed necropsies on all animals taken to determine the bullet's terminal performance, evaluating shot placement and tissue damage. Unfortunately, that information was lost during one of our moves a few years ago.

I started writing for shooting and

My Perfect Deer Rifle

Larry started hunting deer with a Remington Model 33 .22 Long Rifle, here compared to the Mossberg Patriot Predator in 7mm PRC.

O ver my past 70 years of hunting deer, there have been several lever, bolt, and single-shot rifles, which I deemed ideal chambered in .30-30 Winchester, .257 Roberts, 7x57, .270 Winchester, .280 Remington, .30-'06, or .300 Win. Mag. among others. Then, several years ago, Ruger asked me to design my "dream whitetail" rifle. I suggested a 7x57 Mauser, Ruger M77 action, 20-inch barrel, integral muzzle brake, 2-pound trigger, beautifully grained walnut wood stock, topped with a Trijicon 2.5-12.5x50 AccuPoint scope, shooting Hornady's 139-grain SST ammo. Unfortunately, the project was shelved with the introduction of the Ruger American.

That was then. Today, my ideal dream deer rifle would be chambered in Hornady's 7mm PRC using a Remington 700 standard magnum action with a steel hinged floorplate engraved with one of my deer drawings, Timney trigger adjusted to break at 2 pounds, fitted with a 20-inch Proof Research carbon-fiber barrel in 1:8 twist with a Hill Country Rifles muzzle brake to see the bullet strike; finely figured walnut, with classic straight lines and a Hornady buttstock cheek pad to bring my eye immediately to the height of the center of the scope. Because of the lighted reticle, the rifle would be scoped with a Trijicon AccuPoint 4-16x50 30mm tube. My choice of ammo? Hornady's 175-grain ELD-X Precision Hunter.

Why the 7mm PRC? I have long been a 7mm fan, specifically the 7x57 and .280 Remington, two of my all-time favorite deer rounds. The 7mm PRC's Hornady 175-grain ELD-X Precision Hunter is a very efficient, aerodynamic, and powerful round, essentially 3,000 fps and 3,496 ft-lbs of energy. With a 20-inch barrel, it still produces 2,047 ft-lbs of energy at 500 yards. And the round does extremely well in a shorter barrel.

Hunting, to me, means getting as close as possible before pulling the trigger. Sighted in dead-on at 200 yards, the 175-grain ELD-X drops merely 6 inches at 300 yards. With such a sight-in, I would not have to be concerned about holdover or turret ad-

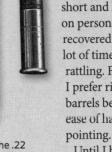

Compared to the .22 Long Rifle cartridge Larry first hunted deer with, he strongly believes the 7mm PRC comes as close to perfect as any round he has ever used on deer.

justments out to nearly 300 yards. Most of my shots at whitetails tend to be 200 yards or less. If farther, I could make appropriate holdover or turret adjustments.

From a 20-inch barrel shooting Hornady's 175-grain ELD-X Precision Hunter, the 7mm PRC's downrange energy does all and more than needed for whitetails and even other big game. It is still producing 1,000 ft-lbs of energy to at least 800 yards. The ELD-X bullet, too, expands well at both extremely short and long ranges, based on personal experience and recovered bullets. I spend a lot of time still hunting and rattling. For that reason, I prefer rifles with short barrels because of their ease of handling and quick pointing.

Until I build my "perfect deer rifle," I'll be content with my Mossberg Patriot Predator 7mm PRC, topped with a Trijicon AccuPoint scope shooting Hornady's 175-grain ELD-X Precision Hunter. It comes close except for barrel length and stock.

During his many years of "buck fever," Weishuhn hunted with various muzzleloaders. Here, he shows off a nearly Boone & Crockett whitetail taken with a .50 using Hornady's 250-grain SST.

The single-shot is no slouch on deer! The author used a .300 Win. Mag. T/C Encore for this nice southern Texas whitetail.

Hodgdon's Pyrodex. With faster twist barrels, we abandoned patched lead balls and started using sabots with bullets. Both increased accuracy and distance capabilities.

During this same time, we saw bolt-action rifles' pretty wood stocks replaced by synthetic and laminated stocks. Riflescopes started changing as well, from fixed power to variable magnification. Change was certainly in the air during the 1980s. Not only did guns, optics and ammo change, but so did our hunting clothes. Very quickly, camo clothing became the deer hunter's uniform with the introduction of Jim Crumley's TreBark, Toxy Haas' Mossy Oak and Bill Jordan's Realtree.

On the handgun front, I had started hunting with a Thompson/Center Contender single-shot, break-action handgun for deer and javelinas in the early 1970s, starting with a .30-30 Winchester Contender built in late 1967, the year that model was introduced. In the early 1980s,

I met J. Wayne Fears, who introduced me to the JDJ wildcat rounds/barrels produced by J.D. Jones (SSK Industries) for the T/C Contender frame. I was smitten with the .309 JDJ, based on the .444 Marlin case; ballistically, it was very similar to a .308 Winchester. That .309 JDJ and I took a lot of deer together. I also shot other SSK barrels and rounds, such as his .375 JDJ, 6.5 JDJ, 7mm JDJ, and .338 Woodstalker.

However, I did not forget about rifles. In 1987, Kenny Jarrett produced one of the first 7mm STW-chambered rifles. The round had started as a wildcat developed by Layne Simpson, but not long after, Remington chambered it in the Model 700. I had the opportunity to shoot a 7 STW while hunting with Jim Bequette, longtime editor of *Shooting Times,* on a hunt in the northern part of Texas. While on the Stasney's Cook Ranch, we shot at targets out to 500 yards.

Bequette became my boss at *Shooting Times,* where I served on staff for several years. Over a campfire, he said, "I've got a feeling we're soon going to see more rounds and rifles, as well as scopes and ammunition, be developed for shooting long range." His words were prophetic, even if they would take a few years to come to fruition.

During the summer of 1995, I got a call from the late Ken French, then with Thompson/Center Arms. I had long been shooting T/C's muzzleloaders and Contender single-shot handguns. "You're coming moose hunting in Maine. Don't bring a gun. I'll have one for you. J. Wayne Fears is also coming." I was thrilled. The gun I hunted with had, at that time, not yet been named. It looked like a beefed-up version of the T/C Contender single-shot handgun, chambered in .308 Winchester. I shot a three-shot group using the Hornady 180-grain soft-point load, all in the same hole.

A few days later, I shot a really nice Maine moose. Two weeks after that, I also took a Shiras moose and a 6x6 elk in Colorado with the same handgun. I did not want to send it back but reluctantly did with the promise to receive the first production gun, which turned out to

be a .30-'06. I broke the story about the new handgun and rifle with a cover story in Shooting Times. Two days before the publication was going to press, T/C named the new gun the "Encore." When the story broke, Thompson/Center hoped for orders of upward of 500 guns. Dealers ordered many times more.

Fears shot a moose in Maine as well, the first person to shoot an animal with the Encore version of the rifle. The Encore rifle had a unique stock design, much like a thumbhole stock but without a "hole." The design placed the shooter's hand naturally when raised rather than canted forward, as with most rifle stocks. You could comfortably shoot it either left- or right-handed. The unique stock design proved to be a bit prophetic since many of today's stocks are similarly designed.

Ruger's falling block single-shot No. 1 was first introduced to the shooting and hunting world in 1967. I have always been enamored with the rifle, and it makes a perfect deer-stalking gun. I love its blued steel, finely-figured walnut stocks, and truly classy lines. Initially, I scrimped, saved, and worked extra jobs

Larry Weishuhn, aka "Mr. Whitetail," used a Ruger M77, .300 Win. Mag., Hornady Precision Hunter to take this Boone & Crockett non-typical while hunting in Alberta, Canada, with Ron Nemetchek's North River Outfitting.

As a Ruger Ambassador for several years, Larry took this excellent whitetail with a Ruger Model 77 chambered in .300 Win. Mag. and using as he often does, Hornady ammo, in this instance, the 200-grain ELD-X Precision Hunter.

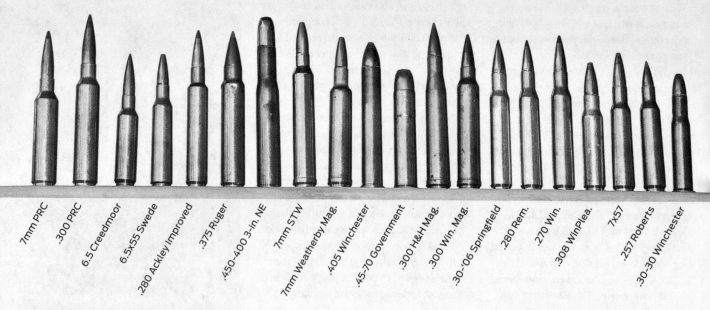

The author has used many different rounds on deer, including (from left to right): 7mm PRC, .300 PRC, 6.5 Creedmoor, 6.5x55 Swede, .280 Ackley Improved, .375 Ruger, .450-400 3-in. NE, 7mm STW, 7mm Weatherby Mag., .405 Winchester, .45-70 Government, .300 H&H Mag., .300 Win. Mag., .30-'06 Springfield, .280 Rem., .270 Win., .308 WinPlea., 7x57, .257 Roberts, and .30-30 Winchester.

to buy my first, a .375 H&H Mag. Others have followed it. The Ruger No. 1 was then—and remains—one of my favorite deer rifles.

As we headed into the 21st century, new cartridges, including the Remington Ultra Magnums, started appearing based on the .404 Jeffery case. The Winchester Short Magnums and Remington Short Action Ultra Magnums soon followed these. I was fortunate to hunt with one of the first .300 Remington Ultra Magnums produced. Using 180-grain Swift Scirocco commercial Remington loads, I shot a 6x6 elk at 12 yards, a Rocky Mountain goat at over 500 yards, and several whitetail bucks.

In 2001, Winchester introduced its line of Winchester Short Magnums (WSM), including the .270 WSM, .300 WSM, and 7mm WSM. These quickly became the rage, and I hunted with them and shot some of the first animals taken with the .270 WSM and .300 WSM. But the popularity of the Ultra and Short Magnums soon faded. Those I owned found their way into the back of my gun safes. I returned to hunting with old favorites such as the .270 Winchester, 7x57 (.275 Rigby), .280 Remington, .30-'06 Springfield, .300 Winchester Magnum,

and the older rounds such as the .45-70 Government, .405 Winchester, .300 H&H Magnum, and .375 H&H Magnum.

With the expiration of the Federal Assault Weapons Ban, interest greatly increased in semi-automatic military-style rifles, even for hunting. They were soon touted as the "Modern Sporting Rifle," or MSR. I am a fan of the more traditional single-shot, double, lever-action, bolt-action hunting rifles, single- and double-action revolvers, and single-shot handguns. I do not personally own an MSR. I have shot them, but not at game. However, this is simply a personal preference because I strongly support those who like shooting and hunting with them.

2007 saw the introduction of the .338 Federal, a round I used with excellent success on deer and deer-sized animals. Mine was a T/C Encore with blued steel stocked in pretty walnut. Sadly, like several other rounds, it appeared and rather quickly disappeared.

The introduction of new cartridges was fairly quiet after the various Ultra Mag. and Short Mag. rounds until 2007, when Hornady introduced the 6.5 Creedmoor and the .375 Ruger, as well as the short-lived .30 T/C (a short magnum, by a different name). I will openly admit that

if I could own only one rifle to hunt the world, it would be a .375 Ruger. With that cartridge, I feel comfortable hunting elephants, buffalo, and lions (which I have taken with the cartridge) down to whitetail deer and smaller animals.

For years, hunters and shooters had touted the value of 6.5mm rounds, but none had ever been popular in the USA; these, among others, included the .264 Win. Mag., 6.5 Rem. Mag., .260 Rem., and 6.5x55 Swedish Mauser. Then, Hornady introduced the 6.5 Creedmoor, based on a .30 T/C case necked down to 6.5. The Creedmoor's popularity built slowly for the first decade but then increased dramatically. New technology allowed ballisticians to learn about bullet travel. This helped Hornady design bullets such as the ELD-X (Extremely Low Drag eXpandable) and loads that have increased long-distance shooting capabilities. All of this boosted interest in long-range shooting. Today, a shot at 400 yards and even farther is often regarded as a "chip shot."

The 6.5 Creedmoor, whether loved or hated—and it is both—has led the way to the current offering of such long-range capable rounds as the 6.5 PRC (Precision Rifle Cartridge), 7mm PRC, and .300

PRC, and the various new Nosler rounds and loads. I have hunted with the long-range capable 7mm PRC and the .300 PRC. While I enjoy shooting steel at long ranges out to 1,000 yards, to me, hunting means getting as close as possible rather than taking long shots at live animals; again, this is a personal decision. I have to admit I like Hornady's new 7mm PRC. Mine is a Mossberg Patriot Predator topped with a Trijicon AccuPoint scope, and it has become one of my favorite hunting rifles.

During my 70 years of buck fever, I have hunted deer with shotguns loaded with buckshot and slugs, muzzleloaders in .45 to .54 caliber, revolvers from

.357 Magnum up to .454 Casull and .500 S&W Magnum, and rifle rounds from .223 Remington to .30-'06 Springfield and .375 JDJ in my single-shot handguns.

I have watched hunters evolve from using primarily iron sights to scopes, starting from low fixed power to variables up to 24x power, and from considering 200 yards as long-range to accurately shooting ranges up and beyond 1,000 yards. I have watched hunting grow from having to guess the range to using modern rangefinders to accurately obtain the target's yardage—even systems complete with computers that link rangefinders to the riflescope. I have also seen the average hunting firearm go from blued steel

with pretty wood stocks to stainless steel and high-tech synthetic. Much has occurred since I started hunting during the middle of the 20th century.

During those same years, I have seen game populations significantly increase to where hunter opportunities, particularly for whitetail deer, have never been better than they are now during the mid-2020s.

With all the changes I have witnessed during my 70 years of buck fever, there are two remaining constants: I still dearly love guns and hunting, and the bullet still goes where the barrel is pointed when the trigger is pulled. **GD**

A Texas desert mule deer taken with a .280 Rem., using Hornady's Precision Hunter ammo.

Gun Store Museum Reveals Historical Gems

This replica of a Gatling gun has five barrels and is fully functional but never has been fired.

In an Alabama "pistol and pawn shop," a display of guns of the last 200 years (or more!) reveals interesting designs, rich history, and more.

❯ALAN CLEMONS

The array of startlingly bright lights gives notice that in the back corner of Larry's Pistol & Pawn, something quite important is on display. Lighting in the rest of the spacious, packed store is good—you can easily make out the signs pointing to a special deal bin of holsters and an ammo rack. Nothing is dim or hard to make out, whether in the pawn area—replete with diamond rings and yard implements—or the firearms and ammo side where, if they don't have it, they can get it. Making your way through either of the North Alabama stores owned by Larry Barnett is often a leisurely pastime for many visitors. They take an hour or so to mosey, saunter, look, examine, stroll, wish, perhaps hold a pistol or revolver or shoulder a long gun on the rack.

Museum creator John Hering used old ammunition boxes and ammo for unique displays amid the firearms exhibits.

Yet, in the back of the 18,000-square-foot store in Madison, a growing city west of sprawling Huntsville—the largest city in Alabama, home to technology geniuses, NASA rocket engineers, biotech wizards and also, many hunters and gun owners—you'll have to make your way to the northeast corner under those bright LED lights. There, after you walk past the gun cleaners and long gun racks and pawn area, you'll find the museum John Hering built. It is large and neatly arranged, with easy-to-read signage and descriptions. Hering, the store's general manager, took his time creating the area for the extraordinary things Barnett has acquired over the years. Tucked away in the large building, it is dwarfed by everything else. But the little well-lit museum in the corner is quite astonishing with its depth of notable and historical items.

Before we get to the firearms—and there are many, so we'll have to parse a few favorites—consider these other gems in the museum:

—Front pages of *The Miami Herald* from 1963, when President John F. Kennedy was assassinated in Dallas, and 1969, when the U.S. landed on the moon.

—Various antique boxes of ammunition to take a stroll down memory lane. Remember Sears-branded shotgun shells? How about these: Dupont Remington Shur Shot "Smokeless Wetproof Shot Shells with Kleanbore Priming" … Western X Center Fire Cartridges … Western Super X "All New Plastic" Mark 5 shotgun shells … Kynoch 9mm Mauser Cartridges … Peters HV Rustless Priming … Mohawk, by Remington .22 Long Rifle.

—A Smith & Wesson Model 270 International Line Thrower for large ships on the ocean. Sailors could fire a hard, wooden missile-shaped projectile attached by a steel cable to a rope, and the ships could connect.

—Various other helmets, ammunition, a pistol-shaped hand-powered drill made by Bill Ruger, old holsters, and more.

Barnett opened the pawn in 1973 after several years of working with one of the area's top outdoor stores. He wanted to focus specifically on firearms and began building his inventory and expanding his network. Barnett was a shrewd business-

man. He believed strongly in customer service, making it known that if he didn't have something, he could order it. His staff was, and still is, knowledgeable about what they sell. Customers come in to ask about a specific firearm or accessory, ammunition, training or self-defense, and they get answers. Sometimes, the answer is, "I don't know, but let me get …" and they will find an employee who knows. Barnett built a reputation that resounds after five decades, including with people who bring him antique firearms.

"I'd guess probably 98 percent of this collection came across the counter," said Hering, who has been with Barnett for almost 30 years. "He's been in business since the early '70s, and we buy, sell and trade a lot of things from people. We also used to buy lots of police trade-ins or confiscation items the (law enforcement) agencies would sell when cases were cleared, things were unclaimed, things like that. We might get a 55-gallon drum of Smith & Wesson revolvers and other makes. So, we might find something in there that was rare, or unique. Or we might have a woman call whose husband died, and she wants to get rid of a gun or some guns.

"Sometimes things might really open your eyes because they're really old, like Civil War or since then. Other times, they could be so rusted or in such bad shape they're not worth anything. It was a crapshoot. The shotguns hanging up here, these all came from this area, the southern Tennessee and northern Alabama farms. He's never sold them because a lot of them have Damascus barrels. Those won't put up with the pressures for today's cartridges, and Larry never wanted to sell them or see somebody get hurt."

Hering spent some time with *Gun Digest* in the museum, reviewing the exhibits. Barnett was unable to visit with us due to some medical rehab. Hering designed it at Barnett's request, with both picking the various rifles, pistols, revolvers and other items to show. Some are grouped by brand, including several cases showing Ruger, Colt, and Smith & Wesson pistols. Others by period, such as Civil War and post-war rifles, or a specif-

ic collection of Civil War pieces, including letters and photos. As expected, with so many cool things, Hering couldn't pick just one or two favorites.

CIVIL WAR PIECES

Among the Civil War-era items are a Harpers Ferry 1844, Springfield Arms 1864 musket, Parker Snow 1861 Contract musket and Springfield 1816 musket. Not much has changed over the years with these designs. Barrel, stock, hammer and cap, trigger … bang. That's simplifying it, of course, but these 160-year-old rifles are incredibly cool.

In another case are two Rappahannock Forge pistols in .69 caliber, each with brass fittings, gorgeous wood, and steel barrels with ample patina. These were designed and made by Scottish immigrant James Hunter, who, in 1759, created

The museum at Larry's Pistol & Pawn in Alabama houses exhibits covering more than 160 years of firearms history.

Bill Ruger created a line of tools like this hand drill before getting into firearms design and manufacturing.

31) Ruger Hand Drill

A machinist and life-long firearms enthusiast, Bill Ruger formed The Ruger Corporation in Southport, Connecticut in 1946. Intending to one day produce his own firearms, Ruger experimented with design and manufacturing methods by producing a line of handheld tools. This rotary drill's grip design was inspired by the classic Japanese Nambu and German Luger pistols, and eventually found its way into [Ruge]r's very first firearm, the Ruger Standard pistol.

Japanese Nambu revolvers were similar in design to the Luger but had some modifications. The Model 26 (on top, in photo) had a design flaw that could cause an unexpected discharge.

Famed designer Almo Lahti designed this Swedish Lahti 9mm Model 40 pistol for the Finnish Armed Forces and later licensed it to the Swedish military.

Hunter's Iron Works—later known as the Rappahannock Forge on the river of the same name. By the outset of the Revolutionary War, he capably built military-grade arms and supplied the Continental Army and Navy. Hunter's works are rare, with examples in the Smithsonian Institute, West Point Museum, and Rock Island Arms Museum.

"These Civil War-era, mid- or early-1800s-era blackpowder rifle … designs haven't changed too much in almost 200 years," Hering said. "The hammer design, obviously it's come from a flintlock, right? And that hammer design didn't change significantly when even the newer Sharps and rolling block rifles or others using metallic cartridges were introduced.

"Those early flintlocks and percussion guns were made on water wheels with leather belts, hand-fed fires, a lot of sweat and effort. Maybe steam engines later on. Everything is hand-fitted. All of that is a huge deal, and to do that for the military contracts some of them had or for everyday use, that's really a big deal."

GATLING GUN

Behind the velvet ropes, like a star, the six-barrel Gatling gun shines and glimmers under the bright lights. While Hering can't pick just one favorite, this is near the top. It's a badass replica of one of the most fierce, shocking and devastating weapons unleashed during the Civil War. Richard Jordan Gatling created it in 1861, offering troops continuous fire. Over the next five decades, it was modified for different calibers and used in multiple wars, including in Africa, South America, Asia, and several domestic conflicts in the United States.

It's hard to imagine taking fire from this gun. It has six barrels, each firing as fast as the gunner can turn the crank. By 1893, it was modified for the .30 Army ammunition and four more barrels. Future modifications included the .30-'03 cartridge and, later, the .30-'06. The one at the museum is a Colt 1877 Bulldog, based on the original design and in .45-70 Gov't. Its rate of fire is 800 rounds per minute.

"This one's on a .45-70 carriage, and I think Colt made 50 of them, and this is No. 6," Hering said. "Colt made this gun

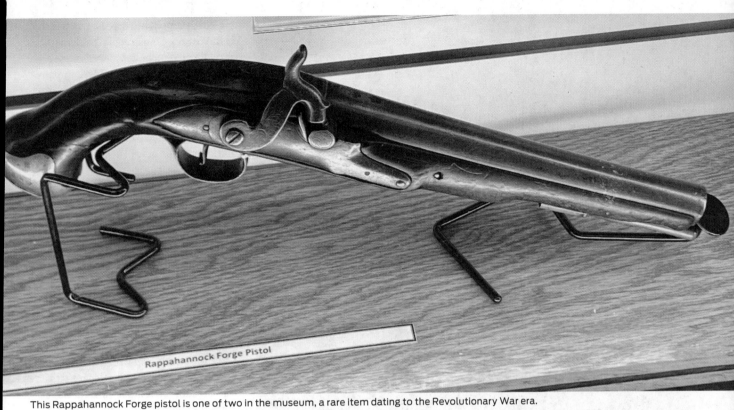

This Rappahannock Forge pistol is one of two in the museum, a rare item dating to the Revolutionary War era.

back about 10 or so years ago. It's a direct reproduction of the ones they used to make. We tried to get Larry to go out and shoot it, but he didn't want to clean it, and I don't blame him.

"You'd have a loader that was loading cartridges in the slots. They would be gravity-fed in, and then one guy in the back just cranked 'em out. Today's version is the mini-gun that's on the A-10 Warthog, and they're in .30-caliber. (*Officially, they're the seven-barrel General Electric GAU-8/A Avenger.*) And they're driven by an electric motor. But, these early Gatling guns, they would hitch this to a horse and with the big wheels, they could take off. I've always liked this one."

VOLCANIC

Titans of the firearms world collaborated to create the Volcanic Repeating Arms Company. In today's firearms industry, we sometimes see these kinds of things: an ammunition company will come up with a new cartridge that works—amazingly, with the rifle being introduced simultaneously or soon after by a manufacturer. *Voilà!* Marketing, production, and sales are all rolled into one big bundle.

That kind of collaboration is noth-

Exhibits showcase a variety of weapons dating to the Revolutionary War era and covering many wars, conflicts, and other innovations since then.

This Gatling gun weighs several hundred pounds but is easy to move thanks to the large wheels. Colt made 50 of them, which are brass and wood, with a gravity-fed magazine. It was revealed during the Civil War, but only a few were put into action. Later, modified versions were used in various wars and conflicts worldwide.

ing new, though. In 1855, Daniel Smith, D.B. Wesson, Benjamin Tyler Henry and Oliver Winchester played roles in the Volcanic Repeating Arms Company. Smith and Wesson were based in Smith's Norwich, Conn., plant, and changed the name of their company—Smith & Wesson—to the Volcanic name and obtained all rights to the new pistol, rifle, and ammunition.

Winchester was an investor in the Volcanic company but forced it into insolvency in 1856. In 1857, he took control, moved it to Connecticut and rebranded it as the New Haven Arms Company. Henry was hired as the plant superintendent. Three years later, Henry got a patent for his innovative lever-action rifle, which was used in the Civil War and made by the New Haven Arms Company.

The Volcanic is a cool pistol. It has a swept wooden grip with an enlarged base, brass action, ample triggerguard with an additional finger hole for better grip, a hexagonal barrel, and an oversized hammer. The latter seems it would be a bit challenging to cock easily. It is a robust gun that fired the .41-caliber Volcanic Rocket Ball, a self-contained cartridge with gunpowder inside the rear of the bullet. It was sealed with a cork wad and a cup containing a primer. Once fired, the projectile left the muzzle, and the cap fell away. It was not very powerful, though, perhaps less than a modern .25-caliber round.

"This is quite unique, yes, and preceded lever-action rifles," Hering said. "With the self-contained cartridge, you could load them in and operate it similar to a lever-action. You can see at the front you pull that lever all the way to the end and turn it, and that opens it. You load the cartridges from the front. Later, of course, they loaded from the side. But this definitely was different, as well as having four major influences in the firearms world being part of this."

MORE CIVIL WAR STUFF

Captain Seth C. Hall was a member of the 8th New York Heavy Artillery, which had an Infantry unit and was involved in 19 battles, including the Spotsylvania Court House, the Siege of Petersburg, and the Appomattox Campaign. Hall was born in North Bergen, N.Y., and after the war, lived near Rochester. Like many on both sides of the war, he did what he believed was necessary and then returned to his life after the conflict ended.

The exhibit is fascinating. It includes Hall's Burnside Carbine, a breechloading rifle that fired bullets from a metal cartridge and separate primer. Ambrose Burnside figured out how to eliminate leaking gases encountered with other breechloading rifles. Thanks to this design, more than 55,000 were made for the Civil War. The Burnside Carbine was the third-most used in the war behind the Sharps and Spencer carbines.

Along with Hall's rifle is a sword with scabbard, a large ledger with detailed information about each company member, a photo of him and his family, and a letter to his sister describing life amid the battles and the surrender at Appomattox in April 1865. Everything is in fine shape, remarkable for 160-year-old documents. The letter describes fighting at Appomattox in April—"Glory sought for one day."—and the surrender by Gens. Longstreet and Lee, which ended the nation's most tumultuous period.

"This book lists the men that he had, ages, and where they were from, if they survived or how they died," Hering said. "You can see that some of them died of typhoid, some were wounded in battle, things like that. And this was a piece of the wrapped cartridge paper from a box of .45-70, or whatever (caliber) it was. The letter—that's quite interesting. Imagine what it took to be able to write that and get it sent home or somewhere else while you're in battle. And he wrote this in April after the surrender, so that's quite interesting."

WEBB PIERCE'S REVOLVERS

Few things in the store exhibit are flashy or blingy. The Gatling gun is, of course, with its polished brass and perhaps the Smith & Wesson four-screw .44 Magnum. That gun was made famous in the movie "Dirty Harry," with Clint Eastwood. It's big and hearty, like a lineman at a Big 10 football powerhouse. Perhaps one or two other guns offer a little bling-blang that catches your eye.

But it's almost impossible to overlook

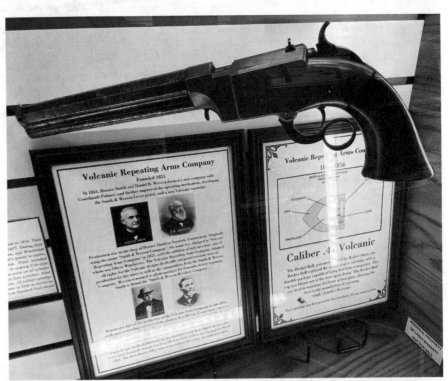

The Volcanic pistol was a collaboration between the founders of Smith & Wesson, with investment from Oliver Winchester. Winchester forced the Volcanic company into insolvency and took control, after which D.B. Wesson and Horace Smith teamed to create Smith & Wesson.

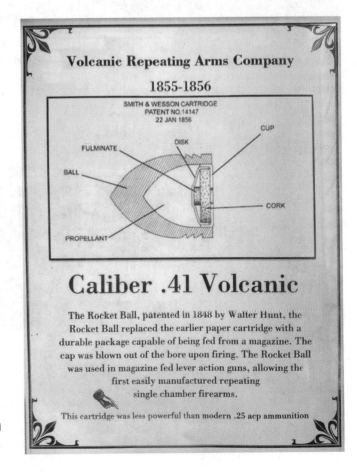

The pistol fired a self-contained cartridge, the .41-caliber Rocket Ball. It was handcrafted with precise fittings and made of brass, steel, and wood.

The exhibit of Civil War memorabilia from a Union soldier is well done. It includes a rifle, sword, ledger, letter to home from Appomattox, and more. Hall's ledger lists soldiers' information, including name and rank, and the date, location, and cause of death.

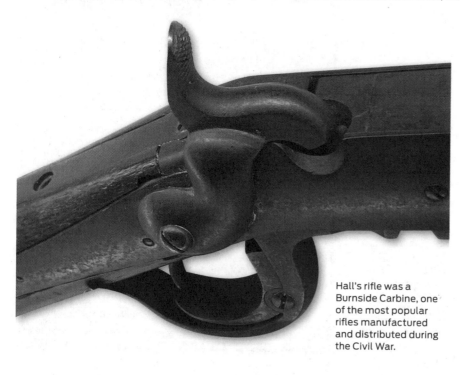

Hall's rifle was a Burnside Carbine, one of the most popular rifles manufactured and distributed during the Civil War.

the two Colt revolvers owned by country music legend Webb Pierce. They shout at you to look, gaze, gawk, or perhaps wrinkle a nose at "Wow, that's … something." They cannot be ignored. And interestingly enough, Barnett and Hering know little about them.

"To be honest, I don't know anything about them, and Larry couldn't remember how or when he got them," he said. "We've had them for quite a while and it's been so long, neither of us remember or know about them. They're definitely interesting to look at, though."

Both revolvers are Colt Single Action Army; one is of .41 caliber, manufactured in 1907, and the other is a .32-20, manufactured in 1904. Initially designed in 1872, the Colt SAA became a staple of the U.S. military for 20 years. Pierce's revolvers have highly detailed filigree engraving along the action, cylinder, hammer, and part of the barrel. The load-

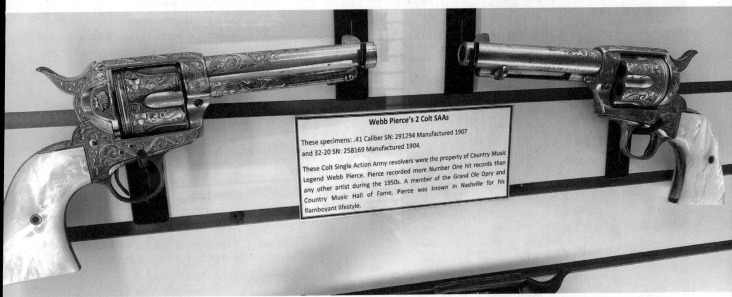

Country Music Hall of Fame singer Webb Pierce owned these two Colt SAA revolvers, which were highly customized and fit the flamboyant star's personality. Both revolvers have pearl handles, contrasting with the vivid gold plating on the metal.

Webb Pierce's 2 Colt SAAs

These specimens: .41 Caliber SN: 291294 Manufactured 1907 and 32-20 SN: 258169 Manufactured 1904.

These Colt Single Action Army revolvers were the property of Country Music Legend Webb Pierce. Pierce recorded more Number One hit records than any other artist during the 1950s. A member of the Grand Ole Opry and Country Music Hall of Fame, Pierce was known in Nashville for his flamboyant lifestyle.

ing gates have a raised relief of an Indian chief in a war bonnet. They are gold-plated, with areas rubbed or scuffed away, and have pearl handles. Chips, dings and imperfections exist, as expected on 120-year-old firearms. These obviously weren't put on a shelf.

Pierce was born in Shreveport, Louisiana, home of the famed "Louisiana Hayride" radio show. Country and honky-tonk singers made their way to that corner of Louisiana to appear on the show, which could launch careers. Pierce was no different, growing up around music and appearing on the show before heading to Nashville, the home of country music and the legendary Grand Ole Opry broadcast every Saturday night on WSM 650-AM. Like the Hayride broadcast, the Opry went wide thanks to the clear-channel signal.

Pierce was the top singer of the 1950s, with 21 charted hits, including "Wondering," which hit No. 1 in 1952. Pierce replaced Hank Williams Sr. on the Opry after the latter's death, furthering his ascent. Other songs charted, but not like "In the Jailhouse Now" in 1955, which was No. 1 for 21 weeks and cemented Pierce as a star. He helped himself, as well, with his wildly flamboyant lifestyle, sparkly rhinestone suits made famous by Nudie Cohen of Hollywood, and can't-miss cars. Cohen customized his 1962 Pontiac Bonneville convertible to include

The loading gate on the revolvers is adorned with a raised relief of an Indian chief in a war bonnet. Each is engraved with detailed filigree, including on the action, cylinder, hammer, and part of the barrel.

$20,000 worth of flashy upgrades, including steer horns, hand-tooled leather upholstery studded with silver dollar coins, a hood ornament, passenger glove box lid, and door handles with Old West revolvers, and a chrome-plated lever-action rifle on the trunk lid.

Pierce was hard to miss around Nashville, similar to fellow star Porter Waggoner in his bright suits and white

convertible with steer horns on the hood. Pierce was inducted into the Country Music Hall of Fame in 1991.

BROWNING AIRCRAFT TRAINER
The big humpback design stands out to anyone who knows about older shotguns or is of a certain age. John Browning's iconic Auto-5 shotgun design is impossible to mistake for anything else. It's

This Remington shotgun, in the design of the famed Browning "Humpback," was used on Jeeps to help gunners prepare for aircraft bomber training. A long, metal rod extending to the rear gunner guiding handles was used to pull the trigger on the Remington bomber training shotgun.

The sled's design to hold the Remington shotgun gave gunners more realism during training sessions before entering an aircraft.

beefy and brawny, an old-school shotgun that, whether in 12- or 20-gauge (or the 10-gauge for those who enjoy a bigger thump), will get the job done, and you'll know you hunted with it.

This one, though, is a Remington design through licensing and was used as a training setup for aircraft bomber gunners in World War II. It's mounted in a steel cage that allows the shooter to look down the sights while guiding it with twin handles behind the butt of the stock. A long metal rod bent at the ends with one over the trigger allowed it to be fired. The one displayed at the museum is on a tripod; a similar setup would've been used for training.

"They would mount this on the rear of a Jeep and then drive through a field with the gunner shooting at clay targets being thrown for him," Hering said. "The gunner would learn to follow the target with this trigger just like they would a machine gun. They could learn to get the lead on a target while the Jeep was bouncing around like a plane being buffeted by the wind. You're talking about 17- and 18-year-olds who, maybe never had touched a shotgun before or definitely a machine gun, for that matter. You're trying to teach them really quickly how to lead the target."

Hering said the shotgun is a real training gun, not a replica. He laughed when asked if he'd shot this one.

"I've shot these (kind of shotguns) many, many, many times," he said. "I was an armorer in the military. But our stuff was a lot more modern."

GERMAN MG-42

This exhibit makes you look twice because, like the Gatling gun, it's impossible to imagine doing battle with a German MG-42 machine gun. It's in a closed case with a detailed setup that includes ammunition boxes and rounds, a metal helmet, and more. It still reeks of death and destruction, of nightmares and the evil we don't want to think about but must remember.

The MG-42 is near another larger training gun atop a case, an oversized rifle Hering says was used for classroom instruction. The trainer "probably is three times the size of the real thing, so everyone could see it easily." The instructor could point out details, show loading with wooden ammunition, and do other tasks for those learning. But it's the MG-42, an 8mm Mauser used extensively in the second half of World War II, that commands your attention. With belt-fed ammunition and a rate of fire of about 1,200 rounds per minute, it was known as Hitler's buzzsaw.

Hering explained that the trainer rifle had a welded tank around the barrel filled with water to cool it. The MG-42 had a slotted barrel shroud, but that did little with such an intense rate of fire. Soldiers trapped under the withering barrage of the machine gun had to wait for a specific moment, hopefully, to move forward or take a shot at the Nazi gunner.

"If you look on this side here, there's a handle latch, and you can actually, if you pop that forward, the barrel would slide and fall out," Hering said. "And then you can just take that extra barrel, slide it in, and close the latch to lock it. Because this thing had such a high rate of fire, they heat up extremely quickly. Our soldiers were up against this gun and could only attack it when the barrel was being changed. When that was going on, you were trying to charge him in maybe 10 to 15 seconds, at the most, because a lot of the Germans had a really fast ability to change (the barrel).

This photo shows gunners in a plane aiming through openings.

Inexpensive to produce and devastating in the field, the MG-42 helped Nazi soldiers wreak havoc in the second half of World War II.

When the barrel became so hot it had to be changed, this latch handle (underneath) was deployed. The unlocked barrel was quickly replaced with another.

This machine gun created by the Germans is a 7.92x57mm (8mm) Mauser with a rate of fire hitting more than 1,200 rounds per minute. Barrels grew so hot they had to be changed, giving a momentary opportunity for troops under fire to move.

"In this configuration, the gun would be up above the bunker, and you wouldn't be able to see the soldier because the soldier would sit back here and look through the scope. The gun might be visible, or part of it, above the bunker or sandbags or whatever, and the scope eyepiece was in the rear. So it was like a periscope."

Hering said the German soldiers were trained to change the hot barrel for a new one quickly, knowing that was when they were vulnerable. Multiple MG-42s could alternate, perhaps, but nothing was easy for either side. The ammunition was on 50-round belts, so they could attach the belts and keep cranking out rounds.

"They called it Hitler's buzzsaw because it's firing so fast. It sounds like you're tearing a sheet," he said. "An example of it is in the Tom Hanks movie "Saving Private Ryan." When they're attacking on the beach, and later in the movie in another scene, they can only move when that barrel change happens."

BORCHARDT C-93

Inside the store's front door is a small case atop a larger display case. If you're in a hurry or aren't paying attention, you'll miss one of the most unique pistols ever made.

In 1893, Hugo Borchardt created the Borchardt C-93, with more than 3,000 of them produced in Germany. It was the first mass-production semi-automatic pistol and was manufactured by Loewe and *Deutsche Waffen und Munitionsfabriken (DWM)*. Borchardt also created the cartridge for it, a 7.65x25mm high-velocity round. His assistant, Georg Luger, asserted that he had input on both, but Borchardt received the credit for the C-93.

The pistol is almost comical in design, like something from a Star Trek movie. Its skinny barrel meets the much larger action and grip, like a soda straw stuck in a wood block. A large, circular magazine with the rear blade sight atop is in the rear. It was accurate, though, and became known among military brass throughout Europe and the United States.

However, testing by the U.S. military revealed it wanted size design changes and ways to lower costs. However, Borchardt wouldn't budge; neither side would give an inch, and that was that.

However, Luger saw an opportunity when DWM appointed him to make the suggested changes. He switched to the 7.65x21mm Parabellum cartridge, which reduced the size. This did not affect the accuracy or rate of fire. The Luger Parabellum was born and became one of the most well-known pistols in history. **GD**

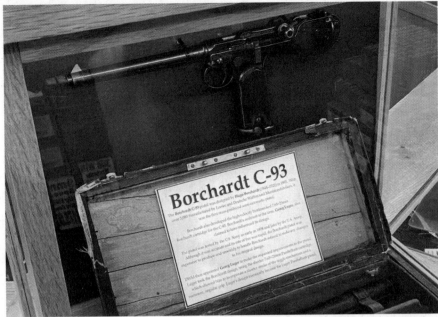

Creator Hugo Borchardt wouldn't modify his pistol after requests from military brass, but his assistant—Georg Luger—agreed to make the changes. Luger's modifications eventually led to the Luger Parabellum pistol.

The Borchardt C-93 was the first mass-produced semi-automatic pistol; it was unique in appearance but clearly showed imagination and a detailed design.

The magazine at the C-93's rear worked well but gave the gun a unique appearance.

Too Much Gun?

Are heavy target rifles and high-powered scopes overkill for backcountry hunting?

❯ THOMAS GOMEZ

Hunting in the Santa Fe National Forest North of the Valles Caldera National Preserve, I was in hot pursuit of elk. My scouting efforts had proved fruitful, locating elk herds feeding in the meadows and on the ridges. Weeks later, when it came time to hunt, the drought had scattered the animals into small herds, which held tight to the trees, even at dusk and dawn. I'd planned to hike several miles and glass the canyons and meadows from multiple vantage points, and I was prepped for a long-range shot.

The author's custom 6.5 PRC Tikka T3 with a SilencerCo Harvester EVO suppressor, Tract Toric UHD scope and MDT XRS Chassis System is excellent for long-range shooting but a tad heavy for 20+ miles of hiking.

Attached to my pack was a custom Tikka T3 chambered in 6.5 PRC with a heavy barrel, MDT XRS Chassis, Tract Toric UHD 4-20x riflescope, and suppressor, the ideal setup for longer shots. On day one, after 14 miles of hiking and glassing numerous valleys and canyons, I didn't see a single herd of elk save for the occasional one I jumped in the oak scrub or aspens. While quietly creeping through the bush, I would hear a commotion as a lone elk would run through, giving me mere seconds to acquire a target and try for an ethical shot. The animals were usually within 50 yards. However, I could not swing the bulky rifle and acquire a target quickly enough, even with the scope dialed down to 4 power. This trend would repeat itself.

After walking nearly 30 miles, I wondered if I was taking too much rifle and scope into the wilderness. Walking back to my SUV in the dark, I spent hours contemplating something like an AR-15 6.5 Grendel build with a 1-8x low-power variable optic (LPVO) or even a lightweight bolt gun with a simple red-dot for hunting the bush.

Fast forward a few weeks, and I was chasing mule deer in the Lincoln National Forest, carrying the same rifle. The terrain was rugged and rocky and had a mixture of cedar, piñon, and juniper trees. After a 6-mile hike, my hunting partner, Mark, and I came across a herd of bucks grazing on the side of a mountain. Using a small pine tree as an improvised monopod, Mark harvested an excellent buck at 270 yards. While walking along a ridge line the following day, we found a small group of deer, and I shot the lone buck at 140 yards.

From the shadows, I took a seated position, deployed my MDT Triple-Pull CKYE-Pod bipod, settled in, found my target, exhaled and sent a 147-grain Hornady round into the cranial vault of the cervid. After securing the rifle, saying prayers, and doing a quick photo shoot, we harvested the meat using the gutless method and hiked back to the truck. Before we hiked out, I took out my rangefinder and ranged the surrounding hills and peaks. Conceivably, my farthest shot would have been 400 yards. Once again, I wondered if I was taking too much rifle into the woods.

THE JOURNEY

My journey into long-range shooting started around 2010 when I picked up a Remington 700 SPS Tactical to get a handle on the coyote population at the family ranch in Central New Mexico.

Since then, I've devoted significant time to mastering precision rifle shooting, and I will readily admit that I see all aspects of shooting, even pistol, through the lens of ultra-precision. I regularly train to 1,000 yards and occasionally shoot steel to 2,500 yards if testing a new cartridge or long-range shooting technology.

Though I don't see myself as a long-range hunter or advocate for long shots on large game, the mastery of a precision rifle and the ability to hit targets at long distances increases confidence. It familiarizes you with all aspects of your rifle system and ancillary gear. The ability to hit targets at medium and long range is a valuable tool in your hunting toolbox. Is a trophy buck standing broadside at 500 yards? Get prone, acquire the range and atmospheric data, and send it. Hit an animal at 300 yards, then have it reappear at 600 yards on the adjacent canyon? Consult your ballistic calculator and send a round with confidence.

I spent years shooting varmints and steel targets at long range before getting serious about hunting big game. Initially, I was obsessed with having a match-grade rifle capable of shooting at least a ½-MOA group. These rifles were usually mated to a Modular Driven Technologies or Kinetic Research Group chassis system and typically weighed around 12 to 14 lbs. The rifles would have a heavy barrel and a large, high-magnification riflescope. I typically used rounds with a high ballistic coefficient, like the 6.5 Creedmoor or 6.5 PRC, and the rifles were capable of sub-MOA groups. How did I manage to lug the weight on long hikes? Fitness, a stable pack, and a good sling helped immensely, though admittedly, after three days into an elk hunt, a heavy rifle was only fun if you had an ATV or horses.

After my elk and deer hunt, I thought about every large game hunt I had been on or guided. All of the deer I have harvested have been within 200 yards. Most of the engagements were quick: I spotted the animal, steadied myself, and took a well-aimed shot from a tripod, trekking poles, or the kneeling position. I assume animals have insanely good vision and sense of smell, but I am astounded by how close I have gotten to deer and elk while hunting.

Varmint hunting is a different story. I've shot prairie dogs and coyotes between 600 and 800 yards. The most incredible shot I attempted was on a coyote at 1,820 yards, though I missed it by mere feet. The antelope hunting clients at our ranch, whom I formally trained in precision rifle and had Kestrel ballistic calculators with data confirmed to 1,200 yards, have made some great shots. However, the farthest to date was 450 yards, a perfect broadside shot with a 6.5 Creedmoor that instantly dropped that animal. Depending on the time and terrain, I will always try to get closer; *I have just never had to.*

Long-range shooting and precision

A client (blurred face as he is active duty military and a member of the Special Operations community) with an impressive pronghorn antelope. This antelope was harvested at 450 yards with one perfect shot.

Getting ready to send a 6.5 PRC round well past a mile (at a steel target, not a game animal).

rifle competition have created many new hunters who often carry something analogous to their competition or long-range rig, which is how I came into the sport. This leads me to ask: Are some sportsmen taking too much rifle into the woods? Do we need the high magnification scopes, 24-inch barrels, and the new-fangled high-BC bullets? On a more personal note, do I need the heavy barrel, suppressor, chassis system, and insane accuracy? Let's explore these questions.

BARREL LENGTH AND WEIGHT

For this section, we'll consider anything below a 20-inch barrel to be a short barrel. There are zero questions about it: A long barrel on a rifle is awesome. It maximizes velocity and kinetic energy and flattens trajectories at typical hunting ranges.

Rifles with sporter or thin-contour barrels don't weigh much. Still, they can have high accuracy when paired with the correct factory load or handload. When shooting groups with an accurate sporter barrel, I can get two rounds to touch, and then the third shot is usually .50 to 1 inch from the first two holes. I'll let the rifle cool for 10 minutes, then shoot another group. This will play out multiple times

before I consider the rifle zeroed. (If you put a muzzle brake on a rifle, hearing protection is mandatory since the sound directed toward the shooter will cause permanent hearing loss, even after one shot.)

Heavy varmint or match barrels have excellent harmonics and, when paired with the proper ammunition, can usually shoot very tight 3- or 5-round groups. They're purpose-built for accuracy but heavy. A rifle with such a barrel is fine for backcountry hunting if you have mobility platforms like E-bikes, horses, or ATVs. The weight can mitigate recoil, though I still like a brake for spotting hits and fast follow-up shots. Heavy barrels are super easy to zero. I've hunted with heavy 16- and 20-inch barrels, which are awesome

to pair with a suppressor.

In theory, a carbon-fiber-wrapped barrel offers the best of both worlds. It features a thin barrel wrapped in carbon fiber, and manufacturers claim it can produce results typical of a heavy contour with reduced weight. My experience with carbon-wrapped barrels has been hit-and-miss. Some shoot excellently with factory ammunition, but when you add a muzzle device, groups open up like crazy. Tuners and handloading are a good idea if you're considering one.

Whether you have a thin sporter or heavy barrel, how much length do you need? To answer this, ask yourself a few questions. What kind of zero do you use? For example, do you zero at 100 yards and dial or use a reticle for longer shots?

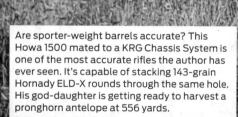

Are sporter-weight barrels accurate? This Howa 1500 mated to a KRG Chassis System is one of the most accurate rifles the author has ever seen. It's capable of stacking 143-grain Hornady ELD-X rounds through the same hole. His god-daughter is getting ready to harvest a pronghorn antelope at 556 yards.

Do you zero 1 or 2 inches high at 100 and point and shoot out no farther than a determined range, such as 300 yards? A long barrel is advantageous if you use the latter because the high velocity will give you a flatter trajectory.

If you zero at 100 yards, dial or hold your shots in your reticle, understand how to use a ballistic calculator, and confirm your data at the distances you intend to harvest animals, barrel length doesn't matter as much. What matters is that you have enough energy and velocity to dispatch your quarry ethically.

SHORT BARRELS

Modern hunting bullets need a certain velocity to expand reliably, causing crush injuries that damage an animal's organs, circulatory, and nervous systems. Your bullet's kinetic energy when making contact with the animal is also vital. How much velocity do modern bullets need to expand reliably? That will vary by manufacturer, but modern hunting projectiles usually need a minimum of 1,700 fps to expand reliably. Though up for debate, a minimum of 1,000 ft-lbs is a decent amount of energy for deer-sized animals and at least 1,500 ft-lbs for elk.

Energy and velocity aside, an important variable is shot placement. This became apparent when I saw a video of my buddy dropping a bull elk at 600 yards while using a 6mm Creedmoor match round fired from his PRS competition rifle. It was a perfect shot through the heart. Do most hunters have the skill, training, and gear to make perfect shots at 600 yards? Probably not. Another variable to contend with is wind, which can be hard to ascertain in certain locations. Also, large game animals are tough and adapted to harsh climates and predators. They are an amalgamation of sinew, bone, water, muscle, and hide. Sometimes, bullets don't perform like they should, especially when they contact bone. Shot placement is critical, but it's nice to back it up with a fast bullet and kinetic energy. With that said, when I run the numbers on my ballistic calculator to determine the performance of a cartridge, I like 1,800 fps at a minimum and 1,000 ft-lbs for deer-sized animals. Now that we have established a baseline for velocity and energy let's look at barrel length, specifically short ones.

I appreciate short barrels for my ranch and hunting rifles. They are handy, com-

pact, and easy to carry. Since I often hunt with suppressors, starting with a shorter barrel doesn't substantially increase the overall length of my rifle system. Suppressors mitigate recoil and allow me to hunt without hearing protection.

I've always liked short barrels due to their compact nature and accuracy. Still, several years ago, I cut one of my Howa 1500 barreled actions chambered in 6.5 Creedmoor down to 16 inches and was curious about its external ballistics. After running some Hornady 143-gr. ELD-X Precision Hunter rounds through my Labradar chronograph, I recorded an anemic average of 2,498 fps. Plugging the data into my Kestrel anemometer, I was surprised by the numbers. Even with the low muzzle velocity, I had 1,800 fps and 1,082 ft-lbs of energy out to 800 yards. I would never shoot at an animal at that range, but even at a realistic distance, like 500 yards, I had 2,078 fps and 1,372 ft-lbs of energy.

Regarding long-range shooting, some bullets can lose gyroscopic stability at the transonic range, which starts at around 1,350 fps. My Kestrel told me I could expect decent performance from my weapon system out to 1,500 yards at

Early morning pronghorn antelope hunt. Heavy rifles are excellent for precise shots prone or off tripods.

Tikka T3 chambered in 6.8 Western—a superb all-around hunting rifle and cartridge.

my density altitude. To test it, I proned out and easily got a second-round hit at 1,000 yards. After hitting steel at 1,000 yards, I aimed at the 12-inch steel target (on which I trued my ballistic coefficient) and had a first-round hit at 1,250 yards.

For comparison, I grabbed another Kestrel with the data for one of my .308 rifles with a 24-inch barrel. The rifle was zeroed and trued for Hornady 178-gr. ELD-X Precision Hunter loads. Consulting the ballistic chart, I was looking for the 1,800 fps and 1,000 ft-lbs band and found it around 800 yards. My .308 had 1,852 fps and 1,356 ft-lbs of energy at that distance. Granted, it had more energy due to the weight of the bullet, but I was impressed by what a slower, higher-BC bullet could do. From this experiment, I found that a 16-inch barrel has plenty of velocity and energy for hunting shots to 600 yards. (For more information about ballistics, I recommend reading *The Ballistics Handbook* by Philip P. Massaro.) Now, it was time to take a deep dive into optics.

OPTICS

Back to my conundrum: Was I taking too much rifle and scope into the woods? To answer this question, I built the perfect rifle for hunting thick forests and aspen

groves. It could also reach across a canyon and hit something at 500 yards if necessary. For the build, I grabbed an old Tikka T3 barreled action chambered in .308 Winchester, with a barrel cut down to 16.1 inches. I dropped the barreled action into an HNT26 Chassis System from MDT and attached a Tract Toric UHD 30mm 1-8x24 LPVO scope. At the end of the muzzle, I attached a SilencerCo Harvester EVO suppressor and, for added stability, the MDT GRND-POD bipod. The System as a whole weighed just under 7 lbs.

Since the Tikka had a 1:11-inch twist rate, I opted for Hornady 168-gr. ELD-M bullets with a G1 BC of .523. Settling behind the rifle, I shot three rounds, made some adjustments, let the rifle cool, and then fired three more rounds. Even though I only had an 8x scope, I could shoot groups of just under 1 MOA, and the Labradar chronograph gave me an average velocity of 2,502 fps.

Satisfied with my zero, I drove to the 2,000-yard range at our ranch, which had a steady left-to-right wind averaging between 12-15 mph that day. I hung a 10-inch steel gong and worked back in 100-yard increments. From 100 to 400 yards, I held in the reticle and had first-round hits on steel. My first miss came at

the 500-yard line. After that miss, I dialed the elevation and made a solid hit. I dialed the 600-yard shot, had a first-round hit, and connected on my second shot at 700 yards. At 800 yards, I had difficulty seeing the target, so I ended the exercise. Consulting the range card in my Kestrel, I noted that at 600 yards, the 168-grain ELD-M traveled at 1,809 fps and had 1,221 ft-lbs of energy. That's plenty for deer, though the rifle was not intended to shoot that far.

THE HUNTING TEST

After drawing a mule deer tag in Unit 37—where I've taken several nice mule deer—I was anxious to carry something other than a 12-pound rifle into the woods. I again pondered an AR-15 6.5 Grendel build with two upper receivers. One upper receiver would have a hunting scope, and the other a simple red-dot optic. However, that was quickly dismissed because of my excellent results with the Tikka T3 and the 1-8x scope. Moreover, the 6.5 Grendel is a tad light for mule deer and runs out of energy past 200 yards. Next, I pondered a Tikka T3x chambered in 6.5 Creedmoor with a red-dot sight, but the precision side of my brain insisted I take at least some magnification. Ultimately, I chose the

Tikka T3 with the MDT HNT26 chassis I had built to see how far I could effectively shoot the 1-8x LPVO.

Due to my hectic schedule, I could only hunt for two days. On day one, I started at first light, creeping up a canyon with the riflescope on 1x. After several hours of careful hiking, I crested a ridge and saw a dozen deer resting in the shadows 50 yards away. I froze and slowly took out my binocular. All of the deer were does, save for one barely legal buck. After watching for 30 minutes, I kept hunting and moved downhill to avoid disturbing them. I worked my way to the top of the canyon, where I settled on a vantage point that allowed me to glass multiple canyons. I saw dozens of deer moving to and from a spring at the bottom of the canyon, but nothing that I could shoot.

Taking out my rangefinder, I noted that the farthest deer was 400 yards away. I looked at the group through the 1-8x scope and was confident that, had a good-sized buck appeared, I could have easily harvested it with that setup. I spent the rest of the day glassing from that point and, with the sun setting, started the hike back to my vehicle.

As I was hiking down, I bumped into a group of deer at 10 yards. I quickly scanned the group but didn't see a single legal buck. I watched as the animals bounded toward the ridgeline and then paused to look back at me. I continued my journey back to my vehicle and noted how lightweight the rifle was. Had a buck presented itself, I could have harvested it with ease. Day two was nearly identical, though a blizzard drove me off the mountain. I saw many deer and one small buck that was legal, though I passed on harvesting it. I hiked 15 miles and felt great because I carried a light-weight, nimble rifle.

Several weeks later, I accompanied some friends in the Chama to pursue mule deer. Due to the terrain and foliage, we found ourselves hunting a mix of sub-alpine forests, meadows, and mixed cedar, piñon, and juniper. One group member had a Howa 1500 chambered in 6.5 Creedmoor with an Arken EPL 4-16x riflescope, and the other member carried my lightweight Tikka. The logic was that we had rifles ideal for close and long shots. Though a deer wasn't harvested, we learned a lot and had a great time.

LOOKING FORWARD

Since I rarely hunt alone, moving forward, I think one member of the team will have a 4-16x or a 6-24x riflescope for precise shots out to 600 yards, and one will carry a lightweight, compact rifle, suppressed, with a 1-8x or 1-10x scope. Why the suppressor? When sneaking through the bush, you want to use all of your senses, and if you have an animal trotting past, you often don't have time to put on hearing protection. Suppressors also mask your sound signature and don't bugger up the general area after you have taken a shot.

I will use my lightweight Tikka T3 with the MDT HNT26 Chassis System, or my heavier custom Tikka T3x chambered in 6.5 PRC for all future hunting. The custom Tikka features a 20-inch carbon-fiber-wrapped barrel from Oregon Mountain Rifle Company. I adore chassis systems and will continue to use them for the foreseeable future. I will usually grab the lightweight Tikka T3 unless I'm hunting plains animals. I like the challenge of the stalk and enjoy creeping through the trees and harvesting animals up close. The lightweight rifle allows me to carry extra food and sleep systems for back-country hunts farther from the trailhead.

It's been challenging not taking a heavy precision rifle capable of insane accuracy into the woods. Even so, my recent hunts showed that a shorter barrel and lower magnification scope can do the job and make close-up shots. If I draw a tag this year, I will once again take a lightweight, short-barreled rifle with a low-powered variable optic. Who knows? You may soon find me hiking around the woods with a red-dot optic or open sights! **GD**

The author's long-range rifle: A custom Tikka chambered in 6.5 PRC with an Oregon Mountain Rifle Company carbon-wrapped barrel.

MAXIMUM LEVERAGE

Running A Pair of Mad Pig Customs Marlins at Gunsite

❯PATRICK MCCARTHY & TOM MARSHALL

In a true case of "what's old is new again," the last several years have seen the lever-action rifle's resurgence—and evolution. Although the platform was once reserved for ranchers and Cowboy Action Shooters, well-known companies like Midwest Industries have committed significant resources to develop accessories to modernize this oft-overshadowed platform. Smaller custom houses like Mad Pig Customs go even further, offering complete boutique builds with selectable furniture, accessories and colorways. With all this effort expended to teach an old gun new tricks, you may be wondering: why?

We're not sure there is a definitive answer. If you only care about practicality and cost-effectiveness, it's impossible to deny the advantages of a modern semi-auto rifle with a detachable 30-round magazine. But there are some genuine merits to an updated lever gun (colloquially known as "the cowboy assault rifle"). Speaking of so-called "assault rifles," a rifle with a manually cycled action and tube magazine can skirt just about any assault weapon restriction in the country. You can forget about fin grips and put flash hiders back on the menu, even in places like California. For those who live in—or frequently travel through—freedom-restricted territory, a tactical lever gun might be a great way to get around draconian legislation while still having an accurate and heavy-hitting rifle with all manner of modern accessories.

Editor Tom Marshall's lever gun (top) started life as an old Marlin 30AW, while editor Patrick McCarthy's (bottom) is a newer 336 Dark Series. Mad Pig Customs modified both.

Caliber options range from rimfire to the behemoth .45-70, which has a documented history of taking down most of the world's biggest and toughest game—Marlin even jokingly advertised it as effective against a T-Rex. The sample guns in this article are in .30-30 Winchester, a highly respectable caliber in its own right for general preparedness. With bullet weights typically ranging from 150 to 170 grains and muzzle velocities around 2,000 fps, this caliber has been used on nearly every game animal on the North American continent, from mule deer to black bears, elk and moose.

Such firepower translates easily to use as a defensive caliber. While not known for its long-range capabilities, it's generally accepted as a 200-yard cartridge, which aligns with most mass-issue military calibers. Its trajectory and ballistic data are similar to arguably the most widely used military caliber on the modern battlefield: 7.62x39mm Russian. While a lever gun lacks the capacity or rate of fire of an AK-type rifle, the .30-30

is in very good ballistic company when it comes to *in extremis* use in mixed terrain environments.

Preparation is an intensely personal pursuit. Some folks have determined that they simply don't require the capacity or fire rate of a modern semi-automatic carbine. But many of them also think it prudent to have a firearm of some kind around for the ever-ominous "just in case" scenario. A lever-action rifle is easier to shoot than a pistol and reaches farther than a shotgun. But, until a few years ago, this choice meant sacrificing easy access to modern enhancements such as suppressors, weapon lights, electronic optics, lasers, modular grips or adjustable stocks. Those days are over, and we're here to prove it.

We're showcasing two rifles built by Mad Pig Customs, each with different furniture and accessories. Mad Pig refinished each rifle in our preferred Cerakote colors, installed its signature lever and trigger parts and performed a complete action job to ensure smooth and reliable functionality. We hope to shed some light on the myriad possible configurations available with a modernized lever-action rifle and prove once and for all that this platform hasn't been relegated to history books.

A lever gun's manual of arms is comparable to a pump shotgun, but the half-cock safe position requires an additional learning curve.

The Marlin 30AW features a traditional sling from Wilderness Tactical attached to studs on the underside of the stock and handguard.

TOM MARSHALL'S SETUP

This rifle started life as a Marlin 30AW. No longer in production, the 30AW was meant to be a budget-friendly alternative to the flagship Marlin 336. With less expensive furniture material and less refinement in the fit and finish, the 30AW was truly a working man's gun. The team at Mad Pig Customs stripped the rifle down to the skeleton and rebuilt it, starting with a Midwest Industries M-LOK handguard and a Form Stocks backend. The MI handguard offers a full-length, seven-sided M-LOK surface with a continuous top rail. This upgrade allowed us to mount a Vortex UH-1 holographic sight (on an ADM riser) and a Holosun LS-321G dual-beam laser/illuminator. Also from Midwest Industries are the universal shell caddies, each holding a pair of .30-30 rounds.

The Form stock retains a modicum of traditional styling with the upgrade of an adjustable-height comb, which comes in handy when using an optics riser. A Surefire Dual-Fuel Scout light gave us low-light ability, with a dual-lead remote switch to run both light and laser from one switch. A pair of Walker Defense NILE grip panels and an Emissary Development Handbrake Mini afforded customization for support hand control. Finally, we mounted a Langolis Rhodesian sling from Wilderness Tactical to the factory sling studs. The muzzle device is a Rearden Manufacturing brake with a Rearden suppressor mount.

PATRICK MCCARTHY'S SETUP

Unlike Tom's rifle, this one has been a "tactical" lever gun since day one. It started as a Marlin 336 Dark Series, a variant that was only available for a short

time before Remington went bankrupt, ceased production of Marlin rifles and sold the brand to Ruger. (Ruger recently announced the re-launch of the Marlin Dark Series, this time with an M-LOK forend and adjustable stock straight from the factory.)

Initially, the Dark Series had a 16.25-inch threaded barrel, XS lever rail with ghost ring sight and black-painted wood furniture. Mad Pig Customs replaced the wood furniture with a machined aluminum stock from Chisel Machining and a LASAI handguard from Hoptic USA. The stock features a soft Kick-Eez recoil pad, adjustable cheek rest, QD sling socket and an attachment point for a six-round Hoptic LongBow ammo carrier. The handguard is equipped with a Hoptic USA Quiver carrying two more rounds of .30-30, a JMac Customs HRD handstop, a Burn Proof Gear heat-resistant rail wrap and a SureFire Mini Scout Light Pro Infrared with selectable white or IR output.

Atop the rifle's original XS sight rail is a Leupold Patrol6 HD 1-6x24mm LPVO in a Midwest Industries 30mm QD scope mount; we mounted a Leupold DeltaPoint Pro NV red dot at the 12 o'clock position on a Reptilia ROF-SAR ring mount. The magnified optic's simple

duplex reticle and illuminated FireDot are ideal for daytime shooting, and the top-mounted, NV-capable DeltaPoint pairs with the IR weapon light to make the rifle usable under night vision, just like our favorite AR-15s. We topped off the rifle with a JK Armament suppressor attached to the threaded Rearden SPB muzzle brake via a Rearden Atlas adapter and added a Blue Force Gear Vickers padded sling.

AMMO CARRIAGE CONSIDERATIONS

One of the downsides of lever guns is their tube magazines, which make their manual of arms more like a shotgun than a modern bolt-action or semi-auto. While we've already touched on the idiosyncrasies of reloading, this also affects ammo carriage and load bearing. You won't be carrying a box magazine in a belt pouch, so you're left with tossing a fistful of loose rounds in your pants pocket—a compromise that will inevitably lead to slow, fumbled reloads or seeking specialized ammo carriage equipment, which is a little harder to source. We found two companies that offer lever-gun-specific ammo pouches.

Wilderness Tactical sells a simple, low-profile solution called the ZipLoader, which is the equivalent of wearing an ammo butt cuff on your belt. It's a simple nylon platform with 10 elastic loops for individual cartridges. We paired it with a small, zippered Bug Pack from Wilderness Tactical, which we used to carry loose rounds to replenish our other ammo carriers between drills.

For those who want a larger supply of organized ammo storage or more flexibility for carrying, Grim Hunter Tactical makes two products we evaluated for this article. The first is the Quick Loader Pouch, a fold-out pouch that carries 24 rounds. There are eight loops hard sewn to the outside. Inside the pouch are two more tear-away "cards" that hold another eight rounds each, which are attached by hook and loop. We like this modular design, as it allows you to attach the cards to other places you might want ammo—stick them to the headliner in your truck, the outside of your range bag or even the sleeve of your combat shirt or jacket. You can order the Quick Loader Pouch with either MOLLE/PALS backing or a belt loop, and it's available in nearly two dozen colors.

If your lever gun is your dedicated bug-out or SHTF rifle, Grim Hunter offers a Lever Gun Chest Rig consisting of two Quick Loader Pouches and a third detachable pouch you can use as a medical or admin kit. On Grim Hunter's website, you can choose to have your ammo pouches biased to the left or right side of the rig based on personal prefer-

ence. It's available in a variety of colors with multiple harness options.

Finally, like a shotgun, carrying a few extra rounds on the gun itself may be advantageous for speed reloads. You can carry these on a traditional fabric or leather butt cuff or attach them to modern M-LOK-mounted carriers such as those seen on our rifles.

While testing and training with our lever guns, we used Sellier & Bellot 150-grain soft-point .30-30 ammo.

HOME ON THE RANGE AT GUNSITE

The effectiveness of any tool is contingent on its user's skill and experience, and our lever-action rifles are no different. The two of us have spent quite a bit of time training with AR-15s, but AR-15s these ain't. Even so, many fundamentals carry over—stance, grip, sight picture, trigger control, etc. However, the manual of arms is drastically different from an AR, in addition to the reloading and ammo management challenges we mentioned earlier. This led us to seek training from Lew Gosnell, an instructor who has amassed a variety of vintage and modern lever-actions and spent many years teaching students about the intricacies of these rifles. Gosnell is a Marine Corps veteran who also spent 31 years working in law enforcement on the streets of East

L.A. These days, he teaches Defensive Lever Gun and other courses at Gunsite Academy in Paulden, Arizona.

In case you're not familiar with Gunsite, it's considered by many to be the Mecca of firearms training in the United States, if not the whole world. In 1976, Lt. Col. Jeff Cooper founded Gunsite as a location to teach his Modern Technique of the Pistol, and it has evolved into an expansive facility with a wide range of pistol, rifle, shotgun and even edged weapon classes. It offers everything from classrooms and traditional range bays to run-and-gun simulator courses, complex shoot houses and vehicle-based training areas. It's like an amusement park for shooting enthusiasts, complete with catered lunches, an on-site campground and a museum built inside Cooper's home.

After traveling to Gunsite and meeting Gosnell, we headed to the 50-yard Hanneken range to start working with our lever guns.

HALF-COCKED

The first order of business was to learn about manipulating the lever guns' safeties. Our Marlin rifles feature manual cross-bolt safeties—Marlin calls it a Hammer Block Safety—but this feature is a relatively recent addition introduced in the early 1980s. Gosnell and many other lever gun users view this manual safety

The Burn Proof Gear Rail-Rap is the latest addition to the rifle. The suppressed barrel heats up quickly with rapid-fire, and the Rail-Rap offers protection for gloved or ungloved hands.

Some may scoff at the idea of using a lever-action for home defense and CQB, but in states and countries where semi-automatic rifles are heavily restricted, it may be one of the best options available.

In addition to our modernized lever guns, instructor Lew Gosnell brought out some of his classics—no matter your preference, they're all fun to shoot.

as redundant and excessive. Historically, the primary safety on an exposed hammer lever gun was the half-cocked position, pulled back halfway to full cock. This prevented the hammer from resting against the firing pin, which could potentially fire a round if an object struck the hammer hard enough. It also prevented users from carrying the gun fully cocked and ready to fire at all times, which could lead to a negligent discharge if a foreign object touched the trigger.

To prepare our lever guns for a drill, we went through the following procedure:

- Half cock the hammer, then engage the manual safety.
- Load the tube magazine.
- Cycle the lever to chamber a round. The hammer is now fully cocked. (Top off the tube magazine with one more round if necessary.)
- With the manual safety still engaged and the gun pointed in a safe direction, place the firing hand thumb on the fully cocked hammer and apply pressure.
- Maintaining firm pressure on the hammer, press the trigger just long enough to lower the hammer into the half-cocked position carefully.
- Index the trigger finger safely on the side of the receiver and disengage the manual safety.

As soon as Gosnell gave the command to fire, we quickly thumbed our hammers back to the fully cocked position and pressed the trigger.

In a way, the manual safety serves as training wheels—if a shooter lets the hammer slip while returning it to half cock, it prevents the gun from firing. But once we had done enough dry and live fire reps of this process to be entirely comfortable with it, we left the manual safety disengaged and carefully returned our guns to half cock after firing.

Always be careful to maintain a good grip on the hammer while returning it to half cock; this is not something that should be rushed. As Gosnell explained, this procedure may feel strange to us today, but it was the standard modus operandi for more than a century before the introduction of cross-bolt safeties.

FEEDING THE BEAST

Loading a lever gun is similar to a shotgun, but the loading gate's placement on the receiver's right side (as opposed to the underside) means you'll have to load with your firing hand. Hold the gun in a low-ready position against your shoulder, and press each round into the tube magazine until the loading gate closes behind it. Alternately, you can use a "violin load" position by resting the buttstock sideways

over your shoulder, leaving the loading gate facing upward. Gosnell reminded us to keep our heads up and our eyes downrange while loading to remain aware of potential threats.

Also, like a shotgun, it's OK to load a round directly into the chamber while the action is open. This can be useful for speed reloads in conjunction with a match-saver-style ammo carrier directly in front of the ejection port (as seen on both our rifles). However, be aware that lever guns can have trouble feeding if they're operated at steep angles. So, don't try to chamber load—or operate the lever—with the muzzle pointed at the ground.

To run the lever, be quick and forceful but deliberate. Babying it or failing to run the lever all the way forward may induce a malfunction. We also found that the angle of hand movement is essential. Depending on your rifle and lever design, you may need to push your hand down, forward, or somewhere in between to achieve the smoothest action.

Numerous ammo carriage solutions are available for today's modern lever-action shooters.

An SPB muzzle brake and Atlas adapter from Rearden Manufacturing allowed quick attachment of the JK Armament suppressor.

TESTING OUR SKILLS

Once comfortable manipulating, loading, and firing our lever guns on the 50-yard range, we moved on to more complex challenges. After all, that manual of arms may feel comfortable on a flat range, but doing it while running, transitioning between multiple targets, and navigating around obstacles is a different story. This wasn't just a lever-gun class; it was a defensive lever-gun class.

We started by setting up a barricade on the range, leaning out from either side to shoot without exposing ourselves more than necessary. Then we ratcheted it up a notch by heading down to The Pit, an indoor simulator course that most of us would call a shoot house. We practiced clearing the structure, "slicing the pie" around doorways and corners to methodically take in every angle before proceeding. Admittedly, we'd prefer a

ing and sitting. Some stations had fallen logs or trees to use for support, but others required unsupported shots. This also tested our ability to load our rifles quickly

semi-auto rifle over a lever gun for these close-quarters applications since thumbing back the hammer before firing and running the action between shots was tougher than simply mashing a trigger. That said, our Mad Pig Marlins had no trouble getting repeatable, accurate hits on the threats in hallways, corners and windows. The tall-mounted red-dot optics on both rifles were helpful for this purpose, offering a wide field of view and fast sight acquisition.

Next, we headed to Gunsite's Military Crest, a winding trail with various natural shooting positions and an array of steel targets at 100 to 200 yards or greater distances. We braced off trees and rocks and used our rifles in standing, kneeling and sitting positions. With a slight holdover for the longer shots, we had no trouble ringing steel from each position. The only challenge we encountered was running the lever in positions where the rifle was rested on a flat surface, such as kneeling behind a stump; it may be necessary to lift or rotate the rifle to make room to move the lever. This is also why lever guns aren't ideal for prone shooting.

For our final challenge, we moved to the Scrambler, a course that continued our work on positional shooting but emphasized speed. With four rounds in our guns and a shot timer running, we sprinted between seven positions and shot steel targets while standing, kneel-

Sources

MAD PIG CUSTOMS
madpigcustoms.com

MIDWEST INDUSTRIES
midwestindustriesinc.com

SELLIER & BELLOT
sellierbellot.us

WILDERNESS TACTICAL
thewilderness.com

GRIM HUNTER TACTICAL
grimhuntertactical.com

GUNSITE ACADEMY
gunsite.com

while moving and to carefully engage the half-cocked position after each hit. Like any other move-and-shoot drill, making your weapon safe before running ahead is essential. By the end of the Scrambler, we were out of breath and grinning.

FINAL THOUGHTS

So, the question remains: is teaching an old gun new tricks worth the effort? We'd give an emphatic yes based on our experience with these two builds and our range time at Gunsite. While we certainly won't deny there are more efficient, ergonomic, and cost-effective defensive weapons on the market, that doesn't mean the venerable lever gun isn't worth owning. And if it's worth owning, it's worth modifying and improving with aftermarket parts, just like your favorite semi-auto carbine.

With expert help from Mad Pig Customs and Midwest Industries, we built these two modernized lever guns to deliberately push the envelope and become as AR-like (or "tactical," if you prefer that term) as possible. They're unabashedly extreme, like classic muscle cars converted into fire-breathing supercharged dragsters. You may not want a full M-

LOK forend and adjustable stock for your lever gun, much less an infrared laser and night-vision-height optic mount, and that's OK. We intended to show what's possible using existing off-the-shelf components and a little fine-tuning in the hands of the lever-gun specialists at Mad Pig Customs. The result is a pair of rifles that never fail to stir up controversy on

social media or draw a crowd at the local range. More importantly, they're much more capable for dynamic shooting and defensive use than they were in unmodified form. Sorry, Grandpa, you may not like it, but the future is now. **GD**

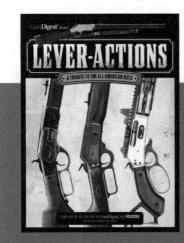

This article is an excerpt from the book Lever-Actions: A Tribute to the All-American Rifle, *available at GunDigestStore.com.*

The .44 Magnum

... One Year Later

The world's most potent handgun cartridge in 1958, its history and development, plus notes on handloading and shooting it, by the man whose dream came true!

❯ELMER KEITH

I
n 1953, while at Camp Perry, Ohio, I had several long sessions with
C. G. Peterson of Remington. He was very much interested when I
asked him to bring out a heavy .44 Special load with my bullet at 1,200
feet. He asked me to come up to the Remington plant and handload
it for pressures and velocity readings. I also had several long talks with Carl
Hellstrom, President of Smith & Wesson, and he also urged me to visit his
plant after Camp Perry. When I finally arrived at the Remington plant, Mr.
Peterson was away on vacation, but Henry Davis took me to Gail Evans, who
made notes on all my work and findings and promised to take it up with Mr.
Peterson as soon as he returned. They promised me nothing except to see
what could be done about a heavy factory .44 Special load.

Right, Keith 250-gr. bullet cast and plated by Marked, compared with a Remington factory 240-gr. gas-check bullet.

They were afraid that the old Triple Lock, even though it had been handling my heavy loads for many years, might, in some instances, blow up. They said, and rightly, that it was made long before the days of heat treatment or magnafluxing, and some could have dangerous flaws.

After several days at Remington, I put in a week at the Smith & Wesson plant, urging them to get together with Remington in the production of a heavy factory .44 Special load with my bullet and, if necessary, make a new gun to hold it. If they were afraid of the old gun's strength, I said a new gun could be made with a longer, recessed-head cylinder, the amount of barrel extension through the frame cut to the minimum, but with room for a gas ring.

During my last day at the Smith & Wesson plant, Mr. Hellstrom told me he could build a safe gun around any heavy .44 Special load that Remington would make. I then suggested that they could lengthen the .44 Special case until it would not enter any of the older .44 Special guns, and again strongly urged them to get together with Remington and bring out a powerful .44 gun and load. I vamosed [sic] then but continued, in letters to both companies, to urge such a load and, if necessary, a gun to handle it.

Actually, all this had been covered in my book, *Sixguns*, years before!

From the late summer of 1953 until early in 1956, I had no word from either company on what they were doing about the heavy .44. In January 1956, Smith & Wesson phoned me one evening to tell me they had built a big .44 and that the first one finished would be sent to me! This was great news, and I learned also that Remington would ship me some of the new ".44 Magnum" ammunition with 240-grain bullet at 1,570-foot seconds velocity. I immediately gave General Hatcher—he was also being sent the new gun—the good news.

Well, that's the story behind the Smith & Wesson .44 Magnum gun and the Remington .44 Magnum cartridge, and it's all well documented. Thousands of shooters the country over, their interest spurred by my writings and the articles of others, created the demand.

Mr. Peterson and the Remington ballisticians put in a lot of hard work designing and perfecting the load, Mr. Hellstrom and his staff of gun makers likewise did endless work on the new gun. At last, my dreams of thirty years are a reality. Today, we have the world's finest big sixgun and load, and my hat is off to every man in both organizations who

had anything at all to do with the development. They did a wonderful job.

First, the men behind the gun. Carl Hellstrom, Bill Gunn, Harold Austin, Walt Sanborn, Fred Miller, Harold Steins and many others at the Smith & Wesson plant had their part in the production of this fine arm.

THE .44 S&W MAGNUM

The new gun employs the heavy N frame regularly made for the .357 Magnum, .38/44 Heavy Duty, .44 Special and .45 Smith & Wessons, but this gun has all major parts made from a premium lot of special alloy steel, perfectly heat treated for greatest strength in the Smith & Wesson furnaces. The hammer and trigger are case hardened to a new high in this treatment, ensuring a perfect and lasting, crisp, clean trigger pull. The heavy barrels are 6½ or 4 inches in length with a wide rib and encased ejector rod. The top of the frame and barrel are grooved along the rib and sandblasted to prevent glare and reflection.

All lockwork parts and bearing surfaces are honed to a mirror finish to ensure maximum smoothness, either single or double action. The hammer has a wide target spur and the trigger has a wide flare that perfectly contours the trigger finger for easy cocking and maximum contact area of finger to trigger. The trigger pull runs from three to four pounds and is as clean and sharp as breaking glass.

The S&W rear sight, fully adjustable for both elevation and windage and of locking micrometer-construction, has a white-outlined rear notch of adequate width to ensure a strip of light on each side of the front sight, a one-eighth-inch red-insert ramp when held at arm's length. The red-insert ramp front shows up well on a black target or game in any shooting light. Stock straps are grooved to prevent slippage. Stocks of Goncalo Alves fancy-figured hardwood are of the S&W Target shape and offer a filler behind the triggerguard as well as covering the front strap and the butt of the gun.

They are hand-filling, and the left stock is hollowed out for the right thumb. They are perfectly shaped to fit and fill the hand and distribute the recoil over as wide a surface as possible. They are also

finely and attractively checkered. The big gun weighs 47 ounces empty. The main spring is the standard S&W long spring with a compression screw in the front strap. Cylinder and barrel clearance are held to a minimum, yet the gun has the smoothest possible action. Cylinder locks tight and lines up perfectly. The cylinder is a full 1.75 inches long and has ample room for my 250-grain bullet reloaded in the one-eighth-inch longer .44 Magnum case, still leaving a sixteenth-of-an-inch clearance when the bullet is crimped in the regular crimping groove.

SHOOTING THE .44 MAGNUM
The new gun is the finest target arm I have ever fired with standard .44 Special factory ammunition or a light reload with my own or any accurate target bullet. It holds steadier than any gun I have used on target. Double-action pull for fast work is superb and for the target shooter the broad hammer spur is ideal for fast cocking in single-action, timed, and

rapid-fire matches.

The rear end of the barrel projects through the frame about 1/8-inch and with the long cylinder adds strength to these, the two weakest parts of a sixgun. The 6½-inch barrel job is ideal for the hills, for target shooting, or for hunting with a sixgun, and a perfect gun for running cougar with hounds. It gives maximum sight radius as well as maximum velocity. It is a great two-hand weapon for game shooting, as it feels muzzle-heavy and hangs well on the object.

In a 4-inch barrel, the weight lies more in the hand and is better balanced for emergency double-action shooting, hip shooting and fast aerial double-action work. The four-inch job will also be the gun for the peace officer as he can stop either man or automobile and yet it is short enough to ride high on the waist belt where it will not poke the seat of a car or chair. It will also be the faster to get into action.

External finish of the new gun is the

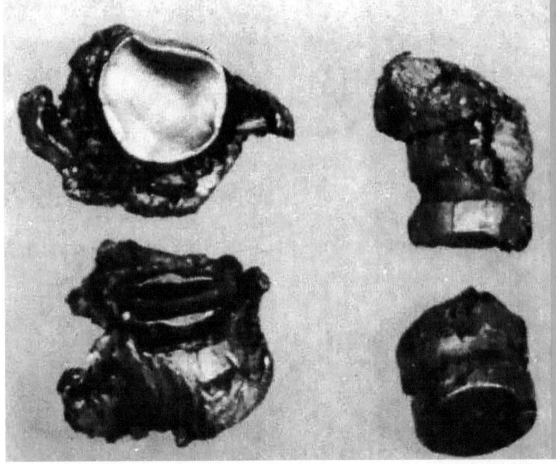

Left, two Remington .44 Magnum bullets found in the necks of a big steer and a 1,400-lb. cow. Right, two Keith 250-gr. Markell-cast bullets (backed by 22 grs. of No. 2400 powder) taken from the necks of two large cows. The skulls were completely penetrated.

The buck mule deer that Keith hit twice out of four shots at over 600 yards, using the S&W .44 Magnum.

traditional Smith & Wesson high bright blue. A new high in polish has been attained on this gun, and even the edges of the triggerguard and the hinge of the crane are polished like a mirror. The ramp front sight is pinned through the rib with two pins before polishing so that careful examination is necessary to detect the two pins. Attractively packaged in a presentation, hinged-lid case of blue leatherette, it sells at $140.00 and is worth every cent of its cost. It all adds up to a finer gun than I thought anyone would ever build.

Remington has produced the greatest and most powerful sixgun cartridge ever made. The new case is an eighth-inch longer than the .44 Special, and it will not fully enter any .44 Special chamber we have so far tried, including S&W, Colt, and Great Western. The solid head case is the heaviest sixgun brass I have ever seen. There are no worthless cannelures to cause the case to stretch when fired and resized. The new case appears to be of the same length as the .357 Magnum brass. The bullet is a modification of my design, with two narrow and shallow grease grooves instead of one heavy, wide and deep grease groove, and with the case crimped down into the soft lead of the forward band, leaving a very small full caliber band in front of the case. The crimp is heavy, and so far, no bullets have jumped their crimp from recoil.

The 240-grain bullet has a shorter nose than my slug, the same wide flat point, slightly larger on the flat surface. It is made of very soft lead, a necessity because it is extruded in long ropes fed to the cutting and swaging machines. The soft bullet requires a gas check cup, not only to prevent deformation of the base but to help hold the soft slug in the rifling at high velocity. The slug upsets to fill the chamber mouths perfectly and the gas check is the best I have ever seen on a bullet, being crimped into the rear grease groove. The factory bullets do not carry as much lubricant in both grooves as my original bullet does in its one grease groove. The slug mikes .431 inch and the groove diameter of my gun is .429 inch. Pressure is high with factory loads; I would estimate it to be at least 40,000 pounds and possibly 42,000.

The gun is made to take it, and the case is made for high pressure; fired cases fall out of my gun with a tap on the extractor rod. Accuracy is high at all ranges and the gun shoots good to a half mile. Once, we managed to put five out of six bullets on a rock one foot high by 18 inches long at over 500 yards (two of us paced it), shooting with both hands out of a car window, which is plenty good enough for any sixgun. They would have hit a buck deer at that range five times out of six.

At close range, it shot quite small groups on targets and, like my original bullet, cut clean, full-caliber holes in the paper. My first shot at game was a big Goshawk in the top of a cottonwood 100 yards away. I used both hands, rested my left arm and shoulder against a post and shot with just his head showing over the front sight. The gas check slug caught him dead center and splattered him all over.

HANDLOADING THE .44 MAGNUM

The powder charge is 22 to 22.2 grains of what looks like Hercules 2400 but may be a duPont version of this powder with similar characteristics. We removed the slugs from a few loads, opened the crimp and put the original charge back in the case with my 250-grain .44 Special bullet, cast hard by Mar-Mur Bullet Co., copper-plated and sized to .429 inch. It seemed to shoot in the same group as the factory load but clearly indicated at least 5,000 pounds less pressure, estimated from primer comparisons. With factory bullets, the primer is well flattened, the firing pin indentation is not deep or full, and the primer flows around the perimeter of the firing pin indentation slightly.

When the Keith 250-grain hard .429-inch slug was fired, the firing pin indentation was deep, and the primer was not flattened to anything like the extent of the factory load. This clearly shows the value of one to 16 tin and lead, or harder bullets, when reloading this cartridge.

We also reloaded the fired factory cases with 22 grains No. 2400 and my 250-grain solid and 235-grain hollow base and hollowpoint bullets, getting, at an estimate, at least 5,000 pounds less pressure. This is a good way to leave it. Let the factory, with its pressure guns

and precision instruments for managing heavy pressures, use the high-pressure load. I'm well satisfied with either the factory load or my handload, which develops far less pressure. It is on the safe side, yet a load substantially as powerful. It penetrates even better in beef, perhaps because it is harder, and gives equal accuracy.

The new .44 Magnum S&W does not group all loads of the same bullet weight to the same point as do many .44 Special guns. The new Magnum lighter loads print high and right at 1 o'clock; my heavy .44 Special loads a bit lower and nearer center; 20 grains No. 2400 with the Keith 250-grain slug in the Magnum case, just out of the black at 7 o'clock, while the full handload of 22 grains 2400 and Keith 250-grain bullet print low and left at 7 o'clock. We settled for the full reload and the factory Remington (as both shoot to the same sighting) and sighted the gun for them. The target shooter wishing to use factory .44 Specials will have to sight for that load and change his sights when using the factory Magnum .44 load. Each load made small groups at all ranges tried. I have fired the big gun at least 600 times, both handloads and factory hulls.

The factory bullet is soft enough to expand readily on impact with flesh and acts just like a soft-nosed bullet from a .45–70 or .38–55. With my hollowpoint 235-grain bullet and 22 grains of No. 2400, expansion is even more rapid than with the factory bullet. It disintegrates on large bones and explodes jackrabbits, chucks, torn cats and similar vermin. The tests prove beyond any doubt that the .44 Magnum factory load will penetrate to the brain of the largest bear on earth or the biggest elk or moose if directed right. It will stop any mad cow or bull on the range with one well-placed shot if the cowpoke gets wound up and has to kill a critter. The fisherman or camera hunter, working the Alaskan streams, now has a gun for protection against a suddenly surprised Brownie with which he can stop the animal if he uses his head and shoots for the brain or spine. The prospector can kill all the meat he needs with this gun and factory loads or my heavy reloads.

Twenty-two grains No. 2400 and Keith 250-grain bullet and also factory loads were tried on car bodies, old cook stoves and motor blocks. They'll penetrate a lot of car body material and even get through the heavier steel braces. Each load cracks up motor heads and will penetrate the block, and ruin a piston. One shot through a radiator un-corks it, and these big heavy slugs placed almost anywhere on a motor will put it out of commission. The peace officer can stop a car with it or stop the criminal in it by shooting through the body of the car. I only asked for a duplication of my old-time tried .44 Special heavy load with 18.5 grains 2400 and the 250-grain Keith bullet, but the boys went me one better by producing a load that is even more powerful!

The big gun is, I would say, pleasant to shoot and does not jar the hand as much as do my heavy .44 Special loads from the much lighter 4-inch barrel .44 Special S&W guns. It is definitely not a ladies' gun, but I have known women who would enjoy shooting it. The recoil has not bothered me in the slightest, nor have several other old sixgun men complained who have fired it extensively,

including Hank Benson and Don Martin. The recoil is not as severe as that of a two-inch Airweight Chiefs' Special with high-speed .38 Specials. With .44 Special factory loads, it is just as pleasant to shoot as a K-22 and with the .44 Magnum loads, which give heaviest recoil, it will not bother a seasoned sixgun man at all. Recoil with my heaviest loads of 22 grains of 2400, and the Keith 250-grain bullet is much less than that of the factory load. The factory load, fired with one hand, flips the barrel up almost to the vertical.

Factory load velocity is claimed to be 1,570 feet with 1,314 pounds energy as against 1,450 feet velocity and 690 pounds energy for the .357 Magnum factory load. We are a bit skeptical about the claimed 1,570 feet velocity. Our own estimate would be somewhere nearer 1,400 feet. We base this on a lot of reloading for the .44 Special with 18.5 grains 2400, which gave the Keith 250-grain slug something over 1,200 feet from 6½-inch barrels. Pressure of the factory load is high, make no mistake on that score. Don't rechamber any .44 Special cylinder to take the big load. Cylinders, as well as guns, should be made especially for this

load, and I certainly won't convert any of my .44 Specials to take the .44 Remington Magnum. A Model 1892 Winchester carbine, however, built to handle this load would make an excellent companion gun, especially useful to the peace officer or to anyone in the backcountry.

The Remington .44 Magnum is the best case to reload I've seen. With the Keith 250-grain slug cast one to 16 tin and lead and sized exact groove diameter, to cut down pressures, the cartridge gives wonderful accuracy with 5 grains of Bullseye and would shoot accurately with even less of this fast powder. With 8½ grains of Unique, it makes a fine, medium load of around 1,000 feet or more; with 20 grains of 2400, one gets a good, fairly heavy load about equal to my old .44 Special heavy load. If you don't reload, you can always buy a box of Remington factory loads and be sure of getting the most powerful and perfect sixgun ammunition ever made anywhere.

I've killed enough beef animals with an 85-pound yew bow and broadheads that went entirely through the beasts to know that an arrow gives a slow, painful death with no shock. Now we have a sixgun and load that is infinitely better in

Remington .44 Magnum, an unfired bullet, and two fired and expanded bullets.

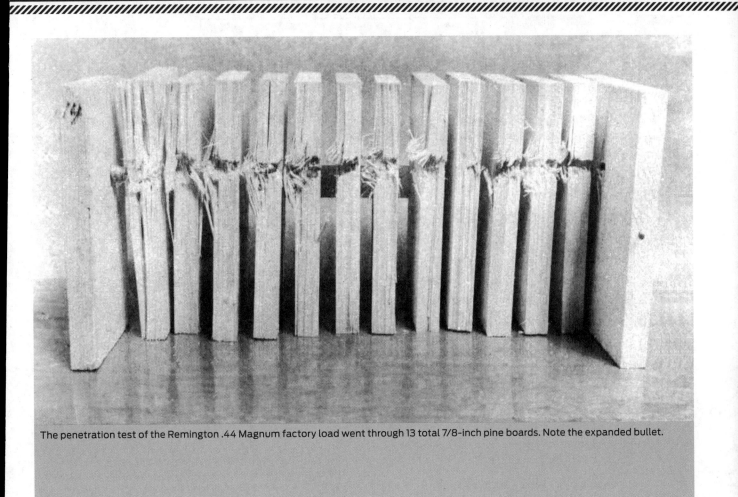

The penetration test of the Remington .44 Magnum factory load went through 13 total 7/8-inch pine boards. Note the expanded bullet.

every respect as a big game weapon than any bow ever drawn. It kills two-year-old steers too dead. They do not bleed well after being hit in the brain with the factory .44 Magnum load. One big porcupine, shot about dead center from the side, was killed instantly, leaving a two-inch exit hole on the far side. This gun and load will kill deer just as dead as a .30-30, up to at least 100 yards, if well placed, and the big slug will leave a better blood trail, as it is so soft it expands on contact and continues to expand as it penetrates. Velocity is high enough to carry considerable shock to any animal.

Friends who returned from Korea after fighting through that unpleasant affair tell me that they encountered many enemy soldiers with body armor which our .45 Auto ammo would not penetrate. The .44 Magnum loads go through quarter-inch dump truck beds like cheese and would penetrate any body armor a soldier would be likely to carry. Loaded with a full metal-jacketed bullet for military use, it would take care of any useful body armor.

After a lifetime of working with all manner of sixguns and loads, answering thousands of letters about them, and the writing of two books on the subject, as well as a great many magazine articles, I consider the .44 Remington Magnum cartridge and the great Smith & Wesson gun that chambers it the greatest sixgun development of our time! I am happy to have had even a small part in its development. **GD**

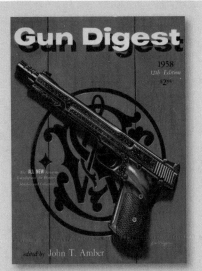

This article originally appeared in the *1958 Gun Digest* edition.

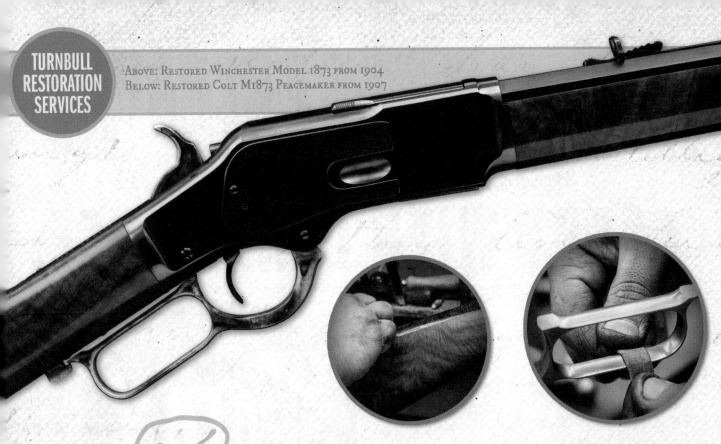

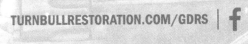

Parkwest Arms
SD-76

The Parkwest Arms custom Legend in its natural environment.

Top talent from the defunct Dakota Arms raises the bar on custom rifles.

›FRED ZEGLIN

I n 1981, I signed up for the gunsmithing program at Lassen College in Susanville, California. More than forty years later, my love for hunting rifles has not waned. I spent more than a few years of that time building custom hunting rifles for clients. You might guess that I have an opinion about rifle design and stocks. I sure do.

One of my hunting buddies likes to tease me about taking a synthetic-stocked rifle out deer hunting. I told him I would prefer to take a nice custom rifle into the field, but my customers kept them all. So, when I had the opportunity to shoot and review this fine custom rifle from Parkwest, I was excited, to

Two-panel hand-cut checkering is a standard feature on the Legend.

Rabackoff and his partner, Tim Land, bought the remains of Dakota Arms out of bankruptcy a few years back. "One of our primary goals was to preserve this group of artisans who had come together building rifles," Rabackoff said. "We had a very short window to make this happen before everyone would all have to move away and find work elsewhere. We were able to hire six of the staff who worked for the old company. My brother Jason was added to the mix as a general manager to oversee the shop. Tim and I are very proud that we provide jobs for 13 very talented craft persons who currently build our custom rifles." Parkwest is in the same factory as the former company in Sturgis, South Dakota.

Why the name change? The Dakota Arms moniker was not for sale with the company's other assets. So, Rabackoff and his team had to devise a new name. Rabackoff said dealers universally stated they could sell the product if the quality remained.

The new company wisely tapped the employees' knowledge base to improve the already great products. These improvements are things the end user will feel but may not be able to identify. The tolerances and fit of many parts were adjusted to reduce the hand-fitting time and tighten the tolerances. Parkwest provided top-quality tools to the machinists, aiding in tighter tolerances on the finished product. "Cheaper tools

would suffice, but the offset in quality far outweighs any savings possible," says Rabackoff. As a result, the customer will be pleased with the fit of the bolt to the action, the trigger's feel, and the overall quality improvement.

FIT OF RIFLE

A few things are critical to the function of a good hunting rifle. First and foremost is the fit of the rifle. Many shooters' experience is limited to "off-the-shelf" rifles for the mythical average-sized shooter.

That works out for most of us because the "average" represents the middle of the road when fitting a rifle. When you order a rifle from a custom maker like Parkwest Arms, you can match the gun to your needs and measurements. While I'm lucky to be an average-sized American male and most factory rifles fit me well, once you shoot a custom-fit gun, going back to average is difficult.

For my test of the Parkwest Arms SD-76, I received a 'Legend' rifle in .300 Winchester Magnum. I was offered a

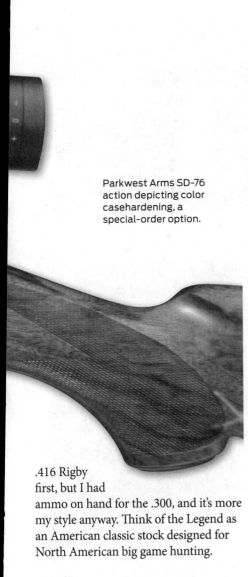

Parkwest Arms SD-76 action depicting color casehardening, a special-order option.

.416 Rigby first, but I had ammo on hand for the .300, and it's more my style anyway. Think of the Legend as an American classic stock designed for North American big game hunting.

BEAUTY

The SD-76 receivers are manufactured in-house using CNC equipment, giving Parkwest total control over quality. It offers receivers of different lengths so the action matches the cartridge. They're machined from pre-hardened billets of 4140 steel, which aids in maintaining dimensional integrity and consistency. The lug ways in the bolt race are wire EDM cut, which improves the control over dimensions and finish. Bolts are one-piece: no welding or brazing of bolt handles. The action has controlled-round feeding and a claw extractor, *à la* the pre-'64 Model 70 Winchester—a three-position safety is standard on all SD-76 actions.

It would have been fun to test the 'Dark Continent' in .416 Rigby; if you're a rifleman, African-style rifles are some-

thing most hunters want in their arsenals. The Parkwest rifles are what I would consider a classic design with a drop-belly magazine, banded ramp front sight, and a quarter rib to carry the rear sight. A mercury recoil reducer cuts the recoil. When I think of rifles for Africa, this is the style I envision, and I would feel safe betting most hunters would agree with me.

The Legend rifle I received was not the standard model. Instead, I thought it had several well-deserved and carefully thought-out upgrades. The color case-hardening of the action and scope mounts immediately jumped out at me. The colors were bright and vibrant, a detail that impressed me right out of the gate. Color case-hardening is all about the preparation of the metal. If it's polished properly, the metal shows off the colors; if poorly polished, it detracts from the colors and reveals imperfections.

Other features included the excellent iron sights, the Howell sling swivel/barrel band, and the ebony forend tip. Checkering on the forend wrapped around instead of two separate panels. All these touches add to the functionality and beauty of the finished rifle.

WORKMANSHIP

As a guy who still builds a stock now and then, I focused next on the inletting, carefully examining the quality of the workmanship. It's difficult to hide inletting mistakes from a gunsmith. Even though an individual gunsmith might have difficulty competing with the quality, most gunsmiths know good work when they see it. The inletting on this rifle was so close to perfect that I have no complaints. The fit of metal and wood was uniform and well executed by expert hands. The stock was made from a nice piece of XXX English Walnut. (Parkwest offers the choice of Turkish, Bastogne, or English Walnut stocks.)

The next detail to draw my eye is always the screw alignment. All the action screws—and those in the oval sling swivel at the toe of the stock—had their

Parkwest's inlet of metal to wood shows superior workmanship, and the detail around the floorplate is uniform, crisp, and well-executed.

Ebony forend tip upgrade and the Howell-style barrel band/swivel make for a classy look.

The shadow line cheekpiece was well-executed, like all the details on this rifle.

PARKWEST ARMS LEGEND SPECIFICATIONS:

Right or left-handed
XXX English, Turkish, or
Bastogne Walnut
Point pattern checkering, 23 LPI,
two panels on the grip and two
panels on the forearm
Premium match-grade barrel
Calibers from .22-250 to .375
H&H
Magazine capacity is 4+1 in
standard calibers, 3+1 with
magnum cartridges
Classic button release floorplate
Classic ball swivel studs
Talley bases and rings
Weight approximately 7.5 lbs
Sub-1-MOA guarantee
MSRP $10,995
parkwestarms.com

slots aligned straight with the stock. Many gunsmiths will do this if you pay for the work, but I expect this detail from a premium gunbuilder like Parkwest. Does it matter if the slots are not aligned? Not at all, but it speaks volumes about the care put into the firearm during the building process.

Iron sights are an added detail. I never object when I have the backup sights available. This is the same setup that is standard on Parkwest's Savanna model. An ebony forearm tip finishes the rifle with a nice, clean detail. I know this should go without saying, but the sights, barrel band and forend tip are all aligned and square to the barreled action as they should be.

EXECUTION
I dug around the shop and found a

Leupold
VX-III Long Range
4.5-14x40mm scope with a Boone & Crockett reticle. Like the scope, the Talley rings supplied with the gun were 30mm, so it was fate. It was time to hit the range with the rig assembled and the scope collimated. I was excited to get this rifle on the target.

The rifle's balance and weight were right on track. Unloaded with the scope installed, it weighed 8.5 pounds. Truthfully, it felt lighter in my hand than I expected—this is not a skinny toothpick-style stock. It fills the hand comfortably.

ACCURACY
According to my gauge, the trigger was crisp and set to under 3 pounds, perfect for a hunting rifle. I never claimed to be any great marksman, but I can

punch holes in paper when the occasion requires proof that a gun can shoot. The first three shots out of the rifle went into a .418-inch group. That's well under the 1 MOA that Parkwest guarantees on all its rifles.

The second group opened up to just under an inch for five shots. The flyer from that group increased the group size; otherwise, it would have been right at a half-inch. We noticed that the primer on that shot looked different than all the rest after firing, so I am willing to attribute it to the ammo. Either way, it still beats the accuracy that Parkwest promises with factory loads.

FUNCTION

Single feeding for accuracy worked flawlessly. After finishing the benchrest work, I wanted to see how the gun functioned in rapid fire. The drill is standing at 50 yards; put five shots on the paper as fast as safely possible. I had a case that failed to fully eject from the port, which caused a jam. I was sure it was just a matter of adjusting the extractor, but I called and talked to Ward, Parkwest's gunsmith, who confirmed that a quick adjustment to the extractor to increase spring tension was the correct solution. The gun functioned flawlessly once I adjusted it.

Brass varies from one maker to the next, and the rim of my lot of brass proved to be at the minimum dimensions for factory ammo. So, this minor

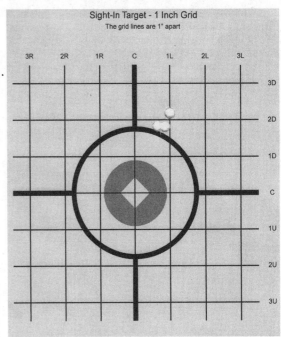

The first group from a cold barrel and factory ammo: .418 inch at 100 yards from a rest.

adjustment does not reflect the rifle's or brass's fit or quality. I spend much of my time teaching clients and students about variations in ammo and tolerances in guns and chambers. Guns are machines; they are not magical wands. Understanding tolerances is an integral part of gun knowledge that is often overlooked.

With careful load development, I am sure it would be easy to tighten up the groups I achieved even further, though most hunters would call this minute-of-elk at 500 to 600 yards with the factory loads. I used ammo from Full Throttle

Arsenal, a Montana manufacturer with a 190-grain HP bullet.

By now, it should be obvious that the Parkwest SD-76 Legend checked all the boxes for me. Keep in mind, as a gunsmith, I handle many guns. My taste in firearms favors ones that I do not have the economic right to own. However, it's all about priorities. A Timex will tell time, but a Rolex does it with style. The same can be said for a fine custom rifle. A $300 rifle will fill the freezer, but a Parkwest Arms rifle delivers the luxury and success inherent in all top-quality products. **GD**

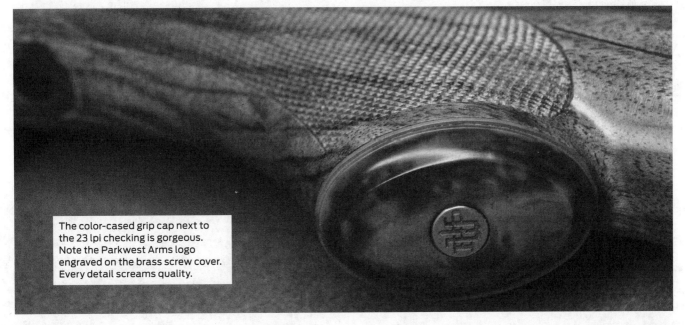

The color-cased grip cap next to the 23 lpi checking is gorgeous. Note the Parkwest Arms logo engraved on the brass screw cover. Every detail screams quality.

This is the finely crafted Anschutz Model 1761 MPR (Multi-Purpose Rimfire) rifle, complete with a Leupold 6X scope.

The Anschutz Model 1761

> STAN TRZONIEC

The target rimfire rifle's upgrades enhance an already nearly perfect plinker.

I n years past, the field between rimfire and centerfire target rifles seemed pretty well matched in models, but with the advent of new cartridges and more rugged guns, the rimfire is the one to pick now. Rimfire rifles are lighter, easier to carry, and use softer-recoiling ammunition, which is less expensive and involves no reloading. Besides that, the .22 rimfire has a greater variety of precision or match ammo for serious target sessions or small game and varmint hunting in the field.

During my 50-plus-year writing career (yep, I'm getting up there), I've used almost every target handgun or rifle available. Handguns from Smith & Wesson, Colt, Walther, and the Ruger Mark IV Target come to mind and rifles, both custom and production, in sporter weight and heavy barrel versions from Remington, Ruger, Savage, or the CZ Model 457 rate high on my list.

Of course, the Anschutz Model 1761 series of guns includes various specialized models, of which one-third can make the grade as target guns, including the MPR (Multi-Purpose Rifle) we feature here due to its features and stock design. Anschutz is well known for catering to shooters who want the best but also appreciate options tailored to a shooting style or budget; in short, I will call these production-custom rifles with further upgrades in wood and engraving available from the Custom Shop.

Anschutz entered the specialized target market with the Model 54 action in the 1950s and, some years later, with the SuperMatch in 1962, when the Winchester Model 52 was considered the .22-caliber rifle for competition sports. However, Anschutz's well-designed trigger, shorter lock time, and heavier receiver placed the Winchester brand on the back burner in these venues almost overnight.

About a decade later, the lighter-weight Model 64-type receiver came about, aimed at the sporting rifle enthusiast. In 2015, Anschutz announced a shorter bolt machined 30mm in overall length to compete with other competition rifles in the same class. With its life cycle closing

in, engineers conceived a new action that could be used for sporting and target-grade rifles. The result was the Model 1761, which incorporates a shorter bolt lift and a smoother operation across several new models.

The new design replaced the 53-degree bolt lift on the Model 54 with a 60-degree one, thus moving the three locking lugs to the middle of the bolt rather than at the rear. This gained the advantage of a single-spring striker system that moved to the bolt's rear with a shorter bolt. Also, a roller bearing reduces the cocking effort. Finally, an oversized bolt knob of 25mm (1-inch) in diameter aids cocking, extraction (via twin opposing extractors on the bolt face), and loading of the cartridge into the chamber, which shows a red indicator at the rear of the shroud when cocked.

With all that going on, the receiver needed to be upgraded. Anschutz went with a flat bottom machined from a solid Chromoly steel billet with an integral recoil lug shortened by 40mm. The conventional 11mm dovetail was kept for scope mounting, as was a 3mm cross-slot at the

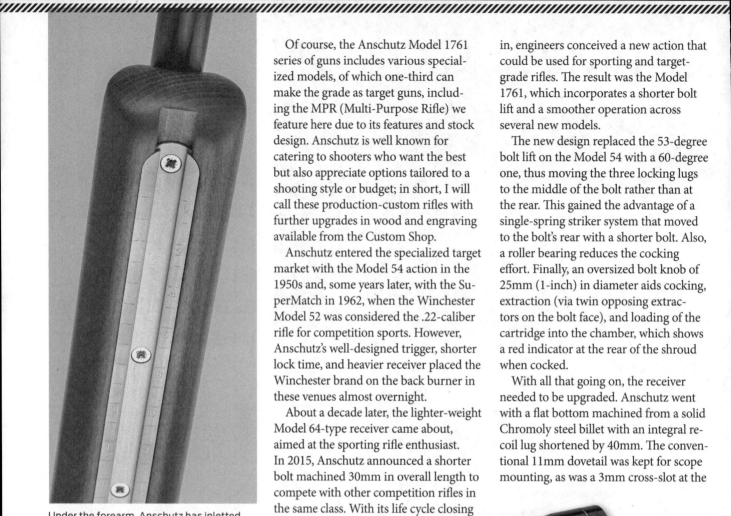

Under the forearm, Anschutz has inletted an accessory rail for those who want to use the MPR for target use. It also keeps the stock from warping.

The MPR's stock was developed for target and small game hunters. It combines the classic look with a wide beavertail forearm and an accessory rail.

The Anschutz Model 1761 MPR is impressive from any angle. The oversized bolt handle is made for all weather conditions, and the safety lever and magazine are within easy reach.

There was never any doubt this gun could shoot! This five-shot group with all touching came in at .240 inch at 50 yards using RWS R50 ammunition.

rear of the receiver for a Picatinny rail. The receiver is not epoxy bedded into the stock; Anschutz engineers reasoned that the larger bottom's flat surface was more than enough to ensure the desired accuracy, having a choice of the .22 Long Rifle, .17 HMR, or the .22 Winchester Magnum Rifle (WMR) cartridge.

Anschutz made this target gun—and the others in the series—to accept interchangeable barrels for precision and hunting duties, with a selection of seven barrels in lengths including 18, 19.3, 20.3, 21.4 and 23 inches in sporter and heavy configurations with or without open sights, barrel threads, or a suppressor. All are changed (Anschutz recommends a gunsmith) via twin barrel locking clamps that allow precision seating and head-space on the receiver. Additionally, the barrels are target-crowned, and on the MPR model, the barrel has been enlarged slightly from a total barrel diameter of .810 to .860 inch at the muzzle with a 3-inch-long 11mm dovetail to accept a competition front sight.

While the guns accept three different calibers, the five-round magazines are dimensionally the same on the outside, allowing them to work seamlessly with one standard style of bottom metal and trigger group. With the addition of an extended pad on the bottom, regardless of the weather or gloves, it's easy to guide it into the gun thanks to a small channel on the triggerguard. You can also remove it via a release on the inside of the trig-gerguard.

Anschutz improved the safety lever by enlarging its surface and smoothing its operation. While there is a detent, it has no detectable click and rides over this notch without any noise—and very smoothly at that.

When I mention custom in describing the Model 1761, trigger options are a significant part of the rifle's accuracy. Both are finely adjustable, with one single-stage affair, including the magazine release with or without a trigger blade that moves forward or rearward on a slide to accommodate a "length of pull" on the trigger shoe. The other option is the one I like since it includes a two-stage trigger, with or without the trigger blade adjustment. Out of the box, the trigger

Like the rest of the gun, the bolt is finely finished for smooth operation. The target ammunition used in the testing is shown.

on my MPR broke at 8 ounces after the initial take-up.

The Multi-Purpose Rifle's stock work is outstanding. The lines are clean and well-defined, the wood is select-grade or above with no knots, and it's finished with a satin-lacquered finish.

Other features include a wide bea-vertail forearm with finger grooves on each side and a 10-inch aluminum rail inletted underneath for target shooting accessories. While the rail may not serve the average varmint shooter, it keeps this part of the wood stock in check against moving or warping—and any varmint or small game hunter would be happy using it as it adapts to any spontaneous rest in the field. There is no checkering here, as the width and finger grooves offer more than enough purchase.

Moving back, the stock tapers inward over the bottom metal holding the

The Model 1761 has a fully adjustable recoil pad with a black spacer. A tool is furnished to adjust it.

On the left side of the photo, note how the wide beavertail forearm tapers into the stock just before the magazine and trigger assembly. The bolt release is under the rear scope base.

TABLE 1. — .22 LONG RIFLE FACTORY LOADS

LOAD (GRAINS)	VELOCITY (FPS)	FIVE-SHOT 50-YARD GROUP (IN.)
40 RWS Rifle Match	1,068	.285
40 RWS R50	1,060	.240
40 S&K Rifle Match	996	.245

Note: This is an Anschutz Model 1761 MPR with a 21-inch barrel. Velocities were chronographed at 10 feet from the muzzle with an Oehler Model 35P Chronograph.

SPECIFICATIONS MODEL 1761

Manufacturer: Anschutz, West Germany
Action: Bolt-action
Caliber Tested: .22 Long Rifle
Barrel: Carbon steel, blued
Barrel Length: From 18 to 23 inches
Barrel Twist Rate: 420mm (1:16.5 inches)
Magazine Capacity: 5
Safety: Two-position, silent
Trigger Pull: Two-stage, 8 ounces
Sights: None, receiver drilled and tapped for scope mounts
MSRP: $2,195
anschutznorthamerica.com

magazine well and triggerguard. The pistol grip is well-formed and curved for comfortable handling. There is no pistol grip cap—watch those prone shooting opportunities—and it's checkered in a pleasing outline on both sides, complete with a custom ribbon cut halfway in the pattern.

The stock wrist is full and offers plenty of room, even with winter gear or heavy gloves. On the buttstock, the comb is high sans a cheekpiece. At the rear is an adjustable recoil pad. Removing the screw allows you to move the rear part up or down to fit your shoulder. Taking it off reveals two holes, which I surmise are for high-tech buttplates that fit in the stock with two rods for length-of-pull adjustments.

I've always enjoyed custom touches on my rifles, and to this end, Anschutz offers four grades of wood with the initial order. Starting at the entry level, you have the Standard Grade (nice wood and finish), and then you move to the

Premium Grade, which has more color, figure, and grain pattern. From there, you get into the fine wood with the Luxus Grade and the Meister Grade, which shows a Grade V or VI class of wood. To further trick out the rifle to your tastes and checkbook, Anschutz has its Custom Shop. Here, you can pick from the best wood, deep-relief engraving, and other details to make your gun a unique family heirloom.

But how does it shoot? Since winter makes it hard to go woodchuckin,' paper targets set up at 50 yards had to do. The company sent three selections of target-grade ammunition from RWS and S&K. I installed a Leupold 6x42mm scope in Bushnell low rings. The mounting was low, with just a bit of air between the objective bell and the barrel.

Settling down at the bench with sandbags, the Model 1761 came to life. With the extra heft of the gun and the near-perfect trigger, I could count on groups with all five shots touching. What you see in the chart is the best of the five-shot groups fired from each box of ammo. Not averages, the best of the best, and to confirm what I saw—and not just dreamed—Anschutz sent six range test targets which, as an aggregate, came in at .326-inch from the factory with the best group of .238 inch. Now, it was my turn.

Up first was the RWS Rifle Match brand. After the smoke cleared, the best was at a curt .285 inch. The RWS Matchless Precision topped all with the best of the morning, with five shots touching at .240 inch. This was also the best ammo the company used for its testing. Rounding up the session, the S&K Rifle Match came in close, but there was no cigar at .245 inch. Velocities were around 1,000 fps plus, typical for this type of ammunition.

As a dedicated small game and chuck hunter, the Anschutz Model 1761 MPR is worthy of a second look. The lines are true; the gun is sound and more than accurate if you do your part. **GD**

The author gives the Mossberg 940 Pro Turkey two thumbs up. The shotgun, which takes cues from the competition world, busts gobblers like there's no tomorrow.

Mossberg 940
PRO SERIES SHOTGUNS

From waterfowl to turkey to self-defense, these gas-operated autoloaders deliver.

›BRAD FENSON

Confession time: I am addicted to wingshooting and shotguns. The old scattergun is a favorite, and my vault holds several smoothbores in various gauges. Every shotgun is different, and paying attention to detail helps me decide what to use on any given day.

I am also a waterfowl aficionado, and fast-cycling shotguns that can keep up with the fast action and even faster-flaring birds are paramount. My passion makes me look for any advantage that produces consistent results.

A waterfowl hunt in Saskatchewan introduced me to a new semi-automatic

The 940 Pro Turkey's features are well thought out and will be appreciated by hunters. For example, not only is it gas-operated (versus inertia) to reduce recoil, but its HIVIZ TriComp sights enhance visibility in the turkey woods and enable precise hits.

waterfowl gun from the Mossberg 940 Pro Series. It was a target-rich environment, and over four days, I emptied more than a dozen boxes of shotshells. The shotgun worked flawlessly, cycled for every shot, and was not cleaned during the entire adventure. It wasn't until the following week that I started to understand the features. The recoil was noticeably more intense when I returned to my regular shotguns to hunt at home. The experience led me to dissect the excellence of the Mossberg 940 series, delving into the Waterfowl and Turkey models and exploring their competitive roots.

The 940 Pro Waterfowl model was fun to shoot and reduced recoil punishment. It shouldered consistently, engaged the target easily, and delivered precise patterns at various ranges. The new waterfowl autoloader is impervious to corrosion and durable enough for the toughest field conditions.

Mossberg is a well-known shotgun manufacturer that has dominated the market for decades. The company's early models were bolt- or pump-action shotguns. In August 1961, Mossberg launched the 500 Series pump-action shotgun, which is still one of the most-produced sporting firearms in the world, with over 10 million sold. What Mossberg has not been known for is semi-automatic shotguns, which is where the story gets interesting. The initial 930 line of semi-autos offered value and clean operation and helped set the stage for Mossberg to catapult into the autoloader world, leading to the 940 advancements.

DESIGN AND ADAPTABILITY

Fit and feel are critical factors for shooting a shotgun accurately and consistently.

Being on target starts with getting the shotgun to your shoulder the same way every time you lift it. The 940 Pro's drop, cast, and length-of-pull adjustability proved a game-changer (the length-of-pull adjustment ranges from 13 to 14.25 inches). I liked the adaptability of wearing heavy clothes and maintaining the same shouldering for consistent down-range results. That adjustability makes the 940 an excellent option for any size shooter. Our waterfowl group consisted of men and women of various statures, and everyone shot well because we could adjust the guns for proper fit.

The front end of the shotgun is just as crucial for shooting consistently, and the 940 has features that work together to make shooters successful. Mossberg's innovative barrel-making process makes it intuitive to look down the rib and shoot consistent point-of-aim and impact patterns. At the same time, the slim-profile forend enhanced the shotgun's nimbleness, ensuring a smooth swing. Having the right length, an easy grip, and being able to draw your eye down the barrel to the target was punishing for the local waterfowl population.

EVOLUTION THROUGH COLLABORATION

A pivotal collaboration with renowned competitive shooters Jerry and Lena Miculek and Mossberg engineers marked the genesis of the 940 series. This partnership generated changes to engineering a shotgun—the 940 JM Pro introduced in 2020, a 12-gauge autoloader tailored for competitive shooting. The results were noticeable, and Mossberg recognized the potential for transferable technology and incorporated these innovations into the Waterfowl and Snow Goose models. I shot one of the first Waterfowl models

The 940 Pro series shotguns' ability to adjust the drop, cast, and length of pull makes them feel tailor-made.

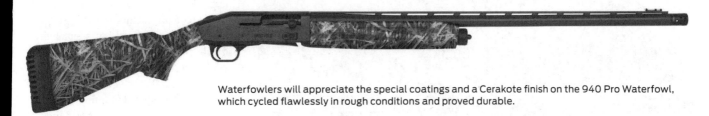

Waterfowlers will appreciate the special coatings and a Cerakote finish on the 940 Pro Waterfowl, which cycled flawlessly in rough conditions and proved durable.

in 2021 and still consider it the lightest-recoil shotgun in my arsenal.

ERGONOMICS AND HANDLING

Loading the firearm, even with gloves, was effortless, thanks to an oversized charging handle and a beveled loading port with an elongated, pinch-free elevator. Even when the bird action was hot and heavy, the gas-operated system ensured rapid and reliable cycling, even in freezing temperatures. Gas systems are not known for reduced recoil, but the 940 line is easy and fun to shoot.

LOW-RECOIL REVELATION

The shotgun industry has been leaning towards inertia-driven guns. However, the 940 series embraced gas operation but has been engineered to reduce recoil, even with big magnums. Its low recoil became evident compared to conventional shotguns, offering a critical advantage in swift target acquisition and shooting. There was little recovery time between shots.

DURABILITY IN ADVERSE CONDITIONS

The 940 Pro Waterfowl's durability was not to be understated. The Cerakote finish, in TrueTimber Prairie camouflage, proved non-reflective and camouflaged, shielding the shotgun against the elements. Further fortifying its robust design, the chrome-lined chamber and bore resisted corrosion and pitting, even in the harshest conditions.

PRECISION IN PERFORMANCE

Mossberg's meticulous attention to coatings, gas operation, and the shell catch translated into flawless cycling. Through 15 boxes of shotshells, the 940 Pro never faltered. Mossberg boasts that the gun will cycle up to 1,500 rounds before

cleaning is required. This performance-enhancing feature could be a game-changer for avid hunters when the action is fast-paced. The special coatings started with the 930 line and have continued to advance in the 940s.

AESTHETICS AND SIGHTS

The camouflage-finished stock, paired with the distinctive Cerakote finish, helped with concealment from keen-eyed ducks and geese without giving up a modern and stylish appearance. There are different colors and patterns in all models.

The first time Fenson shot the 940 Pro Waterfowl, he downed a triple on big northern mallards, which made him pay attention to the fit, feel, and recoil. Anyone considering purchasing a new shotgun needs to try a 940 Pro to feel the difference in recoil and fit.

The 940 Pro shotgun series' advantages and features are attributed to engineering innovations from competition guns. Still, new models, like the 940 Pro Turkey, are specialized for that hunting style.

The author took this ocellated turkey in the Yucatan jungle with the Mossberg 940 Pro Turkey.

attention in the market, the 940 Pro Turkey emerged as the next virtuoso in the series. It aimed to redefine the turkey hunting experience by combining precision, adaptability, and style. But would it deliver?

With adjustability in drop, cast, and length-of-pull, the 940 Pro Turkey echoed the tailored fit found in its predecessors. This adaptability and the new barrel-making process ensured shooters maintained their point-of-aim and impact, offering a customized and comfortable feel.

The 940 Pro Turkey has an optics-ready design with a drilled and tapped receiver, but it still comes fitted with a HIVIZ CompSight Fiber-Optic Sight. This addition enhanced target acquisition, providing a clear advantage in the field. The Pro Turkey uses a clean-running gas-vent system and quick-empty magazine release.

The 940 Pro Turkey is dressed in Mossy Oak Greenleaf camouflage with an X-Factor XX-Full Tky Choke Tube. To cater to the preferences of discerning turkey hunters, you can choose from 18.5- or 24-inch barrels. The MSRP is $1,120.

FORM AND FUNCTION

The Mossberg saga, once synonymous with bolt- and pump-action designs, took a big turn with the 940 series. The series started from competitive roots, but these shotguns emerged as versatile performers, seamlessly blending the needs of hunters, competitive shooters, and those looking for defense.

In the world of shotguns, the Mossberg 940 Pro series has been a breath of fresh air for gas-operated guns, with new technologies and innovation stemming from collaboration and adaptability. The diverse and plentiful bag of ducks and geese taken on the first hunt with the 940 Pro Waterfowl resonated with us wing-shooters. An ocellated turkey from the Yucatan jungle proved the value of the 940 Pro Turkey. In a world of shotguns, the 940 series has carved its niche—a harmonious blend of form and function, poised to leave an indelible mark on the legacy of Mossberg shotguns.

New in 2024, the 940 Pro Turkey, Snow Goose, Waterfowl, and JM are all optics-ready. **GD**

The 940 Pro line includes the HIVIZ TriComp sight from HIVIZ Shooting Systems, with interchangeable LitePipes that enhance target acquisition, adding a touch of sophistication to its design. If you've never tried the HIVIZ sights, you owe it to yourself to see the difference.

SPECIFICATIONS AND PRICING
Decked in TrueTimber Prairie camouflage, the 940 Pro Waterfowl boasts a 28-inch vent rib barrel with an extended, ported choke, which ate more of the recoil but made hearing protection a must. The choke system is Accu-Choke-

compatible. The shotgun features an ambidextrous safety and a five-round capacity, with an MSRP of $1,050. The Snow Goose variant, with a 12-round capacity and unique Battleship Gray Cerakote finish, offers additional options at an MSRP of $1,120.

TURKEY PRO MODEL
The waterfowl model impressed me, and when I tried the turkey model, I couldn't help but wonder if it could eat some of the intense recoil of the hardest-hitting shotshells designed for hammering a big gobbler. As the 940 Pro Waterfowl gained

The Franchi Momentum rifle has an attractive flat dark earth stock with straight lines and Italian flair.

Franchi Momentum in
.350 Legend

The affordable Franchi Momentum rifle is an excellent choice for hunting in states that mandate straight-walled cartridges.

❯ MIKE DICKERSON

Staring at fresh, large grizzly tracks in the snow can wake you up faster than a cold shower, especially when hunting with an unproven prototype rifle from a company that had never made rifles before.

That's the situation I found myself in during an eight-day elk hunt in southern Alberta in 2017. I was there, with five other hunters, to test and provide feedback on a pre-production version of the Momentum bolt-action rifle from Franchi, the Italian manufacturer of fine shotguns. I took no small comfort in the fact that the rifle shot well for me and was chambered in .30-'06 Springfield. Grizzlies were much in evidence during that hunt, and wolves were even more abundant, which likely accounted for the scarcity of elk.

The bolt has a short, 60-degree throw, allowing ample room for mounting optics.

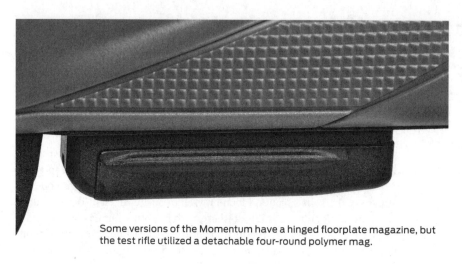

Some versions of the Momentum have a hinged floorplate magazine, but the test rifle utilized a detachable four-round polymer mag.

The prototypes showed a little room for improvement, as you might expect with a company's first-ever rifle. Our group made several suggestions, mainly concerning the barrel and trigger. When Franchi introduced the feature-rich Momentum at the 2018 SHOT Show, I was pleased to see its changes. The relatively thin barrel had been replaced with a heavier one. The plain, fat bolt had been replaced with a weight-reducing spiral-fluted one, and the trigger was much improved. I tested that first production model, chambered in .30-'06, and found it consistently shot 1-MOA groups with various factory ammo.

A few years later, I tested a Momentum Elite Varmint rifle, chambered in .224 Valkyrie, on a Montana hunt. In addition to smoking a considerable number of prairie dogs, I killed a pronghorn at 260 yards. That rifle consistently printed sub-

My hunting partner shot a massive wolf during that hunt, and two of our hunters in the wildlife management unit north of us shot their way out of the middle of a wolf pack during a snow-storm, downing three of the canines. Two of our party, who hunted the northernmost unit and reported no wolf sightings, connected on a pair of nice 6X6 bulls.

MOA groups with ammo it liked.

Given my history with the Momentum rifle, I eagerly jumped at a chance to test one chambered in .350 Legend, an ideal deer cartridge for hunters in states that mandate straight-walled cartridges. I would not be disappointed.

RELIABLE PROPRIETARY ACTION

Franchi builds the Momentum around a proprietary push-feed action that utilizes a full-size, chrome-finished and fluted bolt body with three locking lugs, a plunger ejector, and an extractor built into one of the lugs. The bolt cycles smoothly, with just a bit of chatter, but that disappears if you cycle it forcefully. The bolt has a short, 60-degree throw that allows ample clearance for mounting a scope and lets you run the gun fast. Unlike some short-throw bolts, it does not require excessive force to operate. Functionally, the action worked with nary a hiccup. It fed, fired, and ejected cartridges with monotonous reliability.

In .350 Legend, the Momentum has a 22-inch cold-hammer-forged chrome-moly barrel with a 1:16 twist rate. It is threaded 5/8x24 for attaching muzzle brakes or suppressors and has a knurled thread protector. Both the barrel and action have a nicely executed black anodized finish.

The barreled action is not bedded to the stock with a traditional recoil lug. Instead, it uses machined slots that fit onto small bedding lugs in the stock. This, at least theoretically, can improve accuracy by relieving stress on the action. The barrel is truly free-floated (I checked). The stock forend has a bit more flex in it than I would prefer, but that did not, as you will see, adversely impact the rifle's accuracy.

Basic versions of the Momentum come with a hinged floorplate magazine, but my test gun used a detachable straight-feed, four-round polymer mag that protrudes slightly beneath the bottom of the stock. The magazine proved reliable, but it's one component of the rifle that I'm not entirely fond of. It can be

The smooth-cycling Momentum action uses a full-size, chrome-finished, fluted bolt body with three locking lugs.

difficult to load due to the force required to depress the magazine follower, and it was challenging to insert and fully seat it into the magazine well with the bolt in the closed position. Seating the magazine was much easier with the bolt open. On the plus side, the magazine release button is protected inside the triggerguard, so it's unlikely to release when moving through the brush. The magazine drops freely into the hand when you activate the button release.

UNIQUE STYLING

The Momentum's barreled action is mated to an attractive, flat dark earth synthetic stock (upgraded Momentum Elite versions come with camo pattern stocks for more money). While the stock has straight and mostly classic lines, its styling exhibits some Italian flair.

Franchi says the stock is ergonomically designed to provide an ideal hold in the most frequently used shooting positions. Checkered surfaces below the action and along much of the forend ride atop swells that fill the hand, while the fingertips

tend to wrap around the cutout, somewhat scalloped borders on the top side, providing a solid and comfortable grip. There's additional checkering above the magazine and on the slightly narrowed wrist of the pistol grip, which is not surprising from an Italian shotgun maker. There's even a checkered cutout at the rear bottom of the stock, just ahead of the bottom of the recoil pad, intended to serve as an offhand finger-gripping point when shooting from a bench.

Notably, the stock has recessed swivel studs, so they won't get in the way when shooting from rests at the bench. The stock is also equipped with Franchi's TSA recoil pad. The company says it reduces felt recoil by as much as 50 percent. I don't know how accurate that claim is, but the recoil pad does seem to do a pretty good job of reducing recoil. The pad is slightly grippy with rounded edges so it won't snag on clothing. You would expect these touches from a company that has long made fine shotguns. Transferring some of this technology to rifles makes a lot of sense.

The stock has recessed swivel studs that won't get in the way when shooting from rests at the bench.

The barrel is threaded (5/8x24) to attach muzzle brakes or suppressors.

BALANCED FEEL

The rifle balances nicely in the hands, with a slight weight-forward feel that I like for steadying it for shots. The gun has a 14-inch length of pull and measures 44.25 inches overall. Empty weight, without an optic, is 7.1 pounds. With a scope installed, I measured the weight of my test rifle at 7 pounds, 15 ounces. Unless you plan on toting it up Mount Everest, I would classify the gun's weight as just right. It is neither too heavy nor too light for most hunting purposes.

This gun will also allow you to hunt quietly. Loaded or empty, it does not rattle, making it a good choice as a stalking rifle. The broad, flat bottom of the forend makes it at home on the bench or in a blind, and it can be shot from rests or bags.

The rifle mounts naturally and quickly to the shoulder, and I found I could trigger follow-up shots without taking my eye out of the scope.

A FANTASTIC TRIGGER

One of the best things—and maybe *the* best thing about the Momentum—is the Franchi Relia Trigger. It feels like a premium, upgraded aftermarket trigger—a single-stage design with no creep. Have you heard of triggers that break like glass? This one does. Franchi says it is user-adjustable within a range of 2 to 4 pounds, but the trigger on my test rifle broke cleanly and consistently at a pull weight of 1 pound, 14 ounces as the rifle arrived from the factory. Out of the box, it's one of the best triggers I've ever encountered on a factory rifle, let alone one that's so affordably priced. If you make a poor shot using this rifle, it will not be because of the trigger.

The trigger is paired with a two-position safety located within easy reach of the thumb of the shooting hand. It has a finely knurled surface for operation in inclement weather, making an audible click when engaged or disengaged. It does not lock the bolt down when in the safe position, which may or may not be your cup of tea. It didn't bother me because I always exercise caution when moving through heavy brush, so the bolt is unlikely to snag and open inadvertently.

BY THE NUMBERS

For range testing, I put the Momentum through its paces with a Burris Fullfield E1 .350 Legend 3-9X48 scope, which has a Ballistic Plex reticle with dots on the vertical stadia for trajectory compensation. Mounting a scope was a breeze because the rifle came with two short Picatinny rail sections installed atop the receiver. You can install different bases using the Remington 700 pattern if you wish.

I had only three factory loads, with three bullet weights, available for testing. They produced some surprising results.

First, the two loads' velocities were significantly higher than the factory-stated figures. Hornady's 165-grain FTX load launched at 2,377 fps, 177 fps faster than the factory number. Browning's 124-grain FMJ load stepped out 224 fps faster than the factory-claimed 2,500 fps. I checked spent cases for any signs of excessive pressure and found none. This means these ammo makers use test barrels shorter than 22 inches for testing .350 Legend ammo, which I doubt—or this rifle has a somewhat "fast" barrel. Either way, these higher velocities are, in my book, a good thing. With these loads, you can shoot with a slightly flatter trajectory, and bullets will impact with more authority.

The Momentum is equipped with a fantastic trigger. The adjustable Relia Trigger on the test rifle broke crisply at a pull weight of 1 pound, 14 ounces.

The author tested the Momentum in .350 Legend at 100 yards and was not disappointed with its performance.

The Franchi Momentum in .350 Legend proved surprisingly accurate—all three tested loads produced average groups of 1 MOA or better.

TABLE 1. FRANCHI MOMENTUM .350 LEGEND VELOCITY AND ACCURACY

FACTORY LOAD	VELOCITY (FPS)	STANDARD DEVIATION (FPS)	EXTREME SPREAD (FPS)	AVG. GROUP (IN.)	BEST GROUP (IN.)
Browning 124-gr. FMJ	2,724	11.2	26.8	.88	.81
Hornady 165-gr. FTX	2,377	20.3	48.5	1.0	.60
Winchester 180-gr. Power-Point	2,057	12.4	26.5	.75	.58

Note: Velocities were measured over a Garmin Xero C1 chronograph, and test groups fired in the wind varying 6-11 mph. Accuracy was measured with three three-shot groups.

FRANCHI MOMENTUM .350 LEGEND SPECIFICATIONS

Chambering: .350 Legend
Action: Push-feed bolt-action
Barrel: 22-inches, 1:16 rate of twist
Finish: Anodized black
Stock: FDE synthetic
Magazine: Detachable polymer
Capacity: 4+1
Weight: 7.1 lbs.
Trigger: Franchi Relia Trigger
Length of pull: 14 in.
Overall length: 44.25 in.
MSRP: $799

I measured the load using the heaviest bullet—Winchester's 180-grain Power-Point load—at 2,057 fps. That number is 43 fps slower than the factory-claimed velocity and more in line with expectations.

In accuracy testing with three-shot groups the Momentum positively shined. Straight-walled cartridges don't always produce stellar accuracy, but the Momentum shot surprisingly well with all three tested loads—and it wasn't finicky about bullet weights. Each shot 1 inch or better average groups at 100 yards. Top honors went to Winchester's 180-grain Power-Point load, which produced a .75-inch average group and the best group measuring just .58 inch. Hornady's 165-grain FTX load wasn't far behind,

with a .60-inch best group and a 1-inch average group. Browning's 124-grain FMJ load also shot well, producing .88-inch average groups. It's worth noting that all testing was done when I had to deal with a full-value wind.

FINAL THOUGHTS

The Momentum is a well-thought-out design. It's reliable, accurate, and light enough for most hunting purposes. In the .350 Legend chambering, it's an ideal choice for hunting in straight-walled-cartridge states or for anywhere shot opportunities will be within 150 yards. With an MSRP of just $799, the Momentum is one of the best of the sub-$1,000 rifles, and it's backed with a 7-year warranty. **GD**

Weatherby's 307 Alpine CT

The latest from Sheridan, Wyoming, uses carbon fiber to make a flyweight rifle.

› PHIL MASSARO

The Weatherby Model 307, a new release from the Sheridan, Wyoming, plant is based on the familiar M700 design.

Mention the name Weatherby, and most riflemen envision the venerated Mark V, with its nine-lug bolt action and easily discernible stock design. The latest release from Weatherby is a rifle one might not immediately associate with the Big Cursive W but pays homage to its new home: the Model 307. Named for the area code where Weatherby is now headquartered, the new Model 307 may be the least familiar design ever to bear the Weatherby name; in fact, it's highly reminiscent of another iconic American staple: Remington's Model 700.

Yes, you read that correctly. Weatherby has produced a Remington 700 clone, yet with many useful—maybe necessary—upgrades, which result in a damned fine action. With a half-dozen different models now available and the ability to use the myriad aftermarket parts for that near-universal action, the M307 is surely flexible.

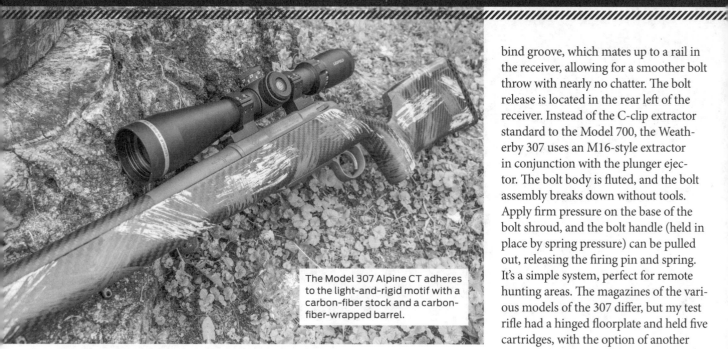

The Model 307 Alpine CT adheres to the light-and-rigid motif with a carbon-fiber stock and a carbon-fiber-wrapped barrel.

The Model 307 Alpine CT uses a Peak 44 Bastion carbon-fiber stock. Photo: Peak 44

bind groove, which mates up to a rail in the receiver, allowing for a smoother bolt throw with nearly no chatter. The bolt release is located in the rear left of the receiver. Instead of the C-clip extractor standard to the Model 700, the Weatherby 307 uses an M16-style extractor in conjunction with the plunger ejector. The bolt body is fluted, and the bolt assembly breaks down without tools. Apply firm pressure on the base of the bolt shroud, and the bolt handle (held in place by spring pressure) can be pulled out, releasing the firing pin and spring. It's a simple system, perfect for remote hunting areas. The magazines of the various models of the 307 differ, but my test rifle had a hinged floorplate and held five cartridges, with the option of another in the chamber. I like the design of the ejections port—it's larger and slightly scooped at the rear, throwing spent cases easily.

The Model 307 Alpine CT has a 22-inch carbon-fiber barrel (not including the 2½-inch brake) from BSF Barrels, again adhering to the light-and-rigid theme. The rifle comes stock with Weatherby's Accubrake DST muzzle brake on the business end. The metalwork is finished in a handsome bronze Cerakote, making the entire package impervious to the elements.

YOU GOTTA SEE IT TO SHOOT IT

Weatherby shipped the rifle with a Peak 44 Picatinny rail; while that design works just fine, I have never been

Upon initial inspection, it's immediately familiar: the cylindrical action, the dual-lug bolt design, the right-side, two-position rocker safety, and, in the case of my test rifle, a hinged floorplate. But that is where the standard M700 features end, and the Weatherby's refinements begin.

Of the six variants, I received the Alpine CT, with a carbon-fiber stock and barrel and a hefty muzzle brake. It is designed for mountain hunting or any situation where weight is an issue. Chambered for the popular 6.5 Creedmoor, this makes a sensible choice for medium game species.

The Alpine CT is stocked in a Peak 44 Bastion carbon-fiber stock with a near-vertical grip, a comb properly designed to mate with modern optics, and a honeycombed 3D Hex

recoil pad to take the sting out of even magnum cartridges. The Model 307 has a well-tuned TriggerTech trigger, which broke cleanly at 3 lbs., 1 oz. on my Lyman trigger gauge, with virtually no creep or overtravel. I much prefer the feel and performance of this trigger to the majority of 700-style triggers I've used, perhaps except the Timney.

Although the two-lug pattern is retained, the Model 307's bolt has some features that differ from your standard Model 700. The right-hand lug has an anti-

The Leupold VX-5HD 3-15x44 was set in Talley's Lightweight Alloy base/ring combo and made an excellent sighting system.

a fan, opting instead for a two-piece design. This test was no different, and as the 700 action has a wide choice of scope mounting systems, I stayed with the lightweight theme and removed the Pic rail in favor of Talley's Lightweight Alloy scope mounts, cradling a Leupold VX-5HD 3-15x44mm riflescope. In addition to giving me the two-piece design that doesn't inhibit the ejection of spent cases, it allowed me to mount that excellent scope nice and low to the bore.

If you notice that I seem to gravitate toward the VX-5HD on my hunting rifles, you wouldn't be wrong. Of late, Leupold's lens coating on this line of scopes is stellar, and the weight of the VX-5 line is perfect for the hunter who wants the best balance of ruggedness, clarity, and portability.

TAKING IT TO THE STREET

I tossed the Weatherby 307 in the truck and packed four 6.5 Creedmoor hunting loads: The uber-popular Hornady Precision Hunter with the 143-grain ELD-X bullet, Federal's 130-grain Barnes

The Model 307 came equipped with Weatherby's large—and very effective—Accubrake DST muzzle brake to mitigate recoil.

TSX, the Federal 140-grain Fusion, and Hornady's 120-grain monometal CX bullet in the Outfitter ammo line. Settling in at the bench with the targets at 100 paces, the 307 was put to work. I had no problems with feeding, extraction, or ejection, and none of the cartridges exhibited any visual symptoms of excessive pressure. Between the Peak 44 recoil pad and that big muzzle brake, the recoil posed no issues, either.

While all the ammunition tested gave acceptable accuracy results for a hunting rifle, the 307 showed a preference for the heavier lead-core projectiles, with the Hornady ELD-X and Fusion bullets printing the tightest average three-shot groups of .68 and .82 inch, respectively.

They were followed by the Hornady CX load coming in at 1.03 inches and the Federal TSX load printing 1.15 inches—the latter being the only one to exceed the 1-MOA mark. Considering that the rifle comes with a 1-MOA guarantee with Weatherby ammunition, I feel this makes the mark; after all, few barrels will digest all bullets equally. My Oehler 35P chronograph indicated that the velocities generated by the 307 were not radically different

The Weatherby 307's bolt is easily disassembled, without tools, for cleaning.

The Weatherby 307 showed a definite preference for the Hornady Precision Hunter load.

pack, or utilizing a good old tree branch, the Weatherby 307 Alpine CT is designed properly for modern hunting/shooting techniques, as the stock design and flat forend work wonderfully when rested.

Is it strange to shoot a rifle with such a familiar feel that is labeled as a Weatherby? I won't lie; it wasn't what I had expected, and it took some time to wrap my head around it. But if Roy Weatherby's vision was to engrave his name into the rock of ballistic history through innovative features such as the double-radius shoulders of his belted cartridges and the nine-lug receiver of the Mark V action, his grandson is working equally hard to bring the Weatherby name to more shooters. Deviating from Roy's signature cartridge features with the pair of Weatherby RPM cartridges of the 21st century and now putting the Weatherby spin on a tried-and-true American classic shows that Adam Weatherby is as bold with his cartridge and rifle designs as he is with his decision to move the company out of California.

Sometimes, change is inevitable, and not all of it is bad. That Mark V action and belted cartridges aren't going anywhere, but I will say the Weatherby lineup got much more diverse with the excellent Model 307. It's available in 14 different chamberings, including many of your Weatherby favorites and the PRC family, with a starting MSRP of $2,199. **GD**

from those advertised on the boxes, with each load running 15 to 25 fps above the printed values. The Hornady 143-grain ELD-X gave the most consistent velocity values of the four.

The Model 307 had the familiar feel of a well-tuned M700 rifle, with all the points of interest located just where they should be. As I put the rifle through its paces, I began to pick up on the subtle differences, such as the smooth action, the ability to work the bolt with the rifle on safe, and that wonderful TriggerTech trigger.

Considering that the rifle weighed 8 lbs., 1 oz. with the scope mounted and four rounds in the magazine, this represents a very portable package without being too light to settle down for the shot. I am all about a rifle that balances properly, and I found the balance point to be just over an inch of the forward action screw. While this made the rifle slightly nose-heavy, it wasn't noticeable when shooting from field positions. The rifle's style will probably see the shooter employing some type of rest. Whether a bipod, set of shooting sticks, leaning across a hunting

WEATHERBY MODEL 307 ALPINE CT SPECIFICATIONS

NEW SKU	CALIBER	WEIGHT (LBS.)	OAL	MAG CAPACITY	BARREL CONTOUR	THREADS	BARREL LENGTH	TWIST	LOP
3WACT240WR4B	240 WBY	6.1	44"	4+1	#4 CARBON	5/8-24	22"	1:7.5"	13.5"
3WACT243NR4B	243 Win	6.1	43.5"	4+1	#4 CARBON	5/8-24	22"	1:7.5"	13.5"
3WACT257WR6B	257 WBY	6.2	46"	3+1	#4 CARBON	5/8-24	24"	1:10"	13.5"
3WACT280AR4B	280 AI	6.1	44"	4+1	#4 CARBON	5/8-24	22"	1:9"	13.5"
3WACT28NOR4B	28 Nosler	6.1	44"	3+1	#4 CARBON	5/8-24	22"	1:9"	13.5"
3WACT300NR4B	300 Win	6.1	44"	3+1	#4 CARBON	5/8-24	22"	1:10"	13.5"
3WACT300PR4B	300 PRC	6.1	44"	3+1	#4 CARBON	5/8-24	22"	1:10"	13.5"
3WACT300WR6B	300 WBY	6.2	46"	3+1	#4 CARBON	5/8-24	24"	1:10"	13.5"
3WACT308NR2B	308 Win	6	41.5"	4+1	#4 CARBON	5/8-24	20"	1:10"	13.5"
3WACT653WR8B	6.5-300 WBY	6.3	48"	3+1	#4 CARBON	5/8-24	26"	1:8"	13.5"
3WACT65CMR4B	6.5 CM	6.1	43.5"	4+1	#4 CARBON	5/8-24	22"	1:8"	13.5"
3WACT65PPR4B	6.5 PRC	6.1	43.5"	3+1	#4 CARBON	5/8-24	22"	1:8"	13.5"
3WACT65RWR4B	6.5 WBY RPM	6.1	44"	4+1	#4 CARBON	5/8-24	22"	1:8"	13.5"
3WACT7MMPR4B	7mm PRC	6.1	44"	3+1	#4 CARBON	5/8-24	22"	1:8"	13.5"

Elvira

Photos: JD Photography

She's not much to look at, but everyone loves this practical Remington 700. ›BILL GABBARD

It wasn't love at first sight, but a relationship born of necessity. I've never been a fan of synthetic stock, stainless rifles, even though I owned one for my "truck gun." I considered myself old school, preferring the feel of a walnut stock and the luster of a quality blued finish. The previous deer season had left me reconsidering those values. Five days of torrential rain spent on an open stand trying to keep my rifle somewhat protected, then wiping it down every night to keep rust from setting in and worrying that the wood stock would be damaged was enough. I made it through the season without the rifle being harmed but decided to start searching for something that I could use during inclement weather without as much worry.

As happens most years, shortly after the close of the modern firearms season for whitetails here in Kentucky, used deer rifles started showing up for sale.

A friend who often took advantage of these bargains called me and told me he had something I might like. He knew my taste in rifles and had a beautiful walnut and blue Remington 700 in 7mm Remington Ultra Magnum that he thought I might like. While looking at it, I noticed a synthetic stainless rifle lying in the back seat of his truck. Remembering my previous season, I asked about it. It turned out to be a Remington 700 BDL SS. He told me it was chambered in 7mm Weatherby Magnum, and he figured he was stuck with it because of the high price of ammo. After a little painful deliberation, I went with the stainless one, knowing that the ammo would be expensive and I couldn't afford both. The 7mm Weath-

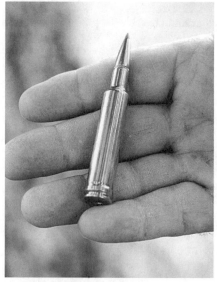

7mm Weatherby cartridge the author reloaded with Hornady brass, Hornady 154-gr. SST bullet and IMR 4350 powder ignited by a Remington 9½ M primer.

erby came home with me. It came with a cheap scope and half a box of ammo.

Before firing it, I removed the scope and installed a new Leupold Vari-X III 4.5-14x50. I paid more for that scope than I did for the rifle, but it was a good investment because it has performed flawlessly ever since.

The ammunition was Hornady Custom 154 grain, and it shot under 1-inch groups, with two shots touching and one flyer. J.J. Reich from Vista Outdoor came down to turkey hunt with us and brought Federal Premium ammo loaded with Nosler 150-gr. bullets that did the same thing. Under an inch should be good enough for a rifle that is only used in inclement weather, right? You would think so, but that flyer and the cost of the 7mm Weatherby Magnum ammo drove me to start down the long and rewarding road of reloading. I had wanted to try my hand at reloading for a long time, and this pushed me over the edge.

The Remington 700 BDL SS rifles were produced from 1993 through 2005, but Remington only chambered the 7mm Weatherby round from 1991 through 1995.

In 2010, Mark Six, Owner of Green's Run Calls, successfully used Elvira for a Kentucky cow elk hunt.

Armed with a good source of brass and a new love of handloading, I went to work to get rid of the flyer. Shortly into load development, and after wearing the phone out and calling my reloading mentor, Paul Johnson, the new rifle was shooting groups under 1/2 inch with no pesky flyer. A load of IMR 4350 ignited by a Remington 9½ M primer pushing a Hornady 154-gr. SST bullet produced a group of .306 inch.

Daniel Boone carried a rifle called "Ticklicker" because he claimed he could shoot the tick from a bear's nose. Davey Crockett carried a flintlock named "Old Betsy." The second year I hunted with this rifle, right at the last minute of shooting light, I killed a beautiful 15-point buck. Someone asked me what I shot that buck with. I jokingly replied, "Elvira, The Mistress of The Darkness." The nickname stuck,

and she has been known by that ever since.

Elvira has accounted for 18 bucks, and the number keeps growing. I killed my largest buck to date with her, a 13-pointer that scored 168 B&C, and numerous others. Many of them are more memorable than the biggest ones. In 2018, I was hunting by myself when a beautiful 9-pointer walked into the field about 600 yards away and made his way

The author and Elvira on the farm where they do most of their hunting now.

to a cedar tree, which he thrashed. He came a little closer and began feeding at around 400 yds. I steadied Elvira and waited for him to come closer, thinking how much the bullet would drop at that range and where I should hold. (I still haven't replaced the Vari-X III with a scope that allows you to dial for range.)

It became apparent that he had no intention of coming any closer, so I steadied the horizontal crosshair level with the top of his back and the vertical one at the back edge of his front leg. I took a deep breath and squeezed Elvira's trigger. I was back on target by the time the bullet made an impact and watched him roll and run. He made it about 50 yards.

I've lost count of the coyotes I have taken over the years with Elvira. Some folks believe that shooting coyotes during deer season will scare off the deer, but I haven't found that true. Song dogs are detrimental to the turkey population and rough on young fawns, so any coyote that presents itself as a target gets a taste of one of Steve Hornady's SST bullets courtesy of Elvira. While they might not be designed to perform as a varmint bullet, the coyotes will never complain if I can do my part. Last year, Elvira and I killed seven coyotes during the firearm season.

In 2010, Mark Six, founder of Greens Run Game Calls, was turkey hunting with us when he discovered he had been drawn for a Kentucky cow elk tag. At the time, Six didn't own a rifle that met the requirements to elk hunt in Kentucky and had no idea where to hunt. I knew some folks who would allow us hunting access and offered the use of Elvira. Since it was a cow-only permit and Six wanted it to eat, we had discussed it and decided that if the opportunity were presented, he would try to harvest a mid-sized cow that wouldn't be too old or tough.

Opening morning found us easing along an old trail on a reclaimed mountaintop removal surface mine. As we rounded a corner, we faced a small herd of cow elk standing about 40 yards above us. One looked twice the size of the rest and wore a tracking collar. Six quickly raised Elvira to his shoulder and pulled the trigger. The elk stood on her back feet, took a few steps backward, and fell with all four feet in the air. I accused him of killing the grandmother of all Kentucky elk. He decided then and there that Elvira was a "stone-cold killer."

While still-hunting nearly ten years ago, my little brother took a nasty fall and landed on his scope. A test shot revealed that his scope wasn't hitting near his point of aim. Since Elvira and I had tagged out, I let him take her hunting. The result was a nice 8-point buck on the ground at a little over 200 yards—his farthest kill then, and Elvira had another admirer.

Steven Asher—whom my wife and I call 'Stepson,' even though he is not related to us—had a similar experience where a huge-bodied mature 8-pointer collapsed in his tracks. The immediate collapse of the buck and ease of felt recoil added him to the long list of people wanting to be the recipient of Elvira in my will.

While hunting alone a few years ago, a small two-year-old 8-point was chasing does, and I was enjoying the show. When he stopped about 60 yards before me, I placed the crosshairs on his shoulder and eased the rifle down. I had no reason to kill him because I knew there were better bucks on the farm. He stopped again and turned at a little over 100 yards at the perfect angle. I settled the crosshairs, then took my finger off the trigger and told Elvira, "That would be a pie shot, but you don't want to kill him." The next time he stopped, he was at 250 yards, facing me head-on. Elvira had already placed the crosshairs of the Leupold dead center on his chest. Once again, I convinced her not to shoot. I told her what a mess the 154-grain SST bullet would make at that angle, and besides, we didn't want to kill that buck.

He then turned, quartering slightly away, and Elvira didn't wait for any of my excuses. The little buck crumpled in his tracks. My cousin Henley McIntosh asked me why I killed such a young deer. I told him my story, and he laughingly replied, "You should have checked it in under Elvira's name; everybody knows how she is!"

Our local sportsman's club holds a "Deer Rifle Match" once a year. The rules require that the gun must be legal to hunt with in Kentucky but cannot be a heavy-barreled rifle. You generally see light-barreled .22-250, .223, .243, and 6.5 Creedmoor rifles. I took Elvira one year to see how she could stack up. While we didn't win the match, we finished in a respectable 3rd place.

I have several other rifles that I am fond of. Trying to satisfy my addiction to reloading, I built hunting loads for them. I have a 7mm Remington Magnum that will shoot groups under 1/4 inch. There are ones in 6.5 Grendel, 6.5 Creedmoor, 7mm-08 Remington, 6.8 Western, .270 Winchester, .25-'06 Remington, and .260 Remington—that all will outshoot Elvira (don't tell her I said that). Most of these are easier to find factory ammo for. Some have newer scopes, which can dial up for longer ranges. A few are stainless, while others have Cerakote. There is no valid reason why they shouldn't be taken to the deer stand each fall.

Over the years, I have bought newer scopes, some with illuminated reticles, and a couple of Leupolds with the CDS system that would eliminate the need to figure out where to hold at longer ranges, but I can't seem to make myself try to fix what isn't broken. A few years ago, a friend offered to "dip" Elvira with a camouflage covering, but since she is a fairly uncommon rifle, I declined his offer, thinking it might adversely affect her value. My wife laughed at my response, saying, "Like you would ever sell Elvira."

Every year, when deer season rolls around, I look over the current residents of the vault, consider the weather conditions along with where I plan to hunt, and, after careful consideration, pick up Elvira and head to the stand.

The value of a rifle depends on many variables: Brand, caliber, scope, condition, rarity, and others. But, its value can sometimes depend on how badly the prospective buyer wants it or the current owner's willingness to sell. Even though Elvira is probably a low-production model based on her chambering, I doubt she would be considered rare or highly collectible. Being chambered in an obscure caliber could either raise her value because of rarity or lower it because of the high price of the ammo and difficulty in finding it.

The primary factor that affects the old Remington's value is the determination of the current owner to keep it. My wife often refers to Elvira as "The other woman in our marriage." I have threatened to have Elvira buried with me, but that would be senseless because I am sure someone would dig me up to get her. There is an old mountain saying that "Every man is entitled to one good gun, one good dog, and one good woman." Living in this politically correct age, we won't discuss the woman, and I have had more than one good dog.

When it comes to guns, I have had more than one good one, but if I had to pick only one, that would be an easy answer. My wife, most of my family members, and numerous friends could quickly answer it for you. Elvira! **GD**

This buck walked into a field 209 yards from the author and Elvira's stand early one morning. That was as far as he walked.

Remembering Dad and the Walther PP

A military bringback recalls the good ol' days.

›BRADLEY JOHNSON

Buffalo Bore 71-gr. hardcast in .32 Auto is a game-changer.

On the hour-long drive across the lake to the south shore, I almost passed out in Dad's old Dodge. We stopped at Dot's Diner in Kenner to get breakfast. My dad loved breakfast, and Dot's was a typical local hole-in-the-wall diner. I couldn't eat a thing; he ordered me waffles and bacon, but I was too excited to eat. As we left the diner, he had bluegrass music on the radio, and I'll never forget Ralph Stanley playing.

The anticipation had built up so much the night before that I could barely sleep. We pulled into the parking lot of a dilapidated indoor range that would soon go out of business, but none of this mattered because that was the day Dad was going to teach me how to shoot a pistol. I had never shot anything up to this point except my single-shot .22 rifle in the backyard.

The episode would become my personal Rubicon, for there was no looking back after crossing it.

We walked inside, and Dad handed me a pair of cheap, clear safety glasses and earmuffs older than him. After a brief safety chat, we reviewed the loading process, sight alignment, and grip. The sense of satisfaction from racking the slide and the tactile feeling of a cartridge getting stripped off the top of the mag and flying home into the chamber was amazing. As the slide flew home, I instantly saw the loaded chamber indicator pop out—something I had never seen before, and it made it feel real.

I fired an entire magazine, and I was instantly hooked.

I'll never forget how the man in the lane beside us was shooting a .50AE Desert Eagle. During a break, he walked over to see what we were shooting, and I puffed my chest out and proudly told him, "My dad brought me here today to shoot the finest pistol a gentleman can own, a Walther model PP."

After the range, I rolled up my target and called my grandfather and Uncle Nicky from Dad's phone on the drive home to tell them about my new marksmanship skills.

Dad helped me tape the target in my bedroom, and we headed to his office. Before I could play with friends that evening and show them my target, he sat me down, and we cleaned the pistol together. He took out an old tackle box where he kept all his gun cleaning equipment and taught me how to field strip the gun. Dad stressed how important it was to clean a gun before putting it up, using it as an example of taking care of your equipment. I can still smell the Hoppes gun oil as he took out his Case Canoe pocket knife to cut up an old t-shirt to use as an oil rag.

As we sat cleaning, he read some lines from "If"—possibly the best poem for boys learning to become honorable men. After reading a line, he would ask me what I thought that meant and explain that particular life lesson.

We were done after the bore was scrubbed, the carbon removed, and the finish wiped down with a light coat of oil. He showed me how to reassemble the pistol, put it back in its thin, black factory box, and set it in his desk drawer.

It was my formal introduction to my now favorite pistol of all time.

Carl Walther invented the Model PP in 1929 and packed it with features ahead of its time. A loaded chamber indicator, double-action/single-action

The Walther PP that the author's
father brought home from Germany.

Companies such as The Attic Imports bring in a good supply of original magazines, so you can keep your Walther running forever.

(DA/SA), and a decocker are all things we take for granted today, but for 1929, they were cutting edge.

You have probably heard of the PPK, the smaller, more compact version of the PP. The PPK was made famous in the James Bond 007 series. While the PPK is insanely cool, and the current ones made by Walther USA are the best, my heart will always have a soft spot for the PP.

The PP was initially designed as a standard-issue sidearm for military and police units. It is slightly larger than the PPK in both grip and slide/barrel lengths. It came in various chamberings, including .22 LR, .32 ACP, and .380 Auto. The .32 ACP was the most prevalent cartridge among police and military across Europe, and more than 30 countries officially adopted the PP. The Swedish police carried them until the mid-2000s.

Volumes have been written on the Walther PP, and if you've read this far

hoping for a more detailed historical piece, I am sorry to disappoint. I would instead like to tell you why this particular gun is special to me.

While my dad enjoyed going to the range and shooting it, he was not a hunter, nor was he a "gun guy" in the sense that he was constantly looking for the next one. He was simply someone who had a few pistols that he enjoyed taking to the range and keeping on hand for things that go bump in the night, his favorite being the Walther PP.

Dad spent 26 years in the Army, mostly in West Germany, stationed with an air defense artillery unit. It was his favorite time in the military, and he spoke of it often and fondly. While stationed there, he attended many events with his landlord, a member of the Heidelberg Rod and Gun Club. This club had a shooting range and served as a school for people applying for German gun licenses. Dad loved shooting

there and even took the German hunting course.

German gun laws were not then what they are now. The local police were changing out to new sidearms. The local club was assisting in selling the surplus Walther PP pistols from a Bavarian police unit. The police mark on the frame even has an X stamped in the middle, indicating it was decommissioned. Dad purchased two—one for himself and a matching one, which he gave to my uncle Nicky upon coming home on leave.

The gun accompanied him across Europe. He spent time between Germany, France, Greece, and Turkey. He was a young officer flush with cash and playing rugby; it was a good time for him, and this gun was his constant companion.

Wiping the pistol down with an oily rag, he would sit with a smile and reminisce about those years. He would recall the bakery he lived above, the rugby tournaments, the pet Saint Bernard he had named Sweets, his friends he attended hunting school with, and his mentors in both the American and West German Army. Why the trip down memory lane?

A part of the human condition fascinates me: how certain senses can trigger key memories in the brain. When we experience these things, it brings us back to memorable moments. Think about it like this: your brain is permanently on record mode your entire life. When you experience a certain feeling—be it the feeling or texture of an object, a taste, or a smell—you can be brought instantly back to the memory. Your brain essentially hits rewind momentarily and plays that moment back.

When Dad held the Walther, it transported him back, and I happily soaked up every minute of the stories he would tell.

We enjoyed the gun together for many years; it was our favorite to shoot. Nothing points like a Walther PP in the hand. Sure, the sights are terrible—designed in the 1920s, they are not easy to pick up. The hammer tends to bite the web of your hand like a Browning Hi Power or Sig P210 (the tang is extended to overcome this issue in the current-production PPKs). This does not matter as the gun is so natural in the hands that the rudimentary sights are not a bother.

Now, let me explain the trigger. As stated, this was one of the first successful DA/SA pistols commercially produced. Also, while the PP is a classic, it was not designed as a target gun but as a service sidearm. The trigger reflects this. The double-action first shot on my example is not light but is smoother than most DA triggers of the same period, such as the Walther P38 and Russian Makarov. While the double-action trigger certainly is not a slicked-up pre-lock Smith & Wesson, it's serviceable and more than adequate for its intended purpose. The single-action is really what sets this pistol apart. Do you like triggers with a mild pull weight, zero travel, and a crisp break? Then, the single-action trigger on the Walther PP will bring you immense joy.

If I had to pick a weak point in the Walther PP, it would be the magazines. For a long time, originals were hard to come by in good condition, and the aftermarket ones I tried were less than stellar. We shot it so much that the spring in one of the magazines gave out. Thankfully, my good friend Garrett Wright from The Attic Imports found me a suitable replacement, an original. For anyone looking, these guys bring in a ton of vintage Walthers, spare parts, and magazines.

I still shoot it often and consider it a backup gun in my carry rotation once I find a good holster. Most holsters available for the Walther PP are military or police surplus; while these are cool, they were not made with concealed carry in mind.

Regarding ammunition, my PP has been the most reliable with the traditional 71-gr. FMJ loading from Sellier & Bellot, as well as the 71-gr. FMJ loading from Federal. I would advise anyone with a .32 ACP to test various types of ammunition as I found factory-loaded ammo varied wildly in reliability and accuracy. I initially tried traditional hollowpoints as a carry load, but they were highly unreliable. After research-

ing various sources, I concluded that .32 ACP is so underpowered that penetration was the key. There were reports of hollowpoint ammunition not having enough velocity to expand reliably. I will be the first to admit I have not tested these loads on ballistic gel or similar media and leaned on the experience of those who had.

Enter Tim Sundles at Buffalo Bore, who is doing excellent things to make the .32 ACP a viable option again. He offers a 71-gr. +P loading at an advertised 1,150 fps. It features a hardcast lead bullet designed to penetrate deeply. This solves two issues: the lack of reliability in feeding hollowpoint bullets and hollowpoints that underperform on target.

With the new reliable magazine from The Attic Imports and the 75-gr. +P load from Buffalo Bore, my Walther PP is in a completely different league. Is it the best choice for a concealed carry gun? Absolutely not. Will carrying it

and using it as a backup gun bring me immense joy? You bet.

On the 4th of July, 2022, I lost my dad unexpectedly. He was the best friend and dad I could have ever hoped for, and for all of that, I am eternally grateful. I will not lie. After losing him, it was difficult to even look at the Walther. The gun sat in my safe for six months before I dared to pull it out. After a while, I was ready, and the feeling of grief and loss was suddenly replaced with an immense respect and cherishing of memories.

Dad and I shared a similar bond with the Walther. For us, it served as the trigger for that switch in the brain that transports us to happier places. For me, this is less about the gun and more about the man who owned it.

Today, when I pick that gun up, I experience the same thing Dad did. I am brought to a good place that always brings joy and a smile. That place is the time I had with my dad. **GD**

The Walther PP has minimal muzzle jump, allowing the shooter to get back on target almost immediately.

Marlin 336RC

Grandpa's brush gun still carries the day—and the memories.

›TRENT MARSH

There's no single recipe for what makes a gun special. Many collectors are drawn to things like scarcity, custom 'smithing, ornate engravings, obscure chamberings, or a new-in-box finish. Those things are fine and even exciting, but for many people, such exotic offerings are a luxury they can't justify. For many shooters, what makes a great gun is the provenance, legacy, and stories it tells. Such is the case with my Marlin 336RC.

The 336RC that lives in my safe does not have its original luster, nor is it flawless or pristine. Its appeal is not for the market; it's a special gun for me because of its origin. My grandfather purchased it new ahead of a mule deer hunt in Colorado. Serialized as a 1968 model, the last for the original RC variant, he purchased it in the early summer of 1969. He and his party of four other hunters made their way west later that year. Of the five, he was the only one to take a mule deer on that trip, a fine 4x4, with that Marlin.

Fast forward almost three decades, and it was the centerfire rifle I learned to shoot. Growing up in Indiana, we didn't have a rifle season for deer. It was shotguns only for the fall seasons. I had learned to shoot rimfires, but when I graduated to a "real" rifle, Grandpa taught me to shoot with that iron-sighted 336.

It was an excellent gun to learn with, looking back. It offered enough heft to help take some of the sting of recoil but was compact and balanced—not unwieldy or awkward, even for a not-quite-teenager. It quickly became one of my favorite guns to shoot.

I don't think anyone of a certain age can help but feel like John Wayne with a lever gun in their hands. For a young boy learning to shoot with his grandfather, I don't think there is a single gun I would pick ahead of that Marlin.

A few years later, Grandpa gave me that rifle.

At the time, I mostly used it for coyotes. Indiana still didn't allow rifles in deer season, and short of groundhogs, there wasn't much else to shoot. I was just out of high school and in college and didn't have the funds for a dedicated predator rifle. More than a few times that .30-30 connected on coyotes harassing the horses or curious enough to investigate the screaming rabbit call in my pocket. Primarily, though, the gun sat.

The author wonders how many miles have been walked by hunters who laid their Marlin 336 down just like this to clean game and pack out their prize, only to return to the woods because they left their rifles behind.

In 2016, Indiana passed a law allowing limited rifle cartridges to be used on private property. The .30-30 was one of them. By then, I had added to my collection, and in those first few years, other rifles in various legal calibers were taken afield. In the meantime, I had gotten the 336 ready for the deer season by adding a lightweight 2-8x32 scope that didn't sacrifice agility and handling but lent some precision to a round known for practical accuracy, if not single-hole groups.

It waited in the safe.

In November 2020, I took the old Marlin to the woods. That morning, I made my way to the stand on the edge of a bedding area. I climbed the stand and laid the lever gun across my lap. This location was made for such a rifle: A low spot that sometimes holds water, maple trees of all sizes, nowhere with more than 80 yards of even obscured visibility. While the "brush gun" moniker is often misapplied, this is precisely the setting in which the .30-30 has thrived for decades.

The sun hadn't even cleared the horizon when I heard footsteps behind me. The grip on my rifle tightened as I turned to peek over my right shoulder. I could see a deer picking its way through the narrow clearing, heading toward me. When I looked over my left shoulder, it had already crossed the cut and stood within bow range. I was looking at him out of the corner of my eye. I knew he was a shooter, but that was all I could tell.

The buck stared a hole in the side of the tree. I did my best to remain motionless. I'm sure my head and shoulder on the side of the tree looked like a fat raccoon, ready to call it a day after a night of foraging. He bobbed his head slightly and took those slow, deliberate steps any hunter knows. His mind was not yet made up. He was curious and aware but unsure how concerned to be. By then, the wind was in my favor. Maybe he would pass me by and offer a shot if I could hold still.

He stopped again, even closer. His head shot up at me. He knew something was there but wasn't sure of what. I was still peeking out the corner of my eye, staring at the fallen leaves below me, doing my best to keep my nerves under control. He was close enough now that even without putting my eyes on him directly, I knew he was an impressive deer.

Grandpa's Marlin lay still across my lap.

It felt like an hour; I doubt more than 20 seconds had passed. The buck broke his gaze from mine and looked at the bedding area. He was undoubtedly there to scent-check it, which is why I was there.

He looked once more up at me.

"This is it. He's had enough. He's too close. He's wheeling out of here."

As I was already trying to comfort myself at the opportunity missed, he dropped his head and started toward the dense underbrush several doe groups called home.

The rifle came to my shoulder almost instantly. He crossed behind a small maple tree. I found him in my scope.

Once clear, I let out a small bleat. The beast stopped, quartering away, and my reticle settled halfway back on his side.

The Marlin barked.

A full 150 grains of lead crashed home, slamming into ribs, liver, and lungs. The buck's back legs buckled. He toppled with barely a twitch and lay in the leaves. Steam rose from the crimson puddle forming below him.

I stowed the rifle and pulled up my binoculars to get a better look. All I could see was a massive beam from his right side reaching toward the sky and a kicker point coming off between his third and fourth points.

I sat in awe.

It took me a while to safely make it from the stand to get a better look at the animal: a mainframe 10 with kickers, a triple brow tine, and a busted triple on his other side. Every inspection offered some new detail or feature I had missed the first time.

I called my grandpa to tell him I would be by directly to show him how my morning had gone.

Grandpa never did a lot of deer hunting. Like much of the country in the 1940s and '50s, the deer population had been decimated. Seeing a deer track while hunting rabbits or foxes was the talk of the town for two weeks after. Though he had killed mule deer in Colorado and hunted other things across the country, he never killed a whitetail in Indiana. It would take more than five decades before that 1968 model Marlin 336RC would kill what has become the most popular big game animal in the country and the only one huntable within 500 miles.

When I got to his house, he came out and looked the deer over. He remarked that it was the biggest buck he'd ever seen in person and congratulated me on my filled tag. We stood at the back of the truck talking about how the hunt had unfolded, how it probably shouldn't have happened that way, and he dropped one of his favorite sayings.

"The cards can change just like that."

Aside from teaching me to shoot a rifle and a shotgun, hunt rabbits, tie fishing knots, filet fish, and myriad other things, Grandpa also taught me

how to play cards, especially Euchre. Rarely could you make it through a drubbing at his hands without hearing that phrase at least once.

Indeed, that day, I drew both bowers and some aces.

It may well be the last time I heard him say that. Just eight weeks later, in January of 2021, he slipped on ice, breaking his hip. At the height of the pandemic, he was in and out of hospitals and rehab facilities until after one surgery. He never woke from the anesthesia.

Indeed, thousands, maybe even tens of thousands, of game animals worldwide have fallen to the Marlin 336 rifle and .30-30 Winchester cartridge. Neither is especially unique or awe-inspiring. They are the workmen of the hunting and shooting world, well-suited for a particular job without fanfare or attention. There is no eye-popping ballistics, gold leaf etching, or flashy curb appeal.

What makes the Marlin 336 one good gun is the sheer volume of stories like mine. It's a rifle passed from generation to generation, among successful hunts, meager seasons, and lessons learned. Chances are you have one in your safe right now. If you don't, someone in your circle does.

Ask about it.

You may be surprised by the stories it can tell. **GD**

While the myth of a "brush gun" has largely been dispelled, that doesn't mean that the dense hardwoods, swampy lowlands, and pine stands from Maine to Minnesota and Missouri to Virginia aren't the perfect home for the 336.

The author says he'll never be able to look at this photo of him recovering the deer with his sons and not seeing his grandfather beside them.

The Winchester Model 69A

It was an excellent .22 rifle then. It still is. › STEVE GASH

The .22 was a Winchester Model 69, a fine bolt-action repeater. It had a nice American walnut stock and was fed from a removable five-round box magazine. Ammo was then 45 cents for a box of 50, and I earned enough hauling hay for the neighbors to keep myself stocked.

In 1934, Winchester's Frank F. Burton designed the Model 69, and Winchester introduced it a year later. Production lasted through 1963, with 355,363 units produced. The rimfire rifle was developed in response to the low sales of Models 56 and 57. Its striker was cocked upon closing of the bolt. The cocking piece was at the end of the bolt, and it could be pulled back and turned as a safety.

The Model 69 fired the .22 Short, Long, and Long Rifle cartridges interchangeably. Interestingly, Winchester's Models 52, 56, 57, and 75 also used its five-round magazine. An optional 10-round mag and a single-shot adapter (called a "single loading adapter") were also available, as were five-round magazines for the .22 Short

only. A push-button on the stock's left side released the magazine.

The front sight was a blade, which was available with a hood, and the rear sight was a drift-adjustable buckhorn. Peep sights were also available.

The Model 69A's stock was of American walnut; it had a pistol grip but no checkering. You could break the rifle down by removing a screw in the bottom of the stock. These features worked fine, but in 1935, the bolt was modified to incorporate a rebounding firing pin. In 1937, the stock was modified so that the takedown screw was flush with the bottom of the stock, the forend was given a semi-beavertail shape, and the grip was enlarged.

In 1937, Winchester offered a telescopic sight in two versions bearing its name. Those with crosshair reticles were available in a 2¾x or 5x power. The latter was also made with a vertical post for aiming. Scope models still came with open sights. The scopes were boxed separately, and integral bases were on the barrel.

THE MODEL 69A APPEARS

While the Model 69 was popular, design improvements continued, and several changes were made in 1937. This resulted in a new version called the Model 69A. Whereas the bolt of the Model 69 cocked on closing, the 69A's cocked on opening. IN addition, a safety was added to the 69A on the right rear of the receiver. Engaging the safety also locked the bolt closed, and there was no longer a protruding cocking piece on the bolt. The trigger had an adjustment screw that varied the pull weight. One reference states that the 25-inch barrel was given a uniform diameter throughout its length rather than the tapered

An original Model 69A magazine is shown to the right of an aftermarket magazine, formerly available from Brownells.

contour of the Model 69.

It could be, but my rifle's barrel, clearly marked "69A," is .621 inch at the muzzle, .729 inch at the end of the forend, and .819 inch at its juncture with the receiver.

In 1940, the "Match" and "Target" models were introduced. These Model 69As had slightly larger stocks than the regular M-69A and were designed to fire .22 Long Rifle cartridges only. The Match model had a Lyman No. 57E rear (peep) sight and a hooded front sight. It also came with a 1-inch leather sling that was changed in 1947

to a 1¼-inch sling. The Target variant featured a Winchester No. 80A aperture sight and a post-style front sight. The scope sight was unpopular, and Winchester dropped it in 1941.

MY MODEL 69A

I frequently visit gun shows but seldom come away with anything more than some books, cleaning supplies, and whatnot. However, in October of 2022, I came across a table with some nice older rifles, some of which were .22 rimfires.

One particular rifle drew my attention. It looked, well, familiar. No, it wasn't the one I used so long ago, but it was close. It was a Model 69A. The condition was pretty good, considering it was at least 53 years old. It contained the original Winchester five-round magazine. (I am told that these original mags are pretty expensive.) After receiving permission to handle it, I worked the bolt, tried the safety. Everything functioned. It had the original Winchester sights. I noted that the left rear of the receiver was drilled and tapped for a receiver sight. Of course, the rifle bore no serial number since they were not required until the Gun Control Act of 1969. A brief dickering period ensued, a deal was struck, and I came home with my very own Winchester Model 69A. It was like meeting an old friend again.

The Model 69A's receiver was grooved for scope mounting, so the next day, I went through my miscellaneous scope bases and rings and found

The Model 69A's barrel bears the name Winchester and the model number.

The front sight is a blade that can be drift-adjusted for windage.

The stock and barreled action can be separated by removing this takedown screw at the bottom of the stock.

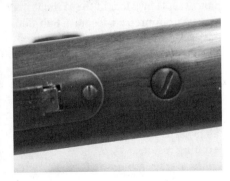

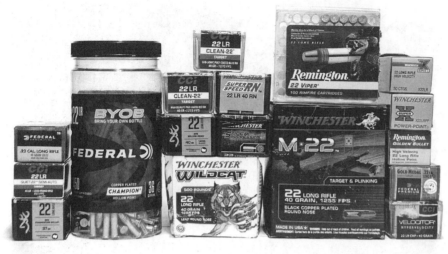

The popularity of the .22 rimfire has led to the introduction of a vast array of ammunition. Here are some of the "everyday" loads the author tested in the Model 69A.

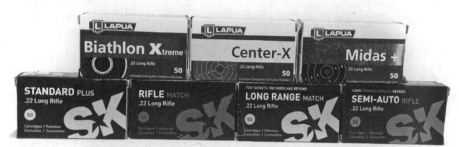

The author tested seven match-grade loads in the Model 69A with excellent results.

a set for 1-inch scopes and grooved receivers. I had a new Sightron 1.75-4x scope for testing, which I mounted. It looked right at home and turned out to be a perfect match. So equipped, the rifle weighed 6 pounds, 9 ounces.

Given the scarcity and cost of original magazines, I checked the Brownells catalog and found exact replacement mags for the rifle. I quickly ordered two. There is even a big "W" on the floorplate. (I regret to report that Brownells no longer lists the mags at this time. I am told that when Winchester stopped making the rifles, a firm in Denver bought the original tooling for the magazines. However, I have been unable to contact them.)

The gun is in excellent shape, considering its age. I checked the barrel with my Gradient Lens Corp. Hawkeye Precision Bore Scope, and the bore looked new. The trigger pull was a delightful 2 pounds, 12.2 ounces. You can bet I didn't touch the adjustment screw!

I had an extensive supply of .22 LR ammo on hand and proceeded to shoot groups over my Oehler M-35P Chronograph. Targets were placed at a laser-measured 50 yards, and five-shot groups fired with a representative assortment of match and what I called "everyday ammo." The outside temperatures on shooting days hovered in the 40s to 50s.

RANGE RESULTS

For a rifle at least 55 years old, the Model 69A shot pretty darn well, with no failures to feed, fire, or eject, with one exception. Most of the Winchester Super-X Suppressed 45-grain Sub-Sonic cases refused to leave the chamber without the assistance of a cleaning rod down the barrel from the muzzle.

I tested seven match-grade loads and 14 everyday or standard loads. Most were fired at 50 yards, but I shot a few at 25 yards just for fun, with some exciting results.

The average group size for the match

loads was .70 inch (both ranges combined), and the 50-yard groups were only 20 percent larger than those shot at 25 yards. The Lapua Midas+ load grouped slightly smaller at 50 yards (.75 vs .83 inch). I am sure this was a function of the shooter, not the rifle or ammo.

The 14 "everyday" loads averaged .92 inch, and the 25-yard groups were 46 percent larger than those shot at 50 yards. But there were plenty of ragged hole groups with both ammo types, and this testing revealed several squirrel loads.

I always consider the coefficient of variation (COV). This is the standard deviation (DV) expressed as the average velocity. Anything under 2 percent is not bad, and anything around 1 inch is darn good. Interestingly, the match ammo's COV was 2.79. That figure for the standard ammo was 1.43, or about twice as large. The muzzle energies of those loads were all over 100 ft-lbs, and the milder match loads were all under 100 ft-lbs.

HOME AGAIN

While many high-quality and accurate .22 rifles are available these days, to come across one with which I had learned many lessons was a step back in time. I don't hunt squirrels or rabbits anymore, but a few rounds of mild .22s downrange at an attacking soda can does wonders to relieve the stress of deadlines, government meddling, and other life intrusions. Getting reacquainted with the Model 69A was like going home again. **GD**

A pair of aces. These two groups were made with Lapua Midas+ (left) and SK Rifle Match (right) loads.

Remington's Golden Bullet load was very accurate in the Model 69A.

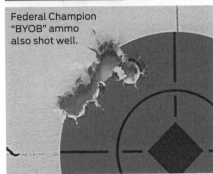

Federal Champion "BYOB" ammo also shot well.

See this, fur-ball?

This is minute-of-squir accuracy!

A pesky squirrel got into Gash's birdfeeders, so he left it a message.

WINCHESTER MODEL 69A

Manufacturer: Winchester Repeating Arms Company

Type: Bolt-action repeater

Caliber: .22 Short, Long, and Long Rifle

Magazine Capacity: 5

Barrel Length: 25 in.

Overall Length: 42 in.

Weight: 6 pounds, 9 ounces (as tested, with scope)

Stock: American Walnut, pistol grip

Length Of Pull: 13-7/8 inches

Finish: Metal, blue, stock smooth oil finish, no checkering

Sights: Drift-adjustable semi-buckhorn rear, with elevator, blade front

Trigger Pull: 2 lbs., 12.2 oz.

Safety: Two-position lever

Table 1. Winchester Model 69A—Match Ammo

Load	Velocity (fps)	Muzzle Energy (ft-lbs)	25-yd. Group (in.)	50-yd. Group (in.)
Lapua Biathlon Xtreme, 40-grain RN	1,043	97	.41	–
Lapua Center-X, 40-grain RN	966	83	.83	–
Lapua Midas+ 40-grain RN	966	83	.83	.75
SK Long Range Match, 40-grain RN	1,036	95	.49	
SK Rifle Match, 40-grain RN	900	72	.67	
SK Semi-Auto Rifle Match, 40-grain RN	922	76	–	.50
SK Standard Plus, 40-grain RN	936	78	–	1.08

Average accuracy: .65 (25 yds.) .78 (50 yds.)

Table 2. Winchester Model 69A—Everyday Ammo

Load	Velocity (fps)	Muzzle Energy (ft-lbs)	25-yd. Group (in.)	50-yd. Group (in.)
Browning Performance Rimfire 37-gr. Fragmenting Bullet	1,245	51	1.18	–
Browning Performance Rimfire 40-gr. Hollowpoint Target & Hunting	1,354	64	.88	–
CCI Clean-22, 40-grain RN	1,184	18	.59	–
CCI Quite-22, 45-grain RN	816	43	–	1.12
CCI Velicitor 40-gr. Copper Plated Hollowpoint	1,276	24	.65	–
Federal Champion 36-gr. Solid Round Nose "BYOB"	1,162	39	–	.92
Federal Gold Medal Target 40-gr. Solid #719	1,175	37	–	1.00
Remington High Velocity 40-gr. Plated Hollowpoint Golden Bullet	1,149	74	–	1.22
Remington Hyper Velocity Viper 36-gr. Truncated Cone Solid	1,271	30	.83	–
Winchester M-22 40-grain Black Copper-Plated Round Nose	1,150	43	–	1.41
Winchester Super-X 40-gr. High-Velocity	1,210	9	–	.79
Winchester Super-X 40-gr. Lead Power-Point	1,151	40	–	1.18
Winchester Super-X Suppressed, 45-grain Sub-Sonic*	1,040	43	.51	–
Winchester Wildcat 40-grain RN	1,120	44	.59	–

*Several failures to eject fired cases.

Average accuracy: .75 (25 yds.) 1.09 (50 yds.)

Overall average: .83

Notes: For all testing, the author used a Winchester Model 69A with a 25-inch barrel and a 16-inch twist. The optic was a Sightron S1 Gen. 2 1.75-4x32 scope set at 4x. Velocity was measured at 10 feet. The accuracy is for a five-shot group at 25 or 50 yards from an indoor benchrest. The range temperatures (outside) were 41 to 58 degrees F.

- REPORTS -
from the Field
RIFLES

> TRENT MARSH

Everything old is new again.
Time is a flat circle.
History repeats itself.

The Springfield Armory Redline sports the Grayboe Trekker stock with a unique cutout, making it easy to identify. The length of pull adjustment ranges from 13.25 to 16 inches. The stock also has an integrated bubble level just behind the action. Chamberings include 6.5 Creedmoor and .308 Winchester.

The Benelli LUPO HPR has a five-shot, ¾-inch sub-MOA factory guarantee.

Looking at the latest rifle offerings from our favorite manufacturers, it's tough not to end up with nostalgia creeping into your thoughts. Of course, there are new and exciting things, and the hybrid precision/hunter platform continues to grow in popularity. What struck me with this year's offerings, though, was just how many makers were addressing rimfire and lever-action options—platforms that for some years seem to have been getting the same treatment as print magazines and linear television.

Talking to my peers, I wasn't the only one who saw the trend and felt the same. Personally, it's something I love to see. Selfishly, as the father of young sons, seeing more rimfire options in the market warms my heart. We know the old standbys won't let us down, but the more platforms we have to experiment with in the rimfire portfolio, the better off we are. Affordability of ammunition is as important now as ever, and being able to train or introduce shooters to different platforms and designs without burning five-dollar bills every time we pull the trigger is a wonderful development.

Solidly in the nostalgia wheelhouse is where we go for the lever-gun love. I grew up watching John Wayne movies with my father and grandfather, so you'll never convince me that a more pure and worthy-of-reverence shooting platform exists. It's a fairly easy cast to make that the lever gun is the tool that saw this nation realize its potential at a time when it could have been lost. So, seeing so many manufacturers embrace and reimagine the platform is something I truly love.

Without further delay, here are some of the latest offerings in the world of rifles.

BENELLI

The Benelli LUPO HPR is the rifle you would expect from a name like Benelli. Holding this rifle at SHOT, it felt like a day at the range wouldn't disappoint. Benelli believes that to be the case with the five-shot, ¾-inch sub-MOA factory guarantee.

While the LUPO HPR is another of a growing class of hybrid competition/hunting rifles, it's hardly an also-ran. I was astounded at the customization level possible in an out-of-the-box rifle. Even for a brand like Benelli, seeing that kind of custom rifle influence in a factory platform was impressive. The stock offers an eight-position adjustable comb, removable bag rider, interchangeable grips, stock shims to adjust for drop and cast, and the Progressive Comfort System to manage recoil. The ergonomics on the forend are comfortable, as well.

The CRIO barrels are threaded and free-floating, with a muzzle brake installed. The action was silky smooth, and I struggled to find something to pick at while handling it.

The LUPO HPR tends toward the bench with the caliber offerings and how the rifle comes together. With barrels of 24 or 26 inches and overall lengths just over 46 and 48 inches, respectively, it's a larger platform than others. Weights for the LUPO HPR range from 9.4 to 10.4 pounds. It's for you to judge if that's a rifle you'll pack into the mountains.

No matter where you put it to work, however, the calibers you have at your disposal should work well for you. Benelli chose 6.5 Creedmoor, .308 Win., .300 Win. Mag., .338 Lapua Mag., .300 PRC, and 6.5 PRC for the LUPO HPR, and I think it's tough to argue with those choices. It's a true crossover rifle with options you'd usually expect only to see from a custom maker. MSRP: $2,949. *benelliusa.com*

BERGARA

It's fun to see something truly unique. Bergara delivers precisely that with the MgMicro Lite. While the skeletonized chassis rifle has been growing in popularity as precision rifle influences breed hybrid options, the confluence of features in the MgMicro Lite should make most shooters sit up and take notice. According to Bergara, pairing the 18-inch Cure carbon barrel with the magnesium micro chassis sheds ounce after ounce of weight but without sacrificing durability or reliability.

The Bergara Premier action is a feature all its own. Paired with the foldable XLR Atom magnesium chassis, carbon-fiber buttstock and grips, and Cure barrel, it's a dynamic shooting platform. While the chassis rifle may not be everyone's cup of tea and may lack some of the warmth of polished walnut furniture, there is an undeniable appeal here. The TriggerTech trigger rounds out the main features quite well. The MgMicro Lite is found in 6.5 Creedmoor, .308 Win., and 6.5 PRC. A detachable AICS magazine feeds the action. MSRP: $3,099.

The Bergara B-14 has garnered considerable attention in recent years, and the latest addition, the B-14 Squared Crest

Carbon, is sure to continue that trend. Thanks to the internal spine, the carbon-fiber stock offers a perfect balance of lightweight and ruggedness. Sniper grey Cerakote on the action reinforces the theme of built-for-the-conditions thinking. The rifle also employs the Bergara Cure carbon-fiber barrel, bringing its own performance history to the platform. The sub-MOA guarantee comes as no surprise.

At just 6.2 pounds, getting into the backcountry seems a little less daunting. It's chambered in 6.5 Creedmoor, .308 Win., .22-250 Rem., 6.5 PRC, .300 Win. Mag., and 7mm PRC, and the barrels range from 20 to 22 inches, depending on your chosen caliber. MSRP? $2,099.

The new Sierra from Bergara offers an option to shooters who prefer a more classic sporter style. At a reasonable 7.4 pounds, the Sierra uses 20- to 22-inch threaded barrels fitted with an omni-directional muzzle brake and the same B-14 action that has become a hallmark of the Bergara offering.

No matter which caliber you choose,

you'll get the sub-MOA promise, and there is plenty with the Sierra available in 6.5 Creedmoor, .308 Win., .22-250 Rem., 6mm Creedmoor, 6.5 PRC, .30-'06 Sprg., .270 Win., 7mm Rem. Mag., .300 Win. Mag., 7 PRC, and .300 PRC. MSRP $1,099.

Few things are as unpleasant as an ill-fitting rifle. Most of us of a certain stature can usually make the rifle we settle behind work, though we've all found exceptions. Shooters of somewhat slighter build don't usually have that luxury. Shooting is manageable but rarely as enjoyable as it should be.

Kudos to Bergara for offering a solution. Enter the new Stoke.

Again, using the B-14 action, the real highlight of the Stoke is its compact and adjustable stock design. With a length of pull of 12.25 inches and three ¼-inch spacers, customization is in hand for a class of shooter that has traditionally had to make due. The barrels also run from 16.25 to 20 inches, keeping the rifle's balance in check. Weights will start right at the 6-pound mark, depending

on barrel length.

The caliber offering makes a great deal of sense as well, with .223 Rem., .300 BLK, .350 Legend, 6.5 Creedmoor, .308 Win., .243 Win., .22-250 Rem., 6.5 PRC, and my favorite of the bunch, 7mm-08, all available. MSRP $899. *bergara.online/us/*

BLACK RAIN ORDNANCE

Don't panic. You didn't skip pages. While you may know Black Rain Ordnance as a maker of modern sporting rifles, there's more happening in Neosho, Missouri, than you might think. BRO has expanded well beyond the world of ARs, with offerings in the semi-auto rimfire, handgun, and bolt-gun market.

Enter the BRO-Contour. The Contour uses the purpose-designed Derecho three-lug action from BRO. It features a 60-degree bolt throw and runs smoothly. I came across this rifle at the range day event at the SHOT Show and helped myself to an empty seat. It was a pleasure to run. At 8.8 lbs., there is enough heft to make for a rock-solid shooting platform but not so much to keep you from toting

The Black Rain Ordnance Contour uses BRO's Derecho three-lug action. A TriggerTech trigger adjusts from 1 lb. to 3.5 lbs. The carbon-fiber-wrapped stainless steel barrels are 22 inches, except for the .308 Win., at 20 inches. The hybrid target/hunting rifle also comes in 6mm Creedmoor, 6.5 Creedmoor, and 6.5 PRC.

Browning's new X-Bolt 2 comes in 10 variants to suit any adventure or discipline.

it around if long-range hunting is in the cards. It fits that hybrid position well.

Black Rain Ordnance went with the TriggerTech Special Flat Straight Adjustable trigger, with pulls from 1 lb. to 3.5 lbs. The carbon-fiber-wrapped stainless steel barrels are 22 inches, except for the .308 Win., at 20 inches. You'll also find the Contour in 6mm Creedmoor, 6.5 Creedmoor, and 6.5 PRC. The barrels are threaded and come with the self-timing Tempest muzzle brake from Black Rain.

The action is married with the Amend2 Modular Chassis stock, which does a fine job tying the whole package together. I noticed the Contour on the firing line after coming from shooting handguns and immediately sat down on a rifle over a 1,000-yard target. My first shot was just off the right side, though I blame the desert wind. The next four found their mark, which is good enough for me. MSRP: $2,589. *blackrainord nance.com*

BROWNING

The new X-Bolt 2 from Browning offers 10 rifle models to suit any adventure or discipline. All models employ the new multiple-lever DLX trigger with an exceptionally crisp break and no take-up. A redesigned receiver promotes bolt operation and features the X-Lock scope mounting system. Rather than using two mounting screws for the optics plates, four screws provide double security. The redesigned bolt is another nice touch, and with a 60-degree lift, there are no worries about not clearing the scope when working the action.

The top tang safety is my preferred location and is adjacent to the bolt unlock button that allows the bolt to be operated while in the safe position. That's a nice touch when you want to ensure your rifle is ready as the moment to shoot approaches or for extra safety when unloading. Numerous model-specific features are also available, such as the move from the Vari-Tech stock to a McMillan or carbon-fiber option, plus carbon-fiber barrel upgrades, or the Target model with a purpose-designed trigger and magazine configuration.

With 10 models and numerous options, prices range from $1,469 for the X-Bolt 2 Speed to $4,069 for the X-Bolt 2 Pro McMillan Carbon Fiber. Chambered offerings include .243 Win., .270 Win., 28 Nosler, .30-'06 Sprfld., .300 PRC, .300 Win. Mag., .308 Win., 6.5 Creedmoor, 6.5 PRC, 6.8 Western, 6mm Creedmoor, 7 PRC, and 7mm Rem Mag. *browning.com*

CHRISTENSEN ARMS

Christensen Arms introduced three new platforms, each catering to a different audience and having its own unique appeal.

The Evoke is a no-nonsense rifle designed for the hunt. The line starts with the base model Evoke, the Christensen Arms action, and a stainless steel barrel ready for a suppressor or to be used with the included RFR-style brake. A three-lug bolt and 60-degree bolt throw work just as you would expect a Christensen Arms rifle. Handling the rifle, I liked the hybrid grip angle. It walks a clean line between a straight grip and the exaggerated, not-quite-pistol grip of so many modern rifles. You find your hand resting right where you want it to be, a minor but welcomed point. All models run from 7.7 to 8.5 lbs and are backed by the Christensen Arms Sub-MOA Guarantee and Limited Lifetime Warranty.

The Evoke Mossy Oak brings the Bottomland camo of its namesake to the base rifle. The Evoke and Evoke Mossy Oak are available in .243 Win., 6.5 Creedmoor, 6.5 PRC, .270 Win., 7mm Rem. Mag., 7mm PRC, .308 Win., .30-'06, .300 Win. Mag., .300 PRC, and .350 Legend, with barrel lengths from 18 to 22 inches. The MSRPs are $899 and $949, respectively.

The Evoke Hunter adds an integrated Pic rail and camo stock, while the Evoke Precision stacks the adjustable carbon-fiber cheek riser and hex-pattern engraved barrel. The Hunter and Precision variants are available in 6.5 Creedmoor, 6.5 PRC, 7mm PRC, .308 Win., .300 Win. Mag., and .300 PRC. The MSRPs are $999 and $1,048, respectively.

The Modern Precision Rifle Rimfire was an absolute treat to handle. The lightweight billet aluminum chassis has a folding stock with cutouts that perfectly encase the bolt to ensure it isn't snagged in a bag or pack. A carbon-fiber tension barrel sends .17 HMR, .22 LR, or .22 WMR bullets downrange while you grip the carbon-fiber handguard and keep your cheek on the adjustable FFT carbon-fiber cheek piece. Not only is the comb height adjustable, but so is the length of pull. The Modern Precision Rifle Rimfire uses Ruger BX-1 magazines, so compatibility isn't a problem. Some guns are just fun. I could feel the smile on my face as soon as I picked it up. Everyone else I saw did the same. MSRP: $1,249 *christensenarms.com*

CVA

The CVA Cascade SR-80 is CVA's take on a scout rifle, with some modern twists. First and foremost, the SR-80 gives you options regarding sights. The factory-installed Williams Gun Sights rear peep and adjustable front post are great out-of-the-box options, but if you prefer to use a scout scope or a red-dot, the forward-mounted Pic rail is ready for your optic of choice. At just 7.3 lbs., the rifle is easy to manipulate, as is the 70-degree bolt throw. The whole thing reeks of maneuverability and fast action. Take your pick of the .308 Win. or .350 Legend, and have fun. MSRP $925.

The CVA Cascade LRH (Long Range Hunter) is best described as stable. The medium-heavy barrel contour and a flat forend with a wide profile pair to bring stability to the shooter quite naturally. The adjustable comb height and length of pull double down on that promise of stability by ensuring a solid fitment. The

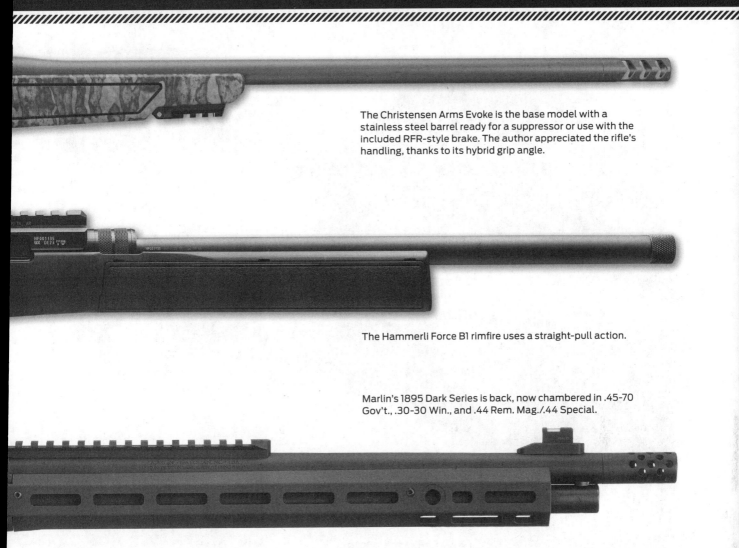

The Christensen Arms Evoke is the base model with a stainless steel barrel ready for a suppressor or use with the included RFR-style brake. The author appreciated the rifle's handling, thanks to its hybrid grip angle.

The Hammerli Force B1 rimfire uses a straight-pull action.

Marlin's 1895 Dark Series is back, now chambered in .45-70 Gov't., .30-30 Win., and .44 Rem. Mag./.44 Special.

LRH leans on calibers you'd expect to see in a long-range rifle. The .308 Win., 6.5 Creedmoor, 6.5 PRC, 7mm Mag, .300 Win. Mag., and 7mm PRC come in a 22- or 24-inch barrel, while the .300 PRC barrel is 26 inches. All barrels are suppressor-ready and equipped with a muzzle brake. Weights start at 8.6 lbs. MSRP: $900.

Cascade VH (Varmint Hunter) takes much of its design inspiration from the LRH above but has some caliber options and features that tend more toward those who focus on chasing varmints. The adjustable stock and fluted, suppressor-ready barrel will look very similar, but a higher capacity magazine is added for when multiple follow-up shots on targets may be needed. While the magazines are larger, the barrels are smaller at 20-22 inches, partly because of the change in calibers, partly to make the rifle easier to negotiate when tracking moving targets.

The VH can be had in .243 Win., .204 Ruger, .22-250 Rem., and .223 Rem., with weights starting at 9 lbs. MSRP? $900. *cva.com*

HAMMERLI

The Hammerli Force B1 rifle is another of the recent rimfire offerings, but it stands apart from most of the rest thanks to its straight-pull action. The oversized throw knob is incredibly easy to grip and operate and can be done more quietly than other actions—not to mention the speed of operation. With a threaded barrel making the addition of a suppressor simple, those who cherish discretion should take particular note.

Also of note is the Quick-Change Barrel System. This tool-less feature allows for a change in barrel length and caliber, moving from .22 LR to .22 WMR. The Adaptable Magwell delivers a seamless fit for whichever magazine you use. The

Hammerli employs the Ruger magazine system, so numerous options are available.

A customizable stock is also tool-less, allowing adjustments to be made on the fly as shooters or conditions dictate.

With a synthetic model coming in just under and wood options at 6 pounds, it's a nimble platform in more ways than one, especially considering the $649 MSRP. *hammerliarms.com*

MARLIN

Marlin is taking us back to the dark ages, and I, for one, am here for it. No, it's not a Marlin trebuchet; it's the Dark Series of lever guns. Three models will be available: a .45-70 Gov't., .30-30 Win., and .44 Rem. Mag./.44 Special.

As someone who has been a vocal proponent of the lever gun in general, but specifically for folks who reside in areas unfriendly to AR-pattern rifles, the Dark

Series is the perfect marriage of technologies separated by more than a century. Modern materials and design concepts, partnered with the trusty lever-action design and tubular magazine that puts more rounds at the shooter's disposal, especially in the handgun calibers, is a big win.

All the models will share the polymer stock, with M-LOK and QD slots and attachments for adding accessories and slings, as well as the anodized aluminum handguard, which is also fitted with M-LOK slots for full platform customization. The barrels are threaded for suppressor use, or you can use the included radial brake.

An extended Pic rail is factory-installed to pair with a traditional optic or dot-style option. If you prefer to stick with iron sights, the rear peep works well with the fiber-optic front sight.

The Dark Series may not be for everyone, but for those who are looking for the niche it fills, it does so admirably. MSRP $1,429 (.45-70 Gov't.).

When Ruger acquired Marlin, shooting enthusiasts were hopeful that the Marlin legacy would live on, and they've largely been happy with how it has been handled. Another reason to be happy is the reintroduction of the 1894 in .357 Mag./.38 Special. When the Model 1894 was first brought back to the market, it was only in the .44 Mag.; now we see the family start to round out. Both calibers share the walnut straight-grip stock and blue finish. The .357 Magnum is slightly shorter than the .44 Magnum model, with a barrel just over 18.5 inches. The tubular magazine will hold nine rounds of .357 Mag. or 10 rounds of .38 Special. The MSRP is $1,239. *marlinfirearms.com*

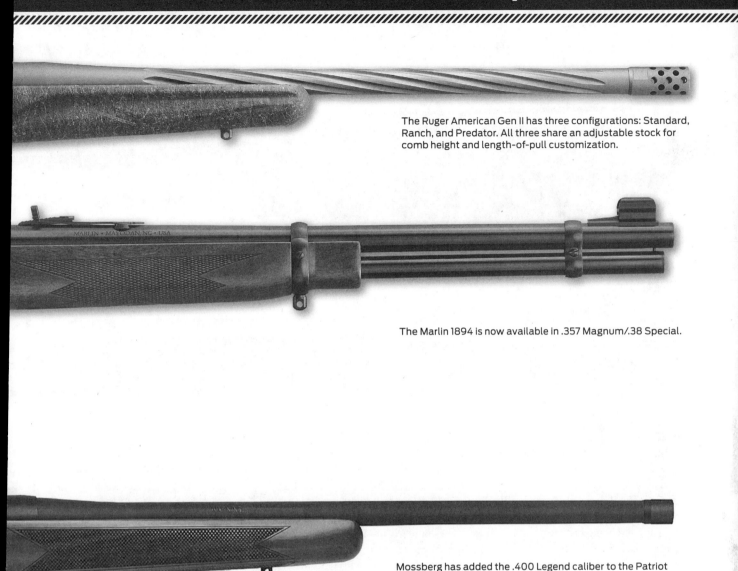

The Ruger American Gen II has three configurations: Standard, Ranch, and Predator. All three share an adjustable stock for comb height and length-of-pull customization.

The Marlin 1894 is now available in .357 Magnum/.38 Special.

Mossberg has added the .400 Legend caliber to the Patriot line in a walnut and synthetic version.

MOSSBERG

Mossberg has added the .400 Legend caliber to the Patriot line in a walnut and synthetic variant. The Patriot series has grown in popularity in recent years because of its value and reliability. The free-floating 20-inch barrel is threaded and comes with weaver bases. Like all Patriot rifles, the .400 Legend models feature the patented LBA (Lightning Bolt Action) and a user-adjustable trigger ranging from 2 to 7 pounds of pull. Paired with the .400 Legend, a round offering increased penetration and reduced recoil, it's another option for hunters nationwide.

The synthetic model (part number 28175) comes in at 6.5 pounds with a $484 MSRP. The walnut (part number 28176) is slightly heavier at 7 pounds and has an MSRP of $669. *mossberg.com*

PARKWEST ARMS

Parkwest Arms, formally Dakota Arms, out of Sturgis, South Dakota, continues to offer shooters an option for that custom rifle build to match exactly what our hearts desire. A wide range of base platforms offer a starting point for a selection process of calibers, actions, finishes, and myriad other selections to choose from to make each rifle our very own. As close as most of us will ever come to forging our own rifle, Parkwest is an incredible option for those discerning shooters looking for a rifle for that once-in-a-lifetime hunt or a heritage piece to put in the family. To truly appreciate the entire offering, visit *parkwestarms.com*.

REMARMS

The RemArms 783 LVX Freedom pairs two legacy brands of the shooting world into one ready-to-hunt package that screams value. The CrossFire trigger system is a highlight of the platform, and paired with the free-floating barrel and dual-pillar bedded stock, shooters and hunters alike will find an incredibly shootable platform. The 783 LVX Freedom has a Leupold 3-9x40 VX Freedom scope already mounted and bore-sighted. A quick trip to the range allows for fine-tuning and peace of mind that the next trip will fill the freezer. It's two bedrock brands of the shooting industry married in one dynamic combo. Calibers include .243 Win., .308 Win., 7mm-08 Rem., 6.5 Creedmoor, .350 Legend, .223 Rem., .270 Win., .30-'06 Springfield, .300 Win. Mag., and 7mm Rem. Mag. MSRP $895. *remarms.com*

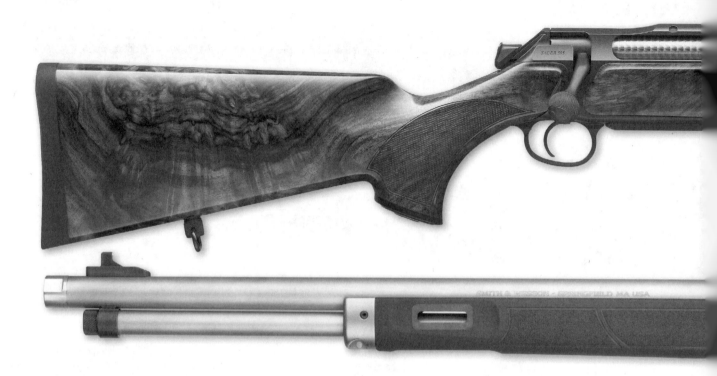

RUGER

The Ruger American made waves in 2010 when it hit the market, changing the reasonably priced bolt-action rifle landscape. The Ruger American Gen II introduction looks poised to do the same thing. Far from being just an expansion of the existing line, American Gen II rifles offer innovative upgrades over the Gen I models, especially at the price point.

The Ruger American Gen II has three configurations: Standard, Ranch, and Predator. All three share an adjustable stock for comb height and length-of-pull customization. There's also an option to add weight to the stock to improve balance with accessories or suppressors installed. Barrels are cold-hammer forged, fluted, Cerakoted, and threaded with a brake installed. All models use the Ruger Marksman adjustable trigger, with a user-adjustable pull weight range from 3-5 lbs. The three-position tang safety allows the rifle to be unloaded without moving the safety into the fire position. The oversized bolt handle is another nice touch for positive grip and control.

Also, depending on your chosen caliber, there are different magazine types across all three families. The Ruger American Gen II uses AI-style, AR-style,

flush fit, and single-stack magazines according to the caliber. For those who value cross-platform functionality, calibers like .223 Rem., 5.56 NATO, or 7.62x39 using the AR-style mags is a nice feature. Count me among that crowd.

The Standard and Predator are similar, with the Standard running 20-inch barrels across the board, with Gun Metal Gray Cerakote, while the Predator barrels run 22 inches with a Burnt Bronze Cerakote. Both variants are also available in the same group of 18 calibers: .350 Legend, .400 Legend, 6mm ARC, 6.5 Grendel, 6mm Creedmoor, 6.5 Creedmoor, .308 Win., 7mm-08 Rem., .243 Win., .223 Rem., .450 Bushmaster, .204 Ruger, .30-'06, .270 Win., .300 Win. Mag., 6.5 PRC, 7mm PRC, and .22 ARC.

The Ranch variant pairs a Cobalt Cerakote with a Flat Dark Earth stock and a 16-inch barrel. It's meant to be lighter, more compact, and maneuverable. The Ranch can be had in the .350 Legend, .400 Legend, 6mm ARC, 6.5 Grendel, 6.5 Creedmoor, .308 Win., .450 Bushmaster, and .22 ARC calibers as Standard and the Predator, with the additional options of 5.56 NATO, .300 BLK, and 7.63x39. The MSRP for all families and calibers is $729. *ruger.com*

SAKO

The Sako 90 family of rifles is built for almost anything but leans into those backcountry adventures we all yearn for. A smooth action in a lightweight platform delivers exactly the feel, fit, and finish you would expect from Sako, while the ergonomics and multiple configurations allow a near-custom fit. The trigger in the Sako 90 family allows the shooter to select one of five preset weight-of-pull settings without disassembling the rifle—a feature we can all appreciate. The bolt and receiver are true to the Sako brand and offer the silky operation we expect. Modern lines are available in the Quest and Quest Ultra variants, while the Peak, Adventure, Hunter, and Varmint variants sport the classic bolt-action appeal. Then there's the Bavarian, with its classically European stylings. The Hogsback stock contour and fast-action setup produce a stunning treat for the eyes. The various models have different caliber offerings but include .22-250 Rem., .243 Win., .270 Win., .300 Win. Mag., .308 Win., .30-'06 Springfield, .338 Win. Mag., .375 H&H Mag, 6.5 Creedmoor, and 7mm Rem. Mag. MSRP: $2,299 to $3,999. *sako.global*

SAUER

The elegance and refinement of the new

The Sauer 505 Elegance's trigger pull weight can be set to an incredible .77 lb. Woods stocks are stunning in Grades 2 to 10.

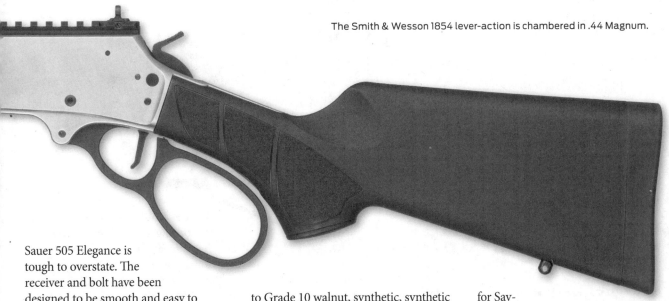

The Smith & Wesson 1854 lever-action is chambered in .44 Magnum.

Sauer 505 Elegance is tough to overstate. The receiver and bolt have been designed to be smooth and easy to operate and include a manual cocking mechanism that ensures the gun is only able to be shot when you want it to be. With the flick of your thumb, virtually silently, the rifle is ready to do its work.

The Sauer 505 uses the adjustable Quattro trigger with four presets, from an incredible .77 lb. to 1.66, 2.2, and 2.75 lbs.

Sights are optional, but Sauer has used the Blaser saddle mount system, which allows you to mount or remove an optic quickly and easily without losing the rifle's zero.

The 505 can be had in an astounding 19 calibers from .222 Rem. on the light side up to the .375 H&H and 10x3x60R on the more robust side. Favorites like the .270 Win., 6.5 Creedmoor .308 Win., .30-'06, 8.5x55, and .300 Win. Mag. are included, among others.

Four stock options include a Grade 2 to Grade 10 walnut, synthetic, synthetic thumbhole, and carbon fiber. Prices start around $3,500. *sauer.de/en/*

SAVAGE

Savage introduces the 110 Ultralite Elite, firmly putting itself in the meaty part of the curve for those looking for that lightweight, long-range crossover rifle. The 110 Ultralight Elite is built on the MDT HNT26 carbon-fiber/magnesium chassis stock, which sheds much weight from a more traditional layout. The stock also collapses, making for easier packing and storing. Coupled with the Proof Research carbon-fiber-wrapped barrel, the lightest variant in the family comes in under 6 pounds, with weights floating right around that 6-pound mark, depending on caliber. The barrel is threaded and equipped with an Omniport muzzle brake.

The 110 action has been wildly popular for Savage and should also be on this platform. The same goes for the adjustable AccuTrigger, with a range of 1.5–4 lbs. A detachable AICS-style magazine feeds it. It is chambered in .300 Win. Mag., .300 WSM, .308 Win., 6.5 Creedmoor, 6.5 PRC, and 7mm PRC. MSRP: $3,299.

Savage also introduced the 110 Klym and Impulse Klym rifles. Both have carbon-fiber thumbhole stocks with adjustable comb height, two-position tang safety, Proof Research carbon-fiber barrels, and Omniport muzzle brakes. They're also available in the same six chamberings. What separates the rifles is that while the 110 Klym uses the 110 action, the Impulse uses the sought-after straight-pull action. Both weigh well under 7 lbs. MSRP: $2,699 (110), $3,309 (Impulse).

The 110 Magpul Scout delivers an

innovative and adaptive competitor to the scout rifle market. Using the popular 110 action and the Magpul Hunter stock, you have a highly adaptable rifle that can be configured in numerous ways. This is primarily thanks to the extended Pic rail that goes from the back of the receiver to the middle of the forend. If you prefer a scout-style or red-dot optic, you can still get it out and away from you, but if you decide a more traditional eye relief LPVO is your preference, you aren't denied that choice. A 10-round AICS-style detachable box magazine feeds .308 Win., .450 Bushmaster, or 6.5 Creedmoor. Savage has made the 110 Magpul Scout available in black or FDE stock finishes, and it's also available in a left-handed configuration. Hunt, shoot, tactical, it doesn't matter. You can find a way to make the 8.4-lb. 110 Magpul Scout fit your needs. MSRP $1,099 *savagearms.com*

SMITH & WESSON

Smith & Wesson has entered the lever-action rifle scene 170 years after founders Horace Smith and Daniel Wesson patented their first lever gun. The Model 1854 series is a stunning homage to the platform. Two models are available featuring 19¼-inch barrels and a maneuverable 36-inch overall length. The Model 1854 Series marries a stainless steel finish with a synthetic stock. While the design is timeless, it also gives a nod to modern design by including M-LOK slots on either side of the forend and an integrated optics plate.

I'll admit, I'm a sucker for the large loop lever and can all but see Robert Mitchum tossing a Model 1854 to John Wayne in "El Dorado," declaring, "I had it set up just like yours. Figured you got lucky with it, thought I'd give it a try."

The Model 1854 series uses a side-loading gate and side ejection, and the removable magazine tube makes unloading a breeze.

There's also a Model 1854 Limited Edition. The Limited model uses a classic blued finish with a walnut stock rather than the more modern stainless and synthetic pairing.

Both the standard and limited models are chambered in .44 Rem. Mag. and use XS Sights' adjustable ghost ring rear and gold bead front.

The Model 1854 Series rifles carry an MSRP of $1,279, while the limited is $3,499. *smith-wesson.com*

SPRINGFIELD ARMORY

The Springfield Armory Model 2020 Redline rifles give you that lightweight, custom rifle feel but remain very approachable. The curb appeal of the Redline series is undeniable, with the Grayboe Trekker stock and unique cutout making it easy to identify. The length of pull adjustment ranges from 13.25 to 14.25 inches, with additional spaces available to take it out to 16

The Weatherby 307 Alpine represents the high-end of the lineup with its folding MDT Carbon stock.

The Winchester Ranger rimfire features a takedown feature for easy cleaning and transport.

inches. The stock also has an integrated bubble level just behind the action, giving you another point of reference to help anchor your accuracy. The forend has not one, but two swivel studs. This gives you options for sling installation if you prefer an attachment point that is not as far out as usual and allows for bipod installation and sling usage without stacking.

The free-floating barrel is wrapped in a carbon-fiber sleeve, helping to keep it cooled and your impacts consistent. While you can't see it, the barrel is also fluted under the carbon, helping to promote temperature management. The barrel is threaded and suppressor-ready with the SA radial brake installed. The series also uses a TriggerTech adjustable trigger with settings from 2.5 to 5 lbs.

The Redline is backed by a .75-MOA Guarantee and is available in a 16- or 20-inch barrel for the 6.5 Creedmoor and .308 Win. MSRP: $2,299. *springfield-armory.com*

WEATHERBY

The new Model 307 from Weatherby offers shooters an adaptable platform. The first new action from Weatherby in more than 50 years, the 2-lug, cylindrical carbon steel design can be paired with any number of available components to make the rifle one's own. As you would expect from Weatherby, the little things make the difference in the Model 307. The redesigned bolt release makes bolt removal a simpler and safer task. Once removed, the tooless bolt takedown removes any excuse for not fully maintaining your action. An adjustable TriggerTech trigger lets you dial your fire control in for your preferred specifications. Five complete Model 307 rifles are available, starting at $1,199 for the Model 307 Range XP and going to $3,499 for the Model 307 Alpine MDT Carbon. Like a DIY project? Weatherby even makes a builder's action available for $749, so you can finish it how you want. A host of calibers are available, varying by model. The usual suspects are in the mix, like .243 Winchester, .308 Winchester, 6.5 Creedmoor, and 7mm PRC, but so too are those venerable Weatherby magnums and more custom calibers so many shooters have come to revere. Fancy something like a .240 Weatherby Mag, .280 Ackley Improved, 6.5 Weatherby RPM, or 28 Nosler? The Model 307 has those available too. *weatherby.com*

WINCHESTER

In a year that seemed to have so many entries in the lever gun and rimfire categories, the unofficial lever rifle brand, Winchester, introduced a new rimfire model. The new Ranger lever-action rimfire has been designed to be a favorite of any shooter. I don't know a more fun platform to run than a lever-action rimfire, and the latest iteration from Winchester is poised to make it a favorite of every shooter in the family.

Winchester's legacy of design and quality shows through with the innovative take-down design to make cleaning easier than ever and allow for multiple storage options. The receiver is machined from aluminum, helping save some weight, which comes in at just 5 pounds, 4 ounces. The Ranger was also engineered with light operating forces, so shooters of all ages and skill levels could operate the rifle. A 20-inch barrel, walnut stock, and forearm make for a traditional look with modernization in operation. MSRP: $419.99. *winchesterguns.com* **GD**

Watchtower Firearms acquired F-1 Firearms, known for its skeletonized AR-15s and AR-10s. Pictured here is a Watchtower Type 10 .308.

- REPORTS -
from the Field
AR-STYLE RIFLES

It's a sign of a successful firearms segment when companies come and go, sad as that may be. But AR-15s and the companies that build them get stronger through 'creative destruction.'

> TODD WOODARD

Yes, Windham Weaponry is back in business, so fans of its A1 20-inch Government shown here can breathe a sigh of relief.

The idea of "creative destruction" in economics is a process in which innovations replace and make older ideas obsolete. Austrian economist Joseph Schumpeter derived the notion from the works of Karl Marx, amazingly enough. Could Herr Schumpeter have arrived at such an audacious insight when looking at today's AR-15 market activity instead of 1940s-era broad-market figures? Why yes, I think it would be obvious if Schumpeter were looking at the comings and goings of companies that build AR-style rifles, but, of course, Schumpeter predates our favorite rifle platform.

But the idea remains—innovation and expansion of ARs doesn't seem to be slowing down. The hard thing to accept is that with creation comes destruction, and there are notable instances of that occurring among AR builders this year.

On the biggest scale, wherein companies come into existence and seem to blink out just as fast, was that Maine gun builder Windham Weaponry announced its "full liquidation"—aka destruction—in September 2023, following the death of its founder Richard Dyke. If you recall, Windham sold the Bushmaster Firearms nameplate to Remington Outdoors, which would go out of business and be remade several times. As late as 2021, Windham Weaponry made more than 20,000 rifles in a year—not chicken feed by any means.

Then, on December 21, 2023, a Facebook post on the Windham page said, "We are back! Windham Weaponry Inc. is pleased to announce our return to the firearms industry. We are under new ownership and a new management team. We have also hired back some of the best gun people in the industry, with many having 20-30 years of experience."

That is a tight cycle of creative destruction—from the ash heap to relaunching "a new revamped website which is now fully operational" in about three months. In recognition of those events, I've modified the Windham listings in the catalog section to reflect the company's current lineup on the new website. When I shopped for Windham rifles online, most products were on backorder or out of stock at retailers. Windham needs a chance to build some guns and get them in the retail pipeline, so here's hoping for the company's successful re-creation.

There are other examples of the business cycle grinding off names we're familiar with. For instance, in March 2023, NEMO (New Evolution Military Ordnance) Arms acquired 2A Armament, which led last year's catalog section because of its numerical name. It looks like the 2A Armament–brand items will be replaced by NEMO-branded products. For example, 2A's builder-series parts line was extremely popular, and NEMO says most of that line will be kept as the NEMO Arms Builder Series. The 2A Palouse will be renamed the NEMO FX, a more affordable AR-15 platform with a forged receiver and builder-series components. And so on, as the 2A Armament brand fades to dusk.

Another style of change can be seen

Watchtower Firearms' Type HSP-H Rifle in 6.5 Creedmoor.

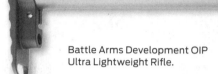

Battle Arms Development OIP Ultra Lightweight Rifle.

Battle Arms Development DARC chambered in 6mm ARC.

in the purchase of the F-1 brand. In May 2023, Jason Colosky, the CEO and founder of Watchtower Firearms, acquired F-1 Firearms, known for its skeletonized AR-15s and AR-10s. Colosky said F-1 had a lot of open machine capacity that he could immediately put to work as part of Watchtower's diversification roadmap. At present, the company builds spec-ops and competition-grade ARs, the Apache double-stack 1911 pistol, the Jedburgh suppressor, and a range of accessories and gear. Watchtower will remain in Spring, Texas, but nothing on the website recalls the F-1 line's existence other than the F-1 logo sitting on a webpage to the left of the Watchtower logo.

There are many other examples of creative destruction in the firearms industry, and while we may miss guns and parts we grew to enjoy, it's a sign of a healthy AR segment that some aren't making it, but many, many others are. I think J. Schumpeter would recognize that and agree that this is classic non-Marxian creative destruction.

Here are some other companies that are building creative products in the AR markets these days:

ANDERSON MANUFACTURING

Anderson Manufacturing's new premium AR-15s are the Frontline series. Known for its affordable AR-15 variants, Anderson, of Hebron, Kentucky, has made AR-15 parts and rifles for nearly 30 years. Anderson started distributing Frontline models in February 2024, with prices starting at $799. That should be ideal pricing for

Anderson Manufacturing's AM-15 Frontline 16 in 5.56 NATO.

entry-level rifles in the burgeoning AR market.

These new Frontline offerings come with either quad rails or Stable Lock M-LOK handguards. The Frontline 16-inch medium-contour 5.56 barrel has a 1:7 twist rate, nitrided finish, and a mid-length gas system under Anderson's TRS 15-inch handguard. The stock is a Magpul SL model fronted by a Magpul K2 Grip. The similar Frontline QR-16 has a 12-inch Free-Float Quad-Rail Handguard with Picatinny rails located at 12, 3, 6 and 9 o'clock and four QD sling sockets at 3 and 6 o'clock positions. Weight: 7 pounds. *andersonmanufacturing.com*

BATTLE ARMS DEVELOPMENT

Battle Arms Development, Inc. (B.A.D. Inc.) is a design, research, and development firm incorporated in 2009 and based in Henderson, Nevada. The company is probably best known for its OIP ultra-lightweight rifle of five years ago. The acronym OIP stands for Ounces Is Pounds, a sub-4-pound unit built from scratch. The current version is only 4.6 pounds and is chambered to shoot full-powered mil-spec 5.56 NATO ammunition.

In 2024, the bad fellows at B.A.D. developed the DARC6 rifle chambered in 6mm ARC. The 6mm Advanced Rifle Cartridge (6×38mm) is a 6mm (.243-caliber) round introduced by Hornady in 2020 as a high-accuracy long-range car-

tridge designed for the AR-15 platform. That round is showing up in more and more rifles as the cartridge proves itself (more than a dozen citations in the 2025 catalog section), and its future looks bright as a 700-plus-yard target choice. At the same time, the .224 Valkyrie seems to be fading from widespread usage—more of that creative destruction. *battlearmsdevelopment.com*

The Pivotal Buttstock from Bilson.

BILSON ARMS

Broussard, Louisiana–based Bilson Arms has some neat items for better AR field function. The Bilson BA-9FC 9mm carbine of 2023 and, for 2025, the company's BA-15FC AR rifles use a forward-mounted pump to charge the weapons, replacing the charging handle of the standard AR-15. The forward charging system in the company's BA-15FC Series in 5.56 NATO, 6 ARC, .300 Blackout, .350 Legend, and .450 Bushmaster functions somewhat like a pump-action rifle or shotgun, with the forward charging handle already in the shooter's hand, ready to recharge the rifle. Press the switch on the left-hand side, pull the forward charging handle back and continue. It's a very intuitive motion.

Already available at retail in the BA-9FC semi-auto 9mm carbine, by 2025, the Bilson device should be in wide retail distribution in the BA-15FC ARs. And perhaps the company's rumored pump-

action rifle (not gas operated) will have appeared to help those shooters who live behind the Blue State Iron Curtain.

Another neat innovation is Bilson's Pivotal Buttstock. Introduced in 2022,

Bilson Arms BA-9FC Upper Assembly.

The Bishop .458 SOCOM AR-15 Hammer Rifle.

Bishop's AR45TC Exodus Subrifle.

the stock is made from anodized aluminum and fits a standard carbine buffer tube. An adjustable ball-and-socket joint allows you to rotate between a standard LPVO on top and an offset red-dot or irons to the side. It also has a small lever lock on the bottom of the stock to adjust LOP. Long story short, the buttpad can rotate and present either set of sights comfortably and consistently. The Gen II version should be out by 2025. Bilson Arms' 9mm Forward-Charging PCC: $1,643. The BA-9FC Upper Assembly, $886. Bilson Arms' BA-15FC 5.56FC Rifle: $1,750. Bilson Arms' Pivotal Buttstock Gen I, $165; Gen II, NA. *bilsonarms.com*

BISHOP AMMUNITION & FIREARMS
I learned about the products of Pocatello, Idaho-based Bishop Ammunition & Firearms, working on several editions of *Cartridges of the World,* most recently covering the .475 Bishop Short Magnum cartridge in

the 17th Edition. Merrisa Bishop says of the round, "This is a high-power round designed for extreme dangerous game or the U.S. military against hardened targets. The cartridge is designed for the AR-10 DPMS rifle platform, and we achieve 2,500 fps with over 5,000 muzzle energy at 65,000 PSI.'" It's available in the company's AR475GAR Rifle for $3,000. That is certainly creative, and it sounds destructive in the right hands, so it's interesting that Bishop decided to make something even more unusual for 2025—the AR45TC Exodus.

Bishop's AR45TC

combines an AR-15 and the Thompson submachine gun. The Exodus rifle has a 16-inch EV-5 match-grade barrel and rifle-length stock and is called a subrifle, not a carbine—shorter than a standard AR but longer than a carbine. Pitched as "the perfect home defense rifle," the Exodus is guaranteed to provide 1-inch or smaller groups at 50 yards with .45 ACP match 230-grain ball ammunition. Other chamberings include 10mm Auto, .40 S&W, and 9mm Luger. If you're a Glock handgun owner already, the use of

The Bilson Arms BA-9FC in Cerakote FDE and anodized black.

Faxon Firearms's ARAK-21 XRS Complete Rifle.

factory Glock magazines in this rifle can be in sync with your sidearm, allowing the same ammunition and magazines to be used in both the rifle and handgun. The receiver is machined from billet aluminum, and the upper receiver is a Gibbz nonreciprocating side charging unit. MSRP: $1,900. *bishopammunition.com*

FAXON FIREARMS

Faxon Firearms' ARAK-21 ("AR-AK") hybrid rifle has resurfaced commercially after refinement to enhance its manufacturing scale, and the product's commercial availability is set to strengthen. The company says there was a lull in the rifle's availability in 2021 while it was being retooled, but now the marque is fully back—and perhaps a little more affordable heading into 2025.

"The demand for the ARAK's return has been constant," said Dustin Wallace, Faxon's director of sales & marketing.

"Faxon Firearms has meticulously improved the model for increased production and lower prices while retaining the features enthusiasts admire."

Founded by brothers Bob and Barry in 2012, Faxon Firearms commercially rolled out the ARAK-21 in 2014. At the time, the rifle was one of the most successful blends of the reliability of the AK-47 with the adaptability of the AR-15, anchored by its upper design and a robust long-stroke gas piston system. Shooters liked the ARAK-21 because of its ambidextrous functionality, straightforward caliber changes, and compatibility with mil-spec AR-15 lowers.

Cincinnati, Ohio-based Faxon Firearms says the ARAK-21 rifles are available in various configurations, including 5.56 NATO, .300 Blackout, and 7.62x39mm. Switching between chamberings takes about three minutes. The ARAK-21's dual reciprocating upper as-

sembly allows the shooter to swap barrels quickly and easily without requiring specialized tools or equipment. This design also eliminates the need for a buffer tube.

The upper receiver is machined from an aircraft-grade 6061-T6 aluminum billet in a one-piece design that incorporates a full-length Picatinny rail (Mil-STD-1913) on the top and three additional rails on the muzzle end of the receiver, making it a full M4-style quad-rail upper. The top Picatinny rail is laser-engraved for repeatable optics placement. The ARAK-21 system also allows for a folding stock to be added because the recoil system does not extend beyond the upper receiver to operate. This eliminates the noise and feel of the buffer tube cycling back and forth. The Faxon ARAK-21 XRS 16-inch Complete 5.56 or 7.62x39 Rifle is $1,600.00. A custom XRS Complete Rifle is $1,900. The custom rifles have choices of colors,

Primary Weapons Systems UXR.

.22 Advanced Rifle CARTRIDGE

In this edition's catalog listings, you can see that several companies have begun chambering rifles in .22 ARC for 2025, which is remarkable considering that Hornady only commercially introduced the round in late 2023. No less a luminary than *Gun Digest* Editor Philip Massaro has written about the round's prospects of becoming the next hot option for AR rifles.

The .22 ARC originates from the 6.5 Grendel, the spawn of the 7.62x39mm, the Soviet AK-47 military cartridge. The 7.62x39 round was necked down and became a 5.6x39, aka the .220 Russian, one of the most successful parent cases in benchrest shooting history. The .22 ARC's design, including a pushed-back shoulder, allows more room for heavy-for-caliber bullets, enhancing its performance in AR-15s.

The .22 ARC is a compact cartridge that fits into your AR-15. Using Hornady's new 62-grain ELD-VT bullet, the .22 ARC in the AR-15 platform can rival the performance of the 22-250 Remington fired from a bolt gun. Utilizing a .441-inch-diameter case head, similar to the 6mm ARC and 6.5 Grendel, it's tailored for long, heavy bullets with high ballistic coefficients. Its optimal overall length of 2.260 inches ensures smooth operation, reliable feeding, and superior performance in AR-15s. The SAAMI-spec twist rate is 1:7 inches.

Partner companies helping to develop .22 ARC chamberings in rifles and barrels include many represented in the 2025 edition's catalog section, including Aero Precision, Christensen Arms, Faxon, IWI, JP Rifles, NEMO Arms, Proof Research, Seekins Precision, and others. Hornady's initial offerings include 62-, 75-, and 88-grain ELD Match loads: Price: $30 per 20-round box.

The .22 ARC's design, including a pushed-back shoulder, allows more room for heavy-for-caliber bullets, enhancing its performance in AR-15s.

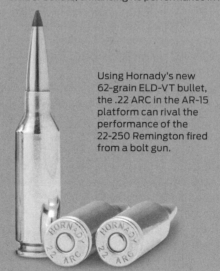

Using Hornady's new 62-grain ELD-VT bullet, the .22 ARC in the AR-15 platform can rival the performance of the 22-250 Remington fired from a bolt gun.

.22 ARC SPECIFICATIONS

Bullet Diameter .... .224 in.
Cartridge Overall Length 2.260 in.
Case Length .... 1.525 in.
Case Head Diameter ...... .441 in.
Shoulder Angle .... 30 degrees
Optimal Barrel Twist 1:7
SAAMI Max Pressure .. 52,000 psi

.22 ARC LOAD BALLISTICS

LOAD	MUZZLE VELOCITY (FPS)
.22 ARC 62-gr. ELD-VT V-Match	3,300
.22 ARC 75-gr. ELD Match Black	3,075
.22 ARC 88-gr. ELD Match	2,820

The Primary Weapons Systems UXR (Universal Exchange Rifle) is a modular AR that can be modified to fire several cartridges.

Primary Weapons Systems UXR R side action.

cartridges, ejection side and other details. *faxonfirearms.com*

PRIMARY WEAPONS SYSTEMS

The new Primary Weapons Systems UXR (Universal Exchange Rifle) is a modular rifle that can be modified Transformers-like to fire several different cartridges, which for early 2025, are 5.56 NATO, .308 Win., and .300 BLK, with 8.6 BLK and other caliber-exchanges coming soon.

For those looking for an AR-type firearm with a lot of flexibility, carrying an extra barrel/magazine well/bolt face is more compact than lugging around another rifle or even uppers. The UXR's upper receiver is the only serialized component of the system, which includes interchangeable magazine wells to accept different magazine types and a barrel-switch assembly to swap chamberings and barrel lengths quickly. Because the upper is the serialized part, everything else can be shipped by mail, depending on your locale. Also, check your municipal and state laws on firearms and parts transfers before receiving products in the mail.

The PWS Long-Stroke Piston System takes the operating system from Kalashnikov's AK design. It merges it with Stoner's AR platform, allowing the rifle to adapt and perform with various ammunition. There is no need to adjust the gas

system each time. Other customizable features include an adjustable cheekpiece, ambi selector switch, magazine release and charging handle, and an adjustable folding buttstock. The UXR's lower includes an Xchange Fire Control Housing with a TriggerTech trigger and XChange Magwell. The interchangeable magwell has different pieces that can accept different magazine patterns, depending on the chambering. A dot-identifier system matches the cartridge with the magwell. The Xchange Barrel Assembly is removed with three torqued screws. The barrel changes are supposed to shift impact less than half MOA. *primaryweapons.com*

SPRINGFIELD ARMORY

Retro ARs continue to appear across the industry, with Springfield Armory adding its SA-16A2 as a salute to the military collectors and shooters wanting simplicity and clean lines. The SA-16A2 5.56mm is inspired by the M16A2 rifle—one of

the most iconic firearms in history. Made from forged 7075 T6 aluminum, the upper receiver features the classic A2-style fixed carry handle with an integrated rear sight. The rear sight is adjustable for windage and elevation, while its dual aperture design facilitates accurate shooting at varying distances.

The forged 7075 T6 aluminum lower receiver features unique "Government Property" markings and a non-functional "burst" selector marking inspired by the three-shot burst modification of the M16A2 rifle. Springfield says its Accu-Tite tensioning system eliminates movement between the upper and lower receivers, enhancing rigidity and precision. The forend houses the 20-inch chrome-lined barrel with a 1:7-inch twist and M4 feed ramps, as well as a rifle-length gas system. The SA-16A2 features an M16-pattern bolt carrier group with a Carpenter 158 steel bolt and staked gas key. *springfield-armory.com* **GD**

The SA-16A2 5.56mm from Springfield Armory is inspired by the M16A2 rifle—one of the most iconic firearms in history. The initial reports from the range are encouraging.

- REPORTS -
from the Field
SEMI-AUTO
PISTOLS

Beefy double-stack 1911s and reintroductions of classics are among this year's autoloading pistols.

›ROBERT SADOWSKI

The Ruger SR1911 75th Anniversary pistol joins a commemorative Mark IV as the company celebrates three-quarters of a century.

Double-stack 1911 platform pistols chambered in 9mm continue to be introduced. VuDoo Gun Works has a premium model with a list price north of $3,000, while the new player in wide-body 1911s, SDS Imports, has introduced a model starting at $800. EAA has upped the caliber ante with the Witness2311 as a double-stack 1911 platform in 10mm Auto and with a 6-inch barrel. There are also many models going through evolutions, some shedding decades-old features for new and improved models like the Beretta Model 92 series, while others like SIG and FN are offering variants based on popular designs, like the P322 and the 509 lines, respectively. Glock continues to apply the Gen5 treatment to its guns. Taurus also reintroduced an older design but chambered it in 10mm Auto. Daniel Defense is now making pistols and brought a recent design that failed—remember the Hudson H9?—from the verge of extinction back to relevance. Here's the new semi-automatic pistol landscape.

The STK100 Ultra (MSRP: $499) is an improved version of the STK100 with more aggressive grip panels, checkering on the backstrap and the forward section of the frame, a straight trigger, and an integrated magazine well.

Beretta's micro-subcompact 30X Tomcat features an improved Trident Trigger with a 35 percent reduction in trigger pull. The magazine capacity is eight rounds, the sights are interchangeable, and the barrel is threaded for a can.

The Beretta 92GTS Launch Edition has a two-tone finish and checkered wood grips.

AMERICAN TACTICAL IMPORTS
The GSG-9 (MSRP $800) is a large-format pistol with a 7.9-inch barrel and a vague resemblance to the H&K MP5. It uses a direct blowback mechanism with a left-side charging handle. Iron sights are standard, but there is a Picatinny rail to mount a red-dot. The grip module looks very much like the MP5. The unique thing about this pistol is that it is compatible with either Glock or SIG P320 mags. Instead of using a magazine well adapter, an adapter fits on the magazine. The GSG-9 comes with both a SIG and Glock adapter. *americantactical.us*

ARMSCOR/ROCK ISLAND ARSENAL
Rock Island's 9mm striker-fire, all-metal STK series has three new models. The STK100 Ultra (MSRP: $499) is an improved version of the STK100 with more aggressive grip panels, checkering on the backstrap and the forward section of the frame, a straight trigger, and an integrated magazine well. The STK150 is a more compact version of the STK100 with a 4-inch barrel and full-size frame. The STK200 is a lightweight compact with a compact slide and frame. *armscor.com*

BERETTA
Beretta has evolved the micro sub-compact Tomcat into the 30X Tomcat (MSRP: $599). It features the tip-up barrel the .32 Auto Tomcat is known for and a new and improved Trident Trigger that offers a 35% reduction in trigger pull. The magazine capacity is eight rounds, the sights are interchangeable, and the barrel is threaded for a can. It comes in a two-

tone finish and checkered wood grips. The 92GTS Full Size Standard (MSRP: $899) features a frame-mounted Type G decocker with a new twin sear design, allowing the user to safely decock the hammer to half cock. The 92GTS starts with a slim Vertex-style frame topped with a full-size slide and 4.7-inch barrel. It also features Beretta's sweet X-Treme S trigger.

The 92GTS Launch Edition (MSRP $1,199) has a two-tone finish and checkered wood grips. The 92XI Squalo (MSRP $1,329) is a slick competition pistol with teeth. "Squalo" is the Italian word for shark and features the X-Treme S DA/SA trigger system, fiber-optic sights, slide cut for optics, extended controls for smooth and fast manipulation, and a flared magwell of a Vertex-style frame. *beretta. com*

CZ-USA

CZ has downsized its competitor favorite, CZ Shadow 2, to create the Shadow 2 Compact (MSRP: $499). This compact version features a 4-inch barrel, a silky smooth DA/SA trigger, fiber-optic sights, and feeds off of 15-round magazines. Available in 9mm. *cz-usa.com*

The CZ Shadow 2 Compact has a 4-inch barrel, silky smooth DA/SA trigger.

EAA's Hunter pistol in 10mm Auto with a 6-inch barrel, 15-round magazine, fully adjustable sights, ambidextrous thumb safety, and an enhanced hunting trigger.

DANIEL DEFENSE

Daniel Defense has introduced its first handgun, the H9 (MSRP $1,299), which might look familiar. Daniel Defense acquired the design from Hudson and made improvements. Features include a low bore axis for

Daniel Defense acquired the H9 design from Hudson and made improvements. Features include a low bore axis for reduced muzzle flip and faster follow-up shots.

reduced muzzle flip and faster follow-up shots. This 9mm pistol has a 1911-style trigger with a trigger safety blade and a straight pull. The H9 feeds from a 15-round magazine. *danieldefense.com*

EAA

New to the Witness2311 line is the Hunter (MSRP

$1,028), chambered in 10mm Auto with a 6-inch barrel, 15-round magazine, fully adjustable sights, ambidextrous thumb safety, and an enhanced hunting trigger. The Influencer series of single-stack 1911s built by Girsan in Turkey

EAA's MC1911 with Liberator treatment.

come optics-ready with either a 5-, 4.4-, or 3.4-inch barrel and are available in 10mm Auto, .38 Super, .45 Auto, or 9mm. The 1911 Untouchable series is an all-business single-stack in .45 Auto or 9mm with a 5-, 4.4-, or 3.4-inch barrel. Girsan-made 1911s feature forged frames and bar stock slides and barrels. The Girsan affordable MC9 Disruptor (MSRP: $379) chambered in 9mm is optics-ready and features a threaded barrel, accessory rail, enhanced striker trigger, Cerakote finishes, and low-profile sights.

The Girsan 1911 and Regard MC get the Liberator treatment to please any shooter with polished steel slides and gold controls. The Girsan 1911 Liberator (MSRP $999) features pearl-like grips engraved with a sugar skull and comes in

.45 Auto. The 9mm Regard MC Liberator (MSRP $691) is adorned with exquisite Santa Muerte-engraved pearl-like grips. The Girsan MC14BDA is chambered in .380 Auto and features a DA/SA trigger, fixed sights and a 13-round magazine capacity. It's available in matte black (MSRP $360) or two-tone (MSRP $381). The Girsan MC14T Tip-Up is also chambered

Ruger's LC Charger pistol is chambered in 5.7x28mm with a 10- or 20-round magazine capacity and has a 10.3-inch barrel.

The FN 509 CC is a tricked-out EDC handgun.

in .380 Auto and features a tip-up barrel design, allowing users to load it quickly without racking the slide. Features fixed sights and a DA/SA trigger. It is available in matte black (MSRP $489) or blue with gold controls (MSRP $680). *eaacorp.com*

FN

FN has expanded the FN 509 series with four new pistols. The 509 CC Edge XL (MSRP $1,629) combines the compact slide of the FN 509 Edge models with a quick-detach compensator barrel and the full-sized that holds a 17-round magazine. Can you say tricked-out everyday

carry? The FN 509 MRD started as a compact pistol, so why not build a full-size model? The FN 509 Full-size MRD (MSRP $834) sports a 4.5-inch barrel and full-size grip and naturally is optics-ready. The FN 509 Compact MRD with Quick Detach Compensator (MSRP $999) is a compact concealed carry pistol with a quick-detach compensator that offers up to 25 percent reduction in muzzle rise. *fnamerica.com*

GLOCK

Glock's subcompact big bores, the G29 (MSRP $620) in 10mm Auto and G30

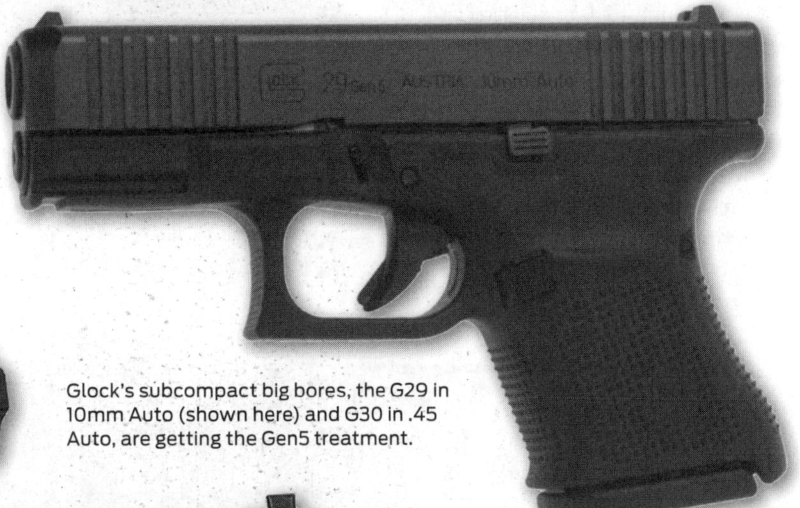

Glock's subcompact big bores, the G29 in 10mm Auto (shown here) and G30 in .45 Auto, are getting the Gen5 treatment.

The KDS9C series of double-stack, single-action 9mm pistols now comes in a rail model.

(MSRP $620) in .45 Auto, are getting the Gen5 treatment. Design upgrades include the Glock Marksman Barrel with enhanced polygonal rifling, and you can say bye-bye to the finger grooves on the front strap. They also get the Glock performance trigger and an ambidextrous slide stop lever. *us.glock.com*

The 75th Anniversary LCP MAX (MSRP $479) carries a laser-engraved commemorative logo on the slide, is chambered in .380 Auto, and has a two-tone finish.

ready (MSRP $734) and optics-installed (MSRP $951). The KDS9C series of double-stack, single-action 9mm pistols now comes in a rail model. The KDS9C Rail (MSRP: $1,903) comes with an integrated Picatinny rail in all matte black or dark gray/black two-tone finishes. *kimberamerica.com*

KAHR

The original innovator of the single-stack, subcompact, polymer-frame pistol, Kahr, has introduced the X9 (MSRP $550)—its first double-stack 9mm pistol. The X9 comes in a 10- or 15-round magazine option and is compatible with SIG P365 magazines. Features include a 3.5-inch barrel and a slide cut for a red-dot optic. *kahr. com*

KIMBER

The new R7 Mako Tactical evolves the R7 series with a total capacity of 15+1 rounds in an extended grip, a threaded barrel for suppressors and a Picatinny rail for a tactical light. It comes in optics-

The 75th Anniversary Mark IV Target .22 LR rimfire features a laser-engraved logo on the receiver and back of the bolt. It's packaged in a throwback-styled 75th Anniversary printed box. That tapered barrel is 6.8 inches.

RUGER

Ruger's larger format LC Charger (MSRP $999) pistol is chambered in 5.7x28mm with a 10- or 20-round magazine capacity. With the 10.3-inch barrel, the overall length is 16 inches. The CNC-

SDS Imports' Tisas Nightstalker DS 2011 features a threaded 5-inch barrel, RMS cut for optics, polymer grip with removable aluminum magwell, and is compatible with Glock-style rear sights.

milled handguard features a bandstop and M-LOK slots to add accessories. To commemorate its 75th anniversary, Ruger offers limited-edition pistols, like the 75th Anniversary SR1911, with laser-engraved slides and custom grip panels. It's chambered in .45 Auto and sports a full-size frame and 5-inch barrel. The 75th Anniversary Mark IV Target (MSRP $599) .22 LR rimfire features a laser-engraved logo on the receiver and back of the bolt. It is packaged in a throwback-styled, 75th Anniversary printed box. It has a 6.8-inch barrel, blued finish and fully checkered wood laminate grips. The 75th Anniversary LCP MAX (MSRP $479) carries a laser-engraved commemorative logo on the slide, is chambered in .380 Auto, and has a two-tone finish. *ruger.com*

SDS IMPORTS

SDS has introduced four new double-stack 1911s in 9mm, poised to disrupt the market with radically affordable prices. SDS imports the 1911s from Turkish manufacturer Tisas. The Nightstalker DS 2011 (MSRP $959) features a threaded 5-inch barrel, RMS cut for optics, polymer grip with removable aluminum magwell, and is compatible with Glock-style rear sights. You won't find cast or MIM parts in this piece; it's just quality manufacturing. The 2011 Duty and 2011 Carry (both MSRP $800) series are built for concealed carry.

Duty series guns have a 5-inch barrel, accessory rail, optics mount, and ambidextrous thumb safety. The Carry has similar features but comes with a 4.25-

inch barrel. The MAC 1911-DS (MSRP $1,100) is the top-of-the-line model with a 4.25-inch forged bull barrel, 17-round capacity magazine, full-length dust rail, optics-cut slide, ambi thumb safety, and removable magazine well. And just when you thought another High Power clone was not possible, MAC has resurrected the World War II-era Inglis

MAC has resurrected the World War II-era Inglis High Power L9A1.

The MAC-5 semi-automatic clone of the famed H&K MP5 with roller-delayed blowback action. It has an 8.9-inch barrel.

High Power L9A1 (MSRP $490) with a black chromate finish, 4.7-inch barrel, ambidextrous thumb safety and polymer grips. Also new to the MAC stable of retro pistols are the MAC-5K (MSRP $1,100) and the MAC-5 (MSRP $1,100), semi-automatic clones of the famed H&K MP5 with roller-delayed blowback action. The MAC-5K is equipped with a 5.8-inch barrel. The MAC-5 has an 8.9-inch barrel. *sdsimports.com*

SIG SAUER

The SIG P322-COMP (MSRP $658) is a tricked-out, competition-ready P322 rimfire featuring a compensator-equipped barrel, a takedown lever that acts like an extended gas pedal, and a RomeoZero red-dot with Elite slide racker. Hence, it's easier and faster to rack the slide. It comes with a 20- and a 25-round mag. Remember to buy plenty of .22 LR ammo to run through this rimfire. *sigsauer.com*

SMITH & WESSON

Smith & Wesson has evolved the affordable SD series with the new SD9 2.0 (MSRP $349) with performance upgrades like the enhanced Self-Defense Trigger with flat face design, and available in 10- and 16-round magazine capacity. The new Performance Center M&P9 Metal M2.0 (MSRP $999) is an all-metal frame pistol with a built-in Faxon compensator to mitigate felt recoil and muzzle rise, custom lightening cuts in the slide

The SIG P322-COMP is a tricked-out, competition-ready P322 rimfire featuring a compensator-equipped barrel, a takedown lever, and a RomeoZero red-dot with Elite slide racker.

The new Smith & Wesson Performance Center M&P9 Metal M2.0 is an all-metal frame pistol with a built-in Faxon compensator to mitigate felt recoil and muzzle rise, custom lightening cuts in the slide to reduce weight, an enhanced sear for a crisper trigger, suppressor height sights, and it comes in an OD Green Cerakote finish. It includes two 23-round magazines, two 17-round mags, the C.O.R.E plate system for mounting optics, a karambit-style knife, and a custom M&P Spec Series Challenge Coin.

hold. The Classic models (MSRP $1,899) are full-size, 5-inch guns and 4.25-inch commander-size pistols. All have a Cerakote finish and magwell, but not all have an accessory rail. If you want to mount a tactical light, the full-size Standard mod-

Springfield Armory's TRP Carry Contour (CC) models have a bobtailed grip for less printing when carrying concealed and sport 4.25-inch barrels.

carbon steel (MSRP $868) or stainless steel finish (MSRP $917). They're available in 9mm or .45 Auto.

Springfield has also updated the classic TRP (Tactical Response Pistol) series 1911s with six new models. All guns are chambered in .45 Auto and feature forged frames and slides. These are

Springfield updated its TRP (Tactical Response Pistol) series 1911s with six new models. All guns are chambered in .45 Auto and feature forged frames and slides. These are semi-custom guns with hand-fitted slides, frames, barrels, bushings, and other key parts, all hand-etched with matching numbers.

semi-custom guns with hand-fitted slides, frames, barrels, bushings, and other key parts, all hand-etched with matching numbers. The rear sights are tactical rack-style, the grips are G10 Hydra-pattern, and there is plenty of front grip strap checkering for a no-slip

The Staccato C is a compact double-stack 1911 chambered in 9mm with a 4-inch bull barrel designed for concealed carry.

els (MSRP: $1,999) come with a built-in rail and are available in coyote brown or black Cerakote finish. The Carry Contour (CC) models (MSRP $1,999) have a bobtailed grip for less printing when carrying concealed and sport 4.25-inch barrels. springfield-*armory.com*

to reduce weight, an enhanced sear for a crisper trigger, suppressor height sights, and it comes in an OD Green Cerakote finish. It includes two 23-round magazines, two 17-round mags, the C.O.R.E plate system for mounting optics, a karambit-style knife, and a custom M&P Spec Series Challenge Coin. *smith-wesson.com*

The TH10, Taurus' first 10mm Auto pistol, features a polymer frame, DA/SA trigger, exposed hammer, and an ambidextrous thumb safety that doubles as a decocker. The barrel length is 4.25 inches, and it includes two 15-round magazines.

STACCATO
The all-new Staccato C (MSRP $2,599) is a compact double-stack 1911 chambered in 9mm with a 4-inch bull barrel designed for concealed

SPRINGFIELD ARMORY
New to Springfield Armory's Garrison line of single-stack 1911s are 4.25-inch-barrel models with classic hot salt-blued

carry. It has a shorter grip for easier concealment and is optics-ready. Staccato includes two 16-round mags, and the gun has an accessory rail and external extractor for better extraction and performance. *staccato2011.com*

TAURUS

The TH10 (MSRP $531) is Taurus' first 10mm Auto pistol. It's built on the TH platform, which features a polymer frame, DA/SA trigger, exposed hammer, and the ambidextrous thumb safety that doubles as a decocker. The barrel length is 4.25 inches and comes with two 15-round magazines. This is an option if you've

The Taurus GX4 Carry gets a larger grip to flush fit a 15-round mag and has an accessory rail for a light or laser. The GX4 Carry T.O.R.O., pictured here, is the optics-ready version.

always wanted to get into a 10mm.

The GX4 Carry (MSRP $485) gets a larger grip to flush fit a 15-round mag and has an accessory rail for a light or laser. The GX4 Carry T.O.R.O. (MSRP $516) is the optics-ready version. Taurus is also reintroducing the compact version of the Taurus 92. The 917C (MSRP $607) is a compact version with a 4.3-inch

Taurus' 917C is a compact version of the 92, with a 4.3-inch barrel, DA/SA trigger, exposed hammer, finger groove frontstrap, accessory rail and frame-mounted thumb safety. It comes with two 19-round magazines.

signed for EDC. Features include Walther's Performance Duty Grip texture for a secure hold, Super-Terrain slide serration for a better grasp, DA/SA trigger, European-style paddle magazine release, ambi slide-mounted safety/decocker, and 9-round capacity. It's available in a matte black finish. *walther-arms.com*

Walther's all-new PD380 is a compact, hammer-fired .380 Auto designed for EDC.

VUDOO GUN WORKS

The Vudoo Priest (MSRP $3,195) is the newest flagship handgun for Vudoo. This double-stack 1911-style pistol offers a precision-fit slide and frame for optimal performance. The barrel length is 5 inches, and the slide is cut for optics. Vudoo also offers custom options so you can fine-tune the Priest to your needs, like flat triggers, standard or full dust cover, and magwell options, and the grip module is available in various finishes and textures. *vudoogunworks.com* GD

The Vudoo Gun Works Priest is a double-stack 1911-style pistol with a precision-fit slide and frame. The barrel length is 5 inches, and the slide is cut for optics. Custom options abound.

barrel, DA/SA trigger, exposed hammer, finger groove front strap, accessory rail and, best of all, a frame-mounted thumb safety. It comes with two 19-round magazines and in a matte black finish. *taurususa.com*

WALTHER

Walther's all-new PD380 (MSRP $479) is a compact, hammer-fired .380 Auto de-

- REPORTS -
from the Field
REVOLVERS
& OTHERS

Super fun .22 wheelgun plinkers and a stunningly engraved Colt Python are among this year's revolvers.

▶ SHANE JAHN

The American Precision Firearms R-1 Revolver is now available in three different barrel lengths, blued or stainless steel, and fixed or adjustable sight models.

This year, the revolver scene grew, evolved, and even returned to the classics. One of the biggest newsmakers at the 2024 SHOT Show was the product of coordination between Smith & Wesson and Lipsey's that fashioned the Ultimate Carry J-Frame revolver. The two companies worked with industry experts to fine-tune this renowned defensive revolver by focusing on an improved action, better sights, and enhanced grips for controlling recoil. In doing so, they have made the good S&W J-Frame revolver excellent. Having examined and shot the Ultimate Carry in .32 H&R Magnum and .38 Special, I am excited for my order of each model to arrive. I am also eager and hopeful that S&W and Lipsey's will continue with what is sure to be a successful line of wheelguns by applying the same creative applications to other models.

Staying with the evolution of the classics, it's fair to say that the Colt Python is currently the most customized factory revolver on the market regarding engraving and adding aftermarket, quality stocks. Several companies offer dressed-up Pythons to fit any want and budget. Looking back at *Gun Digest 2024*, references were made to upcoming models like the Bond Arms Cyclops in .44 Mag. and .50 AE, both currently available. The long-awaited Colt King Cobra in .22 LR finally arrived for review, and I'm happy to report that the small revolver was operated and shot with no disappointment. Ruger brought out a neat "surprise" chambering in the Super Redhawk. Davidson's is offering a couple of classics, and Taurus continued adding wheelguns and others to its ever-growing line of handguns. We also have some new revolvers available to the market from manufacturers like American Precision Firearms (APF), SAR Firearms, and

The Colt Combat Elite 3-inch Python with G-10 grips panels and a non-fluted cylinder.

The engraved Dark Series Colt from Custom & Collectable Firearms with stag handles.

Davidson's Texas Ranger Smith & Wesson honors the 200th Anniversary of the Texas Rangers with the limited production run of a fixed-sight Model 20 Heavy Duty .357 Magnum.

Spohr. So, pour another cup of coffee, then sit back and enjoy reading about all the new options available this year to add to your collection.

AMERICAN PRECISION FIREARMS

The APF R-1 Revolver is now available in three different barrel lengths, blued or stainless steel, and fixed or adjustable sight models. This revolver has been in production in the Czech Republic for over three decades and is now available here. *americanprecisionfirearms.com*

BOND ARMS

Bond Arms delivered on the Cyclops additions in .44 Magnum and the "Thumper" in .50 AE as promised. It also brought out the Honey B in .22 WRM, a fun-to-shoot derringer-style option. Right after the SHOT Show, Bond Arms' Joey Hedberg stopped by with a truckload of guns to shoot, including the big .50. While it's no cream puff, it is still manageable and adds a certain degree of bragging rights to those who own one! Bond Arms has also just announced the Stinger "Fireball," chambered in .22 WMR and .327 Federal. *bondarms.com*

COLT

Colt added the easy-packing 2.5-inch barrel to the Python series, brought back classic blued versions in 4- and 6-inch barrel lengths, and offered a matte-stainless finish option. It also introduced the Combat Elite 3-inch Python with G-10 grips panels and a non-fluted cylinder. Several folks were excited to hear that the blued Pythons were back in action. I think these additions are a good sign that the folks at Colt are listening to their customers by offering these fine revolvers in various finishes. *colt.com*

CUSTOM & COLLECTABLE FIREARMS

Another company offering banquet-quality revolvers with its Dark Series and Deep Engraved limited-edition Colt Pythons is Custom & Collectable Firearms. One of these finely engraved guns in a carved leather rig would make anyone stand out in a crowd of savvy sixgunners! *cncfirearms.com*

DIAMONDBACK FIREARMS

Diamondback Firearms' new Self Defense Revolver (SDR) is a well-thought-out wheelgun with high-visibility sights and a smooth trigger pull. The sixshooter has a bit of a modern look to it and should be a viable competitor in the personal defense scene. *diamond-backfirearms.com*

DAVIDSON'S EXCLUSIVES

Davidson's has a couple of dandy, old-school S&W N-Frames available this year. First is the Model 20, a fixed-sight .357 Magnum with a 4-inch barrel that hearkens back to an era when lawmen transitioned from the Colt Single Action Army to modern double-action revolvers. The other S&W exclusive honors the 200th Anniversary of the Texas Rangers with the limited production run of a fixed-sight Model 20 Heavy Duty .357 Magnum. Only 250 of these fine revolvers will be offered. Handgun hunters will be particularly interested in the 1873 Pietta .44 Magnum, an adjustable sight single-action with a 7.5-inch barrel. *davidsonsinc.com*

Fink's Modern Red Dot Revolver (MRR) uses Moreno's Interchangeable Barrel System (MIBS): Barrels of various lengths are easily swapped out by hand in seconds.

Henry is now in the revolver business, with the Big Boy chambered in .38 Special/.357 Magnum.

The Heritage Settler Mare's Leg in .22 LR.

The Kimer Model K6xs is a double-action-only six-shot with a 2-inch barrel.

EMF COMPANY, INC./PIETTA FIREARMS

Strolling by the EMF booth, I struck up a conversation with the man behind the counter. After a good visit, I asked if anything new for the year was out, and he showed me the 1873 Premier Wood Grip in the display case. If you're looking for a single-action with a little something extra, this might be it. The gun's color-cased finish, bluing and figured wood stocks show extra care and attention that fine firearms connoisseurs will note and appreciate. *emf-company.com*

FINK'S CUSTOM GUNS

Located onsite at the famed Gunsite Academy (gunsite.com), Dave Fink and his crew turn out top-quality work. From simple fix-its to custom guns, they do it all. Two of Fink's custom revolvers caught my attention at first glance, and their smooth actions and accuracy on the range made me pay attention! As the name implies, the Modern Red Dot Revolver (MRR) is just that. We shot this gun on steel at the NRA Whittington Center, and its accuracy, even at long ranges, was impressive. Fink's Moreno Interchangeable Barrel System (MIBS) is simply genius. Barrels of various lengths are easily swapped out by hand in seconds. *finksguns.com*

HENRY

Probably best known for its smooth-cycling lever-action rifles, Henry surprised shooters with an old-school-looking revolver called the Big Boy chambered in .38 Special/.357 Magnum. I spent a little time with one on the range at the Shootists Holiday and found it to be an accurate and reliable revolver. *henryusa.com*

HERITAGE MANUFACTURING CO.

Heritage Manufacturing offers a variety of bargain-priced firearms for shooters. One of the "ya just gotta have one because it's cool" guns is the Settler Mare's Leg. Reminiscent of the star firearm in the old television western, "Wanted Dead or Alive," Heritage's rendition is in .22 LR. *heritagemfg.com*

KIMBER

Kimber continues to add to its line of excellent revolvers with this year's model K6xs, a double-action-only six-shot with a 2-inch barrel. This little gun has a nice action and should be a good option for a small defensive revolver. *kimberamerica. com*

LIPSEY'S

The Lipsey's team is renowned for coordinating with firearms manufacturers to produce some of the most unique and highly sought-after guns on the market. The S&W Ultimate Carry snubbies are already a home run, but that's not the only exclusives up for grabs this year. Lipsey's also worked with Colt and Tyler Gun Works (TGW) to offer a 4.25-inch version of the Premier-Grade Python. Complete with engraving and American elk stag grips, this is one classy sixgun. Its other exclusive stainless steel Python has a 2.5-inch barrel, TGW-applied Nitre Blue PVD Hammer, trigger, sideplate screws and rear sight elevation screw that dress up the revolver. Other additions include Holly grips, complete with Colt medallions. These fine grips are almost indistinguishable from ivory and are handsome on a sixgun. *lipseys.com*

NIGHTHAWK CUSTOM-KORTH

Nighthawk Custom has added some color to its fine Korth revolver line. The NXA 8-Shot has an anodized red aluminum barrel shroud and wooden grips in a

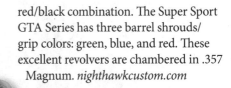

Lipsey's Tyler Gun Works 2.5-inch stainless steel Python with Holly grips and Colt medallions.

The Lipsey's Smith & Wesson J-Frame Ultimate Carry was one of the most notable introductions in the EDC category—the little wheelgun sports aftermarket grips and sights, which are common upgrades that are now standard.

This Lipsey's Tyler Gun Works Premier-Grade Colt Python sports stunning engraving and stag grips.

red/black combination. The Super Sport GTA Series has three barrel shrouds/grip colors: green, blue, and red. These excellent revolvers are chambered in .357 Magnum. *nighthawkcustom.com*

NORTH AMERICAN ARMS

NAA has a trunkload of mini-revolvers and added one more to the collection called The Sentinel. The little stainless shooter will have a swing-out cylinder, be chambered in .22 Winchester Magnum Rimfire with an optional .22 LR conversion cylinder, a 1.5-inch barrel, and an optional white dot or Tritium front sight. *northamericanarms.com*

ROSSI

Another just-because-it's-cool gun is Rossi's Brawler. This single-shot .45 Colt/.410 ga. handgun has real applications for personal defense and can readily handle any varmint problem on the old homestead. *rossiusa.com*

RUGER

Ruger surprised many when it brought out the stout Super Redhawk in .22 Hornet. As soon as I saw the announcement, I ordered one. A fresh shipment of Hornady ammunition just arrived, and I cannot wait to take this combination out for prairie dogs in the coming weeks. *ruger.com*

RW 2 DOGS REAR SIGHTS

Good sights are as important as a crisp trigger for accurate shot placement. Ronnie Wells of RW Grip Frames makes numerous grip frames for single-action revolvers, offering the perfect grip for every size hand. Fermin Garza makes his tough 2 Dogs Custom front sights for various handguns. These two know guns and have decades of ex-

The Nighthawk Custom-Korth NXA 8-Shot has an anodized red aluminum barrel shroud and wooden grips in a red/black combination. Green and blue are also available in the .357 Mag.

perience behind them to turn out quality, functional products. They have combined forces to offer the drop-in RW 2 Dogs rear sights for revolvers. Several rear sight pictures are available, such as Square, "V," "U," and those options with white outlines. Currently available for Ruger revolvers, they make a difference! *rwgripframes.com, fermincgarza.com*

SAR FIREARMS

SAR's new line of double-action revolvers is available in

A Ruger Super Redhawk in .22 Hornet sent revolver fans rushing to their checkbooks to place orders.

black or stainless steel with barrel lengths of 4 and 6 inches. These guns have alloy-forged steel frames, barrels, cylinders, full-length barrel underlugs, adjustable rear sights, and changeable front sights. *sarusa.com*

SPOHR REVOLVERS

I threw the SHOT Show map to the wind and walked up and down each aisle through the maze of the showrooms. Not only did this burn plenty of calories, but it also allowed me to see specific booths and meet different people I might have otherwise missed. The Spohr booth was one. The German revolvers caught my eye as soon as I approached the showcase. Immediately suspecting quality, handling one of the top-shelf revolvers reaffirmed my assessment. I suspect five minutes on the range will do the same. Their engineer explained the inner workings of these guns, and I expect they will outshoot my capabilities, which I intend to find out as soon as possible. Spohr has been providing its revolvers in Germany since 2019 and now offers U.S. shooters a variety of double-action options to meet any need. *spohrguns.com, mmbimports.com*

The North American Arms Sentinel has a swing-out cylinder chambered in .22 Winchester Magnum Rimfire with an optional .22 LR conversion cylinder.

TALO DISTRIBUTOR EXCLUSIVES

Talo has a couple of notable Ruger revolvers. One is the LCRx in 9mm. This lightweight (21.3-ounce) 3-inch double-action revolver is a good idea that will make a superb personal defense/woods gun that is easy to pack. Talo also added a midnight blue Cerakote Wrangler .22 LR with a brass Cerakote trigger-guard and grip frame with a 6.5-inch barrel that is a classy-looking single-action. *taloinc. com*

TAURUS

You can always bet Taurus has new additions to its revolver line, and this year was no different. The slick-actioned 605 Executive Grade is a 3-inch, five-shot .357 Magnum worthy of consideration for a defensive revolver, as is the 327 Defender T.O.R.O. in the potent .327 Federal/.32 H&R Magnum. The Judge Home Defender might be the ticket if you want something a little larger in the defense market. This .45 Colt/.410-gauge revolver with a 13-inch barrel offers plenty of protection when discreet carry isn't concerned. Classic single-action revolver enthusiasts have another option with Taurus' Deputy in .45 Colt or .357 Magnum. The deep satin-black revolver has a transfer bar safety and comes in 4.75- and 5.5-inch barrel lengths. *taurususa.com*

TAYLOR'S & COMPANY

Taylor's & Co. offers a ton of different revolvers from the Old West in various finish-

The Spohr Club Edition, a finely made German revolver, will now be available in the U.S. via MMB Imports.

Taurus' slick-actioned 605 Executive Grade is a 3-inch, five-shot .357 Magnum.

Taylor's & Co. offers the classic 1873 in modern-day Cerakote for shooters looking for a hogleg with a weather-resistant coating.

es like traditional blued, color-cased, distressed, stainless, engraved, and the like. This year, it offers the classic 1873 in modern-day Cerakote for shooters looking for a hogleg with a weather-resistant coating or a single-action revolver slightly different from the other guys'. *taylorsfirearms.com*

TYLER GUN WORKS

Tyler Gun Works is a name you see repeated in this short article. It is not only a premier firearms finishing company offering excellent color-casing, bluing, and multiple other quality firearms finishes, but it's also a leader in gunsmithing and custom projects throughout the industry. Bobby Tyler is a man of vision who sees needs in the industry, and he and his team exceed expectations by fulfilling those demands. One of their current options is offering a TGW Exclusive Custom Adjustable Dovetail Front Sight for former fixed-sight revolvers. Not only does this make dialing in a particular load easy via windage adjustment, but additional blades are also available in different heights that can be purchased to fine-tune your sight for a particular load. This sight also provides an excellent picture for better shooting, especially for those with aging eyesight. Keep an eye on the website; you never know what extraordinary collection is up for sale there or what special run of TGW custom guns come along. *tylergunworks.com*

Classic, modern, large, and small. From wheelguns and others made right here in the USA to quality imports from overseas, there are a variety of good guns available for today's handgunners. The only trouble is deciding which one you will buy first! **GD**

- REPORTS -
from the Field
SHOTGUNS

From Southpaw-friendly to exquisitely engraved to The Age of the 28 Gauge, shotgun innovation marches on.

❯KRISTIN ALBERTS

Connecticut Shotgun Manufacturing Company (CSMS) A10 shotguns at Safari Club International's show in Nashville, Tennessee.

Weatherby shocked Pheasant Fest attendees by introducing its Sorix autoloader—a transformer-meets-inertia-gun ambidextrous-friendly shottie.

We were four ladies off the grid in rustic Sonora, Mexico, armed with Mossberg shotguns. When the dust settled, four gorgeous Gould's wild turkeys had fallen to the 12-gauge 940 Pro and a raging 28-gauge SA-28 Tactical Turkey. And by fall, I mean bang-flop clean, ethical harvests that put sub-gauges on centerstage. If the previous quinquennial was dedicated to all things .410 bore—from ammo to turkey guns to levers—then this is officially The Age of the 28.

This age of smaller bores, lighter guns, and lightning-cycling repeaters comes at the expense of the old guard. Don't get me wrong. I still enjoy a good 10-gauge whooping, and I'd even welcome a punt gun into my collection, but the buyer's market for big 'ol boat anchors is dwindling. It's harder now than ever to find new-manufacture 10s, an unfortunate truth that seems to worsen each year.

That loss goes hand-in-hand with the rise of specialty shot types negating the "need"—not necessarily the want—for magnum 3.5-inch chambers and, by proxy, 10-bores. Can you believe finding a magnum, 3-inch chambered 28-gauge is easier than a basic 10?

Weatherby shocked Pheasant Fest attendees with a transformer-meets-inertia-gun ambidextrous-friendly number. What's more, scattergun companies are also rallying behind smaller-framed shooters with multiple quality entries in that space. Gone are the days of taking a chop saw to the buttstock of granddad's worn pump; these shotguns are built with more than abbreviated length of pull (LOP) metrics for comfort, recoil reduction, and, ultimately, a more enjoyable shooting experience.

In this edition, we're seeing not just budget and solely premium-priced entries but a healthy dose of both, with plenty of middle ground for buyers wanting to stretch their dollars. As another page turns, the mix of classy sporting, attitude tactical, practical hunting, exquisite craftsmanship, and modern engineering converge to offer shotgunners the guns of their dreams. Best of all, we no longer have to smash the poor little piggy bank—or hold up a stagecoach—to have one heckuva good-looking and mean-shooting scattergun.

BENELLI

Sports shooters, competitors, and hunters alike can celebrate Benelli's updated and additional model variants. Smaller-statured hunters—not only youngsters—will flock to the company's workhorse Super Black Eagle 3 (SBE3) Compact. With a length of pull (LOP) reduced to 13-1/8 inches along with a shorter 26-inch barrel and lighter weight, it not only fits better for slighter builds but for waterfowlers layered in bulky gear. The SBE3 Compact can be had in 12-, 20-, and 28-gauges.

In contrast to the camo-ed SBE family stands the young Ethos SuperSport Performance Shop A.I. with high-grade walnut, nickel-plated receiver, and Advanced Impact (AI) components. With Briley's weighted forend cap, extended tubes, enlarged controls, and sharp red accents, this gem will catch the attention of your fellow clay shooters. Still, its performance-forward features are geared toward a serious competition circuit. *benelliusa.com*

BERETTA

Talk about a clash. Beretta swings from one extreme to the other with its duo of newbies. One is a classically styled upland number, while the other is a high-capacity, yeti-dressed, optics-ready monster. You're intrigued now, so let's start with the latter. The A300 Ultima Arctic Fox Snow Goose has a name as long as the gun. There's an extended magazine tube, optics-ready receiver, lower Picatinny rail for a camera or accessory, and features tailored to cold-weather gloved shooters. It marks the company's first entry into the dedicated snow goose space and does so in a big way.

Before you get worried about Beretta turning back on its roots, the innovative Ultraleggero O/U also receives

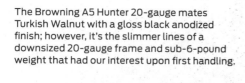

The Browning A5 Hunter 20-gauge mates Turkish Walnut with a gloss black anodized finish; however, it's the slimmer lines of a downsized 20-gauge frame and sub-6-pound weight that had our interest upon first handling.

an upgrade. The trimmed-down O/U with techno-polymer inserts sees the addition of the company's proven recoil-reducing Kick-Off system and a mid-wrist shim kit for further fit customizations. The chance to have both of those upgrades for not much more money or poundage sounds like a no-brainer for those in the 12-gauge Ultraleggero market. *beretta.com*

BROWNING

Ah, my affinity for the white whale of American shotguns gets another boost with the introduction of an A5 in 20-gauge. While I'll argue to no end that there's no replacement for the original round knob Belgian-made Auto-5s of nearly a century hence, I also boldly applaud Browning for not only returning but continuing to expand the "new" A5 family of humpback repeaters. The A5 Hunter 20-gauge mates Turkish Walnut with a gloss black anodized finish; however, it's the slimmer lines of a downsized 20-gauge frame and sub-6-pound weight that had our interest upon first handling. Like the other reborn A5s, the young twenty uses a recoil-operated kinematic drive with a 100,000-round (or five-year) guarantee.

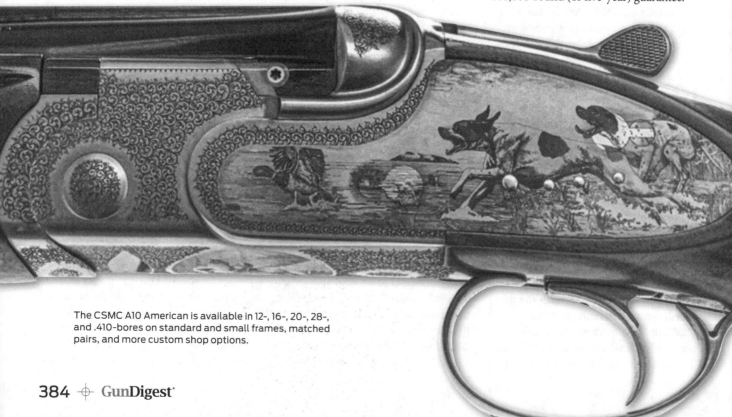

The CSMC A10 American is available in 12-, 16-, 20-, 28-, and .410-bores on standard and small frames, matched pairs, and more custom shop options.

The Benelli Ethos SuperSport Performance Shop A.I. has high-grade walnut, nickel-plated receiver, and Advanced Impact (AI) components.

Sometimes, it's not only what you see but what you don't. A close study of Browning's latest catalog shows new model firearms and some standbys that have gone missing. The big 10s are nearly absent, with only a 10-gauge BPS Field Composite remaining at the time of this writing. It feels like the end of an era we hope isn't forgotten, but rising prices on existing 10-gauges indicate interest in the thumper is far from cold. Likewise, Browning has taken the axe to its slide-action rosters, with BPS listings getting a major chop job, with only the aforementioned Field Composite and a wood-stocked BPS Field remaining from what used to be a laundry list of pump guns. *browning.com*

CONNECTICUT SHOTGUN MANUFACTURING COMPANY

There they were: Rows of tables full of cased sets and the finest shotguns from the likes of Holland & Holland, Parker, Purdy, and W.W. Greener on display at Safari Club International's show in Nashville, Tennessee. But it was no museum exhibition. Oh no. It was Tony Galazan's Connecticut Shotgun Manufacturing

Company (CSMC) booth, where the crazy genius was showing off not only historic models available for sale but, more importantly, for our purposes, the stunning breadth of shotguns of his manufacture. For those unfamiliar with CSMC—and its wildcat offshoot Standard Manufacturing—it does everything in-house at its expansive New Britain, CT, facility.

Galazan and CSMC's current production shotguns grabbed our attention. In addition to stunning one-offs with enameled receivers or drop-dead engraving are the lines of Inverness, Pointer Superlight, G1, Christian Hunter O/U and SxS, its own A.H. Fox SxS and "Winchester" 21. The latest to the party—and believe me, it's a par-tay—is the rapidly growing family of A10 American variants. This burgeoning line of O/Us can be snagged in production guns or otherwise upgraded, customized, and ala-carted to your heart's content. The A10 American is available in 12-, 16-, 20-, 28-, and .410-bores on standard and small frames, matched pairs, and more custom shop options than my favorite bourbon list. *connecticutshotgun.co*

HERITAGE

The name synonymous with the most affordable single-action rimfire revolvers is digging its spurs into the shotgun milieu. No doubt, Heritage is capitalizing on the peaking interest in Old West guns that initially drove them to fame. One need only look as far as the rifle market, with more lever-actions built now than ever, including entries from Heritage.

But Heritage's first shotgun is no lever; it's a coach gun with attitude. The aptly named Badlander is half robber Black Bart, half gentleman Charles Boles, with a sure nod to the Wells Fargo stagecoach days. The American-made 12-gauge looks and feels the part, dressed with Turkish Walnut, built of steel, and finished with a clean black chrome coating, while the hammerless double with its 18.5-inch barrels is ready for serious business. The double-triggered defender measures only 34.8 inches in overall length. Hence, it disappears behind the bedpost yet tips its hat to cowboy attitude with engraved Heritage cattle brand-style engraving on both the buttstock and receiver. *heritagemfg.com*

FRANCHI

Franchi's Affinity 3 series of repeaters continues its stronghold on the company's semi-automatic shotgun catalog. The latest additions include a Sport Trap, and a fully Realtree'd Max-7 camouflage option for waterfowlers. The Affinity 3 Sport Trap bridges the gap between a do-all gun and an entry into competitive clays. The 3-inch-chambered 12-gauge has a 30-inch ported barrel, stepped vent rib, and extended stainless chokes. The inertia-driven autoloader retails for under a grand, and while its blued receiver and black synthetic stock appear basic, that Ergonom-X stock allows for tweaks to drop, cast, and LOP for improved fit and, hopefully, more exploding orange clouds.

Shooters who prefer a more traditional break-action will gravitate to Franchi's O/U's. It's business as usual, with the over/under Instinct family chugging along in Sideplate, SLX, LX, SL, and L variants with options in every gauge from 12- to .410. *franchiusa.com*

KRIEGHOFF

The German-made masterpieces—and yes, some of them surely appear, as the company claims, "art on a metal canvas"—continue to impress. Though we haven't seen any new models with the turning of another calendar, Krieghoff showed off several stunning new engraving patterns on its K-80 and K-20 models. The Eternity, with its diamond-like lines and blue-green hues, marks one of the most modern-meets-unique takes on "engraving," with Safari Club Show onlookers showing a split love-it-or-hate-it reaction on the K-80 Parcours' receiver. Several more traditional, deep relief and gold-accented game scene designs are already winning over hunters and collectors, including a Gold San Remo Nitride with actively flushing game birds in contrasting tones.

Get this. In addition to the 69 engraving patterns that Krieghoff currently shows on its website as cataloged patterns, the Custom Shop makes the sky (and your pocketbook) the limit as you team with one of the company's master engravers. When looks match performance, look out. *krieghoff.com*

MOSSBERG

Brace yourselves. This is a long one because the gloves are off, and O.F. Mossberg is hoisting the title belt for most new shotguns launched in recent years. While most cater to hunters, there's plenty to love for sport shooters and home defenders.

Jerry Miculek makes Mossberg's 940 Pro models—some of which bear his name and design influence—run like a full auto. That youngish 940 Pro family of gas-driven repeaters allows up to 1,500 rounds between cleaning and includes JM Pro, Field, Waterfowl, Tactical, Field, Sporting, Turkey, Snow Goose, and Thunder Ranch variants. The shotgun world's move to optics-readiness is not lost on Mossberg; it's now one of the leaders in both shotgun receivers machined for direct mounting optics and ready-made Holosun combos.

Its Waterfowl and Snow Goose Pros are in on the ground floor of optics use for geese and ducks, which I'm admittedly still scratching my head about, but I won't knock it 'til I've tried it. The same can be said for a team of lower-capacity 940 Pro's with five-shot variants on the Tactical, JM Pro, and Snow Goose, with the latter leaving me with the same bewildered reaction. Seeing those swirling tornadic clouds of Snow Geese makes me want every last round I can stuff into that extended magazine tube, weight be darned.

Believe it or not, the 940 Pros were taking a backseat to onlooker interest at the last Pheasant Fest show, but only because Mossberg's revamped International Silver Series Eventide O/Us are grabbing hunters' attention. The latest models can be had in 12-, 20-, and 28-gauges, with both Waterfowl- and Turkey-specific selections. The former pits a 3.5-inch-chambered 12 with Patriot Brown Cerakote metal and camo stocks. The Eventide Turkeys, with 20-inch barrels and full Mossy Oak coverage, pique my curiosity. At only 37.75 inches in overall length, that

Krieghoff Eternity engraving pattern on display at SCI.

little banger should be a wieldy gobbler buster.

Speaking of 28s, Mossberg has been all over the rise of the 28. Though the Eventide marks the company's first entry into the magnum 3-inch 28-gauge world, I was delighted with the performance of the 2.75-inch-chambered SA-28 Tactical Turkey on the aforementioned Mexican Gould's adventure. If you appreciate the low-recoil-meets-light-weight of .410 gobbler guns, you'll find even greater joy in the equally soft-shooting but significantly increased shotshell capacity of the sub-gauge over the baby bore. *mossberg.com*

POINTER

The latest from Legacy Sports International's portfolio comes from shotgun brand Pointer with the introduction of Acrius over/unders and a line of side-by-sides aptly—if not un-creatively named—Side by Side. Marketing fails aside, the Pointer Side by Side comprises a useful contingent of 12-, 20-, 28-, and .410-bore doubles with 28- or 26-inch barrels, impressive checkered Turkish Walnut stocks, a single trigger, barrel selector, and finish options including case color, nickel, and even Cerakote.

Pointer's Acrius is a practical over-under in the same gauges, each with chrome-lined barrels, a single mechanical trigger, barrel selector, and extractors. The Acrius can be had in the standard silver finish receiver with laser etching or the Acrius Cerakote. The newbies join existing Pointer models, including the single-shot Pup 410, Field Tek semi-autos, and Sport Tek wing of break-actions and repeaters purpose-built for the sporting lifestyle. *pointershotguns.com*

TRISTAR ARMS

Another year, another plethora of reinvigorated offerings from "The Value Experts" at Tristar Arms. The latest O/U listings include an updated look with a Trinity II and an entirely new expression in the Cypher. Tristar goes back to the side-by-side well, doubling down on its recent success with the Bristol double to offer a Phoenix SxS. This 12- or 20-gauge wears 28-inch chrome-lined barrels, a 13-inch LOP, and a single selective trigger

Mossberg SA-28 Tactical Turkey with Federal Custom Shop 28-ga. TSS loads.

against a case-color receiver and glossy Turkish Walnut in a pistol-grip style.

The Cypher O/U can be had in every gauge from .410 to 12, each with 28-inch barrels, auto ejectors, and deluxe walnut furniture with a 14.25-inch LOP. The Cypher is comprised of three distinct variants: the standard Cypher, built with steel mono-block construction; a Cypher X with a lighter-weight aluminum build; and finally, the Cypher SP sporting 12-gauge manufacture of steel, featuring 30-inch ported barrels, a target rib, extended tubes, and an adjustable comb. All three youngsters are built in Turkey, ship with five Beretta-style choke tube set, and carry the company's five-year warranty. *tristararms.com*

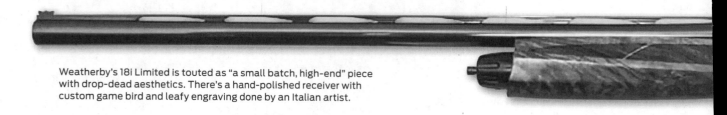

Weatherby's 18i Limited is touted as "a small batch, high-end" piece with drop-dead aesthetics. There's a hand-polished receiver with custom game bird and leafy engraving done by an Italian artist.

STOEGER

The workaday Stoeger family of shotguns gets a slightly fancier upgrade as the brand celebrates a century of gun building. The M3000 Signature Series 100th Anniversary is a 12-gauge repeater that capitalizes on the company's M3000 inertia-driven semi-automatic line but dresses it up for dinner. There's a nickel receiver with scrollwork engraving against a polished blue 28-inch barrel. A red fiber-optic front sight, sling studs, and a set of three chokes round out the package. The two-tone receiver paired with upgraded satin-finish Turkish Walnut pistol grip-style checkered furniture grants more class to what is usually a more utilitarian scattergun.

Celebration aside, Stoeger's exiting lines of M3000, M3020, M3500, Freedom, Condor, Longfowler, Uplander, M3K, Double Defense, Coach Gun, and Grand Series of shotguns all continue, representing pretty much every action—pumps, repeaters, O/Us, SxSs—along with every use from home defense to sporting, do-all-ers, compacts, hunters, and game-specific options in the turkey and waterfowl spaces. *stoegerindustries. com*

WEATHERBY

Since the move to Wyoming, Weatherby has gotten down to business. While only the venerable Mark V and brand new 307 rifles are built in the U.S. in Sheridan, the company hasn't lost its commitment to shotgunners. Weatherby is touting a trio of newfangled, updated, and downright unexpected ones.

First comes surprising innovation with the Sorix, described by the company as "a new era in Weatherby shotguns." The waterfowl-minded autoloader accommodates left-handed shooters with what Weatherby calls the Shift System, an ambidextrously friendly cut receiver that allows the charging handle to be quickly swapped from right- to left-handed operations. In a further Southpaw advancement, the safety can also be reversed easily. While the shape-shifting dominates headlines, other practical features abound, including oversized controls, a drilled and tapped receiver for optics mounting, and aggressive receiver cuts for faster reloads. Three color combinations illuminate the Sorix, with Storm, Midnight Marsh, and Slough in uniquely paired Cerakote metalwork against stocks hand-painted in Sheridan. Each is built in three configurations: 12-gauge or 20-gauge with a 3-inch chamber or a

Tristar Cypher receiver detail.

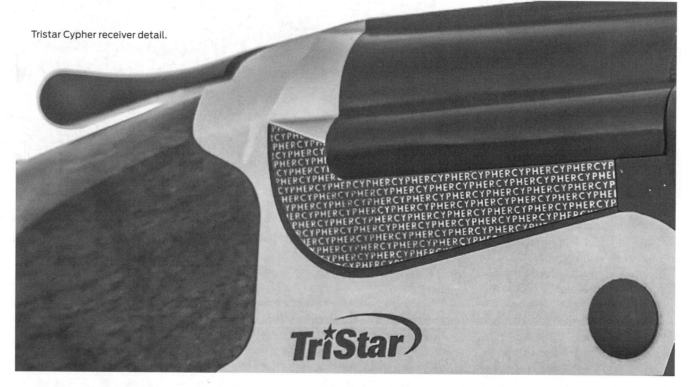

magnum 3.5-inch twelve.

In existing Weatherby shotguns, the 18i Deluxe is nice, but its 18i Limited kin is off the charts in looks. Touted as "a small batch, high-end" piece by Weatherby, the Limited doubles the price tag of its nearest compatriot but pays that back in drop-dead aesthetics. There's a hand-polished receiver with custom game bird and leafy engraving done by a single, named Italian artist. The 24-karat gold inlays, exhibition-grade walnut stock, and high-gloss bluing make it worthy of a black-tie banquet. Exterior aside, the Limited features the same inertia recoil action, machined aluminum triggerguard assembly, and a set of five Crio Plus choke tubes.

The Sorix and the 18i models are crafted in Italy, while the Orions—and most other models, including the Element and SA-08—are built to Weatherby specs in Turkey. *weatherby.com*

WINCHESTER

While newish rounds—looking at you, .350 and .400 Legend—and a Ranger rimfire lever gun steal Winchester's thunder, more than 70 individual shotgun variants are waiting in the wings. At long last, lefties can shop with not just one or two but three variants on the SX4 Hybrid Hunter and Waterfowl Hunter camo-clad scatterguns. The 12-gauges with 3.5-inch chambers chew through even light loads without adjustment, while southpaws can choose from 26- or 28-inch barrel lengths and Cerakote and several camo patterns. In addition, Winchester has added multiple finish options to its SX4 Defender shorter-barreled repeaters. *winchesterguns.com* ⅁Ⅾ

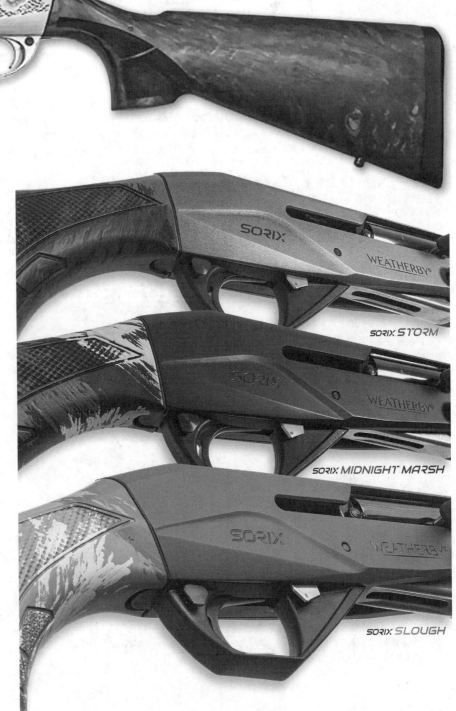

Weatherby's new waterfowl-minded Sorix autoloader accommodates left-handed shooters with what Weatherby calls the Shift System, an ambidextrously friendly cut receiver that allows the charging handle to be quickly swapped from right- to left-handed operations. Three color combinations illuminate the Sorix, with Storm, Midnight Marsh, and Slough in uniquely paired Cerakote metalwork against stocks hand-painted in Sheridan. Available in 12- or 20-gauge with a 3-inch chamber or a magnum 3.5-inch 12-gauge.

- REPORTS -
from the Field
MUZZLELOADERS

Federal's unique ignition system expands to more makes and models, bullets improve, and custom smokepoles abound.

❯ BRAD FENSON

Remington's Accutip MZ Muzzleloader bullet is among the notable new product releases in the blackpowder space.

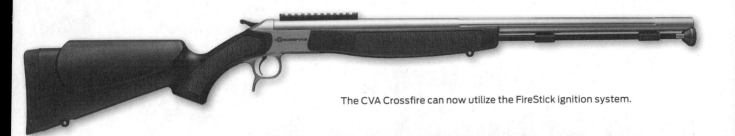

The CVA Crossfire can now utilize the FireStick ignition system.

Muzzleloaders and components continue to advance. Propellants are cleaner and provide more consistent velocity and energy. Fighting the elements is no longer an issue when propellants and ignition are encased in a waterproof polymer self-contained charge. The muzzleloading industry has certainly seen many positive changes in the last 40 years. It's mind-numbing to think of any changes that could make a muzzleloader easier to use and more accurate than it is today. Here's a look at some current and new offerings for smokepole shooters.

ANARCHY OUTDOORS
Are you looking for a soft-shooting muzzleloader? Consider a muzzle brake to take the kick out of the equation. Anarchy Outdoors is making muzzle brakes for popular CVA models. Check out the options to tame your rifle. Anarchy Outdoors also has a Grayboe stock with a compatibility kit for the CVA Paramount Pro and HTR. The Grayboe Eagle Stock is a lightweight, universal fit for hunting. *anarchyoutdoors.com*

ARROWHEAD RIFLES
Arrowhead Rifles' Obsidian Muzzleloader is a custom rifle that can shoot sub-minute-of-angle groups at 500 yards. The smokeless powder Gen 2 Large Rifle Magnum Primer Ignition System is the base for consistency, and a cut-rifled .45-caliber barrel keeps up with performance. There are several custom-built options for serious muzzleloader enthusiasts to check out. *arrowheadrifles.com*

CVA CROSSFIRE
The innovative CVA Crossfire rifle utilizes the groundbreaking FireStick ignition

The new Federal FireStick is a self-contained powder charge housed in a polymer casing designed to load into a Traditions NitroFire and now CVA muzzleloader.

system (see Federal below). This system allows the pre-loaded powder capsules to be inserted into the breech area of the barrel while the projectile is loaded through the muzzle. Paired with CVA's break-action design, the Crossfire offers easy loading and unloading, catering to shooters who prioritize convenience.

The Crossfire comes in two models. The first Crossfire Cerakote Burnt Bronze/Escape has a 26-inch barrel with a 1:28-inch twist. It weighs 8 pounds and is available in .50 caliber. The second is the Crossfire Stainless Steel Black with a 26-inch barrel and 1:28-inch twist. *cvariflesusa.com*

FEDERAL FIRESTICK
Spending three days at the Federal Premium ammunition production facility the week before the world shut down due to COVID-19 was an extraordinary experience. During this time, I had the opportunity to thoroughly evaluate the new Federal FireStick—a self-contained powder charge housed in a polymer casing designed to load into a Traditions NitroFire muzzleloader. My time at the facility was dedicated to testing the rifle's accuracy and velocity with various bullets and propellants.

The testing process involved setting up a chronograph 10 feet from the barrel to capture the velocity of five shots for each of two bullets, utilizing Federal Premium Muzzleloader 209 primers as the ignition source. The results obtained with the Traditions Smackdown Carnivore 250-grain bullet with sabot were impressive, with a mean velocity of 1,973 fps.

It's worth noting that the NitroFire and FireStick systems demonstrated exceptional consistency, surpassing the acceptable industry tolerance of 75

fps variance by nearly 42 percent. The velocities achieved were comparable to popular propellants such as Pyrodex, Blackhorn 209, and Triple Seven. Moreover, the FireStick's convenience, reliability, and resistance to adverse weather conditions make it an ideal choice for hunting applications.

In addition to velocity measurements, the bullet groups obtained during testing were equally impressive. The smallest five-shot group measured a mere 3/8 inch, showcasing the remarkable precision of the Federal Premium 100-grain FireStick in conjunction with the Traditions Smackdown Carnivore 250-grain bullet. The smallest group was 3/8 inch with an average of 1 1/6 inches.

These results underscore the exceptional performance and accuracy achievable with the Federal FireStick system, reaffirming its status as a top-tier option for muzzleloader enthusiasts. The FireStick uses Triple Eight powder, which burns clean and consistent. The propellant is the next step forward for muzzleloading.

Traditions had an exclusive with the FireStick for a couple of years after its initial release. When the door opened to other companies, CVA introduced its first rifle to use the FireStick technology. *federalpremium.com*

HANKINS CUSTOM RIFLES
Suppose you have dreamed of customizing or building the perfect frontstuffer for your passion and needs. In that case, Hankins Custom Rifles will keep you glued to the computer surfing options. Barrels, ramrods, stocks, and accessories will open your mind to build the perfect muzzleloader. You can adapt an existing model or piece one together. *hankinscustomrifles.com*

MCWHORTER RIFLES
A decade of dedication to muzzleloader design resulted in a highly accurate muzzleloader using smokeless powder for McWhorter Rifles. The smokeless 45 XML muzzleloader uses a unique ignition system and custom breech plug design that ignites a magnum charge using a 215 Magnum rifle primer. You can customize your rifle order to shoot your specifications. The 45 XML shoots a Pittman 325-gr. Aeromax at speeds up to 3,100 fps. *mcwhorterrifles.com*

PURE PRECISION CUSTOM MUZZLELOADER
The Pure Precision Muzzleloader is designed to extend the range of a smokepole beyond what is thought possible.

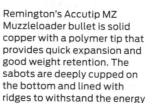

Remington's Accutip MZ Muzzleloader bullet is solid copper with a polymer tip that provides quick expansion and good weight retention. The sabots are deeply cupped on the bottom and lined with ridges to withstand the energy of 200 grains of blackpowder.

The rifle is built on the Summit Muzzleloader action, Altitude carbon-fiber stock, and a Brux barrel. The gun maintains sub-minute of angle accuracy at 600 yards and beyond. The Waypoint trigger from TriggerTech maintains a constant pull at 2.5 to 5.0 pounds. *pureprecision.com*

REMINGTON ARMS
Remington has confirmed that the Model 700 Ultimate Muzzleloader is still in production. The news is good, as it is still a coveted firearm that generates consumer interest and offers long-range shooting with a modern twist on smokepoles. Consumers will find the Model 700 on the shelves by early fall 2024. *remarms.com*

REMINGTON AMMUNITION
Remington recommended using its Premier AccuTip 250-grain bullet and sabot with its muzzleloader. The solid copper bullet with a polymer tip provides quick expansion and good weight retention. The sabots are deeply cupped on the bottom and lined with ridges to withstand the energy of 200 grains of powder.

Remington Ammunition's Premier AccuTip MZ bullet, introduced in 2024,

The Traditions Pursuit XT Pro Series in Veil Alpine. It's also available in a black synthetic stock.

was designed exclusively for muzzleloader hunting. Featuring a bonded bullet guided by the Power Port Tip—the same advanced technology found in Remington's popular Premier AccuTip rifled shotgun slugs—the Premier AccuTip MZ delivers exceptional accuracy and impressive performance on big game, according to Remington.

Upon impact, the Power Port Tip facilitates rapid expansion, ensuring deadly energy transfer. At the same time, the 260-grain bonded bullet ensures optimal penetration and retains over 97 percent of its weight. Compatible with all leading muzzleloading propellants, the Premier AccuTip MZ's bonded bullets pair seamlessly with an easy-loading sabot for speedy reloads. Packaged in convenient 12-bullet packs with quick-loading tubes for easy access in the field or range, the Premier AccuTip MZ is worth looking into for muzzleloader enthusiasts. MSRP: $22.99 *remington.com*

TRADITIONS PRO MODELS
Traditions Performance Firearms launched its Pro Series, catering to avid hunters seeking top-notch features. Available within the NitroFire, Pursuit XT, and Outfitter G3 product lines, the Pro Series boasts an adjustable cheekpiece for enhanced shooting comfort and an adjustable length of pull for customizable fit. The threaded barrel facilitates the easy addition of a muzzle brake for reduced recoil. More accessories are available for different models, offering hunters and shooters various options to enhance their muzzleloading experience. According to Traditions, the Pro Series provides all the desired features in one package, ensuring a

comfortable and optimized shooting experience. MSRP ranges from $469.95 to $749.95.

The Traditions Pursuit continues to be a popular model, and shooters will appreciate the new Pursuit VAPR XT Pro with a revamped stock design and adjustable length of pull and cheekpiece. Personal fit and comfort are paramount to accuracy, and the newest Pursuit in the Pro Series will bring smiles to shooting enthusiasts' faces.

The Pursuit VAPR XT Pro has a threaded barrel to attach a muzzle brake, reducing recoil and enhancing accuracy and overall control. Lightweight, finished with Cerakote, and all the regular features of the Pursuit line provide incredible value in this customizable muzzleloader.

The Pursuit XT Pro is a new model for 2024. There may be confusion around models. Traditions confirmed it does not have a model called the Pursuit VAPR XT Pro. The Pursuit XT and Pursuit XT Pro Series are the models found in stores, and all have VAPR twist barrels, which are a 1:24-inch twist in .50 caliber and a 1:20-inch twist in .45 caliber. *traditionsfirearms.com*

THOMPSON/CENTER
Thompson/Center was established in 1965 when K.W. Thompson made a pistol designed by Warren Center. The company grew quickly, and hunters and shooters welcomed the unique Contender pistol design. T/C was known for novel rifle designs, including the muzzleloading Hawken Rifle introduced in 1970. The T/C designs, created by Warren Center, played an important role in steering the modern blackpowder industry.

Over the years, T/C became known

as the America's Master Gunmaker. In 2007, Smith & Wesson purchased T/C and moved the business from Rochester, New Hampshire to Springfield, Massachusetts. Most firearm enthusiasts know that it didn't take long for T/C to take a backseat in production until the brand was phased out.

On April 30, 2024, the firearms industry received an announcement declaring that Greg Ritz had purchased T/C with plans to revitalize the once-popular firearms manufacturer. Ritz is on record as saying Encore rifles and accessories will return by early 2025. The plan is to make a variety of muzzleloaders in the future, but the exact date is uncertain. Ritz did say that Hawken rifles and more modern designs should be expected.

ULTIMATE FIREARMS CUSTOM MUZZLELOADER
You may have heard of the Safari Club International (SCI) International Muzzleloader Hall of Fame award presented to Ken Johnston and Bob Hodgdon for their work with Ultimate Firearms. The art and science of muzzleloaders, propellants, and projectiles were fine-tuned to create one of the first modern inline-style frontstuffers to shoot 500 yards accurately. *ultimatefirearms.com*

WOODMAN ARMS PATRIOT G3 MUZZLELOADER
The Patriot G3 is not new but holds a soft spot in the hearts of hunters who track big bucks in the big woods. The rifle features a 26-inch, hand-lapped, cut-rifled 1:15 twist barrel with a 1:15-twist cut rifling. The 'loader is designed to be used with bore-sized bullets, not sabots. *woodmanarms.com* **GD**

- REPORTS - from the Field OPTICS

Tack-sharp image stabilization and in-scope hit probability calculation are the tip of this year's proverbial optics iceberg.

› JOE ARTERBURN

Maven's ultra-compact 10x25 binoculars did heavy lifting for the author from spring turkey through waterfowl season. They let him scout flocks from afar, locate longbeards, and spot incoming ducks and geese while they were still on the horizon. Weighing 12 ounces and measuring 2.75 x 4.25 inches, they fit the EDC mode in your pocket, pack, tackle bag, or glove compartment.

Optics manufacturers continue to light up the hunting and shooting world with new and innovative products, reaching levels of performance that only a generation or so ago would have been unimaginable. Rather than rest on their laurels, manufacturers constantly work to improve current products while forging into new optical frontiers as improved and previously unthought-of technology and materials are developed. It's a race to apply those new technologies and materials to products that benefit those who rely on quality optics for work, recreation, or survival. Here's a look at some of the top products making it to the finish line.

AIMPOINT

Aimpoint is making waves with its second-generation shotgun optic, the Acro S-2, which is 30 percent smaller and 50 percent lighter than the popular Micro Series sights. Features include a waterproof, fully enclosed optical system, a small, sleek design with no protruding features to obstruct your view and crisp, clear, 9-MOA red-dot for rapid target acquisition. They say it'll provide 50,000 hours (more than five years) of operation on one commonly available CR2023 battery. Ten intensity settings match various lighting situations, including high-maximum for bright sky conditions. The ultra-low integrated carbon-fiber reinforced shotgun rib mount with interchangeable base plates accommodates most of the ventilated ribs on the market. MSRP: $755. *aimpoint.com*

BURRIS

In 2006, Burris introduced its first effective rangefinding riflescope, giving hunters the advantage of one-source aiming. The Eliminator is now in its sixth generation. It features a new balanced profile, with an aggressively knurled cap and adjustment knob for no-slip handling and convenient parallax and illumination adjustments. It precisely ranges to 2,000

Aimpoint released its second-generation shotgun optic, the Acro S-2, which is 30 percent smaller and 50 percent lighter than the popular Micro Series sights.

yards on reflective targets and 1,400 on deer-hide tests. No more need to go from a handheld rangefinder to your scope; place the reticle on our target, depress the button, and you'll receive your reading. Built-in thermometer, barometer and inclinometer (and manual density altitude) monitor the environment and develop a ballistics solution based on your database in

the BurrisConnect mobile app. An illuminated X177 reticle displays precise holdovers for the ranged distance and windage hold-off points. Other features include new 4-20X magnification, 52mm tube diameter, 60.1mm objective lens, and 44.28mm ocular lens. MSRP: $3,000.

Burris' FastFire C red-dot sight is designed for sub-compact, micro-compact, EDC and deep-concealment handguns. Weighing less than 1 ounce, the FastFire C features "Always On" technology and a Burris Intelligent Auto-Bright system that adjusts reticle brightness to match lighting conditions, so it—and you—are always ready to engage. The low profile allows for co-witness with most standard-height factory open sights, eliminating the need to install elevated sights. The Popular RMSc footprint allows easy mounting. Lastly, the FastFire C boasts an exceptionally clear aspherical glass lens with minimal bluing

The Burris Eliminator 6 features a new balanced profile and precisely ranges to 2,000 yards on reflective targets and 1,400 on deer-hide tests.

and field curvature. This promotes a crisp, undistorted reflective surface for the stable, no-flicker 6-MOA red-dot reticle. MSRP: $276. *burrisoptics.com*

BUSHNELL

Customer demand convinced Bushnell to build an MOA version of its award-winning Match Pro ED 5-30x56 riflescope. It has the same features and high-quality glass as the original and adds a modified reticle and turrets for the Deploy MOA 2 reticle, which has a theme like the Deploy MIL 2 reticle. However, the turrets are in ¼ MOA clicks, and the elevation turret has an extra row of numerals to help keep track of the dial into the second revolution up from zero. The 34mm tube provides room for 100 MOA in elevation and 50 in windage adjustments. The glass-etched first focal plane reticle has 11 brightness settings to adjust to any light conditions. The integral holdover tree allows for instant holdover without dial adjustment. MSRP: $699.99; *bushnell.com*

Burrris' new FastFire C low-profile red-dot optic.

GERMAN PRECISION OPTICS

Don't let the name mislead you. German Precision Optics is an American company that figured out it could incorporate German design and engineering into precision optics; therefore, German Precision Optics is the name and precisely what you get. GPO continues to expand its offerings in the rangefinding binocular, rangefinder and binocular arenas, starting with the new Rangeguide 8x40 and 10x40 rangefinding binoculars, the smallest, most compact premium mid-sized rangefinding binos

available, GPO says, just slightly larger than the 8x32 and 10x32 units in the Rangeguide line. The new 40mm models feature a magnesium frame for lightweight strength and an eye-safe Class 1 laser that can reach targets up to 3,500 yards and produces a fast 0.25 response time. They also measure the angle to the target, giving you precise inclination/declination compensation readings. The Rangeguide 32mm models have a new MSRP of $999.99, and the new 40mm models

A new MOA version of the Bushnell Match Pro ED 5-30x56 riflescope.

have an MSRP of $1,299.99.

GPO also introduced its "ultimate long-range hunting riflescope," the Spectra 6X 4.5-27x50i second-focal plane. The large 50mm objective lens transmits plenty of light, and the 4.5-27x power range provides magnification for close to long-range targets. GPO's iControl microdot illumination makes targeting dark objects easier, and Passiontrac zero-stop-lock turrets assist in any shooting scenario. MSRP: $1249.99; *gpo-usa.com*

KAHLES

With support from professional shooters, Kahles improved its K18i with a wide (150 feet at 100 yards) field of view for faster target acquisition in 3-Gun and IPSC matches and for any shooter desiring to get on target quickly. Kahles' quality throughout it has fine and extra-bright day/night illuminated second focal plane reticle combined with the MaxLight reticle illumination function for extremely backlit situations. Features include an improved, more user-friendly eye box for quick, easy focusing, a rugged 34mm tube and two sizes of individually adjustable throw levers. MSRP: $3,299; *kahles.at*

KONUS

Konus introduced the Eternity 6-24x50mm first focal plane riflescope with two turret knobs. One has zero stop, and the other is for long range, something no other scope offers, they say. The reasoning behind the extra turret is that the zero-stop turret has a pin that must be removed for long-range shooting and that can easily be lost in the field. The extra turret prevents that

German Precision Optics introduced the Spectra 6X 4.5-27x50i second-focal plane scope.

and makes changing the zero-stop turret to a traditional turret quick and easy. Features include a 30mm tube, constant long eye relief at all magnifications, a side parallax wheel, ultra-wideband multi-coated lenses, and an engraved reticle illuminated in red with 11 intensities. MSRP: $699.99. *konususa.com*

LEICA

Question: What would you say to a laser rangefinder that calculates the probability of hitting your target? Answer: Hello, Geovid Pro 10x42 AB+. Leica has enhanced its optics and laser rangefinder with Shot Probability Analysis technology

LEUPOLD

Leupold introduced its Mark 4HD family of riflescopes featuring a 4-to-1 zoom ratio and five magnification ranges, providing options for everything from up-close to long-range engagements. The two lower magnification range models, 1-4.5x24 and 2.5-10x42, have 30mm main tubes. The 1.4.5x24s are in the second focal plane, while the 2.5-10x42 comes in your choice of first or second. The three higher magnification ranges, 4.5-18x52, 6-24x52 and 8-32x56, have 34mm main tubes and are all first focal plane.

All feature Leupold's Professional-Grade Optical system that provides premium light transmission, glare reduction, and crisp resolution. Illuminated reticle options with push-button operation are available. Motion Sensor Technology will shut off the illumination after five minutes of inactivity but instantly restarts as soon as you move the scope. Push-button ZeroLock prevents the accidental movement of dial settings and allows a rapid zero return. Expect retail prices to range from $999.99 to $1,599.99, depending on the model. *leupold.com*

Kahles improved its K18i with a wide (150 feet at 100 yards) field of view for faster target acquisition.

developed by Applied Ballistics, a leading ballistic software manufacturer. After providing input data, you'll receive a hit-probability percentage on the unit's display and the Leica Hunting app. With a maximum range of 3,200 yards-plus and accuracy within a half yard, it's a boon to long-range hunting and shooting applications. The ProTrack feature allows you to plot GPS points in BaseMap and Google Maps. MSRP: $3,499.99. *leica.com*

Leica's Geovid Pro 10x42 AB+ uses statistical modeling to calculate the probability of making your shot. Let that sink in.

MAVEN

I wasn't convinced I needed ultra-compact binoculars until I used Maven's 10x25 model (also available in 8x25) from spring turkey season through waterfowl. Having these along let me scout flocks from afar to locate any longbeards and helped spot incoming ducks and geese while they were still on the horizon. Weighing 12 ounces and measuring 2.75 x 4.25 inches, they fit the EDC mode in your pocket, pack, tackle bag, or glove compartment. If you're familiar with Maven, you know the optics will provide clear, bright, high-contrast images from edge to edge, thanks to features like extra-low dispersion ED glass, fully multi-coated lenses and phase correction coating. Maven sells direct to consumer,

so don't expect to see them in stores; you're paying for quality, not retail profit margin. MSRP: $600.

Maven's RS3.2 5-30x50 first focal plane riflescope is designed for long-range hunters and shooters. It's built on the popular RS.3 scope, enlarging the elevation turret (which is also more tactile for sure grip), improving the zero-stop and capping the windage turret. The wide magnification range and precise dialing capabilities provide confidence at all ranges, from mid- to long-range. Other features include side parallax adjustment, silky focus mechanism, precision-milled adjustments with solid click detents and custom turret options. The anodized construction protects the crystal-clear ED glass for which Maven is known. MSRP: $1,600. *mavenbuilt.com*

Leupold's Mark 4 is back, represented here by the HD 4.5-18x52 M5C3. The new Mark 4HD family of riflescopes features a 4-to-1 zoom ratio and five magnification ranges, providing options for everything from up-close to long-range engagements.

RITON OPTICS

Riton launched its first enclosed-emitter red-dot sight, the 3 Tactix EED, for shooters of every stripe. The enclosed emitter design protects internal components from dust, moisture, impact, and other everyday hazards in challenging situations and environments. This small (1.14 inches high, 1.73 inches long, 1.06 inches wide) and lightweight

Maven's RS3.2 5-30x50 first focal plane riflescope is designed for long-range hunters and shooters.

(1.48 ounces) sight features 1X magnification, a 21.8mm x 15.8mm viewing lens for easy target acquisition of the 3-MOA reticle and a shake-awake battery-saving function. MSRP: $349.99.

And here's the new 5 Primal 15-45x60

spotting scope, Riton's all-new lightweight, compact offering for hunters and shooters who need sharp optics in the field. Designed with a lightweight aluminum-alloy construction and IPX7 waterproof rating, you don't have to coddle this scope. At 12.5 inches long and weighing 2.75 pounds, it's easily packable and, therefore, more likely to be used when needed. Expect optical clarity and resolution and minimalized color fringing. The optical design and multi-coated lens coatings allow maximum light transmission and definition in all lighting and weather conditions. Easy to focus and zoom, with large rubberized and knurled zoom and focus rings. MSRP: $999.99; *ritonoptics.com*

SIG SAUER

Don't be surprised if image stabilization is the next big push in optics. SIG is already

there with its Optical Image Stabilization technology in the ZULU6 HDX binoculars, which electronically cancels shaking and vibration, enhancing the ability to glass offhand. Two modes: Scan mode is for general glassing and scanning and gridding terrain; Target mode increases stability up to 50 percent, allowing you to lock in better on and identify game and targets. Available in new 16x42 and 20x42 models, as well as 10x30 and 12x42. MSRP: $899.99-$1,199.99.

SIG touts the new line of TANGO-DMR riflescopes as blending military-inspired design with

Riton's new 5 Primal 15-45x60 spotting scope is designed with a lightweight aluminum-alloy construction and IPX7 waterproof rating, so you don't have to coddle it. At 12.5 inches long and weighing 2.75 pounds, it's easily packable.

ultralight functionality, blurring the lines between hunting and tactical-precision optics. With a 34mm tube and SIG's new multi-lock zero stop elevation dial, it provides generous elevation adjustment. Available in multiple illuminated reticle configurations that include MRAD and MOA. Other features include low-profile capped windage turrets, locking illumination control and a removable throw lever. Two models. MSRP: 3-18x44, $1,299.99; 5-30x56, $1,499.99. *sigsauer. com*

STEINER

Steiner introduced a new T6Xi riflescope series to cover the spectrum of tactical shooting needs. The series includes a 5-30x56 for long-range and precision shooting, 3-18x56 and 2.5-15x50 for near- to extended-range targets, and 1-6x24 for close-quarters to mid-range engagements. These scopes feature rugged 34mm tubes, Steiner's bright, clear-coated lenses and low-profile Never-Lost turrets that show each mil of elevation through a window so you can easily track adjustments. Three reticles across the series. MSRP: 1,954.99-$2,874.99

Steiner designed the new H6Xi riflescopes with similar military and law-enforcement features as their T6Xi tactical series for big-game hunters who require lightweight optics that can perform in extreme environments. Three models, all with milled 30mm tubes, and Steiner's high-density lenses and MHR (Modern Hunting Reticle) with

duplex crosshairs for fast aiming at lower magnification and precise illuminated denotation reveal wind drift and bullet drop when zoomed in for distant shots. It has low-profile elevation turrets with easy-to-read numbers, tactile detents with audible clicks and zero click stop in your choice of 2-12x42mm, 3-16x50mm, and 5-30x50mm. MSRP: $2,299-$2,874; *steiner-optics.com*

SWAROVSKI

Swarovski also improved its already impressive Z8i riflescope range with the new Z8i+, which features a 34mm tube, a larger field of view, and the ability to pick up game even faster at close ranges. Thanks to the ViewPlus optical system, which provides 150 feet of field of view at 100 yards on 1x magnification, the large, comfortable eye box helps target acquisition, and the new ergonomic throw lever allows faster, easier handling. A shorter 160-degree zoom rotation from 1X to 8X makes for fast magnification adjustments. MSRP: $3,666-$3,999; *swarovskioptik.com*

TRACT OPTICS

Tract released its 4-24x50mm first focal-place riflescope to fulfill the needs of extreme long-range shooters. The scope, in the award-winning Toric line, features a 34mm tube and is adjustable up to 160 MOA or 47 MRAD. (Huge elevation adjustment, the top in the industry, they say, for 34mm tubes.) Thus, ELR and PRS shooters can dial precise adjustments at longer ranges instead of estimating hold. Long-range rimfire and airgun shoot-

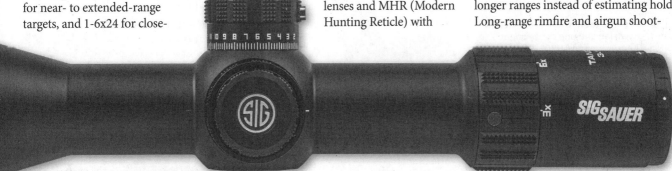

SIG launched a new line of Tango-DMR riflescopes that blend military-inspired design with ultralight functionality. With a 34mm tube and SIG's new multi-lock zero stop elevation dial, they provide generous elevation adjustment. They are available in multiple illuminated reticle configurations that include MRAD and MOA.

Steiner's new H6Xi Series riflescopes with milled 30mm tubes.

VORTEX

The Vortex 3-15x44 is a reliable, accurate workhorse for all shooters, from beginners to tactical experts. With quality glass, good magnification range and an EBR (Enhanced Battle reticle)-7C reticle for fast, precise ranging and windage corrections, it's spot-on for targets up and down the range. The first focal plane design means the reticle's subtensions remain accurate at all magnifications. Other features include the RevStop

ers are on board, too. Expect sharp Schott HT glass with extra-low dispersion lenses and a glass-etched illuminated reticle in your choice of MOA ELR or MRAD ELR Christmas tree-style reticle with a floating center dot that won't obscure the target. Tract's direct-to-consumer business model cuts out retail middlemen, so you're paying for value, not retail markup. MSRP: $1,494. *tractoptics.com*

TRIJICON

Trijicon named its new Made-in-USA pistol red-dot sight RCR for Ruggedized Closed Reflex because that is precisely

recoil, impacts, and protects the lenses from stress. Featuring Trijicon's capstan screw design, the RCR mounts directly on any slide or plate that accepts Trijicon's RMR design. Ten brightness settings are available, including three night-vision options and one super-bright

Trijicon's U.S.-made red-dot sight RCR (Ruggedized Closed Reflex) mounts directly on any RMR-design slide or plate. Ten brightness settings are available, including three night-vision and one super-bright option. The top-loaded CR2032 battery provides up to six years of continuous use; the red dot is 3.25 MOA.

what it is—a durable closed emitter optic that meets the demands of military, law enforcement, and other serious handgunners. Based on Trijicon's award-winning Ruggedized Miniature Reflex sight, the RCR is sealed to keep out the elements, waterproof to 66 feet and is built with a rugged aluminum housing that absorbs

Tract released its Toric 4-24x50mm first focal-place riflescope to fulfill the needs of extreme long-range shooters. It features a 34mm tube and is adjustable up to 160 MOA or 47 MRAD—massive elevation adjustment, the top in the industry for 34mm tubes.

option. The top-loaded, easy-to-change CR2032 battery will provide up to six years of continuous use. The 3.25-MOA red-dot easily adjusts for elevation and windage without special tools. MSRP: $849; *trijicon.com*

Zero System that ensures rapid re-indexing and reliable zero adjustments; single-piece 34mm aluminum tube; rugged capped windage and exposed elevation turrets, the balance between quick adjustments and precise dial control; and a throw lever for on-the-fly zoom adjustments. MSRP: $649.99. *vortexoptics.com* **GD**

Vortex Venom 3-15x44 is an EBR (Enhanced Battle reticle) with a -7C reticle for fast, precise ranging and windage corrections. The tube is 34mm.

- REPORTS -
from the Field
AIRGUNS

From backyard plinkers to heavy thumpers capable of taking predators, today's crop of airguns has something for everybody.

❯ JIM HOUSE

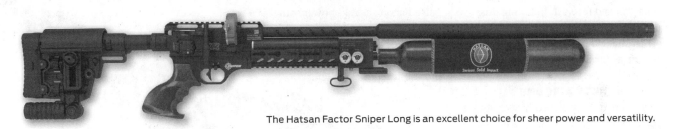

The Hatsan Factor Sniper Long is an excellent choice for sheer power and versatility.

Products develop over time. My first computer had 16K bytes of memory, and my first camera cost 50 cents plus two cereal box tops. Now, I have a computer with many gigabytes and a Nikon. The same sort of metamorphosis has occurred with airguns. Today, we have such options as fully automatic BB machine guns and pre-charged pneumatic (PCP) repeating big bores of .50 caliber. As with almost any hobby, it's easy to see that some airguns of today bear little resemblance to those of the past.

It seems that airguns constitute three large groups. The first group includes low-powered rifles and pistols that fire BBs or .177 pellets at velocities of only 250–400 fps. A single compression stroke or a CO_2 cylinder generally powers these models. A second category includes air rifles of .177, .20, or .22 caliber that give velocities up to 800–1000 fps, making them suitable for general use and eradicating tiny pests. The third category includes models in larger calibers that produce enough energy to be included in the magnum category. Some of the big-bore models are super magnums that are suitable for hunting medium game. Here's a rundown of this year's notable new airguns.

AIRFORCE

AirForce specializes in PCP rifles made in Ft. Worth, TX, except for the Lothar Walther barrels. The Texan CF series represents a group of rifles with various features available in .45 and .50 caliber, and the reservoir can be pressurized to 3,625 psi (250 bar). Advertised to produce up to 800 ft-lbs of energy, these big bores are suitable for hunting applications that involve rather large species. However, with an overall length of 54.25 inches and weighing 8 pounds, such air rifles are not dainty. Carbine models are available that can produce energies up to 620 ft-lbs. *airforceairguns.com*

AIR VENTURI

The Seneca line from Air Venturi includes rifle and shotgun models that can also shoot round balls, flat-point slugs, or arrows. Also included is the multi-pump Dragonfly that is available in .177 and .22 calibers with velocities up to 850 and 730 fps, respectively. Using rotary magazines that hold nine pellets in .177 caliber or seven in .22, the Dragonfly comes with a wood stock with a checkered grip, a grooved forearm, excellent open sights, and a grooved receiver. In testing this rifle, I found it to be an outstanding performer that would make an excellent pest gun. *airventuri.com*

BLACK BUNKER AIRGUNS

Black Bunker Airguns produces a unique break-action rifle that utilizes a gas ram rather than a spring. The rifle has different power levels, making it acceptable for use where airgun power is limited. The most potent version is a .22 caliber, advertised to produce up to 850 fps

with lead pellets or 1,000 fps with alloy pellets. Such specifications may not be impressive. What is unique is that the rifle can be folded into a compact triangular shape!

Moreover, within the triangle can be fitted a hard case that can hold anything from a flashlight to fish hooks. As a result, the rifle is billed as a versatile survival tool. It's available in black and coyote tan colors. This unusual air rifle has an MSRP of $269.95. *black-bunker.com*

CROSMAN-BENJAMIN

Crosman's available products include the Mag-Fire series, which is available with different options, including the Mission, Ultra, Trailhawk, Diamondback, and Extreme models in .177 and .22 calibers.

The rifles feature synthetic stocks and rotary magazines that hold 12 and 10 pellets in these calibers. They also have open sights and a rail for mounting optics. The Shockwave is another Crosman break-action in .177 caliber that features the Nitro Piston gas ram power source.

The American Classic is a multi-pump single-shot pistol available in .177 and .22 calibers. It provides variable power. Both models accept a skeleton

stock so they can be fired from the shoulder and are equipped with open sights.

Some Crosman multi-pump rifles have been produced for many years. One of them, the Model 2100 Legacy, was offered as a 100th-anniversary special in 2023. The 2100 can be used as a single shot with .177 pellets or as a repeater using BBs. I have used a 2100 extensively; it is a fine pest rifle.

Crosman offers a 100th Anniversary limited edition .22 multi-pump with a Turkish walnut stock and pump handle for the connoisseur of multi-pump rifles.

The rifle comes equipped with a Williams peep sight and a blade front sight with a fiber-optic insert, and it has a grooved receiver for attaching optics. It is an elegant rifle, only 36 inches in length and weighing 5.8 pounds. Only 2023 of the rifles have been

The Black Bunker is a gas ram break-action that can be folded for convenient travel or storage.

The Black Bunker folds into a triangle.

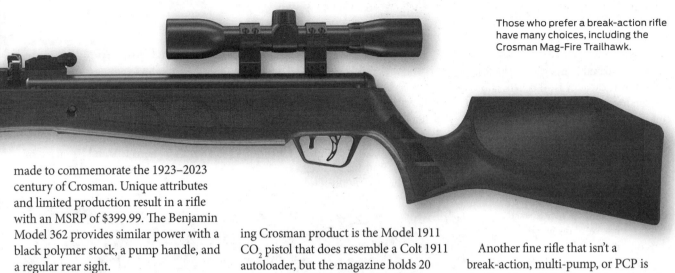

Those who prefer a break-action rifle have many choices, including the Crosman Mag-Fire Trailhawk.

made to commemorate the 1923–2023 century of Crosman. Unique attributes and limited production result in a rifle with an MSRP of $399.99. The Benjamin Model 362 provides similar power with a black polymer stock, a pump handle, and a regular rear sight.

An unusual PCP from Crosman is the Challenger, a competition model in .177 caliber that fires pellets at 600 fps and generates only 5.9 ft-lbs in keeping with its intended use. However, it is a complete target rifle with a fully adjustable stock, outstanding target sights, and a Lothar Walther barrel, making it suitable for entry-level competition. A .22 model from Crosman is the 3622, which resembles a 362 multi-pump but is a PCP rifle. It does not have a pressure gauge or regulator but gives velocities up to 700 fps, making it suitable for plinking and pest control.

Crosman offers a single-action revolver that mimics the Colt Single Action Army. Known as the Fortify, it holds up to 18 BBs in a spring-loaded magazine along the barrel where the ejector rod is located in a Colt. Another interest-ing Crosman product is the Model 1911 CO_2 pistol that does resemble a Colt 1911 autoloader, but the magazine holds 20 BBs. The MSRP of the Fortify is $59.99, whereas that of the Model 1911 is $60.99.

The Crosman PFAM9B resembles a Beretta 92 with fixed sights but fires BBs up to 420 fps from a smoothbore barrel in either single or double action or full-auto mode. At the opposite end of the spectrum is the Model 1701P, a single-shot PCP pistol that gives up to 50 shots with one fill of the air reservoir. It's intended for 10m competition, so it has numerous features to address that use, including a Lothar Walther barrel.

Single-action shooters will enjoy the realism of the Crosman Fortify.

Another fine rifle that isn't a break-action, multi-pump, or PCP is the Sheridan 2260. It is a CO_2-powered, single-shot, bolt-action .22—a classic metal and wood rifle.

Unlike earlier versions, it now has a grooved metal receiver for attaching a scope mount. Although some earlier versions had a sight on the rear of the receiver, it was too close to the eye to be of any real use, but the new Sheridan 2260 has the rear sight mounted on the barrel. Velocity is specified as up to 600 fps, and my earlier model produces 550–575, depending on pellet weight. The 2260 is easy to operate in general use or eliminating small pests.

Carrying the historic Benjamin label is the Akela, a .177-caliber PCP bullpup that features a Turkish walnut stock. It has no sights but an extended rail for

To commemorate its 100th Anniversary, Crosman introduced the elegant 362 multi-pump.

mounting optics. Reservoir pressure can be up to 3,000 psi, which produces velocities up to 1,100 fps. With a slender tank having moderate capacity, the Akela is sleek compared to many other PCPs. Its magazine capacity is 14 pellets, and you can fire up to 60 shots with a full tank. *crosman.com*

DAISY

The Daisy 880 multi-pump has been around since 1972 and can launch BBs or .177 pellets. A 50th Anniversary edition was available with special features. I have tested several versions of the Model 880, and they are easy to pump and generally give fine accuracy. Daisy continues to market the Avanti 753 target rifle intended for entry-level 10m competition, a single shot powered by a single stroke of the pump lever. Noteworthy is that the 753 is provided with a globe front sight that accepts different inserts and a target-style receiver sight with click adjustments and a rubber eye cup.

A Daisy pistol that fires BBs is the Model 426, which outwardly resembles a Ruger SR22 rimfire or a Walther PD380. Its magazine holds 15 BBs and is powered by a CO_2 cylinder. It features fixed sights and a rail under the barrel to attach accessories. This should be a fun gun for getting beginners familiar with handling a handgun. Another of the Daisy models that I like is the 5501, which features blowback action. *daisy.com*

FX AIRGUNS

The FX Maverick Sniper is a short rifle with a length of only 36 inches, and it's a PCP model in .22, .25, and .30 calibers. It features a 27.6-inch barrel, a main air reservoir holding 590cc, and a second-

ary reservoir holding 89cc. You can set the power level using a two-stage regulator. It has no sights, but a Picatinny rail is attached. The .22-caliber version has a magazine that holds 18 rounds, up to 270 shots may be fired before refilling is required, and the muzzle energy is up to 71 ft-lbs. In .25 caliber, the parameters are 16, 170, and 85, respectively, and in .30 caliber they are 13, 90, and 116, respectively. With a weight of only 7.2 pounds, I would use this short rifle on predators. *fxairguns.com*

GAMO

Gamo continues offering a broad line of break-actions, including the Swarm Magnum 10X and Hunter series in .177, .22, and .25 calibers. Looking for something special

The Daisy 426 mimics the size and feel of a Ruger SR22.

The FX Maverick Sniper is a compact rifle with sufficient power to take varmints effectively.

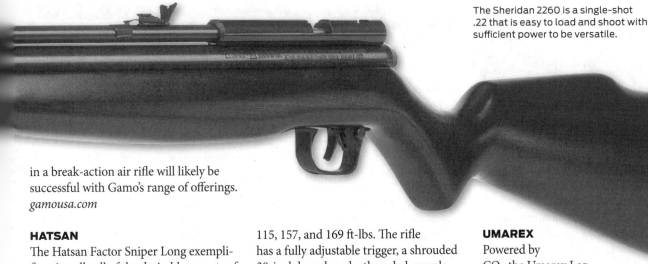

The Sheridan 2260 is a single-shot .22 that is easy to load and shoot with sufficient power to be versatile.

in a break-action air rifle will likely be successful with Gamo's range of offerings. *gamousa.com*

HATSAN

The Hatsan Factor Sniper Long exemplifies virtually all of the desirable aspects of a PCP. It's available in .22, .25, .30, and .35 calibers (magazine capacities are 21, 19, 16, and 13 shots for the various calibers).

This rifle has a 700cc main air reservoir and a secondary tank that holds 100cc. Moreover, the force of the hammer strike and the pressure in the secondary tank can be adjusted for complete control over the power level. This, in turn, provides

115, 157, and 169 ft-lbs. The rifle has a fully adjustable trigger, a shrouded 30-inch barrel, and a threaded muzzle. With these features and sufficient power to make it useful in hunting, the Hatsan Factor Sniper Long is a good choice for serious airgun users. *hatsanusa.com*

SKOUT

Just when you think there could be nothing new comes the Skout Epoch.

You can adjust the Skout Epoch to almost any conceivable configuration using a computer in the grip.

UMAREX

Powered by CO_2, the Umarex Legends Cowboy is a lever-action that fires BBs held in cartridges that eject when the lever is operated. The Legends series also includes a realistic replica of the Luger P08.

Umarex also produces the Gauntlet 30, a .30-caliber model that produces up to 1,000 fps and energies to 100 ft-lbs.

control over the number of shots fired at a desired power level from a single fill. When the secondary reservoir pressure is set at 150 bar (2,176 psi), the .22, .25, .30, and .35 models can give velocities up to 1,050, 1,075, 940, and 970 fps, respectively, with corresponding energies of 81,

This PCP rifle features a computer in the grip section for selecting different firing modes and other options. It has several adjustments to fit the shooter, including length of pull, comb height, etc. You can also change between .177, .22, .25, .30, and .35 calibers by swapping barrels, and the rifle has the M-LOK system for attaching numerous accessories. The rifle is available in 12 colors and barrels of several lengths. High technology has come to airguns but with an MSRP of $2,350. *skoutairguns.com*

Some .30-caliber pellets weigh around 50 grains, so the rifle should be quite effective on predators. The Gauntlet utilizes a seven-round rotary magazine or a tray for single loading with up to 25 shots per fill. Priced at $499.99, it's an economical way to get into high-performance airgunning.

Umarex continues to offer the .50-caliber Hammer that drives a 550-grain pellet at up to 760 fps and generates over 700 ft-lbs of energy. The air tank can be pressurized to 4,500 psi, but shots are regulated to 3,000 psi. It comes without

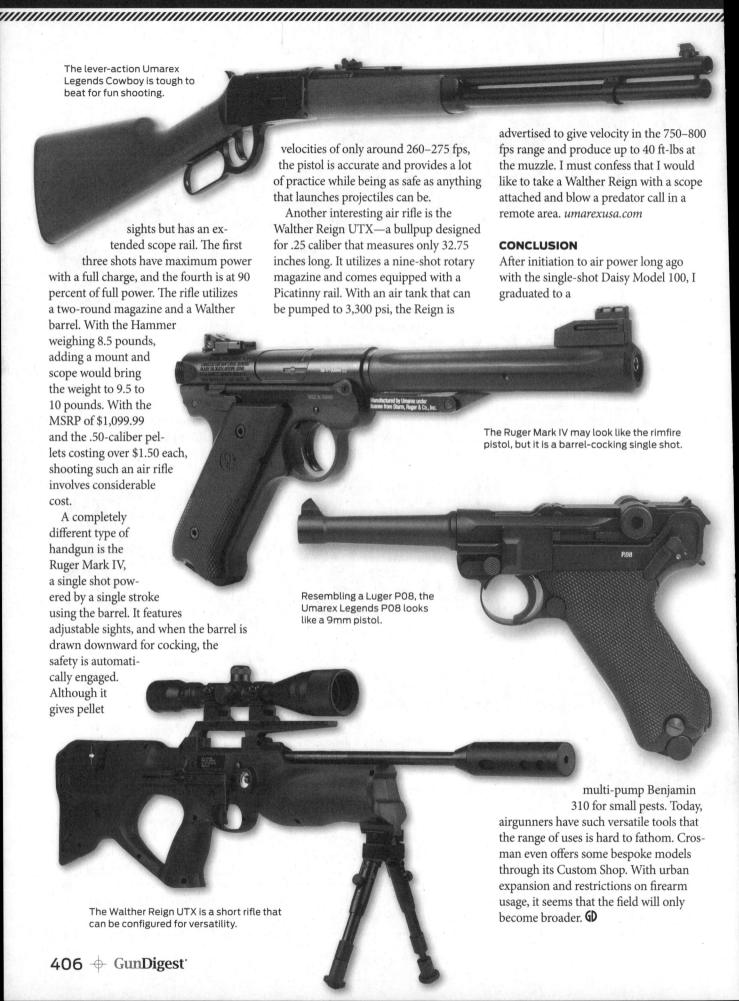

The lever-action Umarex Legends Cowboy is tough to beat for fun shooting.

sights but has an extended scope rail. The first three shots have maximum power with a full charge, and the fourth is at 90 percent of full power. The rifle utilizes a two-round magazine and a Walther barrel. With the Hammer weighing 8.5 pounds, adding a mount and scope would bring the weight to 9.5 to 10 pounds. With the MSRP of $1,099.99 and the .50-caliber pellets costing over $1.50 each, shooting such an air rifle involves considerable cost.

A completely different type of handgun is the Ruger Mark IV, a single shot powered by a single stroke using the barrel. It features adjustable sights, and when the barrel is drawn downward for cocking, the safety is automatically engaged. Although it gives pellet

velocities of only around 260–275 fps, the pistol is accurate and provides a lot of practice while being as safe as anything that launches projectiles can be.

Another interesting air rifle is the Walther Reign UTX—a bullpup designed for .25 caliber that measures only 32.75 inches long. It utilizes a nine-shot rotary magazine and comes equipped with a Picatinny rail. With an air tank that can be pumped to 3,300 psi, the Reign is

advertised to give velocity in the 750–800 fps range and produce up to 40 ft-lbs at the muzzle. I must confess that I would like to take a Walther Reign with a scope attached and blow a predator call in a remote area. *umarexusa.com*

CONCLUSION

After initiation to air power long ago with the single-shot Daisy Model 100, I graduated to a

The Ruger Mark IV may look like the rimfire pistol, but it is a barrel-cocking single shot.

Resembling a Luger P08, the Umarex Legends P08 looks like a 9mm pistol.

The Walther Reign UTX is a short rifle that can be configured for versatility.

multi-pump Benjamin 310 for small pests. Today, airgunners have such versatile tools that the range of uses is hard to fathom. Crosman even offers some bespoke models through its Custom Shop. With urban expansion and restrictions on firearm usage, it seems that the field will only become broader. **GD**

- REPORTS -
from the Field
AMMUNITION

Ammunition remains a rapidly growing sector of the firearms industry!

❯PHIL MASSARO

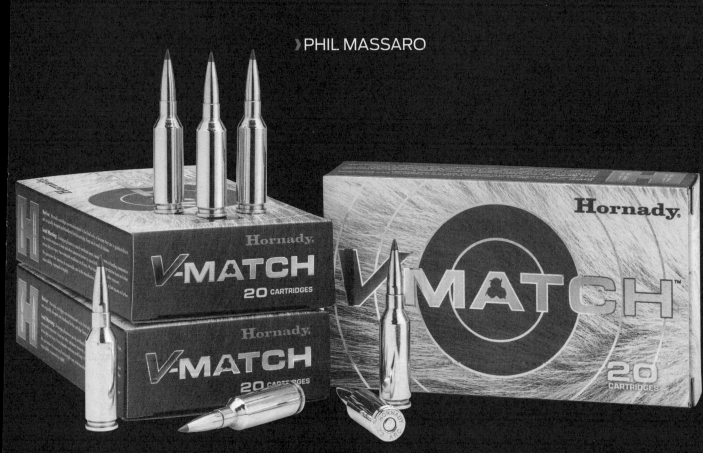

A deadly accurate varmint projectile, the ELD-VT is loaded in Hornady's V-Match ammo line, and predators and varmints should take heed. The new ammo is available in .22 ARC with a 62-grain ELD-VT, 6mm Creedmoor with an 80-grain ELD-VT, and 6.5 Grendel and 6.5 Creedmoor with a 100-grain ELD-VT.

Our ammunition continues evolving as centerfire rifle and pistol, rimfire, and shotgun ammo becomes increasingly consistent and more effective each year. Sadly, it has also come under attack from anti-gun politicians, with New York now requiring a background check for even a simple box of .22 LR or shotshells and California attempting the same idea. Still, our ammunition and component companies continue to push the envelope, creating more efficient cartridges, shot designs, and projectiles each year. We have some new cartridges, ammunition lines, brand crossovers, and interesting line extensions that give plenty of options to the shooter. Let's dive in and see what's new for this year.

APEX AMMUNITION

Apex is extending its Blended TSS Turkey loads to include the Mossy Oak Greenleaf Turkey TSS 28-gauge shells. With a 1½ ounce load of blended TSS—1 ounce of No. 10 and ½ ounce of No. 9 shot—in a 2¾-inch shell, with a muzzle velocity of 1,060 fps. The TSS stuff certainly isn't cheap, but when you want to flatten that tom, nothing works as well. Sold in 5-count boxes. *apexammunition.com*

BLACK HILLS AMMUNITION

South Dakota's Finest offers a quartet of new loads for this year: a pair for the .300 PRC and a pair for the 6mm ARC. The big three hundred gets the proven duo of the ELD-X hunting bullet and ELD Match target bullet in 212 grains at 2,850 fps for the former and 225 grains at 2,800 fps for the latter. These are within 10 to 20 fps of the Hornady ammunition. The 6mm ARC (Advanced Rifle Cartridge) gets the 103-grain Hornady ELD-X at 2,550 fps and the 90-grain Dual Purpose monometal hollowpoint bullet at 2,650 fps (measured from an 18-inch barrel). All loads are sold in 20-count boxes. *black-hills.com*

BROWNING AMMUNITION

For this year, Browning puts the Buckmark on a pair of loads for the esteemed 28 Nosler cartridge. The MaxPoint bullet—designed for rapid expansion and quick energy transfer that handles the

deer species so well—is loaded at 140 grains with a muzzle velocity of 3,315 fps, generating over 3,400 ft-lbs of energy at the muzzle. With its elongated polymer tip, this should make short work of the smaller game species. On the heavier side, Browning uses a simple yet effective plated softpoint bullet in the Silver Series, and for the 28 Nosler, a 175-grain bullet cruising at 3,100 fps for over 3,700 ft-lbs of muzzle energy. If you're looking for a solution for the larger game species of North America and the biggest antelopes of Africa, the Sectional Density of the 175-grain 7mm projectile will be very attractive, and the velocities generated by the 28 Nosler case will offer a flat trajectory. Both come in 20-count boxes. *browningammo.com*

Buffalo Bore jumped into the heavyweight big game stoppers with loads for the .500 Jeffery and the .505 Gibbs.

505 GIBBS
Item 505G - 525 SOLID/5 (525 gr CUTTING EDGE BULLETS Flat Nose Solid 2300 fps/ME 6166 ft lbs)

BUFFALO BORE AMMUNITION

That little ol' ammo company from Idaho, Buffalo Bore Ammunition—the brainchild of Tim Sundles—has embraced a pair of metric classics and several celebrated Nitro Express cartridges. The 8x57 Mauser gets three new bullets, including a 150- and 195-grain cup-and-core softpoint and a 200-grain Barnes TSX. One of my personal favorites, the 9.3x62 Mauser, is also now available at Buffalo Bore, with a 250-grain Barnes TSX at 2,650 fps and a 286-grain lead-core spitzer at 2,450 fps, giving those who love the old German cartridge plenty to be happy about. Both the 8x57 and 9.3x62 are sold in 20-count boxes.

Looking at the larger bores, I am also personally pleased to see my beloved

.404 Jeffery represented in Buffalo Bore's lineup, loaded with a pair of Cutting Edge Bullets' projectiles: the 400-grain flat-nose solid and 375-grain Raptor expanding (actually designed to break apart) bullet. Buffalo Bore loads these on the hotter side, giving 2,375 and 2,425 fps, respectively, yet keeps pressures low to allow for reliable extraction. From there, Buffalo Bore jumps into the heavyweight big game stoppers, starting with the .500 Jeffery and the .505 Gibbs. The former gets a 575-grain Cutting Edge Solid at 2,150 fps, a 525-grain Cutting Edge Solid and a 525-grain Barnes TSX at 2,300 fps. Moving upward from there, the .577 Nitro Express is loaded with the 750-grain Barnes TSX and Cutting Edge Solid of the same weight, both moving at 2,150 fps (the equivalent of the 100-grain

Cordite load, to regulate properly in older double rifles).

Finally, the behemoth .600 Nitro Express is now available from Buffalo Bore, with a pair of loads built around the 900-grain Hammer softpoint and 900-grain Cutting Edge flat-nose solid, with one at the 100-grain Cordite equivalent (1,850 fps) and another at the 110-grain Cordite equivalent (1,950 fps). The .404 Jeffery, .500 Jeffery, .505 Gibbs, .577 Nitro Express, and .600 Nitro Express are sold in 5-count boxes. *buffalobore.com*

CCI

Lewiston, Idaho's CCI, has long been a favorite of rimfire shooters, handgunners, and reloaders alike, and its primers are world-renowned. This year, CCI has four

new products in its catalog. Starting with the Blazer handgun ammunition packaged in the Reduced Recoil 100-grain FMJ 9mm Luger load in reloadable brass cases in 50-count boxes. CCI uses clean-burning propellants and its excellent primers, and with an MSRP of $22.99, this ammunition will keep you at the range longer.

The CCI handgun shotshells have long been a favorite of mine, as they make a perfect tool for garden pests and unwanted rodents and reptiles alike. New for 2024, CCI has extended the Pest Control Shotshell line to include an offering for the 10mm Auto cartridge, featuring 105 grains of No. 9 shot. The case has an integral mock "projectile" to aid in reliable feeding in the autoloaders, whereas the cartridges designed for revolvers use a rounded or squared plastic cap over the shot load. Your favorite 10mm Auto carry gun can easily eradicate pests and potential hazards. They are sold in 10-count boxes.

Further expanding on the handgun shotshell line, CCI offers a Hevi-Bismuth shotshell in six popular cartridges. Completely lead-free and including a lead-free primer, the Bismuth shot weighs in at 9.6g/cc and is cast here in the USA. Using No. 11 shot, the Hevi-Bismuth shotshells will carry farther and hit harder. They are available in 9mm Luger, .38 Special/.357 Magnum, .40 S&W, .44 Special/.44 Remington Magnum, .45 ACP, and .45 Colt, all sold in 10-shot boxes.

Lastly, CCI introduced its Uppercut .22 LR ammunition, designed for optimum performance in the short-barreled handguns. While the .22 LR remains a strong favorite for many applications, the available ammunition isn't ideal for a defensive handgun. Rather than a lead or a plated bullet, CCI developed a 32-grain jacketed hollowpoint, loaded to provide roughly 950 fps from the common barrel lengths of carry guns. Testing has shown that the bullet gives 8 to 10 inches of penetration in bare gel, with the expanded slug having six petals peeling back from the center. Is the .22 LR the optimum carry cartridge? That might be debatable, but it is certainly better than nothing, and if you intend to use it, a specialized load like CCI's Uppercut should be consid-

CCI introduced its Uppercut .22 LR ammunition, designed for short-barreled handguns. Rather than use a lead or a plated bullet, CCI has developed a 32-grain jacketed hollowpoint, loaded to 950 fps. Testing has shown that the bullet gives 8 to 10 inches of penetration in bare gel.

ered. The new load uses the same reliable priming of the CCI rimfire ammo and is loaded in nickel-plated cases. Uppercut is sold in 50-count boxes. *cci-ammunition.com*

DOUBLETAP AMMUNITION

2024 sees Doubletap offering its twist on the snake shot ammunition for revolvers, blending a load of No. 9 shot followed by a wadcutter projectile for ultimate lethality. Because the shot column doesn't come into contact with the rifling, the pattern doesn't expand in a centrifugal pattern. Loaded in 20-count boxes, the DT Snake Shot is available in .32 H&R, .327 Federal, .38 Special, .41 Remington Magnum, .44 Remington Magnum, and .45 Colt. *doubletapammo.com*

FEDERAL PREMIUM

Federal rolls out all sorts of new products and line extensions this year, including an entirely new rifle bullet line, a few new products for shotguns, and new handgun ammunition—plenty for all from the folks in Anoka!

Federal Premium announced its new Fusion Tipped ammunition. Building on the solid reputation of the Fusion line—though I have long felt that projectile is grossly underrated—Federal has added a polymer tip to the bullet to improve the Ballistic Coefficient and keep it as consistent as possible. Now, the original variant of the Fusion gave the hunter a whole lot of appreciable features at a highly attractive price point. The Fusion projectile's copper jacket is electrochemically bonded to the lead core, and that jacket is skived along the ogive to enhance expansion in that portion of the bullet. This results in a bullet that offers a balance of expansion and high weight retention, as the bonding prevents the projectile from shedding too much of its weight. Federal's addition of a polymer tip solves the issue of a marred meplat, increases the BC value, and keeps that BC throughout its flight. Fusion Tipped features bullets on the heavier side of the spectrum for each cartridge offered, presumably to increase the BC figures, reduce wind deflection, increase retained energy, and flatten trajectories. All of the positive attributes of the original Fusion design are there, and I feel this new line will prove more popular than the original.

If you want to take the bonded-core technology out to longer distances, the new Federal Fusion Tipped warrants an audition from your rifle. Available in 6.5 Creedmoor and 6.5 PRC at 140 grains, .270 Winchester at 150 grains, 7mm Remington Magnum and 7mm PRC at 175 grains, .300 Blackout at 190 grains (subsonic), and .308 Winchester, .30-'06 Springfield, and .300 Winchester Magnum at 180 grains.

Extending the Terminal Ascent loaded ammo line, Federal offers the beastly .300 PRC loaded with a 210-grain Terminal Ascent. A cartridge with this type of case capacity is usually best served by a bullet of proper Sectional Density with a sufficient Ballistic Coefficient to retain the energy generated, shoot a flat trajectory, and work best in the wind. The combination of the 210-grain Terminal Ascent and the .300 PRC is a big game hunter's dream: a big case capable of fine accuracy, mated with a damned fine projectile, fully capable of excellent performance at any range. Traveling at 2,850 fps, you've got a hard-hitting, long-range hunting cartridge capable of taking any game animal you'd hunt with a .30 caliber.

Federal has also topped the 7mm PRC with a 170-grain Terminal Ascent, giving the long-action cartridge a high BC bullet, among the strongest produced today. With a muzzle velocity of 2,950 fps, you'll have magnum-level performance with a bullet that works well in windy conditions and retains more energy than conventional designs. Having spent a

Federal topped the 7mm PRC with a 170-grain Terminal Ascent, giving the long-action cartridge a strong, high-BC bullet. With a muzzle velocity of 2,950 fps, you'll have magnum-level performance with a hunting bullet that works well in windy conditions and retains more energy than conventional designs.

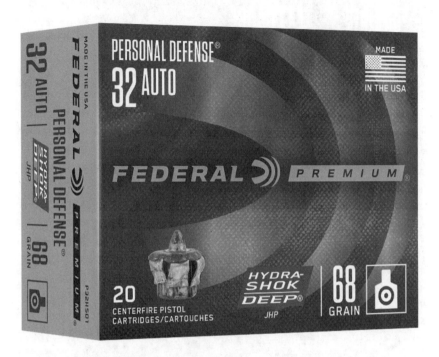

Federal's Personal Defense handgun ammo line expanded with the .32 Auto getting a 68-grain Hydra-Shok Deep bullet.

Waterfowlers get Federal's new Ultra Steel line of shotshells, with the rear-opening Flitecontrol Flex wad, housing zinc-plated steel shot. Blended shot sizes and standard shot payloads are offered in 3-inch magnum configurations. The 12-gauge shells are available in 1¼-ounce shot weight, with BB, BB and No. 2, No. 2, and No. 2 and No. 4 blend, all at 1,450 fps.

good deal of time with the 7mm PRC (which I feel is a great design), I can say it will only benefit from the heavier version of the Terminal Ascent.

Continuing the crossover Federal/ Hornady line, the ELD-X bullet is now loaded in the 6.5 PRC and 7mm PRC. The 6.5 PRC gets the 143-grain ELD-X, while the 7mm PRC gets the heavy-for-caliber 175-grain ELD-X, and both cartridges can take full advantage of the potential of those sleek bullets. Federal supplies nickel-plated cases for this ammunition line, sold in 20-count boxes.

In the Hammerdown line—optimized for lever-action rifles—Federal now offers a 220-grain bonded core bullet for the .360 BuckHammer, cruising at 2,000 fps, thereby adding further dimension to the cartridge that is catching on so quickly. Like the rest of the line, the case edges are chamfered, and the ammunition is designed to best function in the rifles with tubular magazines.

In the Personal Defense handgun ammunition department, the Punch ammo line sees the addition of the .25 Auto with a 45-grain solid to help the little cartridge penetrate. The .32 Auto gets a 68-grain Hydra-Shok Deep in the so-named ammo line. If you haven't considered carrying the Hydra-Shok Deep, you must look at how this bullet performs in the FBI protocol testing; it's an amazing projectile. Federal's Champion handgun ammo, frequently used for training sessions, gets a line extension, offering affordably priced ammunition in reloadable brass cases. Champion is now available in .38 Special with a 130-grain FMJ, .380 Auto with a 95-grain FMJ, and in the relatively new .30 Super Carry with a 90-grain FMJ; all three come in 50-count boxes.

Federal's shotshells have gotten quite a bit of attention this year, with offerings for every shotgunner, from the big game hunters to the defensive crowd to the waterfowlers, turkey hunters, and clay busters.

Federal's new Freight Train Copper Tipped Sabot Slugs are not your grandfather's ammunition. Using a lead-free copper monometal design with a polymer tip over a hollow cavity, the Freight Train Copper gives a massive ballistic advantage over conventional slugs. Federal's ballisticians have seen this ammunition print 4-inch groups at 200 yards, something unheard of in my youth. The slugs sit neatly in a sabot, which aligns perfectly with the shotgun's bore and separates from the slug at the muzzle. And Federal has not skimped in the velocity department; the 300-grain Freight Train in the 3-inch, 12-gauge variant leaves the muzzle at an even 2,000 fps. The polymer tip is used for aerodynamic benefits and to initiate expansion upon striking a game animal. Moreover, the slug is skived along the ogive to further guarantee expansion after impact. And the copper monometal construction is perfect for those areas, States, and provinces where lead and lead-core ammunition is banned by law. The Freight Train Copper Tipped Sabot Slugs are available in 12-gauge 300-grain 3- and 2¾-inch, and 20-gauge 3- and 2¾-inch, in 5-round boxes.

Waterfowlers will be happy about the new Ultra Steel line of shotshells, built around the rear-opening Flitecontrol Flex wad, housing zinc-plated steel shot. There are blended shot sizes and standard shot payloads, all in 3-inch magnum configurations. The 12-gauge shells are available in 1¼-ounce shot weight, with BB, BB and No. 2, No. 2, and No. 2 and No. 4 blend, all at 1,450 fps. The 20-gauge shells come in No. 2, No. 2 and No. 4, and No. 3 and No. 5 blends at 1,400 fps. Ultra Steel is sold in 25-shell boxes.

Federal's Prairie Storm Bismuth Blend offers upland game hunters a lead-free alternative, which is highly effective on distant roosters and fast-flushing timberdoodles alike. The new line also uses the Flitecontrol Flex wad but blends Premium steel shot and HEVI-Bismuth shot in a 70/30 ratio. These shells adhere to the regulations of non-toxic ammunition. Available in 12-gauge 3-inch 1¼ ounces of No. 3 steel/No. 5 Bismuth and No. 4 steel/No. 6 Bismuth; 12-gauge 2¾-inch 1⅛ ounces of No. 3 steel/No. 5 Bismuth and No. 4 steel/No. 6 Bismuth; and in 20-gauge 3-inch 1 ounce of No. 3 steel/No. 5 Bismuth and No. 4 steel/No. 6 Bismuth. Prairie Storm Bismuth Blend is sold in 25-count boxes.

Prairie Storm FS Lead gets a quartet

Federal's Prairie Storm Bismuth Blend offers upland game hunters a lead-free alternative. The new line also uses the Flitecontrol Flex wad but blends Premium steel shot and HEVI-Bismuth shot in a 70/30 ratio.

of new loads using that blend of copper-plated lead and Flitestopper lead pellets in a 70/30 ratio. The trio of new 12-gauge loads are at a reduced velocity of 1,330 fps and use 1¼ ounces of No. 4, No. 5, or No. 6 shot, but I'm most excited about the 3-inch 28-gauge load of 1 ounce of No. 6 FS lead, which takes that little gun to a new level. Sold in 25-count boxes. *federalpremium.com*

FIOCCHI

Extending its Hyperformance ammo line for 2024, Fiocchi now offers the 50-grain Barnes Varmint Grenade bullet in the .223 Remington. With its copper-/tin-powdered metal core inside a thin gilding metal jacket, that frangible bullet leaves the muzzle at 3,300 fps, giving an excellent option for the varmint hunter who wants a lead-free projectile. Sold in 50-count boxes. *fiocchiusa.com*

HEVI-SHOT

I started my hunting career with a Fox Model B-SE SxS .410-bore shotgun, as the lack of recoil was perfect for a young teenager. While the lead-shot No. 4 and

No. 6 loads were good, we now have many loads using alternative shot material, extending the capabilities of the little .410 bore. The TSS Turkey shells with the No. 7 and even No. 9 shot are taking toms out to 50 yards and beyond; in my youth, anything less than a heavy load of large shot from a 12-gauge was considered a gamble.

For 2024, HEVI-Shot has expanded its shotshell line to include its 12g/cc tungsten shot in the .410 bore, with a ½-ounce load of No. 7 at a muzzle velocity of 1,250 fps in the 3-inch magnum shells. This shot is over 50 percent denser than traditional steel, making the HEVI-XII a logical choice for those who like hunting waterfowl with sub-gauge shotguns. Using denser shot material results in the ability to use a finer shot, as the tungsten will retain energy better than other choices, and you can put more pellets on the target. It might not be cheap, but it sure is effective. While HEVI-Shot indicates that these shotshells are intended for waterfowl, I see no reason why they wouldn't work equally well for turkeys.

The .22 ARC (Advanced Rifle Cartridge) is a new Hornady cartridge designed for the AR platform. It uses a 2.260-inch cartridge overall length but with a case length of just 1.525 inches. Loads include the 62-grain ELD-VT at 3,300 fps, a 75-grain ELD Match at 3,000 fps, and an 88-grain ELD Match at 2,825 fps—putting the .22 ARC in the class of the 22 Nosler and the .224 Valkyrie from Federal.

The HEVI-Steel Upland line will have the birds' attention this year, as it offers a 1-ounce load of No. 6 or No. 7 steel shot (weighing 7.8g/cc) at 1,350 fps in a 2¾-inch 12-gauge high brass. HEVI-Shot uses a proprietary wad to keep the shot column tidy and the patterns tight. It is sold in 25-count boxes.

The HEVI-Metal Xtreme line gets an extension, with a 12-gauge load blending No. 2 tungsten shot and BB steel shot in a 3-inch magnum load of 1¼ ounce of shot at 1,450 fps. The Flitecontrol Flex wad keeps that unique shot blend in place and provides a tight pattern for more extended pokes. The steel and tungsten are blended in a 70/30 ratio in the shot column to take down distant geese and high-flying ducks. A hotter primer is used for consistent ignition, no matter the temperature or weather. Sold in 25-count boxes. *hevishot.com*

HORNADY

New for this year is the Hornady V-Match ammunition line, equipped with the ELD-VT varmint bullet. Take the main ingredients of the ELD-X and ELD Match line—the Heat Shield polymer tip, which resists deformation in flight, and the AMP bullet jacket—and modify them to have a thinner, more frangible jacket, and a deep air cavity under that polymer tip and you'll have ELD-VT. A deadly accurate varmint projectile, the ELD-VT is loaded in Hornady's V-Match ammo line, and predators and varmints should take heed. The new ammo is available in .22 ARC with a 62-grain ELD-VT, 6mm Creedmoor with an 80-grain ELD-VT, and 6.5 Grendel and 6.5 Creedmoor with a 100-grain ELD-VT.

The .22 ARC (Advanced Rifle Cartridge) is a new Hornady cartridge designed for the AR platform. Using a 2.260-inch cartridge overall length but with a case length of just 1.525 inches, Hornady has left plenty of room to seat long, heavy-

The HEVI-Steel Upland line offers a 1-ounce load of No. 6 or No. 7 steel shot (weighing 7.8g/cc) at 1,350 fps in a 2¾-inch 12-gauge high brass. HEVI-Shot uses a proprietary wad to keep the shot column tidy and the patterns tight.

for-caliber bullets. The new cartridge gets a 1:7 twist, perfectly capable of stabilizing the three loads Hornady offers: the 62-grain ELD-VT at 3,300 fps, a 75-grain ELD Match at 3,000 fps, and an 88-grain ELD Match at 2,825 fps. These offerings will put the .22 ARC in the class of the 22 Nosler and the .224 Valkyrie from Federal. The .441-inch case head diameter shows the lineage of the 6.5 Grendel—the .22 ARC and its younger, though more popular sibling, the 6mm ARC, is derived from the Grendel—and both ARCs sit comfortably in the AR-15. The 30-degree shoulder handles the headspacing, and the cartridge runs at a relatively high pressure of 52,000 psi. If you're looking for velocities on par with the classic .22-250 Remington but with heavier bullets with a higher Ballistic Coefficient, the .22 ARC might be for you.

Hornady also offers two new loads for the 5.7x28mm, featuring the 40-grain FTX (popular in its lever-action cartridges) in the Critical Defense line and the 40-grain V-Max varmint bullet in the Black ammo line. Both loads run at 1,810 fps (from a 4.8-inch barrel) and are sold in 25-round boxes. *hornady.com*

NOSLER

There are five new ammunition offerings from Nosler, starting with the 7mm PRC loaded with the 175-grain AccuBond Long Range at 3,000 fps. Shooters will benefit from a bonded core bullet, perfect for larger game species or closer shots with higher impact velocities. The .243 Winchester lineup is enhanced with a 70-grain Ballistic Tip Varmint, screaming out of the barrel at 3,500 fps, and the .300 WSM is now equipped with the 165-grain Ballistic Tip bullet at 3,125 fps. Nosler also offers the classic 6.5x55 Swedish with a couple of great options: the 120-grain Expansion Tip—perfect for the lead-free fans—and the 140-grain Ballistic Tip. Nosler's ammo comes in proprietary brass cases and has always proven consistent. *nosler.com*

REMINGTON

There's lots going on over at Big Green, with some new ammunition lines and a whole bunch of line extensions. Big Green has extended the proprietary

Remington's Premier CuT, short for Copper Tipped, uses an opaque green polymer tip, a sleek ogive and a boattail. Expect monometal terminal performance in a conformation perfect for hunting at any sane range.

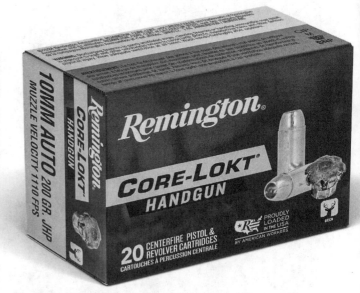

Remington has also extended the Core-Lokt bullet into handgun calibers. Those included the 180-grain .357 Remington Magnum, the 200-grain 10mm Auto, the 210-grain Core-Lokt in the .41 Remington Magnum, and the .44 Remington Magnum loaded with the 240-grain Core-Lokt.

The Remington Nitro Steel Duplex shotshell line sees the revival of blended shot sizes. The line consists of four loads of 12-gauge, 3-inch magnums, all at 1,450 fps.

For waterfowlers toting 28-gauge shotguns, Winchester released a 3-inch steel load in its Xpert shotshell line that features ¾ ounce of No. 4 shot at 1,350 fps.

bullet family—which dates back to 1939 with the Core-Lokt bullet—to include the Premier CuT, short for Copper Tipped. Equipped with an opaque green polymer tip, a sleek ogive and a boattail, Remington says the Premier CuT line will give monometal terminal performance in a conformation perfect for hunting at any sane range. The polymer tip maintains BC values and initiates expansion; there is a hollow cavity underneath into which the tip is driven so that even at lower impact velocities (read longer shot distances), the CuT will expand. Being a lead-free bullet, bullet weights run slightly lighter, especially in the standard, classic cartridges. Available in 6.5 Creedmoor at 120 grains, 6.5 PRC at 130 grains, .270 Winchester at 140 grains, 7mm-08 Remington at 140 grains, 7mm Remington Magnum at 150 grains, 7mm PRC at 160 grains, .308 Winchester and

30-'06 Springfield at 150 grains, and .300 Winchester Magnum at 180 grains. It comes in 20-round boxes.

Core-Lokt Copper is now available in the .360 BuckHammer, making the cartridge compliant with those states and provinces that have banned lead-core ammunition. Though the .360 BuckHammer isn't exactly a speed demon, it's fast enough to open a copper monometal projectile reliably. Core-Lokt Copper is a hollowpoint bullet, and in the .360 Buck-Hammer, it is loaded at 160 grains with a muzzle velocity of 2,500 fps. Despite the lower bullet weight, the Core-Lokt Copper's structural integrity will prevent bullet breakup, though the hollowpoint will ensure reliable expansion, according to Remington. It is sold in 20-count boxes.

Core-Lokt Tipped gets four new additions this year, including a 180-grain load for the .360 Buckhammer, a 140-grain

load for both the 7mm-08 Remington and 6.5 PRC, a 175-grain offering for the 7mm PRC, and a 210-grain load for the big .300 PRC. The green polymer tip increases the Ballistic Coefficient and initiates expansion upon impact. Sold in 20-count boxes.

Remington has also extended the Core-Lokt cup-and-core bullet into handgun calibers, giving handgun hunters the performance of the 'Deadliest Mushroom in the Woods.' Included in the new line are the 180-grain .357 Remington Magnum, the 200-grain 10mm Auto, the 210-grain Core-Lokt in the .41 Remington Magnum, and the .44 Remington Magnum loaded with the 240-grain Core-Lokt. It's loaded in nickel-plated cases and sold in 20-count boxes.

Big Green has a couple of new shot-shell lines out this year, starting with the Low Decibel line. Available in .410-bore in 2¾-inch shells with a ¾-ounce load of No. 9 shot at the subdued velocity of 550 fps. This is a perfect choice for dispatching pests in areas where the report of a firearm is unwanted. It's sold in 25-count boxes.

The Nitro Steel Duplex shotshell line sees the revival of blended shot sizes—who remembers the lead shot Duplex turkey loads of the late 1980s/early '90s?—but this time in steel shot. The line consists of four loads of 12-gauge, 3-inch magnums, all at 1,450 fps. The Nitro Steel Duplex is offered in the following blended loads: BBx2, 2x4, BBx4, and 2x6, available in 25-count boxes. *remington.com*

WINCHESTER

Winchester brings us a trio of 28-gauge shotshells, providing waterfowlers and upland game hunters with some good options. For waterfowlers, a 3-inch steel load in its Xpert shotshell line features ¾ ounce of No. 4 shot at 1,350 fps. However, if steel shot doesn't appeal to you, Winchester has a non-toxic option in the Bismuth line: a 3-inch load stuffed with 1 ounce of No. 5 shot, leaving the muzzle at 1,300 fps. I prefer the terminal performance of Bismuth over steel, as it retains more downrange energy.

And for the upland crowd, Win-

Winchester expanded its .400 Legend lineup with a 190-grain Extreme Point in the Deer Season XP ammunition line. With an oversized polymer tip and a copper jacket with a tapered thickness, the Extreme Point is designed for immediate expansion.

chester adds a 28-gauge option to the Super Pheasant shotshell line. Featuring a 1⅛-ounce load of copper-plated No. 5 shot cradled in a wad designed to optimize the shot pattern, the Super Pheasant load will put smiles on the faces of fans of the 28-gauge, but I'm not exactly sure the birds will be as happy about this. At 1,200 fps, the 3-inch 28-gauge Super Pheasant load will hold distant birds without punishing recoil. Sold in 25-count boxes.

Winchester's Varmint-X line gets three new offerings this year, all featuring the Extreme Point polymer tip varmint bullet. Winchester designed the bullet using a thin alloy jacket to deliver the frangibility and immediate energy transfer that varmint hunters desire. Winchester offers it now in .223 Remington with a 55-grain bullet at 3,240 fps, in .243 Winchester with a 65-grain bullet at 3,620 fps, and in 6.5 Creedmoor with a 95-grain bullet at 3,300 fps. Sold in 20-count boxes.

Winchester also expanded the .400 Legend lineup, this time with a 190-grain Extreme Point in the Deer Season XP ammunition line. With an oversized polymer tip and a copper jacket with a tapered thickness, the Extreme Point is designed to provide immediate expansion, delivering the shock that can switch a whitetail "off" yet still has a good BC value for longer shots. With the .350 Legend and .400 Legend checking the boxes for several Midwestern states, the Extreme Point bullet will make an already sound design perform even better. *winchester.com* 𝗚𝗗

- REPORTS -
from the Field
RELOADING

News from the front
for those who roll their own!

> PHIL MASSARO

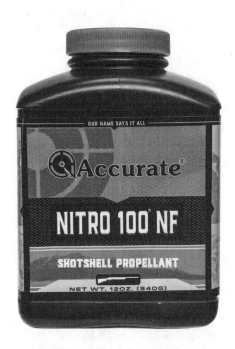

Accurate's Nitro 100 NF—the "NF" for New Formulation—is optimized for more consistent ignition and better flow through a powder thrower. It is a perfect choice for just about all 12-gauge target loads.

The handloading community has been through an awful lot over the last five years, between the COVID-19 pandemic and civil unrest and millions of new shooters coming online, causing a component drought. For the last two years, shelves have been stocked again, and the loading presses are working. But, for reasons unclear at this time, we are experiencing severe price increases and a lack of availability. All components have gone up significantly in price—with rifle powder selling from $45 to $90 per pound, depending on where you're shopping—and many of the main staples going out of stock. Nonetheless, we reloaders are a stubborn lot, and the truly dedicated reloader will not stop participating in their favorite pastime. Looking at the new products out this year for the reloader, there isn't anything earth-shaking, but there are some exciting developments. Let's delve into the new reloading products.

ACCURATE POWDER

Accurate's popular shotgun powder, Nitro 100, gets a facelift this year and is now known as Nitro 100 NF, with the "NF" standing for New Formulation. Now optimized for more consistent ignition and better flow through a powder thrower, Nitro 100 NF is a perfect choice for just about all 12-gauge target loads. Keep an eye on the Hodgdon website (parent company of Accurate Powder) for the latest load data for this new powder. Sold in 12 oz., 4-lb., and 8-lb. canisters. *hodgdon.com*

BERGER BULLETS

For 2024, Berger gives its Hybrid Target line a neat extension, a sleek .375-caliber, weighing in at 410 grains. Featuring the famous Berger J4 jacket, renowned for its concentricity, the new Hybrid Target bullet has a G1 BC of .928 and a G7 BC of .475, making it a fine candidate for serious long-range target work. The

Berger's Hybrid Target line grows with a sleek .375-caliber, weighing 410 grains. It features the famous Berger J4 jacket with a G1 BC of .928 and a G7 BC of .475 for serious long-range target work.

Hodgdon High Gun is a flattened spherical powder designed for light 12-gauge target loads, which could replicate the old Remington Nitro 27 shotshells.

Hybrid ogive blends the best characteristics needed for rifling engagement and resistance to atmospheric drag. Sold in 50-count boxes. *bergerbullets.com*

HODGDON

A couple of new powders are available from Hodgdon: High Gun and Perfect Pattern. Starting with High Gun, we have a flattened spherical powder designed for light 12-gauge target loads, which just so happens to come very close to replicating the old Remington Nitro 27 shotshells. High Gun is available in 1-, 4-, and 8-pound canisters. Perfect Pattern also shares a flattened spherical pattern—this shape makes a big difference in consistent metering—and makes a good choice for the lightest target and field loads for the 12-gauge. Both recoil and report are mild when you load with Perfect Pattern—available in 1- and 8-pound canisters.

Hodgdon also has released its latest manual, which is always loaded with great data and information. The *Annual Manual* includes feature articles by Gun Digest contributors Steve Gash and Frank Melloni, plus load data for the Remington .360 Buckhammer and Winchester's .400 Legend. Hodgdon packed 192 pages with more than 6,000 loads and it makes an affordable, entertaining, and informative read. *hodgdon.com*

HORNADY

The big red H has not been idle, releasing the newest member of the ELD family: the ELD-VT. Available in the V-Match loaded ammo line, Hornady offers the ELD-VT in component form. The new projectile blends the uniformity, aerodynamics, and accuracy of the ELD-X and ELD Match lines with a thinner jacket, resulting in near-explosive expansion. The Hornady AMP bullet jacket is uniform and renowned for its excellent concentricity. Mate the AMP jacket with the proprietary Heat Shield polymer tip—which will maintain its integrity throughout the bullet's flight—and you're looking at the main ingredients of the ELD bullet formula. But, with the ELD-VT projectile, the lead core is significantly shortened, which moves the bullet's center of gravity rearward and leaves a large air void behind the Heat Shield tip.

6000+ LOADS

PERFECT PATTERN & HIGH GUN UPDATES INCLUDED

HODGDON® 2024 ANNUAL MANUAL

RELOADING

HODGDON®
THE GUNPOWDER PEOPLE

FOR HANDGUNS, RIFLES & SHOTSHELLS WITH HODGDON®, IMR®, WINCHESTER®, ACCURATE® & RAMSHOT® POWDERS

DATA FOR NEW
RAMSHOT GRAND
MAGNUM RIFLE POWDER

DATA FOR THE
REMINGTON 360 BUCKHAMMER

WINCHESTER 400 LEGEND

UPDATED DATA FOR
**70+ RIFLE AND PISTOL CARTRIDGES
& 1,000+ 12 GA LOADS**

Hodgdon Manual 2024.

Hornady released its Click-Adjustable Bullet Seating Micrometer, which replaces the standard seating adjustment stem. It's marked in .001-inch increments.

Upon impact, that tip will move rearward into that air cavity, and the compression of the air will violently force the bullet jacket outward; this gives the violent expansion that varmint hunters love. It's available in .224-inch diameter at 62 and 80 grains, 6mm at 80 grains, 6.5mm at 100 grains, and .308-inch diameter at 174 grains.

Hornady has also released its Click-Adjustable Bullet Seating Micrometer. This handy little tool replaces the standard seating adjustment stem, giving the reloader a much more precise means of adjusting bullet seating depth. Marked in .001-inch increments, it gives a click for each adjustment. If you want a simple means of converting your Hornady seating dies to a more accurate tool, here you go. *hornady.com*

LYMAN

Lyman has some handy new products for 2024, including its Pro Headspace gauges, a new electronic scale, and a couple of ultrasonic cleaners. The Digi-Touch 1500 is a neat, compact digital scale that runs on a rechargeable internal battery, charged using your phone charger. Measuring just 3½ x 5¾ inches, the Digi-Touch 1500 is a perfect scale for the range or any other application where portability is needed. With a 1,500-grain capacity and a bright LED display, the Digi-Touch 1500 comes with a plastic cover and a powder scoop.

Lyman's Pro Headspace Gauges are used to set up a sizing die for bottleneck cartridges to ensure your ammunition will function properly. Made of stainless steel, these cylindrical gauges have flats machined into the body to prevent them from rolling off your bench. Each has a pair of rubber O-rings to afford a good grip on the unit. They are available in .223 Remington, 6.5 Creedmoor, .300 AAC Blackout, .308 Winchester, and .30-'06 Springfield.

If you haven't had the opportunity to use an ultrasonic cleaner for your cases, you are missing out; they clean both the inside and outside of the cases, and the interior of your reloading dies. Lyman's new Power Pro Ultrasonic Cleaners are now available in 3- and 6-liter sizes, so not only can your cases be cleaned, but all sorts of gun parts, tools, jewelry, and anything else you can fit in the hopper. The 3L model holds over 100 oz. of fluid, and double that for the 6L model; the Power Pro uses a stainless steel tank and black stainless steel exterior and features a handy drain hose, so you don't have to move the unit with the liquid inside. Temperature-adjustable and offering the choice of 5-, 10-, or 30-minute cleaning cycles, the Lyman Power Pro Ultrasonic Cleaner will make an excellent addition to your reloading room. *lyman.com*

NOSLER

Embracing the new 7mm PRC, Nosler offers its excellent brass cases for the cartridge to the handloader. Having long used Nosler's fully prepped cases for my ammunition, I can attest to the convenience of having cases ready to load straight out of the box. Nosler chamfers, deburrs, sizes and trims all its component cases before inspection, and these have been a part of the most accurate and uniform handloads I've developed. The 7mm PRC cases come 50 to the box.

For those shooting the .308 Winchester and .30-'06 Springfield, Sierra now offers a 180-grain Tipped GameKing engineered to be seated correctly in both cartridges.

Sierra's .30-caliber 205-grain hollowpoint boattail GameKing was designed for subsonic use in the .300 Blackout. With a G1 BC of .480, it's optimized for best expansion results at impact velocities between 900 and 1,150 fps.

Nosler now offers the boattail hollowpoint Custom Competition bullet in .338-caliber, at 250 grains, which will be good news for the fans of the .338 Lapua and .338 Norma. Measuring just under 1.6 inches long, with a G1 BC of .590, this bullet uses Nosler's Custom Competition jacket to create a very accurate projectile. Sold in 100-count boxes. Nosler adds a 150-grain 6.5mm projectile in the RDF (Reduced Drag Factor) projectile line. With a compound ogive designed to reduce sensitivity to seating depth, this 150-grain bullet has a G1 BC of .670 and a G7 BC of .342 and should be an excellent choice for the 6.5 Creedmoor and 6.5 PRC shooters. Sold in 100-count boxes. *nosler.com*

RAMSHOT

New for 2024, Ramshot announces the new Grand rifle powder. Designed to serve the same family of cartridges as Hodgdon's H1000, this spherical, double-based powder is designed for temperature insensitivity and contains a copper-fouling removal agent, so you can spend time shooting instead of cleaning. Right at home in the magnum cartridges

like the Remington Ultra Magnums, the Hornady PRC family, and the Winchester WSM cartridges—including the 6.8 Western—I'm hoping that Ramshot's Grand will fill the void that the lack of H1000 availability has created. *hodgdonpowderco.com/ramshot/*

RCBS

The RCBS Summit Press is a unique design, with the reloading die moving up and down as the case remains stationary. With a small footprint, it makes an excellent choice for those with limited space or who appreciate the economy of space. This year, the Summit Press turns 10 years old, and to celebrate, RCBS is releasing a commemorative red, white, and blue version. Equipped with the Freedom Camo die plate and the shorter handle (perfect for small spaces), you can find the 10th-anniversary Summit Press at *rcbs.com*

REDDING RELOADING

Here's a personal favorite, which will hopefully aid in bringing a wonderful yet nearly obsolete cartridge back to life. Redding has produced a limited number of reloading die sets for the .318 Westley Richards as a custom order. If you are interested in the classic British cartridge, don't hesitate to contact Redding to get your set before they're gone. *redding-reloading.com*

SIERRA BULLETS

New for 2024, Sierra offers a .30-caliber 205-grain hollowpoint boattail GameKing designed for subsonic use in the .300 Blackout. Having a G1 BC of .480 and optimized for best expansion results at impact

velocities between 900 fps and 1,150 fps, this bullet will surely appeal to the subsonic hunting crowd. Sold in 100- or 500-count boxes.

For those shooting the .308 Winchester and .30-'06 Springfield, Sierra offers a 180-grain Tipped GameKing engineered to be seated correctly in both cartridges. (The bullet differs slightly from the earlier No. 4680, which Sierra indicates is better for the .300 Winchester Magnum.) The new bullet is sold in 50-, 100-, and 500-count boxes. Sierra has also extended the Tipped GameKing line to include a 145-grain model engineered explicitly for the velocity and performance of the 6.5 PRC cartridge. Having a G1 BC of .597, this bullet makes a good choice for hunting at longer ranges. Sold in 100- or 500-count boxes. *sierrabullets. com* **GD**

RCBS' 10th-Anniversary Summit Press comes in red, white, and blue.

AUTO-ORDNANCE 1927A-1 THOMPSON

Caliber: .45 ACP. Barrel: 16.5 in. Weight: 13 lbs. Length: About 41 in. overall (Deluxe). Stock: Walnut stock and vertical fore-end. Sights: Blade front, open rear adjustable for windage. Features: Recreation of Thompson Model 1927. Semi-auto only. Deluxe model has finned barrel, adjustable rear sight and compensator; Standard model has plain barrel and military sight. Available with 100-round drum or 30-round stick magazine. Made in USA by Auto-Ordnance Corp., a division of Kahr Arms.

Price: Deluxe w/stick magazine **$1,551.00**
Price: Deluxe w/drum magazine.. **$2,583.00**
Price: Lightweight model w/stick mag **$1,403.00**

AUTO ORDNANCE M1 CARBINE

Caliber: .30 Carbine (15-shot magazine). Barrel: 18 in. Weight: 5.4 to 5.8 lbs. Length: 36.5 in. Stock: Wood or polymer. Sights: Blade front, flip-style rear. Features: A faithful recreation of the military carbine.

Price: **$1,036.00**
Price: Folding stock... **$1,137.00**

BARRETT MODEL 82A-1 SEMI-AUTOMATIC

Calibers: .416 Barret, 50 BMG. Capacity: 10-shot detachable box magazine. Barrel: 29 in. Weight: 28.5 lbs. Length: 57 in. overall. Stock: Composition with energy-absorbing recoil pad. Sights: Scope optional. Features: Semiautomatic, recoil operated with recoiling barrel. Three-lug locking bolt; muzzle brake. Adjustable bipod. Introduced 1985. Made in USA by Barrett Firearms.

Price: **$9,119.00**

BARRETT M107A1

Caliber: 50 BMG. Capacity: 10-round detachable magazine. Barrels: 20 or 29 in. Sights: 27-in. optics rail with flip-up iron sights. Weight: 30.9 lbs. Finish: Flat Dark Earth. Features: Four-port cylindrical muzzle brake. Quick-detachable Barrett QDL Suppressor. Adjustable bipod and monopod.

Price: **$12,281.00**

BERETTA CX4 STORM CARBINE

Calibers: 9mm, 40 S&W, .45 ACP. Barrel: 16.6 in. Stock: Black synthetic with thumbhole. Sights: Ghost ring. Features: Blowback single action, ambidextrous controls, Picatinny quad rail system. Reintroduced in 2017.

Price: **$700.00**

BROWNING BAR SAFARI MARK II

Calibers: Safari: .25-06 Rem., .270 Win., 7mm Rem. Mag., .30-06, .308 Win., .300 Win. Mag., .338 Win. Mag. Barrels: 22–24 in. round tapered. Weights: 7.4–8.2 lbs. Lengths: 43–45 in. overall. Stock: French walnut pistol grip stock and forend, hand checkered. Sights: No sights. Features: Has new bolt release lever; removable trigger assembly with larger triggerguard; redesigned gas and buffer systems. Detachable 4-round box magazine. The scroll-engraved receiver is tapped for scope mounting. The BOSS version was discontinued. Mark II Safari was introduced in 1993. Made in Belgium.

Price: BAR MK II Safari .... **$1,230.00 –$1,849.00**

BROWNING BAR MK III SERIES

Calibers: .243 Win., 7mm-08, .270 Win., .270 WSM, 7mm Rem., .308 Win, .30-06, .300 Win. Mag., .300 WSM. Capacities: Detachable 4 or 5-shot magazine. Barrel: 22, 23 or 24 in.es. Stock: Grade II checkered walnut, shim adjustable. Camo stock with composite gripping surfaces available. Stalker model has composite stock. Weight: 7.5 lbs. Features: Satin nickel alloy with high relief engraving, stylized fore-end.

Price: .... **$1,439.00–$1,599.00**
Price: Stalker .... **$1,389.00–$1,599.00**
Price: Smoked Bronze Cerakote and OVIX camo .... **$1,829.00–$1,929.00**
Price: BAR Safari Tribute Mid-Grade **$2,399.00**
Price: BAR Safari Tribute High-Grade **$4,669.00**

BROWNING BAR MK 3 DBM SERIES

Caliber: 308 Win. Capacity: 10-round "detachable box magazine," so named for the DBM series. Barrel: 18-in. fluted blued. Length: 40-1/8 in. Weight: 7 lbs. 6 oz. Stock: Choice of two model variants. DBM Wood uses Grade II Turkish Walnut with oil finish. DBM Stalker uses black synthetic. Features: Picatinny top rail for optics mounting. Other features comparable to standard BAR Mk 3.

Price: BAR MK3 DBM Wood **$1,779.00**
Price: BAR MK3 DBM Stalker **$1,729.00**

CENTURY INTERNATIONAL AES-10B

Caliber: 7.62x39mm. Capacity: 30-shot magazine. Barrel: 23.2 in. Weight: NA. Length: 41.5 in. overall. Stock: Wood grip, fore-end. Sights: Fixed notch rear, windage-adjustable post front. Features: RPK-style, accepts standard double-stack AK-type mags. Side-mounted scope mount, integral carry handle, bipod. Imported by Century Arms Int'l.

Price: AES-10, From **$1,735.00**

DSA SA58 STANDARD

Caliber: .308 Win. Barrel: 21 in. bipod cut w/threaded flash hider. Weight: 8.75 lbs. Length: 43 in. Stock: Synthetic, X-Series or optional folding para stock. Sights: Elevation-adjustable post front, windage-adjustable rear peep. Features: Fully adjustable short gas system, high-grade steel or 416 stainless upper receiver. Many variants available. Made in USA by DSA, Inc.

Price: From.. **$1,800.00**

DSA SA58 CARBINE

Caliber: .308 Win. Barrel: 16.25 in. bipod cut w/threaded flash hider. Features: Carbine variation of FAL-style rifle. Other features identical to SA58 Standard model. Made in USA by DSA, Inc.

Price: **$1,700.00**

Prices given are believed to be accurate at time of publication however, many factors affect retail pricing so exact prices are not possible.

79TH EDITION, 2025 ⊕ **421**

HECKLER & KOCH MODEL USC

Caliber: .45 ACP. Capacity: 10-round magazine. Barrel: 16 in. Weight: 6.13 lbs. Length: 35.4 in. Features: Polymer construction, adjustable rear sight, ambidextrous safety/selector, optional Picatinny rail. Civilian version of HK UMP submachine gun.

Price: $1,499.00

HENRY HOMESTEADER CARBINE

Calibers: 9mm Luger. Barrel: 16.3 in. round-blued steel. Weight: 6.6 lbs. Stock: American walnut. Features: Henry's first semi-automatic PPC-style rifle. Hard-anodized black receiver finish. Adjustable aperture rear sight and post front. Threaded barrel. Ambidextrous bolt handle. Swivel studs. Tang safety. All models include 5- and 10-round Henry proprietary magazines. Additional magazines and adapters sold separately.

Price: w/ Henry magazine $928.00
Price: w/ addition of Glock mag well $956.00
Price: w/ addition of Sig/S&W M&P mag well $956.00

INLAND M1 1945 CARBINE

Caliber: .30 Carbine. Capacity: 15 rounds. Barrel: 18 in. Weight: 5 lbs. 3 oz. Features: A faithful reproduction of the last model that Inland manufactured in 1945, featuring a type 3 bayonet lug/barrel band, adjustable rear sight, push button safety, and walnut stock. Scout Model has 16.5-in. barrel, flash hider, synthetic stock with accessory rail. Made in the USA.

Price: $1,299.00
Price: Scout Model $1,449.00

KALASHNIKOV USA

Caliber: 7.62x39mm. Capacity: 30-round magazine. AK-47 series made in the USA in several variants and styles. Barrel: 16.25 in. Weight: 7.52 lbs.

Price: KR-9 Side-folding stock $1,249.00
Price: US132S Synthetic stock $799.00
Price: US132W Wood carbine $836.00

RUGER LC CARBINE

Calibers: .45 Auto, 5.7x28mm. Capacity: 13 (.45 ACP), 20 (5.7x28mm) pistol magazines. Barrel: 16.25-in. threaded barrel. Sights Adjustable Ruger Rapid Deploy. Length: 30.6 in. Weight: 7.1 lbs. Stock: Synthetic. Features: Barrel threaded .578"-28. Adjustable length of pull from 12.6-14.6 in. Unique bolt-over-barrel design with the magazine in the grip allows for excellent balance and control. The folding stock is reversible and features an adjustable length of pull, but can easily be replaced with AR-pattern stocks. The rear of the receiver has a Picatinny rail for maximum accessory compatibility. Interchangeable magazine wells for use with common Ruger and Glock magazines.

Price: $1,009.00

RUGER PC CARBINE

Calibers: 9mm or 40 S&W. Capacity: 17 (9mm), 15 (40 S&W) pistol magazines.10-round state-compliant versions available. Barrel: 16-in. cold-hammer forged, threaded, fluted. Sights: Standard model with iron sights;

chassis models with Picatinny optics rail. Length: 32.25–35.5 in. Weight: 7.3 lbs. Stock: Choice of synthetic, fixed, or adjustable aluminum chassis furniture. Features: Aluminum alloy receiver, hardcoat anodized. Utilizes 10/22 trigger components with light, crisp pull. Ergonomic pistol grip with extended trigger reach for precise control. Interchangeable magazine wells for use with common Ruger and Glock magazines.

Price: $779.00
Price: With handguard..................................$879.00
Price: Adjustable Chassis $999.00
Price: State Compliant $999.00
Price: Distributor Exclusives ....$779.00–$999.00

RUGER MINI-14

Calibers: .223 Rem., .300 Blackout (Tactical Rifle). Capacity: 5-shot or 20-shot detachable box magazine. Barrel: 18.5 in. Rifling twist 1:9 in. Weights: 6.75–7 lbs. Length: 37.25 in. overall. Stocks: American hardwood, steel reinforced,or synthetic. Sights: Protected blade front, fully adjustable Ghost Ring rear. Features: Fixed piston gas-operated, positive primary extraction. New buffer system, redesigned ejector system. Ruger S100RM scope rings included on Ranch Rifle. Heavier barrels added in 2008, 20-round magazine added in 2009. For 2024, new stainless-barrel Tactical variant with 18-in. barrel and side-folding stock.

Price: Mini-14, Ranch Rifle ....$1,259.00–$1,449.00
Price: Mini-14 Tactical 16.12 in. barrel with flash hider, black synthetic stock, adjustable sights $1,489.00
Price: Mini-14 Tactical with 18.00 in. barrel, side-folding stock $1,849.00

SIG-SAUER MPX PCC

Caliber: 9mm. 30-round capacity. Barrel: 16 in. Features: M-LOK handguard, 5-position folding telescoping stock. Weight: 6.6 lbs. Sights: none.

Price: From $2,016.00

SPRINGFIELD ARMORY M1A

Caliber: 7.62mm NATO (.308). Capacities: 5- or 10-shot box magazine. Barrel: 25.062 in. with flash suppressor, 22 in. without suppressor. Weight: 9.75 lbs. Length: 44.25 in. overall. Stock: American walnut with walnut-colored heat-resistant fiberglass handguard. Matching walnut handguard available. Also available with fiberglass stock. Sights: Military, square blade front, full click-adjustable aperture rear. Features: Commercial equivalent of the U.S. M-14 service rifle with no provision for automatic firing. From Springfield Armory.

Price: SOCOM 16..$1,987.00
Price: Scout Squad, From $1,850.00
Price: Standard M1A, From $1,685.00
Price: Loaded Standard, From $1,847.00
Price: National Match, From $2,434.00
Price: Super Match (heavy premium barrel) about $2,965.00
Price: Tactical, From ....$3,619.00–$4,046.00

ADAMS ARMS P-SERIES RIFLES

Proprietary gas-piston operating systems mechanically actuate the bolt carrier external of the receiver. P1 model features ergonomic mid-length handguards, standard Picatinny adjustable block piston system, tactical stock and grip with QD mounts, enhanced triggerguard. Barrel lengths and chamberings: 16 in. (5.56). P2 model includes ergonomic free-float rail, P-Series Micro Block piston system. P2 barrel lengths and chamberings: 16 in. (5.56); 16 in. (.300 BLK). P3 line features Proof Research carbon-fiber-wrapped barrel, jet comp, ergonomic free-float rail, and P-Series Micro Block piston system.

Price: P1 Rifle 16 in. $900.00
Price: P2 Rifle 16 in. $1,450.00
Price: P3 Rifle .308 Win. 17 in. $2,800.00
Price: P3 Rifle 6.5 Creedmoor 24 in. $2,800.00

AERO PRECISION M4E1 ENHANCED SERIES RIFLE

Chambering: .223 Wylde for .223 Rem. or 5.56 NATO. 300 BLK. Built on Enhanced Series Upper Receiver, which has an integrated upper receiver and handguard system that's free-floated. Barrel: 16-in. .223 Wylde, mid-length, 1:8 twist, 416 stainless steel, bead-blasted. Handguard: Gen 2 Enhanced Series. Gas System: Low profile gas block and mid-length gas tube. Bolt Carrier Group: M16 Cut, 8620 steel, phosphate finish, staked. Muzzle Device: Standard A2 flash hider. Stock: Magpul STR. Grip: Magpul MOE. Magazine: Magpul 30-round PMAG. Weight: approx. 7 pounds. Spartan Worn rifle comes with 16-in. 5.56 barrel and 15-in. Enhanced M-LOK Gen 2 Handguard. Handguard, upper and lower receivers have Spartan Worn Cerakote hand finishes by Blown Deadline. Pro series ambidextrous model introduced 2024. Controls on either side allow both left- and right-handed shooters to drop magazines and release bolt carrier groups.

Price: ....$974.00–$1,249.00
Price: Spartan Worn $1,340.00

ALEX PRO AR-15 RIFLES

Calibers: .204 Ruger, 22 Nosler, .223 Wylde, 5.56 NATO, 6mm ARC, 6.5 Grendel, 6.8 SPC, .300 BLK, .350 Legend, .450 Bushmaster. Specializes in making nickel-boron bolt-carrier groups and hunting-caliber AR-style rifles in both AR-15 and AR-10 sizes. Established 2013.

Price: AR15 Guardian .300 BLK...$850.00
Price: APF Regulator 5.56 ....$700.00
Price: APF Carbine 2.0 ....$1,375.00
Price: APF .223 Wylde Carbine $1,800.00
Price: APF DMR 2.0 6ARC...$1,750.00
Price: APF Varmint 2.0 22 Nosler $1,920.00
Price: APF Hunter 2.0 6.8 SPC $1,500.00
Price: APF 6.5 Grendel Carbine $1,050.00
Price: APF Valor .450 Bushmaster $950.00

ALEX PRO AR-10 RIFLES

Calibers: .22-250 Rem., .243 Win. 6mm CM, 6.5 CM, .308 Win.

Price: AR-10 Hunter 2.0..$1,800.00

Price: AR-10 DMR 2.0...$2,325.00
Price: AR-10 Varmint .243 Win.....................................$2,400.00

ALEX PRO MLR RIFLES

Calibers: 28 Nosler, 7mm Rem. Mag., .300 PRC, .300 Win. Mag.
Price: MLR .300 Win. Mag. SST $3,200.00

ALEXANDER ARMS AR SERIES

Calibers: .17 HMR, 5.56 NATO, 6.5 Grendel, .300 AAC, .50 Beowulf. Produces a range of AR-15-type rifles and carbines. Barrels: 16, 18, 20 or 24 in. Depending on model, features include forged flattop receiver with Picatinny rail, button-rifled stainless-steel barrels, composite free-floating handguard, A2 flash hider, M4 collapsible stock, gas-piston operating system.

Price: .17 HMR Standard $1,530.00
Price: .17 HMR Tactical $1,700.00
Price: .17 HMR Varmint Predator $2,150.00
Price: 6.5 Grendel Hunter 18 in. $1,570.00
Price: .300 AAC Blackout Standard.................................$1,405.00
Price: .50 Beowulf Classic Laminate $1,770.00

AMERICAN TACTICAL, INC. OMNI SERIES

AR-15-type rifles and carbines. Barrels: 16, 18, 24 in. Builds include CNC-machined 7075 T6 aluminum forgings for uppers and lowers, machined to military specifications and marked "Multi-Cal" to be used with multiple calibers on the AR-15 platform. Proprietary RF85 metal treatment on some rifles. Omni builds have polymer handguards and metal-reinforced polymer receivers.

Price: ATI Omni Hybrid Maxx 16 in. 5.56...........................$490.00
Price: ATI Omni Hybrid Maxx 16 in. 5.56 M-LOK $540.00
Price: ATI Mil-Sport 16 in. 5.56 M-LOK............................$600.00
Price: ATI Mil-Sport 16 in. 6 ARC.....................................$830.00
Price: ATI Mil-Sport 16 in. 300 BLK $540.00
Price: AM-15 M4 5.56, 16 in. HBAR..................................$450.00
Price: AM-15 M4 5.56, 16 in. Pencil, M-LOK $470.00

ANDERSON MANUFACTURING AM-15 RIFLES

Calibers: 5.56 NATO, 6.5 Grendel, .300 BLK, 7.62x39. This manufacturer, based in Hebron, Kentucky, produces a range of AR-15-type rifles and carbines. Barrels: 16, 18, 24 in. Builds include CNC-machined 7075 T6 aluminum forgings for uppers and lowers, machined to military specifications and marked "Multi-Cal" to be used with multiple calibers on the AR-15 platform. Proprietary RF85 metal treatment on some rifles is billed as needing "zero lubrication." Frontline series features Anderson TRS handguards and free-float quad rail systems. M-LOK series has handguards with that fastener. A4 Rifles have A2 "F" stamped front sights. Utility Series rifles have Anderson Stainless Steel Lower Parts Kit, six-position adjustable carbine stock, A2 grip and flash hider.

Price: AM-15 Frontline QR-16 5.56, 16 in. $850.00
Price: AM-15 Frontline 16 5.56, 16 in. $850.00
Price: AM-15 M-LOK Patriot 5.56, 16 in. $950.00
Price: AM-15 M-LOK Marksman 5.56, 16 in. $800.00

Prices given are believed to be accurate at time of publication however, many factors affect retail pricing so exact prices are not possible.

79TH EDITION, 2025 423

Price: AM-15 A4 5.56, 20 in..**$600.00**
Price: AM-15 A4 Carbine 5.56, 16 in. **$600.00**
Price: AM-15 Utility 5.56, 16 in. **$650.00**
Price: AM-15 Utility Long Range 5.56, 20 in........................**$800.00**

ANDERSON MANUFACTURING AM-10 GEN 2 RIFLES
Calibers: .308 Win., Barrels: 16, 18, 24 in. Features common to all AM-10 Gen 2 rifles include Forged 7075-T6 aluminum upper and lower receivers with Type 3 hard anodizing; 8620 steel nitrided bolt carrier; 9310 steel bolt; 4150 chrome-moly vanadium barrels, 1:10 twist rifling; standard charging handles, six-position receiver extensions, enhanced flared magwells. Models include Ranger, Battle Rifle, and Marksman XL. Introduced June 2022.
Price: AM-10 Ranger .308 Win., 18 in. **$1,000.00**
Price: AM-10 Silent Ranger .308 Win., 18 in. **$1,200.00**
Price: AM-10 Marksman XL .308 Win., 20 in.................**$1,075.00**
Price: AM-10 Battle Rifle .308 Win., 20 in. **$950.00**

ANDERSON MANUFACTURING AM-9 PISTOL CALIBER CARBINE
Caliber: 9mm Para. Barrel: 16-in. 4150 Chrome Moly Vanadium, 1:10 twist, 1/2-36 tpi muzzle threads. Anderson Knight Stalker Flash Hider, 15-in. Anderson M-LOK Handguard w/upper-height top Picatinny rail. Magpul furniture, K2 Grip and Black MOE stock, and PMAG 27 GL9 magazine (27 rd). Introduced 2018.
Price: AM-9 PCC **$850.00**
Price: AM-9 Utility-9 Rifle **$800.00**

ARMALITE M-15 AND AR-10 COMPETITION RIFLES
Calibers: .223 Wylde (M-15) or .308 Win. (AR-10). Built for 3-Gun and practical rifle competition. Timney 4-lb. single-stage trigger, Ergo wide grip MBA-1 buttstock with adjustable cheek piece and length-of-pull. Factory ambidextrous safety and Raptor charging handle, adjustable gas block. On 13.5-in. .223 Wylde model, tunable proprietary Armalite muzzle brake is pinned and welded to create an overall length of 16 in.
Price: M-15 Competition Rifle 18 in. **$2,040.00**
Price: AR-10 Competition Rifle 18 in. **$2,627.00**

ARMALITE M-15 AND AR-10 TACTICAL RIFLES
Calibers: 5.56 NATO/.223 Rem., .308 Win. Slim handguard with octagonal profile, full-length MIL-STD 1913 12 o'clock rail. Adjustable gas block, Magpul MBUS flip-up sights. Non-NFA models come in barrel lengths of 14.5, 16, and 18 in. 5.56 and 16, 18, and 20 in. in .308.
Price: M-15 Tactical Rifle 16 in. **$1,896.00**
Price: AR-10 Tactical Rifle 18 in. **$2,524.00**
Price: AR-10 Tactical Rifle 22 in. 6.5 CM......................**$2,524.00**

ARMALITE M-15 LIGHT TACTICAL CARBINE
Caliber: 5.56 NATO. Armalite free-floating tactical M-LOK handguard, low-profile gas block. Weight: 6 lbs.
Price: M-15 Light Tactical Carbine (LTC) 16 in. **$1,215.00**

ARMALITE M-15 AND AR-10 DEFENSIVE SPORTING RIFLES
Caliber: 5.56 NATO or .308 Win. Weight: 6.1 lbs. Forged flat-top receiver with MIL-STD 1913 rail. Optics-ready and pinned Mil-spec A2 front sight base models.
Price: M-15 Defensive Sporting Rifle....................................**$925.00**

ARMALITE AR-10 A-SERIES SUPERSASS GEN II
Caliber: 7.62x51. SuperSASS (Semi-Automatic Sniper System) civilian model has a 15 in. Armalite Gen II M-LOK free-float handguard, Magpul PRS Gen II adjustable stock, an adjustable gas system for suppressed and un-suppressed fire. 20-in. stainless barrel, 1:10 RH twist. 11.4 lbs.
Price: AR-10 A-Series SuperSASS Gen II A10SBF **$3,825.00**

BARRETT REC7 RIFLES
Caliber: 5.56 NATO. Capacity: 30. Short-stroke gas-piston operating system. One-piece 174 stainless piston. Monolithic TB41 DLC coated anti-tilt full-auto bolt carrier. Forged upper and lower receivers, hardcoat anodized and finished in Cerakote. M4 feed ramps, lightweight free-float handguard.

Full-length M1913 Picatinny top rail with Magpul M-LOK accessory mounting slots at 3, 6, and 9 o'clock positions. 7.2 lbs. DI has a lengthened gas system. Magpul furniture. Custom Radian Raptor ambidextrous charging handle; extended slimline Barrett handguard, Sides and bottom have Barrett Rail System positions. 6.7 lbs.
Price: REC7 5.56 16 in...**$2,790.00**
Price: REC7 DI 5.56 16 in. **$1,910.00**

BARRETT REC10
Caliber: .308 Win. Capacity: 20. Direct impingement gas system. Ambidextrous bolt release, mag catch and safety. Chrome moly vanadium barrel is button rifled with a chrome bore and flash hider. Magpul MOE-SL buttstock, Magpul MBUS sights, ALG Defense QMS trigger group, BRS M-LOK handguard. Black cerakote finish.
Price: REC10 16 in. **$2,800.00**
Price: REC10 Carbine 16 in. **$2,850.00**

BLACKOUT DEFENSE QUANTUM DTL
Chamber: .223 Wylde. Barrel: 13.9, 14.5, 16 in., mid-length gas system. Pinned and welded muzzle device to exceed 16.0 in. total overall length as needed. Heavy profile, 416-R stainless steel, gun-drilled and reamed in 5R rifling and 1:8 twist. Stress relieved, precision air gauged. Dual Taper Lock (DTL) system secures and centers the barrel. Quantum-series lower receivers use patented Presslock technology with a linear compression pad for a tight, rattle free fitment, no carrier tilt. Handguard: 7-side M-LOK compatible. Stryker ambidextrous charging handle. Weight: 6.875 lbs. Black anodized is standard receiver color; several other colors are $50-$75 upcharges. Many options for gas block, charging handle, triggers, etc. .300 BLK added 2023.
Price: ....**$2,410.00–$2,875.00**
Price: .300 BLK..**$2,105.00**

BRAVO COMPANY MFG. BCM M4 CARBINES
Caliber: 5.56mm NATO. Capacity: 30 rounds. Barrel: 16 in., standard government profile, 1:7 twist, M4 feed ramp barrel extension. USGI chrome-lined bore and chamber. Mil-Spec 11595E barrel steel, manganese phosphate finish. Stock: BCM Gunfighter. Sights: Flat-top rail, post front. Weight: 6.3 lbs. Overall Length: 32.5 to 35.5 in. MOD 0 has BCM PKMR Handguard. 6.3 pounds. MOD 2 has BCM QRF Handguard. 6.5 lbs.
Price: MOD 0 ....**$1,175.00**
Price: MOD 2 ....**$1,690.00**

BRAVO COMPANY MFG. BCM RECCE CARBINES
Caliber: 5.56mm NATO. Capacity: 30 rounds. Barrels: 14.5 in., 16 in. 1:7 Twist, M4 feed ramp barrel extension. USGI chrome-lined bore and chamber. MIL-SPEC 11595E barrel steel, manganese phosphate finish. Stock: BCM. Sights: M4 feed ramp flat top with laser T-markings. Mid-length gas systems. Five models in RECCE-14 line: KMR-A and KMR-A LW, MCMR and MCMR LW, and QRF. Four additional models in RECCE-16 line: KMR-A Precision, MCMR Precision, and 300 BLK KMR-A and 300 BLK MCMR.
Price: Bravo Co. RECCE-14 KMR-A 5.56 ....**$2,510.00**
Price: Bravo Co. RECCE-16 KMR-A 5.56 ....**$1,680.00**

BRAVO COMPANY MFG. BCM MID16 RIFLES
Caliber: 5.56mm NATO. Mid-length gas systems. MOD 0 has PKMR handguard. MOD 2 has QRF Handguard.
Price: BCM MID16 MOD 0...**$1,355.00**

BRAVO COMPANY MFG. MARKSMAN RIFLES
Caliber: 5.56mm NATO. Based on the U.S. Navy MK12 Mod 0 Special Purpose Rifle (SPR), the BCM MK12 is a heavily modified DMR-type weapon. 18 in. barrels, various contours. Also includes RECCE-18 rifles. Weights: 7-9 lbs.
Price: Bravo Co. RECCE-18 MCMR 5.56 ....**$1,860.00**

BUSHMASTER M4 PATROLMAN'S MOE RIFLE
The venerable Bushmaster brand restarted production under new ownership

Prices given are believed to be accurate at time of publication however, many factors affect retail pricing so exact prices are not possible.

in August 2021 in Carson City, Nevada. Preliminary offerings are variants of the XM15-E2S model, such as the QRC and M4 Patrolman's nameplates. The M4 Patrolman's MOE rifle is the company's staple, with upgraded features, including Magpul furniture, a 16-in. barrel made from 4150 CMV, with a salt bath nitride finish, and a 1:7 twist rate. It comes with Magpul MOE SL handguard, CTR stock, and MOE grip in ODG. The rifle also features a Mil-Spec trigger, a detachable carry handle, and an F-Marked A2 front sight. It uses PMAG Gen M2 30-round black magazines and an A2 flash hider. Made in the USA. Weight w/o magazine: 6.9 lbs. Length: 32.5 to 35.5 in.
Price: **$1,190.00**

BUSHMASTER 450 Bushmaster 20
Caliber: .450 Bushmaster. Snake Charmer muzzle brake, 20-inch barrel, 14-inch BFI free-float handguard, DM2S two-stage trigger, five-round aluminum magazine, fixed A2-style shoulder stock. BOAR version (2023) has Bushmaster Snake Charmer Muzzle Brake and 5-round stainless steel BFI .450 magazine.
Price: **$1,160.00**
Price: BOAR **$1,320.00**

CHRISTENSEN ARMS CA5FIVE6 RIFLE
Chambering: .223 Wylde. Forged aluminum receiver set and a black nitride-finished BCG matched with a Christensen Arms carbon-fiber-wrapped 16-in. 1:8-twist stainless barrel and a carbon-aluminum hybrid handguard. Add $150 for Cerakote finish. Weight: 6.3 lbs. Sub-MOA Guarantee on all Christensen rifles. FFT model has carbon-fiber handguard, add $200. Based in Gunnison, Utah.
Price: CA5five6 black anodized 5.56........................**$1,900.00**

CHRISTENSEN ARMS CA-15 G2 RIFLE
Chamberings: .223 Wylde, 6mm ARC. Custom-built AR-style rifle optimized for weight and accuracy. Features: Matched receiver set with contour-matching carbon-fiber handguard, black nitride-finished BCG, single-stage match-grade trigger assembly. 16-in. stainless-steel barrel, 1:8 twist. Weight: 5.8 lbs. with 16-in. carbon-fiber barrel, 1:7.5 twist.
Price: CA-15 G2 5.56 stainless steel barrel **$1,800.00**
Price: CA-15 G2 5.56 carbon-fiber barrel **$2,400.00**

CHRISTENSEN ARMS CA-10 G2 RIFLE
Chamberings: .308 Win. (18-in. barrel, 1:10 twist) and 6.5 CM (20-in. barrel 1:8 twist) is designed for larger calibers and longer shots. Features: Aerospace-grade carbon-fiber free-floating handguard, billet aluminum receiver set, M-LOK or KeyMod fitments. Carbon-fiber barrel only. Weight: 7.2 lbs.
Price: **$3,200.00**

CHRISTENSEN ARMS CA-10 DMR RIFLE
Chamberings: 6.5 CM (20- or 22-in. barrels, 1:8 twist) and .308 Win. (18- or 20-in. barrels, 1:10 twist). Long-range rifle with an aluminum receiver set, proprietary barrel nut, and aerospace-grade carbon-fiber handguard assembly. Comes with Christensen Arms carbon-fiber-wrapped barrel. Titanium side baffle brake, ⅝×24 threaded muzzle. Weight: 7.8 lbs.
Price: **$3,500.00**

CMMG RESOLUTE RIFLES
Calibers: .22 LR, 5.56 NATO, 5.7x28mm, 6mm ARC, 6.5 Grendel, .300 Blackout, .308 Win., 7.62x39mm, .350 Legend, 9mm Luger, .40 S&W, .45 ACP. The Mk4 is the carbine-length AR-15 direct-impingement platform. The Mk3 platform (AR-10) is based on the LR-308/DPMS Gen 1 high-pattern design. Pistol-caliber-carbine designations include MkG, MkGs, Mk9, Mk17, and Mk57. The Mk47 designation is for the 7.62x39mm chambering. Weight

for the 5.56 MK4 is 6.4 lbs.; length is 32.5 in. Add $150 for 5.7x28mm, 9mm; add $175 for Mk9 9mm with Colt-style SMG magazines.
Price: Resolute MK4 5.56x45mm NATO, 16.1 in. **$1,550.00**

CMMG ENDEAVOR RIFLES
Calibers: 5.56x45mm, 6.5 Creedmoor, .308 Win. Longer and heavier (18, 20, 24 in.) stainless barrels compared to Resolute line. Platforms: Mk3, Mk4. Lengths start at 37.8 in. for 18-in. barrel length, weight 7 lbs. Add $600 for 20-in. barrel; add $650 for 24-in. barrel.
Price: Endeavor MK4 5.56, 18 in. **$1,450.00**
Price: Endeavor MK3 6.5 CM, 20 in. **$1,950.00**
Price: Endeavor MK3 .308 Win., 24 in. **$1,900.00**

CMMG DISSENT RIFLES
Calibers: as listed above. Dissent models have side-folding stock with adjustable LOP and adjustable cheek riser. Forward non-reciprocating charging handle, M-LOK handguard, top Picatinny rail. Cerakote finish options. Introduced 2023.
Price: Dissent Mk4, 5.56, 16.1..**$2,200.00**

COLT LE6920 M4 CARBINE
Caliber: 5.56 NATO. Barrel: 16.1-in. chrome lined. Sights: Adjustable. Based on military M4. Direct gas/locking bolt operating system. Magpul MOE handguard, carbine stock, pistol grip, vertical grip.
Price: M4 Carbine...**$1,100.00**
Price: M4 Carbine Magpul.....................................**$1,200.00**

COLT M16A1 RETRO REISSUE
Caliber: 5.56 NATO. Classic design, unique triangular handguard, 20-inch pencil-profile chrome-lined barrel with a 1:12-inch twist, and recognizable carrying handle.
Price: **$2,500.00**

COLT XM177E2 RETRO CARBINE
Caliber: 5.56 NATO. Built to the Original Colt Model 629 specifications from the 1960s. 11.5-in. barrel with extended flash hider, vinyl-acetate coated aluminum buttstock reproduction, and U.S. Property-marked rollmarks.
Price: **$2,600.00**

DANIEL DEFENSE DD4 RIII RIFLE
Caliber: 5.56 NATO/.223. New ambidextrous DD4 lower and new 12.5-in. RIS III M-LOK rail system rather than Picatinny quad rail. Includes 6-bolt lock-up found on the RIS II, but with less weight. Ambidextrous GRIP-N-RIP Charging Handle. 16-in. cold-hammer-forged Government Profile barrel, mid-length gas system, CMV steel, 1:7 twist. Daniel Defense Flash Suppressor, 17-4 PH stainless steel, salt bath nitride finished. Bolt Carrier Group: M16 Profile, Mil-spec MP tested, chrome lined, properly staked gas key. Daniel Defense buttstock and pistol grip. Weight: 6.52 lbs. Length: 32 1/4 to 35 7/8 in. Introduced: Spring 2022, available 2023. Made in the USA.
Price: **$2,394.00**

DANIEL DEFENSE M4A1 RIII RIFLE
Caliber: 5.56 NATO/.223. Similar to DD4 RIII but with 14.5-in. M4 barrel

Prices given are believed to be accurate at time of publication however, many factors affect retail pricing so exact prices are not possible.

79ᵀᴴ EDITION, 2025 ⊕ **425**

and pinned and welded Daniel Defense flash suppressor. Comes in FDE and black colors. Weight: 6.39 lbs. Length: 31.5 to 34.75 in.

Price: **$2,394.00**

DANIEL DEFENSE DD5 RIFLES

Calibers: 6.5 CM, .260 Rem., 7.62x51mm/.308 Win. Capacity: 20-round Magpul PMAG. Barrel: 16, 18, 20 in. 5/8×24 tpi muzzle thread, S2W barrel profile, 1:11 twist. Stock: Daniel Defense buttstock. Sights: Full-length top rail. Trigger: Daniel Defense Mil-spec. Handguard: Daniel Defense DD5 Rail 15.0, 6061-T6 aluminum, M-LOK. Weight: ~8.3 lbs. Overall Length: 33.375 to 37 in. Features: Intermediate gas system, two-position adjustable gas block, DLC-coated bolt carrier group, cold hammer chrome-lined forged barrel, Mil-spec heavy phosphate coated. 4-Bolt Connection System, ambidextrous controls (bolt catch, magazine release, safety selector, furniture, GRIP-N-RIP charging handle). Daniel Defense Superior Suppression Device, 6-position Mil-spec 7075-T6 aluminum receiver extension. Daniel Defense pistol grip, accepts all SR-25 magazines. Add $460 for Hunter model.

Price: DD5V3 (.308 Win., 16 in.).....................................**$2,731.00**
Price: DD5V4 (6.5 CM, .308 Win. 18 in.) **$2,731.00**
Price: DD5V5 (6.5 CM, .260 Rem. 20 in.)..........................**$2,731.00**

DANIEL DEFENSE AR-15 RIFLES

Caliber: 5.56 NATO/.223., 6.8 SPC, .300 BLK. Non-NFA Barrels: 14.5, 16 or 18 in. Weight: 7.4 lbs. Lengths: 34.75 to 37.85 in. overall. Stock: Glass-filled polymer with SoftTouch overmolding. Sights: None. Features: Lower receiver is Mil-spec with enhanced and flared magazine well, QD swivel attachment point. Upper receiver has M4 feed ramps. Lower and upper CNC machined of 7075-T6 aluminum, hard coat anodized. Add $190 for Cerakote finishes added in 2023.

Price: DDM4V7 ....**$1,964.00**
Price: DDM4V7 Matte Black **$1,964.00**
Price: DDM4V7 Pro...**$2,468.00**
Price: DDM4V7 Pro Rattlecan...**$2,468.00**
Price: DDM4V9 ....**$2,075.00**
Price: DDM4 Hunter 6.8 18 ....**$2,211.00**
Price: DDM4ISR .300 Blackout 9-in. SBR **$3,562.00**
Price: MK12 ....**$2,457.00**
Price: M4A1 ....**$2,240.00**

DANIEL DEFENSE WPSM4A1 SIGNATURE SERIES RIFLE

Caliber: 5.56 NATO. Signature Series rifles designed by well-known names in firearms industry. The WPSM4A1 was designed by John Lovell of Warrior Poet Society. Heavy-duty RIS III rail, Holosun 515 GM, Unity FAST Micro Mount pinned and welded Surefire Warcomp. Radian Raptor charging handle, Radian Talon safety and Railscales components, OD Green Cerakote. Geissele SSA trigger, WPS Rifle sling, signed copy of the Warrior Poet Way, a custom challenge coin, matching hard case. Barrel: 14.5-in. M4 barrel profile. OAL: 31.5 to 34.5 in. Introduced 2024.

Price: **$3,000.00**

DEL-TON INC. AR-15 RIFLES

Chamberings: 5.56 NATO, .223 Wylde, 7.62x39. Del-Ton offers a complete line of AR-15-style modern sporting rifles. Dozens of variations and options. Product lines include Alpha, DT Scout, DT Sport Mod 2, Echo, Sierra, and SXT. Based in Elizabethtown, North Carolina.

Price: 5.56 models, 16, 20 in. barrels ....**$673.00–$918.00**
Price: Alpha 220H, 20 in. heavy profile barrel......................**$918.00**
Price: SXT Dark Earth, 16 in. LW barrel................................**$750.00**

DEL-TON INC. AR-10 RIFLES

Chambering: .308 Win. Echo optics-ready and Alpha sighted models. Upper and lower receivers: Forged 7075 T6 aluminum, integral triggerguard, 18-in. CMV 1x10 barrel, Magpul M-LOK standard length handguard, ERGO Sure Ambi grip, Magpul 20-rd. P-Mag.

Price: Alpha .308 M-LOK, 18 In. **$1,100.00**

DIAMONDBACK DB15 SERIES

Caliber: 5.56 NATO. Barrel: Diamondback Barrels 5.56, 16 in., Medium, 4150 CrMov, Black Nitride, 1:8 RH. Gas System: Carbine-Length. BCG: Shot-Peened, Magnetic Particle Inspected Mil Spec 8620 Carrier. Upper: A3 Flattop Forged 7075 T-6 Aluminum, T-Marked. Lower: 7075 T-6 Aluminum (DB-15 Carbon Lower). Handguard: 15 in. M-LOK Rail. Grip: MOE. Stock/Brace: MOE Carbine Stock. Magazine: Gen3 PMAG 30 Round. Sights: N/A. Muzzle Device: A2 Flash Hider (1/2x28). Trigger: Mil-Spec. Weight: 6.6 lbs. Overall Length: 32.5 to 35.75 in. Introduced 2012. Obsidian Series (2024) rifles have enhanced bolt catch, ambi safety selector and mag release; free-float anti-rotation M-LOK S-Rail with full Picatinny top rail and integrated QD Mounts.

Price: Carbon Series **$750.00**
Price: Obsidian Series...**$1,216.00**

DIAMONDBACK DB10 SERIES

Caliber: 6.5 Creedmoor, .308 Win. Barrel: Diamondback Barrels mid-length 16 in., light, 4150 CrMov, black nitride, 1:10 RH twist: Gas System: Mid-Length. BCG: Shot-Peened, Magnetic Particle Inspected Mil-spec 8620 Carrier. Upper: A3 flattop forged 7075 T-6 aluminum. Lower: Forged 7075 T-6 aluminum. Handguard: 15-in. M-LOK rail. Grip: MOE K Grip. Stock/Brace: MOE Carbine Stock. Magazine: Gen M3 PMAG 20 Rd. Muzzle Device: A2 .30 Cal Flash Hider [5/8x24]. Weight: 8.2 lbs. Length 31-1/8 in. to 33-3/4 in.

Price: DB10CCMLB .308 Win. **$1,146.00**
Price: DB1065CBGB 6.5 CM **$1,600.00**

DSARMS AR15 ZM4 5.56 RIFLES

Caliber: 5.56 NATO. Capacity: Magpul Custom G2 MOE 30-round magazine, black with flat dark earth ribs. Barrels: 14.7, 16, and 20 in., lightweight mid-length. 1:8 twist, M4 feed ramps on both barrel extension and upper receiver. Stock: B5 Systems Custom SOPMOD Stock. Weight: 6.9 lbs. Trigger: ALG Defense Advanced Combat Trigger. Overall Length: 33 to 35 in. Features: Premium match barrel machined from either 416-R stainless steel or 4150-11595 Mil-spec material, 5.56 match chamber. Enhanced A3M4 upper receiver, upgraded fire control group, ambidextrous selector switch and WarZ triggerguard, bolt catch and charging handle. Midwest Industries 15 in. Combat Series M-LOK free float handguard. Magpul Custom MIAD Modular Pistol Grip, flat dark earth with black two-tone. DSArms Enhanced FDE alloy triggerguard, SureFire Pro Comp (1/2x28 tpi).

Price: Flat Top Carbine...**$750.00**

DSARMS AR15 SERVICE SERIES

Caliber: 5.56 NATO. Capacity: ASC 30-round gray alloy magazine. Barrel: 14.5 in. with permanently affixed A2 bird cage flash hider for 16 in. barrel

Prices given are believed to be accurate at time of publication however, many factors affect retail pricing so exact prices are not possible.

O.A.L., or 20" A2 government profile rifle-length barrel. M4-profile, chrome-lined chamber and bore, 4150 - 11595E Mil-spec barrel steel, 1:7 twist. Stock: Mil-spec. M4 style, six-position Mil-spec buffer tube. Sights: Top rail segments. Forged front sight tower (F-Marked). Weight: 6.9 lbs. Features: Carbine-length gas system, M4 feed ramps on both barrel extension and upper receiver. Stainless-steel carbine-length gas tube, Knight's Armament Co. M4 RAS carbine-length handguard assembly. Knight's forward vertical grip. DSArms-forged A3M4 Mil-spec upper receiver, DSArms forged lower receiver, both hardcoat anodized per MIL-A-8625F, Type III, Class 2 finish. Mil-spec M16 complete bolt carrier group. Mil-spec A2-style pistol grip.
Price: **$1,200.00**

FN 15 DMR3 RIFLE
Caliber: 5.56 NATO. The Designated Marksman Rifle (DMR) includes 18-in. barrel, SureFire ProComp muzzle brake, and Geissele two-stage trigger in matte black anodize, flat dark earth (FDE) or tungsten gray Cerakote colors. Barrel: Hybrid profile, cold hammer-forged, chrome-lined, 1:8 twist. Made from FN's proprietary machine-gun-barrel steel. Rifle-length direct-impingement gas system with pinned low-profile gas block. Hodge Defense 14 5/8-inch aluminum handguard free-float barrel. Continuous MIL-STD Picatinny rail at 12 o'clock, multiple M-LOK attachment slots. Mil-spec lower receiver, M16-style bolt carrier group. Ergonomic pistol grip, six-position collapsible carbine stock, 30-rd. magazine, Radian Raptor-LT ambidextrous charging handle and Radian Talon ambidextrous safety selector. Length: 35.2 to 38.5 in. Weight: 7.4 lbs. Introduced May 2022.
Price: **$2,439.00**

FN 15 SERIES
Caliber: 5.56x45. Capacity: 20 or 30 rounds. Barrels: 16 in., 18 in., 20 in. Features: AR-style rifle/carbine series with most standard features and options.
Price: TAC3 Duty 16 in. **$1,700.00**
Price: TAC3 Carbine **$1,890.00**
Price: Guardian 16 in., 6.6 lbs. **$1,000.00**
Price: Military Collector M4 and M16 .... **$1,929.00**

FNH SCAR 16S NRCH
Caliber: 5.56mm/.223. Capacities: 10 or 30 rounds. Barrel: 16.25 in. Weight: 7.25 lbs. Lengths: 27.5–37.5 in. (extended stock). Stock: Telescoping, side-folding polymer. Adjustable cheekpiece, A2 style pistol grip. Sights: Adjustable folding front and rear. Features: Hard anodized aluminum receiver with four accessory rails. Ambidextrous safety and mag release. NRCH (non-reciprocating charging handle) added 2021.
Price: **$3,840.00**

FNH SCAR 17S NRCH
Caliber: 7.62x51 NATO/.308. Capacities: 10 or 30 rounds. Barrel: 16.25 in. Weight: 8 lbs. Lengths: 28.5–38.5 in. (extended stock). Features: Other features same as SCAR 16S NRCH. DMR version not NRCH, chambered in 6.5 CM.
Price: **$4,239.00**
Price: 17S DMR, 6.5 Creedmoor **$4,629.00**

FNH SCAR 20S NRCH
Caliber: 6.5 Creedmoor, 7.62x51mm. Capacities: 10. Barrel: 20 in. Weight: 11.2 lbs. Lengths: 41-42.8 in. (extended stock). Stock: Precision adjustable for LOP, adjustable cheek piece, Hogue rubber pistol grip with finger

grooves. Features: Hard anodized aluminum receiver with four accessory rails, two-stage match trigger. Other features same as 17S NRCH.
Price: **$5,000.00**

FOLDAR MOBETTA CONCEALED CARRY RIFLES
Caliber: 5.56 NATO, .223 Wylde chamber; .300 Blackout, 6.5 Grendel. Lower Receiver: FoldAR FLDR15. FoldAR's patented folding upper offers concealability and easy carry and transport. Folded Length: 17-5/8 in. Folded Width: 4.25 in. Quick-change barrel system, modular M-LOK handguard of three different lengths. Barrels: 9, 10.5, 12.5, 14.5 and 16 in., 4150 alloy steel, QPQ Melonite black nitride finish, 1:7 twist, A2 compensator, muzzle threaded 1/2"-28. Mil-Spec components: BCG, grip, trigger, carbine stock, and non-adjustable gas block (.750 diameter). Overall Length: 32-7/8 in. Weight: 6.15 lbs. Introduced 2023. Victor Marx Signature Series Limited Edition 2024 was a concealment configuration of 100 rifles, backpacks and optics.
Price: MoBetta Concealed Carry Rifle, 16 in. **$2,099.00**
Price: Victor Marx Signature Series **$3,033.00**

FOXTROT MIKE MIKE-15 GEN 2 RIFLE
Chambering: .223 Wylde for 5.56 NATO. FM-15 Gen 2 platform, direct impingement. Barrel: 16-in. lightweight 41V50 steel, black nitride finish. 1:8 twist, A2 flash hider, 1/2x28 muzzle thread. Mid-length gas system, 0.625-in. non-adjustable gas block. Weight: 6.0 lbs. Length: 34 in., 25.75 folded. Hand Guard: 15.5-in. M-LOK free float. Thril competition stock, Thril Rugged Tactical pistol grip. USGI Mil-Spec trigger.
Price: **$800.00**

FOXTROT MIKE RANCH RIFLE 15
Chamber: .223 Wylde. Ranch Rifle 15 lacks a pistol grip and uses a more traditionally styled WOOX Gladiatore 870 Stock instead. Introduced 2024.
Price: **$1,500.00**

FRANKLIN ARMORY F17-L
Caliber: .17 WSM rimfire. Capacity: One 10- or 20-round magazine. Barrel: 20 in. full contour, 1:9 RH twist. 11-degree target crown, ½-28 muzzle thread pitch. Stock: Magpul MOE. Sights: Optic ready 12 o'clock Picatinny rail. Weight: 8.9 lbs. Trigger: FN Combat Trigger, 4.75–7.75 lbs. Overall Length: 30.75 in. Features: Gas piston rimfire rifle, F17 Piston. Rotating locking bolt and piston design. 12-in. TML M-LOK Handguard/Upper, .17 WSN Salt Bath Nitride bolt carrier, Ergo Sure Grip. Libertas lower. Introduced 2014.
Price: **$1,829.00**

FRANKLIN ARMORY F17-X
Similar to F17-L model, but piston-driven function. Barrel: 16-in. M4 Contour. Sights: Fixed front & MBUS. Lower Receiver: FAI. Handguard/Upper: Magpul MOE SL M-LOK Gray. Stock: Magpul SL. Grip: Magpul K2. Stock: A2. Grip: A2. Weight: 6.7 lbs.
Price: **$1,490.00**

Prices given are believed to be accurate at time of publication however, many factors affect retail pricing so exact prices are not possible.

79TH EDITION, 2025 ⊕ **427**

FRANKLIN ARMORY BFSIII M4

Caliber: 5.56mm/.223. Capacities: 30 rounds. AR-type rifles and carbines offered with the BFSIII Binary Trigger. Barrel: 16 in., LTW Contour, 1:7 RH twist, A2 muzzle device. Stock: M4. Sights: Optics ready, 12 o'clock full-length Picatinny rail. Weight: NA. Trigger: BFSIII Binary Trigger. Overall Length: 32.5 to 35.5 in. Features: Standard charging handle, low-profile gas block, 15-in. FST Handguard/Upper, salt bath nitride bolt carrier, A2 Grip. FAI-15 lower.
Price: **$1,070**

FRANKLIN ARMORY M4-HTF R3

Caliber: .350 Legend. Capacity: One 10- or 20-round magazine. Barrel: 16 in. M4 Contour, 1:12 RH twist, Aura XTD muzzle device. Stock: B5 Bravo. Grip: B5. Handguard: 15 in. FSR. Sights: Optics ready 12 o'clock full-length Picatinny rail. Weight: NA. Trigger: BFSIII Binary Trigger or custom tuned. Overall Length: NA. Features: 350 Legend was designed for use in several American states that have specific regulations for deer hunting with straight-walled centerfire cartridges. It has the same rim diameter as a 5.56 case (.378 in.), so it can use the same bolt. Rounds will fit in a modified AR magazine. MFT EVOLV charging handle, mid-length gas system, low-profile gas block, salt bath nitride bolt carrier, FAI-15 lower.
Price: **$1,290.00**

FRANKLIN ARMORY LIBERTAS-L 16

Calibers: 5.56 NATO. Similar to other Franklin Armory offerings but with billet lower. Incorporates integrated ambidextrous, anti-rotational Quick Detach sling mounts. Textured Memory Index Point, enlarged and beveled magazine well, integral over-sized triggerguard. Front of the magazine well is also textured so it can be used as a grip for forward support. Carbine length, 6-position collapsible stock. Barrel: 16 in. M4 Contour 1:7 RH twist. Handguard: 15 in. FSR. Sights: Magpul MBUS. Stock: Magpul CTR. Grip: Ergo Ambi Sure. Add $110 for BFSIII trigger. Add $40 for 14.5-in. barrel with TRIUMVIR muzzle device pinned and welded.
Price: **$1,600.00**

FULTON ARMORY FAR-15 LEGACY RIFLE

Caliber: 5.56 NATO or .223 Rem. Several builds make up the Fulton Armory AR lineup, six with fixed stocks, and five with front sight posts. Legacy specs include the Upper Receiver: M16 Slick Side, with new A1 rear sight (forged, machined, anodized). Retro 601 charging handle. Parts: GI & True Mil Spec, GI Chrome M16/AR15 HPT/MPI Bolt with HD extractor spring, early slip ring. Barrel: 20 in. 1x12, "pencil" profile, match quality, chrome lined, .223/5.56 NATO hybrid match chamber. Handguard: New M16, triangular. Gas Block/Front Sight: Forged, with bayonet lug, taper pinned. Front Sight Post: A1, round. Muzzle Device: 3-prong flash suppressor. Lower Receiver: FA, with Accu-wedge (forged, machined, anodized, & Teflon coated per mil spec). Butt Stock: Fixed, A1 with A1 butt plate. Grip: A1. Trigger: Standard military, single-stage. Included accessories: FA 10-round magazine, OD cotton web sling, and owner's manual. Precision Guarantee: 1.5 MOA with Federal Gold Medal Match Ammunition. Weight: 6.75 lbs. Length: 39 in.
Price: **$1,600.00**

FULTON ARMORY FAR-15 A2 AND A4 SERVICE RIFLES

Similar to FAR-15 Legacy rifle, but with 20 in. barrel, 1x7, A2 Government Profile, match quality, chrome lined, .223/5.56 NATO Hybrid Match Chamber and 12 in. round A2 handguard with heat shields. A2 weight: 8.05 lbs. A4 lacks carrying handle and has a top receiver Picatinny rail.
Price: FAR-15 A2 .... **$1,525.00**
Price: FAR-15 A4 .... **$1,375.00**

FULTON ARMORY FAR-15 PEERLESS NM A4 SERVICE RIFLE

Similar to FAR-15 Legacy rifle, but with 20 in. 1x8 barrel, HBAR profile, match quality, stainless steel, .223/5.56 NATO hybrid match chamber. Handguard: 12 in., round A2, modified for float tube.
Price: **$1,875.00**

FULTON ARMORY FAR-308 GUARDIAN

Chambering: .308 AR M118 chamber. Upper Receiver: A3 style, numbered flat top with M4-style feed ramps. Lower Receiver: FAR-308, DPMS GEN 1 with enhanced triggerguard and bolt stop. Barrel: Criterion 20-in., 1x11 twist, chrome-lined, match grade. Handguard Float Tube: 15-in. Midwest Industries Combat Rail, M-LOK. Buttstock: Fixed, A1 with A2 buttplate. Grip: Ergo SureGrip, ambi. Trigger: Two-stage, non-adjustable, FA factory-tuned match, 4.5 lbs. Extensive options. Weight: 8 lbs. 13 oz. Length: 40.25 in. "SC" model has a side charging bolt carrier group with staked key.
Price: Guardian **$1,900.00**
Price: Guardian SC **$1,975.00**

GEISSELE AUTOMATICS SUPER DUTY RIFLE

Chamberings: 5.56 NATO. Features a Nanoweapon-coated Surefire Closed-Tine Warcomp mounted to a 16-in. mag-phosphate cold hammer-forged, chrome-lined Geissele barrel. Twist: 1:7 in. Gas system: Geissele Length, with Geissele Super Compact Gas Block. Trigger: SSA-E X with Lightning Bow trigger, a nanocoated, two-stage unit. BCG: Machined from mil-spec 8620 steel, properly torqued and staked chrome-lined gas key. Lower: Machined from 7075-T6 aluminum with Geissele's Ultra Duty Lower Parts Kit. Ambidextrous Super Configurable safety and Ultra Precision triggerguard. Mil-spec Geissele Buffer Tube with Super-42 in H2 buffer ensures this rifle is properly tuned out of the box. 15 MK16 Super Modular Rail mates to Super Duty Upper Receiver via a center aligning tab. Sights: None. Grips: Geissele Rifle Grip. Rails: 15 in. MK16 Super Modular. Stock: B5 Enhanced Sopmod. No magazine. Colors: Luna Black, DDC (Desert Dirt Color), ODG (OD Green). Add $225 for 14.5-in. barrel with Nanocoated Surefire Closed-Tine Flash Hider, pinned and welded.
Price: Super Duty **$2,350.00**
Price: Super Duty MOD1 .... **$2,325.00**

GEISSELE AUTOMATICS GFR

Chambering: 6mm ARC. Geissele Freedom Rifle (GFR). Barrel: 14.5, 18, 20 in., chrome-lined, precision machined, cold hammer forged. Geissele

Anti-Strike Super Compact Gas Block, GFR-E trigger. Nanoweapon coated 6mm ARC enhanced bolt carrier group, chrome-lined gas key with staked screws, advanced tool-steel cam pin, extended carrier rails, and 6mm ARC GFR Stressproof Bolt. GFR uppers have properly heat-treated stainless steel cam races. Ambidextrous Geissele Super Charging Handle, HUXWRX Flash Hider-QD 6MM ARC suppressor-ready muzzle device. Nanoweapon-coated HUXWRX Flash Hider-QD muzzle device. MK16 Super Modular Rail, Super 42 Buffer system. One eight-round Geissele 6mm ARC magazine. Introduced 2022.

Price: GFR Maritime Recon,18 in. **$3,400.00**
Price: GFR RECCE, 16 in. **$3,650.00**
Price: GFR Stratomatch, 20 in..**$3,700.00**

GEISSELE AUTOMATICS ALG DEFENSE EL JEFE RIFLE
Caliber: 5.56 NATO. Mil-Spec-class rifle with included sling and Warner & Swasey red-dot sight. ALG V3X hand guard, M-LOK slots. B5 Systems SOPMOD stock, Mil-Spec six-position buffer tube H1 buffer. ALG Defense Advanced Combat Trigger. Barrel: MIL-B-11595E chrome-moly steel, hard-chrome plating. Geissele 17–4 PH stainless steel gas block, Geissele extended mid-length gas tube, A2 flash hider. Warner & Swasey 3-MOA red-dot sight sits 1.54 in. above the bore's centerline.

Price: GFR Stratomatch, 20 in..**$1,200.00**

HECKLER & KOCH MODEL MR556A1
Caliber: .223 Remington/5.56 NATO. Capacity: 10+1. Barrel: 16.5 in. Weight: 8.9 lbs. Lengths: 33.9 to 37.68 in. Stock: Black synthetic adjustable. Features: Uses the gas piston system found on the HK 416 and G26, which does not introduce propellant gases and carbon fouling into the rifle's interior.

Price: **$3,500.00**

HECKLER & KOCH MODEL MR762A1
Caliber: 7.62x51mm/.308 Win. Otherwise, similar to Model MR556A1. Weight: 10 lbs. w/empty magazine. Lengths: 36 to 39.5 in. Features: Variety of optional sights are available. Stock has five adjustable positions.

Price: **$4,300.00**

HK-USA MR762A1 LONG RIFLE PACKAGE III
Caliber: 7.62x51mm. Capacity: 10- or 20-round magazines. Barrel: 16.5 in., four lands and grooves, right twist, 1:11. Stock: Fully adjustable G28 buttstock. Sights: Vortex Viper PSTII 3-15x44 FFP MRAD scope, base, mounts. Weight: 10.42 lbs. Trigger: Two-stage. Overall Length: 36.5 to 40.5 in. Features: MR762 semi-auto rifle with LaRue/Harris bipod, new long 14.7 in. Modular Rail System (MRS) handguard, Blue Force Gear sling and sling mount, one 10-round and one 20-round magazine, OTIS cleaning kit, HK multi-tool, and Pelican Model 1720 case.

Price: **$7,500.00**

IWI ZION Z-15
Caliber: 5.56 NATO. First M4 variant rifle from IWI US. Barrel: 16-in. 4150 Chrome Moly Vanadium HB, 1:8 twist, 6 RH grooves. Gas System: Mid-length direct impingement. Overall Length: 33–36.25 in. Weight: 6.9 lbs. without magazine. 15-in. free-float handguard, B5 Systems Stock and Grip. One 30-round Magpul PMAG. Manufactured and assembled at the IWI US facility in Middletown, Pennsylvania.

Price: **$950.00**

JP ENTERPRISES JP-15 SMALL-FRAME READY RIFLES
Caliber: .223/5.56 or .223 Wylde. Mil-spec forged 7075 receiver set with Magpul MOE triggerguard. Barrel: 16- or 18-in. JP Supermatch 416R barrel, 1:8 twist, black Teflon finish. JP tactical compensator. Hogue Overmolded buttstock, A2 grip, Rapid Configuration hand guard, rifle length, with JPHG-SM QD sling mount. JP Full Mass Operating System with EnhancedBolt assembly. JP LE Enhanced Reliability Fire Control Package, 4.0 to 4.5 lbs. trigger pull weight. Models include Patrol Rifle, Essentials Carbine, Professional Rifle, and Compact Professional Rifle.

Price: ....**$1,650.00–$2,400.00**

JP ENTERPRISES JP-15 LARGE-FRAME READY RIFLE
Caliber: 6.5 Creedmoor, .308 Win. Similar set-up to JP-15 Small-Frame Ready Rifles. 16-in. barrel for .308; 22 in. for 6.5 Creedmoor.

Price: .308 Win. Professional Rifle.....................................**$4,060.00**
Price: 6.5 Creedmoor LR Suppressor Ready **$4,180.00**

JP ENTERPRISES LRP-07 SERIES
Calibers: .308 Win, 6.5 Creedmoor, 6mm Creedmoor. Barrels: 14.5, 16, 18, 20 in., polished stainless with compensator or Proof Research carbon fiber. Every component can be selected in online rifle builder. Receiver choices are LRI-20 side-charge upper receiver with integral hand guard nut (compatible with any existing LRP-07 side-charge lower receiver) or LTI-23, upgraded version of LTC-19 top-charging design that will mate to any DPMS LR-308-pattern lower receiver. Introduced 2019.

Price: Base price...**$3,500.00**

JP ENTERPRISES JP-15 PROFESSIONAL RIFLE
Calibers: .223, 6.5 Grendel, .300 Blackout, .22 LR. Barrels: 18 or 24 in. Buttstock: Synthetic modified thumbhole or laminate thumbhole. Grip: Hogue Pistol grip. Basic AR-type general-purpose rifle with numerous online-ordering options.

Price: Base Price...**$2,100.00**

JP ENTERPRISES ASF-20 AMBIDEXTROUS RIFLE
Caliber: .223/5.56, 6.5 Grendel, .300 AAC Blackout, .22 LR. Combines A-DAC (Ambidextrous Dual Action Catch) system from Radian Weapons with JP Ambi Mag Release. Compatible with any mil-spec pattern upper receiver. Choice of JP Low Mass Operating System, JP Full Mass Operating System, or JP Variable Mass Operating System. Trigger: JP Fire Control Package, 3.0 to 5.0 lbs. Ambi lower receiver introduced 2020.

Price: **$2,500.00**

KEL-TEC RFB
Caliber: 7.62 NATO/.308. 20-round FAL-type magazine. Barrel: 18 in. with threaded muzzle, A2-style flash hider. Weight: 8 lbs. RFB stands for Rifle Forward-ejecting Bullpup. Features: A bullpup short-stroke gas-piston-operated carbine with ambidextrous controls, reversible operating handle, Mil-Spec Picatinny rail. Length: 27.5 in. RFB Hunter has a 24-in. barrel, add $200. Length: 32.5 in.

Price: RFB **$1,800.00**

KEL-TEC SU-16 SERIES

Caliber: 5.56 NATO/.223. Capacity: 10-round magazine. Barrels: 16 or 18.5 in. Minimum length: folded 24.9 in.; overall, 35.9 in. Weights: 4.5 to 5 lbs. Magazine storage stock holds two proprietary 10-round magazines. The forend covers an 18.5-in. barrel and doubles as a bipod. Adjustable sights and an integrated Picatinny-style top rail. Offered in several rifle, carbine, and SBR variations with A, B, C, CA, D9, D12, and E designations. Add $417 for D9 and D12 models. Add $140 for E gas-piston model, which has a threaded muzzle and six-position stock.
Price: **$575.00**

KNIGHTS ARMAMENT CO. SR-15 MOD 2

Caliber: 5.56mm NATO. Barrel: 14.5, 16, 18 in. Chrome-lined mil-spec, proprietary mid-length gas system. Free-floated, hammer forged, 1:7 twist. E3 round-lug bolt design; ambidextrous bolt release, selector, and magazine release. M-LOK handguard. Drop-in two-stage trigger. 3-Prong Flash Eliminator. Models: Carbine (14.5-in. barrel, 6.3 lbs.); MOD 2 M-LOK (16-in. barrel, 6.55 lbs.); LPR (18-in. barrel, 7.4 lbs.). Length: 33 to 36.5 in.
Price: **$2,910.00**

KNIGHTS ARMAMENT CO. SR-25 E2 COMBAT CARBINE

Caliber: 7.62mm NATO/.308 Win. Ambidextrous bolt release, selector, and magazine release. Drop-in 2-stage trigger, 7.62 QDC flash suppressor. Barrel: 16 in., hammer-forged, chrome-lined, 1:10 twist, 5R cut. M-LOK handguard. Weight: 8.4 lbs. Length: 35.75–39.5 in. Add $875 for E2 PC variant.
Price: **$4,900.00**

LARUE TACTICAL PREDATOBR 5.56 RIFLE

Caliber: 5.56 NATO. Barrels: 16.1, 18, or 20 in.; 1/8 twist rate; muzzles threaded 1/2x28. Weights: 7.5 to 9.25 lbs. Manufacturer of several models of AR-style rifles and carbines. Many AR-type options available. Hybrid between OBR and PredatAR 5.56x45 Rifles. May be broken down and stored into the optional Rollup Bag and Toolbox. Handguard has locking stainless-steel QD lever system to slide off the upper assembly in seconds. Barrel can be removed with supplied wrench, no need to remove the gas tube, gas block, or muzzle device. No conventional AR barrel nut; handguard bolts directly to the proprietary upper receiver, free-floating barrel. Zero-MOA upper rail. Adjustable Port Selector Technology gas block for sound suppressor use. LaRue Tactical 6-position Retract Action Trigger (R.A.T.) stock, A-PEG grip. Introduced 2012. Made in the USA.
Price: **$3,200.00**

LARUE TACTICAL PREDATOBR 7.62 RIFLE

Caliber: 7.62 NATO. Barrels: 16.1, 18, or 20 in.; 1/8 twist rate; muzzles threaded 5/8x24. Weights: 7.5 to 9.25 lbs. Chambering in 6.5 Creedmoor has 20 in.; 1:7.5 twist.
Price: **$4,300.00**

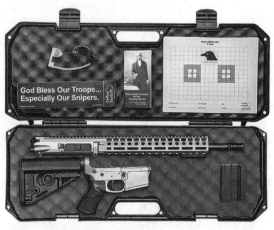

LARUE TACTICAL 16.1 IN. BLACK AND TAN 5.56

Caliber: 5.56 NATO, 6.5 Grendel. Barrels: 16.1, 18 in., 1:8 twist rate; medium-weight contour, mid-length gas tube, M4 Feed Ramps, and 1/2x28 threaded muzzle. CNC machined LaRue Billet Match Grade Upper mated to LaRue Billet. Full-floating upper handguard with M-LOK attach points, LaRue MBT trigger. LaRue Rat Stock, machined buffer tube, birdcage flash hider installed. Comes in compact high-impact-polymer case for easy and discreet carry.
Price: **$2,500.00**

LEWIS MACHINE & TOOL STANDARD PATROL MODEL RIFLES

Caliber: 5.56 NATO/.223. Direct impingement. Features chrome-moly-vanadium 1:7-in. RH twist cryogenically treated barrel and Defender semi-auto lower receiver with six-position Gen 2 M4 or SOPMOD stock. Offered in four lengths: 10.5-, 14.5-, and 16-in. carbine assemblies and 20-in. rifle. Meet current Mil-Spec and STANAG requirements. Made in the USA.
Price: SPM **$2,000.00**

LEWIS MACHINE & TOOL DEFENDER SERIES

Calibers: 5.56 NATO/.223; 7.62 NATO/.308 Win. Come with LMT Monolithic Rail Platform, MRP upper receivers, mil-spec lower. Lacks ambidextrous controls of MARS system. S-A bolt carrier group, Defender lower receiver. 14.5-in. Picatinny top rail, M-LOK-compatible attachment points on other rail faces. Low-profile gas block with straight gas tube; textured grip, M4-style stock, and dry-film-lubricant-coated extension tube.
Price: DEFENDER-L 5.56 16 in. **$2,200.00**
Price: DEFENDER-H 7.62 16 in. **$2,900.00**

LEWIS MACHINE & TOOL MARS RIFLES

Calibers: 5.56 NATO/.223; 7.62 NATO/.308 Win., 6.5 Creedmoor. Modular Ambidextrous Rifle System (MARS) features ambi safety selector, mag-release button, bolt release, and bolt catch. Monolithic Rail Platform upper receiver, ambidextrous charging handle. S-A bolt carrier group. MARS-L has 16-in. 5.56x45 (.223) chrome-lined 1:7 RH twist barrel. Other models include MRP, Quad, Piston, and PDW (10.5-in. barrel). MARS-H has 16-in. 7.62 NATO chrome-lined 1:10 RH twist barrel. Other models include Battle Rifle (13.5-in. lightweight barrel w/pinned LMT 3-prong flash hider),

DMR (with 20-in. 1:11.25 RH twist 5R cut barrel), and 6.5 DMR (20-in. 6.5 Creedmoor stainless-steel 1:8 RH twist barrel).
Price: MARS-L 5.56 ....**$2,700.00**
Price: MARS-H 7.62 ....**$4,100.00**
Price: MARS-H 6.5 DMR **$4,100.00**

LWRC INTERNATIONAL IC-SPR RIFLE
Caliber: 5.56 NATO. Capacity: Magpul PMAG 5.56. Barrel: 14.7, 16.1 in.; 1:7 in. RH twist, 1/2x28 muzzle threads. Cold hammer forged, spiral fluted, NiCorr treated. Stock: LWRC adjustable compact stock. Sights: Low-profile flip-up Skirmish Sights. Weight: 7.0 lbs., 7.3 lbs. In the series, IC stands for Individual Carbine. Add $110 for Billet version.
Price: REPR MKII...**$2,590.00**

LWRC INTERNATIONAL IC-PSD
Caliber: 5.56 NATO. Barrel: 8.5 in. Capacity: Magpul PMAG 30-round magazine. Stock: LWRC adjustable compact stock. Sights: Low-profile, flip-up Skirmish Sights. Weight: 5.9 lbs. Trigger: LWRC Enhanced Fire Control Group. Overall Length: 25-28 in. Features: Personal Security Detail NFA item. LWRCI Monoforge upper receiver with modular 7-in. rail system. Nickel-boron coated bolt carrier, LWRCI High Efficiency 4-Prong Flash Hider.
Price: **$2,590.00**

LWRC INTERNATIONAL SIX8
Caliber: 6.8 SPC II. Capacity: Magpul 20 Round PMAG. Barrel: 10.5, 12.7, 14.7, 16.1 in.; 1:10 RH twist, 5/8x24 muzzle threads. Cold hammer forged, spiral fluted, NiCorr treated. Stock: LWRC adjustable compact stock. Grip: Magpul MOE+. Sights: Low-profile flip-up Skirmish Sights. Weight: 6.5 lbs. Trigger: LWRC Enhanced Fire Control Group. Overall Length: 32-35.25 in. Features: LWRCI proprietary upper and lower receivers optimized for 6.8 SPC II cartridge; adjustable 2-position gas block, Birdcage (A2) Flash Hider; 12-in. user-configurable rail system; ambidextrous charging handle and lower receiver. SIX8 PMAG is slightly wider, with stronger walls and red follower. Add $165 for non-black colors. PSD NFA model has 8.5-in. barrel, 21.25 in. OAL. 5.9 lbs. Razorback II model has hog engraving on magwell. Add $165 for FDE, OD Green, Patriot Brown, and Tungsten Gray colors.
Price: SIX8-A5 ....**$2,865.00**

LWRC INTERNATIONAL REPR MKII
Caliber: 6.5 Creedmoor, 7.62 NATO. Rapid Engagement Precision Rifle. Capacity: Magpul 20 Round PMAG. Barrel: 12.7, 16.1, 20, and 22 in. stainless steel. 1:8 RH twist, 5/8x24 muzzle threads. Stock: Magpul PRS. Grip: Magpul MOE+. Sights: Low-profile flip-up Skirmish Sights. Weight: 10.5 lbs. Trigger: Geissele SSA-E 2-Stage Precision. Overall Length: 43.5 in. Non-reciprocating side charging handle, 20-position tunable gas block, short-stroke gas piston system, Monoforge upper receiver with integrated rail base, removable top rail design, removable barrel, fully ambidextrous lower receiver controls including bolt catch and release, magazine release, and safety selector. LWRCI Advanced Triggerguard, Skirmish Back-Up Iron Sights, Enhanced 4-port Ultra Static muzzle brake. Add $560 for Proof carbon-fiber barrel.
Price: REPR MKII...**$4,485.00**

MIDWEST INDUSTRIES COMBAT RIFLES
Caliber: 5.56 NATO/.223 Rem., .223 Wylde. Barrels: 16, 18, 20 in. Upper receiver: Forged 7075 T6 aluminum, M16/M4 specs, M4 feed ramps, hardcoat anodized Mil 8625 Type-3 Class-2 Finish, .250 takedown pins. MI M16 bolt carrier group, MI-CRM12.625 Combat series handguard, M-LOK compatible. Criterion barrels, mid-Length hybrid profile, 1:8 twist, .223 Wylde chamber, chrome-lined, .625 diameter. A2 flash hider. Lower receiver: Receiver rear takedown pin detent hole threaded for a 4-40 set screw, Mil-Spec-diameter buffer tube. Magpul CTR buttstock, MOE grip, MOE triggerguard. Heavy-duty quick-detach end plate. Lightweight model has MI-ULW14 handguard, M-LOK compatible; titanium barrel nut, screws installed for maximum weight savings;

lightweight Criterion 16-in. barrel. Weight: ~5 lbs. 12 oz.
Price: 16 in. **$1,495.00**
Price: 16 in. Ultra Lightweight, M-LOK **$1,555.00**
Price: 18 in. **$1,300.00**
Price: 20 in. **$1,500.00**

MIDWEST INDUSTRIES MI .308 RIFLES
Caliber: .308 Win. Capacity: (1) Magpul 10 round; accepts SR-25 pattern magazines. Barrel: 16, 18 in.; Criterion 1:10 twist, stainless-nitride finish. Upper/Lower Receivers: Forged 7075 aluminum. Stock: Magpul Gen 3 PRS buttstock. Grip: Magpul MOE. Sights: Optics-ready top rail. Weight: 8.2 lbs. for MI-10F-16M. Features: Midwest Industries .308 Bolt carrier group, 12-in. M-LOK handguard, two-chamber enhanced muzzle brake, mid-length gas system .750-in. gas block, MI-HDEP heavy-duty quick-detach end plate. Add $50 for 18-in. Criterion barrel. Introduced 2015.
Price: **$1,700.00**
Price: Nitride finish, 16 in., M-LOK **$1,500.00**

MIDWEST INDUSTRIES MI TACTICAL RESPONSE RIFLE
Caliber: 5.56 NATO/.223 Rem. Weight: 6.25 lbs. Outfitted with Magpul CTR Stock, MOE grip, MOE triggerguard, heavy duty quick detach end plate MI-HDEP, and has Custom Tactical Response logo laser engraved on receiver. 13.5-in. Night Fighter Handguard, M-LOK compatible. Barrel: 16 in., 1:8 twist. Weight: 6.5 lbs.
Price: **$1,500.00**

MITCHELL DEFENSE STREET LEGAL RAT DOG PCC
Caliber: 9mm. Barrel: 16-in. straight profile, 4150 CMV steel. A2 birdcage, 1:10 twist. Enhanced feed ramp, blowback operated. 15-in. 6061 T6 aluminum handguard. Offset M-LOK slots at 3, 6, and 9 o'clock. Full-length Picatinny top rail. Front and rear anti-rotational QD points on both sides. Established 2019. Veteran-owned. Based in Glenside, Pennsylvania.
Price: **$1,900.00**

MITCHELL DEFENSE DOC MD-15 RIFLES
Chambers: 5.56 NATO/.223 Rem., .223 Wylde, 6 ARC, 300 BLK. 5.56 Barrel: 16 in., 1:7 twist, or or 16-in. 1:8 223 Wylde Hanson profile stainless steel. 6 ARC 18 in. 1:7.5 twist Proof Research full profile. Thermal fit barrel, precision billet upper with flat barrel seat, ArmorLube BCG. Proprietary buffer system with flat wire technology. Lower receiver has right-side bolt release, flared mag well, E series Cerakote finish. GWOT (Global War On Terror) has 16 in. full-profile barrel. SOIDC (Special Operation independent Duty Corpsman) has Proof Research carbon-fiber-wrapped barrel.
Price: GWOT5.56 16 ....**$2,000**
Price: SOIDC 5.56 16 ....**$3,050**

MITCHELL DEFENSE PIPE HITTER RIFLES
Chambers: .308 Win., 6.5 CM, 8.6 BLK. 16, 20 in. barrels.
Price: **$3,900**

Prices given are believed to be accurate at time of publication however, many factors affect retail pricing so exact prices are not possible.

79TH EDITION, 2025 ✛ **431**

NEMO ARMS BATTLE-LIGHT RIFLES

Calibers: .22 LR, .22 ARC, 5.56 NATO/.223 Rem., .223 Wylde, .224 Valkyrie, 6mm ARC, 6.5 Grendel, 7.62x39, .300 BLK. NEMO (New Evolution Military Ordnance) Arms acquired 2A Armament in March 2023. Based in Caldwell, Idaho. NEMO will honor all 2A Armament warranties. Built to order. Nickel boron-coated bolt carrier group. Receivers: Small-frame NEMO matched billet upper and lower receiver set, 7075-T6 aluminum with full ambi (safety, mag and bolt release). Handguard / Forearm: 15-in. 6061 extruded aluminum, M-LOK modular rail. Heat-dissipating barrel nut, 7075-T6 aluminum. Bolt: High-pressure bolt 9310 steel. Heat treated, cryo'd, shot-peened, MPI. Battle-Light SYN-COR is integrally suppressed. Short-stroke piston-driven gas system. Pinned suppressor sleeve keeps rifle NFA/ATF compliant as a rifle, not SBR. 11.5" barrel, 1:8 twist; 416 stainless steel. Overall Length: 35.5 in. Weight: 8 lbs. Battle-Light 22 ARC Steel (2024) has 20-in. barrel, 8.4 lbs. Battle-Light Carbon models have Proof Research carbon-fiber-wrapped barrels. Weight: 7.54 lbs. The Battle-Light .22 LR has 16-in. barrel, 31-in. OAL. 8 lbs.

Price: SYNCOR-556 5.56mm NATO Rifle **$3,700.00**
Price: Battle-Light .22 ARC Steel **$2,550.00**
Price: Battle-Light 6.5 Grendel Carbon **$3,300.00**
Price: Battle-Light 6.5 Grendel Steel **$2,750.00**
Price: Battle-Light AK **$2,450.00**
Price: Battle-Light 22LR **$2,100.00**

NEMO ARMS OMEN SERIES

Caliber: .300 Win. Mag. Magnum frame variant. Billet matched receiver set and nickel boron high pressure, side-charging bolt to patented recoil-reduction bolt, bolt carrier group, and roller bearing cam pin. Introduced 2016. Watchman has 24-in. Proof Research carbon-fiber barrel. 1:8 twist. 10.2 lbs. Match 3.0 has Bartlein-blank 22-in. steel barrel; Magpul PRS rifle stock. Recon has 18-in. 416R stainless steel barrel, 1:8 twist 5R rifling, Bartlein blank. 10.5 lbs. Recon Lite has 18-in. Proof Research carbon-fiber barrel, Magpul CTR stock. 8.75 lbs. M-210 is no-frills option with steel takedown pins and compensator, fixed Magpul rifle stock, standard safety, CMC trigger. 20-in. barrel, 10.2 lbs. Woodsman has 20-in. Proof Research carbon-fiber barrel, Magpul PRS Lite adjustable stock, needle-screw adjustable gas block. 44-in. OAL; 9.25 lbs.

Price: Watchman **$6,200.00**
Price: Match 3.0 .... **$5,100.00**
Price: Recon **$4,900.00**
Price: Recon Lite **$5,790.00**
Price: M-210 .... **$3,900.00**
Price: Woodsman **$5,990.00**

NEMO ARMS XO RIFLES

Calibers: 6.5 Creedmoor, .260 Remington, .308 Win. Common features of Executive Order rifles include Bartlein-blank stainless-steel barrels or Proof Research carbon-fiber-wrapped barrels in 16- or 20-in. barrels. Geissele Super Dynamic Enhanced (SD-E) two-stage trigger. NEMO patented recoil-reducing bolt carrier. XO Carbon Exclusive is 38.5 in. long, 8.2 lbs. XO Steel 16 carbine has 16-in. barrel, 34.25-in. long, 8.2 lbs.

Price: XO Steel 16 .... **$3,625.00**
Price: XO Steel 20 .... **$3,800.00**
Price: XO Steel 6.5 Creedmoor, 22-in. barrel **$3,800.00**
Price: XO Carbon. **$4,300.00**

NOVESKE RIFLEWORKS 4th GEN RIFLES

Calibers: 5.56 NATO. Barrels: Stainless steel cold hammer forged, muzzle thread pitch 1/2×28. Twist: 1:7. Low-profile adjustable gas block, direct impingement. PDW-style collapsible stock. M-LOK free-float handguard, Magpul MBUS PRO folding sights, and a Geissele Super Badass charging handle. Full-length Picatinny rail, ambidextrous safety selector. Colors: Armor Black, Bazooka Green, FDE, Sniper Grey, Tiger Eye.

Price: 14.5-in. Afghan **$3,050.00**
Price: 16-in. Recon **$3,100.00**
Price: 17-in. Rival.. **$3,350.00**
Price: 18-in. SPR **$3,150.00**

NOVESKE RIFLEWORKS CHAINSAW RIFLE

Caliber: 5.56 NATO/.223 Rem. Noveske's forged product offering based on a hybrid of Gen 1 and Gen 4 designs. Barrel: 16 in. 416R stainless, 1:7 twist. Hand-polished Noveske Match Chamber, mid-length gas tube system. Noveske marked gas block: Low profile, .750 in. journal, pinned to barrel. M4 barrel extension w/extended hand-polished feed ramps, ½x28 muzzle threads with an A2 birdcage flash hider. Noveske Chainsaw forged upper receiver w/extended feed ramps. Radian Raptor LT charging handle. Phosphate-coated bolt carrier, full auto compatible, chrome-lined carrier bore and key. Properly staked grade 8 American made gas key bolts. Phosphate bolt made from Carpenter 158 heat-treated steel, MPI tested. GEN 4 NSR-15 (M-LOK) free floating handguard. Flared magazine well. Magpul enhanced aluminum triggerguard. ALG Defense Advanced Combat Trigger. Stock: Magpul MOE SL. Grip: Magpul MOE K2. Length collapsed: 35.25 in. 6.8 lbs. One 30-rd Gen 3 PMAG. Introduced 2022.

Price: **$1,975.00**

PALMETTO STATE ARMORY AR-15 RIFLE

Chamber: 5.56 NATO. Barrel: 16 or 20 in. 4150V Chrome Moly Vanadium Steel, Nitride finish. Barrel Profile: A2 Style. Twist Rate: 1:7 in. M4 extension. Mid-length gas system, low-profile .750-in. gas block. Upper Receiver Style: M4 flat top with feed ramps. Handguard: PSA 13.5 in. Lightweight M-LOK Free Float Rail. Bolt Steel: Carpenter 158. Bolt Carrier Steel: 8620. Staked gas key. PSA AR-15 Enhanced Polished Trigger (EPT). Mil-Spec buffer tube. Magpul MOE Carbine 6-position collapsible stock. (1) 30-round magazine (where available by law). Backup Sights: Magpul MBUS. Length: 32 in.

Price: PSA PA-15 16 in. M4 Classic Black **$470.00**
Price: PSA PA-15 16 in. SS M4 A2 Mid-Length **$520.00**
Price: PSA PA-15 16 in. Premium Classic **$900.00**

PALMETTO STATE ARMORY GEN 3 PA-10

Caliber: 6.5 Creedmoor, .308 Win. Barrels: 16, 18 or 20 in., stainless steel, adjustable gas block. Buttstock: PSA Classic M4 Stock, Black 6-position adjustable. Handguards: PSA Classic Polymer Mid-length Handguard, Keymod or M-LOK compatible free-floated. 38 models in 2024.

Price: **$850.00**

PALMETTO STATE ARMORY H&R M16A1

Caliber: 5.56 NATO. Copy of the gas-operated semi-automatic M16A1

Prices given are believed to be accurate at time of publication however, many factors affect retail pricing so exact prices are not possible.

with a 20-in. barrel. Harrington & Richardson was one of only four manufacturers to have made an official M16 variant for the U.S. military. Fixed synthetic stock, A2 carry handle receiver, smooth rifle-length handguard, A2 front sight. Includes sling swivels, 20-round magazine.
Price: **$1,199.00**

PALMETTO STATE ARMORY SABRE MIL-SPEC

Chamber: 5.56 NATO. Barrel: 16-in. 4150V Nitride, 1:7 twist, M4 barrel extension. Mid-length gas system. Has PSA 15-in. Sabre Lock Up Rail and Sabre Compensator muzzle device. Upper: Forged 7075-T6 A3 AR Mil-Spec upper, hardcoat anodized black and T-marked engraved. Bolt Carrier Group: Father's of Freedom BCG by Microbest. Lower: Sabre-15 lower with FDE B5 Bravo stock and grip. FDE Cerakote finish. Marked multi-caliber. Comes Standard with Springco Buffer Spring, Battle Arms Development Pivot/Takedown Pins, Hiperfire RBT Trigger, JP Reduced Power Springs, and Anti-Walk Pins. Introduced 2023.
Price: **$850.00**

PATRIOT ORDNANCE FACTORY MINUTEMAN RIFLE

Caliber: 5.56 NATO, .300 BLK. Direct Impingement. Nitride heat-treated barrel, 16.5 in., 1:8 RH twist 5R for 5.56; 1:10 RH twist 5R for .300 BLK. Features: Rear QD ambidextrous sling swivel plate, anti-tilt buffer tube, ambidextrous Strike Eagle charging handle. 3.5-lbs. straight match-grade trigger. Mid-length gas system. 6.2 lbs. 34 in. length. Introduced 2019. Add $67 for 13.75-in. barrel or .300 BLK. Add $134 for Patriot Brown or Tungsten finishes.
Price: **$1,613.00**
Price: .300 BLK..**$1,663.00**

PATRIOT ORDNANCE FACTORY P415 EDGE

Caliber: 5.56 NATO, .300 BLK. Gas-piston operation. Barrel: 16.5 in. Rail length: 14.5 in. Weight: 7 lbs. Collapsed length: 34 in. E2 Extraction Technology. Gen4 lower receiver, ambidextrous fire controls, modular free-floating rail platform, redesigned handguard. Add $134 for Burnt Bronze or Tungsten finishes. Introduced 2002. .300 BLK added 2023.
Price: **$2,150.00**

PATRIOT ORDNANCE FACTORY PRESCOTT

Caliber: 6mm CM, 6.5 CM. Built on Rogue platform. Weight: 7 lbs. Barrel: 20 in. Collapsed length: 41 in. Introduced 2021. Add $134 for Patriot Brown or Olive Drab finishes.
Price: **$2,285.00**

PATRIOT ORDNANCE FACTORY ROGUE

Caliber: 7.62x51mm NATO (.308 Win.). Capacity: one Magpul 20-round magazine. Barrel: 13.75 (added 2023, pinned & welded for 16.1 barrel length), 16.5 in., 1:8 twist, 5/8x24 tpi muzzle threads, match-grade stainless steel, Micro-B muzzle brake. Stock: Mission First Tactical. Sights: None, optics ready with top Picatinny rail. Weight: 5.9 lbs. Trigger: 4.5-lbs. POFUSA drop-in trigger system with KNS anti-walk pins. Length: 34 in. Roller cam pin with NP3-coated roller head. Introduced 2020. Add $134 for Patriot Brown or Olive Drab finishes. Add $174 for 13.75-in. barrel.
Price: **$2,097.00**

PATRIOT ORDNANCE FACTORY REVOLUTION DI

Caliber: 7.62x51mm NATO (.308 Win.) or 6.5 Creedmoor. Similar to PD Revolution, but with direct-impingement operation, 9-position adjustable Dictator gas block and Renegade rail. Weight: 6.8 lbs. Barrel: 16.5 in. Gen 4 ambi lower receiver. Add $134 for Burnt Bronze or Tungsten finishes. Introduced 2019.
Price: **$2,769.00**

PATRIOT ORDNANCE FACTORY WONDER RIFLE

Caliber: 5.56 NATO, .300 BLK. Direct impingement. Barrel: 13.75 (added 2023, pinned & welded for 16.1 barrel length), 16.5 in. Match-grade Nitride heat-treated Puritan barrel, 1:8 twist, 1/2x28 barrel threads. Lightweight carbine with some upgrades. Ambidextrous rear sling mount, Renegade Rail with heat sink barrel nut, DI bolt carrier group with Roller Cam Pin, single-stage straight match-grade trigger, Strike Eagle Ambi Charging Handle, Micro B single-port muzzle brake. Weight: 6.18 lbs. Length: 3 in. Introduced 2019. Add $67 for 13.75-in. barrel or .300 BLK.
Price: **$1,775.00**

PRIMARY WEAPONS SYSTEMS UXR

Caliber: .300 BLK (2024). .223 Wylde, .308 Win. Ambidextrous receiver. Folding buttstock with cheek and LOP adjustments, configurable to left- or right-side folding. Mounts on 1913 Picatinny rail attached to trigger housing. 3-position adjustable gas system with dedicated suppressor setting. Other features: 14.5-in. 1:6 twist barrel with pinned and welded PWS FRC Compensator, M-LOK handguard. Compatible with Rearden-type suppressor mounts. Weight: 6.8 lbs. Formed in 2008, based in Boise, Idaho. PWS was purchased by Vigilant Gear, LLC. in 2022.
Price: **$2,650.00**

RED ARROW WEAPONS RIFLES

Caliber: 5.56 NATO (2021), 6.5 CM (2021), .300 BLK (2020), .308 Win. (2020), .350 Legend (2023). Barrels: 16, 18, 20 in. free-floated Melonite-coated 4150 chrome-moly barrel, 1:8 twist, DB15 556 Muzzle Brake, threaded 5/8x24. Stainless barrels Red accents on black anodized hardcoat finish. CMC 2.5-lb single-stage trigger, pistol-length gas system, Magpul CTR stock, Magpul K2+ grip, M-LOK forend. Length: 32.5 to 36.25 in. Weight: 6.9 lbs. Handguard: 15-in. RAW M-LOK Battle Rail. Ambidextrous safety selector, MagPul K2+ Grip, MagPul CTR Stock, Magpul P-Mag 30 rd. Color and other options available. Introduced: 2022. Based in Fork Union, Virginia.
Price: 5.56, 16 in. CMV, Raw S rail..**$900.00**
Price: .223/5.56, 16 in. CMV, M-LOK..**$1,397.00**
Price: 6.5 CM, 22 in. stainless fluted, M-LOK..**$1,850.00**
Price: .308 Win., 18 in. stainless fluted..**$1,690.00**
Price: .350 Legend, 16 in. CMV..**$1,407.00**

ROCK RIVER ARMS ASCENDANT ATH SERIES

Caliber: .223 Wylde, .350 Legend, .450 Bushmaster. All Terrain Hunter (ATH). Length: 38.125 in. (collapsed). Weight: 9.4 lbs. Barrel: 18.0-in. 416R fluted stainless steel, media-blasted, cryo treated. Handguard: RRA 13-in. lightweight, M-LOK, full 12-o'clock Picatinny rail. Trigger: TriggerTech Diamond Single-Stage AR-15 trigger, adjustable from 1.5 to 4 lbs. of pull weight. Magpul PRS Lite stock, Hogue overmolded rubber grip, ambidextrous Radian Raptor charging handle. Options: Vortex Viper HS 4-16X 44mm riflescope or Vortex Strike Eagle 1-6X 24mm optic. Introduced 2023.
Price: AR1562.A .223 Wylde..**$1,950.00**
Price: AR1563.A .223 Wylde w/Viper HS 4-16X..**2,805.00**

Prices given are believed to be accurate at time of publication however, many factors affect retail pricing so exact prices are not possible.

79TH EDITION, 2025 ✦ 433

Price: 350L1562.A .350 Legend **$1,910.00**
Price: 350L1563.A .350 Legend w/Strike Eagle 1-6 .... **$2,550.00**
Price: 450B1562.A .450 Bushmaster **$3,075.00**

ROCK RIVER ARMS LAR-15 SERIES

Calibers: .17 HMR, .22 LR, .223/5.56, .223 Wylde chamber, .243 Win., 6.8 SPC II, .300 BLK, .308 Win., 7.62x39, .350 Legend, .450 Bushmaster, .458 SOCOM. Rifles and carbines available with a wide range of options, including left-hand versions. Individual nameplates include Coyote Carbine, Fred Eichler Series, NM A4, Operator ETR, Predator Pursuit, RRage, X-Series, and others. Added .17 HMR-chambered gas-impingement delayed-blowback model in 2024. No. 17HMR1325, $1,190.
Price: .... **$820.00–$1,950.00**

ROCK RIVER ARMS LAR-BT6 .338 LAPUA MAGNUM

Barrel: 24-in. black nitride stainless steel, 1:10 twist, four port brake. RRA Ultra Match two-stage trigger. Quick takedown design. Weight: 13.5 lbs. Length: 48 in.
Price: **$5,660.00**

ROCK RIVER ARMS LAR-BT3 PREDATOR RIFLE

Caliber: .243 Win., 6.5 CM. Barrel: 20, 24 in. Weight: 8.5-9.7 lbs. Length: 36.5 to 41 in. Introduced 2022.
Price: .... **$1,795–$1,850.00**

ROCK RIVER ARMS OPERATOR ETR CARBINE

Caliber: .308 Win. Barrel: 16-in. chrome lined, 1:10 twist. Weight: 8.2 lbs. Length: 34.5 in. retracted. Stock: RRA six-Position NSP-2 CAR Stock. Hogue Beavertail Grip. Trigger: RRA Two-Stage Ultra Match Trigger. Introduced 2022.
Price: **$1,670.00**

RUGER AR-556 STANDARD

Caliber: 5.56 NATO. Capacity: 30-round magazine. 16.1 in. barrel, 1:8-in. RH twist, 1/2x28 muzzle thread pattern. Features: Basic AR M4-style Modern Sporting Rifle with direct impingement operation, forged aluminum upper and lower receivers, and cold hammer-forged chrome-moly steel barrel with M4 feed ramp cuts. Other features include Ruger Rapid Deploy folding rear sight, milled F-height gas block with post front sight, telescoping six-position stock and one 30-round Magpul magazine. Weight: 6.5 lb. Overall Length: 32.25 to 35.50 in. Introduced 2015. Add $50 for Magpul MOE furniture.
Price: **$1,019.00**

RUGER AR-556 MPR (Multi-Purpose Rifle)

Caliber: 5.56 NATO, .223 Wylde chamber, .350 Legend, .450 Bushmaster. MPR model has 16.1-, 18-, 18.38-, and 18.63-in. barrels with muzzle brake, flat-top upper, 15-in. free-floating handguard with Magpul M-LOK accessory slots, Magpul MOE SL collapsible buttstock and MOE grip. Proof Research carbon-fiber barrel added December 2022.
Price: 5.56 .... **$1,129.00**
Price: .223 Wylde, Proof Research 18 in. **$2,049.00**
Price: .350 Legend, .450 Bushmaster **$1,299.00**

RUGER AR-556 FREE-FLOAT HANDGUARD

Caliber: 5.56 NATO, .300 BLK. 16.1-in. barrel. Similar to MPR model, with 11-in. aluminum free-floated handguard. Magpul M-LOK accessory attachment slots at the 3, 6, and 9 o'clock positions with additional slots on the angled faces near the muzzle. Introduced 2016. .300 BLK chambering added in 2019.
Price: **$1,039.00**

RUGER SMALL-FRAME AUTOLOADING RIFLE (SFAR)

Chambering: 7.62 NATO/.308 Win., 6.5 Creedmoor. The SFAR combines the ballistic advantages of .308 Win. in the size of a traditional MSR. Barrel: 16 in., cold hammer-forged, 5R rifling, 5/8"-24 muzzle thread, tapered lugs, black-nitride finish. Trigger: Ruger Elite 452. Receivers: CNC-machined from 7075-T6 forgings, oversized magazine well, forward assist, dust cover and brass deflector. 4-position regulated gas block, included 3/16-in. ball-end wrench for regulator adjustment, 2-port Boomer muzzle brake. Handguard: Magpul M-LOK accessory attachment slots at the 3:00, 6:00, and 9:00 positions, sockets for QD sling swivels. Model 5610: 16-in. barrel, mid-length gas system, 15-in. Lite free-float handguard. Model 5611: 20-in. barrel, rifle-length gas system, 15-in. handguard with a full Picatinny top rail. Magpul MOE SL stock, MOE grip and one 20-rd. Magpul PMAG magazine. Weight: 6.8 pounds unloaded. Introduced 2022. State-compliant models with 10-rd. magazines added 2023. Add $70 for Magpul PRS Lite buttstock.
Price: **$1,329.00**

SEEKINS PRECISION SP15 DMR

Chamber: Caliber: 223 Wylde/5.56; 6 ARC. A Dedicated Marksman Rifle (DMR) lower receiver has ambidextrous controls. Proprietary upper receiver and 15-in. SP3Rv3 MLOK handguard. Barrel: 16 or 18 in., 1:8 twist 5R 416 stainless steel for 5.56. 6 ARC Barrel: 22-in. 1:8 twist 5R 416 stainless steel. Weight: 8.2 lbs.
Price: **$1,795.00**

SEEKINS PRECISION NX15

Chamber: .223 Wylde/5.56 NATO. Similar to SP15, but with higher-level components, including an upgraded Timney trigger, NX15 skeletonized upper/lower receiver set and NOX handguard, ambidextrous controls. Barrel: 16 in. 1:8 twist 5R 416 stainless steel. Weight: 7 lbs.
Price: **$1,795.00**

SEEKINS PRECISION SP10

Calibers: 6mm Creedmoor/ 1:8 twist; 6.5 Creedmoor/ 1:8 twist. .308 Win./ 1:11.25 twist. Ambidextrous controls, large-frame AR platform. Barrel: .308 18 in.; 6mm Creedmoor and 6.5mm Creedmoor 22 in., 5R 416 stainless steel. Seekins Low-Profile Adjustable Gas Block. IRMT Upper receiver, SP10 lower receiver made from 7075-T6 billet. Handguard: 15-in. SP3R M-LOK. Trigger: single-stage set at 3 lbs. Weight: 10.5 lbs.
Price: **$2,895.00**

SIG SAUER 716i TREAD

Caliber: .308 Win. Capacity: one 20-round magazine, compatible with SR-25 magazines. Barrel: 16 in., 1:10 RH twist, stainless steel. Upper/Lower Receivers: Forged aluminum, hardcoat anodized finish. Stock: Magpul SL-K six-position telescoping stock. Sights: None, optics ready. Weight: 8.5 lbs. Trigger: Two-stage match. Overall Length: 33.8 to 37 in. Features: Direct-impingement operating system, integral QD mount, ambi safety selector, charging handle, free-floating 15-in. M-LOK handguard. Snakebite SE has Elite Cerakote 3-Port Comp, a two-stage SIG Matchlite trigger, free-floating

M-LOK handguard, Cerakote-finished receivers and barrels.
Price: **$1,880.00**
Price: Snakebite SE **$2,080.00**

SIG SAUER MCX-SPEAR
Caliber: 7.62 NATO. Civilian variant of the U.S. Army's 6.8x51 rifle. Features 6-position adjustable folding stock, ambidextrous controls, two-stage match-grade trigger, adjustable gas-piston system. Also includes free-float M-LOK handguard with full-length Picatinny top rail. Barrel: 16 in. long CMV, 1:10 twist, interchangeable. Both non-reciprocating side and rear charging handles, ambidextrous controls. Length: 38.3 in. Height: 8 in. Width: 2.5 in. Weight (w/magazine): 9.2 lbs. Coyote tan. Introduced: Feb. 2023.
Price: **$4,579.00**

SIG SAUER MCX-SPEAR LT
Caliber: 5.56 NATO, 7.62x39mm, 300 BLK (pistol and SBR). 16-in. carbon-steel barrel on rifle; 11.5-in. and 9-in. for SBRs and pistols. Lightened handguard with attachment screws for additional rigidity and a lightened profile barrel. Ambidextrous bolt catch and release, minimalist, AR-15-style trigger compatibility. Interchangeable barrels, Rocksett SIG QD suppressor-ready flash hider. Barrel twist for 7.62x39 is 1:9.5; for 5.56 NATO, 1:7. Length: 34.5 in. Height: 7.5 in w/o magazine. 5/8x24 muzzle threads on 7.62x39mm barrel, 1/2x28 tpi on 5.56. Weight: 7.6 lbs. Introduced: Sept. 2022.
Price: **$2,850.00**

SIG SAUER M400 TREAD
Caliber: 5.56 NATO/.223 Rem. Capacity: one 30-round magazine, comparable with AR-15 types. Barrel: 16 in., 1:8 RH twist, stainless steel. Upper/Lower Receivers: Forged aluminum, hardcoat anodized finish. Stock: Magpul SL-K 6-position telescoping stock. Sights: None, optics-ready. Weight: 7 lbs. Trigger: Single-stage, polished hardcoat trigger. Overall Length: 30.8 in. Features: Direct-impingement operating system, integral QD mount, ambi safety selector, charging handle, free-floating 15-in. M-LOK handguard, mid-length gas system.
Price: **$1,130.00**

SIG SAUER M400 TREAD PREDATOR
Chambering: 5.56 NATO. MSR platform designed for predator hunting. Aluminum frame, Cerakote Elite Jungle finish, lightweight adjustable, 16-in. 1:8-twist stainless threaded barrel with thread protector, lightened free-float M-LOK 15-in. Predator handguard, hardened polished trigger, ambidextrous controls. Ships with five round magazines. Length: 35.5 in. Height: 7.5 in. Width: 2.5 in. Weight (with magazine): 7.4 lbs. Compatible with full line of Tread accessories. Introduced March 2021.
Price: **$1,299.00**

SIG SAUER M400-DH3 RIFLE
Caliber: .223 Rem. or 5.56 NATO (223 Wylde chamber). Specialized version released under world champion 3-Gun competitor and Team SIG Shooter Daniel Horner's DH3 brand. The M400-DH3 Rifle is a SIG Direct Impingement (SDI) aluminum frame rifle with a Cerakote Elite Titanium finish. DH3 fully adjustable competition stock, two-stage adjustable Timney trigger, 16-in. 1:8-twist fluted stainless barrel, three-chamber compensator, low-profile 3-gun handguard with M-LOK mounts, ambidextrous controls including bolt catch/release. Ships with one 30-round magazine. Length: 34.5 in. Height: 7.5 in. Width: 2.5 in. Weight (with magazine): 7 lbs. Introduced June 2022.
Price: **$2,179.00**

SIG SAUER MPX PCC
Caliber: 9mm Luger. Gas-piston operation. Barrel: 16 in., 1:10 twist, carbon steel. M13.5x1mm muzzle threads. Magazine: MPX 30-rd polymer mag. Trigger: Timney Single Stage. Overall Length: 35.25 in. Accessory Rail: M-LOK. Weight: 6.63 lbs.
Price: **$2,180.00**

SMITH & WESSON M&P15 SPORT II SERIES
Caliber: 5.56mm NATO/.223. Capacity: 30-shot steel magazine. Barrel: 16 in., 1:9-in. twist. Weight: 6.74 lbs., w/o magazine. Lengths: 32 to 35 in. overall. Stock: Black synthetic. Sights: Adjustable post front sight, adjustable dual aperture rear sight. Features: 6-position telescopic stock, thermo-set M4 handguard. 14.75 in. sight radius. 7-lb. (approx.) trigger pull. 7075 T6 aluminum upper, 4140 steel barrel. OR (Optics Ready) model has Crimson Trace CTS-103 Red/Green Dot Electronic Sight. Hardcoat black-anodized receiver and barrel finish. Made in USA.
Price: Sport II **$840.00**
Price: Sport II OR **$820.00**

SMITH & WESSON M&P15 VOLUNTEER XV SERIES
Caliber: 5.56mm NATO/.223. Capacity: 30-shot steel magazine. Barrel: 16-in. 4140 steel, 1:8 twist. Flat-faced trigger. BCM Gunfighter forend with M-LOK attachments. Gas block with integral Picatinny-style rail. B5 Systems Bravo Stock and P-Grip 23 pistol grip. Chromed firing pin. Forward assist. A2 flash suppressor. Adjustable A2 front sight post. Forged integral triggerguard. Armornite finish on barrel (internal and external). Weight: 8.8 lbs. Length: 36.25 in. No. 13507. Introduced 2022.
Price: **$1,049.00**

SMITH & WESSON M&P15 VOLUNTEER XV OPTICS READY
Caliber: 5.56mm NATO/.223. Similar to Volunteer XV except has gas block with integral Picatinny-style rail. Weight: 9 lbs. Length: 36.25 in. No. 13510. Introduced 2022.
Price: **$1,049.00**

SMITH & WESSON M&P15 VOLUNTEER XV RED DOT SIGHT
Caliber: 5.56mm NATO/.223. Similar to Volunteer XV except has gas block with integral Picatinny-style rail and includes Crimson Trace red dot sight. Weight: 9.375 lbs. Length: 36.25 in. No. 13513. Introduced 2022.
Price: **$1,100.00**

SMITH & WESSON M&P15 VOLUNTEER XV DMR
Caliber: 5.56mm NATO/.223. Similar to Volunteer XV Pro except rifle-length gas system and 20-in. barrel (No. 13517). Weight: 8.125 lbs. Length: 40.7 in. Introduced 2022.
Price: **$1,609.00**

Prices given are believed to be accurate at time of publication however, many factors affect retail pricing so exact prices are not possible.

79TH EDITION, 2025 ⊕ **435**

SMITH & WESSON M&P15 VOLUNTEER XV PRO
Caliber: 5.56mm NATO/.223. Similar to Volunteer XV except has gas block with integral Picatinny-style rail, B5 SOPMOD stock, and upright B5 grip. Mid-length gas system, 15-in. aluminum S&W M-LOK forend. Primary Weapons Systems muzzle brake, and 5R rifling. Sights: WGS Tactical Folding Sight front and rear. 16-in. target crowned, threaded barrel (No. 13515) or 14.5 in. (No. 13516), the latter with a with a pinned flash hider. Weight: 6.8 lbs. Length: 36.75 in. Introduced 2022. XV Pro M-LOK 6mm ARC (No. 13518) has 20-in. barrel. Overall Length: 37.5-40.75 in. Weight: 7.8 lbs. Introduced 2023.
Price: $1,590.00
Price: 6 ARC 20-in. $1,609.00

SMITH & WESSON M&P10 SPORT OPTICS READY
Caliber: .308 Win. (No. 11532), 6.5 Creedmoor (No. 12606). Capacity: 10 rounds. Barrel: 18 to 20 in. Weight: 7.7 pounds. Features: Magpul MOE stock with MOE Plus grip, 15-in. free-float Troy M-LOK handguard, black hard anodized finish. Camo-finish hunting model available w/5-round magazine.
Price: M&P10 Sport .308 Win. $1,250.00
Price: M&P10 Sport 6.5 Creedmoor $1,250.00

SONS OF LIBERTY GUN WORKS PATROL SL SERIES
Caliber: 5.56 NATO. Barrels: 13.7- and 16-in. Sons of Liberty Gun Works 4150CoMOV 1:7 MPI HPT. 1:7 twist, 1/2-28 threaded muzzle. .750-in. gas block journal with appropriately sized gas port. Other SOL lines include EX03 Series, M4-89 Series, and M4-L89 Series. MK-10 series of large-frame AR-pattern rifles introduced 2024. Based in San Antonio, Texas.
Price: PATROL SL 5.56 16 ....$1,300.00

SPRINGFIELD ARMORY HELLION BULLPUP
Caliber: 5.56 NATO. Ambidextrous controls, including the safety, charging handle, magazine, and bolt releases. Reversible case ejection system. Barrel: 16, 18, 20 in., CMV w/Bayonet Lug. 1:7 rate of twist, Melonite coating. Picatinny top rail, flip-up iron sights. Bravo Company USA BCMGUNFIGHTER Mod 3 grip. Five-position adjustable buttstock. Polymer handguard with nine M-LOK slots, three each at 3, 6 and 9 o'clock positions. Two-position adjustable gas block with "S" suppressed and "N" normal modes. Magazine: 30-round Magpul PMAG. Weight: 8 lbs. Length: 28.25 in. Add $17 for 18-in. barrel, + $32 for 20 in. Introduced January 2023.
Price: $1,999.00

SPRINGFIELD ARMORY SAINT AR-15 RIFLES
Caliber: 5.56 NATO. Introduced 2016. Springfield Armory's first entry into AR category. Capacity: 30-round magazine. Barrel: 16 in., 1:8 twist. Weight: 6 lbs., 11 oz. Sights: A2-style fixed post front or gas block with Pic rail, flip-up aperture rear. Features: Mid-length gas system, BCM 6-position stock, Mod 3 grip PMT KeyMod handguard 7075 T6 aluminum receivers. In 2020, several models with M-LOK handguards were added. Bravo Company handguards have an internal aluminum heat shield.
Price: $1,023.00

SPRINGFIELD ARMORY SAINT EDGE
Caliber: 5.56 NATO. Billet-cut receiver with lightening cuts. Metal flip-up sights, baffled muzzle brake, enhanced Melonite-coated trigger, 16-in. 1:8-twist Melonite-coated barrel. Bravo Company Mod 0 SOPMOD buttstock, Springfield Armory Multi-Port Muzzle Brake. Weight: 6 lbs. 3 oz. Length: 32.5 to 35.75 in.
Price: $1,379.00

SPRINGFIELD ARMORY SAINT VICTOR AR-15 RIFLES
Caliber: 5.56 NATO. Capacity: Includes one 30-round Magpul PMAG Gen M3. Barrel: 16-in., CMV, 1:8 twist, Melonite-finished barrels, Springfield Armory proprietary muzzle brake. Upper/Lower Receivers: Lowers are Accu-Tite tension-bonded to a flat-top forged upper receiver with Melonite finish. Stock: BCMGUNFIGHTER Mod 0. Pistol Grip: BCMGUNFIGHTER Mod 3. Sights: Spring-loaded, flip-up iron sights adjustable for windage and elevation. Weight: 6.9 lbs. Trigger: Enhanced nickel-boron-coated, single-stage flat trigger. Overall Length: 32.25 to 35.5 in. Features: Direct-impingement mid-length gas system. M16 bolt carrier Melonite finished, HPT/MPI tested, shot peened, and houses a 9310 steel bolt. 15-in. M-LOK free-float handguard, pinned, low-profile gas block. QD mounts built into the end plate and stock. Desert FDE color approx. $60 extra. Introduced 2019. Saint Victor Carbine 9mm (add $150) introduced December 2022.
Price: $1,150.00

SPRINGFIELD ARMORY SAINT VICTOR AR-10 RIFLE
Caliber: .308 Win. Capacity: One 20-round Magpul Gen M3. Barrel: 16 in., 1:10 twist, lightweight profile, CMV Melonite finish, SA muzzle brake. Upper/Lower Receivers: Forged Type III hardcoat anodized, 7075 T6 Aluminum. Lower has Accu-Tite Tension System. Stock: Bravo Company 6-Position. Pistol Grip: Bravo Company Mod. 3. Sights: Spring-loaded, flip-ups. Weight: 7.8 lbs. Trigger: Enhanced nickel boron-coated, single-stage flat trigger. Overall Length: 34.5 to 37.5 in. Features: Gas system is direct impingement, mid-length, pinned gas block. Bolt carrier group is MPT, Melonite finish with a 9310 steel bolt; handguard is 15-in. M-LOK aluminum free-float with SA locking tabs. Introduced 2019.
Price: $1,497.00

STAG ARMS STAG 15 RIFLES
Calibers: 5.56 NATO/.223; 6.8 SPC. Capacities: 20- or 30-round magazine. Features: This manufacturer offers many AR-style rifles or carbines with many optional features including barrel length and configurations, stocks, sights, rail systems and both direct-impingement and gas-piston operating systems. Left-hand models are available on some products. Tactical line added 2022. FDE finish added 2023, + $100. Located in Cheyenne, Wyoming.
Price: Stag 15 Tactical 16 ....$1,400.00
Price: Stag 15 Retro $820.00
Price: Stag 15 Super Varminter (6.8 SPC) $760.00
Price: Stag 15 LEO $1,150.00
Price: Stag 15 3Gun Elite $1,900.00

STAG ARMS AR-10 PURSUIT RIFLES
Calibers: .308 Win., 6.5 CM. Barrels: 18 in. 6.5 CM; 16 in. .308. Midnight Bronze Cerakote finish, with black Magpul K2+ Vertical Grip, adjustable CTR stock, Stag Arms branded custom leather piece over the cheek weld. Lightweight Hanson-profile barrel, Timney USA curved short two-stage trigger, BREACH by Aero precision charging handle. Ambidextrous safety selector, VG6 Gamma muzzle brake. Weight: 7.8 lbs. Magpul magazines. LH models available.
Price: $2,200.00

STAG ARMS STAG 10 RIFLES
308 Win. or 6.5 Creedmoor. Tactical model is DPMS .308 platform. .308 Win. chamber on 16-in. 1:10 barrel, VG6 Gamma compensator, 13.5-in. Stag 10 or Stag 10 SL M-LOK handguard. Nitride bolt carrier group, Magpul MOE grip, SL-S stock. Available in either mil-spec hardcoat anodized or FDE Cerakote finishes. We The People Select model has 18-in. nitride-coated Hanson-profile barrel with VG6 muzzle device, 16-in. M-LOK free-float handguard, Hiperfire RBT trigger.
Price: Stag 10 Tactical FDE .308 16 in. $1,800.00
Price: Stag 10 Classic Burnt Bronze .308 16 in. $750.00

Price: Stag 10 We The People 6.5 CM 18 in.......................................**$1,950.00**

STONER TACTICAL ORDNANCE SR-15 MOD 2 RIFLE
Caliber: 5.56mm NATO. Capacity: 30-round magazine. Barrel: 16 in. 1:7 twist, free-floated inside M-LOK URX handguard. Weight: 6.3 lbs. Length: 32 to 35 in. overall. Stock: Magpul MOE. Sights: Post front, fully adjustable rear (300-meter sight). Features: URX-4 upper receiver; two-stage trigger, 30-round magazine. Black finish. Made in USA by Knight's Armament Co.
Price: **$2,910.00**

STONER TACTICAL ORDNANCE SR-15 LPR MOD 2
Caliber: .223. Capacity: 30-round magazine. Barrel: 18 in., free-floated inside M-LOK URSx handguard. Weight: 7.6 lbs. Length: 38 in. overall. Stock: Mag-Pul MOE. Sights: Post front, fully adjustable rear (300m sight). Features: URX-4 upper receiver; two-stage trigger, 30-round magazine. Black finish. Made in USA by Knight's Armament Co.
Price: **$3,200.00**

STONER TACTICAL ORDNANCE SR-25 RIFLE
Caliber: 7.62 NATO. Capacity: 10- or 20-shot steel magazine. Barrel: 16 in. with flash hider. Weight: 8.5 lbs. APC (Carbine) features: Shortened, non-slip handguard; drop-in two-stage match trigger, removable carrying handle, ambidextrous controls, matte-black finish. APR (Rifle) has 20-in. heavy barrel. Made in USA by Knight's Armament Co.
Price: **$5,775.00**

WILSON COMBAT AR-15 RIFLES
Caliber: .204 Ruger, .223 Rem./5.56mm NATO, .223 Wylde, 22 Nosler, .224 Valkyrie, 6mm ARC, 6.5 Grendel, 6.8 SPC, .300 Ham'r, .300 Blackout, .350 Legend, .375 SOCOM, .458 SOCOM, .450 Bushmaster. Capacity: Accepts all M-16/AR-15-style magazines, and includes one 20-round magazine. Barrel: 16.25 in., 1:9-in. twist, match-grade fluted. Weight: 6.9 lbs. Length: 36.25 in. overall. Stock: Fixed or collapsible. Features: Free-float ventilated aluminum quad-rail handguard, mil-spec Parkerized barrel and steel components, anodized receiver, precision CNC-machined upper and lower receivers, 7075 T6 aluminum forgings. Single-stage JP Trigger/Hammer Group, Wilson Combat Tactical muzzle brake, nylon tactical rifle case. Made in USA by Wilson Combat.
Price: Ranger **$2,500.00**
Price: Ultralight Ranger **$2,665.00**
Price: Recon Tactical **$2,450.00**
Price: Protector S Carbine 5.56 16 in. (2023) **$2,050.00**
Price: Protector Carbine 300 BLK **$2,325.00**
Price: Super Sniper..**$2,475.00**
Price: Urban Super Sniper **$2,525.00**

WILSON COMBAT AR-10 RIFLES
Caliber: .243 Win., .260 Rem., 6.5 Creedmoor, 7mm-08 Rem., .308 Win., .338 Federal, .358 Win. Large-format BILLet-AR rifles with precision-machined match-grade barrels, M-LOK handguard rail, Tactical Trigger Units. Barrels: 14.7-in. barrel with pinned muzzle device on Recon Tactical. Also, 16, 18, and 20 in. fluted or standard Medium Recon-profile barrels. Receivers accept metal or polymer SR-25-pattern magazines.
Price: Recon Tactical..**$3,360.00**
Price: Tactical Hunter **$3,360.00**
Price: Ultralight Ranger **$3,400.00**

WILSON COMBAT AR-9 CARBINE
Caliber: 9mm Luger. AR-9 lower receivers with last-round bolt hold open compatible with 9mm service pistol magazines for Glock, Beretta, and Wilson Combat EDC X9. Accepts standard AR accessories. Integral triggerguard, flared magwell. Closed-bolt blowback operating system. Match-grade button-rifled 1:10 twist barrels. Introduced 2016.
Price: $2,100.00

WATCHTOWER FIREARMS TYPE 15 RIFLE
Caliber: 5.56 NATO, .223 Wylde chamber. Receiver set machined from high-grade 7075-T6511 billet aluminum. Ambidextrous charging handle, Watchtower safety selector. Hiperfire EDT2 Heavy Gunner trigger, a single-stage semi-auto LE/SWAT AR style. Tru-Black PVD-coated 5.56 NATO M16 profile MPI tested Durabolt BCG. 16-in. 5.56 NATO cold-hammer-forged or .223 Wylde stainless-steel barrel with 1:8 rifling twist. Mid-length gas system, 13.7-in. S7M free-floating handguard with M-LOK attachments at five positions, 4 QD points, full-length 1913 Picatinny rail. Flat Face compensating muzzle brake finished in Tru-black PVD coating. B5 reinforced polymer pistol grip and buttstock. 7 lbs. CQB has 10.5-in. barrel, + $125. Lifetime warranty. In May 2023, Watchtower Firearms acquired F-1 Firearms. Based in Spring, Texas.
Price: **$1,475.00**

WATCHTOWER FIREARMS TYPE 15M RIFLE
Chamberings: 5.56 NATO or .223 Wylde. Premium forged line meeting military specifications. Black nitride Durabolt BCG. Barrels: 5.56 NATO cold hammer forged or .223 Wylde stainless-steel black nitride, 16-in. with 1:8 rifling and mid-length gas system. 13.7-inch S7M free-floating M-LOK handguard.
Price: **$1,100.00**

WATCHTOWER FIREARMS TYPE 10 RIFLES
Caliber: .308 Win. match-grade chamber. Based on the DPMS high-profile receiver. Stainless-steel 18-in. barrel, 1:8 rifling. Mid-length gas system, 15-in. S7M free-floating handguard. Dragon Slay-AR compensating muzzle brake. Other appointments similar to Type 15.
Price: **$1,819.00**

WATCHTOWER FIREARMS TYPE HSP-H RIFLES
Caliber: 6.5 Creedmoor. Rifle-length gas system. Barrel: 16 in., 5/8 x24 TruBlack Dragon Slay-AR muzzle device. Other specs similar to Type 10 rifle, but with matte-Cerakote camouflage. Geissele SSA-E two-stage trigger.
Price: **$2,500.00**

WINDHAM WEAPONRY 20 VARMINT
Caliber: .223 Rem./5.56mm NATO. Capacity: 5+1, ships with one 5-round magazine (accepts all standard AR-15 sizes). Barrel: 20 in., 1:8 RH twist, fluted 416R stainless steel, matte finish. Upper/Lower Receivers: A4-type flattop upper receiver, forged 7075 T6 aircraft aluminum with aluminum triggerguard. Electroless nickel-plated finish. Forend: 15 in. Windham Weaponry aluminum M-LOK free-float. Pistol Grip: Hogue OverMolded rubber pistol grip. Sights: None, optics-ready, Picatinny top rail. Weight: 8.4 lbs. Length: 38.1 in. Features: Gas-impingement system, Carpenter 158 steel bolt. Compass Lake chamber specification with a matched bolt. LUTH MBA-1 stock. Comes with a hard-plastic case and a black web sling.
Price: R20FSSFTTL **$1,560.00**

WINDHAM WEAPONRY A1 GOVERNMENT
Caliber: .223 Rem./5.56mm NATO. Capacity: 30+1, ships with one 30-round magazine (accepts all standard AR-15 sizes). Barrel: 20 in., A2 profile, chrome-lined with A1 flash suppressor, 4150 chrome-moly Vanadium 11595E steel with M4 feed ramps. Rifling: 1:7 RH twist. Receivers: A1 upper with brass deflector and teardrop forward assist. Forend: Rifle-length triangular handguard with A1 Delta Ring. Pistol Grip: A1 Black Plastic Grip. Rear Sight: A1 dual aperture rear sight. Front Sight: Adjustable-height square post in A2 standard base. Trigger: Standard mil-spec trigger. Stock: A2 Solid Stock with Trapdoor Storage Compartment. Weight: 7.45 lbs. Length: 39.5 in.
Price: R20GVTA1S-7...**$1,450.00**

WINDHAM WEAPONRY DISSIPATOR M4
Caliber: .223 Rem./5.56mm NATO. Similar to Superlight SRC. Barrel: 16 in.,

M4 profile, chrome-lined with A2 flash suppressor. Flattop-type upper receiver with A4 detachable carry handle. Rifle-length heat-shielded handguards. A2 black plastic grip. Rear Sight: A4 dual-aperture elevation and windage adjustable for 300–600m. Front Sight: adjustable-height square post in A2 standard base. Six-position telescoping buttstock. Weight: 7.2 lbs. Length: 32.375 to 36.125 in.
Price: R16DA4T...$1,390.00

WINDHAM WEAPONRY R16SFST-308
Caliber: .308 Win. Capacity: 20+1, ships with one 20-round Magpul PMag magazine. Barrel: 16.5-in., medium profile, chrome lined with A2 flash suppressor; 4150M chrome-moly-vanadium 11595E steel; 1:10 right-hand-twist rifling, 6 lands and grooves. Upper/Lower Receivers: A4-type flattop upper receiver, forged 7075 T6 aircraft aluminum with aluminum triggerguard. Forend: Mid-length tapered shielded handguards. Pistol Grip: Hogue OverMolded rubber pistol grip. Sights: None, optics ready, Picatinny top rail. Weight: 7.55 lbs. Length: 34-38 in. Features: Gas-impingement system, Carpenter 158 steel bolt. Compass Lake chamber specification with matched bolt. Six-position telescoping buttstock. Comes with hard-plastic gun case with black web sling.
Price: R16SFST-308 .308 Win...$1,870.00
Price: R16SFST-300 .300 BLK $1,560.00

CENTERFIRE RIFLES Lever & Slide

BIGHORN ARMORY MODEL 89 BLACK THUNDER /WHITE LIGHTNING
Calibers: .500 S&W Magnum. Capacity: 6-round tubular magazine. Barrel: 16.25 in. steel. Weight: 7 lbs. 6 oz. Length: 36 in. Stock: Black laminate with M-LOK rail on the front of the forend. Sights: Skinner iron sights and factory-installed scout rail. Features: Expansion of the Model 89 lever-action line built as a carbine with a shorter barrel, ideal for hunting, home defense, and survival. Robust stainless steel construction, heat-treated, and coated with a black nitride finish. Bighorn Armory rifles built in Cody, WY. Addition of White Lightning variant with gray laminate stock and matte stainless receiver in 2024.
Price: **$3,850.00**
Price: White Lightning **$3,899.00**

BIG HORN ARMORY MODEL 89 RIFLE AND CARBINE
Caliber: .500 S&W Mag. Capacities: 5- or 7-round magazine. Features: Lever-action rifle or carbine chambered for .500 S&W Magnum. 22- or 18-in. barrel; walnut or maple stocks with pistol grip; aperture rear and blade front sights; recoil pad; sling swivels; enlarged lever loop; magazine capacity 5 (rifle) or 7 (carbine) rounds.
Price: **$2,424.00**

BIG HORN ARMORY MODEL 90 SERIES
Calibers: .460 S&W, .454 Casull. Features similar to Model 89. Several wood and finish upgrades available.
Price: .460 S&W **$2,849.00**
Price: .454 Casull, .45 Colt...**$3,049.00**
Price: .500 Linebaugh **$3,699.00**

BOND ARMS LVRB
Calibers: .223 Wylde, .300 Blackout, .450 Bushmaster, and .350 Legend, but will accept most any chambering using stndard rotating AR-15 bolt. Capacity: 30-round AR-style magazine. Barrel: 16.25 in. Weight: 6.4 lbs. Length: 39.5 in. overall. Stock: Black polymer Magpul / 870 style buttstock with AR-style forend, compatible with most related styles. Features: The first lever-action from Bond Arms with high-capacity magazine-fed design that is compatible with AR-15 uppers and handguards. Rotating bolt design. Ambidextrous controls. Flash hider. Crossbolt safety.
Price: **$1,599.00**

BROWNING BLR
Calibers: .243 Win., 6.5 Creedmoor, .308 Win., .270 Win., .30-06 Spfld., .300 Win. Mag. Capacity: 3–5 round magazine, depending on caliber. Barrel: 20, 22, or 24 in. Length: 40–45 in. Weight: 6 lbs. 8 oz.–7 lbs. 4 oz. Stock: Grade III/IV Walnut stock with Schnabel forearm and brass spacers and rosewood caps. Features: High Grade lever action centerfire limited edition. Gloss finish engraved receiver built of lightweight aluminum. Gloss blued barrel drilled and tapped for optic mounts. Detachable box magazine. Iron sights. Pachmayr Decelerator recoil pad. Gold-plated trigger and gold inlay receiver branding.
Price: Short actions **$1,540.00**
Price: Long actions **$1,630.00**

CHIAPPA MODEL 1892 RIFLE
Calibers: .38 Special/357 Magnum, .38-40, .44-40, .44 Mag., .45 Colt. Barrels: 16 in. (Trapper), 20 in. round and 24 in. octagonal (Takedown). Weight: 7.7 lbs. Stock: Walnut. Sights: Blade front, buckhorn. Trapper model has interchangeable front sight blades. Features: Finishes are blue/case colored. Magazine capacity is 12 rounds with 24 in. bbl.; 10 rounds with 20 in. barrel; 9 rounds in 16 in. barrel. Mare's Leg models have 4-shot magazine, 9- or 12-in. barrel.

Price: **$1,329.00**
Price: Takedown...**$1,435.00**
Price: Trapper **$1,329.00**
Price: Mare's Leg **$1,288.00**

CHIAPPA MODEL 1886
Caliber: .45-70. Barrels: 16, 18.5, 22, 26 in. Replica of famous Winchester model offered in several variants.
Price: Rifle...**$1,709.00**
Price: Carbine **$1,629.00**

CHIAPPA 1892 LEVER-ACTION WILDLANDS
Caliber: .44 Mag. Capacity: 5. Barrel: 16.5 in., stainless steel, Cerakote dark gray or color case finish, heavy. Stock: Wood laminate or hand-oiled walnut. Sights: Fixed fiber-optic front, Skinner peep rear. Weight: 6.3 lbs. Features: Takedown and solid-frame configurations, mag tube fed.
Price: ....**$1,434.00-$1,689.00**

CIMARRON 1873 SHORT RIFLE
Calibers: .357 Magnum, .38 Special, .32 WCF, .38 WCF, .44 Special, .44 WCF, .45 Colt. Barrel: 20 in. tapered octagon. Weight: 7.5 lbs. Length: 39 in. overall. Stock: Walnut. Sights: Bead front, adjustable semi-buckhorn rear. Features: Has half "button" magazine. Original-type markings, including caliber, on barrel and elevator and "Kings" patent. Trapper Carbine (.357 Mag., .44 WCF, .45 Colt). From Cimarron F.A. Co.
Price: **$1,299.00**
Price: Trapper Carbine 16-in. bbl. **$1,352.00**

CIMARRON 1873 DELUXE SPORTING
Similar to the 1873 Short Rifle except has 24-in. barrel with half-magazine.
Price: **$1,485.00**

CIMARRON 1873 LONG RANGE SPORTING
Calibers: .44 WCF, .45 Colt. Barrel: 30 in., octagonal. Weight: 8.5 lbs. Length: 48 in. overall. Stock: Walnut. Sights: Blade front, semi-buckhorn ramp rear. Tang sight optional. Features: Color casehardened frame; choice of modern blued-black or charcoal blued for other parts. Barrel marked "Kings Improvement." From Cimarron F.A. Co.
Price: **$1,385.00**

EMF 1866 YELLOWBOY LEVER ACTIONS
Calibers: .38 Special, .44-40, .45 LC. Barrels: 19 in. (carbine), 24 in. (rifle). Weight: 9 lbs. Length: 43 in. overall (rifle). Stock: European walnut. Sights: Bead front, open adjustable rear. Features: Solid brass frame, blued barrel, lever, hammer, buttplate. Imported from Italy by EMF.
Price: Rifle..**$1,175.00**

EMF MODEL 1873 LEVER-ACTION
Calibers: .32/20, .357 Magnum, .38/40, .44-40, .45 Colt. Barrels: 18 in., 20 in., 24 in., 30 in. Weight: 8 lbs. Length: 43.25 in. overall. Stock: European walnut. Sights: Bead front, rear adjustable for windage and elevation. Features: Color casehardened frame (blued on carbine). Imported by EMF.
Price: **$1,250.00**

FIGHTLITE HERRING MODEL 2024
Calibers: 5.56 NATO & .300 Blackout but can be reconfigured for most any AR-15 chambering. Conversion kit for .22 LR rimfires announced, along with pistol-caliber conversions. Capacity: 5-100 rounds with AR-pattern Stanag magazines. Barrel: 16.25-in. chromemoly steel, threaded at 1/2x28 with protector. Weight: 5.7 lbs. Length: 37.75 in. overall. Stock: High-impact polymer buttstock with AR-style handguard. Sights: Mil-Std 1913. Features: Introduced in 2024 as a modern lever-action rifle. Utilizes standard AR-15 bolts and barrel extensions. M-LOK attachment slots. Ambidextrous controls.
Price: **$1,299.00**

HENRY LEVER ACTION SUPREME

Calibers:. .223 Rem, .300 Blackout. Barrel: free-floated with threaded muzzle. Stock: American Walnut, pistol grip style, with checkering and rubber buttpad. Sights: Choice of standard iron sights or Picatinny optics rail. Features: Debuted in 2024 as an AR-style lever-action with a match-grade adjustable trigger and sub-MOA capability. Ambidextrous controls. Feeds from AR-style MSR detachable box magazines, including P-Mags. Short throw lever with larger loop. Internal hammer. Optimized for use with a suppressor. Sling studs. Built in the USA.
Price: **$1,400.00**

HENRY NEW ORIGINAL RIFLE

Calibers: .44-40 Win, .45 Colt. Capacity: 13-round tubular magazine. Barrel: 24-in. octagonal blued steel. Weight: 9 lbs. Length: 43 in. Stock: Fancy-grade American Walnut with straight-grip buttstock. Sights: Folding ladder rear with blade front. Features: Hardened brass receiver finished in high polish. Essentially identical to the 1860 original, except for caliber. Serial numbers begin with "BTH" prefix in honor of Benjamin Tyler Henry, inventor of the lever action repeating rifle that went on to become the most legendary firearm in American history. Made in the USA. Only this standard model New Original is available in the .45 Colt chambering; all other New Original Models below are .44-40 Win. only.
Price: **$2,590.00**
Price: New Original Deluxe Engraved **$3,810.00**
Price: New Original B.T. Henry 200th Anniv. Edition **$4,286.00**
Price: New Original Rare Carbine **$2,590.00**
Price: New Original Iron Framed **$3,023.00**
Price: New Original Silver Deluxe Engraved **$4,078.00**

HENRY SIDE GATE MODELS

Beginning in 2020, Henry began building the centerfire lever actions listed below with a side loading gate in addition to the tubular magazine charging port. These are not to be confused with the specific Henry Side Gate Model H024. NOTE: All previous Henry centerfire models without the side gate are now discontinued and considered "Legacy" models with slightly lower value at time of publication.
Price: Big Boy Color Case Hardened Side Gate **$1,141.00**
Price: Big Boy Steel Side Gate, Carbine or Rifle **$969.00**
Price: Big Boy Steel Side Gate, Large Loop **$986.00**
Price: Color Case Hardened Side Gate .30-30 and .45-70 ....**$1,141.00**
Price: Steel .30-30 Side Gate **$969.00**
Price: Steel .30-30 Side Gate Large Loop **$986.00**
Price: Steel .45-70 Side Gate **$969.00**
Price: Steel Wildlife Edition Side Gate **$1,618.00**

HENRY MODEL H024 SIDE GATE LEVER ACTION

Calibers: .38-55 Win., .30-30 Win., .45-70 Govt, .35 Rem, .360 Buckhammer. Capacity: 4 or 5-round tubular magazine. Barrel: 20-in. round blued steel. Weight: 7.5 lbs. Length: 38.3 in. Stock: American Walnut straight style with special deep checkering including floral scroll and Henry logo wood detail not found on any other models. Sights: Fully adjustable semi-buckhorn diamond-insert rear. Front ramp with 0.62-in. ivory bead. Drilled and tapped. Features: This H024 is the debut model using Henry's side loading gate design in addition to the standard tubular loading port. These hardened brass receiver centerfires are instantly recognizable with the special engraved and checkered stocks. Polished brass buttplate, barrel band, and swivel stud. Standard-size lever loop. Transfer bar safety.
Price: **$1,100.00**

HENRY LONG RANGER

Calibers: .223 Rem., .243 Win., 6.5 Creedmoor, .308 Win. Capacity: 4 (.243, 6.5CM, .308) or 5 (.223) box magazine. Barrel: 20 or 22 in. (6.5 Creedmoor) round blued steel. Weight: 7 lbs. Length: 40.5–42.5 in. Stock: Straight-grip, checkered, oil-finished American Walnut. Sights: Two models, one sighted with folding fully adjustable rear and ramp ivory bead front. The other does not have iron sights but includes scope bases and hammer extension instead.

Both are drilled and tapped. Features: Geared action with side ejection port. Chromed steel bolt with six lugs. Flush-fit box magazine with side push-button release. Sling studs, rubber recoil pad. Transfer bar safety.
Price: **$1,099.00**
Price: Long Ranger Wildlife Editions **$1,973.00**
Price: Long Ranger Deluxe Engraved................................. **$1,973.00**

HENRY LONG RANGER EXPRESS

Calibers: .223 Rem/5.56 NATO. Capacity: 5-round steel box magazine. Barrel: 16.5-in. threaded round blued steel. Weight: 7 lbs. Length: 37 in. Stock: Birch laminate in black/gray. Sights: Top Picatinny rail. No iron sights. Features: Expansion of the Long Ranger line, this one a more compact platform. Same geared action with side ejection port. Chromed steel bolt with six lugs. Flush fit dropbox magazine with side push-button release. Sling studs, rubber recoil pad. Transfer bar safety. Hammer extension included. Barrel threaded at 5/8x24.
Price: **$1,235.00**

HENRY X-MODELS

Calibers: .30-30 Win., .45-70 Govt., .45 Colt, .44 Mag., .38 Spl./.357 Mag., 360 Buckhammer. Capacity: 4 (.45-70), 5 (.30-30), or 7 (Big Boys) tubular magazine Barrel: 17.4-, 19.8-, 21.375-in. round blued steel. Weight: 7.3–8.07 lbs. Length: 36.3–40.375 in. Stock: Black synthetic with M-LOK attachment points and lower Picatinny rail. Sights: Fully adjustable fiber-optic front and rear. Also drilled and tapped for Weaver 63B base. Features: Blacked-out lever actions built around several of Henry's existing family lines of long guns. Large loop lever. Barrel threaded at 5/8x24 for easy suppressor or brake attachment. Transfer bar safety. Solid rubber recoil pad. Sling studs. Matte blued steel metalwork.
Price: X-Model **$1,091.00**
Price: Big Boy X-Model.. **$1,000.00**
Price: X-Model .30-30 .... **$1,019.00**
Price: X-Model .45-70 .... **$1,000.00**

MARLIN CLASSIC SERIES

Calibers: .30-30 Win., .44 Rem Mag/.44 Spl., .357 Mag./.38 Spl. Barrel: 20.25-in. (.30-30 & .44), 18.63 in. (.357/.38) round blued. Capacity: 6+1 rounds (.30-30), 10/11 rounds (.44 Mag/Spl), 9/10 rounds (.357/.38). Stock: American Black Walnut with checkering and low-profile rubber buttpad. Pistol grip design on 336; straight grip stock on 1894. Features: New model launch under Ruger ownership. Classic lineup pairs walnut stocks with blued steel. Blued metalwork with forward barrel band. Iron sights with hooded front. Crossbolt safety. Gold-plated trigger. Side loading gate. Sling studs. Red and white bullseye stock insert denotes Ruger production Marlins. Built in Mayodan, North Carolina.
Price: 336 Classic .30-30...**$1,279.00**
Price: 1894 Classic .44 Mag/.44 Spl...............................**$1,279.00**
Price: 1894 Classic .357 Mag/38 Spl..............................**$1,279.00**

MARLIN SBL SERIES

Calibers: .45-70 Govt., .30-30 Win. Capacity: 6+1-round tubular magazine. Barrel: 19.10-in. threaded, cold-hammer-forged stainless steel. Weight: 7.3 lbs. Length: 37.25 in. Stock: Gray laminate wood with checkering; pistol grip style. Sights: Adjustable ghost ring rear, Tritium fiber-optic front. Extended Picatinny optics rail. Features: The SBL Series in the Model 1895 was the first launch under Ruger's ownership of the Marlin brand. The SBL is recognizable for its polished stainless metalwork against gray laminate

Prices given are believed to be accurate at time of publication however, many factors affect retail pricing so exact prices are not possible.

furniture. Nickel-plated, spiral-fluted bolt. Barrel threaded at 11/16x24. Black rubber buttpad. Push-button, cross-bolt manual safety and half-cock hammer. Oversized lever loop and slimmed-down forend. Includes swivel studs and offset hammer spur. Marlin horse-and-rider logo laser-engraved on the grip. Ruger-made Marlin rifles begin with the serial prefix "RM." Traditional Marlin stock bullseye is now red/white. Built in Mayodan, North Carolina.

Price: 1895 SBL .45-70 .... **$1,529.00**
Price: 336 SBL .30-30 .... **$1,529.00**

MARLIN GUIDE GUN SERIES
Caliber: .45-70 Gov't. Barrel: 19.10-in. round, cold hammer forged. Weight: 7.4 lbs. Stock: Brown laminate with checkering. Features: The Guide Gun Series is recognized for its satin blued metalwork finish, and brown laminate furniture. Big loop guide gun model variant. Threaded barrel with cap. Semi-buckhorn rear and hooded front sight. Bead blasted satin-blued metalwork finish. Nickel-plated bolt. 6+1 capacity. Black rubber recoil pad. Sling studs. Red/white bullseye stock insert denotes Ruger manufacture. Built in Mayodan, North Carolina.

Price: 1895 Guide Gun .45-70 .... **$1,279.00**

MARLIN TRAPPER SERIES
Calibers: .45-70 Gov't. Capacity: 5+1. Barrel: 16.17 in. stainless round. Weight: 7.1 lbs. Stock: Black laminate with checkering. Features: The Trapper Series is known for its more compact metrics, black laminate furniture, and stainless metalwork. Short-barreled, large loop model variant. Bead blasted matte stainless metalwork. Spiral-fluted bolt. Threaded barrel with cap. Black rubber recoil pad. Sling studs. It comes standard with Skinner Sights receiver-mounted peep and rear sight blank factory-installed. Red/white bullseye stock insert denotes Ruger manufacture. Built in Mayodan, North Carolina.

Price: 1895 Trapper .45-70 .... **$1,499.00**
Price: 336 Trapper .30-30 .... **$1,499.00**

MARLIN DARK SERIES
Calibers: .45-70 Gov't., .30-30 Win., .44 Mag/.44 Spl. Capacity: 5+1 (.45-70). Barrel: 16.17 in. round cold hammer-forged steel with muzzle brake. Weight: 7 lbs. (.45-70). Stock: Black tactical-style nylon-reinforced polymer with adjustable cheek riser and generous rubber recoil pad. Sights: Fiber-optic front with Tritium ring and adjustable ghost ring rear, along with extended optics rail. Features: The Dark Series is the blacked-out variant with more tactical features. M-LOK attachment slots and flush cup sockets for QD mounts. Satin black metalwork. Red/white bullseye stock insert denotes Ruger manufacture. Built in Mayodan, North Carolina.

Price: 1895 Dark .45-70 .... **$1,429.00**
Price: 336 Dark .30-30 .... **$1,429.00**
Price: 1894 Dark .44 Mag./.44 Spl. **$1,429.00**

PEDERSOLI 86/71 BOARBUSTER
Calibers: .45-70 Govt. Capacity: 5-round tubular magazine. Barrel: 19-in. round. Weight: 7.93–8.25 lbs. Length: 37-7/16 in. Stock: Varied by model. Sights: Scout-style Picatinny rail and fiber-optic iron sights. Receiver drilled and tapped for side scope mounts. Features: Big-bore lever action based on the 1886. Several models use two-piece, interchangeable loop loading lever on several models. Pedersoli's Boarbuster line is comprised of five model variants. Mark II wears coated black Walnut with Silicon grip film adjustable

cheek piece and Bronze Cerakote metal finish. HV-1 wears orange and black HV-1 camo stocks with Silicon grip film and black Cerakote. Evolution is a classic model with selected Walnut stocks, Silver Cerakote receiver, and blued barrel. Shadow uses gray techno-polymer stock with adjustable cheek riser and ghost ring sights in place of Picatinny rail. Guidemaster wears camo stocks and fully chromed metalwork.

Price: **$1,792.00**

POF-USA TOMBSTONE
Caliber: 9mm Luger. Barrel: 16.5-in. free-floating, fluted steel. Weight: 5.75 lbs. Stock: Black synthetic Magpul SGA. Features: Accepts the same 10- and 20-round magazines as the company's Phoenix pistols. 10.5-in. Modular Receiver Rail (MRR) with M-LOK slots and Pic rails. Ghost ring iron sights. Crossbolt safety. Threaded muzzle with removable dual port brake. Single-stage 3.5-pound nonadjustable trigger.

Price: Black **$1,962.00**
Price: Tan **$2,097.00**

ROSSI R92 LEVER-ACTION CARBINE
Calibers: .38 Special/.357 Magnum, .44 Magnum., .44-40 Win., .45 Colt. Barrels: 16 or 20 in. with round barrel, 20 or 24 in. octagon barrel. Weight: 4.8–7 lbs. Length: 34–41.5 in. Features: Blued or stainless finish. Various options available in selected chamberings (large lever loop, fiber-optic sights, cheekpiece).

Price: R92 Blued Rifle **$730.00**
Price: R92 Stainless Rifle **$770.00**
Price: R92 Carbine **$725.00**
Price: R92 Stainless Carbine **$770.00**
Price: R92 Octagonal Barrel .... **$830.00–$875.00**
Price: R92 Gold **$810.00**
Price: R92 Triple Black **$925.00**
Price: R92 .454 Casull **$950.00**

ROSSI R95 LEVER-ACTION RIFLE
Calibers: .30-30 Win, .45-70 Govt. Barrels: Varies by model with 16.5 in (Trapper), 20 in. (Stainless laminate), 20 in. (walnut). Capacity: 5+1 rounds tubular magazine. Sights: Drift-adjustable front and buckhorn adjustable rear. Features: Larger centerfire chambering lineup of lever-action rifles with multiple model variants. Thumb safety. Alloy steel frame. Rubber recoil pad. Sling studs. Built in Brazil. Standard walnut with black oxide finish, standard loop, checkered walnut. Trapper wears large loop, threaded barrel, checkered hardwood. Stainless Laminate with large loop, polished stainless, gray laminate.

Price: R95 Walnut **$985.00**
Price: R95 Stainless Laminate **$1,213.00**
Price: R95 Trapper **$1,069.00**

SMITH & WESSON 1854 SERIES
Calibers: .44 Rem. Mag. Capacity: 9-round tubular magazine. Barrel: 19.25 in. .410 stainless. Weight: 6.8 lbs. Length: 36 in. overall. Stock: Black synthetic with textured grip panels and M-LOK slots on forend. Sights: Gold bead front and XS ghost ring rear along with drilled and tapped receiver accepting Marlin 1894 hole patterns. Features: S&W's first modern lever-action built with a 416 stainless receiver. Large loop lever. Flat trigger. Barrel threaded at 11/16x24. Crossbolt safety.

Price: **$1,279.00**
Price: Limited Edition with high-grade walnut and
black PVD metalwork **$3,499.00**

Prices given are believed to be accurate at time of publication however, many factors affect retail pricing so exact prices are not possible.

79TH EDITION, 2025 ◆ 441

SOUTHERN CROSS SMALL ARMS TAIPAN X

Calibers: .223 Wylde. Capacity: 10-round magazine standard; compatible with AR-style magazines. Barrel: 16.5-in. stainless steel, threaded at 1/2x28. Stock: TSP-X buttstock with comb riser, and polymer three-piece pump forend. Sights: None. Full-length Picatinny rail integral to receiver. Features: Spring-assist, pump-action rifle, with a straight-pull "bolt" built on an AR-style platform Built in Australia by SCSA. ARCA/ Swiss rail adapter available, and a folding stock adapter. Glass-filled nylon casing deflector. Enhanced straight trigger. Pistol grip. M-LOK and accessory attachment points on forend. Advertised to be legal in all 50 states due to its unique action design. Colors available in Burnt Bronze, Black, FDE, and Dark Gray. Sold in the U.S. through Legacy Sports International.
Price: $1,299.00

UBERTI 1873 SPORTING RIFLE

Calibers: .357 Magnum, .44-40, .45 Colt. Barrels: 16.1 in. round, 19 in. round or 20 in., 24.25 in. octagonal. Weight: Up to 8.2 lbs. Length: Up to 43.3 in. overall. Stock: Walnut, straight grip and pistol grip. Sights: Blade front adjustable for windage, open rear adjustable for elevation. Features: Color casehardened frame, blued barrel, hammer, lever, buttplate, brass elevator. Imported by Stoeger Industries.
Price: Carbine 19-in. bbl. $1,309.00
Price: Trapper 16.1-in. bbl. $1,329.00
Price: Carbine 18-in. half oct. bbl. $1,379.00
Price: Short Rifle 20-in. bbl. $1,339.00
Price: Sporting Rifle, 24.25-in. bbl. $1,339.00
Price: Special Sporting Rifle, A-grade walnut $1,449.00

UBERTI 150TH ANNIVERSARY 1873 RIFLE

Caliber: .45 Colt, .357 Mag. Capacity: 10+1 rounds. Barrel: 20-in. blued octagonal. Weight: 8.2 lbs. Stock: A-Grade Satin Walnut. Iron sights. Blued crescent buttplate. Features: Special anniversary remake of Winchester's Model 1873, "The gun that won the West." Casehardened receiver finish. Sideplate engraving reproduced from an original Winchester by Atelier Giovanelli of Italy.
Price: $1,799.00

UBERTI 1860 HENRY

Calibers: .44-40, .45 Colt. Barrel: 24.25 in. half-octagon. Weight: 9.2 lbs. Length: 43.75 in. overall. Stock: American walnut. Sights: Blade front, rear adjustable for elevation. Imported by Stoeger Industries.
Price: 1860 Henry Trapper, 18.5-in. barrel, brass frame $1,499.00
Price: 1860 Henry Rifle Iron Frame, 24.25-in. barrel $1,499.00

UBERTI 1866 YELLOWBOY DELUXE

Caliber: .45 Colt. Barrel: 20-in. blued octagonal. Weight: 8.2 lbs. Stock: A-Grade Walnut. Brass crescent buttplate. Blued barrel band. Casehardened lever. Iron sights. Features: Remake of Winchester's famed 1866 Yellowboy. Polished brass frame with classically inspired engraving pattern, including a bugling elk. Blank area on right escutcheon intended for the owner's custom engraving.
Price: $1,799.00

WINCHESTER MODEL 94 SHORT RIFLE

Calibers: .30-30, .38-55, .32 Special. Barrel: 20 in. Weight: 6.75 lbs. Sights: Semi-buckhorn rear, gold bead front. Stock: Walnut with straight grip. Fore-end has black grip cap. Also available in Trail's End takedown design in .450 Marlin or .30-30.
Price: $1,230.00
Price: (Takedown) $1,460.00

WINCHESTER MODEL 94 SPORTER

Calibers: .30-30, .38-55. Barrel: 24 in. Weight: 7.5 lbs. Features: Same features of Model 94 Short Rifle except for crescent butt and steel buttplate, 24 in. half-round, half-octagon barrel, checkered stock.
Price: $1,400.00
Price: Deluxe Sporting 24 in. .30-30 Win., .38-55 Win. $2,169.00

WINCHESTER 1873 SHORT RIFLE

Calibers: .357 Magnum, .44-40, .45 Colt. Capacities: Tubular magazine holds 10 rounds (.44-40, .45 Colt), 11 rounds (.38 Special). Barrel: 20 in. Weight: 7.25 lbs. Sights: Marble semi-buckhorn rear, gold bead front. Tang is drilled and tapped for optional peep sight. Stock: Satin finished, straight-grip walnut with steel crescent buttplate and steel fore-end cap. Tang safety. A modern version of the "Gun That Won the West."
Price: $1,300.00
Price: Deluxe Sporting Rifle.................................$1,800.00
Price: Competition Carbine High Grade 20 in..45 Colt or .357 Mag....$1,839.00
Price: Deluxe Sporting 24 in. .44-40 Win. $2,119.00

WINCHESTER 1873 150TH ANNIVERSARY

Caliber: .44-40 Win. Barrel: 24-in. octagon. Weight: 8.0 lbs. Stock: Grade V/VI Black Walnut straight grip with laser cut 20 LPI checkering. Features: Special anniversary edition of "The gun that won the West." High-gloss blued steel metalwork. Gold-filled 150th-anniversary engraving. Crescent buttplate with engraving detail. Semi buckhorn rear sight with Marble's gold bead front. Receiver drilled and tapped for tang-mounted sight.
Price: $3,659.00

WINCHESTER MODEL 1886 SADDLE RING CARBINE

Calibers: .45-70 Govt., .45-90 Win. Capacity: 7-round tubular magazine. Barrel: 22-in. round polished blued steel. Weight: 8 lbs. Length: 41 in. Stock: Grade I Black Walnut with straight grip and carbine-style forearm, oil finished. Sights: Carbine ladder-style rear and blade front. Features: Full-length magazine tube, steel barrel band. Drilled and tapped for receiver mount sight. Brushed polish receiver finish. Tang safety. Side Saddle Ring.
Price: $1,549.00

WINCHESTER MODEL 1895

Calibers: .30-06 Spfld., .405 Win. Capacity: 4-round internal magazine. Barrel: 24-in. gloss blued steel, button rifled. Weight: 8 lbs. Length: 42 in. Stock: Grade I Black Walnut, straight grip with traditional cut checkering. Sights: Drilled and tapped receiver for side mount sight; Marble Arms gold bead front and Buckhorn rear. Features: Throwback lever gun reminiscent of Teddy Roosevelt's "Big Medicine." Grade I Model 1895 lever action with scalloped receiver, two-piece lever, and Schnabel forend.
Price: .... $1,369.00–$1,439.00
Price: Grade III/IV Black Walnut .30-40 Krag $1,699.00–1,769.00

ARMALITE AR-50A1

Caliber: .50 BMG, .416 Barrett. Capacity: Bolt-action single-shot. Barrel: 30 in. with muzzle brake. National Match model (shown) has 33-in. fluted barrel. Weight: 34.1 lbs. Stock: Three-section. Extruded fore-end, machined vertical grip, forged and machined buttstock that is vertically adjustable. National Match model (.50 BMG only) has V-block patented bedding system, Armalite Skid System to ensure straight-back recoil.
Price: **$3,359.00**

ANSCHUTZ 1782

Calibers: .243 Win., 6.5 Creedmoor, .308 Win., .30-06, 8x57, 9.3x62. Capacity: 3. Barrel: 20.5 to 23.8 in., blued, threaded. Stock: Walnut. Sights: Integrated Picatinny rail. Weight: 8 lbs. Features: Solid-steel milled action, 60-degree bolt lift, sliding safety catch.
Price: **$2,795.00**

BENELLI LUPO

Calibers: .243 Win., 6mm Creedmoor, 6.5 Creedmoor, .308 Win., 6.5 PRC, .30-06 Spfld., .270 Win, 7mm Rem. Mag., .300 Win. Mag. (Addition of .300 PRC and .338 Lapua Mag. to select models). Capacity: 4–5-round box magazine. Barrel: 22 and 24 in. Crio-treated, free-floating, threaded barrel with thread cover. Length: 44.25–46.62 in. Stock: Black Synthetic. Sights: None. Includes two piece Picatinny rail. Weight: 6.9–7.1 lbs. Features: Shims allow stock adjustment. Matte blued metalwork. Progressive comfort recoil reduction system. Sub-MOA guarantee. CombTech cheek pad. Ambidextrous safety. Integral swivel mounts. HPR BE.S.T uses BE.S.T metal finish along with tan synthetic stock with black webbing and adjustable comb, interchangeable grips, removeable bag rider, and 30MOA rail.
Price: **$1,699.00**
Price: BE.S.T. CAMO, Elevated II or Open Country camo **$1,899.00**
Price: Walnut stock, .308 Win. or .30-06..**$2,199.00**
Price: HPR BE.S.T **$2,949.00**

BENELLI LUPO WOOD BE.S.T.

Calibers: 6.5 Creedmoor, .308 Win., .300 Win. Mag. Capacity: 4–5 round box magazine. Barrel: 22- and 24-in. Crio-treated, free-floating, threaded barrel with thread cover. Length: 44.225–46.625 in. Stock: AA-grade satin Walnut. Sights: Two-piece Picatinny bases. No iron sights. Weight: 7.1 lbs. Features: The new model Lupo replaces synthetic furniture with Walnut but keeps most other features. Also adds BE.S.T. surface treatment to metal surfaces for added durability. Trigger reach spacers. Ambidextrous safety. Progressive comfort recoil reduction system. Sub-MOA guarantee.
Price: ....**$1,899.00–$2,199.00**

BARRETT MRAD

Calibers: .260 Rem., 6.5 Creedmoor, .308 Win., .300 Win. Mag., .338 Lapua Magnum. Capacity: 10-round magazine. Barrels: 20 in., 24 in. or 26 in. fluted or heavy. Features: User-interchangeable barrel system, folding stock, adjustable cheekpiece, 5-position length of pull adjustment button, match-grade trigger, 22-in. optics rail.
Price: ....**$5,850.00–$6,000.00**

BARRETT MRADELR

Calibers: .416 Barrett. Capacity: 5-round polymer magazine. Barrel: 36-in. heavy contour, match-grade, single-point cut, hand-lapped stainless. Weight: 23 lbs. Length: 62 in. overall. Stock: Fixed with oversized recoil pad, push-button comb height and LOP adjustment. Choice of tan, gray, or black. Sights: None. Extended 24.6-in.-long 10 MIL top Picatinny rail. Features: Bolt-action repeater with user-changeable barrel system.

Electroless nickel-plated bolt head with 60-degreee throw. High-efficiency three-port muzzle brake is also compatible with QDL brake. Adjustable single-stage trigger.
Price: **$9,995.00**

BERETTA BRX-1

Calibers: 6.5 Creedmoor, .308 Win., .30-'06, .300 Win. Mag. Capacity: 5-round blaze orange magazine standard; higher capacity also available. Barrels: 20- and 22-in. steel. 24-in carbon-fiber, free floating, each with threaded muzzle. Weight: 7.2 lbs. Stock: Polymer stock in choice of either black or OD Green with negative comb angle, modular grip, and customizable LOP. Sights: None. Picatinny optics rail. Features: New straight-pull, linear action debuted to the American market in late 2023. The BRX1 is built entirely by machines, allowing for more reasonable cost. The rotating bolt design uses 8 lugs on standard calibers and 16 lugs on magnums. Reversible bolt handle and a three-position safety. Barrels and chamberings are interchangeable. Single-stage trigger adjustable to three pre-set weights of 2.1, 2.6, and 3.3 pounds. More stock styles, chamberings, and accessories forthcoming.
Price: ....**$1,599.00–$1,899.00**

BERGARA B-14 SERIES

Calibers: 6.5 Creedmoor, .270 Win., 7mm Rem. Mag., .308 Win., .30-06, .300 Win. Mag. Barrels: 22 or 24 in. Weight: 7 lbs. Features: Synthetic with Soft touch finish, recoil pad, swivel studs, adjustable trigger, choice of detachable mag or hinged floorplate. Made in Spain.
Price: **$825.00**
Price: Walnut Stock (Shown, Top) **$945.00**
Price: Premier Series **$2,190.00**
Price: Hunting and Match Rifle (HMR)(Shown, Bottom).................**$1,150.00**

BERGARA B-14 CREST CARBON

Calibers: .22-250 Rem., .308 Win., 6.5 Creedmoor, 6.5 PRC, 7mm PRC, .300 Win. Mag. Capacity: Comes standard with 5-round AICS magazine but uses M5 bottom metal, allowing for conversion to a traditional floorplate. Barrel: 20 or 22 in. Cure Carbon barrel with No. 6 taper, threaded and fitted with Omni brake. Weight: 6.2–6.5 lbs. Length: 40–43.5 in. overall. Stock: Monocoque 100% Carbon fiber with carbon spine with gray accents. Sights: None . Features: Sniper Gray Cerakote metalwork. LOP adjustable with spacers. Spiral fluted bolt with sliding extractor. Bergara Performance Trigger with smooth shoe, adjustable from 1.5 to 3.5 pounds.
Price: **$2,099.00**

BERGARA B-14 STOKE

Calibers: .22-250 Rem., .308 Win., 6.5 Creedmoor, .243 Win., 7mm-08, 6.5 PRC (floorplate); .223 Rem., .300 Blackout, .350 Legend (dropbox magazine). Capacity: 5-round magazine. Barrel: 16.5 or 20 in. 4140 CrMo steel with 4.5 taper. Threaded at 5/8x24. Weight: 6.0–6.4 lbs. Length: 35–38.5 in. overall. Stock: Sporter-style synthetic black with gold web. Sights: None. Features: Built specifically for smaller-framed shooters with Bergara's compact stock with a 12.25 in LOP as well as ¼-in. spacers for further customization. Forend length is also shortened, along with barrel length. Raised negative comb design engineered for smaller shooters to have proper eye-scope alignment, as well as less felt recoil on the face. Graphite Black Cerakote. Most chamberings use an internal box magazine with an M5 hinged floorplate, though several Special Purpose models come

with an AICS detachable magazine. Sub-MOA accuracy guarantee.
Price: $929.00

BERGARA PREMIER CANYON
Calibers: 6.5 Creedmoor, 6.5 PRC, .308 Win., 28 Nosler, .300 Win. Mag., 300 PRC, .375 H&H. Capacity: AICS-style detachable 3-round mag. provided, 5-round long action. 375 uses hinged floorplate with 3-round capacity. Barrel: 20–22 in. No. 4 taper, fluted stainless steel. Weight: 6.2–6.5 lbs. Length: 41–44 in. Stock: AG Composite 100% carbon fiber. Sights: Drilled and tapped for Remington 700 bases with 8-40 screws. Features: Classic style hunting rifle. Bolt uses a non-rotating gas shield, coned bolt nose, and sliding plate extractor. TriggerTech frictionless release trigger with two-position safety. Threaded muzzle with Omni Muzzle Brake. Sniper Grey Cerakote. Guaranteed MOA accuracy.
Price: .... $2,379.00–$2,429.00

BERGARA PREMIER DIVIDE
Calibers: 6.5 Creedmoor, 6.5 PRC, .308 Win., .300 Win. Mag. Capacity: AICS-style detachable, 5 standard, 3 magnum. Barrel: 22 in., 24 in. No. 6 CURE carbon fiber. Weight: 7.2–7.4 lbs. Length: 43–46 in. Stock: AG Composite 100% carbon fiber. Sights: Drilled and tapped for Remington 700 bases with 8-40 screws. Features: Built to bridge the divide between tactical and hunting rifles. Bolt uses a non-rotating gas shield, coned bolt nose, and sliding plate extractor. TriggerTech frictionless release trigger with two-position safety. Threaded muzzle with Omni Muzzle Brake. Patriot Brown Cerakote finish. Guaranteed MOA accuracy.
Price: .... $2,749.00–$2,799.00

BERGARA PREMIER MG LITE
Calibers: 6.5 Creedmoor, 6.5 PRC, .308 Win., .300 Win Mag. Capacity: 5 standard, 3 magnum. Barrel: 22 in. or 24 in. fully free-floated, proprietary CURE carbon fiber. Weight: 6.7–6.8 lbs. Length: 43–45 in. Stock: Ultra-lightweight XLR Element 4.0 magnesium chassis with folding buttstock. Sights: Drilled and tapped for Remington 700 bases with 8-40 screws. Features: Precision bolt-action hunting rifle with a non-rotating gas shield, coned bolt nose, and sliding plate extractor. TriggerTech frictionless release trigger with two-position safety. Threaded muzzle with Omni Muzzle Brake. Graphite Black Cerakote. Guaranteed MOA accuracy.
Price: .... $3,229.00–$3,349.00

BERGARA MG MICRO LITE
Calibers: .308 Win., 6.5 Creedmoor, 6.5 PRC. Capacity: 5-round AICS dropbox magazine. 3-round (6.5 PRC). Barrel: 18 in. CURE carbon-fiber barrel threaded at 5/8x24. Weight: From 5.8 lbs. Length: 37 in. overall. Stock: XLR magnesium Atom chassis with smoke carbon-fiber folding buttstock and adjustable cheek rest. Sights: None. Features: New design for 2024 in a lightweight chassis style. Two-lug bolt with floating head. Sliding plate extractor. Threaded bolt knob. Carbon-fiber skeletonized pistol grip. Limbsaver recoil pad. M-LOK attachment slots. Machined Arca/Swiss dovetail at forend. TriggerTech trigger.
Price: .... $3,099.00–$3,199.00

BERGARA B-14 SQUARED CREST
Calibers: 6.5 Creedmoor, 6.5 PRC, .308 Win., .300 Win. Mag. Barrel: 20 in., (22 in. .300 WM) round steel. Weights: from 6.8–7.2 lbs. Stock: 100% carbon fiber with carbon spine. Features: Addition to the B-14 bolt action family. Sniper Gray Cerakote metalwork. Sub-MOA guarantee. Threaded muzzle with Omni brake. M5 AICS-style magazine.
Price: $1,999.00

BLASER R-8 SERIES
Calibers: Available in virtually all standard and metric calibers from .204 Ruger to .500 Jeffery. Straight-pull bolt action. Barrels: 20.5, 23, or 25.75 in. Weights: 6.375–8.375 lbs. Lengths: 40 in. overall (22 in. barrel). Stocks: Synthetic or Turkish walnut. Sights: None furnished; drilled and tapped for scope mounting. Features: Thumb-activated safety slide/cocking mechanism; interchangeable barrels and bolt heads. Many optional features. Imported from Germany by Blaser USA. *Note, Blaser R8 bolt action series adds a .22 LR rimfire conversion system.*
Price: $3,787.00

BLASER R8 ULTIMATE CARBON
Calibers: Available in wide range of calibers from .22 LR to .500 Jeffery, now including 6.5 Creedmoor and 6.5 PRC. Barrel: 20.5, 23, or 25.75 in. Stock: Hand-laid 100% carbon fiber thumbhole stock with Elastomer grip inserts. An Ultimate Carbon Leather variant is available with dark brown weather-proof leather inserts. Sights: Drilled and tapped. Features: Straight-pull bolt-action hunting rifle with interchangeable barrels and bolt heads. Ultimate Carbon variant designed for max performance and minimum weight. Blaser Precision trigger. Thumb-activated safety slide/cocking mechanism. Optional upgrades include an adjustable comb and recoil absorption system or adjustable recoil pad. Imported from Germany by Blaser Group.
Price: $11,500.00

BROWNING AB3 COMPOSITE STALKER
Calibers: .243, 6.5 Creedmoor, .270 Win., .270 WSM, 7mm-08, 7mm Rem. Mag., .30-06, .300 Win. Mag., .300 WSM or .308 Win. Barrels: 22 in, 26 in. for magnums. Weights: 6.8–7.4 lbs. Stock: Matte black synthetic. Sights: None. Picatinny rail scope mount included.
Price: $600.00
Price: Micro Stalker $600.00
Price: Hunter $670.00

BROWNING X-BOLT 2
Calibers: .243 Win., 6mm Creedmoor, 6.5 Creedmoor, .270 Win., 28 Nosler, 6.5 PRC, 6.8 Western, .30-'06, 7mm Mag., 7mm PRC, .300 PRC, .300 Win. Mag. Capacity: New Plus magazine system adds two rounds to standard capacity. Barrels: 18–26 in. (varies by model variant and chambering) threaded, free-floating. Most models wear muzzle brakes. Weight: Varies by model. Length: Varies by model. Stock: Synthetic Vari-Tech with customizable fit in LOP, comb height, grip angle and more adjustments

with rubber overmolding and camouflage finish. McMillan stocks on select models. Carbon-fiber stocks on select others. Sights: None. Drilled and tapped for X-Lock scope mounts. Features: Second generation of the X-Bolt arrived in 2024 with X-Bolt 2, replacing original X-Bolt models. Select models include a Pic rail. Reconfigured receiver now features bolt guidance area for smoother operation and zero-bind performance. Hand-reamed chambers. Adjustable DLX trigger with zero creep, take-up, or overtravel. Top tang safety, bolt unlock button, rotary magazine, Inflex recoil pad. Vari-Tech stocks are fitted with a thicker 1.25-in recoil pad, though a 1-inch pad is available to further reduced LOP. Many models are ARCA Swiss rail ready.

Price: X-Bolt 2 Speed ....**$1,469.00–$1,549.00**
Price: X-Bolt 2 Speed LR ....**$1,499.00–$1,579.00**
Price: X-Bolt 2 Speed SPR ....**$1,499.00–$1,559.00**
Price: X-Bolt 2 Hell's Canyon McMillan LR ....**$2,599.00–$2,699.00**
Price: X-Bolt 2 Target Competition Lite **$2,739.00**
Price: X-Bolt 2 Mountain Pro Carbon-Fiber ....**$3,739.00–$3,799.00**
Price: X-Bolt 2 Pro McMillan SPR Carbon-Fiber ....**$3,999.00–$4,069.00**
Price: X-Bolt 2 Pro McMillan Carbon-Fiber..................**$3,999.00–$4,069.00**

CADEX DEFENCE CDX-R7 CRBN SERIES

Calibers: 6.5 Creedmoor, 6.5 PRC, .308 Win., .300 WSM, .300 PRC, .338 Lapua Mag. Capacity: Varies by box magazine. Barrel: 24 or 26 in. Proof Research carbon fiber threaded. Weight: 8.2–8.3 lbs. Length: 45.25–48.06 in. Stock: Lightweight Tundra Strike chassis with aluminum bedding blocks available in 14 color combinations. Cadex recoil pad, neoprene cheek pad, and rubberized grip panel. Sights: None. 0 MOA Picatinny rail standard, 20 or 30 MOA rails available. Features: Bolt-action rifle designed with backcountry hunters in mind. Hunting style muzzle brake and bolt knob. Spiral fluted bolt. Cerakote metalwork. DX2 Evo single-/two-stage selectable trigger. Oversized triggerguard and mag release. Hard case included.

Price: **$3,359.00**

CADEX DEFENCE CDX-R7 SPTR SERIES

Calibers: 6.5 Creedmoor, 6.5 PRC, .308 Win., .300 WSM, .300 PRC, 338 Lapua Mag. Capacity: varies by box magazine. Barrel: 24 or 26 in. sporter profile stainless, fluted and threaded. Weight: 8.2–8.5 lbs. Length: 45.25–48.06 in. Stock: Lightweight Tundra Strike chassis with aluminum bedding blocks available in 14 color combinations. Cadex recoil pad, neoprene cheek pad, and rubberized grip panel. Sights: None. 0 MOA Picatinny rail standard, 20 or 30 MOA rails available. Features: Bolt-action rifle similar to the CRBN series, but without the carbon-fiber barrel. Hunting-style muzzle brake and bolt knob. Spiral fluted bolt. DX2 Evo single-/two-stage selectable trigger. Oversized triggerguard and mag release. Hard case included.

Price: **$2,769.00**

CHAPUIS ROLS

Calibers: .30-06 Spfld., .300 Win. Mag., .375 H&H (6.5 Creed & .308 Win. available on Carbon only). Barrel: 24 in., 25.5 in. Weights: 5.3-5.5 lbs. (Carbon); 6.6-7.2 lbs. (Classic & Deluxe) Stock: High-grade Circassian Walnut, pistol grip-style with Schnabel forend on Classic and Deluxe. Carbon-fiber black on Carbon model. Features: Straight-pull bolt action rifle. Sub-MOA accuracy guarantee. Action and locking system tested for up to 123,000 PSI. Manual decocker. Single trigger. Manual safety. Open rifle sights with slots for Recknagel scope mounts. Quick detach rotary magazine. Ready to accept barrels in different calibers. Ships with prestige-grade custom hard case.

Price: Classic w/ bronze receiver, Walnut ....**$5,899.00–$6,299.00**
Price: Deluxe w/ silver engraved receiver, Walnut ....**$6,899.00–$7,399.00**
Price: Carbon w/ carbon-fiber stock, no sights ....**$9,099.00–$9,399.00**

CHEYTAC M-200

Calibers: .357 CheyTac, .408 CheyTac. Capacity: 7-round magazine. Barrel: 30 in. Length: 55 in. stock extended. Weight: 27 lbs. (steel barrel); 24 lbs. (carbon-fiber barrel). Stock: Retractable. Sights: None, scope rail provided. Features: CNC-machined receiver, attachable Picatinny rail M-1913, detachable barrel, integral bipod, 3.5-lb. trigger pull, muzzle brake. Made in USA by CheyTac, LLC.

Price: **$11,700.00**

CHRISTENSEN ARMS RIDGELINE FFT

Calibers: .450 Bushmaster, .22-250 Rem., .243 Rem, 6.5 Creed, 6.5 PRC, 6.5-284, 26 Nosler, .270 Win., 7mm-08, .280 Ackley, 28 Nosler, 7mm Rem. Mag., .308 Win., .30-06, 30 Nosler, .300 WSM, .300 Win. Mag., .300 PRC, .300 RUM. Capacity: FFT hinged floor plate with internal magazine. 4-round standard, 3-round magnum. Barrel: 20 or 22-in. carbon-fiber wrapped stainless, button-rifled, hand-lapped, free-floating. Weight: From 5.3 lbs. Stock: Proprietary Flash Forged Technology (FFT) carbon-fiber sporter style with stainless steel bedding pillars. Choice of black with gray webbing, green with black and tan webbing, Sitka Subalpine camo, or Sitka Elevated II camo. Sights: No iron sights. Drilled and tapped at 6-48 for Remington 700 bases. Features: Upgraded version of the Ridgeline uses the latest in carbon-fiber technology to build the rifle a full pound lighter. New side-baffle brake and stylish paint scheme distinguish the upgraded model. Choice of natural stainless or Burnt Bronze Cerakote metalwork. Enlarged ejection port. Billet aluminum bottom metal. Sub-MOA guarantee, excluding .450 Bushmaster. Multiple calibers available in a left-hand rifle.

Price: **$2,399.00**

CHRISTENSEN ARMS RIDGELINE SCOUT

Calibers: .223 Rem, 6mm ARC, 6.5 Creed, .308 Win., .300 Blackout. Capacity: 10-round AICS box magazine. Barrel: 16-in. carbon-fiber wrapped stainless, button rifled, free-floating. Weight: From 5.9 lbs. Stock: Carbon-fiber composite, sporter style with stainless steel bedding pillars. Tan with black webbing. Sights: No iron sights. 0 MOA rail. Features: Compact, scout-rifle version of the Ridgeline bolt-action hunting rifle. Black nitride-coated action. Flat-shoe TriggerTech trigger. Match chamber. Three-prong flash hider removes for easy suppressor use. Forward mount lower rail with barricade stop. MOA guarantee.

Price: **$2,199.00**

CHRISTENSEN ARMS RIDGELINE TITANIUM EDITION

Calibers: 6.5 Creedmoor, 6.5 PRC, .308 Win., .300 Win. Mag. Capacity: 3 to 4. Barrel: 22 to 24 in., 416R stainless steel, carbon-fiber wrapped. Stock: Carbon-fiber composite, sporter style. Sights: Picatinny rail. Weight: 5.8 lbs. Features: Titanium radial brake, M16-style extractor, LimbSaver recoil pad.

Price: **$2,495.00**

CHRISTENSEN ARMS MODERN HUNTING RIFLE (MHR)

Calibers: 6.5 Creed, 6.5 PRC, 6.8 Western, .308 Win., 7mm PRC, 7mm Rem. Mag., .300 Win. Mag., .300 PRC. Barrel: 22 in., 24 in. carbon-fiber wrapped stainless steel. Weight: 7.4 lbs. Stock: Aluminum mini chassis with FFT carbon-fiber stock. Features: Modular bolt-action design blending chassis rifle design with hunting features. Sub-MOA accuracy guarantee. Removeable side-baffle brake. V-Block bedding. Toolless adjustable comb. Forward Picatinny and M-LOK points. Match chamber. Hand-lapped button-rifled free-floating barrel design. Black nitride action finish. Multiple stock finishes available. TriggerTech trigger. Internal magazine with AICS drop-box compatibility.

Price: **$3,499.00**

Prices given are believed to be accurate at time of publication however, many factors affect retail pricing so exact prices are not possible.

79TH EDITION, 2025 ✦ 445

CHRISTENSEN ARMS EVOKE

Calibers: .243 Win., 6.5 Creedmorr, 6.5 PRC, .270 Win., .308 Win., .30-'06, .350 Legend, 7mm Rem. Mag., 7mm PRC, .300 Win. Mag., .300 PRC. Capacity: 5-round detachable magazine. Barrels: 18, 20, 22 in. 416R stainless #4 contour with Cerakote finish. Included RFR muzzle brake. Weights: from 7.7 lbs. (Hunter 8.1 lbs.; Precision 8.4 lbs.) Stock: Synthetic with hybrid grip angle. Sights: None. Integrated Picatinny rail Features: Christensen's most affordable hunting rifle upon debut in 2024. Sixty-degree bolt throw with three-lug bolt. Adjustable TriggerTech trigger. Sub-MOA guarantee and limited lifetime warranty. Evoke family available in four model variants, each suppressor-ready. Hunter adds a Pic optics rail. Precision model adds ARCA rail, Pic optics rail, and adjustable FFT carbon-fiber cheek riser.

Price: Evoke $899.00
Price: Evoke Mossy Oak. (Bottomland camo) $949.00
Price: Evoke Hunter (Christensen Hunter camo) $999.00
Price: Evoke Precision (Hex pattern engraved barrel/Hex Camo) $1048.00

CVA CASCADE

Calibers: .243 Win., 6.5 Creedmoor, 7mm-08 Rem., .308 Win., .350 Legend, .450 Bushmaster, .22-250 Rem., 6.5 PRC, 7mm Rem. Mag., .300 Win. Mag. Capacity: 3 or 4-round flush-fit detachable magazine Barrel: 22-in. 4140 carbon steel in either matte blue or Cerakote FDE. Weight: 6.85–7.25 lbs. Length: 42.5–45.5 in. Stock: Synthetic, fiber-glass reinforced with SoftTouch finish. Available in either charcoal gray or Veil Wideland camo. Sights: Drilled and tapped for Savage 110 mounts; aftermarket CVA 20-MOA one-piece base available. Features: Bolt designed with 70-degree throw. Two-position safety. Threaded muzzle. Dual front swivel studs. Buttstock has adjustable LOP with removeable spacer. MOA guarantee.

Price: ....$567.00–$658.00
Price: Cascade SB (Short Barrel) Series $670.00

CVA CASCADE XT

Calibers: 6.5 Creedmoor, .308 Win., .450 Bushmaster, .350 Legend, 6.5 PRC, 7mm Rem. Mag., .300 Win. Mag. Barrel: 22, 24, 26 in. #5 Taper fluted, threaded. Stock: Synthetic with Realtree Excape camo and SoftTouch finish. Features: Precision-oriented version of the Cascade bolt action. Heavier barrel with radial muzzle brake. Tactical-style bolt knob. Two-position safety. Dual front swivel studs. Graphite black Cerakote metalwork. MOA guarantee. Flush-fit, dropbox magazine.

Price: $799.00

CVA CASCADE SR-80

Calibers: .308 Win., .350 Legend. Capacity: Higher-capacity dropbox magazine. Barrel: 18 in. with radial muzzle brake threaded at 5/8x24. Stock: Synthetic pistol grip-style in FDE with black web, checkered grip panels, dual forward studs, and black recoil pad. Adjustable LOP with spacer. Sights: Williams rear peep and adjustable front. Forward-mounted Picatinny rail for long eye relief optics. Features: The SR-80 is CVA's entry into a traditional scout-style rifle. Metalwork finished in Graphite Black Cerakote. Oversized bolt knob. Three-lug bolt.

Price: $925.00

CVA CASCADE LRH & VH

Calibers: 6.5 Creedmoor, .308 Win., 6.5 PRC, 7mm Rem. Mag., .300 Win. Mag., .300 PRC (LRH); .204 Ruger, .223 Rem., .22-250 Rem., .243 Win. (VH). Barrel: 20, 22, 24, 26 in. medium-heavy contour threaded with muzzle brake installed. Stock: Synthetic with adjustable LOP and comb height, and dual forward studs. Features: Pair of Long Range Hunter (LRH) and Varmint Hunter (VH) purpose-specific rifles. LRH available in two variants: Smoked Bronze metal w/ Realtree Hillside and Smoked bronze metal w/ black/bronze web stock. Varmint Hunter with smoked bronze and Realtree hillside camo. Higher capacity magazines on Varmint models.

Price: LRH .... $925.00–$950.00
Price: VH $900.00

CZ 600

Calibers: .223 Rem., .243 Win., 6.5 Creedmoor, .308 Win., .270 Win., .30-'06, .300 Win. Mag. (American); .223 Rem., .243 Win., 6mm Creedmoor, 6.5 Creedmoor, 6.5 PRC, .308 Win., 7.62x39, .270 Win., .30-'06, 8x57 IS, .300 Win. Mag., (Alpha); .223 Rem., .308 Win., .30-'06, .300 Win. Mag. (Lux); 6mm Creedmoor and .308 Win. (Range); .223 Rem., .300 AAC, and 7.62x39 (Trail). Capacity: 5-round detachable magazine. Barrel: Varies by model. Weight: Varies by model. Stock: Varies by model. See below. Features: Debuted by CZ in 2021, replacing previous centerfire platforms. Comes in three different receiver sizes: Mini, Medium, and Long with both steel and aluminum receiver options. Smaller actions use a three-lug bolt; magnums have six lugs. Though initially marketed as a switch-barrel design, a full recall noted below has changed the 600 to a fixed-barrel platform. Tang located vertical safety and bolt release button. Short extractor controlled feed. Magazine lock mechanism activates to change the rifle to a fixed magazine configuration. Adjustable single-stage trigger on most models. The 600 family is comprised of five model variants: The American with Turkish Walnut stock, no sights, and threaded barrel. The Alpha with black synthetic stock, lightweight aluminum receiver, and semi-heavy barrel. The Lux with select-grade walnut stock in Bavarian style with iron sights, including hooded front. Range with laminate wood minimalist stock, heavy barrel, and best accuracy guarantee at ¾ MOA. Trail in a lightweight, more AR-style build with collapsible PDW-style stock, available only in .223 Rem., .300 AAC, (AR mags) and 7.62x39 (CZ Bren 2 mags). NOTE: The CZ 600 was initially marketed as a swappable-barrel system, but a mandatory safety recall was issued shortly after launch. The rifle could still be fired even with a barrel improperly installed, so CZ began permanently installing all 600 barrels, including modifying rifles returned under the recall due to potential catastrophic failures. Early production rifles will need to be returned under the recall.

Price: 600 American $849.00
Price: 600 American High Grade introduced 2024 w/ upgraded
    wood and *fleur de lis* checkering...................................$1,499.00
Price: 600 Alpha $649.00
Price: 600 Lux $999.00
Price: 600 Range $1,299.00
Price: 600 Trail $1,079.00

FIERCE FIREARMS RIVAL

Calibers: 6.5 Creedmoor, 6.5 PRC, 7mm Rem., 28 Nosler, .300 Win., .300 PRC, .300 RUM. Capacity: 4 to 5. Barrel: 20 to 26 in., spiral-fluted, match-grade stainless steel or carbon fiber. Stock: Fierce Tech C3 carbon fiber. Sights: None, drilled and tapped. Weight: 6.4 to 7 lbs. Features: Cerakote finish, Trigger Tech trigger, built-in bipod rail.

Price: .... $2,295.00-$2,795.00

FIERCE FIREARMS MTN REAPER
Calibers: 6.5 Creed, 6.5 PRC, 7mm PRC, 7mm Rem. Mag., .308 Win., .300 Win. Mag., .300 PRC. Barrel: 18 or 20 in. (short action), 20 or 22 in. (long action) C3 carbon fiber Weight: 5.8-6.6 lbs. Stock: Ultralite magnesium chassis with push button carbon-fiber fold and lock stock. Features: Precision machined two-lug bolt action. 70-degree bolt throw with tactical knob. Bix'nAndy trigger. AccurateMag box magazine. NIX muzzle brake. Limbsaver buttpad. Spiral fluted bolt. 0-MOA scope rail. Guaranteed 1/2 MOA accuracy.
Price: **$3,399.00**

FRANCHI MOMENTUM
Calibers: .243 Win., 6.5 Creedmoor, .270 Win., .308 Win., .30-06, .300 Win. Mag. Barrels: 22 or 24 in. Weights: 6.5-7.5 lbs. Stock: Black synthetic with checkered gripping surface, recessed sling swivel studs, TSA recoil pad. Sights: None. Features: Available with Burris Fullfield II 3-9X40mm scope.
Price: Varminter..**$609.00**
Price: With Burris 3-9X scope..**$729.00**

FRANCHI MOMENTUM ELITE
Calibers: .223 Rem., 6.5 Creedmoor, 6.5 PRC, .308 Win., .300 Win. Mag., .350 Legend. Capacity: 3 or 4-round box magazine. Barrel: 22- or 24-in. free floating, cold hammer forged with threaded muzzle brake. Weight: 7.1-7.5 lbs. Stock: Synthetic in True Timber Strata, Realtree Excape, and now also available with Sitka Optifade Elevation II camouflage. Sights: Picatinny rail. Features: TSA recoil pad absorbs up to 50 percent of felt recoil. Sling attachment points recessed into stock. One-piece spiral fluted bolt with three locking lugs and 60-degree throw. Two-position safety. RELIA trigger adjustable from 2 to 4 pounds. Cobalt Cerakote metalwork on the Sitka camo models.
Price: **$899.00**

FRANCHI MOMENTUM ELITE VARMINT
Calibers: .223 Rem., .22-250 Rem., .224 Valkyrie, 6.5 Creedmoor, .308 Win. Capacity: 3-4-round flush magazines or 7-8-round extended magazines. Barrel: 24-in. free-floating, heavy, spiral-fluted, threaded. Weight: 9.0-9.4 lbs. Length: 46.75 in. Stock: Evolved EGONOM-X synthetic with removeable cheek rest and checkered-polymer grip, finished in Sitka OptiFade Subalpine camo. Sights: One-piece Picatinny rail. Features: Varmint addition to the Momentum Elite family gets caliber additions for 2022. Stock designed specifically for varmint hunting. Midnight Bronze Cerakote metalwork. RELIA-Trigger adjustable from 2-4 pounds. MOA accuracy guarantee. DEPENDA bolt with three locking lugs and 60-degree throw.
Price: **$999.00**

FRANCHI MOMENTUM ALL TERRAIN ELITE
Caliber: .223 Rem./5.56 NATO, .308 Win./7.62 NATO. Barrel: 18-in. free-floating, threaded. Weight: 7.5 lbs. Stock: Synthetic in True Timber Strata. Features: Specialized version of the Momentum bolt actions. Optimized for carry. Modular stock with a low-rise comb and M-LOK and QD points. Metalwork in Midnight Bronze Cerakote. Extended Picatinny rail. AICS 10-round magazine. Flip-up adjustable iron sights. Relia adjustable single-stage trigger and MOA guarantee. Threaded barrel with muzzle brake. TSA

recoil pad.
Price: **$1,499.00**

GUNWERKS CLYMR
Calibers: 7 LRM, .22-250, 6mm Creed, 6.5 Creed, 6.5-284 Norma, 6.5 PRC, 28 Nosler, 7mm Rem. Mag., 7 SAUM, .300 Win. Mag., 30 Nosler, 300 PRC. Capacity: 3-round capacity in the internal mag. Option to upgrade to dropbox mags. Barrel: Carbon wrapped, threaded, 20- or 22-in. barrel come standard. Upgrade to 18 in. available. Weight: Varies by options selected. Stock: Carbon fiber in choice of ten paint finishes with negative comb and flat toe line. Sights: No sights. Drilled and tapped. Choice of multiple base, scope ring, and scope options direct from the factory. Features: Lightweight, semi-custom, bolt-action hunting rifle built for mountain hunting and available as a user-built rifle system with multiple options. Choice of standard GLR SS action or Titanium action upgrade. Add $150 for Left-hand action. Eleven metal finish colors available, as well as option of directional muzzle brake or thread cap. LOP of 13.5 in. Prices increase significantly as options are added for custom factory builds.
Price: **$5,245.00**

GUNWERKS WERKMAN SYSTEM
Caliber: 6.5 PRC, 7mm PRC, .300 PRC. Barrel: 22-in. stainless steel, cut rifled. Weight: 9.6 lbs. Stock: Gen1 Magnus carbon fiber in tan, gray, or green Fracture paint finish. Features: Bolt-action rifle system with fewer frills. GLR stainless receiver. Threaded barrel with directional brake. TriggerTech trigger. GW floorplate bottom metal. Topped with Revic Werkman RS25 rifle scope. Custom BDC turret matched to Hornady ELD Match ammunition and ballistics data for 1,000 yards. Left-hand action available for +$150.
Price: **$4,950.00**

HEYM EXPRESS BOLT-ACTION RIFLE
Calibers: .375 H&H Mag., .416 Rigby, .404 Jeffery, .458 Lott, .450 Rigby. Capacity: 5. Barrel: 24 in., Krupp steel, hammer-forged. Stock: Custom select European walnut. Sights: Iron, barrel-banded front. Weight: 9 to 10.5 lbs. Features: Caliber-specific action and magazine box, classic English sporting rifle, three-position safety.
Price: **$12,000.00**

HOWA MINI ACTION FULL DIP
Calibers: .223 Rem., 6.5 Grendel, 7.62x39. Capacity: 5. Barrel: 20 in., threaded, heavy. Stock: Hogue pillar-bedded. Sights: 3.5-10x44 scope. Weight: 10 lbs. Features: Full-dipped camo, forged, one-piece bolt with locking lugs.
Price: **$769.00**

HOWA HS CARBON FIBER
Caliber: 6.5 Creedmoor. Capacity: 4. Barrel: 24 in., carbon-fiber wrapped. Stock: Synthetic, CNC-machined aluminum bedding block. Sights: None, drilled and tapped. Weight: 7.8 lbs. Features: Lightweight, hand-finished stock, scope optional.
Price: **$1,819.00**

HOWA CARBON ELEVATE

Calibers: .6.5 Grendel, 6.5 Creedmoor, .308 Win., 6.5 PRC. Capacity: Varies by caliber and depending on flush mount or extended magazine. Barrel: 24-in. heavy threaded barrel. Weight: from 4 lbs. 13 oz. Stock: Stocky's Custom carbon-fiber super lightweight design available in natural carbon fiber or Kryptek Altitude. Sights: No sights. Drilled and tapped. Features: Ultra-lightweight bolt-action hunting rifle with AccuBlock lug bed. Three-position safety. Sub-MOA accuracy assurance. HACT two-stage trigger. LimbSaver buttpad. Suppressor-ready. Sub-MOA guarantee. Manufacturer Lifetime Warranty.

Price: **$1,528.00**

HOWA HERA H7

Calibers: 6.5 Creedmoor, .308 Win.. Capacity: 5 rounds with an AICS-compatible magazine. Barrel: Choice of 22-in. standard; 24-in. heavy steel; or 24-in. carbon fiber. Weight: Varies by model/barrel material. Length: 44.5–47.5 in. Stock: Fiberglass-reinforced polymer Howa H7 chassis system with aluminum forestock with M-LOK in choice of black, tan, OD green, or XK7 Kings Camo. Sights: None. Drilled and tapped. Features: Modern chassis-system, short-action rifle in three distinct variants denoted by barrel type. LOP adjustable with three inserts. Threaded barrel, polymer cheek piece support, and aluminum v-lock bedding. HACT-adjustable trigger.

Price: Standard **$839.00**
Price: Heavy Steel.. **$899.00**
Price: Carbon Fiber... **$1,299.00**

J.P. SAUER & SOHN 404 SYNCHRO XTC

Calibers: .243 Win., .270 Win., 6.5 Creedmoor, 6.5x55, .308 Win., .30-06 Spfld., 7x64, 8x57IS, 9.3x62, 7mm Rem. Mag., .300 Win. Mag., .338 Win. Mag., .404 Jeffery, 10.3x60R. Barrel: 22-in. fluted, cold-hammer forged. Sights: Integral scope bases. Length: 42 in. Weight: 6.1 lbs. Stock: Carbon-fiber XTC thumbhole style with Green/Black/Grey carbon-fiber camo and adjustable comb. Features: Fully modular concept rifle. Adjustable trigger blade and trigger pull, from 1.2–2.7 lbs. Manual cocking. Threaded muzzle. MagLock magazine safety. Matte black hard anodized aluminum receiver. Engineered for changing bolt heads and barrels. SUS combination tool integrated into front sling swivel. Miniature universal tool integrated into rear sling swivel.

Price: **$8,199.00**

J.P SAUER & SOHN 505

Calibers: 19 available calibers interchangeable one system. Mini: .222 Rem., .223 Rem. Medium: .243 Win., .270 Win., 6.5x55 SE, 6.5 Creedmoor, .308 Win., .30-'06, 7x64, 8x57 IS, 9.3x62. Short Magnum: .270 WSM, 6.5 PRC, 8.5x55 Blaser. Magnum: 7mm Rem. Mag., .300 Win. Mag., 8x68S, .375 H&H. Capacity: Flush-mount detachable magazine with capacity varying by chambering. Barrels: 16.5, 18.5, 20, 22 in. cold hammered, threaded. Weight: from 6.1 pounds (carbon) to 7.8 lbs (Walnut). Stock: Choice of multiple materials, including synthetic, synthetic thumbhole, carbon fiber, and high-grade walnut (Grades 2 to 10). Stocks exchange quickly. Sights: None. Blaser quick-detach saddle mount with 100% return to zero. Features: New platform announced in 2024 with steel chassis and interchangeable barrels for caliber changes. Built in Germany. Sixty-degree bolt throw. Trigger adjustable with four pre-set weights from .77 to 2.75 lbs. Manual cocking system. Integrated magazine safety. Adjustable comb on several variants, including Synchro XT and XTC. Detachable sling swivels come standard. Plasma-nitrated metalwork with DLC option.

Price: **$3,500.00**

KENNY JARRETT RIFLES

Calibers: Custom built in virtually any chambering including .223 Rem., .243 Improved, .243 Catbird, 7mm-08 Improved, .280 Remington, .280 Ackley Improved, 7mm Rem. Mag., .284 Jarrett, .30-06 Springfield, .300 Win. Mag., .300 Jarrett, .323 Jarrett, .338 Jarrett, .375 H&H, .416 Rem., .450 Rigby, other modern cartridges. Numerous options regarding barrel type and weight, stock styles and material. Features: Tri-Lock receiver. Talley rings and bases. Accuracy guarantees and custom loaded ammunition. Newest series is the Shikar featuring 28-year aged American Black walnut hand-checkered stock with Jarrett-designed stabilizing aluminum chassis. Accuracy guaranteed to be .5 MOA with standard calibers, .75 MOA with magnums.

Price: Shikar Series **$10,320.00**
Price: Signature Series... **$8,320.00**
Price: Long Ranger Series **$8,320.00**
Price: Ridge Walker Series **$8,320.00**
Price: Wind Walker **$8,320.00**
Price: Original Beanfield (customer's receiver) **$6,050.00**
Price: Professional Hunter **$11,070.00**
Price: SA/Custom **$7,000.00**

KIMBER HUNTER PRO

Calibers: 6.5 Creedmoor, .308 Win., .280 Ackley Improved. Capacity: 3-round box magazine. Barrel: 22 or 24 in. sporter with satin finish and muzzle brake. Weight: 5 lbs. 7oz.–5 lbs. 12 oz. Length: 41.25 in. Stock: Fiber-reinforced polymer in Desolve Blak pattern with pillar bedding. Sights: No iron sights. Drilled and tapped. Features: Full stainless build based on 84M action with Mauser claw extraction. Three-position wing safety. Sling studs. One-inch rubber recoil pad. Match-grade chamber. Factory adjustable trigger set at 3.5–4 lbs. Sub-MOA guarantee.

Price: **$1,006.00**

MAGNUM RESEARCH MOUNTAIN EAGLE

Calibers: Available in most any standard bottlenecked and belted magnum chamberings. Capacity: 3-5 rounds. Dependent on chambering. Barrel: 24, 26, 28 in. linear graphite carbon with Criterion steel inner liner. Weight: Varies by model and barrel length. Stock: Choice of several styles. Sights: None. Integral scope bases. Features: Custom bolt-action rifle with choice of bull barrel or sport taper models, the former with a heavier benchrest-style stock and the latter with a carbon-fiber stock. Adjustable trigger. Available with threaded barrel cap. Dual forward sling studs. Hand-done sponge paint stock on lightweight variant. Built in-house at Pillager, Minnesota, with parts made both in-house and sourced from U.S. manufacturers.

Price: .... **On Request**

MONTANA RIFLE COMPANY JUNCTION

Calibers: 6.5 Creedmoor, .308 Win., 6.5 PRC, 7mm PRC, .375 H&H. (Coming soon: .300 Rem. Ultra Mag., 7mm Rem. Mag., 28 Nosler, .280 Ackley, .270 Win.). Capacity: 4 or 5 rounds, depending on caliber. Barrel: 24-in. hand-lapped, button rifled. Weight: 7.5–7.6 lbs. Length: 42.25 in. overall. Stock: Monte Carlo-style walnut with checkered panels and black grip cap. Sights: None. Integral scope bases. Features: Introduced in 2024 and built on the new MRC 2022 receiver, machined from a 416 stainless blank. Integrated aluminum M-LOK rail at the base of the forend along with QD socket and traditional sling stud. Adaptive controlled-round feed with Mauser-style claw extractor. Three-position safety. Adjustable trigger. Muzzle brake. Built in USA at the new Montana Rifle Co. headquarters in Michigan. Includes a ½-MOA accuracy guarantee.

Price: **$2,495.00**

MONTANA RIFLE COMPANY HIGHLINE

Calibers: 6.5 Creedmoor, .308 Win., 6.5 PRC, 7mm PRC, .375 H&H. (Coming soon: 300 Rem. Ultra. Mag., 7mm Rem. Mag., 28 Nosler, .280 Ackley, .270 Win.). Capacity: 4 or 5 rounds, depending on caliber. Barrel: 24-in. hand-lapped, button rifled. Weight: 6.8–7 lbs. Length: 45.25 in. overall. Stock: McMillan carbon-fiber Game Hunter. Sights: None. Integral scope bases. Features: Introduced in 2024 and built on the new MRC 2022 receiver, machined from a 416 stainless blank. Integrated aluminum M-LOK rail at the base of the forend along with QD socket and traditional sling stud. Adaptive controlled-round feed with Mauser-style claw extractor. Three-position safety. Adjustable trigger. Muzzle brake. Built in USA at the new Montana Rifle Co. headquarters in Michigan. Includes a ½-MOA accuracy guarantee.

Price: **$2,495.00**

MAUSER M-18

Calibers: .223 Rem., .243 Win., 6.5x55, 6.5 PRC, 6.5 Creedmoor, .270 Win., .308 Win., .30-06 Spfld., 8x57IS, 9.3x62, 7mm Rem. Mag., .300 Win. Mag. Capacity: 5-round box magazine. Barrel: 21.75 or 24.5 in. Weight: 6.5–6.8 lbs. Length: 41.7–44.0 in. Stock: Polymer with softgrip inlays. Sights: No iron sights. Drilled and tapped. Features: Adjustable trigger. Three-position safety. Removeable recoil pad section with interior buttstock storage. Budget-priced option tagged "The People's Rifle."

Price: **$699.00**

MAUSER M18 SAVANNA

Calibers: .223 Rem., .243 Win., 6.5 PRC, 6.5 Creedmoor, .270 Win., .308 Win., .30-06 Spfld., 7mm Rem. Mag., .300 Win. Mag. Capacity: 5-round magazine standard; 10-rounders available. Barrel: 21.75 or 24.5-in. cold-hammer forged, German-steel, threaded. Weight: 6.5–6.8 lbs. Length: 41.7–44.0 in. Stock: Savanna Tan Polymer with grip inserts. Sights: No iron sights. Drilled and tapped. Features: Adjustable trigger. Sixty-degree oversized bolt. Three-position safety. Removeable recoil pad section with interior buttstock storage. Sub-MOA guarantee and 10-year warranty.

Price: **$799.00**

MOSSBERG MVP SERIES

Caliber: .223/5.56 NATO. Capacity: 10-round AR-style magazines. Barrels: 16.25-in. medium bull, 20-in. fluted sporter. Weight: 6.5–7 lbs. Stock: Classic black textured polymer. Sights: Adjustable folding rear, adjustable blade front. Features: Available with factory mounted 3-9x32 scope, (4-16x50 on Varmint model). FLEX model has 20-in. fluted sporter barrel, FLEX AR-style 6-position adjustable stock. Varmint model has laminated stock, 24-in. barrel. Thunder Ranch model has 18-in. bull barrel, OD Green synthetic stock.

Price: Patrol Model	**$732.00**
Price: Patrol Model w/scope	**$863.00**
Price: FLEX Model	**$764.00**
Price: FLEX Model w/scope	**$897.00**
Price: Thunder Ranch Model	**$755.00**
Price: Predator Model	**$732.00**
Price: Predator Model w/scope	**$872.00**
Price: Varmint Model	**$753.00**
Price: Varmint Model w/scope	**$912.00**
Price: Long Range Rifle (LR)	**$974.00**

MOSSBERG PATRIOT

Calibers: .22-250, .243 Win., .25-06, .270 Win., 7mm-08, .7mm Rem.,7mm PRC., .308 Win., .30-06, .300 Win. Mag., .38 Win. Mag., .375 Ruger, .350 Legend, .400 Legend. Capacities: 4- or 5-round magazine. Barrels: 22-in. sporter or fluted, 24 in. Stock: Walnut, laminate, camo or synthetic black. Weights: 7.5–8 lbs. Finish: Matte blued. Sights: Adjustable or none. Some models available with 3-9x40 scope. Other features include patented Lightning Bolt Action Trigger adjustable from 2 to 7 pounds, spiral-fluted bolt. Not all variants available in all calibers. Introduced in 2015.

Price: Walnut stock	**$559.00**
Price: Walnut with premium Vortex Crossfire scope	**$649.00**
Price: Synthetic stock	**$396.00**
Price: Synthetic stock with standard scope	**$436.00**
Price: Laminate stock w/iron sights	**$584.00**
Price: Deer THUG w/Mossy Oak Infinity Camo stock	**$500.00**
Price: Bantam	**$396.00**
Price: Patriot Predator FDE	**$536.00**
Price: Predator Cerakote/Camo	**$636.00**

MOSSBERG PATRIOT LR TACTICAL

Caliber: 6.5 Creedmoor, 6.5 PRC, .308 Win. Barrel: 22, 24-in. medium bull threaded. Stock: MDT adjustable for LOP and cheek rest. Features: Latest hunting-meets-long range competition bolt action with the most popular Patriot features plus additional upgrades. M-LOK forend slots. 20 MOA Picatinny rail. Aluminum V-Block bedding. AICS magazine with either a 7- or 10-round capacity.

Price: **$1,085.00**

NOSLER MODEL 48

Calibers: 6mm Creedmoor, 6.5 Creedmoor, 6.5 PRC, 26 Nosler, 27 Nosler, .280 Ackley Improved, 28 Nosler, .300 Win. Mag., 30 Nosler, 33 Nosler. Capacity: 3 or 4-round hinged aluminum floorplate. Barrel: 24-in. light Sendero contour, carbon-fiber wrapped with cut rifling. Sights: No iron sights; contoured to accept any standard two-piece scope base that would otherwise fit a Remington 700. Weight: 6.0 lbs. Length: 44.4–45 in. Stock: Carbon-fiber Mountain Hunter stock in either Granite Green or Shale Gray with textured finish. Features: Built around a Model 48 action. Match-grade, cut-rifled, carbon-wrapped, fully free-floating barrel with guaranteed sub-MOA accuracy. Glass and aluminum pillar bedded into ultra-light Mountain Hunter stock. Steel surfaces coated in Tungsten Grey Cerakote for weather resistance. Timney trigger with two-position safety. Threaded muzzle with knurled thread protector. *Note, Nosler has discontinued all rifles except the Mountain Carbon and Long Range Carbon. Liberty and Heritage are no longer in current production.*

Price: **$3,140.00**

NOSLER MODEL 21

Calibers: 22 Nosler, 6.5 Creedmoor, 6.5 PRC, 26 Nosler, 27 Nosler, .280 Ackley Improved, 28 Nosler, .308 Win., .300 Win. Mag., 30 Nosler, 33 Nosler, .375 H&H Magnum. Capacity: 3 or 4 rounds depending on caliber. Barrel: 22- or 24-in. Shilen match-grade stainless Weight: 6.8–7.1 lbs. Length: 41.625–44.5 in. Stock: McMillian Hunters Edge Sporter 100% carbon fiber painted in all-weather epoxy-style finish. Sights: No iron sights; contoured to accept any standard two-piece scope base that would otherwise fit a Remington 700. Features: Nosler's new rifle design for 2022 with a blueprinted action, wire EDM machined receiver, spriral-fluted, one-piece, nitride coated bolt. TriggerTech Frictionless Release trigger. M16-

Prices given are believed to be accurate at time of publication however, many factors affect retail pricing so exact prices are not possible.

79TH EDITION, 2025 ✛ **449**

style extractor and fire control group feature tool-less takedown. LOP of 13.5-in. with one-inch recoil pad. Threaded barrel with knurled cover.
Price: **$2,795.00**

NULA MODEL 20
Calibers: .243 Win., 6.5 Creedmoor, 7mm-08 Rem., .308 Win., .358 Win. Capacity: 5-round magazine. Barrels: 16, 16.25, 20, and 22-in. button-rifled 416R stainless threaded at 5/8x24. Weight: 4 lbs. 15 oz. to 5 lbs. 4 oz., depending on chambering and barrel length. Stock: Lightweight carbon fiber with a one-inch Pachmayr Decelerator recoil pad. Choice of color options in Canyon Rogue, Charcoal Gray, or Kodiak Rogue. Sights: None. Features: The NULA 20 marks the new era of New Ultralight Arms (now NULA) under Wilson Combat ownership. Designed as a high-quality production version of Melvin Forbes' original hand-built rifle. 4140 receiver with Armorlube DLC coating. Timney Elite Hunter trigger adjustable from 2.75–3.25 lbs. Nitride-coated sling studs. Built in the USA by Wilson Combat.
Price: **$3,295.00**

PARKWEST ARMS PW-LDR
Calibers: Many standard and magnum chamberings available. Capacity: 4+1 (standard); 3+1 (magnum) with hinged floorplate. Detachable magazine available as an upgrade. Barrel: Stainless steel in multiple lengths, threaded with cap. Stock: AG Composite Sportsman carbon fiber. Sights: None. Drilled and tapped for 8-40 screws. Features: Similar to the XTi but built instead with a stainless steel reeiveer and barrel. Black matte Cerakote standard, with custom colors on request. Sub-MOA accuracy guarantee. Includes tactical hard case.
Price: **$10,995.00**

PARKWEST ARMS SD-76
Calibers: Wide variety of centerfire chamberings, covering everything from plains game to dangerous game, from .22-250 Rem. to .450 Rigby. Capacity: Varies by chambering with internal magazine, with most either 4+1 or 3+1. Drop belly mag on Savanna and Dark Continent. Barrel: Multiple lengths available, button-rifled, individually matched to the receiver within .0005 in. Stock: Choice of multiple types and grades of walnut on most models, including English, Turkish, Bastogne, and Claro Walnuts. Bushveld model uses bedded composite stock. Sights: Varies by model. Most include irons. All are drilled and tapped for 8-40 base screws. Features: The SD-76 remains the focal point of ParkWest Arms' catalog, carried over from the original Dakota Arms. All guns built in Sturgis, South Dakota. Most models are available in both right- or left-handed actions. Hand-checkering on all walnut-stocked models, with multiple custom checkering patterns available. Receiver CNC-machined from 4140 billet, one-piece bolt, three-position safety, claw extractor, positive mechanical ejector, and true controlled feed. Sub-MOA guarantee on all models. Matte blue finish comes standard, but casehardening is also available, along with custom engraving. The Take-Down Model allows the barrel and forend to be quickly removed. The Dark Continent is designed for dangerous game hunting with a hand-fit quarter rib, choice of fixed or folding sights regulated to customer specs. The Savanna is designed for plains game hunting with an Island rear sight and flip-up bead front. The Alpine is built for lightweight big game hunting with a 22-inch barrel, XXX-grade walnut with Schnabel forend tip, and included Talley mounts; available in .22-250 Rem. through .30-06. The Bushveld is designed for the Professional Hunter and is available in .300 H&H through .450 Rigby, with green composite stock, match barrel, island sights, and Talley mounts. The Legend is built for a broad range of big game hunting, with XXX-grade walnut, classic ball swivel studs, matte blued finish, and Talley mounts.
Price: **$10,995.00**

PARKWEST ARMS SD-97
Calibers: .257 Roberts through .375 H&H. Capacity: Blind magazine, capacity varies by chambering. 4+1 for standard calibers, 3+1 for magnums.

Barrel: 24-in. standard; 2-in. magnum; button-rifled, free-floated. Stock: Precision composite with aluminum pillar bedding and two-part catalyzed paint textured for grip. Color choices of black, green, tan, white, brown, or gray. Webbing or splatter available in black and tan. Sights: None. Scope bases installed. Features: SD-97 receiver built of either chromoly or stainless steel with two action lengths. CNC machined from 4140 billet or 15-5 stainless. Round body receiver. Designed specifically for synthetic stock applications. All parts hand polished and hand fit.
Price: **$10,995.00**

PARKWEST ARMS XTi
Calibers: Wide range of short- and long-action chamberings available. Capacity: 4+1 (standard), 3+1 (magnum). Varies by chambering, with hinged floorplate. Detachable magazine available as an upgrade. Barrel: Proof Research carbon fiber with threaded muzzle cap. Stock: AG Composite sportsman carbon-fiber stock in multiple color and camo options. Sights: None. Drilled and tapped at 8-40 with a 20 MOA rail. Features: Lightweight, long-range bolt-action built with a titanium reviver. Matte black Cerakote metalwork. Nitrided bolt. Timney Elite Hunter adjustable trigger. M16-style extractor. Side button bolt release. Sub-½ MOA accuracy guarantee. Includes tactical hard case. PW-XTi Youth variant offered in barrel lengths from 16.5–26 in. with an adjustable stock; LOP starting at 10.25 in. for smaller shooters.
Price: **$10,995.00**

PARKWEST ARMS XTi-UL
Calibers: Wide range of short action chamberings available. Capacity: 4+1 (standard) with hinged floorplate. Barrel: Sporter contour fluted premium barrel. Stock: Manners MCS-UC carbon fiber with gray-black camo. Sights: None. Drilled and taped at 8-40. Features: Parkwest's lightest weight rifle starting at 5.5 lbs built on the PW-XTi titanium action. Matte black Cerakote metalwork, with custom colors upon request. Nitrided bolt. Timney Elite Hunter adjustable trigger. Sub-MOA accuracy guarantee. Includes tactical hard case.
Price: **$10,995.00**

PARKWEST ARMS TAC-LDR
Calibers: Multiple options available in both short and long action. Capacity: Varies by detachable AICS magazine. Barrel: 26 in. Lilja Match Premium barrel, threaded with cap. Stock: MDT-ESS chassis with 15-in. handguard and folding buttstock. Sights: None. Full-length Picatinny rail. Features: Right-handed bolt-action built as a long-distance competition rifle with AR-style features including pistol grip, M-LOK attachment points, and modular buttstock. Sub-1 MOA accuracy guarantee. Includes tactical hard case.
Price: **$10,995.00**

PROOF RESEARCH ASCENSION
Caliber: 6.5 Creed, 6.5 PRC, 7mm Rem. Mag., 7mm PRC, 28 Nosler, .308 Win., .300 Win. Mag., .300 WSM, 300 PRC. Barrel: 20 to 26 in. Proof carbon-fiber wrapped, match-grade Sendero weight. Weight: 5 lbs., 5 oz. to 6 lbs., 4 oz. Stock: PROOF carbon-fiber Monte Carlo-style in multiple colors/patterns. Features: High Country Hunter bolt-action rifle built on a titanium Zermatt Arms receiver. TriggerTech trigger. Threaded barrel with protector; brakes available for an upcharge. Multiple Cerakote action colors. Split rail base. BDL-style magazine. 1/2 MOA accuracy guarantee.
Price: **$7,699.00**

Prices given are believed to be accurate at time of publication however, many factors affect retail pricing so exact prices are not possible.

REMARMS MODEL 700 ALPHA 1
Caliber: .223 Rem., .22-250 Rem., .243 Win., 6.5 Creed, 7mm-08 Rem., .270 Win,. .308 Win., .30-06 Spfld., 7mm Rem. Mag., .300 Win. Mag. Barrel: 22, 24 in. fluted 5R w/ Black Cerakote. Stock: AG Composite Gray Speckled Synthetic. Features: First rifle launch from new RemArms. Precision ground recoil lug. Enlarged ejection port. Timney Elite Hunter trigger. Toolless firing pin disassembly. Aluminum Obendorf-style triggerguard. Included Picatinny rail mount. Longer internal magazine for greater case lengths.
Price: **$2,140.00**

RIGBY BIG GAME LIGHTWEIGHT
Calibers: .350 Rigby Magnum. Capacity: 5+1 rounds. Barrel: 24 in. engraved with maker's name in old English font, fitted with barrel band and swivel for sling attachment. Weight: 9.3 lbs. (Stock: Grade 5 Walnut with profile mirroring prewar models. No cheekpiece, large hand-checkered panels, and 14.5 LOP. Sights: Express island-style sights with ramp front and folding blade rear for 65, 150, and 250 yards. Also fitted with quick detachable swing off mounts. Features: Debuted at DSC in 2024 as the lighter weight addition to Rigby's Big Game and Big Game PH models. Built on a Mauser M98 magnum double square bridge action. Three-position side safety. Color-casehardened recoil bar and grip cap. Magazine floorplate engraved with Rigby's double "R" logo.
Price: **$14,075.00**

RUGER AMERICAN GEN II
Calibers: .204 Ruger, .22 ARC, .223 Rem, .243 Win., 6mm ARC, 6mm Creedmoor, 6.5 Grendel, 6.5 Creedmoor, 6.5 PRC, .308 Win., 7mm-08, .30-'06, .270 Win., .350 Legend, .400 Legend, .450 Bushmaster, 7mm PRC, .300 Win. Mag. Capacity: Varies with AI-style dropbox magazine. Most chamberings 3-round cap; 5- and 10-round come standard on select calibers. Barrel: 20-in. spiral fluted with threaded muzzle and installed radial port muzzle brake Weight: 6.1–6.6 lbs. Length: 41.25 in. overall. Stock: Synthetic tan with splatter finish for grip. Comb risers for adjusting height. Sights: None. Picatinny scope base included. Features: Second generation model American launched in 2024 with two distinct variants— the Standard and Ranch. Three-position tang safety. Oversized bolt handle. Integral bedding block and free-floated barrel. Cerakote metalwork. Ruger Marksman adjustable trigger with pull weight adjustable from 3–5 pounds. LOP adjusts from 12–13.75 in. with insert. Standard wears Gray Splatter furniture and Gun Metal Gray Cerakote metalwork with longer barrels.
Price: **$729.00**

RUGER AMERICAN GEN II PREDATOR
Calibers: .204 Ruger, .223 Rem., .22 ARC, 6mm ARC, 6.5 Grendel, .300 Blackout, .243 Win., 6mm Creedmoor, 6.5 Creedmoor, 6.5 PRC, .308 Win., 7mm-08 Rem., .350 Legend, .400 Legend, .30-'06, .270 Win., 7mm PRC, .300 Win. Mag., .450 Bushmaster. Capacity: Varies by chambering with dropbox magazine of 3-, 5-, or 10-round, some AR style, some single stack. Barrel: 22-in. spiral fluted with threaded muzzle and installed radial port muzzle brake Weight: 6.5–6.7 lbs. Length: 43.25–43.75 in. overall. Stock: Synthetic Green with splatter finish for grip. Comb risers for adjusting height. Sights: None. Picatinny scope base included . Features: Second-generation model American launched in 2024. Scout marks the more compact package. Three-position tang safety. Oversized bolt handle. Integral bedding block and free-floated barrel. Cerakote metalwork. Ruger Marksman adjustable trigger with pull weight adjustable from 3–5 pounds. LOP adjusts from 12–13.75 inches with insert. Predator wears green furniture and Burnt Bronze Cerakote metalwork.
Price: **$729.00**

RUGER AMERICAN GEN II RANCH
Calibers: 5.56 NATO, .300 Blackout, 7.62x39, 6mm ARC, 6.5 Grendel, 6.5 Creedmoor, 6.5 PRC, .308 Win., .350 Legend, .400 Legend, .450 Bushmaster. Capacity: Varies by chambering with a dropbox magazine of 3-, 5-, or 10-round, some AR-style, some Mini Thirty, some single stack. Barrel: 16.10–16.4 in. spiral fluted with threaded muzzle and installed radial port muzzle brake Weight: 5.8–6.2 lbs. Length: 37.35–41.25 in. overall. Stock: Synthetic with splatter finish for grip. Comb risers for adjusting height. Sights: None. Picatinny scope base included . Features: Second generation model American launched in 2024. Scout marks the more compact package. Three-position tang safety. Oversized bolt handle. Integral bedding block and free-floated barrel. Cerakote metalwork. Ruger Marksman adjustable trigger with pull weight adjustable from 3–5 pounds. LOP adjusts from 12–13.75 in. with insert. Ranch wears Flat Dark Earth furniture and Cobalt Cerakote metalwork.
Price: **$729.00**

RUGER GUIDE GUN
Calibers: .30-06, .300 Win. Mag., .338 Win. Mag., .375 Ruger, .416 Ruger. Capacities: 3 or 4 rounds. Barrel: 20 in. with barrel band sling swivel and removable muzzle brake. Weights: 8–8.12 pounds. Stock: Green Mountain laminate. Finish: Hawkeye matte stainless. Sights: Adjustable rear, bead front. Introduced 2013.
Price: **$1,269.00**

RUGER HAWKEYE
Calibers: .204 Ruger, .223 Rem., .243 Win., .270 Win., 6.5 PRC, 6.5 Creedmoor, 7mm/08, 7mm Rem. Mag., .308 Win., .30-06, .300 Win. Mag., .338 Win. Mag., .375 Ruger, .416 Ruger. Capacities: 4-round magazine, except 3-round magazine for magnums; 5-round magazine for .204 Ruger and .223 Rem. Barrels: 22 in., 24 in. Weight: 6.75–8.25 lbs. Length: 42–44.4 in. overall. Stock: American walnut, laminate or synthetic. FTW has camo stock, muzzle brake. Long Range Target has adjustable target stock, heavy barrel. Sights: None furnished. Receiver has Ruger integral scope mount base, Ruger 1 in. rings. Features: Includes Ruger LC6 trigger, new red rubber recoil pad, Mauser-type controlled feeding, claw extractor, 3-position safety, hammer-forged steel barrels, Ruger scope rings. Walnut stocks have wrap-around cut checkering on the forearm, and more rounded contours on stock and top of pistol grips. Matte stainless all-weather version features synthetic stock. Hawkeye African chambered in .375 Ruger, .416 Ruger and has 23-in. blued barrel, checkered walnut stock, windage-adjustable shallow V-notch rear sight, white bead front sight. Introduced 2007. *(Note: VT Varmint Target and Compact Magnum are no longer currently produced)*

Price: Standard, right and left hand	**$939.00**
Price: Compact	**$939.00**
Price: Laminate Compact	**$999.00**
Price: Compact Magnum	**$969.00**
Price: Hawkeye Hunter	**$1,099.00**
Price: VT Varmint Target	**$1,139.00**
Price: Predator	**$1,139.00**
Price: Alaskan	**$1,279.00**
Price: Long Range Hunter	**$1,279.00**
Price: African with muzzle brake	**$1,279.00**
Price: FTW Hunter	**$1,279.00**
Price: Long Range Target	**$1,279.00**

Prices given are believed to be accurate at time of publication however, many factors affect retail pricing so exact prices are not possible.

79TH EDITION, 2025 ✛ 451

SAKO TRG-22 TACTICAL RIFLE

Calibers: 6.5 Creedmoor, .308 Winchester (TRG-22). For TRG-22A1 add .260 Rem. TRG-42 only available in .300 Win. Mag., or .338 Lapua. Features: Target-grade Cr-Mo or stainless barrels with muzzle brake; three locking lugs; 60-degree bolt throw; adjustable two-stage target trigger; adjustable or folding synthetic stock; receiver-mounted integral 17mm axial optics rails with recoil stop-slots; tactical scope mount for modern three-turret tactical scopes (30 and 34 mm tube diameter); optional bipod. 22A1 has folding stock with two-hinge design, M-LOK fore-end, full aluminum middle chassis.

Price: TRG-22 ....**$3,495.00**
Price: TRG-22A1 ....**$6,725.00**
Price: TRG-42 ....**$4,550.00**

SAKO S20

Calibers: .243 Win., 6.5 Creedmoor, 6.5 PRC, .270 Win., .308 Win., .30-06 Spfld., 7mm Rem. Mag., .300 Win. Mag. Capacity: 5 (3 Magnum), and 10 (7 magnum) double-stacked magazines, glass-reinforced composite. Barrel: 20- to 24-in. cold-hammer forged, fluted, threaded. Weight: 7.3–8.8 lbs. Length: 42.9–46.9 in. Stock: Choice of two interchangeable injection-molded synthetic stock types — tactical precision or ergonomic hunting thumbhole. Sights: Picatinny rail integral to receiver. Features: Designed as a hybrid rifle for both hunters and precision shooters. Full aluminum rifle chassis. Takedown-style stock design allows user configuration. Adjustable recoil pad for LOP and adjustable cheek piece. QD sling attachments. Two-stage multi-adjustable trigger. Five-shot sub MOA guarantee.

Price: **$1,598.00**

SAKO 90

Calibers: .22-250 Rem., .243 Win., .308 Win., 6.5 Creedmoor (Quest); .22-250 Rem., .243 Win., 7mm-08, .308 Win., 6.5 Creedmoor, 7mm Mag., .300 Win. Mag. (Adventure); .22-250 Rem., .243 Win., 7mm-08, .308 Win., 6.5 Creedmoor, 7mm Mag., .300 Win. Mag., .338 Win. Mag., .375 H&H (Bavarian); .222 Rem., .22-250 Rem., .243 Win., 6.5 Creedmoor, 7mm-08, .308 Win., 6.5x55 SE, .270 Win., .30-'06, 8x57 IS, 9.3x62, .270 WSM, .300 WSM, 7mm Rem. Mag., .300 Win. Mag., .338 Win. Mag., .375 H&H. (Hunter); .22-250 Rem., .243 Win., 6.5 Creedmoor, 7mm-08 Rem., .308 Win. (Varmint). Capacity: 5-round magazine on most models. Barrel: 20, 22, 24 in. varies by model and composition. Weight: Varies by model variant. Stock: Varies by model variant, including synthetic, carbon fiber, walnut, and laminate. Sights: Most with no iron sights. Integral Picatinny scope bases on most models. Models with Optilock receiver enable clear view through open sights. Features: Purpose built for mountain and backcountry hunters. Push feed bolt-action. Multi-adjustable trigger mechanism with five pre-set weight settings. Trigger blade position is also adjustable. Multiple model variants. Quest with carbon-fiber dark gray synthetic stock adjustable for LOP and comb height. Quest Ultra with adjustable two-tone gray/brown stock. Peak lightweight with silver metal and black synthetic sporter-style stock. Adventure black carbon fiber with adjustable combi and black metal. Bavarian with Central European style designed for high-seat hunting. Hunter with high-grade wood in classic style. Varmint with heavy fluted barrel and laminate birch wood furniture. Hunter model available in left-hand variant.

Price: 90 Quest **$3,999.00**

Price: 90 Quest Ultra **$4,995.00**
Price: 90 Peak **$3,499.00**
Price: 90 Adventure **$2,699.00**
Price: 90 Bavariian **$2,399.00**
Price: 90 Hunter **$2,299.00**
Price: 90 Hunter LH **$2,399.00**
Price: 90 Varmint **$2,299.00**

SAVAGE IMPULSE BIG GAME

Calibers: .243 Win., .308 Win., 6.5 Creedmoor, 7mm PRC, .308 Win., .300 Win. Mag., .300 WSM. Capacity: 2, 3, or 4-round flush-fit detachable box magazine. Barrel: 22- or 24-in. medium contour, carbon steel, fluted, and threaded. Sights: Single piece 20 MOA rail machined into receiver. Length: 43.5–45.5 in. Weight: 8.8–8.9 lbs. Stock: Sporter-style AccuStock with AccuFit user-adjustable system and Kuiu Verde 2.0 camouflage finish. Features: New straight-pull bolt action uses HexLock bolt system. Ambidextrous rotary bolt handle. Tang safety. Free-floating, tool-free, interchangeable bolt head. Four-bolt barrel clamp system. Adjustable AccuTrigger. Hazel Green Cerakote aluminum receiver. Removeable and user-adjustable round bolt knob handle.

Price: $1,449.00

SAVAGE IMPULSE HOG HUNTER

Calibers: 6.5 Creedmoor, .308 Win., .30-06 Spfld., .300 Win. Mag. Capacity: 3- or 4-round flush-fit detachable box magazine. Barrel: 18-, 20-, or 24-in. medium contour, carbon steel, threaded. Sights: Single piece 20 MOA rail machined into receiver. Length: 39.25–44.25 in. Weight: 8.41–9.1 lbs. Stock: OD Green Sporter-style AccuStock with AccuFit user-adjustable system. Features: New straight pull bolt action uses HexLock bolt system. Ambidextrous rotary bolt handle. Tang safety. Free-floating, tool-free, interchangeable bolt head. Four-bolt barrel clamp system. Adjustable AccuTrigger. Matte black aluminum receiver. Removeable and user adjustable round bolt knob handle.

Price: $1,379.00

SAVAGE IMPULSE PREDATOR

Calibers: .22-250 Rem., .243 Win., 6.5 Creedmoor, .308 Win. Capacity: 10-round AICS-style magazine with ambidextrous release. Barrel: 20-in. medium contour, threaded. Sights: Single piece 20 MOA rail machined into receiver. Length: 41.25 in. Weight: 8.75 lbs. Stock: Mossy Oak Terra Gila camouflage AccuStock with AccuFit user-adjustable system. Features: New straight-pull bolt action uses HexLock bolt system. Ambidextrous rotary bolt handle. Tang safety. Free-floating, tool-free, interchangeable bolt head. Four-bolt barrel clamp system. Adjustable AccuTrigger. Matte black aluminum receiver. Removeable and user adjustable round bolt knob handle.

Price: $1,379.00

SAVAGE IMPULSE MOUNTAIN HUNTER

Caliber: 6.5 Creedmoor, 6.5 PRC, .308 Win., 28 Nosler, 7mm PRC, .300 WSM, .300 Win. mag. Barrel: 22, 24-in. Proof Research carbon-fiber-wrapped stainless steel. Weight: 7.16 to 7.44 lbs. Stock: Synthetic gray with AccuFit system. Features: Latest addition to the straight-pull family. Aluminum receiver with integral 20 MOA rail. Carbon-fiber barrel. Threaded muzzle with included brake. Detachable box magazine. Ambidextrous, removable, multi-position bolt handle.

Price: $2,437.00

SAVAGE ARMS IMPULSE KLYM

Calibers: 6.5 Creedmoor, 6.5 PRC, .308 Win., 7mm PRC, .300 WSM, .300 Win. Mag. Capacity: 2- or 3-round magazine, depending on caliber. Barrel: 22–24 in. Proof Research carbon fiber with threaded muzzle and Omniport brake installed. Weight: 6.6–6.73 lbs. Length: 45.5–47.5 in. overall. Stock: Custom FBT carbon fiber with push button comb height adjustment and thumbhole design. Sights: None. One-piece 20-MOA Pic rail. Features: Lighter weight addition to savage's Impulse straight-pull bolt-action rifle line. Ambidextrous, removeable, multi-positional threaded bolt handle with a carbon-fiber knob. Two sling studs with Magnaswitch system installed. LOP measures 13.75 in. Adjustable AccuTrigger, two-position tang safety.
Price: Impulse Straight Pull KLYM **$3,309.00**

SAVAGE MODEL 110

Caliber: The models below now include 7mm PRC in addition to standard chamberings. Numerous model variants and features.
Price: 110 ULTRALITE **$1,649.00**
Price: 110 ULTRALITE HD **$1,649.00**
Price: 110 ULTRALITE CAMO **$1,699.00**
Price: 110 HIGH COUNTRY **$1,239.00**
Price: 110 Timberline LH **$1,239.00**
Price: 110 APEX HUNTER XP..**$709.00**
Price: 110 APEX STORM XP...**$819.00**
Price: 110 APEX HUNTER XP LH...**$709.00**

SAVAGE 110 CARBON TACTICAL

Calibers: 6.5 Creedmoor, .308 Win., 6.5 PRC. Capacity: 10-round AICS magazine. Barrel: 22-in. Proof Research stainless steel, carbon-fiber wrapped, threaded. Length: 42 in. Weight: 7.65 lbs. Stock: Synthetic AccuFit with included interchangeable LOP spacers and comb risers. Features: Factory blueprinted Model 110 bolt action. User-adjustable AccuTrigger. Tactical knurled bolt handle. One-piece 20MOA rail. Beavertail forend with three sling studs.
Price: **$1,789.00**

SAVAGE MODEL 110 PRECISION

Calibers: .308 Win., .300 Win. Mag., .338 Lapua, 6.5 Creedmoor. Capacity: 5, 8/10. Barrel: 20 to 24 in., carbon steel, heavy, threaded. Stock: Aluminum chassis. Sights: Picatinny rail. Weight: 8.9 lbs. Features: BA muzzle brake, skeletonized stock with adjustable comb height and LOP.
Price: **$1,499.00**

SAVAGE MODEL 110 PREDATOR

Calibers: .204 Ruger. .223, .22-250, .243, .260 Rem., 6.5 Creedmoor. Capacity: 4-round magazine. Barrels: 22 or 24 in. threaded heavy contour. Weight: 8.5 lbs. Stock: AccuStock with Mossy Oak Max-1 camo finish, soft grip surfaces, adjustable length of pull.
Price: **$899.00**

SAVAGE MODEL 110 CARBON PREDATOR

Caliber: .223 Rem., .22-250 Rem., 6mm ARC, 6.5 Creedmoor, .308 Win., .300 Blackout. Barrel: 16, 18, 22-in. Proof Research carbon-fiber-wrapped stainless steel. Weight: 6.5 to 7.2 lbs. Stock: Synthetic gray with AccuFit system. Features: Latest addition to the 110 bolt-action family, now with lighter weight carbon-fiber barrel. AICS detachable box magazine. Spiral-fluted bolt. Threaded barrel. Swivel studs. Two-piece Weaver bases included.
Price: **$1,695.00**

SAVAGE MODEL 110 TACTICAL

Caliber: .308 Win. Capacity: 10-round magazine. Barrels: 20 or 24 in. threaded and fluted heavy contour. Weight: 8.65 lbs. Stock: AccuStock with soft-grip surfaces, AccuFit system. Features: Top Picatinny rail, right- or left-hand operation.
Price: **$784.00**
Price: Tactical Desert (6mm, 6.5 Creedmoor, FDE finish **$769.00**

SAVAGE ARMS 110 ULTRALITE ELITE

Calibers: 6.5 Creedmoor, 6.5 PRC, .308 Win., 7mm PRC, .300 WSM, .300 Win. Mag. Capacity: 3-round low-profile AICS detachable box magazine. Barrel: 18 or 20 in. Proof Research carbon-fiber wrapped stainless cut-rifled with threaded muzzle with Omniport brake installed. Weight: 5.8–6.0 lbs. Length: 38.5–41.1 in overall. Stock: MDT HNT26 chassis with folding carbon-fiber forend, pistol grip, and buttstock. Sights: None. Drilled and tapped receiver with one-piece 20-MOA Pic rail. Features: Debuted in 2024 as Savage's lightest weight centerfire rifle yet. Built around a blueprinted action. Adjustable LOP and comb height, with four ¼-inch LOP spacers. Diamond-fluted bolt coated with Blackout Cerakote. Threaded bolt handle with carbon-fiber bolt knob.
Price: **$3,299.00**

SAVAGE ARMS 110 KLYM

Calibers: 6.5 Creedmoor, 6.5 PRC, .308 Win., 7mm PRC, .300 WSM, .300 Win. Mag. Capacity: 3- or 4-round magazine, depending on caliber. Barrel: 22–24 in. Proof Research carbon fiber with threaded muzzle and Omniport brake installed. Weight: 6.0–6.4 lbs. Length: 44.5–46.75 in. overall. Stock: Custom FBT carbon fiber with push button comb height adjustment and thumbhole design. Sights: None. One-piece 20-MOA Pic rail. Features: Built on factory blueprinted action. Diamond-fluted bolt coated with Blackout Cerakote. Threaded bolt handle with a carbon-fiber knob. Two sling studs with Magnaswitch system installed. LOP measures 13.75 in. Adjustable AccuTrigger, three-position tang safety.
Price: 110 KLYM **$2,699.00**

SAVAGE AXIS II PRECISION

Calibers: .243 Win., .223 Rem., .270 Win., .30-06, .308 Win., 6.5 Creedmoor. Capacity: 5 to 10. Barrel: 22 in., carbon steel, button-rifled heavy, threaded w/cap. Stock: Aluminum MDT chassis. Sights: Picatinny rail. Weight: 9.9 lbs. Features: AccuTrigger, adjustable comb height and LOP spacers, AICS magazine.
Price: **$949.00**

SEEKINS PRECISION HAVAK ELEMENT

Calibers: 28 Nosler, 6mm Creedmoor, 6.5 Creedmoor, .308 Win., 6.5 PRC, .300 Win. Mag., .300 PRC. Capacity: 3 or 5-round detachable Magpul PMAG or carbon-fiber magazine, depending on caliber. Barrel: 21- or 22-in. Mountain Hunter spiral fluted, built of 5R 416 stainless steel. Sights: 20 MOA rail. Weight: 5.5 lbs. short actions; long actions at 6.0 lbs. Stock: Element camouflage Carbon Composition stock. Features: Drawing on years of precision AR-rifle experience comes the bolt action, hybrid, ultra-lightweight Havak Element. Aerospace-grade 7075 aluminum encases stainless steel on a Mountain Hunter barrel. Four locking lugs on 90-degree bolt with removable head. ATC muzzle brake on long actions. M-16-style extractor. Muzzle threaded at 5/8x24. Integrated recoil lug, and bubble level.
Price: **$2,795.00**

SEEKINS PRECISION HAVAK PRO HUNTER PH2

Calibers: 6mm Creedmoor, 6.5 Creedmoor, 6.5 PRC, .308 Win., 28 Nosler, 7mm Rem. Mag., .300 Win. Mag., 300 PRC, .338 Win. Mag. Capacity: 5, short action; 3, long action detachable magazine. Barrel: 24 in. short action; 26 in. long action built of 5R 416 stainless steel. Weight: 6.9–7.2 lbs. Stock: Seekins carbon composite in Charcoal Gray. Sights: 20 MOA Picatinny rail with 8-32 screws. Features: Timney Elite Hunter trigger set at 2.5 lbs. Bead-blasted barreled action. Threaded muzzle. Integrated recoil lug and M16-style extractor. Bolt with four locking lugs and 90-degree throw. Removeable bolt head. Extended cartridge overall length with Seekins carbon-fiber magazines.

Price: **$1,895.00**

SPRINGFIELD ARMORY 2020 WAYPOINT

Calibers: Short actions: 6mm Creedmoor, 6.5 Creedmoor, .308 Win., 6.5 PRC, long actons: 7mm Rem. Mag., 7mm PRC, .300 Win. Mag., 300 PRC, .270 Win. and .30-06. Capacity: 3 or 5-round AICS-pattern magazine. Barrel: 20, 22, or 24 in. Option of steel or carbon fiber. Weight: 6 lbs. 10 oz.–7 lbs. 6 oz. Length: 41.5–45.5 in. Stock: Choice of two stock configurations, premium AG Composites carbon fiber with custom camo in Evergreen or Ridgeline. Features: Stainless steel receiver. Dual locking lugs on a fluted bolt. Picatinny rail. 90-degree bolt handle with removeable knob. Enlarged ejection port and sliding extractor. Hybrid dual-plane feed ramp. Adjustable Trigger Tech trigger. Five QD stock mounts. SA Radial muzzle brake. Cerakote metalwork in Desert Verde or Mil-Spec Green. Pachmayr Decelerator recoil pad. Available in two stock configurations, one with three-axis adjustable cheek comb and two barrel choices. Accuracy guarantee of .75 MOA. New for 2024, long-action calibers added.

Price: Steel barrel, standard stock **$1,699.00**
Price: Steel barrel, adjustable stock **$1,825.00**
Price: Carbon-fiber barrel, standard stock **$2,275.00**
Price: Carbon-fiber barrel, adjustable stock **$2,399.00**

STAG ARMS PURSUIT

Calibers: 6.5 Creedmoor, 6.5 PRC, .308 Win. Capacity: 3- or 5-round AICS/AIAW short-action magazine, depending on chambering. Barrel: 18, 20, 22 in. threaded, sporter fluted. Weight: 8 lbs. 9 oz.–8 lbs. 14 oz. Stock: Synthetic Hybrid Hunter with choice of FDE, OD Green, and Black stock coloration. Sights: None, includes bolt-on 20-MOA rail. Features: First bolt-action rifle from Stag Arms built on a Remington 700 footprint. Interchangeable three-lug bolt head, 60-degree throw, and tool-less bolt disassembly. Fitted with a Picatinny spigot, Arca/Swiss plate, and attachable bag rider. TriggerTech Primary adjustable trigger. Backed with a lifetime transferable warranty and sub-MOA guarantee.

Price: Synthetic **$1,899.00**

STEVENS MODEL 334

Calibers: .243 Win., .308 Win., 6.5 Creedmoor. Barrel: 20-in. free-floating button rifled. Stock: Walnut or black synthetic. Features: The first centerfire rifle under the Stevens by Savage name in decades. Budget bolt action built completely in Turkey. Two-stage trigger, 60-degree bolt throw, three-position safety. Three-round box magazine. Drilled and tapped with Savage 110 spacing.

Price: Synthetic **$389.00**
Price: Walnut **$489.00**

STEYR PRO HUNTER II

Calibers: .223 Rem., 7mm-08 Rem., 6.5 Creedmoor, .308 Win. Capacity: 4 to 5. Barrel: 20 in., hammer-forged stainless steel. Stock: Wood laminate, Boyds. Sights: None, drilled and tapped. Weight: 7 lbs. Features: Three-position safety, crisp 3-lb. trigger.

Price: **$1,199.00**

STEYR SSG08

Calibers: .243 Win., 7.62x51 NATO (.308Win), 7.62x63B (.300 Win Mag)., .338 Lapua Mag. Capacity: 10-round magazine. Barrels: 20, 23.6 or 25.6 in. Stock: Dural aluminum folding stock black with .280 mm long UIT-rail and various Picatinny rails. Sights: Front post sight and rear adjustable. Features: High-grade aluminum folding stock, adjustable cheekpiece and buttplate with height marking, and an ergonomical exchangeable pistol grip. Versa-Pod, muzzle brake, Picatinny rail, UIT rail on stock and various Picatinny rails on fore-end, and a 10-round HC-magazine. SBS rotary bolt action with four frontal locking lugs, arranged in pairs. Cold-hammer-forged barrels are available in standard or compact lengths.

Price: **$5,899.00**

STEYR SM 12

Calibers: .243, 6.5x55SE, .270 Win., 7mm-08 Rem., .308 Win., .30-06, .300 Win. Mag, .300 WSM, 9.3x62mm. Barrels: 20-in. blue or 25-in. stainless. Stock: Walnut with checkered grip and fore-end. Available in half or full-length configurations. Sights: Adjustable rear, ramp front with bead. Stainless barrel has no sights. Features: Sling swivels, Bavarian cheekpiece, hand-cocking system operated by thumb manually cocks firing mechanism.

Price: Standard-length stock **$2,545.00**
Price: Full length (Mannlicher) **$2,750.00**

STRASSER RS 14 EVOLUTION STANDARD

Calibers: .222 Rem., .223 Rem., .300 AAC Blackout, .22-250 Rem., .243 Win., 6 XC, 6.5 Creedmoor, .284 Norma, 6.5x55SE, 6.5x65RWS, .270 Win., 7x64, 7mm-08 Rem, .308 Win., .30-06, 8x57 IS, 8.5x63, 9.3x62, 9.3x57, 7mm Rem. Mag., .300 Win. Mag., .375 Ruger, .338 Win. Mag., .458 Win. Mag., 10.3x68. Capacity: 3 to 7. Barrel: 22 to 24 in., blued. Stock: Grade-1 wood, grade-2 wood, standard or thumbhole. Sights: Integrated Picatinny rail. Weight: 6.75 to 7.725 lbs. Features: Barrel-exchange system, adjustable trigger with trigger set, plasma-hardened bolt.

Price: .... **$3,452.00-$4,033.00**

TAURUS EXPEDIITION

Calibers: .308 Win. Capacity: 5-round detachable AICS-pattern magazine. Barrel: 18-in. hammer-forged, threaded. Weight: 7.05 lbs. Length: 37.9 in. overall. Stock: Injection-molded polymer black, with scalloped cut for gun saddles and vertical grip style. Sights: None. Drilled and tapped at 6-48. Features: Taurus' entry into the bolt-action rifle market based on the Remington 700 action and compatible with aftermarket accessories. Stainless steel frame and barrel with Black DLC finish. M-LOK attachment point at the bottom of the stock, along with Spartan Precision point user-adjustable trigger. Thick rubber recoil pad and sling studs.

Price: **$985.00**

TIKKA T3X SERIES

Calibers: Virtually any popular chambering including .204 Ruger .222 Rem., .223 Rem., .243 Win., .25-06, 6.5x55 SE, .260 Rem, .270 Win., .260 WSM, 7mm-08, 7mm Rem. Mag., .308 Win., .30-06, .300 Win. Mag., .300 WSM. Barrels: 20, 22.4, 24.3 in. Stock: Checkered walnut, laminate or modular synthetic with interchangeable pistol grips. Newly designed recoil pad. Features: Offered in a variety of different models with many options. Left-hand models available. One minute-of-angle accuracy guaranteed. Introduced in 2016. Made in Finland by Sako. Imported by Beretta USA.

Prices given are believed to be accurate at time of publication however, many factors affect retail pricing so exact prices are not possible.

Price: Hunter **$875.00**
Price: Lite (shown) **$725.00**
Price: Varmint **$950.00**
Price: Laminate stainless.. **$1,050.00**
Price: Forest **$1,000.00**
Price: Tac A1 (shown) **$1,899.00**
Price: Compact Tactical Rifle **$1,150.00**

WEATHERBY BACKCOUNTRY 2.0

Replaces the original Backcountry family. Upgraded with carbon-fiber Peak44 Blacktooth stock that weights under 20 oz. Other improvements include: second generation 3DHEX recoil pad, the first printed pad made. Deeper spiral fluting on the bolt and threaded bolt handle. Fit with Accubrake ST. Patriot Brown Cerakote finish. Weight from only 5.2 lbs. Carbon models include a carbon-fiber barrel. Ti models are built on a titanium action.

Price: Mark V Backcountry 2.0 .... **$2,699.00–$2,799.00**
Price: Mark V Backcountry 2.0 Carbon .... **$3,299.00–$3,399.00**
Price: Mark V Backcountry 2.0 Ti .... **$3,449.00–$3,599.00**
Price: Mark V Backcountry Ti Carbon .... **3,849.00–$3,949.00**

WEATHERBY MARK V

This classic action goes back more than 60 years to the late '50s. Several significant changes were made to the original design in 2016. Stocks have a slimmer fore-end and smaller grip, which has an added palm swell. The new LXX trigger is adjustable down to 2.5 lbs. and has precision ground and polished surfaces and a wider trigger face. All new Mark V rifles come with sub-MOA guarantee. Range Certified (RC) models are range tested and come with a certified ballistic data sheet and RC engraved floorplate. **Calibers:** Varies depending on model. **Barrels:** 22 in., 24 in., 26 in., 28 in. **Weight:** 5 3/4 to 10 lbs. **Stock:** Varies depending on model. **Sights:** None furnished. **Features:** Deluxe version comes in all Weatherby calibers plus .243 Win., .270 Win., 7mm-08 Rem., .30-06, .308 Win. Lazermark same as Mark V Deluxe except stock has extensive oak leaf pattern laser carving on pistol grip and fore-end; chambered in Wby. Magnums .257, .270 Win., 7mm., .300, .340, with 26 in. barrel. Sporter is same as the Mark V Deluxe without the embellishments. Metal has low-luster blue, stock is Claro walnut with matte finish, Monte Carlo comb, recoil pad. Chambered for these Wby. Mags: .257, .270 Win., 7mm, .300, .340. Other chamberings: 7mm Rem. Mag., .300 Win. Introduced 1993. Six Mark V models come with synthetic stocks. Ultra Lightweight rifles weigh 5.75 to 6.75 lbs.; 24 in., 26 in. fluted stainless barrels with recessed target crown. Bell & Carlson stock with CNC-machined aluminum bedding plate and tan "spider web" finish, skeletonized handle and sleeve. Available in .243 Win., .25-06 Rem., .270 Win., 7mm-08 Rem., 7mm Rem. Mag., .280 Rem, .308 Win., .30-06, .300 Win. Mag. Wby. Mag chamberings: .240, .257, .270 Win., 7mm, .300. Accumark uses Mark V action with heavy-contour 26 in. and 28 in. stainless barrels with black oxidized flutes, muzzle diameter of .705 in. No sights, drilled and tapped for scope mounting. Stock is composite with matte gel-coat finish, full-length aluminum bedding block. Weighs 8.5 lbs. Chambered for these Wby. Mags: .240, .257, .270, 7mm, .300, .340, .338-378, .30-378. Other chamberings: 6.5 Creedmoor, .270 Win., .308 Win., 7mm Rem. Mag., .300 Win. Mag. Altitude has 22-, 24-, 26-, 28-in. fluted stainless steel barrel, Monte Carlo carbon fiber composite stock with raised comb, Kryptek Altitude camo. Tacmark has 28-in. free floated fluted barrel with Accubrake, fully adjustable stock, black finish. Safari Grade has fancy grade checkered French walnut stock with ebony fore-end and grip cap, adjustable express rear and hooded front sights, from the Weatherby Custom Shop. Camilla series is lightweight model designed to fit a woman's anatomy. Offered in several variations chambered for .240 Wby. Mag., 6.5 Creedmoor, .270 Win., .308 Win., .30-06. Arroyo is available in Weatherby Magnums from .240 to .338-378, plus 6.5 Creedmoor, .300 Win. Mag., and .338 Lapua Mag. Finish is two-tone Cerakote with Brown Sand and FDE added flutes. Carbonmark has 26in. Proof Research carbon fiber threaded barrel and is chambered for .257 and .300 Wby. Mags. Outfitter is chambered for .240-.300 Wby. Magnums plus most popular calibers. Stock has Spiderweb accents. KCR model comes with Krieger Custom Match-

grade barrel in .257, 6.5-300, .300 and .30-378 Wby. Magnums. Altitude is lightweight model (5 3/4-6 3/4 lbs.) and comes in Wby. Magnums from .240 to.300, plus 6.5 Creedmoor, .270 Win., .308, .30-06. Dangerous Game Rifle is offered in all Wby. Magnums from .300 to .450, plus .375 H&H. Hand laminated Monte Carlo composite stock. High Country built as a mountain rifle with Peak44 carbon-fiber stock and vertical grip, Wyo brown and cream sponge pattern stock, and starts at 5.7 lbs Note: Most Mark V rifles are available in 6.5 Wby. RPM and 6.5-300 Wby. Mag. chamberings. All Weatherby Mark V rifles built since 2019 are made in Sheridan, Wyoming.

Price: Mark V Backcountry **$2,499.00**
Price: Mark V Backcountry Ti .... **$3,349.00–$3,449.00**
Price: Mark V Deluxe **$2,700.00**
Price: Mark V Hunter **$1,499.00**
Price: Mark V Lazermark.. **$2,800.00**
Price: Mark V Sporter **$1,800.00**
Price: Mark V Ultra Lightweight **$2,300.00**
Price: Mark V Accumark .... **$2,300.00–$2,700.00**
Price: Mark V Altitude .... **$3,000.00–$3,700.00**
Price: Mark V Safari Grade Custom .... **$6,900.00–$7,600.00**
Price: Mark V Tacmark **$4,100.00**
Price: Mark V Camilla Series .... **$2,300.00–$2,700.00**
Price: Mark V Arroyo **$2,800.00**
Price: Mark V Carbonmark **$4,100.00**
Price: Mark V Outfitter .... **$2,600-$2,800.00***
Price: Mark V Krieger Custom Rifle (KCR)............... **$3,600-$4,100.00***
Price: Mark V Altitude **$2,700.00***
Price: Mark V Dangerous Game Rifle **$3,600.00**
Price: Mark V Weathermark .... **$1,549.00–$1,749.00**
Price: Mark V Weathermark Bronze .... **$1,549.00–$1,749.00**
Price: Mark V Carbonmark Pro .... **$2,999.00–$3,099.00**
Price: Mark V Carbonmark Elite .... **$3,299.00–$3,399.00**
Price: Mark V Apex Right Hand **$2,799.00**
Price: Mark V Apex Left Hand **$2,899.00**
Price: Mark V High Country .... **$2,699.00–$2,799.00**
*Add ....$500 for optional Range Certified (RC) model with guaranteed sub-MOA accuracy certificate and target.

WEATHERBY VANGUARD II SERIES

Calibers: Varies depending on model. Most Weatherby Magnums and many standard calibers. **Barrels:** 20, 24, or 26 in. **Weights:** 7.5–8.75 lbs. **Lengths:** 44–46.75 in. overall. **Stock:** Raised comb, Monte Carlo, injection-molded composite stock. **Sights:** None furnished. **Features:** One-piece forged, fluted bolt body with three gas ports, forged and machined receiver, adjustable trigger, factory accuracy guarantee. Vanguard Stainless has 410-Series stainless steel barrel and action, bead blasted matte metal finish. Vanguard Deluxe has raised comb, semi-fancy-grade Monte Carlo walnut stock with maplewood spacers, rosewood fore-end and grip cap, polished action with high-gloss blued metalwork. Sporter has Monte Carlo walnut stock with satin urethane finish, fineline diamond point checkering, contrasting rosewood fore-end tip, matte-blued metalwork. Sporter SS metalwork is 410 Series bead-blasted stainless steel. Vanguard Youth/Compact has 20 in. No. 1 contour barrel, short action, scaled-down nonreflective matte black hardwood stock with 12.5-in. length of pull, full-size, injection-molded composite stock. Chambered for .223 Rem., .22-250 Rem., .243 Win., 7mm-08 Rem., .308 Win. Weighs 6.75 lbs.; OAL 38.9 in. Sub-MOA Matte and Sub-MOA Stainless models have pillar-bedded Fiberguard composite stock (Aramid, graphite unidirectional fibers and fiberglass) with 24-in. barreled action; matte black metalwork, Pachmayr Decelerator recoil pad. Sub-MOA Stainless metalwork is 410 Series bead-blasted stainless steel. Sub-MOA Varmint guaranteed to shoot 3-shot group of .00 in. or less when used with specified Weatherby factory or premium (non-Weatherby calibers) ammunition. Hand-laminated, tan Monte Carlo composite stock with black spiderwebbing; CNC-machined aluminum bedding block, 22 in. No. 3 contour barrel, recessed target crown. Varmint Special has tan injection-molded Monte Carlo composite stock, pebble grain finish, black spiderwebbing. 22 in. No. 3 contour barrel (.740-in. muzzle dia.), bead blasted matte black finish, recessed target crown. Back Country has two-stage trigger, pillar-bedded Bell & Carlson stock, 24-in. fluted barrel, three-position safety. Vanguard rifles are built in Japan by Howa to Weatherby specs.

Price: Vanguard Synthetic **$649.00**
Price: Vanguard Stainless **$799.00**
Price: Vanguard Deluxe, 7mm Rem. Mag., .300 Win. Mag..............**$1,149.00**
Price: Vanguard Sporter **$849.00**
Price: Laminate Sporter.. **$849.00**
Price: Vanguard Youth/Compact...................................... **$599.00**

Price: Vanguard S2 Back Country $1,399.00
Price: Vanguard RC (Range Certified) $1,199.00
Price: Vanguard Varmint Special $849.00
Price: Camilla (designed for women shooters) $849.00
Price: Camilla Wilderness $899.00
Price: Lazerguard (Laser carved AA-grade walnut stock) $1,199.00
Price: H-Bar (tactical series) .... $1,149.00–$1,449.00
Price: Weatherguard $749.00
Price: Modular Chassis $1,519.00
Price: Dangerous Game Rifle (DGR) .375 H&H $1,299.00
Price: Safari (.375 or .30-06) $1,199.00
Price: First Lite Fusion Camo $1,099.00
Price: Badlands Camo $849.00
Price: Accuguard $1,099.00
Price: Select $599.00
Price: Wilderness $999.00
Price: High Country $999.00

WEATHERBY 307 RANGE XP
Calibers: .240 Wby. Mag., .243 Win., .257 Wby. Mag., .270 Win., .280 Ackley Imp., .30-'06, .300 Win. Mag., .308 Win., 6.5 Creedmoor, 6.5 Wby. RPM, 7mm PRC, 7mm Rem. Capacity: 5-round magazine. Barrel: 24, 26, 28 in., depending on caliber. Graphite Black Cerakote finish. Weight: 7.3–7.5 lbs. Length: 41.5–45.75 in. overall. Stock: Adjustable Range XP synthetic OD Green with textured touch points. LOP from 13.5–14 in. Sights: None. PEAK44 optics rail. Features: Introduced in 2024, Weatherby's first new bolt-action rifle built in-house in decades. Named 307 for the area code at the Wyoming company headquarters. The Range XP is compatible with Remington 700 platform parts. Two-lug bolt, fully cylindrical action. Barrel threaded at 1/2x28 and fitted with 2-in. muzzle brake. Guaranteed Sub-MOA accuracy for two years.
Price: Range XP $1,199.00

WEATHERBY 307 MEATEATER EDITION
Calibers: .240 Wby. Mag., .243 Win., .257 Wby. Mag., .270 Win., .280 Ackley Imp., .30-'06, .300 Win., .308 Win., 6.5 Creedmoor, 6.5 Wby. RPM, 7mm PRC, 7mm Rem. Capacity: 5-round magazine. Barrel: 24, 26, 28 in., depending on caliber. Patriot Brown Cerakote finish. Weight: 7.4–7.5 lbs. Length: 41.5–45.75 in. overall. Stock: Synthetic tan base with green and brown sponge paint accents. Black adjustable cheekpiece. Vertical grip stock style. Sights: None. PEAK44 rail. Features: Introduced in 2024, Weatherby's first new bolt-action rifle built in-house in decades. Named 307 for the area code at the Wyoming company headquarters. Compatible with Remington 700 platform parts. Two-lug bolt, fully cylindrical action. Barrel threaded at 1/2x28 and fitted with 2-in. muzzle brake. Guaranteed Sub-MOA accuracy for two years. MeatEater Edition available at Scheels & Sportsman's Warehouse in select calibers.
Price: Meateater $1,299.00

WEATHERBY 307 ALPINE MDT
Calibers: .240 Wby. Mag., .243 Win., .257 Wby. Mag., .270 Win., .280 Ackley Imp., 28 Nosler, .300 Win. Mag., .300 Wby. Mag., 6.5 Creedmoor, 6.5 Wby. RPM, 6.5-300 Wby. Mag., 7mm PRC, 7mm Rem. Mag., .300 PRC. Capacity: 3-round AICS magazine. Barrel: 24, 26, 28 in., depending on caliber. Graphite Black Cerakote finish. Weight: 6.8–6.9 lbs. Length: 31.25–48.25 in. overall from folded to open. Stock: MDT carbon-fiber HNT26 Chassis System foldable. Sights: None. PEAK 44 Picatinny optics rail . Features: Introduced in 2024, Weatherby's first new bolt-action rifle built in-house in decades. Named 307 for the area code at the Wyoming company headquarters. Two-lug bolt, fully cylindrical action. Alpine MDT model partners Weatherby with MDT for a more compact lightweight chassis option. Barrel threaded at 1/2x28 and fitted with 2-in. muzzle brake. Bolt equipped with M16-style extractor. Magnesium alloy chassis and carbon-fiber forend, pistol grip, and buttstock. Externally adjustable TriggerTech trigger. The forend wears an integral ARCA rail. Guaranteed Sub-MOA accuracy for two years.
Price: Alpine MDT $2,999.00

WINCHESTER MODEL 70 SUPER GRADE
Calibers: .270 Win., .270 WSM, 7mm Rem. Mag., .30-06, .300 Win Mag., .300 WSM, .338 Win. Mag. Capacities: 5 rounds (short action) or 3 rounds (long action). Barrels: 24 in. or 26 in. blued. Weights: 8–8.5 lbs. Features: Full fancy Grade IV/V walnut stock with shadow-line cheekpiece, controlled round feed with claw extractor, Pachmayr Decelerator pad. No sights but drilled and tapped for scope mounts.
Price: .... $1,679.00–$1,719.00

WINCHESTER MODEL 70 ALASKAN
Calibers: .30-06, .300 Win. Mag., .338 Win. Mag., .375 H&H Magnum. Barrel: 25 in Weight: 8.8 lbs. Sights: Folding adjustable rear, hooded brass bead front. Stock: Satin finished Monte Carlo with cut checkering. Features: Integral recoil lug, Pachmayr Decelerator recoil pad.
Price: .... $1,569.00–$1,629.00

WINCHESTER MODEL 70 FEATHERWEIGHT
Calibers: .22-250, .243, 6.5 Creedmoor, 7mm-08, .308, .270 WSM, 7mm WSM, .300 WSM, .325 WSM, .25-06, .270, .30-06, 7mm Rem. Mag., .300 Win. Mag., .338 Win. Mag. Capacities: 5 rounds (short action) or 3 rounds (long action). Barrels: 22-in. blued (24 in. in magnum chamberings). Weights: 6.5–7.25 lbs. Length: NA. Features: Satin-finished checkered Grade I walnut stock, controlled round feeding. Pachmayr Decelerator pad. No sights but drilled and tapped for scope mounts.
Price: .... $1,279.00–$1,299.00

WINCHESTER MODEL 70 SAFARI EXPRESS
Calibers: .375 H&H Magnum, .416 Remington, .458 Win. Mag. Barrel: 24 in. Weight: 9 lbs. Sights: Fully adjustable rear, hooded brass bead front. Stock: Satin finished Monte Carlo with cut checkering, deluxe cheekpiece. Features: Forged steel receiver with double integral recoil lugs bedded front and rear, dual steel crossbolts, Pachmayr Decelerator recoil pad.
Price: $1,759.00

WINCHESTER MODEL 70 LONG RANGE MB
Calibers: .22-250 Rem., .243 Win., 6.5 Creedmoor, .308 Win., 6.5 PRC, .270 WSM, .300 WSM, 6.8 Western. Capacity: 3, 4, or 5-round internal magazine with hinged floorplate. Barrel: 24-in. matte blued, light varmint contour, fluted with muzzle brake. Weight: 7 lbs. Length: 44 in. Stock: Bell & Carlson composite with tan/black spider web and Pachmayr Decelerator recoil pad. Sights: Drilled and tapped. Features: Bolt-action short action designed for long-range hunting and target shooting. Aluminum bedding block. Matte black finish. Controlled round feed with claw extractor. Three-position safety. Flat, bench-rest style fore-end with dual sling studs. Jeweled bolt. Recessed target crown.
Price: .... $1,759.00–$1,789.00

WINCHESTER XPR
Calibers: .243, 6.5 Creedmoor, .270 Win., .270 WSM, 7mm-08, 7mm Rem. Mag., .308 Win., .30-'06, .300 Win. Mag., .300 WSM, .325 WSM, .338 Win. Mag., .350 Legend, 6.8 Western, .400 Legend, .450 Bushmaster. Capacities: Detachable box magazine holds 3 to 5 rounds, depending on chambering. Barrels: 18, 20, 22, 24 or 26 in. button-rifled with recessed target crown. Stock: Varies by model, with choice of synthetic in a variety of finishes as well as wood and laminate, each with Inflex Technology recoil pad. Weight: Varies by model. Finish: Matte blue. Features: Receiver machined from solid steel along with steel recoil lug. Bolt unlock button, nickel-coated Teflon bolt. Two-position thumb safety. MOA trigger system.
Price: .... $569.00–$1,239.00

C. SHARPS ARMS 1874 BRIDGEPORT SPORTING
Calibers: .38-55 to .50-3.25. Barrel: 26 in., 28 in., 30-in. tapered octagon. Weight: 10.5 lbs. Length: 47 in. Stock: American black walnut; shotgun butt with checkered steel buttplate; straight grip, heavy fore-end with Schnabel tip. Sights: Blade front, buckhorn rear. Drilled and tapped for tang sight. Features: Double-set triggers. Made in USA by C. Sharps Arms.
Price: **$1,995.00**

C. SHARPS ARMS NEW MODEL 1885 HIGHWALL
Calibers: .22 LR, .22 Hornet, .219 Zipper, .25-35 WCF, .32-40 WCF, .38-55 WCF, .40-65, .30-40 Krag, .40-50 ST or BN, .40-70 ST or BN, .40-90 ST or BN, .45-70 Govt. 2-1/10 in. ST, .45-90 2-4/10 in. ST, .45-100 2-6/10 in. ST, .45-110 2-7/8 in. ST, .45-120 3-1/4 in. ST. Barrels: 26 in., 28 in., 30 in., tapered full octagon. Weight: About 9 lbs., 4 oz. Length: 47 in. overall. Stock: Oil-finished American walnut; Schnabel-style fore-end. Sights: Blade front, buckhorn rear. Drilled and tapped for optional tang sight. Features: Single trigger; octagonal receiver top; checkered steel buttplate; color casehardened receiver and buttplate, blued barrel. Many options available. Made in USA by C. Sharps Arms Co.
Price: **$1,975.00**

CIMARRON BILLY DIXON 1874 SHARPS SPORTING
Calibers: .45-70, .45-90, .50-70. Barrel: 32-in. tapered octagonal. Weight: NA. Length: NA. Stock: European walnut. Sights: Blade front, Creedmoor rear. Features: Color casehardened frame, blued barrel. Hand-checkered grip and fore-end; hand-rubbed oil finish. Made by Pedersoli. Imported by Cimarron F.A. Co.
Price: **$2,141.70**
Price: Officer's Trapdoor Carbine w/26-in. round barrel.................**$2,616.00**

CIMARRON ADOBE WALLS ROLLING BLOCK
Caliber: .45-70 Govt. Barrel: 30-in. octagonal. Weight: 10.33 lbs. Length: NA. Stock: Hand-checkered European walnut. Sights: Bead front, semi-buckhorn rear. Features: Color casehardened receiver, blued barrel. Curved buttplate. Double-set triggers. Made by Pedersoli. Imported by Cimarron F.A. Co.
Price: **$1,740.00**

EMF PREMIER 1874 SHARPS
Calibers: .45-70, .45-110, .45-120. Barrel: 32 in., 34 in.. Weight: 11–13 lbs. Length: 49 in., 51 in. overall. Stock: Pistol grip, European walnut. Sights: Blade front, adjustable rear. Features: Superb quality reproductions of the 1874 Sharps Sporting Rifles; casehardened locks; double-set triggers; blue barrels. Imported from Pedersoli by EMF.
Price: Business Rifle...**$1,585.00**
Price: Down Under Sporting Rifle, Patchbox, heavy barrel **$2,405.00**
Price: Silhouette, pistol-grip...**$1,899.90**
Price: Super Deluxe Hand Engraved **$3,600.00**
Price: Competition Rifle..**$2,200.00**

HENRY SINGLE SHOT BRASS
Calibers: .44 Mag./.44 Spl., .357 Mag./.38 Spl., .45-70 Govt. Capacity: Single shot. Barrel: 22-in. round blued steel. Weight: 7.01–7.14 lbs. Length: 37.5 in. Stock: American Walnut with English-style straight buttstock. Sights: Fully adjustable folding leaf rear and brass bead front. Also drilled and tapped. Features: Polished brass receiver single-shot break actions built in a limited number of calibers. Sling studs. Brass buttplate. Rebounding hammer safety. Break-action lever can be moved either left or right to open, making it friendly for lefties.
Price: **$646.00**

HENRY SINGLE SHOT STEEL
Calibers: .223 Rem., .243 Win., .308 Win., .357 Mag./.38 Spl., .44 Mag., .30-

30 Win., .45-70 Govt., .350 Legend, 360 Buckhammer, .450 Bushmaster. Capacity: Single-shot. Barrel: 22-in. round blued steel. Weight: 6.73–6.96 lbs. Length: 37.5 in. Stock: Checkered American Walnut, pistol grip style. Sights: Fully adjustable folding leaf rear and brass front. Also drilled and tapped. Features: Blued steel receiver single-shot rifles. Solid rubber recoil pad. Rebounding hammer safety. Sling studs. Break-action lever can be moved either left or right to open, making it friendly for lefties. Youth model uses shorter 13-inch LOP, standard model LOP is 14 inches.
Price: **$580.00**

KRIEGHOFF HUBERTUS SINGLE-SHOT
Calibers: .222, .22-250, .243 Win., .270 Win., .308 Win., .30-06, 5.6x50R Mag., 5.6x52R, 6x62R Freres, 6.5x57R, 6.5x65R, 7x57R, 7x65R, 8x57JRS, 8x75RS, 9.3x74R, 7mm Rem. Mag., .300 Win. Mag. Barrels: 23.5 in. Shorter lengths available. Weight: 6.5 lbs. Length: 40.5 in. Stock: High-grade walnut. Sights: Blade front, open rear. Features: Break-open loading with manual cocking lever on top tang; takedown; extractor; Schnabel forearm; many options. Imported from Germany by Krieghoff International Inc.
Price: Hubertus single shot **$7,295.00**
Price: Hubertus, magnum calibers **$8,295.00**

MERKEL K1 MODEL LIGHTWEIGHT STALKING
Calibers: .243 Win., .270 Win., 7x57R, .308 Win., .30-06, 7mm Rem. Mag., .300 Win. Mag., 9.3x74R. Barrel: 23.6 in. Weight: 5.6 lbs. unscoped. Stock: Satin-finished walnut, fluted and checkered; sling-swivel studs. Sights: None (scope base furnished). Features: Franz Jager single-shot break-open action, cocking/uncocking slide-type safety, matte silver receiver, selectable trigger pull weights, integrated, quick detach 1 in. or 30mm optic mounts (optic not included). Extra barrels are an option. Imported from Germany by Merkel USA.
Price: Jagd Stalking Rifle **$3,795.00**
Price: Jagd Stutzen Carbine **$4,195.00**
Price: Extra barrels **$1,195.00**

PARKWEST ARMS LITTLE SHARPS
Calibers: Virtually any caliber from Rimfire to .38-55 Win. Barrel: 26-in. premium octagonal barrel standard, with option of ½ round, ½ octagon. Stock: XXX-grade English Walnut with straight grip. Many options and upgrades are available. Sights: Tang rear sight with front bead sight combinations. Features: Parkwest's 80% scale version of the original 1874 Sharps rifle. Matte blue barrel finish and color-casehardened receiver. Smooth steel buttplate. Blueprinted action. Scaled historical trigger design with choice of standard trigger or set trigger configurations.
Price: ....**Custom**

PARKWEST ARMS PW-ACE
Calibers: From .17 Fireball to 6mm BR. Capacity: Single-shot. Barrel: 24-in. stainless steel match grade with multiple options in both heavy or lite barrel.. Stock: XXX-grade Claro Walnut. Sporter forend on Lite models, Semi-beavertail forend on Heavy barrel. Weight:7.75 lbs. (Lite), 8.75 lbs. Heavy Barrel. Sights: None. Custom bases to accommodate Talley rings. Features: Single-shot bolt-action target rifle. Timney Elite Hunter adjustable trigger. Eleven-degree target crown. Right- or left-handed actions available. Sliding plate extractor. Side bolt release. Three standard bolt face diameters.
Price: ....**Custom**

PARKWEST ARMS SD-10
Calibers: Available in rimfire calibers through 7mm Rem. Mag. Capacity: Varied by chambering. Barrel: Match grade with multiple length options available. Stock: XXX-grade Walnut selected by customer. Sights: None. Custom bases to accommodate Talley rings. Weight: from 6.25 lbs.

Features: Don Allen designed single-shot, falling block action built as a lightweight stalking rifle. Tang safety for ambidextrous use. CNC machined from 4140 billet. All parts hand polished. Accuracy guarantee. Built in Sturgis, South Dakota.
Price: ....**Custom**

ROSSI LWC (LIGHTWEIGHT CARBINE) SINGLE-SHOT SERIES
Calibers: 5.56 Nato, .300 BLK, .350 Legend, .357 Mag., 6.5 Creedmoor. **Barrel:** 16.5 in. **Weight:** 6.25 lbs. **Stocks:** Black Synthetic with recoil pad and removable cheek piece. **Sights:** Adjustable rear, fiber optic front, scope rail. Some models have scope rail only. **Features:** Single-shot break open, positive ejection, internal transfer bar mechanism, manual external safety, trigger block system, Taurus Security System, Matte blue finish.
Price: $333.00

SHILOH CO. SHARPS 1874 LONG RANGE EXPRESS
Calibers: .38-55, .40-50 BN, .40-70 BN, .40-90 BN, .40-70 ST, .40-90 ST, .45-70 Govt. ST, .45-90 ST, .45-110 ST, .50-70 ST, .50-90 ST. **Barrel:** 34-in. tapered octagon. **Weight:** 10.5 lbs. **Length:** 51 in. overall. **Stock:** Oil-finished walnut (upgrades available) with pistol grip, shotgun-style butt, traditional cheek rest, Schnabel fore-end. **Sights:** Customer's choice. **Features:** Re-creation of the Model 1874 Sharps rifle. Double-set triggers. Made in USA by Shiloh Rifle Mfg. Co.
Price: $2,059.00
Price: Sporter Rifle No. 1 (similar to above except with 30-in. barrel, blade front, buckhorn rear sight) $2,059.00
Price: Sporter Rifle No. 3 (similar to No. 1 except straight-grip stock, standard wood) $1,949.00

SHILOH CO. SHARPS 1874 QUIGLEY
Calibers: .45-70 Govt., .45-110. **Barrel:** 34-in. heavy octagon. **Stock:** Military-style with patch box, standard-grade American walnut. **Sights:** Semi-buckhorn, interchangeable front and midrange vernier tang sight with windage. **Features:** Gold inlay initials, pewter tip, Hartford collar, case color or antique finish. Double-set triggers.
Price: $3,533.00

SHILOH CO. SHARPS 1874 SADDLE
Calibers: .38-55, .40-50 BN, .40-65 Win., .40-70 BN, .40-70 ST, .40-90 BN, .40-90 ST, .44-77 BN, .44-90 BN, .45-70 Govt. ST, .45-90 ST, .45-100 ST, .45-110 ST, .45-120 ST, .50-70 ST, .50-90 ST. **Barrels:** 26 in. full or half octagon. **Stock:** Semi-fancy American walnut. Shotgun style with cheek rest. **Sights:** Buckhorn and blade. **Features:** Double-set trigger, numerous custom features can be added.
Price: $2,044.00

SHILOH CO. SHARPS 1874 MONTANA ROUGHRIDER
Calibers: .38-55, .40-50 BN, .40-65 Win., .40-70 BN, .40-70 ST, .40-90 BN, .40-90 ST, .44-77 BN, .44-90 BN, .45-70 Govt. ST, .45-90 ST, .45-100 ST, .45-110 ST, .45-120 ST, .50-70 ST, .50-90 ST. **Barrels:** 30 in. full or half octagon. **Stock:** American walnut in shotgun or military style. **Sights:** Buckhorn and blade. **Features:** Double-set triggers, numerous custom features can be added.
Price: $2,059.00

SHILOH CO. SHARPS CREEDMOOR TARGET
Calibers: .38-55, .40-50 BN, .40-65 Win., .40-70 BN, .40-70 ST, .40-90 BN, .40-90 ST, .44-77 BN, .44-90 BN, .45-70 Govt. ST, .45-90 ST, .45-100 ST, .45-110 ST, .45-120 ST, .50-70 ST, .50-90 ST. **Barrel:** 32 in. half round-half octagon. **Stock:** Extra fancy American walnut. Shotgun style with pistol grip. **Sights:** Customer's choice. **Features:** Single trigger, AA finish on stock, polished barrel and screws, pewter tip.
Price: $3,105.00

UBERTI 1874 SHARPS SPORTING
Caliber: .45-70 Govt. **Barrels:** 30 in., 32 in., 34 in. octagonal. **Weight:** 10.57 lbs. with 32 in. barrel. **Lengths:** 48.9 in. with 32 in. barrel. **Stock:** Walnut. **Sights:** Dovetail front, Vernier tang rear. **Features:** Cut checkering, case-colored finish on frame, buttplate, and lever. Imported by Stoeger Industries.
Price: Standard Sharps **$1,919.00**
Price: Special Sharps...**$2,019.00**
Price: Deluxe Sharps **$3,269.00**
Price: Down Under Sharps **$2,719.00**
Price: Long Range Sharps **$2,719.00**
Price: Buffalo Hunter Sharps **$2,620.00**
Price: Sharps Cavalry Carbine **$2,020.00**
Price: Sharps Extra Deluxe...**$5,400.00**
Price: Sharps Hunter...**$1,699.00**

UBERTI 1885 HIGH-WALL SINGLE-SHOT
Calibers: .45-70 Govt., .45-90, .45-120. **Barrels:** 28–32 in. **Weights:** 9.3–9.9 lbs. **Lengths:** 44.5–47 in. overall. **Stock:** Walnut stock and fore-end. **Sights:** Blade front, fully adjustable open rear. **Features:** Based on Winchester High-Wall design by John Browning. Color casehardened frame and lever, blued barrel and buttplate. Imported by Stoeger Industries.
Price: .... **$1,079.00–$1,279.00**

UBERTI 1885 COURTENEY STALKING RIFLE
Calibers: .303 British, .45-70 Gov't. **Capacity:** Single shot. **Barrel:** 24-in. round blued steel. **Weight:** 7.1 lbs. **Length:** 37.5 in. **Stock:** A-Grade Walnut, Prince of Wales buttstock and slim fore-end with African heartwood. **Sights:** Hooded front and V-style express rear with quarter-rib slot for Weaver rings. **Features:** Named after English hunter Frederick Courteney Selous, this single shot shows traditional British style. Casehardened receiver. Checkered pistol grip. Rubber buttpad. Sling swivels including barrel-mounted front.
Price: **$1,689.00**

UBERTI SPRINGFIELD TRAPDOOR RIFLE/CARBINE
Caliber: .45-70 Govt., single shot **Barrel:** 22 or 32.5 in. **Features:** Blued steel receiver and barrel, casehardened breechblock and buttplate. **Sights:** Creedmoor style.
Price: Springfield Trapdoor Carbine, 22 in. barrel **$1,749.00**
Price: Springfield Trapdoor Army, 32.5 in. barrel **$2,019.0**

Prices given are believed to be accurate at time of publication however, many factors affect retail pricing so exact prices are not possible.

CHAPUIS ARMES X4 DOUBLE RIFLE
Caliber: 9.3x74R, .30-06 Spfld. Barrel: 22 in. Weight: 6 lbs. Stock: AAA-grade Circassian Walnut with English-style cheekpiece. Features: The double can be re-regulated for new loads. Built on a Progress 28-gauge scalloped receiver. Intricate engraving. Double triggers and ejectors. Adjustable rear and ramp front sights. Machined for Recknagel scope mounts.
Price: 9.3x74R $7,299.00
Price: 30.06 Spfld $7,599.00

CHAPUIS ARMES IPHISI DOUBLE RIFLE
Caliber: .375 H&H. Barrel: 26 in. Weight: 9.3 lbs. Stock: AAA-grade Walnut with satin finish and pistol grip design. Features: The Iphisi (Zulu for 'big game hunter') is an express double. Border engraving, case-color receiver, ejectors. Express sights and rib machined to accept Talley rings. Barrels are regulated for 300-grain Hornady DGX loads but can be tuned by a gunsmith to new loads. Length of pull of 15.3 in. Double triggers. Includes Prestige-grade custom-fit hard case.
Price: $9,999.00

FAUSTI CLASS EXPRESS
Calibers: .243 Win., 6.5x55, 6.5x57R, 7x57R, .308 Win., .270 Win., .30-06, .30R Blaser, .45-70, .444 Marlin, 9.3x74, 8x57 JRS. Barrel: 24 in. Weight: 7.6 lbs. average. Stock: A-Grade Walnut with oil finish. Pistol grip style. Sights: Fiber-optic sight on ramp, adjustable for elevation. Features: O/U double rifle in a wide range of chamberings. LOP of 14.49 in. Choice of single or double triggers, no selector. Automatic ejectors. Includes VL151 gun case.
Price: $4,990.00
Price: CLASS SL EXPRESS $5,690.00

FAUSTI DEA EXPRESS
Calibers: .243 Win., 7x57R, .308 Win., .270 Win., .30-06, .30R Blaser, .45-70, .444 Marlin, 9.3x74, 8x57 JRS. Barrel: 24 in. Weight: 7 lbs. average. Stock: A-Grade Walnut with oil finish. Pistol grip style. Sights: Fiber-optic sight on ramp, adjustable for elevation. Features: SxS double rifle in a wide range of chamberings. LOP of 14.49 in. Choice of single or double triggers, no selector. Automatic ejectors. Includes VL151 gun case.
Price: $6,800.00

HEYM MODEL 88B SXS DOUBLE RIFLE
Calibers/Gauge: .22 Hornet, .300 Win. Mag., .375 H&H Belted Mag., .375 H&H Flanged Mag., .416 Rigby, .416/500 NE, .450/400 NE 3-in., .450 NE 3.25-in., .470 NE, .500 NE, .577 NE, .600 NE, 20 gauge, and more. Barrel: Up to 26 in., Krupp steel, hammer-forged. Stock: Custom select European walnut. Sights: V rear, bead front. Weight: 9 to 13 lbs. Features: Automatic ejectors, articulated front trigger, stocked-to-fit RH or LH, cocking indicators, engraving available.
Price: $18,000.00

HEYM MODEL 89B SXS DOUBLE RIFLE
Calibers/Gauge: .22 Hornet, .300 Win. Mag., .375 H&H Belted Mag., .375 H&H Flanged Mag., .416 Rigby, .416/500 NE, .450/400 NE 3-in., .450 NE 3.25-in., .470 NE, .500 NE, .577 NE, .600 NE, 20 gauge, and more. Barrel: Up to 26 in., Krupp steel, hammer-forged. Stock: Custom select European walnut. Sights: V rear, bead front. Weight: 9-13 lbs. Features: Five frame sizes, automatic ejectors, intercepting sears, stocked-to-fit RH or LH, engraving available.
Price: $23,000.00

KRIEGHOFF CLASSIC DOUBLE
Calibers: 7x57R, 7x65R, .308 Win., .30-06, 8x57 JRS, 8x75RS, 9.3x74R, .375NE, .500/.416NE, .470NE, .500NE. Barrel: 23.5 in. Weight: 7.3–11 lbs. Stock: High grade European walnut. Standard model has conventional rounded cheekpiece, Bavaria model has Bavarian-style cheekpiece. Sights: Bead front with removable, adjustable wedge (.375 H&H and below), standing leaf rear on quarter-rib. Features: Boxlock action; double triggers; short opening angle for fast loading; quiet extractors; sliding, self-adjusting wedge for secure bolting; Purdey-style barrel extension; horizontal firing pin placement. Many options available. Introduced 1997. Imported from Germany by Krieghoff International.
Price: $10,995.00
Price: Engraved sideplates, add $4,000.00
Price: Extra set of rifle barrels, add $6,300.00
Price: Extra set of 20-ga., 28 in. shotgun barrels, add $4,400.00

KRIEGHOFF CLASSIC BIG FIVE DOUBLE RIFLE
Similar to the standard Classic except available in .375 H&H, .375 Flanged Mag. N.E., .416 Rigby, .458 Win., 500/416 NE, 470 NE, 500 NE. Has hinged front trigger, nonremovable muzzle wedge, Universal Trigger System, Combi Cocking Device, steel triggerguard, specially weighted stock bolt for weight and balance. Many options available. Introduced 1997. Imported from Germany by Krieghoff International.
Price: $13,995.00
Price: Engraved sideplates, add $4,000.00
Price: Extra set of 20-ga. shotgun barrels, add $5,000.00
Price: Extra set of rifle barrels, add $6,300.00

MERKEL BOXLOCK DOUBLE
Calibers: 5.6x52R, .243 Winchester, 6.5x55, 6.5x57R, 7x57R, 7x65R, .308 Win., .30-06, 8x57 IRS, 9.3x74R. Barrel: 23.6 in. Weight: 7.7 oz. Length: NA. Stock: Walnut, oil finished, pistol grip. Sights: Fixed 100 meter. Features: Anson & Deeley boxlock action with cocking indicators, double triggers, engraved color casehardened receiver. Introduced 1995. Imported from Germany by Merkel USA.
Price: Model 140-2 .... $13,255.00
Price: Model 141 Small Frame SXS Rifle; built on smaller frame, chambered for 7mm Mauser, .30-06, or 9.3x74R $11,825.00
Price: Model 141 Engraved; fine hand-engraved hunting scenes on silvered receiver. $13,500.00

BROWNING SA-22 SEMI-AUTO 22

Caliber: .22 LR. Capacity: Tubular magazine in buttstock holds 11 rounds. Barrel: 19.375 in. Weight: 5 lbs. 3 oz. Length: 37 in. overall. Stock: Checkered select walnut with pistol grip and semi-beavertail fore-end. Sights: Gold bead front, folding leaf rear. Features: Engraved receiver with polished blue finish; crossbolt safety; easy takedown for carrying or storage. The Grade VI is available with either grayed or blued receiver with extensive engraving with gold-plated animals: right side pictures a fox and squirrel in a woodland scene; left side shows a beagle chasing a rabbit. On top is a portrait of the beagle. Stock and fore-end are of high-grade walnut with a double-bordered cut checkering design. Introduced 1956. Made in Belgium until 1974. Currently made in Japan by Miroku.
Price: .... **$799.00–$1,799.00**

H&K 416-22

Caliber: .22 LR. Capacity: 10- or 20-round magazine. Features: Blowback semi-auto rifle styled to resemble H&K 416 with metal upper and lower receivers; rail interface system; retractable stock; pistol grip with storage compartment; on-rail sights; rear sight adjustable for wind and elevation; 16.1-in. barrel. Also available in pistol version with 9-in. barrel. Made in Germany by Walther under license from Heckler & Koch and imported by Umarex.
Price: **$599.00**

H&K MP5 A5

Caliber: .22 LR. Capacity: 10- or 25-round magazine Features: Blowback semi-auto rifle styled to resemble H&K MP5 with metal receiver; compensator; bolt catch; NAVY pistol grip; on-rail sights; rear sight adjustable for wind and elevation; 16.1-in. barrel. Also available in pistol version with 9-in. barrel. Also available with SD-type fore-end. Made in Germany by Walther under license from Heckler & Koch. Imported by Umarex.
Price: **$599.00**

HENRY AR-7 SURVIVAL RIFLE

Caliber: .22 LR. Capacity: 8, detachable steel magazine. Barrel: 16.125-in. steel covered with ABS plastic. Weight: 3.5 lbs. Length: 35 in. Stock: ABS plastic, floating, hollow design allowing rifle to be disassembled and packed inside buttstock. Choice of Black, True Timber Kanati, or Viper Western camo. Sights: Peep rear with blaze orange blade front. Also 3/8-in. grooved receiver. Features: Henry's version of the AR-7 takedown rifle issued to U.S. Air Force pilots. Receiver, barrel, and spare mags stow inside the buttstock. Rubber buttpad. 14-inch LOP. Two 8-round magazines included. The US Survival Pack includes a black synthetic AR-7 rifle, zippered soft case, and a wide variety of survival gear, including a Henry-branded Buck knife.
Price: AR-7 Black **$319.00**
Price: AR-7 Camo **$388.00**
Price: AR-7 Survival Pack **$577.00**

HOWA M1100

Calibers: .22 LR, .22 WMR, .17 HMR. Capacity: 10. Barrel: 18 in., threaded, blued. Stock: Composite Hogue over-molded. Sights: Picatinny rail. Weight: 9.35 lbs. Features: Guaranteed sub-MOA, two-stage HACT trigger.
Price: **$699.00**

KEL-TEC SU-22CA

Caliber: .22 LR. Capacity: 26-round magazine. Barrel: 16.1 in. Weight: 4 lbs. Length: 34 in. Features: Blowback action, crossbolt safety, adjustable front and rear sights with integral Picatinny rail. Threaded muzzle.
Price: **$547.00**

MAGNUM RESEARCH MAGNUM LITE RIMFIRE

Calibers: .22 LR or .22 WMR Capacity: 10 (.22 LR), 9 (.22 WMR) rotary magazine. Barrel: 17-, 18-, 18.5-, or 19-in. lengths with options of carbon, aluminum-tensioned, threaded, and integrally suppressed TTS-22. Weight: 4 lbs.–4 lbs. 8 oz. Length: 36-5/8–38-5/8 in. Stock: Multiple options including Hogue Overmolded and laminated Barracuda style. Sights: Integral scope base. Features: The Magnum Lite Rimfire (MLR) uses a one-piece forged 6061-T6 receivers that are black hardcoat anodized. Custom barrels. Integral Picatinny rail for easy optics mounting. Upgraded trigger. Multiple stock style and material options, as well as barrel types and lengths. Crossbolt safety and manual bolt hold-open catch. Made in the USA.
Price: Hogue Overmolded **$764.00**
Price: MLR .22 LR w/ aluminum-tensioned barrel **$641.00**
Price: MLR .22 WMR w/ Barracuda stock **$935.00**
Price: MLR .22 LR with Ultra barrel **$596.00**
Price: MLR .22 LR with TTS-22 suppressed barrel **$860.00**

MAGNUM RESEARCH SWITCHBOLT

Caliber: .22 LR. Capacity: 10-round rotary magazine. Barrel: 17-in. carbon. Weight: 4.25 lbs. Length: 35-1/8–35-1/2 in. Stock: Two models, one with Hogue Overmolded Black and the other with colored Ambidextrous Evolution laminate. Sights: Integral scope base. Features: Unique gas-assisted blowback operation. An extension of the lightweight MLR rifles, the Switchbolt was tested and perfected on the professional speed shooting circuit. Built in the USA. Integral Picatinny rail. Machined from 6061-T6, hardcoat anodized. Equipped with a bolt handle on the left side of a right-handed bolt, built for right-handed shooters so the trigger hand never has to leave the stock. Custom-designed Switchbolts are available from the Magnum Research Custom Shop.
Price: Hogue overmolded black stock **$731.00**
Price: Ambidextrous Evolution laminate stock **$893.00**
Price: Blaze 47 wood stock **$420.00**

MOSSBERG MODEL 702 PLINKSTER

Caliber: .22 LR. Capacity: 10-round magazine. Barrel: 18 in. free-floating. Weights: 4.1–4.6 lbs. Sights: Adjustable rifle. Receiver grooved for scope mount. Stock: Wood or black synthetic. Features: Ergonomically placed magazine release and safety buttons, crossbolt safety, free gun lock. Made in USA by O.F. Mossberg & Sons, Inc.
Price: **$245.00**

MOSSBERG MODEL 715T SERIES

Caliber: .22 LR. Capacity: 10- or 25-round magazine. Barrel: 16.25 or 18 in. with A2-style muzzle brake. Weight: 5.5 lbs. Features: AR style offered in several models. Flattop or A2 style carry handle.
Price: Black finish **$406.00**
Price: Black finish, Red Dot sight **$462.00**

ROSSI RS22

Caliber: .22 LR. Capacity: 10-round detachable magazine. Barrel: 18 in. Weight: 4.1 lbs. Length: 36 in. Stock: Black synthetic with impressed checkering. Sights: Adjustable fiber optic rear, hooded fiber optic front. Made in Brazil, imported by Rossi USA.
Price: Standard model, synthetic stock **$139.00**

RUGER 10/22 AUTOLOADING CARBINE

Caliber: .22 LR. Capacity: 10-round rotary magazine. Barrel: 18.5 in. round tapered (16.12 in. compact model). Weight: 5 lbs. (4.5, compact). Length: 37.25 in., 34 in. (compact) overall. Stock: American hardwood with pistol grip and barrel band, or synthetic. Sights: Brass bead front, folding leaf rear adjustable for elevation. Features: Available with satin black or stainless finish on receiver and barrel. Detachable rotary magazine fits flush into stock, crossbolt safety, receiver tapped and grooved for scope blocks or tip-off mount. Scope base adaptor furnished with each rifle. Made in USA by Sturm, Ruger & Co.
Price: Wood stock **$389.00**
Price: Synthetic stock **$389.00**
Price: Stainless, synthetic stock **$439.00**
Price: Compact model, fiber-optic front sight **$379.00**

Prices given are believed to be accurate at time of publication however, many factors affect retail pricing so exact prices are not possible.

RUGER 10/22 TAKEDOWN RIFLE

Caliber: .22 LR. Capacity: 10-round rotary magazine. Barrels: 18.5 in. stainless, or 16.6 in. satin black threaded with suppressor. Easy takedown feature enables quick separation of the barrel from the action by way of a recessed locking lever, for ease of transportation and storage. Stock: Black synthetic. Sights: Adjustable rear, gold bead front. Weight: 4.66 pounds. Comes with backpack carrying bag.

Price: Stainless..**$559.00**
Price: Satin black w/flash suppressor................................**$579.00**
Price: Threaded barrel...**$799.00**

RUGER 10/22 SPORTER

Same specifications as 10/22 Carbine except has American walnut stock with hand-checkered pistol grip and fore-end, straight buttplate, sling swivels, 18.9-in. barrel, and no barrel band.

Price: **$529.00**

SAVAGE A17 SERIES

Calibers: .17 HMR, . Capacity: 10-round rotary magazine. Barrel: 22 in. Weight: 5.4–5.6 lbs. Features: Delayed blowback action, Savage AccuTrigger, synthetic or laminated stock. Target model has heavy barrel, sporter or thumbhole stock. Introduced in 2016.

Price: Standard model **$473.00**
Price: Sporter (Gray laminate stock) **$574.00**
Price: Target Sporter..**$571.00**
Price: Target Thumbhole **$631.00**
Price: A17 Pro Varmint **$739.00**
Price: A17 Overwatch camo **$599.00**
Price: A17 HM2 chambered for 17HM2 with black synthetic stock **$409.00**

SAVAGE A22 SERIES

Caliber: .22 LR, .22 WMR. Capacity 10-round magazine. Similar to A17 series except for caliber.

Price: **$284.00**
Price: A22 SS stainless barrel **$419.00**
Price: Target Thumbhole stock, heavy barrel **$449.00**
Price: Pro Varmint w/Picatinny rail, heavy bbl., target stock **$409.00**
Price: 22 WMR **$479.00**
Price: A22 Pro Varmint **$569.00**
Price: A22 Pro Varmint Magnum in .22 WMR.....................**$739.00**
Price: A22 FV-SR Overwatch Camo **$429.00**
Price: A22 Precision with MDT Chassis **$659.00**
Price: A22 Precision Lite with carbon-fiber stainless barrel **$949.00**

SAVAGE A22 BNS-SR

Caliber: .22 LR. Capacity: 10. Barrel: 18 in., carbon steel. Stock: Laminated wood. Sights: Two-piece Weaver bases, no scope included. Weight: 6.6 lbs. Features: Ergonomic stock, AccuTrigger, straight blowback semi-auto.

Price: **$479.00**

SAVAGE A22 TAKEDOWN

Calibers: .22 LR. Barrel: 18 in. Weight: 6.3 lbs. Stock: Black synthetic adjustable. Features: Latest addition to the semi-auto A22 family now in takedown. Breaks in half with a twist. Threaded barrel with low-profile sights. Crossbolt safety, adjustable AccuTrigger. Storage compartment in

pistol grip and magazine compartment in cheek riser. Has 0 MOA rail with a see-through iron sight channel. Includes 10-round rotary magazine.

Price: **$479.00**

SAVAGE B-SERIES PRECISION

Calibers: .22 LR, .22 WMR, .17 HMR. Capacity: 10-round detachable magazine. Barrel: 18 in heavy carbon steel, threaded. Weight: from 5 lbs. 5 oz. Stock: MDT one-piece billet aluminum chassis with adjustable LOP and comb height. Sights: None. One-piece Picatinny rail. Features: B-Series Precision rifles are built for target performance. They include the B22 in .22 LR, B22 Magnum in .22 WMR, and B17 in .17 HMR. Adjustable AccuTrigger with red trigger detail.

Price: **$659.00**
Price: B-Series Precision Lite 18 in. carbon fiber bbl. wrap **$949.00**

SMITH & WESSON M&P15-22 SERIES

Caliber: .22 LR. Capacities: 10- or 25-round magazine. Barrel: 15.5 in., 16 in. or 16.5 in. Stock: 6-position telescoping or fixed. Features: A rimfire version of AR-derived M&P tactical autoloader. Operates with blowback action. Quad-mount Picatinny rails, plain barrel or compensator, alloy upper and lower, matte black metal finish. Kryptek Highlander or Muddy Girl camo finishes available.

Price: Standard **$449.00**
Price: Kryptek Highlander or Muddy Girl camo **$499.00**
Price: MOE Model with Magpul sights, stock and grip.............**$609.00**
Price: Performance Center upgrades, threaded barrel **$789.00**
Price: M&P 15 Sport w/Crimson Trace Red Dot sight.................**$759.00**

VOLQUARTSEN CLASSIC

Calibers: .22 LR, .22 WMR, .17 HMR. Capacity: 10-round rotary magazine. Barrel: .920-in. stainless bull barrel threaded into receiver. Weight: from 5 lbs. 5oz. Stock: Choice of multiple options, including black Hogue or colored laminate wood sporter style. Sights: Integral Picatinny rail Features: Classic semi-automatic is the foundation of all subsequent models. Match bore and chamber tolerances for bolt-action accuracy from a repeater. Stainless steel CNC-machined receiver. TG2000 for crisp 2.25-lb. trigger pull.

Price: **$1,504.00**

VOLQUARTSEN VF-ORYX

Caliber: 22 LR Capacity: 10-round magazine. Barrel: 18.5-in. free-floating, snake-fluted. Weight: 9 lbs. 3 oz. Stock: MDT Oryx one-piece aluminum chassis. Sights: Integral 20 MOA rail. Features: CNC-machined stainless steel receiver. Barrel threaded into receiver for rigidity. CNC'ed bolt with round titanium firing pin and tuned extractor. TG2000 trigger group with crisp 2.25-lb. pull. Stock tailored for bench, bipod, and prone shooting. Adjustable cheek riser, overmolded pistol grip, and LOP spacer.

Price: **$1,944.00**
Price: VF-ORYX-S package with Zeiss Conquest...........................**$3,269.00**

WINCHESTER WILDCAT 22 SR (SUPPRESSOR READY)

Caliber: .22 LR. Capacity: 10-round rotary magazine. Barrel: 16.5-in. precision button-rifled chromoly steel with threaded muzzle, thread protector, and recessed target crown. Weight: 4.0 lbs. Length: 34.75 in. Stock: Black polymer ambidextrous skeletonized buttstock with textured grip panels. Sights: Fully adjustable ghost ring rear and ramped post front. Also, integral Picatinny rail. Features: Suppressor-ready version of the company's lightweight repeating rimfire. Rotary magazine system with last round bolt hold open. Dual ambidextrous magazine releases. Reversible manual safety button. Suppressor not included.

Price: ....**$269.00–$369.00**

Prices given are believed to be accurate at time of publication however, many factors affect retail pricing so exact prices are not possible.

79TH EDITION, 2025 461

BERGARA B-14 RIMFIRE

Caliber: .22 LR. Capacity: 10. Barrel: 18 in., 4140 Bergara. Stock: HMR composite. Sights: None. Weight: 9.25 lbs. Features: Threaded muzzle, B-14R action, Remington 700 accessories compatible.
Price: **$1,150.00**

BROWNING BL-22

Caliber: .22 LR. Capacity: Tubular magazines, 15+1. Action: Short-throw lever action, side ejection. Rack-and-pinion lever. Barrel: Recessed muzzle. Stock: Walnut, two-piece straight-grip Western style. Trigger: Half-cock hammer safety; fold-down hammer. Sights: Bead post front, folding-leaf rear. Steel receiver grooved for scope mount. Weight: 5–5.4 lbs. Length: 36.75–40.75 in. overall. Features: Action lock provided. Introduced 1996. FLD Grade II Octagon has octagonal 24-in. barrel, silver nitride receiver with scroll engraving, gold-colored trigger. FLD Grade I has satin-nickel receiver, blued trigger, no stock checkering. FLD Grade II has satin-nickel receivers with scroll engraving; gold-colored trigger, cut checkering. Both introduced 2005. Grade I has blued receiver and trigger, no stock checkering. Grade II has gold-colored trigger, cut checkering, blued receiver with scroll engraving. Imported from Japan by Browning.
Price: BL-22 Grade I/II, From ....**$620.00–$700.00**
Price: BL-22 FLD Grade I/II, From ....**$660.00–$750.00**
Price: BL-22 FLD, Grade II Octagon **$980.00**

BROWNING T-BOLT RIMFIRE

Calibers: .22 LR, .17 HMR, .22 WMR. Capacity: 10-round rotary box double helix magazine. Barrel: 22-in. free-floating, semi-match chamber, target muzzle crown. Weight: 4.8 lbs. Length: 40.1 in. overall. Stock: Walnut, maple or composite. Sights: None. Features: Straight-pull bolt action, three-lever trigger adjustable for pull weight, dual action screws, sling swivel studs. Crossbolt lockup, enlarged bolt handle, one-piece dual extractor with integral spring and red cocking indicator band, gold-tone trigger. Top-tang, thumb-operated two-position safety, drilled and tapped for scope mounts. Varmint model has raised Monte Carlo comb, heavy barrel, wide forearm. Introduced 2006. Imported from Japan by Browning. Left-hand models added in 2009.
Price: .22 LR, From..**$750.00–$780.00**
Price: Composite Target ....**$780.00–$800.00**
Price: .17 HMR/.22 WMR, From ....**$790.00–$830.00**

BROWNING T-BOLT TARGET W/ MUZZLE BRAKE

Calibers: .22 LR, .22 WMR, .17 HMR. Capacity: 10-round Double Helix box magazine. Barrel: 16.5-in. heavy bull. Sights: No iron sights. Drilled and tapped. Length: 34.75 in. Weight: 6 lbs. 2 oz. Stock: Black Walnut with satin-finish, checkered, Monte Carlo style. Features: Precision straight-pull bolt-action rimfire. Extra-wide fore-end. Free floating heavy bull target barrel threaded at 1/2x28. Includes removeable muzzle brake. Steel receiver with blued finish. Semi-match chamber and target crown. Top tang safety. Adjustable trigger. Sling studs. Plastic buttplate. Cut checkering at 20 LPI. Gold-plated trigger.
Price: ....**$699.00–$739.00**

BROWNING T-BOLT MAPLE

Caliber: .22 LR. Barrel: 20-in. threaded (Target SR); 22-in. sporter weight (Sporter). Weight: 4 lbs. 14 oz. (Sporter) 6 lbs. 2 oz. (Target SR). Stock: AAA-Grade Maple with a gloss finish and cut checkering at 20 LPI. Features: Straight-pull bolt action operation in special maple furniture. Double helix 10-round magazine. Adjustable trigger. Polished chamber. Polymer buttplate. Swivel studs. Receiver drilled and tapped.
Price: Maple Sporter **$929.00**
Price: Maple Target SR **$899.00**

CHIAPPA LITTLE BADGER

Caliber: .22 LR. Barrel: 16.5-in. blued steel. Weight: 2.9 lbs. Stock: Folding steel rod system. Features: Ultralight, minimalist, folding Take Down Xteme (TDX) version of the skeletonized break-action rimfire. Single shot with shell holder and quad Picatinny forend. OAL of 31 in. Alloy frame. Barrel threaded at 1/2x28. Fixed M1 military-style front sight and adjustable rear. Half cock hammer safety. Picatinny rail behind triggerguard. Ships with polymer tube for storage.
Price: TDX **$280.00**

CHRISTENSEN MODERN PRECISON RIFLE - RIMFIRE (MPR-R)

Calibers: .22 LR, .22 WMR, .17 HMR. Capacity: 10-round Ruger BX-1 magazine standard, with optional Ruger BX-15 mag. Barrel: 16, 18, 20 in. Weight: 6.2 lbs. Stock: Folding buttstock with Magnelock technology. FFT carbon-fiber handguard with M-LOK attachment points. AR-compatible pistol grip. Sights: None. 0-MOA Pic rail standard with optional 20-MOA, 40-MOA, or 60-MOA. Features: New for 2024 rimfire version of the MPR with a lightweight billet aluminum chassis. TriggerTech Remington 700-style trigger. Six QD flushcup mounts. Adjustable comb height and LOP. Sub-MOA accuracy guarantee at 50 yards.
Price: **$1,249.00**

CHIPMUNK SINGLE SHOT

Caliber: .22 Short, Long and Long Rifle or .22 WMR. Manually cocked single-shot bolt-action youth gun. Barrel: 16.125 in. blued or stainless. Weight: 2.6 lbs. Length: 30 in., LOP 11.6 in. Stock: Synthetic, American walnut or laminate. Barracuda model has ergonomic thumbhole stock with raised comb, accessory rail. Sights: Adjustable rear peep, fixed front. From Keystone Sporting Arms.
Price: Synthetic..**$163.00-$250.00**
Price: Walnut ....**$209.00-$270.00**
Price: Barracuda ....**$258.00-$294.00**

COOPER MODEL 57-M REPEATER

Calibers: .22 LR, .22 WMR, .17 HMR, .17 Mach. Barrel: 22 in. or 24 in. Weight: 6.5–7.5 lbs. Stock: Claro walnut, 22 LPI hand checkering. Sights:

None furnished. Features: Three rear locking lug, repeating bolt-action with 5-round magazine for .22 LR; 4-round magazine for .22 WMR and 17 HMR. Fully adjustable trigger. Left-hand models add $150 to base rifle price. 0.250-in. group rimfire accuracy guarantee at 50 yards; 0.5-in. group centerfire accuracy guarantee at 100 yards. Options include wood upgrades, case-color metalwork, barrel fluting, custom LOP, and many others.

Price: Classic	$2,495.00
Price: Custom Classic	$2,995.00
Price: Western Classic	$3,795.00
Price: Schnabel	$2,595.00
Price: Jackson Squirrel	$2,595.00
Price: Jackson Hunter	$2,455.00
Price: Mannlicher	$4,755.00

CZ 457 AMERICAN
Calibers: .17 HMR, .22 LR, .22 WMR. Capacity: 5-round detachable magazine. Barrel: 24.8 in. Weight: 6.2 lbs. Stock: Turkish walnut American style with high flat comb. Sights: None. Integral 11mm dovetail scope base. Features: Adjustable trigger, push-to-fire safety, interchangeable barrel system.

Price:	$476.00
Price: .17 HMR .22 WMR	$496.00
Price: Varmint model	$660.00-$762.00

CRICKETT SINGLE SHOT
Caliber: .22 Short, Long and Long Rifle or .22 WMR. Manually cocked single-shot bolt-action. Similar to Chipmunk but with more options and models. Barrel: 16.125 in. blued or stainless. Weight: 3 lbs. Length: 30 in., LOP 11.6 in. Stock: Synthetic, American walnut or laminate. Available in wide range of popular camo patterns and colors. Sights: Adjustable rear peep, fixed front. Drilled and tapped for scope mounting using special Chipmunk base. Alloy model has AR-style buttstock, XBR has target stock and bull barrel, Precision Rifle has bipod and fully adjustable thumbhole stock.

Price: Alloy	$300.00
Price: XBR	$380.00-$400.00
Price: Precision Rifle	$316.00-$416.00
Price: Adult Rifle	$240.00-$280.00

HAMMERLI FORCE B1
Caliber: .22 LR, .22 WMR. Capacity: 10-round detachable Ruger magazine. Barrel: 16.1-in. standard. threaded at 1/2x28. (20-in. coming soon). Weight: 5.75 lbs. Length: 35.5–37.4 in. overall. Stock: Black polymer with vertical grip style. Laminate wood option. Adjustable for LOP and comb height. Sights: None. Picatinny optic rail. Features: Toggle-style straight-pull action with quick-change barrel system. Crossbolt safety. Adaptable magwell system facilitates use of the correct Ruger rotary mag. M-LOK slots and quick-detach sling pockets. Adjustable trigger compatible with Ruger 10/22 groups.

Price:	$649.00

HENRY LEVER-ACTION RIFLES
Caliber: .22 Long Rifle (15 shot), .22 Magnum (11 shots), .17 HMR (11 shots). Barrel: 18.25 in. round. Weight: 5.5–5.75 lbs. Length: 34 in. overall (.22 LR). Stock: Walnut. Sights: Hooded blade front, open adjustable rear. Features: Polished blue finish; full-length tubular magazine; side ejection; receiver grooved for scope mounting. Introduced 1997. Made in USA by Henry Repeating Arms Co.

Price: H001 Carbine .22 LR	$378.00
Price: H001L Carbine .22 LR, Large Loop Lever	$394.00
Price: H001Y Youth model (33 in. overall, 11-round .22 LR)	$378.00
Price: H001M .22 Magnum, 19.25 in. octagonal barrel, deluxe walnut stock	$525.00

Price: H001V .17 HMR, 20 in. octagonal barrel, Williams Fire Sights	$578.00
Price: Frontier Threaded Barrel, Suppressor-Ready .22 LR	$552.00
Price: Frontier Threaded Barrel, Suppressor-Ready .22 WMR	$656.00

HENRY LEVER-ACTION OCTAGON FRONTIER MODEL
Same as lever rifles except chambered in .17 HMR, .22 Short/Long/LR, .22 Magnum. Barrel: 20 in. octagonal. Sights: Marble's fully adjustable semi-buckhorn rear, brass bead front. Weight: 6.25 lbs. Made in USA by Henry Repeating Arms Co.

Price: H001T Lever Octagon .22 S/L/R	$473.00
Price: H001TM Lever Octagon .22 Magnum, .17 HMR	$578.00

HENRY GOLDEN BOY SERIES
Calibers: .17 HMR, .22 LR (16-shot), .22 Magnum. Barrel: 20 in. octagonal. Weight: 6.25 lbs. Length: 38 in. overall. Stock: American walnut. Sights: Blade front, open rear. Features: Brasslite receiver, brass buttplate, blued barrel and lever. Introduced 1998. Made in USA from Henry Repeating Arms Co.

Price: H004 .22 LR	$578.00
Price: H004M .22 Magnum	$625.00
Price: H004V .17 HMR	$641.00
Price: H004DD .22 LR Deluxe, engraved receiver	$1,575.00-1,654.00

HENRY SILVER BOY
Calibers: 17 HMR, .22 S/L/LR, .22 WMR. Capacities: Tubular magazine. 12 rounds (.17 HMR and .22 WMR), 16 rounds (.22 LR), 21 rounds (.22 Short). Barrel: 20 in. Stock: American walnut with curved buttplate. Finish: Nickel receiver, barrel band and buttplate. Sights: Adjustable buckhorn rear, bead front. Silver Eagle model has engraved scroll pattern from early original Henry rifle. Offered in same calibers as Silver Boy. Made in USA from Henry Repeating Arms Company.

Price: .22 S/L/LR	$630.00
Price: .22 WMR	$682.00
Price: .17 HMR	$709.00
Price: Silver Eagle	$892.00–$945.00

HENRY PUMP ACTION
Caliber: .22 LR. Capacity: 15 rounds. Barrel: 18.25 in. Weight: 5.5 lbs. Length: NA. Stock: American walnut. Sights: Bead on ramp front, open adjustable rear. Features: Polished blue finish; receiver grooved for scope mount; grooved slide handle; two barrel bands. Introduced 1998. Made in USA from Henry Repeating Arms Co.

Price: H003T .22 LR	$578.00
Price: H003TM .22 Magnum	$620.00

MEACHAM LOW-WALL
Calibers: Any rimfire cartridge. Barrels: 26–34 in. Weight: 7-15 lbs. Sights: none. Tang drilled for Win. base, .375 in. dovetail slot front. Stock: Fancy eastern walnut with cheekpiece; ebony insert in forearm tip. Features: Exact copy of 1885 Winchester. With most Winchester factory options available including double-set triggers. Introduced 1994. Made in USA by Meacham T&H Inc.

Price: From	$4,999.00

MOSSBERG INTERNATIONAL MODEL 802
Caliber: .22 LR Capacity: 10-round magazine. Barrel: 18 in. free-floating. Weight: 4.1 lbs. Sights: Adjustable rifle or scope combo variant. Receiver grooved for scope mount. Stock: Black synthetic. Features: Ergonomically placed magazine release and safety buttons, crossbolt safety.

Prices given are believed to be accurate at time of publication however, many factors affect retail pricing so exact prices are not possible.

79TH EDITION, 2025 ⊕ 463

Price: Plinkster **$231.00**
Price: Scope combo **$245.00**

PEDERSOLI BLACK WIDOW

Calibers: .22 LR. Capacity: Single shot. Barrel: 19-in. round steel. Weight: 3.3 lbs. Stock: Black techno-polymer folder with skeletonized buttstock and removeable forend. Sights: Iron sights. Drilled and tapped for Picatinny rail mounting. Features: Folding-style, single-shot rimfire. Threaded barrel with knurled thread protector cap. Integral ammo storage along buttstock. Forward Picatinny rail at base of forend. Built to fit into medium-sized backpack. European model threaded at ½-20 UNF. American version threaded at ½"-28 TPI.
Price: **$400.00**

ROSSI GALLERY

Caliber: 22 LR. Capacity: 15-round tubular magazine. Barrel: 18-in. round. Weight: 5.3 lbs. Length: 36 in. Stock: Choice of either German Beechwood or black synthetic. Sights: Traditional Buckhorn iron sights on wood model; fiber optics on synthetic model. Features: Pump action reminiscent of classic gallery guns of the 1890s. Polished black metalwork. Hammer fired with cross-bolt safety. Sling studs.
Price: German Beechwood........................**$360.00**
Price: Black Polymer...............................**$315.00**

ROSSI RIO BRAVO

Caliber: 22 LR. Capacity: 15-round tubular magazine. Barrel: 18-in. round. Weight: 5.5 lbs. Length: 36 in. Stock: Choice of either German Beechwood or black synthetic. Sights: Traditional Buckhorn iron sights on wood model; fiber optics on synthetic model. Features: Lever action rimfire based on the company's R92 centerfires. Polished black metal finish. Hammer fired with cross-bolt safety. Sling studs.
Price: German Beechwood........................**$370.00**
Price: Black Polymer...............................**$370.00**

ROSSI RIO BRAVO GOLD

Caliber: .22 LR. Capacity: 15-round tubular magazine. Barrel: 18-in. round. Weight: 5.5 lbs. Length: 36 in. Stock: German Beechwood. Sights: Traditional Buckhorn iron sights. Features: New "Gold" version of Rossi's lever-action rimfire based on the R92 centerfire. PVD gold receiver and lever finish with polished black on remaining metalwork. Hammer fired with cross-bolt safety. Sling studs.
Price: **$465.00**

RUGER AMERICAN RIMFIRE RIFLE

Calibers: .17 HMR, .22 LR,.22 WMR. Capacity: 10-round rotary magazine. Barrels: 22-in., or 18-in. threaded. Sights: Williams fiber optic, adjustable. Stock: Composite with interchangeable comb adjustments, sling swivels. Adjustable trigger.
Price: **$359.00**

RUGER PRECISION RIMFIRE RIFLE

Calibers: .17 HMR, .22 LR, .22 HMR. Capacity: 9 to 15-round magazine. Barrel: 18 in. threaded. Weight: 6.8 lbs. Stock: Quick-fit adjustable with AR-pattern pistol grip, free-floated handguard with Magpul M-LOK slots. Features: Adjustable trigger, oversized bolt handle, Picatinny scope base.
Price: **$529.00**

SAVAGE MARK II BOLT-ACTION

Calibers: .22 LR, .17 HMR. Capacity: 10-round magazine. Barrel: 20.5 in. Weight: 5.5 lbs. Length: 39.5 in. overall. Stock: Camo, laminate, thumbhole or OD Green stock available Sights: Bead front, open adjustable rear. Receiver grooved for scope mounting. Features: Thumb-operated rotating safety. Blue finish. Introduced 1990. Made in Canada, from Savage Arms, Inc.
Price: ....**$228.00–$280.00**
Price: Varmint w/heavy barrel **$242.00**
Price: Camo stock **$280.00**
Price: OD Green stock.. **$291.00**
Price: Multi-colored laminate stock **$529.00**
Price: Thumbhole laminate stock **$469.00**

SAVAGE MODEL 93FVSS MAGNUM

Similar to Model 93FSS Magnum except 21-in. heavy barrel with recessed target-style crown, satin-finished stainless barreled action, black graphite/fiberglass stock. Drilled and tapped for scope mounting; comes with Weaver-style bases. Introduced 1998. Imported from Canada by Savage Arms, Inc.
Price: **$364.00**

SAVAGE B SERIES

Calibers: .17 HMR, .22 LR, 22 WMR. Capacity: 10-round rotary magazine. Barrel: 21 in. (16.25 in. threaded heavy barrel on Magnum FV-SR Model). Stock: Black synthetic with target-style vertical pistol grip. Weight: 6 lbs. Features include top tang safety, Accutrigger. Introduced in 2017.
Price: ....**$281.00–$445.00**

SAVAGE MARK II MINIMALIST

Choice of Green or Brown Boyd's Minimalist laminate stock design.
Price: **$379.00**

SAVAGE MODEL 42

Calibers/Gauges: Break-open over/under design with .22 LR or .22 WMR barrel over a .410 shotgun barrel. Under-lever operation. Barrel: 20 in. Stock: Synthetic black matte. Weight: 6.1 lbs. Sights: Adjustable rear, bead front. Updated variation of classic Stevens design from the 1940s.
Price **$509.00**

SAVAGE RASCAL

Calibers: .22 LR. Capacity: Single shot. Barrel: 16.125-in. carbon steel.

Weight: 2.71 lbs. Length: 30.6 in. Stock: Synthetic sporter. Upgraded models available with different stock options. Sights: Adjustable peep sights. Features: Micro-rimfire bolt action with short 11.25-inch length of pull for the smallest framed shooters. Cocks by lifting the bolt and unloads without pulling the trigger. User-adjustable AccuTrigger. Feed ramp. Manual safety.

Price **$199.00**
Price Rascal FV-SR Left Hand **$249.00**
Price Rascal Target **$339.00**
Price Rascal Target XP **$429.00**

SAVAGE RASCAL MINIMALIST
Caliber: .22 LR. Capacity: single shot. Barrel: 16.125-in. carbon steel, threaded with protector. Length: 30.625 in. Weight: 3.5 lbs. Stock: Minimalist hybrid laminate design in two color options. Features: Addition to the micro-sized Rascal single shot, bolt-action family. Blued carbon steel receiver. Manual safety. Cocks by lifting the bolt. Unloads without pulling the trigger. 11-degree target crown. Adjustable peep sight. Sling studs. User-adjustable AccuTrigger. Feed ramp. ChevCore Laminate technology with Boyd's stock in two color options: Pink/Purple or Teal/Gray. Short 11.5-in length of pull. Package includes ear plugs and firearms lock.
Price: **$289.00**

SPRINGFIELD ARMORY MODEL 2020 RIMFIRE CLASSIC
Calibers: .22 LR. Capacity: 10-rd. rotary mag. Barrel: 20-in No. 1 sporter contour, 1:16, matte blued, threaded 1/2x28. Stock: Walnut in four options from select through Grades A-AAA. Sights: Interupted Picatinny rail. Weight: 6 lbs., 3 oz. Features: Adjustable Remington 700-style trigger group w/ Hanger System for compatibility.
Price: .... **$529.00–$1,099.00**

TIKKA T1x MTR
Calibers: .22 LR or .17 HMR. Capacity: 10-round polymer magazine. Barrel: 20-in. cold hammer forged, crossover profile. Weight: 5.7 lbs. Length: 39.6 in. Stock: Modular Black synthetic. Sights: No iron sights. Dovetailed and tapped. Features: Stainless steel bolt for smooth movement and weather resistance. Compatible with most T3x accessories. Action shares same bedding surfaces and inlay footprint with the T3x centerfire rifles. Threaded muzzle. Adjustable single-stage trigger.
Price **$529.00**

VOLQUARTSEN SUMMIT
Calibers: .22 LR or .17 Mach2. Capacity: 10-round rotary magazine. Barrel: 16.5-in. lightweight carbon fiber with threaded muzzle. Stainless steel tapered barrel also available. Weight: 4 lbs. 13 oz.–7 lbs. 11 oz. Stock: Available with multiple stock options, including black Hogue, colored Magpul, McMillan Sporter, or Laminated Silhouette Wood sporter. Sights: Integral 20 MOA Picatinny rail. Features: Unique straight-pull bolt-action rimfire inspired by the 10/22 platform. Built for both competition shooting and small game hunting. CNC-machined receiver with integral rail. Suppressor ready. Accepts 10/22-style magazines. Crisp 1.75-lb. trigger

pull. Made in the USA.
Price **$1,252.00**

WINCHESTER RANGER
Calibers: .22 LR . Capacity: 15-round tubular magazine. Barrel: 20.5 in. round steel sporter contour. Weight: 5 lbs., 4 oz. Length: 37.75 in. overall. Stock: Straight grip style finish Grade 1 Turkish Walnut with satin oil and cut checkering. Sights: Iron sights along with grooved receiver. Features: New for 2024 version of the lever-action Ranger rimfire. Receiver machined from solid aluminum billet and finished in matte black. Steel triggerguard and plastic buttplate. LOP of 13 in. Trigger is adjustable for overtravel. Carbine-style handguard with steel barrel band. Single receiver action screw for quick takedown and cleaning. Built in Turkey for Winchester.
Price **$419.00**

WINCHESTER XPERT
Calibers: .22 LR. Capacity: 10-round rotary detachable magazine, interchangeable with both Wildcat and Ruger 10/22. Barrel: 18-in. precision button rifled with recessed target crown. Weight: 4 lbs. 8 oz. Length: 36.25 in. Stock: Gray Synthetic skeletonized with optional LOP spacers and cheek riser. Sights: Adjustable rear and ramped post front. Drilled and tapped. Features: Bolt-action precision cousin to the Wildcat line of semi-auto rimfires. Xpert uses a rimfire version of the M.O.A. trigger found on Model 70 and XPR rifles. Semi-match Bentz chamber and hemispherical firing pin. Extended bolt handle. Ambidextrous side-mounted mag releases. Plastic butt plate.
Price: **$319.00**
Price: Xpert Suppressor Ready **$349.00**
Price: Xpert True Timber Strata **$359.00**
Price: True Timber Strata Suppressor Ready **$389.00**
Price: Forged Carbon Gray Suppressor-Ready **$399.00**

Prices given are believed to be accurate at time of publication however, many factors affect retail pricing so exact prices are not possible.

79TH EDITION, 2025 ✦ **465**

ANSCHUTZ 1903 MATCH

Caliber: .22 LR. Capacity: Single-shot. Barrel: 21.25 in. Weight: 8 lbs. Length: 43.75 in. overall. Stock: Walnut-finished hardwood with adjustable cheekpiece; stippled grip and fore-end. Sights: None furnished. Features: Uses Anschutz Match 64 action. A medium weight rifle for intermediate and advanced Junior Match competition. Available from Champion's Choice.

Price: Right-hand **$1,195.00**

ANSCHUTZ 1912 SPORT

Caliber: .22 LR. Barrel: 26 in. match. Weight: 11.4 lbs. Length: 41.7 in. overall. Stock: Non-stained thumbhole stock adjustable in length with adjustable buttplate and cheekpiece adjustment. Flat fore-end raiser block 4856 adjustable in height. Hook buttplate. Sights: None furnished. Features: in. Free rifle in. for women. Smallbore model 1907 with 1912 stock: Match 54 action. Delivered with: Hand stop 6226, fore-end raiser block 4856, screwdriver, instruction leaflet with test target. Available from Champion's Choice.

Price: **$2,995.00**

ANSCHUTZ 1913 SUPER MATCH RIFLE

Same as the Model 1911 except European walnut International-type stock with adjustable cheekpiece, or color laminate, both available with straight or lowered fore-end, adjustable aluminum hook buttplate, adjustable hand stop, weighs 13 lbs., 46 in. overall. Stainless or blued barrel. Available from Champion's Choice.

Price: Right-hand, blued, no sights, walnut stock............................**$3,799.00**

ANSCHUTZ 1907 STANDARD MATCH RIFLE

Same action as Model 1913 but with 0.875-in. diameter 26-in. barrel (stainless or blues). Length: 44.5 in. overall. Weight: 10.5 lbs. Stock: Choice of stock configurations. Vented fore-end. Designed for prone and position shooting ISU requirements; suitable for NRA matches. Also available with walnut flat-forend stock for benchrest shooting. Available from Champion's Choice.

Price: Right-hand, blued, no sights..**$2,385.00**

BROWNING X-BOLT TARGET MAX COMPETITION

Caliber: 6mm Creed, 6mm GT, 6.5 Creedmoor, .308 Win. Barrel: 26-in. heavy stainless bull (Heavy model), 22-in. fluted sporter weight (Lite model). Weights: 9 to 12 lbs. Stock: Nylon-filled MAX with vertical grip and adjustable comb. Features: Specialized bolt-action target rifles aimed at competitions. Built on stiffer, heavier receivers. Factory ARCA/Swiss rail. Threaded barrel with Recoil Hawg brake. Textured grip panels. Gold-plated trigger. Extra capacity magazine.

Price: Competition Lite **$1,779.00**
Price: Competition Heavy **$1,799.00**

CADEX DEFENCE CDX-R7 CPS SERIES

Calibers: 6.5 Creedmoor, .308 Win. Capacity: Multiple magazine sleeves to fit most mags on the market. Barrel: 16.5-in. Bartlein heavy, straight-taper, fluted, threaded. Weight: 10.49 lbs. Length: 33.5 in. Stock: Lightweight with small contour forend tube and rail placement at 3, 6, and 9 o'clock. Takedown QD skeleton buttstock. Available in 14 color combinations. Cadex recoil pad, neoprene cheek pad, and rubberized grip panel. Sights: None. 0 MOA Picatinny rail standard, 20 or 30 MOA rails available. Features: Military-quality bolt-action platform for the civilian market. Spiral fluted bolt. DX2 Evo single-/two-stage selectable trigger. Optional MX2 muzzle brake. Hard case included.

Price: **$4,479.00**

COLT CBX

Caliber: 6.5 Creedmoor, .308 Win. Barrel: 24 in. (.308), 26 in. (6.5) Weight: 10.75 lbs. Stock: Aluminum chassis with adjustable LOP and cheek riser. Features: Precision bolt-action chassis rifle system. Flat bottom receiver. AICS magazine compatible. User-adjustable trigger. Extended forend with ARCA

rail and M-LOK slots. Picatinny rail. 60-degree bolt throw. Black nitride barrel finish. Pistol grip with thumb shelf and ambidextrous magazine latch.

Price: **$1,899.00**

CZ 457 VARMINT PRECISION CHASSIS

Caliber: .22 LR. Capacity: 5. Barrel: 16.5 or 24 in., suppressor ready, cold hammer-forged, heavy. Stock: Aluminum chassis. Sights: None, integral 11mm dovetail. Weight: 7 lbs. Features: Fully adjustable trigger, receiver mounted push-to-fire safety, swappable barrel system.

Price: **$999.00**

CZ 457 VARMINT PRECISION TRAINER MTR

Caliber: .22 LR. Capacity: 5-round detachable box magazine. Barrel: 16.2-in. cold hammer forged Varmint weight. Sights: No iron sights, integral 11mm Dovetail. Length: 33.5 in. Weight: 7.1 lbs. Stock: Manners carbon-fiber stock with colored highlights. Forearm is recessed, drilled, and threaded for ARCA rail. Features: The upgraded Varmint Precision Trainer makes use of a barrel borrowed from the Match Target Rifle (MTR). Match chamber. Heavy barrel threaded at 1/2x28. Designed to provide the same look and feel as a full-size tactical rifle but with more economical training. American-style, two position, push-to-fire safety. 60-degree bolt rotation. Fully adjustable trigger. Same swappable barrel system as the Model 455. Competition-grade rimfire rifle.

Price: **$1,635.00**

GUNWERKS HAMR 2.0

Calibers: .375 CheyTac. Barrel: 30 in. Carbon wrapped, threaded, with aggressive Cadex MX1 muzzle brake. Weight: 21.25 lbs. standard, total package. Stock: Cadex Defence Dual Strike tactical folding chassis-style with adjustable LOP. Sights: Comes standard with user option of scope (Kahles K525i, Leupold Mk 5HD, Revic PMR 428) on a 40 MOA mount. Features: Bolt-action ultra-long-range rifle built as a complete ELR system capable of shooting over two miles. The upgraded 2.0 version includes a carbon-wrapped barrel, new optic choices, and finish options. Included Elite Iron bipod encircles the centerline of the bore. Timney trigger set at 2.5 lbs. Prices increase significantly as options are added for custom factory builds. Long-range data package available.

Price: **$9,150.00**

HEYM HIGH PERFORMANCE PRECISION RIFLE (HPPR)

Calibers: Standard: .308 Win., 7mm Rem. Mag., .300 Win. Mag. Additional calibers available in 6.5 Creedmoor, 6.5x55, .270 Win., 7x64, .30-06 Spfld., and 8.5x63. Capacity: Detachable box magazine, varies by caliber. Barrel: 26-in. Krupp Steel, hammer forged, threaded, with protector. Sights: Top rail; available paired with Schmidt & Bender Precision Hunter scope. Weight: 8.0 lbs. Stock: PSE Carbon Precision with adjustable comb. Features: Precision shooting bolt actions from Heym built around two models, one SR21 with three-locking-lug turn bolt and the other SR30 straight pull. Single-stage trigger set at 3-lbs. with no creep or overtravel. Guaranteed 5-shot 20mm groups at 100 meters. Sling studs. Rubber recoil pad.

Price: **$4,750.00**

MASTERPIECE ARMS MPA BA PMR COMPETITION RIFLE

Calibers: .308 Win., 6mm Creedmoor, 6.5 Creedmoor. Capacity: 10. Barrel: 26 in., M24 stainless steel, polished. Stock: Aluminum chassis. Sights: None, optional package with MPA 30mm mount and Bushnell scope. Weight: 11.5 lbs. Features: Built-in inclinometer, MPA/Curtis action, match-grade chamber.

Price: ....**$2,999.00-$3,459.00**

Prices given are believed to be accurate at time of publication however, many factors affect retail pricing so exact prices are not possible.

PARKWEST ARMS SD-22
Calibers: .22 LR. Capacity: 5-round flush-mount detachable magazine. Barrel: Shilen Premium Match Grade. Stock: Choice of multiple high grades of walnut, including XXX-Claro Walnut with hand-rubbed oil finish. Sights: None. Drilled and tapped for Talley mounts. Features: ParkWest's rimfire version of a full-size bolt-action rifle with weight and feel similar to the SD-76 series. Dual extractors. Choice of matte blued or color-casehardened finish. TriggerTech adjustable trigger. Choice of uncheckered or hand checkered stocks with multiple design patterns. Accuracy guarantee.
Price: ....**Custom**

ROCK RIVER ARMS RBG-1S
Calibers: .308 Win./7.62X51 NATO or 6.5 Creedmoor. Capacity: AICS/Magpul compatible box magazine. Barrel: 20-, 22-, or 24-in. stainless steel air-gauged, cryo-treated. Weight: 10.2 lbs. Length: 39.5–43.5 in. Stock: KRG adjustable chassis in tan, black or green. Sights: 20 MOA rail. Also has standard scope base holes drilled for use with conventional ring mounts. Features: Rock River's first precision bolt-action rifles series. Precision aluminum bedding. One-piece, interchangeable two-lug bolt. Oversized knurled handle. TriggerTech trigger standard, with option of Timney upgrade. Toolless field adjustability. Guaranteed sub-MOA accuracy.
Price: **$4,235.00**

SAKO TRG-22 BOLT-ACTION
Calibers: .308 Win., .260 Rem, 6.5 Creedmoor, .300 Win Mag, .338 Lapua. Capacity: 5-round magazine. Barrel: 26 in. Weight: 10.25 lbs. Length: 45.25 in. overall. Stock: Reinforced polyurethane with fully adjustable cheekpiece and buttplate. Sights: None furnished. Optional quick-detachable, one-piece scope mount base, 1 in. or 30mm rings. Features: Resistance-free bolt, free-floating heavy stainless barrel, 60-degree bolt lift. Two-stage trigger is adjustable for length, pull, horizontal or vertical pitch. TRG-42 has similar features but has long action and is chambered for .338 Lapua. Imported from Finland by Beretta USA.
Price: TRG-22 ....**$3,495.00**
Price: TRG-22 with folding stock **$6,400.00**
Price: TRG-42 ....**$4,445.00**
Price: TRG-42 with folding stock **$7,400.00**

SAVAGE 110 ELITE PRECISION *(now adds LH)*
Calibers: .223 Rem., 6mm Creedmoor, 6.5 Creedmoor, .308 Win., .300 Win. Mag., .300 PRC, .338 Lapua. Capacity: 5- or 10-round AICS-pattern detachable box magazine. Barrel: 26 or 30 in stainless steel. Weight: 12.6–14.95 lbs. Stock: Modular Driven Technologies (MDT) Adjustable Core Competition aluminum chassis with Grey Cerakote finish. Sights: 20 MOA rail. Features: Factory blueprinted action. ARCA Rail along entire length of chassis. Titanium Nitride bolt body. User adjustable AccuTrigger. MDT vertical grip. Self-timing taper aligned muzzle brake on short action calibers only.
Price: ....**$1,999.00–$2,199.00**
Price: Left-hand model **$2,199.00**

SAVAGE IMPULSE ELITE PRECISION
Calibers: 6mm Creedmoor, 6.5 Creedmoor, .308 Win., 6.5 PRC, .300 Win. Mag., .300 PRC, .338 Lapua. Capacity: 5- or 10-round AICS magazine with ambidextrous release. Barrel: 26 or 30 in. precision button-rifled, stainless steel, modified Palma contour, with muzzle brake. Sights: Integral 20 MOA rail. Weight: 13.7 lbs. Stock: MDT Adjustable Core Competition chassis. Features: The straight-pull bolt action moves to Savage's Precision series rifles for faster split times. Action uses HexLock bolt system. Ambidextrous rotary bolt handle. Adjustable AccuTrigger. Matte black aluminum receiver. Removeable and user-adjustable round bolt knob handle. ARCA rail forend with M-LOK slots.
Price: **$2,499.00**

SEEKINS PRECISION HAVAK BRAVO
Calibers: 6mm Creedmoor, 6.5 Creedmoor, 6.5 PRC, .308 Win. Capacity: 5-round box magazine. Barrel: 24-in. 5R 416 stainless steel with threaded muzzle. Weight: 9.8 lbs. Stock: KRG Bravo Chassis in Black. OD Green, FDE, or Stealth Gray. Sights: 20 MOA Picatinny rail with five 8-32 screws. Features: Specialty bolt-action rifle built for hard-running, from SWAT to precision shooting. Matte black Cerakoted barreled action. Integrated recoil lug and M16-style extractor. Bolt with four locking lugs and 90-degree throw. Removeable bolt head. Extended magazine release.
Price: **$1,950.00**

SEEKINS PRECISION HAVAK ELEMENT
Calibers: .308 Win., 6mm Creedmoor, 6.5 PRC, 6.5 Creedmoor. Capacity: 3 to 5. Barrel: 21 in., Mountain Hunter contour, spiral fluted, threaded. Stock: Carbon composite. Sights: 20 MOA picatinny rail. Weight: 5.5 lbs. Features: Timney Elite Hunter trigger, M16-style extractor, 7075 aerospace aluminum/stainless steel body.
Price: **$2,795.00**

SEEKINS PRECISION HAVAK HIT
Calibers: 6mm GT, 6mm Creedmoor, 6.5 Creedmoor, .308 Win., 6.5 PRC. Capacity: Varies by chambering, compatible with single- or double-stack AICS magazines. Barrel: 24 in. 416 SS LT Tactical contour, threaded, with 5R rifling. Sights: 20 MOA rail. Length: 43.5 in; 34.5 in. folded. Weight: 11.5 lbs. Stock: Chassis-style, folding, available in black and FDE. Features: Bolt-action chassis rifle. A Pro version for competition is planned to follow. Changeable bolt head, M16-style extractor, integrated recoil lug. Quick-change barrel system. R700 trigger compatibility. Integral 20 MOA Picatinny rail. Carbon-fiber cheek piece, fully adjustable recoil pad, and toolless LOP adjustment.
Price: **$2,100.00**

SIG SAUER CROSS RIFLE
Calibers: .277 Sig Fury, .308 Win., 6.5 Creedmoor. Capacity: 5. Barrel:16 to 18 in., stainless steel. Stock: Sig precision, polymer/alloy, folding. Sights: Picatinny rail. Weight: 6.5 to 6.8 lbs. Features: Compact bolt action series rifles. M-LOK rail, two- stage match trigger. Trax uses minimalist folding stock. Magnum in 300 Win Mag with Coyote color receiver and stock. STX with Sig Precision Stock and 20 in barrel. PRS with steel frame folding stock and 24 in barrel with 14.2 lb weight.
Price: **$1,599.00**
Price: Cross Trax **$1,529.00**
Price: Cross Magnum **$2,649.00**
Price: Cross STX **$2,195.00**
Price: Cross PRS **$2,679.00**

SPRINGFIELD ARMORY M1A/M-21 TACTICAL MODEL
Similar to M1A Super Match except special sniper stock with adjustable cheekpiece and rubber recoil pad. Weighs 11.6 lbs. From Springfield Armory.
Price: **$3,619.00**
Price: Krieger stainless barrel **$4,046.00**

SPRINGFIELD ARMORY MODEL 2020 RIMFIRE TARGET
Calibers: .22 LR. Capacity: 10-rd. rotary mag. Barrel: 20-in. heavy target profile, straight taper contour, 1:16, matte blued, threaded 1/2x28. Stock: Synthetic target reinforced polymer. New for 2024 are two rimfire color variants—a Coyote stock with black webbing, and OD-Green with black webbing. Sights: Interupted Picatinny rail. Weight: 7 lbs., 7 oz. Features: Adjustable Remington 700-style trigger group w/ Hanger System for compatibility.
Price: **$499.00**

Prices given are believed to be accurate at time of publication however, many factors affect retail pricing so exact prices are not possible.

79TH EDITION, 2025 ✦ **467**

AMERICAN TACTICAL IMPORTS HGA FXH-45

Caliber: .45 ACP. Capacity: 7+1 magazine. Barrel: 4.25 or 5 in. Grips: Textured polymer. Sights: Fixed, fiber-optic front. Finish: Black. Hybrid polymer and steel frame with 1911-style action.
Price: **$459.00**

AMERICAN TACTICAL IMPORTS GSG-9

Caliber: 9mm. Capacity: 30 magazine. Barrel: 7.9 in. Compatible with Glock and SIG magazines us-ing magazine adpter.
Price: **$799.00**

AMERICAN TACTICAL IMPORTS GSG 1911

Caliber: .22 LR. Capacity: 10+1 magazine. Weight: 34 oz. Other features and dimensions similar to centerfire 1911.
Price: .... **$379.00–$389.00**

AMERICAN TACTICAL IMPORTS GSG Firefly HGA

Caliber: .22 LR. Capacity: 10+1 magazine. Weight: 34 oz. Other features and dimensions similar to centerfire SIG P226.
Price: **$299.00**

AMERICAN TACTICAL IMPORTS GSG-MP40P

Caliber: 9mm. Capacity: 30+1 magazine. Barrel: 10.8 in. Weight: 8.3 lbs. Other features and dimensions similar to WWII-era MP-40.
Price: **$689.00**

AMERICAN TACTICAL IMPORTS Omni Hybrid Maxx

Caliber: .5.56 NATO, .300 BLK. Capacity: 30+1 magazine. Barrel: 7.5 or 8.5 in. Weight: 4.8 lbs. AR-15-style action.
Price: .... **$400.00–$500.00**

ANDERSON KIGER-9C

Caliber: 9mm. Capacity: 15-round magazine. Barrel: 3.1 in. Weight: 20.6 oz. Length: 7.35 in. overall. Sights: fixed. Features: Polymer frame, striker fire. 9C Pro model has lightweight slide, enhanced controls, and suppressor height sights. Made in USA.
Price: 9C **$429.00**
Price: 9C Pro.. **$539.00**

AUTO-ORDNANCE 1911A1

Caliber: 45 ACP. Capacity: 7-round magazine. Barrel: 4.25 or 5 in. Weight: 39 oz. Length: 8.5 in. overall. Grips: Brown checkered plastic with medallion. Sights: Blade front, rear drift-adjustable for windage. Features: Same specs as 1911A1 military guns-parts interchangeable. Frame and slide blued; each radius has non-glare finish. Introduced 2002. Made in USA by Kahr Arms.
Price: 1911BKO Parkerized, plastic grips **$984.00**
Price: 1911BKOW Black matte finish, wood grips **$963.00**
Price: 1911BKOCW Black matte finish, wood grips, Commander **$1,023.00**
Price: 1911GCH Case hardened finish, wood grips **$1,593.00**
Price: Stainless steel finish, G10 grips, cut slide .... **$1,278.00–$1,402.00**

BERETTA MODEL 21A BOBCAT

Calibers: .22 LR. Capacities: 9-round magazine. Barrel: 2.5 in. Weight: 11.8 oz. Sights: Round post front, square notch rear. Grip: G10, wood, or plastic. Finish: Blued, Inox, or FDE. Features: Tip-up barrel, DA/SA trigger, Covert model is suppressor-ready.
Price: **$649.00**

BERETTA MODEL 80X CHEETAH

Calibers: .380 Auto. Capacities: 13-round magazine. Barrel: 3.9 in. Weight: 25 oz. Sights: Post front, square notch rear. Grip: Textured plastic. Finish: Blued or two-tone bronze/black. Features: X-treme DA/SA trigger, optic ready.
Price: .... **$819.00–$999.00**

BERETTA 92/96 A1 SERIES

Calibers: 9mm, .40 S&W. Capacities: 15-round magazine; .40 S&W, 12 rounds (M96 A1). Barrel: 4.9 in. Weight: 33-34 oz. Length: 8.5 in. Sights: Fiber-optic front, adjustable rear. Features: Same as other models in 92/96 family except for addition of accessory rail.
Price: **$849.00**

BERETTA MODEL 92FS

Caliber: 9mm. Capacity: 10-round magazine. Barrels: 4.9 in., 4.25 in. (Compact). Weight: 34 oz. Length: 8.5 in. overall. Grips: Checkered black plastic. Sights: Blade front, rear adjustable for windage. Tritium night sights available. Features: Double action. Extractor acts as chamber loaded indicator, squared triggerguard, grooved front and backstraps, inertia firing pin. Matte or blued finish. Introduced 1977. Made in USA

Prices given are believed to be accurate at time of publication however, many factors affect retail pricing so exact prices are not possible.

Price:	$799.00
Price: Inox	$909.00
Price: Brigadier	$949.00
Price: Bronze/Gray finish	$819.00

BERETTA MODEL 92GTS FULL SIZE STANDARD

Calibers: 9mm. Capacities: 10-, 15-, or 18-round magazine. Barrel: 4.7 in. Weight: 33.3 oz. Length: 8.5 in. Sights: Fiber-optic front, square notch rear. Features: Vertec-style frame, front and rear serra-tions, skeletonized hammer, Type G frame mounted decocker, X-Treme S trigger, optics-ready.

Price:	$899.00
Price: Centurion, 4.25-in. barrel	$899.00

BERETTA MODEL 92X RDO/RDO COMPACT/CENTURION

Calibers: 9mm. Capacities: 15-round magazine. Barrel: 4.3 or 4.7 in. Weight: 33.2 oz. Sights: Fiber-optic front, square notch rear. Features: Vertec style frame, frame-mounted ambi thumb safety, oversized mag release button, Picatinny rail.

Price: RDO	$799.00
Price: RDO Compact	$799.00
Price: Centurion	$799.00
Price: Performance Defense series	$1,649.00
Price: Performance Carry Optic	$1,799.00

BERETTA MODEL 92XI SAO

Caliber: 9mm. Capacities: 15-round magazine. Barrel: 4.7 in. Weight: 33.2 oz. Sights: Fiber-optic front, square notch rear. Features: Vertec-style frame, frame-mounted ambi thumb safety, single action only trigger, Picatinny rail.

Price:	$969.00
Price: Tactical	$1,069.00
Price: Squalo	$1,280.00
Price: camo finishes	$996.00

BERETTA MODEL 3032 TOMCAT

Calibers: .32 Auto. Capacities: 7-round magazine. Barrel: 2.45 in. Weight: 14.8 oz. Sights: Round post front, square notch rear. Grip: G10, wood or plastic. Features: Tip-up barrel, DA/SA trigger. 30X model with Trident trigger, 8-round magazine.

Price:	$649.00
Price: 30X	$549.00–$599.00

BERETTA M9/M9A1/92FSR .22 LR

Caliber: .22 LR. Capacity: 10 or 15-round magazine. Features: Black Brunitron finish, interchangeable grip panels. Similar to centerfire 92/M9 with same operating controls, lighter weight (26 oz.).

Price:	$469.00

BERETTA MODEL PX4 STORM

Calibers: 9mm, 40 S&W. Capacities: 17 (9mm Para.); 14 (40 S&W). Barrel: 4 in. Weight: 27.5 oz. Grips: Black checkered w/3 interchangeable backstraps. Sights: 3-dot system coated in Superlumi-nova; removable front and rear sights. Features: DA/SA, manual safety/hammer decocking lever (ambi) and automatic firing pin block safety. Picatinny rail. Comes with two magazines (17/10 in 9mm Para. and 14/10 in 40 S&W). Removable hammer unit. American made by Beretta. Introduced 2005. G-SD model with 20-round magazine and decocker. Compact Carry 2 model with 3.2-inch barrel.

Price: 9mm or .40	$699.00
Price: .45 ACP	$799.00
Price: .45 ACP SD (Special Duty)	$1,149.00
Price: G SD	$875.00
Price: Compact Carry 2	$875.00

BERETTA MODEL PX4 STORM SUB-COMPACT

Calibers: 9mm, 40 S&W. Capacities: 13 (9mm); 10 (40 S&W). Barrel: 3, 3.27, or 4 in. Weight: 26.1 oz. Length: 6.2 in. overall. Grips: NA. Sights: 3-dot night sights. Features: Ambidextrous manual safety lever, interchangeable backstraps included, lock breech and tilt barrel system, stainless steel barrel, Picatinny rail.

Price:	$699.00

BERETTA MODEL APX SERIES

Calibers: 9mm, 40 S&W. Capacities: 10, 17 (9mm); 10, 15 (40 S&W). Barrel: 4.25, 3.7 (Compact), 3.0 in. (Carry). Weight: 28, 29 oz. Length: 7.5 in. Sights: Fixed. Features: Striker fired, 3 inter-changeable backstraps included, reversible mag release button, ambidextrous slide stop. Centurion is mid-

size with shorter grip and barrel. Magazine capacity is two rounds shorter than standard model. Tactical model is full size with threaded barrel.

Price: Full	$499.00
Price: Carry	$409.00
Price: Compact	$499.00
Price: Tactical	$549.00

BERETTA MODEL M9

Caliber: 9mm. Capacity: 15. Barrel: 4.9 in. Weights: 32.2-35.3 oz. Grips: Plastic. Sights: Dot and post, low profile, windage adjustable rear. Features: DA/SA, forged aluminum alloy frame, delayed locking-bolt system, manual safety doubles as decocking lever, combat-style triggerguard, loaded chamber indicator. Comes with two magazines (15/10). American made by Beretta. Introduced 2005.

Price:	$459.00

BERETTA MODEL M9A1

Caliber: 9mm. Capacity: 15. Barrel: 4.9 in. Weights: 32.2-35.3 oz. Grips: Plastic. Sights: Dot and post, low profile, windage adjustable rear. Features: Same as M9, but also includes integral Mil-Std-1913 Picatinny rail, has checkered front and backstrap. Comes with two magazines (15/10). American made by Beretta. Introduced 2005.

Price:	$469.00

BERETTA M9A4

Caliber: 9mm. Capacity: 10 or 15. Features: Same general specifications as M9A1 with safety lever able to be converted to decocker configuration. Flat Dark Earth finish. Comes with three magazines, Vertec-style thin grip.

Price:	$1,199.00

BRG-USA BRG9 SERIES

Caliber: 9mm. Capacity: 16- or 20-round magazine. Barrel: 4 in. Weight: 30 oz. Sights: Fixed. Finish: Matte black or two-tone. Features: Striker fire. Interchangeable backstraps. Tactical model has threaded barrel and magwell.

Price: BRG9 Elite	$249.00
Price: BRG9 Tactical	$499.00

Prices given are believed to be accurate at time of publication however, many factors affect retail pricing so exact prices are not possible.

79TH EDITION, 2025 ⬦ 469

BERSA THUNDER 380 SERIES
Caliber: .380 ACP. Barrel: 3.5 in. Weight: 20.5 oz. Length: 6.6 in. overall. Capacity: Thunder 380 8-round, Thunder 380 Plus 15-round. Features: DA/SA trigger, CC model is DAO trigger. X models have threaded muzzles. Imported from Argentina by Eagle Imports, Inc.
Price: .... $324.00–$421.00

BERSA FIRESTORM
Caliber: .380 ACP. Capacity: 7 rounds. Barrel: 3.5 in. Weight: 20.5 oz. Length: 6.6 in. overall. Grip: Rubber wraparound with finger grooves. Features: DA/SA tigger, combat rear sight.
Price: $339.00

BERSA THUNDER 22
Caliber: .22 LR. Capacity: 10-round magazine. Weight: 19 oz. Features: Similar to Thunder .380 Se-ries except for caliber. Alloy frame and slide. Finish: Matte black, satin nickel or duo-tone. 22X model with threaded barrel.
Price: .... $324.00–$369.00

BERSA BP SERIES
Caliber: 9mm. Capacity: 8-round magazine. Barrel: 3.3 in. Weight: 21.5 oz. Sights: Fixed or optics-ready. Features: Striker-fire trigger, polymer frame, accessory rail. Threaded barrel model available.
Price: .... $354.00–$361.00

BERSA TRP SERIES
Caliber: 9mm. Capacity: 13- or 17-round magazine. Barrel: 3.5 or 5 in. Weight: 23-33.9 oz. Grips: Checkered black polymer. Sights: Adjustable or fixed rear, dovetail fiber-optic front. Finish: Matte black or duo-tone. Features: Traditional double/single action trigger.
Price: .... $494.00–$518.00

BERSA THUNDER PRO XT
Caliber: 9mm. Capacity: 17-round magazine. Barrel: 5 in. Weight: 34 oz. Grips: Checkered black polymer. Sights: Adjustable rear, dovetail fiber optic front. Features: Available with matte or duo-tone finish. Traditional double/single action design developed for competition. Comes with five magazines.
Price: $899.00

BROWNING 1911-22 COMPACT
Caliber: .22 LR Capacity: 10-round magazine. Barrel: 3.625 in. Weight: 15 oz. Length: 6.5 in. overall. Grips: Brown composite. Sights: Fixed. Features: Slide is machined aluminum with alloy frame and matte blue finish. Blowback action and single action trigger with manual thumb and grip safeties. Works, feels and functions just like a full-size 1911. It is simply scaled down and chambered in the best of all practice rounds: .22 LR for focus on the fundamentals.
Price: $749.00

BROWNING 1911-22 A1
Caliber: .22 LR, Capacity: 10-round magazine. Barrel: 4.25 in. Weight: 16 oz. Length: 7.0625 in. overall. Grips: Brown composite. Sights: Fixed. Features: Slide is machined aluminum with alloy frame and matte blue finish. Blowback action and single action trigger with manual thumb and grip safeties. Works, feels and functions just like a full-size 1911. It is simply scaled down and chambered in the best of all practice rounds: .22 LR for focus on the fundamentals.
Price: .... $749.00–$879.00

BROWNING 1911-22 BLACK LABEL
Caliber: .22 LR. Capacity: 10-round magazine. Barrels: 4.25 in. or 3.625 in. (Compact model). Weight: 14 oz. overall. Features: Other features are similar to standard 1911-22 except for this model's composite/polymer frame, extended grip safety, stippled black laminated grip, skeleton trigger and hammer. Available with accessory rail (shown). Suppressor Ready model has threaded muzzle protector, 4.875-inch barrel.
Price: $799.00
Price: With Rail $799.00
Price: Suppressor Ready model $879.00

BROWNING 1911-380 SERIES
Caliber: .380 Auto. Capacity: 8-round magazine. Barrels: 3.62 or 4.25 in. Weight: 16 oz. Features: Similar to 1911-22 series and variants.
Price: $799.00

BROWNING BUCK MARK CAMPER UFX
Caliber: .22 LR. Capacity: 10-round magazine. Barrel: 5.5-in. tapered bull. Weight: 34 oz. Length: 9.5 in. overall. Grips: Overmolded Ultragrip Ambidextrous. Sights: Pro-Target adjustable rear, ramp front. Features: Matte blue receiver, matte blue or stainless barrel.
Price: Camper UFX $499.00

Prices given are believed to be accurate at time of publication however, many factors affect retail pricing so exact prices are not possible.

BROWNING BUCK MARK HUNTER
Caliber: .22 LR. Capacity: 10-round magazine. Barrel: 7.25-in. heavy tapered bull. Weight: 38 oz. Length: 11.3 in. overall. Grips: Cocobolo target. Sights: Pro-Target adjustable rear, Tru-Glo/Marble's fiber-optic front. Integral scope base on top rail. Scope in photo not included. Features: Matte blue.
Price: .... **$629.00–$899.00**

BROWNING BUCK PRACTICAL URX
Caliber: .22 LR. Capacity: 10-round magazine. Barrels: 5.5-in. tapered bull. Weight: 34 oz. Length: 9.5 in. overall. Grips: Ultragrip RX Ambidextrous. Sights: Pro-Target adjustable rear, Tru-Glo/ Mar-ble's fiber-optic front. Features: Matte gray receiver, matte blue barrel.
Price: **$549.00**

BROWNING BUCK MARK MEDALLION ROSEWOOD
Caliber: .22 LR. Capacity: 10-round magazine. Barrel: 5.5-in. Grips: Laminate rosewood colored with gold Buckmark. Sights: Pro-Target adjustable rear, TruGlo/Marble's fiber-optic front, or Vortex Crossfire red-dot. Finish: Matte black receiver, blackened stainless barrel with polished flats. Gold-plated trigger.
Price: .... **$629.00–$929.00**

BROWNING BUCK MARK CONTOUR STAINLESS URX
Caliber: .22 LR. Capacity: 10-round magazine. Barrel: 4 (Micro), 5.5, 5.9 or 7.25-in. special con-tour. Grips: Checkered, textured. Sights: Pro-Target adjustable rear, Pro- Target front. Integral scope base on top rail. Finish: Matte black receiver, blackened stainless barrel with polished flats. Gold-plated trigger.
Price: .... **$699.00–$739.00**
Price: Micro **$579.00**

BROWNING BUCK MARK FIELD TARGET SUPPRESSOR READY
Caliber: .22 LR. Capacity: 10-round magazine. Barrel: 5.5-in. heavy bull, suppressor-ready model available. Grips: Cocobolo target. Sights: Pro-Target adjustable rear, Tru-Glo/Marble's fiber-optic front. Integral scope base on top rail. Scope in photo not included. Features: Matte blue.
Price: **$729.00**

BROWNING BUCK MARK PLUS SERIES
Caliber: .22 LR. Capacity: 10-round magazine. Barrel: 4.4 (Micro), 5.5, 5.8, or 6-in. Grips: Polymer. Sights: Pro-Target adjustable rear, Tru-Glo/Marble's fiber- optic front, Crimson Trace optic (Practi-cal). Integral scope base on top rail. Features: Matte blue. Some suppressor ready. Vision variant has alloy sleeve barrel.
Price: .... **$579.00–$829.00**

CANIK TP9 SERIES
Caliber: 9mm. Capacity: 15- or 18-round magazine. Barrel: 3.5, 4.07, or 4.7-in. Grip: Textured pol-ymer, modular backstraps. Sights: White dot front, u-notch rear, some with red-dot optic. Length: 7.1 in. overall. Weight: 27.8 oz. unloaded. Finish: Matte black, FDE. Features: DA/SA trigger with decocker.
Price: TP9SA Mod.2 .... **$404.00**
Price: TP9SF Elite SC .... **$439.00–$594.00**
Price: TP9SF Elite **$429.00**
Price: TP9SFx .... **$549.00–$689.00**
Price: TP9 Elite Combat .... **$749.00–$901.00**

CANIK METE SERIES
Caliber: 9mm. Capacity: 10, 18- or 20-round magazine. Barrel: 3.1, 4.46, or 5.2-in. Grip: Textured polymer, modular backstraps. Sights: White dot 3-dot, optics ready; factory red-dot on some mod-els. Length: 7.56 in. overall. Weight: 27.8 oz. unloaded. Finish: Matte black, FDE. Features: Striker fire. MC9 model is compact with 3.1-inch barrel.
Price: Mete SFT .... **$519.00–$679.00**
Price: Mete SFX .... **$574.00–$729.00**
Price: Mete MC9 .... **$439.00–$619.00**

CANIK RIVAL SERIES
Caliber: 9mm. Capacity: 18-round magazine. Barrel: 5-in. Grip: Textured polymer, modular back-straps. Sights: Fiber-optic front, adj. rear, optics ready. Length: 8.1 in. overall. Weight: 29.5 oz. un-loaded. Finish: Matte black, black with gold accents. Features: Striker fire. Rival-S and Rival-S Darkside have an all-metal frame.
Price: SFX .... **$679.00–$849.00**
Price: SFX Rival-S .... **$949.00–$1,099.00**
Price: SFX Rival-S Darkside .... **$899.00–$1,049.00**

Prices given are believed to be accurate at time of publication however, many factors affect retail pricing so exact prices are not possible.

79TH EDITION, 2025 ✛ 471

CHIAPPA MODEL 1911

Caliber: .45 ACP. Barrel: 5 in. Weight: 37.5 oz. Length: 8.5 in. overall. Grips: Checkered walnut or G10. Features: 1911 platform with case hardened or gold finish.

Price: **$1,000.00**

CHIAPPA 1911-22

Caliber: .22 LR. Capacity: 10-round magazine. Barrel: 5 in. Weight: 33.5 oz. Length: 8.5 in. Grips: Two-piece wood. Sights: Fixed. Features: A faithful replica of the famous John Browning 1911A1 pistol. Fixed barrel design. Available in black, OD green or tan finish. Target and Tactical models have adjustable sights.

Price: .... **$305.00–$428.00**

CHIAPPA M9-22 STANDARD

Caliber: .22 LR. Barrel: 5 in. Weight: 2.3 lbs. Length: 8.5 in. Grips: Black molded plastic. Sights: Fixed front sight and windage adjustable rear sight. Features: The M9 9mm has been a U.S. stand-ard-issue service pistol since 1990. Chiappa's M9-22 is a replica of this pistol in 22 LR. The M9-22 has the same weight and feel as its 9mm counterpart but has an affordable 10-shot magazine for the .22 Long Rifle cartridge, which makes it a true rimfire reproduction. Comes standard with steel trig-ger and hammer assembly.

Price: **$309.00**

CHIAPPA CBR-9 BLACK RHINO

Caliber: 9mm. Barrel: 8.8in. Weight: 2.2 lb. Length: 16.9 in. overall. Grips: Textured polymer. Fea-tures: Semi-automatic large pistol format.

Price: Aluminum frame **$2,265.00**

CIMARRON MODEL 1911

Caliber: .45 ACP. Barrel: 4.25 (One Ranger) or 5 in. Weight: 37.5 oz. Length: 8.5 in. overall. Grips: Checkered walnut. Features: A faithful reproduction of the original pattern of the Model 1911 with Parkerized finish and lanyard ring. Polished or nickel finish available.

Price: .... **$622.00–$929.00**
Price: One Ranger... **$747.00**

CITADEL M-1911

Calibers: .45 ACP, 9mm. Capacity: 7. Barrels: 4.2 or 5 in. Weight: 37.9 oz. Length: 8.5 in. Grips: Cocobolo. Sights: Low-profile combat fixed rear, blade front. Finish: Matte black. Features: Extended grip safety, lowered and flared ejection port, beveled mag well, Series 70 firing system. Built by Armscor (Rock Island Armory) in the Philippines and imported by Legacy Sports.

Price: **$599.00**
Price: Flag models **$1,030.00**

COLT MODEL 1911 CLASSIC

Caliber: .45 ACP. Capacity: 7-round magazine. Barrel: 5 in. Weight: 38 oz. Length: 8.5 in. overall. Grips: Checkered black composition. Sights: Ramped blade front, fixed square notch rear, high profile. Features: Matte finish. Continuation of serial number range used on original G.I. 1911A1 guns. Comes with one magazine and molded carrying case. Introduced 1991. Series 80 firing system.

Price: Blue .... **$899.00–$1,299.00**
Price: Bright Stainless .... **$1,499.00–$1,549.00**
Price: Stainless .... **$999.00–$1,046.00**
Price: Royal Blue **$1,499.00**

COLT COMBAT ELITE SERIES

Caliber: 9mm or .45 ACP. Capacity: 8-round magazine. Barrel: 3, 4.2, or 5 in. Grips: Checkered, G10. Sights: Three white-dot Novak. Features: Brushed stainless receiver with blued slide; adjusta-ble, two-cut aluminum trigger; extended ambidextrous thumb safety; upswept beavertail with palm swell; elongated slot hammer.

Price: **$1,399.00**

COLT COMBAT UNIT SERIES

Caliber: 9mm or .45 ACP. Capacity: 8-round magazine. Barrel: 4.2 or 5 in. Grips: Checkered G10. Sights: Three white-dot Novak. Features: Matte black finish; extended ambidextrous thumb safety; upswept beavertail; Series 80 firing system; National Match Barrel.

Price: .... **$1,499.00–$1,599.00**

COLT COMMANDER SERIES

Calibers: .38 Super, 9mm, or .45 ACP, 8-shot, 9mm (9 shot). Barrel: 4.25 in. Weight: 26 oz. alloy frame, 33 oz. (steel frame). Length: 7.75 in. overall. Grips: G10 Checkered Black Cherry. Sights: Novak White Dot front, Low Mount Carry rear. Features: Blued slide, black anodized frame. Alumi-num alloy (Lightweight Commander) or steel frame (Combat Commander).

Price: Lightweight... **$999.00**
Price: Combat................................... **$999.00–$1,049.00**
Price: Custom Carry.. **$1,099.00**

COLT DEFENDER

Caliber: .45 ACP (7-round magazine), 9mm (8-round). Barrel: 3 in. Weight: 22.5 oz. Length: 6.75 in. overall. Grips: Pebble-finish rubber wraparound with finger grooves. Sights: White dot front, snag-free Colt competition rear. Features: Stainless or blued finish; aluminum frame; combat-style hammer; Hi-Ride grip safety, extended manual safety, disconnect safety. Introduced 1998. Made in USA by Colt's Mfg. Co., Inc.

Price: **$999.00**

COLT SERIES 70 SERIES

Caliber: .45 ACP. Barrel: 5 in. Weight: 37.5 oz. Length: 8.5 in. Grips: Rosewood with double diamond checkering pattern. Sights: Fixed. Features: Custom replica of the Original Series 70 pistol with a Series 70 firing system, original roll marks. Introduced 2002. Made in USA by Colt's Mfg. Co., Inc.

Price: Blued **$999.00**

COLT M45A1 MARINE PISTOL

Caliber: .45 ACP. Variant of Rail Gun series with features of that model plus Decobond Brown Coating, dual recoil springs system, Novak tritium front and rear 3-dot sights. Selected by U.S. Marine Corps as their Close Quarters Battle Pistol (CQBP).

Price: **$1,699.00**

COLT DELTA ELITE SERIES

Caliber: 10 mm. Capacity: 8+1. Barrel: 5 in. Grips: Black composite with Delta Medallions. Sights: Novak Low Mount Carry rear, Novak White Dot front. Finish: Two-tone stainless frame, black matte slide. Features: Up-swept beavertail safety, extended thumb safety, 3-hole aluminum trigger. Accessory rail on some models.

Price: .... **$1,199.00–$1,299.00**

COLT WILEY CLAPP SERIES

Calibers: 9mm or .45 Auto. Barrel: 4.25 in. Weight: 26 oz. alloy frame.

Length: 7.75 in. overall. Grips: Oval grips with fingerprint checkering. Sights: Novak brass bead front, Low Mount Carry rear. Features: Blued slide, black anodized frame. Aluminum alloy frame. Steel slide.
Price: **$1,130.00**

CZ 75 B
Calibers: 9mm. Capacity: 16-round magazine. Barrel: 4.7 in. Weight: 34.3 oz. Length: 8.1 in. overall. Grips: High impact checkered plastic. Sights: Square post front, rear adjustable for windage; 3-dot system. Features: Single action/double action; firing pin block safety; choice of black polymer, matte or high-polish blue finishes. All-steel frame. B-SA is a single action with a drop-free magazine. Imported from the Czech Republic by CZ-USA.
Price: 75 B **$630.00**

CZ 75 BD DECOCKER
Similar to the CZ 75B except has a decocking lever in place of the safety lever. All other specifications are the same. Introduced 1999. Imported from the Czech Republic by CZ-USA.
Price: **$649.00**

CZ 75 B COMPACT
Similar to the CZ 75 B except has 14-round magazine in 9mm, 3.9-in. barrel and weighs 32 oz. Has removable front sight, non-glare ribbed slide top. The triggerguard is squared and serrated; combat hammer; steel or alloy (D PCR and P-01) frame; black polymer finish. Introduced 1993. Imported from the Czech Republic by CZ-USA. D CPR and P-01 are decocker models.
Price: Compact **$649.00**
Price: D PCR Compact **$649.00**
Price: P-01 .... **$649.00**

CZ P-07
Calibers: 9mm. Capacity: 15. Barrel: 3.8 in. Weight: 27.2 oz. Length: 7.3 in. overall. Grips: Polymer black Polycoat. Sights: Blade front, fixed groove rear. Features: The ergonomics and accuracy of the CZ 75 with a totally new trigger system. The new Omega trigger system simplifies the CZ 75 trigger system, uses fewer parts and improves the trigger pull. In addition, it allows users to choose between using the handgun with a decocking lever (installed) or a manual safety (included) by a simple parts change. The polymer frame design and a new sleek slide profile (fully machined from bar stock) reduce weight, making the P-07 a great choice for concealed carry.
Price: **$489.00**

CZ SHADOW 2 COMPACT
Calibers: 9mm. Capacity: 15-round magazine. Barrel: 4.0 in. Weight: 30 oz. Length: 7.5 in. overall. Grips: Checkered aluminum. Sights: Fiber optic front, adjustable rear. Features: Single action/double action; hammer fire. Matte blue finish. Aluminum frame. Imported from the Czech Republic by CZ-USA.
Price: **$1,430.00**

CZ P-09 DUTY SUPRESSOR READY
Calibers: 9mm. Capacity: 19. Features: High-capacity version of P-07. 5.1-inch threaded. Accessory rail, interchangeable grip backstraps, ambidextrous decocker can be converted to manual safety.
Price: **$529.00**

CZ 75 SP-01
Similar to NATO-approved CZ 75 Compact P-01 model. Features an integral 1913 accessory rail on the dust cover, rubber grip panels, black Polycoat finish, extended beavertail, new grip geometry with checkering on front and back straps, and double or single action operation. Introduced 2005. The Tactical model has an ambidextrous decoker. Imported from the Czech Republic by CZ-USA.
Price: SP-01 .... **$799.00**

CZ P-01
Caliber: 9mm. Capacity: 14-round magazine. Barrel: 3.85 in. Weight: 27 oz. Length: 7.2 in. overall. Grips: Checkered rubber. Sights: Blade front with dot, white outline rear drift adjustable for windage. Features: Based on the CZ 75, except with forged aircraft-grade aluminum alloy frame. Hammer forged barrel, decocker, firing-pin block, M3 rail, dual slide serrations, squared triggerguard, re-contoured trigger, lanyard loop on butt. Serrated front and backstrap. Introduced 2006. Imported from the Czech Republic by CZ-USA.
Price: CZ P-01 .... **$649.00**

CZ P-10 SERIES
Caliber: 9mm. Capacity: 19- or 21-round magazine. Barrel: 4.5-5.10 in. Weight: 26-29.4 oz. Length: 8 in. overall. Grips: Textured. Polymer frame.

Prices given are believed to be accurate at time of publication however, many factors affect retail pricing so exact prices are not possible.

79TH EDITION, 2025 ⊕ **473**

Sights: Fixed, 3-dot. Features: Striker fire. Suppres-sor-ready and optics ready on some models.

Price: CZ P-10 F $499.00
Price: CZ P-10 C...$399.00
Price: CZ P-10 S ....$399.00–$499.00
Price: CZ P-10 C or F Suppressor Ready.............................$499.00

CZ BREN 2 MS

Caliber: .223 Rem. or 7.62×39mm. Capacity: 30-round magazine. Barrel: 14.7 in. Features: Pistol version of the 805 Bren rifle.
Price: $1,799.00

CZ SCORPION 3+ MICRO

Caliber: 9mm. Capacity: 20-round magazine. Barrel: 4.2 in. Features: Next generation of CZ Scorpion Evo semi-automatic gun. Ambidextrous controls, adjustable sights, accessory rails.
Price: $1,200.00

DAN WESSON DWX SERIES

Calibers: 9mm. Capacity: 15 or 19-round magazine. Barrel: 4 or 5 in. Grips: Checkered red alumi-num. Sights: Fixed fiber-optic front/adjustable rear. Length: 8.52 in. overall. Weight: 43 oz. unload-ed. Finish: Black Duty Coat. Features: Hybrid pistol built using the single-action fire control group of a Dan Wesson 1911 and frame of a CZ 75 pistol. Compatible with CZ P-09 and CZ P-10 F maga-zines. Bull barrel and full dust cover with accessory rail. Flat red aluminum trigger. Oversized con-trols.
Price: .... $1,999.00–$2,159.00

DAN WESSON BRUIN

Caliber: 10mm. Capacity: 8-round magazine. Barrel: 6.03 in. Grips: Textured G10. Sights: Fixed, fiber-optic front/adjustable rear. Length: 9.7 in. overall. Weight: 47.1 oz. unloaded. Finish: Black or bronze. Features: 1911 platform with coarse slide serrations, mag well and ambidextrous safety.
Price: $2,359.00

DAN WESSON ECP

Calibers: 9mm, .45 ACP. Capacity: 8 (.45) or 9 (9mm). Barrel: 4 in. Features: Forged aluminum frame with flat-top slide, serrated tactical rear and brass bead front sight, checkered frontstrap and backstrap, G10 grips, V-Bob frame, flat trigger.
Price: $1,739.00

DAN WESSON GUARDIAN

Calibers: 9mm, .38 Super, .45 ACP. Capacity: 8- or 9-round magazine. Barrel: 5 in. Length: 8.5 in. Grips: Wood. Sights: Fixed night sights. Features: Undercut triggerguard, serrated front strap, V-Bob frame.
Price: $1,739.00

DAN WESSON KODIAK

Caliber: 10mm. Capacity: 8-round magazine. Barrel: 6.03 in. Grips: Textured G10. Sights: Fixed, fiber-optic front/adjustable rear. Length: 9.7 in. overall. Weight: 47.1 oz. unloaded. Finish: Black or tri-tone. Features: 1911 platform

with coarse slide serrations, mag well and ambidextrous safety. Black version has bronzed controls and barrel, and tri-tone with a matte gray slide.
Price: .... **$2,499.00–$2,699.00**

DAN WESSON SPECIALIST

Caliber: 9mm, 10mm, or .45 ACP. Capacity: 8 or 10-round magazine. Barrel: 5 in. Grips: G10 VZ Operator II. Sights: Single amber tritium dot rear, green lamp with white target ring front sight. Fea-tures: Integral Picatinny rail, 25 LPI frontstrap checkering, undercut triggerguard, ambidextrous thumb safety, extended mag release and detachable two-piece magwell.
Price: .... **$1,849.00–$2,279.00**

DAN WESSON V-BOB

Caliber: .45 ACP. Capacity: 8-round magazine. Barrel: 4.25 in. Weight: 34 oz. Length: 8 in. Grips: Slim Line G10. Sights: Heinie Ledge Straight-Eight Night Sights. Features: Black matte or stainless finish. Bobtail forged grip frame with 25 LPI checkering front and rear.
Price: .... $1,969.00–$2,299.00

DAN WESSON POINTMAN

Calibers: 9mm, .45 ACP. Capacity: 8 or 9-round magazine. Barrel: 5 in. Length: 8.5 in. Grips: Double-diamond cocobolo. Sights: Adjustable rear and fiber-optic front. Features: Undercut triggerguard, checkered front strap, serrated rib on top of slide.
Price: $1,799.00

DAN WESSON RAZORBACK

Calibers: 10mm. Capacity: 9-round magazine. Barrel: 5 in. Length: 8.5 in. Grips: Double-diamond Cocobolo. Sights: Novak rear and post front. Features: Serrated rib on top of slide.
Price: $1,799.00

DAN WESSON TCP

Calibers: 9mm, .45 ACP. Capacity: 8 (.45) or 9 (9mm). Barrel: 4 in. Features: Forged aluminum frame with flat-top slide, serrated tactical rear and brass bead front sight, checkered frontstrap and backstrap, G10 grips, magwell, flat trigger.
Price: $1,849.00

DAN WESSON VALOR

Caliber: .45 ACP. Capacity: 8-round magazine. Barrel: 5 in. Grips: Textured G10. Sights: Fixed, night-sight front/U-notch rear. Length: 8.75 in. overall. Weight: 39.7 oz. unloaded. Finish: Matte stainless or black Duty Coat. Features: 1911 platform with GI style slide serrations, Stan Chen SI mag well, tapered grip and tactical ambidextrous safety.
Price: .... $1,969.00–$2,299.00

DANIEL DEFENSE H9
Caliber: 9mm. Capacity: 15-round magazine. Barrel: 4.28 in. Grips: Textured G10. Sights: Fixed, optics-ready. Length: 7.6 in. overall. Weight: 29.6 oz. unloaded. Finish: DLC coating. Features: 1911-style trigger with blade safety. Aluminum frame. Based on Hudson H9 design.
Price: $1,600.00

DIAMONDBACK DB380
Caliber: .380 ACP. Capacity: 6+1. Barrel: 2.8 in. Weight: 8.8 oz. Features: ZERO-Energy striker firing system with a mechanical firing pin block, steel magazine catch, windage-adjustable sights. Frames available with several color finish options.
Price: .... $282.00–$288.00

DIAMONDBACK DB9
Caliber: 9mm. Capacity: 6+1. Barrel: 3 in. Weight: 11 oz. Length: 5.60 in. Features: Other features similar to DB380 model.
Price: .... $305.00–$322.00

DIAMONDBACK FIREARMS DBX
Caliber: 5.7x28mm. Capacity: 20-round magazine. Barrel: 8 in. Grips: Magpul MOE-K. Sights: Op-tic-ready, Picatinny rail. Length: 16.9 in. overall, brace folded. Weight: 3 lbs. unloaded. Finish: Black hardcoat-anodized or bronze, grey. Features: DBX muzzle brake, compatible with FN Five-seveN, side-folding brace. Uses AR-15 Mil-Spec trigger.
Price: ....$1,128.00–$1,193.00

DIAMONDBACK FIREARMS DBAM29/AM29
Caliber: 9mm. Capacity: 12- or 17-round magazine. Barrel: 3.5 in. Grips: Textured grip. Sights: Fixed, 3-dot. Length: 6.6 in. overall. Weight: 21 oz. unloaded. Finish: Black.
Price: .... $415.00–$425.00

DOUBLESTAR 1911 SERIES
Caliber: .45 ACP. Capacity: 8-round magazine. Barrels: 4.25 in., 5 in. Weights: 33–40 oz. Grips: Co-cobolo wood. Sights: Novak LoMount 2 white-dot rear, Novak white-dot front. Features: Single ac-tion, M1911-style with forged frame and slide of 4140 steel, stainless steel barrel machined from bar stock by Storm Lake, funneled mag well, accessory rail, black Nitride or bronze finish. Optional features include bobtail grip frame, accessory rail.
Price: .... $1,369.00–$2,309.00

EAA GIRSAN MC9 DISRUPTOR
Caliber: 9mm. Capacity: 17-round magazine. Barrel: 4.6, in. Weight: 22.4 oz. Length: 7.9 in. overall. Features: Full-size polymer frame with accessory rail. Striker-fire trigger. Manufactured by Girsan and imported by EAA.
Price: $394.00

EAA GIRSAN MC14BDA SERIES
Caliber: .380 Auto. Capacity: 13-round magazine. Barrel: 4.8 in. Weight: 24 oz. Length: 6.8 in. over-all. Features: Full slide model or open slide model similar to Beretta Model 84, black or two-tone finish. Manufactured by Girsan and imported by EAA.
Price: .... $360.00–$369.00

EAA GIRSAN MC 14T SERIES
Caliber: .380 Auto. Capacity: 13-round magazine. Barrel: 4.5 in. Weight: 22.4 oz. Length: 6.8 in. overall. Features: Compact Beretta Cheetah-style pistols with tip-up barrel. Manufactured by Girsan and imported by EAA.
Price: .... $489.00–$699.00

Prices given are believed to be accurate at time of publication however, many factors affect retail pricing so exact prices are not possible.

79TH EDITION, 2025 ✦ 475

EAA GIRSAN INFLUENCER MC1911 SERIES

Caliber: .38 Super, 9mm, .45 ACP, 10mm Auto. Capacity: 6-, 8- or 9-round magazine. Barrel: 3, 4.2, or 5 in. Weight: 32-51.2 oz. Length: 8.58-9.63 in. overall. Sights: Fixed, low profile, optic ready. Features: Compact, Full-size, and long barrel 1911-style pistol with steel frame with accesso-ry rail and mag well. Three-hole trigger. Manufactured by Girsan and imported by EAA.
Price: .... **$500.00–$740.00**

EAA GIRSAN UNTOUCHABLE MC1911 SERIES

Caliber: 9mm, .45 ACP. Capacity: 6-, 8- or 9-round magazine. Barrel: 3, 4.2, or 5 in. Weight: 32-51.2 oz. Length: 8.58-9.63 in. overall. Features: Compact, Full-size, and long barrel 1911-style pis-tol with steel frame. Solid trigger. Manufactured by Girsan and imported by EAA.
Price: .... **$400.00–$440.00**

EAA GIRSAN REGARD MC SERIES

Caliber: 9mm. Capacity: 15-round magazine. Barrel: 3.8 or 4.8 in. Weight: 25.6–28.8 oz. Length: 8.6 in. overall. Features: Full-size Beretta 92-style pistols. Manufactured by Girsan and imported by EAA.
Price: .... **$600.00–$1,099.00**

EAA GIRSAN MC P35 SERIES

Caliber: 9mm. Capacity: 18-round magazine. Barrel: 3.8 or 4.9 in. Weight: 34.4 oz. Length: 6.25–7.75 in. overall. Features: Compact and full-size Browning Hi Power-style pistols. Finish: Black, two-tone, FDE, or gold. Manufactured by Girsan and imported by EAA.
Price: .... **$585.00–$1,075.00**

EAA GIRSAN WITNESS 2311 SERIES

Caliber: 9MM, 10MM, OR .45 ACP. Capacity: 11-, 15- or 17-round magazine. Barrel: 4.2, 5, or 6 in. Weight: 32-51.2 oz. Length: 8.58-9.63 in. overall. Features: 1911-style pistol with polymer double-stack magazine frame. Manufactured by Girsan and imported by EAA.
Price: Steel frame .... **$999.00–$1,029.00**

ED BROWN CLASSIC CUSTOM

Caliber: .45 ACP, 9mm, .38 Super. Capacity: 7-round magazine. Barrel: 5 in. Weight: 40 oz. Grips: Cocobolo wood. Sights: Bo-Mar adjustable rear, dovetail front. Features: Single action, M1911 style, custom made to order, stainless frame and slide available. Special mirror-finished slide.
Price: **$3,995.00**

ED BROWN FX2

Caliber: 9mm. Capacity: 9-round magazine. Barrels: 4.25 in. Weight: 37 oz. Grips: Textured G10. Sights: Trijicon RMRcc sight 3.25 MOA with Ed Brown designed co-witness rear sight, and Ameri-glo orange front sight. Features: Snakeskin pattern serrations on forestrap and American flag pattern on slide, dehorned edges, beavertail grip safety, Bobtail frame.
Price: .45 ACP .... **$3,995.00–$4,595.00**

ED BROWN EVO-E9 SERIES

Caliber: 9mm. Capacity: 9-round magazine. Barrels: 4 in. Weight: 35 oz. Grips: Textured G10. Sights: orange front sight, tactical edge U-notch rear. Features: Snakeskin pattern serrations on forestrap and housing, dehorned edges, beavertail grip safety, external extractor, full-size Bobtail frame. Some models equipped with red-dot optic.
Price: .... **$3,295.00–$3,395.00**
Price: LW .... **$3,545.00–$3,895.00**

ED BROWN EVO-KC9 SERIES

Caliber: 9mm. Capacity: 9-round magazine. Barrels: 4 in. Weight: 34 oz. Grips: Textured G10. Sights: orange front sight, tactical edge U-notch rear. Features: Snakeskin pattern serrations on forestrap and housing, dehorned edges, beavertail grip safety, external extractor, Bobtail frame.
Price: G4 .... **$2,995.00–$3,095.00**
Price: LW .... **$3,295.00–$3,395.00**
Price: SS .... **$2,995.00–$3,095.00**
Price: VTX .... **$3,045.00–$3,395.00**

ED BROWN KOBRA CARRY

Caliber: 9mm or .45 ACP. Capacity: 7-round magazine. Barrels: 4.25 in. Weight: 34 oz. Grips: Hogue exotic wood. Sights: Ramp, front; fixed Novak low-mount night sights, rear. Features: Snake-skin pattern serrations on forestrap and mainspring housing, dehorned edges, beavertail grip safety.
Price: .... **$3,195.00–$3,295.00**

ED BROWN SPECIAL FORCES

Similar to other Ed Brown products, but with ChainLink treatment on forestrap and mainspring housing. Entire gun coated with Gen III finish. Square cut serrations on rear of slide only. Dehorned. Introduced 2006. Available with various finish, sight and grip options.
Price: .... **$3,150.00–$3,295.00**

FMK 9C1 G2

Caliber: 9mm. Capacity: 10+1 or 14+1. Barrel: 4 in. Overall length: 6.85 in. Weight: 23.45 oz. Finish: Black, Flat Dark Earth or pink. Sights: Interchangeable Glock compatible. Features: Available in either single action or double action only. Polymer frame, high-carbon steel slide, stainless steel barrel. Very low bore axis and shock absorbing backstrap are said to result in low felt recoil. DAO model has Fast Action Trigger (FAT) with shorter pull and reset. Made in the USA.
Price: **$299.00**

Prices given are believed to be accurate at time of publication however, many factors affect retail pricing so exact prices are not possible.

FN 502 SERIES
Caliber: 22 LR. Capacity: 10- and 15- round magazine. Barrel: 4.6 in. threaded. Grip: Textured polymer. Sights: Suppressor height, fixed front and rear sights. Length: 7.6 in. overall. Weight: 23.7 oz. unloaded. Finish: Matte black or FDE. Features: Hammer-fire, accessory rail.
Price: MRD $469.00
Price: Tactical... $559.00

FN 509 SERIES
Caliber: 9mm. Capacity: 10-, 12- or 15-round magazine. Barrel: 3.7 or 4.5 in. Grips: Textured grip, interchangeable backstraps. Sights: Fixed, tall co-witness; FN Low-Profile Optics Mounting System. Length: 6.8 in. overall. Weight: 25.5 oz. unloaded. Finish: Black or FDE. Compact, midsize, and tac-tical model sizes.
Price: .... $754.00–$1,104.00
Price: CC Edge XL... $1,399.00

FN FNX SERIES
Calibers: 9mm, .45 Auto. Capacities: 17-round magazine, .45 ACP (10 or 14 rounds). Barrels: 4 in. (9mm), 4.5 in. .45. Weights: 22–32 oz. (.45). Lengths: 7.4, 7.9 in. (.45). Features: DA/SA operation with decocking/manual safety lever. Has external extractor with loaded-chamber indicator, front and rear cocking serrations, fixed 3-dot combat sights.
Price: 9mm $824.00
Price: .45 ACP $919.00

FN FNX .45 TACTICAL
Similar to standard FNX .45 except with 5.3-in. barrel with threaded muzzle, polished chamber and feed ramp, enhanced high-profile night sights, slide cut and threaded for red-dot sight (not included), MIL-STD 1913 accessory rail, ring-style hammer.
Price: $1,379.00

FN FIVE-SEVEN
Caliber: 5.7x28mm. Capacity: 10- or 20-round magazine. Barrel: 4.8 in. Weight: 23 oz. Length: 8.2 in. Features: Adjustable three-dot system. Single-action polymer frame, chambered for low-recoil 5.7x28mm cartridge.
Price: $1,409.00
Price: MRD $1,509.00

FN HIGH POWER
Caliber: 9mm. Capacity: 17-round magazine. Barrel: 4.7 in. Grip: Textured G10. Sights: Steel fixed front and rear. Length: 8 in. overall. Weight: 40 oz. unloaded. Finish: Matte black or FDE. Features: Hammer-fire, based on classic High Power pistol.
Price: $1,155.00

GLOCK 17/17L
Caliber: 9mm. Capacities: 17/19/33-round magazines. Barrel: 4.49 in. Weight: 22.04 oz. (without magazine). Length: 7.32 in. overall. Grips: Black polymer. Sights: Dot on front blade, white outline rear adjustable for windage. Features: Polymer frame, steel slide; double-action trigger with Safe Action system; mechanical firing pin safety, drop safety; simple takedown without tools; locked breech, recoil operated action. ILS designation refers to Internal Locking System. Adopted by Austrian armed forces 1983. NATO approved 1984. Model 17L has 6-inch barrel, ported or non-ported, slotted and relieved slide, checkered grip with finger grooves, no accessory rail. Imported from Austria by Glock, Inc. USA. Gen 4 pistols are law enforcement only.
Price: G17 Gen 5 .... $647.00
Price: G17L Gen 5 MOS $851.00

GLOCK 19
Caliber: 9mm. Capacities: 15/17/19/33-round magazines. Barrel: 4.02 in. Weight: 20.99 oz. (without magazine). Length: 6.85 in. overall. Compact version of Glock 17. 19X model has 17 frame and 19 slide in Coyote Tan finish. Imported from Austria by Glock, Inc. Gen 4 pistols are law enforcement only.
Price: G19 Gen 5 .... $647.00
Price: G19 Gen 5 MOS $745.00
Price: G19X $707.00

GLOCK 20
Caliber: 10mm. Capacity: 15-round magazine. Barrel: 4.6 in. Weight: 27.68 oz. (without magazine). Length: 7.59 in. overall. Features: Otherwise similar to Model 17. Imported from Austria by Glock, Inc. Introduced 1990.
Price: G20 Gen 5 MOS $745.00

GLOCK 21
Caliber: .45 ACP. Capacity: 13-round magazine. Barrel: 4.6 in. Weight: 26.28 oz. (without magazine). Length: 7.59 in. overall. Features: Otherwise similar to the Model 17. Imported from Austria by Glock, Inc. Introduced 1991. SF version has tactical rail, smaller diameter grip, 10-round magazine capacity. Introduced 2007.
Price: G21 Gen 5 MOS $745.00

Prices given are believed to be accurate at time of publication however, many factors affect retail pricing so exact prices are not possible.

79TH EDITION, 2025 ✦ 477

GLOCK 22

Caliber: .40 S&W. Capacities: 15/17-round magazine. Barrel: 4.49 in. Weight: 22.92 oz. (without magazine). Length: 7.32 in. overall. Features: Otherwise similar to Model 17, including pricing. Im-ported from Austria by Glock, Inc. Introduced 1990. Gen 4 pistols are law enforcement only.

Price: G22 Gen 5 .... **$647.00**
Price: G22 Gen 5 MOS... **$745.00**

GLOCK 23

Caliber: .40 S&W. Capacities: 13/15/17-round magazine. Barrel: 4.02 in. Weight: 21.16 oz. (without magazine). Length: 6.85 in. overall. Features: Otherwise similar to the Model 22, including pricing. Compact version of Glock 22. Imported from Austria by Glock, Inc. Introduced 1990. Gen 4 pistols are law enforcement only.

Price: G23 Gen 5 .... **$647.00**
Price: G23 Gen 5 MOS... **$745.00**

GLOCK 24

Caliber: .40 S&W. Capacities: 10/15/17 or 22-round magazine. Features: Similar to Model 22 except with 6.02-inch barrel, ported or non-ported, trigger pull recalibrated to 4.5 lbs.

Price: G24 Gen 3 .... **$729.00**

GLOCK 26

Caliber: 9mm. Capacities: 10/12/15/17/19/33-round magazine. Barrel: 3.46 in. Weight: 19.75 oz. Length: 6.29 in. overall. Subcompact version of Glock 17. Imported from Austria by Glock, Inc. Gen 4 pistols are law enforcement only.

Price: G26 Gen 5 .... **$647.00**
Price: G26 Gen 5 MOS... **$745.00**

GLOCK 27

Caliber: .40 S&W. Capacities: 9/11/13/15/17-round magazine. Barrel: 3.46 in. Weight: 19.75 oz. Length: 6.29 overall. Features: Otherwise similar to the Model 22, including pricing. Subcompact version of Glock 22. Imported from Austria by Glock, Inc. Introduced 1996. Gen 4 pistols are law enforcement only.

Price: G27 Gen 5 .... **$647.00**

GLOCK 28

Caliber: .380 Auto. Capacities: 10-round magazine. Barrel: 3.5 in. Weight: 21 oz. Length: 6.2 in. overall. Features: Otherwise similar to the Model

26. Originally introduced for law enforcement on-ly. Commercial variant introduced 2023.

Price: G28 Gen 3 .... **$649.00**

GLOCK 29

Caliber: 10mm. Capacities: 10/15-round magazine. Barrel: 3.78 in. Weight: 24.69 oz. (without magazine). Length: 6.77 in. overall. Features: Otherwise similar to the Model 20, including pricing. Subcompact version of the Glock 20. SF (Short Frame) model has short frame design. Imported from Austria by Glock, Inc. Introduced 1997.

Price: G29 Gen 5 .... **$647.00**

GLOCK 30

Caliber: .45 ACP. Capacities: 9/10/13-round magazines. Barrel: 3.78 in. Weight: 23.99 oz. (without magazine). Length: 6.77 in. overall. Features: Otherwise similar to the Model 21, including pricing. Subcompact version of the Glock 21. Imported from Austria by Glock, Inc. Introduced 1997. SF version has tactical rail, octagonal rifled barrel with a 1:15.75 rate of twist, smaller diameter grip, 10-round magazine capacity. SF (Short Frame) model has short frame design. Introduced 2008.

Price: G30 Gen 5 .... **$647.00**

GLOCK 30S

Caliber: .45 ACP. Capacity: 10-round magazine. Barrel: 3.78 in. Weight: 20 oz. Length: 7 in. Features: Variation of Glock 30 with a Model 36 slide on a Model 30SF frame (short frame).

Price: G30S **$655.00**

GLOCK 31

Caliber: .357 Auto. Capacities: 15/17-round magazine. Barrel: 4.49 in. Weight: 23.28 oz. (without magazine). Length: 7.32 in. overall. Features: Otherwise similar to the Model 17. Imported from Austria by Glock, Inc.

Price: G31 Gen 3 .... **$599.00**

GLOCK 32

Caliber: .357 Auto. Capacities: 13/15/17-round magazine. Barrel: 4.02 in. Weight: 21.52 oz. (without magazine). Length: 6.85 in. overall. Features: Otherwise similar to the Model 31. Compact. Imported from Austria by Glock, Inc.

Price: G32 Gen 3 .... **$599.00**

GLOCK 33

Caliber: .357 Auto. Capacities: 9/11/13/15/17-round magazine. Barrel: 3.46 in. Weight: 19.75 oz. (without magazine). Length: 6.29 in. overall. Features: Otherwise similar to the Model 31. Subcompact. Imported from Austria by Glock, Inc.

Price: G33 Gen 3... **$599.00**

GLOCK 34

Caliber: 9mm. Capacities: 17/19/33-round magazine. Barrel: 5.32 in. Weight: 22.9 oz. Length: 8.15 in. overall. Features: Competition version of Glock 17 with extended barrel, slide, and sight radius dimensions. Available with MOS (Modular Optic System). Gen 4 pistols are law enforcement only.

Price: G34 Gen 5 MOS... **$851.00**

GLOCK 35

Caliber: .40 S&W. Capacities: 15/17-round magazine. Barrel: 5.32 in. Weight: 24.52 oz. (without magazine). Length: 8.15 in. overall. Sights: Adjustable. Features: Otherwise similar to the Model 22. Competition version of the Glock 22 with extended barrel, slide and sight radius dimensions. Avail-able with MOS (Modular Optic System). Introduced 1996. Gen4 pistols are law enforcement only.

Price: G35 Gen 3 .... **$716.00**

Prices given are believed to be accurate at time of publication however, many factors affect retail pricing so exact prices are not possible.

GLOCK 36

Caliber: .45 ACP. Capacity: 6-round magazine. Barrel: 3.78 in. Weight: 20.11 oz. (without magazine). Length: 6.77 overall. Sights: Fixed. Features: Single-stack magazine, slimmer grip than Glock 21/30. Subcompact. Imported from Austria by Glock, Inc. Introduced 1997.
Price: G36 .... **$655.00**

GLOCK 37

Caliber: .45 GAP. Capacity: 10-round magazine. Barrel: 4.49 in. Weight: 25.95 oz. (without magazine). Length: 7.32 overall. Features: Otherwise similar to the Model 17. Imported from Austria by Glock, Inc. Introduced 2005.
Price: G37 Gen 3 .... **$620.00**

GLOCK 38

Caliber: .45 GAP. Capacities: 8/10-round magazine. Barrel: 4.02 in. Weight: 24.16 oz. (without magazine). Length: 6.85 overall. Features: Otherwise similar to the Model 37. Compact. Imported from Austria by Glock, Inc.
Price: G38 Gen 3 .... **$620.00**

GLOCK 39

Caliber: .45 GAP. Capacities: 6/8/10-round magazine. Barrel: 3.46 in. Weight: 19.33 oz. (without magazine). Length: 6.3 overall. Features: Otherwise similar to the Model 37. Subcompact. Imported from Austria by Glock, Inc.
Price: G39 Gen 3 .... **$620.00**

GLOCK 40

Caliber: 10mm. Features: Similar features as the Model 41 except for 6.01-in. barrel. Includes MOS optics.
Price: G40 Gen 4 MOS.. **$840.00**

GLOCK 41

Caliber: .45 ACP. Capacity: 13-round magazine. Barrel: 5.31 in. Weight: 27 oz. Length: 8.9 in. overall. Features: This is a long-slide .45 ACP Gen4 model introduced in 2014. Operating features are the same as other Glock models. Available with MOS (Modular Optic System).
Price: G41 Gen 4.. **$716.00**
Price: G41 Gen 4 MOS.. **$800.00**

GLOCK 42

Caliber: .380 ACP. Capacity: 6-round magazine. Barrel: 3.25 in. Weight: 13.8 oz. Length: 5.9 in. overall. Features: This single-stack, slimline sub-compact is the smallest pistol Glock has ever made. This is also the first Glock pistol made in the USA.
Price: G42 Gen 4.. **$479.00**

GLOCK 43

Caliber: 9mm. Capacity: 6+1. Barrel: 3.39 in. Weight: 17.95 oz. Length: 6.26 in. Height: 4.25 in. Width: 1.02 in. Features: Newest member of Glock's Slimline series with single-stack magazine.
Price: G43 Gen 4.. **$538.00**

GLOCK 43X

Caliber: 9mm. Capacity: 17+1. Barrel: 4.02 in. Weight: 24.5 oz. Length: 7.4 in. Height: 5.5 in. Width: 1.3 in. Combines compact slide with full-size frame. MOS variant model available.
Price: G43X Gen 5 .... **$538.00**
Price: G43X Gen 5 MOS.. **$582.00**

GLOCK 44

Caliber: .22 LR. Capacity: 10-round magazine. Barrel: 4.02 in. Grips: Textured grip, interchangeable backstraps. Sights: Fixed, dot front/notch rear. Length: 7.28 in. overall. Weight: 14.6 oz. unloaded. Finish: Black. Features: Same size as Glock G19, hybrid slide of polymer and steel.
Price: G44 Gen 5.. **$430.00**

GLOCK 45

Caliber: 9mm. Capacity: 17+1. Barrel: 3.41 in. Weight: 18.7 oz. Length: 6.5 in. Height: 5.04 in. Width: 1.1 in. Combines Glock 19 slide with G17 frame. MOS variant.
Price: G45 .... **$647.00**
Price: G45 MOS **$745.00**

GLOCK 47

Caliber: 9mm. Capacity: 17+1. Barrel: 4.49 in. Weight: 25.93 oz. Length: 7.95 in. Height: 5.47 in. Width: 1.34 in. Features MOS.
Price: **$745.00**

GLOCK 48

Caliber: 9mm. Capacity: 10. Barrel: 3.41 in. Weight: 18.7 oz. Length: 6.05 in. Height: 5.04 in. Width: 1.1 in. Features: Silver-colored PVD-coated slide with front serrations. Similar length and height as Model 19 with width reduced to 1.1 inch. MOS variant model available.
Price: G48 Gen 5... **$538.00**
Price: G48 Gen 5 MOS.. **$582.00**

GLOCK 49

Caliber: 9mm. Capacity: 17+1. Barrel: 4.49 in. Weight: 25.93 oz. Length: 7.95 in. G17-size slide and barrel on a G19-size fraem. Features MOS.
Price: G49 .... **$745.00**

GRAND POWER P-1 MK7

Caliber: 9mm. Capacity: 15+1 magazine. Barrel: 3.7 in. Weight: 26 oz. Features: Compact DA/SA pistol featuring frame-mounted safety, steel slide and frame and polymer grips. Offered in several variations and sizes. Made in Slovakia
Price: **$449.00**

Prices given are believed to be accurate at time of publication however, many factors affect retail pricing so exact prices are not possible.

79TH EDITION, 2025 ⊕ **479**

GRAND POWER STRIBOG SERIES

Caliber: .22 LR, 9mm, .45 Auto, or 10mm. Capacity: 30-round magazine. Barrel: 5 or 8 in. Weight: 3.9 lb. Overall Length: 7.9 in. Features: Large format pistol with or without brace. Offered in several variations and sizes. Made in Slovakia.

Price: SP9A3 .... **$1,100.00**
Price: SP45A3 .... **$1,500.00**
Price: SP10A3 .... **$1,700.00**
Price: TR22 .... **$700.00**

GUNCRAFTER INDUSTRIES

Calibers: 9mm, .38 Super, .45 ACP or .50 GI. Capacity: 7- or 8-round magazine. Features: 1911-style series of pistols best known for the proprietary .50 GI chambering. Offered in approximately 30 1911 variations. No. 1 has 5-inch heavy match-grade barrel, Parkerized or hard chrome finish, checkered grips and frontstrap, numerous sight options. Other models include Commander-style, Officer's Model, Long Slide w/6-inch barrel and several 9mm and .38 Super versions.

Price: .... **$4,230.00–$5,110.00**

HECKLER & KOCH USP

Calibers: 9mm, .40 S&W, .45 ACP. Capacities: 15-round magazine; .40 S&W, 13-shot magazine; 45 ACP, 12-shot magazine. Barrels: 4.25–4.41 in. Weight: 1.65 lbs. Length: 7.64–7.87 in. overall. Grips: Non-slip stippled black polymer. Sights: Blade front, rear adjustable for windage. Features: New HK design with polymer frame, modified Browning action with recoil reduction system, single control lever. Special "hostile environment" finish on all metal parts. Available in SA/DA, DAO, left- and right-hand versions. Introduced 1993. .45 ACP Introduced 1995. Imported from Germany by Heckler & Koch, Inc.

Price: .... **$1,159.00–$1,309.00**

HECKLER & KOCH USP COMPACT

Calibers: 9mm, .357 SIG, .40 S&W, .45 ACP. Capacities: 13-round magazine; .40 S&W and .357 SIG, 12-shot magazine; .45 ACP, 8-shot magazine. Features: Similar to the USP except the 9mm, .357 SIG and .40 S&W have 3.58-in. barrels, measure 6.81 in. overall and weigh 1.47 lbs. (9mm). Introduced 1996. .45 ACP measures 7.09 in. overall. Introduced 1998. Imported from Germany by Heckler & Koch, Inc.

Price: .... **1,189.00–$1,309.00**

HECKLER & KOCH USP TACTICAL

Calibers: 9mm, .45 ACP. Capacities: 13-round magazine; .45 ACP, 12-round magazine. Barrels: 4.90-5.09 in. Weight: 1.9 lbs. Length: 8.64 in. overall. Grips: Non-slip stippled polymer. Sights: Blade front, fully adjustable target rear. Features: Has extended threaded barrel with rubber O-ring; adjustable trigger; extended magazine floorplate; adjustable trigger stop; polymer frame. Introduced 1998. Imported from Germany by Heckler & Koch, Inc.

Price: .... **$1,609.00–$1,729.00**

HECKLER & KOCH USP ELITE

Calibers: .45 ACP. Capacities: 10-round magazine. Barrels: 6.02 in. Weight: 25.6 oz. Length: 8.7 in. overall. Grips: Non-slip stippled polymer. Sights: Blade front, fully adjustable target rear. Features: Ambi thumb safety and decocker, with or with out Jet Funnel magazine funnel.

Price: .... **$1,309.00–$1,729.00**

HECKLER & KOCH USP EXPERT

Calibers: 9mm or .45 ACP. Capacities: 10- or 18-round magazine. Barrels: 5.2 in. Weight: 33.6 oz. Length: 8.7 in. overall. Grips: Non-slip stippled polymer. Sights: Blade front, fully adjustable target rear. Features: Ambi thumb safety and decocker, with or with out Jet Funnel magazine funnel.

Price: .... **$1,309.00–$1,789.00**

HECKLER & KOCH HK45

Caliber: .45 ACP. Capacity: 10-round magazine. Barrel: 4.53 in. Weight: 1.73 lbs. Length: 7.52 in. overall. Grips: Ergonomic with adjustable grip panels. Sights: Low profile, drift adjustable. Features: Polygonal rifling, ambidextrous controls, operates on improved Browning linkless recoil system. Available in Tactical and Compact variations. Tactical models come with threaded barrel, adjustable TruGlo high-profile sights, Picatinny rail.

Price: HK45 .... **$849.00–$949.00**
Price: HK45 Compact .... **$849.00–$949.00**
Price: HK45 Compact Tactical **$1,029.00**
Price: HK45 Tactical **$1,029.00**

HECKLER & KOCH MARK 23 SPECIAL OPERATIONS

Caliber: .45 ACP. Capacity: 12-round magazine. Barrel: 5.87 in. Weight: 2.42 lbs. Length: 9.65 in. overall. Grips: Integral with frame; black polymer. Sights: Blade front, rear drift adjustable for windage; 3-dot. Features:

Civilian version of the SOCOM pistol. Polymer frame; double action; exposed hammer; short recoil, modified Browning action. Introduced 1996. Imported from Germany by Heckler & Koch, Inc.
Price: **$2,729.00**

HECKLER & KOCH P30 SERIES
Calibers: 9mm, .40 S&W. Capacities: 13- or 15-round magazines. Barrels: 3.2 (P30SK), 3.86 or 4.45 in. (P30L) Weight: 26–27.5 oz. Length: 6.95, 7.56 in. overall. Grips: Interchangeable panels. Sights: Open rectangular notch rear sight with contrast points. Features: Ergonomic features include a special grip frame with interchangeable backstrap inserts and lateral plates, allowing the pistol to be individually adapted to any user. Browning-type action with modified short recoil operation. Ambidextrous controls include dual slide releases, magazine release levers and a serrated decocking button located on the rear of the frame (for applicable variants). A Picatinny rail molded into the front of the frame. The extractor serves as a loaded-chamber indicator.
Price: P30 .... **$869.00–$979.00**
Price: P30L .... **$869.00–$979.00**
Price: P30L .... **$869.00–$979.00**
Price: P30SK .... **$869.00–$979.00**

HECKLER & KOCH P2000
Calibers: 9mm, .40 S&W. Capacities: 13-round magazine; .40 S&W, 12-shot magazine. Barrel: 3.62 in. Weight: 1.5 lbs. Length: 7 in. overall. Grips: Interchangeable panels. Sights: Fixed Patridge style, drift adjustable for windage, standard 3-dot. Features: Incorporates features of HK USP Compact pistol, including Law Enforcement Modification (LEM) trigger, double-action hammer system, ambidextrous magazine release, dual slide-release levers, accessory mounting rails, recurved, hook triggerguard, fiber-reinforced polymer frame, modular grip with exchangeable backstraps, nitro-carburized finish, lock-out safety device. Introduced 2003. Imported from Germany by Heckler & Koch, Inc.
Price: .... **$959.00–$1,079.00**

HECKLER & KOCH P2000 SK
Calibers: 9mm, .40 S&W. Capacities: 10-round magazine; .40 S&W, 9-round magazine. Barrel: 3.27 in. Weight: 1.3 lbs. Length: 6.42 in. overall. Sights: Fixed Patridge style, drift adjustable. Features: Standard accessory rails, ambidextrous slide release, polymer frame, polygonal bore profile. Smaller version of P2000. Introduced 2005. Imported from Germany by Heckler & Koch, Inc.
Price: .... **$959.00–$1,079.00**

HECKLER & KOCH VP SERIES
Calibers: 9mm, .40 S&W. Capacities: 10- or 15-round magazine. .40 S&W (10 or 13). Barrel: 4.09 in. Weight: 25.6 oz. Length: 7.34 in. overall. Sights: Fixed 3-dot, drift adjustable. Features: Striker-fired system with HK enhanced light pull trigger. Ergonomic grip design with interchangeable back-straps and side panels. VP9SK is compact model with 3.4-in. barrel. Tactical model with threaded barrel.
Price: VP9/VP40 .... **$869.00–$979.00**

Price: VP9 Match **$1,199.00**
Price: VP9L OR .... **$1,029.00–$1,159.00**
Price: VP9SK .... **$869.00–$1,269.00**
Price: VP9SK OR .... **$929.00–$1,029.00**
Price: VP9 Tactical OR... **$1,099.00**

HI-POINT FIREARMS MODEL C-9
Caliber: 9mm. Capacity: 8-round magazine. Barrel: 3.5 in. Weight: 25 oz. Length: 6.75 in. overall. Grips: Textured plastic. Sights: Combat-style adjustable 3-dot system; low profile. Features: Single-action design; frame-mounted magazine release; polymer frame offered in black or several camo finishes. Scratch-resistant matte finish. Introduced 1993. Comps are similar except they have a 4-in. barrel with muzzle brake/compensator. Compensator is slotted for laser or flashlight mounting. Introduced 1998. Made in USA by MKS Supply, Inc.
Price: C-9 .... **$209.00–$229.00**
Price: Yeet Cannon **$226.00**

HI-POINT FIREARMS MODEL CF380
Caliber: .380 ACP. Capacities: 10- and 8-round magazine. Weight: 25 oz. Features: Similar to the 9mm Compact model except chambered for adjustable 3-dot sights. Polymer frame with black or camo finish. Action locks open after last shot. Trigger lock.
Price: CF-380 .... **$196.00–$228.00**
Price: YC-380 .... **$215.00**

HI-POINT FIREARMS JCP 40 AND JCP 45
Calibers: .40 S&W, .45 ACP. Capacities: .40 S&W, 8-round magazine; .45 ACP, 9 rounds. Barrel: 4.5 in. Weight: 32 oz. Length: 7.72 in. overall. Sights: Adjustable 3-dot. Features: Polymer frames, offered in black or several camo finishes, last round lock-open, grip-mounted magazine release, magazine disconnect safety, integrated accessory rail, trigger lock. Introduced 2002. Made in USA by MKS Supply, Inc.
Price: JCP 40 .... **$215.00–$249.00**
Price: JCP 45 .... **$215.00–$249.00**

HI-POINT FIREARMS JXP10
Caliber: 10mm. Capacity: 10-round magazine. Similar to .40 S&W and .45 ACP models.
Price: **$225.00**

ITHACA 1911

Caliber: .45 ACP. Capacity: 7-round capacity. Barrels: 4.25 or 5 in. Weight: 35 or 40 oz. Sights: Fixed combat or fully adjustable target. Grips: Checkered cocobolo with Ithaca logo. Classic 1911A1 style with enhanced features including match-grade barrel, lowered and flared ejection port, extended beavertail grip safety, hand-fitted barrel bushing, two-piece guide rod, checkered front strap.
Price: .... **$1,599.00–$2,399.00**

IVER JOHNSON EAGLE

Calibers: 9mm, .45 ACP, 10mm. Features: Series of 1911-style pistols made in typical variations including full-size (Eagle), Commander (Hawk), Officer's (Thrasher) sizes.
Price: .... **$716.00–$1,827.00**

IWI JERICHO 941 FULL SIZE/COMPACT

Caliber: 9mm. Capacity: 16-round magazine. Barrels: 4.4 in. Weight: 36.8 oz. Sights: Fixed combat. Features: Steel frame based on CZ-75, hammer-fire, DA/SA trigger.
Price: **$615.00**

IWI JERICHO SERIES

Caliber: 9mm. Capacity: 17-round magazine. Barrels: 4.4 in. Weight: 26.8 oz. Sights: Fixed combat. Features: Polymer frame with modular backstops, based on CZ-75, hammer-fire, DA/SA trigger. Mid-size model has 3.8-in. barrel.
Price: .... **$599.00–$659.00**

IWI MASADA

Caliber: 9mm. Capacity: 17-round magazine. Barrels: 4.1 in. Weight: 22.8 oz. Sights: Fixed combat. Features: Polymer frame, striker-fire. Slim model has 3.4-in. barrel.
Price: **$534.00**
Price: Slim.. **$450.00**

IWI UZI PRO

Caliber: 9mm. Capacity: 20- and 25-round magazine. Barrels: 4.5 in. Weight: 3.6 lb. Sights: Fixed combat. Features: Polymer frame, threaded barrel.
Price: **$3,999.00**

KAHR CM SERIES

Calibers: 9mm, .45 ACP. Capacities: 9mm (6+1), .45 ACP (5+1). CM45 Model is shown. Barrels: 3 in., 3.25 in. (45) Weights: 15.9–17.3 oz. Length: 5.42

in. overall. Grips: Textured polymer with integral steel rails molded into frame. Sights: Pinned in polymer sight; drift-adjustable, white bar-dot combat. Features: A conventional rifled barrel instead of the match-grade polygonal barrel on Kahr's PM series; the CM slide stop lever is MIM (metal-injection-molded) instead of machined; the CM series slide has fewer machining operations and uses simple engraved markings instead of roll marking. The CM series are shipped with one magazine instead of two. The slide is machined from solid 416 stainless with a matte finish, each gun is shipped with one 6-round stainless steel magazine with a flush baseplate. Magazines are U.S.-made, plasma welded, tumbled to remove burrs and feature Wolff springs. The magazine catch in the polymer frame is all metal and will not wear out on the stainless steel magazine after extended use.
Price: **$528.00**

KAHR CT SERIES

Calibers: 9mm, .45 ACP. Capacities: 9mm (8+1), .45 ACP (7+1). Barrel: 4 in. Weights: 20–25 oz. Length: 5.42 in. overall. Grips: Textured polymer with integral steel rails molded into frame. Sights: Drift adjustable, white bar-dot combat.
Price: **$494.00**

KAHR CT 380

Caliber: .380 ACP. Capacity: (7+1). Barrel: 3 in. Weight: 14 oz. Other features similar to CT 9/40/45 models.
Price: **$457.00**

KAHR K SERIES

Calibers: 9mm, 7-shot magazine. Barrel: 3.5 in. Weight: 25 oz. Length: 6 in. overall. Grips: Wraparound textured soft polymer. Sights: Blade front, rear drift adjustable for windage; bar-dot combat style or tritium night sights. Features: Trigger-cocking double-action mechanism with passive firing pin block. Made of 4140 ordnance steel with matte black finish. Introduced 1994. Made in USA by Kahr Arms.
Price: **$1,013.00**

KAHR MK SERIES

Similar to the K9 except is 5.35 in. overall, 4 in. high, with a 3.08 in. barrel. Weighs 23.1 oz. Has snag-free bar-dot sights or tritium night sights, polished feed ramp, dual recoil spring system, DAO trigger. Comes with 5-round flush baseplate and 6-shot grip extension magazine. Introduced 1998. Made in USA by Kahr Arms.
Price: **$1,020.00**

KAHR P SERIES

Calibers: 9mm, .40 S&W, 45 ACP. Capacity: 7-shot magazine. Features: Similar to K9/K40 steel frame pistol except has polymer frame, matte stainless steel slide. Barrel length 3.5 in.; overall length 5.8 in.; weighs 17 oz. Includes two 7-shot magazines, hard polymer case, trigger lock. Introduced 2000. Made in USA by Kahr Arms.
Price: .... **$539.00–$776.00**

KAHR PM SERIES

Calibers: 9mm, .40 S&W, .45 ACP. Capacity: 7-round magazine. Features: Similar to P-Series pistols except has smaller polymer frame (Polymer Micro). Barrel length 3.08 in.; overall length 5.35 in.; weighs 17 oz. Includes two 7-shot magazines, hard polymer case, trigger lock. Introduced 2000. Made in USA by Kahr Arms.

Price: $762.00

KAHR CW SERIES

Caliber: 9mm or .45 ACP. Capacities: 9mm, 7-round magazine; .45 ACP, 6-round magazine. Barrels: 3.5 and 3.64 in. Weight: 17.7–18.7 oz. Length: 5.9–6.36 in. overall. Grips: Textured polymer. Similar to the P-Series, but CW Series have conventional rifling, metal-injection-molded slide stop lever, no front dovetail cut, one magazine. Made in USA.

Price: $762.00

KAHR P380

Caliber: .380 ACP. Capacity: 6+1. Features: Very small DAO semi-auto pistol. Features include 2.5-in. Lothar Walther barrel; black polymer frame with stainless steel slide; drift adjustable white bar/dot combat/sights; optional tritium sights; two 6+1 magazines. Overall length 4.9 in., weight 10 oz. without magazine.

Price: Standard sights .... $539.00–$776.00

KAHR CW380

Caliber: .380 ACP. Capacity: 6-round magazine. Barrel: 2.58 in. Weight: 11.5 oz. Length: 4.96 in. Grips: Textured integral polymer. Sights: Fixed white-bar combat style. Features: DAO. Black or purple polymer frame, stainless slide.

Price: .... $457.00–$504.00

KEL-TEC P15

Caliber: 9mm. Capacity: 15-round magazine. Barrel: 4-in. bull. Grip: Textured polymer. Sights: Adjustable tritium and fiber optic. Length: 5.6 in. overall. Weight: 14 ozs. unloaded. Finish: Matte black. Features: Striker-fire, accessory rail, grip safety

Price: $450.00
Price: Metal frame $800.00

KEL-TEC P17

Caliber: .22 LR. Capacity: 16-round magazine. Barrel: 3.8 in. Grips: Textured polymer. Sights: Fixed. Length: 6.7 in. overall. Weight: 11.2 oz. unloaded. Finish: Matte black, OD green, tan.

Price: .... $199.00–$214.00

KEL-TEC P32

Caliber: .32 ACP. Capacity: 7-round magazine. Barrel: 2.68. Weight: 6.6 oz. Length: 5.07 overall. Grips: Checkered composite. Sights: Fixed. Features: Double-action-only mechanism with 6-lb. pull; internal slide stop. Textured composite grip/frame.

Price: .... $360.00–$382.00

KEL-TEC P50

Caliber: 5.7 x 28mm. Capacity: 20 round magazine. Barrel: 5-in. bull. Grip: Textured aluminum. Sights: Optic ready. Length: 15 in. overall. Weight: 3.2 lbs. unloaded. Finish: Matte black. Features: Uses FN P90 50-round double stack magazines, QD mount in butt.

Price: $795.00

KEL-TEC PLR16

Caliber: 5.56mm NATO. Capacity: 10-round magazine. Weight: 51 oz. Sights: Rear sight adjustable for windage, front sight is M-16 blade. Barrel: 9.2 in. Length: 18.5 in. Features: Muzzle is threaded 1/2x28 to accept standard attachments such as a muzzle brake. Except for the barrel, bolt, sights and mechanism, the PLR-16 pistol is made of high-impact glass fiber reinforced polymer. Gas-operated semi-auto. Black, tan or green finish. Conventional gas-piston operation with M-16 breech locking system. MIL-STD-1913 Picatinny rail. Made in USA by Kel-Tec CNC Industries, Inc.

Price: Blued .... $600.00–$650.00

KEL-TEC PLR22

Caliber: .22 LR. Capacity: 26-round magazine. Length: 18.5 in. overall. 40 oz. Features: Semi-auto pistol based on centerfire PLR-16 by same maker. Blowback action. Open sights and Picatinny rail for mounting accessories; threaded muzzle. Black, tan or green finish.

Price: .... $440.00–$530.00

KEL-TEC PMR30

Caliber: .22 Magnum (.22WMR). Capacity: 30 rounds. Barrel: 4.3 in. Weight:

13.6 oz. Length: 7.9 in. overall. Grips: Glass reinforced Nylon (Zytel). Sights: Dovetailed aluminum with front & rear fiber optics. Features: Operates on a unique hybrid blowback/locked-breech system. It uses a double-stack magazine of a new design that holds 30 rounds and fits completely in the grip of the pistol. Dual opposing extractors for reliability, heel magazine release to aid in magazine retention, Picatinny accessory rail under the barrel, Urethane recoil buffer, captive coaxial recoil springs. The barrel is fluted for light weight and effective heat dissipation. PMR30 disassembles for cleaning by removal of a single pin.
Price: .... $495.00–$525.00

KIMBER MICRO SERIES
Caliber: .380 ACP. Capacity: 6-round magazine. Barrel: 2.75 in. Weight: 17 oz. Finish: Various fin-ishes and grip material. Mini 1911-style single-action with no grip safety.
Price: Two Tone $713.00
Price: Desert Night $742.00
Price: Desert Tan $860.00
Price: Eclipse $860.00
Price: Raptor... $995.00
Price: Raptor Stainless...................................... $995.00
Price: Stainless $713.00
Price: Amethyst $1,210.00
Price: Sapphire $1,210.00
Price: Bel Air $1,025.00

KIMBER 1911 COVERT SERIES
Caliber: .45 ACP Capacity: 7-round magazine. Barrels: 3, 4 or 5 in. Weight: 25–31 oz. Grips: Crimson Trace laser with camo finish. Sights: Tactical wedge 3-dot night sights. Features: Made in the Kimber Custom Shop. Finish: Kimber Gray frame, matte black slide, black small parts. Carry Melt treatment. Available in three frame sizes: Custom, Pro and Ultra.
Price: $1,692.00

KIMBER 1911 CUSTOM II
Caliber: 9mm, .45 ACP. Barrel: 5 in. Weight: 38 oz. Length: 8.7 in. overall. Grips: Checkered black rubber, walnut, rosewood. Sights: Dovetailed front and rear, Kimber low profile adjustable or fixed sights. Features: Slide, frame and barrel machined from steel or stainless steel. Match-grade barrel, chamber and trigger group. Extended thumb safety, beveled magazine well, beveled front and rear slide serrations, high ride beavertail grip safety, checkered flat mainspring housing, kidney cut under triggerguard, high cut grip, match-grade stainless steel barrel bushing, polished breechface, Commander-style hammer, lowered and flared ejection port, Wolff springs, bead blasted black oxide or matte stainless finish. Introduced in 1996. Made in USA by Kimber Mfg., Inc.
Price: $1,046.00
Price: Two-Tone $980.00

KIMBER 1911 CUSTOM TLE II
Caliber: .45 ACP or 10mm. Features: TLE (Tactical Law Enforcement) version of Custom II model plus night sights, frontstrap checkering, threaded barrel, Picatinny rail.
Price: .... $1,190.00–$1,211.00

KIMBER MICRO 9 SERIES
Caliber: 9mm. Capacity: 7-round magazine. Barrel: 3.15 in. Weight: 15.6 oz. Features: The easily concealed Micro 9 features mild recoil, smooth trigger

pull and the intuitive operation of a 1911 platform. Micro 9 slides are made to the tightest allowable tolerances, with barrels machined from stainless steel for superior resistance to moisture. All Micro 9 frames are shaped from the finest aluminum for integrity and strength. Lowered and flared ejection ports for flawless ejection and a beveled magazine well for fast, positive loading. In 2020, Kimber offered 15 different Micro 9 models with a total of 26 variations.
Prices:... $679.00–$1,250.00

KIMBER 1911 STAINLESS II
Same features as Custom II except has stainless steel frame.
Price: .... $1,022.00–$1,220.00

KIMBER 1911 PRO CARRY II
Calibers: 9mm, .45 ACP. Features: Similar to Custom II, has aluminum frame, 4-in. bull barrel fitted directly to the slide without bushing. Introduced 1998. Made in USA by Kimber Mfg., Inc.
Price: .... $1,120.00–$1,331.00

KIMBER 1911 SAPPHIRE ULTRA II
Caliber: 9mm or .45 Auto. Capacity: 8-round magazine. Features: Similar to Pro Carry II, 3-inch match-grade barrel. Striking two-tone appearance with satin silver aluminum frame and high polish bright blued slide. Grips are blue/ black G-10 with grooved texture. Fixed Tactical Edge night sights. From the Kimber Custom Shop.
Price: .... $1,449.00–$1,508.00

KIMBER 1911 RAPTOR II
Caliber: .45 ACP. Capacities: .45 ACP (8-round magazine, 7-round (Ultra and Pro models). Barrels: 3, 4 or 5 in. Weight: 25–31 oz. Grips: Thin milled rosewood. Sights: Tactical wedge 3-dot night sights. Features: Made in the Kimber Custom Shop. Matte black or satin silver finish. Available in three frame sizes: Custom (shown), Pro and Ultra.
Price: .... $1,548.00–$1,641.00

KIMBER 1911 RAPIDE SERIES
Caliber: 9mm, .45 ACP, or 10mm Auto. Capacities: .45 ACP and 10mm Auto 8-round magazine, 9mm 8-round magazine. Barrel: 5 in. Weight: 38 oz. Grips: Textured G10. Sights: Tru-Glo TFX Pro Day Night with orange ring front. Features: Stepped cocking serrations, slide lightening cuts.
Price: .... $1,816.00–$1,918.00

KIMBER 1911 ULTRA CARRY II
Calibers: 9mm, .45 ACP. Features: Lightweight aluminum frame, 3-in. match-grade bull barrel fitted to slide without bushing. Grips 0.4-in.

shorter. Light recoil spring. Weighs 25 oz. Introduced in 1999. Made in USA by Kimber Mfg., Inc.
Price: .... **$980.00–$1,316.00**

KIMBER 1911 CDP II SERIES
Calibers: 9mm, .45 ACP. Features: Similar to Custom II but designed for concealed carry. Aluminum frame. Standard features include stainless steel slide, fixed Meprolight tritium 3-dot (green) dovetail-mounted night sights, match-grade barrel and chamber, 30 LPI frontstrap checkering, two-tone finish, ambidextrous thumb safety, hand-checkered double diamond rosewood grips. Introduced in 2000. Made in USA by Kimber Mfg., Inc.
Price: .... **$1,399.00–$1,622.00**

KIMBER 1911 ECLIPSE II SERIES
Calibers: .38 Super, 10 mm, .45 ACP. Features: Similar to Custom II and other stainless Kimber pistols. Stainless slide and frame, black oxide, two-tone finish. Gray/black laminated grips. 30 LPI frontstrap checkering. All models have night sights; Target versions have Meprolight adjustable Bar/Dot version. Made in USA by Kimber Mfg., Inc.
Price: .... **$1,477.00–$1,600.00**

KIMBER ULTRA CDP II
Calibers: 9mm, .45 ACP. Capacities: 7-round magazine (9 in 9mm). Features: Compact 1911-style pistol; ambidextrous thumb safety; carry melt profiling; full-length guide rod; aluminum frame with stainless slide; satin silver finish; checkered frontstrap; 3-inch barrel; rosewood double diamond Crimson Trace laser grips; tritium 3-dot night sights.
Price: **$1,603.00**

KIMBER STAINLESS ULTRA TLE II
Caliber: .45 ACP. Capacity: 7-round magazine. Features: 1911-style semi-auto pistol. Features include full-length guide rod; aluminum frame with stainless slide; satin silver finish; checkered frontstrap; 3-in. barrel; tactical gray double diamond grips; tritium 3-dot night sights.
Price: **$1,136.00**

KIMBER 1911 SUPER JAGARE
Caliber: 10mm. Capacity: 8+1. Barrel: 6 in, ported. Weight: 42 oz. Finish: Stainless steel KimPro, Charcoal gray frame, diamond-like carbon coated slide. Slide is ported. Sights: Delta Point Pro Optic. Grips: Micarta. Frame has rounded heel, high cut triggerguard. Designed for hunting.
Price: **$3,012.00**

KIMBER 1911 KHX SERIES

Calibers: .45 ACP, 9mm. Capacity: 8+1. Features: This series is offered in Custom, Pro and Ultra sizes. Barrels: 5-, 4- or 3-inch match-grade stainless steel. Weights: 25–38 oz. Finishes: Stainless steel frame and slide with matte black KimPro II finish. Stepped hexagonal slide and top-strap serrations. Sights: Green and red fiber optic and Hogue Laser Enhanced MagGrip G10 grips and matching mainspring housings. Pro and Ultra models have rounded heel frames. Optics Ready (OR) models available in Custom and Pro sizes with milled slide that accepts optics plates for Vortex, Trijicon and Leupold red-dot sights.
Price: .... **$1,318.00–$1,512.00**

KIMBER 1911 AEGIS ELITE SERIES
Calibers: 9mm, .45 ACP. Features: Offered in Custom, Pro and Ultra sizes with 5-, 4.25- or 3-in. barrels. Sights: Green or red fiber optic or Vortex Venom red dot on OI (Optics Installed) models (shown). Grips: G10. Features: Satin finish stainless steel frame, matte black or gray slide, front and rear AEX slide serrations.
Price: .... **$1,233.00–$1,722.00**

KIMBER EVO SERIES
Caliber: 9mm. Capacity: 7 rounds. Barrel: 3.16 in. Sights: Tritium night sights. Weight: 19 oz. Grips: G10. Features: Offered in TLE, CDP, Two Tone variants with stainless slide, aluminum frame.
Price: CDP **$800.00**
Price: Two Tone **$860.00**

KIMBER KDS9C SERIES
Calibers: 9mm. Capacity: 15-round magazine. Frame: Aluminum. Barrel: 4-in. barrels. Weight: 25.3 oz unloaded. Sights: Green red fiber optic front/adjustable rear, optic ready. Grips: G10. Features: Stainless steel, matte black, front and rear slide serrations. Rail model available. SAO trigger.
Price: .45 ACP Compensated .... **$1,495.00–$1,903.00**

KIMBER R7 MAKO SERIES
Calibers: 9mm. Capacity: 15-round magazine. Frame: Polymer. Barrel: 3.3- or 3.9-in. barrels. Weight: 24.2 oz unloaded. Sights: 3-dot iron sight, optic ready or factory red-dot. Striker-fire trigger. Tactical model with threaded barrel.
Price: .... **$679.00–$815.00**

Prices given are believed to be accurate at time of publication however, many factors affect retail pricing so exact prices are not possible.

79TH EDITION, 2025 ✦ **485**

KRISS VECTOR SDP SERIES

Calibers: .22 LR, 9mm, 10mm, or .45 Auto. Capacity: 10- or 30-round magazine. Barrel: 5.5 in. Weight: 5.9 lb. Sights: Low-profile, flip-up, optics-ready. Grip/Stock: Polymer. Features: Large for-mat pistol, delayed blowback, Super V recoil mitigation, single-stage trigger, threaded barrel.
Price: .... **$799.00–$1,749.00**

LES BAER 1911 ULTIMATE MASTER COMBAT

Calibers: .38 Super, 400 Cor-Bon, .45 ACP (others available). Capacity: 10-shot magazine. Barrels: 5, 6 in. Baer National Match. Weight: 37 oz. Length: 8.5 in. overall. Grips: Checkered cocobolo. Sights: Baer dovetail front, low-mount Bo-Mar rear with hidden leaf. Features: Full-house competition gun. Baer forged NM blued steel frame and double serrated slide; Baer triple port, tapered cone compensator; fitted slide to frame; lowered, flared ejection port; Baer reverse recoil plug; full-length guide rod; recoil buff; beveled magazine well; Baer Commander hammer, sear; Baer extended ambidextrous safety, extended ejector, checkered slide stop; beavertail grip safety with pad, extended magazine release button; Baer speed trigger. Made in USA by Les Baer Custom, Inc.
Price: .... **$4,233.00–$4,574.00**

LES BAER 1911 AMERICAN HANDGUNNER SPECIAL EDITION

Caliber: .45 ACP. Capacity: 8+1 capacity. Barrel: 5 in. Length: 8.5 in. overall. Grips: G10 blue/black. Sights: Low-Mount LBC Adj. Finish: Blued slide, matte stainless frame.
Price: .... **$2,989.00–$3,391.00**

LES BAER 1911 BLACK BEAR

Caliber: 9mm. Capacity: 9+1 capacity. Barrel: 4.25 in. Grips: G10. Sights: Combat night sights.
Price: **$3,950.00**

LES BAER 1911 BOSS .45

Caliber: .45 ACP. Capacity: 8+1 capacity. Barrel: 5 in. Weight: 37 oz. Length: 8.5 in. overall. Grips: Premium Checkered Cocobolo Grips. Sights: Low-Mount LBC Adj. Sight, red fiber-optic front. Features: Speed Trigger, Beveled Mag Well, Rounded for Tactical. Rear cocking serrations on the slide, Baer fiber-optic front sight (red), flat mainspring housing, checkered at 20 LPI, extended combat safety, Special tactical package, chromed complete lower, blued slide, (2) 8-round premium magazines.
Price: **$3,559.00**

LES BAER 1911 CUSTOM CARRY

Caliber: .38 Super, 9mm, 10mm, or .45 ACP. Capacity: 7- or 10-round magazine. Barrel: 5 in. Weight: 37 oz. Length: 8.5 in. overall. Grips: Checkered walnut. Sights: Baer improved ramp-style dovetailed front, Novak low-mount rear. Features: Baer forged NM frame, slide and barrel with stainless bushing. Baer speed trigger with 4-lb. pull. Made in USA by Les Baer Custom, Inc.
Price: Custom Carry 5, Blued **$2,845.00**
Price: Custom Carry 5, Stainless **$2,908.00**
Price: Custom Carry 5, 9mm or .38 Super **$3,380.00**
Price: Custom Carry 4 Commanche-length, blued **$3,380.00**
Price: Custom Carry 4 Commanche-length,
     .38 Super 10mm .... **$4,187.00–$4,321.00**

LES BAER 1911 PREMIER II

Calibers: .38 Super, .45 ACP. Capacity: 7- or 10-round magazine. Barrel: 5 in. Weight: 37 oz. Length: 8.5 in. overall. Grips: Checkered rosewood, double diamond pattern. Sights: Baer dovetailed front, low-mount Bo-Mar rear with hidden leaf. Features: Baer NM forged steel frame and barrel with stainless bushing, deluxe Commander hammer and sear, beavertail grip safety with pad, extended ambidextrous safety; flat mainspring housing; 30 LPI checkered front strap. Made in USA by Les Baer Custom, Inc.
Price: 5 in. .45 ACP **$2,757.00**
Price: 5 in. .38 Super, 9mm.. **$3,372.00**
Price: 6 in. .45 ACP, .38 Super, 9mm.............................. **$3,829.00**
Price: Super-Tac, .45 ACP, .38 Super **$3,949.00**
Price: 6-in Hunter 10mm **$3,945.00**

LES BAER 1911 STINGER

Calibers: .45 ACP or .38 Super. Capacity: 7-round magazine. Barrel: 5 in. Weight: 34 oz. Length: 8.5 in. overall. Grips: Checkered cocobolo. Sights: Baer dovetailed front, low-mount Bo-Mar rear with hidden leaf. Features: Baer NM frame. Baer Commanche slide, Officer's style grip frame, beveled mag well. Made in USA by Les Baer Custom, Inc.
Price: .... **$2,845.00–$2,917.00**

LES BAER HEMI 572

Caliber: .45 ACP. Based on Les Baer's 1911 Premier I pistol and inspired by Chrysler 1970 Hemi Cuda muscle car. Features: Double serrated slide, Baer fiber-optic front sight with green insert, VZ black recon grips with hex-head screws, hard chrome finish on all major components, Dupont S coating on barrel, trigger, hammer, ambi safety and other controls.
Price: **$3,559.00**

LES BAER ULTIMATE MASTER COMBAT

Calibers: .45 ACP, 9mm, or .38 Super. A full house competition 1911 offered in 8 variations in-cluding 5 or 6-inch barrel, PPC Distinguished or Open class, Bullseye Wadcutter class and others. Features include double serrated slide, fitted slide to frame, checkered front strap and triggerguard, serrated rear of slide, extended ejector, tuned extractor, premium checkered grips, blued finish and two 8-round magazines.
Price: .... **$4,233.00–$4,574.00**

LES BAER 1911 MONOLITH STINGER

Calibers: 10mm, .45 ACP, .38 Super, 9mm, .40 S&W. A full house competition 1911 offered in 14 variations. Unique feature is extra-long dust cover that matches the length of the slide and reduces muzzle flip. Features include flat-bottom double serrated slide, low mount LBC adjustable sight with hidden rear leaf, dovetail front sight, flat serrated mainspring housing, premium checkered grips, blued finish and two 8-round magazines.
Price: .... **$3,887.00–$4,273.00**

LES BAER KENAI SPECIAL

Caliber: 10mm. Capacity: 9-round magazine. Barrel: 5 in. Features: Hardchrome finish, double serrated slide, Baer fiber-optic front sight with green or red insert, low-mount LBC adjustable rear sight, Baer black recon

grips, special bear paw logo, flat serrated mainspring housing, lowered and flared ejection port, extended safety.
Price: **$3,530.00**

LES BAER GUNSITE PISTOL
Calibers: .45 ACP. Capacity: 8-round magazine. Barrel: 5 in. Features: double serrated slide, fitted slide to frame, flat serrated mainspring housing, flared and lowered ejection port, extended tactical thumb safety, fixed rear sight, dovetail front sight with night sight insert, all corners rounded, extended ejector, tuned extractor, premium checkered grips, blued finish and two 8-round magazines. Gunsite Raven logo on grips and slide.
Price: **$2,750.00**

MAGNUM RESEARCH DESERT EAGLE 1911 G
Caliber: 9mm or .45 ACP. Capacity: 8-round magazine. Barrels: 5 in. or 4.33 in. (DE1911C Com-mander size), or 3.0 in. (DE1911U Undercover). Grips: Double diamond checkered wood. Features: Extended beavertail grip safety, checkered flat mainspring housing, skeletonized hammer and trig-ger, extended mag release and thumb safety, stainless full-length guide road, enlarged ejection port, beveled mag well and high-profile sights. Comes with two 8-round magazines.
Price: .... **$1,025.00–$1,099.00**

MAGNUM RESEARCH DESERT EAGLE MARK XIX
Calibers: .357 Mag., 9 rounds; .44 Mag., 8 rounds; .50 AE, 7 rounds. Barrels: 6 in., 10 in., interchangeable. Weight: 62 oz. (.357 Mag.); 69 oz. (.44 Mag.); 72 oz. (.50 AE) Length: 10.25-in. overall (6-in. bbl.). Grips: Polymer; rubber available. Sights: Blade-on-ramp front, combat-style rear. Adjustable available. Features: Interchangeable barrels; rotating three-lug bolt; ambidextrous safety; adjustable trigger. Military epoxy finish. Satin, bright nickel, chrome, brushed, matte or black-oxide finishes available. 10-in. barrel extra. Imported from Israel by Magnum Research, Inc.
Price: .... **$1,480.00–$2,210.00**

MAGNUM RESEARCH BABY DESERT EAGLE III
Calibers: 9mm, .40 S&W, .45 ACP. Capacities: 10-, 12- or 15-round magazines. Barrels: 3.85 in. or 4.43 in. Weights: 28–37.9 oz. Length: 7.25–8.25 overall. Grips: Ergonomic polymer. Sights: White 3-dot system. Features: Choice of steel or polymer frame with integral rail; slide-mounted decocking safety. Upgraded design of Baby Eagle II series.
Price: **$739.00**

MAGNUM RESEARCH DESERT EAGLE L5/L6
Caliber: .357 Magnum, .44 Magnum, .50 AE. Capacity: 7, 8 or 9+1. Barrel: 5 in. or 6 in (L6). Weight: 50 to 70 oz. Length: 9.7 in. (L5), 10.8, (L6). Features: Steel barrel, aluminum frame and stainless steel slide with full Weaver-style accessory rail and integral muzzle brake. Gas-operated rotating bolt, single-action trigger, fixed sights.
Price: .... **$1,926.00–$2,451.00**

MILITARY ARMAMENT CORP 1911MAC
Caliber: .45 ACP. Capacity: 8-round magazine. Barrels: 5 in. Grips: Double-checkered wood. Fea-tures: Extended beavertail grip safety, checkered flat mainspring housing, skeletonized hammer and trigger, ambi thumb safety, enlarged ejection port, beveled magwell and adjustable sights.
Price: **$747.00**

MILITARY ARMAMENT CORP MAC 9 DS
Caliber: 9mm. Capacity: 17-round magazine. Barrels: 4.25 in. Grips: Synthetic. Features: Extended beavertail grip safety, checkered flat mainspring housing, skeletonized hammer and trigger, ambi thumb safety, enlarged ejection port, magwell and fixed sights, optics-ready.
Price: **$1,099.00**

MILITARY ARMAMENT CORP MAC 5 AND 5K
Caliber: 9mm. Capacity: 30-round magazine. Barrels: 5.8 or 8.9 in. Grips: Synthetic. Features: HK MP5 clones.
Price: **$1,099.00**

MILITARY ARMAMENT CORP INGLIS SERIES
Caliber: 9mm. Capacity: 15-round magazine. Barrels: 4.7 in. Grips: Synthetic or wood. Features: Browning Hi-Power clone.
Price: .... **$489.00–$649.00**

MOSSBERG MC1
Caliber: 9mm Capacity: 6+1 magazine. Barrel: 3.4 in. Sights: Three white-dot, snag-free. TruGlo tritium Pro sights or Viridian E-Series Red Laser available as an option. Weight: 22 oz., loaded. Grips: Integral with aggressive texturing and with palm swell. Features: Glass-reinforced polymer frame, stainless steel slide with multi-angle front and rear serrations, flat-profile trigger with integrated blade safety, ships with one 6-round and one 7-round magazine. Optional cross-bolt safety.
Price: **$435.00**

MOSSBERG MC2C
Caliber: 9mm. Capacity: 10, 13- or 15-round magazine. Barrel: 3.9 in. Grips: Textured polymer. Sights: Fixed, 3-dot, some models optics-ready. Length: 7.1 in. overall. Weight: 21 oz. unloaded. Finish: Matte black. Features: Accessory rail, forward-slide serrations.
Price: .... **$505.00–$662.20**

MOSSBERG MC2SC
Caliber: 9mm. Capacity: 11- or 14-round magazine. Barrel: 3.4 in. Grips: Textured polymer. Sights: Fixed, 3-dot, optics-ready. Length: 6.2 in. overall. Weight: 19.5 oz. unloaded. Finish: Matte black. Features: Accessory rail, forward-slide serrations.
Price: .... **$505.00–$662.00**

NIGHTHAWK CUSTOM AGENT 2 SERIES
Calibers: 9mm, .45 ACP. Capacity: 10-round magazine. Barrel: 4.25 in. Grips: G10 Railscale texture. Sights: Fixed, Heinie Ledge Black rear/gold-bead front. Length: 7.85 in. overall. Weight: 38.6 oz. unloaded. Finish: Smoke Cerakote. Features: Accessory rail, faceted slide with side windows, one-piece mainspring housing/mag well, ultra-high-cut front grip strap.
Price: **$5,199.00**

NIGHTHAWK CUSTOM BULL SERIES
Caliber: 9mm. Capacity: 8-round magazine. Barrel: 3.8, 4.25, or 5 in. Grips: Textured carbon fiber. Sights: Fixed, Heinie Ledge Black rear/fiber-optic front. Length: 7.85 in. overall. Weight: 38.2 oz. unloaded. Finish: Black nitride. Features: Bull nose and French border on slide, ultra-high-cut front grip strap, dehorned.
Price: **$4,199.00**

Prices given are believed to be accurate at time of publication however, many factors affect retail pricing so exact prices are not possible.

79TH EDITION, 2025 ⊕ **487**

NIGHTHAWK CUSTOM CHAIRMAN

Calibers: 9mm, .45 ACP. Barrel: 6 in. Weights: 40.9 oz. Features: Slide cuts. CLC finish with gold titanium nitride barrel.
Price: $4,799.00

NIGHTHAWK CUSTOM COUNSELOR

Calibers: 9mm. Barrel: 3.5 in. Weights: 27.9 oz. Features: Slide cuts, aluminum frame, Officer size.
Price: $4,499.00

NIGHTHAWK CUSTOM DELEGATE

Calibers: 9mm or .45 Auto. Barrel: 4.25 in. Weights: 38.2 oz. Features: Steel frame, Commander size.
Price: $4,499.00

NIGHTHAWK CUSTOM ENVOY

Calibers: 9mm or .45 Auto. Barrel: 5 in. Weights: 40.8 oz. Features: Steel frame, Full size.
Price: $4,499.00

NIGHTHAWK CUSTOM GRP/GRP RECON

Calibers: 9mm, .45 ACP. Capacity: 8-round magazine. Features: Global Response Pistol (GRP). Black, Sniper Gray, green, Coyote Tan or Titanium Blue finish. Match-grade barrel and trigger, choice of Heinie or Novak adjustable night sights.
Price: $3,699.00
Price: Recon.. $3,799.00

NIGHTHAWK CUSTOM LADY HAWK SERIES

Calibers: 9mm or .45 Auto. Barrel: 4.25 in. Weights: 36 oz. Features: Slim-profile steel frame, Commander size, Hiene Straight Eight Slant Pro sights.
Price: $4,399.00
Price: 2.0 .... $5,399.00

NIGHTHAWK CUSTOM PREDATOR SERIES

Calibers: 9mm or .45 Auto. Barrel: 4.25 or 5 in. Weights: 35.8–40.3 oz. Features: Engineered to minimize felt recoil, Full and Commander sizes, Hiene Straight Eight Slant Pro sights.
Price: $4,499.00
Price: II $4,499.00
Price: III $4,499.00

NIGHTHAWK CUSTOM T4

Calibers: 9mm, .45 ACP Capacities: .45 ACP, 7- or 8-round magazine; 9mm, 9 or 10 rounds; 10mm, 9 or 10 rounds. Barrels: 3.8, 4.25 or 5 in. Weights: 28–41 ounces, depending on model. Features: Manufacturer of a wide range of 1911-style pistols in Government Model (full-size), Commander and Officer's frame sizes. Shown is T4 model, introduced in 2013 and available only in 9mm.
Price: $4,199.00

NIGHTHAWK CUSTOM THUNDER RANCH

Caliber: 9mm, .45 ACP. Capacity: 8-round (.45 ACP), 10-round (9mm) magazine. Barrel: 5 in. Grips: Textured linen micarta. Sights: Fixed, Heinie Black Ledge rear/gold-bead front. Length: 8.6 in. overall. Weight: 41.3 oz. unloaded. Finish: Smoked nitride. Features: Custom front- and rear-cocking serrations, lanyard-loop mainspring housing, GI-Style nub thumb safety and custom engraving.
Price: $3,999.00

NIGHTHAWK CUSTOM SHADOW HAWK

Caliber: 9mm or .45 Auto. Barrels: 4.25, 5, or 6-in. Features: Stainless steel frame with black Nitride finish, flat-faced trigger, high beavertail grip safety, checkered frontstrap, Heinie Straight Eight front and rear titanium night sights.
Price: .... $4,199.00–$4,499.00

NIGHTHAWK CUSTOM VICE PRESIDENT

Caliber: 9mm. Capacity: 10-round magazine. Barrel: 4.25 in. Grips: G10 Railscale Ascend texture. Sights: Fixed, Heinie Straight Eight Ledge rear/tritium front. Length: 7.4 in. overall. Weight: 32 oz. unloaded. Finish: Black DLC. Features: Gold titanium nitride barrel, heavy angle slide-lightening cuts, one-piece mainspring housing/mag well, ultra-high-cut front grip strap, dehorned.
Price: $4,799.00

NIGHTHAWK CUSTOM HEINIE LONG SLIDE

Calibers: .45 ACP. Barrel: Long slide 6-in. Features: Cocobolo wood grips, black Perma Kote finish, adjustable or fixed sights, frontstrap checkering.
Price: $4,499.00

NIGHTHAWK CUSTOM BORDER SPECIAL

Caliber: 9mm or .45 ACP Capacity: 8+1 magazine. Barrel: 4.25-in. match grade. Weight: 34 oz. Sights: Heinie Black Slant rear, gold bead front. Grips: Cocobolo double diamond. Finish: Cerakote Elite Midnight black. Features: Commander-size steel frame with bobtail concealed carry grip. Scal-loped frontstrap and mainspring housing. Serrated slide top. Rear slide serrations only. Crowned barrel flush with bushing.
Price: $4,199.00

NIGHTHAWK CUSTOM VIP BLACK

Caliber: .45 ACP. Capacity: 8+1 magazine. Hand built with all Nighthawk 1911 features plus deep hand engraving throughout, black DLC finish, custom vertical frontstrap and mainspring serrations, 14k solid gold bead front sight, crowned barrel, giraffe bone grips, custom walnut hardwood presentation case.
Price: $8,999.00

NORTH AMERICAN ARMS GUARDIAN DAO

Calibers: .32 ACP, .380 ACP. Capacity: 6-round magazine. Barrel: 2.49 in. Weight: 20.8 oz. Length: 4.75 in. overall. Grips: Black polymer. Sights: Low-profile fixed. Features: DAO mechanism. All stainless steel construction. Introduced 1998. Made in USA by North American Arms.
Price: .... $409.00–$520.00

ORACLE ARMS 2311

Caliber: 9mm. Capacity: 15-, 17- or 21-round magazine. Barrels: 4.25 or 5 in. Features: 1911-style platform. Compatible with SIG P320 magazines. Modular grip and magwell. Optics-ready.
Price: .... $2,299.00–$2,349.00

PHOENIX ARMS HP22, HP25

Calibers: .22 LR, .25 ACP. Capacities: .22 LR, 10-shot (HP22), .25 ACP, 10-shot (HP25). Barrel: 3 in. Weight: 20 oz. Length: 5.5 in. overall. Grips: Checkered composition. Sights: Blade front, adjustable rear. Features: Single action, exposed hammer; manual hold-open; button magazine release. Available in satin nickel,matte blue finish. Introduced 1993. Made in USA by Phoenix Arms.

Price: With gun lock **$162.00**
Price: HP Range kit with 5-in. bbl., locking case and
      accessories (1 Mag) **$207.00**
Price: HP Deluxe Range kit with 3- and 5-in. bbls., 2 mags, case **$248.00**

REPUBLIC FORGE 1911

Calibers: .45 ACP, 9mm, .38 Super, .40 S&W, 10mm. Features: A manufacturer of custom 1911-style pistols offered in a variety of configurations, finishes and frame sizes, including single- and double-stack models with many options. Made in Texas.
Price: From .... **$3,680.00–$4,280.00**

ROCK ISLAND ARMORY GI STANDARD SERIES

Calibers: 9mm, .38 Super, .45 ACP. Capacities: 7-, 8-, or 10-round. Grips: Hard rubber or smooth wood. Finish: Parkerized or nickel. Sights: Round post front, fixed rear. Features: 1911 GI-style semi-auto pistol. FS models have 5-in. barrels, MS models have 4.4-in. barrels, CS models have 3.5-in. barrels.
Price: .... **$474.00–$845.00**

ROCK ISLAND ARMORY ROCK SERIES

Calibers: 9mm, .38 Super, .45 ACP. Capacities: 7-, 8-, 10-, or 16-round. Grips: Hard rubber or G10 grips. Barrel: 3.6-, 4.25, or 5-inch. Finish: Blued, Duracoat or two-tone finish, matte stainless, or nickel. Sights: Post front, fixed or adjustable rear. Features: 1911-style semi-auto pistol. Rock Ultra has fiber-optic front sight and adjustable rear sight. Some with double-stack magazines.
Price: Rock Standard .... **$599.00–$759.00**
Price: Rock Ultra.. **$849.00–$1,169.00**

ROCK ISLAND ARMORY TCM/ARMOR SERIES

Caliber: .22 TCM. Capacity: 17-round magazine. Barrel: 4.25 or 5 in. Weight: 36 oz. Length: 8.5 in. Grips: Polymer. Sights: Adjustable rear. Features: 1911 platform, chambered for high-velocity .22 TCM rimfire cartridge. TCM Premium FS has magwell.
Price: TCM Standard MS and Standard FS... **$749.00**
Price:TCM Premium FS **$949.00**

ROCK ISLAND ARMORY TAC ULTRA SERIES

Caliber: 9mm, .40 S&W, .45 Auto, 10mm. Capacity: 8-, 16-, or 17-round magazine. Barrel: 3.6, 4.25, or 5.5 in. Weight: 40 oz. Length: 8.5 in. Grips: VZ G10. Sights: Fiber-optic front, adjustable rear. Features: Two magazines, accessory rails, extended beavertail safety. CS, FS and MS models use single-stack magazines, HC models use double-stack magazines.
Price: .... **$699.00–$899.00**

ROCK ISLAND ARMORY MAPP

Caliber: 9mm. Capacity: 10-round magazine. Barrel: 3.75 or 4.6 in. Browning short recoil action-style pistols with: integrated front sight; snag-free rear sight; DA/SA trigger; thumb safety; polymer frame with accessory rail. FS models has 4.60-inch barrel, MS model has 3.7-inch barrel.
Price: MAPP FS/MS.. **$499.00**

ROCK ISLAND ARMORY XT22

Calibers: .22 Magnum. Capacities: 14-round magazine. Barrel: 5 in. Weight: 38 oz. Features: The XT-22 is the only .22 Magnum 1911 with a forged 4140 steel slide and a one-piece 4140 chrome-moly barrel.

PRICE: XT22 Magnum **$599.00**
PRICE: XT22 Magnum Target **$649.00**
PRICE: XT22 Magnum Pro **$749.00**

ROCK ISLAND ARMORY BBR SEIES

Caliber: .380 ACP, 9mm or .45 ACP. Capacity: 7- or 10-round magazine. Barrel: 3.1 or 3.7 inches. Features: Smaller 1911-A1 design with features identical to full-size model.
Price: .... **$399.00–$699.00**

ROCK ISLAND ARMORY LI380

Caliber: .380 ACP. Capacity: 8-round magazine. Barrel: 3.5 in. Features: Blowback operation. DA/SA trigger.
Price: **$299.00**

ROCK ISLAND ARMORY STK100 SERIES

Caliber: 9mm. Capacity: 17-round magazine. Barrel: 4.5 in. Features: Striker-fire trigger. Metal frame. STK150 model has 4-in. Barrel. STK200 is a compact model.
Price: **$499.00**

ROCK ISLAND ARMORY RIA 5.0

Caliber: 9mm. Capacity: 17-round magazine. Barrel: 4.5 inch. Features: Striker-fire trigger. Polymer frame. Patented RVS recoil system that maximizes barrel mass and linear movement for softer felt recoil.
Price: **$1,998.00**

ROCK RIVER ARMS LAR-15/LAR-9

Calibers: .223/5.56mm NATO, 9mm. Barrels: 7 in., 10.5 in. Wilson chrome moly, 1:9 twist, A2 flash hider, 1/2x28 thread. Weights: 5.1 lbs. (7-in. barrel), 5.5 lbs. (10.5-in. barrel). Length: 23 in. overall. Stock: Hogue rubber grip. Sights: A2 front. Features: Forged A2 or A4 upper, single-stage trigger, aluminum free-float tube, one magazine. Similar 9mm Para. LAR-9 also available. From Rock River Arms, Inc.
Price: .... **$760.00–$1,310.00**

ROCK RIVER ARMS BASIC LIMITED

Caliber: .45 ACP. Features: Standard-size 1911 pistol with rosewood grips, adjustable sights, Lus-trous-blued finish, guaranteed 2.5-inch groups at 50 yards.
Price: **$3,565.00**

ROCK RIVER ARMS TACTICAL PISTOL

Caliber: .45 ACP. Features: Standard-size 1911 pistol with rosewood grips, Heinie or Novak sights, Black Cerakote finish.
Price: **$3,730.00**

ROCK RIVER ARMS LIMITED MATCH

Calibers: .45 ACP, 40 S&W, .38 Super, 9mm. Barrel: 5 in. Sights: Adjustable rear, blade front. Finish: Hard chrome. Features: National Match frame with beveled magazine well, front and rear slide serrations, Commander Hammer, G10 grips.
Price: **$3,600.00**

ROCK RIVER ARMS CARRY PISTOL

Caliber: .45 ACP. Barrel: 5 in. Sights: Heinie. Finish: Parkerized. Grips: Rosewood. Weight: 39 oz.
Price: **$2,925.00**

ROCK RIVER ARMS 1911 POLY

Caliber: .45 ACP. Capacity: 7-round magazine. Barrel: 5 in. Weight: 33 oz. Sights: Fixed. Features: Full-size 1911-style model with polymer frame and steel slide.
Price: **$2,085.00**

Prices given are believed to be accurate at time of publication however, many factors affect retail pricing so exact prices are not possible.

79TH EDITION, 2025 ✦ **489**

RUGER-57

Caliber: 5.7x28mm. Capacity: 20-round magazine. Barrel: 4.94 in. Grips: Textured polymer. Sights: Adjustable rear/fiber-optic front, optic ready. Length: 8.65 in. overall. Weight: 24.5 oz. unloaded. Finish: Black oxide. Features: 1911-style ambidextrous manual safety, Picatinny-style accessory rail, drilled and tapped for optics with adapter plate. Made in the USA.
Price: **$899.00**

RUGER AMERICAN PISTOL

Calibers: 9mm, .45 ACP. Capacities: 10 or 17 (9mm), 10 (.45 ACP). Barrels: 4.2 in. (9), 4.5 in. (.45). Lengths: 7.5 or 8 in. Weights: 30–31.5 oz. Sights: Novak LoMount Carry 3-Dot. Finish: Stainless steel slide with black Nitride finish. Grip: One-piece ergonomic wrap-around module with adjustable palm swell and trigger reach. Features: Short take-up trigger with positive re-set, ambidextrous mag release and slide stop, integrated trigger safety, automatic sear block system, easy takedown. Introduced in 2016.
Price: ....**$669.00–$689.00**

RUGER AMERICAN COMPACT PISTOL

Caliber: 9mm. Barrel: 3.5 in. Features: Compact version of American Pistol with same general specifications.
Price: **$669.00**

RUGER EC9S

Caliber: 9mm. Capacity: 7+1. Barrel: 3.12 in. Grips: Glass-filled nylon. Sights: Fixed. Features: Black glass-filled grip frame. Multiple finishes. Striker-fired operation with smooth trigger pull. Integral safety plus manual safety.
Price: ....**$349.00–$389.00**

RUGER MAX-9

Caliber: 9mm. Capacity: 12+1. Barrel: 3.2 in. Grips: Glass-filled nylon. Sights: Fixed tritium front or factory red-dot. Features: Black glass-filled grip frame. Multiple finishes. Striker-fired operation with smooth trigger pull. Integral safety plus manual safety.
Price: ....**$439.00–$489.00**

RUGER SECURITY-9 PRO

Caliber: 9mm. Capacity: 15-round magazine. Barrel: 4 in. Grips: Textured polymer. Sights: Fixed-steel tritium. Length: 7.24 in. overall. Weight: 23.8 oz. unloaded. Finish: Black oxide. Features: Rug-ged construction with black oxide, through-hardened, alloy-steel slide and barrel and high-performance, glass-filled nylon grip frame. Made in the USA.
Price: ....**$369.00–$389.00**

RUGER SECURITY-9 COMPACT PRO

Caliber: 9mm. Capacity: 10-round magazine. Barrel: 3.42 in. Grips: Textured polymer. Sights: Fixed-steel tritium. Length: 6.52 in. overall. Weight: 21.9 oz. unloaded. Finish: Black oxide. Features: Similar to Ruger Security-9 Pro. Precision-machined, hard-coat, anodized aluminum chassis with full-length guide rails. Made in the USA.
Price: **$529.00**

RUGER SECURITY-380

Caliber: .380 Auto. Capacity: 10- or 15-round magazine. Similar to Security-9 but with Lite Rack system, which consists of slide serrations, cocking ears and a lighter recoil spring.
Price: **$369.00**

RUGER SECURITY-9

Caliber: 9mm. Capacity: 10- or 15-round magazine. Barrel: 4 or 3.4 in. Weight: 21 oz. Sights: Drift-adjustable 3-dot or factory red-dot. Viridian E-Series Red Laser available. Striker-fired polymer-frame compact model. Uses the same Secure Action as LCP II. Bladed trigger safety plus external manual safety.
Price: ....**$369.00–$389.00**

RUGER LC380

Caliber: .380 ACP. Capacity: 7+1. Barrel: 3.12 in. Grips: Glass-filled nylon. Sights: Adjustable 3-dot. Features: Brushed stainless slide, black glass-filled grip frame, blue alloy barrel finish. Striker-fired operation with smooth trigger pull.
Price: **$679.00**

RUGER LCP

Caliber: .380. Capacity: 6-round magazine. Barrel: 2.75 in. Weight: 9.4 oz. Length: 5.16 in. Grips: Glass-filled nylon. Sights: Fixed, drift adjustable or integral Crimson Trace Laserguard. MAX model has 10-round magazine.
Price: ....**$259.00–$529.00**

Prices given are believed to be accurate at time of publication however, many factors affect retail pricing so exact prices are not possible.

RUGER LCP II
Caliber: .22 LR. Capacity: 10-round magazine. Barrel: 2.75 in. Weight: 11.2 oz. Length: 5.16 in. Grips: Glass-filled nylon. Sights: Fixed. Features: Lite Rack system. Larger grip frame surface provides better recoil distribution. Finger grip extension included. Improved sights for superior visibility. Sights are integral to the slide, hammer is recessed within slide.
Price: .... **$439.00–$449.00**

RUGER EC9S
Caliber: 9mm. Capacity: 7-shot magazine. Barrel: 3.125 in. Striker-fired polymer frame. Weight: 17.2 oz.
Price: .... **$349.00–$389.00**

RUGER LC CHARGER
Caliber: 5.7x28mm. Capacity: 20-round magazine. Barrel: 10.3 in. Weight: 66.5 oz. Features: Based on Ruger-5.7 design design with pistol grip stock and forend, scope rail.
Price: **$999.00**

RUGER PC CHARGER
Caliber: 9mm. Capacity: 17-round magazine. Barrel: 6.5 in. Weight: 5.2 lb. Features: Based on PC rifle design with pistol grip stock and forend, scope rail. Interchangeable mag well for Ruger Ameri-can/Security-9 or Glock magazines. Takedown.
Price: **$899.00**

RUGER 22 CHARGER
Caliber: .22 LR. Capacity: 15-round BX-15 magazine. Features: Based on famous 10/22 rifle design with pistol grip stock and forend, scope rail, bipod. Black laminate stock. Silent-SR Suppressor available. Add $449. NFA regulations apply. Reintroduced with improvements and enhancements in 2015.
Price: Standard .... **$399.00–$489.00**
Price: Takedown .... **$529.00–$739.00**

RUGER MARK IV SERIES
Caliber: .22 LR. Capacity: 10-round magazine. Barrels: 4.75, 5.5, or 6.8 in. Target model has 5.5-in. bull barrel, Hunter model 6.88-in. fluted bull, Competition model 6.88-in. slab-sided bull. Weight: 33–46 oz. Grips: Checkered or target laminate. Sights: Adjustable rear, blade or fiber-optic front (Hunter). Features: Updated design of Mark III series with one-button takedown. Introduced 2016. Modern successor of the first Ruger pistol of 1949.
Price: Standard .... **$569.00–$599.00**
Price: Hunter .... **$729.00–$1,069.00**
Price: Limited **$699.00**
Price: Tactical **$749.00**
Price: Target .... **$679.00–$899.00**
Price: Competition **$969.00**

RUGER 22/45 MARK IV SERIES
Caliber: .22 LR. Features: Similar to other .22 Mark IV autos except has Zytel grip frame that matches angle and magazine latch of Model 1911 .45 ACP pistol. Available in 4.4-, 5.5-in. bull barrels. Comes with extra magazine, plastic case, lock. Molded polymer or replaceable laminate grips. Weight: 25–33 oz. Sights: Adjustable. Updated design of Mark III with one-button takedown. Introduced 2016. LITE models features aluminum barrel sleeve.
Price: Standard **$529.00**
Price: Tactical.. **$669.00**
Price: Lite.. **$739.00**

RUGER SR22
Caliber: .22 LR. Capacity: 10-round magazine. Barrel: 3.5 or 4.5 in. Weight: 17.5 oz. Length: 6.4 in. Sights: Adjustable 3-dot. Features: Ambidextrous manual safety/decocking lever and mag release. Comes with two interchangeable rubberized grips and two magazines. Black or silver anodized finish. Available with threaded barrel. DA/SA trigger.
Price: .... **$559.00–$619.00**

RUGER SR1911 SERIES
Caliber: 9mm, .45 Auto or 10mm Auto. Capacity: 7-, 8- or 9-round

---

magazine. Barrel: 4.2 or 5 in. Weight: 36.4–39 oz. Length: 8.6 in., 7.1 in. Grips: Slim checkered hardwood. Sights: Novak Lo-Mount Carry rear, standard front or adjustable rear (Target). Frame: Stainless or aluminum. Fea-tures: Based on Series 70 design. Flared and lowered ejection port. Extended mag release, thumb safety and slide-stop lever, oversized grip safety, checkered backstrap on the flat mainspring hous-ing. Comes with one 7-round and one 8-round magazine.
Price: .... **$799.00–$1,299.00**

RUGER SR1911 OFFICER
Caliber: .45 ACP, 9mm. Capacity: 8-round magazine. Barrel: 3.6 in. Weight: 27 oz. Features: Com-pact variation of SR1911 Series. Black anodized aluminum or matte stainless frame, stainless slide, skeletonized trigger, Novak 3-dot Night Sights, G10 deluxe checkered G10 grips.
Price: **$1,279.00**

SAR K2 SERIES
Caliber: .45 Auto. Based on metal frame variation of the CZ 75 design. Full size and compact mod-els. Manufactured by Sarsilmaz in Turkey.
Price: .... **$629.00–$689.00**

SAR P8S SERIES
Caliber: 9mm. Based on metal frame variation of the CZ 75 design. Full size and compact models. Manufactured by Sarsilmaz in Turkey.
Price: .... **$555.00–$619.00**

SAR SAR9
Caliber: 9mm. Polymer frame striker-fire. Sub compact, compact, and full size models. Manufac-tured by Sarsilmaz in Turkey.
Price: .... **$419.00–$519.00**

SAVAGE 1911
Caliber: .45 ACP, 9mm. Capacity: 8-round magazine. Barrel: 5 in. Weight: 39 oz. Features: 1911 style platform. Multiple finishes. G10 grips.
Price: .... **$1,349.00–$1,499.00**

SAVAGE STANCE
Calibers: 9mm. Capacity: 7-, 8- or 10-rounds. Barrel: 3-in. Grip: Textured polymer. Sights: 3 white-dot system. Finishes: Cerakote Black, gray or FDE. Features: Polymer frame with chassis system.
Price: .... **$449.00–$559.00**

SCCY CPX
Caliber: 9mm. Capacity: 10-round magazine. Barrel: 3.1 in. Weight: 15 oz.

Length: 5.7 in. overall. Grips: Integral with polymer frame. Sights: 3-dot system, rear adjustable for windage. Features: Zytel polymer frame, steel slide, aluminum alloy receiver machined from bar stock. DAO with consistent 9-pound trigger pull. Concealed hammer. Available with (CPX-1) or without (CPX-2) manual thumb safety. Introduced 2014. CPX-3 is chambered for .380 ACP. Made in USA by SCCY Industries.
Price: CPX-1 .... **$284.00**
Price: CPX-2 .... **$270.00**
Price: CPX-3 .... **$305.00**

SCCY DVG SERIES
Caliber: 9mm. Capacity: 10-round magazine. Barrel: 3.1 in. Weight: 15.5 oz. Length: 6 in. overall. Grips: Integral with polymer frame. Sights: white dot front and optic ready. Features: Zytel polymer frame, steel slide, aluminum alloy receiver machined from bar stock. Striker-fire with 5.5-pound trigger pull. Made in USA.
Price: DVG-1 .... **$289.00**

SDS IMPORTS 1911 ISSUED SERIES
Calibers: 9mm or .45 ACP. Capacity: 7-round (.45 ACP) or 9-round (9mm) magazine. Barrel: 5-in. Grips: Checkered wood or G10. Sights: Ramp front, low-profile rear. Length: 8.5 in. overall. Weight: 39.5 oz. unloaded. Finish: Cerkaote matte grey or parkerized. Features: Similar to 1911A1 pistols. Series 70 mechanism.
Price: .... **$479.00–$529.00**

SDS IMPORTS 1911 DUTY SERIES
Calibers: 9mm or .45 ACP. Capacity: 7-round (.45 ACP) or 9-round (9mm) magazine. Barrel: 5-in. Grips: Checkered rubber. Sights: Ramp front, low-profile rear. Length: 8.5 in. overall. Weight: 39.5 oz. unloaded. Finish: Cerkaote black or matte stainless. Features: Series 70 mechanism. Models with accessory rail.
Price: .... **$579.00–$699.00**

SDS IMPORTS 1911 CARRY SERIES
Calibers: 9mm or .45 ACP. Capacity: 7-round (.45 ACP) or 9-round (9mm) magazine. Barrel: 4.2-in. Grips: Checkered rubber. Sights: Ramp front, low-profile rear. Finish: Cerkaote black or matte stainless. Features: Series 70 mechanism. Models with accessory rail. Commander size.
Price: .... **$549.00–$719.00**

SDS IMPORTS 1911 CONCEALMENT SERIES
Calibers: 9mm, 10mm Auto or .45 ACP. Capacity: 7-round (.45 ACP or 10mm Auto) or 9-round (9mm) magazine. Barrel: 4.2-in. Grips: Checkered rubber. Sights: Ramp front, low-profile rear. Fin-ish: Cerkaote black or two-tone. Features: Series 70 mechanism. Models with accessory rail. Com-mander-size with bobbed grip.
Price: .... **$579.00–$619.00**

SDS IMPORTS 1911 PINNACLE SERIES
Calibers: 9mm, 10mm Auto or .45 ACP. Capacity: 7-round (.45 ACP or 10mm

Prices given are believed to be accurate at time of publication however, many factors affect retail pricing so exact prices are not possible.

Auto) or 17-round (9mm) magazine. Barrel: 4.2-in. Grips: Checkered rubber. Sights: Ramp front, low-profile rear. Fin-ish: Cerkaote black or two-tone. Features: Series 70 mechanism. Models with accessory rail. Single- and double-stack models.

Price: Single-stack **$799.00**
Price: Double-stack .... **$799.00–$959.00**

SEECAMP LWS 32/380 STAINLESS DA
Calibers: .32 ACP, .380 ACP. Capacity: 6-round magazine. Barrel: 2 in., integral with frame. Weight: 10.5 oz. Length: 4.125 in. overall. Grips: Glass-filled nylon. Sights: Smooth, no-snag, contoured slide and barrel top. Features: Aircraft quality 17-4 PH stainless steel. Inertia-operated firing pin. Hammer fired DAO. Hammer automatically follows slide down to safety rest position after each shot, no manual safety needed. Magazine safety disconnector. Polished stainless and Cerakote finishes. Introduced 1985.

Price: .32 .... **$579.00–$695.00**
Price: .380 .... **$665.00–$775.00**

SIG SAUER 1911
Calibers: .45 ACP. Capacities: 8-round magazine. Barrel: 5 in. Weight: 40.3 oz. Length: 8.65 in. overall. Grips: Checkered wood grips. Sights: Novak night sights. Blade front, drift adjustable rear for windage. Features: Single-action 1911. Hand-fitted dehorned stainless steel frame and slide; match-grade barrel, hammer/sear set and trigger; 25-LPI front strap checkering, 20-LPI mainspring housing checkering. Beavertail grip safety with speed bump, extended thumb safety, firing pin safety and hammer intercept notch. Introduced 2005. XO series has contrast sights, Ergo Grip XT textured polymer grips. STX line available from Sig Sauer Custom Shop; two-tone 1911, non-railed, Nitron slide, stainless frame, burled maple grips. Polished cocking serrations, flat-top slide, mag well. Carry line has Siglite night sights, lanyard attachment point, gray diamondwood or rosewood grips, 8+1 capacity. Compact series has 6+1 capacity, 7.7 OAL, 4.25-in. barrel, slim-profile wood grips, weighs 30.3 oz. Ultra Compact in 9mm or .45 ACP has 3.3-in. barrel, low-profile night sights, slim-profile gray diamondwood or rosewood grips. 6+1 capacity. 1911 C3 is a 6+1 compact .45 ACP, rosewood custom wood grips, two-tone and Nitron finishes. Weighs 30 oz. unloaded, lightweight alloy frame. Length is 7.7 in. Now offered in more than 30 different models with numerous options for frame size, grips, finishes, sight arrangements and other features. From SIG Sauer, Inc.

PRICE: STX.. **$1,300.00**
PRICE: Stainless **$1,429.00**
PRICE: Fastback Nightmare Carry **$1,700.00**
PRICE: Emperor Scorpion Full-Size **$1,400.00**
PRICE: Fastback Emperor Scorpion Carry **$1,429.00**
PRICE: X **$1,649.00**

SIG SAUER P210 CARRY SERIES
Caliber: 9mm. Capacity: 8-round magazine. Barrel: 4.1 in. Grip: Checkered G10. Sights: SIGLITE night sights. Length: 7.5 in. overall. Weight: 32 ozs. unloaded. Finish: Nitron. Features: Conceal car-ry version of iconic P210.
Price: **$2,179.00**

SIG SAUER P220
Caliber: .45 ACP, 10mm. Capacity: 7- or 8-round magazine. Barrel: 4.4 in. Weight: 27.8 oz. Length: 7.8 in. overall. Grips: Checkered black plastic. Sights: Blade front, drift adjustable rear for windage. Optional Siglite night sights. Features: Double action. Stainless steel slide, Nitron finish, alloy frame, M1913 Picatinny rail; safety system of decocking lever, automatic firing pin safety block, safety intercept notch, and trigger bar disconnector. Squared combat-type triggerguard. Slide stays open after last shot. Introduced 1976. P220 SAS Anti-Snag has dehorned stainless steel slide, front Siglite night sight, rounded triggerguard, dust cover, Custom Shop wood grips. Equinox line is Custom Shop product with Nitron stainless slide with a black hard-anodized alloy frame, brush-polished flats and nickel accents. Truglo tritium fiber-optic front sight, rear Siglite night sight, gray laminated wood grips with checkering and stippling. From SIG Sauer, Inc.

Price: Elite **$1,099.00**
Price: Legion .45 ACP.. **$1,429.00**
Price: Legion 10mm.. **$1,779.00**

SIG SAUER P226
Calibers: 9mm, .40 S&W. Barrel: 4.4 in. Length: 7.7 in. overall. Features: Similar to the P220 pistol except has 4.4-in. barrel, measures 7.7 in. overall, weighs 34 oz. DA/SA or DAO. Many variations available. Snap-on modular grips. Legion series has improved short reset trigger, contoured and shortened beavertail, relieved triggerguard, higher grip, other improvements. From SIG Sauer, Inc. Five model has SAO trigger. ZEV model comes with red dot optic and threaded barrel.

Price: Nitron **$1,099.00**
Price: Elite **$1,099.00**
Price: Equinox.. **$1,449.00**
Price: Legion **$1,429.00**
Price: MK25 Navy Version **$1,199.00**
Price: Pro-Cut **$1,599.00**
Price: XFive **$2,499.00**
Price: XFive Legion **$2,779.00**
Price: ZEV **$2,199.00**

SIG SAUER P229
Caliber: Similar to the P220 except chambered for 9mm (10- or 15-round magazines). Barrels: 3.86-in. barrel, 7.1 in. overall length and 3.35 in. height. Weight: 32.4 oz. Features: Introduced 1991. Snap-on modular grips. Frame made in Germany, stainless steel slide assembly made in U.S.; pistol assembled in U.S. Many variations available. Legion series has improved short reset trigger, contoured and shortened beavertail, relieved triggerguard, higher grip, other improvements. Select has Nitron slide, Select G10 grips, Emperor Scorpion has accessory rail, FDE finish, G10 Piranha grips.

Price: Nitron **$1,099.00**
Price: Elite **$1,099.00**
Price: Legion **$1,429.00**

Prices given are believed to be accurate at time of publication however, many factors affect retail pricing so exact prices are not possible.

79TH EDITION, 2025 ✦ **493**

Price: Legion SAO $1,429.00
Price: M11-A1 .... $1,199.00

SIG SAUER SP2022

Calibers: 9mm. Capacities: 10- or 15-round magazines. Barrel: 3.9 in. Weight: 30.2 oz. Length: 7.4 in. overall. Grips: Composite and rubberized one-piece. Sights: Blade front, rear adjustable for windage. Features: Polymer frame, stainless steel slide; integral frame accessory rail; replaceable steel frame rails; left- or right-handed magazine release, two interchangeable grips.
Price: $570.00

SIG SAUER P238

Caliber: .380 ACP. Capacity: 6-round magazine. Barrel: 2.7 in. Weight: 15.4 oz. Length: 5.5 in. overall. Grips: Hogue G-10 and Rosewood grips. Sights: Contrast/Siglite night sights. Features: All-metal beavertail-style frame.
Price: Two Tone $779.00

SIG SAUER P320 NITRON

Calibers: 9mm, .45 ACP. Capacities: 15 or 16 rounds. Barrels: 3.6 in. (Subcompact), 3.9 in. (Carry model) or 4.7 in. (Full size). Weights: 26–30 oz. Lengths: 7.2 or 8.0 in overall. Grips: Interchangeable black composite. Sights: Blade front, rear adjustable for windage. Optional Siglite night sights. Features: Striker-fired DAO, Nitron finish slide, black polymer frame. Frame size and calibers are interchangeable. Introduced 2014. Made in USA by SIG Sauer, Inc.
Price: Full Size $579.00
Price: Compact $579.00

SIG SAUER P320 AXG SERIES

Calibers: 9mm. Capacities: 10 or 17 rounds. Similar to P320 series except with metal frame.
Price: Carry $1,199.00
Price: Legion $1,529.00
Price: Pro $1,299.00

SIG SAUER P320 XCOMPACT SERIES

Calibers: 9mm. Capacities: 10 or 15 rounds. Barrel: 3.6 in. Similar to P320 Compact except with tungsten infused heavy XFULL grip module with a flat skeletonized trigger. Fixed or Romeo-X op-tics models.
Price: .... $779.00–$1,149.00

SIG SAUER P320 X SERIES

Calibers: 9mm or 10mm. Capacities: 10 or 17 rounds. Similar to P320 series except with X-series polymer frame. Ten models chambered in 10mm Auto.
Price: X-Carry Legion $1,149.00
Price: XFive Legion $1,149.00
Price: XFive Max $1,749.00
Price: XFive Full $799.00
Price: XFive Full Romeo-X.. $1,149.00

Price: X-Full RXP $1,079.00
Price: XTen $929.00
Price: XTen Carry Comp $1,049.00
Price: XTen Endure $1,099.00

SIG SAUER P365

Caliber: 9mm. Barrel: 3.1 in. Weight: 17.8 oz. Features: Micro-compact striker-fired model with 10-, 12, or 15-round magazine, stainless steel frame and slide, XRAY-3 day and night sights fully tex-tured polymer grip. ROMEOZero Elite model with red-dot optics. P365X models have XSERIES-style grip module and flat trigger. SAS model has SIG Anti-Snag treatment.
Price: P365 NITRON...................................... $579.00–$779.00
Price: P365 ROMEOZero Elite $799.00
Price: P365X $650.00
Price: P365-AXG Legion $1,299.00
Price: P365 Rose $1,029.00

SIG SAUER P365 XL

Caliber: 9mm. Capacity: 12-round magazine. Barrel: 3.7 in. Grips: Textured polymer. Sights: Optics-ready, Day/Night sights. Length: 6.6 in. overall. Weight: 20.7 oz. unloaded. Finish: Nitron. Features: Grip with integrated carry magwell and extended beavertail, flat trigger and optic-ready slide. P365 XL ROMEOZERO model with red-dot optic. X-MACRO model has built-in barrel compensator. Spectre model has a laser engraved grip module and aggressive slide serrations.
Price: P365 XL $679.00
Price: P365 XL ROMEOZERO... $999.00
Price: P365 XL X-MACRO $749.00
Price: P365 XL X-MACRO TACOPS $849.00

SIG SAUER P365-380

Caliber: .380 Auto. Similar to P365.
Price: P365-380 NITRON $659.00

SIG SAUER M17/M18

Caliber: 9mm. Capacity: 17-round magazine. Barrel: 3.9 in. Grips: Textured polymer. Sights: Siglite front/night rear, optic ready. Length: 7.2 in. overall. Weight: 28.1 oz. unloaded. Finish: Coyote tan. Features: Commercial version of U.S. Military M18, manual thumb safety. M17X and M18X have factory-mounted Romeo-X optics.
Price: M17 .... $799.00
Price: M17X $1,549.00
Price: M18 .... $679.00
Price: M18X $1,549.00

SIG SAUER P322

Caliber: .22 LR. Capacity: 10 or 20-round magazine. Barrel: 4 in. Grips: Textured polymer. Sights: Fiber-optic front/adjustable rear or Romeo1Pro red dot. Length: 7 in. Weight: 17.1 oz. unloaded. Finish: Nitron. Ambidextrous controls.
Price: .... $449.00–$699.00

Prices given are believed to be accurate at time of publication however, many factors affect retail pricing so exact prices are not possible.

SIG SAUER MPX SERIES
Calibers: 9mm. Capacities: 35-round magazine. Barrel: 8 in. Weight: 5 lbs. Features: Semi-auto AR-style gun with closed, fully locked short-stroke pushrod gas system. Copperhead model with 3.5-in. barrel and 20-round magazine. K Model with 4.5-inch barrel.

Price: MPX Copperhead K .... **$2,179.00–$2,299.00**
Price: MPX Copperhead **$2,079.00**

SIG SAUER P938
Calibers: 9mm. Capacities: 6-shot mag. Barrel: 3.0 in. Weight: 16 oz. Length: 5.9 in. Grips: Hogue Extreme, Hogue Diamondwood. Sights: Siglite night sights or Siglite rear with Tru-Glo front. Features: Slightly larger version of P238.

Price: Nitron **$779.00**
Price: Legion **$829.00**
Price: Scorpion **$913.00**

SMITH & WESSON CSX SERIES
Calibers: 9mm. Capacities: 10 and 12 rounds. Barrel: 3.1 in. Weights: 19.5 oz. Lengths: 6.1 in. Grips: Polymer. Sights: 3 white-dot system with low-profile rear. Features: Metal alloy frame with stainless steel slide. Ambidextrous controls. Single-action trigger.

Price: **$619.00**

SMITH & WESSON M&P SHIELD M2.0 SERIES
Calibers: 9mm, .30 Super Carry, .40 S&W, .45 Auto. Capacities: 7- and 8-rounds (9mm), 6- and 7-rounds (.40). Barrel: 3.1-in. Weights: 18.3 oz. Lengths: 6.1 in. Grips: Polymer. Sights: 3 white-dot system with low-profile rear. Finishes: Armornite Black. Features: Polymer frame, micro-compact size. Plus model has .30 Super Carry double stack 12- or 15-round magazine.

Price: **$519.00**
Price: Performance Center Edition **$629.00**
Price: Plus model.. **$499.00**

SMITH & WESSON M&P 5.7 SERIES
Calibers: 5.7x28mm. Capacitiy: 22 rounds. Barrels: 5-in. Weights: 26.7 oz. Lengths: 8.5 in. Grips: Polymer. Sights: 3 white-dot system and optic ready. Finish: Armornite Black. Features: Polymer frame with stainless steel slide, barrel and structural components. Flat-face trigger. Picatinny rail.

Price: **$699.00**

SMITH & WESSON MODEL SD SERIES
Calibers: .40 S&W, 9mm. Capacities: 10+1, 14+1 and 16+1 Barrel: 4 in. Weight: 39 oz. Length: 8.7 in. Grips: Wood or rubber. Sights: Front: Tritium Night Sight, Rear: Steel Fixed 2-Dot. Features: SDT (Self Defense Trigger) for optimal, consistent pull first round to last, standard Picatinny-style rail, slim ergonomic textured grip, textured finger locator and aggressive front and backstrap texturing with front and rear slide serrations.

Price: **$349.00**

SMITH & WESSON SDVE SERIES
Similar to SD Series except with stainless steel slide.

Price: **$399.00**

SMITH & WESSON MODEL SW1911
Calibers: .45 ACP, 9mm. Capacities: 8 rounds (.45), 7 rounds (subcompact .45), 10 rounds (9mm). Barrels: 3, 4.25, 5 in. Weights: 26.5–41.7 oz. Lengths: 6.9–8.7 in. Grips: Wood, wood laminate or synthetic. Crimson Trace Lasergrips available. Sights: Low-profile white dot, tritium night sights or adjustable. Finish: Black matte, stainless or two-tone. Features: Offered in three different frame siz-es. Skeletonized trigger. Accessory rail on some

models. Compact models have round-butt frame. Pro Series have 30 LPI checkered frontstrap, oversized external extractor, extended mag well, full-length guide rod, ambidextrous safety. SC model with scandium frame, PC with slide ported lighting cuts, TA with stainless frame with accessory rail, PCRB with slide ported lighting cuts and bobtail frame.

Price: Standard **$1,129.00**
Price: PC **$1,849.00**
Price: PCRB **$1,849.00**
Price: Pro Series **$1,619.00**
Price: SC **$1,679.00**
Price: TA **$1,679.00**

SMITH & WESSON PERFORMANCE CENTER M&P9 AND M&P40 M2.0 COMPETITOR SERIES
Calibers: 9mm, .40 S&W, 10mm. Capacity: 17-round (9mm) or 15-round (.40 S&W) magazine. Barrel: 5 in. Grips: Four interchangeable palm-swell inserts. Sights: Fixed, fiber-optic front and rear. Length: 8.5 in. overall. Weight: 23 oz. unloaded. Finish: Black Armornite. Features: Metal frame with accessory rail, reversible magazine release, ported barrel and slide and tuned action with audi-ble trigger reset.

Price: **$999.00**

SMITH & WESSON SHIELD EZ M2.0
Caliber: 9mm or 30 Super Carry. Capacity: 8-round (9mm) 10-round (30 Super Carry) magazine. Barrel: 3.67 in. Grips: Textured polymer. Sights: Fixed, 3-dot. Length: 6.8 in. overall. Weight: 23.2 oz. unloaded. Finish: Black Armornite. Features: Accessory rail and reversible magazine release, with or without manual thumb safety.

Price: **$459.00**

SMITH & WESSON SHIELD EZ M2.0 PERFORMANCE CENTER
Caliber: 9mm or .380 Auto. Capacity: 8-round magazine. Barrel: 3.83 in. Grips: Textured polymer. Sights: Fixed, HI-VIZ sights. Length: 7 in. overall. Weight: 23.1 oz. unloaded. Finish: Black Ar-mornite frame and black, silver or gold accents. Features: Easy to rack slide, grip safety, manual thumb safety, accessory rail, reversible magazine release, ported barrel and lightening cuts in slide, accessory rail, reversible magazine release, flat trigger, tuned action.

Price: **$579.00**

SMITH & WESSON BODYGUARD 380
Caliber: .380 Auto. Capacity: 6+1. Barrel: 2.75 in. Weight: 11.85 oz. Length: 5.25 in. Grips: Polymer. Sights: Integrated laser plus drift-adjustable front and rear. Features: The frame of the Bodyguard is made of reinforced polymer, as is the magazine base plate and follower, magazine catch and trigger. The slide, sights and guide rod are made of stainless steel, with the slide and sights having a Melonite hardcoating.

Price: .... **$399.00–$479.00**

Prices given are believed to be accurate at time of publication however, many factors affect retail pricing so exact prices are not possible.

79TH EDITION, 2025 ✦ **495**

SMITH & WESSON EQUALIZER

Caliber: 9mm. Capacity: 10, 13 or 15-round magazine. Barrel: 3.6 in. Weight: 22.9 oz. Length: 6.7 in. Grips: Polymer. Sights: Fixed white 3-dot. Features: Easy rack slide, manual thumb safety, sin-gle-action trigger.

Price: **$599.00**

SPHINX SDP

Caliber: 9mm. Capacity: 15-shot magazine. Barrel: 3.7 in. Weight: 27.5 oz. Length: 7.4 in. Sights: Defiance Day & Night Green fiber/tritium front, tritium 2-dot red rear. Features: DA/SA with ambidextrous decocker, integrated slide position safety, aluminum MIL-STD 1913 Picatinny rail, Blued alloy/steel or stainless. Aluminum and polymer frame, machined steel slide. Offered in several variations. Made in Switzerland and imported by Kriss USA.

Price: **$1,295.00**

SPRINGFIELD ARMORY 1911 GARRISON

Calibers: 9mm or .45 ACP. Capacity: 7-round magazine. Barrel: 4.2 or 5 in. Grips: Thinline check-ered wood. Sights: Low profile, 3-dot. Length: 7.9–8.4 in. overall. Weight: 34–37 oz. unloaded. Fin-ish: Blued or stainless. Features: Heirloom-quality 1911.

Price: Blued **$868.00**
Price: Stainless **$917.00**

SPRINGFIELD ARMORY 1911 DS PRODIGY

Caliber: 9mm. Capacity: 17- and 20-round magazine. Barrel: 4.25 or 5 in. Weight: 32.5 or 34 oz. Length: 7.8 or 8.6 in. overall. Double-stack magazine 1911 platform. Sights: Fiber-optic front, black serrated rear, optics-ready. Some models with HEX Dragonfly red dot. Ambidextrous safety. Picatinny rail.

Price: Standard model **$1,499.00**
Price: HEX optic **$1,699.00**

SPRINGFIELD ARMORY 1911 EMISSARY

Calibers: 9mm or .45 ACP. Capacity: 7-round (.45 ACP) or 9-round (9mm) magazine. Barrel: 4.25- or 5-in. Grips: Textured G10. Sights: Tactical Rack rear/tritium front sights. Length: 8.4 in. overall. Weight: 40 oz. unloaded. Finish: Two-tone, black slide/stainless frame. Features: Square triggerguard, custom milled slide, flat trigger.

Price: **$1,378.00**

SPRINGFIELD ARMORY EMP ENHANCED MICRO

Calibers: 9mm. Capacity: 9-round magazine. Barrel: 3-inch stainless steel match grade, fully supported ramp, bull. Weight: 26 oz. Length: 6.5 in. overall. Grips: Thinline cocobolo hardwood. Sights: Fixed low-profile combat rear, dovetail front, 3-dot tritium. Features: Two 9-round stainless steel magazines with slam pads, long aluminum match-grade trigger adjusted to 5 to 6 lbs., forged aluminum alloy frame, black hardcoat anodized finish; dual spring full-length guide rod, forged satin-finish stainless steel slide. Introduced 2007.

Price: **$1,313.00**

SPRINGFIELD ARMORY ECHELON

Caliber: 9mm. Capacity: 17- and 20-round magazine. Barrel: 4.5 in. Grip: Textured polymer with modular back strap. Sights: Fixed, Tritium/luminescent front, Tactical Rack U-Notch rear; optics-ready. Length: 8 in. overall. Weight: 23.9 oz. unloaded with flush magazine. Finish: Matte black. Features: Central Operating Group. Threaded barrel model.

Price: .... **$679.00–$739.00**

SPRINGFIELD ARMORY HELLCAT 3" MICRO COMPACT

Caliber: 9mm. Capacity: 11- and 13-round magazine. Barrel: 3 in. Grip: Textured polymer. Sights: Fixed, Tritium/Luminescent front, Tactical Rack U-Notch rear. Length: 6 in. overall. Weight: 18.3 oz. unloaded with flush magazine. Finish: Matte black or Desert FDE. Features: Dual captive recoil spring w/ full-length guide rod. With or without manual thumb safety.

Price: **$599.00**
Price: OSP with Optical Sight mount **$843.00**

SPRINGFIELD ARMORY HELLCAT PRO

Caliber: 9mm. Capacity: 15-round magazine. Barrel: 3.7 in. Grip: Textured polymer. Sights: Fixed, Tritium/Luminescent front, Tactical Rack U-Notch rear. Length: 6.6 in. overall. Weight: 21 oz. unloaded. Finish: Matte black or Desert FDE. Features: Dual captive recoil spring w/ full-length guide rod.

Price: **$649.00**
Price: OSP with Optical Sight mount **$859.00**

SPRINGFIELD ARMORY HELLCAT RDP (RAPID DEFENSE PACKAGE)

Caliber: 9mm. Capacity: 11- and 13-round magazine. Barrel: 3.8 in. Grip: Textured polymer. Sights: Fixed, Springfield Armory HEX micro red dot. Length: 7 in. overall. Weight: 19.3 oz. unloaded with flush magazine. Finish: Matte black. Features: Self-indexing single port compensator, with or without manual thumb safety.

Price: .... **$778.00–$983.00**

SPRINGFIELD ARMORY XD SERIES

Calibers: 9mm, .40 S&W, .45 ACP. Barrels: 3, 4, 5 in. Weights: 20.5-31 oz. Lengths: 6.26-8 overall. Grips: Textured polymer. Sights: Varies by model; Fixed sights are dovetail front and rear steel 3-dot units. Features: Three sizes in X-Treme Duty (XD) line: Sub-Compact (3-in. barrel), Service (4-in. barrel), Tactical (5-in. barrel). Three ported models available. Ergonomic polymer frame, hammer-forged barrel, no-tool disassembly, ambidextrous magazine release, visual/tactile loaded chamber indicator, visual/tactile striker status indicator, grip safety, XD gear system included. Compact is shipped with one extended magazine (13) and one compact magazine (10). XD Mod.2 Sub-Compact has newly contoured slide and redesigned serrations, stippled grip panels, fiber-optic front sight.

Price: Sub-Compact .... **$440.00–$540.00**
Price: Compact **$592.00**
Price: Service .... **$440.00–$585.00**
Price: Tactical **$590.00**

Prices given are believed to be accurate at time of publication however, many factors affect retail pricing so exact prices are not possible.

SPRINGFIELD ARMORY XD(M) ELITE SERIES

Calibers: 9mm, 10mm, .45 ACP. Barrels: 3.8, 4.5, or 5.2 in. Sights: Fiber-optic front with interchangeable red and green filaments, fixed rear and optic ready or HEX Dragonfly red-dot optic. Grips: Integral polymer with three optional backstrap designs. Removable magwell. Features: Variation of XD design with improved ergonomics, deeper and longer slide serrations, slightly modified grip contours and texturing. Black polymer frame, forged steel slide. Available with compact or full size grip. Precision model with 5.2-in. barrel.

Price: Compact	$653.00–$837.00
Price: Service	$603.00–$633.00
Price: OSP	$653.00–$695.00

SPRINGFIELD ARMORY RONIN OPERATOR

Calibers: 9mm, 10mm, or .45 ACP. Capacity: 7-round (.45 ACP) or 9-round (9mm) magazine. Barrel: 3-, 4-, 4.25- or 5-in. Grips: Checkered wood. Sights: Fiber-optic front, tactical rack, white-dot rear. Length: 8.6 in. overall. Weight: 40 oz. unloaded. Finish: Two-tone, black slide/stainless frame.

Price:	$917.00
Price: Operator	$917.00
Price: EMP	$917.00

SPRINGFIELD ARMORY SA-35

Calibers: 9mm. Capacity: 13-round magazine. Barrel: 4.7 in. Grips: Checkered walnut. Sights: White dot front, tactical-rack rear. Length: 7.8 in. overall. Weight: 31.5 oz. unloaded. Finish: Matte blued. Features: Clone of Iconic Hi-Power pistol.

Price:	$799.00

SPRINGFIELD ARMORY TRP

Caliber: .45 ACP. Barrels: 4.25 or 5 in. Features: Similar to 1911A1, except checkered frontstrap and mainspring housing, Novak Night Sight combat rear sight and matching dovetailed front sight, tuned, polished extractor, oversize barrel link; lightweight speed trigger and combat action job, match barrel and bushing, extended ambidextrous thumb safety and fitted beavertail grip safety. Textured G10 grips. Finish: Blued or stainless. Classic model is full or commander size with Hydro G10 grips and no accessory rail. CC model has bobbed frame. Operator model has full dust cover and adjustable sights.

Price:	$1,732.00
Price: Operator	$1,818.00
Price: Classic	$1,899.00
Price: CC	$1,999.00

SPRINGFIELD ARMORY 1911 LOADED

Caliber: .45 ACP. Capacity: 7-round magazine. Barrel: 5 in. Weight: 34 oz. Length: 8.6 in. overall. Similar to Mil-Spec 1911A1 with the following additional features: Lightweight Delta hammer, ex-tended and ergonomic beavertail safety, ambidextrous thumb safety, and other features depending on the specific model. Match-grade barrels, low-profile 3-dot combat sights. Marine Corps Operator has black OD green Cerakote finish. Target model has adjustable sights.

Price: Parkerized	$999.00
Price: Stainless	$1,055.00
Price: Marine Corps Operator (shown	$1,374.00
Price: Target	$1,119.00

STACCATO 2011 SERIES

Calibers: 9mm, .40 S&W, .38 Super. Capacity: 9-, 17- or 21-round magazine. Barrels: 3.9- or 5-in., match-grade. Sights: Optic-ready, Dawson Precision Perfect Impact. Weight: 38–46.5 oz. Finish: Carbon black. Grips: Textured polymer. Features: 4-lb. trigger pull, ambidextrous safety levers, single- or double-stack magazine.

Price: Staccato-CS	$2,499.00
Price: Staccato-C2	$2,299.00
Price: Staccato-P	$2,499.00
Price: Staccato-XC	$4,299.00
Price: Staccato-XL	$3,599.00

SPRINGFIELD ARMORY MIL-SPEC 1911A1

Caliber: .45 ACP. Capacity: 7-round magazine. Barrel: 5 in. Weights: 35.6–39 oz. Lengths: 8.5–8.625 in. overall. Finish: Stainless steel. Features: Similar to Government Model military .45.

Price: Parkerized	$822.00
Price: Stainless Steel	$915.00
Price: Defend Your Legacy	$725.00

Prices given are believed to be accurate at time of publication however, many factors affect retail pricing so exact prices are not possible.

79TH EDITION, 2025 ✦ 497

STANDARD MANUFACTURING 1911 SERIES

Caliber: .45 ACP. Capacity: 7-round magazine. Barrel: 5-inch stainless steel match grade. Weight: 38.4 oz. Length: 8.6 in. Grips: Checkered rosewood double diamond. Sights: Fixed, Warren Tactical blade front/U-notch rear. Finish: Blued, case color, or nickel. Features: Forged frame and slide, beavertail grip safety, extended magazine release and thumb safety, checkered mainspring housing and front grip strap.

Price: Blued .... $1,200.00–$1,700.00
Price: Case Color .... $1,699.00–$2,349.00
Price: Nickel.. $1,999.00–$2,649.00
Price: Titanium Nitride PVD Gold $3,995.00
Price: Damascus $7,999.00

STANDARD MANUFACTURING SG22 SERIES

Caliber: .22 LR. Capacity: 10-round magazine. Barrel: 5.6 inch. Features: Colt Woodsman clone.

Price: Blued $1,299.00
Price: Case Color $1,599.00

STANDARD MANUFACTURING JACKHAMMER

Caliber: .22 LR. Capacity: 10- or 50-round magazine. Barrel: 5.3 inch. Features: Blowback action, optional 50-round drum magazine.

Price: .... $625.00–$599.00

STEYR L9-A2 MF

Calibers: 9mm. Capacities: 10 or 17-round. Barrels: 4.5 in. Weight: 27.2 oz. Sights: Trapizoid. Grips: Polymer, textured grip modules. Features: DAO striker-fired operation.

Price: $679.00

STOEGER STR-9 COMPACT

Caliber: 9mm. Capacity: 13-round magazine. Barrel: 3.8, 4, or 4.5 in. Grips: Three interchangeable backstraps. Sights: 3-dot sights or tritium night sights. Length: 6.9 in. overall. Weight: 24 oz. un-loaded. Finish: Matte black. Features: Compact version of the STR-9 striker-fire pistol. Aggressive forward and rear slide serrations and accessory rail. Made in Turkey.

Price: STR-9 .... $329.00
Price: STR-9C $329.00
Price: STR-9S Combat $629.00
Price: STR-9S Combat X $599.00
Price: STR-9MC.. $399.00
Price: STR-9F... $329.00

TAURUS G2 SERIES

Caliber: 9mm. Capacity: 6+1. Barrel: 3.2 in. Weight: 20 oz. Length: 6.3 in. Sights: Adjustable rear, fixed front. Features: Double/Single Action, polymer frame in blue with matte black or stainless slide, accessory rail, manual and trigger safeties. S models have single-stack magazines, C models have double-stack magazines.

Price: C models... $303.00
Price: S models.. $295.00

TAURUS G3 SERIES

Caliber: 9mm. Capacity: 17-round magazine. Barrel: 4.0-in. Grip: Textured polymer. Sights: White dot front, notch rear. Length: 7.28 in. overall. Weight: 24.8 oz. unloaded. Finish: Matte black, gray, tan. Features: Re-strike trigger, accessory rail.

Price: $340.00
Price: T.O.R.O. $413.00
Price: G3c Compact $325.00
Price: G3X $348.00
Price: G3XL $348.00
Price: Tactical $583.00

TAURUS GX4 SERIES

Caliber: 9mm. Capacity: 10, 11, and 13-round magazines. Barrel: 3.0-in. Grip: Textured polymer with modular backstrap. Sights: White dot front, notch rear. Length: 7.28 in. overall. Weight: 18.5 oz. unloaded. Finish: Matte black. Striker-fire trigger. T.O.R.O. model comes with red-dot optic. XL models have 3.7-in. barrels.

Price: GX4... $393.00
Price: GX4 T.O.R.O. $424.00
Price: GX4 XL $437.00
Price: GX4 XL T.O.R.O. $515.00

TAURUS TH SERIES

Caliber: 9mm, 10mm Auto or .40 S&W. Capacity: 13 or 17 round (9mm), 11 or 15 round (.40 S&W or 10mm Auto). Barrel: 3.5 or 4.3 in. Weight: 28 oz. Length: 7.7 in. Sights: Novak drift ad-justable. Features: Full-size 9mm double-stack model with SA/DA action. Polymer frame has inte-gral grips with finger grooves and stippling panels. C model has 3.8-in. barrel, 6.8-in. overall length.

Price: .... $381.00–$530.00

TAURUS TX22

Caliber: .22 LR. Capacity: 10- or 16-round magazine. Barrel: 4.1-in. Grip: Textured polymer, wrap around. Sights: Adjustable rear, white dot front. Length: 7.06 in. overall. Weight: 17.3 oz. unloaded. Finish: Matte black to tan. Compact model has 3.06-in. barrel.

Price: Standard $348.00
Price: Compact $393.00

TAURUS MODEL 1911

Calibers: 9mm, .45 ACP. Capacities: .45 ACP 8+1, 9mm 9+1. Barrel: 5 in. Weight: 33 oz. Length: 8.5 in. Grips: Checkered black. Sights: Heinie straight 8. Features: SA. Blued, stainless steel, duotone blue and blue/gray finish. Standard/Picatinny rail, standard frame, alloy frame and alloy/Picatinny

rail. Introduced in 2007. Imported from Brazil by Taurus International. Commander model has a 4.25-in. barrel. Officer model has a 3.2-in. barrel.
Price: 1911B, Blue **$719.00**
Price: 1911SS, Stainless Steel **$886.00**
Price: Blue w/rail **$810.00**
Price: Stainless Steel w/rail **$878.00**
Price: 1911 Commander .... **$677.00–$719.00**
Price: 1911 Officer **$677.00**

TAURUS MODEL 92
Caliber: 9mm. Capacity: 17-round magazine. Barrel: 5 in. Weight: 34 oz. Length: 8.5 in. overall. Grips: Checkered rubber. Sights: Fixed notch rear. 3-dot sight system. Also offered with micrometer-click adjustable night sights. Features: Beretta Model 92 platform. DA, ambidextrous 3-way hammer drop safety, allows cocked and locked carry. Blued, stainless steel, blued with gold highlights, stainless steel with gold highlights, forged aluminum frame, integral key-lock. Imported from Brazil by Taurus International.
Price: 92B .... **$606.00–$621.00**

TAURUS MODEL 917C
Caliber: 9mm. Capacity: 18-round magazine. Barrel: 4.3 in. Weight: 33.5 oz. Length: 7.9 in. overall. Grips: Checkered polymer. Sights: Fixed notch rear. Finish: Matte black. Features: Beretta Model 92 platform. DA/SA trigger, ambidextrous safety mounted on frame.
Price: **$606.00**

TRISTAR AMERICAN CLASSIC 1911
Calibers: 9mm, 10mm, or .45 ACP. Capacity: 7-round (.45 ACP) or 9-round (9mm) magazine. Bar-rel: 4.25- or 5-in. Grips: Checkered wood. Sights: Ramp front, low-profile rear. Length: 8.5 in. overall. Weight: 39.5 oz. unloaded. Finish: Hard chrome or blued.
Price: Government .... **$730.00–$825.00**
Price: Commander .... **$795.00–$900.00**
Price: Trophy **$1,020.00**

TRISTAR AMERICAN CLASSIC II 1911
Calibers: 9mm, 10mm, or .45 ACP. Capacity: 7-round (.45 ACP) or 9-round (9mm) magazine. Bar-rel: 5-in. Grips: Checkered wood. Sights: Ramp front, low-profile rear. Length: 8.5 in. overall. Weight: 39.5 oz. unloaded. Finish: Hard chrome or blued. Front slide serrations.
Price: .... **$780.00–$885.00**

WALTHER PD380
Caliber: .380 ACP. Capacity: 9-round magazine. Barrel: 3.7 in. Weight: 20.6

oz. Length: 6.4 in. Sights: Three-dot system, drift adjustable rear. Finish: Matte black. Features: DA/SA trigger, ham-mer-fired, ambidextrous mag release and manual safety/decoker. Picatinny rail.
Price: **$479.00**

WALTHER PDP SERIES
Caliber: 9mm. Capacity: 18-round magazine. Barrel: 4, 4.5 or 5 in. Grip: Textured polymer, modular backstrap. Sights: 3-dot, optics ready. Length: 8 in. overall. Weight: 25.4 ozs. unloaded. Finish: Black. Features: Accessory rail. Compact model has a 15-round magazine, 4-in. barrel. SF Compact has steel frame. Pro SD models have threaded barrel and flat trigger.
Price: Full Size... **$649.00**
Price: Compact **$640.00**
Price: Pro SD Full Size **$899.00**
Price: Pro SD Compact **$899.00**
Price: SF Compact **$1,699.00**

WALTHER PDP F-SERIES
Caliber: 9mm. Capacity: 15-round magazine. Barrel: 3.5 or 4 in. Grip: Textured polymer, modular backstrap. Sights: 3-dot, optics ready. Length: 7.25 in. (4-in. barrel) overall. Weight: 24 ozs. (4-in. barrel) unloaded. Finish: Black. Features: Accessory rail. Reduced grip circumference, trigger reach, and slide force.
Price: **$649.00**

WALTHER PPK, PPK/S
Caliber: .22 LR, .32 Auto or .380 ACP. Capacities: 6+1 (PPK), 7+1 (PPK/s). Barrel: 3.3 in. Weight: 21-26 oz. Length: 6.1 in. Grips: Checkered plastic. Sights: Fixed. New production in 2019. Made in Fort Smith, AR with German-made slide.
Price: PPK **$969.00**
Price: PPK/S **$969.00**
Price: PPK/S .22 LR **$449.00**

WALTHER PPQ 22 M2
Calibers: .22 LR. Capacities: 10 or 12 rounds. Barrels: 4 or 5 in. Weight: 19 oz. Lengths: 7.1, 8.1 in. Sights: Drift-adjustable. Features: Quick Defense trigger, firing pin block, ambidextrous slidelock and mag release, Picatinny rail. Comes with two interchangeable frame backstraps and hard case. Tactical model has threaded barrel.
Price: M2 .22 .... **$449.00–$479.00**
Price: M2 Tactical **$479.00**

WALTHER CCP M2
Caliber: 9mm. Capacity: 8-round magazine. Barrel: 3.5 in. Weight: 22 oz. Length: 6.4 in. Features: Thumb-operated safety, reversible mag release, loaded chamber indicator. Delayed blowback gas-operated action provides less recoil and muzzle jump, and easier slide operation. Available in all black or black/stainless two-tone finish.
Price: **$499.00**

WALTHER PPS M2 SERIES

Caliber: 9mm. Capacity: 6-, 7- or 8-round magazine. Barrel: 3.2 in. Sights: Optic-ready, fixed 3-dot, fixed 3-dot tritium or Crimson Trace Laserguard or factory mounted red-dot optic. Weight: 19.4 oz. Length: 6.3 in. Finish: Carbon black. Grips: Textured polymer. Features: Striker-fire, 6.1-lb. trigger pull.

Price: .... $479.00–$599.00

WALTHER P22/P22Q

Caliber: .22 LR. Barrel: 3.4 in. Weight: 19.6 oz. Length: 6.26 in. Sights: Interchangeable white dot, front, 2-dot adjustable, rear. Features: A rimfire version of the Walther P99 pistol, available in nick-el slide with black frame, Desert Camo or Digital Pink Camo frame with black slide. Military models has black/OD finish.

Price: $329.00
Price: Military $329.00

WALTHER Q4 STEEL FRAME

Caliber: 9mm. Capacity: 15-round magazine. Barrel: 4 or 4.5 in. Grips: Textured polymer, wrap around. Sights: 3-dot night. Length: 7.4 in. overall. Weight: 39.7 oz. unloaded. Finish: Matte black Tenifer. Features: Duty optimized beaver tail, Quick Defense trigger, accessory rail, oversized controls.

Price: $1,699.00

WALTHER WMP

Caliber: .22 WMR. Barrel: 4.5 in. Weight: 27.8 oz. Length: 8.2 in. Sights: Fiber-optic front, adjustable, rear and optics-ready.

Price: $549.00

WILSON COMBAT 1911 SERIES

Calibers: 9mm, .38 Super, .40 S&W; .45 ACP. Barrel: Compensated 4.1-in. hand-fit, heavy flanged cone match grade. Weight: 36.2 oz. Length: 7.7 in. overall. Grips: Cocobolo. Sights: Combat Tactical yellow rear tritium inserts, brighter green tritium front insert. Features: High-cut frontstrap, 30 LPI checkering on frontstrap and flat mainspring housing, High-Ride Beavertail grip safety. Dehorned, ambidextrous thumb safety, extended ejector, skeletonized ultralight hammer, ultralight trigger, Armor-Tuff finish on frame and slide. Introduced 1997. Made in USA by Wilson Combat. This manufacturer offers more than 100 different 1911 models ranging in price

from about $2,800 to $5,000. XTAC and Classic 6-in. models shown. Prices show a small sampling of available models.

Price: .45 ACP	$3,285.00
Price: Supergrade Commander Special	$6,130.00
Price: X-Tac Supergrade	$5,460.00
Price: X-Tac Elite	$4,380.00
Price: X-Tac Carry Comp	$4,610.00
Price: CQB	$3,430.00
Price: CQB Elite	$4,120.00
Price: Tactical Supergrade	$5,740.00

WILSON COMBAT DOUBLE-STACK SERIES

Calibers: 9mm. Capacity: 15 or 18 rounds. Barrel: 3.25, 4, or 5-in. match grade. Weight: 33.4 oz. Length: 8.7 in. overall. Grips: G10. Sights: Tactical Adjustable Battlesight rear, fiber optic. Features: High-capacity compact size Aluminum X-Frame, X-TAC frontstrap/backstrap treatment, Concealment Bullet Proof hammer, Bullet Proof thumb safety, magazine release. STF Model has aluminum TRAK-frame.

Price: EDX X9	$3,315.00
Price: STF9	$3,160.00
Price: eXperior	$3,465.00
Price: SFX9	$3,160.00

BROWNING BUCK MARK PLUS VISION AMERICANA SUPPRESSOR READY
Caliber: .22 LR. Capacity: 10-round magazine. Barrel: 5.875-in. Grip: UFX rubber overmolded grips. Sights: Optics-ready, adjustable Pro-Target with fiber-optic front sight. Length: 9.9 in. overall. Weight: 27 oz. unloaded. Finish: anodized red, white and blue. Features: Blowback operating system, aluminum barrel sleeve with lightening cuts, removable muzzle brake.
Price: **$799.00**

BROWNING BUCK MARK PLUS VISION BLACK/GOLD SUPPRESSOR READY
Caliber: .22 LR. Capacity: 10-round magazine. Barrel: 5.875-in. Grip: UFX rubber overmolded grips. Sights: Optics-ready, adjustable Pro-Target with fiber-optic front sight. Length: 9.9 in. overall. Weight: 27 oz. unloaded. Finish: anodized black and gold. Features: Blowback operating system, aluminum barrel sleeve with lightening cuts, removable muzzle brake.
Price: **$749.00**

CHIAPPA FAS 6007
Caliber: .22 LR. Capacity: 5-round magazine. Barrel: 5.63 in. Weight: 36.8 oz. Length: 13.3 in. Grips: Adjustable right-hand wood. Sights: 2-position front, adjustable target rear. Features: Aluminum receiver. Adjustable trigger.
Price: **$1,850.00**

COLT COMPETITION SERIES
Calibers: .45 ACP, .38 Super or 9mm Para. Full-size Government Model with a 5-in. national match barrel, dual-spring recoil operating system, adjustable rear and fiber-optic front sights, custom G10 Colt logo grips blued or stainless steel finish.
Price: **$949.00**

COLT GOLD CUP SERIES
Caliber: .38 Super, 9mm, or .45 ACP. Capacity: 7- or 9-round magazine. Barrel: 5 in. Weight: 38 oz. Length: 8.5 in. overall. Grips: Textured G10 or double diamond checkered walnut with gold medallion. Sights: Fiber-optic or post front, fully adjustable rear. Features: Royal blue (Gold Cup National Match) or matte stainless (Gold Cup and Gold Cup Trophy) finish. Gold Cup Trophy has magazine funnel. Comes with one magazine. Series 70 firing system.
Price: Gold Cup **$1,199.00–1,249.00**
Price: Gold Cup Trophy **$1,699.00–1,729.00**
Price: Gold Cup National Match **$1,299.00–1,349.00**

CZ 75 TS 2 SERIES
Caliber: 9mm or .40 S&W. Capacity: 17- or 20-round magazine. Barrel: 5.28 in. Weight: 48.5 oz. Length: 8.86 in. overall. Features: The handgun is built by CZ's Custom Shop. Ergonomic blue aluminum grip. Adjustable sights. TS 2 Orange is designed for competing in the IPSC Standard division and USPSA Limited division.
Price: **$1,500.00**
Price: TS 2 Orange **$2,100.00**

CZ ACCUSHADOW 2
Calibers: 9mm. Capacities: 17-round magazines. Barrel: 4.89 in. Features: Similar to Shadow 2 except with 1911-style AccuBushing for enhanced accuracy.
Price: **$2,050.00**

CZ P-10 F COMPETITION READY
Caliber: 9mm. Capacity: 19-round magazine. Barrel: 5 in. Sights: Fiber-optic front, fixed rear; optics-ready. Length: 8.5 in. overall. Weight: 30 oz. unloaded.

Finish: Nitride black with gold accents. Features: Striker-fire trigger.
Price: **$855.00**

CZ SHADOW 2 SERIES
Caliber: 9mm. Capacity: 17-round magazine. Barrel: 4.89 in. Grips: Textured blue aluminum. Sights: Fiber-optic front, HAJO rear. Length: 8.53 in. overall. Weight: 46.5 oz. unloaded. Finish: Nitride black. Features: Single-action only or DA/SA trigger. Swappable magazine release with adjustable, extended button with three settings. Ambidextrous manual thumb safety.
Price: **$1,235.00**

KEL-TEC CP33
Caliber: .22 LR. Capacity: 33-round magazine. Barrel: 5.5-in. Grip: Textured polymer. Sights: Op-tics-ready. Length: 10.6 in. overall. Weight: 24 oz. unloaded. Finish: Matte black.
Price: **$530.00**

KIMBER SUPER MATCH II
Caliber: .45 ACP. Capacity: 8-round magazine. Barrel: 5 in. Weight: 38 oz. Length: 8.7 in. overall. Grips: Rosewood double diamond. Sights: Blade front, Kimber fully adjustable rear. Features: Guaranteed to shoot 1-in. groups at 25 yards. Stainless steel frame, black KimPro slide; two-piece magazine well; premium aluminum match-grade trigger; 30 LPI frontstrap checkering; stainless match-grade barrel; ambidextrous safety; special Custom Shop markings. Introduced 1999. Made in USA by Kimber Mfg., Inc.
Price: **$2,313.00**

LES BAER 1911 NATIONAL MATCH HARDBALL
Caliber: .45 ACP. Capacity: 7-round magazine. Barrel: 5 in. Weight: 37 oz. Length: 8.5 in. overall. Grips: Checkered walnut. Sights: Baer dovetail front with under-cut post, low-mount Bo-Mar rear with hidden leaf. Features: Baer NM forged steel frame, double serrated slide and barrel with stainless bushing; slide fitted to frame; Baer match trigger with 4-lb. pull; polished feed ramp, throated barrel; checkered frontstrap, arched mainspring housing; Baer beveled magazine well; lowered, flared ejection port; tuned extractor; Baer extended ejector, checkered slide stop; recoil buff. Made in USA by Les Baer Custom, Inc.
Price: **$2,989.00**

LES BAER 1911 PPC OPEN CLASS
Caliber: .45 ACP, 9mm. Barrel: 6 in, fitted to frame. Sights: Adjustable PPC rear, dovetail front. Grips: Checkered Co-cobola. Features: Designed for NRA Police Pistol Combat matches. Lowered and flared ejection port, extended ejec-tor, polished feed ramp, throated barrel, frontstrap checkered at 30 LPI, flat serrated mainspring housing, Com-mander hammer, front and rear slide serrations. 9mm has supported chamber.
Price: **$3446.00**
Price: 9mm w/supported chamber **$3,949.00**

LES BAER 1911 BULLSEYE WADCUTTER
Similar to National Match Hardball except designed for wadcutter loads only. Polished feed ramp and barrel throat; Bo-Mar rib on slide; full-length recoil rod; Baer speed trigger with 3.5-lb. pull; Baer deluxe hammer and sear; Baer beavertail grip safety with pad; flat mainspring housing checkered 20 LPI. Blue finish; checkered walnut grips. Made in USA by Les Baer Custom, Inc.
Price: **$2,461.00**

Prices given are believed to be accurate at time of publication however, many factors affect retail pricing so exact prices are not possible.

79TH EDITION, 2025 ⊕ 501

ROCK ISLAND ARMORY PRO ULTRA MATCH SERIES

Caliber: 9mm, .40 S&W, .45 Auto, 10mm. Capacity: 8-, 16-, or 17-round magazine. Barrel: 5 or 6 in. Weight: 40 oz. Length: 8.5 in. Grips: VZ G10. Sights: Fiber-optic front, adjustable rear. Features: Two magazines, upper and lower accessory rails, extended beavertail safety. HC models use double stack magazines.
Price: .... $859.00–$1,319.00

ROCK RIVER ARMS WADCUTTER

Caliber: .45 ACP. Barrel: 5 in. Sights: Bullseye rib. Finish: Parkerized. Grips: Rosewood. Weight: 39 oz. Features: 1911 style platform.
Price: $2,995.00

ROCK RIVER ARMS BULLSEYE WADCUTTER

Caliber: 9mm or .45 ACP. Features: Standard-size 1911 pistol with rosewood grips, adjustable sights or slide mount, Lustrous blued finish, guaranteed 1.5-inch groups at 50 yards.
Price: .... $3,790.00–$4,160.00

ROCK RIVER ARMS NM HARDBALL

Caliber: .45 ACP. Features: Standard-size 1911 pistol with walnut grips, adjustable sights, Lustrous blued finish, guaranteed 2.5-inch groups at 50 yards.
Price: .... $3,835.00–$4,045.00

ROCK RIVER ARMS LIMITED MATCH

Calibers: .45 ACP, 40 S&W, .38 Super, 9mm. Barrel: 5 in. Sights: Adjustable rear, blade front. Fin-ish: Hard chrome. Features: National Match frame with beveled magazine well, front and rear slide serrations, Commander Hammer, G10 grips.
Price: $5,565.00

ROCK RIVER ARMS UNLIMITED POLICE COMPETITION

Calibers: 9mm. Barrel: 6 in. Sights: Adjustable rear, blade front. Finish: Hard chrome. Features: Guaranteed 2-inch groups at 50 yards.
Price: $5,950.00

RUGER AMERICAN COMPETITION

Caliber: 9mm. Capacity: 17-round magazine. Barrel: 5 in. Grips: Three interchangeable grip inserts. Sights: Adjustable rear, fiber-optic front, optic ready. Length: 8.3 in. overall. Weight: 34.1 oz. unloaded. Finish: Black Nitrite. Features: Slide is drilled and tapped for mounting red-dot reflex optics, ported stainless steel slide. Made in the USA.
Price: $689.00

RUGER MARK IV COMPETITION

Caliber: .22 LR. Capacity: 10-round magazine. Barrel: 6.8-in. slab-side heavy bull. Weight: 45.8 oz. Grips: Checkered laminate. Sights: .125 blade front, micro-click adjustable rear. Finish: Blued or stainless. Features: Loaded Chamber indicator; integral lock, magazine disconnect.
Price: Competition $969.00

RUGER MARK IV TARGET

Caliber: .22 LR. Capacity: 10-round magazine. Barrel: 5.5- or 10-in. heavy bull. Weight: 35.6 oz. Grips: Checkered synthetic or laminate. Sights: .125 blade front, micro-click rear, adjustable for windage and elevation.

Features: Loaded Chamber indicator; integral lock, magazine disconnect. Plastic case with lock included.
Price: Target .... $679.00–$899.00

RUGER SR1911 TARGET

Calibers: 9mm, 10mm, .45 ACP. Capacities: .45 and 10mm (8-round magazine), 9mm (9 shot). Barrel: 5 in. Weight: 39 oz. Sights: Bomar adjustable. Grips: G10 Deluxe checkered. Features: Skeletonized hammer and trigger, satin stainless finish. Introduced in 2016.
Price: $1,299.00

RUGER SR1911 COMPETITION

Calibers: 9mm. Capacities: .10+1. Barrel: 5 in. Weight: 39 oz. Sights: Fiber-optic front, adjustable target rear. Grips: Hogue Piranha G10 Deluxe checkered. Features: Skeletonized hammer and trigger, satin stainless finish, hand-fitted frame and slide, competition trigger, competition barrel with polished feed ramp. From Ruger Competition Shop. Introduced in 2016.
Price: $2,849.00

SIG SAUER P210 TARGET

Caliber: 9mm. Capacity: 8-round magazine. Barrel: 5 in. Grip: Checkered wood. Sights: Adjustable. Length: 8.4 in. overall. Weight: 36.9 ozs. unloaded. Finish: Nitron.
Price: $2,179.00

SMITH & WESSON MODEL 41 TARGET

Caliber: .22 LR. Capacity: 10-round magazine. Barrels: 5.5 in., 7 in. Weight: 41 oz. (5.5-in. barrel). Length: 10.5 in. overall (5.5-in. barrel). Grips: Checkered walnut with modified thumb rest, usable with either hand. Sights: .125 in. Patridge on ramp base; micro-click rear-adjustable for windage and elevation. Features: .375 in. wide, grooved trigger; adjustable trigger stop drilled and tapped. Top rail on some models.
Price: .... $1,759.00–$2,079.00

TAURUS TX22 COMPETITION

Caliber: .22 LR. Capacity: 10- or 16-round magazine. Barrel: 5.25 in. Grip: Textured polymer, wrap around. Sights: Adjustable rear, optics-ready. Length: 8.21 in. overall. Weight: 17.3 oz. unloaded. Finish: Matte black. Features: Red-dot optics-ready with mounting plates. The compact model has a 3.06-in. barrel. Steel Challenge Ready (SCR) model has a compensator. Competition models are op-tics-ready.
Price: Competition $537.00
Price: Competition SCR $590.00

TRISTAR S.P.S. PANTERA

Calibers: 9mm. Capacity: 18-round magazine. Barrel: 5-in., match-grade. Sights: Bomar-type, fully adjustable rear, fiber-optic front. Weight: 36.6 oz. Finish: Black, black chrome, chrome. Grips: Pol-ymer. Features: Polymer frame, checkered frontstrap serrations, skeletonized trigger and hammer, flared and lowered ejection port, ambidextrous safety, wide mag well, full dust cover. Imported from Spain by TriStar.
Price: .... $2,135.00–$2,290.00

WALTHER P22 TARGET

Caliber: .22 LR. Barrel: 5 in. Weight: 20 oz. Length: 6.26 in. Sights: Interchangeable white dot, front, 2-dot adjustable, rear. Features: Black frame.
Price: $399.00

WALTHER PDP MATCH SERIES

Caliber: 9mm. Capacity: 20-round magazine. Barrel: 5 in. Grip: Textured polymer. Sights: 3-dot, optics ready. Length: 8.3 in. overall. Weight: 26.9 ozs. unloaded. Finish: Black. Features: Accessory rail, Dynamic Performance Trigger, magwell. SF model has steel frame.
Price: $1,099.00
Price: SF $1,899.00

WALTHER Q5 MATCH STEEL FRAME

Caliber: 9mm. Capacity: 15-round magazine. Barrel: 5 in. Grips: Textured polymer. Sights: LPA fi-ber-optic front, adj. rear. Length: 8.7 in. overall. Weight: 41.6 oz. unloaded. Finish: Matte black. Features: Metal frame, optic ready, accessory rail.
Price: $1,899.00

Prices given are believed to be accurate at time of publication however, many factors affect retail pricing so exact prices are not possible.

AMERICAN PRECISION FIREARMS R-1 3"
Caliber: .357 Magnum, 3-in. barrel, fixed sights, wooden grips.
Price:..$1,410.00
Price: Blued...$1,270.00

AMERICAN PRECISION FIREARMS R-1 4"
Caliber: .357 Magnum, 4-in. barrel, stainless steel, adjustable sights.
Price:..$1,480.00
Price: Blued $1,330.00

AMERICAN PRECISION FIREARMS R-1 6"
Caliber: .357 Magnum, 6-in. barrel, adjustable sights, stainless steel.
Price:..$1,560.00
Price: Blued $1,410.00

CHARTER ARMS BOOMER
Caliber: .44 Special. Capacity: 5-round cylinder. Barrel: 2 in., ported.
Weight: 20 oz. Grips: Full rubber combat. Sights: Fixed.
Price: Blued $443.00

CHARTER ARMS CHIC LADY & CHIC LADY DAO
Caliber: .38 Special. Capacity: 5-round cylinder. Barrel: 2 in. Weight: 12 oz.

Grip: Combat. Sights: Fixed. Features: 2-tone pink or lavender & stainless with aluminum frame. American made by Charter Arms.
Price: Chic Lady $473.00
Price: Chic Lady DAO $483.00

CHARTER ARMS OFF DUTY
Caliber: .38 Special. Barrel: 2 in. Weight: 12.5 oz. Sights: Blade front, notch rear. Features: 5-round cylinder, aluminum casting, DAO with concealed hammer. Also available with semi-concealed hammer. American made by Charter Arms.
Price: Aluminum $404.00
Price: Crimson Trace Laser grip $657.00

CHARTER ARMS MAG PUG
Caliber: .357 Mag. Capacity: 5-round cylinder. Barrel: 2.2 in. Weight: 23 oz. Sights: Blade front, notch rear. Features: American made by Charter Arms.
Price: Blued or stainless $400.00
Price: 4.4-in. full-lug barrel.. $470.00
Price: Crimson Trace Laser Grip.. $609.00

CHARTER ARMS PITBULL
Calibers: 9mm, 40 S&W, .45 ACP. Capacity: 5-round cylinder. Barrel: 2.2 in. Weights: 20–22 oz. Sights: Fixed rear, ramp front. Grips: Rubber. Features: Matte stainless steel frame or Nitride frame. Moon clips not required for 9mm, .45 ACP.
Price: 9mm $502.00
Price: .40 S&W $489.00
Price: .45 ACP $489.00
Price: 9mm Black Nitride finish $522.00
Price: .40, .45 Black Nitride finish.. $509.00

CHARTER ARMS PATHFINDER
Calibers: .22 LR or .22 Mag. Capacity: 6-round cylinder. Barrel: 2 in., 4 in. Weights: 20 oz. (12 oz. Lite model). Grips: Full. Sights: Fixed or adjustable (Target). Features: Stainless finish and frame.
Price .22 LR $365.00
Price .22 Mag $367.00
Price: Lite $379.00
Price: Target $409.00

CHARTER ARMS THE PINK LADY
Caliber: .38 Special. Capacity: 6-round cylinder. Barrel: 2.2 in. Grips: Full. Sights: Fixed rear, LitePipe front. Weight: 12 oz. Features: As the name indicates, the Pink Lady has a pink and stainless steel finish. This is an aluminum-framed revolver from the Undercover Lite series.
Price: $357.00

CHARTER ARMS UNDERCOVER
Caliber: .38 Special +P. Capacity: 6-round cylinder. Barrel: 2 in. Weight: 12 oz. Sights: Blade front, notch rear. Features: American made by Charter Arms.
Price: Blued $346.00

CHARTER ARMS UNDERCOVER LITE
Caliber: .38 Special. Capacity: 6-round cylinder. Barrel: 2.2 in. Grips: Full.
Sights: Fixed rear, LitePipe front. Weight: 12 oz. Features: Aluminum-
framed lightweight revolver with anodized finish. Lots of power in a
feather-weight package.
Price: $357.00

CHIAPPA RHINO
Calibers: .357 Magnum, 9mm, .40 S&W. Features: 2-, 4-, 5- or 6-inch barrel;
fixed or adjustable sights; visible hammer or hammerless design. Weights:
24–33 oz. Walnut or synthetic grips with black frame; hexagonal-shaped
cylinder. Unique design fires from bottom chamber of cylinder.
Price: From .... $1,090.00-$1,465.00

**CHIAPPA RHINO REVOLVER 30DS NEBULA .357 MAG/3-INCH BBL
(30SAR-CALIFORNIA COMPLIANT)**
Type of Gun: Revolver, Caliber: .357 Magnum, Action: Single/Double, Barrel
Length: 3 in. (76mm) Capacity: 6. Feed In: manual, Trigger System: Single.
Grips: Blue laminate medium. Front Sight: Fixed red fiber optic. Rear Sight:
Adjustable elevation and windage green fiber optic, Safety: Internal, Weight:
1.7 lbs. Length: 7.5 in. (190 mm) Material: Machined 7075-T6 alloy frame/
steel cylinder and barrel finish: Muti-Color PVD. Extraction: Manual. Notes:
Includes three moon clips, removal tool, gun lock and black leather holster.
Price: $1,912.00

CHIAPPA RHINO 60DS STORMHUNTER
Caliber: 357 Magnum. Capacity: 6. Action: Double, Barrel Length: 6-in.
Trigger System: Single, Grips: Stippled walnut. Sights: Black. Rear Sight: Adj.
fiber optic. Safety: Cylinder block, cylinder rotation, hammer block. Specs:
1:19 twist rate. Total Length: 10.5 in. Material: Machined 7075-T6 alloy
frame, steel cylinder and barrel. Net Weight: 2.1 lbs. Finishes: Storm Hunter.
Extraction: Manual. Ships with manual and three moon clips. Note: Special
Edition.
Price: $1,820.00

COBRA SHADOW
Caliber: .38 Special +P. Capacity: 5 rounds. Barrel: 1.875 in. Weight: 15 oz.
Aluminum frame with stainless steel barrel and cylinder. Length: 6.375
in. Grips: Rosewood, black rubber or Crimson Trace Laser. Features: Black
anodized, titanium anodized or custom colors including gold, red, pink and
blue.
Price: $369.00
Price: Rosewood grips $434.00
Price: Crimson Trace Laser grips........................... $625.00

COLT COBRA
Caliber: .38 Special. Capacity: 6 rounds. Sights: Fixed rear, fiber optic
red front. Grips: Hogue rubbed stippled with finger grooves. Weight: 25
oz. Finish: Matte stainless. Same name as classic Colt model made from
1950–1986 but totally new design. Introduced in 2017. King Cobra has a
heavy-duty frame and 3-inch barrel.
Price: $699.00
Price: King Cobra... $899.00

COLT NIGHT COBRA
Caliber; .38 Special. Capacity: 6 rounds. Grips: Black synthetic VC G10.
Sight: Tritium front night sight. DAO operation with bobbed hammer.
Features a linear leaf spring design for smooth DA trigger pull.
Price: $899.00

COLT PYTHON
Caliber: .357 Magnum. Capacity: 6-round cylinder. Barrels: 4.25 and 6 in.
Grips: Walnut. Sights: Fully adjustable rear, fixed red ramp interchangeable
front. Weights: 42 oz. (4.25 in.), 46 oz. (6 in.). Features: New and improved
and available only in stainless steel. Has recessed target crown and user-
interchangeable front sight.
Price: $1,499.00
Price: 2.5-in. bbl stainless................................$1,500.00
Price: 4.25-, 6-in. bbl blued..............................$1,600.00
Price: 3-, 4.25-, 6-in. bbl matte stainless.........$1,300.00

COLT PYTHON 3-INCH BARREL
Caliber: .357 Magnum. Capacity: 6-round cylinder. Barrels: 3, 4.25 and 6 in.
Grips: Walnut. Sights: Fully adjustable rear, fixed red ramp interchangeable
front. Weight: 42 oz. (4.25 in.), 46 oz. (6 in.). Features: New and improved
and available only in stainless steel. Has recessed target crown and user-
interchangeable front sight.
Price: $1,499.00

COLT PYTHON COMBAT ELITE

Caliber: .357 Magnum/.38 Special. Barrel: 3-in. polished stainless steel w/ recessed target crown. Capacity: 6 Rounds. Sights: Front night sight with adjustable target rear. Grips: Combat-style G10. Cylinder: Polished, unfluted. Frame: Stainless steel. Overall Weight: 2.5 lbs. Overall Length: 8.5 in.

Price...$1,500.00

LIPSEY'S EXCLUSIVE COLT PYTHON (TYLER GUN WORKS)

Caliber: .357 Magnum/.38 Special, 3-in. barrel. Tyler Gun Works Premier Grade-Engraved with stag grips.

Price: $2,400.00
Price: 4-in. TGW Premier Grade-engraved w/ stag grips.............$2,400.00

LIPSEY'S EXCLUSIVE COLT PYTHON 2.5" (TYLER GUN WORKS)

Caliber: 357 Mag./.38 Special. 2.5-in. barrel, polished stainless steel. Grips: American holly. Nitre Blue PVD accents.

Price:..$1,900.00

COLT ANACONDA

Caliber: .44 Magnum. Capacity: 6 rounds. Barrel: 6 and 8 in. Grip: Hogue Overmolded. Sights: Fully adjustable rear, fixed red ramp interchangeable front. Weight: 53 oz. (6 in.), 59 oz. (8 in.) Features: New and improved and available in stainless steel only. Has recessed target crown and user-interchangeable front sight.

Price: $1,499.00

COMANCHE II-A

Caliber: .38 Special. Capacity: 6-round cylinder. Barrels: 3 or 4 in. Weights: 33, 35 oz. Lengths: 8, 8.5 in. overall. Grips: Rubber. Sights: Fixed. Features:

Blued finish, alloy frame. Distributed by SGS Importers.
Price: $220.00

DAN WESSON 715

Caliber: .357 Magnum. Capacity: 6-round cylinder. Barrel: 6-inch heavy barrel with full lug. Weight: 38 oz. Lengths: 8, 8.5 in. overall. Grips: Hogue rubber with finger grooves. Sights: Adjustable rear, interchangeable front blade. Features: Stainless steel. Interchangeable barrel assembly. Reintroduced in 2014. 715 Pistol Pack comes with 4-, 6- and 8-in. interchangeable barrels.

Price: From $1,558.00
Price: Pistol Pack...$1,999.00

DIAMONDBACK SIDEKICK

Caliber: .22 LR/.22 Mag. Convertible. Action: Single & Double Grips: Checkered glass filled Nylon. Capacity: 9 rounds., Front Sight: Blade., Rear Sight: Integral., Barrel length: 4.5 inch. Overall Length: 9.875 in. Frame & Handle Material: Zinc., Frame & Handle Finish: Black Cerakote. Weight: 32.5 oz., Twist: 1:16 RH. Grooves: 6. The Sidekick is chambered in both .22 LR and .22 Mag with 9-shot cylinders. It has a 9-round capacity and weighs 32.5 ounces. Swing-out cylinders allow the user to switch between .22 LR and .22 Mag in seconds.

Price: $320.00

DIAMONDBACK SDR

Caliber: .357 Mag./.38 Special +P. Capacity: 6. Length: 6.53 in. Width: 1.38 in. Height: 4.44 in. Weight: 21.20 oz. Frame Material: Forged stainless steel. Frame Finish: Polished. Barrel Length: 2.0 in. Barrel Material: Stainless steel. Barrel Finish: Polished. Twist: 1:18.75 RH. Length: 6.53 in. Action: DA/SA. Trigger Pull: 9–11.5 lbs., non-stacking. Sights: Front fixed fiber optic orange. Rear Sight: Low-profile dovetail fiber optic green. Grip: Black rubber w/ Diamondback logo.

Price:...$780.00

EAA WINDICATOR

Calibers: .38 Special, .357 Mag Capacity: 6-round cylinder. Barrels: 2 in., 4 in. Weight: 30 oz. (4 in.). Length: 8.5 in. overall (4 in. bbl.). Grips: Rubber with finger grooves. Sights: Blade front, fixed rear. Features: Swing-out cylinder; hammer block safety; blue or nickel finish. Introduced 1991. Imported from Germany by European American Armory.

Price: .38 Spec. from $354.00
Price: .357 Mag, steel frame from $444.00

Prices given are believed to be accurate at time of publication however, many factors affect retail pricing so exact prices are not possible.

79TH EDITION, 2025 ◈ 505

HENRY BIG BOY REVOLVER

Caliber: .357 Mag./.38 Spl. Capacity: 6. Action Type: Traditional Double-Action. Additional Specifications: Barrel Length: 4 in. Barrel Type: Round blued steel. Rate of Twist: 1:16. Overall Length: 9 in. Weight: 34 oz.(birdshead), 35 oz. (gunfighter). Receiver Finish: Polished blued steel. Rear Sight: Fixed notch. Front Sight: Screw-on post. Stock Material: American Walnut. Safety: Transfer Bar. Embellishments/Extras: Interchangeable high/medium/low front sights, birdshead or gunfighter grip options.
Price: **$930.00**

KIMBER K6S

Caliber: .357 Magnum. Capacity: 6-round cylinder. Barrel: 2-inch full lug. Grips: Gray rubber. Finish: Satin stainless. Kimber's first revolver, claimed to be world's lightest production 6-shot .357 Magnum. DAO design with non-stacking match-grade trigger. Introduced 2016. CDP model has laminated checkered rosewood grips, Tritium night sights, two-tone black DLC/brushed stainless finish, match grade trigger.

Price:	**$878.00**
Price: 3-in. Barrel	**$899.00**
Price: Deluxe Carry w/Medallion grips	**$1,088.00**
Price: Custom Defense Package	**$1,155.00**
Price: Crimson Trace Laser Grips	**$1,177.00**
Price: TLE	**$999.00**
Price: DA/SA	**$949.00**

KIMBER K6s DASA TARGET

Caliber: .357 Magnum. Capacity: 6-round cylinder. Barrel: 4 in. Grips: Walnut laminate, oversized. Sights: Fully adjustable rear, fiber-optic front. Features: The DASA is the next evolution of the K6s. The DASA is outfitted with a double- and single-action trigger mechanism. Kimber's K6s revolvers feature the purportedly smallest cylinder capable of housing 6 rounds of .357 Magnum at 1.39-inch diameter, making for a very slim and streamlined package.
Price: **$989.00**

KIMBER K6s DASA COMBAT

Caliber: .357 Magnum. Capacity: 6-round cylinder. Barrel: 4 in. Grips: Walnut laminate, oversized with finger grooves. Sights: Fixed front and rear with white dots. Features: The DASA Combat is outfitted with a double- and single-action trigger mechanism. Kimber's K6s DASA revolvers have a smooth no-stack double-action trigger and a crisp 3.25- to 4.25-lb. single-action pull. The K6s DASA revolvers are equipped with knurled hammer spur.
Price: **$989.00**

KIMBER K6s DASA TEXAS EDITION

Caliber: .357 Magnum. Capacity: 6-round cylinder. Barrel: 2 in. Grips: Ivory G10. Sights: Fixed front and rear with white dots. Features: The Texas Edition is adorned with ivory G10 grips with the state moto, name and flag on this special edition. The satin finish has American Western cut scroll engraving on the barrel, frame and cylinder. The K6s DASA Texas Edition revolvers are equipped with knurled hammer spur.
Price: **$1,359.00**

KIMBER K6s ROYAL

Caliber: .357 Magnum. Capacity: 6-round cylinder. Barrel: 2 in. Grips: Walnut. Sights: Fixed brass-bead front and rear with white dots. Features: The K6s Royal features a 2-inch barrel for easy concealment. The dovetailed white-dot rear sight complements the brass-bead front sight. The Royal's stainless steel is hand polished to a high shine and a Dark Oil DLC is applied for a unique look.
Price: **$1,699.00**

KIMBER K6XS

Caliber: .38 Special. Capacity: 6. Barrel Length: 2-in. Overall Length: 6.8 in. Lightweight aluminum frame, stainless steel barrel with glass bead finish. 5R rifling. Non-stacking trigger. Action: DAO. Finish: Silver KimPro II. Grips: Houge black rubber with Kimber logo. Sights: Orange dot front; fixed rear.
Price: **$680.00**

KORTH USA

Calibers: .22 LR, .22 WMR, .32 S&W Long, .38 Special, .357 Mag., 9mm. Capacity: 6-shot. Barrels: 3, 4, 5.25, 6 in. Weights: 36–52 oz. Grips: Combat, Sport: Walnut, Palisander, Amboina, Ivory. Finish: German Walnut, matte with oil finish, adjustable ergonomic competition style. Sights: Adjustable Patridge (Sport) or Baughman (Combat), interchangeable and adjustable rear w/Patridge front (Target) in blue and matte. Features: DA/SA, 3 models, over 50 configurations, externally adjustable trigger stop and weight, interchangeable cylinder, removable wide-milled trigger shoe on Target model. Deluxe models are highly engraved editions. Available finishes

include high polish blued finish, plasma coated in high polish or matte silver, gold, blue or charcoal. Many deluxe options available. From Korth USA.
Price: From **$8,000.00**
Price: Deluxe Editions, from **$12,000.00**

KORTH SKYHAWK
Caliber: 9mm. Barrels: 2 or 3 in. Sights: Adjustable rear with gold bead front. Grips: Hogue with finger grooves. Features: Polished trigger, skeletonized hammer. Imported by Nighthawk Custom.
Price: **$1,699.00**

NIGHTHAWK CUSTOM/KORTH-WAFFEN NXR
Caliber: .44 Magnum. Capacity: 6-round cylinder Barrel: 6 in. Grips: Ivory G10. Sights: Adjustable rear, fast-changeable front. Weight: 3.05 lbs. Features: The NXR is a futuristic looking stainless steel double-action revolver that is black DLC finished. Comes equipped with a removable under-barrel balancing lug/weight. Picatinny rail on top of barrel and underneath for easy accessory mounting.
Price: **$5,299.00**

KORTH-NIGHTHAWK CUSTOM MONGOOSE
Caliber: .357 Mag. Optional 9mm cyl. Barrel lengths: 2.75, 3, 4, 5.25, and 6 in. Full-lug with black DLC finish A silver DLC-finished .357 Magnum Mongoose is available with 4-, 5.25-, or 6-in. barrel configurations.
Price: .... **$3,699.00–$4,999.00**

KORTH-NIGHTHAWK CUSTOM VINTAGE
Caliber: .357 Magnum. Barrel: 4- or 6-in. half-lug. Color-casehardened frame and barrel and charcoal blue cylinder.
Price: **$8,999.00**

KORTH-NIGHTHAWK CUSTOM NXA
Caliber: .357 Magnum. Capacity: 8. Weight Empty: 2.75 lbs., Barrel Length: 6 in. Overall Length: 11.65 in. Width: 1.72 in. Height: 6.38 in. Barrel: 416R, Features: DLC finish, anodized, red aluminum barrel shroud. Hammer-forged precision barrel. Fully adjustable rear sight. Removable side panels on front sight. Single-/double-action trigger. Wood grip in red/black, integrated Picatinny rail in the frame. Cylinder release classic back left. Easy reload via wide-swinging cylinder. Cylinder is moon clip cut, changeable cylinder in 9mm Luger w/ moon clip cut (available).
Price: **$5,300.00**

KORTH-NIGHTHAWK CUSTOM SUPER SPORT GTA SERIES
Caliber: .357 Magnum. Capacity: 6. Weight Empty: 41.19 oz. Barrel Length: 6 in. Overall Length: 11.35 in. Width: 1.72 in. Height: 6.25 in. Barrel: 416R. Features: DLC finish, anodized, blue, red, or green aluminum barrel shroud. Hammer-forged precision barrel. Fully adjustable rear sight. Removable side panels on front sight. Single-/double-action trigger. Wood grip in blue/gray, red/black, or green/black. New style cylinder release. Integrated Picatinny rail for scope/red-dot mount. Ventilated barrel shroud for faster cooling. Easy reload via wide-swinging cylinder. Modern. Cylinder includes moon clip cut.
Price: **$6,200.00**

ROSSI RM66
Caliber: 357 Magnum. Capacity: 6 rounds. Rear Sight: Adjustable. Front Sight: Removable Serrated Blade. Finish: Stainless Steel. Barrel Length: 6 inches. Grips: wrap-around rubber. Medium-sized frame. Overall Length: 11.14 in. Overall Height: 5.47 in. Overall Width 1.46 in. Overall Weight: 34.40 oz. (unloaded). Safety: Hammer Block.
Price: **$620.00**

ROSSI RP63
Caliber: .357 Magnum. Capacity: 6 rounds. Rear Sight: Fixed. Front Sight: Removable Serrated blade. Finish: Stainless steel. Barrel Length: 3-in. Grips: Rubber. Small-sized frame. Overall Length: 7.95 in. Overall Height: 5.20 in. Overall Width 1.46 in. Overall Weight: 27.30 oz. (unloaded). Safety: Hammer Block.
Price: **$460.00**

RUGER (CUSTOM SHOP) SUPER GP100 COMPETITION REVOLVER
Calibers: .357 Magnum, 9mm. Capacity: 8-round cylinder. Barrels: 5.5 and 6 in. Grips: Hogue hand-finished hardwood. Sights: Adjustable rear, fiber-optic front. Weights: 47 oz., 45.6 oz. Features: Designed for competition, the new Super GP100 is essentially a Super Redhawk with the frame extension removed and replaced by a shrouded, cold hammer-forged barrel. The Super GP utilizes the superior action of the Super Redhawk. The high-strength stainless steel cylinder has a PVD finish and is extensively fluted for weight reduction. Comes with high-quality, impact-resistant case.
Price: **$1,549.00**

Prices given are believed to be accurate at time of publication however, many factors affect retail pricing so exact prices are not possible.

79TH EDITION, 2025 ⊕ **507**

RUGER GP-100

Calibers: .357 Mag., .327 Federal Mag, .44 Special Capacities: 6- or 7-round cylinder, .327 Federal Mag (7-shot), .44 Special (5-shot), .22 LR, (10-shot). Barrels: 3-in. full shroud, 4-in. full shroud, 6-in. full shroud. (.44 Special offered only with 3-in. barrel.) Weights: 36–45 oz. Sights: Fixed; adjustable on 4- and 6-in. full shroud barrels. Grips: Ruger Santoprene Cushioned Grip with Goncalo Alves inserts. Features: Uses action, frame features of both the Security-Six and Redhawk revolvers. Full-length, short ejector shroud. Satin blue and stainless steel.

Price: Blued **$769.00**
Price: Satin stainless **$799.00**
Price: .22 LR **$829.00**
Price: .44 Spl. **$829.00**
Price: 7-round cylinder, 327 Fed or .357 Mag **$899.00**

RUGER GP-100 MATCH CHAMPION

Calibers: 10mm Magnum, .357 Mag. Capacity: 6-round cylinder. Barrel: 4.2-in. half shroud, slab-sided. Weight: 38 oz. Sights: Fixed rear, fiber optic front. Grips: Hogue Stippled Hardwood. Features: Satin stainless steel finish.
Price: Blued **$969.00**

RUGER LCR

Calibers: .22 LR (8-round cylinder), .22 WMR, .327 Fed. Mag., .38 Special and .357 Mag., 5-round cylinder. Barrel: 1.875 in. Weights: 13.5–17.10 oz. Length: 6.5 in. overall. Grips: Hogue Tamer or Crimson Trace Lasergrips. Sights: Pinned ramp front, U-notch integral rear. Features: The Ruger Lightweight Compact Revolver (LCR), a 13.5 ounce, small frame revolver with a smooth, easy-to-control trigger and highly manageable recoil.
Price: .22 LR, .22 WMR, .38 Spl., iron sights **$579.00**
Price: 9mm, .327, .357, iron sights..................................... **$669.00**
Price: .22 LR, .22WMR, .38 Spl. Crimson Trace Lasergrip.................... **$859.00**
Price: 9mm, .327, .357, Crimson Trace Lasergrip **$949.00**

RUGER LCRX

Calibers: .38 Special +P, 9mm, .327 Fed. Mag., .22 WMR. Barrels: 1.875

in. or 3 in. Features: Similar to LCR except this model has visible hammer, adjustable rear sight. The 3-inch barrel model has longer grip. 9mm comes with three moon clips.
Price: **$579.00**
Price: .327 Mag., .357 Mag., 9mm **$669.00**

TALO EXCLUSIVE RUGER LCRX

Caliber: 9mm Luger. Capacity: 5. Barrel Length: 3 in. Twist: 1:16 inch RH. Weight: 21.6 oz. Height: 5.80 in. Overall Length: 7.5 in. Features: TALO distributor exclusive: Limited availability. Grip: Hogue Tamer Monogrip. Front Sight: Replaceable, pinned ramp. Cylinder finish: PVD. Rear Sight: Adjustable black blade. Finish: Matte black.
Price:.. **$865.00**

RUGER SP-101

Calibers: .22 LR (8 shot); .327 Federal Mag. (6-shot), 9mm, .38 Spl, .357 Mag. (5-shot). Barrels: 2.25, 3 1/16, 4.2 in (.22 LR, .327 Mag., .357 Mag). Weights: 25–30 oz. Sights: Adjustable or fixed, rear; fiber-optic or black ramp front. Grips: Ruger Cushioned Grip with inserts. Features: Compact, small frame, double-action revolver. Full-length ejector shroud. Stainless steel only.
Price: Fixed sights **$719.00**
Price: Adjustable rear, fiber optic front sights **$769.00**
Price: .327 Fed Mag 3-in bbl **$769.00**
Price: .327 Fed Mag **$749.00**

RUGER REDHAWK

Calibers: .44 Rem. Mag., .45 Colt and .45 ACP/.45 Colt combo. Capacity: 6-round cylinder. Barrels: 2.75, 4.2, 5.5, 7.5 in. (.45 Colt in 4.2 in. only.) Weight: 54 oz. (7.5 bbl.). Length: 13 in. overall (7.5-in. barrel). Grips: Square butt cushioned grip panels. TALO Distributor exclusive 2.75-in. barrel stainless model has round butt, wood grips. Sights: Interchangeable Patridge-type front, rear adjustable for windage and elevation. Features: Stainless steel, brushed satin finish, blued ordnance steel. 9.5 sight radius. Introduced 1979.
Price: **$1,079.00**
Price: Hunter Model 7.5-in. bbl... **$1,159.00**
Price: TALO 2.75 in. model **$1,069.00**

Prices given are believed to be accurate at time of publication however, many factors affect retail pricing so exact prices are not possible.

RUGER SUPER REDHAWK
Calibers: 10mm, .44 Rem. Mag., .454 Casull, .480 Ruger. Capacities: 5- or 6-round cylinder. Barrels: 2.5 in. (Alaskan), 5.5 in., 6.5 in. (10mm), 7.5 in. or 9.5 in. Weight: 44–58 oz. Length: 13 in. overall (7.5-in. barrel). Grips: Hogue Tamer Monogrip. Features: Similar to standard Redhawk except has heavy extended frame with Ruger Integral Scope Mounting System on wide topstrap. Wide hammer spur lowered for better scope clearance. Incorporates mechanical design features and improvements of GP-100. Ramp front sight base has Redhawk-style interchangeable insert sight blades, adjustable rear sight. Alaskan model has 2.5-inch barrel. Satin stainless steel and low-glare stainless finishes. Introduced 1987.
Price: .44 Magnum, 10mm **$1,159.00**
Price: .454 Casull, .480 Ruger **$1,199.00**
Price: Alaskan, .44 Mag, .454 Casull, .480 Ruger **$1,189.00**

RUGER SUPER REDHAWK 22 HORNET
Caliber: .22 Hornet. Capacity: 8. Overall Length: 15 in. Barrel Length: 9.50 in. Twist: 1:9. Weight: 66 oz. RH Grip: Hogue Tamer Monogrip. Finish: Satin stainless. Front Sight: HiViz Green. Rear Sight: Adjustable.
Price: **$1,500.00**

SMITH & WESSON GOVERNOR
Calibers: .410 Shotshell (2.5 in.), .45 ACP, .45 Colt. Capacity: 6 rounds. Barrel: 2.75 in. Length: 7.5 in., (2.5 in. barrel). Grip: Synthetic. Sights: Front: Dovetailed tritium night sight or black ramp, rear: fixed. Grips: Synthetic. Finish: Matte black or matte silver (Silver Edition). Weight: 29.6 oz. Features: Capable of chambering a mixture of .45 Colt, .45 ACP and .410 gauge 2.5-inch shotshells, the Governor is suited for both close and distant encounters, allowing users to customize the load to their preference. Scandium alloy frame, stainless steel cylinder. Packaged with two full moon clips and three 2-shot clips.
Price: **$869.00**
Price: w/Crimson Trace Laser Grip **$1,179.00**

SMITH & WESSON J-FRAME
The J-frames are the smallest Smith & Wesson wheelguns and come in a variety of chamberings, barrel lengths and materials as noted in the individual model listings.

SMITH & WESSON 60LS/642LS LADYSMITH
Calibers: .38 Special +P, .357 Mag. Capacity: 5-round cylinder. Barrels: 1.875 in. (642LS); 2.125 in. (60LS) Weights: 14.5 oz. (642LS); 21.5 oz. (60LS); Length: 6.6 in. overall (60LS). Grips: Wood. Sights: Black blade, serrated ramp front, fixed notch rear. 642 CT has Crimson Trace Laser Grips. Features: 60LS model has a Chiefs Special-style frame. 642LS has Centennial-style frame, frosted matte finish, smooth combat wood grips. Introduced 1996. Comes in a fitted carry/storage case. Introduced 1989. Made in USA by Smith & Wesson.

Price: (642LS) **$499.00**
Price: (60LS) **$759.00**
Price: (642 CT) **$699.00**

SMITH & WESSON MODEL 63
Caliber: .22 LR Capacity: 8-round cylinder. Barrel: 3 in. Weight: 26 oz. Length: 7.25 in. overall. Grips: Black synthetic. Sights: Hi-Viz fiber optic front sight, adjustable black blade rear sight. Features: Stainless steel construction throughout. Made in USA by Smith & Wesson.
Price: **$769.00**

SMITH & WESSON MODEL 442/637/638/642 AIRWEIGHT
Caliber: .38 Special +P. Capacity: 5-round cylinder. Barrels: 1.875 in., 2.5 in. Weight: 15 oz. Length: 6.375 in. overall. Grips: Soft rubber. Sights: Fixed, serrated ramp front, square notch rear. Features: A family of J-frame .38 Special revolvers with aluminum-alloy frames. Model 637; Chiefs Special-style frame with exposed hammer. Introduced 1996. Models 442, 642; Centennial-style frame, enclosed hammer. Model 638, Bodyguard style, shrouded hammer. Comes in a fitted carry/storage case. Introduced 1989. Made in USA by Smith & Wesson.
Price: From **$469.00**
Price: Laser Max Frame Mounted Red Laser sight **$539.00**

SMITH & WESSON MODELS 637 CT/638 CT
Similar to Models 637, 638 and 642 but with Crimson Trace Laser Grips.
Price: **$699.00**

SMITH & WESSON MODEL 317 AIRLITE
Caliber: .22 LR. Capacity: 8-round cylinder. Barrel: 1.875 in. Weight: 10.5 oz. Length: 6.25 in. overall (1.875-in. barrel). Grips: Rubber. Sights: Serrated ramp front, fixed notch rear. Features: Aluminum alloy, carbon and stainless steels, Chiefs Special-style frame with exposed hammer. Smooth combat trigger. Clear Cote finish. Model 317 Kit Gun has adjustable rear sight, fiber optic front. Introduced 1997.
Price: **$759.00**

SMITH & WESSON MODEL 340/340PD AIRLITE SC CENTENNIAL
Calibers: .357 Mag., 38 Special +P. Capacity: 5-round cylinder. Barrel:

Prices given are believed to be accurate at time of publication however, many factors affect retail pricing so exact prices are not possible.

79TH EDITION, 2025 ⬦ **509**

1.875 in. Weight: 12 oz. Length: 6.375 in. overall (1.875-in. barrel). Grips: Rounded butt rubber. Sights: Black blade front, rear notch Features: Centennial-style frame, enclosed hammer. Internal lock. Matte silver finish. Scandium alloy frame, titanium cylinder, stainless steel barrel liner. Made in USA by Smith & Wesson.
Price: **$1,019.00**

SMITH & WESSON MODEL 351PD
Caliber: .22 Mag. Capacity: 5-round cylinder. Barrel: 1.875 in. Weight: 10.6 oz. Length: 6.25 in. overall (1.875-in. barrel). Sights: HiViz front sight, rear notch. Grips: Wood. Features: 7-shot, aluminum-alloy frame. Chiefs Special-style frame with exposed hammer. Nonreflective matte-black finish. Internal lock. Made in USA by Smith & Wesson.
Price: **$759.00**

SMITH & WESSON MODEL 360/360PD AIRLITE CHIEF'S SPECIAL
Calibers: .357 Mag., .38 Special +P. Capacity: 5-round cylinder. Barrel: 1.875 in. Weight: 12 oz. Length: 6.375 in. overall (1.875-in. barrel). Grips: Rounded butt rubber. Sights: Red ramp front, fixed rear notch. Features: Chief's Special-style frame with exposed hammer. Internal lock. Scandium alloy frame, titanium cylinder, stainless steel barrel. Model 360 has unfluted cylinder. Made in USA by Smith & Wesson.
Price: 360 .... **$770.00**
Price: 360PD **$1,019.00**

SMITH & WESSON BODYGUARD 38
Caliber: .38 Special +P. Capacity: 5-round cylinder. Barrel: 1.9 in. Weight: 14.3 oz. Length: 6.6 in. Grip: Synthetic. Sights: Front: Black ramp, Rear: fixed, integral with backstrap. Plus: Integrated laser sight. Finish: Matte black. Features: The first personal protection series that comes with an integrated laser sight.
Price: **$539.00**

SMITH & WESSON MODEL 640 CENTENNIAL DA ONLY
Calibers: .357 Mag., .38 Special +P. Capacity: 5-round cylinder. Barrel: 2.125 in. Weight: 23 oz. Length: 6.75 in. overall. Grips: Uncle Mike's Boot grip. Sights: Tritium Night Sights. Features: Stainless steel. Fully concealed hammer, snag-proof smooth edges. Internal lock.
Price: **$839.00**

SMITH & WESSON MODEL 649 BODYGUARD
Caliber: .357 Mag., .38 Special +P. Capacity: 5-round cylinder. Barrel: 2.125 in. Weight: 23 oz. Length: 6.625 in. overall. Grips: Uncle Mike's Combat. Sights: Black pinned ramp front, fixed notch rear. Features: Stainless steel construction, satin finish. Internal lock. Bodyguard style, shrouded

hammer. Made in USA by Smith & Wesson.
Price: **$729.00**

LIPSEY'S EXCLUSIVE-SMITH & WESSON ULTIMATE CARRY 32 H&R MAGNUM
Caliber: 32 H&R Mag. Capacity: 6. Barrel: 1 7/8 in. Overall Length: 6.3 in. 432/632 Series. Action: Double-action-only. Finish: Matte black/matte stainless. Frame: Aluminum. Stock/Grips: VZ Blk Cherry G10 UC High Horn/ VZ Grey G10. Grip Type: Synthetic. Sights: XS Front NS/Blk U-notch rear. Sights: Fixed. Weight: 16 oz. Titanium pins/enhanced trigger. Chamfered charge holes, beveled cylinder edges.
Price: **$760.00**

LIPSEY'S EXCLUSIVE-SMITH & WESSON ULTIMATE CARRY 38 SPECIAL
Caliber: 38 Special. Capacity: 5. Barrel: 1 7/8 in. Overall Length: 6.3 in. Weight: 16 oz. 442/642 Series. Action: Double-action-only. Finish: Matte black/matte stainless. Frame: Aluminum. Stock/Grips: VZ Blk Cherry/Grey G10 UC High Horn. Grip Type: Synthetic. Sights: XS Front NS/Blk U-Notch Rear. Sight Type: Fixed. Titanium pins/enhanced trigger. Beveled cylinder edges, chamfered charge holes.
Price: **$760.00**

SMITH & WESSON K-FRAME/L-FRAME
The K-frame series are mid-size revolvers and the L-frames are slightly larger.

SMITH & WESSON MODEL 10 CLASSIC
Caliber: .38 Special. Capacity: 6-round cylinder. Features: Bright blued steel frame and cylinder, checkered wood grips, 4-inch barrel and fixed sights. The oldest model in the Smith & Wesson line, its basic design goes back to the original Military & Police Model of 1905.
Price: **$739.00**

SMITH & WESSON MODEL 17 MASTERPIECE CLASSIC
Caliber: .22 LR. Capacity: 6-round cylinder. Barrel: 6 in. Weight: 40 oz. Grips: Checkered wood. Sights: Pinned Patridge front, micro-adjustable rear. Updated variation of K-22 Masterpiece of the 1930s.
Price: **$989.00**

SMITH & WESSON MODEL 19 CLASSIC
Caliber: .357 Magnum. Capacity: 6-round cylinder Barrel: 4.25 in. Weight: 37.2 oz. Grips: Walnut. Sights: Adjustable rear, red ramp front. Finish: Polished blue. Classic-style thumbpiece. Reintroduced 2019.
Price: **$826.00**

DAVIDSON'S SMITH & WESSON MODEL 20
Caliber: .357 Mag./.38 Special. Capacity: 6. Double-/Single-Action. Safety: Internal lock. Frame Finish: Blue. Grips: Wood. Features: Forged hammer. Trigger: Forged.
Price: **$1,550.00**

DAVIDSON'S SMITH &WESSON MODEL 20 TEXAS RANGER COMMEMORATIVE
Caliber: .357 Mag./.38 Special. Capacity: 6. Safety: Internal lock. Frame Finish: Blue. Double/single-action. Embellishments: Gold inlays, 200th TX Ranger. Grips: Wood. Features: Engraved w/ gold inlays, wooden display box. One Riot, One Ranger. Finish: blued. Trigger: Forged.
Price: **$2,950.00**

SAR FIREARMS 357 MAGNUM
Caliber: .357 Mag./.38 Special. Barrel Length: 4 and 6 in. Single-action/double-action. Synthetic grip w/finger grooves. Alloy-forged steel frame, barrel and cylinder.
Price: Black 4 in **$650.00**
Price: Black 6 in **$680.00**
Price: Stainless 4 in **$800.00**
Price: Stainless 6 in **$850.00**

SMITH & WESSON MODEL 48 CLASSIC
Same specifications as Model 17 except chambered in .22 Magnum (.22 WMR) and is available with a 4- or 6-inch barrel.
Price: .... **$949.00–$989.00**

SMITH & WESSON MODEL 64/67
Caliber: .38 Special +P. Capacity: 6-round cylinder Barrel: 3 in. Weight: 33 oz. Length: 8.875 in. overall. Grips: Soft rubber. Sights: Fixed, .125-in. serrated ramp front, square notch rear. Model 67 is similar to Model 64 except for adjustable sights. Features: Satin finished stainless steel, square butt.
Price: From .... **$689.00–$749.00**

SMITH & WESSON MODEL 66
Caliber: .357 Magnum. Capacity: 6-round cylinder. Barrel: 4.25 in. Weight: 36.6 oz. Grips: Synthetic. Sights: White outline adjustable rear, red ramp front. Features: Return in 2014 of the famous K-frame "Combat Magnum" with stainless finish.
Price: **$849.00**

SMITH & WESSON MODEL 69
Caliber: .44 Magnum. Capacity: 5-round cylinder. Barrel: 4.25 in. Weight: 37 oz. Grips: Checkered wood. Sights: White outline adjustable rear, red ramp front. Features: L-frame with stainless finish, 5-shot cylinder, introduced in 2014.
Price: **$989.00**

SMITH & WESSON MODEL 610
Caliber: 10mm. Capacity: 6-round cylinder. Barrels: 4.25 and 6 in. Grips: Walnut. Sights: Fully adjustable rear, fixed red ramp interchangeable front. Weights: 42.6 oz. (4.25 in.), 50.1 oz (6 in.). Features: Built on Smith & Wesson's large N-frame in stainless steel only. Will also fire .40 S&W ammunition. Comes with three moon clips.
Price: **$987.00**

SMITH & WESSON MODEL 617
Caliber: .22 LR. Capacity: 10-round cylinder. Barrel: 6 in. Weight: 44 oz. Length: 11.125 in. Grips: Soft rubber. Sights: Patridge front, adjustable rear. Drilled and tapped for scope mount. Features: Stainless steel with satin finish. Introduced 1990.
Price: From **$829.00**

SMITH & WESSON MODEL 648
Caliber: .22 Magnum. Capacity: 8-round cylinder. Barrel: 6 in. Grips: Walnut. Sights: Fully adjustable rear, Patridge front. Weight: 46.2 oz. Features: This reintroduction was originally released in 1989 and produced until 2005. Ideal for target shooting or small-game hunting.
Price: **$752.00**

SMITH & WESSON MODEL 686/686 PLUS
Caliber: .357 Mag/.38 Special. Capacity: 6 (686) or 7 (Plus). Barrels: 6 in. (686), 3 or 6 in. (686 Plus), 4 in. (SSR). Weight: 35 oz. (3 in. barrel). Grips: Rubber. Sights: White outline adjustable rear, red ramp front. Features: Satin stainless frame and cylinder. Stock Service Revolver (SSR) has tapered underlug, interchangeable front sight, high-hold ergonomic wood grips, chamfered charge holes, custom barrel w/recessed crown, bossed mainspring.
Price: 686 .... **$829.00**
Price: Plus **$849.00**
Price: SSR **$999.00**

SMITH & WESSON MODEL 986 PRO
Caliber: 9mm. Capacity: 7-round cylinder Barrel: 5-in. tapered underlug. Features: SA/DA L-frame revolver chambered in 9mm. Features similar to

686 PLUS Pro Series with 5-inch tapered underlug barrel, satin stainless finish, synthetic grips, adjustable rear and Patridge blade front sight.
Price: **$1,149.00**

SMITH & WESSON M&P R8

Caliber: .357 Mag. Capacity: 8-round cylinder. Barrel: 5-in. half lug with accessory rail. Weight: 36.3 oz. Length: 10.5 in. Grips: Black synthetic. Sights: Adjustable v-notch rear, interchangeable front. Features: Scandium alloy frame, stainless steel cylinder.
Price: **$1,329.00**

SMITH & WESSON N-FRAME

These large-frame models introduced the .357, .41 and .44 Magnums to the world.

SMITH & WESSON MODEL 25 CLASSIC

Calibers: .45 Colt or .45 ACP. Capacity: 6-round cylinder. Barrel: 6.5 in. Weight: 45 oz. Grips: Checkered wood. Sights: Pinned Patridge front, micro-adjustable rear.
Price: **$1,019.00**

SMITH & WESSON MODEL 27 CLASSIC

Caliber: .357 Magnum. Capacity: 6-round cylinder. Barrels: 4 or 6.5 in. Weight: 41.2 oz. Grips: Checkered wood. Sights: Pinned Patridge front, micro-adjustable rear. Updated variation of the first magnum revolver, the .357 Magnum of 1935.
Price: (4 in.) **$1,019.00**
Price: (6.5 in.) **$1,059.00**

SMITH & WESSON MODEL 29 CLASSIC

Caliber: .44 Magnum Capacity: 6-round cylinder. Barrel: 4 or 6.5 in. Weight: 48.5 oz. Length: 12 in. Grips: Altamont service walnut. Sights: Adjustable white-outline rear, red ramp front. Features: Carbon steel frame, polished-blued or nickel finish. Has integral key lock safety feature to prevent accidental discharges. Original Model 29 made famous by "Dirty Harry" character played in 1971 by Clint Eastwood.
Price: .... **$999.00–$1,169.00**

SMITH & WESSON MODEL 57 CLASSIC

Caliber: .41 Magnum. Capacity: 6-round cylinder. Barrel: 6 in. Weight: 48 oz. Grips: Checkered wood. Sights: Pinned red ramp, micro-adjustable rear.
Price: **$1,009.00**

SMITH & WESSON MODEL 329PD ALASKA BACKPACKER

Caliber: .44 Magnum. Capacity: 6-round cylinder. Barrel: 2.5 in. Weight: 26 oz. Length: 9.5 in. Grips: Synthetic. Sights: Adj. rear, HiViz orange-dot front. Features: Scandium alloy frame, blue/black finish, stainless steel cylinder.
Price: From **$1,159.00**

SMITH & WESSON MODEL 625/625JM

Caliber: .45 ACP. Capacity: 6-round cylinder. Barrels: 4 in., 5 in. Weight: 43 oz. (4-in. barrel). Length: 9.375 in. overall (4-in. barrel). Grips: Soft rubber; wood optional. Sights: Patridge front on ramp, S&W micrometer click rear adjustable for windage and elevation. Features: Stainless steel construction with .400-in. wide semi-target hammer, .312-in. smooth combat trigger; full lug barrel. Glass beaded finish. Introduced 1989. Jerry Miculek Professional (JM) Series has .265-in. wide grooved trigger, special wooden Miculek Grip, five full moon clips, gold bead Patridge front sight on interchangeable front sight base, bead blast finish. Unique serial number run. Mountain Gun has 4-in. tapered barrel, drilled and tapped, Hogue Rubber Monogrip, pinned black ramp front sight, micrometer click-adjustable rear sight, satin stainless frame and barrel weighs 39.5 oz.
Price: 625 or 625JM **$1,074.00**

SMITH & WESSON MODEL 629

Calibers: .44 Magnum, .44 S&W Special. Capacity: 6-round cylinder. Barrels: 4 in., 5 in., 6.5 in. Weight: 41.5 oz. (4-in. bbl.). Length: 9.625 in. overall (4-in. bbl.). Grips: Soft rubber; wood optional. Sights: .125-in. red ramp front, white outline rear, internal lock, adjustable for windage and elevation. Classic similar to standard Model 629, except Classic has full-lug 5-in. barrel, chamfered front of cylinder, interchangeable red ramp front sight with adjustable white outline rear, Hogue grips with S&W monogram, drilled and tapped for scope mounting. Factory accurizing and endurance packages. Introduced 1990. Classic Power Port has Patridge front sight and adjustable rear sight. Model 629CT has 5-in. barrel, Crimson Trace Hoghunter Lasergrips, 10.5 in. OAL, 45.5 oz. weight. Introduced 2006.
Price: From **$949.00**

SMITH & WESSON MODEL 350

Caliber: .350 Legend. Capacity: 7. Width: 1.92 in. Height: 6.37 in. Weight: 71.5 oz. Action: SA/DA. Barrel Length: 7.5 in. Material: Stainless steel. Sight: Red ramp. Grips: Synthetic.
Price: **$1,680.00**

SMITH & WESSON MODEL 500

Caliber: 500 S&W Magnum. Capacity: 5-round cylinder. Barrels: 4 in., 6.5 in., 8.375 in. Weight: 72.5 oz. Length: 15 in. (8.375-in. barrel). Grips: Hogue Sorbothane Rubber. Sights: Interchangeable blade, front, adjustable rear. Features: Recoil compensator, ball detent cylinder latch, internal lock. 6.5-in.-barrel model has orange-ramp dovetail Millett front sight, adjustable black rear sight, Hogue Dual Density Monogrip, .312-in. chrome trigger with overtravel stop, chrome tear-drop hammer, glass bead finish. 10.5-in.-barrel model has red ramp front sight, adjustable rear sight, .312-in. chrome trigger with overtravel stop, chrome teardrop hammer with pinned sear, hunting sling. Compensated Hunter has .400-in. orange ramp dovetail front sight, adjustable black blade rear sight, Hogue Dual Density Monogrip, glass bead finish w/black clear coat. Made in USA by Smith & Wesson.
Price: From **$1,299.00**

SMITH & WESSON MODEL 460V

Caliber: 460 S&W Magnum (Also chambers .454 Casull, .45 Colt). Capacity: 5-round cylinder. Barrels: 7.5 in., 8.375-in. gain-twist rifling. Weight: 62.5 oz. Length: 11.25 in. Grips: Rubber. Sights: Adj. rear, red ramp front. Features: Satin stainless steel frame and cylinder, interchangeable compensator. 460XVR (X-treme Velocity Revolver) has black blade front sight with interchangeable green Hi-Viz tubes, adjustable rear sight. 7.5-in.-barrel version has Lothar-Walther barrel, 360-degree recoil compensator, tuned Performance Center action, pinned sear, integral Weaver base, non-glare surfaces, scope mount accessory kit for mounting full-size scopes, flashed-chromed hammer and trigger, Performance Center gun rug and shoulder sling. Interchangeable Hi-Viz green dot front sight, adjustable black rear sight, Hogue Dual Density Monogrip, matte-black frame and shroud finish with glass-bead cylinder finish, 72 oz. Compensated Hunter has teardrop chrome hammer, .312-in. chrome trigger, Hogue Dual Density Monogrip, satin/matte stainless finish, HiViz interchangeable front sight, adjustable black rear sight. XVR introduced 2006.
Price: 460V **$1,369.00**
Price: 460XVR, fr **$1,369.00**

SPOHR 283/284 CARRY

Caliber: .357 Magnum. Barrel length: 3 in. (Model 283) 4 in. (Model 284). Capacity: 6. Weight: 39 oz. (Model 283), 42 oz. (284). Features: Stainless. Integrated Picatinny rail, cold hammer-forged polygon match barrel (300mm twist length). Trigger weight:. 2.8 lbs. Wire-EDM trigger system: solid hammer LX-V1 & solid trigger LX-V2, adjustable trigger stop. Fluted cylinder, match cylinder release. Walnut combat grips. LPA red fiber front sight and adjustable green fiber rear sight. Delivered in premium gun case. Optional: Black PVD coating. Exchange-cylinder cal. 9x19 (uses moon clips).
Price: **$2,800.00**

SPOHR 285 UNIVERSAL

Caliber: .357 Magnum. Capacity: 6. Barrel Length: 5 in. Weight: 46 oz. Features: Completely stainless. Integrated Picatinny rail, cold hammer-forged polygon match barrel (300mm twist length). Trigger Weight: 2.8 lbs. Wire-EDM trigger system: solid hammer LX-V1 & solid trigger LX-V2, adjustable stop. Fluted cylinder, match cylinder release. Walnut match grips. LPA TXT rear sight, red fiber front sight. Delivered in premium gun case. Optional: Black PVD coating. Exchange-cylinder cal. 9x19 (uses moon clips).
Price: **$2,800.00**

SPOHR 286 COMPETITION

Caliber: .357 Magnum. Capacity: 6. Barrel Length: 6 in. Weight: 49 oz. Features: Completely stainless. Integrated Picatinny rail, cold hammer-forged polygon match barrel (300mm twist length). Trigger Weight: 2.8 lbs. Wire-EDM trigger system: solid hammer LX-V1 & solid trigger LX-V2, adjustable stop. Fluted cylinder, match cylinder release. Walnut match grips. LPA TXT rear sight, two-stage match front sight. Delivered in premium gun case. Optional: Black PVD coating. Exchange-cylinder cal. 9x19 (uses moon clips).
Price: **$2,900.00**

SPOHR CLUB EDITIONS (3.0, 4.0, 5.0, 6.0 IN.)

Caliber: .357 Magnum. Capacity: 6. Barrel Lengths: 3, 4, 5, 6 in. Weight: 38, 42, 46, 40 oz. Features: Completely stainless. Integrated Picatinny rail, cold hammer-forged polygon match barrel (300mm twist length). Trigger weight: 2.8 lbs. Skeletonized hammer and trigger. Club Edition cylinder release. Adjustable trigger stop. Fluted cylinder in Club design. Walnut match grips. Integrated, adjustable LPA rear sight, Gold-Dot front sight. Delivered in premium gun case, Optional: Black PVD coating. Exchange-cylinder cal. 9x19 (uses moon clips).
Price: .... **$3,800.00–$3,900.00**

SPOHR L562 STANDARD 4.0 AND 6.0

Caliber: .357 Magnum. Capacity: 6. Barrel Length: 4 and 6 in. Weight: 42 and 49 oz. Features: Completely stainless. Cold hammer-forged polygon match barrel (300mm twist length). Trigger Weight: 2.8 lbs. Wire-EDM trigger system: solid hammer LX-V1 & solid trigger LX-V2, adjustable stop. Fluted cylinder, match cylinder release. Walnut combat grips. Black front sight with LPA TXT rear sight. Delivered in premium gun case. Optional: Black PVD coating. Exchange-cylinder cal. 9x19 (uses moon clips).
Price: .... **$2,700.00–$2,800.00**

SPOHR L562 TACTICAL DIVISION

Caliber: .357 Magnum. Capacity: 6. Barrel Length: 6 in. Weight: 51 oz. Features: Completely stainless. Integrated Picatinny rail on and under the barrel. Cold hammer-forged polygon match barrel (300mm twist length).

Prices given are believed to be accurate at time of publication however, many factors affect retail pricing so exact prices are not possible.

79TH EDITION, 2025 ⊕ **513**

Trigger weight: 2.8 lbs. Wire-EDM trigger system: solid hammer LX-V1 & solid trigger LX-V2, adjustable stop. Unfluted cylinder, match cylinder release. Walnut match grips. Black front sight with LPA TXT rear sight. Delivered in premium gun case. Optional: Black PVD coating. Exchange-cylinder cal. 9x19 (uses moon clips).
Price: $3,000.00

STANDARD MANUFACTURING S333 THUNDERSTRUCK
Caliber: .22 Magnum. Capacity: 8-round cylinder. Barrel: 1.25 in. Grips: Polymer. Sights: Fixed front and rear. Weight: 18 oz. Features: Designed to be the ultimate in personal protection and featuring two-barrels that fire simultaneously with each trigger pull. The DA revolver has an 8-round, .22 Magnum capacity. Frame is constructed of 7075 aircraft-grade aluminum with anodized finish.
Price: $429.00

SUPER SIX CLASSIC BISON BULL
Caliber: .45-70 Government. Capacity: 6-round cylinder. Barrel: 10in. octagonal with 1:14 twist. Weight: 6 lbs. Length: 17.5 in. overall. Grips: NA. Sights: Ramp front sight with dovetailed blade, click-adjustable rear. Features: Manganese bronze frame. Integral scope mount, manual cross-bolt safety.
Price: $1,500.00

TAURUS 327
The new Taurus 327 is a double-action/single-action revolver, available with a 2- or 3-inch barrel that is multi-cartridge compatible, can accept .32 H&R Magnum and .32 S&W Long cartridges. The matte black carbon steel or stainless steel barrel, cylinder and frame are backed by a recoil-absorbing rubber grip that is comfortable and provides excellent retention in a compact handgun platform. The Taurus 327's front serrated ramp sight and no-snag rear sight channel provide quick and clear target acquisition.
Price: $371.00
Price: $388.00

TAURUS 327 DEFENDER T.O.R.O.
Caliber: 327 Federal. Capacity: 6. Action Type: DAO. Firing System: Hammer. Front Sight: Night sight with orange outline. Rear Sight: Fixed. Grip: Hogue. Frame Size: Small. Barrel Length: 3 in. Overall Length: 7.5 in. Overall Height: 4.80 in. Overall Width: 1.41 in. Weight: 23.52 oz. unloaded. Frame Material: Stainless steel. Finish: Matte black.
Price: $554.00

TAURUS 942
Caliber: .22 LR. Capacity: 8-round cylinder. Barrels: 2 and 3 in. Grips: Soft

rubber. Sights: Drift-adjustable rear, serrated-ramp front. Weight: 17.8, 25 oz. Features: The 942 is based closely on the Taurus 856 revolver, but chambered in .22 LR with an 8-shot cylinder. Eight models are available: 2- and 3-inch-barrel models with a steel-alloy frame and cylinder in matte-black finish, 2- and 3-inch-barrel models with an ultralight aluminum-alloy frame in hard-coat, black-anodized finish, 2- and 3-inch-barrel models with a stainless steel frame and cylinder in a matte finish, and 2- and 3-inch-barrel models with an ultralight aluminum-alloy frame in a stainless-matte finish. Imported by Taurus International.
Price: .... $369.52 - $384.97

TAURUS 605 DEFENDER
Capacity: 5 Rounds, Action Type: Double Action/Single Action, Firing System: Hammer, Front Sight: Night Sight with orange outline, Rear Sight: Fixed, Grip: Hogue Rubber grips, VZ, Altamont. Caliber: .38 Spl. +P, .357 Mag, Frame Size: Small, Barrel Length: 3 in., Overall Length: 7.50 in., Overall Height: 4.80 in., Overall Width: 1.41 in. Weights: 23.52 to 25.52 oz., Features: Extended ejector rod, night sights, Safety: Transfer Bar. Finishes: Matte black oxide, matte stainless steel, tungsten Cerakote.
Price: .... $472.00–$540.00

TAURUS 605 EXECUTIVE GRADE
Caliber: 357 Mag. Capacity: 5. Action Type: DA/SA. Front Sight: Brass insert. Rear Sight: Fixed. Grip: Presentation wood. Frame Size: Small. Barrel Length: 3 in. Overall Length: 7.5 in. Weight: 23.52 oz. unloaded. Width: 1.41 in. Height: 4.80 in. Stainless steel, hand-tuned trigger.
Price: $758.00

TAURUS DEFENDER 856
Caliber: .38 Special +P. Capacity: 6-round cylinder. Barrel: 3 in. Grips: Hogue rubber, VZ black/gray, walnut. Sights: Fixed rear, tritium night sight with bright orange outline. Features: The Defender 856 is built on Taurus' small frame, making for a compact defensive revolver. Four standard models are available to include a stainless steel frame with matte finish, an ultralight aluminum-alloy frame with matte finish, stainless steel frame with black Tenifer finish, and an aluminum-alloy frame with hard-coat, black-anodized finish. Two upgrade versions are available with special grips and finish treatments. Imported by Taurus International.
Price: .... $429.00 - $477.00

TAURUS MODEL 17 TRACKER
Caliber: .17 HMR. Capacity: 7-round cylinder. Barrel: 6.5 in. Weight: 45.8 oz. Grips: Rubber. Sights: Adjustable. Features: Double action, matte stainless, integral key-lock.
Price: From $539.00

TAURUS MODEL 992 TRACKER
Calibers: .22 LR with interchangeable .22 WMR cylinder. Capacity: 9-round cylinder. Barrel: 4 or 6.5 in with ventilated rib. Features: Adjustable rear sight, blued or stainless finish.
Price: Blue $640.00
Price: Stainless $692.00

Prices given are believed to be accurate at time of publication however, many factors affect retail pricing so exact prices are not possible.

TAURUS MODEL 44SS

Caliber: .44 Magnum. Capacity: 5-round cylinder. Barrel: Ported, 4, 6.5, 8.4 in. Weight: 34 oz. Grips: Rubber. Sights: Adjustable. Features: Double action. Integral key-lock. Introduced 1994. Finish: Matte stainless. Imported from Brazil by Taurus International Manufacturing, Inc.
Price: From .... **$648.00-$664.00**

TAURUS MODEL 65

Caliber: .357 Magnum. Capacity: 6-round cylinder. Barrel: 4-in. full underlug. Weight: 38 oz. Length: 10.5 in. overall. Grips: Soft rubber. Sights: Fixed. Features: Double action, integral key-lock. Matte blued or stainless. Imported by Taurus International.
Price: Blued **$539.00**
Price: Stainless **$591.00**

TAURUS MODEL 66

Similar to Model 65, 4 in. or 6 in. barrel, 7-round cylinder, adjustable rear sight. Integral key-lock action. Imported by Taurus International.
Price: Blue **$599.00**
Price: Stainless **$652.00**

TAURUS MODEL 82 HEAVY BARREL

Caliber: .38 Special. Capacity: 6-round cylinder. Barrel: 4 in., heavy. Weight: 36.5 oz. Length: 9.25 in. overall. Grips: Soft black rubber. Sights: Serrated ramp front, square notch rear. Features: Double action, solid rib, integral key-lock. Imported by Taurus International.
Price: From **$521.00**

TAURUS MODEL 85FS

Caliber: .38 Special. Capacity: 5-round cylinder. Barrel: 2 in. Weights: 17–24.5 oz., titanium 13.5–15.4 oz. Grips: Rubber, rosewood or mother of pearl. Sights: Ramp front, square notch rear. Features: Spurred hammer. Blued, matte stainless, blue with gold accents, stainless with gold accents; rated for +P ammo. Integral keylock. Some models have titanium frame. Introduced 1980. Imported by Taurus International.
Price: From **$379.00**

TAURUS MODEL 856 ULTRALIGHT

Caliber: .38 Special. Capacity: 6-round cylinder. Barrel: 2 in. Matte black or stainless. Weights: 15.7 oz., titanium 13.5–15.4 oz. Grips: Rubber, rosewood or mother of pearl. Sights: Serrated ramp front, square notch rear. Features: Aluminum frame, matte black or stainless cylinder, azure blue, bronze, burnt orange or rouge finish.
Price: .... **$364.00-$461.00**

TAURUS 380 MINI

Caliber: .380 ACP. Capacity: 5-round cylinder w/moon clip. Barrel: 1.75 in. Weight: 15.5 oz. Length: 5.95 in. Grips: Rubber. Sights: Adjustable rear, fixed front. Features: DAO. Available in blued or stainless finish. Five Star

(moon) clips included.
Price: Blued **$478.00**
Price: Stainless **$514.00**

TAURUS MODEL 45-410 JUDGE

Calibers: 2.5-in. .410/.45 Colt, 3-in. .410/.45 Colt. Barrels: 3 in., 6.5 in. (blued finish). Weights: 35.2 oz., 22.4 oz. Length: 7.5 in. Grips: Ribber rubber. Sights: Fiber Optic. Features: DA/SA. Matte stainless and ultra-lite stainless finish. Introduced in 2007. Imported from Brazil by Taurus International.
Price: From **$511.00**

TAURUS JUDGE HOME DEFENDER

Caliber: .45 Colt/.410 Mag. Capacity: 5. Frame Size: Medium. Frame Material: Alloy steel. Frame Finish: Matte black. Cylinder Material: Alloy steel. Cylinder Finish: Matte black. Barrel Material: Alloy steel. Barrel Finish: Matte black. Action Type: DA/SA. Overall Width: 1.9 in. Overall Height: 5.8 in. Overall Weight: 58.6 oz. Barrel Length: 13 in. Overall Length: 19.5 in. Rear Sight: Picatinny rail. Grip Material: Rubber. Firing System: Hammer. Safety: Transfer bar.
Price: **$758.00**

TAURUS JUDGE PUBLIC DEFENDER POLYMER

Caliber: .45 Colt/.410 (2.5 in.). Capacity: 5-round cylinder. Barrel: 2.5-in. Weight: 27 oz. Features: SA/DA revolver with 5-round cylinder; polymer frame; Ribber rubber-feel grips; fiber-optic front sight; adjustable rear sight; blued or stainless cylinder; shrouded hammer with cocking spur; blued finish.
Price: From **$469.00**

TAURUS EXECUTIVE GRADE JUDGE

Caliber: .45 Colt/.410 Capacity: 5 Rounds. Finish: Hand-polished Stainless steel satin. Tuned action. Presentation-grade wood grips and brass bead front sight on a 3-in. barrel. Frame Size: Tracker. Overall Length: 9.50 in. Overall Height: 5.10 in. Overall Width: 1.50 in. Weight: 36 oz. (unloaded). Transfer bar safety.
Prce: **$949.00**

TAURUS DEFENDER 856 T.O.R.O.

Caliber: .38 Special (+P) Capacity: 6 rounds. Barrel length: 3 in. Finish: Stainless steel matte. Optics-ready, accepts compact red-dot sights that fit the Holosun K-footprint. Front Sight: Removable. Rear Sight: Fixed. Small frame. Overall Length 7.50 in. Overall Height: 4.80 in. Overall Width: 1.40 in. Overall Weight: 23.50 oz. (unloaded).
Prce: **$460.00**

TAURUS 605 T.O.R.O.

Caliber: .357 Mag. Capacity: 5 rounds. Otherwise nearly identical to the 856.
Prce: **$470.00**

Prices given are believed to be accurate at time of publication however, many factors affect retail pricing so exact prices are not possible.

79TH EDITION, 2025 ✛ 515

TAURUS RAGING HUNTER

Calibers: .357 Magnum, .44 Magnum, .454 Casull, .460 Smith & Wesson Magnum. Capacity: 7 (.357), 6 (.44) and 5 (.454) rounds. Barrels: 5.12, 6.75, 8.37 in. Grips: Cushioned rubber. Sights: Adjustable rear, fixed front. Weight: 49 - 59.2 oz. Features: This is a DA/SA big-game-hunting revolver, available in three calibers and three barrel lengths, each featuring a Picatinny rail for easy optic mounting without removing the iron sights. All Raging Hunter models come with factory porting and cushioned rubber grips. Two finishes are available: matte black and two-tone matte stainless. Imported by Taurus International.
Prce: Black $968.00
Prce: Two Tone $983.00

TAURUS RAGING HUNTER TWO TONE

Caliber: .460 S&W. Barrel: 10.5-in. w/ compensator. Capacity: 5 rounds. Lower Picatinny rail to attach bipods and shooting sticks. A top rail allows for additional sight/scope options. Fixed front sight, fully adjustable rear. Frame Size: Large. Overall length: 16.22 in. Overall height: 6.40 in. Overall width: 1.80 in. Weight: 71.26 oz. (unloaded).
Prce: Black $1,269.00

TAURUS RAGING HUNTER 500

Caliber: .500 S&W Magnum. Capacity: 5 rounds. Barrel Length: 5.12, 6.75, and 8.37 in. Finish: Matte black or two-tone. Picatinny rail, ported barrel. Sights: Fixed front. Fully adjustable rear.
Prce: Black .... $1,069.00–$1,089.00

TAURUS MODEL 627 TRACKER

Caliber: .357 Magnum. Capacity: 7-round cylinder. Barrels: 4 or 6.5 in. Weights: 28.8, 41 oz. Grips: Rubber. Sights: Fixed front, adjustable rear. Features: Double-action. Stainless steel, Shadow Gray or Total Titanium; vent rib (steel models only); integral key-lock action. Imported by Taurus International.
Price: From $577.00

TAURUS MODEL 444 ULTRA-LIGHT

Caliber: .44 Magnum. Capacity: 5-round cylinder. Barrels: 2.5 or 4 in. Weight: 28.3 oz. Grips: Cushioned inset rubber. Sights: Fixed red-fiber optic front, adjustable rear. Features: UltraLite titanium blue finish, titanium/

alloy frame built on Raging Bull design. Smooth trigger shoe, 1.760-in. wide, 6.280-in. tall. Barrel rate of twist 1:16, 6 grooves. Introduced 2005. Imported by Taurus International.
Price: $944.00

TAURUS MODEL 444/454 RAGING BULL SERIES

Calibers: .44 Magnum, .454 Casull. Barrels: 2.25 in., 5 in., 6.5 in., 8.375 in. Weight: 53–63 oz. Length: 12 in. overall (6.5 in. barrel). Grips: Soft black rubber. Sights: Patridge front, adjustable rear. Features: DA, ventilated rib, integral key-lock. Most models have ported barrels. Introduced 1997. Imported by Taurus International.
Price: 444 .... $900.00
Price: 454 .... $1,204.00

TAURUS MODEL 605 PLY

Caliber: .357 Magnum. **Capacity:** 5-round cylinder. **Barrel:** 2 in. **Weight:** 20 oz. **Grips:** Rubber. **Sights:** Fixed. **Features:** Polymer frame steel cylinder. Blued or stainless. Introduced 1995. Imported by Taurus International.
Price: Blued $393.00
Price: Stainless $410.00

TAURUS MODEL 905

Caliber: 9mm. **Capacity:** 5-round cylinder. **Barrel:** 2 in. **Features:** Small-frame revolver with rubber boot grips, fixed sights, choice of exposed or concealed hammer. Blued or stainless finish.
Price: Blued $531.00
Price: Stainless $583.00

TAURUS MODEL 692

Calibers: .38 Special/.357 Magnum or 9mm. **Capacity:** 7-round cylinder. **Barrels:** 3 or 6.5 in, ported. **Sights:** Adjustable rear, fixed front. **Grip:** "Ribber" textured. **Finish:** Matte blued or stainless. **Features:** Caliber can be changed with a swap of the cylinders which are non-fluted.
Price: $659.00

Prices given are believed to be accurate at time of publication however, many factors affect retail pricing so exact prices are not possible.

CIMARRON BISLEY MODEL SINGLE-ACTION
Calibers: .357 Magnum, .44 WCF, .44 Special, .45. Features: Similar to Colt Bisley, special grip frame and triggerguard, knurled wide-spur hammer, curved trigger. Introduced 1999. Imported by Cimarron F.A. Co.
Price: From **$636.00**

CIMARRON LIGHTNING SA
Calibers: .22 LR, .32-20/32 H&R dual cyl. combo, .38 Special, .41 Colt. Barrels: 3.5 in., 4.75 in., 5.5 in. Grips: Smooth or checkered walnut. Sights: Blade front. Features: Replica of the Colt 1877 Lightning DA. Similar to Cimarron Thunderer, except smaller grip frame to fit smaller hands. Standard blued, charcoal blued or nickel finish with forged, old model, or color casehardened frame. Dual cylinder model available with .32-30/.32 H&R chambering. Introduced 2001. From Cimarron F.A. Co.
Price: From .... **$503.00–$565.00**
Price: .32-20/.32 H&R dual cylinder **$649.00**

CIMARRON MODEL P SAA
Calibers: .32 WCF, .38 WCF, .357 Magnum, .44 WCF, .44 Special, .45 Colt and .45 ACP. Barrels: 4.75, 5.5, 7.5 in. Weight: 39 oz. Length: 10 in. overall (4.75-in. barrel). Grips: Walnut. Sights: Blade front. Features: Old model black-powder frame with Bullseye ejector, or New Model frame. Imported by Cimarron F.A. Co.
Price: From **$550.00**

CIMARRON MODEL "P" JR.
Calibers: .22 LR, .32-20, .32 H&R, 38 Special Barrels: 3.5, 4.75, 5.5 in. Grips: Checkered walnut. Sights: Blade front. Features: Styled after 1873 Colt Peacemaker, except 20 percent smaller. Blue finish with color case-hardened frame; Cowboy action. Introduced 2001. From Cimarron F.A. Co.
Price: From **$480.00**

CIMARRON U.S.V. ARTILLERY MODEL SINGLE-ACTION
Caliber: .45 Colt. Barrel: 5.5 in. Weight: 39 oz. Length: 11.5 in. overall. Grips: Walnut. Sights: Fixed. Features: U.S. markings and cartouche, casehardened frame and hammer. Imported by Cimarron F.A. Co.
Price: Blued finish.. **$594.00**
Price: Original finish **$701.00**

CIMARRON BAD BOY
Calibers: .44 Magnum, 10mm. Capacity: 6-round cylinder. Barrel: 8 in. Grips: Walnut. Sights: Fully adjustable rear, fixed front. Features: Built on a replica Single Action Army Pre-War frame with an 1860 Army-style, one-piece walnut grip. The carbon-alloy steel frame is covered in a classic blue finish and it is fitted with an 8-inch octagon barrel and adjustable sights, and chambered in the popular semi-auto 10mm round in 2020.
Price: **$726.05**

COLT SINGLE ACTION ARMY
Calibers: .357 Magnum, .45 Colt. Capacity: 6-round cylinder. Barrels: 4.75, 5.5, 7.5 in. Weight: 40 oz. (4.75-in. barrel). Length: 10.25 in. overall (4.75-in. barrel). Grips: Black Eagle composite. Sights: Blade front, notch rear. Features: Available in full nickel finish with nickel grip medallions, or Royal Blue with color casehardened frame. Reintroduced 1992. Additional calibers available through Colt Custom Shop.
Price: Blued **$1,599.00**
Price: Nickel... **$1,799.00**

EAA BOUNTY HUNTER SA
Calibers: .22 LR/.22 WMR, .357 Mag., .44 Mag., .45 Colt. Capacities: 6. 10-round cylinder available for .22LR/.22WMR. Barrels: 4.5 in., 7.5 in. Weight: 2.5 lbs. Length: 11 in. overall (4.625 in. barrel). Grips: Smooth walnut. Sights: Blade front, grooved topstrap rear. Features: Transfer bar safety; 3-position hammer; hammer-forged barrel. Introduced 1992. Imported by European American Armory
Price: Centerfire, blued or case-hardened **$478.00**
Price: Centerfire, nickel **$515.00**
Price: .22 LR/.22 WMR, blued **$343.00**
Price: .22LR/.22WMR, nickel **$380.00**
Price: .22 LR/.22WMR, 10-round cylinder **$465.00**

Prices given are believed to be accurate at time of publication however, many factors affect retail pricing so exact prices are not possible.

79TH EDITION, 2025 ✦ **517**

EMF 1875 OUTLAW

Calibers: .357 Magnum, .44-40, .45 Colt. Barrels: 7.5 in., 9.5 in. Weight: 46 oz. Length: 13.5 in. overall. Grips: Smooth walnut. Sights: Blade front, fixed groove rear. Features: Authentic copy of 1875 Remington with firing pin in hammer; color casehardened frame, blued cylinder, barrel, steel backstrap and triggerguard. Also available in nickel, factory engraved. Imported by E.M.F. Co.

Price: All calibers **$520.00**
Price: Laser Engraved **$800.00**

EMF 1873 GREAT WESTERN II

Calibers: .357 Magnum, .45 Colt, .44/40. Barrels: 3.5 in., 4.75 in., 5.5 in., 7.5 in. Weight: 36 oz. Length: 11 in. (5.5-in. barrel). Grips: Walnut. Sights: Blade front, notch rear. Features: Authentic reproduction of the original 2nd Generation Colt single-action revolver. Standard and bone casehardening. Coil hammer spring. Hammer-forged barrel. Alchimista has case-hardened frame, brass backstrap, longer and wider 1860 grip.

Price: 1873 Californian .... **$545.00–$560.00**
Price: 1873 Custom series, bone or nickel, ivory-like grips **$689.90**
Price: 1873 Stainless steel, ivory-like grips **$589.90**
Price: 1873 Paladin **$560.00**
Price: Deluxe Californian with checkered walnut grips stainless......... **$780.00**
Price: Buntline **$605.00**
Price: Alchimista... **$675.00**

EMF 1873 DAKOTA II

Caliber: .357 Magnum, 45 Colt. Barrel: 4.75 in. Grips: Walnut. Finish: black.
Price: **$460.00**

FREEDOM ARMS MODEL 83 PREMIER GRADE

Calibers: .357 Magnum, 41 Magnum, .44 Magnum, .454 Casull, .475 Linebaugh, .500 Wyo. Exp. Capacity: 5-round cylinder. Barrels: 4.75 in., 6 in., 7.5 in., 9 in. (.357 Mag. only), 10 in. (except .357 Mag. and 500 Wyo. Exp.) Weight: 53 oz. (7.5-in. bbl. in .454 Casull). Length: 13 in. (7.5 in. bbl.). Grips: Impregnatedhardwood. Sights: Adjustable rear with replaceable front sight. Fixed rear notch and front blade. Features: Stainless steel construction with brushed finish; manual sliding safety bar. Micarta grips optional. 500 Wyo. Exp. Introduced 2006. Lifetime warranty. Made in USA by Freedom Arms, Inc.

Price: From **$2,738.00**

FREEDOM ARMS MODEL 83 FIELD GRADE

Calibers: .22 LR, .357 Magnum, .41 Magnum, .44 Magnum, .454 Casull, .475 Linebaugh, .500 Wyo. Exp. Capacity: 5-round cylinder. Barrels: 4.75 in., 6 in., 7.5 in., 9 in. (.357 Mag. only), 10 in. (except .357 Mag. and .500 Wyo. Exp.) Weight: 56 oz. (7.5-in. bbl. in .454 Casull). Length: 13.1 in. (7.5 in. bbl.). Grips: Pachmayr standard, impregnated hardwood or Micarta optional. Sights: Adjustable rear with replaceable front sight. Model 83 frame. All stainless steel. Introduced 1988. Made in USA by Freedom Arms Inc.

Price: From **$2,332.00**

FREEDOM ARMS MODEL 97 PREMIER GRADE

Calibers: .17 HMR, .22 LR, .32 H&R, .327 Federal, .357 Magnum, 6 rounds; .41 Magnum, .44 Special, .45 Colt. Capacity: 5-round cylinder. Barrels: 4.25 in., 5.5 in., 7.5 in., 10 in. (.17 HMR, .22 LR, .32 H&R). Weight: 40 oz. (5.5 in. .357 Mag.). Length: 10.75 in. (5.5 in. bbl.). Grips: Impregnated hardwood; Micarta optional. Sights: Adjustable rear, replaceable blade front. Fixed rear notch and front blade. Features: Stainless steel construction, brushed finish, automatic transfer bar safety system. Introduced in 1997. Lifetime warranty. Made in USA by Freedom Arms.

Price: From **$2,148.00**

HERITAGE ROUGH RIDER

Calibers: .22 LR, 22 LR/22 WMR combo, .357 Magnum .44-40, .45 Colt. Capacity: 6-round cylinder. Barrels: 3.5 in., 4.75 in., 5.5 in., 7.5 in. Weights: 31–38 oz. Grips: Exotic cocobolo laminated wood or mother of pearl; bird's head models offered. Sights: Blade front, fixed rear. Adjustable sight on 4.75 in. and 5.5 in. models. Features: Hammer block safety. Transfer bar with Big Bores. High polish blue, black satin, silver satin, casehardened and stainless finish. Introduced 1993. Made in USA by Heritage Mfg., Inc.

Price: Rimfire calibers, From **$200.00**
Price: Centerfire calibers, From... **$450.00**

HERITAGE MANUFACTURING BARKEEP REVOLVER

Caliber: .22 LR. Capacity: 6 rounds. Barrel: 2, 3 in. Grip: Custom scroll wood or gray pearl. Sights: Fixed front and rear. Weight: 2.2 lbs. Features: Heritage Manufacturing's take on the 19th-Century "Storekeeper" single-action revolver. The new Barkeep is chambered in the economical .22 LR but is compatible with an optional interchangeable .22 WMR six-shot cylinder. Available with a black oxide or case-hardened finish. Two grips are also available — custom scroll wood or gray pearl.

Price: Custom wood scroll grips **$180.00**
Price: Gray pearl grips **$189.00**

HERITAGE MANUFACTURING BARKEEP BOOT

Caliber: .22 LR. Capacity: 6 Rounds. Finish: Black standard. Action Type: Single Action Only. Safety: Thumb/Hammer. Grips: Black, gray pearl, custom wood burnt snake. Weight: 25.5 oz. Barrel Length: 1.68 in. Overall Length: 6.38 in.

Price: .... **$196.00–$205.00**

Prices given are believed to be accurate at time of publication however, many factors affect retail pricing so exact prices are not possible.

HERITAGE ROUGH RIDER TACTICAL COWBOY
Chambered in .22 LR, is also compatible with the .22 WMR cylinder allowing you to shoot either .22 LR or .22 WMR ammo. The new Heritage Rough Rider Tactical Cowboy features modern day technology into an old classic world. The barrel is threaded for compensators and suppressors. Caliber: .22 LR, Capacity: 6 Rounds, Finish: Black standard. Action Type: Single Action Only. Lands & Grooves: 6. Front Sight: Fiber optic. Rear Sight: Picatinny rail. Safety: Thumb/hammer. Grips: Carbon fiber. Weight: 32.10 oz., Barrel Length: 6.5 in. Overall Length: 11.85 in.
Price: **$212.00**

MAGNUM RESEARCH BFR 20TH ANNIVERSARY
Each hand-crafted 20th Anniversary BFR is part of a limited series, with only 20 pistols to be produced. This custom gun is based on a .45-70 Government long frame model, the first production caliber. A full octagon barrel is added with a custom E-Rod Housing and base pin. Plow-style white polymer grips are hand fit. Exterior surfaces engraved with elegant scrollwork by the artists at Tyler Gun Works. Ships in a beautiful wood case, includes a signed letter of authenticity. Capacity: 5. Caliber: .45/70 Gov't. Barrel: 7.5 in. full octagon. Overall Length: 15-in. Height: 6 in. Cylinder Width: 1.75 in. Finish: Brushed stainless steel. Weight: 4.3 lbs. Sights: Factory black fixed front/rear adjustable. Grip: Plow-style white polymer.
Price: From **$7,000.00**

MAGNUM RESEARCH BFR SINGLE ACTION
Calibers: .44 Magnum, .444 Marlin, .45-70, .45 Colt/.410, .450 Marlin, .454 Casull, .460 S&W Magnum, .480 Ruger/.475 Linebaugh, .500 Linebaugh, .500 JRH, .500 S&W, .30-30. Barrels: 6.5 in., 7.5 in. and 10 in. Weights: 3.6–5.3 lbs. Grips: Black rubber. Sights: Rear sights are the same configuration as the Ruger revolvers. Many aftermarket rear sights will fit the BFR. Front sights are machined by Magnum in four heights and anodized flat black. The four heights accommodate all shooting styles, barrel lengths and calibers. All sights are interchangeable with each BFR's. Features: Crafted in the USA, the BFR single-action 5-shot stainless steel revolver frames are CNC machined inside and out from a pre-heat treated investment casting. This is done to prevent warping and dimensional changes or shifting that occurs during the heat treat process. Magnum Research designed the frame with large calibers and substantial recoil in mind, built to close tolerances to handle the pressure of true big-bore calibers. The BFR is equipped with a transfer bar safety feature that allows the gun to be carried safely with all five chambers loaded.
Price: ....**$1,218.00-$1,302.00**

MAGNUM RESEARCH BFR SHORT FRAME
Caliber: .357 Magnum, .44 Magnum. Capacity: 6-round cylinder. Barrels: 5

and 7.5 in. Grips: Standard rubber, Bisley, white polymer or black micarta. Sights: Adjustable rear, fixed front. Weights: 3.5, 3.65 lbs. Features: Made entirely of super tough 17-4PH stainless steel, BFRs are made in the United States and were designed from the outset to handle powerful revolver cartridges. The pre-eminent single-action hunting revolver. Two grip frame options available: a standard plow handle with rubber grip, and Magnum Research iteration of a Bisley with white polymer or black micarta grips.
Price: **$1,302.00**

MAGNUM RESEARCH BFR LONG FRAME
Caliber: .350 Legend, .360 Buckhammer. Capacity: 6-round cylinder. Barrels: 7.5 and 10 in. Grips: Standard rubber, Bisley, white polymer or black micarta. Sights: Adjustable rear, fixed front. Weights: 4.8, 5 lbs. Features: Built on Magnum Research's long frame and made entirely of 17-4PH stainless steel. The first long frame in six-shot configuration. Two grip frame options available: a standard plow handle with rubber grip, and Magnum Research iteration of a Bisley with white polymer or black micarta grips.
Price: **$1,302.00**

NORTH AMERICAN ARMS MINI
Calibers: .22 Short, 22 LR, 22 WMR. Capacity: 5-round cylinder. Barrels: 1.125 in., 1.625 in. Weight: 4–6.6 oz. Length: 3.625 in., 6.125 in. overall. Grips: Laminated wood. Sights: Blade front, notch fixed rear. Features: All stainless steel construction. Polished satin and matte finish. Engraved models available. From North American Arms.
Price: .22 Short, .22 LR **$226.00**
Price: .22 WMR **$236.00**

NORTH AMERICAN ARMS MINI-MASTER
Calibers: .22 LR, .22 WMR. Capacity: 5-round cylinder. Barrel: 4 in. Weight: 10.7 oz. Length: 7.75 in. overall. Grips: Checkered hard black rubber. Sights: Blade front, white outline rear adjustable for elevation, or fixed. Features: Heavy vented barrel; full-size grips. Non-fluted cylinder. Introduced 1989.
Price: .... **$284.00-$349.00**

NORTH AMERICAN ARMS BLACK WIDOW
Similar to Mini-Master, 2-in. heavy vent barrel. Built on .22 WMR frame. Non-fluted cylinder, black rubber grips. Available with Millett low-profile fixed sights or Millett sight adjustable for elevation only. Overall length 5.875 in., weighs 8.8 oz. From North American Arms.
Price: Adjustable sight, .22 LR or .22 WMR **$352.00**
Price: Fixed sight, .22 LR or .22 WMR **$288.00**

NORTH AMERICAN ARMS "THE EARL" SINGLE-ACTION

Calibers: .22 Magnum with .22 LR accessory cylinder. Capacity: 5-round cylinder. Barrel: 4 in. octagonal. Weight: 6.8 oz. Length: 7.75 in. overall. Grips: Wood. Sights: Barleycorn front and fixed notch rear. Features: Single-action mini-revolver patterned after 1858-style Remington percussion revolver. Includes a spur trigger and a faux loading lever that serves as cylinder pin release.

Price: .... **$298.00, $332.00 (convertible)**

DAVIDSON'S PIETTA ADJUSTABLE SIGHT 1873

Caliber: .44 Rem. Mag. Capacity: 6. Barrel Length: 7.5 in. Maker: Pietta, Model Series: 1873. Safety: Transfer bar. Finish: Blued. Front Sight: Ramp. Rear Sight: Adjustable. Grips: Walnut. Features: Unfluted cylinder. Firing System: External hammer. Triggerguard: Round. Barrel configuration: Single, cold hammer forged.

Price: **$1,100.00**

RUGER NEW MODEL SINGLE-SIX SERIES

Calibers: .22 LR, .17 HMR. Convertible and Hunter models come with extra cylinder for .22 WMR. Capacity: 6. Barrels: 4.62 in., 5.5 in., 6.5 in. or 9.5 in. Weight: 35–42 oz. Finish: Blued or stainless. Grips: Black checkered hard rubber, black laminate or hardwood (stainless model only). Single-Six .17 Model available only with 6.5-in. barrel, blue finish, rubber grips. Hunter Model available only with 7.5-in. barrel, black laminate grips and stainless finish.

Price: (blued) **$629.00**
Price: (stainless) **$699.00**

RUGER SINGLE-TEN AND RUGER SINGLE-NINE SERIES

Calibers: .22 LR, .22 WMR. Capacities: 10 (.22 LR Single-Ten), 9 (.22 Mag Single-Nine). Barrels: 5.5 in. (Single-Ten), 6.5 in. (Single-Nine). Weight: 38–39 oz. Grips: Hardwood Gunfighter. Sights: Williams Adjustable Fiber Optic.

Price: **$699.00**

RUGER NEW MODEL BLACKHAWK/ BLACKHAWK CONVERTIBLE

Calibers: .30 Carbine, .357 Magnum/.38 Special, .41 Magnum, .44 Special, .45 Colt. Capacity: 6-round cylinder. Barrels: 4.625 in., 5.5 in., 6.5 in., 7.5 in. (.30 carbine and .45 Colt). Weights: 36–45 oz. Lengths: 10.375 in. to 13.5 in. Grips: Rosewood or black checkered. Sights: .125-in. ramp front, micro-click rear adjustable for windage and elevation. Features: Rosewood grips, Ruger transfer bar safety system, independent firing pin, hardened chrome-moly steel frame, music wire springs through-out. Case and lock included. Convertibles come with extra cylinder.

Price: Blued **$669.00**
Price: Convertible, .357/9mm **$749.00**
Price: Convertible, .45 Colt/.45 ACP **$749.00**
Price: Stainless, .357 only **$799.00**

RUGER BISLEY SINGLE ACTION

Calibers: .44 Magnum. and .45 Colt. Barrel: 7.5-in. barrel. Length: 13.5 in. Weight: 48–51 oz. Similar to standard Blackhawk, hammer is lower with smoothly curved, deeply checkered wide spur. The trigger is strongly curved with wide smooth surface. Longer grip frame. Adjustable rear sight, ramp-style front. Unfluted cylinder and roll engraving, adjustable sights. Plastic lockable case. Orig. fluted cylinder introduced 1985; discontinued 1991. Unfluted cylinder introduced 1986.

Price: **$899.00**

RUGER NEW MODEL SUPER BLACKHAWK

Caliber: .44 Magnum/.44 Special. Capacity: 6-round cylinder. Barrel: 4.625 in., 5.5 in., 7.5 in., 10.5 in. bull. Weight: 45–55 oz. Length: 10.5 in. to 16.5 in. overall. Grips: Rosewood. Sights: .125-in. ramp front, micro-click rear adjustable for windage and elevation. Features: Ruger transfer bar safety system, fluted or unfluted cylinder, steel grip and cylinder frame, round or square back triggerguard, wide serrated trigger, wide spur hammer. With case and lock.

Price: **$829.00**

RUGER NEW MODEL SUPER BLACKHAWK HUNTER

Caliber: .44 Magnum. Capacity: 6-round cylinder. Barrel: 7.5 in., full-length solid rib, unfluted cylinder. Weight: 52 oz. Length: 13.625 in. Grips: Black laminated wood. Sights: Adjustable rear, replaceable front blade. Features: Reintroduced Ultimate SA revolver. Includes instruction manual, high-impact case, set of medium scope rings, gun lock, ejector rod as standard. Bisley-style frame available.

Price: (Hunter, Bisley Hunter) **$959.00**

RUGER NEW VAQUERO SINGLE-ACTION

Calibers: .357 Magnum, .45 Colt. Capacity: 6-round cylinder. Barrel: 4.625 in., 5.5 in., 7.5 in. Weight: 39–45 oz. Length: 10.5 in. overall (4.625 in. barrel). Grips: Rubber with Ruger medallion. Sights: Fixed blade front, fixed notch rear. Features: Transfer bar safety system and loading gate interlock. Blued model color casehardened finish on frame, rest polished and blued. Engraved model available. Gloss stainless. Introduced 2005.

Price: **$829.00**

RUGER NEW MODEL BISLEY VAQUERO

Calibers: .357 Magnum, .45 Colt. Capacity: 6-round cylinder. Barrel: 5.5-in. Length: 11.12 in. Weight: 45 oz. Features: Similar to New Vaquero but with Bisley-style hammer and grip frame. Simulated ivory grips, fixed sights.

Price: **$899.00**

RUGER NEW BEARCAT SINGLE-ACTION
Caliber: .22 LR. Capacity: 6-round cylinder. Barrel: 4 in. Weight: 24 oz. Length: 9 in. overall. Grips: Smooth rosewood with Ruger medallion. Sights: Blade front, fixed notch rear. Distributor special edition available with adjustable sights. Features: Reintroduction of the Ruger Bearcat with slightly lengthened frame, Ruger transfer bar safety system. Available in blued finish only. Rosewood grips. Introduced 1996 (blued), 2003 (stainless). With case and lock.
Price: SBC-4, blued **$639.00**
Price: KSBC-4, satin stainless **$689.00**

RUGER WRANGLER
Caliber: .22 LR. Capacity: 6-round cylinder. Barrel: 3.75, 4.62, 6.5, and 7.5 in. Grips: Checkered synthetic. Sights: Fixed front and rear. Weight: 30 oz. Features: Inexpensive to own and inexpensive to shoot, this SA revolver is built on an aluminum alloy frame and fitted with a cold hammer-forged barrel. Available in three models with three different finishes: Black Cerakote, Silver Cerakote or Burnt Bronze Cerakote. Equipped with a transfer-bar mechanism and a freewheeling pawl, allowing for easy loading and unloading.
Price: **$269.00**

RUGER SUPER WRANGLER
Caliber: .22 LR/.22 WMR. Capacity: 6. Barrel: 5.5-in. Sights: adjustable. New family of single-action revolvers. A steel cylinder frame. The Super Wrangler is a convertible model that ships with two cylinders, one for inexpensive .22 LR and one for powerful .22 WMR ammunition.
Price: **$329.00**

RUGER WRANGLER BIRDSHEAD
Caliber: .22 LR, Grips: Birdshead synthetic. Capacity: 6. Front Sight: Blade. Barrel Length: 3.75 in. Overall Length: 8.62 in. Weight: 28 oz. Finish: Black Cerakote, silver Cerakote, burnt bronze Cerakote, Cylinder Frame Material: Aluminum alloy. Rear Sight: Integral. Twist 1:14 in. RH. Grooves: 6
Price: **$279.00**

STANDARD MANUFACTURING NICKEL SINGLE ACTION

Calibers: .38 Special, .45 Colt. Capacity: 6-round cylinder. Barrels: 4.75, 5.5 and 7.5 in. Grips: Walnut. Sights: Fixed front and rear. Weight: 40 oz. Features: This is one of the finest Single Action Army reproductions ever built, with great attention to detail. Made entirely from 4140 steel, the new nickel-plated revolvers are available in .38 special and the iconic .45 Colt. You can also opt for C-coverage engraving, making for a truly remarkable firearm. One- or two-piece walnut grips available.
Price: .... **$1,995.00 - $3,495.00**

TAURUS DEPUTY
Caliber: .45 Colt/.357 Magnum. Capacity: 6. Barrel Length: 4.75 and 5.5 in. Overall Length: 10.27 and 11.04 in. Overall Height: 5.11 in. Overall Width: 1.65 in. Weight: 36.4 oz./38.2 oz. (.45 Colt), 40.5 oz./41.6 oz. (.357 Mag.). Single-Action. Firing System: Hammer. Front Sight: Blade. Rear Sight: Fixed. Grips: Polymer. Frame Size: Medium. Frame Material: Steel. Barrel Material: Steel. Cylinder Material: Steel. Finish: Polished black. Safety: Transfer bar.
Price: **$610.00**

TAYLOR'S CATTLEMAN SERIES
Calibers: .357 Magnum or 45 Colt. Barrels: 4.75 in., 5.5 in., or 7.5 in. Features: Series of Single Action Army-style revolvers made in many variations.
Price: Gunfighter w/blued & color case finish...................... **$556.00**
Price: Stainless **$720.00**
Price: Nickel... **$672.00**
Price: Charcoal blued **$647.00**
Price: Bird's Head 3.5- or 4.5-in. bbl., walnut grips **$603.00**
Price: Engraved (shown)... **$925.00**

TAYLOR'S & COMPANY TC9 1873 CATTLEMAN
Caliber: 9mm. Barrel: 4.74- and 5.5-in. barrel lengths. The TC9 9mm pistol is offered in two styles; a large army-size, walnut checkered grip and a black checkered standard-size grip. The 9mm revolver clone has a steel frame with a rear frame notch and fixed front blade sight. This iconic 9mm 1873 Cattleman revolver is offered in a black checkered grip, casehardened frame, with a blued steel finish. Add 7% for the color-casehardened version.
Price: Walnut **$546.00**

TAYLOR'S & COMPANY GUNFIGHTER
Caliber: .357 Magnum, .45 Colt. Capacity: 6 rounds. Barrel: 4.75, 5.5 in. Grip: Walnut. Checkered or smooth. Sights: Fixed front and rear. Weight: 2.4 lbs. Features: This 1873 Colt Single Action Army replica features an Army-sized grip for users with large hands. Casehardened finish. Available with Taylor Tuned action for additional cost.
Price: Smooth grip.. **$599.00**
Price: Checkered grip **$629.00**

TAYLOR'S & COMPANY GUNFIGHTER DEFENDER
Caliber: .357 Mag., .45 LC Capacity: 6. Weight: 4.75 in. 2.45 lb., 5.5 in. 2.50 lb. Finish: Blue with case hardened frame. Grip/Stock: Checkered walnut. Manufacturer: Uberti. Sights: Fixed front blade. Rear Frame Notch. Overall Length: 4.75 in. (10.35 in.), 5.5 in. (11.10 in.), Action: Taylor tuning available. The Gunfighter Defender with lowered Runnin' Iron hammer, 1860 Army grip is longer and slightly wider than the smaller Navy grip usually found on 1873 single-action models.
Price: .... **$695.00–$847.00**

TAYLOR'S & COMPANY 1860 ARMY SNUB NOSE
Caliber: .36 Caliber, .44 Caliber. Capacity: 6 rounds. Barrel: 3 in. Grip: Checkered flattop birdshead grip. Sights: Fixed front and rear. Weight: 2.3 lbs. Features: 1860 Army Snub Nose blackpowder percussion replica revolver. It features a steel frame, shoulder stock frame cuts and screws, and a round barrel. Barrel and cylinder are blued while the frame is casehardened. A conversion cylinder is available to shoot smokeless ammunition. Manufactured exclusively by Pietta for Taylor's & Company.
Price: **$379.00**

UBERTI 1851–1860 CONVERSION
Calibers: .38 Special, .45 Colt. Capacity: 6-round engraved cylinder. Barrels: 4.75 in., 5.5 in., 7.5 in., 8 in. Weight: 2.6 lbs. (5.5-in. bbl.). Length: 13 in. overall (5.5-in. bbl.). Grips: Walnut. Features: Brass backstrap, triggerguard; color casehardened frame, blued barrel, cylinder. Introduced 2007.
Price: 1851 Navy **$569.00**
Price: 1860 Army **$589.00**

UBERTI 1871–1872 OPEN TOP
Calibers: .38 Special, .45 Colt. Capacity: 6-round engraved cylinder. Barrels: 4.75 in., 5.5 in., 7.5 in. Weight: 2.6 lbs. (5.5-in. bbl.). Length: 13 in. overall (5.5-in. bbl.). Grips: Walnut. Features: Blued backstrap, triggerguard; color casehardened frame, blued barrel, cylinder. Introduced 2007.
Price: .... **$539.00–$569.00**

UBERTI 1873 CATTLEMAN SINGLE-ACTION
Caliber: .45 Colt. Capacity: 6-round cylinder. Barrels: 4.75 in., 5.5 in., 7.5 in. Weight: 2.3 lbs. (5.5-in. bbl.). Length: 11 in. overall (5.5-in. bbl.). Grips: Styles: Frisco (pearl styled); Desperado (buffalo horn styled); Chisholm (checkered walnut); Gunfighter (black checkered), Cody (ivory styled), one-piece walnut. Sights: Blade front, groove rear. Features: Steel or brass

backstrap, triggerguard; color casehardened frame, blued barrel, cylinder. NM designates New Model plunger-style frame; OM designates Old Model screw cylinder pin retainer.
Price: 1873 Cattleman Frisco **$869.00**
Price: 1873 Cattleman Desperado (2006) **$889.00**
Price: 1873 Cattleman Chisholm (2006) **$599.00**
Price: 1873 Cattleman NM, blued 4.75 in. barrel **$669.00**
Price: 1873 Cattleman NM, Nickel finish, 7.5 in. barrel **$689.00**
Price: 1873 Cattleman Cody **$899.00**

UBERTI 1873 CATTLEMAN BIRD'S HEAD SINGLE ACTION
Calibers: .357 Magnum, .45 Colt. Capacity: 6-round cylinder. Barrels: 3.5 in., 4 in., 4.75 in., 5.5 in. Weight: 2.3 lbs. (5.5-in. bbl.). Length: 10.9 in. overall (5.5-in. bbl.). Grips: One-piece walnut. Sights: Blade front, groove rear. Features: Steel or brass backstrap, triggerguard; color casehardened frame, blued barrel, fluted cylinder.
Price: **$569.00**

UBERTI CATTLEMAN .22
Caliber: .22 LR. Capacity: 6- or 12-round cylinder. Barrel: 5.5 in. Grips: One-piece walnut. Sights: Fixed. Features: Blued and casehardened finish, steel or brass backstrap/triggerguard.
Price: (brass backstrap, triggerguard) **$539.00**
Price: (steel backstrap, triggerguard) **$559.00**
Price: (12-round model, steel backstrap, triggerguard) **$589.00**

UBERTI 1873 CATTLEMAN BRASS 9MM
Delivering the same performance and standout features as the 1873 Cattleman Brass 9mm, the 1873 Cattleman Brass Dual Cylinder ups the ante with two included cylinders — one chambered in 9mm Luger and the other in .357 Magnum.
Price: **$599.00**

UBERTI 1873 CATTLEMAN BRASS DUAL CYLINDER 9MM/.357 MAGNUM
Delivering the same performance and standout features as the 1873 Cattleman Brass 9mm, the 1873 Cattleman Brass Dual Cylinder ups the ante with two included cylinders — one chambered in 9mm Luger and the other in .357 Magnum.
Price: **$749.00**

UBERTI DALTON REVOLVER
Caliber: .45 Colt. Capacity: 6-round cylinder. Barrel: 5.5 in. Grips: Simulated pearl. Sights: Fixed front and rear. Weight: 2.3 lbs. Features: Uberti USA

Prices given are believed to be accurate at time of publication however, many factors affect retail pricing so exact prices are not possible.

expands its Outlaws & Lawmen Series of revolvers with the addition of the Dalton Revolver, a faithful reproduction of the Colt Single Action Army revolver used by Dalton Gang leader Bob Dalton. Features hand-chased engraving from famed Italian engraving company, Atelier Giovanelli, on the receiver, grip frame and cylinder.
Price: $1,109.00

UBERTI 1873 BISLEY SINGLE-ACTION
Calibers: .357 Magnum, .45 Colt (Bisley); .22 LR and .38 Special. (Stallion), both with 6-round fluted cylinder. Barrels: 4.75 in., 5.5 in., 7.5 in. Weight: 2–2.5 lbs. Length: 12.7 in. overall (7.5-in. barrel). Grips: Two-piece walnut. Sights: Blade front, notch rear. Features: Replica of Colt's Bisley Model. Polished blued finish, color casehardened frame. Introduced 1997.
Price: 1873 Bisley, 7.5-in. barrel $619.00

UBERTI 1873 BUNTLINE AND REVOLVER CARBINE SINGLE-ACTION
Caliber: .357 Magnum, .44-40, .45 Colt. Capacity: 6. Barrel: 18 in. Length: 22.9–34 in. Grips: Walnut pistol grip or rifle stock. Sights: Fixed or adjustable.
Price: 1873 Revolver Carbine, 18-in. bbl., 34 in. OAL $729.00
Price: 1873 Cattleman Buntline Target, 18-in. bbl. 22.9 in. OAL $639.00

UBERTI 1873 EL PATRÓN 9MM
Presented with checkered walnut grips, case-hardened frame, 5.5-inch blued barrel, numbered cylinder, and EasyView sights, the El Patrón has the classic profile of the Old West SAA revolvers.
Price: $729.00

UBERTI 1870 SCHOFIELD-STYLE TOP BREAK
Calibers: .38 Special, .44 Russian, .44-40, .45 Colt. Capacity: 6-round cylinder. Barrels: 3.5 in., 5 in., 7 in. Weight: 2.4 lbs. (5-in. barrel) Length: 10.8 in. overall (5-in. barrel). Grips: Two-piece smooth walnut or pearl. Sights: Blade front, notch rear. Features: Replica of Smith & Wesson Model 3 Schofield. Single-action, top break with automatic ejection. Polished blued finish (first model). Introduced 1994.
Price: ....$1,189.00-$1,599.00

UBERTI STAINLESS STEEL SHORT STROKE CMS PRO
Caliber: .45 Colt. Capacity: 6-round cylinder. Barrel: 3.5 in. Grips: Synthetic traditional. Sights: Fixed front and rear. Weight: 2.1 lbs. Features: Made specifically for the rigors of Cowboy Mounted Shooting competition, and built entirely of stainless steel. Good for quick, one-handed shooting while riding a horse. Features low-profile, short-stroke hammer with 20-percent less travel. Extra-wide, deeply grooved hammer, and chambered in the classic .45 Colt.
Price: $909.00

UBERTI STAINLESS STEEL SHORT STROKE CMS KL PRO
Caliber: .45 Colt. Capacity: 6-round cylinder. Barrel: 3.5 in. Grips: Synthetic bird's head. Sights: Fixed front and rear. Weight: 2.1 lbs. Features: Made specifically for the rigors of Cowboy Mounted Shooting competition, and

built entirely of stainless steel. This model is the result of the partnership between Uberti USA and legendary Cowboy Mounted Shooter competitor Kenda Lenseigne, winner of multiple world and national mounted shooting championships. It features a modified bird's-head grip with Lenseigne's brand on the grip and her signature engraved on the barrel. Features low-profile, short-stroke hammer with 20-percent less travel. Extra-wide, deeply grooved hammer, and chambered in the classic .45 Colt.
Price: $909.00

UBERTI USA DALTON
Caliber: .357 Magnum. Capacity: 6 rounds. Barrel: 5.5 in. Grip: Simulated pearl. Sights: Fixed front and rear. Weight: 2.3 lbs. Features: Uberti USA Outlaw & Lawmen Series of revolvers adds the Dalton — a faithful reproduction of the Colt Single Action Army revolver used by Dalton Gang leader Bob Dalton. Features hand-chased engraving from famed Italian engraving company, Atelier Giovanelli on the receiver, grip frame, and cylinder. This new version is chambered in .357 Magnum.
Price: $1,109.00

UBERTI USA FRANK
Caliber: .357 Magnum. Capacity: 6 rounds. Barrel: 7.5 in. Grip: Simulated ivory. Sights: Fixed front and rear. Weight: 2.3 lbs. Features: Uberti USA Outlaw & Lawmen Series of revolvers adds a .357 Magnum version of the Frank revolver, a faithful reproduction of the outlaw Frank James' 1875 Remington. Finished in nickel plating, the grip is simulated ivory with a lanyard loop.
Price: $949.00

UBERTI USA HARDIN
Caliber: .45 Colt. Capacity: 6 rounds. Barrel: 7 in. Grip: Simulated bison horn. Sights: Fixed front and rear. Weight: 2.6 lbs. Features: Uberti USA Outlaw & Lawmen Series adds the Hardin, a faithful reproduction of the Smith & Wesson Top-break revolver used by John Wesley Hardin. Features a case-colored frame and charcoal blue barrel and cylinder along with simulated bison-horn grip, chambered in .45 Colt.
Price: $1,479.00

UBERTI USA TEDDY
Caliber: .45 Colt. Capacity: 6 rounds. Barrel: 5.5 in. Grip: Simulated ivory. Sights: Fixed front and rear. Weight: 2.3 lbs. Features: Replica of the revolver Theodore Roosevelt carried on many of his adventures. A replica 1873 Colt, this one is chambered in .45 Colt, and features a nickel finish, full laser engraving along the frame, cylinder, and barrel, and simulated ivory grips.
Price: $1,249.00

Prices given are believed to be accurate at time of publication however, many factors affect retail pricing so exact prices are not possible.

79TH EDITION, 2025 ✦ 523

AMERICAN DERRINGER MODEL 1
Calibers: All popular handgun calibers plus .45 Colt/.410 Shotshell. Capacity: 2, (.45-70 model is single shot). Barrel: 3 in. Overall length: 4.82 in. Weight: 15 oz. Features: Manually operated hammer-block safety automatically disengages when hammer is cocked. Texas Commemorative has brass frame and is available in .38 Special, .44-40. or .45 Colt.
Price: .... $635.00–$735.00
Price: Texas Commemorative $835.00

AMERICAN DERRINGER MODEL 8
Calibers: .45 Colt/.410 shotshell. Capacity: 2. Barrel: 8 in. Weight: 24 oz.
Price: $915.00
Price: High polish finish $1,070.00

AMERICAN DERRINGER DA38
Calibers: .38 Special, .357 Magnum, 9mm Luger. Barrel: 3.3 in. Weight: 14.5 oz. Features: DA operation with hammer-block thumb safety. Barrel, receiver and all internal parts are made from stainless steel.
Price: .... $690.00–$740.00

BOND ARMS TEXAS DEFENDER DERRINGER
Calibers: Available in more than 10 calibers, from .22 LR to .45 LC/.410 shotshells. Barrel: 3 in. Weight: 20 oz. Length: 5 in. Grips: Rosewood. Sights: Blade front, fixed rear. Features: Interchangeable barrels, stainless steel firing pins, cross-bolt safety, automatic extractor for rimmed calibers. Stainless steel construction, brushed finish. Right or left hand.
Price: $543.00
Price: Interchangeable barrels, .22 LR thru .45 LC, 3 in. $139.00
Price: Interchangeable barrels, .45 LC, 3.5 in. .... $159.00–$189.00

BOND ARMS RANGER II
Caliber: .45 LC/.410 shotshells or .357 Magnum/.38 Special. Barrel: 4.25 in. Weight: 23.5 oz. Length: 6.25 in. Features: This model has a triggerguard. Intr. 2011. From Bond Arms.
Price: $673.00

BOND ARMS CENTURY 2000 DEFENDER
Calibers: .45 LC/.410 shotshells. or .357 Magnum/.38 Special. Barrel: 3.5 in. Weight: 21 oz. Length: 5.5 in. Features: Similar to Defender series.
Price: $517.00

BOND ARMS COWBOY DEFENDER
Calibers: From .22 LR to .45 LC/.410 shotshells. Barrel: 3 in. Weight: 19 oz. Length: 5.5 in. Features: Similar to Defender series. No triggerguard.
Price: $493.00

BOND ARMS GRIZZLY
Calibers: .45 Colt/.410 bore. Capacity: 2 rounds. Barrel: 3 in. Grips: Rosewood. Sights: Fixed front and rear. Features: Similar to other Bond Arms derringers, this model is chambered in .45 Colt and 2.5-inch, .410-bore shotshells. Vibrant rosewood grips with grizzly-bear artwork adorn the Grizzly. It includes a matching leather holster embossed with a grizzly bear.
Price: $377.00

BOND ARMS SNAKE SLAYER
Calibers: .45 LC/.410 shotshell (2.5 in. or 3 in.). Barrel: 3.5 in. Weight: 21 oz. Length: 5.5 in. Grips: Extended rosewood. Sights: Blade front, fixed rear. Features: Single-action; interchangeable barrels; stainless steel firing pin. Introduced 2005.
Price: $603.00

BOND ARMS ROUGHNECK
Calibers: 9mm, .357 Magnum, .45 ACP. Capacity: 2 rounds. Barrel: 2.5 in. Grips: Textured rubber. Sights: Fixed front and rear. Weight: 22 oz. Features: A member of the new Bond Arms Rough series of derringers that includes the premium features found in all Bond guns, including stainless steel barrel, cross-bolt safety, retracting firing pin, spring-loaded, cam-lock lever and rebounding hammer. Each gun of the new series undergoes a quick clean up and deburring and then is bead-blasted, giving it a rough finish. This lightweight tips the scales at 22 ounces.
Price: $269.00

BOND ARMS ROWDY XL
Caliber: .45 Colt/.410. Barrel: 3.5 in. Extended grip size. Length: 5.75 in. Weight 22 oz. Grip: B6 Resin.
Price: $349.00

BOND ARMS CYCLOPS
Caliber: .45-70 Govt., .44 Rem. Mag., .50 AE. Barrel: 4.25 in. Length: 6.75 in. Grip: B6 Nylon. Weight: 28 oz. Extended grip. Trigger pull: 7 lbs.
Price: $699.00
Price: .44 Rem. Mag./.50 AE $650.00

BOND ARMS SNAKE SLAYER IV
Calibers: .45 LC/.410 shotshell (2.5 in. or 3 in.). Barrel: 4.25 in. Weight: 22 oz. Length: 6.25 in. Grips: Extended rosewood. Sights: Blade front, fixed rear. Features: Single-action; interchangeable barrels; stainless steel firing pin. Introduced 2006.
Price: $648.00

BOND ARMS STINGER
Calibers: 9mm, .380 ACP. The All-New Stinger has the same quality as Bond Arms' regular models but has half the weight and a slimmer profile. Features:

Prices given are believed to be accurate at time of publication however, many factors affect retail pricing so exact pricing are not possible.

Stainless steel matte barrel, 7075 anodized aluminum frame. Total weight: 12 oz. Rebounding hammer, retracting firing pins, cross-bolt safety. Comes with standard rubber grips and a slimmer set of polymer grips.
Price: **$379.00**

BOND ARMS STUBBY
Caliber: .22 LR, .380 ACP, 9mm. Barrel: 2.2 in. Thin nylon grip. Fixed sight. Length: 4.5 in. Height: 3.75 in. Weight: 13.3 oz. Trigger pull: 7 lbs. Width: 5/16 in.
Price: **$297.00**

BOND ARMS HONEY B
Caliber: .22 LR, .22 Magnum, 9mm, .38 Special. Capacity: 2. Barrel Length: 3 in. Grip Material: B6 Resin. Grip Size: Extended. Sights: Fixed. Length: 5.5 in. Height: 4.19 in. Weight: 17.5 oz. Action: Single Action. Trigger Pull Weight: 7 lb. Triggerguard: Yes. Frame Material: Stainless steel. Frame Type: Stinger RS.
Price: **$320.00**

DOUBLETAP DERRINGER
Calibers: .45 Colt or 9mm Barrel: 3 in. Weight: 12 oz. Length: 5.5 in. Sights: Adjustable. Features: Over/under, two-barrel design. Rounds are fired individually with two separate trigger pulls. Tip-up design, aluminum frame.
Price: **$499.00**

HEIZER PAK1
Caliber: 7.2x39. Similar to Pocket AR but chambered for 7.62x39mm. Single shot. Barrel: 3.75 in., ported or unported. Length: 6.375 in. Weight: 23 oz.
Price: **$339.00**

HEIZER PS1 POCKET SHOTGUN
Calibers: .45 Colt or .410 shotshell. Single-shot. Barrel: Tip-up, 3.25 in. Weight: 22 oz. Length: 5.6 in. Width: .742 in Height: 3.81 in. Features: Available in several finishes. Standard model is matte stainless or black. Also offered in Hedy Jane series for the women in pink or in two-tone combinations of stainless and pink, blue, green, purple. Includes interchangeable AR .223 barrel. Made in the USA by Heizer Industries.
Price: **$499.00**

HEIZER POCKET AR
Caliber: .223 Rem./5.56 NATO. Single shot. Barrel: 3.75 in., ported or non-ported. Length: 6.375 in. Weight: 23 oz. Features: Similar to PS1 pocket shotgun but chambered for .223/5.56 rifle cartridge.
Price: **$339.00**

HENRY MARE'S LEG
Calibers: .22 LR, .22 WMR, .357 Magnum, .44 Magnum, .45 Colt. Capacities: 10 rounds (.22 LR), 8 rounds (.22 WMR), 5 rounds (others). Barrel: 12.9 in. Length: 25 in. Weight: 4.5 lbs. (rimfire) to 5.8 lbs. (centerfire calibers). Features: Lever-action operation based on Henry rifle series and patterned after gun made famous in Steve McQueen's 1950s TV show, "Wanted: Dead or Alive." Made in the USA.
Price: .22 LR **$462.00**
Price: .22 WMR **$473.00**
Price: Centerfire calibers **$1,024.00**

HERITAGE MARE'S LEG
Caliber: .22 LR. Capacity: 10. Frame Material: Aluminum alloy. Barrel Material: Alloy steel. Finish: Polished black oxide. Stock Material: Wood. Action Type: Lever-action. Overall Width: 1.55 in. Overall Height: 7.35 in.
Price: .22 LR...**$485.00**

MAXIMUM SINGLE-SHOT
Calibers: .22 LR, .22 Hornet, .22 BR, .22 PPC, 223 Rem., .22-250, 6mm BR, 6mm PPC, .243, .250 Savage, 6.5mm-35M, .270 MAX, .270 Win., 7mm TCU, 7mm BR, 7mm-35, 7mm INT-R, 7mm-08, 7mm Rocket, 7mm Super-Mag., .30 Herrett, .30 Carbine, .30-30, .308 Win., 30x39, .32-20, .350 Rem. Mag., .357 Mag., .357 Maximum, .358 Win., .375 H&H, .44 Mag., .454 Casull. Barrel: 8.75 in., 10.5 in., 14 in. Weight: 61 oz. (10.5-in. bbl.); 78 oz. (14-in. bbl.). Length: 15 in., 18.5 in. overall (with 10.5- and 14-in. bbl., respectively). Grips: Smooth walnut stocks and fore-end. Also available with 17-finger-groove grip. Sights: Ramp front, fully adjustable open rear. Features: Falling block action; drilled and tapped for M.O.A. scope mounts; integral grip frame/receiver; adjustable trigger; Douglas barrel (interchangeable). Introduced 1983. Made in USA by M.O.A. Corp.
Price: **$1,062.00**

NOSLER MODEL 48 CUSTOM HANDGUN (NCH)
Calibers: 22 Nosler, 7mm-08, 6mm Creedmoor, 6.5 Creedmoor, .308 Winchester. Standard barrel length 15 in. 12- to 18-inch barrels available upon request. Stock: CNC machined 6061-T6 aircraft-grade aluminum. Bedded action. Free-floated barrel. Finish: Variety of Cerakote colors and combinations. Action: single-shot, solid bottom receiver. Brake: Harrell's Precision Tactical 4-Port is available. Grip: Accepts standard AR-15 grips. Ships with Hogue OverMolded rubber grip with finger grooves. Barrel: Shilen 416R stainless heavy contour. Threaded at the muzzle, supplied with

Prices given are believed to be accurate at time of publication however, many factors affect retail pricing so exact prices are not possible.

79TH EDITION, 2025 ⊕ **525**

thread protector. Barrel fluting is available for an additional charge.

Price: **$2,495.00**

ROSSI BRAWLER

Caliber: .45 Colt/.410 ga (2.5- and 3-in. shells). Single shot. Frame Material: Polymer. Frame Finish: Black. Barrel Material: Alloy steel. Barrel Finish: Matte black. Overall Width: 1.30 in. Overall Height: 5.90 in. Overall Weight: 36.80 oz. Barrel Length: 9.00 in. Overall Length: 14.00 in. Front Sight: Fixed. Rear Sight: Serrated. Grip Material: Rubber. Firing System: Hammer. Safety: Thumb safety, transfer bar.

Price: **$258.00**

SAVAGE ARMS 110 PCS (PISTOL CHASSIS SYSTEM)

Calibers: 6.5 Creedmoor, .308 Win., .350 Legend, .300 AAC BLK., .223 Rem. Features: Carbon steel, matte black, barrel and receiver. Medium-contour 10.5-in. barrel, with threaded muzzle (5/8x24). Machined aluminum, 1-piece chassis with 7-in. free-floating modular forend with M-LOK slots and Cerakote finish. 1-Piece 0 MOA rail. Left-hand bolt, right-side eject. Spiral fluted bolt body. 2.5 to 6-lb. user-adjustable AccuTrigger, Picatinny rail at rear of chassis. Accepts most AR-15 pistol grips. Barricade grooves milled into the front of the magazine well, ambidextrous magazine release and AICS magazine.

Price: From **$999.00**

BENELLI ETHOS
Gauges: 12 ga., 20 ga., 28 ga. 3 in. Capacity: 4+1. Barrel: 26 in. or 28 in. (Full, Mod., Imp. Cyl., Imp. Mod., Cylinder choke tubes). Weights: 6.5 lbs. (12 ga.), 5.3–5.7 (20 & 28 ga.). Length: 49.5 in. overall (28 in. barrel). Stock: Select AA European walnut with satin finish. Sights: Red bar fiber optic front, with three interchangeable inserts, metal middle bead. Features: Utilizes Benelli's Inertia Driven system. Recoil is reduced by Progressive Comfort recoil reduction system within the buttstock. Twelve and 20-gauge models cycle all 3-inch loads from light 7/8 oz. up to 3-inch magnums. Also available with nickel-plated engraved receiver. Imported from Italy by Benelli USA, Corp.
Price: **$1,999.00**
Price: Engraved nickel-plated (shown)...........................**$2,149.00**
Price: 20 or 28 ga. (engraved, nickel plated only) **$2,149.00**

BENELLI ETHOS BE.S.T.
Benelli expands its Ethos line with the new BE.S.T. model, so named for the Benelli Surface Treatment, a proprietary coating that protects steel from rust and corrosion and was tested over several months in saltwater with no signs of corrosion. Parts treated with BE.S.T. are backed with a 25-year warranty against rust and corrosion.
Price: **$2,199.00**

BENELLI ETHOS CORDOBA BE.S.T.
Gauge: 12 ga. 3in., 20ga. 3in, 28ga. 3in. Barrel: 28 in. or 30 in. ventilated wide rib. Length: 49.5 –51.5 in. Weight: 5.4–7.0 lbs. Stock: Black Synthetic. Features: Benelli expands their Ethos line of Inertia-Driven semi-autos with the new BE.S.T. (Benelli Surface Treatment). This Cordoba version is designed for high-volume shooting like that of dove hunting in Argentina — the gun's namesake location. Specialty features include ported barrels, ComforTech recoil-reducing system, and lighter weight. Fiber optic front sight with mid-rib bead on a wide broadway sight channel. Shell View system places small windows in the magazine tube for quickly visualizing remaining shell count. Advertised to handle 3-inch magnum rounds down to the lightest 7/8-ounce loads. Ships with five extended Crio chokes (C, IC, M, IM, F).
Price: **$2,349.00**

BENELLI ETHOS SPORT
Gauges: 12 ga., 20 ga., 28 ga. 3 in. Capacity: 4+1. Barrel: Ported, 28 in. or 30 in. (12 ga. only). Full, Mod., Imp. Cyl., Imp. Mod., Cylinder extended choke tubes. Wide rib. Other features similar to Ethos model.
Price: **$2,269.00**

BENELLI ETHOS SUPER SPORT
Gauge: 12 ga. 3in., 20ga. 3in. Barrel: 26 in. or 28 in. ventilated wide rib. Length: 49.5–51.5 in. Weight: 5.4–7.0 lbs. Stock: Carbon-fiber finish composite stock and fore-end. Features: Benelli expands their Ethos semi-automatic line with the Super Sport competition-ready model. Lightweight, weather-resistant carbon-fiber finish furniture. Inertia-Driven semi-automatic with ComforTech recoil-reducing system. Ported Crio barrel. Fiber optic front sight and mid-barrel bead. Nickel-plated receiver. Capacity of 4+1 rounds. Ships with five extended Crio chokes (C, IC, M, IM, F).
Price: **$2,299.00**

BENELLI ETHOS SUPERSPORT PERFORMANCE SHOP AI
Gauge: 12 ga. 3 in. Barrel: 30 in. with carbon-fiber ventilated rib, ported. Stock: Carbon-fiber ComfortTech3. Length: 51.5 in. Weight: 7 lbs. Features: Performance Shop edition with nickel-plated receiver, gloss blued barrel, and red controls. Oversized Briley bolt handle and bolt release, and Briley

6-oz. weighted forend cap for forward balance. Briley Spectrum extended, color-coded choke tubes. Advanced Impact (AI) denotes an AI Crio barrel and extended AI Crio choke tubes.
Price: **$3,339.00**

BENELLI M2 FIELD
Gauges: 12 ga., 20 ga. Barrel: 24, 26, and 28 in. Crio treated. Stock: Black synthetic, Mossy Oak Bottomland, Gore Optifade, Realtree Max-7. Features: The workhorse Field line gets a full redesign for 2023, including sleeker stock dimensions, a longer forend grip surface, an oversized bolt release button, and a new MicroCell recoil unit. A revised bolt touts improved smoothness of cycling with Benelli's Inertia Drive system. Ships with Crio chokes. Available in both standard and compact models.
Price: Black **$1,399.00**
Price: Camo **$1,499.00**

BENELLI M2 TURKEY EDITION
Gauges: 12 ga. and 20 ga., Full, Imp. Mod, Mod., Imp. Cyl., Cyl. choke tubes. Barrel: 24 in. Weight: 6-7 lbs. Stock: 12 ga. model has ComfortTech with pistol grip, Bottomland/Cerakote finish. 20 ga. has standard stock with Realtree APG finish. Features: From the Benelli Performance Shop.
Price: 20 ga. standard stock **$3,199.00**
Price: 12 ga. pistol grip stock **$3,399.00**

BENELLI MONTEFELTRO
Now updated with Benelli's Inertia-Drive bolt system. 12 and 20 ga. 24, 26, 28 in gloss blued barrels. Anodized black receiver. Three Crio chokes. Satin A-Grade Walnut stocks. Red fiber optic front sight. Standard and compact versions available. The Ultra Light variant introduced in 2024 with weight starting at 5.3 pounds with a shortened mag tube and carbon-fiber rib. The Sporting also debuted at the same time with a 30-inch barreled 12-gauge and 28-inch 20-gauge, each with barrel porting, extended Crio chokes, and a high-profile stepped rib.
Price: **$1,499.00**
Price: Ultra Light...**$1,949.00**
Price: Sporting **$1,649.00**

BENELLI SUPER BLACK EAGLE III (SBE3)
Gauge: 12 ga. 3 in., 20 ga. 3 in., 28 ga. 3 in. Barrel: 26, 28 or 30-in. ventilated rib. Length: 47.5–49.5 in. Weight: 5.8–6.9 lbs. Stock: Synthetic with multiple finish choices. Features: Benelli expands their inertia-driven semi-automatic SBE III line by adding a 3-inch chambered 28-gauge model for 2022, which will have slimmer lines. Models available in Black synthetic, Realtree MAX-5, Gore OptiFade Timber, and Mossy Oak Bottomland. ComforTech stock for recoil reduction, Easy Locking bolt, and beveled loading port. Realtree Max-7 camo available across the line on both right- and left-hand models. 28-Gauge additions: 3-in. chambers now available in variants with black synthetic and all camos. 26- or 28-in. barrels. Addition of Compact Series models for 2024 with 26-inch barrel and shorter 13-1/8 inch LOP.
Price: **$1,999.00–2,199.00**
Price: 28 ga. Black **$1,899.00**
Price: 28 ga. Camo **$1,999.00**
Price: Compact 12, 20, 28 ga....................................**$1,949.00**

BENELLI SUPER BLACK EAGLE III BE.S.T.
Benelli expands its SBE III line with the new BE.S.T. model, so named for the

Prices given are believed to be accurate at time of publication however, many factors affect retail pricing so exact prices are not possible.

79TH EDITION, 2025 ⊕ **527**

Benelli Surface Treatment, a proprietary coating that protects steel from rust and corrosion and was tested over several months in saltwater with no signs of corrosion. Parts treated with BE.S.T. are backed with a 25-year warranty against rust and corrosion. The BE.S.T. package will be available on select SBE III models.

Price: **$2,199.00**

BENELLI SUPERSPORT & SPORT II

Gauges: 20 ga., 12 ga., 3-in. chamber. Capacity: 4+1. Barrels: 28 in., 30 in., ported, 10mm sporting rib. Weight: 7.2–7.3 lbs. Lengths: 49.6–51.6 in. Stock: Carbon fiber, ComforTech (Supersport) or walnut (Sport II). Sights: Red bar front, metal midbead. Sport II is similar to the Legacy model except has nonengraved dual tone blued/silver receiver, ported wide-rib barrel, adjustable buttstock, and functions with all loads. Walnut stock with satin finish. Introduced 1997. Features: Designed for high-volume sporting clays. Inertia-driven action, Extended CrioChokes. Ported. Imported from Italy by Benelli USA.

Price: SuperSport **$2,199.00**
Price: Sport II **$1,899.00**

BENELLI SUPER VINCI

Gauge: 12 ga.. 2 3/4 in., 3 in. and 3 1/2 in. Capacity: 3+1. Barrels: 26 in., 28 in. Weights: 6.9–7 lbs. Lengths: 48.5–50.5 in. Stock: Black synthetic, Realtree Max4 and Realtree APG. Features: Crio Chokes: C,IC,M,IM,F. Length of Pull: 14.375 in. Drop at Heel: 2 in. Drop at Comb: 1.375 in. Sights: Red bar front sight and metal bead mid-sight. Minimum recommended load: 3-dram, 1 1/8 oz. loads (12 ga.). Receiver drilled and tapped for scope mounting. Imported from Italy by Benelli USA., Corp.

Price: Black Synthetic Comfortech **$1,799.00**
Price: Camo **$1,899.00**

BERETTA A300 ULTIMA TURKEY

Gauges: 12 ga., 20 ga. Barrels: 24 in. Stock: Synthetic in Realtree Edge or Mossy Oak DNA. Features: New turkey hunting-specific addition to A300 Ultima family of semi-autos. Low-profile receiver with oversized loading port. Enlarged controls. Picatinny top rail. Mid bead and fiber optic front sight. KickOff recoil system comes standard. Extended Mobil choke.

Price: Black Synthetic Comfortech **$999.00**

BERETTA A300 ULTIMA SNOW GOOSE ARCTIC FOX

Gauges: 12 ga., 3 in. Barrel: 28 in. Stock: Synthetic. Features: New high-capacity snow goose addition to the A300 Ultima family of semi-autos. Low-profile receiver with oversized loading port. Enlarged controls. Fiber-optic front sight with receiver cut out for optic. Special gloved-finger groove cut in receiver. Lower Picatinny rail for mounting a camera or accessories. Extended magazine tube. Entire gun covered in snow camouflage.

Price: **$1,399.00**

BERETTA A400 UPLAND 28

Gauges: 28 ga. Barrels: 28 in. with 5x5 top rib. Stock: Wood, pistol grip style. Features: Latest addition to the A400 Upland family of gas-operated semi-autos. Nickel-plated receiver with unique "28" gauge-specific receiver engraving. Magnum, 3-in. chamber. Field strip without tools. Extralight recoil pad. Ships with three OPHC flush chokes.

Price: Black Synthetic Comfortech **$1,829.00**

BROWNING A5

Gauges: 12 ga, 3 or 3.5 in.; 16 ga., 2.75 in. Barrel: 26, 28, or 30 in. Weight: 5.95–7.0 lbs. Stock: Dependent on model, but current listings include high-gloss Walnut, black synthetic, or camouflage variants. Features: Operates

on Kinematic short-recoil system, different from the classic Auto-5 long-recoil action built since 1903 and discontinued in the 1990's. New model features lengthened forcing cone, interchangeable choke tubes, and ventilated rib with multiple front sight options depending on model. A5 Full Camo: Composite stock models with complete camo coverage.

Price: ....**$2,049.00–$2,129.00**
Price: A5 Wicked Wing with Vintage Tan camo ....**$2,279.00–$2,379.00**
Price: A5 in Vintage Tan camo **$1,939.00**
Price: A5 Lightning Sweet 16 w/lightweight black anodized receiver ..**$1,819.00**
Price: A5 Sweet 16 w/ brushed nickel receiver & oil finish Walnut.**$2,029.00**
Price: A5 Sweet 16 with Mossy Oak Shadow Grass Habitat camo ..**$1,999.00**

BROWNING A-5 HUNTER 20-GAUGE

Gauges: 20 ga., 3 in. Barrel: 26 or 28-in. steel. Weight: 5 lbs., 9 oz. to 5 lbs., 10 oz. Stock: High-gloss Grade 1 Turkish Walnut with 18 LPI cut checkering. Features: The 20-gauge variant is new for 2024 and built on a smaller frame. Operates on Kinematic short-recoil system, different from the classic Auto-5 long- recoil action built since 1903 and discontinued in the 1990s. Chrome-plated chamber, anodized black receiver, flush Invector DS- choke tubes. Interchangeable choke tubes. Inflex 2 recoil pad, Speed Load Plus system, Brushed Nickel bolt slide finish.

Price: **$1,979.00**

BROWNING MAXUS II

Gauge: 12 ga. With models in both 3 or 3.5 in. Barrel: 26, 28, or 30 in. Weight: 7.0–7.3 lbs. Stock: Dependent on model, but current listings include black synthetic and camouflaged variants. Features: Builds on Browning's Power Drive gas-operated Maxus autoloader in a II version with enhancements. Chrome chamber and bore. Ramped triggerguard for easier loading. Composite stock can be trimmed and is shim adjustable for cast, drop, and LOP. Rubber overmolding on the stock, including SoftFlex cheek pad and Inflex recoil pad. Oversized controls. New screw-on magazine cap design. Includes Invector-Plus choke tubes, extended on most models, as well as an ABS hard case.

Price: Maxus II Ultimate with nickel receiver & Grade III Walnut ...**$2,129.00**
Price: Maxus II Wicked Wing Camo.............................**$2,099.00–$2,249.00**
Price: Maxus II Camo **$1,949.00–2,049.00**
Price: Maxus II Hunter in matte black/ Satin finish Walnut.............**$1,729.00**
Price: Maxus II Stalker all black ....**$1,729.00–$1,929.00**
Price: Maxus II Upland in nickel/ Walnut **$1,799.00**
Price: Maxus II Hunter Maple w/ Maple stock............................**$1,869.00**
Price: Maxus II Sporting Carbon Fiber..**$1,999.00**
Price: Maxus II Sporting in matte black/ Walnut **$2,269.00**

BROWNING SILVER

Gauges: 12 ga., 3 in. or 3 1/2 in.; 20 ga., 3 in. chamber. Barrels: 26 in., 28 in., 30 in. Invector Plus choke tubes. Weights: 7 lbs., 9 oz. (12 ga.), 6 lbs., 7 oz. (20 ga.). Stock: Satin finish walnut or composite. Features: Active Valve gas system, semi-humpback receiver. Invector Plus choke system, three choke tubes. Imported by Browning.

Price: Silver Field, 12 ga....................................**$1,279.00–$1,329.00**
Price: Silver Field, 20 ga....................................**$1,069.00–$1,329.00**
Price: Silver Field Composite, 12 ga., 3 in. **$1,199.00**
Price: Silver Field Composite, 12 ga., 3 1/2 in............................**$1,279.00**
Price: Silver Field Rifled Deer Matte..**$1,379.00**
Price: Silver Field Rifled Deer OVIX Camo.. ....**$1,479.00**
Price: Silver Field Camo.. ....**$1,349.00**

CHARLES DALY MODEL 600

Gauges: 12 ga. or 20 ga. (3 in.) or 28 ga. (2 3/4 in.). Capacity: 5+1. Barrels: 26 in., 28 in. (20 and 28 ga.), 26 in., 28 in. or 30 in. (12 ga.). Three choke tubes provided

(Rem-Choke pattern). Stock: Synthetic, wood or camo. Features: Comes in several variants including Field, Sporting Clays, Tactical and Trap. Left-hand models available. Uses gas-assisted recoil operation. Imported from Turkey.

Price: Field 12, 20 ga. **$480.00**
Price: Field 28 ga. **$531.00**
Price: Sporting **$858.00**
Price: Tactical **$685.00**

CZ-USA 712 G3
Gauges: 12 ga. Barrels: 20, 26, 28 in. with 7mm flat-vent rib. Stock: Turkish Walnut, synthetic camo Terra. Features: Redesign third-generation gas-operated gun chambering 2.75- or 3-in. shells. Two interchangeable pistons are included for light and heavy loads. Chrome-lined barrel. Ships with five extra-long Active-Choke tubes.

Price: G3 Standard or Utility (20 in.) **$579.00**
Price: G3 Camo **$679.00**

CZ 1012
Gauge: 12 ga., 3 in. Capacity: 4+1. Barrel: 28 in., 8mm flat ventilated rib. Weight: 6.5-6.9 lbs. Length: 47 in. Stock: Options in either Turkish walnut or black synthetic. Features: The company's first gas-less, inertia-driven semi-automatic wears a gloss-black chrome barrel finish along with a choice of three receiver finishes: standard blued, bronze or gray. Oversized controls ideal for use when wearing gloves. Cross-bolt safety located at front of triggerguard. Addition of 26-inch barreled models to the existing 1012 inertia-driven repeater lineup. Includes two camouflaged synthetic stock options as well as checkered Walnut, consistent with the existing 1012 family. Includes five chokes (F, IM, M, IC, C).

Price: **$645.00**

EUROPEAN AMERICAN ARMORY (EAA) MC312 GOBBLER
Gauge: 12 ga., 3.5 in. Barrel: 24 in., with ventilated turkey rib. Length: 50 in. Stock: Synthetic camouflage with either straight or pistol-grip options. Features: The MC312 inertia-driven semi-auto produced by Girsan gets a turkey upgrade with a shorter barrel, mid-bead, Picatinny rail cut into the receiver, Cerakote finish receiver and barrel, cross-bolt safety, sling studs, rubber buttpad, fiber-optic front sight, and field-tested reflex optic. Includes flush mount choke tubes.

Price: **$600.00**

EUROPEAN AMERICAN ARMORY (EAA) AKKAR CHURCHILL 220
Gauge: 20 ga. Barrel: 18.5 in. Length: 37.5 in. Weight: 5.0 lbs. Stock: Black synthetic pistol grip style. Features: This Turkish-made semi-automatic springs from the Churchill 220 series of gas-driven repeaters is now re-vamped for home defense and tactical use. Optics rail machined into receiver for easy target acquisition with included red-dot optic on quick-release mount. Semi-enhanced loading port. Accessible controls. 5+1 round capacity. Checkered pistol grip stock. Black rubber recoil pad, sling swivels. Door-breaching choke tube and shrouded red fiber-optic front sight.

Price: **$561.00**

EAA/GIRSAN MC312
Gauge: 12 ga. Barrel: 28 in. vent rib. Length: 50 in. Weight: 6.95 lbs. Stock: Polymer in choice of either black or camo. Features: Inertia-driven single-action hunting autoloader. Lightweight aircraft aluminum receiver 5+1 round capacity. Fiber-optic front sight. Passed EAA's 5,000-round test with no cleaning and 10,000-round test with no parts replacement.

Price: .... **$431.00–$499.00**

EAA/GIRSAN MC312 GOOSE
Gauge: 12 ga. Barrel: 30-in. vent rib. Length: 52 in. Weight: 6.75 lbs. Stock:

Black polymer. Features: Goose variant of the inertia-driven MC312 line. Lightweight aircraft aluminum receiver with machined integral accessory rail for the included red-dot optic. Fiber-optic front sight. Ships with five extended choke tubes. Same 5+1 capacity as the standard MC312.

Price: **$627.00**

FRANCHI AFFINITY 3
Gauge: 12 ga. 3 in., 20 ga. Barrel: 26 in., 28 in. vent rib. Length: 49.25 in. Weight: 6 lbs. to 6.8 lbs. Stock: Synthetic with various finishes and walnut options. Features: Re-designed line of inertia-driven shotguns launched in 2017, upgrade from the original Affinity. Omni-stock with shims for adjustable fit. TSA recoil pad for up to 50% felt recoil reduction over previous design. Set of three choke tubes come standard. Receiver drilled and tapped for optics mounting. Oversized controls, beveled loading port, and one-piece removeable trigger group.

Price: **$949.00**
Price: Camo and Cerakote 12-ga. models **$1, 179.00**
Price: Left-Hand Models in 12 or 20 Ga **$949.00**
Price: Compact 20ga. **$999.00**
Price: Turkey **$1,049.00**
Price: Sporting **$1,099.00**
Price: Catalyst **$1,049.00**
Price: Sport Trap **$999.00**

FRANCHI AFFINITY 3 ELITE
Gauges: 12ga. 3 in., 12ga. 3.5in., 20ga. 3 in. Barrel: 26 or 28 in. ventilated rib. Length: 48.5–50.75 in. Weight: 6.0–7.1 lbs. Stock: Synthetic with OptiFade Marsh or OptiFade Timber camo. Features: The Affinity Elite lineup offers semi-customized features building on the Affinity Italian-made family of Inertia-Drive semi-autos. Cerakote and OptiFade camo finishes. Oversized controls, lengthened forcing cone, TruGlo front sight. Oversized loading port, ambidextrous safety, chrome lined barrel. Drilled and tapped for optics mounting. Twin Shock Absorber (TSA) recoil pad allows for LOP adjustments. Capacity of 4+1 rounds. Includes shims for fitting drop and cast. Ships with three extended waterfowl chokes (Close, Mid, Long-Range).

Price: Upland Elite **$1,279.00**
Price: Waterfowl Elite **$1,349.00**
Price: Turkey Elite **$1,349.00**

FRANCHI AFFINITY 3.5
Magnum 3.5-inch chambered versions of the Affinity repeater, as well as 3.5 Elite models.

Price: **$1,129.00**
Price: Cerakote **$1,349.00**
Price: 3.5 Turkey Elite **$1,529.00**
Price: 3.5 Waterfowl Elite **$1,529.00**

J.P. SAUER & SOHN SL5 TURKEY
Gauge: 12 ga. 3 in. Barrel: 18.5-in. deep-drilled, chrome-lined, with stepped rib. Weight: 7 lbs. Stock: Fixed synthetic pistol-grip style in choice of three Mossy Oak camo patterns: Obsession, Bottomland, or New Bottomland. Features: Durable inertia-driven semi-automatic with black anodized receiver. Oversized bolt handle and release button. Removeable Picatinny rail. Cervellati recoil pad and sling attachments. Red single-bead LPA front fiber-optic sight. Made in Italy and backed by 10-year warranty. Ships with three chokes: flush Cylinder, extender CRIO Plus Modified, and Carlson extended Turkey choke.

Price: **$1,199.00**

Prices given are believed to be accurate at time of publication however, many factors affect retail pricing so exact prices are not possible.

79TH EDITION, 2025 529

J.P. SAUER & SOHN SL-5 WATERFOWL

Gauges: 12 ga. Barrels: 26, 28, 30-in. chrome-lined with stepped rib Stock: Synthetic with choice of black or Fred Bear Old School camouflage. Features: Latest addition to the inertia-driven semi-automatic line. Steel upper receiver and aluminum lower. Magnum 3.5-in. chamber. Extended bolt handle and release button. Cervellati recoil pad. Rubberized comb. Ships with five Crio Plus extended chokes.

Price: Black Synthetic **$1,579.00**
Price: Fred Bear Old School Camo **$1,679.00**
Price: Fred Bear Camo/Cerakote **$1,779.00**

MOSSBERG MODEL 935 MAGNUM

Gauge: 12 ga. 3 in. and 3 1/2-in., interchangeable. Barrels: 22 in., 24 in., 26 in., 28in. Weights: 7.25–7.75 lbs. Lengths: 45–49 in. overall. Stock: Synthetic. Features: Gas-operated semi-auto models in blued or camo finish. Fiber-optics sights, drilled and tapped receiver, interchangeable Accu-Mag choke tubes.

Price: 935 Magnum Turkey Pistol grip; full pistol grip stock **$924.00**
Price: 935 Magnum Grand Slam: 22 in. barrel **$756.00**
Price: 935 Magnum Waterfowl: 26 in. or 28 in. barrel .... **$660.00–$735.00**
Price: 935 Pro Series Waterfowl **$875.00**

MOSSBERG 940 JM PRO

Gauge: 12 ga., 3 in. Capacity: 9+1. Barrel: 24 in., ventilated rib. Weight: 7.75 lbs. Length: 44.75 in. Stock: Choice of either black synthetic or Black Multicam. Features: Created in conjunction with speed shooter Jerry Miculek, the new 940 JM Pro uses a redesigned gas system built for fast-cycling competition. Adjustable for length of pull, cast and drop. Hi-Viz green front fiber-optic sight, oversized controls. Nickel-boron coated internal parts and anodized receivers in either tungsten gray or black. Competition-level loading port allows for quad loading, elongated pinch-free elevator, and anodized bright orange follower. Black synthetic model uses gold finish appointments and a tungsten-gray receiver. Multicam model wears black-anodized receiver. Ships with Briley Extended choke tube set.

Price: **$1,015.00**
Price: JM Pro 5-Shot **$1,274.00**
Price: JM Pro Optics-Ready **$1,260.00**

MOSSBERG 940 PRO FIELD

Gauge: 12 ga. 3 in. Barrel: 28-in. vent rib. Length: 47.5 in. Weight: 7.75 lbs. Stock: Black synthetic, adjustable for LOP, cast and drop. Features: Field hunting variant of the 940 Pro lineup. Includes an Accu-Set of choke tubes. Fiber-optic front sight, matte blue metalwork finish. Oversized controls. Sling studs. LOP adjustable from 13–14.25 inches. 4+1-round capacity.

Price: **$903.00**

MOSSBERG 940 PRO FIELD WALNUT

Gauges: 12 ga. Barrel: 28in. Stock: Walnut with LOP spacers.
Price: **$1,061.00**

MOSSBERG 940 PRO SPORTING

Gauges: 12 ga. Barrel: 30-in. blued. Weight: 8.5 lbs. Length: 50.5 in. Stock: Walnut cream stock adjustable for LOP. Features: Competition-grade autoloader with specialized feaures. Drilled and tapped receiver, shims for drop at comb/cast. Hi-Viz CompSight front fiber optic. 4+1-round capacity. Briley extended choke tubes.

Price: **$1,225.00**

MOSSBERG 940 PRO SUPER BANTAM SPORTING

Gauges: 12 ga. Barrel: 26 in. Stock: Black synthetic with reduced LOP and spacers. Briley extended choke tubes.

Price: **$1,050.00**

MOSSBERG 940 PRO TACTICAL

Gauge: 12 ga. 3 in. Barrel: 18.5-in. vent rib. Length: 37 in. Weight: 7.75 lbs. Stock: Black synthetic, adjustable for LOP, cast and drop. Choice of either FDE or OD Green Cerakoted metalwork. Features: Tactical variant of the 940 Pro lineup with optics-ready receiver. Accu-Choke system with Cylinder bore tube installed. Fiber-optic front sight. Oversized controls. LOP adjustable from 12.5 to 14.25 in. 7+1-round capacity. Barrel clamp with M-LOK mounting slots. Thunder Ranch edition with specific engraving, full Cerakote Patriot Brown coverage.

Price: **$1,281.00**
Price: Thunder Ranch **$1,295.00**

MOSSBERG 940 PRO TURKEY

Gauge: 12 ga. 3 in. Barrel: 18.5 or 24-in. vent rib. Length: 39.25–44.75 in. Weight: 7.25–7.5 lbs. Stock: Synthetic in Mossy Oak Greenleaf camo, adjustable for LOP, cast and drop. Features: Turkey-specific variants of the 940 Pro lineup, these with shorter barrels, Greenleaf camo, and fitted with X-Factor XX-Full Turkey choke tubes. Optics-ready cutout. Compsight fiber optics. LOP adjustable from 13–14.25 in. Both models carry 4+1-round capacity. Addition of a Holosun Micro Dot Combo with a pre-mounted reflex sight.

Price: **$1,120.00**
Price: Pro Turkey Holosun Micro Dot Combo **$1,406.00**

MOSSBERG 940 PRO WATERFOWL

Gauge: 12 ga. 3 in. Barrel: 28-in. vent rib. Length: 48.75 in. Weight: 7.75 lbs. Stock: Synthetic in True Timber Prairie camo, adjustable for LOP, cast and drop. Features: Waterfowl-specific variant of the 940 Pro lineup. Includes a set of X-Factor extended choke tubes, TriComp fiber-optic front sight. Oversized controls. LOP adjustable from 13–14.25 inches. 4+1-round capacity.

Price: **$1,246.00**

MOSSBERG 940 PRO WATERFOWL SNOW GOOSE

Gauge: 12 ga. 3 in. Barrel: 28-in. vent rib. Length: 50.75 in. Weight: 8.25 lbs. Stock: Synthetic in True Timber Viper Snow camo, adjustable for LOP, cast and drop. Features: Optics-ready, higher-capacity, Snow Goose-specific variant of the 940 Pro lineup. Includes a set of X-Factor extended choke tubes, TriComp fiber-optic front sight. Oversized controls. Chrome lined chambers and bores. Stainless steel return spring, self-draining stock. LOP adjustable from 13–14.25 in. 12+1-round extended magazine tube capacity on standard model; limited 4+1-round capacity on 5-Shot Model sans extended mag tube.

Price: **$1,323.00**
Price: Snow Goose 5-Shot **$1,323.00**

MOSSBERG SA-20

Gauge: 20 or 28 ga. Barrels: 20 in. (Tactical), 26 in. or 28 in. Weight: 5.5–6 lbs. Stock: Black synthetic. Gas operated action, matte blue finish. Tactical model has ghost-ring sight, accessory rail.

Price: 20 ga. .... **$592.00–$664.00**
Price: 28 ga. .... **$588.00–$675.00**

MOSSBERG SA-410 FIELD

Gauge: .410 bore, 3 in. Capacity: 4+1. Barrel: 26 in., ventilated rib. Weight: 6.5 lbs. Length: 46 in. Stock: Black synthetic. Features: Mossberg offers the baby bore for small-game and field hunters as well as light recoiling plinking with this lightweight gas-driven autoloader. Metalwork is finished in matte blue. Brass front bead, fixed 13.75 in. length of pull, ventilated rubber buttpad. Cross-bolt safety, easy-load elevator. Includes Sport Set flush fit chokes (F, IM, M, IC, C).

Price: $616.00

MOSSBERG SA-410 TURKEY
Gauge: .410 bore, 3 in. Capacity: 4+1. Barrel: 26 in., ventilated rib. Weight: 6.5 lbs. Length: 46 in. Stock: Synthetic stock with Mossy Oak Bottomland camouflage. Features: Mossberg expands its baby-bore turkey lineup with this gas-driven semi-automatic. Both the stocks and metalwork wear full camouflage coverage. Rear fiber-optic ghost-ring sight and front green fiber-optic. Top Picatinny rail for easy optics mounting. Cross-bolt safety, easy-load elevator. Ships with an XX-Full Extended Turkey choke.

Price: $735.00

RETAY GORDION
Gauge: 12 ga., 3 in. Barrels: 26 in., 28 in., ventilated rib. Weight: 6.5-6.75 lbs. Stock: Choice of black synthetic, several Realtree camo patterns, or Turkish walnut. Features: The Turkish-made Gordion line of semi-automatics uses an inertia-plus action and bolt system. Oversized SP controls, quick unload system, TruGlo red front sight. Choice of matte or polished black receiver and barrel, or full camouflage coverage. Easy-Load port as well as Easy Unload system that allows the magazine tube to be emptied without racking the action. Includes a stock adjustment ship kit, TSA airline-approved hard case, and five flush choke tubes (F, IM, M, IC, S).

Price: ....$799.00–$899.00
Price: Gordion Turkey 24-in. barrel, Realtree or Mossy Oak camo ... $925.00

RETAY MASAI MARA
Gauges: 12 ga., 3.5 in., 20 ga., 3 in. Barrels: 26 in., 28 in., ventilated rib. Weight: 6.5-6.75 lbs. Stock: Choice of synthetic in black or numerous camouflage patterns or two grades of Turkish walnut. Features: The Turkish-made Masai Mara line of semi-automatics uses an inertia-plus action and bolt system. Oversized controls, Easy Unload system, TruGlo red fiber-optic front sight. Options in Cerakote metalwork or anodized finishes. Push-button removeable trigger group for both safety and easy field cleaning. Microcell rubber recoil pad. Includes a TSA airline-approved hard case and ships with five flush choke tubes (F, IM, M, IC, S).

Price:	$1,099.00
Price: Upland Grade 2	$1,399.00
Price: Upland Grade 3	$1,900.00
Price: Comfort Grade 2	$1,399.00
Price: Comfort Grade 4	$1,999.00
Price: SP Air King Waterfowl Camo/Cerakote	$1,600.00
Price: SP Air King Waterfowl Cerakote	$1,600.00

SAVAGE RENEGAUGE FIELD
Gauges: 12 ga. 3 in. Barrel: 26 or 28 in. fluted carbon steel with ventilated rib. Weight: 7.9–8.0 lbs. Length: 47.5–49.5 in. Stock: Grey synthetic stock with Monte Carlo-style cheekpiece. Adjustable for length of pull, comb height, drop and cast with included inserts. Features: American-made D.R.I.V. (Dual Regulating Inline Valve) gas system. Single-piece, chrome-plated action bar assembly and chrome-plated reciprocating components. Melonite-finished external metalwork. Stock rod buffer to reduce felt recoil. Red fiber-optic sight, competition-ready easy-loading port, oversized controls. 4+1 round capacity. Includes three Beretta/Benelli style chokes (IC, M, F) and hard case. For 2025, Savage announced all Renegauge receivers would be drilled and tapped for optics mounting.

Price: $1,489.00

SAVAGE RENEGAUGE TURKEY
Gauge: 12 ga. 3 in. Barrel: 24-in. fluted carbon steel with ventilated rib. Weight: 7.8 lbs. Length: 49.5 in. Stock: Camo synthetic stock with Monte Carlo-style cheekpiece, adjustable for length of pull, comb height, drop and cast with included inserts. Choice of Mossy Oak Bottomland or Mossy Oak Obsession camouflage finishes. Features: American-made D.R.I.V. (Dual Regulating Inline Valve) gas system. Single-piece, chrome-plated action bar assembly and chrome-plated reciprocating components. Stock rod buffer to reduce felt recoil. Red fiber-optic front sight, competition-ready loading port, oversized controls. 4+1 round capacity. Includes four Beretta/Benelli style chokes (EF, F, IC, M) and hard case. For 2024, Savage announced all Renegauge receivers would be drilled and tapped for optics mounting.

Price: $1,599.00

SAVAGE RENEGAUGE WATERFOWL
Gauge: 12 ga. 3 in. Barrel: 26- or 28-in. fluted carbon steel with ventilated rib. Weight: 7.8 lbs. Lengths: 47.5–49.5 in. Stock: Camouflage synthetic stock with Monte Carlo-style cheekpiece, adjustable for length of pull, comb height, drop and cast with included inserts. Mossy Oak Shadow Grass Blades camouflage. Features: American-made D.R.I.V. (Dual Regulating Inline Valve) gas system. Single-piece, chrome-plated action bar assembly and chrome-plated reciprocating components. Stock rod buffer to reduce felt recoil. Red fiber-optic sight, competition-ready easy loading port, oversized controls. 4+1 round capacity. Includes three Beretta/Benelli style chokes (IC, M, F) and hard case. For 2024, Savage announced all Renegauge receivers would be drilled and tapped for optics mounting.

Price: $1,959.00

SAVAGE RENEGAUGE COMPETITION
Gauge: 12 ga. 3in. Barrel: 24-in. fluted carbon steel with ventilated rib. Weight: 8.2 lbs. Length: 46.2 in. Stock: Black synthetic Monte Carlo style, adjustable for length of pull, comb height, drop and cast. Features: American-made D.R.I.V. (Dual Regulating Inline Valve) gas system. Single-piece, chrome-plated action bar assembly and chrome-plated reciprocating components. Stock rod buffer to reduce felt recoil. Extended magazine tube with 9+1 capacity. Melonite finished barrel and Red Cerakote receiver. Hi-Viz Tri-Comp front sight. Competition-ready loading port, oversized controls. Extended Skeet2 Light Mod (.015-in.) choke tube of Beretta/Benelli-style. For 2024, Savage announced all Renegauge receivers would be drilled and tapped for optics mounting.

Price: $1,959.00

SAVAGE RENEGAUGE PRAIRIE
Gauge: 12 ga. 3 in. Barrel: 28 in. fluted carbon steel with ventilated rib. Weight: 7.9 lbs. Length: 49.5 in. Stock: Camo synthetic sporter style, adjustable for length of pull, comb height, drop and cast with included inserts. Features: American-made D.R.I.V. (Dual Regulating Inline Valve) gas system. Single-piece, chrome plated action bar assembly and chrome-plated reciprocating components. True Timber Prairie camouflage stock finish with Brown Sand Cerakote metalwork. Stock rod buffer to reduce felt recoil. Red fiber-optic sight, competition-ready easy-loading port, oversized controls. 4+1 round capacity. Includes three Beretta/Benelli style chokes (IC, M, F) and hard case. For 2024, Savage announced all Renegauge receivers would be drilled and tapped for optics mounting.

Price: $1,599.00

STANDARD MANUFACTURING SKO-12
Gauge: 12 ga., 3 in. Capacity: 5-round magazine. Barrel: 18-7/8-in. Weight: 7 lbs., 10 oz. Length: 38 in. Stock: Synthetic with six-position buttstock and will accept any Mil-Spec buttstock. Features: Gas-operated semi-automatic. Receivers machined from aircraft-grade aluminum and Mil-Spec hard anodized. Extended 22-inch Picatinny rail. Ambidextrous safety, AR-style mag and bolt release. MOE slots on fore-end. Tru-Choke thread pattern.

Price: $1,100.00

STANDARD MANUFACTURING SKO SHORTY
Gauge: 12 ga., 3 in. Capacity: 5-round magazine. Barrel: 18-7/8-in. Weight: 7.14 lbs. Length: 28.75 in. Stock: Black synthetic with forward vertical grip, but without a buttstock. Features: Gas-operated semi-automatic. Receivers machined from aircraft-grade aluminum and Mil-Spec hard anodized. Ambidextrous safety, AR-style mag and bolt release. MOE slots on fore-end. No sights or top rail. Tru-Choke thread pattern. Buttstock conversion kit available from manufacturer.

Price: $599.00

STEVENS MODEL 560
Gauges: 12 ga. Barrels: 28 in black matte. Stock: Turkish Walnut, checkered with a satin finish. Features: New budget autoloader built in Turkey for

Stevens by Savage. Gas operated with 3-inch chamber and aluminum alloy receiver. Hard chrome-lined barrel. Oversized controls. Fiber-optic front sight. Available in both standard and compact variants at the same price. Ships with three flush choke tubes.
Price: **$499.00**

STOEGER M3K

Gauges: 12 ga. Barrels: 24 in. Stock: Black synthetic. Features: Race-ready factory semi-automatic build for 3-Gun competitors. Oversized controls with contrasting blue anodizing. Enlarged loading port and elongated carrier. A 3-inch chamber and 4+1-round capacity. Uses the Inertia-Drive system. Upgraded recoil pad and integrated cheek pad. Ships with three choke tubes.
Price: **$669.00**

STOEGER M3020

Gauges: 20 ga. Barrels: 18.5, 24, 26, 28 in. Stock: Black synthetic, Gloss Walnut, Camo. Features: Inertia-driven semi-automatic 20-gauge family chambered for 2.75- and 3-in. shells. Fiber-optic front sight. Includes numerous model variants and styles. A shim kit comes standard.
Price: Standard or Compact Black.............................. **$559.00**
Price: Defense ghost ring sights 20 in. **$619.00**
Price: Upland Walnut/Cerakote................................. **$669.00**
Price: Turkey w/Camo 24 in. **$619.00**
Price: Hunter w/Camo/Cerakote............................... **$669.00**

STOEGER M3000

Gauges: 12 ga. Barrels: 24, 26, 28 in. Stock: Black synthetic, Camo, Walnut. Features: Redesigned in 2023 as a 3-inch chambered 12-gauge semi-auto. New recoil pad and removable cheek pieces on all except satin walnut models. Stock grip areas are trimmer with an overall less boxy look. Oversized controls, slimmer magazine cap, and beveled loading port. Red fiber-optic front sight. Ships with three choke tubes. Signature Series M3000 100th Anniversary introduced in 2024, with nickel and scrollwork receiver, polished 28-inch barrel, and upgraded satin Walnut stocks.
Price: Black Synthetic **$559.00**
Price: Satin Walnut **$619.00**
Price: Camo.. **$619.00**
Price: Camo/Cerakote.. **$669.00**
Price: Walnut/Cerakote... **$669.00**
Price: Signature Series **$749.00**

STOEGER M3500

Redesigned for 2023 with slimmer stock dimensions, oversized controls, and an easy-grip magazine cap. View from receiver to rib is lower. Upgraded recoil pad. Addition of cheek pad on all but walnut models.
Price: Black.. **$669.00**
Price: Camo **$769.00**
Price: Camo/Cerakote **$799.00**
Price: Waterfowl Special **$849.00**
Price: Snow Goose **$929.00**

STOEGER M3500 PREDATOR/TURKEY

Gauge: 12 ga., 3.5 in. Capacity: 4+1. Barrel: 24 in., ventilated rib. Length: 46 in. Weight: 7.5 lbs. Stock: Synthetic Mossy Oak Overwatch. Features: Stoeger expands its M3500 line of inertia-driven autoloaders with a predator- and turkey-specific model with a shorter barrel and rubber pistol grip. Red bar fiber-optic front sight. Receiver drilled and tapped for optics mounting. Ships with a paracord sling and five extended chokes, including MOJO Predator and MOJO Turkey tubes.

Price: **$929.00**

STOEGER M3500 WATERFOWL

Gauge: 12 ga. 3.5 in. Barrel: 28 in. ventilated rib. Length: 50 in. Weight: 8.2 lbs. Stock: Synthetic with distressed white Cerakote finish. Features: Stoeger combines the M3500 Waterfowl semi-auto with the 922R-compliant extended magazine Freedom Series to create the higher-capacity M3500 Snow Goose. Full 10+1 capacity. Inertia-driven autoloader with oversized controls. Beveled loading port. Distressed white Cerakote finish on stock, fore-end, receiver, and barrel act as winter camo. Red bar front sight. Includes paracord sling and shim kit for adjusting drop and cast. Ships with five extended choke tubes (IC, M, XFT, Close Range, Mid Range).
Price: **$899.00**

TRISTAR VIPER G2

Gauges: 12 ga., 20 ga. 2 3/4 in. or 3 in. interchangeably. Capacity: 5-round magazine. Barrels: 26 in., 28 in. (carbon fiber only offered in 12-ga. 28 in. and 20-ga. 26 in.). Stock: Wood, black synthetic, Mossy Oak Duck Blind camouflage, faux carbon fiber finish (2008) with the new Comfort Touch technology. Features: Magazine cutoff, vent rib with matted sight plane, brass front bead (camo models have fiber-optic front sight), shot plug included, and 3 Beretta-style choke tubes (IC, M, F). Viper synthetic, Viper camo have swivel studs. Five-year warranty. Viper Youth models have shortened length of pull and 24 in. barrel. Sporting model has ported barrel, checkered walnut stock with adjustable comb. Imported by Tristar Sporting Arms Ltd.
Price: **$549.00**
Price: Camo models **$640.00**
Price: Silver Model.................................... **$670.00–$715.00**
Price: Youth Model **$565.00**
Price: Sporting Model.. **$825.00**

TRISTAR VIPER G2

Gauges: 12 ga., 20ga. 28 ga., .410 bore Barrels: 26, 28, (30-in. Snow Camo only). Stock: Depending on model, premium-select walnut (Pro Bronze), select walnut (Silver), synthetic (Camo). Features: Gas-operated autoloader with 3-inch chambers. Last shot bolt hold open. Rubber recoil pad. Chrome-lined barrel. Shim kits included. Fiber-optic front sight. Manual E-Z load magazine cutoff. Oversized controls. Triangular safety. Enlarged mag well. Ships with three Beretta/Benelli Mobil choke tubes.
Price: G2 Pro Camo (12, 20)....................................... **$855.00**
Price: G2 Pro Silver (12, 20, 28, .410) .... **$870.00–$900.00**
Price: G2 Pro Bronze (12, 20, 16 28, .410) ...... **$990.00–$1,050.00**

TRISTAR VIPER MAX

Gauge: 12. 3 1/2 in. Barrel: 24–30 in., threaded to accept Benelli choke tubes. Gas-operated action. Offered in several model variants. Introduced in 2017.
Price: .... **$630.00–$730.00**

WEATHERBY SA-SERIES

Gauges: 12 ga., 20 ga., 3 in. Barrels: 26 in., 28 in. flat ventilated rib. Weight: 6.5 lbs. Stock: Wood and synthetic. Features: The SA-08 is a reliable workhorse that lets you move from early season dove loads to late fall's heaviest waterfowl loads in no time. Available with wood and synthetic stock options in 12- and 20-gauge models, including a scaled-down youth model to fit 28 ga. Comes with 3 application-specific choke tubes (SK/IC/M). Made in Turkey.
Price: SA-08 Synthetic **$649.00**
Price: SA-08 Synthetic Youth **$649.00**
Price: SA-08 Deluxe **$849.00**

WEATHERBY 18I WATERFOWLER

Gauges: 12 ga. Barrels: 28 in. Stock: Synthetic camo. Features: 3.5 inch "Super Magnum" chamber.
Price: .... **$1,239.00–$1,249.00**

WEATHERBY 18I LIMITED

Gauge: 12 ga. 3 in., 20 ga. 3 in. Barrel: 28 in. ventilated rib. Length: 49.5 in. Weight: 6–7 lbs. Stock: Exhibition-grade wood with shims for adjustment. Features: Billet aluminum receiver with hand-polished brushed nickel, with custom engraving and 24-Karat gold inlay and upland bird detail. LPA fiber-optic front sight. Set of five Crio Plus choke tubes. Machined aluminum triggerguard. Built in Italy and imported by Weatherby. Available in limited quantities.

Price: $3,099.00

WEATHERBY SORIX

Gauge: 12 ga. 3.5 in.; 12 ga. 3 in., 20 ga. 3 in. Barrel: 28 in. with stepped ventilated rib and finished in Cerakote. Length: 49 in. Weight: 6.5 lbs (20 ga.) to 7.1 lbs (12 ga.). Stock: Synthetic with molded textured grip panels in choice of three hand-painted color tones. Features: Italian-built inertia gun launched in 2024 using Weatherby's new Shift System, allowing the charging handle to be quickly swapped from right to left hand operations. Safety can also be swapped from right to left. Receiver drilled and tapped for optics mounting. Oversized controls, aggressive receiver cut for faster reloading, and LPA red fiber-optic front sight. LOP of 14.3-in. with rubber recoil pad. Ships with set of five flush Crio Plus choke tubes in a hard case plus shims for stock adjustment. Color variants are Storm (silver/black), Slough (tan/brown), and Marsh (black/brown) with Cerakote metalwork matching stock coloration. Stocks are finished in-house in Sheridan, WY.

Price: $1,499.00

WINCHESTER SX-4

Gauge: 12 ga., 3 in. and 3 1/2 in. Capacity: 4-round magazine. Barrels: 22 in., 24 in., 26 in. or 28 in. Invector Plus Flush choke tubes. Weight: 6 lbs. 10 oz. Stock: Synthetic with rounded pistol grip and textured gripping surfaces, or satin finished checkered grade II/III Turkish walnut. Length-of-pull spacers. Several camo finishes available. Features: TruGlo fiber optic front sight, Inflex Technology recoil pad, active valve system, matte blue barrel, matte black receiver. Offered in Standard, Field, Compact, Waterfowl, Cantilever Buck, Cantilever Turkey models. Addition of left-hand models in 2024.

Price: Synthetic..$940.00
Price: Field...$940.00–$1,070.00
Price: Upland Field $1,100.00
Price: Waterfowl Hunter ....$940.00–$1,070.00
Price: Waterfowl Hunter in Mossy Oak Shadow Grass Habitat $1,099.00
Price: Waterfowl Hunter Compact in Mossy Oak Shadow Grass Habitat ...$959.00
Price: Hybrid Hunter..$1,040.00
Price: Hybrid Hunter in Mossy Oak Shadow Grass Habitat $1,079.00
Price: NWTF Cantilever Turkey, Mossy Oak Obsession $1,070.00
Price: 20-gauge, 3-inch models $939.00
Price: Universal Hunter in MOBU camo $1,069.00
Price: Universal Hunter 12 and 20 ga. in Mossy Oak DNA camo.....$1,149.00
Price: SX4 Left Hand 12 ga. in multiple variants $1,129.00

ARMSCOR/ROCK ISLAND ARMORY ALL GENERATION SERIES

Gauge: 12 ga. 3 in., 20 ga. 3 in., .410 bore 3 in. **Barrel:** 18.5, 26, 28 in. smoothbore contoured. **Length:** 41.0–48.2 in. **Weight:** 7.10–8.82 lbs. **Stock:** Black polymer with LOP spacers and adjustable cheek rest for customized fit. **Features:** Pump-action shotgun designed to accommodate a wide range of ages and physical sizes of shooters. The All Generation Series includes multiple models designed to customize the fit. Comes packaged with multiple stock spacers and an adjustable comb and ergonomic forend. Lightweight aluminum receiver with anodized finish. Magazine tube capacity 5+1 rounds in all chamberings. Bead front sight. Black rubber recoil pad. Interchangeable chokes (F, M, IM) except 18.5-inch barreled option, which has a Slug Choke.
Price: $299.00

BENELLI SUPERNOVA

Gauge: 12 ga. 3 1/2 in. **Capacity:** 4-round magazine. **Barrels:** 24 in., 26 in., 28 in. **Lengths:** 45.5–49.5 in. **Stock:** Synthetic; Max-4, Timber, APG HD (2007). **Sights:** Red bar front, metal midbead. **Features:** 2 3/4 in., 3 in. chamber (3 1/2 in. 12 ga. only). Montefeltro rotating bolt design with dual action bars, magazine cutoff, synthetic trigger assembly, adjustable combs, shim kit, choice of buttstocks. Introduced 2006. Imported from Italy by Benelli USA.
Price: $549.00
Price: Camo stock $669.00
Price: Rifle slug model ....$829.00–$929.00
Price: Tactical model................................$519.00–$549.00

BENELLI NOVA

Gauges: 12 ga., 20 ga. **Capacity:** 4-round magazine. **Barrels:** 24 in., 26 in., 28 in. **Stock:** Black synthetic, Max-4, Timber and APG HD. **Sights:** Red bar. **Features:** 2 3/4 in., 3 in. (3 1/2 in. 12 ga. only). Montefeltro rotating bolt design with dual action bars, magazine cut-off, synthetic trigger assembly. Introduced 1999. Field & Slug Combo has 24 in. barrel and rifled bore; open rifle sights; synthetic stock; weighs 8.1 lbs. Imported from Italy by Benelli USA.
Price: Field Model...$449.00
Price: Max-5 camo stock $559.00
Price: H20 model, black synthetic, matte nickel finish $669.00
Price: Tactical, 18.5-in. barrel, Ghost Ring sight.................$459.00
Price: Black synthetic youth stock, 20 ga. $469.00

BENELLI NOVA TURKEY

Gauge: 20 ga. 3 in. **Barrel:** 24 in. with ventilated rib. **Length:** 45.5 in. **Weight:** 6.5 lbs. **Stock:** Synthetic with full Mossy Oak Bottomland camouflage. **Features:** Benelli's new addition to the Nova family targets run-and-gun hunters seeking a lighter-built and -recoiling turkey gun. Ergonomic forend. Red bar fiber-optic front sight. Magazine cutoff button. Ships with three chokes (IC, M, F).
Price: $559.00

BROWNING BPS

Gauges: 10 ga., 12 ga., 3 1/2 in.; 12 ga., 16 ga., or 20 ga., 3 in. (2 3/4 in. in target guns), 28 ga., 2 3/4 in., 5-shot magazine, .410, 3 in. chamber. **Barrels:** 10 ga. 24 in. Buck Special, 28 in., 30 in., 32 in. Invector; 12 ga., 20 ga. 22 in., 24 in., 26 in., 28 in., 30 in., 32 in. (Imp. Cyl., Mod. or Full), .410 26 in. (Imp. Cyl., Mod. and Full choke tubes.) Also available with Invector choke tubes, 12 or 20 ga. Upland Special has 22-in. barrel with Invector tubes. BPS 3 in. and 3 1/2 in. have back-bored barrel. **Weight:** 7 lbs., 8 oz. (28 in. barrel). **Length:** 48.75 in. overall (28 in. barrel). **Stock:** 14.25 in. x 1.5 in. x 2.5 in. Select walnut, semi-beavertail fore-end, full pistol grip stock. **Features:** All 12 ga. 3 in. guns except

Buck Special and game guns have back-bored barrels with Invector Plus choke tubes. Bottom feeding and ejection, receiver top safety, high post vent rib. Double action bars eliminate binding. Vent rib barrels only. All 12 and 20 ga. guns with 3 in. chamber available with fully engraved receiver flats at no extra cost. Each gauge has its own unique game scene. Introduced 1977. Stalker is same gun as the standard BPS except all exposed metal parts have a matte blued finish and the stock has a black finish with a black recoil pad. Available in 10 ga. (3 1/2 in.) and 12 ga. with 3 in. or 3 1/2 in. chamber, 22 in., 28 in., 30 in. barrel with Invector choke system. Introduced 1987. Rifled Deer Hunter is similar to the standard BPS except has newly designed receiver/magazine tube/barrel mounting system to eliminate play, heavy 20.5-in. barrel with rifle-type sights with adjustable rear, solid receiver scope mount, "rifle" stock dimensions for scope or open sights, sling swivel studs. Gloss or matte finished wood with checkering, polished blue metal. Medallion model has additional engraving on receiver, polished blue finish, AA/AAA grade walnut stock with checkering. All-Purpose model has Realtree AP camo on stock and fore-end, HiVis fiber optic sights. Introduced 2013. Imported from Japan by Browning.
Price: Field Composite models ....$779.00–$799.00
Price: Field...$799.00–$879.00

BROWNING BPS 10 GAUGE SERIES

Similar to the standard BPS but in the upsized 10-gauge chambering. Available with either 26- or 28-in. barrel. Introduced 1999. Standard Invector choke system. Inflex recoil pad offers LOP adjustment.
Price: Field Composite $879.00

BROWNING BPS MICRO MIDAS

Gauges: 12 ga, 20 ga., 28 ga. or .410 bore. **Barrels:** 24 or 26 in. Three Invector choke tubes for 12 and 20 ga., standard tubes for 28 ga. and .410. **Stock:** Walnut with pistol grip and recoil pad. Satin finished and scaled down to fit smaller statured shooters. Length of pull is 13.25 in. Two spacers included for stock length adjustments. **Weights:** 7–7.8 lbs.
Price: ....$779.00–$799.00

CZ 612

Gauge: 12 ga. Chambered for all shells up to 3 1/2 in. **Capacity:** 5+1, magazine plug included with Wildfowl Magnum. **Barrels:** 18.5 in. (Home Defense), 20 in. (HC-P), 26 in. (Wildfowl Mag.) **Weights:** 6–6.8 pounds. **Stock:** Polymer. **Finish:** Matte black or full camo (Wildfowl Mag.) HC-P model has pistol grip stock, fiber optic front sight and ghost-ring rear. Home Defense Combo comes with extra 26-in. barrel.
Price: Wildfowl Magnum $428.00
Price: Home Defense ....$304.00–$409.00
Price: Target $549.00

CZ MODEL 620/628 Field Select

Gauges: 20 ga. or 28 ga. **Barrel:** 28 inches. **Weight:** 5.4 lbs. **Features:** Similar to Model 612 except for chambering. Introduced in 2017.
Price: $429.00

ESCORT FIELDHUNTER TURKEY

Gauges: 12 ga., 3 in., 20 ga., 3 in., .410 bore, 3 in. **Capacity:** 4+1. **Barrels:** 22 in., 24 in., 26 in., ventilated rib. **Length:** 42-46 in. **Weight:** 6.0-6.9 lbs. **Stock:** Synthetic with camo finish. **Features:** The pump-action Turkey model addition to the FieldHunter family is built of aircraft alloy with a black chrome-finished steel barrel that is camo coated. Cantilever Weaver optics rail, fully adjustable green rear fiber-optic sight with windage-adjustable front red fiber-optic sight. Cross-bolt safety, rubber butt pad, sling studs. Includes three chokes (Ext Turkey, F, IM).
Price: $399.00

EUROPEAN AMERICAN ARMORY (EAA) AKKAR CHURCHILL 620

Gauge: 20 ga. **Barrel:** 18.5 in. **Length:** 37.5 in. **Weight:** 5.0 lbs. **Stock:** Black Synthetic pistol grip style. **Features:** This Turkish-made pump builds on the Churchill 620 series of slide actions now re-vamped for home defense and tactical use. Optics rail machined into receiver for easy target acquisition with included red-dot optic on quick-release mount. Semi-enhanced loading port. Accessible controls. Checkered pistol grip stock. Black rubber recoil pad, sling swivels. Door-breaching choke tube and shrouded red fiber-optic front sight.
Price: $427.00

Prices given are believed to be accurate at time of publication however, many factors affect retail pricing so exact prices are not possible.

ITHACA MODEL 37 FEATHERLIGHT
Gauges: 12 ga., 20 ga., 16 ga., 28 ga. Capacity: 4+1. Barrels: 26 in., 28 in. or 30 in. with 3-in. chambers (12 and 20 ga.), plain or ventilated rib. Weights: 6.1–7.6 lbs. Stock: Fancy-grade black walnut with Pachmayr Decelerator recoil pad. Checkered fore-end made of matching walnut. Features: Receiver machined from a single block of steel or aluminum. Barrel is steel shot compatible. Three Briley choke tubes provided. Available in several variations including turkey, home defense, tactical and high-grade.

Price: 12 ga., 16 ga. or 20 ga. From	**$895.00**
Price: 28 ga.	**$1,149.00**
Price: Turkey Slayer w/synthetic stock	**$925.00**
Price: Trap Series 12 ga.	**$1,020.00**
Price: Waterfowl	**$885.00**
Price: Home Defense 18- or 20-in. bbl	**$784.00**

ITHACA DEERSLAYER III SLUG
Gauges: 12 ga., 20 ga. 3 in. Barrel: 26 in. fully rifled, heavy fluted with 1:28 twist for 12 ga. 1:24 for 20 ga. Weights: 8.14–9.5 lbs. with scope mounted. Length: 45.625 in. overall. Stock: Fancy black walnut stock and fore-end. Sights: NA. Features: Updated, slug-only version of the classic Model 37. Bottom ejection, blued barrel and receiver.

Price: **$1,350.00**

KEYSTONE SPORTING ARMS 4200 MY FIRST SHOTGUN
Gauges: .410 bore. 3 in. Barrel: 18.5 in. Length: 37 in. Stock: Turkish Walnut. Features: Marketed as a Crickett "My First Shotgun," this pump-action baby bore holds 5+1 rounds of 2.75-inch shells or 4+1 rounds of 3 inch. Aluminum receiver with matte blue metalwork. MC-1 choke. Blade-style front sight. Checkered stocks with rubber recoil pad. Length of pull built for small-frame shooters at only 12 in.

Price: **$399.00**

MAVERICK 88 FIELD
Gauges: 12ga., 20 ga. Barrels: 22, 26, 28-in. ventilated rib. Stock: Synthetic Mossy Oak Bottomland camo. Features: Three new All-Purpose Field camo variants. A 3-inch chamber, 5+1-round capacity. Dual extractors, twin action bars, steel-to-steel lockup, and anti-jam elevator for reliable operation. The 22-in. Bantam model shortens LOP to 12 in. Modified choke tube included, but Maverick 88 accessories interchangeable with Mossberg 500.

Price: **$293.00**

MOSSBERG MODEL 835 ULTI-MAG
Gauge: 12 ga., 3 1/2 in. Barrels: Ported 24 in. rifled bore, 24 in., 28 in., Accu-Mag choke tubes for steel or lead shot. Combo models come with interchangeable second barrel. Weight: 7.75 lbs. Length: 48.5 in. overall. Stock: 14 in. x 1.5 in. x 2.5 in. Dual Comb. Cut-checkered hardwood or camo synthetic; both have recoil pad. Sights: White bead front, brass mid-bead; fiber-optic rear. Features: Shoots 2 3/4-, 3- or 3 1/2-in. shells. Back-bored and ported barrel to reduce recoil, improve patterns. Ambidextrous thumb safety, twin extractors, dual slide bars. Mossberg Cablelock included. Introduced 1988.

Price: Turkey	**$601.00–$617.00**
Price: Waterfowl	**$518.00–$603.00**
Price: Turkey/Deer combo	**$661.00–$701.00**
Price: Turkey/Waterfowl combo	**$661.00**
Price: Tactical Turkey	**$652.00**

MOSSBERG 835 ULTI-MAG TURKEY
Gauges: 12 ga. Barrels: 20 in., 24 in. Stock: Synthetic in Mossy Oak

Greenleaf camo. Features: Turkey-specific, optics-ready. Receiver machined for direct mounting of RMSc-pattern optics. A 5+1-round capacity. Magnum 3.5-inch chamber. Interchangeable chokes. Overbored barrel, dual extractors, tang safety. Full Mossy Oak Greenleaf coverage. Addition of a Holosun Micro Dot Combo model with an HS407K reflex sight pre-mounted.

Price:	**$693.00**
Price: Holosun Micro Dot Combo	**$899.00**

MOSSBERG MODEL 500 SPORTING SERIES
Gauges: 12 ga., 20 ga., .410 bore, 3 in. Barrels: 18.5 in. to 28 in. with fixed or Accu-Choke, plain or vent rib. Combo models come with interchangeable second barrel. Weight: 6.25 lbs. (.410), 7.25 lbs. (12). Length: 48 in. overall (28-in. barrel). Stock: 14 in. x 1.5 in. x 2.5 in. Walnut-stained hardwood, black synthetic, Mossy Oak Advantage camouflage. Cut-checkered grip and fore-end. Sights: White bead front, brass mid-bead; fiber-optic. Features: Ambidextrous thumb safety, twin extractors, disconnecting safety, dual action bars. Quiet Carry fore-end. Many barrels are ported. FLEX series has many modular options and accessories including barrels and stocks. From Mossberg. Left-hand versions (L-series) available in most models.

Price: Turkey	**$486.00**
Price: Waterfowl	**$537.00**
Price: Combo	**$593.00**
Price: FLEX Hunting	**$702.00**
Price: FLEX All Purpose	**$561.00**
Price: Field	**$419.00**
Price: Slugster	**$447.00**
Price: FLEX Deer/Security combo	**$787.00**
Price: Home Security 410	**$477.00**
Price: Tactical	**$486.00–$602.00**

MOSSBERG 500 TURKEY
Gauges: 20 ga., .410 bore. Barrels: 22 to 24 in. Stock: Synthetic Mossy Oak Greenleaf camo. Features: Two new optics-ready turkey hunting variants. Receiver machined for direct mounting of RMSc-pattern optics. 5+1-round capacity. Fiber-optic front sight. Has a 3-inch chamber. X-Factor ported choke tube.

Price: **$644.00**

MOSSBERG 590S
Gauge: 12 ga. 3 in. with 1.75-in. short shell and 2.75 in. capability. Barrel: 18.5 or 20 in., matte blued. Length: 39.5–41 in. Weight: 6.75–7.25 lbs. Stock: Black Synthetic with fixed LOP; Model with Ghost ring sights uses tactical stock with M-LOK attachment points. Features: Standard model with 18.5-in. barrel allows capacities of 9+1, 6+1, or 5+1. Model with 20-in. barrel and ghost ring sights has capacities of 13+1, 8+1, or 7+1. The former uses a fixed cylinder bore. The latter features the Accu-Choke system with cylinder bore choke included. Both models cycle all length of shells without adapters or adjustment.

Price: Standard 18.5 in.	**$623.00**
Price: Ghost Ring 20 in.	**$731.00**

MOSSBERG SHOCKWAVE SERIES
Gauges: 12, 20 ga. or .410 cylinder bore, 3-inch chamber. Barrel: 14 3/8, 18.5 in. Weight: 5 – 5.5 lbs. Length: 26.4 - 30.75 in. Stock: Synthetic or wood. Raptor bird's-head type pistol grip. Nightstick has wood stock and fore-end.

Price:	**$455.00**
Price: CTC Laser Saddle Model	**$613.00**
Price: Ceracote finish	**$504.00**
Price: Nightstick (shown)	**$539.00**
Price: Mag-Fed	**$721.00**
Price: SPX w/heatshield	**$560.00–$710.00**

REMARMS FIELDMASTER

Gauges: 12 ga., 20 ga. Barrels: 26, 28 in. (21-in. Compact 20-ga. model available). Stock: Standard-grade American Walnut. Features: New RemArms pump action in the old Express style, now called Fieldmaster. Milled steel receiver. Twin action bars. Matte black metalwork. Ventilated rib barrel with single front bead. Drilled and tapped receiver. Left-hand 12-gauge model available. Includes three flush Rem chokes.
Price: $609.00

REMARMS FIELDMASTER SYNTHETIC

Gauges: 12 ga. (20 ga. Compact only). Barrels: 26, 28 (12 ga.), 21 in. (20 ga.) Stock: Black synthetic. Features: New RemArms pump action in the old Express style, now called Fieldmaster Synthetic. Milled steel receiver. Twin action bars. Matte black metalwork. Adjustable comb insert available. Drilled and tapped receiver. Includes three flush Rem chokes.
Price: $559.00

RETAY GPS

Gauges: 12 ga. 3 in. Barrel: 18.5 in. Weight: 6 lbs. 9 oz. Stock: Black ABS synthetic. Features: Retay's first pump-action shotgun is the GPS, short for Geometric Pump System. Extra-short travel pump action. Anodized aluminum receiver. 5+1-round capacity. Chrome-lined barrel with elongated, back-bored forcing cones. Crossbolt safety. Milled aluminum trigger housing and guard. Integral sling swivel mounts. Beavertail adapter for optics mounting. High visibility front blade sight. Comfort rubber recoil pad. Ships with removeable MaraPro chokes (S, M, F).
Price: $349.00

RETAY GPS XL

Gauge: 12 ga. 3.5 in. Barrel: 28 in. Weight: oz. Stock: Black or camo ABS synthetic. Features: Retay's pump-action GPS expands to the XL, chambering magnum rounds. GPS, short for Geometric Pump System, uses a short-travel pump action with a frictionless forend design. Anodized aluminum receiver, chrome-lined barrel with elongated, back-bored forcing cones. Crossbolt safety. Milled aluminum trigger housing and guard. Integral sling swivel mounts. Red fiber-optic front sight. Rubber recoil pad. Ships with MaraPro chokes.
Price: $419.00

STEVENS MODEL 320

Gauges: 12 ga., or 20 ga. with 3-in. chamber. Capacity: 5+1. Barrels: 18.25 in., 20 in., 22 in., 26 in. or 28 in. with interchangeable choke tubes. Features include all-steel barrel and receiver; bottom-load and ejection design; black synthetic stock.
Price: Security Model $276.00
Price: Field Model 320 with 28-inch barrel........................$251.00
Price: Combo Model with Field and Security barrels $307.00

STEVENS 320 SECURITY THUMBHOLE

Gauges: 12 ga. 3 in., or 20 ga. 3in. Barrel: 18.5-in. chrome alloy steel matte black. Weight: 7.0–7.3 lbs. Length: 39.1 in. Stock: Black matte synthetic with thumbhole cutout. Features: Pump action with dual slide bars and rotary bolt. Thumbhole stock design with ambidextrous cheek riser and grip texture. Swivel studs. Bottom-loading tubular magazine with 5+1-round capacity. Black rubber recoil pad. Ghost Ring Sight or Front Bead Sight models available in both chamberings.
Price: 12-ga. Front Bead Sight Model $275.00
Price: 12-ga. Ghost Ring Sight Model $305.00
Price: 20-ga. Front Bead Sight Model $275.00
Price: 20-ga. Ghost Ring Sight Model $305.00

STEVENS 320 TURKEY THUMBHOLE

Gauges: 12 ga. 3 in., or 20 ga. 3 in. Barrel: 22-in. chrome alloy steel matte black with ventilated rib. Weight: 7.6 lbs. Length: 43.4 in. Stock: Olive drab green matte synthetic with thumbhole cutout. Features: Pump action with dual slide bars and rotary bolt. Thumbhole stock design with ambidextrous cheek riser and grip texture. Swivel studs. Bottom-loading tubular magazine with 5+1-round capacity. Black rubber recoil pad. Adjustable fiber-optic turkey sights. Extended Win-Choke-style Extra Full choke tube.
Price: 12-ga. Front Bead Sight Model $323.00

STOEGER P3000

Gauges: 12 ga. Barrels: 28 in. Stock: Synthetic in Realtree Max-7 camo Features: Redesigned in 2023 as a 3-inch chambered 12-gauge pump action. Improved ergonomics. Barrel extension reaches deeper into the receiver for greater longevity of the action. Pistol grip inset with Stoeger logo cap. Integrated swivel studs.
Price: $389.00

STOEGER P3500

Gauges: 12 ga. Barrels: 26, 28 in. Stock: Synthetic in Realtree Max-7 camo. Features: Redesigned in 2023 as a hunting gun with checkered synthetic stocks, integrated swivel studs, and slimmer stock lines. Twin steel action bars, no-stick pump action, and rotating bolt head. Cycles 2.75-, 3-, and 3.5-inch shells.
Price: $439.00

TRISTAR COBRA III FIELD

Gauges: 12 ga., 3 in., 20 ga., 3 in. Barrels: 26 in., 28 in., ventilated rib. Weight: 6.7-7.0 lbs. Length: 46.5-48.5 in. Stock: Field models available with either Turkish walnut or black synthetic furniture. Features: Third model upgrade to the Cobra pump-action line with extended fore-end. Rubber buttpad, cross-bolt safety, chrome-lined barrel, high-polish blue metalwork, sling studs. Includes three Beretta Mobil-style choke tubes (IC, M, F).
Price: ....$305.00—$335.00

TRISTAR COBRA III YOUTH

Gauge: 20 ga., 3 in. Barrel: 24 in., ventilated rib. Weight: 5.4-6.5 lbs. Length: 37.7 in. Stock: Version III youth models available with black synthetic, Realtree Max-5 camo or Turkish-walnut furniture. Features: Third iteration of the Cobra pump-action with extended fore-end. Ventilated rubber buttpad, cross-bolt safety, chrome-lined barrel, sling studs. Shorter length of pull on Youth model. Includes three Beretta Mobil-style choke tubes (IC, M, F).
Price: ....$305.00—$365.00

WINCHESTER SUPER X (SXP)

Gauges: 12 ga., 3 in. or 3 1/2 in. chambers; 20 ga., 3 in. Barrels: 18 in., 26 in., 28 in. Barrels .742-in. back-bored, chrome plated; Invector Plus choke tubes. Weights: 6.5–7 lbs. Stocks: Walnut or composite. Features: Rotary bolt, four lugs, dual steel action bars. Walnut Field has gloss-finished walnut stock and forearm, cut checkering. Black Shadow Field has composite stock and forearm, non-glare matte finish barrel and receiver. SXP Defender has composite stock and forearm, chromed plated, 18-in. cylinder choked barrel, non-glare metal surfaces, five-shot magazine, grooved forearm. Some models offered in left-hand versions. Reintroduced 2009. Made in USA by Winchester Repeating Arms Co.
Price: Black Shadow Field, 3 in. $380.00
Price: Black Shadow Field, 3 1/2 in. $430.00
Price: SXP Defender..........................$350.00—$400.00
Price: SXP Universal Hunter 12 and 20 ga. Mossy Oak DNA camo.....$509.00
Price: Hybrid Hunter in Mossy Oak Shadow Grass Habitat $449.00
Price: Waterfowl Hunter 3 in. $460.00
Price: Waterfowl Hunter 3 1/2 in. $500.00
Price: Waterfowl Hunter in Mossy Oak Shadow Grass Habitat $499.00
Price: Turkey Hunter 3 1/2 in. $520.00
Price: Black Shadow Deer $520.00
Price: Trap $480.00
Price: Field, walnut stock..........................$400.00—$430.00
Price: 20-ga., 3-in. models..........................$379.00
Price: Extreme Defender FDE $549.00

AMERICAN TACTICAL INC (ATI) CRUSADER

Gauges: 12 ga., 3 in., 20 ga., 3 in., 28 ga., 2.75 in., .410 bore, 3 in. Barrels: 26 in., 28 in., 30 in., ventilated rib. Weight: 6.0-6.5 lbs. Stock: Turkish walnut with oil finish. Features: ATI's new O/U line has both Field and Sport models. Made from 7075 aluminum with laser engraving on the receiver. Single selective trigger, fiber-optic front sight, extractors, chrome-moly steel barrel. Ships with five chokes: flush on the Field, extended on the Sport.

Price: Crusader Field **$499.00**
Price: Crusader Sport **$549.00**

BENELLI 828U

Gauges: 12 ga. 3 in. Barrels: 26 in., 28 in. Weights: 6.5–7 lbs. Stock: AA-grade satin walnut, fully adjustable for both drop and cast. Features: New patented locking system allows use of aluminum frame. Features include carbon fiber rib, fiber-optic sight, removable trigger group, and Benelli's Progressive Comfort recoil reduction system.

Price: Matte black... **$2,699.00**
Price: Nickel... **$3,199.00**
Price: 20-gauge Nickel **$3,199.00**

BENELLI 828U STEEL BE.S.T.

Gauges: 12 ga., 20 ga. Barrels: 26, 28, 30 in. Stock: AA-grade satin walnut with Progressive Comfort system. Features: Sleek steel receiver that is slightly heavier yet balanced for a smooth swing. Red fiber-optic front sight. Progressive comfort stock system. Gloss-blued barrel finish with satin BE.S.T steel corrosion-resistant treatment. Dual ejectors. Has 3-in. chambers. Ships with five Crio chokes. 6.85-7.65 pounds.

Price: **$3,399.00**

BENELLI 828U LIMITED EDITION

With nickel-plated steel frame, elegant engraved and gold inlayed game scene, and AA-grade Walnut. This 12 ga. with 28-in. barrel shows metalwork finished in B.E.S.T. coating. Limited to 200 units.

Price: **$6,499.00**

BERETTA 686/687 SILVER PIGEON SERIES

Gauges: 12 ga., 20 ga., 28 ga., 3 in. (2 3/4 in. 28 ga.). .410 bore, 3 in. Barrels: 26 in., 28 in. Weight: 6.8 lbs. Stock: Checkered walnut. Features: Interchangeable barrels (20 ga. and 28 ga.), single selective gold-plated trigger, boxlock action, auto safety, Schnabel fore-end.

Price: 686 Silver Pigeon Grade I **$2,350.00**
Price: 686 Silver Pigeon Grade I, Sporting **$2,400.00**
Price: 687 Silver Pigeon Grade III **$3,430.00**
Price: 687 Silver Pigeon Grade V **$4,075.00**

BERETTA 687 SILVER PIGEON III

Gauges: 12 ga. 3 in., 20 ga. 3 in., 28 ga. 2.75 in., .410 bore, 3 in. Barrels: 26, 28, 30 in. with 6x6 windowed rib. Stock: Class 2.5 Walnut with gloss finish. Features: The 687 Silver Pigeon III stems from the 680 series design. Trapezoid shoulders and dual conical locking lugs. Fine engraving with game scenes and floral motif done with 5-axis laser. MicroCore 20mm buttpad. The 28-gauge and .410-bore doubles are built on a smaller frame. Gold-colored single selective trigger. Tang safety selector. Steelium barrels. The 12, 20, and 28 gauges use 70mm Optima HP choke tubes while the .410 is equipped with 50mm Mobil Chokes.

Price: **$2,699.00**

BERETTA MODEL 687 EELL

Gauges: 12 ga., 20 ga., 28 ga., 410 bore. Features: Premium-grade model with decorative sideplates featuring lavish hand-chased engraving with a classic game scene enhanced by detailed leaves and flowers that also cover the triggerguard, trigger plate and fore-end lever. Stock has high-grade, specially selected European walnut with fine-line checkering. Offered in three action sizes with scaled-down 28 ga. and .410 receivers. Combo models are available with extra barrel sets in 20/28 or 28/.410.

Price: **$7,995.00**
Price: Combo model **$9,695.00**

BERETTA 687 EELL DIAMOND PIGEON

Gauges: 12, 20 ga. , 28 ga., .410 bore. Barrels: 26, 28, 30 in. cold hammer-forged with top rib. Stock: Select Grade 3 Walnut with choice of English or pistol grip stock. Features: Low-profile box lock O/U action with full side plates hand-engraved with wild game scenes and floral motifs, signed by the engraver. Handfit wood buttpads. Schnabel forend on sporting model; semi-beavertail on field model. MGS trigger. Fixed or interchangeable chokes available. Ships with Beretta hard case.

Price: **$7,549.00**

BERETTA MODEL 690

Gauge: 12 ga. 3 in. Barrels: 26 in., 28 in., 30 in. with OptimaChoke HP system. Features: Similar to the 686/687 series with minor improvements. Stock has higher grade oil-finished walnut. Re-designed barrel/fore-end attachment reduces weight.

Price: .... **$2,650.00–$3,100.00**

BERETTA MODEL 692 SPORTING

Gauge: 12 ga., 3 in. Barrels: 30 in. with long forcing cones of approximately 14 in.. Skeet model available with 28- or 30-in. barrel, Trap model with 30 in or 32 in. Receiver is .50-in. wider than 682 model for improved handling. Stock: Hand rubbed oil finished select walnut with Schnabel fore-end. Features include selective single adjustable trigger, manual safety, tapered 8mm to 10mm rib.

Price: **$4,800.00**
Price: Skeet **$5,275.00**
Price: Trap **$5,600.00**

BERETTA DT11

Gauge: 12 ga. 3 in. Barrels: 30 in., 32 in., 34 in. Top rib has hollowed bridges. Stock: Hand-checkered buttstock and fore-end. Hand-rubbed oil, Tru-Oil or wax finish. Adjustable comb on skeet and trap models. Features: Competition model offered in Sporting, Skeet and Trap models. Newly designed receiver, top lever, safety/selector button.

Price: Sporting **$8,650.00**
Price: Skeet **$8,650.00**
Price: Trap **$8,999.00**

BERETTA ULTRALEGGERO

Gauges: 12 ga. Barrels: 26, 28 in. Steelium Optima-Bore HP with 6x6 rib. Weight: 6.4-6.6 pounds. Stock: Wood with Schnabel forend Features: Built to be the lightest steel receiver shotgun on the market, using techno-polymer receiver inserts. Extralight recoil pad. Single mechanical trigger. Includes ABS hard case and OCHP choke tubes. Addition of model variant with Kick-Off recoil system and buttstock shims in 2024.

Price: **$2,999.00**
Price: w/ KickOff Recoil System.......................**$3,199.00**

BLASER F3 SUPERSPORT

Gauge: 12 ga., 3 in. Barrel: 32 in. Weight: 9 lbs. Stock: Adjustable semi-

Prices given are believed to be accurate at time of publication however, many factors affect retail pricing so exact prices are not possible.

79TH EDITION, 2025 ✦ **537**

custom, Turkish walnut wood grade: 4. Features: The latest addition to the F3 family is the F3 SuperSport. The perfect blend of overall weight, balance and weight distribution make the F3 SuperSport the ideal competitor. Briley Spectrum-5 chokes, free-floating barrels, adjustable barrel hanger system on o/u, chrome plated barrels full length, revolutionary ejector ball system, barrels finished in a powder coated nitride, selectable competition trigger.

Price: SuperSport..$9,076.00
Price: Competition Sporting...$7,951.00
Price: Superskeet..$9,076.00
Price: American Super Trap...$9,530.00

BROWNING CYNERGY

Gauges: .410 bore, 12 ga., 20 ga., 28 ga. Barrels: 26 in., 28 in., 30 in., 32 in. Stocks: Walnut or composite. Sights: White bead front most models; HiViz Pro-Comp sight on some models; mid bead. Features: Mono-Lock hinge, recoil-reducing interchangeable Inflex recoil pad, silver nitride receiver; striker-based trigger, ported barrel option. Imported from Japan by Browning.

Price: Field Grade Model, 12 ga. $1,910.00
Price: CX composite..$1,710.00
Price: CX walnut stock...$1,780.00
Price: Field, small gauges...$1,940.00
Price: Ultimate Turkey, Mossy Oak Breakup camo $2,390.00
Price: Ultimate Turkey in Mossy Oak Bottomland camo $2,549.00
Price: Micro Midas...$1,979.00
Price: Feather...$2,269.00
Price: Wicked Wing...$2,339.00
Price: Wicked Wing in Vintage Tan camo w/ Cerakote barrels $2,499.00

BROWNING CITORI SERIES

Gauges: 12 ga., 20 ga., 28 ga. .410 bore. Barrels: 26 in., 28 in. in 28 ga. and .410 bore. Offered with Invector choke tubes. All 12- and 20-ga. models have back-bored barrels and Invector Plus choke system. Weights: 6 lbs., 8 oz. (26 in. .410) to 7 lbs., 13 oz. (30 in. 12 ga.). Length: 43 in. overall (26-in. bbl.). Stock: Dense walnut, hand checkered, full pistol grip, beavertail fore-end. Field-type recoil pad on 12 ga. field guns and trap and skeet models. Sights: Medium-raised beads, German nickel silver. Features: Barrel selector integral with safety, automatic ejectors, three-piece takedown. Imported from Japan by Browning.

Price: White Lightning $2,670.00
Price: Feather Lightning...$2,870.00
Price: Gran Lightning $3,300.00
Price: Crossover (CX) $2,140.00
Price: Crossover (CX) w/adjustable comb $2,560.00
Price: Crossover (CXS)...$2,140.00
Price: Crossover Target (CXT)..$2,260.00
Price: Crossover Target (CXT) w/adjustable comb.........................$2,660.00
Price: Crossover (CXS)...$2,190.00
Price: Crossover (CXS) w/adjustable comb $2,590.00
Price: Crossover (CXS Micro) $2,140.00
Price: Hunter Deluxe $2,699.00
Price: White Lightning .410 bore and 28 ga. ....$2,669.00–$2,739.00
Price: CX White...$2,379.00
Price: CX White Adjustable..$2,939.00
Price: CX Micro $2,469.00
Price: CXS 20/28 Ga. Combo $3,939.00
Price: CXS White...$2,439.00
Price: CXT White...$2,499.00

BROWNING CITORI TRAP MAX

Gauge: 12 ga., 2.75 in. Barrels: 30 in., 32 in., ported with 5/16 to 7/16 adjustable ventilated rib. Weight: 9.0-9.2 lbs. Length: 47.75-49.75 in. Stock: Grade V/VI black walnut with gloss-oil finish. Features: Graco adjustable Monte Carlo comb. Buttplate adjusts for location and angle. GraCoil recoil reduction system increases comfort and offers length-of-pull adjustment. Adjustable rib allows for 50/50 or 90/10 POI. Semi-beavertail forearm with finger grooves, Pachmayr Decelerator XLT recoil pad. Close radius grip and palm swell. Triple Trigger System with three trigger shoes, gold-plated trigger, Hi-Viz Pro Comp sight, ivory mid-bead, polished blue barrels, Silver-Nitride receiver, chrome-plated chamber. Five Invector DS Extended choke tubes ideal for trap (F, LF, M, IM, IM).

Price: $5,859.00

BROWNING 725 CITORI

Gauges: 12 ga., 20 ga., 28 ga. or .410 bore. Barrels: 26 in., 28 in., 30 in. Weights: 5.7–7.6 lbs. Length: 43.75–50 in. Stock: Gloss oil finish, grade II/III walnut. Features: New receiver that is significantly lower in profile than other 12-gauge Citori models. Mechanical trigger, Vector Pro lengthened forcing cones, three Invector-DS choke tubes, silver nitride finish with high relief engraving.

Price: 725 Field (12 ga. or 20 ga.) $2,560.00
Price: 725 Field (28 ga. or .410 bore) $2,590.00
Price: 725 Feather (12 ga. or 20 ga.)....................................$2,670.00
Price: 725 Sporting $3,270.00
Price: 725 Sporting Left-Hand $3,529.00
Price: 725 Sporting w/adjustable comb $3,600.00
Price: 725 Sporting Golden Clays $5,440.00
Price: 725 Trap $3,400.00
Price: 725 Trap Left-Hand..$3,749.00
Price: 725 Sporting Maple $3,699.00
Price: 725 Trap Maple..$3,749.00

BROWNING CITORI 725 SPORTING MEDALLION HIGH GRADE

Gauge: 12 ga. 3 in. Barrels: 30 or 32 in., steel with floating 5/16 to 7/16-in. rib. Weight: 7 lbs. 8 oz.–7 lbs. 10 oz. Length: 48–50 in. Stock: Grade IV Turkish Walnut with gloss oil finish. Features: Browning expands the higher end of the Citori family. Extensive receiver engraving with gold enhancement. Cut checkering at 20 LPI and right-hand palm swell. HiViz Pro-Comp front sight. Chrome-plated chamber. Tapered locking bolt and full-width hinge pin. Triple trigger system with three included shoes. Blued receiver finish and polished blued barrels. Inflex recoil pad. Gold-plated trigger. Name plate inlay for owner's initials. Includes five Invector DS extended choke tubes (F, IM, M, IC, SK) and Negrini locking hard case.

Price: $7,069.00

BROWNING CITORI HIGH GRADE 50TH ANNIVERSARY

Gauges: 12 ga. Barrels: 30, 32 in. Stock: Grade IV Turkish Walnut with premium gloss oil finish. Features: Limited edition O/U commemorating the 50th anniversary. Built for hunting and target shooting. Silver nitride receiver extensive engraving with gold accents. HiViz Pro-Comp front sight. Checkering cut at 20 LPI. Ships with five Midas choke tubes.

Price: $8,399.00

BROWNING CITORI COMPOSITE

Gauges: 12 ga. Barrels: 26, 28, 30 in. Stock: Black composite with adjustable comb. Features: Synthetic stocked addition to the Citori O/U family. Has 3-inch chambers. Polished blue metalwork with non-glare stock finish. Ivory front bead. Inflex 2 recoil pad. Overmolded grip panels. Gold-plated trigger. Ships with three InvectorPlus flush choke tubes.

Price: $2,199.00

CAESAR GUERINI

Gauges: 12 ga., 20 ga., 28 ga., also 20/28 gauge combo. Some models are available in .410 bore. Barrels: All standard lengths from 26–32 inches. Weights: 5.5–8.8 lbs. Stock: High-grade walnut with hand-rubbed oil finish. Features: A wide range of over/under models designed for the field, sporting clays, skeet and trap shooting. The models listed below are representative of some of the different models and variants. Many optional features are offered including high-grade wood and engraving, and extra sets of barrels. Made it Italy and imported by Caesar Guerini USA.

Price: Summit Sporting...$3,995.00
Price: Summit Limited $4,895.00

Prices given are believed to be accurate at time of publication however, many factors affect retail pricing so exact prices are not possible.

Price: Summit Ascent	$5,135.00
Price: Tempio	$4,325.00
Price: Ellipse	$4,650.00
Price: Ellipse Curve	$7,500.00
Price: Ellipse Curve Gold	$8,900.00
Price: Ellipse EVO Sporting	$6,950.00
Price: Magnus	$5,075.00
Price: Maxum	$6,825.00
Price: Forum	$11,500.00
Price: Woodlander	$3,795.00
Price: Invictus Sporting	$7,400.00
Price: Maxum Trap	$9,295.00
Price: Maxum Sporting	$7,150.00

CAESAR GUERINI REVENANT

Addition of a new combo set to the high-grade 2019 Revenant O/U with a tapered, solid rib and highly engraved maple leaf and branch design receiver. Now with a 20/28-gauge combo barrel set.

Price: $13,495.00

CAESAR GUERINI REVENANT SPORTING

Gauge: 20 ga. 3 in., 28 ga. 2.75 in. Barrels: 28 or 30 in. with non-ventilated center rib, tapered from 8–6mm. Weight: 6 lbs. 6 oz.–6 lbs. 11 oz. Stock: Extra-deluxe wood grade with hand-rubbed oil finish. Left-hand stock option available by special order. Features: Fine-grade over-under Sporting version of the Revenant. Hand-polished coin finish with Invisalloy protective finish. Long-tang triggerguard. Anson rod fore-end escutcheon. Intricate engraving and gold inlay that takes over 40-hours to produce each Revenant action. Wood butt plate. Silver front bead. Checkered at 26 LPI. Premium Revenant gun case included. Ships with five nickel-plated flush-fitting chokes.

Price: $14,750.00

CAESAR GUERINI SYREN JULIA SPORTING

Gauges: 12 ga. 2.75 in. Barrels: 30 in. ventilated rib tapered from 10–8mm. Weight: 7 lbs. 15 oz. Stock: Deluxe Turkish Walnut with hand-rubbed, semi-gloss oil finish. Left-hand stock option and adjustable comb (RH) available by special order Features: Named after Julia, daughter of Julius Caesar, as a top-tier, competition-grade target gun in the Syren line of shotguns for women. Fantasy-style receiver engraving depicting a woman's face evolving from floral scrollwork. Rich case color hardened finish. Checking cut at 26 LPI. Black rubber recoil pad. DuoCon forcing cones. White Bradley style front sight and silver center bead. DTS trigger system with take-up, over-travel, and LOP adjustments. Manual safety. Includes six MAXIS competition chokes as well as plastic hard case, combination locks, and velvet sleeves.

Price: $6,050.00

CHAPUIS FAISAN

Gauges: 12 ga., 20 ga., 28 ga., (.410 bore on Classic only). Barrels: 28 in. with ventilated rib. Weight: 5.5 to 6.2 pounds. Stock: Grade-3 Walnut (Classic), Grade-5 Circassian Walnut (Artisan). Features: Fine over-under line built on an all-steel action. "Faisan" French for "pheasant." Receivers scaled to gauges. Low profile keeps barrels closer to the supporting hand to make pointing intuitive. Round action. Single trigger. Automatic safety and auto ejectors. Brass front bead. Pistol grip-style buttstock. Classic receiver is laser engraved; Artisan is hand-engraved, both with coin finish and game scenes. Ships with five choke tubes and custom hard case.

Price: Classic 12-ga.	$5,299.00
Price: Classic 20-ga.	$5,599.00
Price: Classic 28-ga.	$6,699.00
Price: Classic .410	$6,199.00
Price: Artisan 12-ga.	$10,899.00
Price: Artisan 20-ga.	$11,099.00
Price: Artisan 28-ga.	$12,229.00

CHARLES DALY 202

Gauges: 12 ga., 3 in., 20 ga., 3 in., .410 bore, 3 in. Barrels: 26 in., 28 in., ventilated rib. Length: 43-45 in. Weight: 6.2-7.3 lbs. Stock: Checkered walnut. Features: The new Charles Daly 202 line of O/U shotguns are built of aluminum alloy. Silver receivers are engraved with a dog scene. Single selective mechanical reset trigger, fixed fiber-optic front sight, extractors, rubber buttpad. Includes five extended Mobil style chokes (SK, IC, M, IM, F).

Price: $499.00

CHARLES DALY TRIPLE MAGNUM

Gauges: 12 ga. Barrels: 28 in. Stock: Addition of True Timber DRT or Prairie camouflage synthetic. Features: Triple-barreled break-action shotgun with full camo coverage of barrels and stocks. Set of five Interchangeable MC-5 Rem chokes. Distributed by Chiappa Firearms. Magnum 3.5-inch chambers. Single non-selective mechanical trigger with right, left, top firing sequence.

Price: $2,073.00–2,159.00

CONNECTICUT SHOTGUN A-10 AMERICAN

Gauge: 12 ga., 16 ga., 20 ga., 28 ga., .410 bore. Barrel: 26 in., 28 in., 30 in. ventilated rib. Stock: Select walnut comes standard with upgrade options in 3x, 4x and Exhibition-grade and pistol or Prince of Wales grip, short or long tang. Features: Patented design with the lowest profile sidelock built and shallowest frame design. Extensive hand engraving. Internal parts have trademarked HardGold coating for rust prevention. Multiple stock options available, each with hand-cut checkering. Single selective trigger. Custom shop options available include solid rib, fixed chokes, drop points, checkered butt, heel and toe plates, skeleton butt, cut lock plates, chiseled fences, cut frame, round body, and extra sets of barrels. Each shotgun is built completely in-house at New Britain, Connecticut.

Price: Standard 12 & 16 ga	$18,000.00
Price: 20 ga. & 28 ga. Small Frame	$20,000.00
Price: .410 on Standard Frame	$23,000.00

CONNECTICUT SHOTGUN MODEL 21 O/U

Gauge: 20 ga., 3 in. Barrels: 26–32 in. chrome-lined, back-bored with extended forcing cones. Weight: 6.3 lbs. Stock: A Fancy (2X) American walnut, standard point checkering, choice of straight or pistol grip. Higher grade walnut is optional. Features: The over/under version of Conn. Shotgun's replica of the Winchester Model 21 side-by-side, built using the same machining, tooling, techniques and finishes. Low-profile shallow frame with blued receiver. Pigeon and Grand American grades are available. Made in the USA by Connecticut Shotgun Mfg. Co.

Price: $4,545.00

CZ ALL TERRAIN SERIES

Gauges: 12 ga., 3 in., 20 ga., 3 in. Barrels: 28 in. 30 in. Stock: Walnut, various styles. Features: CZ's new All-Terrain series encompasses five existing shotgun models. The new package includes upgraded wood, OD Green Cerakote finish on all metalwork, as well as a set of rare earth magnets added to the extractor/ejectors of the SxS and O/U models to keep shells from dropping out while handling a dog or working in the blind.

Price: Upland Ultralight All-Terrain 12 ga. or 20 ga.	$890.00
Price: Redhead Premier All-Terrain 12 ga. or 20 ga.	$1,123.00
Price: Drake All-Terrain 12 ga. or 20 ga.	$791.00

CZ REDHEAD PREMIER

Gauges: 12 ga., 20 ga., (3 in. chambers), 28 ga. (2 3/4 in.). Barrel: 28 in. Weight: 7.4 lbs. Length: NA. Stock: Round-knob pistol grip, Schnabel fore-end, Turkish walnut. Features: Single selective triggers and extractors (12 & 20 ga.), screw-in chokes (12 ga., 20 ga., 28 ga.) choked IC and Mod (.410), coin-finished receiver, multi chokes. From CZ-USA.

Price: Deluxe	$953.00
Price: Mini (28 ga., .410 bore)	$1,057.00
Price: Target	$1,389.00
Price: 16 ga., 28 in. barrel	$988.00

CZ REDHEAD PREMIER PROJECT UPLAND

Gauge: 12, 20, 28 ga. Barrel: 28 in. with 8mm flat vent rib. Length: 43.75 in. Weight: 6.9–7.7 lbs. Stock: Grade III Turkish Walnut. Features: Project Upland hunting O/U with silver satin chrome receiver finish. One piece CNC'd action, 3-in. chamber. Gloss black chrome barrel finish. Brass front bead. Single mechanical trigger selectable for barrels. Manual tang safety. Patent pending magnetic chambers. Includes five chokes (F, IM, M, IC, C).
Price: 12 & 20 ga. **$1,509.00**
Price: 28 ga. **$1,609.00**

FABARM ELOS 2 ELITE

Gauge: 12 ga. 3 in., 20 ga. 3 in. Barrels: 28 in. ventilated rib. Stock: Deluxe-grade European Walnut with matte oil finish and pistol grip design. Features: Left-handed stock option available by special order. Rich case-colored action with gold inlay of sporting birds. Hand-cut checkering. Brass front bead. Single gold-plated trigger. TriBore HP barrel and Inner HP flush-fitting chokes. Ships with Integrale case.
Price: **$3,325.00**

FABARM ELOS N2 ALLSPORT COMBO

Gauge: 12 ga. Barrels: 30 in. O/U with 34 in. Unsingle combo; 32 in. O/U with 34 in. Unsingle combo. Stock: Turkish Walnut with TriWood enhanced finish. Available with left-hand stock option or Modified Compact Stock with shorter LOP. Features: The Elos N2 Allsport Type T Combo is built for competition shooting. Microcell 22mm recoil pad. Quick Release Rib (QRR) rib on O/U barrels. Adjustable competition trigger. Adjustable comb. TriBore HP barrel. Hand-cut checkering. Single trigger. Includes five EXIS HP Competition extended choke tubes. Ships with hard case.
Price: **$3,325.00**

F.A.I.R. CARRERA ONE

Gauge: 12 ga. 3 in. Barrels: 30 in. chrome-lined with flat 11mm vent rib. Optional 28, 30 in. Weight: 7 lbs. Stock: Selected European Walnut with ergonomic sporting design and XR-Stock adjustment system (comb/heel) in bright oil finish. Features: FAIR's latest sporting O/U with oversize cross-locking bolt on double lugs. Black bright action with golden clay pigeon and model names. Triple-depth laser engraving, black selective single trigger, top tang manual safety. Long-stroke automatic ejectors. Oil-resistant ventilated rubber recoil pad. Fine-pitch laser checkering. Red fiber-optic front sight. Technichoke XP70 system with 5 tubes. Packed in V500SP case.
Price: **$1,988.00**

F.A.I.R. CARRERA ONE HR

Gauge: 12 ga. 3 in. Barrels: 30 in. chrome-lined with 15mm wide high vent rib. Optional 28, 30 in. Weight: 7.5 lbs. with mounted chokes. Stock: Selected European Walnut with ergonomic sporting design and XR-Stock adjustment system (comb/heel) Monte Carlo style, in bright oil finish. Features: FAIR's latest sporting O/U with oversize cross-locking bolt on double lugs, this HR variant with a high rib. Black bright action with golden clay pigeon and model names. Triple-depth laser engraving, black selective single trigger, top tang manual safety, long-stroke automatic ejectors. Oil-resistant ventilated rubber recoil pad. Fine-pitch laser checkering. Fiber-optic front sight. Technichoke XP70 system with 5 tubes (F, IM, M, IC, C). Packed in V500SP case.
Price: **$2,198.00**

FAUSTI CLASS ROUND BODY

Gauges: 16 ga., 20 ga., 28 ga.. Barrels: 28 or 30 in. Weights: 5.8–6.3 lbs. Lengths: 45.5–47.5 in. Stock: Turkish walnut Prince of Wales style with oil finish. Features include automatic ejectors, single selective trigger, laser-engraved receiver.
Price: **$4,199.00**

FAUSTI CALEDON

Gauges: 12 ga., 16 ga., 20 ga., 28 ga. and .410 bore. Barrels: 26 in., 28 in., 30 in. Weights: 5.8–7.3 lbs. Stock: Turkish walnut with oil finish, round pistol grip. Features: Automatic ejectors, single selective trigger, laser-engraved receiver. Coin finish receiver with gold inlays.
Price: 12 ga. or 20 ga. **$1,999.00**
Price: 16 ga., 28 ga., .410 bore **$2,569.00**

FRANCHI INSTINCT SERIES

Gauges: 12 ga., 16 ga., 20 ga., 28 ga., .410 bore, 2 1/5 in. 2 3/4 in., in 3 in." Barrels: 26 in., 28 in. Weight: 5.3–6.4 lbs. Lengths: 42.5–44.5 in. Stock: AA-grade satin walnut (LS), A-grade (L) with rounded pistol grip and recoil pad. Single trigger, automatic ejectors, tang safety, choke tubes. L model has steel receiver, SL has aluminum alloy receiver. Sporting model has higher grade wood, extended choke tubes. Catalyst model is designed for women, including stock dimensions for cast, drop, pitch, grip and length of pull.
Price: L **$1,299.00**
Price: SL **$1,599.00**
Price: Sporting...**$1,999.00**
Price: Catalyst..**$1,469.00**
Price: SL 28 ga. and .410 bore **$1,699.00**

FRANCHI INSTICT SIDEPLATE

Gauges: 16 ga., 28 ga Barrels: 28 in. Stock: AA-Grade Walnut with Prince of Wales grip and Schnabel forend. Features: Addition of two gauges to the upland O/U family. Three-inch chambers. Gold-inlaid game scenes and blued barrels. Auto ejectors and auto safety. Ships with five extended choke tubes and a custom-fitted hard case.
Price: **$2,399.00**

KOLAR SPORTING CLAYS

Gauge: 12 ga., 2 3/4 in. Barrels: 30 in., 32 in., 34 in.; extended choke tubes. Stock: 14.625 in. x 2.5 in. x 1.875 in. x 1.375 in. French walnut. Four stock versions available. Features: Single selective trigger, detachable, adjustable for length; overbored barrels with long forcing cones; flat tramline rib; matte blue finish. Made in U.S. by Kolar.
Price: Standard **$11,995.00**
Price: Prestige..**$14,190.00**
Price: Elite Gold **$16,590.00**
Price: Legend **$17,090.00**
Price: Select..**$22,590.00**
Price: Custom .... **Price on request**

KOLAR AAA COMPETITION TRAP

Gauge: 12 ga. Similar to the Sporting Clays gun except has 32 in. O/U 34 in. Unsingle or 30 in. O/U 34 in. Unsingle barrels as an over/under, unsingle, or combination set. Stock dimensions are 14.5 in. x 2.5 in. x 1.5 in.; American or French walnut; step parallel rib standard. Contact maker for full listings. Made in USA by Kolar.
Price: Single bbl. **$8,495.00**
Price: O/U **$11,695.00**

KOLAR AAA COMPETITION SKEET

Similar to the Sporting Clays gun except has 28 in. or 30 in. barrels with Kolarite AAA sub-gauge tubes; stock of American or French walnut with matte finish; flat tramline rib; under barrel adjustable for point of impact. Many options available. Contact maker for complete listing. Made in USA by Kolar.
Price: Max Lite **$13,995.00**

Prices given are believed to be accurate at time of publication however, many factors affect retail pricing so exact prices are not possible.

KRIEGHOFF K-80 SPORTING CLAYS

Gauge: 12 ga. Barrels: 28 in., 30 in., 32 in., 34 in. with choke tubes. Weight: About 8 lbs. Stock: #3 Sporting stock designed for gun-down shooting. Features: Standard receiver with satin nickel finish and classic scroll engraving. Selective mechanical trigger adjustable for position. Choice of tapered flat or 8mm parallel flat barrel rib. Free-floating barrels. Aluminum case. Imported from Germany by Krieghoff International, Inc.

Price: Standard grade with five choke tubes **$12,395.00**

KRIEGHOFF K-80 SKEET

Gauge: 12 ga., 2 3/4 in. Barrels: 28 in., 30 in., 32 in., (skeet & skeet), optional choke tubes. Weight: About 7.75 lbs. Stock: American skeet or straight skeet stocks, with palm-swell grips. Walnut. Features: Satin gray receiver finish. Selective mechanical trigger adjustable for position. Choice of ventilated 8mm parallel flat rib or ventilated 8–12mm tapered flat rib. Introduced 1980. Imported from Germany by Krieghoff International, Inc.

Price: Standard, skeet chokes **$11,795.00**

KRIEGHOFF K-80 TRAP

Gauge: 12 ga., 2 3/4 in. Barrels: 30 in., 32 in. (Imp. Mod. & Full or choke tubes). Weight: About 8.5 lbs. Stock: Four stock dimensions or adjustable stock available; all have palm-swell grips. Checkered European walnut. Features: Satin nickel receiver. Selective mechanical trigger, adjustable for position. Ventilated step rib. Introduced 1980. Imported from Germany by Krieghoff International, Inc.

Price: K-80 O/U (30 in., 32 in., Imp. Mod. & Full **$11,795.00**
Price: K-80 Unsingle (32 in., 34 in., Full), standard **$13,995.00**
Price: K-80 Combo (two-barrel set), standard **$17,995.00**

KRIEGHOFF K-20

Similar to the K-80 except built on a 20-ga. frame. Designed for skeet, sporting clays and field use. Offered in 20 ga., 28 ga. and .410; Barrels: 28 in., 30 in. and 32 in. Imported from Germany by Krieghoff International Inc.

Price: K-20, 20 ga. **$11,695.00**
Price: K-20, 28 ga. **$12,395.00**
Price: K-20, .410 .... **$12,395.00**
Price: K-20 Sporting or Parcours... **$12,395.00**
Price: K-20 Victoria **$12,395.00**

MERKEL MODEL 2001EL O/U

Gauges: 12 ga., 20 ga., 3 in. 28 ga. 2-3/4 in. chambers. Barrels: 12 ga. 28 in.; 20 ga., 28 ga. 26.75 in. Weight: About 7 lbs. (12 ga.). Stock: Oil-finished walnut; English or pistol grip. Features: Self-cocking Blitz boxlock action with cocking indicators; Kersten double cross-bolt lock; silver-grayed receiver with engraved hunting scenes; coil spring ejectors; single selective or double triggers. Imported from Germany by Merkel USA.

Price: **$13,255.00**

MERKEL MODEL 2000CL

Similar to Model 2001EL except scroll-engraved casehardened receiver; 12 ga., 20 ga., 28 ga. Imported from Germany by Merkel USA.

Price: **$12,235.00**

MOSSBERG INTERNATIONAL SILVER RESERVE EVENTIDE

Gauge: 12 ga., 20 ga., 28 ga. Barrels: 20 in., 26 in., 28 in. with ventilated rib, choke tubes. Stock: Synthetic. Coloration varies by model with Mossy Oak Greenleaf on Turkey; Mossy Oak Vintage Shadowgrass on Waterfowl; Black Synthetic on base model. Sights: Front fiber optic. Available with extractors. Magnum 3.5-inch chamber on 12-gauge models. Logo engraved receiver. Five choke field set. Chrome-lined barrels and chambers. Dual locking lugs.

Price: Turkey 20-in. 12, 20, 28 ga **$927.00**
Price: Waterfowl 28-in. 12 ga **$956.00**
Price: Standard Black. 26-in. 20 ga...................................... **$756.00**
Price: HS12 18.5-in. 12 ga **$770.00**

MOSSBERG INTERNATIONAL SILVER RESERVE II

Gauge: 12 ga., 3 in. Barrels: 28 in. with ventilated rib, choke tubes. Stock: Select black walnut with satin finish. Sights: Metal bead. Available with extractors or automatic ejectors. Also offered in Sport model with ported barrels with wide rib, fiber optic front and middle bead sights. Super Sport has extra wide high rib, optional adjustable comb.

Price: Field **$773.00**
Price: Sport **$950.00**
Price: Sport w/ejectors **$1,070.00**
Price: Super Sport w/ejectors **$1,163.00**
Price: Super Sport w/ejectors, adj. comb **$1,273.00**

MOSSBERG INTERNATIONAL SILVER RESERVE FIELD SERIES

Gauge: Options depend on model, but include 12 ga. 3 in., 20 ga. 3 in., 28 ga. 2.75 in., and .410 bore 3 in., as well as a 20-ga. Youth. Barrels: 26- or 28-in. ventilated rib. Weight: 6.5–7.5 lbs. Length: 42.25–45 in. Stock: Choice satin Black Walnut, depending upon model, as well as a Youth-sized model with shorter LOP. Features: Matte blue barrel finish. Satin silver receiver on all except the synthetic model with a matte blue receiver. Dual shell extractors. Tang-mounted safety/barrel selector. Includes flush-mount Field set of five chokes (Cyl, IC, M, IM, F).

Price: Black Walnut Price 12, 20, 28 ga., .410 and 20-ga. Youth **$692.00**

MOSSBERG INTERNATIONAL GOLD RESERVE

Gauge: 12 ga. 3 in., 20 ga. 3 in., and .410 bore 3 in. Barrels: 28 or 30 in. ventilated rib. Weight: 6.5–7.5 lbs. Length: 45.0–48.0 in. Stock: Grade-A Satin Black Walnut. Adjustable stock on Super Sport model. Features: Dual locking lugs and Jeweled action. Chrome-lined bores and chambers. Competition-ready dual shell ejectors. Tang-mounted safety/barrel selector with scroll engraving. Polished silver receiver with scroll-engraved receiver with 24-Karat gold inlay on the underside receiver. Black Label variants wear polished black receiver with same embellishments. Includes set of five Extended Sport chokes (SK, IC, M, IM, F).

Price: Black Walnut 12 or 20 ga., .410 .... **$983.00**
Price: Black Label 12 & 20 ga. **$1,135.00**
Price: Super Sport in 12 ga with fully adjustable stock **$1,221.00**

PERAZZI HIGH TECH 2020

Gauge: 12 ga., 3 in. Barrels: 27-9/16 in., 28-3/8 in., 29-1/2 in., 30-3/4 in., 31-1/2 in., flat ramped stepped 9/32 x 3/8 in. rib. Weight: 8 lbs.-8 lbs., 8 oz. Stock: Oil-finish, high-grade walnut, HT design standard or custom adjustable. Features: The competition grade High Tech 2020 is made in Italy. Logo engraving across silver-finish receiver. Hand-cut checkering, blued-steel barrels. Removable trigger group with coil or flat springs and selector. Ventilated mid-rib. Interchangeable chokes available on demand.

Price: **$21,075.00**

PERAZZI MX8/MX8 TRAP/SKEET

Gauge: 12 ga., 20 ga. 2 3/4 in. Barrels: Trap: 29.5 in. (Imp. Mod. & Extra Full), 31.5 in. (Full & Extra Full). Choke tubes optional. Skeet: 27.625 in. (skeet & skeet). Weights: About 8.5 lbs. (trap); 7 lbs., 15 oz. (skeet). Stock: Interchangeable and custom made to customer specs. Features: Has detachable and interchangeable trigger group with flat V springs. Flat .4375 in. vent rib. Many options available. Imported from Italy by Perazzi USA, Inc.

Price: Trap **$11,760.00**
Price: Skeet **$11,760.00**

PERAZZI MX8

Gauge: 12 ga., 20 ga. 2 3/4 in. Barrels: 28.375 in. (Imp. Mod. & Extra Full), 29.50 in. (choke tubes). Weight: 7 lbs., 12 oz. Stock: Special specifications. Features: Has single selective trigger; flat .4375 in. x .3125 in. vent rib. Many options available. Imported from Italy by Perazzi USA, Inc.

Price: Standard **$11,760.00**
Price: Sporting **$11,760.00**
Price: SC3 Grade (variety of engraving patterns) **$21,000.00**
Price: SCO Grade (more intricate engraving/inlays) **$36,000.00**

PIOTTI BOSS

Gauges: 12 ga., 16 ga., 20 ga., 28 ga., .410 bore. Barrels: 26–32 in., chokes as specified. Weight: 6.5–8 lbs. Stock: Dimensions to customer specs. Best quality figured walnut. Features: Essentially a custom-made gun with many options. Introduced 1993. SportingModel is production model with many features of custom series Imported from Italy by Wm. Larkin Moore.

Price: $78,000.00
Price: Sporting Model..$27,200.00

POINTER ACRIUS

Gauges: 12 ga., 20 ga., 28 ga., .410. Barrels: 26, 28 in. with raised vent rib. Weights: 5.4 lbs. (.410) to 7.6 lbs (12 ga). Length: 43–45 in. Stock: Turkish Walnut, checkered, with rubber buttpad. Synthetic camouflage available on Cerakote variants. Features: Laser-etched receiver. Single mechanical trigger. Barrel selector, extractors. Fiber-optic front sight. Set of five chokes included with extended tubes on most models. Standard LOP at 14 in. and a Youth model available in 20 ga. and .410 bore with 26-in. barrel and 12.5-in. LOP. Built in Turkey and imported by Legacy Sports International.

Price: $699.00

RIZZINI AURUM

Gauges: 12 ga., 16 ga., 20 ga., 28 ga., .410 bore. Barrels: 26, 28, 29 and 30, set of five choke tubes. Weight: 6.25 to 6.75 lbs. (Aurum Light 5.5 to 6.5 lbs.) Stock: Select Turkish walnut with Prince of Wales grip, rounded fore-end. Hand checkered with polished oil finish. Features: Boxlock low-profile action, single selective trigger, automatic ejectors, engraved game scenes in relief, light coin finish with gold inlay. Aurum Light has alloy receiver.

Price: 12, 16, 20 ga..$3,425.00
Price: 28, .410 bore..$3,625.00
Price: Aurum Light 12, 16, 20 ga........................$3,700.00
Price: Aurum Light 28, .410 bore........................$3,900.00

RIZZINI ARTEMIS

Gauges: 12 ga., 16 ga., 20 ga., 28 ga., .410 bore. Same as Upland EL model except dummy sideplates with extensive game scene engraving. Fancy European walnut stock. Fitted case. Introduced 1996. Imported from Italy by Fierce Products and by Wm. Larkin Moore & Co.

Price: $3,975.00
Price: Artemis Light $4,395.00

RIZZINI BR 460

Gauge: 12 ga., 3 in. Barrels: 30 in., 32 in., with 10mm x 6mm ventilated rib. Length: 43-45 in. Weight: 8.3 lbs. Stock: Walnut with hand-rubbed oil finish and adjustable comb. Features: These Rizzini O/U Competition guns are produced in Skeet, Sporting, Trap, and Double Trap, each with different characteristics. Choice of fixed or interchangeable chokes and fixed, adjustable or ramped rib. Stock checkered at 28 LPI. White rounded style front sight with silver mid-bead. Rubber buttpad. Either standard or long forcing cones depending on model. Ships with hard case and velvet stock sleeve.

Price: $7,045.00

RIZZINI FIERCE 1 COMPETITION

Gauges: 12 ga., 20 ga., 28 ga. Barrels: 28, 30 and 32 in. Five extended completion choke tubes. Weight: 6.6 to 8.1 lbs. Stock: Select Turkish walnut, hand checkered with polished oil finish. Features: Available in trap, skeet or sporting models. Adjustable stock and rib available. Boxlock low-profile action, single selective trigger, automatic ejectors, engraved game scenes in relief, light coin finish with gold inlay. Aurum Light has alloy receiver.

Price: $4,260.00

RIZZINI VENUS SPORT

Gauges: 20 ga., 28 ga., .410. Barrels: 28, 30 and 32 in. Five extended nickel-coated choke tubes. Weight: 6.2-6.8 lbs. Stock: Grade 2.5 Turkish Walnut designed for women, with 26 LPI checkering. Features: Steel roundbody frame O/U designed for women with adjustments to frame, stock, and forearm. Floral engraved receiver with Venus logo and coin finish. Single selective trigger and automatic ejectors. Engraved triggerguard. Includes Venus-designed ABS hard case.

Price: $5,695.00

SKB 90TSS

Gauges: 12 ga., 20 ga., 2 3/4 in. Barrels: 28 in., 30 in., 32 in. Three SKB Competition choke tubes (SK, IC, M for Skeet and Sporting Models; IM, M, F for Trap). Lengthened forcing cones. Stock: Oil finished walnut with Pachmayr recoil pad. Weight: 7.1-7.9 lbs. Sights: Ventilated rib with target sights. Features: Boxlock action, bright blue finish with laser engraved receiver. Automatic ejectors, single trigger with selector switch incorporated in thumb-operated tang safety. Sporting and Trap models have adjustable comb and buttpad system. Imported from Turkey by GU, Inc.

Price: Skeet $1,470.00
Price: Sporting Clays, Trap....................................$1,800.00

SKB MODEL 690 FIELD

Gauge: 12, 20, 28 ga., .410 bore. Barrel: 26, 28 in. Weight: 6 lbs. 10 oz. –7 lbs. 14 oz. Stock: Grade II Turkish Walnut with pistol grip butt and Schnabel forend with high-gloss poly finish. Features: The 690 Field is built on a box lock receiver, cut with CNC machines from a solid billet of chrome-moly steel. White chrome receiver finish. Chrome lined barrels with 3-in. chambers and lengthened forcing cones and automatic ejectors. Also available as a 28-ga./.410 bore multi-gauge set. Youth model available in 12 and 20 ga. with 26-in. barrels and 13-in. LOP. Includes chokes in F, IM, M, IC, S.

Price: $1,369.00
Price: Multi-Gauge Set $2,169.00
Price: Youth Model $1,369.00

SKB MODEL 720 FIELD

Gauge: 12, 20, 28 ga., .410 bore. Barrel: 26, 28, 30 in. Weight: 6 lbs. 10 oz. –7 lbs. 14 oz. Stock: Select Grade II Turkish Walnut. Features: The 720 Field is built on a boxlock receiver, cut with CNC machines from a solid billet of chrome-moly steel. Brushed white chrome receiver is laser engraved with upland and waterfowl scenes and gold scroll. Chrome-lined barrels with 3-in. chambers (except 28 ga.) and lengthened forcing cones and automatic ejectors. Mechanical trigger. Also available as a 28-ga./.410-bore multi-gauge set with 28-in. barrels. Youth model available in 20 ga. with 26-in. barrels and 13-in. LOP. Includes top-thread internal chokes in F, IM, M, IC, S.

Price: $1,569.00
Price: Multi-Gauge Set $2,369.00
Price: Youth Model $1,569.00

STEVENS MODEL 555

Gauges: 12 ga., 20 ga., 28 ga., .410; 2-3/4 and 3 in. Barrels: 26 in., 28 in. Weights: 5.5–6 lbs. Stocks: Semi-gloss finish Turkish Walnut. Features: Lightweight aluminum alloy receiver scaled to gauge. Five screw-in choke tubes with 12 ga., 20 ga., and 28 ga.; .410 has fixed M/IC chokes. Schnabel forend. Single selective mechanical trigger with extractors. Manual safety. Chrome-lined barrels. Sporting model with adjustable comb height and extended tubes.

Price: $705.00
Price: Enhanced Model..$879.00
Price: Sporting Model..$989.00

STOEGER CONDOR

Gauge: 12 ga., 20 ga., 2 3/4 in., 3 in.; 16 ga., .410. Barrels: 22 in., 24 in., 26 in., 28 in., 30 in. Weights: 5.5–7.8 lbs. Sights: Brass bead. Features: IC, M, or F screw-in choke tubes with each gun. Oil finished hardwood with pistol grip and fore-end. Auto safety, single trigger, automatic extractors.

Price:	$449.00–$669.00
Price: Combo with 12 and 20 ga. barrel sets	$899.00
Price: Competition	$669.00

SYREN JULIA FIELD

Gauges: 20 ga., 28 ga. Barrels: 28 in. Stock: Deluxe-grade Turkish Walnut with semi-gloss oil finish. Features: Designed specifically for women as part of Caesar Guerini's Syren division is built as a field gun. Side plate action with fantasy-style engraving depicting a woman's face evolving from a floral scroll. Color-casehardened finish. Single selective trigger, silver front bead, and manual safety. Left-hand stock option and 20/28 combo sets available by special order. Ships with a hard case, velvet sleeves, and five flush choke tubes.

Price:	$6,250.00

TRISTAR CYPHER

Gauge: 12 ga., 16 ga., 20 ga., 28 ga., .410 bore. 3-in. Barrel: 28 in. ventilated rib. Weight: 5.9–7 lbs. Stock: Deluxe Turkish Walnut with oil finish. Features: Solid frame O/U with steel mono-block barrel construction. Auto ejectors. Fiber-optic front sight. Set of five extended color-coded choke tubes. Top tan safety selector. Cypher X uses lighter weight aluminum mono-block construction. Cypher SP has adjustable comb, 30-in. ported sporting barrels, target rib, and blued receiver.

Price: 12, 16, 20 ga	$960.00
Price: 28 ga. & .410	$975.00
Price: Cypher X 12, 16, 20 ga	$960.00
Price: Cypher X 28 ga. & .410	$975.00
Price: Cypher SP	$1,025.00

TRISTAR HUNTER MAG CAMO

Gauge: 12 ga., 3.5 in. Barrels: 26 in., 28 in., 30 in., ventilated rib. Length: 44-48 in. Weight: 7.3-7.9 lbs. Stock: Synthetic, with choice of black or numerous Mossy Oak patterns. Features: The 3.5-inch magnum chambered Hunter Mag O/U expands with the addition of Cerakote/Mossy Oak combination models. Steel mono-block construction, extractors, rubber recoil pad, fiber-optic front sight, single selective trigger, chrome-lined barrel, swivel studs. Includes five Mobil-style choke tubes (SK, IC, M, IM, F).

Price:	$655.00–$760.00

TRISTAR SETTER

Gauge: 12 ga., 20 ga., 3-in. Barrels: 28 in. (12 ga.), 26 in. (20 ga.) with ventilated rib, three Beretta-style choke tubes. Weights: 6.3–7.2 pounds, Stock: High gloss wood. Single selective trigger, extractors.

Price:	$535.00–$565.00
Price: Sporting Model	$824.00–$915.00

TRISTAR TT-15 FIELD

Gauges: 12 ga., 3 in., 20 ga., 3 in., 28 ga., 2.75 in., .410 bore, 3 in. Barrel: 28 in., ventilated rib. Length: 45 in. Weight: 5.7-7.0 lbs. Stock: Turkish walnut. Features: Field hunting O/U model with steel mono-block construction, mid-rib, top-tang barrel selector and safety. Chrome-lined barrel and chamber, engraved silver receiver, single selective trigger, fiber-optic front sight, auto ejectors. Includes five Mobil-style extended, color-coded chokes (SK, IC, M, IM, F).

Price:	$855.00

TRISTAR TRINITY

Gauges: 12 ga., 3 in., 16 ga., 2.75 in., 20 ga., 3 in. Barrels: 26 in., 28 in., steel ventilated rib. Weight: 6.3-6.9 lbs. Length: 43.5-45.5 in. Stock: Oil-finished Turkish walnut with checkering. Features: The CNC-machined all-steel receiver Trinity wears 24-karat gold inlay on the silver-finish engraved receiver. Barrels are blued steel. Single selective trigger, red fiber-optic front sight, rubber buttpad, dual extractors. Includes five Beretta Mobil-style chokes (SK, IC, M, IM, F).

Price:	$685.00

TRISTAR TRINITY LT

Gauges: 12 ga., 3 in., 20 ga., 3 in., 28 ga., 2.75 in., .410 bore, 3 in. Barrels: 26 in.,

28 in, ventilated rib. Weight: 5.3-6.3 lbs. Length: 43.5-45.5 in. Stock: Oil-finished Turkish walnut with checkering. Features: The CNC-machined lightweight aluminum-alloy receiver Trinity LT is engraved and wears a silver finish. Barrels are blued steel. Single selective trigger, red fiber-optic front sight, rubber buttpad, dual extractors. Includes five Beretta Mobil-style chokes (SK, IC, M, IM, F).

Price:	$685.00–$700.00

TRISTAR TRINITY II

Gauge: 12 ga., 16 ga., 20 ga., 28 ga.,. 410 bore. 3 in. Barrel: 28 in. ventilated rib. Weight: 6.1–6.8 lbs. Stock: Turkish Walnut with oil finish. Features: Solid frame with sealed actions, self-adjusting locking lugs, and steel mono-block barrel construction. Acid etched receiver with 24K gold inlay. Top tang safety selector. Rubber recoil pad. Single selective trigger, extractors, fiber-optic front sight. Set of five Beretta/Benelli Mobil style choke tubes. LT variant built with lighter weight aluminum alloy frame with steel inserts at contact points.

Price: 12, 16, 20 ga	$855.00
Price: 28 ga. & .410	$870.00
Price: LT 12, 16, 20 ga	$855.00
Price: LT 28 ga. & .410	$870.00

WEATHERBY ORION

Gauge: 12, 20 ga. Barrel: 26, 28 in. ventilated rib. Weight: 6.2–7.0 lbs. Stock: Gloss-finished A-Grade Turkish Walnut. Features: The new line of Orion O/U shotguns are built at the new factory in Sheridan, WY. Ambidextrous top tang safety. Low-profile receiver, chrome-lined bores with automatic ejectors. Each ships with three interchangeable chokes (F, M, IC). 20-ga. versions introduced to each line in 2022. Sporting variant uses 30-in. barrels, adjustable comb, ported barrels, and five extended choke tubes.

Price: Orion I	$1,049.00
Price: Orion Matte Blue	$1,049.00
Price: Orion Sporting	$1,149.00

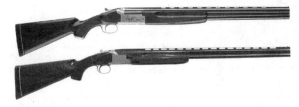

WINCHESTER MODEL 101

Gauge: 12 ga., 2 3/4 in., 3 in. Barrels: 28 in., 30 in., 32 in., ported, Invector Plus choke system. Weights: 7 lbs. 6 oz.–7 lbs. 12. oz. Stock: Checkered high-gloss grade II/III walnut stock, Pachmayr Decelerator sporting pad. Features: Chrome-plated chambers; back-bored barrels; tang barrel selector/safety; Signature extended choke tubes. Model 101 Field comes with solid brass bead front sight, three tubes, engraved receiver. Model 101 Sporting has adjustable trigger, 10mm runway rib, white mid-bead, Tru-Glo front sight, 30 in. and 32 in. barrels. Model 101 Pigeon Grade Trap has 10mm steel runway rib, mid-bead sight, interchangeable fiber-optic front sight, porting and vented side ribs, adjustable trigger shoe, fixed raised comb or adjustable comb, Grade III/IV walnut, 30 in. or 32 in. barrels, molded ABS hard case. Reintroduced 2008. Made in Belgium by FN. Winchester 150th Anniversary Commemorative model has grade IV/V stock, deep relief scrolling on a silver nitride finish receiver.

Price: Field	$1,900.00
Price: Sporting	$2,380.00

ARRIETA SIDELOCK DOUBLE

Gauges: 12 ga., 16 ga., 20 ga., 28 ga., .410 bore. Barrels: Length and chokes to customer specs. Weight: To customer specs. Stock: To customer specs. Straight English with checkered butt (standard), or pistol grip. Select European walnut with oil finish. Features: Essentially custom gun with myriad options. H&H pattern hand-detachable sidelocks, selective automatic ejectors, double triggers (hinged front) standard. Some have self-opening action. Finish and engraving to customer specs. Imported from Spain by Quality Arms, Wm. Larking Moore and others.

Price: Model 557..**$6,970.00**
Price: Model 570..**$7,350.00**
Price: Model 578..**$12,200.00**
Price: Model 600 Imperial..**$14,125.00**
Price: Model 803..**$17,000.00**
Price: Model 931..**$40,000.00**

BERETTA 486 PARALELLO

Gauges: 12 ga., 20 ga., 3 in., or 28 ga. 2 3/4 in. Barrels: 26 in., 28 in., 30 in. Weight: 7.1 lbs. Stock: English-style straight grip, splinter fore-end. Select European walnut, checkered, oil finish. Features: Round action, Optima-Choke Tubes. Automatic ejection or mechanical extraction. Firing-pin block safety, manual or automatic, open top-lever safety. Imported from Italy by Beretta USA

Price: **$5,350.00**

CHAPUIS CHASSEUR

Gauges: 12 ga., 20 ga., 28 ga. Barrels: 28 in. with wide solid rib. Weight: 5.5 to 6.2 pounds. Stock: AAA-Grade Walnut (Classic), Grade-5 Circassian Walnut (Artisan). Features: Fine side-by-side built on a scalloped boxlock action. Extensive receiver engraving of game scenes and acanthus scrolls. Laser engraving on Classic; hand engraving on Artisan. Classic straight grip stock style. Automatic safety. Double triggers. Auto ejectors. Brass front bead. Snag-free checkered wood buttplate. Ships with five choke tubes and a custom hard case.

Price: Classic 12-ga. **$5,449.00**
Price: Classic 20-ga. **$5,699.00**
Price: Classic 28-ga. **$6,899.00**
Price: Artisan 12-ga. **$10,899.00**
Price: Artisan 20-ga. **$11,199.00**
Price: Artisan 28-ga. **$12,499.00**

CHARLES DALY 500

Gauge: .410 bore, 3 in. Barrel: 28 in. Length: 43.25 in. Weight: 4.4 lbs. Stock: Checkered walnut English-style buttstock. Features: Charles Daly's new pair of baby-bore SxS Model 500 includes two versions, both steel, one with a black engraved receiver and the other black engraved with gold accents. Double triggers, extractors, manual safety, brass front bead. Includes five Mobil-style chokes (SK, IC, M, IM, F).

Price: ....**$725.00–$875.00**

CIMARRON 1878 COACH GUN

Gauge: 12 ga. 3 in. Barrels: 20 in., 26 in. Weights: 8–9 lbs. Stock: Hardwood. External hammers, double triggers. Finish: Blue, Cimarron "USA", Cimarron "Original."
Price: Blue ....**$597.00 (20 in.)–$623.00 (26 in.)**

CIMARRON DOC HOLLIDAY MODEL

Gauge: 12 ga. Barrels: 20 in., cylinder bore. Stock: Hardwood with rounded pistol grip. Features: Double triggers, hammers, false sideplates.
Price: **$1,581.00**

CONNECTICUT SHOTGUN MANUFACTURING CO. RBL

Gauges: 12 ga., 16 ga., 20 ga.. Barrels: 26 in., 28 in., 30 in., 32 in. Weight: NA. Length: NA. Stock: NA. Features: Round-action SxS shotguns made in the USA. Scaled frames, five TruLock choke tubes. Deluxe fancy grade walnut buttstock and fore-end. Quick Change recoil pad in two lengths. Various dimensions and options available depending on gauge.

Price: 12 ga. **$3,795.00**
Price: 16 ga. **$3,795.00**
Price: 20 ga. Special Custom Model...............................**$7,995.00**

CONNECTICUT SHOTGUN MANUFACTURING CO. MODEL 21

Gauges: 12 ga., 16 ga., 20 ga., 28 ga., .410 bore. Features: A faithful re-creation of the famous Winchester Model 21. Many options and upgrades are available. Each frame is machined from specially produced proof steel. The 28 ga. and .410 guns are available on the standard frame or on a newly engineered small frame. These are custom guns and are made to order to the buyer's individual specifications, wood, stock dimensions, barrel lengths, chokes, finishes and engraving.

Price: 12 ga., 16 ga. or 20 ga **$15,000.00**
Price: 28 ga. or .410 ....**$18,000.00**

CZ ALL TERRAIN SERIES

Gauges: 12 ga., 3 in., 20 ga., 3 in. Barrels: 28 in., 30 in. Stock: Walnut, various styles. Features: CZ's new All-Terrain series encompasses five existing shotgun models. The new package includes upgraded wood, OD Green Cerakote finish on all metalwork, as well as a set of rare earth magnets added to the extractor/ejectors of the SxS and O/U models to keep shells from dropping out while handling a dog or working in the blind.
Price: Bobwhite G2 All-Terrain 12 ga. or 20 ga. **$828.00**

CZ BOBWHITE G2 INTERMEDIATE

Built on the Bobwhite G2 but with more compact dimensions for smaller-framed shooters.
The 26-in. barrel is 2 in. shorter than standard. Length of pull is also shorter at 14 in. even. Available only in 20 ga. Built for teens/smaller-stature shooters, as well as handling in tight spaces. All other features remain the same.
Price: **$709.00**

CZ BOBWHITE G2 PROJECT UPLAND

Gauge: 12, 20, 28 ga. Barrel: 28 in. with 8mm flat rib.Weight: 6.25–7.15 lbs. Stock: English-style straight grip with Grade III Turkish Walnut. Features: Project Upland hunting SxS designed with crowd-sourced input. Lovely color casehardened receiver finish, dual extractors, and gloss black chrome barrel finish. Splinter forend. Dual triggers and manual tang safety. Hand-engraving borrowed from Sharp Tail model. Includes five chokes (F, IM, M, IC, C).
Price: 12 & 20 ga. **$1,429.00**
Price: 28 ga. **$1,529.00**

CZ BOWWHITE G2 SOUTHPAW

Built on the Bobwhite G2 but the stock is "cast-on," or built in the opposite direction so it properly fits when brought up to the left shoulder. All other features remain, with the Southpaw using 28-in. barrels and available in 12 or 20 ga.
Price: **$709.00**

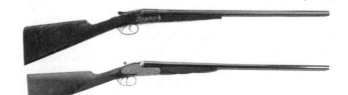

CZ SHARP-TAIL

Gauges: 12 ga., 20 ga., 28 ga., .410. (5 screw-in chokes in 12 and 20 ga. and fixed chokes in IC and Mod in .410). Barrels: 26 in. or 28 in. Weight: 6.5 lbs. Stock: Hand-checkered Turkish walnut with straight English-style grip and single selective trigger.

Price: Sharp-Tail **$1,022.00**
Price: Sharp-Tail Target..**$1,298.00**

CZ HAMMER COACH
Gauge: 12 ga., 3 in. Barrel: 20 in. Weight: 6.7 lbs. Features: Following in the tradition of the guns used by the stagecoach guards of the 1880s, this cowboy gun features double triggers, 19th-century color casehardening and fully functional external hammers.

Price: **$922.00**
Price: Classic model w/30-in. bbls. **$963.00**

EMF MODEL 1878 WYATT EARP
Gauge: 12. Barrel: 20 in.. Weight: 8 lbs. Length: 37 in. overall. Stock: Smooth walnut with steel butt place. Sights: Large brass bead. Features: Colt-style exposed hammers rebounding type; blued receiver and barrels; cylinder bore. Based on design of Colt Model 1878 shotgun. Made in Italy by Pedersoli.

Price: **$1,590.00**
Price: Hartford Coach Model...................................**$1,150.00**

EUROPEAN AMERICAN ARMORY (EAA) CHURCHILL 512
Gauges: 12 ga., 3in., 20 ga., 3 in., 28 ga., 3 in., .410 bore. Barrels: 26 in., 28 in. Length: 45-47 in. Stock: Standard Turkish walnut. Features: These Turkish made Akkar side-by-sides have a Nitride-silver receiver, rubber buttpad, checkered stock, single selective gold-plated trigger, front bead, manual safety, chrome-lined barrels, extractors. Ships with three choke tubes.

Price: **$1,355.00**

FABARM AUTUMN
Gauges: 20 ga. 3 in. Barrels: 28 or 30 in. with textured top rib. Weight: 5 lbs. 9 oz.–6 lbs. 2 oz. Stock: Deluxe Turkish Walnut with hand-oiled matte finish. Available in either English-style straight stock or standard pistol grip style. Left-hand option available by special order. Features: Fine grade side-by-side built in Italy. Color casehardened receiver finish with ornamental scroll engraving. Four lug locking system. Monolithic action design machined from steel forging. Splinter fore-end with English stock or Semi-beavertail with pistol-grip stock. Hand-fit walnut buttplate. Single trigger, tang-mounted safety/selector, auto-ejectors. Ships with Integrale case. Includes five INNER HP long choke tubes.

Price: **$4,095.00**

FAUSTI DEA SERIES
Gauges: 12 ga., 16 ga., 20 ga., 28 ga., .410. Barrels: 26 in., 28 in., 30 in. Weight: 6–6.8 lbs. Stock: AAA walnut, oil finished. Straight grip, checkered butt, classic fore-end. Features: Automatic ejectors, single non-selective trigger. Duetto model is in 28 ga. with extra set of .410 barrels. Made in Italy and imported by Fausti, USA.

Price: 12 ga. or 20 ga. **$5,590.00**
Price: 16 ga., 28 ga., .410 ....**$6,260.00**
Price: Duetto **$5,790.00**

FOX, A.H.
Gauges: 16 ga., 20 ga., 28 ga., .410. Barrels: Length and chokes to customer specifications. Rust-blued Chromox or Krupp steel. Weight: 5.5–6.75 lbs. Stock: Dimensions to customer specifications. Hand-checkered Turkish Circassian walnut with hand-rubbed oil finish. Straight, semi or full pistol grip; splinter, Schnabel or beavertail fore-end; traditional pad, hard rubber buttplate or skeleton butt. Features: Boxlock action with automatic ejectors; double or Fox single selective trigger. Scalloped, rebated and color case-hardened receiver; hand finished and hand-engraved. Grades differ in engraving, inlays, grade of wood, amount of hand finishing. Introduced 1993. Made in U.S. by Connecticut Shotgun Mfg.

Price: CE Grade **$19,500.00**
Price: XE Grade **$22,000.00**
Price: DE Grade **$25,000.00**
Price: FE Grade...**$30,000.00**
Price: 28 ga./.410 CE Grade..................................**$21,500.00**
Price: 28 ga./.410 XE Grade..................................**$24,000.00**
Price: 28 ga./.410 DE Grade..................................**$27,000.00**
Price: 28 ga./.410 FE Grade..................................**$32,000.00**

HERITAGE BADLANDER
Gauge: 12 ga. 3 in. Barrel: 18.5 in. with fixed cylinder chokes. Length: 34.85 in. Weight: 6.4 lbs. Stock: Turkish Walnut with checkering and dark stain finish. Features: Old West coach gun-style hammerless break-action built with an alloy steel frame and barrel with Black Chrome finish. Double triggers. Brass bead front sight and tang safety. Heritage logo brand engraving on receiver sides and right-side buttstock toe.

Price: **$983.00**

MERKEL MODEL 147SL
H&H style sidelock action with cocking indicators, ejectors. Silver-grayed receiver and sideplates have arabesque engraving, fine hunting scene engraving. Limited edition. Imported from Germany by Merkel USA.

Price: Model 147SL **$13,255.00**

MERKEL MODEL 280EL, 360EL
Similar to Model 47E except smaller frame. Greener crossbolt with double under-barrel locking lugs, fine engraved hunting scenes on silver-grayed receiver, luxury-grade wood, Anson and Deeley boxlock action. H&H ejectors, single-selective or double triggers. Introduced 2000. Imported from Germany by Merkel USA.

Price: Model 280EL (28 ga., 28 in. barrel, Imp. Cyl.
and Mod. chokes) **$8,870.00**
Price: Model 360EL (.410, 28 in. barrel, Mod. and Full chokes).......**$8,870.00**

MERKEL MODEL 280SL AND 360SL
Similar to Model 280EL and 360EL except has sidelock action, double triggers, English-style arabesque engraving. Introduced 2000. Imported from Germany by Merkel USA.

Price: Model 280SL (28 ga., 28 in. barrel, Imp. Cyl.
and Mod. chokes) **$13,255.00**
Price: Model 360SL (.410, 28 in. barrel, Mod. and Full chokes) **$13,255.00**

MERKEL MODEL 1620
Gauge: 16 ga. Features: Greener crossbolt with double under-barrel locking lugs, scroll-engraved casehardened receiver, Anson and Deeley boxlock action, Holland & Holland ejectors, English-style stock, single selective or double triggers, or pistol grip stock with single selective trigger. Imported from Germany by Merkel USA.

Price: Model 1620EL **$8,870.00**
Price: Model 1620EL Combo: 16- and 20-ga. two-barrel set **$13,255.00**

MERKEL MODEL 40E
Gauges: 12 ga., 20 ga. Barrels: 28 in. (12 ga.), 26.75 in. (20 ga.). Weight: 6.2 lbs. Features: Anson & Deeley locks, Greener-style crossbolt, automatic ejectors, choice of double or single trigger, blue finish, checkered walnut stock with cheekpiece.

Price: **$4,795.00**

PIOTTI KING NO. 1
Gauges: 12 ga., 16 ga., 20 ga., 28 ga., .410. Barrels: 25–30 in. (12 ga.), 25–28 in. (16 ga., 20 ga., 28 ga., .410). To customer specs. Chokes as specified. Weight: 6.5–8 lbs. (12 ga. to customer specs.). Stock: Dimensions to customer specs. Finely figured walnut; straight grip with checkered butt with classic splinter fore-end and hand-rubbed oil finish standard. Pistol grip, beavertail fore-end. Features: Holland & Holland pattern sidelock action, automatic ejectors. Double trigger; non-selective single trigger optional. Coin finish standard; color case-hardened optional. Top rib; level, file-cut; concave, ventilated optional. Very fine, full coverage scroll engraving with small floral bouquets. Imported from Italy by Wm. Larkin Moore.

Price: **$42,800.00**

PIOTTI LUNIK SIDE-BY-SIDE SHOTGUN
Similar to the Piotti King No. 1 in overall quality. Has Renaissance-style large scroll engraving in relief. Best quality Holland & Holland-pattern sidelock ejector double with chopper lump (demi-bloc) barrels. Other mechanical specifications remain the same. Imported from Italy by Wm. Larkin Moore.

Price: **$46,000.00**

PIOTTI PIUMA

Gauges: 12 ga., 16 ga., 20 ga., 28 ga., .410. Barrels: 25–30 in. (12 ga.), 25–28 in. (16 ga., 20 ga., 28 ga., .410). Weights: 5.5–6.25 lbs. (20 ga.). Stock: Dimensions to customer specs. Straight grip stock with walnut checkered butt, classic splinter fore-end, hand-rubbed oil finish are standard; pistol grip, beavertail fore-end, satin luster finish optional. Features: Anson & Deeley boxlock ejector double with chopper lump barrels. Level, file-cut rib, light scroll and rosette engraving, scalloped frame. Double triggers; single non-selective optional. Coin finish standard, color case-hardened optional. Imported from Italy by Wm. Larkin Moore.

Price: **$25,000.00**

POINTER SIDE BY SIDE

Gauges: 12 ga., 20 ga., 28 ga., .410. Barrels: 26, 28 in. Weights: 5.6 lbs. (.410) to 6.9 lbs (12 ga.). Stock: Turkish Walnut, checkered, with rubber buttpad. Features: Single trigger. Barrel selector, extractors. Three finish options available: black, nickel, and case color, as well as a 12-ga/28-ga. configuration in a Cerakote variant with OD Green. Bead front sight. Built in Turkey for Legacy Sports Intreational.

Price: **$699.00**

RIZZINI BR550

Gauges: 12 ga., 16 ga., 20 ga., 28 ga., .410. Barrels: 26, 28, 29, 30 in. with choice of fixed ramp rib or adjustable rib. Weights: 5.6 lbs. (.410) to 6.9 lbs. (12 ga.). Stock: Grade 2.5 Turkish Walnut with 26 LPI checkering. Splinter forend and pistol grip butt. Features: Roundbody monolithic steel frame SxS. Coin finish receiver with ornamental scroll engraving. Automatic ejectors and single selective trigger. Set of five flush-fit nickel-coated chokes. Ships with Rizzini ABS case.

Price: **$5,590.00**

RIZZINI BR552

Gauges: 12 ga., 16 ga., 20 ga., 28 ga., .410. Barrels: 26, 28, 29, 30 in. with choice of fixed ramp or adjustable rib. Weights: 5.6 lbs. (.410) to 6.9 lbs. (12 ga.). Stock: Grade 2.5 Turkish Walnut with 26 LPI checkering. Splinter forend and pistol grip butt. Features: Roundbody monolithic steel frame with sideplates. Choice of coin or case color finish receiver with ornamental scroll engraving on both frame and side. Plates. Automatic ejectors and single selective trigger come standard, with a double trigger option available by special order. Set of five flush-fit nickel-coated chokes. Ships with Rizzini ABS case.

Price: **$5,875.00**

SAVAGE FOX A-GRADE

Gauge: 12 or 20. Barrels: 26 or 28 in. with solid rib and IC, M, and F choke tubes. Features: Straight-grip American walnut stock with splinter fore-end, oil finish and cut checkering. Anson & Deeley-style boxlock action, Holland & Holland-style ejectors, double triggers and brass bead sight. A re-creation of the famous Fox double gun, presented by Savage and made at the Connecticut Shotgun Manufacturing Co. plant.

Price: **$5,375.00**

SKB 200 SERIES

Gauges: 12 ga., 20 ga., .410, 3 in.; 28 ga., 2 3/4 in. Barrels: 26 in., 28 in. Five choke tubes provided (F, IM, M, IC, SK). Stock: Hand checkered and oil finished Turkish walnut. Prince of Wales grip and beavertail fore-end. Weight: 6–7 lbs. Sights: Brass bead. Features: Boxlock with platform lump barrel design. Polished bright blue finish with charcoal color case hardening on receiver. Manual safety, automatic ejectors, single selective trigger. 200 HR target model has high ventilated rib, full pistol grip. 250 model has decorative color casehardened sideplates. Imported from Turkey by GU, Inc.

Price: 12 ga., 20 ga..**$2,100.00**

Price: 28 ga., .410..**$2,250.00**
Price: 200 28 ga./.410 Combo **$3,300.00**
Price: 200 HR 12 ga., 20 ga. **$2,500.00**
Price: 200 HR 28 ga., .410 ....**$2,625.00**
Price: 200 HR 28 ga./.410 combo **$3,600.00**
Price: 250 12 ga., 20 ga. **$2,600.00**
Price: 250 28 ga., .410...**$2,725.00**
Price: 250 28 ga./.410 Combo..**$3,700.00**

SKB 7000SL SIDELOCK

Gauges: 12 ga., 20 ga. Barrels: 28 in., 30 in. Five choke tubes provided (F, IM, M, IC, SK). Stock: Premium Turkish walnut with hand-rubbed oil finish, fine-line hand checkering, Prince of Wales grip and beavertail fore-end. Weights: 6–7 lbs. Sights: Brass bead. Features: Sidelock design with Holland & Holland style seven-pin removable locks with safety sears. Bison Bone Charcoal casehardening, hand engraved sculpted sidelock receiver. Manual safety, automatic ejectors, single selective trigger. Available by special order only. Imported from Turkey by GU, Inc.

Price: **$6,500.00**

STOEGER UPLANDER

Gauges: 12 ga., 20 ga., .410, 3 in.; 28 ga., 2 3/4. Barrels: 22 in., 24 in., 26 in., 28 in. Weights: 6.5–7.3 lbs. Sights: Brass bead. Features: Double trigger, IC & M choke tubes included with gun. Other choke tubes available. Tang auto safety, extractors, black plastic buttplate. Imported by Benelli USA.

Price: Standard **$449.00**
Price: Supreme (single trigger, AA-grade wood) **$549.00**
Price: Longfowler (12 ga., 30-in. bbl.) **$449.00**
Price: Home Defense (20 or 12 ga., 20-in. bbl., tactical sights) **$499.00**
Price: Double Defense (20 ga.) fiber-optic sight, accessory rail **$499.00**

STOEGER COACH GUN

Gauges: 12 ga., 20 ga., 2 3/4 in., 3 in., .410 bore, Barrel: 20 in. Weight: 6.5 lbs. Stock: Brown hardwood, classic beavertail fore-end. Sights: Brass bead. Features: Double or single trigger, IC & M choke tubes included, others available. Tang auto safety, extractors, black plastic buttplate. Imported by Benelli USA.

Price: **$549.00**
Price: **$449.00**
Price: .410 bore, 3-inch, 20-in. barrel....................................**$449.00**
Price: Black-finished hardwood/polished-nickel model **$549.00**

TRISTAR BRISTOL

Gauges: 12 ga. 3 in., 20 ga. 3 in., 28 ga. 2.75 in., .410 bore 3 in. Barrels: 28 in. Weight: 5.08–6.74 lbs. Stock: Select Turkish Walnut with oil finish, English style. Features: Side-by-side double available in four gauges, each built on a true steel frame. Laser-engraved detail. Features an English-style straight stock paired with case colored receiver. Dual-purpose tang safety/barrel selector. Auto-ejectors, brass front sight, single selective trigger. Chrome-lined chamber and barrel. Includes five Beretta-style choke tubes (SK, IC, M, IM, F).

Price: ....**$1,065.00–$1,100.00**

TRISTAR BRISTOL

Gauge: 12 ga. 3 in., 16 ga., 20 ga. 3 in., 28 ga. 2.75 in., .410 bore 3 in. Barrels: 28 in. Weight: 5.08–6.74 lbs. Stock: Select Turkish Walnut with oil finish, English style. Features: Side-by-side double available in four gauges,

Prices given are believed to be accurate at time of publication however, many factors affect retail pricing so exact prices are not possible.

each built on a true steel frame. Laser engraved detail. Features an English-style straight stock paired with case colored receiver. Dual purpose tang safety/barrel selector. Auto-ejectors, brass front sight, single selective trigger. Chrome-lined chamber and barrel. Includes five Beretta-style choke tubes (SK, IC, M, IM, F).
Price: 12 and 20 ga. $1,160.00
Price: 16, 28 ga., and .410 bore $1,190.00

TRISTAR BRISTOL SILVER
Gauge: 12 ga. 3 in., 16 ga., 20 ga. 3 in., 28 ga. 2.75 in., .410 bore 3 in. Barrels: 28 in. Weight: 5.08–6.74 lbs. Stock: Select Turkish Walnut with oil finish, pistol grip style. Features: Side-by-side double available in four gauges, each built on a true steel frame. Laser engraved detail. Features a nickel-finished receiver with 24-Karat gold inlay on the bottom of the receiver, as well as semi-pistol grip-style stock. Dual-purpose tang safety/barrel selector. Auto-ejectors, brass front sight, single selective trigger. Chrome-lined chamber and barrel. Includes five Beretta-style choke tubes (SK, IC, M, IM, F).
Price: 12 and 20 ga. $1,100.00
Price: 16, 28 ga., and .410 bore $1,130.00

TRISTAR PHOENIX
Gauge: 12 ga., 20 ga. 3 in. Barrels: 28 in.. Weight: 6.6 lbs. (20 ga.) 6.9 lbs. (12 ga.). Stock: Select Turkish Walnut with high-gloss finish. Features: Side by side built on steel frame with precision laser engraved detail and case color receiver. Single selective trigger. Chrome-lined chamber and barrel. Brass bead front sight and selective tang safety. Length of pull measures 13 in. Set of five Berretta Mobil-style choke tubes.
Price: $795.00

WEATHERBY ORION SXS
Gauge: 12 ga., 20 ga., .410 bore 3 in. Barrel: 28 in. with swamp rib. Length: 46 in. Weight: 6.1–7.3 lbs. Stock: Oil-rubbed Grade-A walnut. Features: Matte blued barrel and receiver. Set of five Yildiz extended choke tubes. Brass front bead. Classic English-style straight stock and splinter forend. Mechanical double triggers in long tang triggerguard. Ambidextrous tang safety. Built in Turkey to Weatherby specs.
Price: $1,099.00

YILDIZ ELEGANT
Gauge: .410 bore, 3 in. Barrels: 26 in., 28 in., 30 in., with 7mm or 8mm rib. Weight: 4.8-6.0 lbs. Stock: Oil-finish selected walnut from standard through Grades 3 and 5, some pistol grip and others straight English-style. Features: Built of 4140 Steel, with varying degrees of receiver engraving. Manual or automatic safety, extractors or ejectors, depending on model. Single selective trigger, front bead, full black rubber recoil pad. Models include: A1, A3, A4, A5, and Special Lux. Includes five Mobil chokes. Manufactured in Turkey and imported/sold through Academy.
Price: $479.00

BROWNING BT-99 TRAP

Gauge: 12 ga. Barrels: 30 in., 32 in., 34 in. Stock: Walnut; standard or adjustable. Weights: 7 lbs. 11 oz.–9 lbs. Features: Back-bored single barrel; interchangeable chokes; beavertail forearm; extractor only; high rib.
Price: BT-99 w/conventional comb, 32- or 34-in. barrel..................**$1,470.00**
Price: BT-99 w/adjustable comb, 32- or 34-in. barrel......................**$1,840.00**
Price: BT-99 Max High Grade w/adjustable comb, 32- or
34-in. barrel..**$5,340.00**
Price: Micro Adjustable LOP Model.................................. **$1,669.00**

CHARLES DALY 101

Gauges: 12 ga., 3 in., 20 ga., 3in., .410 bore. Barrels: 26 in., 28 in. Weight: 5.0-8.1 lbs. Length: 41.75-43.75 in. Stock: Choice of either checkered walnut or black synthetic stocks. Features: These updated break-action single shots have become more affordable than ever. Though built of steel, they're still quite light. Brass front bead, manual safety, single trigger, extractor, rubber butt pad. Includes a Modified Beretta/Benelli Mobil choke tube.
Price: ....**$119.00-$129.00**

HENRY .410 LEVER-ACTION SHOTGUN

Gauge: .410, 2 1/2 in. Capacity: 5. Barrels: 20 or 24 in. with either no choke (20 in.) or full choke (24 in.). Stock: American walnut. Sights: Gold bead front only. Finish: Blued. Introduced in 2017. Features: Design is based on the Henry .45-70 rifle.
Price: 20-in. bbl...**$893.00**
Price: 24-in. bbl..**$947.00**

HENRY SIDE GATE LEVER ACTION 410 MODEL H018G-410R

Gauge: .410 bore 2.5in. Barrel: 19.75 in. smoothbore, round blued steel. Weight: 7.09 lbs. Length: 38.1 in. Stock: American Walnut with checkering. Features: This model launches as a blued steel companion to Henry's polished brass version last year. This is the more compact of the pair of lever action 410's. Has Henry's new side-loading gate in addition to the tubular loading port and magazine capacity of six rounds. Adjustable semi-buckhorn rear sight with diamond insert and brass bead front post sight. Black ventilated rubber recoil pad, transfer bar safety, sling swivel studs. Fixed cylinder bore choke.
Price: **$969.00**

HENRY X-MODEL 410

Gauges: .410 bore 2.5 in. Barrel: 19.8 in. smoothbore, round blued steel. Weight: 7.5 lbs. Length: 38.6 in. Stock: Black synthetic with textured panels. Features: Henry's first blacked-out model with matte blued steel receiver. Side loading gate in addition to tubular port with magazine capacity of 6+1 rounds. Black solid rubber recoil pad. Green fiber-optic front sight, transfer bar safety, swivel studs, large loop lever. Tactical features include lower Picatinny rail and M-LOK attachment points at fore-end. Drilled and tapped for a Weaver 63B optics mount. Includes Invector choke.
Price: **$1,000.00**

HENRY SINGLE-SHOT SHOTGUN

Gauges: 12 ga., 20 ga. or .410 bore, 3 1/2 in. (12 ga.), 3 in. (20 ga. and 410). Barrels: 26 or 28 in. with either modified choke tube (12 ga., 20 ga., compatible with Rem-Choke tubes) or fixed full choke (.410). Stock: American walnut, straight or pistol grip. Sights: Gold bead front only. Weight: 6.33 lbs. Finish: Blued or brass receiver. Features: Break-open single-shot design. Introduced in 2017.
Price: **$448.00**
Price: Brass receiver, straight grip...**$576.00**

HENRY SINGLE SHOT SLUG

Gauges: 12 ga. 3 in. Barrel: 24-in. round blued steel. Weight: 6.88 lbs.

Length: 39.5 in. Stock: American Walnut. Features: The company's first slug-hunting shotgun, with a fully-rifled 1:35 twist barrel. This single shot is finished in traditional blued steel and checkered walnut with a black rubber recoil pad. Buttstock has a 14-inch LOP. Sling studs. Rebounding hammer safety. Fiber optic sights. Drilled and tapped for a Weaver 82 base.
Price: **$560.00**

HENRY AXE

Gauge: .410 bore 2.5 in. Barrel: 15.14 in. smoothbore, round blued steel. Weight: 5.75 lbs. Length: 26.4 in. Stock: American Walnut with unique axe-handle-style rear grip. Features: Henry's Axe is most closely related to the handgun-chambered Mare's Leg platform, but this time with a slightly different design and firing .410 shotshells. Both the standard Steel and Brass Axe have a 5-round capacity with the addition of a loading gate. Short barrel takes interchangeable Invector-style chokes and ships with a full tube. Brass front bead, swivel studs, transfer bar safety. Drilled and tapped for optics mounting.
Price: **$1,049.00**
Price: Brass Axe **$1,132.00**

HENRY SINGLE SHOT TURKEY

Gauges: 12 ga. 3.5 in. Barrel: 24-in. round. Weight: 6.78 lbs. Length: 39.5 in. Stock: American Walnut covered in Mossy Oak Obsession camo. Features: The company's first dedicated turkey-hunting shotgun wears full-coverage Mossy Oak Obsession, the official camouflage pattern of the National Wild Turkey Federation. Fiber-optic front and rear sights. Drilled and tapped for a Weaver 82 base. Black solid rubber recoil pad creates a 14-inch LOP. Swivel studs. Rebounding hammer safety. Includes an extended Turkey choke.
Price: **$687.00**

KEYSTONE SPORTING ARMS 4100 My First Shotgun

Gauges: .410 bore 3 in. Barrel: 18.5 in. Length: 32 in. Weight: 4.2 lbs. Stock: Turkish Walnut. Features: Marketed as a Crickett "My First Shotgun," this single-shot baby bore uses a folding design. Recoil reducing chamber and soft rubber recoil pad. Aluminum receiver with matte blue metalwork. Blade-style front sight. Checkered stock. Length of pull built for small-frame shooters at 11 inches. Fixed modified choke.
Price: **$179.00**

KRIEGHOFF K-80 SINGLE BARREL TRAP GUN

Gauge: 12 ga., 2 3/4 in. Barrel: 32 in., 34 in. Unsingle. Fixed Full or choke tubes. Weight: About 8.75 lbs. Stock: Four stock dimensions or adjustable stock available. All hand-checkered European walnut. Features: Satin nickel finish. Selective mechanical trigger adjustable for finger position. Tapered step vent rib. Adjustable point of impact.
Price: Standard Grade Full Unsingle..............................**$12,995.00**

KRIEGHOFF KX-6 SPECIAL TRAP GUN

Gauge: 12 ga., 2 3/4 in. Barrel: 32 in., 34 in.; choke tubes. Weight: About 8.5 lbs. Stock: Factory adjustable stock. European walnut. Features: Ventilated tapered step rib. Adjustable position trigger, optional release trigger. Fully adjustable rib. Satin gray electroless nickel receiver. Fitted aluminum case. Imported from Germany by Krieghoff International, Inc.
Price: **$5,995.00**

LJUTIC MONO GUN SINGLE BARREL

Gauge: 12 ga. Barrel: 34 in., choked to customer specs; hollow-milled rib, 35.5-in. sight plane. Weight: Approx. 9 lbs. Stock: To customer specs. Oil finish, hand checkered. Features: Custom gun. Pull or release trigger; removable triggerguard contains trigger and hammer mechanism; Ljutic pushbutton opener on front of triggerguard. From Ljutic Industries.
Price: Std., med. or Olympic rib, custom bbls., fixed choke. **$7,495.00**
Price: Stainless steel mono gun................................**$8,495.00**

LJUTIC LTX PRO 3 DELUXE MONO GUN
Deluxe, lightweight version of the Mono gun with high-quality wood, upgrade checkering, special rib height, screw-in chokes, ported and cased.
Price: $8,995.00
Price: Stainless steel model..............................$9,995.00

PANZER ARMS EG-220 TACTICAL
Gauge: 12 ga. 3 in. Barrel: 20 in. plain. Length: 39 in. Weight: 7.2 lbs. Stock: Checkered walnut buttstock with rubber recoil pad and full metal tactical forend. Features: Tactical lever-action scattergun with five-round tubular magazine capacity. Enlarged loop lever and extra large lower loading port. M-LOK-compatible forend and Pic rail attachment points. Crossbolt safety. Set of three flush-mount choke tubes in F, M, C.
Price: $479.00

REVOLUTION ARMORY REV410
Gauge: .410 bore. 3 in. Barrel: 20 in., 24 in. Stock: Checkered Turkish Walnut. Features: Revolver-shotgun design. Five-round cylinder. Ships with two removeable cylinder plugs to limit capacity for hunting. Interchangeable chokes in Full, Mod, IC. Rubber recoil pad. Fiber-optic adjustable sights or a ventilated rib barrel with brass bead front. Made in Turkey and imported by Canadian-based Revolution Armory.
Price: $839.00

ROSSI CIRCUIT JUDGE
Revolving shotgun chambered in .410 (2 1/2- or 3-in./.45 Colt. Based on Taurus Judge handgun. Features include 18.5-in. barrel; fiber-optic front sight; 5-round cylinder; hardwood Monte Carlo stock.
Price: $689.00

ROSSI TUFFY SINGLE SHOT 410 TURKEY
Gauge: .410 bore 3 in. Barrel: 26 in. Length: 41 in. Weight: 58.80 oz. Stock: Olive drab green polymer thumbhole-style with integral buttstock shell holders. Features: Part of Rossi's single-shot, break-action Tuffy family, the new 410 Turkey has an extended barrel length and gobbler-specific choke. Polymer receiver with steel frame structure. Matte black finish metalwork. Bead front sight. Picatinny top rail for easy optics mounting. Sling swivels. Black rubber buttpad. Transfer bar safety. Extended Extra Full Turkey choke.
Price: Standard Grade Full Unsingle $220.00

SAVAGE 212/220
Gauges: 12 ga., 3 in., 20 ga., 3 in. Barrel: 22 in., carbon steel. Weight: 7.34-7.75 lbs. Length: 43 in. Stock: Synthetic AccuFit stock with included LOP and comb inserts. Thumbhole model uses gray wood laminate. Features: The bolt-action Savage models 212 and 220, so named for their chamberings, are available in Slug, Slug Camo, Thumbhole, Left-Handed and Turkey models. Choice of button-rifled slug barrels or smoothbore. Detachable box magazine, thread-in barrel headspacing. User adjustable AccuTrigger and AccuStock internal chassis. Oversized bolt handle, Picatinny optics rail, sling studs, rubber buttpad.
Price: .... $629.00–$799.00
Price: 212 Turkey w/extended X-Full choke......................... $779.00
Price: 220 Turkey w/extended X-Full choke......................... $695.00

STEVENS 301 TURKEY XP
Gauges: 20 ga., 3 in., .410 bore, 3 in. Barrel: 26 in., black matte. Weight: 5.07 lbs. Length: 41.5 in. Stock: Camouflage synthetic stock and fore-end with either Mossy Oak Obsession or Mossy Oak Bottomland pattern. Features: Single-shot break action with removable one-piece rail. XP variant includes mounted and bore-sighted 1x30 red-dot optic. Barrel optimized for Federal Premium TSS Heavyweight turkey loads. Swivel studs, front bead, manual hammer block safety, rubber recoil pad. Includes Winchoke pattern Extra Full turkey choke.
Price: $239.00

STEVENS 301 TURKEY THUMBHOLE
Gauges: .410 bore 3 in. Barrel: 26 in. chrome alloy steel black matte. Weight: 5.07 lbs. Length: 41.5 in. Stock: Olive drab green matte synthetic thumbhole style. Features: Continuation of the 301 single-shot break-action line with a removeable one-piece rail and gobbler-specific features. Ambidextrous cheek riser. Barrel optimized for Federal Premium Heavyweight TSS turkey loads. Swivel studs, front bead sight, manual hammer block safety, rubber recoil pad. Includes Win-Choke pattern Extra Full turkey choke.
Price: $229.00

STEVENS 555 TRAP
Gauges: 12 ga., 3 in., 20 ga., 3 in. Barrel: 30 in., raised ventilated rib. Weight: 6.6-6.8 lbs. Length: 47.5 in. Stock: Turkish walnut stock and fore-end with adjustable comb and oil finish. Features: Lightweight silver aluminum receiver scaled to gauge with steel breech reinforcement. Top single barrel with shell extractor. Manual tang safety, front bead, chrome-lined barrel, semi-gloss metalwork finish. Includes three chokes.
Price: $689.00

STEVENS 555 TRAP COMPACT
Gauges: 12 ga., 3 in., 20 ga., 3 in. Barrel: 26 in., raised ventilated rib. Weight: 7.3-7.5 lbs. Length: 42.5 in. Stock: Turkish walnut stock and fore-end with adjustable comb and oil finish. Features: Lightweight silver aluminum receiver scaled to gauge with steel breech reinforcement. Top single barrel with shell extractor. Manual tang safety, front bead, chrome-lined barrel, semi-gloss metalwork finish. Compact 13.5 in. length of pull. Includes three chokes.
Price: $689.00

TAR-HUNT RSG-12 PROFESSIONAL RIFLED SLUG GUN
Gauge: 12 ga., 2 3/4 in., 3 in., Capacity: 1-round magazine. Barrel: 23 in., fully rifled with muzzle brake. Weight: 7.75 lbs. Length: 41.5 in. overall. Stock: Matte black McMillan fiberglass with Pachmayr Decelerator pad. Sights: None furnished; comes with Leupold windage or Weaver bases. Features: Uses rifle-style action with two locking lugs; two-position safety; Shaw barrel; single-stage, trigger; muzzle brake. Many options available. All models have area-controlled feed action. Introduced 1991. Made in U.S. by Tar-Hunt Custom Rifles, Inc.
Price: 12 ga. Professional model $3,495.00
Price: Left-hand model $3,625.00

TAR-HUNT RSG-20 MOUNTAINEER SLUG GUN
Similar to the RSG-12 Professional except chambered for 20 ga. (2 3/4 in. and 3 in. shells); 23 in. Shaw rifled barrel, with muzzle brake; two-lug bolt; one-shot blind magazine; matte black finish; McMillan fiberglass stock with Pachmayr Decelerator pad; receiver drilled and tapped for Rem. 700 bases. Right- or left-hand versions. Weighs 6.5 lbs. Introduced 1997. Made in USA by Tar-Hunt Custom Rifles, Inc.
Price: $3,495.00

TRISTAR LR94
Gauges: .410 bore. Barrels: 22, 24 in. Stock: Turkish Walnut, checkered and oil finished. Features: The company's first lever-action firearm. Top safety, blade/bead front sight and rifle-style rear sight. 2.5-inch chamber. Side-loading gate and tubular magazine. Leather-wrapped lever. Accepts CT-1 interchangeable choke tubes. Choice of three finish options.
Price: Matte walnut $990.00
Price: Case Color/walnut $1,100.00
Price: Nickel/walnut $1,070.00

Prices given are believed to be accurate at time of publication however, many factors affect retail pricing so exact prices are not possible.

79TH EDITION, 2025 ◆ 549

AMERICAN TACTICAL BULLDOG

Gauge: 12 ga. 3 in., 20 ga. 3 in. Barrel: 16 and 18.5 in. with ported shroud. Length: 23.5–26 in. Weight: 4.5 lbs. Stock: Black synthetic with fixed bullpup style with adjustable cheek riser. Features: Gas-operated tactical bullpup shotgun with AR-style charging handle, adjustable cheek rest, and both Picatinny and M-LOK rails. Housing for spare five-round magazine. Extra magazine can also be attached to the bottom rail and used as a fore grip. Includes quick acquisition flip-up sights and three choke tubes.
Price: $359.00

ARMSCOR VRF-14

Gauge: 12 ga. Barrel: 14 in. Length: 26 in. Weight: 6.6 lbs. Stock: Black polymer with full-top forend and sling adapter rear. Features: Semi-automatic short-barreled firearm in 12-ga. Pistol-grip style designed to be fired from the hip. Built with a 7075 aluminum receiver, Bufferbolt system, and full-length top Picatinny rail. Flip-up front and rear sights. Five-round magazine included, but also compatible with VR-Series 9 and 19-round mags.
Price: $599.00

BENELLI M2 TACTICAL

Gauge: 12 ga., 2 3/4 in., 3 in. Capacity: 5-round magazine. Barrel: 18.5 in. IC, M, F choke tubes. Weight: 6.7 lbs. Length: 39.75 in. overall. Stock: Black polymer. Standard or pistol grip. Sights: Rifle type ghost ring system, tritium night sights optional. Features: Semi-auto inertia recoil action. Cross-bolt safety; bolt release button; matte-finish metal. Introduced 1993. Imported from Italy by Benelli USA.
Price: ....$1,239.00–$1,359.00

BENELLI M3 TACTICAL

Gauge: 12 ga., 3 in. Barrel: 20 in. Stock: Black synthetic w/pistol grip. Sights: Ghost ring rear, ramp front. Convertible dual-action operation (semi-auto or pump).
Price: $1,599.00

BENELLI M4 TACTICAL

Gauge: 12 ga., 3 in. Barrel: 18.5 in. Weight: 7.8 lbs. Length: 40 in. overall. Stock: Synthetic. Sights: Ghost Ring rear, fixed blade front. Features: Auto-regulating gas-operated (ARGO) action, choke tube, Picatinny rail, standard and collapsible stocks available, optional LE tactical gun case. Introduced 2006.
Price: $1,999.00
Price: M4 H20 Cerakote Finish $2,269.00

BENELLI NOVA TACTICAL

Gauge: 12 ga., 3 in. Barrel: 18.5 in. Stock: Black synthetic standard or pistol grip. Sights: Ghost ring rear, ramp front. Pump action.
Price: $439.00

BENELLI VINCI TACTICAL

Gauge: 12 ga., 3 in. Barrel: 18.5 in. Semi-auto operation. Stock: Black synthetic. Sights: Ghost ring rear, ramp front.
Price: $1,349.00
Price: ComforTech stock...$1,469.00

BERETTA A300 ULTIMA PATROL

Gauges: 12 ga., 20 ga. Barrel: 19.1 in. Stock: Synthetic. Features: New defense-style addition to A300 Ultima family of semi-autos. Low profile receiver with oversized loading port. Enlarged controls. Wide 7x7 stepped rib with mid bead. KickOff recoil system included as standard configuration on most models. Tactical sights with fiber optic front. Thinner forend with M-LOK and QD points. 7+1 round extended magazine tube secured with barrel clamp.
Price: Black or Gray $1,099.00
Price: Tiger Stripe $1,199.00

CHARLES DALY AR 410 UPPER

Gauge: .410 bore 2.5 in. Barrel: 19 in. Length: 26.75 in. Weight: 4.9 lbs. Stock: Upper only with quad Picatinny rail fore-end. Features: Charles Daly enters the AR market with a .410 bore shotgun upper. Built of black anodized aluminum. Auto-ejection, gas-operated system. Windage-adjustable rear sight and elevation adjustable rear flip-up sights. Ships with a five-round magazine but compatible with 10 and 15 rounders. This upper must be used with a Mil-Spec lower and carbine-length buffer tube.
Price: $415.00

ESCORT BULLTAC

Gauge: 12 ga., 20 ga., .410 bore, 3in. Barrel: 18 in. Length: 27.75 in. Weight: 6.7 lbs (.410), 6.8 lbs. (20 ga.), 7.0 lbs. (12 ga.). Stock: Black synthetic pistol grip bullpup design. Features: Hatsan Escort's bullpup-style pump-action shotgun with an alloy upper receiver and synthetic lower. Shell deflector directs spent shells downward. Capacity of 5+1 rounds of either shot or slugs. Detachable carry handle with side accessory rails, removeable Picatinny optics rail. Quick-disconnect sling mount and manual cross button safety. Fixed cylinder choke.
Price: $249.00

GARAYSAR FEAR 116

Gauge: 12 ga. 3 in. Barrel: 20 in. 4140 steel. Length: 39 in. Weight: 8.8 lbs. Stock: Synthetic available in a variety of colors and finishes. Features: Gas-operated semi-automatic with an aluminum receiver. Adjustable cheek rest. Front and rear flip-up sights. Ships with two five-round magazines, but also accepts 10-round mags. Includes five choke tubes (F, IM, M, IC, C), choke tube case, and hard case.
Price: $589.00

GARAYSAR FEAR BULLPUP

Gauge: 12 ga. 3 in. Barrel: 18.5 in. Length: 28.34 in. Stock: Black synthetic, with both green and FDE to follow. Features: Gas-regulated, semi-automatic bullpup-style shotgun. Built on an aluminum receiver with 4140 steel barrel. Bullpup family available in multiple model variants including 104, 105, 106, and 109, each with different options on a similar build. Ships with two five-round magazines, but also accepts 10- and 15-round mags. Adjustable cheek riser. Multiple choke options dependent on model; some fixed, others interchangeable.
Price: $489.00

IVER JOHNSON STRYKER-12

Gauge: 12 ga., 3 in. Barrel: 20 in., smoothbore with muzzle brake. Length: 43 in. Stock: Black synthetic two-piece, pistol-grip stock. Features: This AR15-style semi-auto shotgun uses a standard AR15 bolt and mag release. A2-style detachable carry handle with adjustable sight, fiber-optic front sight. Light rails on both sides and bottom of fore-end. Push button releases the stock and leaves the pistol grip for a modular platform. Cross-bolt safety, thick rubber buttpad. Ships with two MKA 1919 5-round box magazines.
Price: $495.00

IWI TAVOR TS-12

Gauge: 12 ga. 3 in. Barrel: 18.5 in. Length: 28.34 in. Weight: 8.9 lbs. Stock: Synthetic fixed bullpup style, with Black, OD green and FDE color options.

Prices given are believed to be accurate at time of publication however, many factors affect retail pricing so exact prices are not possible.

Features: Gas-driven semi-automatic bullpup design that feeds from one of three magazine tubes. Each tube holds four 3-in. shells or five 2.75-in. rounds. Max capacity 15 rounds. Includes four sling attachment points, M-LOK rails, and extended Picatinny top rail. Crossbolt safety. Bullhead bolt system. Uses Benelli/Beretta-style Mobil choke tubes.
Price: **$1,399.00**

KALASHNIKOV KOMP12
Gauge: 12 ga. 3 in. Barrel: 18.25 in. with external threading. Weight: 17 lbs. Stock: Synthetic skeleton-style, collapsible. Features: The Kalashnikov USA x Dissident Arms KOMP12 is an American-made semi-automatic based on the Russian Saiga series. Adjustable gas system. Extended charging handle, aluminum handguard rail, enhanced safety lever. Flared magazine well, tuned trigger. Top Picatinny rail for optics. Threaded flash suppressor. Magpul AK pistol grip. Zinc phosphate parkerized undercoat with Dissident Arms Black, Red, and Sniper Grey color scheme. Ships with Dissident SGM 12-round magazine.
Price: **$1,499.00**

KEL-TEC KSG BULL-PUP TWIN-TUBE
Gauge: 12 ga. Capacity: 13+1. Barrel: 18.5 in. Overall Length: 26.1 in. Weight: 8.5 lbs. (loaded). Features: Pump-action shotgun with two magazine tubes. The shotgun bears a resemblance to the South African designed Neostead pump-action gun. The operator is able to move a switch located near the top of the grip to select the right or left tube, or move the switch to the center to eject a shell without chambering another round. Optional accessories include a factory installed Picatinny rail with flip-up sights and a pistol grip. KSG-25 has 30-in. barrel and 20-round capacity magazine tubes.
Price: **$990.00**
Price: KSG-25 .... **$1400.00**

KELTEC KSG410
Gauge: .410 bore. Barrel: 18.5 in. Stock: Synthetic bullpup style in Black or FDE. Features: Baby bore bullpup touted as "sidekick with no kick." Only 1.7 inches wide with two magazine tubes. Capacity of 5+5+1 rounds. Fiber-optic sights, top carry handle/sight rail. Overall length of 26.1 in. keeps it legal as a shotgun. Three-inch chamber.
Price: **$495.00**

KEL-TEC KS7 BULLPUP
Gauge: 12 ga., 3 in. Capacity: 6+1. Barrel: 18.5 in. Length: 26.1 in. Weight: 5.9 lbs. Stock: Black synthetic bullpup. Features: The pump-action KS7 Bullpup is a compact self-defense shotgun. Carry handle, Picatinny rail, M-LOK mounting points. Rear loading, downward ejection, ambidextrous controls. Cylinder choke.
Price: **$495.00**

MOSSBERG MAVERICK 88 CRUISER
Gauges: 12 ga., 3 in., 20 ga., 3in. Capacity: 5+1 or 7+1 capacity. Barrels: 18.5 in., 20 in. Length: 28.125-30.375 in. Weight: 5.5-6.0 lbs. Stock: Black synthetic pistol grip. Features: Fixed cylinder bore choke, blued metalwork, bead front sight, cross-bolt safety.
Price: **$231.00**

MOSSBERG MODEL 500 SPECIAL PURPOSE
Gauges: 12 ga., 20 ga., .410, 3 in. Barrels: 18.5 in., 20 in. (Cyl.). Weight: 7 lbs. Stock: Walnut-finished hardwood or black synthetic. Sights: Metal bead front. Features: Slide-action operation. Available in 6- or 8-round models. Top-mounted safety, double action slide bars, swivel studs, rubber recoil pad. Blue, Parkerized, Marinecote finishes. Mossberg Cablelock included. The HS410 Home Security model chambered for .410 with 3 in. chamber; has pistol grip fore-end, thick recoil pad, muzzle brake and has special spreader choke on the 18.5-in. barrel. Overall length is 37.5 in. Blued finish; synthetic field stock. Mossberg Cablelock and video included. Mariner model has Marinecote metal finish to resist rust and corrosion. Synthetic field stock; pistol grip kit included. 500 Tactical 6-shot has black synthetic tactical stock. Introduced 1990. Holosun optic combo variants introduced in 2024.
Price: 500 Mariner **$636.00**
Price: HS410 Home Security **$477.00**
Price: Home Security 20 ga. **$631.00**
Price: FLEX Tactical **$672.00**
Price: 500 Chainsaw pistol grip only; removable top handle **$547.00**
Price: JIC (Just In Case) with storage tube **$500.00**
Price: Thunder Ranch **$553.00**
Price: 500 Turkey Holosun Micro Dot Combo **$844.00**
Price: 500 Super Bantam Turkey Holosun Micro Dot Combo **$844.00**

MOSSBERG 590S SHOCKWAVE
Gauge: 12 ga. 1.7–3 in. Barrel: 14.375 and 18.5 in. Length: 26.37–30.75 in. Weight: 5.3–5.5 lbs. Stock: Black synthetic with Raptor grip and corn-cob forend with strap. Features: The upgraded 590S version of the pistol grip Shockwave is built to cycle any length shells without adapter or adjustment, from 1.75 to 3-in. Bead front sight, matte blued metalwork, shorter-barreled model uses heavy-walled barrel. Both feature fixed cylinder bore choke.
Price: Shockwave .... **$455.00–$721.00**

MOSSBERG MODEL 590 SPECIAL PURPOSE
Gauges: 12 ga., 20 ga., .410 3 in. Capacity: 9-round magazine. Barrel: 20 in. (Cyl.). Weight: 7.25 lbs. Stock: Synthetic field or Speedfeed. Sights: Metal bead front or Ghost Ring. Features: Slide action. Top-mounted safety, double slide action bars. Comes with heat shield, bayonet lug, swivel studs, rubber recoil pad. Blue, Parkerized or Marinecote finish. Shockwave has 14-inch heavy walled barrel, Raptor pistol grip, wrapped fore-end and is fully BATFE compliant. Magpul model has Magpul SGA stock with adjustable comb and length of pull. Mossberg Cablelock included. From Mossberg.
Price: **$559.00**
Price: Flex Tactical **$672.00**
Price: Tactical Tri-Rail Adjustable **$879.00**
Price: Mariner **$756.00**
Price: MagPul 9-shot **$836.00**
Price: Compact Optics-Ready **$727.00**
Price: Magpul Holosun Micro Dot Combo **$1,035.00**

MOSSBERG 930 SPECIAL PURPOSE SERIES
Gauge: 12 ga., 3 in. Barrel: 18.5-28 in. flat ventilated rib. Weight: 7.3 lbs. Length: 49 in.. Stock: Composite stock with close radius pistol grip; Speed Lock forearm; textured gripping surfaces; shim adjustable for length of pull, cast and drop; Mossy Oak Bottomland camo finish; Dura-Touch Armor Coating. Features: 930 Special Purpose shotguns feature a self-regulating gas system that vents excess gas to aid in recoil reduction and eliminate stress on critical components. All 930 autoloaders chamber both 2 3/4 inch and 3-in. 12-ga. shotshells with ease — from target loads, to non-toxic magnum loads, to the latest sabot slug ammo. Magazine capacity is 7+1 on models with extended magazine tube, 4+1 on models without. To complete the package, each Mossberg 930 includes a set of specially designed spacers for

Prices given are believed to be accurate at time of publication however, many factors affect retail pricing so exact prices are not possible.

79TH EDITION, 2025 ◆ **551**

quick adjustment of the horizontal and vertical angle of the stock, bringing a custom-feel fit to every shooter. All 930 Special Purpose models feature a drilled and tapped receiver, factory-ready for Picatinny rail, scope base or optics installation. 930 SPX models conveniently come with a factory-mounted Picatinny rail and LPA/M16-Style Ghost Ring combination sight right out of the box. Other sighting options include a basic front bead, or white-dot front sights. Mossberg 930 Special Purpose shotguns are available in a variety of configurations; 5-round tactical barrel, 5-round with muzzle brake, 8-round pistol-grip, and even a 5-round security/field combo.

Price: Tactical 5-Round $612.00
Price: Home Security $662.00
Price: Standard Stock $787.00
Price: Pistol Grip 8-Round $1,046.00
Price: 5-Round Combo w/extra 18.5-in. barrel $693.00
Price: Chainsaw $564.00

MOSSBERG 940 PRO TACTICAL-HOLOSUN COMBO

Gauges: 12 ga. Barrels: 18.5 in. Stock: Black synthetic. Features: Same system as 940 Pro family with the receiver machined for direct micro-dot optics mounting and a Holosun HS407K along with a fiber-optic front.
Price: $1,333.00

PANZER ARMS M4

Gauge: 12 ga. 3 in. Barrel: 18.5 in. Length: 39 in. Weight: 7.2 lbs. Stock: Option of fixed standard and adjustable skeleton stocks in Turkish Walnut or synthetic. Features: Semi-automatic family of hunting, tactical, and sporting shotguns built as a clone to the Benelli M4. Parts are interchangeable with the original M4. Buffer tube is notched in three positions. Ghost ring sights and optics rail. Available in multiple color options and patterns, including a Marine Tactical with electroless nickel-phosphorus plating.
Price: $649.00
Price: Marine Tactiical $699.00

RETAY MASAI MARA WARDEN

Gauge: 12 ga., 3 in. Barrel: 18.5 in. Weight: 6.6 lbs. Stock: Black Synthetic. Features: The Turkish-made Masai Mara line of semi-automatics uses an inertia-plus action and bolt system. Oversized controls, quick unload system, Picatinny rail, extended charging handle, ghost-ring sights. Push-button removeable trigger group. Microcell rubber recoil pad. Includes a hard case and ships with five MaraPro choke tubes.
Price: $1,099.00

ROCK ISLAND ARMORY/ARMSCOR VRBP-100

Gauge: 12 ga., 3 in. Capacity: 5+1. Barrel: 20 in. contoured. Length: 32 in. Weight: 7.94 lbs. Stock: Black polymer bullpup design with pistol grip. Features: Semi-automatic bullpup design. Compatible with all VR Series magazines. Matte-black anodized finish. Includes rubber spacers to adjust length of pull. Full length top rail with flip-up sights, right-sided Picatinny accessory rail. Ships with three interchangeable chokes.
Price: $774.00

ROCK ISLAND ARMORY/ARMSCOR VRPA-40

Gauge: 12 ga., 3 in. Capacity: 5+1. Barrel: 20 in., contoured. Length: 55.11 in. Weight: 6.9 lbs. Stock: Black synthetic. Features: The VRPA40 marks the more affordable pump action addition to the VR family of shotguns. Magazine fed, aluminum heat shield, fiber-optic front sight, adjustable rear sight, Picatinny rail. Marine black anodized, compatible with VR series 9-round magazines. Mobil chokes.
Price: $399.00

ROCK ISLAND ARMORY/ARMSCOR VR82

Gauge: 20 ga. 3 in. Barrel: 18 in. contoured. Length: 38 in. Weight: 7.5 lbs. Stock: Black polymer thumbhole style. Features: The semi-automatic VR82 is the little brother of the VR80. Built of 7075 T6 aluminum for lighter weight. Magazine fed with 5+1 capacity but also accepts VR-series 10- and 20-round mags. Ambidextrous controls, flip-up sights, barrel shroud. Fore-end accepts most aftermarket accessories. Compatible with most buffer tube stocks and pistol grips. Black anodized finish. Mobil choke.
Price: $729.00

ROCK ISLAND PF14

Gauges: 12 ga. Barrel: 14.1 in. Stock: Black synthetic with F-Grip. Features: Handheld pump-action defense shotgun with five-round capacity. Bead front sight. Overall length of 26.1 inches. Includes sling adapter and forend strap. Chambered for 2.75- or 3-inch loads.
Price: $369.00

ROCK ISLAND VRPF14

Gauges: 12 ga. Barrel: 14.1 in. Stock: Black synthetic with F-Grip. Features: Handheld pump-action defense shotgun. Like other VR series, is magazine-fed, and mags are interchangeable. Bead front sight. Overall length of 26.1 inches. Includes sling adapter and forend strap. Chambered for 2.75- or 3-inch loads.
Price: $449.00

SAVAGE RENEGAUGE SECURITY

Gauge: 12 ga. 3 in. Barrel: 18.5 in. Melonite-treated, fluted, with ventilated rib. Length: 40 in. Weight: 7.3 lbs. Stock: Matte gray synthetic with adjustable LOP, comb height, and drop/cast. Features: Savage's self-regulating DRIV gas system. One-piece chrome-plated action bar and reciprocating components. Stock rod buffer to reduce recoil. Adjustable ghost ring sights and one-piece rail. Oversized controls. Includes three flush choke tubes (IC, M, F) and hard case.
Price: $1,499.00

SMITH & WESSON M&P-12

Gauge: 12 ga. 3 in. Barrel: 19 in. Length: 27.8 in. Weight: 8.3 lbs. Stock: Black synthetic with fixed stock. Features: Single barrel pump-action shotgun with two independent magazine tubes. Capacity of seven rounds of 2-3/4-in. shells or six rounds of 3-in. shells per tube. Vertical foregrip, action lock lever button, and push button mag tube selector. Ships with four interchangeable pistol grip palm swell inserts. Picatinny top rail, M-LOK barrel slots. Includes Rem-Choke-style choke tubes (M, C), choke wrench, and foam-lined hard gun case.
Price: $1,185.00

STANDARD MANUFACTURING DP-12 PROFESSIONAL

Gauge: 12 ga. 3 in. Barrels: 18-7/8 in. Length: 29.5 in. Weight: 9 lb. 12 oz. Stock: Synthetic with anodized aluminum. Features: Upgraded Professional version of the pump-action DP-12 high-capacity defense shotgun. Additions include an aluminum rail with front grip, which wears an integral laser and flashlight. Precision-honed bores and chambers finished with hand-lapping. PVD coating on all critical wear areas. Mil-spec hard anodized finish with accents in either Blue or OD Green. Includes Reflex Sight with multiple brightness levels. Ships with both soft and hard cases
Price: $3,250.00

WINCHESTER SXP EXTREME DEFENDER

Gauge: 12 ga., 3 in. Barrel: 18 in., with Heat Shield. Length: 38.5 in. Weight: 7.0 lbs. Stock: Flat Dark Earth composite with textured grip panels and pistol grip. Features: Aluminum-alloy receiver, hard-chrome chamber and bore, Picatinny rail with ghost-ring sight, blade front sight. Two interchangeable comb pieces and two quarter-inch length-of-pull spacers for custom fit. Side-mounted Picatinny accessory rails, sling studs, Inflex recoil pad. Includes one Invector Plus cylinder choke and one Door Breacher choke.
Price: $529.00

CHIAPPA LE PAGE PERCUSSION DUELING PISTOL
Caliber: .45. Barrel: 10 in. browned octagon, rifled. Weight: 2.5 lbs. Length: 16.6 in. overall. Stock: Walnut, rounded, fluted butt. Sights: Blade front, open-style rear. Features: Double set trigger. Bright barrel, silver-plated brass furniture. External ramrod. Made by Chiappa.
Price: $779.00

CVA OPTIMA PISTOL
Caliber: .50. Barrel: 14 in., 1:28-in. twist, Cerakote finish. Weight: 3.7 lbs. Length: 19 in. Stock: Black synthetic, Realtree Xtra Green. Sights: Scope base mounted. Features: Break-open action, all stainless construction, aluminum ramrod, quick-removal breech plug for 209 primer. From CVA.
Price: PP222SM Stainless/Realtree Xtra, rail mount $354.00
Price: PP221SM Stainless/black, rail mount $307.00

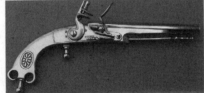

DIXIE MURDOCK SCOTTISH HIGHLANDER'S PISTOL
Caliber: .352. Barrel: 7.5 in., blued steel finish, round. Weight: 3.75 lbs. Length: 18.25 in. overall. Stock: Steel frame. Sights: None. Features: Flintlock, steel ramrod. An exact copy of an Alexander Murdock Scottish pistol of the 1770s. Made in India. Imported by Dixie Gun Works.
Price: $425.00

DIXIE MODEL 1855 U.S. DRAGOON PISTOL
Caliber: .58. Barrel: 12 in., bright finish, round. Weight: 2.25 lbs. Length: 16.75 in. overall. Stock: Walnut. Sights: Fixed rear and front sights. Features: Percussion, swivel-style, steel ramrod. Made by Palmetto Arms. Imported by Dixie Gun Works.
Price: $650.00

LYMAN PLAINS PISTOL
Caliber: .50 or .54. Barrel: 8 in.; 1:30-in. twist, both calibers. Weight: 3.1 lb. Length: 15 in. overall. Stock: Walnut. Sights: Blade front, square-notch rear adjustable for windage. Features: Polished brass triggerguard and ramrod tip, color case-hardened coil spring lock, spring-loaded trigger, stainless steel nipple, blackened iron furniture. Hooked patent breech, detachable belt hook. Introduced 1981. From Lyman Products.
Price: 6010608 .50-cal. $426.00
Price: 6010609 .54-cal. $426.00
Price: 6010610 .50-cal Kit $349.00
Price: 6010611 .54-cal. Kit $349.00

PEDERSOLI CARLETON UNDERHAMMER MATCH PERCUSSION PISTOL
Caliber: .36. Barrel: 9.5 in., browned octagonal, rifled. Weight: 2.25 lbs. Length: 16.75 in. overall. Stock: Walnut. Sights: Blade front, open rear, adjustable for elevation. Features: Percussion, under-hammer ignition, adjustable trigger, no half cock. No ramrod. Made by Pedersoli. Imported by Dixie Gun Works.
Price: $925.00

PEDERSOLI CHARLES MOORE ENGLISH DUELING PISTOL
Caliber: .45. Barrel: 11 in., 1:18 twist Weight: 2.5 lbs. Length: 16.5 in. overall. Stock: Walnut. Sights: Fixed. Features: Flintlock or percussion. Single set, adjustable trigger. Blued barrel and lock, steel furniture left in the white. Wooden ramrod. Replica of a fine British dueling pistol made by Charles Moore in London. Made by Pedersoli. Imported by Dixie Gun Works.
Price: Flintlock $795.00
Price: Percussion $610.00

PEDERSOLI FRENCH AN IX NAPOLEONIC PISTOL
Caliber: .69. Barrel: 8.25 in. Weight: 3 lbs. Length: 14 in. overall. Stock: Walnut. Sights: None. Features: Flintlock, case-hardened lock, brass furniture, buttcap, lock marked "Imperiale de S. Etienne." Steel ramrod. Made by Pedersoli. Imported by Dixie Gun Works.
Price: $740.00

PEDERSOLI FRENCH AN IX GENDARMERIE NAPOLEONIC PISTOL
Caliber: .69. Barrel: 5.25 in. Weight: 3 lbs. Length: 14 in. overall. Stock: Walnut. Sights: None. Features: Flintlock, case-hardened lock, brass furniture, buttcap, lock marked "Imperiale de S. Etienne." Steel ramrod. Imported by Dixie Gun Works.
Price: $725.00

PEDERSOLI FRENCH AN XIII NAPOLEONIC PISTOL
Caliber: .69. Barrel: 8.25 in. Weight: 3 lbs. Length: 14 in. overall. Stock: Walnut half-stock. Sights: None. Features: Flintlock, case-hardened lock, brass furniture, butt cap, lock marked "Imperiale de S. Etienne." Steel ramrod. Made by Pedersoli. Imported by Dixie Gun Works.
Price: $725.00

PEDERSOLI HARPER'S FERRY 1805 PISTOL
Caliber: .58. Barrel: 10 in. Weight: 2.5 lbs. Length: 16 in. overall. Stock: Walnut. Sights: Fixed. Features: Flintlock or percussion. Case-hardened lock, brass-mounted German silver-colored barrel. Wooden ramrod. Replica of the first U.S. government made flintlock pistol. Made by Pedersoli. Imported by Dixie Gun Works.
Price: Flint $565.00
Price: Flint Kit $450.00
Price: Percussion $565.00
Price: Percussion Kit $395.00

PEDERSOLI HOWDAH HUNTER PISTOLS
Caliber: .50, 20 gauge, .58. Barrels: 11.25 in., blued, rifled in .50 and .58 calibers. Weight: 4.25 to 5 lbs. Length: 17.25 in. Stock: American walnut with checkered grip. Sights: Brass bead front sight. Features: Blued barrels, swamped barrel rib, engraved, color case-hardened locks and hammers, captive steel ramrod. Available with detachable shoulder stock, case, holster and mold. Made by Pedersoli. Imported by Dixie Gun Works, Cabela's, Taylor's and others.
Price: 50X50 .... $895.00
Price: 58XD58 .... $895.00
Price: 20X20 gauge $850.00
Price: 50X20 gauge $850.00
Price: 50X50, Kit $640.00
Price: 50X20, Kit $675.00
Price: 20X20, Kit $640.00

Prices given are believed to be accurate at time of publication however, many factors affect retail pricing so exact prices are not possible.

79TH EDITION, 2025 ✦ **553**

PEDERSOLI KENTUCKY PISTOL

Caliber: .45, .50, .54. Barrel: 10.33 in. Weight: 2.5 lbs. Length: 15.4 in. overall. Stock: Walnut with smooth rounded birds-head grip. Sights: Fixed. Features: Available in flint or percussion ignition in various calibers. Case-hardened lock, blued barrel, drift-adjustable rear sights, blade front. Wooden ramrod. Kit guns of all models available from Dixie Gun Works. Made by Pedersoli. Imported by Dixie Gun Works, EMF and others.

Price: .45 Percussion $395.00
Price: .45 Flint $437.00
Price: .45 Flint, Kit $325.00
Price: .50 Flint $495.00
Price: .50 Percussion $450.00
Price: .54 Flint $495.00
Price: .54 Percussion $450.00
Price: .54 Percussion, Kit $325.00
Price: .45, Navy Moll, brass buttcap, Flint $650.00
Price: .45, Navy Moll, brass buttcap, Percussion $595.00

PEDERSOLI LE PAGE PERCUSSION DUELING PISTOL

Caliber: .44. Barrel: 10 inches, browned octagon, rifled. Weight: 2.5 lbs. Length: 16.75 inches overall. Stock: Walnut, rounded checkered butt. Sights: Blade front, open-style rear. Features: Single set trigger, external ramrod. Made by Pedersoli. Imported by Dixie Gun Works.

Price: $950.00

PEDERSOLI MANG TARGET PISTOL

Caliber: .38. Barrel: 11.5 in., octagonal, browned; 1:15-in. twist. Weight: 2.5 lbs. Length: 17. in. overall. Stock: Walnut with fluted grip. Sights: Blade front, open rear adjustable for windage. Features: Browned barrel, polished breech plug, remainder color case-hardened. Made by Pedersoli. Imported by Dixie Gun Works.

Price: $1,795.00

PEDERSOLI MORTIMER TARGET PISTOL

Caliber: .44. Barrel: 10 in., bright octagonal on Standard, browned on Deluxe, rifled. Weight: 2.55 lbs. Length: 15.75 in. overall. Stock: Walnut, checkered saw-handle grip on Deluxe. Sights: Blade front, open-style rear. Features: Percussion or flint, single set trigger, sliding hammer safety, engraved lock on Deluxe. Wooden ramrod. Made by Pedersoli. Imported by Dixie Gun Works.

Price: Flint $1,175.00
Price: Percussion $1,095.00
Price: Deluxe $2,220.00

PEDERSOLI PHILADELPHIA DERRINGER

Caliber: .45. Barrel: 3.1 in., browned, rifled. Weight: 0.5 lbs. Length: 6.215 in. Stock: European walnut checkered. Sights: V-notch rear, blade front. Features: Back-hammer percussion lock with engraving, single trigger. Made by Pedersoli. Imported by Dixie Gun Works.

Price: $550.00
Price: Kit $385.00

PEDERSOLI QUEEN ANNE FLINTLOCK PISTOL

Caliber: .50. Barrel: 7.5 in., smoothbore. Stock: Walnut. Sights: None. Features: Flintlock, German silver-colored steel barrel, fluted brass triggerguard, brass mask on butt. Lockplate left in the white. No ramrod. Introduced 1983. Made by Pedersoli. Imported by Dixie Gun Works.

Price: $495.00
Price: Kit $375.00

PEDERSOLI REMINGTON RIDER DERRINGER

Caliber: 4.3 mm (BB lead balls only). Barrel: 2.1 in., blued, rifled. Weight: 0.25 lbs. Length: 4.75 in. Grips: All-steel construction. Sights: V-notch rear, bead front. Features: Fires percussion cap only – no powder. Available as case-hardened frame or polished white. Made by Pedersoli. Imported by Dixie Gun Works.

Price: Case-hardened. $210.00

PEDERSOLI SCREW BARREL PISTOL

Caliber: .44. Barrel: 2.35 in., blued, rifled. Weight: 0.5 lbs. Length: 6.5 in. Grips: European walnut. Sights: None. Features: Percussion, boxlock with center hammer, barrel unscrews for loading from rear, folding trigger, external hammer, combination barrel and nipple wrench furnished. Made by Pedersoli. Imported by Dixie Gun Works.

Price: $225.00

TRADITIONS KENTUCKY PISTOL

Caliber: .50. Barrel: 10 in., 1:20 in. twist. Weight: 2.75 lbs. Length: 15 in. Stock: Hardwood full stock. Sights: Brass blade front, square notch rear fixed. Features: Polished brass finger spur-style triggerguard, stock cap and ramrod tip, color case-hardened leaf spring lock, springloaded trigger, No. 11 percussion nipple, brass furniture. From Traditions, and as kit from Bass Pro and others.

Price: P1060 Finished $309.00
Price: KPC50602 Kit $279.00

TRADITIONS TRAPPER PISTOL

Caliber: .50. Barrel: 9.75 in., octagonal, blued, hooked patent breech, 1:20 in. twist. Weight: 2.75 lbs. Length: 15.5 in. Stock: Hardwood, modified saw-handle style grip, halfstock. Sights: Brass blade front, rear sight adjustable for windage and elevation. Features: Percussion or flint, double set triggers, polished brass triggerguard, stock cap and ramrod tip, color case-hardened leaf spring lock, spring-loaded trigger, No. 11 percussion nipple, brass furniture. From Traditions and as a kit from Bass Pro and others.

Price: P1100 Finished, percussion.................................... $399.00
Price: P1090 Finished, flint $459.00
Price: KPC51002 Kit, percussion $399.00
Price: KPC50902 Kit, flint $429.00

Prices given are believed to be accurate at time of publication however, many factors affect retail pricing so exact prices are not possible.

DANCE AND BROTHERS PERCUSSION REVOLVER

Caliber: .44. Barrel: 7.4 in., round. Weight: 2.5 lbs. Length: 13 in. overall. Grips: One-piece walnut. Sights: Brass blade front, hammer notch rear. Features: Reproduction of the C.S.A. revolver. Brass triggerguard. Color case-hardened frame Made by Pietta. Imported by Dixie Gun Works and others.
Price: **$350.00**

GRISWOLD AND GUNNISON PERCUSSION REVOLVER

Caliber: .36. Barrel: 7.5 in., round. Weight: 2.5 lbs. Length: 13.25 in. Grips: One-piece walnut. Sights: Fixed. Features: Reproduction of the C.S.A. revolver. Brass frame and triggerguard. Made by Pietta. Imported by EMF, Cabela's and others.
Price: **$235.00**

NORTH AMERICAN COMPANION PERCUSSION REVOLVER

Caliber: .22. Barrel: 1-1/8 in. Weight: 5.1 oz. Length: 4 in. overall. Grips: Laminated wood. Sights: Blade front, notch rear. Features: All stainless steel construction. Uses No. 11 percussion caps. Comes with bullets, powder measure, bullet seater, leather clip holster, gun rag. Long Rifle frame. Introduced 1996. Made in U.S. by North American Arms.
Price: NAA-22LR-CB Long Rifle frame................................. **$251.00**

NORTH AMERICAN SUPER COMPANION PERCUSSION REVOLVER

Caliber: .22. Barrel: 1-5/8 in. Weight: 7.2 oz. Length: 5-1/8 in. Grips: Laminated wood. Sights: Blade font, notched rear. Features: All stainless steel construction. No. 11 percussion caps. Comes with bullets, powder measure, bullet seater, leather clip holster, gun rag. Introduced 1996. Larger "Magnum" frame. Made in U.S. by North American Arms.
Price: NAA-Mag-CB Magnum frame.................................... **$296.00**

PEDERSOLI REMINGTON PATTERN TARGET REVOLVER

Caliber: .44. Barrel: 8 in., tapered octagon progressive twist. Weight: 2.75 lbs. Length: 13-3/4 in. overall. Grips: One-piece hardwood. Sights: V-notch on top strap, blued steel blade front. Features: Brass triggerguard, Non-reflective coating on the barrel and a wear resistant coating on the cylinder, blued steel frame, case-hardened hammer, trigger and loading lever. Made by Pedersoli. Imported by EMF, Dixie Gun Works, Cabela's and others.
Price: **$1,010.00**

PIETTA TEXAS PATTERSON PERCUSSION REVOLVER

Caliber: .36. Barrel: 9 in. tapered octagon. Weight: 2.75 lbs. Length: 13.75 in. Grips: One-piece walnut. Sights: Brass pin front, hammer notch rear.

Features: Folding trigger, blued steel furniture, frame and barrel; engraved scene on cylinder. Ramrod: Loading tool provided. Made by Pietta. Imported by E.M.F, Dixie Gun Works.
Price: **$610.00**

PIETTA 1851 NAVY MODEL PERCUSSION REVOLVER

Caliber: .36, .44, 6-shot. Barrel: 7.5 in. Weight: 44 oz. Length: 13 in. overall. Grips: Walnut. Sights: Post front, hammer notch rear. Features: Available in brass-framed and steel-framed models. Made by Pietta. Imported by EMF, Dixie Gun Works, Cabela's, Cimarron, Taylor's, Traditions and others.
Price: Brass frame.. **$230.00**
Price: Steel frame **$275.00**

PIETTA 1851 NAVY LONDON MODEL PERCUSSION REVOLVER

Caliber: .36, 6-shot. Barrel: 7.5 in. Weight: 44 oz. Length: 13 in. overall. Grips: Walnut. Sights: Post front, hammer notch rear. Features: steel frame and steel triggerguard and back strap. Available with oval triggerguard or squared back triggerguard. Made by Pietta. Imported by EMF, Dixie, Gun Works, Cabela's, Cimarron, Taylor's, Traditions and others.
Price: **$275.00**

PIETTA 1851 NAVY SHERIFF'S MODEL PERCUSSION REVOLVER

Caliber: .44, 6-shot. Barrel: 5.5 in. Weight: 40 oz. Length: 11 in. overall. Grips: Walnut. Sights: Post front, hammer notch rear. Features: Available in brass-framed and steel-framed models. Made by Pietta. Imported by EMF, Dixie, Gun Works, Cabela's.
Price: Brass frame.. **$235.00**
Price: Steel frame **$275.00**

PIETTA 1851 NAVY CAPTAIN SCHAEFFER MODEL PERCUSSION REVOLVER

Caliber: .36, 6-shot. Barrel: 4 in. Weight: 40 oz. Length: 9.5 in. overall. Grips: Grips Ultra-ivory (polymer). Sights: Post front, hammer notch rear. Features: Polished steel finish, completely laser engraved. Made by Pietta. Imported by EMF
Price: **$395.00**

PIETTA 1851 NAVY YANK PEPPERBOX MODEL PERCUSSION REVOLVER

Caliber: .36, 6-shot. Barrel: No Barrel. Weight: 36 oz. Length: 7 in. overall. Grips: One-piece walnut. Sights: Post front, hammer notch rear. Features: There is no barrel. Rounds fire directly out of the chambers of the elongated cylinder. Made by Pietta. Imported by EMF, Dixie Gun Works and Taylor's & Co.
Price: **$235.00**

PIETTA 1851 NAVY BUNTLINE MODEL PERCUSSION REVOLVER

Caliber: .44, 6-shot. Barrel: 12 in. Weight: 36 oz. Length: 18.25 in. overall. Grips: Walnut. Sights: Post front, hammer notch rear. Features: Available in brass-framed and steel-framed models. Made by Pietta. Imported by EMF, Dixie Gun Works (Brass only).
Price: Brass frame.. **$245.00**
Price: Steel frame **$295.00**

Prices given are believed to be accurate at time of publication however, many factors affect retail pricing so exact prices are not possible.

79TH EDITION, 2025 ⊕ **555**

PIETTA 1851 NAVY SNUBNOSE MODEL PERCUSSION REVOLVER

Caliber: .44, 6-shot. Barrel: 3 in. Weight: 36 oz. Length: 8.25 in. overall. Grips: Birds-head grip frame, one-piece checkered walnut. Sights: Post front, hammer notch rear. Features: Color case-hardened, steel-frame. Made by Pietta. Imported by Dixie Gun Works.
Price: $395.00

PIETTA 1858 GENERAL CUSTER

Caliber: .44, 6-shot. Barrel: 8 in., blued. Grips: Two-piece wood. Sights: Open. Weight: 2.7 lbs. Features: Nickel-plated triggerguard, color case-hardened hammer, laser engraving.
Price: $360.00

PIETTA 1860 ARMY MODEL PERCUSSION REVOLVER

Caliber: .44. Barrel: 8 in. Weight: 2.75 lbs. Length: 13.25 in. overall. Grips: One-piece walnut. Sights: Brass blade front, hammer notch rear. Features: Models available with either case-hardened, steel frame, brass triggerguard, or brass frame, triggerguard and backstrap. EMF also offers a model with a silver finish on all the metal. Made by Pietta. Imported by EMF, Cabela's, Dixie Gun Works, Taylor's and others.
Price: Brass Frame... $260.00
Price: Steel Frame $295.00
Price: Steel Frame Old Silver finish............................. $325.00
Price: Steel Frame Old Silver finish Deluxe Engraved $350.00

PIETTA 1860 ARMY SHERIFF'S MODEL PERCUSSION REVOLVER

Caliber: .44. Barrel: 5.5in. Weight: 40 oz. Length: 11.5 in. overall. Grips: One-piece walnut. Sights: Brass blade front, hammer notch rear. Features: Case-hardened, steel frame, brass triggerguard. Made by Pietta. Imported by EMF, Cabela's, Dixie Gun Works and others.
Price: $295.00

PIETTA 1860 ARMY SNUBNOSE MODEL PERCUSSION REVOLVER

Caliber: .44. Barrel: 3 in. Weight: 36 oz. Length: 8.25 in. overall. Grips: Birds-head grip frame, one-piece, checkered walnut. Sights: Brass blade front, hammer notch rear. Features: Fluted cylinder, case-hardened, steel frame, brass triggerguard, Made by Pietta. Imported by EMF.
Price: $385.00

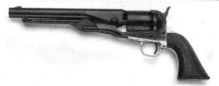

PIETTA NAVY 1861 PERCUSSION REVOLVER

Caliber: .36. Barrel: 8 in. Weight: 2.75 lbs. Length: 13.25 in. overall. Grips: One-piece walnut. Sights: Brass blade front, hammer notch rear. Features: Steel, case-hardened frame, brass-grip frame, or steel-grip frame (London Model), case-hardened creeping loading lever. Made by Pietta. Imported by EMF, Dixie Gun Works, Cabela's and others.
Price: Brass Triggerguard.. $300.00
Price: Steel Triggerguard $300.00

PIETTA 1858 REMINGTON ARMY REVOLVER

Caliber: .44. Barrel: 8 in., tapered octagon. Weight: 2.75 lbs. Length: 13.5 in.

overall. Grips: Two-piece walnut. Sights: V-notch on top strap, blued steel blade front. Features: Brass triggerguard, blued steel backstrap and frame, case-hardened hammer and trigger. Also available, a brass-framed model, and an all stainless steel model. Made by Pietta. Imported by EMF, Dixie Gun Works, Cabela's and others.
Price: Steel Frame $290.00
Price: Brass Frame... $250.00
Price: Stainless Steel.. $430.00

PIETTA 1858 REMINGTON TARGET REVOLVER

Caliber: .44. Barrel: 8 in., tapered octagon. Weight: 2.75 lbs. Length: 13.5 in. overall. Grips: Two-piece walnut. Sights: Adjustable rear, ramped blade front. Features: Brass triggerguard, blued steel frame, case-hardened hammer, and trigger. Also available, a brass-framed model. Made by Pietta. Imported by EMF, Dixie Gun Works, Cabela's and others.
Price: $350.00

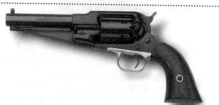

PIETTA 1858 REMINGTON SHIRIFF'S MODEL REVOLVER

Caliber: .36 and .44. Barrel: 5.5in., tapered octagon. Weight: 2.75 lbs. Length: 11.5 in. overall. Grips: Two-piece checkered walnut. Sights: V-notch on top strap, blued steel blade front. Features: Brass triggerguard, blued steel backstrap and frame, case-hardened hammer and trigger. Also available in a color case-hardened-framed model, and in an all stainless steel model. Made by Pietta. Imported by EMF, and others.
Price: Blued Steel Frame $290.00
Price: Color-Case-Hardened frame................................ $395.00
Price: Stainless Steel.. $490.00

PIETTA 1858 REMINGTON BUFFALO BILL COMMEMORATIVE REVOLVER

Caliber: .44. Barrel: 8 in., tapered octagon. Weight: 2.75 lbs. Length: 13-3/4 in. overall. Grips: Two-piece walnut. Sights: V-notch on top strap, blued steel blade front. Features: Gold-filled engraving over dark blue steel. A higher-grade gun commemorating the life of Buffalo Bill Cody. Made by Pietta. Imported by EMF.
Price: $695.00

PIETTA REMINGTON BELT MODEL REVOLVER

Caliber: .36. Barrel: 6.5 in., octagon. Weight: 44 oz. Length: 12.5 in. overall. Grips: Two-piece walnut. Sights: V-notch on top strap, blued steel blade front. Features: Brass triggerguard, blued steel backstrap and frame, case-hardened hammer and trigger. Made by Pietta. Imported by Dixie Gun Works.
Price: $295.00

PIETTA 1863 REMINGTON POCKET MODEL REVOLVER

Caliber: .31, 5-shot. Barrel: 3.5 in. Weight: 1 lb. Length: 7.6 in. Grips: Two-piece walnut. Sights: Pin front, groove-in-frame rear. Features: Spur trigger, iron-, brass- or nickel-plated frame. Made by Pietta. Imported by EMF (Steel Frame), Dixie Gun Works, Taylor's and others.
Price: Brass frame.. $260.00
Price: Steel frame $295.00
Price: Nickel-plated $315.00

PIETTA LEMATT REVOLVER

Caliber: .44/20 Ga. Barrel: 6.75 in. (revolver); 4-7/8 in. (single shot). Weight: 3 lbs., 7 oz. Length: 14 in. overall. Grips: Hand-checkered walnut. Sights: Post front, hammer notch rear. Features: Exact reproduction with all-steel construction; 44-cal., 9-shot cylinder, 20-gauge single barrel; color case-hardened hammer with selector; spur triggerguard; ring at butt; lever-type barrel release. Made by Pietta. Imported by EMF, Dixie Gun Works and others.
Price: Navy $1,075.00
Price: Cavalry.. $1,100.00
Price: Army $1,100.00

Prices given are believed to be accurate at time of publication however, many factors affect retail pricing so exact prices are not possible.

PIETTA SPILLER & BURR PERCUSSION REVOLVER
Caliber: .36. Barrel: 7 in., octagon. Weight: 2.5 lbs. Length: 12.5 in. overall.
Grips: Two-piece walnut. Sights: V-notch on top strap, blued steel blade front.
Features: Reproduction of the C.S.A. revolver. Brass frame and triggerguard.
Also available as a kit. Made by Pietta. Imported by Dixie Gun Works,
Traditions, Midway USA and others.
Price: **$275.00**
Price: Kit **$235.00**

PIETTA STARR DOUBLE-ACTION ARMY REVOLVER
Caliber: .44. Barrel: 6 in. tapered round. Weight: 3 lbs. Length: 11.75 in.
Grips: One-piece walnut. Sights: Hammer notch rear, dovetailed front.
Features: Double-action mechanism, round tapered barrel, all blued frame
and barrel. Made by Pietta. Imported by Dixie Gun Works and others.
Price: **$565.00**

PIETTA STARR SINGLE-ACTION ARMY REVOLVER
Caliber: .44. Barrel: 8 in. tapered round. Weight: 3 lbs. Length: 13.5 in. Grips:
One-piece walnut. Sights: Hammer notch rear, dovetailed front. Features:
Single-action mechanism, round tapered barrel, all blued frame and barrel.
Made by Pietta. Imported by Cabela's, Dixie Gun Works and others.
Price: **$550.00**

PIETTA 1873 PERCUSSION REVOLVER
Caliber: .44. Barrel: 5.5 in. Weight: 40 oz. Length: 11.25 in. overall. Grips:
One-piece walnut. Sights: V-notch on top strap, blued steel blade front.
Features: A cap-and-ball version of the Colt Single Action Army revolver.
Made by Pietta. Imported by EMF, Cabela's, Dixie Gun Works and others.
Price: **$360.00**

TRADITIONS U.S. MARSHAL
Caliber: .36, 6-shot. Barrel: 8 in., blued. Grips: One-piece walnut. Sights:
Open, hammer/blade. Weight: 2.61 lbs. Features: Case-hardened frame,
single action, U.S. Marshal logo on grips.
Price: **$351.00**

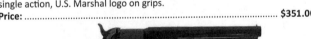

TRADITIONS WILDCARD
Caliber: .36, 6-shot. Barrel: 7.5 in., blued octagon. Grips: Simulated stag.
Sights: Open, hammer/blade. Weight: 2.75 lbs. Features: 1851 "Gunfighter,"
13.5-in. overall length, case-hardened frame.
Price: **$499.00**

UBERTI 1847 WALKER PERCUSSION REVOLVER
Caliber: .44. Barrel: 9 in. Weight: 4.5 lbs. Length: 15.7 in. overall. Grips: One-
piece hardwood. Sights: Brass blade front, hammer notch rear. Features: Copy
of Sam Colt's first U.S. contract revolver. Engraved cylinder, case-hardened
hammer and loading lever. Blued finish. Made by Uberti. Imported by Cabela's,
Cimarron, Dixie Gun Works, EMF, Taylor's, Uberti U.S.A. and others.
Price: Standard Model, Blued................................... **$429.00**

UBERTI DRAGOON PERCUSSION REVOLVERS
Caliber: .44. Barrel: 7.5 in. Weight: 4.1 lbs. Grips: One-piece walnut. Sights:
Brass blade front, hammer notch rear. Features: Four models of the big .44
caliber revolvers that followed the massive Walker model and pre-dated the
sleek 1860 Army model. Blued barrel, backstrap and triggerguard. Made by
Uberti. Imported by Uberti USA, Dixie Gun Works, Taylor's and others.
Price: Whitneyville Dragoon..................................... **$429.00**
Price: First Model Dragoon...................................... **$429.00**
Price: Second Model Dragoon................................... **$429.00**
Price: Third Model Dragoon **$429.00**

UBERTI 1849 POCKET MODEL WELLS FARGO PERCUSSION REVOLVER
Caliber: .31. Barrel: 4 in., seven-groove, RH twist. Weight: About 24 oz. Grips:
One-piece walnut. Sights: Brass pin front, hammer notch rear. Features:
Unfluted cylinder with stagecoach holdup scene, cupped cylinder pin, no
grease grooves, one safety pin on cylinder and slot in hammer face. Made by
Uberti. Imported by Uberti USA, Cimarron, Dixie Gun Works and others.
Price: **$349.00**

UBERTI 1849 WELLS FARGO PERCUSSION REVOLVER
Caliber: .31. Barrel: 4 in.; seven-groove; RH twist. Weight: About 24 oz. Grips:
One-piece walnut. Sights: Brass pin front, hammer notch rear. Features:
No loading lever, Unfluted cylinder with stagecoach holdup scene, cupped
cylinder pin, no grease grooves, one safety pin on cylinder and slot in
hammer face. Made by Uberti. Imported by Uberti USA, Cimarron, Dixie Gun
Works and others.
Price: **$349.00**

UBERTI NAVY MODEL 1851 PERCUSSION REVOLVER
Caliber: .36, 6-shot. Barrel: 7.5 in. Weight: 44 oz. Length: 13 in. overall. Grips:
One-piece walnut. Sights: Post front, hammer notch rear. Features: Brass
backstrap and triggerguard, or steel backstrap and triggerguard (London
Model), engraved cylinder with navy battle scene; case-hardened hammer,
loading lever. Made by Uberti and Pietta. Imported by Uberti USA, Cabela's,
Cimarron, and others.
Price: Brass grip...**$329.00**
Price: London Model...**$369.00**

UBERTI 1860 ARMY REVOLVER
Caliber: .44. Barrel: 8 in. Weight: 44 oz. Length: 13.25 in. overall. Grips: One-
piece walnut. Sights: Brass blade front, hammer notch rear. Features: Steel
or case-hardened frame, brass triggerguard, case-hardened creeping loading
lever. Many models and finishes are available for this pistol. Made by Uberti.
Imported by Cabela's, Cimarron, Dixie Gun Works, EMF, Taylor's, Uberti
U.S.A. and others.
Price: Roll engraved cylinder **$349.00**
Price: Full fluted cylinder **$369.00**

UBERTI 1861 NAVY PERCUSSION REVOLVER

Caliber: .36 Barrel: 7.5 in. Weight: 44 oz. Length: 13.25 in. overall. Grips: One-piece walnut. Sights: Brass blade front, hammer notch rear. Features: Brass backstrap and triggerguard, or steel backstrap and triggerguard (London Model), engraved cylinder with navy battle scene; case-hardened hammer, loading lever. Made by Uberti. Imported by Uberti USA, Cabela's, Cimarron, Dixie Gun Works, Taylor's and others.

Price: Brass grip $349.00
Price: London Model $349.00

UBERTI 1862 POLICE PERCUSSION REVOLVER

Caliber: .36, 5-shot. Barrel: 5.5 in., 6.5 in., 7.5 in. Weight: 26 oz. Length: 12 in. overall (6.5 in. bbl.). Grips: One-piece walnut. Sights: Fixed. Features: Round tapered barrel; half-fluted and rebated cylinder; case-hardened frame, loading lever and hammer; brass triggerguard and backstrap. Made by Uberti. Imported by Cimarron, Dixie Gun Works, Taylor's, Uberti U.S.A. and others.

Price: $369.00

UBERTI 1862 POCKET NAVY PERCUSSION REVOLVER

Caliber: .36, 5-shot. Barrel: 5.5 in., 6.5 in. Weight: 26 oz. Length: 12 in. overall (6.5 in. bbl.). Grips: One-piece walnut. Sights: Fixed. Features: Octagon barrel; case-hardened frame, loading lever and hammer; silver or brass triggerguard and backstrap; also available in an all stainless steel version. Made by Uberti. Imported by Uberti USA, Cimarron, Dixie Gun Works, Taylor's and others.

Price: $369.00

UBERTI LEACH AND RIGDON PERCUSSION REVOLVER

Caliber: .36. Barrel: 7.5 in., octagon to round. Weight: 2.75 lbs. Length: 13 in. Grips: One-piece walnut. Sights: Hammer notch and pin front. Features: Steel frame. Reproduction of the C.S.A. revolver. Brass backstrap and triggerguard. Made by Uberti. Imported by Uberti USA, Dixie Gun Works and others.

Price: $349.00

UBERTI NEW ARMY REMINGTON PERCUSSION REVOLVER

Caliber: .44, 6-shot. Barrel: Tapered octagon 8 in. Weight: 32 oz. Length: Standard 13.5 in. Grips: Two-piece walnut. Sights: Standard blade front, groove-in-frame rear; adjustable on some models. Features: Many variations of this gun are available. Target Model (Uberti U.S.A.) has fully adjustable target rear sight, target front, .36 or .44. Made by Uberti. Imported by Uberti USA, Cimarron F.A. Co., Taylor's and others.

Price: $369.00
Price: Stainless $449.00

ARMI SPORT ENFIELD THREE-BAND P1853 RIFLE

Caliber: .58. Barrel: 39 in. Weight: 10.25 lbs. Length: 52 in. overall. Stock: European walnut. Sights: Blade front, flip-up rear with elevator marked to 800 yards. Features: Reproduction of the original three-band rifle. Percussion musket-cap ignition. Blued barrel with steel barrelbands, brass furniture. Case-hardened lock. Lockplate marked "London Armory Co. and Crown." Made by Euro Arms, Armi Sport (Chiappa). Imported by Dixie Gun Works and others.
Price: Rifled bore $895.00
Price: Smooth bore $750.00

CVA ACCURA IN-LINE BREAK-ACTION RIFLE

Caliber: .50. Barrel: 28 in. fluted. Weight: 7.5 lbs. Length: Standard 45 in. Stock: Ambidextrous solid composite in standard or thumbhole. Sights: Adj. fiber-optic. Features: Break-action, quick-release breech plug, aluminum loading rod, cocking spur, lifetime warranty. By CVA.
Price: CVA PR3120NM (Accura MR Nitride with Black Stocks and Scope Mount)...$493.00

CVA ACCURA V2 LR NITRIDE "SPECIAL EDITION" IN-LINE BREAK-ACTION RIFLE

Caliber: .50. Barrel: 30 in. fluted. Weight: 7.5 lbs. Length: Standard 45 in. Stock: Ambidextrous solid composite. Sights: Adj. fiber-optic. Features: Break-action, quick-release breech plug, aluminum loading rod, cocking spur, equipped with a genuine, Nitride treated, 30-inch Bergara Barrel, and a deep pistol grip stock decorated in APG camo. Lifetime warranty. By CVA.
Price: CVA PR6124NM $449.00

CVA ACCURA LR

Caliber: .45, .50. Barrel: 30 in., Nitride-treated, 416 stainless steel Bergara. Stock: Ambidextrous thumbhole camo. Sights: DuraSight Dead-On one-piece scope mount, scope not included. Weight: 6.75 lbs. Features: Reversible hammer spur, CrushZone recoil pad, quick-release breech plug.
Price: $605.00

CVA ACCURA MR (MOUNTAIN RIFLE) IN-LINE BREAK-ACTION RIFLE

Caliber: .50. Barrel: 25 in. Weight: 6.35 lbs. Length: Standard 45 in. Stock: Ambidextrous solid composite. Sights: DuraSight DEAD-ON One-Piece Scope Mount. Features: Break-action, quick-release breech plug, aluminum loading rod, cocking spur, and a deep pistol grip stock decorated in Realtree APG camo. Lifetime warranty. By CVA.
Price: CVA PR3121SNM $546.00

CVA ACCURA MR-X

Caliber: .50. Barrel: 26 in., 1:28 in. twist, Nitride-treated stainless steel. Drilled and tapped for a scope and sights. Weight: 8.75 lbs. Features: 3/4x24 threaded barrel, adjustable comb, carbon-fiber collapsable loading rod, Quake sling, free-floating barrel, True Timber Strata camo.
Price: CVA PR3121SNM $730.00

CVA ACCURA LRX

Caliber: .45 and .50. Barrel: 30 in. Nitride-treated stainless steel Bergara barrel. Comes with a carbon-fiber collapsible field rod, which you carry on your hip, a configuration that allows the barrel to be completely free-floated. The stock also wears a height-adjustable comb. Utilizes CVA's screw-in/out breech plug system.
Price: $675.00

CVA PLAINS RIFLE

Caliber: .50. Barrel: 28 in., Nitride, fluted, stainless steel Bergara. Stock: Ambidextrous composite Realtree MAX-1 XT. Sights: DuraSight Dead-On one-piece scope mount, scope not included. Weight: 7.2 lbs. Features: Solid aluminum PalmSaver ramrod, reversible cocking spur, Quake Claw sling.
Price: $593.00

CVA OPTIMA V2

Caliber: .50. Barrel: 26 in., 1:28 in. twist, Nitride-treated stainless steel. Free-floating barrel, drilled and tapped for a scope and sights. Weight: 8.75 lbs. Features: Triggerguard actuated breeching lever, ambidextrous stock, Crush Zone recoil pad, DuraSight DEAD-ON one-piece scope mount or DuraSight fiber-optic sight, aluminum PalmSaver ramrod, Realtree Escape or True Timber Strata camo.
Price: PR2037NM LR TH Cerakote Burnt Bronze/Nitride/
Realtree Escape 28-in. Barrel..$520.00
Price: PR2038SM LR TH Stainless Steel/Realtree
Escape 28-in. Barrel...$435.00
Price: PR2039N Nitride/Realtree Escape 26-in. Barrel. $455.00
Price: PR2039NM Nitride/Realtree Escape 26-in. Barrel. $450.00
Price: PR2040S Stainless Steel/Realtree Escape 26-in. Barrel. $415.00
Price: PR2040SM Stainless Steel/Realtree Escape 26-in. Barrel..........$405.00
Price: PR2041NW NORTHWEST Nitride/Realtree
Escape 26-in. Barrel. $455.00
Price: PR6022SM Stainless Steel/True Timber Strata 26-in. Barrel. $405.00

CVA WOLF V2

Caliber: .50. Barrel: 26 in., 1:28 in. twist, Nitride-treated stainless steel. Free-floating barrel, drilled and tapped for a scope and sights. Weight: 8.75 lbs. Features: breeching button, ambidextrous LOP adjustable stock, Quick-Release Breech Plug, aluminum PalmSaver ramrod, True Timber Strata camo.
Price: $340.00

CVA PARAMOUNT PRO V2

Caliber: .45 and .50. Barrel: 26 in., 1:22-in. twist, nitride-treated stainless steel. Drilled and tapped for a scope and sights. Weight: 8.2–8.75 lbs. Features: fully adjustable TriggerTech trigger, custom Greyboe stock, and CeraKote/nitride finish on the barrel, removable stock spacers, 3/4x24 threaded barrel, adjustable comb, carbon-fiber collapsible loading rod, Quake sling, free-floating barrel, True Timber Strata camo.
Price: .50-Cal. CVA PR3521N $1,999.00
Price: .45-Cal. CVA PR3514N $1,899.00

CVA PARAMOUNT LONG-RANGE MUZZLELOADER .45 CAL.

Caliber: .45. Barrel: 26 in., 1:22-in. twist, nitride-treated stainless steel. Drilled and tapped for a scope and sights. Weight: 8.75 lbs. Features: 3/4x24 threaded barrel, fully adjustable stock, aluminum chassis, carbon-fiber collapsible loading rod, Quake sling, free-floating barrel, Realtree Hillside camo.
Price: CVA PR3507N $1,062.00

CVA CROSSFIRE

Caliber: .50. Barrel: 28 in., 1:28-in. twist, nitride-treated stainless steel. Drilled and tapped for a scope and sights. Weight: 8.0 lbs. Features: FireStick Ignition, nitride-treated, ambidextrous stock, solid aluminum loading rod, Quake sling, free-floating barrel, black synthetic.
Price: CVA CR3801SSC Stainless Steel/Black $450.00
Price: CVA CR3801SM Cerakote Burnt Bronze/Escape $595.00

DIXIE DELUXE CUB RIFLE

Caliber: .32, .36. Barrel: 28 in. octagonal. Weight: 6.5 lbs. Length: 44 in. overall. Stock: Walnut. Sights: Fixed. Features: Each gun available in either flint or percussion ignition. Short rifle for small game and beginning shooters. Brass patchbox and furniture. Made by Pedersoli for Dixie Gun Works.
Price: Dixie Gun Works (.32-cal. flint) PR3130.....................$890.00
Price: Dixie Gun Works (.36-cal. flint) FR3135......................$890.00
Price: Dixie Gun Works (.32-cal. Percussion kit) PK3360.....................$690.00
Price: Dixie Gun Works (.36-cal. Percussion kit) PK3365.....................$690.00
Price: Dixie Gun Works (.32-cal. Flint kit) PK3350 ....$710.00
Price: Dixie Gun Works (.36-cal. Flint kit) PK335 ....$710.00
Price: Dixie Gun Works (.32-cal. percussion) PR3140.........................$850.00
Price: Dixie Gun Works (.36 cal. percussion) PR3145.........................$850.00

DIXIE PENNSYLVANIA RIFLE

Caliber: .45 and .50. Barrel: 41.5 in. octagonal, .45/1:48, .50/1:56 in. twist. Weight: 8.5, 8.75 lbs. Length: 56 in. overall. Stock: European walnut, full-length stock. Sights: Notch rear, blade front. Features: Flintlock or percussion, brass patchbox, double-set triggers. Also available as kit guns for both calibers and ignition systems. Made by Pedersoli for Dixie Gun Works.
Price: Dixie Gun Works (.45-cal. flint) FR1060..................................$1,100.00
Price: Dixie Gun Works (.50-cal. flint) FR3200..................................$1,100.00
Price: Dixie Gun Works (.45-cal. Percussion kit) PR1075....................$910.00
Price: Dixie Gun Works (.50-cal. Percussion kit) PK3365....................$910.00

Price: Dixie Gun Works (.45-cal. Flint kit) FR1065 .... **$910.00**
Price: Dixie Gun Works (.50-cal. Flint kit) FK3420 .... **$910.00**
Price: Dixie Gun Works (.45-cal. percussion) FR1070 .... **$1,050.00**
Price: Dixie Gun Works (.50-cal. percussion) PR3205 .... **$1,050.00**

EUROARMS 1803 HARPER'S FERRY FLINTLOCK RIFLE
Caliber: .54. Barrel: 35.5 in., smoothbore. Weight: 9.5 lbs. Length: 50.5 in. overall. Stock: Half-stock, walnut w/oil finish. Sights: Blade front, notched rear. Features: Color case-hardened lock, browned barrel, with barrel key. Made by Euroarms. Imported by Dixie Gun Works.
Price: **$795.00**

EUROARMS J.P. MURRAY ARTILLERY CARBINE
Caliber: .58. Barrel: 23.5 in. Weight: 8 lbs. Length: 39.5 in. Stock: European walnut. Sights: Blade front, fixed notch rear. Features: Percussion musket-cap ignition. Reproduction of the original Confederate carbine. Lock marked "J.P. Murray, Columbus, Georgia." Blued barrel. Made by Euroarms. Imported by Dixie Gun Works and others.
Price: **$1,100.00**

EUROARMS ENFIELD MUSKETOON P1861
Caliber: .58. Barrel: 24 in. Weight: 9 lbs. Length: 40 in. overall. Stock: European walnut. Sights: Blade front, flip-up rear with elevator marked to 700 yards. Features: Reproduction of the original cavalry version of the Enfield rifle. Percussion musket-cap ignition. Blued barrel with steel barrelbands, brass furniture. Case-hardened lock. Euroarms version marked London Armory with crown. Pedersoli version has Birmingham stamp on stock and Enfield and Crown on lockplate. Made by Euroarms. Imported by Dixie Gun Works and others.
Price: **$1,050.00**

KNIGHT DISC EXTREME
Caliber: .52. Barrel: 26 in., fluted stainless, 1:28 in. twist. Weight: 7 lbs. 14 oz. to 8 lbs. Length: 45 in. overall. Stock: Carbon Knight straight or thumbhole with blued or SS; G2 thumbhole; left-handed Nutmeg thumbhole. Ramrod: Solid brass extendable jag. Sights: Fully adjustable metallic fiber optics. Features: Bolt-action rifle, full plastic jacket ignition system, #11 nipple, musket nipple, bare 208 shotgun primer. With recommended loads, guaranteed to have 4-inch, three-shot groups at 200 yards. Also available as a Western gun with exposed ignition. Made in the U.S. by Knight Rifles.
Price: **$591.00**

KNIGHT LITTLEHORN IN-LINE RIFLE
Caliber: .50. Barrel: 22 in., 1:28 in. twist. Weight: 6.7 lbs. Length: 39 in. overall. Stock: 12.5-in. length of pull, G2 straight or pink Realtree AP HD. Ramrod: Carbon core with solid brass extendable jag. Sights: Fully adjustable Williams fiber optic. Features: Uses four different ignition systems (included): Full Plastic Jacket, #11 nipple, musket nipple or bare 208 shotgun primer; vented breech plug, striker-fired with one-piece removable hammer assembly. Finish: Stainless steel. With recommended loads, guaranteed to have 4-inch, three-shot groups at 200 yards. Also available as Western gun with exposed ignition. Made in U.S. by Knight Rifles.
Price: **$390.00**

KNIGHT MOUNTAINEER IN-LINE RIFLE
Caliber: .45, .50, .52. Barrel: 27 in. fluted stainless steel, free floated. Weight: 8 lbs. (thumbhole stock), 8.3 lbs. (straight stock). Length: 45.5 inches. Sights: Fully adjustable metallic fiber optic. Features: Bolt-action rifle, adjustable match-grade trigger, aluminum ramrod with carbon core, solid brass extendable jag, vented breech plug. Ignition: Full plastic jacket, #11 nipple, musket nipple, bare 208 shotgun primer. With recommended loads, guaranteed to have 4-inch, three-shot groups at 200 yards. Also available as Western gun with exposed ignition. Made in U.S. by Knight Rifles.
Price: **$1,016.00**

KNIGHT ULTRA-LITE IN-LINE RIFLE
Caliber: .45 or .50. Barrel: 24 in. Stock: Black, tan or olive-green Kevlar spider web. Weight: 6 lbs. Features: Bolt-action rifle. Ramrod: Carbon core with solid brass extendable jag. Sights: With or without Williams fiber-optic sights, drilled and tapped for scope mounts. Finish: Stainless steel. Ignition: 209

Primer with Full Plastic Jacket, musket cap or #11 nipple, bare 208 shotgun primer; vented breech plug. With recommended loads, guaranteed to have 4-inch, three-shot groups at 200 yards. Also available as Western version with exposed ignition. Made in U.S. by Knight Rifles.
Price: **$1,217.00**

KNIGHT PEREGRINE
Caliber: .40, Barrel: 28 in. Green Mountain stainless helical-fluted barrel, 1:16 in. twist. Weight 7.4 lbs. Overall Length 46.25 in. Designed and built for increased velocities and accuracy at greater distances. Features: solid carbon fiber w/aluminum bed block for free-floating barrel design, Sage Brush Camo, Bare Primer Tungsten Carbide Inserted Breech Plug, Timney Match-Grade Trigger. Included is a Lee Hand Press with adjustable sizing die for bullets.
Price: **$1,569.00**

LYMAN DEERSTALKER RIFLE
Caliber: .50, .54. Barrel: 28 in. octagon, 1:48 in. twist. Weight: 10.8 lbs. Length: 45 in. overall. Stock: European walnut with black rubber recoil pad. Sights: Lyman's high visibility, fiber-optic sights. Features: Fast-twist rifling for conical bullets. Blackened metal parts to eliminate glare, stainless steel nipple. Hook breech, single trigger, coil spring lock. Steel barrel rib and ramrod ferrules. From Lyman.
Price: .50-cal /.54-cal. flint **$448.00**
Price: .50-cal /.54-cal. percussion **$398.00**

LYMAN GREAT PLAINS RIFLE
Caliber: .50, .54. Barrel: 32 in., 1:60 in. twist. Weight: 11.6 lbs. Stock: Walnut. Sights: Steel blade front, buckhorn rear adjustable for windage and elevation, and fixed notch primitive sight included. Features: Percussion or flint ignition. Blued steel furniture. Stainless steel nipple. Coil spring lock, Hawken-style triggerguard and double-set triggers. Round thimbles recessed and sweated into rib. Steel wedge plates and toe plate. Introduced 1979. From Lyman.
Price: 6031102/3 .50-cal./.54-cal percussion **$784.00**
Price: 6031105/6 .50-cal./.54-cal flintlock **$839.00**
Price: 6031125/6 .50-ca./.54-cal left-hand percussion **$824.00**
Price: 6031137 .50-cal. left-hand flintlock **$859.00**
Price: 6031111/2 .50/.54-cal. percussion kit **$639.00**
Price: 6031114/5 .50/.54-cal. flintlock kit **$689.00**

LYMAN GREAT PLAINS HUNTER MODEL
Similar to Great Plains model except 1:32 in. twist, shallow-groove barrel for conicals or sabots, and comes drilled and tapped for Lyman 57GPR peep sight.
Price: 6031120/1 .50-cal./.54-cal percussion **$791.00**
Price: 6031148/9 .50-cal./.54-cal flintlock **$839.00**
Price: 6031112 .50-cal./.54-cal percussion kit **$669.00**
Price: 6031115 .50-cal/.54-cal flintlock kit **$729.00**

LYMAN TRADE RIFLE
Caliber: .50, .54. Barrel: 28 in. octagon, 1:48 in. twist. Weight: 10.8 lbs. Length: 45 in. overall. Stock: European walnut. Sights: Blade front, open rear adjustable for windage, or optional fixed sights. Features: Fast-twist rifling for conical bullets. Polished brass furniture with blue steel parts, stainless steel nipple. Hook breech, single trigger, coil spring percussion lock. Steel barrel rib and ramrod ferrules. Introduced 1980. From Lyman.
Price: 6032125/6 .50-cal./.54-cal. percussion **$565.00**
Price: 6032129/30 .50-cal./.54-cal. flintlock **$583.00**

PEDERSOLI 1777 CHARLEVILLE MUSKET
Caliber: .69. Barrel: 44.75 in. round, smoothbore. Weight: 10.5 lbs. Length: 57 in. Stock: European walnut, fullstock. Sights: Steel stud on upper barrelband. Features: Flintlock using one-inch flint. Steel parts all polished armory bright, brass furniture. Lock marked Charleville. Made by Pedersoli. Imported by Cabela's, Dixie Gun Works, others.
Price: **$1,450.00**

Prices given are believed to be accurate at time of publication however, many factors affect retail pricing so exact prices are not possible.

PEDERSOLI 1795 SPRINGFIELD MUSKET

Caliber: .69. Barrel: 44.75 in., round, smoothbore. Weight: 10.5 lbs. Length: 57.25 in. Stock: European walnut, fullstock. Sights: Brass stud on upper barrelband. Features: Flintlock using one-inch flint. Steel parts all polished armory bright, brass furniture. Lock marked US Springfield. Made by Pedersoli. Imported by Cabela's, Dixie Gun Works, others.
Price: **$1,495.00**

PEDERSOLI POTSDAM 1809 PRUSSIAN MUSKET

Caliber: .75. Barrel: 41.2 in. round, smoothbore. Weight: 9 lbs. Length: 56 in. Stock: European walnut, full stock. Sights: Brass lug on upper barrelband. Features: Flintlock using one-inch flint. Steel parts all polished armory bright, brass furniture. Lock marked "Potsdam over G.S." Made by Pedersoli Imported by Dixie Gun Works.
Price: **$1,575.00**

PEDERSOLI 1816 FLINTLOCK MUSKET

Caliber: .69. Barrel: 42 in., smoothbore. Weight: 9.75 lbs. Length: 56-7/8 in. overall. Stock: Walnut w/oil finish. Sights: Blade front. Features: All metal finished in "National Armory Bright," three barrel bands w/springs, steel ramrod w/button-shaped head. Made by Pedersoli. Imported by Dixie Gun Works.
Price: Percussion conversion **$1,495.00**

PEDERSOLI 1841 MISSISSIPPI RIFLE

Caliber: .54, .58. Barrel: 33 inches. Weight: 9.5 lbs. Length: 48.75 in. overall. Stock: European walnut. Sights: Blade front, notched rear. Features: Percussion musket-cap ignition. Reproduction of the original one-band rifle with large brass patchbox. Color case-hardened lockplate with browned barrel. Made by Pedersoli. Imported by Dixie Gun Works, Cabela's and others.
Price: (.54 caliber) **$1,200.00**
Price: (.58 caliber) **$1,100.00**

PEDERSOLI 1854 LORENZ RIFLE

Caliber: .54. Barrel: 37 in. Weight: 9 lbs. Length: 49 in. overall. Stock: European walnut. Sights: Blade front, rear steel open, flip-up style. Features: Percussion musket-cap ignition. Armory bright lockplate marked "Konigi. Wurt Fabrik." Armory bright steel barrel. Made by Pedersoli. Imported by Dixie Gun Works.
Price: **$1,500.00**

PEDERSOLI 1857 MAUSER RIFLE

Caliber: .54. Barrel: 39.75 in. Weight: 9.5 lbs. Length: 52 in. overall. Stock: European walnut. Sights: Blade front, rear steel adjustable for windage and elevation. Features: Percussion musket-cap ignition. Color case-hardened lockplate marked "Konigi. Wurt Fabrik." Armory bright steel barrel. Made by Pedersoli. Imported by Dixie Gun Works.
Price: **$1,695.00**

PEDERSOLI 1861 RICHMOND MUSKET

Caliber: .58. Barrel: 40 inches. Weight: 9.5 lbs. Length: 55.5 in. overall. Stock: European walnut. Sights: Blade front, three-leaf military rear. Features: Reproduction of the original three-band rifle. Percussion musket-cap ignition. Lock marked C. S. Richmond, Virginia. Armory bright. Made by Pedersoli. Imported by Dixie Gun Works and others.
Price: **$1,150.00**

PEDERSOLI 1861 SPRINGFIELD RIFLE

Caliber: .58. Barrel: 40 inches. Weight: 10 lbs. Length: 55.5 in. overall. Stock: European walnut. Sights: Blade front, three-leaf military rear. Features: Reproduction of the original three-band rifle. Percussion musket-cap ignition. Lockplate marked 1861 with eagle and U.S. Springfield. Armory bright steel. Made by Armi Sport/Chiappa, Pedersoli. Imported by Cabela's, Dixie Gun Works, others.
Price: **$1,199.00**

PEDERSOLI BAKER CAVALRY SHOTGUN

Gauge: 20. Barrels: 11.25 inches. Weight: 5.75 pounds. Length: 27.5 in. overall. Stock: American walnut. Sights: Bead front. Features: Reproduction of shotguns carried by Confederate cavalry. Single non-selective trigger, back-action locks. No. 11 percussion musket-cap ignition. Blued barrel with steel furniture. Case-hardened lock. Pedersoli also makes a 12-gauge coach-length version of this back-action-lock shotgun with 20-inch barrels, and a full-length version in 10, 12 and 20 gauge. Made by Pedersoli. Imported by Cabela's and others.
Price: **$1,099.00**

PEDERSOLI BRISTLEN MORGES AND WAADTLANDER TARGET RIFLES

Caliber: .44, .45. Barrel: 29.5 in tapered octagonal, hooked breech. Weight: 15.5 lbs. Length: 48.5 in. overall. Stock: European walnut, halfstock with hooked buttplate and detachable palm rest. Sights: Creedmoor rear on Morges, Swiss Diopter on Waadtlander, hooded front sight notch. Features: Percussion back-action lock, double set, double-phase triggers, one barrel key, muzzle protector. Specialized bullet molds for each gun. Made by Pedersoli. Imported by Dixie Gun Works and others.
Price: .44 Bristlen Morges **$2,995.00**
Price: .45 Waadtlander **$2,995.00**

PEDERSOLI BROWN BESS

Caliber: .75. Barrel: 42 in., round, smoothbore. Weight: 9 lbs. Length: 57.75 in. Stock: European walnut, fullstock. Sights: Steel stud on front serves as bayonet lug. Features: Flintlock using one-inch flint with optional brass flash guard (SCO203), steel parts all polished armory bright, brass furniture. Lock marked Grice, 1762 with crown and GR. Made by Pedersoli. Imported by Cabela's, Dixie Gun Works, others.
Price: Complete Gun **$1,350.00**
Price: Kit Gun...**$1,050.00**
Price: Trade Gun, 30.5-in. barrel **$1,495.00**
Price: Trade Gun Kit **$975.00**

PEDERSOLI COOK & BROTHER CONFEDERATE CARBINE/ARTILLERY/RIFLE

Caliber: .58 Barrel: 24/33/39 inches. Weight: 7.5/8.4/8.6 lbs. Length: 40.5/48/54.5 in. Stock: Select oil-finished walnut. Features: Percussion musket-cap ignition. Color case-hardened lock, browned barrel. Buttplate, triggerguard, barrelbands, sling swivels and nose cap of polished brass. Lock marked with stars and bars flag on tail and Athens, Georgia. Made by Pedersoli. Imported by Dixie Gun Works, others.
Price: Carbine **$995.00**
Price: Artillery/Rifle...**$995.00**

PEDERSOLI COUNTRY HUNTER

Caliber: .50. Barrel: 26 in. octagonal. Weight: 6 lbs. Length: 41.75 in. overall. Stock: European walnut, halfstock. Sights: Rear notch, blade front. Features: Percussion, one barrel key. Made by Pedersoli. Imported by Dixie Gun Works.
Price: Percussion, .50 ....**$675.00**
Price: Flint, .50..**$688.00**

PEDERSOLI ENFIELD MUSKETOON P1861

Caliber: .58. Barrel: 33 in. Weight: 9 lbs. Length: 35 in. overall. Stock: European walnut. Sights: Blade front, flip-up rear with elevator marked to 700 yards. Features: Reproduction of the original cavalry version of the Enfield rifle. Percussion musket-cap ignition. Blued barrel with steel barrelbands, brass furniture. Case-hardened lock. Euroarms version marked London Armory with crown. Pedersoli version has Birmingham stamp on stock and Enfield and Crown on lockplate. Made by Euroarms, Pedersoli. Imported by Cabela's and others.
Price: **$1,099.00**

PEDERSOLI FRONTIER RIFLE

Caliber: .32, .36, .45, .50, .54. Barrel: 39 in., octagon, 1:48 twist. Weight: 7.75 lbs. Length: 54.5 in. overall. Stock: American black walnut. Sights: Blade front, rear drift adjustable for windage. Features: Color case-hardened lockplate and cock/hammer, brass triggerguard and buttplate; double set, double-phased triggers. Made by Pedersoli. Imported by Dixie Gun Works, and by Cabela's (as the Blue Ridge Rifle)
Price: Percussion **$599.00**
Price: Flintlock **$649.00**

PEDERSOLI ENFIELD THREE-BAND P1853 RIFLE

Caliber: .58. Barrel: 39 in. Weight: 10.25 lbs. Length: 52 in. overall. Stock: European walnut. Sights: Blade front, flip-up rear with elevator marked to 800 yards. Features: Reproduction of the original three-band rifle. Percussion musket-cap ignition. Blued barrel with steel barrelbands, brass furniture. Case-hardened lock. Lockplate marked "London Armory Co. and Crown." Made by Pedersoli. Imported by Cabela's.
Price: **$1,149.00**

PEDERSOLI INDIAN TRADE MUSKET

Gauge: 20. Barrel: 36 in., octagon to round, smoothbore. Weight: 7.25 lbs. Length: 52 in. overall. Stock: American walnut. Sights: Blade front sight, no

Prices given are believed to be accurate at time of publication however, many factors affect retail pricing so exact prices are not possible.

79TH EDITION, 2025 ✧ 561

rear sight. Features: Flintlock. Kits version available. Made by Pedersoli. Imported by Dixie Gun Works.

Price: **$1,095.00**
Price: Kit **$995.00**

PEDERRSOLI JAEGER RIFLE

Caliber: .54. Barrel: 27.5 in. octagon, 1:24 in. twist. Weight: 8.25 lbs. Length: 43.5 in. overall. Stock: American walnut; sliding wooden patchbox on butt. Sights: Notch rear, blade front. Features: Flintlock or percussion. Conversion kits available, and recommended converting percussion guns to flintlocks using kit LO1102 at $209.00. Browned steel furniture. Made by Pedersoli. Imported by Dixie Gun Works.

Price: Percussion **$1,350.00**
Price: Flint **$1,450.00**
Price: Percussion, kit **$1,075.00**
Price: Flint, kit **$1,100.00**

PEDERSOLI KENTUCKY RIFLE

Caliber: .32, .45 and .50. Barrel: 35.5 in. octagonal. Weight: 7.5 (.50 cal.) to 7.75 lbs. (.32 cal.) Length: 51 in. overall. Stock: European walnut, full-length stock. Sights: Notch rear, blade front. Features: Flintlock or percussion, brass patchbox, double-set triggers. Also available as kit guns for all calibers and ignition systems. Made by Pedersoli. Imported by Dixie Gun Works.

Price: Percussion, .32 .... **$750.00**
Price: Flint, .32 .... **$775.00**
Price: Percussion, .45 .... **$750.00**
Price: Flint, .45 .... **$775.00**
Price: Percussion, .50 .... **$750.00**
Price: Flint, .50 .... **$775.00**

PEDERSOLI KODIAK DOUBLE RIFLES AND COMBINATION GUN

Caliber: .50, .54 and .58. Barrel: 28.5 in.; 1:24/1:24/1:48 in. twist. Weight: 11.25/10.75/10 lbs. Stock: Straight grip European walnut. Sights: Two adjustable rear, steel ramp with brass bead front. Features: Percussion ignition, double triggers, sling swivels. A .72-caliber express rifle and a .50-caliber/12-gauge shotgun combination gun are also available. Blued steel furniture. Stainless steel nipple. Made by Pedersoli. Imported by Dixie Gun Works and some models by Cabela's and others.

Price: Rifle 50X50 .... **$1,525.00**
Price: Rifle 54X54 .... **$1,525.00**
Price: Rifle 58X58 .... **$1,525.00**
Price: Combo 50X12 gauge **$1,350.00**
Price: Express Rifle .72 Cal **$1,550.00**

PEDERSOLI MAGNUM PERCUSSION SHOTGUN & COACH GUN

Gauge: 10, 12, 20 Barrel: Chrome-lined blued barrels, 25.5 in. Imp. Cyl. and Mod. Weight: 7.25, 7, 6.75 lbs. Length: 45 in. overall. Stock: Hand-checkered walnut, 14-in. pull. Features: Double triggers, light hand engraving, case-hardened locks, sling swivels. Made by Pedersoli. From Dixie Gun Works, others.

Price: 10-ga. **$1,250.00**
Price: 10-ga. Kit **$975.00**
Price: 12-ga. **$1,175.00**
Price: 12-ga. Kit **$875.00**
Price: 12-ga. Coach gun, CylXCyl **$1,150.00**
Price: 20-ga. **$1,175.00**

PEDERSOLI MORTIMER RIFLE & SHOTGUN

Caliber: .54, 12 gauge. Barrel: 36 in., 1:66 in. twist, and cylinder bore. Weight: 10 lbs. rifle, 9 lbs. shotgun. Length: 52.25 in. Stock: Halfstock walnut. Sights: Blued steel rear with flip-up leaf, blade front. Features: Percussion and flint ignition. Blued steel furniture. Single trigger. Lock with hammer safety and "waterproof pan" marked Mortimer. A percussion .45-caliber target version

of this gun is available with a peep sight on the wrist, and a percussion shotgun version is also offered. Made by Pedersoli. Imported by Dixie Gun Works.

Price: Flint Rifle **$1,575.00**
Price: Flint Shotgun **$1,525.00**

PEDERSOLI OLD ENGLISH SHOTGUN

Gauge: 12 Barrels: Browned, 28.5 in. Cyl. and Mod. Weight: 7.5 lbs. Length: 45 in. overall. Stock: Hand-checkered American maple, cap box, 14-in. pull. Features: Double triggers, light hand engraving on lock, cap box and tang, swivel studs for sling attachment. Made by Pedersoli. From Dixie Gun Works, others.

Price: **$1,750.00**

PEDERSOLI ROCKY MOUNTAIN & MISSOURI RIVER HAWKEN RIFLES

Caliber: .54 Rocky Mountain, .45 and .50 in Missouri River. Barrel: 34.75 in. octagonal with hooked breech; Rocky Mountain 1:65 in. twist; Missouri River 1:47 twist in .45 cal., and 1:24 twist in .50 cal. Weight: 10 lbs. Length: 52 in. overall. Stock: Maple or walnut, halfstock. Sights: Rear buckhorn with push elevator, silver blade front. Features: Available in Percussion, with brass furniture and double triggers. Made by Pedersoli. Imported by Dixie Gun Works and others.

Price: Rocky Mountain, Maple **$1,395.00**
Price: Rocky Mountain, Walnut **$1,195.00**
Price: Missouri River, .50 Walnut **$1,275.00**
Price: Missouri River, .45 Walnut **$1,275.00**

PEDERSOLI PENNSYLVANIA RIFLE

Caliber: .32, .45 and .50. Barrel: 41.5 in. browned, octagonal, 1:48 in. twist. Weight: 8.25 lbs. Length: 56 in. overall. Stock: American walnut. Sights: Rear semi-buckhorn with push elevator, steel blade front. Features: Available in flint or percussion, with brass furniture, and double triggers. Also available as a kit. Made by Pedersoli. Imported by Dixie Gun Works and others.

Price: Flint .32 .... **$950.00**
Price: Percussion .32 .... **$900.00**
Price: Flint .45 .... **$950.00**
Price: Percussion .45 .... **$900.00**
Price: Flint .50 .... **$950.00**
Price: Percussion .50 .... **$900.00**
Price: Flint Kit .32 .... **$750.00**
Price: Percussion kit .32 .... **$695.00**
Price: Flint kit .45 .... **$750.00**
Price: Percussion kit .45 .... **$695.00**
Price: Flint kit .50 .... **$750.00**
Price: Percussion kit .50 .... **$695.00**

PEDERSOLI SHARPS NEW MODEL 1859 MILITARY RIFLE AND CARBINE

Caliber: .54. Barrel: 30 in., 6-groove, 1:48 in. twist. Weight: 9 lbs. Length: 45.5 in. overall. Stock: Oiled walnut. Sights: Blade front, ladder-style rear. Features: Blued barrel, color case-hardened barrelbands, receiver, hammer, nose cap, lever, patchbox cover and buttplate. Introduced in 1995. Rifle made by Pedersoli. Rifle imported from Italy by Dixie Gun Works and others.

Price: Rifle **$1,650.00**
Price: Carbine (22-in. barrel) **$1,400.00**

PEDERSOLI SHARPS MODEL 1863 SPORTING RIFLE

Caliber: .45. Barrel: 32 in., octagon, 6-groove, 1:18 in. twist. Weight: 10.75 lbs. Length: 49 in. overall. Stock: Oiled walnut. Sights: Silver blade front, flip-up rear. Features: Browned octagon barrel, color case-hardened receiver, hammer and buttplate. Rifle made by Pedersoli. Imported by Dixie Gun Works and others.

Price: Rifle **$1,500.00**

PEDERSOLI SHARPS CONFEDERATE CARBINE

Caliber: .54. Barrel: 22 in., 6-groove, 1:48 in. twist. Weight: 8 lbs. Length: 39 in. overall. Stock: Oiled walnut. Sights: Blade front, dovetailed rear. Features: Browned barrel, color case-hardened receiver, hammer, and lever. Brass buttplate and barrel bands. Rifle made by Pedersoli. Imported by Dixie Gun Works and others.

Price: Carbine **$1,395.00**

PEDERSOLI TRADITIONAL HAWKEN TARGET RIFLE

Caliber: .50 and .54. Barrel: 29.5 in. octagonal, 1:48 in. twist. Weight: 9 or 8.5 lbs. Length: 45.5 in. overall. Stock: European walnut, halfstock. Sights: Rear click adjustable for windage and elevation, blade front. Features: Percussion and flintlock, brass patchbox, double-set triggers, one barrel key. Flint gun available for left-handed shooters. Both flint and percussion guns available as kit guns. Made by Pedersoli. Imported by Dixie Gun Works.
Price: Percussion, .50 .... **$650.00**
Price: Percussion, .54 .... **$650.00**
Price: Flint, .50 .... **$725.00**
Price: Flint, .54 .... **$725.00**

PEDERSOLI TRYON RIFLE

Caliber: .50. Barrel: 32 in. octagonal, 1:48 in. twist. Weight: 9.5 lbs. Length: 49 in. overall. Stock: European walnut, halfstock. Sights: Elevation-adjustable rear with stair-step notches, blade front. Features: Percussion, brass patchbox, double-set triggers, two barrel keys. Made by Pedersoli. Imported by Dixie Gun Works.
Price: Percussion **$1,100.00**

PEDERSOLI VOLUNTEER RIFLE

Caliber: .451. Barrel: 33 in., round interior bore 1:21 in. twist. Weight: 9.5 lbs. Length: 49 in. Stock: Oiled Grade 1 American walnut. Sights: Blade front, ladder-style rear. Features: Checkered stock wrist and fore-end. Blued barrel, steel ramrod, bone charcoal case-hardened receiver and hammer. Designed for .451 conical bullets. Compare to hexagonal-bored Whitworth Rifle below. Hand-fitted and finished.
Price: **$1,295.00**

PEDERSOLI WHITWORTH RIFLE

Caliber: .451. Barrel: 36 in., hexagonal interior bore 1:20 in. twist. Weight: 9.6 lbs. Length: 52.5 in. Stock: Oiled Grade 1 American walnut. Sights: Blade front, ladder-style rear. Features: Checkered stock wrist and fore-end. Blued barrel, steel ramrod, bone charcoal case-hardened receiver and hammer. Designed for .451 conical hexagonal bullet. Compare to round-bored Volunteer Rifle above. Hand-fitted to original specifications using original Enfield arsenal gauges.
Price: **$1,750.00**

PEDERSOLI ZOUAVE RIFLE

Caliber: .58 percussion. Barrel: 33 inches. Weight: 9.5 lbs. Length: 49 inches. Stock: European walnut. Sights: Blade front, three-leaf military rear. Features: Percussion musket-cap ignition. One-piece solid barrel and bolster. Brass-plated patchbox. Made in Italy by Pedersoli. Imported by Dixie Gun Works, others.
Price: **$975.00**

REMINGTON MODEL 700 ULTIMATE MUZZLELOADER

Caliber: .50 percussion. Barrel: 26 in., 1:26 in. twist, satin stainless steel, fluted. Length: 47 in. Stock: Bell & Carlson black synthetic. Sights: None on synthetic-stocked model. Ramrod: Stainless steel. Weight: 8.5 lbs. Features: Remington single shot Model 700 bolt action, re-primable cartridge-case ignition using Remington Magnum Large Rifle Primer, sling studs.
Price: **$1,015.00**

TRADITIONS BUCKSTALKER XT

Caliber: .50. Barrel: 24 in. Twist rate: 1:28 in. Ignition: 209 primer. Features: Elite XT™ Trigger System, Chromoly steel, Premium CeraKote or Blued finish, Accelerator Breech Plug™, Dual Safety System, Speed Load System, etc. Variants include a G2 Vista camo or black stock, various finish options, and scoped and non-scoped versions.
Price: .... **$269.00–$469.00**

TRADITIONS BUCKSTALKER XT NORTHWEST MAGNUM

Caliber: 50. Barrel: 24 in. 1:28 in. twist, CeraKote finish barrel and action.

Overall length: 40 in. Drilled and tapped for a scope. Weight: 6 lbs. Features: Chromoly tapered, fluted barrel, Musket cap ignition, Elite XT Trigger System, Accelerator breech plug, Speed Load System, Dual Safety System, Quick-T Ramrod Handle, sling swivel studs, solid aluminum ramrod. Comes with sight. Available in Black/SS Cerakote.
Price: **$335.00**

TRADITIONS CROCKETT RIFLE

Caliber: .32. Barrel: 32 in., 1:48 in. twist. Weight: 6.75 lbs. Length: 49 in. overall. Stock: Beech, inletted toe plate. Sights: Blade front, fixed rear. Features: Set triggers, hardwood halfstock, brass furniture, color case-hardened lock. Percussion. Imported by Traditions.
Price: R26128101 .32-cal. Percussion, finished **$619.00**
Price: RK52628100 .32-cal. Percussion, kit................... **$549.00**

TRADITIONS HAWKEN WOODSMAN RIFLE

Caliber: .50. Barrel: 28 in. 1:48-in. twist, blued, 15/16 in. flats. Weight: 7 lbs., 11 oz. Length: 44.5 in. overall. Stock: Select hardwood. Sights: fixed blade. Features: Brass patchbox and furniture. Double-set triggers. Flint or percussion. Imported by Traditions.
Price: R2390801 .50-cal. Flintlock **$619.00**
Price: R24008 .50-cal. Percussion **$569.00**

TRADITIONS KENTUCKY DELUXE

Caliber: .50. Barrel: 33.5 in. 1:66-in. twist, blued octagon. Overall length 49 in. Stock: Select hardwood. Sights: Fixed blade. Weight: 7 lbs. Features: Double set trigger, brass patch box, available as a kit, authentic wooden ramrod.
Price: .... **$559.00–$629.00**

TRADITIONS KENTUCKY RIFLE

Caliber: .50. Barrel: 33.5 in., 7/8 in. flats, 1:66 in. twist. Weight: 7 lbs. Length: 49 in. overall. Stock: Select hardwood. Sights: Blade front, fixed rear. Features: Full-length, two-piece stock; brass furniture; color-casehardened lock. Flint or percussion. Imported by Traditions.
Price: R2010 .50-cal. Flintlock,1:66 twist **$589.00**
Price: R2020 .50-cal. Percussion, 1:66 twist...................... **$519.00**
Price: KRC52206 .50-cal. Percussion, kit........................... **$419.00**

TRADITIONS MOUNTAIN RIFLE

Caliber: .50. Barrel: 32 in., octagon with brown Cerakote finish. Stock: Select hardwoods. Sights: Primitive, adjustable rear. Weight: 8.25 lbs. Features: Available in percussion or flintlock, case-hardened lock, wooden ramrod, available as a kit.
Price: .... **$569.00–$749.00**

TRADITIONS NITROFIRE

Caliber: .50. Barrel: 26 in., 1:24 in. VAPR twist, CeraKote finish barrel and action. Overall length: 42 in. Drilled and taped for scope and for sights. Weight: 6.6 lbs. (rifle only). Uses Federal Premium Firestick System, Chromoly steel tapered and fluted barrel, Elite XT Trigger system, Speed Load System, available scoped or non-scoped in various finishes.
Price: .... **$569.00–$729.00**

TRADITIONS NITROFIRE PRO SERIES

Caliber: .50, 26 in. chromoly steel barrel, 1:24 in. VAPR Twist. Overall Length:

Prices given are believed to be accurate at time of publication however, many factors affect retail pricing so exact prices are not possible.

79TH EDITION, 2025 ✛ **563**

42 in. Drilled and tapped for a scope. Weight: 7.1 lbs. (gun only). Features: Adjustable cheekpiece, adjustable length of pull, threaded barrel, uses Federal Premium Firestick System, tapered and fluted barrel, Elite XT Trigger system, Speed Load System, available scoped or non-scoped in various finishes. Some models come with a one-piece base.
Price: ....**$639.00–$729.00**

TRADITIONS PA PELLET ULTRALIGHT
Caliber: .50. Barrel: 26 in., chrome-moly steel, 1:28 in. twist., Cerakote. Weight: 7 lbs. Length: 45 in. Stock options: synthetic in black or various camo patters, select hardwoods. Fiber-optic sights. Features: Improved harden frizzen, single or double set trigger options, removable Accelerator Breech Plug, left-hand model available.
Price: .... **$519.00–$699.00**

TRADITIONS DEERHUNTER
Caliber: .50, 24-in. octagonal barrel, 1:48-in. twist. Overall Length: 40 in. Percussion models drilled and tapped for a scope. Weight: 6 lbs. (gun only). Features: lightweight, fiber-optic sights, crisp hunting trigger, upgraded rubber buttpad, blued finish. Available in select hardwood or black synthetic stock; percussion or flintlock ignition.
Price: .... **$325.00–$479.00**

TRADITIONS PENNSYLVANIA RIFLE
Caliber: .50. Barrel: 33.5 in., 7/8 in. flats, 1:66 in. twist, octagon. Weight: 7 lbs. Length: 49 in. overall. Stock: Walnut. Sights: Blade front, adjustable rear. Features: Single-piece walnut stock, brass patchbox and ornamentation. Double-set triggers. Flint or percussion. Imported by Traditions.
Price: R2090C .50-cal. Flintlock **$999.00**
Price: R2100C .50-cal. Percussion **$949.00**

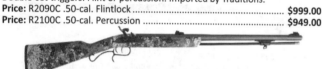

TRADITIONS SHEDHORN SIDELOCK MUZZLELOADERS
Caliber: .50. Barrel: 26 in. 1:28 in. twist, CeraKote finish barrel and action. Overall length: 45 in. Drilled and tapped for a scope. Weight: 6 lbs. Features: Chromoly tapered, fluted barrel, Musket cap ignition, fires loose blackpowder or Pyrodex, double set trigger system, Accelerator breech plug, sling swivel studs, solid aluminum ramrod. Drilled and tapped for scope. Available in camo, wood or black and various color finishes.
Price: .... **$479.00–$589.00**

TRADITIONS PURSUIT XT .50 CALIBER
Caliber: 50. Barrel: 26 in. 1:24" VAPR Twist, CeraKote finish barrel and action. Overall length: 42 in. Drilled and tapped for a scope. Weight: 5.75 lbs (rifle only). Features: Chromoly steel tapered and fluted barrel, Elite XT trigger system, Accelerator Breech Plug, Dual Safety System, Speed Load System. Available scoped or non-scoped in various camo patterns and CeraKote finishes
Price: ....**$399.00–$549.00**

TRADITIONS PURSUIT XT NORTHWEST MAGNUM
Caliber: .50. Barrel: 26 or 30 in. 1:24 in. VAPR Twist, CeraKote finish barrel and action. Overall length: 42 or 46 in. Drilled and tapped for a scope. Weight: 5.75 or 6.1 lbs (rifle only). Features: Chromoly tapered, fluted barrel, Musket cap ignition, Elite XT trigger system, Accelerator Breech Plug, wider forend for better grip, LT-1 alloy frame, Speed Load System, Dual Safety System, Quick-T Ramrod Handle, sling swivel studs, solid aluminum ramrod. Comes with sights—available in various finishes.
Price: ....**$419.00–$479.00**

TRADITIONS PURSUIT XT PRO SERIES
Caliber: .50 or .45, 26 in. chromoly steel barrel, 1:24 in. (or 1:20 in. .45-cal. models) VAPR Twist. Overall Length: 42 in. Drilled and tapped for a scope. Weight: 6.5 lbs. (gun only). Features: Adjustable cheekpiece, adjustable length of pull, threaded barrel, tapered and fluted barrel, Elite XT trigger system, Accelerator Breech Plug, Dual Safety System, Speed Load System. Available scoped or non-scoped in various finishes.
Price: ....**$469.00–$619.00**

TRADITIONS VORTEK STRIKERFIRE .50 CALIBER
Caliber: .50. Barrel: 28 or 30 in. VAPR 1:24 in. VAPR twist, CeraKote finish barrel and action. Overall length: 44 or 46 in. Drilled and tapped for a scope. Weight: 6-6.25 lbs (rifle only). Features: Chromoly tapered, fluted barrel, Strikerfire System and button, recessed De-Cocking button, TAC2 Trigger System, Accelerator Breech Plug, recoil-reducing buttstock and buttpad, LT-1 alloy frame, Hogue Comfort-Grip Overmolding, Speed Load System, Dual Safety System, Quick-T Ramrod Handle, sling swivel studs, 209 shotgun primer ignition, solid aluminum ramrod. Available scoped or non-scoped, various camo patterns and finishes.
Price: ....**$459.00–$638.00**

TRADITIONS VORTEK STRIKERFIRE .45 CALIBER
Caliber: .45. Barrel: 28 or 30 in. 1:20 in. twist, CeraKote finish barrel, and action. Overall length: 44 or 46 in. Drilled and tapped for a scope. Weight: 6–6.25 lbs (rifle only). Features: Chromoly tapered, fluted barrel, Strikerfire System and button, recessed De-Cocking button, TAC2 Trigger System, Accelerator Breech Plug, recoil-reducing buttstock and buttpad, LT-1 alloy frame, Hogue Comfort-Grip Overmolding, Speed Load System, Dual Safety System, Quick-T Ramrod Handle, sling swivel studs, 209 shotgun primer ignition, solid aluminum ramrod. Available scoped or non-scoped, various camo patterns and finishes.
Price: ....**$459.00–$474.00**

WOODMAN ARMS PATRIOT
Caliber: .45, .50. Barrel: 24 in., nitride-coated, 416 stainless, 1:24 twist in .45, 1:28 twist in .50. Weight: 5.75 lbs. Length: 43-in. Stocks: Laminated, walnut or hydrographic dipped, synthetic black, over-molded soft-touch straight stock. Finish: Nitride black and black anodized. Features: Break-open action, hammerless cocking mechanism, match-grade patented trigger assembly, speed load system, recoil pad. Sights: Picatinny rail with built-in rear and 1-inch or 30 mm scope mounts, red fiber-optic front bead.
Price: Patriot .45 or .50-cal...**$899.00**

UBERTI 1858 NEW ARMY REMINGTON TARGET CARBINE REVOLVER
Caliber: .44, 6-shot. Barrel: Tapered octagon, 18 in. Weight: 70.4 oz. Length: Standard 35.3 in. Stock: Walnut. Sights: Standard blade front, adjustable rear. Features: Replica of Remington's revolving rifle of 1866. Made by Uberti. Imported by Uberti USA, Cimarron F.A. Co., Taylor's and others.
Price: **$559.00**

Prices given are believed to be accurate at time of publication however, many factors affect retail pricing so exact prices are not possible.

AIRFORCE TALON P PCP AIR PISTOL

Caliber: .25. Barrel: Rifled 12.0 in. Weight: 4.3 lbs. Length: 27.75–32.25 in. Sights: None, grooved for scope. Features: Quick-detachable air tank with adjustable power. Match-grade Lothar Walther barrel, massive power output in a highly compact size, two-stage trigger, single shot, open sights optional. Velocity: 500–900 fps.
Price: $570.00

AIR VENTURI V10 MATCH AIR PISTOL

Caliber: .177 pellets. Barrel: Rifled. Weight: 1.95 lbs. Length: 12.6 in. Power: Single-stroke pneumatic. Sights: Front post, fully adjustable rear blade. Features: 10m competition class pistol, fully adjustable trigger, 1.5-lb. trigger pull. Velocity: 400 fps.
Price: $300.00

ASG 1911 US-C BLOWBACK CO_2 PISTOL

Caliber: .177 BBs. Barrel: Smoothbore, 4.5 in. Weight: 1.93 lbs. Length: 8.7 in. Power: CO_2. Sights: Fixed. Features: Blowback semi-automatic action, single CO_2 cylinder, 18-round magazine, functional thumb and grip safeties, metal frame and slide, polymer grip inserts. Velocity: 420 fps.
Price: $130.00

ASG STI DUTY ONE CO_2 BB PISTOL

Caliber: .177 steel BBs. Barrel: Smoothbore Weight: 1.82 lbs. Length: 8.66 in. Power: CO_2. Sights: Fixed. Features: Blowback, accessory rail, and metal slide. Velocity: 383 fps.
Price: $120.00

BARRA BLACK OPS CO_2 REVOLVER

Caliber: .177 BBs. Barrel: Smoothbore, 2.5 in. Weight: 1.92 lbs. Length: 7.25 in. Power: CO_2. Sights: Fixed front, adjustable rear. Features: 6-round cylinder with realistic shells, Weaver-style scope rail, operates either double or single action, working ejector rod, black metal frame with black plastic grips, available with 2.5-in. barrel and chrome finish. Velocity: 435 fps.
Price: $85.00

BEEMAN 2004 (P17) PISTOL

Caliber: .177 pellet. Barrel: Rifled. Weight: 1.7 lbs. Length: 9.25 in. Power: Single-stroke pneumatic. Sights: Adjustable fiber-optic. Features: Polymer frame, recoilless. Velocity: 410 fps.
Price: $65.00

BEEMAN 2027 PCP PISTOL

Caliber: .177 Barrel: Rifled. Weight: 1.7 lbs. Length: 9.25 in. Power: Precharged pneumatic. Sights: Adjustable open sights. Features: Textured

grip, 12-round magazine, adjustable velocity, 60 shots per fill (at 600 fps), adjustable trigger. Velocity: 600 fps.
Price: $190.00

BENJAMIN MARAUDER PCP PISTOL

Caliber: .22 Barrel: Rifled. Weight: 2.7-3 lbs. Length: Pistol length 18 in./ Carbine length 29.75 in. Power: Precharged pneumatic Sights: None. Grooved for optics. Features: Multi-shot (eight-round rotary magazine), bolt action, shrouded steel barrel, two-stage adjustable trigger, includes both pistol grips and a carbine stock and is built in America. Velocity: 700 fps.
Price: $430.00

BENJAMIN MARAUDER WOODS WALKER PCP PISTOL

Caliber: .22 Barrel: Rifled. Weight: 2.7 lbs. Length: Pistol length 18 in./ Carbine length 29.75 in. Power: Precharged pneumatic Sights: Includes CenterPoint Multi-TAC Quick Aim Sight. Features: Multi-shot (8-round rotary magazine) bolt action, shrouded steel barrel, two-stage adjustable trigger, includes both pistol grips and a carbine stock and is built in America. Velocity: 700 fps.
Price: $510.00

BENJAMIN TRAIL MARK II NP AIR PISTOL

Caliber: .177 pellets. Barrel: Rifled. Weight: 3.43 lbs. Length: 16 in. Power: Single cock, nitro piston. Sights: Fiber-optic front, fully adjustable rear. Features: Grooved for scope, Velocity: To 625 fps.
Price: $127.00

BERETTA APX BLOWBACK CO_2 PISTOL

Caliber: .177 steel BBs. Barrel: Smoothbore. Weight: 1.47 lbs. Length: 7.48 in. Power: CO_2. Sights: Fixed. Features: Highly accurate replica action pistol, 19-shot capacity, front accessory rail, metal and ABS plastic construction. Velocity: 400 fps.
Price: $75.00

BERETTA M84FS CO_2 PISTOL

Caliber: .177 steel BBs. Barrel: Smoothbore Weight: 1.4 lbs. Length: 7 in. Power: CO_2. Sights: Fixed. Features: Highly realistic replica action pistol, blowback operation, full metal construction. Velocity: To 360 fps.
Price: $110.00

Prices given are believed to be accurate at time of publication however, many factors affect retail pricing so exact prices are not possible.

79TH EDITION, 2025 ✛ 565

BERETTA PX4 STORM CO₂ PISTOL
Caliber: .177 pellet /.177 steel BBs. Barrel: Rifled Weight: 1.6 lbs. Length: 7.6 in. Power: CO_2. Sights: Blade front sight and fixed rear sight. Features: Semi-automatic, 16-shot capacity with a maximum of 40 shots per fill, dual ammo capable. Velocity: To 380 fps.
Price: $120.00

BERETTA ELITE II CO₂ PISTOL
Caliber: .177 steel BBs. Barrel: Smoothbore Weight: 1.5 lbs. Length: 8.5 in. Power: CO_2. Sights: Blade front sight and fixed rear sight. Features: Semi-automatic, 19-shot capacity. Velocity: Up to 410 fps.
Price: $60.00

BERETTA M9A3 FULL AUTO BB PISTOL
Caliber: .177 steel BBs. Barrel: Smoothbore Weight: NA. Length: NA. Power: CO_2. Sights: Blade front sight and fixed rear sight. Features: Can operate as semi-automatic or fully automatic, full size 18-shot magazine, blowback slide, single/double action, ambidextrous safety. Velocity: To 380 fps.
Price: $160.00

BERETTA 92A1 CO₂ FULL AUTO BB PISTOL
Caliber: .177 steel BBs. Barrel: Smoothbore Weight: 2.4 lbs. Length: 8.5 in. Power: CO_2. Sights: Fixed. Features: Highly realistic replica action pistol, 18-shot semi-automatic, full metal construction, selectable fire semi-automatic and full-automatic. Velocity: To 330 fps.
Price: $170.00

BERETTA 92FS CO₂ PELLET GUN
Caliber: .177 pellets. Barrel: Rifled Weight: 2.75 lbs. Length: 8.0 in. Power: CO_2. Sights: Fixed front sight, rear adjustable for windage. Features: Highly realistic replica-action pistol, eight-shot semi-automatic, full metal construction, available in various finishes and grips. Velocity: To 425 fps.
Price: .... $240.00–$334.00

BERSA THUNDER 9 PRO BB PISTOL
Caliber: .177 steel BBs. Barrel: Smoothbore Weight: 1.17 lbs. Length: 7.56 in. Power: CO_2. Sights: Fixed, 3 white dot system. Features: Highly realistic replica action pistol, 19-shot semi-automatic, composite/synthetic construction Velocity: To 400 fps.
Price: $55.00

BERSA BP9CC BLOWBACK CO₂ PISTOL
Caliber: .177 steel BBs. Barrel: Smoothbore. Weight: 1.35 lbs. Length: 6.61 in. Power: CO_2. Sights: Fixed 3-dot system. Features: Blowback, metal slide, weaver accessory rail, is also available in a nonblowback version. Velocity: 350 fps.
Price: $100.00

BROCOCK ATOMIC XR PCP PISTOL
Calibers: .177, .22, .25. Barrel: Rifled, match grade. Weight: 4 lbs. Length: 14 in. Power: Precharged pneumatic. Sights: None, 11mm rail. Features: Optional Picatinny top and side rail, side lever action, single-shot tray or 11-shot magazine, weight and position adjustable trigger, shrouded barrel with adaptor for second-stage silencer, side power adjustor. Up to 30–33 shots and 16–18 ft-lbs of energy at full power depending on caliber. Velocities: Adjustable.
Price: $1,599.00

BROWNING BUCK MARK URX

BROWNING BUCK MARK AIR PISTOL
Caliber: .177 pellets. Barrel: Rifled Weight: 1.5 lbs. Length: 12.0 in. Power: Single cock, spring-piston. Sights: Front ramp sight, fully adjustable rear notch sight. Features: Weaver rail for scope mounting, light cocking force. Velocity: 360 fps.
Price: $56.00

CHIAPPA FAS 6004 PNEUMATIC PISTOL
Caliber: .177 pellets. Barrel: Rifled. Weight: 2 lbs. Length: 11.0 in. Power: Single stroke pneumatic. Sights: Fully adjustable target rear sight. Features: Walnut ambidextrous grip, fully adjustable trigger. Also available with an adjustable target grip. Velocity: 330 fps.
Price: .... $443.00–$569.00

COBRAY INGRAM M11 CO₂ BB SUBMACHINE GUN
Caliber: .177 BBs. Barrel: Smoothbore. Weight: 1.2 lbs. Length: 10.0 in. Power: CO₂. Sights: Fixed sights. Features: Semi-automatic, 39-shot capacity, folding metal stock. Velocity: 394 fps.
Price: $90.00

COLT DEFENDER BB PISTOL
Caliber: .177 steel BBs. Barrel: Smoothbore Weight: 1.6 lbs. Length: 6.75 in. Power: CO₂. Sights: Fixed with blade ramp front sight. Features: Semi-automatic, 16-shot capacity, all metal construction, realistic weight and feel. Velocity: 410 fps.
Price: $65.00

COLT 1911 A1 CO₂ PELLET PISTOL
Caliber: .177 pellets. Barrel: Rifled Weight: 2.4 lbs. Length: 9.0 in. Power: CO₂. Sights: Blade ramp front sight and adjustable rear sight. Features: Semi-automatic, 8-shot capacity, all metal construction, realistic weight and feel. Velocity: 425 fps.
Price: $260.00

COLT COMMANDER CO₂ PISTOL
Caliber: .177 steel BBs. Barrel: Smoothbore. Weight: 2.1 lbs. Length: 8.5 in. Power: CO₂. Sights: Blade front sight and fixed rear sight. Features: Semi-automatic, blowback action, 18-shot capacity, highly realistic replica pistol. Velocity: 325 fps.
Price: $130.00

CROSMAN MK45 BB PISTOL
Caliber: .177 steel BBs. Barrel: Smoothbore. Weight: 1.1 lbs. Length: 7.5 in. Power: CO₂. Sights: Fixed. Features: 20-round drop-out magazine, accessory rail. Velocity: 480 fps.
Price: $49.00

COLT M45 CQBP CO₂ PISTOL
Caliber: .177 steel BBs. Barrel: Smoothbore. Weight: 1.75 lbs. Length: 8.75 in. Power: CO₂. Sights: Fixed three-dot sights, rear sight adjustable for windage. Features: Blowback action, 19-round drop-free magazine, desert tan steel slide, polymer frame, under-barrel Picatinny rail. Velocity: 400 fps.

Price: $89.00

COLT PYTHON CO₂ PISTOL
Caliber: .177 steel BBs. Barrel: Smoothbore Weight: 1.1 lbs. Length: 11.5 in. Power: CO₂. Sights: Fixed front, adjustable rear. Features: Includes three 10-round removable clips, double/single action. Velocity: 410 fps.
Price: $50.00

COLT SAA CO₂ PELLET REVOLVER
Caliber: .177 pellets. Barrel: Rifled. Weight: 2.1 lbs. Length: 11 in. Power: CO₂. Sights: Blade front sight and fixed rear sight. Features: Full metal revolver with manual safety, realistic loading, six individual shells, highly accurate, full metal replica pistol, multiple finishes and grips available. Velocity: 380 fps.
Price: $150.00

JOHN WAYNE "DUKE" COLT SINGLE ACTION ARMY CO₂ PELLET REVOLVER
Caliber: .177 steel BBs. Barrel: Smoothbore. Weight: 2.1 lbs. Length: 11 in. Power: CO₂. Sights: Blade front sight and fixed rear sight. Features: Officially licensed "John Wayne Duke" imagery and signature, full metal revolver with manual safety, realistic loading, six individual shells, highly accurate, full metal replica pistol, multiple finishes and grips available. Velocity: 380 fps.
Price: $167.00

COMETA INDIAN AIR PISTOL
Caliber: .177 pellets. Barrel: Rifled. Weight: 2.43 lbs. Length: 10.43 in. Power: Spring Powered. Sights: Blade front sight and adjustable rear sight. Features: Single shot, cold hammer-forged barrel, textured grips. Velocity: 492 fps.
Price: .... $199.00–$219.00

CROSMAN 2240 CO₂ PISTOL
Caliber: .22. Barrel: Rifled. Weight: 1.8 lbs. Length: 11.13 in. Power: CO₂. Sights: Blade front, rear adjustable. Features: Single-shot bolt action, ambidextrous grip, all metal construction. Velocity: 460 fps.
Price: $86.00

CROSMAN 2300S TARGET PISTOL
Caliber: .177 pellets. Barrel: Rifled. Weight: 2.66 lbs. Length: 16 in. Power: CO₂. Sights: Front fixed sight and Williams notched rear sight. Features: Meets IHMSA rules for Production Class Silhouette Competitions. Lothar Walter match-grade barrel, adjustable trigger, adjustable hammer, stainless steel bolt, 60 shots per CO₂ cartridge. Velocity: 520 fps.
Price: $333.00

Prices given are believed to be accurate at time of publication however, many factors affect retail pricing so exact prices are not possible.

79TH EDITION, 2025 ⬥ **567**

CROSMAN 2300T CO₂ PISTOL

Caliber: .177 pellets. Barrel: Rifled. Weight: 2.66 lbs. Length: 13.25 in. Power: CO₂. Sights: fixed front sight and LPA rear sight. Features: Single-shot, bolt action, adjustable trigger, designed for shooting clubs and organizations that teach pistol shooting and capable of firing 40 shots per CO₂ cartridge. Velocity: 420 fps.
Price: **$235.00**

CROSMAN 1701P SILHOUETTE PCP AIR PISTOL

Caliber: .177 pellets. Barrel: Rifled Lothar Walther Match. Weight: 2.5 lbs. Length: 14.75 in. Power: precharged pneumatic. Sights: fixed front sight rear sight not included. Features: Adjustable trigger, designed for shooting silhouette competition, 50 shots per fill. Velocity: 450 fps.
Price: **$510.00**

CROSMAN 1720T PCP TARGET PISTOL

Caliber: .177 pellets. Barrel: Rifled Lothar Walther Match. Weight: 2.96 lbs. Length: 18.00 in. Power: Precharged Pneumatic. Sights: Not included. Features: Adjustable trigger, designed for shooting silhouettes, fully shrouded barrel, 50 shots per fill. Velocity: 750 fps.
Price: **$522.00**

CROSMAN SNR357 BB CO₂ REVOLVER

Caliber: .177 steel BBs/.177 pellets. Barrel: Smoothbore, 2.5 in. Weight: 1.9 lbs. Length: 6.75 in. Power: CO₂. Sights: Fixed front, adjustable rear sight. Features: six-shot capacity, full metal construction, swing-out cylinder, double or single action, comes with reusable shells. Velocity: Up to 500 fps with alloy pellets.
Price: **$101.00**

CROSMAN SR357 BB CO₂ REVOLVER

Caliber: .177 steel BBs. Barrel: Smoothbore Weight: 2.00 lbs. Length: 11.73 in. Power: CO₂. Sights: Adjustable rear sight, fixed front blade. Features: Full metal revolver in "stainless steel" finish. Swing-out cylinder. Double or single action. Comes with shells for BBs. Velocity: Up to 450 fps.
Price: **$156.00**

CROSMAN FULL AUTO A4P PISTOL

Caliber: .177 steel BBs. Barrel: Smoothbore. Weight: 6 lbs. Length: 21.2 in. Power: CO₂. Sights: None, comes with red-dot sight. Features: Tactical-style AR full-/semi-auto pistol, blowback action, AR-compatible pistol grip, quad rail forearm for accessory mounting, 25-round removable magazine, uses two 12-gram CO₂ cylinders. Velocity: Up to 400 fps.
Price: **$236.00**

CROSMAN FULL AUTO P1 PISTOL

Caliber: .177 steel BBs. Barrel: Smoothbore Weight: 2.5 lbs. Length: 8.5 in. Power: CO₂. Sights: Fixed, rail-mounted laser included. Features: Full-/semi-auto pistol, blowback action, metal frame and slide, single/double action, 20-round removable magazine, Picatinny rail. Velocity: 400 fps.
Price: **$211.00**

CROSMAN FORTIFY CO₂ REVOLVER

Caliber: .177 BB. Barrel: Smoothbore. Weight: 1 lb. Length: 10.5 in. Power: CO₂. Sights: Fixed. Features: 18 BB capacity, functional hammer, crossbolt safety. Velocity: 420 fps.
Price: **$60.00**

CROSMAN TRIPLE THREAT CO₂ REVOLVER

Caliber: .177 steel BBs/.177 pellets. Barrel: Rifled. Weight: Variable. Length: Variable. Power: CO₂. Sights: Adjustable rear sight. Features: Comes with three barrels (3, 6, and 8 in.) and six-shot BB clip and 10-shot .177 lead pellet clip, single/double action, diecast full metal frame. Velocity: Up to 425 fps. with steel BBs.
Price: **$123.00**

CROSMAN C11 CO₂ BB GUN

Caliber: .177 steel BBs. Barrel: Smoothbore Weight: 1.4 lbs. Length: 7.0 in. Power: CO₂. Sights: Fixed. Features: Compact semi-automatic BB pistol, front accessory rail. Velocity: 480 fps.
Price: **$61.00**

CROSMAN CM9B MAKO BB PISTOL

Caliber: .177 BBs. Barrel: Smoothbore. Weight: 1.7 lbs. Length: 8.6 in. Power: CO₂. Sights: Fiber optic. Blowback action, tricolor, accessory rail. Velocity: 425 fps.
Price: **$73.00**

CROSMAN PFM16 FULL METAL CO₂ BB PISTOL

Caliber: .177 steel BBs. Barrel: Smoothbore Weight: 1.6 lbs. Length: 6.5 in. Power: CO₂. Sights: Fixed. Features: Compact semi-automatic BB pistol, full metal construction, 20-shot capacity, kit includes: CO₂, BBs, and holster. Velocity: 400 fps.
Price: **$61.00**

CROSMAN PFAM9B FULL AUTO PISTOL

Caliber: .177 steel BBs. Barrel: Smoothbore Weight: 1.6 lbs. Length: 6.5 in. Power: CO₂. Sights: Fixed. Features: Full metal construction, full-auto, blowback slide, 20-shot capacity. Velocity: 400 fps.
Price: **$159.00**

CROSMAN AMERICAN CLASSIC P1377/1322 AIR PISTOL

Caliber: .177 or .22. Barrel: Rifled Weight: 2 lbs. Length: 13.63 in. Power: Multi-pump pneumatic. Sights: front blade and ramp, adjustable rear. Features: Single shot, bolt action, available with brown (.177 only) or black grips, pistol grip shoulder stock available separately. Velocities: To 695 fps (.177); to 460 fps (.22).
Price: .... **$80.00–$98.00**

CROSMAN VIGILANTE CO₂ REVOLVER

Caliber: .177 steel BBs/.177 pellets. Barrel: Rifled. Weight: 2 lbs. Length: 11.38 in. Power: CO₂. Sights: Blade front, rear adjustable. Features: Single- and double-action revolver (10-shot pellet/six-shot BBs) synthetic frame and finger-molded grip design. Velocity: 465 fps.
Price: **$59.00**

CROSMAN 1911 CO₂ BB PISTOL

Caliber: .177 steel BBs. Barrel: Smoothbore. Weight: 0.88 lbs. Length: 7.9 in. Power: CO₂. Sights: Fixed. Features: 20-round capacity, double-action-only, Picatinny under-rail. Velocity: 480 fps.
Price: **$61.00**

CZ P-09 DUTY CO₂ PISTOL

Caliber: .177 BBs/.177 flat-head pellets. Barrel: Rifled. Weight: 1.6 lbs. Length: 8.2 in. Power: CO₂. Sights: Three-dot fixed sights. Features: Blowback action, manual safety, double-action-only trigger, 16-round capacity in a 2x8 shot stick magazine, Weaver-style accessory rail, threaded muzzle, blue or two-tone finish, ambidextrous safety with decocker. Velocity: 492 fps.
Price: **$123.00**

CZ-75 CO₂ PISTOL

Caliber: .177 BBs. Barrel: Smooth. Weight: 2.1 lbs. Length: 8.2 in. Power: CO₂. Sights: Fixed sights. Features: Blowback action, manual safety, full metal construction, single-action trigger, removable 17-round BB magazine, Weaver-style accessory rail, also available as a non-blowback compact version. Velocity: 312 fps.
Price: **$220.00**

CZ 75 SP-01 SHADOW CO₂ BB PISTOL

Caliber: .177 steel BBs. Barrel: Smoothbore threaded for barrel extension. Power: CO₂. Weight: 1.3 lbs. Length: 8.4 in. Sights: Fiber optics front and rear. Features: Non-blowback, double action, accessory rail, 21-round capacity, also available in a heavier-weight, blowback version. Velocity: 380 fps.
Price: **$65.00**

CZ SHADOW 2 CO₂ BB PISTOL

Caliber: .177 steel BBs. Barrel: Smoothbore. Weight: 2.7 lbs. Length: 8.5 in. Power: CO₂. Sights: Fiber optic, adjustable rear. Features: Full metal construction, adjustable travel trigger, adjustable hop up, double action, checkered grip, individual serial number, blowback, 18-round dropout magazine, uses one 12-gram CO₂ cylinder, under-barrel accessory rail, adjustable magazine release. Velocity: 285 fps.
Price: **$300.00**

CZ 75 P-07 DUTY PISTOL

Caliber: .177 steel BBs. Barrel: Smoothbore. Weight: 1.81 lbs. Length: 7.5 in. Power: CO₂. Sights: Fixed. Features: Full metal construction, accessory rail, blowback, 20-round dropout magazine, threaded barrel, blue or two-tone finish. Also available in a non-blowback, lower-priced version. Velocity: 342 fps.
Price: **$120.00**

CZ 75D COMPACT CO₂ BB PISTOL

Caliber: .177 steel BBs. Barrel: Smoothbore. Weight: 1.5 lbs. Length: 7.4 in. Power: CO₂. Sights: Adjustable rear sight and blade front sight. Features: Compact design, non-blowback action, blue or two-tone finish, accessory rail. Velocity: 380 fps.
Price: **$63.00**

Prices given are believed to be accurate at time of publication however, many factors affect retail pricing so exact prices are not possible.

79TH EDITION, 2025 ✦ **569**

DAISY POWERLINE 340 AIR PISTOL

Caliber: .177 steel BBs. Barrel: Smoothbore. Weight: 1.0 lbs. Length: 8.5 in. Power: Single cock, spring-piston. Sights: Rear sight fixed, front blade. Features: Spring-air action, 200-shot BB reservoir with a 13-shot Speed-load Clip located in the grip. Velocity: 240 fps.
Price: $30.00

DAISY POWERLINE 415 CO$_2$ BB PISTOL

Caliber: .177 steel BBs. Barrel: Smoothbore. Weight: 1.0 lbs. Length: 8.6 in. Power: CO$_2$. Sights: Front blade, Rear fixed open rear. Features: Semi-automatic 21-shot BB pistol. Velocity: 500 fps.
Price: $39.00

DAISY 426 PISTOL

Caliber: .177 steel BBs. Barrel: Smoothbore. Weight: 1 lbs. Length: 6.8 in. Power: CO$_2$. Sights: Front blade, rear fixed open. Features: Semi-automatic, eight-shot removable clip, lower accessory rail Velocity: 430 fps.
Price: $33.00

DAISY POWERLINE 5501 CO$_2$ PISTOL

Caliber: .177 steel BBs. Barrel: Smoothbore. Weight: 1.0 lbs. Length: 6.8 in. Power: CO$_2$. Sights: Blade and ramp front, fixed rear. Features: CO$_2$ semi-automatic blowback action. 15-shot clip. Velocity: 430 fps.
Price: $77.00

DAN WESSON 2.5/4/6/8 IN. REVOLVER

Caliber: .177 BBs or .177 pellets. Barrel: Smoothbore (BB version) or Rifled (Pellet version). Weights: 1.65–2.29 lbs. Lengths: 8.3–13.3 in. Power: CO$_2$. Sights: Blade front and adjustable rear sight. Features: Highly realistic replica revolver with swing out 6-shot cylinder, Weaver-style scope rail, multiple finishes and grip configurations, 6 realistic cartridges, includes a speed loader. Also available as a kit with a holster, speedloader and additional cartridges. Velocities: 318–426 fps.
Price: ....$150.00–$210.00

DAN WESSON 715 2.5/4 /6 IN. REVOLVER

Caliber: .177 BBs or .177 pellets. Barrel: Smoothbore (BB version) or Rifled (pellet version). Weights: 2.2–2.7 lbs. Lengths: 8.3–11.7 in. Power: CO$_2$. Sights: Blade front and adjustable rear. Features: Highly realistic replica

revolver, accessory rail, multiple finishes and grip configurations, six realistic cartridges, includes a speedloader. Velocities: 318–426 fps.
Price: $160.00

DAN WESSON VALOR 1911 PISTOL

Caliber: .177 pellets. Barrel: Rifled. Weight: 2.2 lbs. Length: 8.7 in. Power: CO$_2$. Sights: Non-adjustable. Features: Non-blowback, full metal construction, 12-round capacity in two six-round drum magazines. Velocities: 332 fps.
Price: $140.00

DIANA AIRBUG CO$_2$ PISTOL

Caliber: .177, .22 pellets. Barrel: Rifled, 8.3 in. Weight: 2 lbs. Length: 14 in. Power: CO$_2$. Sights: Front post, adjustable rear. Features: Hardwood, ambidextrous grip, bolt action, nine-shot (.117), seven-shot (.22), or single shot, comes with a soft-sided case. Velocities: 525 fps (.177), 460 fps (.22).
Price: $180.00

DIANA BANDIT PCP PISTOL

Caliber: .177, .22 pellets. Barrel: Rifled, 9.5 in. Weight: 2.2 lbs. Length: 20.1 in. Power: Precharged pneumatic. Sights: Front post, adjustable rear, 11mm dovetail under rear sight. Features: Hardwood, ambidextrous grip, bolt action, nine-shot (.117), seven-shot (.22), or single shot, two-stage adjustable Diana Improved Trigger (DIT), comes with a soft-sided case. Velocities: 725 fps (.177), 630 fps (.22).
Price: $250.00

DIANA LP 8 PISTOL

Caliber: .177 pellets. Barrel: Rifled. Weight: 3.20 lbs. Length: 7.00 in. Power: Spring powered. Sights: Fixed front sight with fully adjustable rear sight. Features: Powerful spring-powered air pistol, single cock delivers full power, exceptional design and build quality. Velocity: 700 fps.
Price: $350.00

EVANIX AR6-P PCP PISTOL

Caliber: .22 pellets. Barrel: Rifled, 10 in. Weight: 3.1 lbs. Length: 17.3 in. Power: Precharged pneumatic. Sights: None, 11mm dovetail rail. Features: Ambidextrous walnut target-style grips, six-shot magazine, spare mag included. Velocity: Up to 900 fps.
Price: $660.00

FEINWERKBAU P11 PICCOLO AIR PISTOL

Caliber: .177 pellets. Barrel: Rifled. Weight: 1.6 lbs. Length: 13.58 in. Power: Precharged pneumatic. Sights: Front post, fully adjustable rear blade, Features: 10m competition class pistol, meets ISSF requirements, highly adjustable match trigger, Velocity: 492 fps.
Price: $1,600.00

FEINWERKBAU P8X PCP 10-METER AIR PISTOL

Caliber: .177 pellets. Barrel: Rifled, 8.6 in. Weight: 2.09 lbs. Length: 16.33 in. Power: Precharged pneumatic. Sights: Front post, fully adjustable rear blade. Features: 10m competition class pistol with highly customizable grip system, meets ISSF requirements, highly adjustable match trigger. Also available with a shorter barrel. Velocity: 508 fps.
Price: $2,100.00

Prices given are believed to be accurate at time of publication however, many factors affect retail pricing so exact prices are not possible.

GAMO C-15 BONE COLLECTOR CO₂ PISTOL
Caliber: .177 BB/.177 pellets. Barrel: Smooth. Weight: 1.5 lbs. Length: 10 in. Power: CO₂. Sights: Fixed. Features: Blowback action, approx. 80 shots per CO₂ cylinder, single/double action, manual safety, has two side-by-side eight-shot magazines Velocity: 450 fps with PBA pellets.
Price: **$94.00**

GAMO GP-20 COMBAT CO₂ BB PISTOL
Caliber: .177 BBs. Barrel: Smooth. Weight: 1 lb. Length: 10 in. Power: CO₂. Sights: Fixed with fiber-optic rear. Features: Single/double action, manual safety, 20 BB magazine. Velocity: 400 fps.
Price: **$40.00**

GAMO P-900 IGT AIR PISTOL
Caliber: .177 pellets. Barrel: Rifled. Weight: 1.3 lbs. Length: 12.6 in. Power: Single cock, gas pistol. Sights: Fiber-optic front and fully adjustable fiber-optic rear. Features: Break-barrel single-shot, ergonomic design, rubberized grip. Velocity: 508 fps.
Price: **$84.00**

GAMO P-25 AIR PISTOL
Caliber: .177 pellets. Barrel: Rifled. Weight: 1.5 lbs. Length: 7.75 in. Power: CO₂. Sights: Fixed. Features: Semi-automatic, 16-shot capacity, realistic blowback action. Velocity: 450 fps.
Price: **$84.00**

GAMO P-27 AIR PISTOL
Caliber: .177 BB/.177 pellets. Barrel: Smooth. Weight: 1.5 lbs. Length: 7 in. Power: CO₂. Sights: Fixed with white dots. Features: Single/double action, semi-automatic, 16-shot capacity in two eight-round clips, non-blowback action, rail under barrel. Velocity: 400 fps.
Price: **$63.00**

GAMO PR-776 CO₂ REVOLVER
Caliber: .177 pellets. Barrel: Rifled. Weight: 2.29 lbs. Length: 11.5 in. Power: CO₂. Sights: Fixed front sight with fully adjustable rear sight. Features: All metal frame, comes with two eight-shot clips, double- and single-action. Velocity: 438 fps.
Price: **$110.00**

GAMO PT-85 CO₂ PISTOL
Caliber: .177 pellets. Barrel: Rifled. Weight: 1.5 lbs. Length: 7.8 in. Power: CO₂. Sights: Fixed. Features: Semi-automatic, 16-shot capacity, realistic blowback action. Velocity: 450 fps.
Price: **$95.00**

GLETCHER NGT F CO₂ BB REVOLVER
Caliber: .177 steel BBs. Barrel: Smoothbore. Weight: 1.54 lbs. Length: 9.00 in. Power: CO₂. Sights: Fixed. Features: Full metal frame, highly realistic replica, seven-shot cylinder with realistic "shells," double action and single action, available in blued and polished silver finishes, also available in a pellet version with a rifled barrel ($170–$200). Velocity: 403 fps.
Price: .... **$170.00–$190.00**

GLOCK 17 GEN 3/GEN 4/GEN 5 CO₂ PISTOL
Caliber: .177 BBs. Barrel: Smoothbore. Weight: 1.6 lbs. Length: 7.75 in. Power: CO₂. Sights: Fixed. Features: Blowback action, metal slide and magazine, 18-BB capacity, manual safety, double-action trigger, replica of the Glock 17 firearm. Velocity: 365 fps.
Price: .... **$123.00–$170.00**

GLOCK 19 GEN3 CO₂ PISTOL
Caliber: .177 BBs. Barrel: Smoothbore. Weight: 1.6 lbs. Length: 7.25 in. Power: CO₂. Sights: Fixed Features: Non-blowback action, manual safety, 16-BB capacity, integrated Weaver-style accessory rail, double-action trigger, replica of the Glock 19 firearm. Velocity: 410 fps.
Price: **$90.00**

GLOCK 19 X CO₂ PISTOL
Caliber: .177 BBs. Barrel: Smoothbore. Weight: 1.6 lbs. Length: 7.5 in. Power: CO₂. Sights: Fixed. Features: Blowback action, desert tan, metal slide, manual safety, 18-BB magazine, integrated Weaver-style accessory rail, double-action trigger, replica of the Glock 19 firearm. Velocity: 377 fps.
Price: **$115.00**

HAMMERLI AP-20 AIR PISTOL
Caliber: .177 pellets. Barrel: Rifled, match. Weight: 2.2 lbs. Length: 16.34 in. Power: Precharged pneumatic. Sights: Fully adjustable micrometer. Features: Two-stage adjustable trigger factory set to 500-gram pull weight, single shot, bolt action, up to 180 shots per fill, walnut grip with 3D adjustment, tunable front sight with three widths, adjustable width rear sight, comes with six barrel jackets in different colors. Velocity: 492 fps.
Price: **$1,000.00**

Prices given are believed to be accurate at time of publication however, many factors affect retail pricing so exact prices are not possible.

79TH EDITION, 2025 ✛ **571**

HATSAN USA JET II PCP PISTOL/CARBINE COMBO
Calibers: .177, .22, .25. Barrel: Rifled, 7.9 in. Weight: 2 lbs. without buttstock. Length: 15 in. without buttstock. Power: Precharged pneumatic. Stock: Ambidextrous synthetic. Sights: Three integrated flip-up sights, Picatinny rail for scope mounting. Features: Easily converts from pistol to carbine with a removable and adjustable buttstock, 22.8 – 24.6 in. with buttstock, side lever cocking, removable dual black air cylinders with built-in pressure gauge, replacement air cylinders also available in red, blue, or green, two Picatinny side rails, shrouded barrel, two 6-8 shot magazines (depending on caliber) included, 30-48 shots per fill depending on caliber. Velocities: .177/788 fps, .22/700 fps, .25/600 fps with lead pellets.
Price: $340.00

HATSAN SORTIE TACT PISTOL/RIFLE
Caliber: .177, .22, or .25 pellets. Barrel: Rifled, 7.9 in. Weight: 4.7 lbs. Length: 18.1 in. folded, 25 in. extended. Power: Precharged pneumatic. Sights: Removable fiber-optic sights. Features: Synthetic removable folding buttstock to convert from rifle to pistol, semi-automatic, combination 11mm and 22mm rail for mounting accessories, molded right-handed grips, two-stage trigger, three 14 (.177), 12 (.22), 10 (.25) round magazines included, fully shrouded and choked barrel. Velocities: 850 (.177), 700 (.22), 625 (.25) fps.
Price: $380.00

HATSAN MODEL 25 SUPERCHARGER QE AIR PISTOL
Caliber: .177 or .22 pellets. Barrel: Rifled. Weight: 3.9 lbs. Length: 20 in. Power: Single cock, air piston. Sights: Fiber-optic front and fully adjustable fiber-optic rear. Features: Molded right-handed grips, fully adjustable "Quattro" two-stage trigger, Quiet Energy-integrated sound moderator, 11mm dovetail grooves, XRS recoil reduction system. Velocity: 800 fps.
Price: $140.00

H&K VP9 BB CO₂ PISTOL
Caliber: .177 steel BBs. Barrel: Smoothbore. Weight: 1.42 lbs. Length: 7.2 in. Power: CO_2. Sights: Fixed. Features: Highly realistic replica, blowback action, integrated front weaver accessory rail, 18-round magazine. Velocity: 350 fps.
Price: $95.00

H&K HK45 CO₂ BB PISTOL
Caliber: .177 steel BBs. Barrel: Smoothbore. Weight: 1.4 lbs. Length: 8.0 in. Power: CO_2. Sights: Fixed. Features: Highly realistic replica, integrated front weaver accessory rail, 20-shot capacity, double-action-only. Velocity: 400 fps.
Price: $55.00

H&K USP CO₂ BB PISTOL
Caliber: .177 BBs. Barrel: Smoothbore. Weight: 2.15 lbs. Length: 7.75 in.

Power: CO_2. Sights: Fixed white dot. Features: Highly realistic replica, blowback, integrated front weaver accessory rail, single action/double action, realistic hammer movement, 16-shot drop-free magazine, metal barrel and slide. Also available in a less expensive non-blowback version. Velocity: 325 fps.
Price: $88.00

ISSC M22 CO₂ PISTOL
Caliber: .177 BBs. Barrel: Smoothbore, 4 in. Weight: 1.3 lbs. Length: 6.75 in. Power: CO_2. Sights: Fixed front, windage adjustable rear. Features: Semi-automatic blowback action, molded finger grooves, under barrel rail, manual trigger safety, built-in trigger lock, blowback action, 18-shot capacity. Velocity: 400 fps.
Price: $110.00

MORINI MOR-162EL AIR PISTOL
Caliber: .177 pellets. Barrel: Rifled. Weight: 2.25 lbs. Length: 16.14 in. Power: Precharged pneumatic. Sights: Front post, rear adjustable for windage. Features: Adjustable electronic trigger, single-shot bolt action, extreme match-grade accuracy, over 200 regulated shots per 200 bar fill, available with different grip sizes. Velocity: 500 fps.
Price: $2,250.00

MORINI CM 200EI AIR PISTOL
Caliber: .177 pellets. Barrel: Lothar Walther rifled. Weight: 2.17 lbs. Length: 15.75 in. Power: Precharged pneumatic. Sights: Front post, rear diopter/micrometer adjustable. Features: Adjustable electronic trigger, single-shot bolt action, digital manometer, battery life of 15,000 shots, match-grade accuracy, available with medium or large grip size, muzzle compensator, 150 regulated shots per 200 bar fill, comes with two air cylinders. Velocity: 492 fps.
Price: $2,600

RUGER MARK IV PELLET PISTOL
Caliber: .177 pellets. Barrel: Rifled. Weight: 2.15 lbs. Length: 11 in. Power: Spring piston. Sights: Fiber-optic fixed front, adjustable rear. Features: Single shot, single-stage trigger, single stroke cocking. Velocity: 369 fps.
Price: $60.00

SCHOFIELD NO. 3 REVOLVER, FULL METAL
Caliber: .177 steel BBs or .177 pellets. Barrel: Smoothbore. Weight: 2.4 lbs. Length: 12.5 in. Power: CO_2. Sights: Fixed. Features: Highly detailed replica top-break revolver, six-shot capacity, realistic reusable cartridges,

available in distressed black with imitation wood grips and plated steel with imitation ivory grips. Velocity: Up to 430 fps.
Price: **$155.00**

SIG SAUER X-FIVE ASP .177 CO₂ PISTOL
Caliber: .177 pellets. Barrel: Smoothbore. Weight: 2.75 lbs. Length: 8.7 in. Power: CO_2. Sights: Adjustable. Features: Realistic replica action pistol, 20-shot capacity, front accessory rail, black or silver finish, full metal construction, metal slide with blowback action. Velocity: 430 fps.
Price: **$160.00**

SIG SAUER 1911 METAL BLOWBACK CO₂ BB PISTOL
Caliber: .177 steel BBs. Barrel: Smoothbore. Weight: 2.0 lbs. Length: 8.75 in. Power: CO_2. Sights: Fixed. Features: Extremely Realistic replica action pistol, 18-shot capacity, front accessory rail, full metal construction, metal slide with blowback action, functioning takedown lever for field stripping. Velocity: 330 fps.
Price: **$140.00**

SIG SAUER P226 CO₂ PELLET PISTOL
Caliber: .177 pellets. Barrel: Rifled. Weight: 2.35 lbs. Length: 8.25 in. Power: CO_2. Sights: Fixed. Features: Highly detailed replica action pistol, 16-shot capacity, front accessory rail, full metal construction, metal slide with blowback action, available in dark earth and black, 16-round 8x2 rotary magazine. Velocity: 450 fps.
Price: **$130.00**

SIG SAUER P320 CO₂ PISTOL
Caliber: .177 BBs/.177 pellets. Barrel: Rifled. Weight: 2.2 lbs. Length: 9.6 in. Power: CO_2. Sights: Fixed, white dot. Features: 30-round belt-fed magazine, front accessory rail, polymer frame, metal slide with blowback action, black or coyote tan finish. Velocity: 430 fps.
Price: **$140.00**

SIG SAUER P365 CO₂ PISTOL
Caliber: .177 BBs. Barrel: Smoothbore. Weight: .8 lbs. Length: 5.75 in. Power: CO_2. Sights: Fixed, white dot. Features: 12-round magazine, metal slide with blowback action, black finish, slide locks back after last shot. Velocity: 295 fps.
Price: **$130.00**

SMITH & WESSON MODEL 29 CO₂ REVOLVER
Caliber: .177 BBs. Barrel: Smoothbore, 8.375 in. Weight: 2.65 lbs. with cartridges. Length: 12.14 in. Power: CO_2. Sights: Fixed front, adjustable rear. Features: Brown faux wood grip, single/double action, approximately 60 shots per 12-gram cartridge, removable bullet casings. Velocity: 425 fps.
Price: **$180.00**

SMITH & WESSON M&P 9 M2.0 CO₂ PISTOL
Caliber: .177 steel BBs. Barrel: Smoothbore. Weight: 1.45 lbs. Length: 7.5 in. Power: CO_2. Sights: Fixed front sight, fully adjustable rear sight. Features: Blowback action, full-size drop-free magazine with 18-round capacity, comes with three interchangeable backstraps, double- and single-action trigger, Picatinny accessory rail, last-round hold open, ambidextrous slide release. Velocity: 400 fps.
Price: **$130.00**

SMITH & WESSON 327 TRR8 CO₂ BB PISTOL
Caliber: .177 steel BBs. Barrel: Smoothbore. Weight: 2.0 lbs. Length: 12 in. Power: CO_2. Sights: Fiber-optic front sight, fully adjustable fiber-optic rear sight. Features: High-quality replica, top-mounted weaver scope rail, weaver accessory rail under the barrel, swing-out cylinder, removable casings and functioning ejector. Velocity: 400 fps.
Price: **$100.00**

SPRINGFIELD ARMORY 1911 MIL-SPEC C0₂ BB PISTOL
Caliber: .177 BBs. Barrel: Smoothbore, 4.1 in. Weight: 2.0 lbs. Length: 8.6 in. Power: CO_2. Sights: Fixed 3-dot. Features: Full metal construction, blowback slide, 18-round magazine, single action, checkered grips, approximately 65 shots per fill, slide locks back after last shot, functioning grip safety. Velocity: 320 fps.
Price: **$130.00**

SPRINGFIELD ARMORY XDE C0₂ BB PISTOL
Caliber: .177 BBs. Barrel: Smoothbore, 4.3 in. Weight: 1.95 lbs. Length: 7.75 in. Power: CO_2. Sights: Fixed fiber optic. Features: Full metal construction, blowback slide, 18-round drop-free magazine, double/single action, functional takedown lever, ambidextrous safety and magazine release, checkered grips, single slot Picatinny rail, front and rear slide serrations. Velocity: 380 fps.
Price: **$120.00**

SPRINGFIELD ARMORY XDM C0₂ BB PISTOL
Caliber: .177 BBs. Barrel: Smoothbore. Weight: 1.9 lbs. Length: 8 in. Power:

Prices given are believed to be accurate at time of publication however, many factors affect retail pricing so exact prices are not possible.

79TH EDITION, 2025 ⬦ **573**

CO_2. Sights: Fixed fiber optic. Features: Blowback metal slide, polymer frame, interchangeable backstraps, grip safety and trigger safety, functional striker status indicator, 20-round drop-free magazine, functional slide stop lever, field strips like real XDM, Picatinny accessory rail, functional takedown lever, ambidextrous magazine release, slide locks back after last shot, available with 3.8- or 4.5-in. barrel, blue or two tone. Velocity: 325 fps.
Price: .... **$140.00–$170.00**

STEYR M9-A1 PISTOL
Caliber: .177 BBs. Barrel: Smoothbore Weight: 1.2 lbs. Length: 7.5 in. Power: CO_2. Sights: Fixed. Features: Non-blowback, accessory rail, metal slide, two-tone or blue finish, 19-round capacity. Velocity: 449 fps.
Price: Blue **$55.00**

Price: Two-tone **$110.00**

STI DUTY ONE CO₂ BB PISTOL
Caliber: .177 BBs. Barrel: Smoothbore. Weight: 1.2 lbs. Length: 8.8 in. Power: CO_2. Sights: Fixed. Features: Blowback, accessory rail, metal slide, threaded barrel, 20-round magazine. Velocity: 397 fps.
Price: **$120.00**

SWISS ARMS SA92 BB PISTOL
Caliber: .177 BBs. Barrel: Smoothbore. Weight: 2.5 lbs. Length: 8.5 in. Power: CO_2. Sights: Fixed. Features: Blowback, accessory rail, full metal construction, stainless finish with brown grips, 20-round magazine. Velocity: 312 fps.
Price: **$150.00**

SWISS ARMS SA 1911 BB PISTOL
Caliber: .177 BBs. Barrel: Smoothbore. Weight: 2 lbs. Length: 8.6 in. Power: CO_2. Sights: Fixed. Features: Blowback, slide locks back when empty, metal construction, single-action-only, desert tan, checkered grips, functional grip safety, accessory rail on some models, 18-round magazine. Velocity: 320 fps.
Price: **$120.00**

TANFOGLIO WITNESS 1911 CO₂ BB PISTOL, BROWN GRIPS
Caliber: .177 steel BBs. Barrel: Smoothbore. Weight: 1.98 lbs. Length: 8.6 in. Power: CO_2. Sights: Fixed. Features: Often recognized as the "standard" for 1911 replica action pistols, 18-shot capacity, full metal construction with metal slide with blowback action. Velocity: 320 fps.
Price: **$150.00**

UMAREX LEGENDS MAKAROV ULTRA BLOWBACK CO₂ BB PISTOL
Caliber: .177 steel BBs. Barrel: Smoothbore. Weight: 1.40 lbs. Length: 6.38 in. Power: CO_2. Sights: Fixed. Features: Highly realistic replica, all-metal construction with blowback action, semi-automatic and full-auto capable, 16-round capacity. Velocity: 350 fps.
Price: **$65.00**

UMAREX LEGENDS M712 BROOM HANDLE FULL-AUTO CO₂ BB PISTOL
Caliber: .177 steel BBs. Barrel: Smoothbore. Weight: 3.10 lbs. Length: 12.00 in. Power: CO_2. Sights: Fixed front sight with rear sight adjustable for elevation. Features: Highly realistic replica that functions as the original, all-metal construction with blowback action, semi- and full-auto capable, 18-round capacity. Velocity: 360 fps.
Price: **$140.00**

UMAREX LEGENDS P08 BLOWBACK CO₂ BB PISTOL
Caliber: .177 steel BBs. Barrel: Smoothbore. Weight: 1.90 lbs. Length: 8.75 in. Power: CO_2. Sights: Fixed. Features: Highly realistic replica that functions as the original, all-metal construction with blowback action, 21-round capacity. Also available in a less expensive, non-blowback version. Velocity: 300 fps.
Price: **$133.00**

UMAREX BRODAX BB REVOLVER
Caliber: .177 steel BBs. Barrel: Smoothbore. Weight: 1.52 lbs. Length: 10.0 in. Power: CO_2. Sights: Fixed. Features: Aggressively styled BB revolver, 10-shot capacity, top accessory rail, front accessory rail, synthetic construction. Velocity: 375 fps.
Price: **$44.00**

UMAREX D17 BB PISTOL
Caliber: .177 BBs. Barrel: Smoothbore. Weight: 1.6 lbs. Length: 9.5 in. Power: Spring piston. Sights: Fixed fiber optic. Features: Integrated accessory rail, 15-shot capacity. Velocity: 200 fps.
Price: **$22.00**

UMAREX SA10 CO₂ PISTOL
Caliber: .177 pellet or steel BBs. Barrel: 5.0 in. rifled. Weight: 2.05 lbs. Length: 9.25 in. Power: CO_2. Sights: Fixed. Features: Full metal slide with polymer grips, blowback action, ported slide with gold-look barrel and breech block, threaded muzzle, magazine holds the CO_2 cylinder, an eight-shot rotary clip, and three additional clips, under-barrel accessory rail. Velocity: 420 fps.
Price: **$100.00**

Prices given are believed to be accurate at time of publication however, many factors affect retail pricing so exact prices are not possible.

UMAREX STEEL STORM CO_2 PISTOL
Caliber: .177 steel BBs. Barrel: Smooth, 7.5 in. Weight: 2.7 lbs. Length: 15 in. Power: CO_2. Sights: Fixed, Picatinny accessory rail. Features: Submachine gun styling, blowback action, uses two 12-gram CO_2 cylinders, 30-round nonremovable magazine, 300-round reservoir, full or semi-automatic modes, six-shot bursts in full-auto mode, up to 300 shots per fill, CO_2 housed in a drop-out magazine, can be bulk filled with an adapter (not included). Velocity: 430 fps.
Price: $123.00

UMAREX STRIKE POINT PELLET MULTI-PUMP AIR PISTOL
Caliber: .177 pellets. Barrel: Rifled. Weight: 2.6 lbs. Length: 14.00 in. Power: Multi-pump pneumatic. Sights: Adjustable rear sight, fixed fiber-optic front sight. Features: Variable power based on the number of pumps, bolt action, includes integrated "Silenceair" moderator for quiet shooting. Velocity: Up to 650 fps.
Price: $56.00

UMAREX TAC BB PISTOL WITH FOLDING STOCK
Caliber: .177 BB. Barrel: Smooth bore. Weight: 1.85 lbs. Length: 22.5 in. Power: CO_2. Sights: Rear adjustable for windage, blade front. Features: Four Picatinny rails, foldable shoulder stock, semi-automatic. Velocity: 410 fps.
Price: $64.00

UMAREX TDP 45 BB PISTOL
Caliber: .177 BB. Barrel: Smoothbore. Weight: 1 lb. Length: 6.5 in. Power: CO_2. Sights: Fixed. Features: 19-round drop-free magazine, double-action-only, under-barrel accessory rail, semi-automatic. Velocity: 410 fps.
Price: $40.00

UMAREX TREVOX AIR PISTOL
Caliber: .177 pellets. Barrel: Rifled. Weight: 3.5 lbs. Length: 18.25 in. Power: Gas piston. Sights: Adjustable rear sight, fixed fiber-optic front sight. Features: Full power from a single cock, suitable for target practice and plinking, includes integrated "Silenceair" moderator for quiet shooting. Velocity: 540 fps.
Price: $100.00

UMAREX XBG CO_2 PISTOL
Caliber: .177 steel BBs. Barrel: Smoothbore. Weight: 0.7 lbs. Length: 6.75 in. Power: CO_2. Sights: Fixed. Features: 19-shot capacity, under-barrel accessory rail, double-action-only. Velocity: 410 fps.
Price: $35.00

UZI (KWC) MINI CARBINE
Caliber: .177 steel BBs. Barrel: Smoothbore. Weight: 4.8 lbs. Length: 24/25 in. Power: CO_2. Sights: Adjustable. Features: Realistic replica airgun, 25-shot capacity, foldable stock, semi-automatic with realistic blowback system, heavy bolt provides realistic "kick" when firing. Velocity: 344 fps.
Price: $210.00

WALTHER LP500 COMPETITION PCP AIR PISTOL
Caliber: .177 pellets. Barrel: Rifled, match grade. Weight: 2 lbs. Length: 16.5 in. Power: Precharged pneumatic. Sights: Adjustable for windage and elevation. Features: Mechanical trigger, carbon-fiber air cylinder, up to 150 shots per fill, adjustable sight radius, walnut grip with adjustable palm shelf, single shot, five-way adjustable match trigger. Velocity: 500 fps.
Price: $2,200.00

WALTHER CP88 CO_2 PISTOL
Caliber: .177 pellets. Barrel: Rifled. Weight: 2.3-2.5 lbs. Length: 7-9 in. Power: CO_2. Sights: Blade ramp front sight and adjustable rear sight. Features: Manual safety, semi-auto repeater, single or double action, available with 4- or 6-in. barrel, available in multiple finishes and grip materials, eight-shot capacity. Velocity: 450 fps.
Price: $230.00

WALTHER CP99 CO_2 PISTOL
Caliber: .177 pellets. Barrel: Rifled Weight: 1.6 lbs. Length: 7.1 in. Power: CO_2. Sights: Fixed front and fully adjustable rear sight. Features: Extremely realistic replica pistol, single and double action, eight-shot rotary magazine. Velocity: 360 fps.
Price: $190.00

WALTHER CP99 COMPACT PISTOL
Caliber: .177 steel BBs. Barrel: Smoothbore. Weight: 1.7 lbs. Length: 6.6 in. Power: CO_2. Sights: Fixed front and rear. Features: Extremely realistic replica pistol, semi-automatic 18-shot capacity, available in various configurations, including a nickel slide. Velocity: 345 fps.
Price: $86.00

WALTHER PPQ M2 CO_2 PISTOL
Caliber: .177 pellets. Barrel: Rifled. Weight: 1.4 lbs. Length: 7.0 in. Power: CO_2. Sights: Fixed front and rear sight adjustable for elevation. Features: Extremely realistic replica pistol, blowback action, 20-shot drop-free magazine, metal slide, polymer frame. Velocity: 380 fps.
Price: $150.00

WALTHER P38 CO_2 BB PISTOL

Prices given are believed to be accurate at time of publication however, many factors affect retail pricing so exact prices are not possible.

79TH EDITION, 2025 · 575

Caliber: .177 steel BBs. Barrel: Smoothbore. Weight: 1.9 lbs. Length: 8.5 in. Power: CO_2. Sights: Fixed. Features: Authentic replica action pistol, blowback action, semi-automatic 20-shot magazine. Velocity: 400 fps.
Price: **$110.00**

WALTHER PPK/S CO_2 PISTOL

Caliber: .177 steel BBs. Barrel: Smoothbore. Weight: 3.7 lbs. Length: 6.1 in. Power: CO_2. Sights: Fixed. Features: Authentic replica action pistol, blowback slide locks back after last shot, stick-style magazine with 15-shot capacity. Velocity: 295 fps.
Price: **$84.00**

WALTHER PPS M2 BLOWBACK COMPACT CO_2 PISTOL

Caliber: .177 steel BBs. Barrel: Smoothbore. Weight: 1.2 lbs. Length: 6.38 in. Power: CO_2. Sights: Fixed. Features: Authentic replica action pistol, blowback action, semi-automatic 18-shot capacity. Velocity: 390 fps.
Price: **$90.00**

WEBLEY AND SCOTT MKVI REVOLVER

Caliber: .177 pellets. Barrel: Rifled, 6 in. Weight: 2.4 lbs. Length: 11.25 in. Power: CO_2. Sights: Fixed. Features: Authentic replica pistol, single/double action, can be field stripped, full metal construction, six-shot capacity, available in silver or distressed finish. Also available with a 2.5- or 4-in. barrel. Velocity: 430 fps.
Price: **$175.00**

WEBLEY AND SCOTT NEMESIS CO_2 PISTOL

Caliber: .177 OR .22 pellets. Barrel: Rifled. Weight: 2 lbs. Length: 10.25 in. Power: CO_2. Sights: Fiber-optic fixed. Features: Bolt action, the bolt can be swapped from right to left, tandem self-indexing magazine system (2x7 in .177 or 2x6 in .22), single-shot tray included, storage for magazine in grip, Picatinny rail for accessories, 3/8-in. dovetail for optics mounting, ambidextrous grip, 1/2-inch UNF threaded barrel, approximately 40 shots per CO_2 cylinder, two-stage adjustable trigger. Velocities: 450 fps (.177), 370 fps (.22).
Price: **$130.00**

WEIHRAUCH HW 40 PCA AIR PISTOL

Caliber: .177, .20, .22. Barrel: Rifled. Weight: 1.7 lbs. Length: 9.5 in. Power: Single-stroke spring piston. Sights: Fiber optic, fully adjustable. Features: Automatic safety, two-stage trigger, single shot. Velocity: 400 fps.
Price: **$324.00**

WEIHRAUCH HW 44 AIR PISTOL, FAC VERSION

Caliber: .177, .22. Barrel: Rifled. Weight: 2.9 lbs. Length: 19 in. Power: Precharged pneumatic. Sights: None. Features: Ambidextrous safety, two-stage adjustable match trigger, built-in suppressor, Weaver-style scope rail, 10-shot magazine, built-in air cartridge with quick fill, internal pressure gauge. Velocity: 750 (.177), 570 (.22) fps.
Price: **$1,200.00**

WEIHRAUCH HW 45 AIR PISTOL

Caliber: .177, .20, .22. Barrel: Rifled. Weight: 2.5 lbs. Length: 10.9 in. Power: Single-stroke spring piston. Sights: Fiber optic, fully adjustable. Features: Automatic safety, two-stage trigger, single shot, two power levels, blued or two tone. Velocity: 410/558 (.177), 394/492 (.20), 345/427 (.22) fps.
Price: **$578.00**

WEIHRAUCH HW 75 AIR PISTOL

Caliber: .177. Barrel: Rifled. Weight: 2.3 lbs. Length: 11 in. Power: Single-stroke spring piston. Sights: Micrometer adjustable rear. Features: Ambidextrous, adjustable match-type trigger, single shot. Velocity: 410 fps.
Price: **$616.00**

WINCHESTER MODEL 11 BB PISTOL

Caliber: .177 steel BBs. Barrel: Smoothbore. Weight: 1.9 lbs. Length: 8.5 in. Power: CO_2. Sights: Fixed. Features: All-metal replica action pistol, blowback action, 4-lb. two-stage trigger, semi-automatic 15-shot capacity. Velocity: 410 fps.
Price: **$100.00**

AIR ARMS TX200 MKIII AIR RIFLE
Calibers: .177, .22. Barrel: Rifled, Lothar Walter match-grade, 13.19 in. Weight: 9.3 lbs. Length: 41.34 in. Power: Single cock, spring-piston. Stock: Various; right- and left-handed versions, multiple wood options. Sights: 11mm dovetail. Features: Fixed barrel, heirloom-quality craftsmanship, holds the record for the most winning spring-powered airgun in international field target competitions. Velocities: .177, 930 fps/.22, 755 fps.
Price: **$975.00**

AIR ARMS PRO-SPORT RIFLE
Calibers: .177, .22. Barrel: Rifled, Lothar Walter match-grade, 9.5 in. Weight: 9.03 lbs. Length: 40.5 in. Power: Single cock, spring-piston. Stock: Various; right- and left-handed versions, multiple wood options. Sights: 11mm dovetail. Features: Fixed barrel, heirloom-quality craftsmanship, unique inset cocking arm. Velocities: .177, 950 fps/.22, 750 fps.
Price: .... **$1,033.00–$1,230.00**

AIR ARMS XTI-50 FT PCP AIR RIFLE
Caliber: .177. Barrel: Rifled, custom match-grade, 19.7 in. Weight: 10.4 lbs. Length: 37.6–39.0 in. Power: Precharged pneumatic. Stock: Highly adjustable laminate. Sights: 11mm dovetail with MOA droop built in. Features: Designed for field target competition, fully regulated, approximately 100 shots per fill, titanium 2,900 psi air cylinder, one-touch to adjust hamster, adjustable mechanical energy adsorber, match-grade trigger, wind indicator and built in level, single shot, side-lever action, fully adjustable and extendable butt hook. Comes with case. Velocity: 802 fps with 8.4 grain pellet.
Price: **$4,500.00**

AIRFORCE CONDOR SS RIFLE
Calibers: .177, .20, .22, .25. Barrel: Rifled, Lothar Walther match-grade, 18 or 24 in. Weight: 6.1 lbs. Length: 38.1-38.75 in. Power: Precharged pneumatic. Stock: Synthetic pistol grip, tank acts as the buttstock. Sights: Grooved for scope mounting. Features: Single shot, adjustable power, automatic safety, large 490cc tank volume, extended scope rail allows easy mounting of the largest airgun scopes, optional CO_2 power system available, manufactured in the USA. Velocities: .177, 1,450 fps/.20, 1,150 fps/.22, 1,250 fps/.25, 1,100 fps.
Price: **$1,093.00**

AIRFORCE ESCAPE/SS/UL AIR RIFLE
Calibers: .22, .25. Barrel: Rifled, Lothar Walther match-grade, 12, 18, or 24 in. Weight: 4.3-5.3 lbs. Length: 32.3-39.00 in. Power: Precharged pneumatic. Stock: Synthetic pistol grip, tank acts as the buttstock. Sights: Grooved for scope mounting. Features: Single shot, adjustable power, automatic safety, extended scope rail allows easy mounting of the largest airgun scopes, manufactured in the USA. Velocities: .22, 1,300 fps/.25, 1,145 fps.
Price: .... **$750.00–$830.00**

AIRFORCE TALON SS PCP RIFLE
Calibers: .177, .20, .22, 25. Barrel: Rifled, Lothar Walther match-grade, 12

in. Weight: 5.25 lbs. Length: 32.75in. Power: Precharged pneumatic, Stock: Synthetic pistol grip. Sights: None, grooved for scope mounting. Features: Single shot, removable moderator to reduce noise, adjustable power, can be easily broken down for compact transport, red or blue anodized frame, automatic safety, two-stage nonadjustable trigger, 490cc air tank, up to 50 ft-lbs of energy, manufactured in the USA. Velocities: 1,000 fps (.177), 800 fps (.20), 800 fps (.22), 665 fps (.25).
Price: **$745.00**

AIRGUN TECHNOLOGY URAGAN 2 KING RIFLE
Calibers: .177, .22, .25 or .30. Barrel: Hammer-forged, 23.6 or 27.6 in. Weight: 9.6 lbs. Length: 35.4 – 39.4 in. Power: Precharged pneumatic. Stock: Ambidextrous walnut, synthetic, or laminate bullpup stock. Sights: None, 20 MOA Picatinny rail for scope mounting. Features: Reversible biathlon side lever, under-barrel Picatinny accessory rail, 1060cc composite dual air cylinders, 9 to 15-shot magazine depending on caliber, and sound moderator.
Price: .... **$1,295.00–$1,350.00**

AIRGUN TECHNOLOGY VULCAN 3 - 500 BULLPUP RIFLE
Calibers: .177, .22, .25 or .30. Barrel: 19.7. Weight: 7.5 lbs. Length: 31.4. Power: Precharged pneumatic. Stock: Ambidextrous walnut bullpup stock with polymer cheekpiece. Sights: None, 20 MOA sloped Weaver-style rail for scope mounting. Features: Ambidextrous biathlon-style side lever, Picatinny under-rail, improved trigger and safety system, modified sound moderator, adjustable power, two 9 to 15-shot magazines depending on caliber, 480cc carbon-fiber air bottle, soft case. Also available with a 27.6-in. barrel with a 580cc air bottle (Vulcan 3 - 700 model).
Price: .... **$1,495.00–$1,595.00**

AIR VENTURI AVENGER RIFLE
Caliber: .177, .22, .25. Barrel: Rifled, 22.75 in. Weight: 6.0 lbs. Length: 42.75 in. Power: Precharged pneumatic. Stock: Ambidextrous synthetic or wood stock. Sights: None, Picatinny rail. Features: Side-lever cocking, externally adjustable regulator, hammer spring adjustment screw, two-stage adjustable trigger, shrouded barrel, easy access degassing screw, includes two magazines and a single-shot loading tray, 8 (.25) or 10 shot (.177 and .22) capacity. Velocities: .177, 1,000 fps; .22, 930 fps; .25, 900 fps.
Price: **$400.00**

AIR VENTURI SENECA DOUBLE SHOT .50 CAL DOUBLE BARREL AIR SHOTGUN
Caliber: No. 8 shot or .50 slug. Barrel: Smooth, double barrel, 20.9 in. Weight: 8.55 Length: 43.5 in. Power: Precharged pneumatic. Stock: Ambidextrous wood stock. Sights: Front bead with no rear sight. Features: Up to five shots per fill, shoots shotshells, airbolts, or round balls. Thread on chokes, optional dovetail rail, two-stage non-adjustable trigger. Velocity: Up to 1,130 fps with shotshells.
Price: **$950.00**

AIR VENTURI SENECA DRAGON CLAW PCP AIR RIFLE
Caliber: .50-cal. pellet or airbolt. Barrel: Rifled 21.65 in. Weight: 8.5 Length:

Prices given are believed to be accurate at time of publication however, many factors affect retail pricing so exact prices are not possible.

79TH EDITION, 2025 ✦ 577

42.1 in. Power: Precharged pneumatic. Stock: Right-handed wood stock. Sights: Fixed front sight with fully adjustable rear sight. Features: Massive 500cc reservoir delivers several powerful shots, 230 ft-lbs of energy at the muzzle on high setting, two power levels, dual air chambers, build-in manometer, 11mm scope rail. Velocity: 639 fps.
Price: **$800.00**

AIR VENTURI SENECA DRAGONFLY MK2 MULTI-PUMP AIR RIFLE

Calibers: .177, .22. Barrel: Rifled 22.75 in. Weight: 6.5 lbs. Length: 40 in. Power: Multi-pump pneumatic. Stock: Ambidextrous wood. Sights: Fixed front sight with fully adjustable rear. Features: Butterfly High-Efficiency Pump System, threaded muzzle adapter, 11mm dovetail optics rail, variable power based on the number of pumps. Bolt action, single shot, and multi-shot capability. Velocities: 850 fps (.177), 730 fps (.22).
Price: **$230.00**

AIR VENTURI SENECA WING SHOT II SHOTGUN

Caliber: .50. Barrel: Smoothbore 22.5 in. Weight: 7.4 lbs. Length: 43.0 in. Power: Precharged pneumatic. Stock: Ambidextrous wood. Sights: Fixed bead shotgun-style. Features: 244cc reservoir delivers several powerful shots, shoots shot cartridges and round ball, exceptionally reliable. Use as a shotgun to hunt birds or small game or as a slug gun to hunt larger game. Velocity: 760 fps (with slug), 1,130 fps.
Price: **$925.00**

AMERICAN AIR ARMS EVOL SPORT CARBINE

Calibers: .22 or .30. Barrel: Hammer forged, rifled, threaded, 15 in. (.22), 18 in (.30). Weight: 6.2 (.22)–7.2 lbs. (.30). Length: 36 (.22) or 39 in. (.30) with moderator. Power: Precharged pneumatic. Stock: Magpul synthetic. Sights: None, Picatinny rail. Features: Upper and lower chassis made from aluminum, titanium air cylinder, shrouded chrome moly tensioned barrel, Picatinny underside accessory rail, adjustable two-stage target trigger set to 10 ounces, aluminum self-indexing 9 (.30) or 13 round (.22) rotary magazine or single-shot loading tray, 45–120 .22 shots per fill, rear velocity adjustment, 4,000 psi pressure, custom manufactured in the USA in very limited quantities. Also available in other versions with longer and shorter barrels. Velocity: Adjustable.
Price: **$2,795.00**

AMERICAN AIR ARMS SLAYER HI-POWER BULLPUP RIFLE

Calibers: .308 or .357. Barrel: Rifled, threaded, 24 in (.357) or 26 in. (.308). Weight: 7.2 lbs. Length: 36-40 in with moderator. Power: Precharged pneumatic. Stock: Synthetic adjustable length stock. Sights: None, Picatinny rail. Features: Titanium reservoir, 3-lb. cocking effort, six- (.357 caliber) or seven- (.308 caliber) round rotary magazine, adjustable two-stage trigger, underside accessory rail, rear velocity adjuster, available in right or left hand, manufactured in the USA in very limited quantities. Velocity: 950 fps.
Price: **$2,795.00**

ANSCHUTZ 9015 AIR RIFLE

Caliber: .177. Barrel: Rifled, 16.5 in. Weight: Variable from 8.1 to 11 pounds. Length: Variable from 39.0 to 47 in. Power: Precharged pneumatic. Stock: Fully adjustable variable composition. Sights: Fully adjustable target sights with interchangeable inserts. Features: Single shot, ambidextrous grip, adjustable match trigger, exchangeable air cylinder with integrated manometer, approximately 200 shots per fill, available with a bewildering array of options. Also available in lower-priced Club and Junior versions. Velocity: 560 fps.
Price: .... **$3,095.00–$4,795.00**

ASELKON MX6 PCP RIFLE

Caliber: .177, .22, .25. Barrel: Rifled, 21.7 in. Weight: 68.3 pounds. Length: 43.3 in. Power: Precharged pneumatic. Stock: Turkish Walnut. Sights: None, Picatinny rail. Features: 10 (.25), 12 (.22) or 14 (.177) shot magazine. 500cc fill volume, adjustable trigger, side lever cocking, approximately 65–90 shots per fill, depending on caliber. Velocities: Up to 1,100 (.177), 1,000 (.22), 900 (.25) fps.
Price: **$510.00**

ASELKON MX10 PCP RIFLE

Caliber: .177, .22, .25. Barrel: Rifled, 21.7 in. Weight: 6.3 lbs. Length: 33.5 in. Power: Precharged pneumatic. Stock: Camo, wood, or black synthetic. Sights: None, Picatinny rail. Features: 10- (.25), 12- (.22) or 14- (.177) shot magazine, 275cc fill volume, adjustable trigger, side lever cocking, approximately 55-70 shots per fill depending on caliber. Velocities: Up to 950 fps (.177 or .22), 850 fps (.25).
Price: .... **$440.00–$490.00**

ASG TAC-4.5 CO₂ BB RIFLE

Caliber: .177 steel BBs. Barrel: Smoothbore. Weight: 3.5 lbs. Length: 36.0 in. Power: CO_2 Stock: Synthetic thumbhole stock. Sights: Fixed fiber-optic front sight and fully adjustable fiber-optic rear sight/weaver rail for optics. Features: Semi-automatic action, includes bipod, 21-shot capacity. Velocity: 417 fps.
Price: **$120.00**

ATAMAN BULLPUP M2R PCP RIFLE

Calibers: .25, .357. Barrel: Lothar Walther rifled match-grade free-floating, 20.5 in. Weight: 7.7-8.4 lbs. Length: 32.3 in. Power: Precharged pneumatic. Stock: Ambidextrous bullpup stock available in walnut or "soft touch" synthetic. Sights: Integrated Picatinny rails for scope mounting. Features: Multi-shot side-level action, shot capacity varies on caliber, adjustable match trigger, finely tuned regulator matched to optimal velocity in each caliber for maximum accuracy. Velocities: .25, 985 fps/.35, 900 fps.
Price: .... **$1,700.00–$2,000.00**

ATAMAN M2R ULTRA-COMPACT CARBINE

Calibers: .177, .22, .25. Barrel: Lothar Walther rifled match-grade, 11.2 in. Weight: 6.2 lbs. Length: 32.3 in. Power: Precharged pneumatic. Stock: Ambidextrous folding stock available in various configurations and finishes. Sights: None, Picatinny rail for scope mounting. Features: Also available in bullpup and tactical configurations, shrouded, 8- to 12-shot magazine dependent on caliber, adjustable match trigger. Velocities: .177, 850 fps/.22, 850 fps/.25, 900 fps.
Price: .... **$1,395.00–$1,600.00**

BARRA 400 E ELECTRIC RIFLE

Caliber: .177 BB. Barrel: Smoothbore, 19 in. Weight: 7.5 lbs. Length: 42.25 in. Power: AEG (electric). Stock: Black synthetic tactical style. Sights: Removable flip-up front and rear peep, Picatinny rail. Features: Ambidextrous elect fire semi- or full-automatic, lithium battery gives over 1,000 shots per charge, 50-round BB repeater, CNC-machined aluminum handguard and receiver, six-position adjustable buttstock, AR-style pistol grip, QD sling mount, speedloader, M-LOK slots on forearm sides. Velocity: 410 fps.
Price: $400.00

BARRA 1100 Z PCP RIFLE

Caliber: .177 or .22 pellet. Barrel: Rifled, 19 in. Weight: 7.5 lbs. Length: 42.25 in. Power: Precharged pneumatic. Stock: Synthetic, black or camo. Sights: None, Picatinny rail. Features: Includes two rotary magazines (12-shot .177 or 10-shot .22) and two single-shot trays, side-lever cocking, shrouded barrel, ambidextrous comb with height adjustment, adjustable trigger, 3,000 psi maximum fill, adjustable hammer spring to adjust power level, noise, and shot count, single-stage trigger. Velocities: Up to 1,100 fps (.177), 1,000 fps (.22).
Price: $250.00

BARRA 1866 JUNIOR RIFLE

Caliber: .177 BBs or pellets. Barrel: Smoothbore, 16.5 in. Weight: 4.1 lbs. Length: 36 in. Power: Single-stroke pneumatic. Stock: Synthetic. Sights: Fixed front, adjustable rear. Features: Single pump pneumatic, bolt-action, 50-shot BB capacity or single-shot pellet, scaled for smaller shooters, gold-toned receiver, automatic safety. Also available in an adult-sized version. Velocity: 350 fps.
Price: $40.00

BARRA 1866 CO₂ RIFLE

Caliber: .177 pellet. Barrel: Smoothbore, 18 in. Weight: 6.5 lbs. Length: 38.4 in. Power: CO_2. Stock: Synthetic wood. Sights: Fixed front, adjustable rear, Picatinny rail. Features: Lever-action, pellets held in shells loaded into the side of the rifle and ejected upon cycling lever. The magazine holds 10 shells. Powered by two CO_2 cylinders. Also available are .177 and .22 rifled barrel conversion kits. Velocity: 600 fps.
Price: $220.00

BEEMAN R9 AIR RIFLE

Calibers: .177, .20, .22. Barrel: Rifled 16.33 in. Weight: 7.3 lbs. Length: 43 in. Power: Break-barrel, spring-piston. Stock: Ambidextrous walnut-stained beech, cut-checkered pistol grip, Monte Carlo comb and rubber buttpad. Sights: None, grooved for scope. Features: German quality, limited lifetime warranty, highly adjustable match-grade trigger, extremely accurate. Velocities: .177, 935 fps/.20, 800 fps/.22, 740 fps.
Price: $625.00

BEEMAN AR2078A CO₂ RIFLE

Calibers: .177, .22 pellets. Barrel: Rifled, 21.50 in. Weight: 7.5 lbs. Length: 38 in. Power: CO_2. Stock: Beech. Sights: Competition diopter peep sight, 11mm dovetail. Features: Bolt action, single shot, operates on two standard 12-gram CO_2 cylinders or with tank adapter and connector, adjustable trigger, approximately 60 shots per fill. Velocities: .177, 650/.22, 500 fps.
Price: $260.00

BEEMAN COMMANDER PCP RIFLE

Calibers: .177, .22 pellets. Barrel: Rifled. Weight: 8 lbs. Length: 43 in. Power: Precharged pneumatic. Stock: Hardwood thumbhole. Sights: Adjustable fiber optic, comes with a 4x32 scope. Features: Up to 100 shots per fill, 10-shot magazine, built-in noise suppressor. Velocities: .177, 1,100/.22, 1,000 fps.
Price: $270.00

BEEMAN COMPETITION PCP RIFLE

Caliber: .177 pellets. Barrel: Rifled. Weight: 8.8 lbs. Length: 41.7 in. Power: Precharged pneumatic. Stock: Adjustable hardwood. Sights: None, dovetail grooves. Features: Side lever cocking, up to 200 shots per fill, single shot, built-in noise suppressor, 10m competition, adjustable trigger, adjustable pistol grip, comb, and buttplate. Velocity: 550 fps.
Price: $1,059.00

BENJAMIN 392 / 397 AIR RIFLE

Calibers: .177, .22. Barrel: Rifled 19.25 in. Weight: 5.5 lbs. Length: 36.25 in. Power: Multi-pump pneumatic. Stock: Ambidextrous wood or synthetic stock. Sights: Front ramp and adjustable rear sight. Features: Multi-pump system provides variable power, single-shot bolt action. Velocities: .177, 800 fps/.22, 685 fps.
Price: $242.00

BENJAMIN ARMADA PCP RIFLE

Calibers: .177, .22, .25. Barrel: Rifled, 20 in. Weight: 7.3 lbs. (10.3 lbs. with scope and bipod). Length: 42.8 in. Power: Precharged pneumatic. Stock: Adjustable mil-spec AR-15-style buttstock, all metal M-LOK-compatible handguard with 15 in. of Picatinny rail space. Sights: None, Weaver/Picatinny rail for scope mounting. Features: Fully shrouded barrel with integrated suppressor, dampener device, bolt action, multi-shot, choked barrel for maximum accuracy. Velocities: .177, 1,100 fps/.22, 1,000 fps/.25, 900 fps.
Price: $707.00

BENJAMIN AKELA PCP AIR RIFLE

Calibers: .22. Barrel: Rifled. Weight: 7.7 lbs. Length: 32.9 in. Power: Precharged pneumatic. Stock: Bullpup-style Turkish walnut stock. Sights: None, Picatinny rail for scope mounting. Features: Side cocking lever, adjustable trigger shoe, 3,000 psi pressure, up to 60 shots per fill, 12-shot rotary magazine. Velocity: 1,000 fps.
Price: .... $556.00–$661.00

BLACK BUNKER BM8 FOLDING RIFLE

Calibers: .177, .22 pellets. Barrel: Rifled. Weight: 7.5 lbs. Length: 42.7

Prices given are believed to be accurate at time of publication however, many factors affect retail pricing so exact prices are not possible.

79TH EDITION, 2025 ✦ **579**

in. Power: Gas ram. Stock: Ambidextrous reinforced synthetic. Sights: Adjustable rear, Picatinny rail for scope mounting. Features: Single-shot, Picatinny side rails for accessories, folds down for compact storage and transport, coyote tan or black, available in lower-powered versions. Comes with a triangular waterproof storage case for accessories. Velocities: 1,200 fps (.177), 1,000 fps (.22) with alloy pellets.
Price: $350.00

BLACK OPS TACTICAL SNIPER GAS-PISTON AIR RIFLE
Calibers: .22. Barrel: Rifled. Weight: 9.6 lbs. Length: 44.0 in. Power: Break-barrel, gas-piston. Stock: Ambidextrous pistol grip synthetic stock. Sights: none, Weaver rail for scope mounting, includes a 4x32 scope. Features: Muzzle brake helps with cocking force, single-shot, single cock delivers maximum power, adjustable single-stage trigger. Velocities: .177, 1,250 fps/.22, 1,000 fps.
Price: $250.00

BROCOCK GHOST HP PCP RIFLE
Calibers: .177, .22, .25, .30. Barrel: Rifled, 23 in. Weight: 7.5 lbs. Length: 33.7 in. Power: Precharged pneumatic. Stock: Ambidextrous polymer. Sights: None, adjustable Picatinny rail. Features: Titanium chassis to maximize rigidity, quick and easy interchangeable barrel system, finger-adjustable power settings, swappable side lever, adjustable check and buttpad, left- or right-hand magazine feed, comes with a hard case, fully adjustable match trigger, shrouded barrel with 1/2-inch UNF threads, three accessory rails. Up to 21 (.30) to 190 (.177) shots and 26 (.177) to 95 ft-lbs (.30) of energy at full power, depending on caliber. Also available in lower-powered Carbine and Plus versions. Velocities: Adjustable.
Price: $2,300.00

BROCOCK SNIPER XR MAGNUM PCP RIFLE
Calibers: .22, .25. Barrel: Rifled, Lothar Walther, 22 in. Weight: 7.3 lbs. Length: 39 in. Power: Precharged pneumatic. Stock: Black or sand-colored ballistic nylon thumbhole. Sights: None, 11mm rail. Features: Hi-Lo power adjuster, breech block made of aircraft-grade alloy, Huma regulator for shot-to-shot consistency, side lever, adjustable cheek and buttpad, 10-shot rotary magazine or single-shot tray, match-grade trigger, full-length built-in baffled silencer with adaptor for second-stage silencer, two pressure gauges, three-position power adjustor. Up to 45-50 shots and 46-55 ft-lbs of energy at full power, depending on caliber. Velocities: Adjustable.
Price: ....$1,654.00–$1,899.00

BSA R-10 SE PCP RIFLE
Calibers: .177, .22, .25. Barrel: Rifled, BSA-made cold hammer-forged precision barrel, 15 in. Weight: 7.4 lbs. Length: 40 in. Power: Precharged pneumatic. Stock: Available right- or left-hand, walnut, laminate, camo or black synthetic. Sights: None, grooved for scope mounting. Features: Adjustable buttpad, customer configurable shroud, up to 52-63 shots per fill depending on caliber, adjustable two-stage trigger, comes with two 10-shot magazines (eight-shot for .25 caliber), with last-shot indicator, fully regulated valve for maximum accuracy and shot consistency, also available with lower power/velocity and as a shorter carbine. Velocities: 950 fps (.177)/800 fps (.22)/665 fps (.25).
Price: ....$1,300.00–$1,496.00

BSA DEFIANT BULLPUP AIR RIFLE
Calibers: .177, .22. Barrel: Rifled, cold hammer-forged precision barrel, 18.5 in. Weight: 9 lbs. Length: 31 in. Power: Precharged pneumatic. Stock: Ambidextrous Walnut, black soft-touch or black pepper laminate with adjustable buttpad. Sights: None, grooved for scope mounting. Features: Multi-shot bolt action, two 10-shot magazines, enhanced valve system for maximum shot count and consistency, integrated suppressor, adjustable two-stage trigger. Velocities: 825 fps (.177)/570 fps (.22).
Price: ....$1,600.00–$1,700.00

BUSHMASTER MPW FULL-AUTO BB RIFLE
Caliber: .177 BB. Barrel: Smoothbore. Weight: 6.5 lbs. Length: 21 in. Power: CO_2. Stock: six-position adjustable nylon stock with AR-compatible pistol grip. Sights: None, comes with a red dot and Picatinny rail. Features: AR platform with mock suppressor, accepts AR stocks, AR-compatible buffer tube and pistol grip, full- or semi-auto modes, two-tone black/flat dark earth, blowback action, quad rail forearm for accessory mounting, 25-round drop-out magazine, uses two 12-gram CO_2 cylinders, fully auto with up to 1,400 rounds per minute. Also comes in a dual-action semi-/full-auto version. Velocity: 430 fps.
Price: $251.00

COMETA FENIX 400 PREMIER STAR AIR RIFLE
Calibers: .177, .22, .25. Barrel: Rifled. Weight: 7.5 lbs. Length: 39.4 in. Power: Gas power piston. Stock: Walnut. Sights: Adjustable, grooved for scope mounting. Features: Single shot. Velocities: 1,080 fps (.177)/900 fps (.22)/700 fps (.25).
Price: $330.00

COMETA FUSION PREMIER STAR AIR RIFLE
Calibers: .177, .22. Barrel: Cold hammer-forged, rifled. Weight: 7.5 lbs. Length: 44.9 in. Power: Gas power piston. Stock: Walnut. Sights: None, grooved for scope mounting. Features: Single shot, bull barrel, checkered stock, adjustable riser, adjustable trigger. Velocities: 1,080 fps (.177)/900 fps (.22).
Price: $500.00

CROSMAN CHALLENGER PCP COMPETITION AIR RIFLE
Caliber: .177. Barrel: Match-grade Lothar Walther rifled barrel. Weight: 7 lbs. Length: 41.75 in. Power: Precharged pneumatic. Stock: Highly adjustable ambidextrous synthetic competition stock. Sights: Globe front sight and Precision Diopter rear sight. Features: Redesigned in 2022, built-in regulator for shot-to-shot consistency, 3,000 psi reservoir to give more shots per fill, single-shot, adjustable two-stage match-grade trigger with an adjustable shoe, approved by the Civilian Marksmanship Program (CMP) for 3-position air rifle Sporter Class competition, swappable side-lever cocking handle. Velocity: 580 fps.
Price: $800.00

CROSMAN FULL-AUTO AK1 RIFLE
Caliber: .177 BBs. Barrel: Smooth. Weight: 8 lbs. Length: 34.5 in. Power: CO_2. Stock: Synthetic adjustable/folding five-position buttstock. Sights: Open, Picatinny rail. Features: Releasable magazine holds two CO_2 cartridges and spring feeds 28 BBs, shoots full or semiauto with blowback,

Prices given are believed to be accurate at time of publication however, many factors affect retail pricing so exact prices are not possible.

AK-compatible pistol grip, quad-rail forearm for accessory mounting. Velocity: 430 fps.

Price: **$219.00**

CROSMAN FULL AUTO R1 CO₂ RIFLE

Caliber: .177 BBs. Barrel: Smooth, 10 in. Weight: 6 lbs. Length: 26.25-29.5 in. Power: CO_2. Stock: Synthetic six-position adjustable buttstock. Sights: None, Picatinny rail, comes with a red-dot sight. Features: 25-round drop-free magazine, full- or semi-auto with blowback, powered by two CO_2 cartridges, AR-compatible buffer tube and pistol grip, quad-rail forearm for accessory mounting, speedloader included, also available as a semi-automatic version. Velocity: 430 fps.

Price: **$208.00**

CROSMAN M4-177 RIFLE

Caliber: .177 steel BBs, .177 pellets. Barrel: Rifled 17.25 in. Weight: 3.75 lbs. Length: 33.75 in. Power: Multi-pump pneumatic. Stock: M4-style adjustable plastic stock. Sights: Weaver/Picatinny rail for scope mounting and flip-up sights. Features: Single-shot bolt action, lightweight and very accurate, multiple colors available. "Ready to go" kits are available complete with ammo, safety glasses, targets, and extra five-shot pellet magazines. Velocity: 660 fps.

Price: **$79.00**

CROSMAN 362 MULTIPUMP AIR RIFLE

Caliber: .22 pellets. Barrel: Rifled. Weight: 4.5 lb. Length: 35.6 in. Power: Multi-pump pneumatic. Stock: Synthetic stock. Sights: Adjustable rear sight. Features: Single-shot, bolt action. Velocity: Up to 850 fps.

Price: **$112.00**

CROSMAN 3622/3677 PCP AIR RIFLE

Caliber: .177 or .22 pellets. Barrel: Rifled. Weight: 3.9 lb. Length: 36.6 in. Power: Precharged pneumatic. Stock: Synthetic stock. Sights: Adjustable rear sight. Features: Single-shot, bolt-action, 2,000 psi reservoir. Velocity: Up to 850 fps with alloy pellets.

Price: **$139.00**

CROSMAN 760 PUMPMASTER AIR RIFLE

Caliber: .177 steel BBs, .177 pellets. Barrel: Rifled 16.75 in. Weight: 2.75 lbs. Length: 33.5 in. Power: Multi-pump pneumatic. Stock: Ambidextrous plastic stock. Sights: Blade and ramp, rear sight adjustable for elevation, grooved for scope mounting. Features: Single-shot pellet, BB repeater, bolt action, lightweight, accurate and easy to shoot. Multiple colors available and configurations are available. "Ready to go" kits are available complete with ammo, safety glasses, targets and extra five-shot pellet magazines. Velocity: 625 fps.

Price: **$42.00**

CROSMAN FIRE NITRO PISTON AIR RIFLE

Caliber: .177. Barrel: Rifled. Weight: 6.0 lbs. Length: 43.5 in. Power: Break-barrel, Nitro-piston. Stock: Synthetic thumbhole style. Sights: None,

dovetail for scope mounting, includes CenterPoint 4x32 scope and rings. Features: Integrated muzzle brake for reduced recoil and noise, single-shot, adjustable two-stage trigger. Velocities: 1,200 fps.

Price: **$158.00**

CROSMAN ICON PCP RIFLE

Caliber: .177 or .22 pellets. Barrel: Rifled, 21 in. Weight: 7 lbs. Length: 38.5 in. Power: Precharged pneumatic. Stock: Ambidextrous tactical all-weather synthetic. Sights: Fiber-optic front and fully adjustable rear with 11mm dovetail optics rail. Features: Bolt action, threaded muzzle, 2,000 psi pressure gauge with up to 30 effective shots per fill, 12-shot (.177) or 10-shot (.22) auto-indexing magazine, textured pistol grip and forearm, raised cheekpiece, rear sling loop, 1/2x20 UNF muzzle threads for moderator, two-stage adjustable trigger. Velocity: Up to 1,000 fps (.177) or 900 fps (.22).

Price: **$306.00**

DAISY 1938 RED RYDER AIR RIFLE

Caliber: .177 steel BBs. Barrel: Smoothbore 10.85 in. Weight: 2.2 lbs. Length: 35.4 in. Power: Single-cock, lever action, spring-piston. Stock: Solid wood stock and forend. Sights: Blade front sight, adjustable rear sight. Features: 650 BB reservoir, single-stage trigger. Velocity: 350 fps.

Price: **$44.00**

DAISY ADULT RED RYDER BB RIFLE

Caliber: .177 steel BBs. Barrel: Smoothbore 10.85 in. Weight: 2.95 lbs. Length: 36.75 in. Power: Single-cock, lever action, spring-piston. Stock: Solid wood stock and forend. Sights: Blade front sight, adjustable rear sight. Features: A larger, adult-size version of the classic youth Red Ryder with 650 shot reservoir, 18-lb. cocking effort. Velocity: 350 fps.

Price: **$55.00**

DAISY MODEL 499B CHAMPION COMPETITION RIFLE

Caliber: .177 BBs. Barrel: Smoothbore, 20.88 in. Weight: 3.1 lbs. Length: 36.25. Power: Lever-action spring piston. Stock: Hardwood. Sights: Hooded front with aperture inserts and adjustable rear peep sight. Features: Single shot, 5m competition rifle. Velocity: 240 fps.

Price: **$186.00**

DAISY MODEL 599 COMPETITION AIR RIFLE

Caliber: .177 pellets. Barrel: Rifled, cold hammer-forged BSA barrel, 20.88 in. Weight: 7.1 lbs. Length: 34.35–37.25 in. Power: Precharged pneumatic. Stock: Ambidextrous beech wood stock with vertical and length of pull adjustment, adjustable comb. Sights: Hooded front and diopter rear sight. Features: Trigger weight adjustable down to 1.5 lbs, rotating trigger adjustment for positioning right or left, straight-pull T-bolt handle, removable power cylinder. Velocity: 520 fps.

Price: **$1,000.00**

DAISY MODEL 25 PUMP GUN

Caliber: .177 steel BBs. Barrel: Smoothbore. Weight: 3 lbs. Length: 37 in. Power: pump action, spring-air. Stock: Solid wood buttstock. Sights: Fixed front and rear sights. Features: 50-shot BB reservoir, removable screw-out shot tube, decorative engraving on receiver, rear sight can be flipped over to change from open to peep sight. Velocity: 350 fps.

Price: **$44.00**

Prices given are believed to be accurate at time of publication however, many factors affect retail pricing so exact prices are not possible.

79TH EDITION, 2025 ✦ **581**

DAISY MODEL 105 BUCK AIR RIFLE

Caliber: .177 steel BBs. Barrel: Smoothbore 7.97 in. Weight: 1.6 lbs. Length: 29.8 in. Power: Single-cock, lever action, spring-piston. Stock: Solid wood buttstock. Sights: Fixed front and rear sights. Features: 400-BB reservoir, single-stage trigger. Velocity: 275 fps.
Price: $36.00

DAISY AVANTI MODEL 753S MATCH GRADE AVANTI

Caliber: .177 pellets. Barrel: Rifled, Lothar Walther, 19.5 in. Weight: 7.3 lbs. Length: 38.5 in. Power: Single-stroke pneumatic. Stock: Ambidextrous wood or synthetic. Sights: Globe front sight and Precision Diopter rear sight. Features: Full-size wood stock, additional inserts available for the front sight, fully self-contained power system, excellent "first" rifle for all 10m shooting disciplines. Velocity: 495 fps.
Price: $290.00

DAISY POWERLINE MODEL 35 AIR RIFLE

Caliber: .177 steel BBs, .177 pellets. Barrel: Smoothbore. Weight: 2.25 lbs. Length: 34.5 in. Power: Multi-pump pneumatic. Stock: Ambidextrous plastic stock, available in black and pink camo. Sights: Blade and ramp, rear sight adjustable for elevation, grooved for scope mounting. Features: Single-shot pellet, BB repeater, lightweight, accurate, and easy to shoot. Velocity: 625 fps.
Price: $44.00

DAYSTATE DELTA WOLF RIFLE

Calibers: .177, .22, .25, .30. Barrel: Rifled, 17 in. (.177 or .22) or 23 in. (.177, .22, .25, .30). Weight: 7.4–7.8 lbs. Length: 28.4–33.1 in. Power: Precharged pneumatic. Stock: AR style. Sights: None, 22mm Picatinny rail. Features: Advanced Velocity Technology with display touchscreen, multi-caliber with fast-change barrel system, factory set power profiles for each caliber, built-in chronograph that allows the shooter to dial in their preferred velocity, OEM Huma-Air regulated, large-capacity (8- to 13-shot) magazine, Bluetooth connectivity, switchable side lever action, carbon-fiber shroud and optional silencer, removable air tank. Velocity: Adjustable.
Price: ....$2,695.00–$2,895.00

DAYSTATE HUNTSMAN REVERE AIR RIFLE

Calibers: .177, .22, .25. Barrel: Match grade, rifled, 17 in. Weight: 6.4 lbs. Length: 36.5 in. Power: Precharged pneumatic. Stock: Right-handed Monte Carlo walnut. Sights: None, 11mm grooved dovetail for scope mounting. Features: Side-lever action, HUMA air regulator, 13- (.177), 11- (.22) or 10- (.25) shot rotary magazine, single-shot loading tray, 20–46 shots per fill depending on caliber, adjustable two-stage trigger, shrouded barrel, available in a left-handed version. Velocity: Adjustable.
Price: $1,500.00

DIANA CHASER CO₂ AIR RIFLE/PISTOL KIT

Caliber: .177, .22. Barrel: Rifled, 17.7 in. Weight: 3.1 lbs. Length: 38.4 in. Power: CO_2. Stock: Ambidextrous synthetic. Sights: Front fiber-optic and adjustable rear, 11mm dovetail for scope mounting. Features: Shrouded barrel, two-stage adjustable trigger, single-shot (can use indexing 7–9 shot magazines from the Stormrider), approximately 50 shots per CO_2 cylinder, kit includes a soft case, Chaser pistol, buttstock, and rifle barrel. Velocities: 642 fps (.177 rifle), 500 fps (.22 rifle).
Price: $200.00

DIANA 34 EMS BREAK-BARREL AIR RIFLE

Caliber: .177, .22. Barrel: Rifled, 19.5 in. Weight: 7.85 lbs. Length: 46.3 in. Power: Break-barrel, spring-piston, convertible to N-TEC gas piston. Stock: Ambidextrous wood or thumbhole synthetic. Sights: Front fiber-optic and micrometer adjustable rear, 11 mm dovetail. Features: Two-stage adjustable trigger, single-shot, removable 1/2 in UNF threaded barrel, EMS (easy modular system) allows for easy changing of barrels, adjustable barrel alignment, two-piece cocking lever. Velocities: 890 fps (.177), 740 fps (.22).
Price: ....$450.00–$500.00

DIANA 54 AIRKING PRO LAMINATE AIR RIFLE

Caliber: .177, .22. Barrel: Rifled, 17.3 in. Weight: 10.25 lbs. Length: 44in. Power: Spring piston side lever. Stock: Red and black laminated or beechwood. Sights: Adjustable rear, 11 mm dovetail. Features: Two-stage adjustable trigger, single-shot, forearm swivel stud to attach a bipod, adjustable barrel weight, checkered grip and forearm. Velocities: 1,100 fps (.177), 990 fps (.22).
Price: $850.00

DIANA XR200 PREMIUM PCP RIFLE

Calibers: .177, .22, .25, .30 pellet. Barrel: Rifled, Lothar Walther, 21.6 in. Weight: 6.5 lbs. Length: 42.9 in. Power: Precharged pneumatic. Stock: Green synthetic or beech wood, ambidextrous with adjustable cheekpiece. Sights: None, 11mm dovetail grove. Features: Optional slug barrel, rotatable manometer for easy reading, 8-14 shot magazine depending on caliber, includes two-shot adapter, adjustable two-stage trigger, ALTAROS regulator for shot-to-shot consistency, built-in compensator, under-rail for bipod, case included. Velocities: Adjustable.
Price: $1,135.00

DPMS SBR FULL-AUTO BB RIFLE

Caliber: .177 BB. Barrel: Smoothbore. Weight: 6.2 lbs. Length: 26.5 in. Power: CO_2. Stock: Adjustable six-position buttstock with AR-compatible pistol grip. Sights: Folding BUIS front and rear with Picatinny rail. Features: Blowback action, quad-rail forearm for accessory mounting, 25-round drop-out magazine, fully auto with up to 1,400 rounds per minute. Also comes in a dual-action semi-/full-auto version. Velocity: 430 fps.
Price: $225.00

EDGUN LELYA 2.0 PCP RIFLE
Calibers: .177, .22, or .25 pellet. Barrel: Rifled, Alfa Precision, 15.4 in. Weight: 6.4 lbs. Length: 23.5 in. Power: Precharged pneumatic. Stock: Walnut ambidextrous bullpup style. Sights: None, Weaver-style rail for scope mounting. Features: Dual side-lever cocking for ambidextrous cocking, adjustable hammer spring tension, two-stage adjustable trigger, 35–50 shots per fill depending on caliber, 10-round (in .177 or .22) or nine-round magazine (.25), sling loop in the rear of the stock, fully shrouded barrel. Velocities: Approximately 920 fps (.177), 900 fps (.22), 880 fps (.25).
Price: **$2,400.00**

EDGUN LESHIY 2 STANDARD PCP AIR RIFLE
Calibers: .177, .22, .25, or .30 pellets. Barrel: Rifled, 9.85 in. Weight: 5 lbs. Length: 25.5 in. overall. Power: Precharged pneumatic. Stock: Ambidextrous adjustable. Sights: None, Weaver-style rail for scope mounting. Features: Semi-automatic, folding stock that is compact to carry (13.5 inches when folded), red and grey laminate AR pistol grip, includes two eight-round magazines, single-stage trigger, Picatinny forearm accessory rail, unique hammerless design, 18–36 shots per fill depending on caliber. Velocities: 900 fps (.177), 870 fps (.22), 800 fps (.25), 740 fps (.30).
Price: **$2,700.00**

EDGUN MATADOR R5M STANDARD PCP RIFLE
Calibers: .177, .22, or .25. Barrel: Rifled, Lothar Walther, 18.75 in. Weight: 6.75 lbs. Length: 27.5 in. Power: Precharged pneumatic. Stock: Ambidextrous walnut thumbhole or synthetic. Sights: None, Weaver rail for scope mounting. Features: Adjustable trigger, adjustable hammer spring tension, designed and manufactured in Russia, 40–60 shots per fill depending on caliber, also available with a longer barrel, ambidextrous safety. Velocities: 950 fps (.177), 920 fps (.22 and .25).
Price: **$2,400.00**

EVANIX AR6K PCP RIFLE
Calibers: .177, .22, .25. Barrel: Rifled, 21.7 in. Weight: 6 lbs. Length: 35.4 in. Power: Precharged Pneumatic. Stock: Ambidextrous wood. Sights: None, 21mm Weaver-style rail. Features: Single-/double-action, external hammer, 4-lb. single-action trigger pull, six-round magazine, 3,000 psi fill, unchoked barrel. Velocities: 800–900 fps.
Price: **$650.00**

EVANIX CLOUD ULTRA PCP RIFLE
Calibers: .177, .22, .25, .30. Barrel: Rifled, 21.7 in. or 23.6 in. (.30 cal.). Weight: 7.3–7.7 lbs. Length: 32.9 in. or 35.4 in. (.30) overall. Power: Precharged pneumatic. Stock: Ambidextrous metal and synthetic. Sights: None, 22mm Picatinny rail. Features: Multi-shot semi-automatic, 10-round magazine, 580cc carbon-fiber removable reservoir, two-stage adjustable trigger, available in red, blue, or black. Velocities: Variable.
Price: **$1,620.00**

FEINWERKBAU 500 AIR RIFLE
Caliber: .177. Barrel: Rifled 13.8 in. Weight: 7.05 lbs. Length: 43.7 in. Power: Precharged pneumatic. Stock: Ambidextrous beech stock with adjustable cheekpiece and buttstock. Sights: Globe front sight and diopter rear. Features: Meets requirements for ISSF competition, trigger pull weight adjusts from 3.9 to 7.8 ounces, bolt action, competition grade airgun. Also available with an aluminum stock. Velocity: 574 fps.
Price: **$1,900.00**

FEINWERKBAU 800X FIELD TARGET AIR RIFLE
Caliber: .177. Barrel: Rifled 16.73 in. Weight: 11.7–15.05 lbs. Length: 49.76 in. Power: Precharged pneumatic. Stock: Highly adaptable field target competition stock. Sights: None, 11mm grooved for scope mounting. Features: Approximately 100+ shots per fill, adjustable trigger shoe, adjustable hand rest, vertically adjustable butt pad, adjustable butt hook, vertically and laterally adjustable comb, five-way adjustable match trigger, bolt action, competition-grade airgun. Also available in a smaller, lower-priced model for Junior competition. Velocity: 825 fps.
Price: **$3,500.00**

FEINWERKBAU 900 ALU RIFLE
Caliber: .177. Barrel: Rifled. Power: Precharged pneumatic. Stock: Highly adjustable silver or black field target competition stock. Sights: Adjustable Vario, 11mm grooved for scope mounting. Features: Adjustable absorber, maintenance-free pressure reducer, 13 different color options available, Centra sights optional, mesh pro grips, right- or left-hand grips in S, M, or L, adjustable trigger shoe, adjustable hand rest, vertically adjustable butt pad, adjustable butt hook, vertically and laterally adjustable comb, five-way adjustable match trigger, competition-grade airgun.
Price: **$4,280.00**

FEINWERKBAU P75 BIATHLON AIR RIFLE
Caliber: .177. Barrel: Rifled 16.73 in. Weight: 9.26 lbs. Length: 42.91 in. Power: Precharged pneumatic. Stock: Highly adaptable laminate wood competition. Sights: Front globe with aperture inserts and diopter micrometer rear. Features: Bolt action, competition-grade airgun, five-way adjustable match trigger. Velocity: 564 fps.
Price: **$3,900.00**

FX IMPACT AIR RIFLE
Calibers: .25, .30. Barrel: Rifled 24.4 in. Weight: 7.0 lbs. Length: 34.0 in. Power: Pre-charged pneumatic. Stock: Compact bullpup stock in various materials and finishes Sights: None, 11mm grooved for scope mounting. Features: Premium airgun brand known for exceptional build quality and accuracy, regulated for consistent shots, adjustable two-stage trigger, FX smooth twist barrel, multi-shot side lever action, fully moderated barrel, highly adjustable and adaptable air rifle system. Velocities: .25, 900 fps/.30, 870 fps.
Price: ....**$1,800.00–$2,100.00**

FX CROWN MK II PCP RIFLE
Calibers: .177, .22, .25, .30. Barrel: Rifled, 15, 19.7, 23.6, or 27.6 in. Weight: 6.2–6.8 lbs. Length: 38.5–43 in. Power: Precharged pneumatic. Stock: Ambidextrous stock in walnut, laminate, or synthetic. Sights: None, 20-MOA Picatinny rail. Features: Optional adjustable laminated GRS stock, Smooth Twist X barrels that can be swapped to change caliber and twist rate, adjustable 15-oz. two-stage trigger, externally adjustable regulator, adjustable power wheel and hammer spring, side-lever cocking, removable carbon-fiber tank, 45–200 shots per fill depending on caliber, dual manometers, built-in muzzle shroud, multiple-shot magazine (13–22

shots depending on caliber), 28–70 ft-lbs of energy depending on caliber. Velocities: .177, 1,000 fps/.22, 920 fps/.25, 900 fps/.30, 870 fps.
Price: ....$2,050.00–$2,100.00

FX DREAMLINE CLASSIC PCP RIFLE

Calibers: .177, .22, .25, .30. Barrel: Rifled, match grade, 19.7 or 23.6 in. Weight: 5.7–6.4 lbs. Length: 38.4–42.9 in. Power: Precharged pneumatic. Stock: Ambidextrous in walnut, laminate, or synthetic. Sights: None, 11 mm dovetail. Features: Optional adjustable laminated GRS stock, Smooth Twist X barrels that can be swapped to change caliber and twist rate, free-floating barrel, 1/2-inch UNF threaded, adjustable match trigger, AMP externally adjustable regulator, adjustable power wheel and hammer spring, side-lever cocking, dual manometers, removable multiple-shot magazine (13–22 shots depending on caliber), 18–45 ft-lbs of energy depending on caliber (.30 TBA). Can be converted to bullpup or tactical models by changing barrels and stocks. Velocities: .177, 940 fps/.22, 920 fps/.25, 890 fps/.30, TBA.
Price: $1,250.00–1,800.00

FX IMPACT MK III PCP RIFLE

Calibers: .177, .22, .25, .30, .35. Barrel: Rifled, 19.7–31.5 in. Weight: 6.1–7.35 lbs. Length: 25–44 in. Power: Precharged pneumatic. Stock: Compact synthetic bullpup stock. Sights: None, 20-MOA Picatinny rail. Features: Dual regulated for consistent shots, tool-free Quick Tune adjustment system, 16-step power wheel, ambidextrous short-throw cocking lever, dual manometers, 18- to 34-shot magazine depending on caliber, AR-style grip, built-in shroud, match trigger, carbon-fiber-wrapped air tank, Smooth Twist X barrels that can be swapped to change caliber and twist rate, highly adjustable and adaptable air rifle system. Velocities: Adjustable.
Price: ....$2,200.00–$2,300.00

FX MAVERICK SNIPER PCP AIR RIFLE

Calibers: .22, .25, .30. Barrel: Rifled 27.6 in. Weight: 7.2 lbs. Length: 36 in. Power: Precharged pneumatic. Stock: Tactical style with AR-style grip. Sights: None, 20-MOA Picatinny rail for scope mounting. Features: Three Picatinny rails for accessories, adjustable match trigger, threaded barrel shroud, side lever action, dual AMP regulators, 580cc carbon-fiber air cylinder, dual manometers, 90 (.30), 170 (.25), 270 (.22) maximum shots per fill, 18- (.22), 16- (.25), 13- (.30) shot magazine, includes one magazine and a hard case, also available in a compact version. Velocities: .22, 1,000 fps/.25, 1,000 fps/.30, 900 fps.
Price: $2,000.00

* scope not included

GAMO COYOTE WHISPER FUSION PCP AIR RIFLE

Calibers: .177, .22. Barrel: Cold hammer-forged match-grade rifled barrel, 24.5 in. Weight: 6.6 lbs. Length: 42.9 in. Power: Precharged pneumatic. Stock: Ambidextrous hardwood stock. Sights: None, grooved for scope mounting. Features: European class airgun, highly accurate and powerful, adjustable two-stage trigger, integrated moderator, 10-shot bolt action. Velocities: .177, 1,200 fps/.22, 1,000 fps.
Price: $400.00

GAMO DELTA FOX JUNIOR RIFLE KIT

Calibers: .177 pellet. Barrel: Rifled. Weight: 4.6 lbs. Length: 39.7 in. Power: Single-stroke spring piston. Stock: Synthetic. Sights: Adjustable fiber optic. Features: 19-lb. cocking effort, comes with pellets and targets, single shot, designed as an introductory pellet rifle. Velocity: 750 fps with alloy pellets.
Price: $110.00

GAMO WILDCAT WHISPER BREAK-BARREL AIR RIFLE

Calibers: .177, .22. Barrel: Rifled, 19.1 in. Weight: 5.6 lbs. Length: 44.5 in. Power: Gas piston, break barrel. Stock: Ambidextrous synthetic stock. Sights: Fixed, grooved for scope mounting, includes a 4x32 scope. Features: Single shot, Inert Gas Technology (IGS), 30-lb. cocking effort, Whisper noise suppression. Velocities: .177, 1,350 fps/.22, 975 fps.
Price: $136.00

GAMO SWARM MAGNUM 10X GEN 3I MULTI-SHOT AIR RIFLE

Caliber: .177, .22 pellet. Barrel: Rifled 21.3 in. Weight: 6.88 lbs. Length: 49.2 in. Power: Break-barrel, gas-piston. Stock: Ambidextrous lightweight nylon thumbhole. Sights: None, grooved for scope mounting, includes recoil-reducing rail, 3-9x40 scope and mounts. Features: 10-shot multi-shot system allows for inertia-feed automatic loading with each cock of the barrel, checkering on grip and forearm, adjustable two-stage trigger, features Whisper Fusion integrated suppressor technology, Shock Wave Absorber recoil pad. Velocity: 1,300 fps with alloy pellets.
Price: $320.00

GLETCHER MOSIN NAGANT M1891 CO$_2$ BB RIFLE

Caliber: .177 BBs. Barrel: Smooth, 16 in. Weight: 5.6 lbs. Length: 22.44 in. Power: CO_2. Stock: Imitation wood. Sights: Adjustable rear with a removable front globe. Features: Reproduction of the Mosin-Nagant sawed-off rifle, working sliding metal bolt action, built-in hex wrench for changing CO_2 cylinders, 16-BB capacity, approximately 120 shots per fill. Velocity: 427 fps.
Price: $280.00

GLETCHER MOSIN NAGANT M1944 CO$_2$ BB RIFLE

Caliber: .177 BBs. Barrel: Smooth, 16 in. Weight: 8.21 lbs. Length: 40.5 in with bayonet folded. Power: CO_2. Stock: Imitation wood. Sights: Adjustable rear with a removable front globe. Features: Reproduction of the Russian Mosin-Nagant rifle, working sliding metal bolt action, built-in hex wrench for changing CO_2 cylinders, 16-BB capacity, approximately 120 shots per fill, integral folding bayonet, reproduction sling included. Velocity: 427 fps.
Price: $360.00

HAMMERLI AR20 SILVER AIR RIFLE

Calibers: .177. Barrel: Rifled Lothar Walther 19.7 in. Weight: 8.75 lbs. Length: 41.65–43.66 in. Power: Precharged pneumatic. Stock: Ambidextrous aluminum stock with vertically adjustable buttpad and spacers for adjusting the length. Sights: Globe front and fully adjustable diopter rear, grooved for scope mounting. Features: Single shot, ambidextrous cocking piece, removable aluminum air cylinder, meets ISSF requirements. The stock is available in several colors. Velocity: 557 fps.
Price: $1,000.00

H&K HK416 CO$_2$ BB RIFLE

Caliber: .177 BBs. Barrel: Smoothbore, 14 in. Weight: 5.3 lbs. Length: 28.5 in. Power: CO_2. Sights: Flip-up front and rear. Stock: Polymer. Features: 500-round BB reservoir with 36 BBs in the feeding portion, semi-automatic, uses two 12-gram CO_2 cylinders, six-shot burst mode, Picatinny accessory rails on all sides, collapsible stock, AR-style grip. Velocity: 450 fps.
Price: $180.00

H&K MP5 K-PDW CO₂ BB COMPACT SUBMACHINE GUN

Caliber: .177 BBs. Barrel: Smoothbore. Weight: 2.4 lbs. Length: 24.5 in. Power: CO_2. Sights: Post globe front, adjustable rear. Features: 40-round removable banana-style magazine, semi-automatic, recoils like a firearm, folding stock, forward grip. Velocity: 400 fps.
Price: $130.00

H&K MP7 BREAK-BARREL PELLET GUN

Caliber: .177 pellets. Barrel: Rifled. Weight: 6.0 lbs. Length: 23.0–31.5 in. Power: Spring piston. Stock: Collapsible wire. Sights: None, Axeon Optics 1xRDS red dot. Features: Single shot, adjustable length of pull, Picatinny rails on top and sides, faux suppressor. Velocity: 490 fps.
Price: $150.00

HATSAN USA EDGE CLASS AIRGUNS

Calibers: .177, .22, .25. Barrel: Rifled 17.7 in. Weight: 6.4–6.6 lbs. Length: 43 in. Power: Break-barrel, spring-piston and gas-spring variations. Stock: Multiple synthetic and synthetic skeleton stock options. Available in different colors such as black, muddy girl camo, moon camo, etc. Sights: Fiber-optic front and fully adjustable fiber-optic rear, grooved for scope mounting, includes 3-9x32 scope and mounts. Features: European manufacturing with German steel, single-shot, adjustable two-stage trigger, performance tested at the factory with lead pellets for accurate velocity specifications. Velocities: .177, 1,000 fps/.22, 800 fps/.25, 650 fps.
Price: .... $140.00–$180.00

HATSAN USA AIRMAX PCP AIR RIFLE

Calibers: .177, .22, .25. Barrel: Rifled 23.0 in. Weight: 10.8 lbs. Length: 37 in. Power: Precharged pneumatic. Stock: Ambidextrous wood bullpup. Sights: None, combination Picatinny rail and 11mm dovetail for scope mounting. Features: Multi-shot side-lever action, 10-shot .177 and .22 magazines/nine-shot .25 magazine, "Quiet Energy" barrel shroud with an integrated suppressor, removable air cylinder, fully adjustable two-stage "Quattro" trigger, "EasyAdjust" elevation comb, sling swivels, includes two magazines. Velocities: .177, 1,170 fps/.22, 1,070 fps/.25, 970 fps.
Price: $630.00

HATSAN USA BULLBOSS QE AIR RIFLE

Calibers: .177, .22, .25. Barrel: Rifled 23.0 in. Weight: 8.6 lbs. Length: 36.8 in. Power: Precharged pneumatic. Stock: Ambidextrous synthetic or hardwood bullpup. Sights: None, innovative dual-rail 11mm dovetail and Weaver compatible for scope mounting. Features: Multi-shot side-lever action, 10-shot .177 and .22 magazines/nine-shot .25 magazine, "Quiet Energy" barrel shroud with an integrated suppressor, European manufacturing with German steel, removable air cylinder, fully adjustable two-stage "Quattro" trigger, performance tested at the factory with lead pellets for accurate velocity specifications. Velocities: .177, 1,170 fps/.22, 1,070 fps/.25, 970 fps.
Price: .... $530.00–$550.00

HATSAN BLITZ FULL AUTO PCP AIR RIFLE

Calibers: .22, .25, .30. Barrel: Rifled 23 in. Weight: 8.8 lbs. Length: 45.2 in. Power: Precharged pneumatic. Stock: Synthetic. Sights: Adjustable, innovative dual-rail 11mm dovetail and Weaver compatible for scope mounting. Features: Full/semi-automatic selector switch, 1,000 rounds per minute cyclic rate, includes two 21- (.22), 19- (.25), or 16-round (.30) SwingLoad magazines, 100–130 shots per fill depending on the rate of fire and caliber, gas-operating cycling mechanism does not require batteries, "Quiet Energy" barrel shroud, adjustable cheekpiece and buttpad, carry handle, three Picatinny forearm accessory rails. Velocities: 1,050 fps (.22), 970 fps (.25), 730 fps (.30).
Price: $1,000.00

HATSAN USA FLASH QE PCP RIFLE

Calibers: .177, .22, .25. Barrel: Rifled, 17.7 in. Weight: 5.9 lbs. Length: 42.3 in. Power: Precharged pneumatic. Stock: Ambidextrous synthetic or hardwood thumbhole. Sights: None, innovative dual-rail 11mm dovetail and Weaver-compatible for scope mounting. Features: Very lightweight, multi-shot side-lever action, multi-shot magazine (shot count varies by caliber). "Quiet Energy" barrel shroud with an integrated suppressor, European manufacturing with German steel, fully adjustable two-stage "Quattro" trigger, performance tested at the factory with lead pellets for accurate velocity specifications. Velocities: .177, 1,250 fps/.22, 1,100 fps/.25, 900 fps.
Price: .... $290.00–$390.00

HATSAN USA PILEDRIVER BIG BORE PCP AIR RIFLE

Calibers: .45, .50. Barrel: Rifled 33 in. Weight: 10 lbs. Length: 46.5 in. Power: Precharged pneumatic. Stock: Bullpup-style synthetic thumbhole stock with adjustable cheekpiece. Sights: None, dual-rail 11mm dovetail and Weaver-compatible for scope mounting. Features: 480cc carbon-fiber tank, long side lever for easy cocking, three Picatinny accessory rails, 4–6 shots in .45 caliber, 3–5 shots in .50 caliber, fully adjustable two-stage "Quattro" trigger. Velocities: .45, 900 fps/.50, 850 fps.
Price: $1,100.00

HATSAN USA VECTIS LEVER ACTION PCP AIR RIFLE

Calibers: .177, .22, .25. Barrel: Rifled 17.7 in. Weight: 7.1 lbs. Length: 41.3 in. Power: Precharged pneumatic. Stock: Synthetic all-weather stock. Sights: Fiber-optic front and rear, combination dual 11mm dovetail and Weaver-compatible for scope mounting. Features: Multi-shot lever action, 14-shot .177 magazine, 12-shot .22 magazine, 10-shot .25 magazine, "Quiet Energy" barrel shroud with integrated suppressor, fully adjustable two-stage "Quattro" trigger, Picatinny under-barrel accessory rail. Velocities: .177, 1,150 fps/.22, 1,000 fps/.25, 900 fps.
Price: $350.00

HATSAN ZADA BREAK-ACTION RIFLE

Calibers: .177, .22, .25. Barrel: Rifled, 14.5 in. Weight: 6.2 lbs. Length: 45 in. Power: Spring piston. Stock: Synthetic tactical style. Sights: Fiber-optic front and adjustable rear, 4x32 scope included. Features: Single shot, "Quiet Energy" barrel shroud with an integrated suppressor, fully adjustable trigger, checkered grip and forearm. Velocities: .177, 1,100 fps/.22, 800 fps/.25, 700 fps with lead pellets.
Price: $130.00

Prices given are believed to be accurate at time of publication however, many factors affect retail pricing so exact prices are not possible.

79TH EDITION, 2025 **585**

HELLRAISER HELLBOY RIFLE

Caliber: .177 BB. Barrel: 14.5 in. Weight: 5.2 lbs. Length: 30–33.5 in. Power: CO_2 cartridge. Stock: Synthetic, tactical style. Sights: Open sights adjustable for windage and elevation, Picatinny rail for scope mounting. Features: Based on the M4 carbine, full-metal construction of barrel, magazine, and receiver, stock adjustable for length of pull, semi-automatic, 18-round magazine, removable carry handle, integrated sling swivels. Velocity: 495 fps.
Price: $180.00

JEFFERSON STATE ROGUE RAPTOR AIR RIFLE

Calibers: .177, .22, .25, .30. Barrel: TJ Hammer forged, 22 in. Weight: 8 lbs. Length: 43 in. Power: Precharged pneumatic. Stock: Highly adjustable. Sights: None, with Picatinny rail for scope mounting. Features: Side lever cocking, interchangeable barrel and probe for quick caliber changes, high-capacity magazine, externally adjustable regulator, 500cc carbon-fiber bottle, two-stage four-way adjustable trigger, shrouded barrel, built-in power adjuster, compatible with AR-15 stocks and grips, spare magazines store in Picatinny rail, 26-in. barrel available as an option. Also available in a Mini Raptor version (34 in. OAL, 7 lbs.) Velocities: Adjustable.
Price: $1,600.00

KALIBRGUN CRICKET 2 BULLPUP PCP AIR RIFLE

Caliber: .177 .22, .25, .30. Barrel: Rifled, Lothar Walther or CZ barrel (depending on caliber), 23.6 in. Weight: 7.5 lbs. Length: 33.1 in. Power: Precharged pneumatic. Stock: Ambidextrous wood or synthetic bullpup with synthetic cheek piece. Sights: None, Weaver rail for scope mounting. Features: Switchable (left/right) side lever cocking system, adjustable power, 14-shot (.177 or .22), 12-shot (.25) or 10-shot magazine (.30), 35–75 shots per fill depending on caliber, stock has integral magazine holder, adjustable two-stage trigger, also available in a tactical version. Velocity: Up to 915–970 fps depending on caliber.
Price: $1,895.00

KALIBRGUN SPRINGBOK PCP RIFLE

Caliber: .22. Barrel: Rifled, 23.5 in. Weight: 8.8 lbs. Length: 34.5 in. Power: Precharged pneumatic. Stock: Ambidextrous wood or laminate bullpup stock. Sights: None, Weaver rail for scope mounting. Features: Semi-automatic, interchangeable carbon-fiber 610cc air reservoir, 4,350 psi, external regulator, ambidextrous side-lever cocking system, adjustable power, 13-shot magazine, up to 160 shots per fill, adjustable two-stage trigger. Velocity: Up to 1,050 fps.
Price: $2,300.00

KRAL ARMS PUNCHER MEGA PCP AIR RIFLE

Calibers: .177, .22, .25. Barrel: Rifled 21.0 in. Weight: 8.35 lbs. Length: 42.0 in. Power: Precharged pneumatic. Stock: Ambidextrous stock available in synthetic with adjustable cheek piece, and Turkish walnut. Sights: None, 11mm grooved dovetail for scope mounting. Features: Multi-shot side-lever action, 14-shot .177 magazine, 12-shot .22 magazine, 10-shot .25 magazine, half-shrouded barrel with integrated suppression, available in blue and satin marine finish, adjustable two-stage trigger. Velocities: .177, 1,070 fps/.22, 975 fps/.25, 825 fps.
Price: $600.00

KRAL ARMS PUNCHER PRO 500 PCP AIR RIFLE

Calibers: .177, .22, .25. Barrel: Rifled, 20.9 in. Weight: 8.5 lbs. Length: 41.3 in. Power: Precharged pneumatic. Stock: Monte Carlo hardwood right-handed. Sights: None, 11mm grooved dovetail for scope mounting. Features: Multi-shot rear bolt action, 14-shot .177 magazine, 12-shot .22 magazine, 10-shot .25 magazine, fully shrouded barrel with integrated suppression, two-stage adjustable trigger, 70–80 shots per fill depending on caliber. Velocities: .177, 1,100 fps/.22, 900 fps/.25, 850 fps.
Price: $725.00

KRAL ARMS PUNCHER BREAKER PCP AIR RIFLE

Calibers: .177, .22, .25. Barrel: Rifled 21 in. Weight: 7.4 lbs. Length: 29 in. Power: Precharged pneumatic. Stock: Ambidextrous bullpup available in synthetic and Turkish walnut. Sights: None, 11mm grooved dovetail for scope mounting. Features: Multi-shot side-lever action, 14-shot .177 magazine, 12-shot .22 magazine, 10-shot .25 magazine, half-shrouded barrel with integrated suppression, available in blue and satin marine finish, adjustable two-stage trigger. Velocities: .177, 1,100 fps/.22, 975 fps/.25, 825 fps.
Price: $600.00

LCS AIR ARMS SK19 FULL-AUTO AIRGUN

Calibers: .22, .25. Barrel: Lothar Walther match grade, 23 in. Weight: 7.75 lbs. Length: 35.0 in. Power: Precharged pneumatic. Stock: Laminate with adjustable cheek piece. Sights: None, Picatinny rail for scope mounting. Features: Made in USA, selector for semi- or full-auto fire, tunable regulated action, carbon-fiber barrel shroud, 480cc or 580cc removable tank, optional 580cc tank available, hard case, 19-shot magazine. Velocity: 890–910 fps.
Price: $2,300.00

MARKSMAN 2066 BREAK-BARREL RIFLE

Caliber: .177 or .22 pellet. Barrel: Rifled. Weight: 6.3 lbs. Length: 43.25 in. Power: Spring piston, 11mm rail. Stock: Wood. Sights: Fiber optic. Features: Built-in noise suppressor, single shot, comes with a 4x32 scope. Velocities: 800 (.177)/600 (.22) fps.
Price: $110.00

PBBA PRO 20-GAUGE AIR SHOTGUN

Calibers: 20 gauge. Barrel: 32 in. Weight: 9.5. Length: 53.5 in. Power: Precharged pneumatic. Stock: Laminate with adjustable cheek piece. Sights: None, rail for scope mounting. Features: Tip-up barrel for loading or barrel swap, pattern mimics a 20-gauge shotgun, separate cocking knob, sling studs, made in USA, 20-in. .457-caliber barrel available as an accessory.
Price: $1,850.00

Prices given are believed to be accurate at time of publication however, many factors affect retail pricing so exact prices are not possible.

RAPID AIR WORX RAW HM1000X LRT RIFLE

Calibers: .22, .25, .30, .357. Barrel: Lothar Walther match grade with polygonal rifling, 24 in. Weight: 7 lbs., 13 oz. Length: 45.4 in. Power: Precharged pneumatic. Stock: Laminate with adjustable cheek piece. Sights: Grooved for scope mounting. Features: Picatinny rail and M-LOK mounting slots, match-grade trigger, multi-shot rotary magazine, adjustable power, side-lever cocking, regulated, quick-fill system, available with right- or left-hand actions. Velocities: .22, 950 fps/.25, 900 fps/.30, NA/.357, NA.
Price: $2,200.00

RAPID AIR WORX RAW HM1000X CHASSIS RIFLE

Calibers: .22, .25. Barrel: Lothar Walther match grade with polygonal rifling, 24 in. Weight: 7 lbs., 13 oz. Length: 43–47 in. Power: Precharged pneumatic. Stock: Synthetic AR-15 style. Sights: Grooved for scope mounting. Features: Chassis constructed from aluminum, designed to accept all AR-15 buttstocks, buffer tubes, and pistol grips, Picatinny rail and M-LOK mounting slots, match-grade trigger, 12-shot rotary magazine, adjustable power, side-lever cocking, regulated, quick-fill system. Velocities: .22, 950 fps/.25, 920 fps.
Price: $2,000.00

RAPID AIR WORX RAW TM1000 BENCHREST RIFLE

Calibers: .177, .22. Barrel: Lothar Walther match grade with polygonal rifling, 24 in. Weight: 9.2–10.5 lbs. Length: 44 in. Power: Precharged pneumatic. Stock: Walnut or black laminate. Sights: Grooved for scope mounting. Features: Built to specifications, target model, internally fitted regulator, fixed bottle, quick fill coupling, approximately 80 shots depending on settings and caliber, Picatinny rail and M-LOK mounting slots, stainless steel ported shroud, adjustable cheek piece and buttpad, match-grade trigger, single shot, 10-in. long accessory rail under barrel, side-lever cocking, right- or left-handed action. Velocities: Dependent on settings and caliber.
Price: $2,200.00

RUGER 10/22 CO₂ RIFLE

Calibers: .177 pellets. Barrel: Rifled 18 in. Weight: 4.5 lbs. Length: 37.1 in. Power: Two 12-gram CO_2 cylinders. Stock: Synthetic stock. Sights: Rear sight adjustable for elevation, accepts aftermarket rail. Features: 10-shot Ruger-style rotary magazine, bolt cocks rifle, 3-lb. single-action trigger pull, sling attachments. Velocity: 650 fps.
Price: $150.00

RUGER AIR MAGNUM COMBO

Calibers: .177, .22. Barrel: Rifled 19.5 in. Weight: 9.5 lbs. Length: 48.5 in. Power: Break-barrel, spring piston. Stock: Ambidextrous Monte Carlo synthetic stock with textured grip and forend. Sights: Fiber-optic front and fully adjustable fiber-optic rear, Weaver scope rail, includes 4x32 scope and mounts. Features: Single-shot, two-stage trigger. Velocities: .177, 1,400 fps/.22, 1,200 fps.
Price: $235.00

RUGER EXPLORER RIFLE

Caliber: .177 pellets. Barrel: Rifled 15 in. Weight: 4.45 lbs. Length: 37.12 in. Power: Break-barrel, spring piston. Stock: Ambidextrous synthetic skeleton stock. Sights: Fiber-optic front and fully adjustable fiber-optic rear, grooved for scope mounting. Features: Designed as an entry-level youth break-barrel rifle, easy to shoot and accurate, single-shot, two-stage trigger. Velocity: 495 fps.
Price: $100.00

RUGER IMPACT MAX ELITE RIFLE

Caliber: .22. Barrel: Rifled 15 in. Weight: 7.5 lbs. Length: 44.75 in. Power: Break-barrel, TNT gas-piston. Stock: Ambidextrous wood, includes rifle sling. Sights: Fiber-optic front and fully adjustable fiber-optic rear, Picatinny optics rail, includes scope and mounts. Features: Integrated "SilencAIR" suppressor. Velocity: 800 fps with lead pellets.
Price: $169.00

RUGER TARGIS HUNTER MAX AIR RIFLE COMBO

Caliber: .22. Barrel: Rifled 18.7 in. Weight: 9.85 lbs. Length: 44.85 in. Power: Break-barrel, spring piston. Stock: Ambidextrous synthetic stock with texture grip and forend, includes rifle sling. Sights: Fiber-optic front and fully adjustable fiber-optic rear, Picatinny optics rail, includes scope and mounts. Features: Integrated "SilencAIR" suppressor, single shot, two-stage trigger. Velocity: 1,000 fps.
Price: $199.00

SHERIDAN/CROSMAN 2260 MB CO₂ RIFLE

Caliber: .22. Barrel: Rifled. Weight: 4.80 lbs. Length: 39.75 in. Power: CO_2. Stock: Ambidextrous wood. Sights: Fixed front, adjustable rear sight, 11mm grooves for scope mounting. Features: Single-shot, metal breech, bolt-action. Velocity: Up to 600 fps.
Price: $250.00

SIG SAUER MCX CO₂ RIFLE, GEN 2

Caliber: .177. Barrel: Rifled, 17.7 in. Weight: 7.2 lbs. Length: 34.75 in. Power: CO_2. Stock: Synthetic. Sights: Flip-up adjustable, Picatinny rail. Features: M-LOK handguard, 30-round semi-automatic, ambidextrous safeties, uses 88 or 90 gram CO_2 cartridges, belt-fed magazine system. Velocity: Up to 545 fps.
Price: $230.00

SIG SAUER MPX GEN 2 CO₂ RIFLE

Caliber: .177 pellet. Barrel: Rifled, 8 in. Weight: 6.2 pounds. Length: 25.8 in. Power: CO_2. Stock: Synthetic stock. Sights: Adjustable folding dual-aperture open sights. Features: Picatinny accessory rail, M-LOK system handguard, flat-blade trigger, 30-round semi-automatic, Roto Belt magazine, ambidextrous safety levers, very realistic replica. Velocity: 450 fps.
Price: $230.00

SKOUT EPOCH PCP RIFLE

Calibers: .177, .22, .25, .30, .357 pellets. Barrel: Rifled, shrouded, 25 in. (.177, .22, .25, .30), 35 in. (.357) Weight: 10.1 lbs. Length: Adjustable. Power: Precharged pneumatic. Stock: Ambidextrous adjustable synthetic. Sights: None, Picatinny rail. Features: Computer control to adjust firing mode, firing timer, and valve timing, dual externally adjustable regulators, 500cc carbon-fiber reservoir, adjustable match-grade two-stage trigger with adjustable trigger shoe height, pre- and post-travel, M-LOK accessory rails, three manometers that show the pressure of the air cylinder, the pilot valve, and the valve pressure, available in 12 different colors, built-in sound suppressor, tool-less barrel removal, interchangeable barrel system to switch calibers,

Teflon-coated barrel. Includes Plano hard case. Magazine capacities: 36 (.177), 30 (.22), 25 (.25), 22 (.30), 18 (.357). Velocities: Up to 1,100 fps (.177), 1,093 fps (.22), 1,096 fps (.25), 1,093 fps (.30), 988 fps (.357).
Price: ....**$2,450.00–$2,500.00**

SPRINGFIELD ARMORY M1A UNDER-LEVER RIFLE
Caliber: .177 or .22. Barrel: Rifled 18.9 in. Weight: 9.9 pounds. Length: 45.6 in. Power: Spring piston under-lever. Stock: Ambidextrous wood. Sights: Fixed front, rear peep adjustable for windage and elevation. Features: Fixed barrel, single shot, realistic replica of the National Match firearm, 35-lb. cocking effort, two-stage non-adjustable trigger. Velocity: 1,000 fps (.177), 750 fps (.22).
Price: **$246.00**

SPRINGFIELD ARMORY M1A CO_2 BB CARBINE
Caliber: .177 BBs. Barrel: Smoothbore, 17.25 in. Weight: 5.7 lbs. Length: 35.8 in. Power: CO_2. Stock: Ambidextrous synthetic wood. Sights: Fixed front, rear peep adjustable for windage. Features: 15-round drop-free magazine, blowback action, approximately 40 shots per CO_2 cylinder, semi-automatic, realistic replica of the M1 carbine, two-stage non-adjustable trigger. Velocity: 425 fps.
Price: **$250.00**

STOEGER S4000-E SUPPRESSED PCP RIFLE COMBO
Caliber: .177 or .22 pellets. Barrel: Rifled, 18.5 in. Weight: 7.65 lbs. Length: 44.25 in. Power: Break-action gas ram. Stock: Black or camo synthetic or hardwood. Sights: Adjustable fiber optic, 11mm dovetail. Features: Automatic ambidextrous safety, interchangeable blue and orange embossed grips, includes a 4X32 scope, fully shrouded suppressed barrel, adjustable two-stage trigger, single shot. Velocities: 1,000 fps (.177), 800 fps (.22).
Price: ....**$150.00–$200.00**

STOEGER XM1 PCP RIFLE
Caliber: .177 or .22 pellets. Barrel: Rifled, 22 in. Weight: 5.7 lbs. Length: 39 in. Power: Precharged pneumatic. Stock: Black or camo thumbhole synthetic. Sights: Adjustable fiber optic, 11 mm dovetail. Features: Approximately 50 shots per charge, nine-shot (.177) or seven-shot (.22) removable rotary magazine, available as a kit with a 4x32 scope, checkered stock, interchangeable cheekpiece, pistol grip, and buttpad, adjustable trigger, available as a suppressed model, Picatinny rails on each side, bolt action. Velocities: 1,200 fps (.177), 1,000 fps (.22).
Price: ....**$250.00–$300.00**

UMAREX EMBARK AIR RIFLE
Caliber: .177. Barrel: Rifled 15 in. Weight: 4.45 lbs. Length: 37.25 in. Power: Spring piston. Stock: Ambidextrous neon green thumbhole synthetic. Sights: Fully adjustable micrometer rear, grooved 11mm dovetail for scope mounting. Features: Official air rifle for the Student Air Rifle program, 12-in. length of pull, muzzle brake, 16.5-lb. cocking effort, 4.25-lb. trigger pull, automatic safety. Velocity: 510 fps.
Price: **$125.00**

UMAREX EMERGE AIR RIFLE
Caliber: .177 or .22. Barrel: Rifled, 21 in. Weight: 9 lbs. Length: 47 in. Power: Break barrel, gas piston. Stock: Synthetic. Sights: Fiber-optic front and rear, Picatinny rail, comes with a 4x32 scope. Features: 12-shot auto-advancing rotary magazine, integrated SilencAir technology, textured grip and forearm. Velocities: 1,000 (.177)/800 (.22) fps.
Price: **$190.00**

UMAREX FUSION 2 CO_2 RIFLE
Calibers: .177 pellets. Barrel: Rifled, 18.5 in. Weight: 5.95 lbs. Length: 40.55 in. Power: CO_2. Stock: Ambidextrous, synthetic, thumbhole. Sights: None, Picatinny rail for scope mounting. Features: SilencAir noise dampening, uses two 12-gram cylinders or one 88-gram cylinder, nine-shot rotary magazine, bolt action, M-LOK slots on both sides, single-stage trigger. Velocity: 700 fps.
Price: **$160.00**

UMAREX GAUNTLET 2 PCP AIR RIFLE
Caliber: .22, .25, .30. Barrel: Rifled 28.25 in. Weight: 8.5 lbs. Length: 47 in. Power: Precharged pneumatic. Stock: Ambidextrous synthetic. Sights: None, grooved 11mm dovetail for scope mounting. Features: 10-shot (.177), eight-shot (.25) or seven-shot (.30) magazine, 25 (.30), 50 (.25), or 70 (.22) shots per fill, removable aluminum air cylinder, multi-shot bolt action, four baffle sound reduction, height-adjustable cheek comb, M-LOK accessory slots on sides and bottom or forearm, adjustable single-stage trigger. Available in a lower-powered version for the Canadian market. Velocities: 1,075 fps (.177), 985 fps (.25), 950 fps (.30).
Price: ....**$450.00–$530.00**

UMAREX HAMMER AIR RIFLE
Caliber: .50. Barrel: Rifled 29.5 in. Weight: 8.5 Length: 43.75 in. Power: Precharged pneumatic. Stock: Nymax synthetic. Sights: None, Picatinny rail for scope mounting. Features: Fires three full-power shots, 2-lb. straight-pull bolt cocks the rifle and advances the magazine, 4,500 psi built-in carbon-fiber tank with quick disconnect Foster fitting, trigger-block safety, will not fire without magazine, Magpul AR grip, full-length composite barrel shroud, comes with two double chamber magazines. Also available in a shorter, lighter carbine version and lower-powered version for the Canadian market. Velocities: 1,130 fps (180-grain non-lead bullet), 760 fps (550-grain lead slug).
Price: **$1,100.00**

UMAREX LEGENDS COWBOY LEVER ACTION RIFLE
Calibers: .177 BBs. Barrel: 19.25 in smoothbore. Weight: 7.75 lbs. Length: 38.0 in. Power: CO_2. Stock: Faux wood polymer. Sights: Blade front sight with rear sight adjustable for elevation. Features: Lever action, 10-shot capacity, ejectable cartridges, full metal frame, powered by two CO_2 capsules, saddle ring. Velocity: 600 fps.
Price: **$225.00**

WALTHER LG400 UNIVERSAL AIR RIFLE, AMBI GRIP
Caliber: .177. Barrel: Advanced match-grade rifled barrel 16.53 in. Weight: 8.6 lbs. Length: 43.7 in. Power: Precharged pneumatic. Stock: Ambidextrous competition, highly adjustable wood stock. Sights: Olympic-grade, match Diopter/Micrometer adjustable. Features: Professional-class 10m target rifle, meets ISSF requirements. Velocity: 557 fps.
Price: **$2,000.00**

WALTHER MAXIMATHOR AIR RIFLE
Calibers: .22, .25. Barrel: Advanced match-grade rifled barrel, 23.5 in. Weight: 9.6 lbs. Length: 41.75 in. Power: Precharged pneumatic. Stock: Ambidextrous wood stock. Sights: None, grooved 11mm dovetail for scope mounting. Features: Bolt-action eight-shot magazine. Velocities: .22, 1,260 fps/.25, 1,000 fps.
Price: **$850.00**

WALTHER LEVER-ACTION CO₂ RIFLE, BLACK
Caliber: .177. Barrel: Rifled 18.9 in. Weight: 6.2 lbs. Length: 39.2 in. Power: CO_2 Stock: Ambidextrous wood stock. Sights: Blade front, adjustable rear. Features: Lever-action repeater, eight-shot rotary magazine, Wild West replica airgun. Velocity: 600 fps.
Price: $480.00

WEIHRAUCH HW50S SPRING PISTON RIFLE
Caliber: .177, .22. Barrel: Rifled, 15.5 in. Weight: 6.8 lbs. Length: 40.5 in. Power: Spring piston. Stock: Checkered beech wood. Sights: Front globe and adjustable rear. Features: Single shot, 24-lb. cocking effort, two-stage adjustable Rekord trigger. Velocity: 820 fps (.177), 574 fps (.22).
Price: $470.00

WEIHRAUCH HW90 SPRING PISTON RIFLE
Caliber: .177, .22, .25. Barrel: Rifled, 19.7 in. Weight: 6.8 lbs. Length: 45.3 in. Power: Spring piston. Stock: Checkered beech wood. Sights: Front globe and adjustable rear, 11 mm dovetail for scope mounting. Features: Single shot, 46-lb. cocking effort, two-stage adjustable Rekord trigger. Velocity: 1,050 fps (.177), 853 fps (.22), 625 fps (.25).
Price: $835.00

WEIHRAUCH HW97K/KT AIR RIFLE
Caliber: .177, .20, .22. Barrel: Rifled, 11.81 in. Weight: 8.8 lbs. Length: 40.1 in. Power: Under-lever, spring-piston. Stock: Various, beech wood, blue-grey laminated, or synthetic, with or without thumbhole. Sights: None, grooved for scope. Features: Silver or blue finish, highly adjustable match-grade trigger. Extremely accurate fixed barrel design. Velocity: 820 fps (.177), 755 fps (.22).
Price: $800.00

WEIHRAUCH HW100 SK PCP RIFLE
Caliber: .177, .22. Barrel: Rifled, 15.7 in. Weight: 8.6 lbs. Length: 38.4 in. Power: Precharged pneumatic. Stock: Monte Carlo walnut stock with a raised cheekpiece. Sights: Grooved for scope mounting. Features: Multi-shot side lever, includes two 14-round magazines, shrouded barrel, two-stage adjustable match trigger. Also available in a longer barrel (S) and a thumbhole stock (T) version. Velocity: 1,135 fps (.177), 870 fps (.22).
Price: $1,645.00

WEIHRAUCH HW110 ST PCP RIFLE, FAC VERSION
Caliber: .177, .20, .22. Barrel: Rifled 30.5 in. Weight: 7.5 lbs. Length: 46 in. Power: Precharged pneumatic. Stock: Black Soft Touch coated wood. Sights: None, Picatinny rail grooved for scope mounting. Features: Includes two 10-shot magazines, side lever action, fully regulated, internal pressure gauge, two-stage adjustable match trigger, available in a shorter carbine version. Velocities: 1,050 fps (.177), 965 fps (.20), 1,025 fps (.22).
Price: $1,180.00

WESTERN BIG BORE BUSHBUCK 45 PCP RIFLE
Caliber: .45. Barrel: Rifled, 30 in. Weight: 10.25 lbs. Length: 49.5 in. Power: Precharged pneumatic. Stock: Walnut or laminate. Sights: None, Picatinny rail for scope mounting. Features: One-piece aluminum receiver and Picatinny rail, all-steel air cylinder, accuracy tested to 250 yards, two 600 ft-lb or four 400 ft-lb shots per fill, accommodates extra-long bullets, approximately 3-lb. trigger pull, sling studs, single shot, also available in a shorter carbine version, made in USA.
Price: $1,895.00

WESTERN BIG BORE SIDEWINDER PCP RIFLE
Caliber: .22, .25, .30. Barrel: Rifled, TJ hammer-forged, 23 in. Weight: 8 lbs. Length: 35 in. Power: Precharged pneumatic. Stock: Synthetic, tactical style. Sights: None, Picatinny rail for scope mounting. Features: Select-fire semi- or full-auto, removable magazine, 15 (.22 or .25) or 12 (.30) shots, Picatinny under-rail for accessory mounting, accepts additional side rails, 580cc removable air bottle for quick changes in the field, adjustable regulator, quick and easy power adjustments, AR-compatible grip, 50–75 shots per fill, 50–90 ft-lbs of energy depending on caliber, made in USA. Velocity: Adjustable.
Price: $2,260.00

WESTERN JUSTICE ANNIE OAKLEY LIL SURE SHOT/JOHN WAYNE LIL DUKE BB RIFLE
Caliber: .177 steel BBs. Barrel: Smooth. Weight: 2.6 lbs. Length: 34 in. Power: Spring piston, lever action. Stock: Hardwood. Sights: Adjustable for elevation, 11mm dovetail mount. Features: 550-round BB reservoir, single-stage trigger, 16-lb. cocking effort, manual safety, available embossed with either Annie Oakley or John Wayne likeness. Velocity: 350 fps.
Price: .... $55.00–$70.00

WINCHESTER 77XS MULTI-PUMP AIR RIFLE
Caliber: .177 steel BBs, .177 pellet. Barrel: Rifled 20.8 in. Weight: 3.1 lbs. Length: 37.6 in. Power: Multi-pump pneumatic. Stock: Ambidextrous synthetic thumbhole stock. Sights: Blade front, adjustable rear, grooved for scope mounting, includes 4x32 scope and mounts. Features: Single-shot pellet, 50-round BB repeater, bolt action, lightweight, accurate and easy to shoot. Velocity: 800 fps.
Price: $140.00

ZBROIA HORTIZIA PCP RIFLE
Calibers: .177, .22. Barrel: Rifled, 13, 17.7, or 21.7 in. Weight: 6.8, 7.1, or 7.5 lbs. Length: 28, 31.7, or 43.7 in. Power: Precharged pneumatic. Stock: Black-stained ash Monte Carlo-style wood stock. Sights: None, grooved for scope mounting. Features: Up to 100 shots per fill in .177 caliber or 60 shots in .22 caliber, free-floated barrel with 12 grooves, two-stage adjustable trigger that is detachable, side-lever cocking, 10- or 12-shot repeater, built-in manometer with 4,351 psi fill, available in three barrel lengths, made in Ukraine. Velocities: .177, 1,000 fps/.22, 980 fps.
Price: $875.00

ZBROIA KOZAK TACTICAL PCP RIFLE
Calibers: .177, .22. Barrel: Rifled, 13, 17.7, or 21.7 in. Weight: 6.6 lbs. Length: 30, 32.7, or 36.6 in. Power: Precharged pneumatic. Stock: Black-stained ash wood semi-bullpup design with adjustable cheekpiece. Sights: None, grooved for scope mounting. Features: Up to 100 shots per fill (.22 caliber), free-floated barrel with 12 grooves, two-stage adjustable trigger, side-lever cocking, 10- or 12-shot repeater, built-in manometer with 4,351 psi fill, available in three barrel lengths, made in Ukraine. Velocities: .177, 1,000 fps/.22, 980 fps.
Price: $990.00

Prices given are believed to be accurate at time of publication however, many factors affect retail pricing so exact prices are not possible.

79TH EDITION, 2025 ✦ 589

Average Centerfire Rifle Cartridge Ballistics

An * after the cartridge means these loads are available with Nosler Partition or Swift A-Frame bullets.
Wea. Mag.= Weatherby Magnum. Spfd. = Springfield. A-Sq. = A-Square. N.E.=Nitro Express.

Cartridge	Bullet Wgt. Grs.	VELOCITY (fps)					ENERGY (ft. lbs.)					TRAJ. (in.)			
		Muzzle	100 yds.	200 yds.	300 yds.	400 yds.	Muzzle	100 yds.	200 yds.	300 yds.	400 yds.	100 yds.	200 yds.	300 yds.	400 yds.
17, 22															
17 Hornet	15.5	3860	2924	2159	1531	1108	513	294	160	81	42	1.4	0	-9.1	-33.7
17 Hornet	20	3650	3078	2574	2122	1721	592	421	294	200	131	1.1	0	-6.4	-20.6
17 Remington Fireball	20	4000	3380	2840	2360	1930	710	507	358	247	165	1.6	1.5	-2.8	-13.5
17 Remington Fireball	25	3850	3280	2780	2330	1925	823	597	429	301	206	0.9	0	-5.4	NA
17 Remington	20	4200	3544	2978	2477	2029	783	558	394	272	183	0	-1.3	-6.6	-17.6
17 Remington	25	4040	3284	2644	2086	1606	906	599	388	242	143	2	1.7	-4	-17
4.6x30 H&K	30	2025	1662	1358	1135	1002	273	184	122	85	66	0	-12.7	-44.5	—
4.6x30 H&K	40	1900	1569	1297	1104	988	320	218	149	108	86	0	-14.3	-39.3	—
204 Ruger (Hor)	24	4400	3667	3046	2504	2023	1032	717	494	334	218	0.6	0	-4.3	-14.3
204 Ruger (Fed)	32 Green	4030	3320	2710	2170	1710	1155	780	520	335	205	0.9	0	-5.7	-19.1
204 Ruger	32	4125	3559	3061	2616	2212	1209	900	666	486	348	0	-1.3	-6.3	—
204 Ruger	32	4225	3632	3114	2652	2234	1268	937	689	500	355	0.6	0	-4.2	-13.4
204 Ruger	40	3900	3451	3046	2677	2336	1351	1058	824	636	485	0.7	0	-4.5	-13.9
204 Ruger	45	3625	3188	2792	2428	2093	1313	1015	778	589	438	1	0	-5.5	-16.9
5.45x39mm	60	2810	2495	2201	1927	1677	1052	829	645	445	374	1	0	-9.2	-27.7
221 Fireball	40	3100	2510	1991	1547	1209	853	559	352	212	129	0	-4.1	-17.3	-45.1
221 Fireball	50	2800	2137	1580	1180	988	870	507	277	155	109	0	-7	-28	0
22 Hornet (Fed)	30 Green	3150	2150	1390	990	830	660	310	130	65	45	0	-6.6	-32.7	NA
22 Hornet	34	3050	2132	1415	1017	852	700	343	151	78	55	0	-6.6	-15.5	-29.9
22 Hornet	35	3100	2278	1601	1135	929	747	403	199	100	67	2.75	0	-16.9	-60.4
22 Hornet	40	2800	2397	2029	1698	1413	696	510	366	256	177	0	-4.6	-17.8	-43.1
22 Hornet	45	2690	2042	1502	1128	948	723	417	225	127	90	0	-7.7	-31	0
218 Bee	46	2760	2102	1550	1155	961	788	451	245	136	94	0	-7.2	-29	0
222 Rem.	35	3760	3125	2574	2085	1656	1099	759	515	338	213	1	0	-6.3	-20.8
222 Rem.	50	3345	2930	2553	2205	1886	1242	953	723	540	395	1.3	0	-6.7	-20.6
222 Remington	40	3600	3117	2673	2269	1911	1151	863	634	457	324	1.07	0	-6.13	-18.9
222 Remington	50	3140	2602	2123	1700	1350	1094	752	500	321	202	2	-0.4	-11	-33
222 Remington	55	3020	2562	2147	1773	1451	1114	801	563	384	257	2	-0.4	-11	-33
222 Rem. Mag.	40	3600	3140	2726	2347	2000	1150	876	660	489	355	1	0	-5.7	-17.8
222 Rem. Mag.	50	3340	2917	2533	2179	1855	1238	945	712	527	382	1.3	0	-6.8	-20.9
222 Rem. Mag.	55	3240	2748	2305	1906	1556	1282	922	649	444	296	2	-0.2	-9	-27
22 PPC	52	3400	2930	2510	2130	NA	1335	990	730	525	NA	2	1.4	-5	0
223 Rem.	35	3750	3206	2725	2291	1899	1092	799	577	408	280	1	0	-5.7	-18.1
223 Rem.	35	4000	3353	2796	2302	1861	1243	874	607	412	269	0.8	0	-5.3	-17.3
223 Rem.	64	2750	2368	2018	1701	1427	1074	796	578	411	289	2.4	0	-11	-34.1
223 Rem.	75	2790	2562	2345	2139	1943	1296	1093	916	762	629	1.5	0	-8.2	-24.1
223 Remington	40	3650	3010	2450	1950	1530	1185	805	535	340	265	2	1	-6	-22
223 Remington	40	3800	3305	2845	2424	2044	1282	970	719	522	371	0.84	0	-5.34	-16.6
223 Remington (Rem)	45 Green	3550	2911	2355	1865	1451	1259	847	554	347	210	2.5	2.3	-4.3	-21.1
223 Remington	50	3300	2874	2484	2130	1809	1209	917	685	504	363	1.37	0	-7.05	-21.8
223 Remington (Win)	52/53	3330	2882	2477	2106	1770	1305	978	722	522	369	2	0.6	-6.5	-21.5
223 Remington	55 Green	3240	2747	2304	1905	1554	1282	921	648	443	295	1.9	0	-8.5	-26.7
223 Remington	55	3240	2748	2305	1906	1556	1282	922	649	444	296	2	-0.2	-9	-27
223 Remington	60	3100	2712	2355	2026	1726	1280	979	739	547	397	2	0.2	-8	-24.7
223 Remington	62	3000	2700	2410	2150	1900	1240	1000	800	635	495	1.6	0	-7.7	-22.8
223 Remington	64	3020	2621	2256	1920	1619	1296	977	723	524	373	2	-0.2	-9.3	-23
223 Remington	69	3000	2720	2460	2210	1980	1380	1135	925	750	600	2	0.8	-5.8	-17.5
223 Remington	75	2790	2554	2330	2119	1926	1296	1086	904	747	617	2.37	0	-8.75	-25.1
223 Rem. Super Match	75	2930	2694	2470	2257	2055	1429	1209	1016	848	703	1.2	0	-6.9	-20.7
223 Remington	77	2750	2584	2354	2169	1992	1293	1110	948	804	679	1.93	0	-8.2	-23.8
223 WSSM	55	3850	3438	3064	2721	2402	1810	1444	1147	904	704	0.7	0	-4.4	-13.6
223 WSSM	64	3600	3144	2732	2356	2011	1841	1404	1061	789	574	1	0	-5.7	-17.7
5.56 NATO	55	3130	2740	2382	2051	1750	1196	917	693	514	372	1.1	0	-7.3	-23
5.56 NATO	75	2910	2676	2543	2242	2041	1410	1192	1002	837	693	1.2	0	-7	-21
224 Wea. Mag.	55	3650	3192	2780	2403	2057	1627	1244	943	705	516	2	1.2	-4	-17
225 Winchester	55	3570	3066	2616	2208	1838	1556	1148	836	595	412	2	1	-5	-20
22-250 Rem.	35	4450	3736	3128	2598	2125	1539	1085	761	524	351	6.5	0	-4.1	-13.4
22-250 Rem.	40	4000	3320	2720	2200	1740	1420	980	660	430	265	2	1.8	-3	-16
22-250 Rem.	40	4150	3553	3033	2570	2151	1530	1121	817	587	411	0.6	0	-4.4	-14.2
22-250 Rem.	45 Green	4000	3293	2690	2159	1696	1598	1084	723	466	287	1.7	1.7	-3.2	-15.7

Cartridge	Bullet Wgt. Grs.	VELOCITY (fps)					ENERGY (ft. lbs.)					TRAJ. (in.)			
		Muzzle	100 yds.	200 yds.	300 yds.	400 yds.	Muzzle	100 yds.	200 yds.	300 yds.	400 yds.	100 yds.	200 yds.	300 yds.	400 yds.
22-250 Rem.	50	3725	3264	2641	2455	2103	1540	1183	896	669	491	0.89	0	-5.23	-16.3
22-250 Rem.	52/55	3680	3137	2656	2222	1832	1654	1201	861	603	410	2	1.3	-4	-17
22-250 Rem.	60	3600	3195	2826	2485	2169	1727	1360	1064	823	627	2	2	-2.4	-12.3
22-250 Rem.	64	3425	2988	2591	2228	1897	1667	1269	954	705	511	1.2	0	-6.4	-20
220 Swift	40	4200	3678	3190	2739	2329	1566	1201	904	666	482	0.51	0	-4	-12.9
220 Swift	50	3780	3158	2617	2135	1710	1586	1107	760	506	325	2	1.4	-4.4	-17.9
220 Swift	50	3850	3396	2970	2576	2215	1645	1280	979	736	545	0.74	0	-4.84	-15.1
220 Swift	50	3900	3420	2990	2599	2240	1688	1298	992	750	557	0.7	0	-4.7	-14.5
220 Swift	55	3800	3370	2990	2630	2310	1765	1390	1090	850	650	0.8	0	-4.7	-14.4
220 Swift	55	3650	3194	2772	2384	2035	1627	1246	939	694	506	2	2	-2.6	-13.4
220 Swift	60	3600	3199	2824	2475	2156	1727	1364	1063	816	619	2	1.6	-4.1	-13.1
22 ARC	62	3300	3044	2803	2574	2357	1499	1275	1081	912	765	1.1	0	-5.6	-16.4
22 ARC	75	3075	2868	2672	2483	2302	1575	1370	1189	1027	883	1.4	0	-6.2	-18.1
22 ARC	88	2820	2652	2491	2335	2185	1554	1375	1212	1066	933	1.7	0	-7.3	-21.1
22 Savage H.P.	70	2868	2510	2179	1874	1600	1279	980	738	546	398	0	-4.1	-15.6	-37.1
22 Savage H.P.	71	2790	2340	1930	1570	1280	1225	860	585	390	190	2	-1	-10.4	-35.7
6mm (24)															
6mm BR Rem.	100	2550	2310	2083	1870	1671	1444	1185	963	776	620	2.5	-0.6	-11.8	0
6mm Norma BR	107	2822	2667	2517	2372	2229	1893	1690	1506	1337	1181	1.73	0	-7.24	-20.6
6mm PPC	70	3140	2750	2400	2070	NA	1535	1175	895	665	NA	2	1.4	-5	0
6mm ARC	80	3020	2788	2569	2359	2160	1620	1381	1172	989	829	1.5	0	-6.8	-19.8
6mm ARC	103	2800	2623	2452	2288	2130	1793	1573	1375	1197	1038	1.8	0	-7.6	-21.8
6mm ARC	105	2750	2580	2417	2260	2108	1763	1552	1362	1190	1036	1.9	0	-7.8	-22.4
6mm ARC	108	2750	2582	2420	2265	2115	1813	1599	1405	1230	1072	1.9	0	-7.8	-22.4
6mm Creedmoor	80	3300	3053	2820	2599	2388	1934	1655	1412	1200	1013	1.1	0	-5.5	-16.2
6mm Creedmoor	87	3210	2962	2727	2505	2292	1990	1694	1437	1212	1015	1.2	0	-5.9	-17.4
6mm Creedmoor	90	3325	3081	2851	2632	2424	2209	1897	1624	1385	1174	1.1	0	-5.4	-15.8
6mm Creedmoor	103	3050	2862	2687	2514	2348	2127	1874	1651	1446	1261	1.4	0	-6.2	-17.9
6mm Creedmoor	105	2960	2872	2612	2447	2289	2043	1805	1590	1396	1221	1.5	0	-6.6	-19
6mm Creedmoor	108	2960	2784	2615	2453	2296	2101	1859	1640	1443	1264	1.5	0	-6.6	-19
243 Winchester	55	4025	3597	3209	2853	2525	1978	1579	1257	994	779	0.6	0	-4	-12.2
243 Win.	58	3925	3465	3052	2676	2330	1984	1546	1200	922	699	0.7	0	-4.4	-13.8
243 Winchester	60	3600	3110	2660	2260	1890	1725	1285	945	680	475	2	1.8	-3.3	-15.5
243 Win.	70	3400	3020	2672	2350	2050	1797	1418	1110	858	653	0	-2.5	-9.7	—
243 Winchester	70	3400	3040	2700	2390	2100	1795	1435	1135	890	685	1.1	0	-5.9	-18
243 Winchester	75/80	3350	2955	2593	2259	1951	1993	1551	1194	906	676	2	0.9	-5	-19
243 Win.	80	3425	3081	2763	2468	2190	2984	1686	1357	1082	852	1.1	0	-5.7	-17.1
243 Win.	87	2800	2574	2359	2155	1961	1514	1280	1075	897	743	1.9	0	-8.1	-23.8
243 Win.	95	3185	2908	2649	2404	2172	2140	1784	1480	1219	995	1.3	0	-6.3	-18.6
243 W. Superformance	80	3425	3080	2760	2463	2184	2083	1684	1353	1077	847	1.1	0	-5.7	-17.1
243 Winchester	85	3320	3070	2830	2600	2380	2080	1770	1510	1280	1070	2	1.2	-4	-14
243 Winchester	90	3120	2871	2635	2411	2199	1946	1647	1388	1162	966	1.4	0	-6.4	-18.8
243 Winchester*	100	2960	2697	2449	2215	1993	1945	1615	1332	1089	882	2.5	1.2	-6	-20
243 Winchester	105	2920	2689	2470	2261	2062	1988	1686	1422	1192	992	2.5	1.6	-5	-18.4
243 Light Mag.	100	3100	2839	2592	2358	2138	2133	1790	1491	1235	1014	1.5	0	-6.8	-19.8
243 WSSM	55	4060	3628	3237	2880	2550	2013	1607	1280	1013	794	0.6	0	-3.9	-12
243 WSSM	95	3250	3000	2763	2538	2325	2258	1898	1610	1359	1140	1.2	0	-5.7	-16.9
243 WSSM	100	3110	2838	2583	2341	2112	2147	1789	1481	1217	991	1.4	0	-6.6	-19.7
6mm Remington	80	3470	3064	2694	2352	2036	2139	1667	1289	982	736	2	1.1	-5	-17
6mm R. Superformance	95	3235	2955	2692	2443	3309	2207	1841	1528	1259	1028	1.2	0	-6.1	-18
6mm Remington	100	3100	2829	2573	2332	2104	2133	1777	1470	1207	983	2.5	1.6	-5	-17
6mm Remington	105	3060	2822	2596	2381	2177	2105	1788	1512	1270	1059	2.5	1.1	-3.3	-15
240 Wea. Mag.	87	3500	3202	2924	2663	2416	2366	1980	1651	1370	1127	2	2	-2	-12
240 Wea. Mag.	100	3150	2894	2653	2425	2207	2202	1860	1563	1395	1082	1.3	0	-6.3	-18.5
240 Wea. Mag.	100	3395	3106	2835	2581	2339	2559	2142	1785	1478	1215	2.5	2.8	-2	-11
25-20 Win.	86	1460	1194	1030	931	858	407	272	203	165	141	0	-23.5	0	0
25-45 Sharps	87	3000	2677	2385	2112	1859	1739	1384	1099	862	668	1.1	0	-7.4	-22.6
25-35 Win.	117	2230	1866	1545	1282	1097	1292	904	620	427	313	2.5	-4.2	-26	0
250 Savage	100	2820	2504	2210	1936	1684	1765	1392	1084	832	630	2.5	0.4	-9	-28
257 Roberts	100	2980	2661	2363	2085	1827	1972	1572	1240	965	741	2.5	-0.8	-5.2	-21.6
257 Roberts	122	2600	2331	2078	1842	1625	1831	1472	1169	919	715	2.5	0	-10.6	-31.4
257 Roberts+P	100	3000	2758	2529	2312	2105	1998	1689	1421	1187	984	1.5	0	-7	-20.5
257 Roberts+P	117	2780	2411	2071	1761	1488	2009	1511	1115	806	576	2.5	-0.2	-10.2	-32.6
257 Roberts+P	120	2780	2560	2360	2160	1970	2060	1750	1480	1240	1030	2.5	1.2	-6.4	-23.6
257 R. Superformance	117	2946	2705	2478	2265	2057	2253	1901	1595	1329	1099	1.1	0	-5.7	-17.1
25-06 Rem.	87	3440	2995	2591	2222	1884	2286	1733	1297	954	686	2	1.1	-2.5	-14.4
25-06 Rem.	90	3350	3001	2679	2378	2098	2243	1790	1434	1130	879	1.2	0	-6	-18.3

Cartridge	Bullet Wgt. Grs.	VELOCITY (fps)					ENERGY (ft. lbs.)					TRAJ. (in.)			
		Muzzle	100 yds.	200 yds.	300 yds.	400 yds.	Muzzle	100 yds.	200 yds.	300 yds.	400 yds.	100 yds.	200 yds.	300 yds.	400 yds.
25-06 Rem.	90	3440	3043	2680	2344	2034	2364	1850	1435	1098	827	2	1.8	-3.3	-15.6
25-06 Rem.	100	3230	2893	2580	2287	2014	2316	1858	1478	1161	901	2	0.8	-5.7	-18.9
25-06 Rem.	117	2990	2770	2570	2370	2190	2320	2000	1715	1465	1246	2.5	1	-7.9	-26.6
25-06 Rem.*	120	2990	2730	2484	2252	2032	2382	1985	1644	1351	1100	2.5	1.2	-5.3	-19.6
25-06 Rem.	122	2930	2706	2492	2289	2095	2325	1983	1683	1419	1189	2.5	1.8	-4.5	-17.5
25-06 R. Superformance	117	3110	2861	2626	2403	2191	2512	2127	1792	1500	1246	1.4	0	-6.4	-18.9
25 WSSM	85	3470	3156	2863	2589	2331	2273	1880	1548	1266	1026	1	0	-5.2	-15.7
25 WSSM	115	3060	2844	2639	2442	2254	2392	2066	1778	1523	1398	1.4	0	-6.4	-18.6
25 WSSM	120	2990	2717	2459	2216	1987	2383	1967	1612	1309	1053	1.6	0	-7.4	-21.8
257 Wea. Mag.	87	3825	3456	3118	2805	2513	2826	2308	1870	1520	1220	2	2.7	-0.3	-7.6
257 Wea. Mag.	90	3550	3184	2848	2537	2246	2518	2026	1621	1286	1008	1	0	-5.3	-16
257 Wea. Mag.	100	3555	3237	2941	2665	2404	2806	2326	1920	1576	1283	2.5	3.2	0	-8
257 Wea. Mag.	110	3330	3069	2823	2591	2370	2708	2300	1947	1639	1372	1.1	0	-5.5	-16.1
257 Scramjet	100	3745	3450	3173	2912	2666	3114	2643	2235	1883	1578	2.1	2.77	0	-6.93
6.5															
6.5 Grendel	123	2590	2420	2256	2099	1948	1832	1599	1390	1203	1037	1.8	0	-8.6	-25.1
6.5x47 Lapua	123	2887	NA	2554	NA	2244	2285	NA	1788	NA	1380	NA	4.53	0	-10.7
6.5x50mm Jap.	139	2360	2160	1970	1790	1620	1720	1440	1195	985	810	2.5	-1	-13.5	0
6.5x50mm Jap.	156	2070	1830	1610	1430	1260	1475	1155	900	695	550	2.5	-4	-23.8	0
6.5x52mm Car.	139	2580	2360	2160	1970	1790	2045	1725	1440	1195	985	2.5	0	-9.9	-29
6.5x52mm Car.	156	2430	2170	1930	1700	1500	2045	1630	1285	1005	780	2.5	-1	-13.9	0
6.5x52mm Carcano	160	2250	1963	1700	1467	1271	1798	1369	1027	764	574	3.8	0	-15.9	-48.1
6.5x55mm Swe.	93	2625	2350	2090	1850	1630	1425	1140	905	705	550	2.4	0	-10.3	-31.1
6.5x55mm Swe.	123	2750	2570	2400	2240	2080	2065	1810	1580	1370	1185	1.9	0	-7.9	-22.9
6.5x55mm Swe.*	139/140	2850	2640	2440	2250	2070	2525	2170	1855	1575	1330	2.5	1.6	-5.4	-18.9
6.5x55mm Swe.	140	2550	NA	NA	NA	NA	2020	NA	NA	NA	NA	0	0	0	0
6.5x55mm Swe.	140	2735	2563	2397	2237	2084	2325	2041	1786	1556	1350	1.9	0	-8	-22.9
6.5x55mm Swe.	156	2650	2370	2110	1870	1650	2425	1950	1550	1215	945	2.5	0	-10.3	-30.6
260 Rem.	100	3200	2917	2652	2402	2165	2273	1889	1561	1281	1041	1.3	0	-6.3	-18.6
260 Rem.	130	2800	2613	2433	2261	2096	2262	1970	1709	1476	1268	1.8	0	-7.7	-22.2
260 Remington	125	2875	2669	2473	2285	2105	2294	1977	1697	1449	1230	1.71	0	-7.4	-21.4
260 Remington	140	2750	2544	2347	2158	1979	2351	2011	1712	1448	1217	2.2	0	-8.6	-24.6
6.5 Creedmoor	100	3200	2978	2768	2568	2376	2274	1970	1702	1464	1253	1.5	0	-5.7	-16.8
6.5 Creedmoor	120	3020	2815	2619	2430	2251	2430	2111	1827	1574	1350	1.4	0	-6.5	-18.9
6.5 Creedmoor	120	3050	2850	2659	2476	2300	2479	2164	1884	1634	1310	1.4	0	-6.3	-18.3
6.5 Creedmoor	140	2550	2380	2217	2060	1910	2021	1761	1527	1319	1134	2.3	0	-9.4	-27
6.5 Creedmoor	140	2710	2557	2410	2267	2129	2283	2033	1805	1598	1410	1.9	0	-7.9	-22.6
6.5 Creedmoor	140	2820	2654	2494	2339	2190	2472	2179	1915	1679	1467	1.7	0	-7.2	-20.6
6.5 C. Superformance	129	2950	2756	2570	2392	2221	2492	2175	1892	1639	1417	1.5	0	-6.8	-19.7
6.5x52R	117	2208	1856	1544	1287	1104	1267	895	620	431	317	0	-8.7	-32.2	—
6.5x57	131	2543	2295	2060	1841	1638	1882	1532	1235	986	780	0	-5.1	-18.5	-42.1
6.5-284 Norma	142	3025	2890	2758	2631	2507	2886	2634	2400	2183	1982	1.13	0	-5.7	-16.4
6.71 (264) Phantom	120	3150	2929	2718	2517	2325	2645	2286	1969	1698	1440	1.3	0	-6	-17.5
6.5 Rem. Mag.	120	3210	2905	2621	2353	2102	2745	2248	1830	1475	1177	2.5	1.7	-4.1	-16.3
264 Win. Mag.	100	3400	3104	2828	2568	2322	2566	2139	1775	1464	1197	1.1	0	-5.4	-16.1
264 Win. Mag.	125	3200	2978	2767	2566	2373	2841	2461	2125	1827	1563	1.2	0	-5.8	-16.8
264 Win. Mag.	130	3100	2900	2709	2526	2350	2773	2427	2118	1841	1594	1.3	0	-6.1	-17.6
264 Win. Mag.	140	3030	2782	2548	2326	2114	2854	2406	2018	1682	1389	2.5	1.4	-5.1	-18
6.5 Nosler	129	3400	3213	3035	2863	2698	3310	2957	2638	2348	2085	0.9	0	-4.7	-13.6
6.5 Nosler	140	3300	3118	2943	2775	2613	3119	2784	2481	2205	1955	1	0	-5	-14.6
6.71 (264) Blackbird	140	3480	3261	3053	2855	2665	3766	3307	2899	2534	2208	2.4	3.1	0	-7.4
6.8mm Rem.	115	2775	2472	2190	1926	1683	1966	1561	1224	947	723	2.1	0	-3.7	-9.4
27															
270 Win. (Rem.)	115	2710	2482	2265	2059	NA	1875	1485	1161	896	NA	0	4.8	-17.3	0
270 Win.	120	2675	2288	1935	1619	1351	1907	1395	998	699	486	2.6	0	-12	-37.4
270 Win.	140	2940	2747	2563	2386	2216	2687	2346	2042	1770	1526	1.8	0	-6.8	-19.8
270 Win. Supreme	130	3150	2881	2628	2388	2161	2865	2396	1993	1646	1348	1.3	0	-6.4	-18.9
270 Win. Supreme	150	2930	2693	2468	2254	2051	2860	2416	2030	1693	1402	1.7	0	-7.4	-21.6
270 W. Superformance	130	3200	2984	2788	2582	2393	2955	2570	2228	1924	1653	1.2	0	-5.7	-16.7
270 Winchester	100	3430	3021	2649	2305	1988	2612	2027	1557	1179	877	2	1	-4.9	-17.5
270 Winchester	130	3060	2776	2510	2259	2022	2702	2225	1818	1472	1180	2.5	1.4	-5.3	-18.2
270 Winchester	135	3000	2780	2570	2369	2178	2697	2315	1979	1682	1421	2.5	1.4	-6	-17.6
270 Winchester*	140	2940	2700	2480	2260	2060	2685	2270	1905	1590	1315	2.5	1.8	-4.6	-17.9
270 Winchester*	150	2850	2585	2336	2100	1879	2705	2226	1817	1468	1175	2.5	1.2	-6.5	-22
270 WSM	130	3275	3041	2820	2609	2408	3096	2669	2295	1564	1673	1.1	0	-5.5	-16.1
270 WSM	140	3125	2865	2619	2386	2165	3035	2559	2132	1769	1457	1.4	0	-6.5	-19
270 WSM	150	3000	2795	2599	2412	2232	2997	2601	2250	1937	1659	1.5	0	-6.6	-19.2

Cartridge	Bullet Wgt. Grs.	VELOCITY (fps)					ENERGY (ft. lbs.)					TRAJ. (in.)			
		Muzzle	100 yds.	200 yds.	300 yds.	400 yds.	Muzzle	100 yds.	200 yds.	300 yds.	400 yds.	100 yds.	200 yds.	300 yds.	400 yds.
270 WSM	150	3120	2923	2734	2554	2380	3242	2845	2490	2172	1886	1.3	0	-5.9	-17.2
270 Wea. Mag.	100	3760	3380	3033	2712	2412	3139	2537	2042	1633	1292	2	2.4	-1.2	-10.1
270 Wea. Mag.	130	3375	3119	2878	2649	2432	3287	2808	2390	2026	1707	2.5	-2.9	-0.9	-9.9
270 Wea. Mag.	130	3450	3194	2958	2732	2517	3435	2949	2525	2143	1828	1	0	-4.9	-14.5
270 Wea. Mag.*	150	3245	3036	2837	2647	2465	3507	3070	2681	2334	2023	2.5	2.6	-1.8	-11.4
6.8 REM SPC	90	2840	2444	2083	1756	1469	1611	1194	867	616	431	2.2	0	-3.9	-32
6.8 REM SPC	110	2570	2338	2118	1910	1716	1613	1335	1095	891	719	2.4	0	-6.3	-20.8
6.8 REM SPC	120	2460	2250	2051	1863	1687	1612	1349	1121	925	758	2.3	0	-10.5	-31.1
7mm															
7mm BR	140	2216	2012	1821	1643	1481	1525	1259	1031	839	681	2	-3.7	-20	0
7mm Mauser*	139/140	2660	2435	2221	2018	1827	2199	1843	1533	1266	1037	2.5	0	-9.6	-27.7
7mm Mauser	139	2740	2556	2379	2209	2046	2317	2016	1747	1506	1292	1.9	0	-8.1	-23.3
7mm Mauser	154	2690	2490	2300	2120	1940	2475	2120	1810	1530	1285	2.5	0.8	-7.5	-23.5
7mm Mauser	175	2440	2137	1857	1603	1382	2313	1774	1340	998	742	2.5	-1.7	-16.1	0
7x30 Waters	120	2700	2300	1930	1600	1330	1940	1405	990	685	470	2.5	-0.2	-12.3	0
7mm-08 Rem.	120	2675	2435	2207	1992	1790	1907	1579	1298	1057	854	2.2	0	-9.4	-27.5
7mm-08 Rem.	120	3000	2725	2467	2223	1992	2398	1979	1621	1316	1058	2	0	-7.6	-22.3
7mm-08 Rem.	139	2840	2608	2387	2177	1978	2489	2098	1758	1463	1207	1.8	0	-7.9	-23.2
7mm-08 Rem.*	140	2860	2625	2402	2189	1988	2542	2142	1793	1490	1228	2.5	0.8	-6.9	-21.9
7mm-08 Rem.	154	2715	2510	2315	2128	1950	2520	2155	1832	1548	1300	2.5	1	-7	-22.3
7-08 R. Superformance	139	2950	2857	2571	2393	2222	2686	2345	2040	1768	1524	1.5	0	-6.8	-19.7
7x64mm	173	2526	2260	2010	1777	1565	2452	1962	1552	1214	941	0	-5.3	-19.3	-44.4
7x64mm Bren.	140	2950	2710	2483	2266	2061	2705	2283	1910	1597	1320	1.5	0	-2.9	-7.3
7x64mm Bren.	154	2820	2610	2420	2230	2050	2720	2335	1995	1695	1430	2.5	1.4	-5.7	-19.9
7x64mm Bren.*	160	2850	2669	2495	2327	2166	2885	2530	2211	1924	1667	2.5	1.6	-4.8	-17.8
7x64mm Bren.	175	2650	2445	2248	2061	1883	2728	2322	1964	1650	1378	2.2	0	-9.1	-26.4
7x65mmR	173	2608	2337	2082	1844	1626	2613	2098	1666	1307	1015	0	-4.9	-17.9	-41.9
275 Rigby	139	2680	2456	2242	2040	1848	2217	1861	1552	1284	1054	2.2	0	-9.1	-26.5
284 Winchester	150	2860	2595	2344	2108	1886	2724	2243	1830	1480	1185	2.5	0.8	-7.3	-23.2
280 R. Superformance	139	3090	2890	2699	2516	2341	2946	2578	2249	1954	1691	1.3	0	-6.1	-17.7
280 Rem.	139	3090	2891	2700	2518	2343	2947	2579	2250	1957	1694	1.3	0	-6.1	-17.7
280 Remington	140	3000	2758	2528	2309	2102	2797	2363	1986	1657	1373	2.5	1.4	-5.2	-18.3
280 Remington*	150	2890	2624	2373	2135	1912	2781	2293	1875	1518	1217	2.5	0.8	-7.1	-22.6
280 Remington	160	2840	2637	2442	2556	2078	2866	2471	2120	1809	1535	2.5	0.8	-6.7	-21
280 Remington	165	2820	2510	2220	1950	1701	2913	2308	1805	1393	1060	2.5	0.4	-8.8	-26.5
280 Ack. Imp.	140	3150	2946	2752	2566	2387	3084	2698	2354	2047	1772	1.3	0	-5.8	-17
280 Ack. Imp.	150	2900	2712	2533	2360	2194	2800	2450	2136	1855	1603	1.6	0	-7	-20.3
280 Ack. Imp.	160	2950	2751	2561	2379	2205	3091	2686	2331	2011	1727	1.5	0	-6.9	-19.9
7x61mm S&H Sup.	154	3060	2720	2400	2100	1820	3200	2520	1965	1505	1135	2.5	1.8	-5	-19.8
7mm Dakota	160	3200	3001	2811	2630	2455	3637	3200	2808	2456	2140	2.1	1.9	-2.8	-12.5
7mm Rem. Mag.	139	3190	2986	2791	2605	2427	3141	2752	2405	2095	1817	1.2	0	-5.7	-16.5
7mm Rem. Mag. (Rem.)	140	2710	2482	2265	2059	NA	2283	1915	1595	1318	NA	0	-4.5	-1.57	0
7mm Rem. Mag.*	139/140	3150	2930	2710	2510	2320	3085	2660	2290	1960	1670	2.5	2.4	-2.4	-12.7
7mm Rem. Mag.	150/154	3110	2830	2568	2320	2085	3221	2667	2196	1792	1448	2.5	1.6	-4.6	-16.5
7mm Rem. Mag.*	160/162	2950	2730	2520	2320	2120	3090	2650	2250	1910	1600	2.5	1.8	-4.4	-17.8
7mm Rem. Mag.	165	2900	2699	2507	2324	2147	3081	2669	2303	1978	1689	2.5	1.2	-5.9	-19
7mm Rem Mag.	175	2860	2645	2440	2244	2057	3178	2718	2313	1956	1644	2.5	1	-6.5	-20.7
7 R.M. Superformance	139	3240	3033	2836	2648	2467	3239	2839	2482	2163	1877	1.1	0	-5.5	-15.9
7 R.M. Superformance	154	3100	2914	2736	2565	2401	3286	2904	2277	1927	1620	1.3	0	-6	-17.7
7mm Rem. SA ULTRA MAG	140	3175	2934	2707	2490	2283	3033	2676	2188	1782	1437	2.5	2.1	-3.6	-15.8
7mm Rem. SA ULTRA MAG	150	3110	2828	2563	2313	2077	3221	2663	2235	1957	1706	1.7	0	-7.2	-20.7
7mm Rem. SA ULTRA MAG	160	2950	2676	2508	2347	2192	2885	2543	2350	2029	1743	2.6	2.2	-3.6	-15.4
7mm Rem. SA ULTRA MAG	160	2960	2762	2572	2390	2215	3112	2709	2430	2106	1812	1.2	0	-5.6	-16.4
7mm Rem. WSM	140	3225	3008	2801	2603	2414	3233	2812	2430	2106	1812	1.2	0	-5.6	-16.4
7mm Rem. WSM	160	2990	2744	2512	2081	1883	3176	2675	2241	1864	1538	1.6	0	-7.1	-20.8
7mm Wea. Mag.	139	3300	3091	2891	2701	2519	3361	2948	2580	2252	1958	1.1	0	-5.2	-15.2
7mm Wea. Mag.	140	3225	2970	2729	2501	2283	3233	2741	2315	1943	1621	2.5	2	-3.2	-14
7mm Wea. Mag.	140	3340	3127	2925	2732	2546	3467	3040	2659	2320	2016	0	-2.1	-8.2	-19
7mm Wea. Mag.	150	3175	2957	2751	2553	2364	3357	2913	2520	2171	1861	0	-2.5	-9.6	-22
7mm Wea. Mag.	154	3260	3023	2799	2586	2382	3539	3044	2609	2227	1890	2.5	2.8	-1.5	-10.8
7mm Wea. Mag.*	160	3200	3004	2816	2637	2464	3637	3205	2817	2469	2156	2.5	2.7	-1.5	-10.6
7mm Wea. Mag.	165	2950	2747	2553	2367	2189	3188	2765	2388	2053	1756	2.5	1.8	-4.2	-16.4
7mm Wea. Mag.	175	2910	2693	2486	2288	2098	3293	2818	2401	2033	1711	2.5	1.2	-5.9	-19.4
7.21(.284) Tomahawk	140	3300	3118	2943	2774	2612	3386	3022	2693	2393	2122	2.3	3.2	0	-7.7
7mm STW	140	3300	3086	2889	2697	2513	3384	2966	2594	2261	1963	0	-2.1	-8.5	-19.6
7mm STW	140	3325	3064	2818	2585	2364	3436	2918	2468	2077	1737	2.3	1.8	-3	-13.1
7mm STW	150	3175	2957	2751	2553	2364	3357	2913	2520	2171	1861	0	-2.5	-9.6	-22

Cartridge	Bullet Wgt. Grs.	VELOCITY (fps)					ENERGY (ft. lbs.)					TRAJ. (in.)			
		Muzzle	100 yds.	200 yds.	300 yds.	400 yds.	Muzzle	100 yds.	200 yds.	300 yds.	400 yds.	100 yds.	200 yds.	300 yds.	400 yds.
7mm STW	175	2900	2760	2625	2493	2366	3267	2960	2677	2416	2175	0	-3.1	-11.2	-24.9
7mm STW Supreme	160	3150	2894	2652	2422	2204	3526	2976	2499	2085	1727	1.3	0	-6.3	-18.5
7mm Rem. Ultra Mag.	140	3425	3184	2956	2740	2534	3646	3151	2715	2333	1995	1.7	1.6	-2.6	-11.4
7mm Rem. Ultra Mag.	160	3225	3035	2854	2680	2512	3694	3273	2894	2551	2242	0	-2.3	-8.8	-20.2
7mm Rem. Ultra Mag.	174	3040	2896	2756	2621	2490	3590	3258	2952	2669	2409	0	-2.6	-9.9	-22.2
7mm Firehawk	140	3625	3373	3135	2909	2695	4084	3536	3054	2631	2258	2.2	2.9	0	-7.03
7.21 (.284) Firebird	140	3750	3522	3306	3101	2905	4372	3857	3399	2990	2625	1.6	2.4	0	-6
30															
300 ACC Blackout	110	2150	1886	1646	1432	1254	1128	869	661	501	384	0	-8.3	-29.6	-67.8
300 AAC Blackout	125	2250	2031	1826	1636	1464	1404	1145	926	743	595	0	-7	-24.4	-54.8
30 Carbine	110	1990	1567	1236	1035	923	977	600	373	262	208	0	-13.5	0	0
30 Carbine	110	2000	1601	1279	1067	—	977	626	399	278	—	0	-12.9	-47.2	—
300 Whisper	110	2375	2094	1834	1597	NA	1378	1071	822	623	NA	3.2	0	-13.6	NA
300 Whisper	208	1020	988	959	NA	NA	480	451	422	NA	NA	0	-34.1	NA	NA
303 Savage	190	1890	1612	1327	1183	1055	1507	1096	794	591	469	2.5	-7.6	0	0
30 Remington	170	2120	1822	1555	1328	1153	1696	1253	913	666	502	2.5	-4.7	-26.3	0
7.62x39mm Rus.	123	2360	2049	1764	1511	1296	1521	1147	850	623	459	3.4	0	-14.7	-44.7
7.62x39mm Rus.	123/125	2300	2030	1780	1550	1350	1445	1125	860	655	500	2.5	-2	-17.5	0
30-30 Win.	55	3400	2693	2085	1570	1187	1412	886	521	301	172	2	0	-10.2	-35
30-30 Win.	125	2570	2090	1660	1320	1080	1830	1210	770	480	320	-2	-2.6	-19.9	0
30-30 Win.	140	2500	2198	1918	1662	—	1943	1501	1143	858	—	2.9	0	-12.4	—
30-30 Win.	150	2390	2040	1723	1447	1225	1902	1386	989	697	499	0	-7.5	-27	-63
30-30 Win. Supreme	150	2480	2095	1747	1446	1209	2049	1462	1017	697	487	0	-6.5	-24.5	0
30-30 Win.	160	2300	1997	1719	1473	1268	1879	1416	1050	771	571	2.5	-2.9	-20.2	0
30-30 Win. Lever Evolution	160	2400	2150	1916	1699	NA	2046	1643	1304	1025	NA	3	0.2	-12.1	NA
30-30 PMC Cowboy	170	1300	1198	1121	—	—	638	474	—	—	—	0	-27	0	0
30-30 Win.*	170	2200	1895	1619	1381	1191	1827	1355	989	720	535	2.5	-5.8	-23.6	0
300 Savage	150	2630	2354	2094	1853	1631	2303	1845	1462	1143	886	2.5	-0.4	-10.1	-30.7
300 Savage	150	2740	2499	2272	2056	1852	2500	2081	1718	1407	1143	2.1	0	-8.8	-25.8
300 Savage	180	2350	2137	1935	1754	1570	2207	1825	1496	1217	985	2.5	-1.6	-15.2	0
30-40 Krag	180	2430	2213	2007	1813	1632	2360	1957	1610	1314	1064	2.5	-1.4	-13.8	0
7.65x53mm Arg.	180	2590	2390	2200	2010	1830	2685	2280	1925	1615	1345	2.5	0	-27.6	0
7.5x53mm Argentine	150	2785	2519	2269	2032	1814	2583	2113	1714	1376	1096	2	0	-8.8	-25.5
308 Marlin Express	140	2800	2532	2279	2040	1818	2437	1992	1614	1294	1207	2	0	-8.7	-25.8
308 Marlin Express	160	2660	2430	2226	2026	1836	2513	2111	1761	1457	1197	3	1.7	-6.7	-23.5
307 Winchester	150	2760	2321	1924	1575	1289	2530	1795	1233	826	554	2.5	-1.5	-13.6	0
7.5x55 Swiss	180	2650	2450	2250	2060	1880	2805	2390	2020	1700	1415	2.5	0.6	-8.1	-24.9
7.5x55mm Swiss	165	2720	2515	2319	2132	1954	2710	2317	1970	1665	1398	2	0	-8.5	-24.6
30 Remington AR	123/125	2800	2465	2154	1867	1606	2176	1686	1288	967	716	2.1	0	-9.7	-29.4
308 Winchester	55	3770	3215	2726	2286	1888	1735	1262	907	638	435	-2	1.4	-3.8	-15.8
308 Win.	110	3165	2830	2520	2230	1960	2447	1956	1551	1215	938	1.4	0	-6.9	-20.9
308 Win. PDX1	120	2850	2497	2171	NA	NA	2164	1662	1256	NA	NA	0	-2.8	NA	NA
308 Winchester	150	2820	2533	2263	2009	1774	2648	2137	1705	1344	1048	2.5	0.4	-8.5	-26.1
308 W. Superformance	150	3000	2772	2555	2348	1962	2997	2558	2173	1836	1540	1.5	0	-6.9	-20
308 Win.	155	2775	2553	2342	2141	1950	2650	2243	1887	1577	1308	1.9	0	-8.3	-24.2
308 Win.	155	2850	2640	2438	2247	2064	2795	2398	2047	1737	1466	1.8	0	-7.5	-22.1
308 Winchester	165	2700	2440	2194	1963	1748	2670	2180	1763	1411	1199	2.5	0	-9.7	-28.5
308 Winchester	168	2680	2493	2314	2143	1979	2678	2318	1998	1713	1460	2.5	0	-8.9	-25.3
308 Win. Super Match	168	2870	2647	2462	2284	2114	3008	2613	2261	1946	1667	1.7	0	-7.5	-21.6
308 Win. (Fed.)	170	2000	1740	1510	NA	NA	1510	1145	860	NA	NA	0	0	0	0
308 Winchester	178	2620	2415	2220	2034	1857	2713	2306	1948	1635	1363	2.5	0	-9.6	-27.6
308 Win. Super Match	178	2780	2609	2444	2285	2132	3054	2690	2361	2064	1797	1.8	0	-7.6	-21.9
308 Winchester*	180	2620	2393	2178	1974	1782	2743	2288	1896	1557	1269	2.5	-0.2	-10.2	-28.5
30-06 Spfd.	55	4080	3485	2965	2502	2083	2033	1483	1074	764	530	2	1.9	-2.1	-11.7
30-06 Spfd. (Rem.)	125	2660	2335	2034	1757	NA	1964	1513	1148	856	NA	0	-5.2	-18.9	0
30-06 Spfd.	125	2700	2412	2143	1891	1660	2023	1615	1274	993	765	2.3	0	-9.9	-29.5
30-06 Spfd.	125	3140	2780	2447	2138	1853	2736	2145	1662	1279	953	2	1	-6.2	-21
30-06 Spfd.	150	2910	2617	2342	2083	1853	2820	2281	1827	1445	1135	2.5	0.8	-7.2	-23.4
30-06 Superformance	150	3080	2848	2617	2417	2216	3159	2700	2298	1945	1636	1.4	0	-6.4	-18.9
30-06 Spfd.	152	2910	2654	2413	2184	1968	2858	2378	1965	1610	1307	2.5	1	-6.6	-21.3
30-06 Spfd.*	165	2800	2534	2283	2047	1825	2872	2352	1909	1534	1220	2.5	0.4	-8.4	-25.5
30-06 Spfd.	168	2710	2522	2346	2169	2003	2739	2372	2045	1754	1497	2.5	0.4	-8	-23.5
30-06 M1 Garand	168	2710	2523	2343	2171	2006	2739	2374	2048	1758	1501	2.3	0	-8.6	-24.6
30-06 Spfd. (Fed.)	170	2000	1740	1510	NA	NA	1510	1145	860	NA	NA	0	0	0	0
30-06 Spfd.	178	2720	2511	2311	2121	1939	2924	2491	2111	1777	1486	2.5	0.4	-8.2	-24.6
30-06 Spfd.*	180	2700	2469	2250	2042	1846	2913	2436	2023	1666	1362	-2.5	0	-9.3	-27
30-06 Superformance	180	2820	2630	2447	2272	2104	3178	2764	2393	2063	1769	1.8	0	-7.6	-21.9

Cartridge	Bullet Wgt. Grs.	VELOCITY (fps)					ENERGY (ft. lbs.)					TRAJ. (in.)			
		Muzzle	100 yds.	200 yds.	300 yds.	400 yds.	Muzzle	100 yds.	200 yds.	300 yds.	400 yds.	100 yds.	200 yds.	300 yds.	400 yds.
30-06 Spfd.	220	2410	2130	1870	1632	1422	2837	2216	1708	1301	988	2.5	-1.7	-18	0
30-06 High Energy	180	2880	2690	2500	2320	2150	3315	2880	2495	2150	1845	1.7	0	-7.2	-21
30 T/C	150	2920	2696	2483	2280	2087	2849	2421	2054	1732	1450	1.7	0	-7.3	-21.3
30 T/C Superformance	150	3000	2772	2555	2348	2151	2997	2558	2173	1836	1540	1.5	0	-6.9	-20
30 T/C Superformance	165	2850	2644	2447	2258	2078	2975	2560	2193	1868	1582	1.7	0	-7.6	-22
300 Rem SA Ultra Mag	150	3200	2901	2622	2359	2112	3410	2803	2290	1854	1485	1.3	0	-6.4	-19.1
300 Rem SA Ultra Mag	165	3075	2792	2527	2276	2040	3464	2856	2339	1898	1525	1.5	0	-7	-20.7
300 Rem SA Ultra Mag	180	2960	2761	2571	2389	2214	3501	3047	2642	2280	1959	2.6	2.2	-3.6	-15.4
300 Rem. SA Ultra Mag	200	2800	2644	2494	2348	2208	3841	3104	2761	2449	2164	0	-3.5	-12.5	-27.9
7.82 (308) Patriot	150	3250	2999	2762	2537	2323	3519	2997	2542	2145	1798	1.2	0	-5.8	-16.9
300 RCM	150	3265	3023	2794	2577	2369	3550	3043	2600	2211	1870	1.2	0	-5.6	-16.5
300 RCM Superformance	150	3310	3065	2833	2613	2404	3648	3128	2673	2274	1924	1.1	0	-5.4	-16
300 RCM Superformance	165	3185	2964	2753	2552	2360	3716	3217	2776	2386	2040	1.2	0	-5.8	-17
300 RCM Superformance	180	3040	2840	2649	2466	2290	3693	3223	2804	2430	2096	1.4	0	-6.4	-18.5
300 WSM	150	3300	3061	2834	2619	2414	3628	3121	2676	2285	1941	1.1	0	-5.4	-15.9
300 WSM	180	2970	2741	2524	2317	2120	3526	3005	2547	2147	1797	1.6	0	-7	-20.5
300 WSM	180	3010	2923	2734	2554	2380	3242	2845	2490	2172	1886	1.3	0	-5.9	-17.2
300 WSM	190	2875	2729	2588	2451	2319	3486	3142	2826	2535	2269	0	3.2	-11.5	-25.7
308 Norma Mag.	180	2975	2787	2608	2435	2269	3536	3105	2718	2371	2058	0	-3	-11.1	-25
308 Norma Mag.	180	3020	2820	2630	2440	2270	3645	3175	2755	2385	2050	2.5	2	-3.5	-14.8
300 Dakota	200	3000	2824	2656	2493	2336	3996	3542	3131	2760	2423	2.2	1.5	-4	-15.2
300 H&H Mag.	180	2870	2678	2494	2318	2148	3292	2866	2486	2147	1844	1.7	0	-7.3	-21.6
300 H&H Magnum*	180	2880	2640	2412	2196	1990	3315	2785	2325	1927	1583	2.5	0.8	-6.8	-21.7
300 H&H Mag.	200	2750	2596	2447	2303	2164	3357	2992	2659	2355	2079	1.8	0	-7.6	-21.8
300 H&H Magnum	220	2550	2267	2002	1757	NA	3167	2510	1958	1508	NA	-2.5	-0.4	-12	0
300 Win. Mag.	150	3290	2951	2636	2342	2068	3605	2900	2314	1827	1424	2.5	1.9	-3.8	-15.8
300 WM Superformance	150	3400	3150	2914	2690	2477	3850	3304	2817	2409	2043	1	0	-5.1	-15
300 Win. Mag.	165	3100	2877	2665	2462	2269	3522	3033	2603	2221	1897	2.5	2.4	-3	-16.9
300 Win. Mag.	178	2900	2760	2568	2375	2191	3509	3030	2606	2230	1897	2.5	1.4	-5	-17.6
300 Win. Mag.	178	2960	2770	2588	2413	2245	3463	3032	2647	2301	1992	1.5	0	-6.7	-19.4
300 WM Super Match	178	2960	2770	2587	2412	2243	3462	3031	2645	2298	1988	1.5	0	-6.7	-19.4
300 Win. Mag.*	180	2960	2745	2540	2344	2157	3501	3011	2578	2196	1859	2.5	1.2	-5.5	-18.5
300 WM Superformance	180	3130	2927	2732	2546	2366	3917	3424	2983	2589	2238	1.3	0	-5.9	-17.3
300 Win. Mag.	190	2885	1691	2506	2327	2156	3511	3055	2648	2285	1961	2.5	1.2	-5.7	-19
300 Win. Mag.	195	2930	2760	2596	2438	2286	3717	3297	2918	2574	2262	1.5	0	-6.7	-19.4
300 Win. Mag.*	200	2825	2595	2376	2167	1970	3545	2991	2508	2086	1742	-2.5	1.6	-4.7	-17.2
300 Win. Mag.	220	2680	2448	2228	2020	1823	3508	2927	2424	1993	1623	2.5	0	-9.5	-27.5
300 Rem. Ultra Mag.	150	3450	3208	2980	2762	2556	3964	3427	2956	2541	2175	1.7	1.5	-2.6	-11.2
300 Rem. Ultra Mag.	150	2910	2686	2473	2279	2077	2820	2403	2037	1716	1436	1.7	0	-7.4	-21.5
300 Rem. Ultra Mag.	165	3350	3099	2862	2938	2424	4110	3518	3001	2549	2152	1.1	0	-5.3	-15.6
300 Rem. Ultra Mag.	180	3250	3037	2834	2640	2454	4221	3686	3201	2786	2407	2.4	0	-3	-12.7
300 Rem. Ultra Mag.	180	2960	2774	2505	2294	2093	3501	2971	2508	2103	1751	2.7	2.2	-3.8	-16.4
300 Rem. Ultra Mag.	200	3032	2791	2562	2345	2138	4083	3459	2916	2442	2030	1.5	0	-6.8	-19.9
300 Rem. Ultra Mag.	210	2920	2790	2665	2543	2424	3975	3631	3311	3015	2740	1.5	0	-6.4	-18.1
300 Wea. Mag.	100	3900	3441	3038	2652	2305	3714	2891	2239	1717	1297	2	2.6	-0.6	-8.7
300 Wea. Mag.	150	3375	3126	2892	2670	2459	3794	3255	2786	2374	2013	1	0	-5.2	-15.3
300 Wea. Mag.	150	3600	3307	3033	2776	2533	4316	3642	3064	2566	2137	2.5	3.2	0	-8.1
300 Wea. Mag.	165	3140	2921	2713	2515	2325	3612	3126	2697	2317	1980	1.3	0	-6	-17.5
300 Wea. Mag.	165	3450	3210	3000	2792	2593	4360	3796	3297	2855	2464	2.5	3.2	0	-7.8
300 Wea. Mag.	178	3120	2902	2695	2497	2308	3847	3329	2870	2464	2104	2.5	-1.7	-3.6	-14.7
300 Wea. Mag.	180	3330	3110	2910	2710	2520	4430	3875	3375	2935	2540	1	0	-5.2	-15.1
300 Wea. Mag.	190	3030	2830	2638	2455	2279	3873	3378	2936	2542	2190	2.5	1.6	-4.3	-16
300 Wea. Mag.	220	2850	2541	2283	1964	1730	3967	3155	2480	1922	1471	2.5	0.4	-8.5	-26.4
300 Pegasus	180	3500	3319	3145	2978	2817	4896	4401	3953	3544	3172	2.28	2.89	0	-6.79
31															
32-20 Win.	100	1210	1021	913	834	769	325	231	185	154	131	0	-32.3	0	0
303 British	150	2685	2441	2211	1993	1789	2401	1985	1628	1323	1066	2.2	0	-9.3	-27.4
303 British	180	2460	2124	1817	1542	1311	2418	1803	1319	950	687	2.5	-1.8	-16.8	0
303 Light Mag.	150	2830	2570	2325	2094	1884	2667	2199	1800	1461	1185	2	0	-8.4	-24.6
7.62x54mm Rus.	146	2950	2730	2520	2320	NA	2820	2415	2055	1740	NA	2.5	2	-4.4	-17.7
7.62x54mm Rus.	174	2800	2607	2422	2245	2075	3029	2626	2267	1947	1664	1.8	0	-7.8	-22.4
7.62x54mm Rus.	180	2580	2370	2180	2000	1820	2650	2250	1900	1590	1100	2.5	0	-9.8	-28.5
7.7x58mm Jap.	150	2640	2399	2170	1954	1752	2321	1916	1568	1271	1022	2.3	0	-9.7	-28.5
7.7x58mm Jap.	180	2500	2300	2100	1920	1750	2490	2105	1770	1475	1225	2.5	0	-10.4	-30.2
8mm															
8x56 R	205	2400	2188	1987	1797	1621	2621	2178	1796	1470	1196	2.9	0	-11.7	-34.3
8x57mm JS Mau.	165	2850	2520	2210	1930	1670	2965	2330	1795	1360	1015	2.5	1	-7.7	0

Cartridge	Bullet Wgt. Grs.	VELOCITY (fps)					ENERGY (ft. lbs.)					TRAJ. (in.)			
		Muzzle	100 yds.	200 yds.	300 yds.	400 yds.	Muzzle	100 yds.	200 yds.	300 yds.	400 yds.	100 yds.	200 yds.	300 yds.	400 yds.
32 Win. Special	165	2410	2145	1897	1669	NA	2128	1685	1318	1020	NA	2	0	-13	-19.9
32 Win. Special	170	2250	1921	1626	1372	1175	1911	1393	998	710	521	2.5	-3.5	-22.9	0
8mm Mauser	170	2360	1969	1622	1333	1123	2102	1464	993	671	476	2.5	-3.1	-22.2	0
8mm Mauser	196	2500	2338	2182	2032	1888	2720	2379	2072	1797	1552	2.4	0	-9.8	-27.9
325 WSM	180	3060	2841	2632	2432	2242	3743	3226	2769	2365	2009	1.4	0	-6.4	-18.7
325 WSM	200	2950	2753	2565	2384	2210	3866	3367	2922	2524	2170	1.5	0	-6.8	-19.8
325 WSM	220	2840	2605	2382	2169	1968	3941	3316	2772	2300	1893	1.8	0	-8	-23.3
8mm Rem. Mag.	185	3080	2761	2464	2186	1927	3896	3131	2494	1963	1525	2.5	1.4	-5.5	-19.7
8mm Rem. Mag.	220	2830	2581	2346	2123	1913	3912	3254	2688	2201	1787	2.5	0.6	-7.6	-23.5
33															
338 Federal	180	2830	2590	2350	2130	1930	3200	2670	2215	1820	1480	1.8	0	-8.2	-23.9
338 Marlin Express	200	2565	2365	2174	1992	1820	2922	2484	2099	1762	1471	3	1.2	-7.9	-25.9
338 Federal	185	2750	2550	2350	2160	1980	3105	2660	2265	1920	1615	1.9	0	-8.3	-24.1
338 Federal	210	2630	2410	2200	2010	1820	3225	2710	2265	1880	1545	2.3	0	-9.4	-27.3
338 Federal MSR	185	2680	2459	2230	2020	1820	2950	2460	2035	1670	1360	2.2	0	-9.2	-26.8
338-06	200	2750	2553	2364	2184	2011	3358	2894	2482	2118	1796	1.9	0	-8.22	-23.6
330 Dakota	250	2900	2719	2545	2378	2217	4668	4103	3595	3138	2727	2.3	1.3	-5	-17.5
338 Lapua	250	2900	2685	2481	2285	2098	4668	4002	2416	2899	2444	1.7	0	-7.3	-21.3
338 Lapua	250	2963	2795	2640	2493	NA	4842	4341	3881	3458	NA	1.9	0	-7.9	0
338 RCM Superformance	185	2980	2755	2542	2338	2143	3647	3118	2653	2242	1887	1.5	0	-6.9	-20.3
338 RCM Superformance	200	2950	2744	2547	2358	2177	3846	3342	2879	2468	2104	1.6	0	-6.9	-20.1
338 RCM Superformance	225	2750	2575	2407	2245	2089	3778	3313	2894	2518	2180	1.9	0	-7.9	-22.7
338 WM Superformance	185	3080	2850	2632	2424	2226	3896	3337	2845	2413	2034	1.4	0	-6.4	-18.8
338 Win. Mag.	200	3030	2820	2620	2429	2246	4077	3532	3049	2621	2240	1.4	0	-6.5	-18.9
338 Win. Mag.*	210	2830	2590	2370	2150	1940	3735	3130	2610	2155	1760	2.5	1.4	-6	-20.9
338 Win. Mag.*	225	2785	2517	2266	2029	1808	3871	3165	2565	2057	1633	2.5	0.4	-8.5	-25.9
338 WM Superformance	225	2840	2758	2582	2414	2252	4318	3798	3331	2911	2533	1.5	0	-6.8	-19.5
338 Win. Mag.	230	2780	2573	2375	2186	2005	3948	3382	2881	2441	2054	2.5	1.2	-6.3	-21
338 Win. Mag.*	250	2660	2456	2261	2075	1898	3927	3348	2837	2389	1999	2.5	0.2	-9	-26.2
338 Ultra Mag.	250	2860	2645	2440	2244	2057	4540	3882	3303	2794	2347	1.7	0	-7.6	-22.1
338 Lapua Match	250	2900	2760	2625	2494	2366	4668	4229	3825	3452	3108	1.5	0	-6.6	-18.8
338 Lapua Match	285	2745	2623	2504	2388	2275	4768	4352	3966	3608	3275	1.8	0	-7.3	-20.8
8.59(.338) Galaxy	200	3100	2899	2707	2524	2347	4269	3734	3256	2829	2446	3	3.8	0	-9.3
340 Wea. Mag.*	210	3250	2991	2746	2515	2295	4924	4170	3516	2948	2455	2.5	1.9	-1.8	-11.8
340 Wea. Mag.*	250	3000	2806	2621	2443	2272	4995	4371	3812	3311	2864	2.5	2	-3.5	-14.8
338 A-Square	250	3120	2799	2500	2220	1958	5403	4348	3469	2736	2128	2.5	2.7	-1.5	-10.5
338-378 Wea. Mag.	225	3180	2974	2778	2591	2410	5052	4420	3856	3353	2902	3.1	3.8	0	-8.9
338 Titan	225	3230	3010	2800	2600	2409	5211	4524	3916	3377	2898	3.07	3.8	0	-8.95
338 Excalibur	200	3600	3361	3134	2920	2715	5755	5015	4363	3785	3274	2.23	2.87	0	-6.99
338 Excalibur	250	3250	2922	2618	2333	2066	5863	4740	3804	3021	2370	1.3	0	-6.35	-19.2
34, 35															
348 Winchester	200	2520	2215	1931	1672	1443	2820	2178	1656	1241	925	2.5	-1.4	-14.7	0
357 Magnum	158	1830	1427	1138	980	883	1175	715	454	337	274	0	-16.2	-33.1	0
35 Remington	150	2300	1874	1506	1218	1039	1762	1169	755	494	359	2.5	-4.1	-26.3	0
35 Remington	200	2080	1698	1376	1140	1001	1921	1280	841	577	445	2.5	-6.3	-17.1	-33.6
35 Remington	200	2225	1963	1722	1505	—	2198	1711	1317	1006	—	3.8	0	-15.6	—
35 Rem. Lever Evolution	200	2225	1963	1721	1503	NA	2198	1711	1315	1003	NA	3	-1.3	-17.5	NA
356 Winchester	200	2460	2114	1797	1517	1284	2688	1985	1434	1022	732	2.5	-1.8	-15.1	0
356 Winchester	250	2160	1911	1682	1476	1299	2591	2028	1571	1210	937	2.5	-3.7	-22.2	0
358 Winchester	200	2475	2180	1906	1655	1434	2720	2110	1612	1217	913	2.9	0	-12.6	-37.9
358 Winchester	200	2490	2171	1876	1619	1379	2753	2093	1563	1151	844	2.5	-1.6	-15.6	0
358 STA	275	2850	2562	2292	2039	NA	4958	4009	3208	2539	NA	1.9	0	-8.6	0
350 Rem. Mag.	200	2710	2410	2130	1870	1631	3261	2579	2014	1553	1181	2.5	-0.2	-10	-30.1
35 Whelen	200	2675	2378	2100	1842	1606	3177	2510	1958	1506	1145	2.5	-0.2	-10.3	-31.1
35 Whelen	200	2910	2585	2283	2001	1742	3760	2968	2314	1778	1347	1.9	0	-8.6	-25.9
35 Whelen	225	2500	2300	2110	1930	1770	3120	2650	2235	1870	1560	2.6	0	-10.2	-29.9
35 Whelen	250	2400	2197	2005	1823	1652	3197	2680	2230	1844	1515	2.5	-1.2	-13.7	0
358 Norma Mag.	250	2800	2510	2230	1970	1730	4350	3480	2750	2145	1655	2.5	1	-7.6	-25.2
358 STA	275	2850	2562	2292	2039	1764	4959	4009	3208	2539	1899	1.9	0	-8.58	-26.1
9.3mm															
9.3x57mm Mau.	286	2070	1810	1590	1390	1110	2710	2090	1600	1220	955	2.5	-2.6	-22.5	0
370 Sako Mag.	286	3550	2370	2200	2040	2880	4130	3570	3075	2630	2240	2.4	0	-9.5	-27.2
9.6x62mm	232	2625	2302	2002	1728	-	2551	2731	2066	1539	-	2.6	0	-11.3	-
9.3x62mm	250	2550	2376	2208	2048	—	3609	3133	2707	2328	—	0	-5.4	-17.9	-
9.3x62mm	286	2360	2155	1961	1778	1608	3537	2949	2442	2008	1642	0	-6	-21.1	-47.2
9.3x62mm	286	2400	2163	1941	1733	—	3657	2972	2392	1908	—	0	-6.7	-22.6	—

Cartridge	Bullet Wgt. Grs.	VELOCITY (fps)					ENERGY (ft. lbs.)					TRAJ. (in.)			
		Muzzle	100 yds.	200 yds.	300 yds.	400 yds.	Muzzle	100 yds.	200 yds.	300 yds.	400 yds.	100 yds.	200 yds.	300 yds.	400 yds.
9.3x64mm	286	2700	2505	2318	2139	1968	4629	3984	3411	2906	2460	2.5	2.7	-4.5	-19.2
9.3x72mmR	193	1952	1610	1326	1120	996	1633	1112	754	538	425	0	-12.1	-44.1	—
9.3x74mmR	250	2550	2376	2208	2048	—	3609	3133	2707	2328	—	0	-5.4	-17.9	—
9.3x74Rmm	286	2360	2136	1924	1727	1545	3536	2896	2351	1893	1516	0	-6.1	-21.7	-49
375															
375 Winchester	200	2200	1841	1526	1268	1089	2150	1506	1034	714	527	2.5	-4	-26.2	0
375 Winchester	250	1900	1647	1424	1239	1103	2005	1506	1126	852	676	2.5	-6.9	-33.3	0
376 Steyr	225	2600	2331	2078	1842	1625	3377	2714	2157	1694	1319	2.5	0	-10.6	-31.4
376 Steyr	270	2600	2372	2156	1951	1759	4052	3373	2787	2283	1855	2.3	0	-9.9	-28.9
375 Dakota	300	2600	2316	2051	1804	1579	4502	3573	2800	2167	1661	2.4	0	-11	-32.7
375 N.E. 2-1/2"	270	2000	1740	1507	1310	NA	2398	1815	1362	1026	NA	2.5	-6	-30	0
375 Flanged	300	2450	2150	1886	1640	NA	3998	3102	2369	1790	NA	2.5	-2.4	-17	0
375 Ruger	250	2890	2675	2471	2275	2088	4636	3973	3388	2873	2421	1.7	0	-7.4	-21.5
375 Ruger	260	2900	2703	2514	2333	—	4854	4217	3649	3143	—	0	-4	-13.4	—
375 Ruger	270	2840	2600	2372	2156	1951	4835	4052	3373	2786	2283	1.8	0	-8	-23.6
375 Ruger	300	2660	2344	2050	1780	1536	4713	3660	2800	2110	1572	2.4	0	-10.8	-32.6
375 H&H Magnum	250	2670	2450	2240	2040	1850	3955	3335	2790	2315	1905	2.5	-0.4	-10.2	-28.4
375 H&H Magnum	270	2690	2420	2166	1928	1707	4337	3510	2812	2228	1747	2.5	0	-10	-29.4
375 H&H Mag.	270	2800	2562	2337	2123	1921	4700	3936	3275	2703	2213	1.9	0	-8.3	-24.3
375 H&H Magnum*	300	2530	2245	1979	1733	1512	4263	3357	2608	2001	1523	2.5	-1	-10.5	-33.6
375 H&H Mag.	300	2660	2345	2052	1782	1539	4713	3662	2804	2114	1577	2.4	0	-10.8	-32.6
375 H&H Hvy. Mag.	270	2870	2628	2399	2182	1976	4937	4141	3451	2150	1845	1.7	0	-7.2	-21
375 H&H Hvy. Mag.	300	2705	2386	2090	1816	1568	4873	3793	2908	2195	1637	2.3	0	-10.4	-31.4
375 Rem. Ultra Mag.	270	2900	2558	2241	1947	1678	5041	3922	3010	2272	1689	1.9	2.7	-8.9	-27
375 Rem. Ultra Mag.	260	2950	2750	2560	2377	—	5023	4367	3783	3262	—	0	-3.8	-12.9	—
375 Rem. Ultra Mag.	300	2760	2505	2263	2035	1822	5073	4178	3412	2759	2210	2	0	-8.8	-26.1
375 Wea. Mag.	260	3000	2798	2606	2421	—	5195	4520	3920	3384	—	0	-3.6	-12.4	—
375 Wea. Mag.	300	2700	2420	2157	1911	1685	4856	3901	3100	2432	1891	2.5	-0.04	-10.7	0
378 Wea. Mag.	260	3100	2894	2697	2509	—	5547	4834	4199	3633	—	0	-4.2	-14.6	—
378 Wea. Mag.	270	3180	2976	2781	2594	2415	6062	5308	4635	4034	3495	2.5	2.6	-1.8	-11.3
378 Wea. Mag.	300	2929	2576	2252	1952	1680	5698	4419	3379	2538	1881	2.5	1.2	-7	-24.5
375 A-Square	300	2920	2626	2351	2093	1850	5679	4594	3681	2917	2281	2.5	1.4	-6	-21
38-40 Win.	180	1160	999	901	827	764	538	399	324	273	233	0	-33.9	0	0
40, 41															
400 Legend	215	2250	1872	1540	1270	NA	2416	1673	1132	770	NA	1.8	-4.9	-26.4	NA
400 A-Square DPM	400	2400	2146	1909	1689	NA	5116	2092	3236	2533	NA	2.98	0	-10	NA
408 CheyTac	419	2850	2752	2657	2562	2470	7551	7048	6565	6108	5675	-1.02	0	1.9	4.2
405 Win.	300	2200	1851	1545	1296		3224	2282	1589	1119		4.6	0	-19.5	0
450/400-3"	400	2050	1815	1595	1402	NA	3732	2924	2259	1746	NA	0	NA	-33.4	NA
416 Ruger	400	2400	2151	1917	1700	NA	5116	4109	3264	2568	NA	0	-6	-21.6	0
416 Dakota	400	2450	2294	2143	1998	1859	5330	4671	4077	3544	3068	2.5	-0.2	-10.5	-29.4
416 Taylor	400	2350	2117	1896	1693	NA	4905	3980	3194	2547	NA	2.5	-1.2	15	0
416 Hoffman	400	2380	2145	1923	1718	1529	5031	4087	3285	2620	2077	2.5	-1	-14.1	0
416 Rigby	350	2600	2449	2303	2162	2026	5253	4661	4122	3632	3189	2.5	-1.8	-10.2	-26
416 Rigby	400	2370	2210	2050	1900	NA	4990	4315	3720	3185	NA	2.5	-0.7	-12.1	0
416 Rigby	400	2400	2115	1851	1611	—	5115	3973	3043	2305	—	0	-6.5	-21.8	—
416 Rigby	400	2415	2156	1915	1691	—	5180	4130	3256	2540	—	0	-6	-21.6	—
416 Rigby	410	2370	2110	1870	1640	NA	5115	4050	3165	2455	NA	2.5	-2.4	-17.3	0
416 Rem. Mag.*	350	2520	2270	2034	1814	1611	4935	4004	3216	2557	2017	2.5	-0.8	-12.6	-35
416 Rem. Mag.	400	2400	2142	1901	1679	—	5116	4076	3211	2504	—	3.1	0	-12.7	—
416 Wea. Mag.*	400	2700	2397	2115	1852	1613	6474	5104	3971	3047	2310	2.5	0	-10.1	-30.4
10.57 (416) Meteor	400	2730	2532	2342	2161	1987	6621	5695	4874	4147	3508	1.9	0	-8.3	-24
500/416 N.E.	400	2300	2092	1895	1712	—	4697	3887	3191	2602	—	0	-7.2	-24	—
404 Jeffery	400	2150	1924	1716	1525	NA	4105	3289	2614	2064	NA	2.5	-4	-22.1	0
404 Jeffery	400	2300	2053	1823	1611	—	4698	3743	2950	2306	—	0	6.8	-24.1	—
404 Jeffery	400	2350	2020	1720	1458	—	4904	3625	2629	1887	—	0	-6.5	-21.8	—
425, 44															
425 Express	400	2400	2160	1934	1725	NA	5115	4145	3322	2641	NA	2.5	-1	-14	0
44-40 Win.	200	1190	1006	900	822	756	629	449	360	300	254	0	-33.3	0	0
44 Rem. Mag.	210	1920	1477	1155	982	880	1719	1017	622	450	361	0	-17.6	0	0
44 Rem. Mag.	240	1760	1380	1114	970	878	1650	1015	661	501	411	0	-17.6	0	0
444 Marlin	240	2350	1815	1377	1087	941	2942	1753	1001	630	472	2.5	-15.1	-31	0
444 Marlin	265	2120	1733	1405	1160	1012	2644	1768	1162	791	603	2.5	-6	-32.2	0
444 Mar. Lever Evolution	265	2325	1971	1652	1380	NA	3180	2285	1606	1120	NA	3	-1.4	-18.6	NA
444 Mar. Superformance	265	2400	1976	1603	1298	NA	3389	2298	1512	991	NA	4.1	0	-17.8	NA
45															
45-70 Govt.	250	2025	1616	1285	1068	—	2276	1449	917	634	—	6.1	0	-27.2	—

Cartridge	Bullet Wgt. Grs.	VELOCITY (fps)					ENERGY (ft. lbs.)					TRAJ. (in.)			
		Muzzle	100 yds.	200 yds.	300 yds.	400 yds.	Muzzle	100 yds.	200 yds.	300 yds.	400 yds.	100 yds.	200 yds.	300 yds.	400 yds.
45-70 Govt.	300	1810	1497	1244	1073	969	2182	1492	1031	767	625	0	-14.8	0	0
45-70 Govt. Supreme	300	1880	1558	1292	1103	988	2355	1616	1112	811	651	0	-12.9	-46	-105
45-70 Govt.	325	2000	1685	1413	1197	—	2886	2049	1441	1035	—	5.5	0	-23	—
45-70 Lever Evolution	325	2050	1729	1450	1225	NA	3032	2158	1516	1083	NA	3	-4.1	-27.8	NA
45-70 Govt. CorBon	350	1800	1526	1296			2519	1810	1307			0	-14.6	0	0
45-70 Govt.	405	1330	1168	1055	977	918	1590	1227	1001	858	758	0	-24.6	0	0
45-70 Govt. PMC Cowboy	405	1550	1193	—	—	—	1639	1280	—	—	—	0	-23.9	0	0
45-70 Govt. Garrett	415	1850	—	—	—	—	3150	—	—	—	—	3	-7	0	0
45-70 Govt. Garrett	530	1550	1343	1178	1062	982	2828	2123	1633	1327	1135	0	-17.8	0	0
450 Bushmaster	250	2200	1831	1508	1480	1073	2686	1860	1262	864	639	0	-9	-33.5	0
450 Dakota	500	2,450	2219	2000	1796	1607	6663	5466	4440	3581	2867	0	-5.6	-20	-45.1
450 Dakota	600	2,350	2169	1997	1833	1679	7356	6267	5312	4476	3755	0	-5.9	-20.6	-45.6
450 Marlin	325	2225	1887	1587	1332	—	3572	2570	1816	1280	—	4.2	0	-18.1	—
450 Marlin	350	2100	1774	1488	1254	1089	3427	2446	1720	1222	922	0	-9.7	-35.2	0
450 Mar. Lever Evolution	325	2225	1887	1585	1331	NA	3572	2569	1813	1278	NA	3	-2.2	-21.3	NA
457 Wild West Magnum	350	2150	1718	1348	NA	NA	3645	2293	1413	NA	NA	0	-10.5	NA	NA
450/500 N.E.	400	2050	1820	1609	1420	—	3732	2940	2298	1791	—	0	-9.7	-32.8	—
450 N.E. 3-1/4"	465	2190	1970	1765	1577	NA	4952	4009	3216	2567	NA	2.5	-3	-20	0
450 N.E.	480	2150	1881	1635	1418	—	4927	3769	2850	2144	—	0	-8.4	-29.8	—
450 N.E. 3-1/4"	500	2150	1920	1708	1514	NA	5132	4093	3238	2544	NA	2.5	-4	-22.9	0
450 No. 2	465	2190	1970	1765	1577	NA	4952	4009	3216	2567	NA	2.5	-3	-20	0
450 No. 2	500	2150	1920	1708	1514	NA	5132	4093	3238	2544	NA	2.5	-4	-22.9	0
450 Ackley Mag.	465	2400	2169	1950	1747	NA	5947	4857	3927	3150	NA	2.5	-1	-13.7	0
450 Ackley Mag.	500	2320	2081	1855	1649	NA	5975	4085	3820	3018	NA	2.5	-1.2	-15	0
450 Rigby	500	2350	2139	1939	1752	—	6130	5079	4176	3408	—	0	-6.8	-22.9	—
450 Rigby	550	2100	1866	1651	-	-	5387	4256	3330	-	-	-	-	-	-
458 Win. Magnum	400	2380	2170	1960	1770	NA	5030	4165	3415	2785	NA	2.5	-0.4	-13.4	0
458 Win. Magnum	465	2220	1999	1791	1601	NA	5088	4127	3312	2646	NA	2.5	-2	-17.7	0
458 Win. Magnum	500	2040	1823	1623	1442	1237	4620	3689	2924	2308	1839	2.5	-3.5	-22	0
458 Win. Mag.	500	2140	1880	1643	1432	—	5084	3294	2996	2276	—	0	-8.4	-29.8	—
458 Win. Magnum	510	2040	1770	1527	1319	1157	4712	3547	2640	1970	1516	2.5	-4.1	-25	0
458 Lott	465	2380	2150	1932	1730	NA	5848	4773	3855	3091	NA	2.5	-1	-14	0
458 Lott	500	2300	2029	1778	1551	—	5873	4569	3509	2671	—	0	-7	-25.1	—
458 Lott	500	2300	2062	1838	1633	NA	5873	4719	3748	2960	NA	2.5	-1.6	-16.4	0
460 Short A-Sq.	500	2420	2175	1943	1729	NA	6501	5250	4193	3319	NA	2.5	-0.8	-12.8	0
460 Wea. Mag.	500	2700	2404	2128	1869	1635	8092	6416	5026	3878	2969	2.5	0.6	-8.9	-28

475

Cartridge	Bullet Wgt. Grs.	Muzzle	100 yds.	200 yds.	300 yds.	400 yds.	Muzzle	100 yds.	200 yds.	300 yds.	400 yds.	100 yds.	200 yds.	300 yds.	400 yds.
500/465 N.E.	480	2150	1917	1703	1507	NA	4926	3917	3089	2419	NA	2.5	-4	-22.2	0
470 Rigby	500	2150	1940	1740	1560	NA	5130	4170	3360	2695	NA	2.5	-2.8	-19.4	0
470 Nitro Ex.	480	2190	1954	1735	1536	NA	5111	4070	3210	2515	NA	2.5	-3.5	-20.8	0
470 N.E.	500	2150	1885	1643	1429	—	5132	3945	2998	2267	—	0	-8.9	-30.8	—
470 Nitro Ex.	500	2150	1890	1650	1440	1270	5130	3965	3040	2310	1790	2.5	-4.3	-24	0
475 No. 2	500	2200	1955	1728	1522	NA	5375	4243	3316	2573	NA	2.5	-3.2	-20.9	0

50, 58

Cartridge	Bullet Wgt. Grs.	Muzzle	100 yds.	200 yds.	300 yds.	400 yds.	Muzzle	100 yds.	200 yds.	300 yds.	400 yds.	100 yds.	200 yds.	300 yds.	400 yds.
50 Alaskan	450	2000	1729	1492	NA	NA	3997	2987	2224	NA	NA	0	-11.25	NA	NA
500 Jeffery	570	2300	1979	1688	1434	—	6694	4958	3608	2604	—	0	-8.2	-28.6	—
505 Gibbs	525	2300	2063	1840	1637	—	6166	4922	3948	3122	NA	2.5	-3	-18	0
500 N.E.	570	2150	1889	1651	1439	—	5850	4518	3450	2621	—	0	-8.9	-30.6	—
500 N.E.-3"	570	2150	1928	1722	1533	NA	5850	4703	3752	2975	NA	2.5	-3.7	-22	0
500 N.E.-3"	600	2150	1927	1721	1531	NA	6158	4947	3944	3124	NA	2.5	-4	-22	0
495 A-Square	570	2350	2117	1896	1693	NA	5850	4703	3752	2975	NA	2.5	-1	-14.5	0
495 A-Square	600	2280	2050	1833	1635	NA	6925	5598	4478	3562	NA	2.5	-2	-17	0
500 A-Square	600	2380	2144	1922	1766	NA	7546	6126	4920	3922	NA	2.5	-3	-17	0
500 A-Square	707	2250	2040	1841	1567	NA	7947	6530	5318	4311	NA	2.5	-2	-17	0
500 BMG PMC	660	3080	2854	2639	2444	2248	13688	500 yd. zero	3.1	3.9	4.7	2.8	NA		
577 Nitro Ex.	750	2050	1793	1562	1360	NA	6990	5356	4065	3079	NA	2.5	-5	-26	0
577 Tyrannosaur	750	2400	2141	1898	1675	NA	9591	7633	5996	4671	NA	3	0	-12.9	0

600, 700

Cartridge	Bullet Wgt. Grs.	Muzzle	100 yds.	200 yds.	300 yds.	400 yds.	Muzzle	100 yds.	200 yds.	300 yds.	400 yds.	100 yds.	200 yds.	300 yds.	400 yds.
600 N.E.	900	1950	1680	1452	NA	NA	7596	5634	4212	NA	NA	5.6	0	0	0
700 N.E.	1200	1900	1676	1472	NA	NA	9618	7480	5774	NA	NA	5.7	0	0	0

50 BMG

Cartridge	Bullet Wgt. Grs.	Muzzle	100 yds.	200 yds.	300 yds.	400 yds.	Muzzle	100 yds.	200 yds.	300 yds.	400 yds.	100 yds.	200 yds.	300 yds.	400 yds.
50 BMG	624	2952	2820	2691	2566	2444	12077	11028	10036	9125	8281	0	-2.9	-10.6	-23.5
50 BMG Match	750	2820	2728	2637	2549	2462	13241	12388	11580	10815	10090	1.5	0	-6.5	-18.3

Notes: Blanks are available in 32 S&W, 38 S&W and 38 Special. "V" after barrel length indicates test barrel was vented to produce ballistics similar to a revolver with a normal barrel-to-cylinder gap. Not all loads are available from all ammo manufacturers. Listed loads are those made by Remington, Winchester, Federal, and others. DISC. is a discontinued load.

Cartridge	Bullet Wgt. Grs.	VELOCITY (fps)			ENERGY (ft. lbs.)			Mid-Range Traj. (in.)		Bbl. Lgth. (in).
		Muzzle	50 yds.	100 yds.	Muzzle	50 yds.	100 yds.	50 yds.	100 yds.	
22, 25										
221 Rem. Fireball	50	2650	2380	2130	780	630	505	0.2	0.8	10.5"
25 Automatic	35	900	813	742	63	51	43	NA	NA	2"
25 Automatic	45	815	730	655	65	55	40	1.8	7.7	2"
25 Automatic	50	760	705	660	65	55	50	2	8.7	2"
30										
7.5mm Swiss	107	1010	NA	NA	240	NA	NA	NA	NA	NA
7.62x25 Tokarev	85	1647	1458	1295	512	401	317	0	-3.2	4.75
7.62mmTokarev	87	1390	NA	NA	365	NA	NA	0.6	NA	4.5"
7.62 Nagant	97	790	NA	NA	134	NA	NA	NA	NA	NA
7.63 Mauser	88	1440	NA	NA	405	NA	NA	NA	NA	NA
30 Luger	93	1220	1110	1040	305	255	225	0.9	3.5	4.5"
30 Carbine	110	1790	1600	1430	785	625	500	0.4	1.7	10"
30-357 AeT	123	1992	NA	NA	1084	NA	NA	NA	NA	10"
32										
32 NAA	80	1000	933	880	178	155	137	NA	NA	4"
32 S&W	88	680	645	610	90	80	75	2.5	10.5	3"
32 S&W Long	98	705	670	635	115	100	90	2.3	10.5	4"
32 Short Colt	80	745	665	590	100	80	60	2.2	9.9	4"
32 H&R	80	1150	1039	963	235	192	165	NA	NA	4"
32 H&R Magnum	85	1100	1020	930	230	195	165	1	4.3	4.5"
32 H&R Magnum	95	1030	940	900	225	190	170	1.1	4.7	4.5"
327 Federal Magnum	85	1400	1220	1090	370	280	225	NA	NA	4-V
327 Federal Magnum	100	1500	1320	1180	500	390	310	-0.2	-4.5	4-V
32 Automatic	60	970	895	835	125	105	95	1.3	5.4	4"
32 Automatic	60	1000	917	849	133	112	96			4"
32 Automatic	65	950	890	830	130	115	100	1.3	5.6	NA
32 Automatic	71	905	855	810	130	115	95	1.4	5.8	4"
8mm Lebel Pistol	111	850	NA	NA	180	NA	NA	NA	NA	NA
8mm Steyr	112	1080	NA	NA	290	NA	NA	NA	NA	NA
8mm Gasser	126	850	NA	NA	200	NA	NA	NA	NA	NA
9mm, 38										
380 Automatic	60	1130	960	NA	170	120	NA	1	NA	NA
380 Automatic	85/88	990	920	870	190	165	145	1.2	5.1	4"
380 Automatic	90	1000	890	800	200	160	130	1.2	5.5	3.75"
380 Automatic	95/100	955	865	785	190	160	130	1.4	5.9	4"
38 Super Auto +P	115	1300	1145	1040	430	335	275	0.7	3.3	5"
38 Super Auto +P	125/130	1215	1100	1015	425	350	300	0.8	3.6	5"
38 Super Auto +P	147	1100	1050	1000	395	355	325	0.9	4	5"
9x18mm Makarov	95	1000	930	874	211	182	161	NA	NA	4"
9x18mm Ultra	100	1050	NA	NA	240	NA	NA	NA	NA	NA
9x21	124	1150	1050	980	365	305	265	NA	NA	4"
9x21 IMI	123	1220	1095	1010	409	330	281	-3.15	—	5
9x23mm Largo	124	1190	1055	966	390	306	267	0.7	3.7	4"
9x23mm Win.	125	1450	1249	1103	583	433	338	0.6	2.8	NA
9mm Steyr	115	1180	NA	NA	350	NA	NA	NA	NA	NA
9mm Luger	88	1500	1190	1010	440	275	200	0.6	3.1	4"
9mm Luger	90	1360	1112	978	370	247	191	NA	NA	4"
9mm Luger	92	1325	1117	991	359	255	201	-3.2	—	4
9mm Luger	95	1300	1140	1010	350	275	215	0.8	3.4	4"
9mm Luger	100	1180	1080	NA	305	255	NA	0.9	NA	4"
9mm Luger Guard Dog	105	1230	1070	970	355	265	220	NA	NA	4"
9mm Luger	115	1155	1045	970	340	280	240	0.9	3.9	4"
9mm Luger	123/125	1110	1030	970	340	290	260	1	4	4"
9mm Luger	124	1150	1040	965	364	298	256	-4.5	—	4
9mm Luger	135	1010	960	918	306	276	253	—	—	4

Cartridge	Bullet Wgt. Grs.	VELOCITY (fps) Muzzle	50 yds.	100 yds.	ENERGY (ft. lbs.) Muzzle	50 yds.	100 yds.	Mid-Range Traj. (in.) 50 yds.	100 yds.	Bbl. Lgth. (in.)
9mm Luger	140	935	890	850	270	245	225	1.3	5.5	4"
9mm Luger	147	990	940	900	320	290	265	1.1	4.9	4"
9mm Luger +P	90	1475	NA	NA	437	NA	NA	NA	NA	NA
9mm Luger +P	115	1250	1113	1019	399	316	265	0.8	3.5	4"
9mm Federal	115	1280	1130	1040	420	330	280	0.7	3.3	4"V
9mm Luger Vector	115	1155	1047	971	341	280	241	NA	NA	4"
9mm Luger +P	124	1180	1089	1021	384	327	287	0.8	3.8	4"
38										
38 S&W	146	685	650	620	150	135	125	2.4	10	4"
38 S&W Short	145	720	689	660	167	153	140	-8.5	—	5
38 Short Colt	125	730	685	645	150	130	·115	2.2	9.4	6"
39 Special	100	950	900	NA	200	180	NA	1.3	NA	4"V
38 Special	110	945	895	850	220	195	175	1.3	5.4	4"V
38 Special	110	945	895	850	220	195	175	1.3	5.4	4"V
38 Special	130	775	745	710	175	160	120	1.9	7.9	4"V
38 Special Cowboy	140	800	767	735	199	183	168			7.5" V
38 (Multi-Ball)	140	830	730	505	215	130	80	2	10.6	4"V
38 Special	148	710	635	565	165	130	105	2.4	10.6	4"V
38 Special	158	755	725	690	200	185	170	2	8.3	4"V
38 Special +P	95	1175	1045	960	290	230	195	0.9	3.9	4"V
38 Special +P	110	995	925	870	240	210	185	1.2	5.1	4"V
38 Special +P	125	975	929	885	264	238	218	1	5.2	4"
38 Special +P	125	945	900	860	250	225	205	1.3	5.4	4"V
38 Special +P	129	945	910	870	255	235	215	1.3	5.3	4"V
38 Special +P	130	925	887	852	247	227	210	1.3	5.5	4"V
38 Special +P	147/150	884	NA	NA	264	NA	NA	NA	NA	4"V
38 Special +P	158	890	855	825	280	255	240	1.4	6	4"V
357										
357 SIG	115	1520	NA	NA	593	NA	NA	NA	NA	NA
357 SIG	124	1450	NA	NA	578	NA	NA	NA	NA	NA
357 SIG	125	1350	1190	1080	510	395	325	0.7	3.1	4"
357 SIG	135	1225	1112	1031	450	371	319	—	—	4
357 SIG	147	1225	1132	1060	490	418	367	—	—	4
357 SIG	150	1130	1030	970	420	355	310	0.9	4	NA
356 TSW	115	1520	NA	NA	593	NA	NA	NA	NA	NA
356 TSW	124	1450	NA	NA	578	NA	NA	NA	NA	NA
356 TSW	135	1280	1120	1010	490	375	310	0.8	3.5	NA
356 TSW	147	1220	1120	1040	485	410	355	0.8	3.5	5"
357 Mag., Super Clean	105	1650								
357 Magnum	110	1295	1095	975	410	290	230	0.8	3.5	4"V
357 (Med.Vel.)	125	1220	1075	985	415	315	270	0.8	3.7	4"V
357 Magnum	125	1450	1240	1090	585	425	330	0.6	2.8	4"V
357 Magnum	125	1500	1312	1163	624	478	376	—	—	8
357 (Multi-Ball)	140	1155	830	665	420	215	135	1.2	6.4	4"V
357 Magnum	140	1360	1195	1075	575	445	360	0.7	3	4"V
357 Magnum FlexTip	140	1440	1274	1143	644	504	406	NA	NA	NA
357 Magnum	145	1290	1155	1060	535	430	360	0.8	3.5	4"V
357 Magnum	150/158	1235	1105	1015	535	430	360	0.8	3.5	4"V
357 Mag. Cowboy	158	800	761	725	225	203	185			
357 Magnum	165	1290	1189	1108	610	518	450	0.7	3.1	8-3/8"
357 Magnum	180	1145	1055	985	525	445	390	0.9	3.9	4"V
357 Magnum	180	1180	1088	1020	557	473	416	0.8	3.6	8"V
357 Mag. CorBon F.A.	180	1650	1512	1386	1088	913	767	1.66	0	
357 Mag. CorBon	200	1200	1123	1061	640	560	500	3.19	0	
357 Rem. Maximum	158	1825	1590	1380	1170	885	670	0.4	1.7	10.5"
40, 10mm										
40 S&W	125	1265	1102	998	444	337	276	-3	—	4
40 S&W	135	1140	1070	NA	390	345	NA	0.9	NA	4"
40 S&W Guard Dog	135	1200	1040	940	430	325	265	NA	NA	4"
40 S&W	155	1140	1026	958	447	362	309	0.9	4.1	4"
40 S&W	165	1150	NA	NA	485	NA	NA	NA	NA	4"
40 S&W	175	1010	948	899	396	350	314	—	—	4

Cartridge	Bullet Wgt. Grs.	VELOCITY (fps)			ENERGY (ft. lbs.)			Mid-Range Traj. (in.)		Bbl. Lgth. (in).
		Muzzle	50 yds.	100 yds.	Muzzle	50 yds.	100 yds.	50 yds.	100 yds.	
40 S&W	180	985	936	893	388	350	319	1.4	5	4"
40 S&W	180	1000	943	896	400	355	321	4.52	—	4
40 S&W	180	1015	960	914	412	368	334	1.3	4.5	4"
400 Cor-Bon	135	1450	NA	NA	630	NA	NA	NA	NA	5"
10mm Automatic	155	1125	1046	986	436	377	335	0.9	3.9	5"
10mm Automatic	155	1265	1118	1018	551	430	357	—	—	5
10mm Automatic	170	1340	1165	1145	680	510	415	0.7	3.2	5"
10mm Automatic	175	1290	1140	1035	650	505	420	0.7	3.3	5.5"
10mm Auto. (FBI)	180	950	905	865	361	327	299	1.5	5.4	4"
10mm Automatic	180	1030	970	920	425	375	340	1.1	4.7	5"
10mm Auto H.V.	180	1240	1124	1037	618	504	430	0.8	3.4	5"
10mm Automatic	200	1160	1070	1010	495	510	430	0.9	3.8	5"
10.4mm Italian	177	950	NA	NA	360	NA	NA	NA	NA	NA
41 Action Exp.	180	1000	947	903	400	359	326	0.5	4.2	5"
41 Rem. Magnum	170	1420	1165	1015	760	515	390	0.7	3.2	4"V
41 Rem. Magnum	175	1250	1120	1030	605	490	410	0.8	3.4	4"V
41 (Med. Vel.)	210	965	900	840	435	375	330	1.3	5.4	4"V
41 Rem. Magnum	210	1300	1160	1060	790	630	535	0.7	3.2	4"V
41 Rem. Magnum	240	1250	1151	1075	833	706	616	0.8	3.3	6.5V
44										
44 S&W Russian	247	780	NA	NA	335	NA	NA	NA	NA	NA
44 Special	210	900	861	825	360	329	302	5.57	—	6
44 Special FTX	165	900	848	802	297	263	235	NA	NA	2.5"
44 S&W Special	180	980	NA	NA	383	NA	NA	NA	NA	6.5"
44 S&W Special	180	1000	935	882	400	350	311	NA	NA	7.5"V
44 S&W Special	200	875	825	780	340	302	270	1.2	6	6"
44 S&W Special	200	1035	940	865	475	390	335	1.1	4.9	6.5"
44 S&W Special	240/246	755	725	695	310	285	265	2	8.3	6.5"
44-40 Win.	200	722	698	676	232	217	203	-3.4	-23.7	4
44-40 Win.	205	725	689	655	239	216	195	—	—	7.5
44-40 Win.	210	725	698	672	245	227	210	-11.6	—	5.5
44-40 Win.	225	725	697	670	263	243	225	-3.4	-23.8	4
44-40 Win. Cowboy	225	750	723	695	281	261	242			
44 Rem. Magnum	180	1610	1365	1175	1035	745	550	0.5	2.3	4"V
44 Rem. Magnum	200	1296	1193	1110	747	632	548	-0.5	-6.2	6
44 Rem. Magnum	200	1400	1192	1053	870	630	492	0.6	NA	6.5"
44 Rem. Magnum	200	1500	1332	1194	999	788	633	—	—	7.5
44 Rem. Magnum	210	1495	1310	1165	1040	805	635	0.6	2.5	6.5"
44 Rem. Mag. FlexTip	225	1410	1240	1111	993	768	617	NA	NA	NA
44 (Med. Vel.)	240	1000	945	900	535	475	435	1.1	4.8	6.5"
44 R.M. (Jacketed)	240	1180	1080	1010	740	625	545	0.9	3.7	4"V
44 R.M. (Lead)	240	1350	1185	1070	970	750	610	0.7	3.1	4"V
44 Rem. Magnum	250	1180	1100	1040	775	670	600	0.8	3.6	6.5"V
44 Rem. Magnum	250	1250	1148	1070	867	732	635	0.8	3.3	6.5"V
44 Rem. Magnum	275	1235	1142	1070	931	797	699	0.8	3.3	6.5"
44 Rem. Magnum	300	1150	1083	1030	881	781	706	—	—	7.5
44 Rem. Magnum	300	1200	1100	1026	959	806	702	NA	NA	7.5"
44 Rem. Magnum	330	1385	1297	1220	1406	1234	1090	1.83	0	NA
44 Webley	262	850	—	—	—	—	—	—	—	—
440 CorBon	260	1700	1544	1403	1669	1377	1136	1.58	NA	10"
45, 50										
450 Short Colt/450 Revolver	226	830	NA	NA	350	NA	NA	NA	NA	NA
45 S&W Schofield	180	730	NA	NA	213	NA	NA	NA	NA	NA
45 S&W Schofield	230	730	NA	NA	272	NA	NA	NA	NA	NA
45 G.A.P.	165	1007	936	879	372	321	283	-1.4	-11.8	5
45 G.A.P.	185	1090	970	890	490	385	320	1	4.7	5"
45 G.A.P.	230	880	842	NA	396	363	NA	NA	NA	NA
45 Automatic	150	1050	NA	NA	403	NA	NA	NA	NA	NA
45 Automatic	165	1030	930	NA	385	315	NA	1.2	NA	5"
45 Automatic Guard Dog	165	1140	1030	950	475	390	335	NA	NA	5"
45 Automatic	185	1000	940	890	410	360	325	1.1	4.9	5"
45 Auto. (Match)	185	770	705	650	245	204	175	2	8.7	5"

Cartridge	Bullet Wgt. Grs.	VELOCITY (fps)			ENERGY (ft. lbs.)			Mid-Range Traj. (in.)		Bbl. Lgth. (in).
		Muzzle	50 yds.	100 yds.	Muzzle	50 yds.	100 yds.	50 yds.	100 yds.	
45 Auto. (Match)	200	940	890	840	392	352	312	2	8.6	5"
45 Automatic	200	975	917	860	421	372	328	1.4	5	5"
45 Automatic	230	830	800	675	355	325	300	1.6	6.8	5"
45 Automatic	230	880	846	816	396	366	340	1.5	6.1	5"
45 Automatic +P	165	1250	NA	NA	573	NA	NA	NA	NA	NA
45 Automatic +P	185	1140	1040	970	535	445	385	0.9	4	5"
45 Automatic +P	200	1055	982	925	494	428	380	NA	NA	5"
45 Super	185	1300	1190	1108	694	582	504	NA	NA	5"
45 Win. Magnum	230	1400	1230	1105	1000	775	635	0.6	2.8	5"
45 Win. Magnum	260	1250	1137	1053	902	746	640	0.8	3.3	5"
45 Win. Mag. CorBon	320	1150	1080	1025	940	830	747	3.47		
455 Webley MKII	262	850	NA	NA	420	NA	NA	NA	NA	NA
45 Colt FTX	185	920	870	826	348	311	280	NA	NA	3"V
45 Colt	200	1000	938	889	444	391	351	1.3	4.8	5.5"
45 Colt	225	960	890	830	460	395	345	1.3	5.5	5.5"
45 Colt + P CorBon	265	1350	1225	1126	1073	884	746	2.65	0	
45 Colt + P CorBon	300	1300	1197	1114	1126	956	827	2.78	0	
45 Colt	250/255	860	820	780	410	375	340	1.6	6.6	5.5"
454 Casull	250	1300	1151	1047	938	735	608	0.7	3.2	7.5"V
454 Casull	260	1800	1577	1381	1871	1436	1101	0.4	1.8	7.5"V
454 Casull	300	1625	1451	1308	1759	1413	1141	0.5	2	7.5"V
454 Casull CorBon	360	1500	1387	1286	1800	1640	1323	2.01	0	
460 S&W	200	2300	2042	1801	2350	1851	1441	0	-1.6	NA
460 S&W	260	2000	1788	1592	2309	1845	1464	NA	NA	7.5"V
460 S&W	250	1450	1267	1127	1167	891	705	NA	NA	8.375-V
460 S&W	250	1900	1640	1412	2004	1494	1106	0	-2.75	NA
460 S&W	300	1750	1510	1300	2040	1510	1125	NA	NA	8.4-V
460 S&W	395	1550	1389	1249	2108	1691	1369	0	-4	NA
475 Linebaugh	400	1350	1217	1119	1618	1315	1112	NA	NA	NA
480 Ruger	325	1350	1191	1076	1315	1023	835	2.6	0	7.5"
50 Action Exp.	300	1475	1251	1092	1449	1043	795	-	-	6"
50 Action Exp.	325	1400	1209	1075	1414	1055	835	0.2	2.3	6"
500 S&W	275	1665	1392	1183	1693	1184	854	1.5	NA	8.375
500 S&W	300	1950	1653	1396	2533	1819	1298	—	—	8.5
500 S&W	325	1800	1560	1350	2340	1755	1315	NA	NA	8.4-V
500 S&W	350	1400	1231	1106	1523	1178	951	NA	NA	10"
500 S&W	400	1675	1472	1299	2493	1926	1499	1.3	NA	8.375
500 S&W	440	1625	1367	1169	2581	1825	1337	1.6	NA	8.375
500 S&W	500	1300	1178	1085	1876	1541	1308	—	—	8.5
500 S&W	500	1425	1281	1164	2254	1823	1505	NA	NA	10"

Rimfire Ammunition Ballistics

Note: The actual ballistics obtained with your firearm can vary considerably from the advertised ballistics. Also, ballistics can vary from lot to lot with the same brand and type load.

Cartridge	Bullet Wt. Grs.	Velocity (fps) 22-1/2" Bbl.		Energy (ft. lbs.) 22-1/2" Bbl.		Mid-Range Traj. (in.)	Muzzle Velocity
		Muzzle	100 yds.	Muzzle	100 yds.	100 yds.	6" Bbl.
17 Aguila	20	1850	1267	NA	NA	NA	NA
17 Hornady Mach 2	15.5	2050	1450	149	75	NA	NA
17 Hornady Mach 2	17	2100	1530	166	88	0.7	NA
17 HMR Lead Free	15.5	2550	1901	NA	NA	0.9	NA
17 HMR TNT Green	16	2500	1642	222	96	NA	NA
17 HMR	17	2550	1902	245	136	NA	NA
17 HMR	20	2375	1776	250	140	NA	NA
17 Win. Super Mag.	20 Tipped	3000	2504	400	278	0	NA
17 Win. Super Mag.	20 JHP	3000	2309	400	237	0	NA
17 Win. Super Mag.	25 Tipped	2600	2230	375	276	0	NA
5mm Rem. Rimfire Mag.	30	2300	1669	352	188	NA	24
22 Short Blank	—	—	—	—	—	—	—
22 Short CB	29	727	610	33	24	NA	706
22 Short Target	29	830	695	44	31	6.8	786
22 Short HP	27	1164	920	81	50	4.3	1077
22 Colibri	20	375	183	6	1	NA	NA
22 Super Colibri	20	500	441	11	9	NA	NA
22 Long CB	29	727	610	33	24	NA	706
22 Long HV	29	1180	946	90	57	4.1	1031
22 LR Pistol Match	40	1070	890	100	70	4.6	940
22 LR Shrt. Range Green	21	1650	912	127	NA	NA	NA
CCI Quiet 22 LR	40	710	640	45	36	NA	NA
22 LR Sub Sonic HP	38	1050	901	93	69	4.7	NA
22 LR Segmented HP	40	1050	897	98	72	NA	NA
22 LR Standard Velocity	40	1070	890	100	70	4.6	940
22 LR AutoMatch	40	1200	990	130	85	NA	NA
22 LR HV	40	1255	1016	140	92	3.6	1060
22 LR Silhoutte	42	1220	1003	139	94	3.6	1025
22 SSS	60	950	802	120	86	NA	NA
22 LR HV HP	40	1280	1001	146	89	3.5	1085
22 Velocitor GDHP	40	1435	0	0	0	NA	NA
22 LR Segmented HP	37	1435	1080	169	96	2.9	NA
22 LR Hyper HP	32/33/34	1500	1075	165	85	2.8	NA
22 LR Expediter	32	1640	NA	191	NA	NA	NA
22 LR Stinger HP	32	1640	1132	191	91	2.6	1395
22 LR Lead Free	30	1650	NA	181	NA	NA	NA
22 LR Hyper Vel	30	1750	1191	204	93	NA	NA
22 LR Shot #12	31	950	NA	NA	NA	NA	NA
22 WRF LFN	45	1300	1015	169	103	3	NA
22 Win. Mag. Lead Free	28	2200	NA	301	NA	NA	NA
22 Win. Mag.	30	2200	1373	322	127	1.4	1610
22 Win. Mag. V-Max BT	33	2000	1495	293	164	0.6	NA
22 Win. Mag. JHP	34	2120	1435	338	155	1.4	NA
22 Win. Mag. JHP	40	1910	1326	324	156	1.7	1480
22 Win. Mag. FMJ	40	1910	1326	324	156	1.7	1480
22 Win. Mag. Dyna Point	45	1550	1147	240	131	2.6	NA
22 Win. Mag. JHP	50	1650	1280	300	180	1.3	NA
22 Win. Mag. Shot #11	52	1000	—	NA	—	—	NA

Shotshell Loads

Variations and number of rounds per box can occur with type and brand of ammunition.
Not every brand is available in all shot size variations. # = new load spec this year; "C" indicates a change in data.

10 Gauge 3-1/2" Magnum

Dram Equiv.	Shot Ozs.	Load Style	Shot Sizes	Brands	Velocity (fps)
Max	2-3/8	magnum blend	5, 6, 7	Hevi-shot	1200
4-1/2	2-1/4	premium	BB, 2, 4, 5, 6	Win., Fed., Rem.	1205
Max	2	premium	4, 5, 6	Fed., Win.	1300
4-1/4	2	high velocity	BB, 2, 4	Rem.	1210
Max	18 pellets	premium	00 buck	Fed., Win.	1100
Max	1-7/8	Bismuth	BB, 2, 4	Bis.	1225
Max	1-3/4	high density	BB, 2	Rem.	1300
4-1/4	1-3/4	steel	TT, T, BBB, BB, 1, 2, 3	Win., Rem.	1260
Mag	1-5/8	steel	T, BBB, BB, 2	Win.	1285
Max	1-5/8	Bismuth	BB, 2, 4	Bismuth	1375
Max	1-1/2	hypersonic	BBB, BB, 2	Rem.	1700
Max	1-1/2	heavy metal	BB, 2, 3, 4	Hevi-Shot	1500
Max	1-1/2	steel	T, BBB, BB, 1, 2, 3	Fed.	1450
Max	1-3/8	steel	T, BBB, BB, 1, 2, 3	Fed., Rem.	1500
Max	1-3/8	steel	T, BBB, BB, 2	Fed., Win.	1450
Max	1-3/4	slug, rifled	slug	Fed.	1280

12 Gauge 3-1/2" Magnum

Dram Equiv.	Shot Ozs.	Load Style	Shot Sizes	Brands	Velocity (fps)
Max	2-1/4	premium	4, 5, 6	Fed., Rem., Win.	1150
	2 1/4	TSS	7	Fed	1200
	2 1/4	TSS	9	Fed	1200
Max	2	Lead	4, 5, 6	Fed.	1300
Max	2	Copper plated turkey	4, 5	Rem.	1300
Max	18 pellets	premium	00 buck	Fed., Win., Rem.	1100
Max	1-7/8	Wingmaster HD	4, 6	Rem.	1225
Max	1-7/8	heavyweight	5, 6	Fed.	1300
Max	1-3/4	high density	BB, 2, 4, 6	Rem.	1300
Max	1-7/8	Bismuth	BB, 2, 4	Bis.	1225
Max	1-5/8	blind side	Hex, 1, 3	Win.	1400
Max	1-5/8	Hevi-shot	T	Hevi-shot	1350
Max	1-5/8	Wingmaster HD	T	Rem.	1350
Max	1-5/8	high density	BB, 2	Fed.	1450
Max	1-5/8	Blind side	Hex, BB, 2	Win.	1400
Max	1-3/8	Heavyweight	2, 4, 6	Fed.	1450
Max	1-3/8	steel	T, BBB, BB, 2, 4	Fed., Win., Rem.	1450
Max	1-1/2	FS steel	BBB, BB, 2	Fed.	1500
Max	1-1/2	Supreme H-V	BBB, BB, 2, 3	Win.	1475
Max	1-3/8	H-speed steel	BB, 2	Rem.	1550
Max	1-1/4	Steel	BB, 2	Win.	1625
Max	24 pellets	Premium	1 Buck	Fed.	1100
Max	54 pellets	Super-X	4 Buck	Win.	1050

12 Gauge 3" Magnum

Dram Equiv.	Shot Ozs.	Load Style	Shot Sizes	Brands	Velocity (fps)
4	2	premium	BB, 2, 4, 5, 6	Win., Fed., Rem.	1175
	2	TSS	7 & 9	Fed	1150
4	1-7/8	premium	BB, 2, 4, 6	Win., Fed., Rem.	1210
4	1-7/8	duplex	4x6	Rem.	1210
Max	1-3/4	turkey	4, 5, 6	Fed., Fio., Win., Rem.	1300
Max	1-3/4	high density	BB, 2, 4	Rem.	1450
Max	1-5/8	high density	BB, 2	Fed.	1450
	1 3/4	TSS	7	Fed	1200
	1 3/4	TSS	9	Fed	1200
Max	1-5/8	Wingmaster HD	4, 6	Rem.	1227
Max	1-5/8	high velocity	4, 5, 6	Fed.	1350
4	1-5/8	premium	2, 4, 5, 6	Win., Fed., Rem.	1290
Max	1-1/2	Wingmaster HD	T	Rem.	1300
Max	1-1/2	Hevi-shot	T	Hevi-shot	1300
Max	1-1/2	slug	slug	Bren.	1604
Max	1-5/8	Bismuth	BB, 2, 4, 5, 6	Bis.	1250
4	24 pellets	buffered	1 buck	Win., Fed., Rem.	1040

12 Gauge 3" Magnum (cont.)

Dram Equiv.	Shot Ozs.	Load Style	Shot Sizes	Brands	Velocity (fps)
4	10 pellets	buffered	000 buck	Win., Fed., Rem.	1225
4	41 pellets	buffered	4 buck	Win., Fed., Rem.	1210
Max	1-3/8	heavyweight	5, 6	Fed.	1300
Max	1-3/8	high density	B, 2, 4, 6	Rem. Win.	1450
Max	1-3/8	slug	slug	Bren.	1476
Max	1-3/8	blind side	Hex, 1, 3, 5	Win.	1400
Max	1-1/4	slug, rifled	slug	Fed.	1600
Max	1-3/16	saboted slug	copper slug	Rem.	1500
Max	7/8	slug, rifled	slug	Rem.	1875
Max	1-1/8	low recoil	BB	Fed.	850
Max	1-1/8	steel	BB, 2, 3, 4	Fed., Win., Rem.	1550
Max	1-1/16	high density	2, 4	Win.	1400
Max	1	steel	4, 6	Fed.	1330
Max	1-3/8	buckhammer	slug	Rem.	1500
Max	1	TruBall slug	slug	Fed.	1700
Max	1	slug, rifled	slug, magnum	Win., Rem.	1760
Max	1	saboted slug	slug	Rem., Win., Fed.	1550
Max	385 grs.	partition gold	slug	Win.	2000
Max	1-1/8	Rackmaster	slug	Win.	1700
Max	300 grs.	XP3	slug	Win.	2100
3-5/8	1-3/8	steel	BBB, BB, 1, 2, 3, 4	Win., Fed., Rem.	1275
Max	1-1/8	snow goose FS	BB, 2, 3, 4	Fed.	1635
Max	1-1/8	steel	BB, 2, 4	Rem.	1500
Max	1-1/8	steel	T, BBB, BB, 2, 4, 5, 6	Fed., Win.	1450
Max	1-1/8	steel	BB, 2	Fed.	1400
Max	1-1/8	FS lead	3, 4	Fed.	1600
Max	1-3/8	Blind side	Hex, BB, 2	Win.	1400
Max	1-1/8	steel	BB, 2, 4	Rem.	1500
Max	1-1/8	steel	T, BBB, BB, 2, 4, 5, 6	Fed., Win.	1450
Max	1-1/8	steel	BB, 2	Fed.	1400
Max	1-1/8	FS lead	3, 4	Fed.	1600
Max	1-3/8	Blind side	Hex, BB, 2	Win.	1400

12 Gauge 2-3/4"

Dram Equiv.	Shot Ozs.	Load Style	Shot Sizes	Brands	Velocity (fps)
Max	1-5/8	magnum	4, 5, 6	Win., Fed.	1250
Max	1-3/8	lead	4, 5, 6	Fiocchi	1485
Max	1-3/8	turkey	4, 5, 6	Fio.	1250
Max	1-3/8	steel	4, 5, 6	Fed.	1400
Max	1-3/8	Bismuth	BB, 2, 4, 5, 6	Bis.	1300
3-3/4	1-1/2	magnum	BB, 2, 4, 5, 6	Win., Fed., Rem.	1260
Max	1-1/4	blind side	Hex, 2, 5	Win.	1400
Max	1-1/4	Supreme H-V	4, 5, 6, 7-1/2	Win., Rem.	1400
3-3/4	1-1/4	high velocity	BB, 2, 4, 5, 6	Win., Fed., Rem., Fio.	1330
Max	1-1/4	high density	B, 2, 4	Win.	1450
Max	1-1/4	high density	4, 6	Rem.	1325
3-1/4	1-1/4	standard velocity	6, 7-1/2, 8, 9	Win., Fed., Rem., Fio.	1220
Max	1-1/8	Hevi-shot	5	Hevi-shot	1350
3-1/4	1-1/8	standard velocity	4, 6, 7-1/2, 8, 9	Win., Fed., Rem., Fio.	1255
Max	1-1/8	steel	2, 4	Rem.	1390
Max	1	steel	BB, 2	Fed.	1450
3-1/4	1	standard velocity	6, 7-1/2, 8	Rem., Fed., Fio., Win.	1290
3-1/4	1-1/4	target	7-1/2, 8, 9	Win., Fed., Rem.	1220
3	1-1/8	spreader	7-1/2, 8, 8-1/2, 9	Fio.	1200
3	1-1/8	target	7-1/2, 8, 9, 7-1/2x8	Win., Fed., Rem., Fio.	1200
2-3/4	1-1/8	target	7-1/2, 8, 8-1/2, 9, 7-1/2x8	Win., Fed., Rem., Fio.	1145
2-3/4	1-1/8	low recoil	7-1/2, 8	Rem.	1145
2-1/2	26 grams	low recoil	8	Win.	980
2-1/4	1-1/8	target	7-1/2, 8, 8-1/2, 9	Rem., Fed.	1080

12 Gauge 2-3/4" (cont.)

Dram Equiv.	Shot Ozs.	Load Style	Shot Sizes	Brands	Velocity (fps)
12 Gauge 2-3/4" (cont.)					
3-1/4	28 grams (1oz)	target	7-1/2, 8, 9	Win., Fed., Rem., Fio.	1290
3	1	target	7-1/2, 8, 8-1/2, 9	Win., Fio.	1235
2-3/4	1	target	7-1/2, 8, 8-1/2, 9	Fed., Rem., Fio.	1180
3-1/4	24 grams	target	7-1/2, 8, 9	Fed., Win., Fio.	1325
3	7/8	light	8	Fio.	1200
3-3/4	8 pellets	buffered	000 buck	Win., Fed., Rem.	1325
4	12 pellets	premium	00 buck	Win., Fed., Rem.	1290
3-3/4	9 pellets	buffered	00 buck	Win., Fed., Rem., Fio.	1325
3-3/4	12 pellets	buffered	0 buck	Win., Fed., Rem.	1275
4	20 pellets	buffered	1 buck	Win., Fed., Rem.	1075
3-3/4	16 pellets	buffered	1 buck	Win., Fed., Rem.	1250
4	34 pellets	premium	4 buck	Fed., Rem.	1250
3-3/4	27 pellets	buffered	4 buck	Win., Fed., Rem., Fio.	1325
		PDX1	1 oz. slug, 3-00 buck	Win.	1150
Max	1 oz	segmenting,slug	slug	Win.	1600
Max	1	saboted slug	slug	Win., Fed., Rem.	1450
Max	1-1/4	slug, rifled	slug	Fed.	1520
Max	1-1/4	slug	slug	Lightfield	1440
Max	1-1/4	saboted slug	attached sabot	Rem.	1550
Max	1	slug, rifled	slug, magnum	Rem., Fio.	1680
Max	1	slug, rifled	slug	Win., Fed., Rem.	1610
Max	1	sabot slug	slug	Sauvestre	1640
Max	7/8	slug, rifled	slug	Rem.	1800
Max	400 grains	plat. tip	sabot slug	Win.	1700
Max	385 grains	Partition Gold Slug	slug	Win.	1900
Max	385 grains	Core-Lokt bonded	sabot slug	Rem.	1900
Max	325 grains	Barnes sabot	slug	Fed.	1900
Max	300 grains	SST Slug	sabot slug	Hornady	2050
Max	3/4	Tracer	#8 + tracer	Fio.	1150
Max	130 grains	Less Lethal	.73 rubber slug	Lightfield	600
Max	3/4	non-toxic	zinc slug	Win.	NA
3	1-1/8	steel target	6-1/2, 7	Rem.	1200
2-3/4	1-1/8	steel target	7	Rem.	1145
3	1#	steel	7	Win.	1235
3-1/2	1-1/4	steel	T, BBB, BB, 1, 2, 3, 4, 5, 6	Win., Fed., Rem.	1275
3-3/4	1-1/8	steel	BB, 1, 2, 3, 4, 5, 6	Win., Fed., Rem., Fio.	1365
3-3/4	1	steel	2, 3, 4, 5, 6, 7	Win., Fed., Rem., Fio.	1390
Max	7/8	steel	7	Fio.	1440
16 Gauge 2-3/4"					
3-1/4	1-1/4	magnum	2, 4, 6	Fed., Rem.	1260
3-1/4	1-1/8	high-velocity	4, 6, 7-1/2	Win., Fed., Rem., Fio.	1295
Max	1-1/8	Bismuth	4, 5	Bis.	1200
2-3/4	1-1/8	standard velocity	6, 7-1/2, 8	Fed., Rem., Fio.	1185
2-1/2	1	dove	6, 7-1/2, 8, 9	Fio., Win.	1165
2-3/4	1		6, 7-1/2, 8	Fio.	1200
Max	15/16	steel	2, 4	Fed., Rem.	1300
Max	7/8	steel	2, 4	Win.	1300
3	12 pellets	buffered	1 buck	Win., Fed., Rem.	1225
Max	4/5	slug, rifled	slug	Win., Fed., Rem.	1570
Max	.92	sabot slug	slug	Sauvestre	1500
20 Gauge 3" Magnum					
	1 5/8	TSS	7 & 9	Fed	1000
	1 5/8	TSS	8 & 10	Fed	1000
	1 1/2	TSS	7	Fed	1100
	1 1/2	TSS	9	Fed	1100
3	1-1/4	premium	2, 4, 5, 6, 7-1/2	Win., Fed., Rem.	1185
Max	1-1/4	Wingmaster HD	4, 6	Rem.	1185
3	1-1/4	turkey	4, 6	Fio.	1200
Max	1-1/4	Hevi-shot	2, 4, 6	Hevi-shot	1250
Max	1-1/8	high density	4, 6	Rem.	1300
Max	18 pellets	buck shot	2 buck	Fed.	1200
Max	24 pellets	buffered	3 buck	Win.	1150
2-3/4	20 pellets	buck	3 buck	Rem.	1200

Dram Equiv.	Shot Ozs.	Load Style	Shot Sizes	Brands	Velocity (fps)
20 Gauge 3" Magnum (cont.)					
Max	1	hypersonic	2, 3, 4	Rem.	TBD
3-1/4	1	steel	1, 2, 3, 4, 5, 6	Win., Fed., Rem.	1330
Max	1	blind side	Hex, 2, 5	Win.	1300
Max	7/8	steel	2, 4	Win.	1300
Max	7/8	FS lead	3, 4	Fed.	1500
Max	1-1/16	high density	2, 4	Win.	1400
Max	1-1/16	Bismuth	2, 4, 5, 6	Bismuth	1250
Mag	5/8	saboted slug	275 gr.	Fed.	1900
Max	3/4	TruBall slug	slug	Fed.	1700
20 Gauge 2-3/4"					
2-3/4	1-1/8	magnum	4, 6, 7-1/2	Win., Fed., Rem.	1175
2-3/4	1	high velocity	4, 5, 6, 7-1/2, 8, 9	Win., Fed., Rem., Fio.	1220
Max	1	Bismuth	4, 6	Bis.	1200
Max	1	Hevi-shot	5	Hevi-shot	1250
Max	1	Supreme H-V	4, 6, 7-1/2	Win. Rem.	1300
Max	1	FS lead	4, 5, 6	Fed.	1350
Max	7/8	Steel	2, 3, 4	Fio.	1500
2-1/2	1	standard velocity	6, 7-1/2, 8	Win., Rem., Fed., Fio.	1165
2-1/2	7/8	clays	8	Rem.	1200
2-1/2	7/8	promotional	6, 7-1/2, 8	Win., Rem., Fio.	1210
2-1/2	1	target	8, 9	Win., Rem.	1165
Max	7/8	clays	7-1/2, 8	Win.	1275
2-1/2	7/8	target	8, 9	Win., Fed., Rem.	1200
Max	3/4	steel	2, 4	Rem.	1425
2-1/2	7/8	steel - target	7	Rem.	1200
1-1/2	7/8	low recoil	8	Win.	980
Max	1	buckhammer	slug	Rem.	1500
Max	5/8	Saboted Slug	Copper Slug	Rem.	1500
Max	20 pellets	buffered	3 buck	Win., Fed.	1200
Max	5/8	slug, saboted	slug	Win.,	1400
28 Gauge 3"					
Max	7/8	tundra tungsten	4, 5, 6	Fiocchi	TBD
28 Gauge 2-3/4"					
2	1	high velocity	6, 7-1/2, 8	Win.	1125
2-1/4	3/4	high velocity	6, 7-1/2, 8, 9	Win., Fed., Rem., Fio.	1295
2	3/4	target	8, 9	Win., Fed., Rem.	1200
Max	3/4	sporting clays	7-1/2, 8-1/2	Win.	1300
Max	5/8	Bismuth	4, 6	Bis.	1250
Max	5/8	steel	6, 7	NA	1300
Max	5/8	slug		Bren.	1450
410 Bore 3"					
	13/16	TSS	9	Fed	1100
Max	11/16	high velocity	4, 5, 6, 7-1/2, 8, 9	Win., Fed., Rem., Fio.	1135
Max	9/16	Bismuth	4	Bis.	1175
Max	3/8	steel	6	NA	1400
		judge	5 pellets 000 Buck	Fed.	960
		judge	9 pellets #4 Buck	Fed.	1100
Max	Mixed	Per. Defense	3DD/12BB	Win.	750
410 Bore 2-1/2"					
Max	1/2	high velocity	4, 6, 7-1/2	Win., Fed., Rem.	1245
Max	1/5	slug, rifled	slug	Win., Fed., Rem.	1815
1-1/2	1/2	target	8, 8-1/2, 9	Win., Fed., Rem., Fio	1200
Max	1/2	sporting clays	7-1/2, 8, 8-1/2	Win.	1300
Max		Buckshot	5-000 Buck	Win.	1135
		judge	12-bb's, 3 disks	Win.	TBD
Max	Mixed	Per. Defense	4DD/16BB	Win.	750
Max	42 grains	Less lethal	4/.41 rubber balls	Lightfield	1150

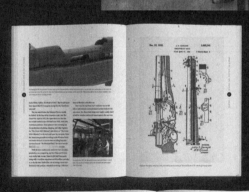
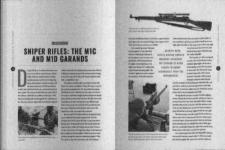

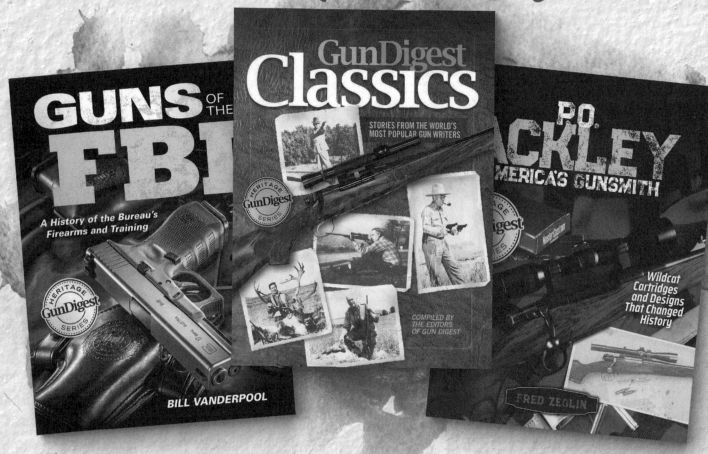